McGraw-Hill
netw○rks™

**MEETS YOU ANYWHERE —
TAKES YOU EVERYWHERE**

GO online

1. Go to *connected.mcgraw-hill.com*.

2. Get your User Name and
   Password from your teacher
   and enter them.

3. Click on your **Networks** book.

4. Select your chapter
   and lesson.

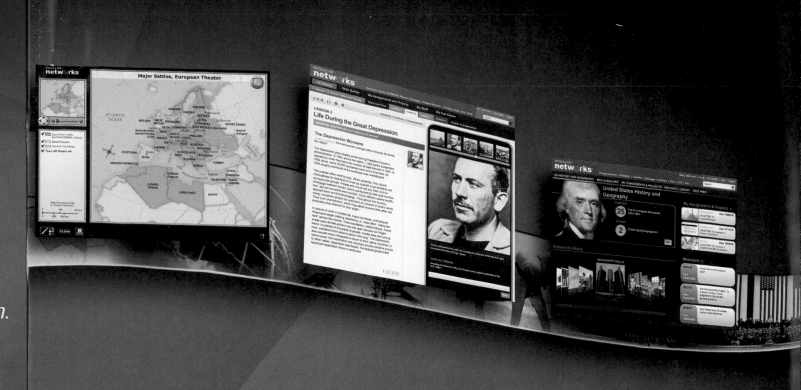

HOW do you learn?

Read • Reflect • Watch • Listen • Connect • Discover • Interact

start netw○rking

WHAT do you learn?

History • Geography • Economics • Government • Culture

start **netw⚙rk**ing

McGraw-Hill
netw⊙rks™

MEETS YOU ANYWHERE — TAKES YOU EVERYWHERE

HOW do you make **Networks** yours?

Organize • Take Notes • Study • Submit • Message

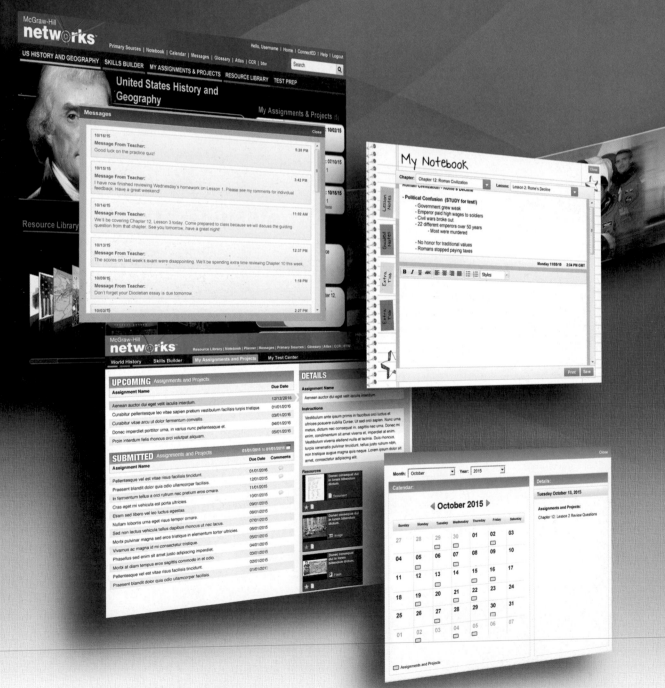

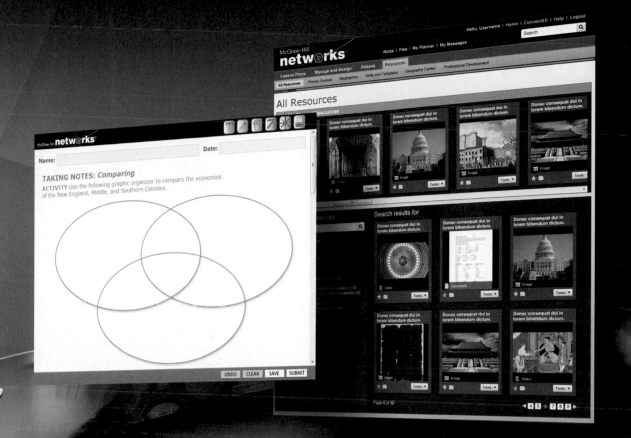

WHAT do you use?

Graphic Organizers • Primary Sources • Videos • Games • Photos

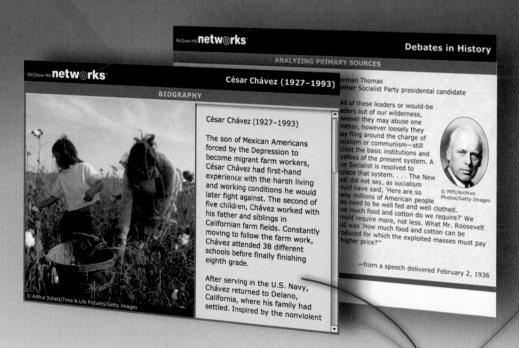

start network ing

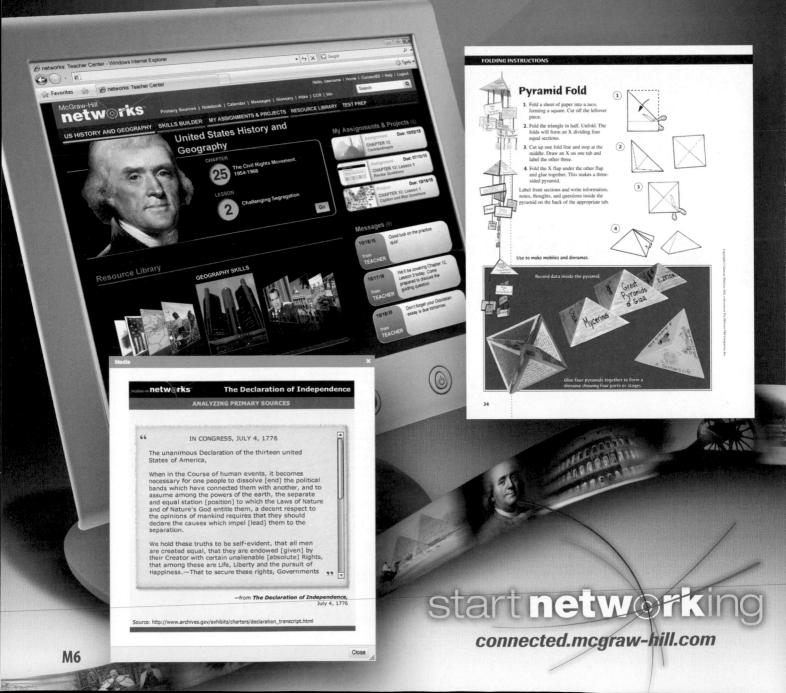

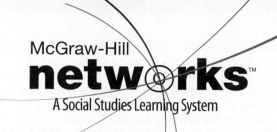

McGraw-Hill
netw⊙rks™
A Social Studies Learning System

UNITED STATES
HISTORY
& GEOGRAPHY

Joyce Appleby, Ph.D.

Alan Brinkley, Ph.D.

Albert S. Broussard, Ph.D.

James M. McPherson, Ph.D.

Donald A. Ritchie, Ph.D.

Mc Graw Hill Education

Bothell, WA • Chicago, IL • Columbus, OH • New York, NY

Cover Photo Credits: (Thomas Jefferson) Superstock/Getty Images, **(thumbnail images l to r, t to b) (2)** Geostock/Getty Images, **(3)** Visions of America, **(4)** LLC/Alamy, **(5)** Library of Congress, Prints and Photographs Division (LC-USZC4-678), **(6)** S. Meltzer/ PhotoLink/Getty Images, **(7)** Library of Congress, Prints and Photographs Division (LC-DIG-fsa-8b29516), **(8)** Library of Congress, Prints and Photographs Division (LC-USZC4-2920), **(9)** Library of Congress, Prints and Photographs Division (LC-USZ62-101445), **(10)** Royalty-Free/CORBIS, Library of Congress Prints & Photographs Division (LC-USZ62-42476), **(11)** NASA Headquarters - GReatest Images of NASA (NASA-HQ-GRIN), **(12)** Royalty-Free/CORBIS, **(13)** U.S. Air Force photo by Airman 1st Class Jesse Shipps, **(14)** Library of Congress, Prints and Photographs Division (LC-USZ62-63360), **(15)** Royalty-Free/CORBIS, **(16)** Library of Congress Prints & Photographs Division (LC-USZC4-1538), **(17)** Library of Congress, Prints and Photographs Division (LC-USZC4-6466), **(18)** NASA Headquarters - GReatest Images of NASA (NASA-HQ-GRIN), **(19)** McGraw-Hill Companies, Inc./Jill Braaten, photographer.

More About the Photos Main Image: Thomas Jefferson; Thumbnails left to right, top to bottom: Mount Rushmore detail, digital composite of three American sailors, Ulysses S. Grant, United States flag, "Migrant Mother", Christopher Columbus, President Woodrow Wilson, Space Shuttle *Endeavour*, Mary McLeod Bethune, *Apollo 11* crew, irrigation sprinklers, President George W. Bush, suffragists, policeman, President Andrew Jackson, astronaut Sally Ride, President Bill Clinton

McGraw-Hill networks ™ A Social Studies Learning System. Meets you anywhere—takes you everywhere. Go online. 1. Go to connected.mcgraw-hill.com. 2. Get your User Name and Password from your teacher and enter them. 3. Click on your *networks* book. 4. Select your chapter and lesson.

The McGraw·Hill Companies

www.mheonline.com/networks

 **Education**

Copyright © 2013 by The McGraw-Hill Companies, Inc.

All rights reserved. No part of this publication may be reproduced or distributed in any form or by any means, or stored in a database or retrieval system, without the prior written consent of The McGraw-Hill Companies, Inc., including, but not limited to, network storage or transmission, or broadcast for distance learning.

Send all inquiries to:
McGraw-Hill Education
8787 Orion Place
Columbus, OH 43240

ISBN: 978-0-07-893568-8
MHID: 0-07-893568-7

Printed in the United States of America.

3 4 5 6 7 8 9 DOW 15 14 13

AUTHORS

Joyce Appleby, Ph.D., is Professor Emerita of History at UCLA. She is the author of several books, including *Economic Thought and Ideology in Seventeenth-Century England*, which won the Berkshire Prize. She served as president of both the Organization of American Historians and the American Historical Association, and chaired the Council of the Institute of Early American History and Culture at Williamsburg. Dr. Appleby has been elected to the American Philosophical Society and the American Academy of Arts and Sciences, and is a Corresponding Fellow of the British Academy.

Alan Brinkley, Ph.D., is Allan Nevins Professor of American History at Columbia University. His published works include *Voices of Protest: Huey Long, Father Coughlin, and the Great Depression*, which won the 1983 National Book Award. He received the Levenson Memorial Teaching Prize at Harvard University.

Albert S. Broussard, Ph.D., is Professor of History at Texas A&M University, where he was selected as the Distinguished Faculty Lecturer for 1999–2000. He also served as the Langston Hughes Professor of American Studies at the University of Kansas in 2005. Before joining the Texas A&M faculty, Dr. Broussard was Assistant Professor of History and Director of the African American Studies Program at Southern Methodist University. Dr. Broussard has also served as president of the Oral History Association.

James M. McPherson, Ph.D., is George Henry Davis Professor Emeritus of American History at Princeton University. Dr. McPherson is the author of 11 books about the Civil War era. Including *Abraham Lincoln as Commander in Chief*, for which he won the 2009 Lincoln Prize. Dr. McPherson is a member of many professional historical associations, including the Civil War Preservation Trust.

Donald A. Ritchie, Ph.D. is Historian of the United States Senate. Dr. Ritchie received his doctorate in American history from the University of Maryland after service in the U.S. Marine Corps. He has taught American history at various levels, from high school to university. He edits the Historical Series of the Senate Foreign Relations Committee and is the author of several books, including *Press Gallery: Congress and the Washington Correspondents*, which received the Organization of American Historians' Richard W. Leopold Prize. Dr. Ritchie has served as president of the Oral History Association and as a council member of the American Historical Association.

Contributing Author

Jay McTighe has published articles in a number of leading educational journals and has co-authored ten books, including the best-selling *Understanding By Design* series with Grant Wiggins. McTighe also has an extensive background in professional development and is a featured speaker at national, state, and district conferences and workshops. He received his undergraduate degree from the College of William and Mary, earned a Masters degree from the University of Maryland and completed post-graduate studies at Johns Hopkins University.

ACADEMIC CONSULTANTS

David Berger, Ph.D.
Ruth and I. Lewis Gordon Professor of Jewish History
Dean, Bernard Revel Graduate School
Yeshiva University
New York, New York

Steven Cunha, Ph.D.
Professor of Geography
Humboldt State University
Arcata, California

Linda Clemmons, Ph.D.
Assistant Professor of History
Illinois State University
Normal, Illinois

Neil Foley, Ph.D.
Associate Professor of History
University of Texas at Austin
Austin, Texas

Shawn Johansen, Ph.D.
Professor of History
Brigham Young University-Idaho
Rexburg, Idaho

K. Austin Kerr, Ph.D.
Emeritus Professor of History
The Ohio State University
Columbus, Ohio

Jeffrey Ogbar, Ph.D.
Associate Dean for the Humanities
University of Connecticut, Storrs
Storrs, Connecticut

William Bruce Wheeler, Ph.D.
Emeritus Professor of History
University of Tennessee
Knoxville, Tennessee

Tom Daccord
Educational Technology Specialist
Co-Director, EdTechTeacher
Boston, Massachusetts

Justin Reich
Educational Technology Specialist
Co-Director, EdTechTeacher
Boston, Massachusetts

TEACHER REVIEWERS

Marsha Baugh
Montgomery Public Schools
Brewbaker Technology Magnet High School
Montgomery, Alabama

Terry L. Cherry
Garland Independent School District
Naaman Forest High School
Garland, Texas

Brian P. Dowd
Massapequa Public Schools
Massapequa High School
Massapequa, New York

Jennifer L. Flores
Francis Howell School District
Francis Howell High School
St. Charles, Missouri

Dr. Robert A. Handy
Bel Air High School
Bel Air, Maryland

Karl R. Johnson
Paradise Valley Unified School District
Pinnacle High School
Phoenix, Arizona

Mark Kuhl
School District #115
Lake Forest High School
Lake Forest, Illinois

Julie M. Lasowski
Orange County Public Schools
Olympia High School
Orlando, Florida

CONSULTANTS AND REVIEWERS

TEACHER REVIEWERS

Kevin McCaffrey
Evanston Township High School
Evanston, Illinois

Michael McLaughlin
Hazelwood School District
Hazelwood East High School
St. Louis, Missouri

Kelly M. Machala
Harford County Public Schools
Patterson Mill Middle/High School
Bel Air, Maryland

James May
Harford County Public Schools
Patterson Mill High School
Bel Air, Maryland

Steven "Duff" Pace
Enterprise School District # 21
Enterprise High School
Enterprise, Oregon

Christa Martell Schneider
Francis Howell School District
Francis Howell High School
St. Charles, Missouri

John A. Toronski
Pinellas County
Lakewood High School
St. Petersburg, Florida

Heather McGraw Verdi
Consolidated School District of New Britain
New Britain High School
New Britain, Connecticut

Andrew White
Montgomery County Public Schools
Paint Branch High School
Burtonsville, Maryland

Brandon J. Woodrome, Ed.S.
Belleville Township High School District 201
Belleville West High School
Belleville, Illinois

CONTENTS

There's More Online . . .

BIOGRAPHIES Dekanawida (1425?–1475?) • Amerigo Vespucci (1454–1512) • Bartolomé de Las Casas (1474–1566) • Anne Hutchinson (1591–1643) • Roger Williams (1603?–1683) • John Locke (1632–1704) • Nathaniel Bacon (1647–1676) • James Oglethorpe (1696–1785) • Phillis Wheatley (1753?–1784)

IMAGES Maya Temple • Tepee Village • Technological Advances in Sea Travel • Advertisement for Settlers

MAPS Ethnic Diversity • The Economy of New England and the Middle Colonies • The Economy of the Colonial South • Typical New England Town • Triangular Trade

VIDEOS North America Before Columbus • Europe Begins to Explore • Founding the Thirteen Colonies • Population and Economy • Governance and New Ideas

SELF-CHECK QUIZZES Lesson 1 Interactive Self-Check Quiz • Lesson 2 Interactive Self-Check Quiz • Lesson 3 Interactive Self-Check Quiz • Lesson 4 Interactive Self-Check Quiz • Lesson 5 Interactive Self-Check Quiz

There's More Online . . .

BIOGRAPHIES Samuel Adams (1722–1803) • George Washington (1732–1799) • Thomas Paine (1737–1809) • Abigail Adams (1744–1818) • George Rogers Clark (1752–1818) • Marquis de Lafayette (1757–1834)

GRAPHIC NOVEL "From Revolution to Declaration"

IMAGES The Death of General Braddock • Battle of Lexington • Treaty of Paris • Noah Webster's *American Spelling Book*

PRIMARY SOURCE The Declaration of Independence

VIDEOS The Colonies Fight for Their Rights • The Revolution Begins • The War for Independence • The War Changes American Society

SELF-CHECK QUIZZES Lesson 1 Interactive Self-Check Quiz • Lesson 2 Interactive Self-Check Quiz • Lesson 3 Interactive Self-Check Quiz • Lesson 4 Interactive Self-Check Quiz

There's More Online . . .

BIOGRAPHIES Patrick Henry (1736–1799) • Alexander Hamilton (1755–1804)

CHARTS/GRAPHS Imports from Britain • Structure of the Constitution

GRAPHIC ORGANIZERS Comparing the Two Plans • Origins of the Bill of Rights

MAP British Forts in the United States

PRIMARY SOURCE Ratifying the Constitution Political Cartoon

VIDEOS The Confederation • A New Constitution • Ratifying the Constitution

SELF-CHECK QUIZZES Lesson 1 Interactive Self-Check Quiz • Lesson 2 Interactive Self-Check Quiz • Lesson 3 Interactive Self-Check Quiz

There's More Online . . .

BIOGRAPHIES John Adams (1735–1826) • Thomas Jefferson (1743–1826) • Aaron Burr (1756–1836) • John Marshall (1755–1835) • Meriwether Lewis (1774–1809) and William Clark (1770–1838) • Sacagawea (1787?–1812?) • Francis Scott Key (1779–1843) • Dolley Madison (1768–1849)

IMAGES Election Banner • Burr-Hamilton Duel • "The Star-Spangled Banner"

MAP The Louisiana Purchase

PRIMARY SOURCE "Ograbme" Political Cartoon

VIDEOS Washington and Congress • Partisan Politics • Jefferson in Office • The War of 1812

SELF-CHECK QUIZZES Lesson 1 Interactive Self-Check Quiz • Lesson 2 Interactive Self-Check Quiz • Lesson 3 Interactive Self-Check Quiz • Lesson 4 Interactive Self-Check Quiz

CONTENTS

CHAPTER 5
Growth and Division .. 137

CHAPTER 6
The Spirit of Reform ... 159

There's More Online . . .

BIOGRAPHIES Robert Fulton (1765–1815) • Eli Whitney (1765–1825) • John Quincy Adams (1767–1848) • Andrew Jackson (1767–1845) • Henry Clay (1777–1852) • Osceola (1800?–1838) • Nat Turner (1800–1831)

CHART/GRAPH Cotton Production

IMAGE Escaped Slave Reward Poster

MAPS Cotton Production and Enslaved Population • An Economy Built on Enslaved Labor • Presidential Election of 1828

SLIDE SHOW Technology Innovations

VIDEOS American Nationalism • Early Industry • The Land of Cotton • Growing Sectionalism

SELF-CHECK QUIZZES Lesson 1 Interactive Self-Check Quiz • Lesson 2 Interactive Self-Check Quiz • Lesson 3 Interactive Self-Check Quiz • Lesson 4 Interactive Self-Check Quiz

There's More Online . . .

BIOGRAPHIES Sarah Hale (1788–1879) • James Fenimore Cooper (1789–1851) • Sojourner Truth (1797?–1883) • Prudence Crandall (1803–1890) • William Lloyd Garrison (1805–1879) • Margaret Fuller (1810–1850) • Elizabeth Cady Stanton (1815–1902) • Henry David Thoreau (1817–1862) • Susan B. Anthony (1820–1906)

GRAPHIC NOVEL "The Seneca Falls Convention"

IMAGES Andrew Jackson Campaign Poster • Andrew Jackson Speaking • Irish Famine • Drunkard's Progress • American Anti-Slavery Society

MAP Emancipation in the United States

VIDEOS Jacksonian America • A Changing Culture • Reforming Society • The Abolitionist Movement

SELF-CHECK QUIZZES Lesson 1 Interactive Self-Check Quiz • Lesson 2 Interactive Self-Check Quiz • Lesson 3 Interactive Self-Check Quiz • Lesson 4 Interactive Self-Check Quiz

CHAPTER 7
Manifest Destiny ... 181

CHAPTER 8
Sectional Conflict Intensifies 201

There's More Online . . .

BIOGRAPHIES Winfield Scott (1786–1866) • Sam Houston (1793–1863) • Antonio López de Santa Anna (1794–1876) • Brigham Young (1801–1877) • Kit Carson (1809–1868)

CHART/GRAPH Texans vs. Mexicans

GRAPHIC NOVEL "Westward Ho!"

INFOGRAPHIC Spanish Mission

MAPS Spanish Missions • Boundaries of the U.S. and Mexico, 1844 and 1848

PRIMARY SOURCE Polk's Victory Political Cartoon

VIDEOS The Western Pioneers • The Hispanic Southwest • Independence for Texas • The War With Mexico

SELF-CHECK QUIZZES Lesson 1 Interactive Self-Check Quiz • Lesson 2 Interactive Self-Check Quiz • Lesson 3 Interactive Self-Check Quiz • Lesson 4 Interactive Self-Check Quiz

There's More Online . . .

BIOGRAPHIES John C. Calhoun (1782–1850) • Daniel Webster (1782–1852) • John Brown (1800–1859) • Jefferson Davis (1808–1889) • Abraham Lincoln (1809–1865) • Harriet Beecher Stowe (1811–1896) • Harriet Tubman (1820?–1913)

GRAPHIC NOVEL "Fort Sumter's Last Stand"

IMAGE Underground Railroad

MAPS Presidential Election of 1856 • United States, 1819–1854

VIDEOS Slavery and Western Expansion • John Brown • The Crisis Deepens • The Union Dissolves

SELF-CHECK QUIZZES Lesson 1 Interactive Self-Check Quiz • Lesson 2 Interactive Self-Check Quiz • Lesson 3 Interactive Self-Check Quiz

CONTENTS

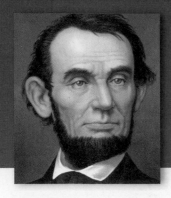

There's More Online . . .

BIOGRAPHIES Helen Hunt Jackson (1830–1885) • Sitting Bull (1831?–1890) • Chief Joseph (1840–1904)

CHARTS/GRAPHS Gold and Silver Production • Major Native American Treaties

GRAPHIC NOVEL "The Importance of the Buffalo"

IMAGES "Old West" Miners • Chinese Immigrant Miners • Women Branding Cattle • Nat Love • Farming in the West • Sod House

INFOGRAPHIC Uses of the Buffalo

MAP Cattle Ranching and the Long Drive

VIDEOS Miners and Ranchers • Farming the Plains • Native Americans

SELF-CHECK QUIZZES Lesson 1 Interactive Self-Check Quiz • Lesson 2 Interactive Self-Check Quiz • Lesson 3 Interactive Self-Check Quiz

There's More Online . . .

BIOGRAPHIES Leland Stanford (1824–1893) • Andrew Carnegie (1835–1919) • Jay Gould (1836–1892) • J. P. Morgan (1837–1913) • "Mother Jones" (1837–1930) • Josephine Cochrane (1839–1913) • John D. Rockefeller (1839–1937) • Lewis Latimer (1848–1928) • Leonora Marie Kearney Barry (1849–1930) • Samuel Gompers (1850–1924) • Eugene V. Debs (1855–1926) • Wilbur (1867–1912) & Orville Wright (1871–1948)

CHARTS/GRAPHS U.S. Businesses • Comparing Major Strikes

INFOGRAPHIC Steel Mill

PRIMARY SOURCE Communist Party Manifesto

VIDEOS The Rise of Industry • The Railroads • Big Business • Unions

SELF-CHECK QUIZZES Lesson 1 Interactive Self-Check Quiz • Lesson 2 Interactive Self-Check Quiz • Lesson 3 Interactive Self-Check Quiz • Lesson 4 Interactive Self-Check Quiz

CONTENTS

PHOTOS: (l)PhotoLink/Photodisc/Getty Images; (r)The Granger Collection, New York

CONTENTS

There's More Online . . .

BIOGRAPHIES Andrew Mellon (1855–1937) • Clarence Darrow (1857–1938) • Charles Evan Hughes (1862–1948) • Henry Ford (1863–1947) • Warren G. Harding (1865–1923) • Calvin Coolidge (1872–1933) • Willa Cather (1873–1947) • Margaret Sanger (1879–1966) • Marcus Garvey (1887–1940) • Jim Thorpe (1888–1953) • Nicola Sacco (1891–1927) and Bartolomeo Vanzetti (1888–1927) • Zora Neale Hurston (1891–1960) • F. Scott (1896–1940) & Zelda Fitzgerald (1900–1948) • Ernest Hemingway (1899–1961) • John Scopes (1900–1970) • Langston Hughes (1902–1967) • Charles Lindbergh (1902–1974)

CHARTS/GRAPHS U.S. Budget • Unemployment • Average Hourly Earnings • African American Population

SLIDE SHOWS The Car Changes America • Artists and Entertainers

VIDEOS The Politics of the 1920s • A Growing Economy • A Clash of Cultures • Cultural Innovations • African American Culture and Politics

SELF-CHECK QUIZZES Lesson 1 Interactive Self-Check Quiz • Lesson 2 Interactive Self-Check Quiz • Lesson 3 Interactive Self-Check Quiz • Lesson 4 Interactive Self-Check Quiz • Lesson 5 Interactive Self-Check Quiz

There's More Online . . .

BIOGRAPHIES Alfred E. Smith (1873–1944) • Herbert Hoover (1874–1964) • William Faulkner (1897–1962) • John Steinbeck (1902–1968)

CHARTS/GRAPHS Income and Spending • Unemployment • Value of Exports

IMAGES Bonus Army • Milk Protest

MAPS Presidential Election of 1928 • Dust Bowl

VIDEOS The Causes of the Great Depression • Life During the Great Depression • Hoover's Response to the Depression

SELF-CHECK QUIZZES Lesson 1 Interactive Self-Check Quiz • Lesson 2 Interactive Self-Check Quiz • Lesson 3 Interactive Self-Check Quiz

CHAPTER **19**
Roosevelt and the New Deal 439

CHAPTER **20**
A World in Flames 457

There's More Online . . .

There's More Online . . .

CONTENTS

CHAPTER 21
America and World War II 477

CHAPTER 22
The Cold War Begins 509

There's More Online . . .

BIOGRAPHIES George C. Marshall (1880–1959) • Henry Kaiser (1882–1967) • Chester W. Nimitz (1885–1966) • George Patton (1885–1945) • A. Philip Randolph (1889–1979) • Omar Bradley (1893–1981) • Oveta Culp Hobby (1905–1995)

IMAGES Battle of Tarawa • Kamikaze Pilots

MAPS Japanese Relocation Camps • Migration in the United States • Axis Expansion and Retreat • Japanese Entrenchment on Iwo Jima • The Battle of Stalingrad • The Atomic Bomb at Hiroshima

SLIDE SHOWS Japanese Internment • The Real Rosie

VIDEOS Wartime America • The War in the Pacific • The War in Europe • The War Ends

SELF-CHECK QUIZZES Lesson 1 Interactive Self-Check Quiz • Lesson 2 Interactive Self-Check Quiz • Lesson 3 Interactive Self-Check Quiz • Lesson 4 Interactive Self-Check Quiz

There's More Online . . .

BIOGRAPHIES Winston Churchill (1874–1965) • Joseph Stalin (1878–1953) • Douglas MacArthur (1880–1964) • Harry S. Truman (1884–1972) • Dwight Eisenhower (1890–1963) • Mao Zedong (1893–1976) • Nikita Khrushchev (1894–1971) • Luis Muñoz Marín (1898–1980) • Alger Hiss (1904–1996) • Julius (1918–1953) & Ethel Rosenberg (1915–1953)

CHART/GRAPH NATO Members

GRAPHIC NOVEL "Seeking Shelter"

IMAGES Postwar Poland • Berlin Airlift • Chinese Propaganda Poster

MAPS Divided Berlin • The Early Cold War in Europe • The Korean War • The Spread of Communism

SLIDE SHOW *Sputnik*

VIDEOS The Origins of the Cold War • The Early Cold War Years • The Cold War and American Society • Eisenhower's Cold War Policies

SELF-CHECK QUIZZES Lesson 1 Interactive Self-Check Quiz • Lesson 2 Interactive Self-Check Quiz • Lesson 3 Interactive Self-Check Quiz • Lesson 4 Interactive Self-Check Quiz

There's More Online . . .

BIOGRAPHIES Vladimir K. Zworykin (1889–1982) • Walt Disney (1901–1966) • Ralph Ellison (1914–1994) • Jack Kerouac (1922–1969) • Flannery O'Connor (1925–1964) • Elvis Presley (1935–1977)

CHARTS/GRAPHS New Home Construction • Native Americans

IMAGES Computer Technology • Suburban Housing • Television

MAPS Interstate Highway Construction • Appalachia

VIDEOS Truman and Eisenhower • The Affluent Society • The Other Side of American Life

SELF-CHECK QUIZZES Lesson 1 Interactive Self-Check Quiz • Lesson 2 Interactive Self-Check Quiz • Lesson 3 Interactive Self-Check Quiz

There's More Online . . .

BIOGRAPHIES Earl Warren (1891–1974) • Esther Peterson (1906–1997) • Robert Weaver (1907–1997) • Barry Goldwater (1909–1998) • John Glenn (1921–) • Michael Harrington (1928–1989) • Buzz Aldrin (1930–) • Neil Armstrong (1930–)

CHART/GRAPH Warren Court Decisions

MAP Presidential Election of 1960

PRIMARY SOURCE Kennedy's Inaugural Address

SLIDE SHOW The Space Race

VIDEOS The New Frontier • JFK and the Cold War • The Great Society

SELF-CHECK QUIZZES Lesson 1 Interactive Self-Check Quiz • Lesson 2 Interactive Self-Check Quiz • Lesson 3 Interactive Self-Check Quiz

PHOTOS: (l)Sunset Boulevard/Historical/CORBS; (r)SuperStock/Getty Images

CONTENTS

There's More Online . . .

BIOGRAPHIES Thurgood Marshall (1908–1993) • Rosa Parks (1913–2005) • Malcolm X (1925–1965) • Martin Luther King, Jr. (1929–1968) • James Meredith (1933–) • Bobby Seale (1936–) • Stokely Carmichael (1941–1998) • Linda Brown Thompson (1942–)

IMAGES Montgomery Bus Boycott • Lunch Counter Sit-ins • Freedom Riders • Black Power

PRIMARY SOURCES Excerpt from *Brown* v. *Board of Education* • Excerpt from *Coming of Age in Mississippi* • Watts Riot

TIME LINE Key Events of the Civil Rights Movement

VIDEOS The Movement Begins • Challenging Segregation • New Civil Rights Issues

SELF-CHECK QUIZZES Lesson 1 Interactive Self-Check Quiz • Lesson 2 Interactive Self-Check Quiz • Lesson 3 Interactive Self-Check Quiz

There's More Online . . .

BIOGRAPHIES Ho Chi Minh (1890–1969) • Ngo Dinh Diem (1901–1963) • William Westmoreland (1914–2005) • Henry Kissinger (1923–) • Robert F. Kennedy (1925–1968) • Maya Lin (1959–)

GRAPHIC NOVELS "The Lottery" • "May Day"

PRIMARY SOURCES Vietnam Political Cartoons • Excerpts from *New York Times* v. *United States*

VIDEOS Going to War in Vietnam • Vietnam Divides the Nation • The War Winds Down

SELF-CHECK QUIZZES Lesson 1 Interactive Self-Check Quiz • Lesson 2 Interactive Self-Check Quiz • Lesson 3 Interactive Self-Check Quiz

There's More Online . . .

BIOGRAPHIES Henry B. Gonzalez (1916–2000) • Betty Friedan (1921–2006) • Shirley Chisholm (1924–2005) • Phyllis Schlafly (1924–) • Dolores Huerta (1930–) • Gloria Steinem (1934–) • Tom Hayden (1939–) • Bob Dylan (1941–) • Mario Savio (1942–1996)

IMAGE Billie Jean King

MAP Latino Immigration

PRIMARY SOURCES Counterculture Political Cartoon • Excerpts from *Roe* v. *Wade*

SLIDE SHOW Migrant Workers

VIDEOS Students and the Counterculture • The Feminist Movement • Latino Americans Organize

SELF-CHECK QUIZZES Lesson 1 Interactive Self-Check Quiz • Lesson 2 Interactive Self-Check Quiz • Lesson 3 Interactive Self-Check Quiz

There's More Online . . .

BIOGRAPHIES Rachel Carson (1907–1964) • John Dean (1938–) • Jesse Jackson (1941–) • Bob Woodward (1943–) and Carl Bernstein (1944–)

CHART/GRAPH Watergate's Key Figures

IMAGES Nixon Visits China • Watergate Political Cartoon • Wounded Knee Protests • Pro-Busing and Anti-Busing

MAPS Presidential Election of 1972 • Environmental Disasters

PRIMARY SOURCE Excerpts from *United States* v. *Nixon*

SLIDE SHOW Endangered Species List

VIDEOS The Nixon Administration • The Watergate Scandal • Ford and Carter • New Approaches to Civil Rights • Environmentalism

SELF-CHECK QUIZZES Lesson 1 Interactive Self-Check Quiz • Lesson 2 Interactive Self-Check Quiz • Lesson 3 Interactive Self-Check Quiz • Lesson 4 Interactive Self-Check Quiz • Lesson 5 Interactive Self-Check Quiz

PHOTOS: (l)Bettmann/CORBIS; (r)Bettmann/CORBIS

CONTENTS

There's More Online . . .

BIOGRAPHIES Billy Graham (1918–) • Sam Walton (1918–1992) • William F. Buckley (1925–2008) • Sandra Day O'Connor (1930–) • Mikhail Gorbachev (1931–) • Norman Y. Mineta (1931–) • Toni Morrison (1931–) • Saddam Hussein (1937–2006) • Colin Powell (1937–) • Boris Yeltsin (1937–2007) • Ted Turner (1938–) • Amy Tan (1952–)

CHART/GRAPH Tax Rates

IMAGES Higher Taxes Protest • Moral Majority

SLIDE SHOW Space Shuttle Launch

VIDEOS The New Conservatism • The Reagan Years • Life in the 1980s • The End of the Cold War

SELF-CHECK QUIZZES Lesson 1 Interactive Self-Check Quiz • Lesson 2 Interactive Self-Check Quiz • Lesson 3 Interactive Self-Check Quiz • Lesson 4 Interactive Self-Check Quiz

There's More Online . . .

BIOGRAPHIES Ruth Bader Ginsburg (1933–) • Janet Reno (1938–) • Newt Gingrich (1943–) • Hillary Rodham Clinton (1947–) • Bill Gates (1955–) • Steve Jobs (1955–2011)

CHART/GRAPH Illegal Border Crossing Deaths

GRAPHIC NOVEL "All Work and No Play"

IMAGES Soldiers and Serbians • Jorge Urbina

VIDEOS The Clinton Years • A New Wave of Immigration • Technology and Globalization

SELF-CHECK QUIZZES Lesson 1 Interactive Self-Check Quiz • Lesson 2 Interactive Self-Check Quiz • Lesson 3 Interactive Self-Check Quiz

CHAPTER **31**
America's Challenges for a New Century... 691

There's More Online . . .

BIOGRAPHIES Ralph Nader (1934–) • Nancy Pelosi (1940–) •
George W. Bush (1946–) • Al Gore (1948–) • Condoleezza
Rice (1954–)

CHARTS/GRAPHS Unemployment • S & P 500 Stock Index •
GDP

GRAPHIC NOVEL "Life of Chad"

IMAGES Desolate Iraq • Patriotic Rally • PATRIOT Act
Protests • Hurricane Katrina

MAPS Presidential Election of 2000 • Presidential Election
of 2008

SLIDE SHOW BP Oil Spill

TIME LINE The Global War on Terror

VIDEOS Bush's Global Challenges • Focusing on Afghanistan
and Iraq • Domestic Challenges • The Obama Presidency

SELF-CHECK QUIZZES Lesson 1 Interactive Self-Check Quiz •
Lesson 2 Interactive Self-Check Quiz • Lesson 3 Interactive
Self-Check Quiz • Lesson 4 Interactive Self-Check Quiz

PHOTO: Pete Souza/Obama Transition Team/Handout/Corbis News/CORBIS

MAPS, CHARTS, AND GRAPHS

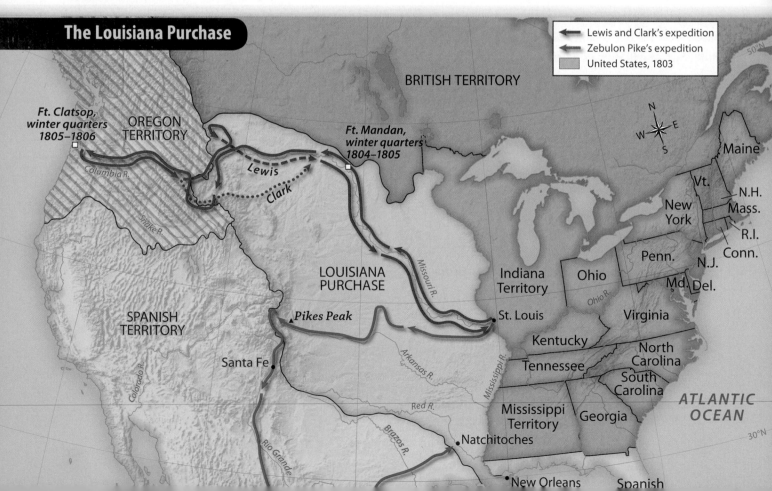

MAPS, CHARTS, AND GRAPHS

MAPS, CHARTS, AND GRAPHS

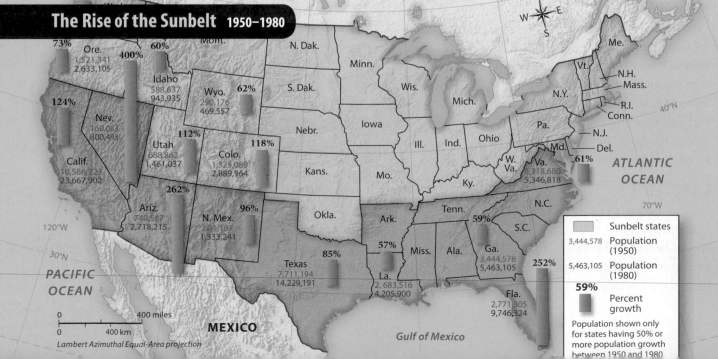

The Rise of the Sunbelt 1950–1980

Ore. 73% 1,521,341 2,633,105
400% 60% Mont.
N. Dak.
Minn.
Me.
Idaho 588,637 943,935
Wyo. 290,176 469,557 62%
S. Dak.
Wis.
Mich.
Vt.
N.H.
Mass.
N.Y.
R.I.
Conn.
124% Nev. 160,083 800,493
Utah 688,862 1,461,037 112%
Colo. 1,325,089 2,889,964 118%
Nebr.
Iowa
Ill. Ind. Ohio
Pa.
N.J.
Md. Del.
W. Va. Va. 3,318,680 5,346,818 61%
ATLANTIC OCEAN
Calif. 10,586,223 23,667,902
Kans.
Mo.
Ky.
Ariz. 749,587 2,718,215 262%
N. Mex. 681,187 1,333,241 96%
Okla.
Ark.
Tenn. 59%
N.C.
S.C.
Texas 7,711,194 14,229,191 85%
Miss. Ala.
Ga. 3,444,578 5,463,105 252%
La. 2,683,516 4,205,900 57%
Fla. 2,771,305 9,746,324

PACIFIC OCEAN

0 ___ 400 miles
0 ___ 400 km
Lambert Azimuthal Equal-Area projection

MEXICO

Gulf of Mexico

Legend:
- Sunbelt states
- 3,444,578 Population (1950)
- 5,463,105 Population (1980)
- 59% Percent growth

Population shown only for states having 50% or more population growth between 1950 and 1980

PRIMARY SOURCES AND POLITICAL CARTOONS

SCAVENGER HUNT

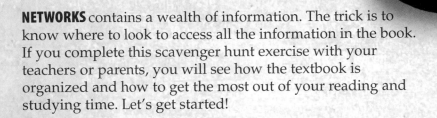

NETWORKS contains a wealth of information. The trick is to know where to look to access all the information in the book. If you complete this scavenger hunt exercise with your teachers or parents, you will see how the textbook is organized and how to get the most out of your reading and studying time. Let's get started!

1 How many chapters and how many lessons are in this book?

2 Where do you find the glossary and the index? What is the difference between them?

3 Where can you find primary sources in the textbook?

4 If you want to quickly find all the maps, charts, and graphs about World War I, where do you look?

5 How can you find information about civil rights leader Dr. Martin Luther King, Jr.?

6 Where can you find a graphic organizer that lists the causes of the Great Depression discussed in Chapter 18?

7 Where and how do you find the content vocabulary for Chapter 24, Lesson 3?

8 What are the online resources listed for Chapter 21, Lesson 4?

9 You want to read the Declaration of Independence. How will you find it?

10 What time period does Chapter 17 cover? How do you know?

Colonizing America

Prehistory to 1754

ESSENTIAL QUESTIONS • *How did the movement of people, goods, and ideas cause social changes over time?* • *How were the colonies affected by global conflicts?* • *How did the colonies develop identities independent of Great Britain?*

networks

There's More Online about the European colonization of the Americas.

CHAPTER 1

Lesson 1
North America Before Columbus

Lesson 2
Europe Begins to Explore

Lesson 3
Founding the Thirteen Colonies

Lesson 4
Population and Economy

Lesson 5
Governance and New Ideas

The Story Matters...

Scientists believe the first people in the Americas arrived from Asia more than 10,000 years ago. Their descendants spread across the Americas, developing distinct cultures. Centuries later, Europeans began exploring overseas, hoping to find a new route to Asia.

In 1492 Queen Isabella and King Ferdinand of Spain financed a voyage by Christopher Columbus. That fateful journey initiated the European colonization of North America and South America.

◄ The marriage of Queen Isabella of Castile (left) and King Ferdinand of Aragon led to the unification of Spain. Their support for Columbus's voyages then gave Spain the basis to claim a vast new empire in the Americas.

PHOTO: The Granger Collection, New York

1

Place and Time: Colonizing America 1492–1707

The arrival of the Europeans in the Americas set in motion a series of complex interactions between peoples and environments. These interactions, called the Columbian Exchange, permanently altered the world's ecosystem and changed nearly every culture around the world. The effects of this exchange still shape the world today.

Step Into the Place

Read the quotes and look at the information presented on the map.

 How did the arrival of Europeans affect both Native American and European cultures?

PRIMARY SOURCE

❝This land is very populous, and full of inhabitants, and of numberless rivers, [and] animals; few [of which] resemble ours . . . they have no horses nor mules . . . nor any kind of sheep or oxen: but so numerous are the other animals which they have. . . . The soil is very pleasant and fruitful. . . . The fruits are so many that they are numberless and entirely different from ours.❞

—Amerigo Vespucci, from *Account of His First Voyage*, 1497

PRIMARY SOURCE

❝While the Spaniards were in Tlaxcala, a great plague broke out here in Tenochtitlan. . . . Sores erupted on our faces, our breasts, our bellies; we were covered with agonizing sores from head to foot. The illness was so dreadful that no one could walk or move.

A great many died from this plague, and many others died of hunger. They could not get up to search for food, and everyone else was too sick to care for them, so they starved to death in their beds.❞

—an Aztec observer, from *The Broken Spears: The Aztec Account of the Conquest of Mexico*, 1959

Horses allowed some Native Americans to become nomadic hunters.

Horses

Peppers

Step Into the Time

Choose an event from the time line and write a paragraph predicting the general social, political, or economic consequences that event might have on the European colonization of the Americas.

UNITED STATES

1492 Christopher Columbus reaches the Americas

1519 Hernán Cortés begins Spanish invasion of the Aztec Empire

1539 Hernando de Soto lands in Florida to begin Spain's exploration of the Southeast

1500

WORLD

1550

1498 Vasco da Gama sails around Africa to India, locating a water route to Asia from Europe

1517 Martin Luther nails his Ninety-Five Theses to the church door in Wittenberg, starting the Protestant Reformation

1520 Ferdinand Magellan sails into Pacific Ocean

1534 Henry VIII breaks with the Catholic Church

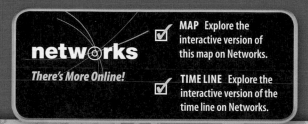

networks
There's More Online!

☑ **MAP** Explore the interactive version of this map on Networks.

☑ **TIME LINE** Explore the interactive version of the time line on Networks.

The Columbian Exchange

The Columbian Exchange Native Americans introduced Europeans to new crops such as corn, cocoa, and tomatoes. Europeans introduced Native Americans to various grains, fruits, and other foods. Europeans also became familiar with other Native American inventions such as canoes, moccasins, and toboggans. When Europeans arrived in North America, however, they brought with them infectious diseases to which the Native Americans had no resistance.

Pigs

European diseases decimated Native American populations.

Disease

Citrus Fruit

Grains

Sugarcane planters brought millions of enslaved Africans to the Americas.

Sugarcane

Cattle

Honeybees

Bananas

Coffee

Potatoes increased northern Europe's population and changed Ireland's diet.

Potatoes

Corn

Beans

Squash and Pumpkins

Peanuts improved people's health in West Africa by providing protein.

Peanuts

Cocoa

Tobacco use killed tens of millions in only a few hundred years.

Disease

Tobacco

Tomatoes became popular in Europe and greatly changed the cuisine of Italy.

Tomatoes

1607 The English found Jamestown in Virginia

1619 First Africans brought to Virginia via Dutch traders

1630 Puritans leave Europe to establish Massachusetts Bay Colony

1660 British use Navigation Acts to regulate American colonial trade

1600

1650

1700

1588 The English navy defeats the Spanish Armada

1642 English Civil War begins

1688 Glorious Revolution establishes limited monarchy in England

1707 Act of Union creates Great Britain

netw☉rks
There's More Online!

- ☑ **BIOGRAPHY** Dekanawida
- ☑ **IMAGES** Maya Temple
- ☑ **IMAGES** Tepee Village
- ☑ **VIDEO** North America Before Columbus
- ☑ **INTERACTIVE SELF-CHECK QUIZ**

Reading **HELP**DESK

Content Vocabulary

- **agricultural revolution**
- **tribute**
- **kiva**
- **pueblo**

Academic Vocabulary

- **decline**   • **eventually**
- **technology**

TAKING NOTES: *Categorizing*

ACTIVITY As you read, complete a chart similar to the one below by filling in the names of the Native American cultures that lived in each region.

Region	Groups
Mesoamerica	
West	
Southeast	
Northeast	

LESSON 1
North America Before Columbus

ESSENTIAL QUESTIONS • *How did the movement of people, goods, and ideas cause social changes over time?* • *How were the colonies affected by global conflicts?* • *How did the colonies develop identities independent of Great Britain?*

IT MATTERS BECAUSE
Before 1492, the peoples of the Americas had almost no contact with the rest of the world. The societies and languages that developed varied widely. In North America, some Native Americans lived as nomadic hunters, while others lived in large, complex cities.

Mesoamerican Cultures

GUIDING QUESTION *What were the most important characteristics of the Mesoamerican cultures?*

Many Native American origin stories tell how their people arrived in the world through the intervention of animals or from nature. For example, Native Americans of the Northwest Coast emerged from a clam that appeared on the beach. The Kiowa passed into the world through a hollow log. While the particulars of these stories are different, there is a common theme of emerging from the natural world or being connected to the environment.

Scientists use other methods to investigate these matters, and while no one knows for certain when the first people arrived in the Americas, current scientific evidence suggests that the first humans arrived between 15,000 and 30,000 years ago. Based on DNA tests and other evidence, some scientists think the earliest Americans came from northeast Asia. Some may have arrived during the last Ice Age, when much of the Earth's water became frozen and created a land bridge between Alaska and Asia along the Bering Strait. Along this stretch of land, known as Beringia, nomadic hunters may have crossed to the Americas as they followed large prey, such as the wooly mammoth, antelope, and caribou. These people did not come all at once, and some may have come by boat.

Over time, the descendants of these early people spread southward and eastward across the Americas. Between 7,500 and 9,500 years ago, some early Americans learned to plant and raise crops. This **agricultural revolution** began in Mesoamerica, the region that today includes central and southern Mexico and Central America. The agricultural revolution made possible the rise of Mesoamerica's first civilizations.

agricultural revolution period when early peoples learned how to plant and raise crops

The Olmec

Anthropologists think the first people to develop a civilization in Mesoamerica were the Olmec. Olmec culture emerged between 1500 B.C. and 1200 B.C., near where Veracruz, Mexico, is located today. The Olmec developed a sophisticated society with large villages, temple complexes, and pyramids.

Olmec ideas spread throughout Mesoamerica, influencing other peoples. One of these peoples constructed the first large city in the Americas, called Teotihuacán (TAY•oh•TEE•wah•KAHN), about 30 miles northeast of where Mexico City is today. The people of Teotihuacán built up a trade network which influenced the development of Mesoamerica. The city lasted from about 300 B.C. to about A.D. 650.

At the top, an Aztec family sits in their home in the front of the hearth, which was sacred to them. Below, an Aztec cooks over a fire.

▶ CRITICAL THINKING
Interpreting Significance Why would the hearth be sacred to the Aztec?

The Maya

Around A.D. 200, the Maya civilization emerged in the Yucatán Peninsula and expanded into what is now Central America and southern Mexico. The Maya had a talent for engineering and mathematics. They developed complex and accurate calendars linked to the positions of the stars. They also built temple pyramids. These pyramids formed the centerpieces of Maya cities, such as Tikal and Chichén Itzá. Marvels of engineering, some pyramids were 200 feet (61 m) high. At the top of each pyramid was a temple where priests performed ceremonies dedicated to the many Maya gods.

Although trade and a common culture linked the Maya, they were not unified. Each city-state controlled its own territory. Because of the fragmented nature of their society, the different cities frequently went to war.

The Maya continued to thrive until the A.D. 900s, when they abandoned their cities in the Yucatán for unknown reasons. Some anthropologists believe Maya farmers may have exhausted the region's soil. This in turn would have led to famine, riots, and the collapse of the cities. Others believe that invaders from the north devastated the region. Maya cities in what is today Guatemala flourished for several more centuries, although by the 1500s they, too, were in **decline.**

decline a change to a lower state or level

The Toltec and the Aztec

North of the Maya civilization, the Toltec people built a large city called Tula. Master architects, the Toltec built large pyramids and huge palaces with pillared halls. They were among the first American peoples to use gold and copper in art and jewelry.

Around A.D. 1150, Tula fell to invaders from the north, known as the Chichimec. One group of Chichimec, called the Mexica, founded the city of Tenochtitlán (tay•NAWCH•teet•LAHN) around 1325 on the site of what is today Mexico City. The Mexica took the name *Aztec* for themselves from the name of their original homeland, Aztlán. Aztlán is thought to have been located in the American Southwest.

The Aztec created an empire by conquering neighboring cities. Using their military power, they controlled trade in the region and demanded **tribute,** or payment, from the cities they conquered. They also brought some of the people they conquered to Tenochtitlán to sacrifice in their religious ceremonies. By the 1500s, an estimated 5 million people were living under Aztec rule.

tribute a payment by one ruler or nation to another in acknowledgment of submission or as the price of protection

✓ PROGRESS CHECK

Identifying What structures did both the Maya and the Olmec build?

Western Cultures

GUIDING QUESTION *How did Native American cultures adapt their way of life to the geographic and climatic conditions of the regions they settled in?*

technology the manner of accomplishing a task using specialized methods, processes, or knowledge

North of Mesoamerica, other peoples developed their own cultures. Many anthropologists think that agricultural **technology** spread from Mesoamerica into the American Southwest and up the Mississippi River. There, it transformed many hunter-gatherer societies—who obtained food by hunting, fishing, and collecting—into farming societies.

The Hohokam

By A.D. 700, in what is now south-central Arizona, a group called the Hohokam was developing a large system of irrigation canals. The Hohokam used the Gila and Salt Rivers as their water supply. Their canals carried water for miles to their farms.

The Hohokam grew corn, cotton, beans, and squash. They also made decorative red-on-buff-colored pottery and turquoise pendants, and used cactus juice to etch shells. Hohokam culture flourished for more than 1,000 years, but in the 1300s, they began to abandon their irrigation systems, likely due to floods and increased competition for farmland. By the 1500s, the Hohokam disappeared from the historical record.

The Anasazi

Descendants of the Anasazi, the Pueblo peoples of the Southwest built multistory complexes out of adobe.

▶ **CRITICAL THINKING**
Drawing Inferences How did their buildings reflect how the Pueblo peoples interacted with their environment?

Between A.D. 700 and A.D. 900, the people living in what is now called the Four Corners area—where Utah, Colorado, Arizona, and New Mexico now meet—developed a unique culture. We know these people by the name the Navajo gave them—*Anasazi*, or "ancient ones." In the harsh desert, the Anasazi accumulated water by building networks of basins and ditches to channel rain into stone-lined depressions.

PHOTO: The Granger Collection, New York

Native American Cultures c.1500

Legend:
- Pacific Coast
- Great Plains
- Southwest
- Northeast
- Mexico
- Mountains and plateau
- Southeast
- Subarctic
- **HOPI** Native American group
- *MAYA* Pre-1500 civilization

PACIFIC OCEAN

ATLANTIC OCEAN

Gulf of Mexico

0 — 400 miles
0 — 400 km
Lambert Azimuthal Equal-Area projection

GEOGRAPHY CONNECTION

Many Native American groups populated North America before the arrival of Europeans.

1. **THE WORLD IN SPATIAL TERMS** *In what locations are the greatest numbers of Native American cultures concentrated?*

2. **ENVIRONMENT AND SOCIETY** *Why are there fewer Native American cultures located in the southern half of the Mountains and plateau region?*

Between A.D. 850 and 1250, the Anasazi living in Chaco Canyon, in what is now northwest New Mexico, constructed multistory buildings of adobe and cut stone, with connecting passageways and circular ceremonial rooms called **kivas.** Spanish explorers called these structures **pueblos,** the Spanish word for "villages." These pueblos were built at junctions where streams of rainwater ran together. One pueblo, called Pueblo Bonito, had more than 600 rooms and probably housed at least 1,000 people.

✔ **PROGRESS CHECK**

Drawing Conclusions What enabled the transformation from hunter-gatherer societies to farming societies?

kiva circular ceremonial room built by the Anasazi

pueblo Spanish for "village"; term used by early Spanish explorers to denote large housing structures built by the Anasazi

The Cherokee established permanent settlements throughout the Southeast.

► **CRITICAL THINKING**

Drawing Conclusions Why did the Cherokee establish permanent settlements as opposed to temporary settlements?

Mississippian Culture and Its Descendants

GUIDING QUESTION *What were the distinctive features of Mississippian culture?*

Between A.D. 700 and A.D. 900, the Mississippian culture emerged. It began in the Mississippi River valley, where the rich soil of the floodplains was well suited to the intensive cultivation of maize and beans. The Mississippians were great builders of cities. One, named Cahokia by anthropologists, covered about 5 square miles (13 sq. km), contained more than 100 flat-topped pyramids and mounds, and was home to an estimated 16,000 people. The largest pyramid, named Monks Mound, was nearly 100 feet (30.5 m) high, had four levels, and covered about 17 acres (7 ha).

As it expanded across the American South, Mississippian culture led to the rise of at least four large cities with flat-topped mounds. These settlements were at what is now St. Louis, Missouri; Spiro, Oklahoma; Moundville, Alabama; and Etowah, Georgia.

Peoples of the Southeast

The population of Cahokia mysteriously declined around A.D. 1300. The city may have been attacked by other Native Americans, or its population may have become too large to support, resulting in famine and emigration. Another possibility is that the city was struck by an epidemic.

Many aspects of the Mississippian culture survived in the Southeast until the Europeans arrived. Most people lived in towns, with the buildings arranged around a central plaza. Women did most of the farming, while men hunted deer, bear, and wildfowl.

Of all the Mississippian cultural groups in the Southeast, the Cherokee were the largest. They were located in what is today western North Carolina, eastern Tennessee, and northeastern Georgia. About 20,000 Cherokee lived in some 60 towns when Europeans arrived there.

The Great Plains

When Europeans arrived, the people of the Great Plains were nomads, who had only recently abandoned farming. Prior to about 1500, the societies of the Great Plains had been shaped by Mississippian culture. The people of the region lived near rivers, where they could easily irrigate their fields of corn and fell trees to build their homes.

Around the year 1500, many people of the western Plains abandoned their villages and became nomads, possibly because of war or drought. These people's nomadic way of life centered around following and hunting migrating buffalo herds. However, some Native American groups in the eastern Plains, including the Pawnee, continued to farm, as well as hunt.

eventually at an unspecified time or day; in the end

Life for the Native Americans on the Great Plains changed dramatically after they began taming horses. The Spanish brought horses to North America in the 1500s. Over the next few centuries, as horses either escaped or were stolen, the animals spread northward, **eventually** reaching the Great Plains. There, Plains groups such as the Lakota Sioux encountered and mastered them. The Sioux soon became some of the world's greatest mounted hunters and warriors.

☑ **PROGRESS CHECK**

Analyzing How did life change for the people of the Great Plains after the Europeans arrived?

Northeastern Peoples

GUIDING QUESTION *What characteristics were common among the peoples of the Northeast?*

Almost a million square miles of woodlands lay east of the Mississippi River and south of the Great Lakes. Most of the peoples of the Northeast provided for themselves by combining hunting and fishing with farming. Deer meat regularly supplemented the corn, beans, and squash the people planted. To create more fields for farming, a method of cultivation often used was slash-and-burn agriculture, where areas of forest are burned and cleared for planting.

The Algonquian Peoples

Most peoples in the Northeast belonged to one of two language groups: those who spoke Algonquian languages and those who spoke Iroquoian languages. The Algonquian-speaking peoples included most of the groups living in the area known today as New England. Farther south, in what is today Virginia, lived the Algonquian-speaking peoples of the Powhatan Confederacy. Native Americans in New England and Virginia were among the first to encounter English settlers.

The Iroquois Confederacy

Stretching west from the Hudson River across what is today New York and southern Ontario and north to Georgian Bay, in Canada, lived the Iroquoian-speaking peoples. They included the Huron, Neutral, Erie, Wenro, Seneca, Cayuga, Onondaga, Oneida, and Mohawk. All the Iroquoian peoples had similar cultures. Extended families, or kinship groups, lived in longhouses in large towns, which they protected by building stockades. Iroquois men did the hunting, while women were responsible for planting and harvesting crops. Women also headed the kinship groups and selected the ruling councilmen.

War often erupted among the Iroquoians. Five of the nations—the Seneca, Cayuga, Onondaga, Oneida, and Mohawk—formed an alliance, probably sometime during the 1500s. According to Iroquoian tradition, Dekanawidah, a shaman or tribal elder, and Hiawatha, a chief of the Mohawk, founded the confederacy. The five nations agreed to the Great Binding Law, an oral constitution that defined how the alliance worked. This alliance was later called the Iroquois Confederacy.

☑ **PROGRESS CHECK**

Identifying Who were among the first to encounter English settlers?

The peoples living in the woodlands of the Northeast settled in permanent, well-defended communities.

▶ **CRITICAL THINKING**
Drawing Conclusions How did the Eastern Woodlands peoples use their resources efficiently?

PHOTO: The Granger Collection, New York

LESSON 1 REVIEW

Reviewing Vocabulary
1. *Describing* Describe the significance of: agricultural revolution, tribute, kiva, and pueblo.

Using Your Notes
2. *Categorizing* Using your notes, list the cultures found in the Northeast.

Answering the Guiding Questions
3. *Evaluating* What were the most important characteristics of the Mesoamerican cultures?

4. *Drawing Conclusions* How did Native American cultures adapt their way of life to the geographic and climatic conditions of the regions they settled in?

5. *Analyzing Information* What were the distinctive features of Mississippian culture?

6. *Making Generalizations* What characteristics were common among the peoples of the Northeast?

Writing Activity
7. EXPOSITORY Write an essay that introduces the reader to the major peoples in each region of what is today the United States. Be sure to describe the political and geographic issues facing each people prior to the European explorations of the fifteenth through the seventeenth centuries.

Reading HELPDESK

Content Vocabulary

• astrolabe
• caravel
• circumnavigate
• conquistador

Academic Vocabulary

• route   • labor
• acquire

TAKING NOTES: *Organizing*

ACTIVITY Complete a note-taking chart similar to the one below by filling in the outcome of each exploration listed.

Exploration	Outcome
Columbus	
Vespucci	
Cortés	
La Salle	

LESSON 2
Europe Begins to Explore

ESSENTIAL QUESTIONS • *How did the movement of people, goods, and ideas cause social changes over time?* • *How were the colonies affected by global conflicts?* • *How did the colonies develop identities independent of Great Britain?*

IT MATTERS BECAUSE
Scientific advances by Muslim scholars aided Europeans in making oceanic exploration possible and desirable. Without the technology to sail the ocean—and the desire to do so—European exploration of the Americas would not have begun in the fifteenth century.

European Explorations

GUIDING QUESTION *What were the political, religious, and economic changes that pushed Europeans to explore and colonize other parts of the world?*

For centuries, the Roman Empire dominated Europe, imposing a unified and stable social and political order. By A.D. 500, however, the Roman political and economic system had collapsed, disconnecting western Europe from the rest of the world. Without a central authority, the region experienced a decline in trade, and the political system became fragmented. Most people lived on manors or in villages ruled by local lords, who kept the peace only in the lands they controlled. This period, lasting from roughly A.D. 500 to A.D. 1500, is known as the Middle Ages.

Expanding Horizons

In 1095 Pope Urban II called for Christians to free their religion's holy places in the Middle East from Muslim control. The resulting expeditions, later called the Crusades, brought western Europeans into contact with the Arab civilization of the Middle East. This new cultural contact helped end the isolation of the Middle Ages. The Europeans began trading with the Arabs and buying luxury goods that Arab traders obtained from East Asia: spices, sugar, melons, tapestries, silk, and other items. As demand for East Asian goods increased, Italian city-states such as Venice, Pisa, and Genoa grew wealthy moving goods between the Middle East and western Europe. By 1200, Italian and Arab merchants controlled most of the trade in the eastern Mediterranean and charged high prices for the goods that

PHOTOS: (l to r)/Encyclopedia/CORBIS, The Granger Collection, New York, Ariadne Van Zandbergen/Lonely Planet Images/Getty Images, HIP/Art Resource, NY, E. Boyd Smith/Blue Lantern Studio/Corbis Art/CORBIS

western Europeans wanted. Yet the flow of goods from the East was a long, land-based **route** through Asia that was often unpredictable. Such uncertainty increased the need to find another way to acquire trade goods from the East.

By the 1300s, Europeans had a strong economic motive to begin exploring the world for a route to Asia that bypassed the Italian city-states and the Arab kingdoms. Yet western Europe did not have the wealth or technology to begin exploring. All that began to change as the rise of towns and the merchant class provided kings and queens a new source of wealth they could tax. They sought to protect trade routes and enforce trade laws and worked to establish a common currency within their kingdoms. Increasingly, rulers began to unify their kingdoms and create strong central governments. By the mid-1400s, four strong states—Portugal, Spain, England, and France—had emerged. Starting with Portugal in the early 1400s, all four began financing exploration in the hope of expanding their trade by finding a new route to Asia.

Scientific Advances

The political and economic changes that encouraged western Europeans to explore the world would not have mattered if they had lacked the technology necessary to launch their expeditions. In order to find a water route to Asia, western Europeans needed navigational instruments and ships capable of long-distance travel. Fortunately, at about the same time that the new, unified kingdoms were emerging in western Europe, European scholars rediscovered the works of ancient poets, philosophers, geographers, and mathematicians. They also read the teachings of Arab scholars. This explosion of learning was called the Renaissance.

By studying Arab texts, western Europeans **acquired** the knowledge of a key navigational instrument, the **astrolabe**—a device invented by the ancient Greeks and refined by Arab navigators. An astrolabe uses the position of the sun to determine direction, latitude, and local time. Europeans also acquired the compass from Arab traders. Invented in China, the compass reliably shows the direction of magnetic north.

Late in the 1400s, European shipwrights began to make technological advances to their ships. They outfitted ships with triangular-shaped lateen sails perfected by Arab traders. These sails made it possible to sail against the wind and used multiple masts with several smaller sails hoisted one above the other, which improved the ship's speed. They also moved the rudder from the side to the stern, making ships easier to steer and maneuver. All of these advances made a ship faster and easier to sail. In the 1400s, a Portuguese ship called the **caravel** incorporated many of these improvements.

Portuguese Exploration

Sailing their caravels, Portuguese explorers became the first Europeans to search for a sea route to Asia. Portugal's Prince Henry dispatched ships to explore Africa's west coast. In 1488 a Portuguese ship commanded by Bartholomeu Dias reached the southern tip of Africa. A decade later, four ships commanded by Vasco da Gama sailed from Portugal, rounded Africa, and reached the southwest coast of India. The long-sought water route to eastern Asia had been found.

✓ **PROGRESS CHECK**

Summarizing What texts were rediscovered during the Renaissance, and what impact did some of them have on navigation and exploration?

route an established or selected course of travel or action

acquire to get as one's own; to come into possession or control of

astrolabe a device used to determine direction, latitude, and local time

caravel sailing ship capable of long-distance exploration

The caravel was perfect for exploration. These small ships ranged in length from 70 to 90 feet (23 to 27 m). They were highly maneuverable and very fast. Their smaller size enabled them to sail along shallow coastlines and explore up rivers farther than larger ships.

▶ **CRITICAL THINKING**
Interpreting Significance How do you think caravels affected trade for European countries?

Mansa Musa ruled the empire of Mali during the early 1300s. His empire's wealth was based on the trading of gold and salt.

▶ **CRITICAL THINKING**
Identifying Central Issues How could control of the salt and gold trade lead to an increase in wealth for African rulers?

labor an action that produces a good or service

African Cultures

GUIDING QUESTION *How did trade influence the development of African empires?*

Three great empires arose in West Africa between the A.D. 400s and the 1400s. All three gained wealth and power by controlling the trade in gold and salt. Between the third and fifth centuries, Berber nomads began using camels to transport salt, gold, ivory, ostrich feathers, and furs from regions south of the Sahara to North Africa.

In the A.D. 400s, the empire of Ghana emerged. Located between the salt mines of the Sahara and the gold mines to the south, Ghana prospered by taxing trade goods. Ghana became a Muslim kingdom in the 1100s but frequent wars with the Muslims of the Sahara took their toll. Equally damaging was a decline in food production. Intensive cultivation had left Ghana's land exhausted and its farmers unable to feed its people. At the same time, new gold mines opened to the east. Trade routes to these mines bypassed Ghana, and by the early 1200s the empire had collapsed.

East of Ghana, the empire of Mali arose. Like Ghana, Mali built its wealth and power by controlling the salt and gold trade. Mali reached its peak in the 1300s. By that time, the opening of new gold mines had shifted the trade routes farther east and helped make the city of Timbuktu, now known as Tombouctou, a great center of trade and Muslim scholarship.

Along the Niger River, the empire of Songhai emerged. When Mali began to decline, the ruler of Songhai, Sonni Ali, seized Timbuktu in 1468. Songhai remained powerful until 1591, when Moroccan troops shattered its army.

As in other parts of the world, slavery existed in African society. Most of the people enslaved in African societies had been captured in war. Many African societies would either ransom captives back to their people or absorb them into their society. West African slavery began to change with the arrival of European and Arab traders, who exchanged goods for enslaved people.

Sugar growers from Spain and Portugal also sought enslaved Africans. In the 1300s and 1400s, Spain and Portugal established sugarcane plantations on the Canary and Madeira Islands, off the northwest coast of Africa. The climate and soil there were favorable for growing sugarcane, a crop that requires rigorous manual **labor.** Sugarcane must be chopped with heavy knives. Sugar growers brought in enslaved Africans to do the difficult work.

✓ **PROGRESS CHECK**

Analyzing Why did Europeans begin to seek the labor of enslaved Africans?

São Jorge da Mina (now Elmina Castle) in Ghana was built in 1482 by the Portuguese to control the gold trade and later became a depot for the slave trade.

Exploring America

GUIDING QUESTION *How did the desire for trade with Asia encourage the exploration of the Americas?*

By the 1400s, most educated Europeans knew that the world was round. On European maps of the time, only the Mediterranean, Europe, the Middle East, and Africa's northern coast were shown in any detail. At that time, Europeans rediscovered the works of Claudius Ptolemy, written in the A.D. 100s. His *Geography* became very influential. His basic system of lines of latitude and longitude is still used today.

European mariners also consulted the work of a twelfth-century Arab geographer named al-Idrīsī. By studying the maps of Ptolemy and al-Idrīsī, Western mariners obtained an idea of the geography of the eastern African coast and the Indian Ocean. Based on these sources, Italian navigator Christopher Columbus believed it was possible to **circumnavigate** the Earth to find a trade route to Asia by sailing west. He predicted that "the end of Spain and the beginning of India are not far apart." Beginning in 1484, Columbus sought financial backing from the king of Portugal to make a voyage. Portuguese scholars, however, determined that Columbus had greatly underestimated the distance to Asia. When the Portuguese navigator Bartholomeu Dias successfully rounded the southern tip of Africa in 1488, the Portuguese lost all interest in supporting Columbus's explorations.

circumnavigate to sail around

Spain Claims America

In 1492 Spain's King Ferdinand and Queen Isabella agreed to finance Columbus's venture. Columbus and his three ships—the *Niña,* the *Pinta,* and the *Santa María*—left Spain in August 1492. He sailed westward across the uncharted Atlantic Ocean until he reached the Bahamas in October. He then headed farther into the Caribbean, searching for gold. He found the islands of Cuba and Hispaniola.

In March 1493, Columbus made a triumphant return to Spain with gold, parrots, spices, and Native Americans. Ferdinand and Isabella were pleased with Columbus's findings, but it put them in conflict with Portugal, which had claimed control over the Atlantic route to Asia. To resolve the rivalry, the two nations appealed to the pope. In 1493 Pope Alexander VI established a line of demarcation, an imaginary line running down the middle of the Atlantic. Spain would control everything west of the line; Portugal would control everything to the east. In 1494 the Treaty of Tordesillas moved the line of demarcation to about 320 miles (515 km) west of the Cape Verde Islands. The treaty confirmed Portugal's right to control the route around Africa to India. It also recognized Spain's claim to most of the Americas.

Columbus sailed back across the Atlantic with 17 ships and more than 1,200 Spanish colonists, hoping to find more gold. He made two more trips, mapping part of the coastline of South America and Central America.

Naming America

In 1499 an Italian named Amerigo Vespucci repeated Columbus's attempt to sail west to Asia. Exploring the coast of South America, Vespucci assumed he had reached outermost Asia. In 1501 he made another voyage. After sailing along the coast of South America, he realized that this landmass could not be part of Asia. In 1507 a German mapmaker proposed that the new continent be named *America* for "Amerigo, the discoverer."

☑ **PROGRESS CHECK**

Identifying How was the conflict between Portugal and Spain resolved, and by whom?

Analyzing
PRIMARY SOURCES

Columbus's Views of Hispaniola

"Here there is only wanting a settlement and the order to the people to do what is required. For I, with the force I have under me, . . . could march over all these islands without opposition. . . . They have no arms, and are without warlike instincts; . . . and are so timid that a thousand would not stand before three of our men. So that they are good to be ordered about, to work and sow, and do all that may be necessary, and to build towns, . . . and to adopt our customs."

—from the journal of Christopher Columbus, December 16, 1492

DBQ *DRAWING INFERENCES*
What benefit to Spain did Columbus see in the native people of Hispaniola?

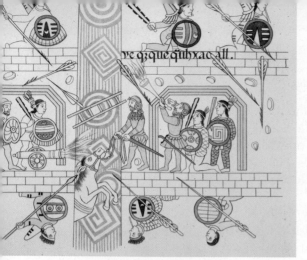

This image depicts the battle for Tenochtitlán between the Aztec and the Spanish in 1519.

▶ **CRITICAL THINKING**

Drawing Conclusions What does this image tell you about the Aztec view of the battle?

conquistador Spanish for "conqueror;" the men who led the expeditions to conquer the Americas

New Spain

GUIDING QUESTION *What was the impact of Spain's settlement in the Americas?*

In 1519 a Spaniard named Hernán Cortés sailed from Cuba to explore the Yucatán Peninsula. He brought 11 ships, 550 men, and 16 horses with him. From local rulers, Cortés learned that the Aztec had conquered many people in the Yucatán Peninsula and were at war with others, including the powerful Tlaxcalan. Cortés wanted the Tlaxcalan to join him against the Aztec. His army helped him gain their support. The local people had never seen horses before. Their foaming muzzles and glistening armor astonished them. Impressed, the Tlaxcalan agreed to ally with Cortés against the Aztec.

The Aztec emperor, Montezuma, tried to ambush the Spanish and the Tlaxacan at the city of Cholula. Warned in advance, the Spanish struck first, killing some 6,000 Cholulans. Believing Cortés was unstoppable, Montezuma then allowed the Spanish troops to enter Tenochtitlán peacefully.

Sitting on an island in the center of a lake, the Aztec city of Tenochtitlán impressed the Spanish. Larger than most European cities, Tenochtitlán had more than 200,000 residents and an elaborate system of canals.

Surrounded by thousands of Aztec, Cortés decided to take Montezuma hostage. Following orders from Cortés, Montezuma had statues of the Aztec gods replaced with Christian crosses and images of the Virgin Mary. In June 1520, the Aztec in Tenochtitlán rebelled. The battle raged for days before the Spanish retreated to Tlaxcala. At least 450 Spaniards and more than 4,000 Aztec died in the rebellion, including Montezuma himself. Meanwhile, smallpox erupted in the region, devastating the defenders of Tenochtitlán.

In 1521 Cortés returned with reinforcements and destroyed Tenochtitlán. On its ruins, the Spanish built Mexico City, which became the capital of the colony of New Spain. Cortés then sent several expeditions to conquer the rest of Central America. The men who led these expeditions became known as **conquistadors,** or "conquerors."

☑ **PROGRESS CHECK**

Identifying What impact did Cortés have on the Aztec?

French and Dutch Settlements

GUIDING QUESTION *What differences are seen among Spanish, French, and Dutch settlement patterns in the Americas?*

Both France and the Netherlands sent explorers to the Americas and claimed land for colonies. These European nations placed their own mark on the Americas with colonies aimed more at profit than settlement.

New France
In 1524 King Francis I of France sent Giovanni da Verrazano to find the Northwest Passage—the hoped-for northern route through North America to the Pacific Ocean. Verrazano explored the Atlantic Coast but found no sign of a passage. Ten years later, Jacques Cartier made three trips to North America, exploring and mapping the St. Lawrence River.

In 1602 King Henry IV of France authorized a group of French merchants to establish a colony in what is today Canada. The merchants hired Samuel de Champlain to help them. In 1608 Champlain founded Quebec, which became the capital of the colony of New France.

The company that founded New France wanted to make money from the fur trade, so they did not need settlers to clear the land and build farms. As a result, the colony grew slowly. Most of the fur traders preferred to make their homes among the Native Americans with whom they traded. In 1663 King Louis XIV made New France a royal colony and the French government began sending new settlers. By the 1670s, New France had nearly 7,000 colonists.

As their colony grew, the French continued to explore North America. In 1673 a fur trader named Louis Jolliet and a Jesuit priest named Jacques Marquette began searching for a waterway the Algonquian people called the "big river." The two men finally found it—the Mississippi. In 1682 René-Robert Cavelier de La Salle followed the Mississippi all the way to the Gulf of Mexico. He claimed the region for France and named the territory Louisiana in honor of King Louis XIV.

The first permanent French settlement in the region was Biloxi, founded in 1699. The French in Louisiana realized that the crops that could be grown in the South, such as sugar, rice, and indigo, required abundant labor. As a result, they began importing enslaved Africans to work on their plantations. The arrival of the French at the mouth of the Mississippi River convinced the Spanish in 1690 to build their first mission in East Texas, San Francisco de los Tejas. Spanish settlers arrived in 1716 to secure Spain's claim and block French expansion in the area.

New Netherland

In 1609 the Dutch East India Company hired English navigator Henry Hudson to locate a passage to Asia through North America, in order to benefit the company's spice trade. Instead, Hudson's search led him to the wide river that came to bear his name, located in what is now New York. The Dutch claimed the region, named it New Netherland, and established the settlement of New Amsterdam on Manhattan Island. The settlers depended on fur trading for their livelihood.

Like New France, the economy of New Netherland was focused on the fur trade and the population grew slowly. As late as 1646, New Netherland only had about 1,500 people.

✓ **PROGRESS CHECK**

Explaining Why do you think the French established settlements in Louisiana?

French explorer René-Robert Cavelier de La Salle was the first European to follow the Mississippi River to the Gulf of Mexico.

▶ **CRITICAL THINKING**
Interpreting Significance Why would La Salle's exploration of the Mississippi be so important to France?

LESSON 2 REVIEW

Reviewing Vocabulary
1. *Explaining* Explain the significance of: astrolabe, caravel, circumnavigate, and conquistador.

Using Your Notes
2. *Organizing* Review the notes you completed throughout the lesson to explain which explorer had the greatest impact on European exploration. Cite reasons for your answer.

Answering Guiding Questions
3. *Analyzing* What were the political, religious, and economic changes that pushed Europeans to explore and colonize other parts of the world?

4. *Assessing* How did trade influence the development of African empires?

5. *Making Connections* How did the desire for trade with Asia encourage the exploration of the Americas?

6. *Examining* What was the impact of Spain's settlement in the Americas?

7. *Contrasting* What differences are seen among Spanish, French, and Dutch settlement patterns in the Americas?

Writing Activity
8. **DESCRIPTIVE** Take on the role of an Aztec priest during the time of Cortés's arrival. Write a journal entry about what you see happening around you.

netw⊚rks

There's More Online!

- ☑ **BIOGRAPHY** Anne Hutchinson
- ☑ BIOGRAPHY James Oglethorpe
- ☑ **BIOGRAPHY** Roger Williams
- ☑ **IMAGE** Advertisement for Settlers
- ☑ **VIDEO** Founding the Thirteen Colonies
- ☑ **INTERACTIVE SELF-CHECK QUIZ**

Reading **HELP**DESK

Content Vocabulary

- **joint-stock company**
- **headright**
- **proprietary colony**

Academic Vocabulary

- **migration** • **grant**

TAKING NOTES: *Organizing*

ACTIVITY Complete a graphic organizer similar to the note-taking chart below by listing the English colonies in chronological order of their founding and the reasons for their founding.

English Colonies in America		
Colony	Founding Year	Reason for Founding

LESSON 3
Founding the Thirteen Colonies

ESSENTIAL QUESTIONS • *How did the movement of people, goods, and ideas cause social changes over time?* • *How were the colonies affected by global conflicts?* • *How did the colonies develop identities independent of Great Britain?*

IT MATTERS BECAUSE

English settlers who came to New England in the early 1600s formed the first successful English colonies in the Americas. These determined men and women endured hard winters in an unfamiliar land and set up democratic forms of government that helped establish a new nation.

England's First Colonies

GUIDING QUESTION *What led England to establish colonies in North America?*

The first English expedition to arrive in North America was led by Italian navigator John Cabot in 1497. For the next 80 years, the English made no effort to settle in America. Cabot had not found a sea route to Asia, nor had he found any riches to encourage **migration.** In the late 1500s, however, dramatic religious, economic, and political changes in England encouraged the founding of the first English colonies in North America.

The Protestant Reformation

At the time Cabot sailed to America, most of western Europe was Roman Catholic. This unity began to break apart in 1517, when a German monk named Martin Luther published a call for reform of the Catholic Church. Luther's call launched the Protestant Reformation.

In England the rebellion against Catholicism began in 1527, when Henry VIII asked the pope to annul his marriage to Catherine of Aragon. The pope refused. Infuriated, Henry broke with the Church and declared himself the head of England's church in 1534. The new church, the Anglican Church, was Protestant, but its organization and rituals retained many Catholic elements.

Some English people supported the new church, but others wanted more reform. Puritans wanted to "purify" the Anglican Church of any remaining Catholic elements. They also disapproved of the monarch having the power to appoint bishops to run the church. In their view, each congregation should elect its own leaders.

PHOTOS: (l to r) McGraw-Hill Companies, The Granger Collection, New York, Private Collection, DEA PICTURE LIBRARY/De Agostini Picture Library/Getty Images

The Puritan cause suffered a serious setback in 1603, when James I became king. Although King James was Protestant, he refused to tolerate any changes in the Anglican Church. His refusal to institute reforms eventually caused many Puritans to decide to leave England—some for America.

Economic Changes in England

During the 1500s, England's population was rising rapidly. Many English leaders concluded that colonies in America were necessary to provide land and work for England's rising number of unemployed.

During the same period, the wool cloth trade grew in importance. Eager to find new markets to sell their wool, merchants began organizing **joint-stock companies.** By joining together and issuing stock to investors, merchants were able to raise large amounts of money to fund major projects. They could also afford to trade with, and colonize, other parts of the world.

English colonization was not easy, nor was it always successful. Sir Walter Raleigh sent settlers to Roanoke Island, off the coast of what is now North Carolina, in 1585 and again in 1587. The first group returned to England after a difficult winter. The fate of the second group is a mystery. When English ships finally returned in 1590, the colonists had vanished.

The Chesapeake Colonies

In 1606 King James I **granted** a charter to the Virginia Company, giving its stockholders permission to start colonies in Virginia. The company sent three small ships and 144 men to Virginia in late 1606. After a difficult trip, the ships sailed into Chesapeake Bay in the spring of 1607. The 104 men who survived the trip founded a settlement on the James River, which they named Jamestown.

Early Troubles Winters were hard for the Jamestown colonists. In late 1607, Captain John Smith began bartering goods for food with the Powhatan Confederacy. This trade helped the colony survive. The winter of 1609–1610 was excruciatingly hard. By spring, only about 60 settlers were still alive. Fortunately, three English ships arrived bringing supplies, 150 more settlers, and the new governor, Lord De La Warr, who convinced them to stay.

Tobacco Saves the Colony The colony still had to find a way to make a profit. The solution was a cash crop: tobacco. In 1614 the colony sent its first tobacco shipment to England. It sold for a good price, and the colonists began planting large quantities of it.

In 1618 the Virginia Company granted the colonists the right to elect a lawmaking body. The elected representatives were called burgesses, and the assembly was called the House of Burgesses. The company also introduced the system of **headrights.** Settlers who paid their own passage to Virginia received 50 acres of land. Settlers also received 50 acres of land for each family member over 15 years of age and each servant they brought to Virginia.

In 1619 the first Africans were brought to Virginia. A Dutch slave ship stopped to trade for supplies, and the Jamestown settlers purchased 20 African men as "Christian servants," not slaves. Within a few years, however, enslaved Africans were being brought to the colony.

By 1622, about 4,500 settlers had arrived in Virginia. Alarmed, Native Americans attacked Jamestown in March 1622. More than 300 settlers were killed. An English court blamed the Virginia Company and revoked its charter. Virginia became a royal colony with a governor appointed by the king.

Maryland Is Founded The persecution of his fellow Catholics convinced Englishman George Calvert, who held the title Lord Baltimore, to found a colony where they could practice their religion freely. After Calvert's death in 1632, King Charles granted Calvert's son a large area of land northeast of Virginia. The new colony was named Maryland.

Maryland was a **proprietary colony.** The proprietor, or owner, had almost unlimited authority over the colony, except that he could do nothing that was contrary to English law. Although founded as a Catholic refuge, most of Maryland's settlers were Protestant. To reduce friction between the two groups, the colonial assembly passed the Toleration Act in 1649. This act mandated religious toleration for all Christians but made denying the divinity of Jesus a crime punishable by death.

proprietary colony
a colony owned by an individual

☑ **PROGRESS CHECK**

Explaining What economic reasons prompted the English to establish colonies?

Pilgrims and Puritans

GUIDING QUESTION *How did the English colonies organize themselves, and what were the colonists' early goals?*

In England, a group of Puritans called Separatists concluded that the Anglican Church was too corrupt to be reformed. They formed their own congregations, and in 1608 one group fled to the Netherlands to escape persecution. These Separatists, later known as Pilgrims, sailed to America in 1620.

Plymouth Colony

Before crossing the Atlantic, the Pilgrims returned to England, where they joined other emigrants aboard a ship called the *Mayflower*. On September 16, 1620, 102 passengers set sail for Virginia. In November, well off course, they reached the Cape Cod area and finally came ashore near what is today Plymouth, Massachusetts. While still aboard the ship, 41 colonists signed the Mayflower Compact, a written framework of government.

PRIMARY SOURCE

❝We whose names are underwritten . . . having undertaken, for the glory of God, and advancement of the Christian faith, and honour of our king and country, a voyage to plant the first colony in the northern parts of Virginia; do by these presents solemnly and mutually in the presence of God, and one another, covenant and combine our selves together into a civil body politick, for our better ordering and preservation and furtherance of the ends aforesaid; and by virtue hereof to enact, constitute, and frame such just and equal laws, ordinances, acts, constitutions, and offices, from time to time, as shall be thought most meet and convenient for the general good of the colony, unto which we promise all due submission and obedience.❞
—from the Mayflower Compact, 1620

After constructing a "common house," the settlers built modest homes. Soon, however, a plague swept through the colony, sparing only about 50 settlers. The surviving Pilgrims might have perished had it not been for Squanto, a Wampanoag man who helped them grow corn and showed them where to fish. The following autumn, the Pilgrims joined with the Wampanoag in a three-day festival to celebrate the harvest and give thanks to God. This celebration later became the basis for the Thanksgiving holiday.

Massachusetts Bay Colony

In 1625 Charles I took the throne, and persecution of the Puritans increased. At the same time, a depression struck England's wool industry. The depression caused high unemployment, particularly in counties where large numbers of Puritans lived.

BIOGRAPHY

Squanto (1580?–1622)

In 1621 Squanto was brought to the Pilgrim settlement in Plymouth, and soon became a member of the Plymouth Colony. In addition to serving as an interpreter and a guide, Squanto helped the English settlers by advising them on planting crops and showing them good places to go fishing.

▶ **CRITICAL THINKING**
Interpreting Significance Why was Squanto such an asset to the English settlers?

PHOTO: The Granger Collection, New York

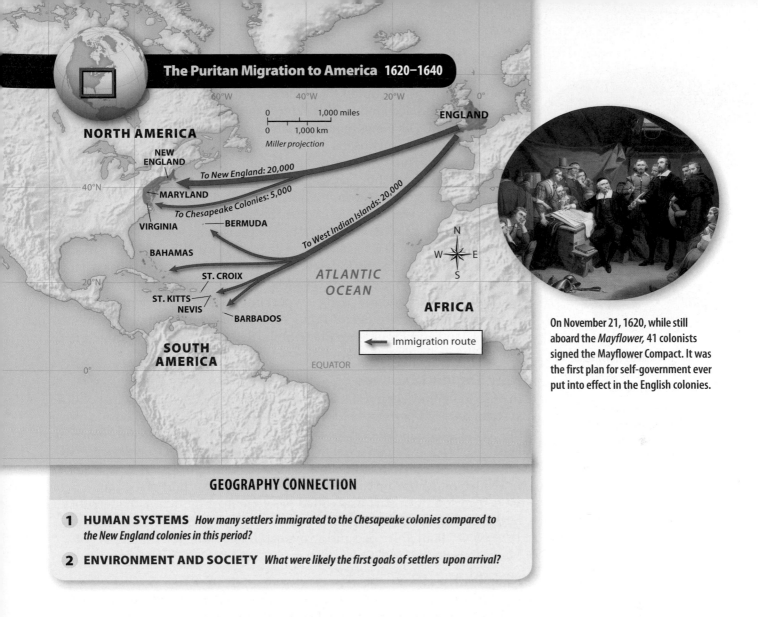

The Puritan Migration to America 1620–1640

NORTH AMERICA

NEW ENGLAND

To New England: 20,000

MARYLAND

To Chesapeake Colonies: 5,000

VIRGINIA

BERMUDA

BAHAMAS

To West Indian Islands: 20,000

ST. CROIX

ST. KITTS
NEVIS

BARBADOS

SOUTH
AMERICA

ATLANTIC
OCEAN

ENGLAND

AFRICA

EQUATOR

Miller projection

1,000 miles
1,000 km

← Immigration route

On November 21, 1620, while still aboard the *Mayflower,* 41 colonists signed the Mayflower Compact. It was the first plan for self-government ever put into effect in the English colonies.

GEOGRAPHY CONNECTION

1. **HUMAN SYSTEMS** *How many settlers immigrated to the Chesapeake colonies compared to the New England colonies in this period?*

2. **ENVIRONMENT AND SOCIETY** *What were likely the first goals of settlers upon arrival?*

As he watched his fellow Puritans suffering both religious and economic hardships, John Winthrop grew concerned. Winthrop and several other wealthy Puritans were stockholders in the Massachusetts Bay Company. The company had already received a charter from King Charles to create a colony in New England, so Winthrop decided to turn his business investment into a refuge for Puritans in America.

Other Puritans embraced the idea, and in 1630, 11 ships carrying the first main group of settlers set sail. En route, in a sermon titled "A Model of Christian Charity," Winthrop preached that the new colony should be an example to the world.

The colony of Massachusetts Bay grew quickly. As conditions in England worsened, more people began to leave in what was later called the Great Migration. By 1643, an estimated 20,000 settlers had arrived in New England.

The charter of the Massachusetts Bay Company defined the new colony's government and established a General Court, which named John Winthrop as the first governor. Puritans kept the governance of church and state separate. They did not tolerate the expression of different religious ideas, however. Heretics—people who disagree with established religious beliefs—were routinely banished. Eventually, Puritan intolerance sparked conflicts that led to the founding of other colonies.

William Penn called Pennsylvania a "holy experiment" because it allowed religious freedom.

▶ **CRITICAL THINKING**
Predicting Consequences How could the religious diversity of Pennsylvania lead it to become a place of greater tolerance?

Rhode Island and Dissent

In 1631 a minister named Roger Williams arrived in Massachusetts. Williams believed Puritans corrupted themselves by staying within the Anglican Church. He also declared that the king had no right to give away Native American land. His views angered many people.

In 1635 the Massachusetts General Court ordered him to be deported back to England, but Williams escaped south with a few followers. He then purchased land from the Narragansett and founded the town of Providence in 1636. The town's government had no authority over religious matters. Religious beliefs were tolerated rather than suppressed.

A year later, a Puritan named Anne Hutchinson questioned the authority of several ministers. The General Court charged her with heresy and banished her. Hutchinson and a few followers headed south and settled near what is now Portsmouth, Rhode Island. Massachusetts later banished other dissenters, who headed south and founded Newport in 1639 and Warwick in 1643. These towns joined Portsmouth and Providence to become the single colony of Rhode Island and Providence Plantations. Religious freedom became a key part of the new colony's charter.

New England Expands

In 1636 Reverend Thomas Hooker, frustrated by the Massachusetts political system, received permission from the Massachusetts General Court to move his congregation to the Connecticut River valley. They founded the town of Hartford. Hooker helped write the Fundamental Orders of Connecticut. This constitution, adopted in 1639, allowed all adult men to vote.

Much of the territory north of Massachusetts was part of a grant to two men. The southern part was called New Hampshire, while the territory farther north was called Maine. Massachusetts claimed them both, but in 1679 New Hampshire became a royal colony. Maine remained part of Massachusetts until 1820.

King Philip's War

After a 1637 war between the English and the Pequot of New England, relative peace ensued for a few decades through trade. Tensions renewed in the 1670s as the fur trade declined and as colonial governments demanded that Native Americans follow English law and customs. In 1675 Plymouth Colony arrested, tried, and executed three Wampanoag men for murder. This act touched off what came to be called King Philip's War, named after the Wampanoag leader, Metacomet, whom the settlers called King Philip. Colonists killed Metacomet in 1676 and then mounted his head on a pike and paraded it through their settlements. By the time the war ended in 1678, few Native Americans were left in New England.

☑ **PROGRESS CHECK**

Summarizing Summarize the goals that John Winthrop and Roger Williams had for their colonies.

England's Civil War and New Colonies

GUIDING QUESTION *How were the English colonies affected by events occurring in Europe?*

The English Civil War arose from a power struggle between King Charles I and Parliament. In 1642 the king sent troops to arrest Puritan leaders who dominated the governing body. Parliament responded with its own army. Battles between the king's troops and Parliament's troops resulted in the king's capture and beheading in 1649. The leader of Parliament's troops,

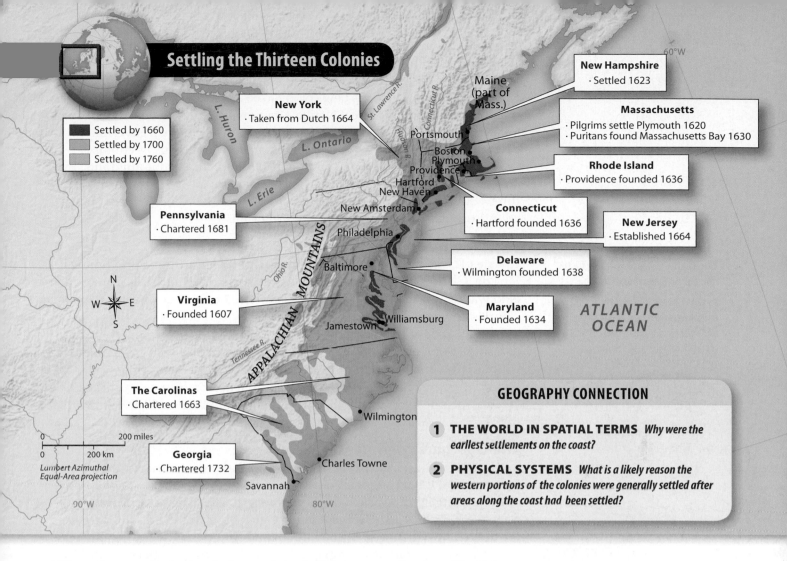

Settling the Thirteen Colonies

Settled by 1660
Settled by 1700
Settled by 1760

New York
· Taken from Dutch 1664

New Hampshire
· Settled 1623

Massachusetts
· Pilgrims settle Plymouth 1620
· Puritans found Massachusetts Bay 1630

Rhode Island
· Providence founded 1636

Connecticut
· Hartford founded 1636

New Jersey
· Established 1664

Pennsylvania
· Chartered 1681

Delaware
· Wilmington founded 1638

Virginia
· Founded 1607

Maryland
· Founded 1634

The Carolinas
· Chartered 1663

Georgia
· Chartered 1732

Maine (part of Mass.)
Portsmouth
Boston
Plymouth
Providence
Hartford
New Haven
New Amsterdam
Philadelphia
Baltimore
Williamsburg
Jamestown
Wilmington
Charles Towne
Savannah

L. Huron
L. Ontario
L. Erie
St. Lawrence R.
Connecticut R.
Hudson R.
Ohio R.
Tennessee R.
APPALACHIAN MOUNTAINS
ATLANTIC OCEAN

N W E S

0   200 miles
0   200 km
Lambert Azimuthal Equal-Area projection

90°W   80°W   60°W

GEOGRAPHY CONNECTION

1 **THE WORLD IN SPATIAL TERMS** *Why were the earliest settlements on the coast?*

2 **PHYSICAL SYSTEMS** *What is a likely reason the western portions of the colonies were generally settled after areas along the coast had been settled?*

Oliver Cromwell, then ruled as a virtual dictator over the new English Commonwealth. After Cromwell died in 1658 and his son unsuccessfully tried to rule in his place, Parliament invited King Charles's son, Charles II, to take the throne. With the monarchy restored in 1660, the English government began backing a new round of colonization in America.

New York and New Jersey

The Dutch colony of New Netherland grew slowly during the early 1600s. To aid the colony's growth, the Dutch allowed anyone to buy land. By 1664, New Netherland had more than 10,000 people, with immigrants from the Netherlands, Britain, Scandinavia, Germany, and France.

England and the Netherlands were commercial rivals. In 1664, King Charles II successfully took New Netherland from the Dutch and granted the land to his brother, James, the Duke of York. James renamed the colony New York. He also received and granted to others a large parcel of land between Delaware Bay and the Connecticut River, naming it New Jersey. To attract settlers, the New Jersey colony offered generous land grants, religious freedom, and the right to have a legislative assembly.

Pennsylvania and Delaware

The origins of the colony of Pennsylvania lay in a persecuted religious group and a large unpaid debt. The religious group was the Society of Friends, also known as the Quakers. William Penn was a member of the Quakers. The Quakers saw no need for ministers and believed in religious toleration.

They also believed in pacifism, or opposition to war. Many people viewed these as radical beliefs. In 1681, to settle the debt owed to William Penn's father, Charles II granted Penn a large tract of land between New York and Maryland. Penn wanted his new colony to be a place of political and religious freedom. He also tried to treat Native Americans fairly. Penn named the capital *Philadelphia,* Greek for "city of brotherly love." The colony's government provided for an elected assembly and guaranteed religious freedom.

Greater religious freedom and available land attracted immigrants. By 1684, Pennsylvania had more than 7,000 residents. In 1682 Penn acquired three counties south of Pennsylvania from the Duke of York. These "lower counties" later became the colony of Delaware.

The Carolinas

Charles II was also interested in the land between Virginia and Spanish Florida. Charles awarded much of this territory to eight friends in 1663. The land was named *Carolina*—Latin for "Charles." The first settlement was named Charles Towne. Although Carolina was not divided into two distinct colonies until 1729, it developed as two separate regions. North Carolina was home to a small population of farmers that grew tobacco as a cash crop. Colonists in South Carolina hoped to cultivate sugarcane, but it did not grow well there. Instead they exported deerskins obtained from nearby Native Americans. The colonists also developed a profitable trade shipping enslaved Native Americans to the West Indies.

The Georgia Experiment

In the 1720s, James Oglethorpe, a member of Parliament, was appalled to find that many of the imprisoned people in England were debtors, not strictly criminals. Oglethorpe asked the king for a colony where poor people could start over. In 1732 King George II made Oglethorpe and 19 others the trustees for the territory between the Savannah and Altamaha Rivers. Oglethorpe named the new colony Georgia, in honor of the king. Settlers arrived in 1733, and in 1752 Georgia became a royal colony.

By 1775, roughly 2.5 million people lived in England's thirteen American colonies. Despite the stumbling starts in Roanoke and Jamestown, the English had succeeded in building a large and prosperous society on the east coast of North America.

✓ **PROGRESS CHECK**

Identifying Cause and Effect How did powerful people in Europe affect the settlement of the Carolinas and Georgia?

King Charles II was responsible for the founding of several colonies.

▶ **CRITICAL THINKING**
Drawing Inferences What do you think was King Charles's goal in helping establish colonies in North America?

LESSON 3 REVIEW

Reviewing Vocabulary

1. *Explaining* Explain the significance of: joint-stock company, grant, headright, and proprietary colony.

Using Your Notes

2. *Comparing and Contrasting* Review the notes you completed through the lesson to compare and contrast the various colonists' motives.

Answering the Guiding Questions

3. *Determining Cause and Effect* What led England to establish colonies in North America?

4. *Describing* How did the English colonies organize themselves, and what were the colonists' early goals?

5. *Making Connections* How were the English colonies affected by events occurring in Europe?

Writing Activity

6. **EXPOSITORY** Write an essay explaining the ways in which the following people helped the colonies develop identities independent of Great Britain: Captain John Smith, George Calvert, John Winthrop, Roger Williams, Anne Hutchinson, William Penn, James Oglethorpe.

networks

There's More Online!

- ☑ **BIOGRAPHY** Nathaniel Bacon
- ☑ **MAP** Ethnic Diversity
- ☑ **MAP** New England and Middle Colonies
- ☑ **MAP** Southern Colonies
- ☑ **MAP** Triangular Trade
- ☑ **MAP** Typical New England Town
- ☑ **VIDEO** Population and Economy
- ☑ **INTERACTIVE SELF-CHECK QUIZ**

Reading **HELP**DESK

Content Vocabulary

- **town meeting**
- **indentured servant**
- **triangular trade**

Academic Vocabulary

- **distinct** • **reliable**

TAKING NOTES: *Comparing*

ACTIVITY Use the following graphic organizer to compare the economies of the New England, Middle, and Southern Colonies.

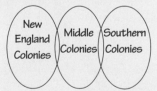

New England Colonies | Middle Colonies | Southern Colonies

LESSON 4
Population and Economy

ESSENTIAL QUESTIONS • *How did the movement of people, goods, and ideas cause social change over time?* • *How were the colonies affected by global conflicts?* • *How did the colonies develop identities independent of Great Britain?*

IT MATTERS BECAUSE

The colonies developed in different ways because of differences in the geography of each region. While the South's warm climate lent itself to plantation farming, the New England area offered rich opportunities for whaling and fishing. The economies that developed in each region were the result of how the settlers made use of the natural environment.

Colonial Society Develops

GUIDING QUESTION *How did the three colonial regions reflect geographic and social differences?*

Between 1650 and 1700, the colonial population increased from about 50,000 to more than 250,000. The rapidly developing colonies took on distinctive regional characteristics. Each of the three regions—the New England Colonies, the Middle Colonies, and the Southern Colonies—had its own social structure, geography, and economy.

New England Society

New England society was centered on small towns. Most New Englanders were subsistence farmers, producing just enough food to support their own families. In the early days of colonial New England, the General Court appointed town officials and managed the town's affairs. Over time, however, townspeople began discussing local problems and issues at town meetings. These developed into local governments, with landowners holding the right to vote and pass laws. They elected selectmen to oversee town matters and appoint clerks, constables, and other officials. Any resident could attend a **town meeting** and express an opinion.

Colonists in New England, unlike English tenants, were allowed to participate in local government. As a result, they developed a strong belief in their right to govern themselves. Town meetings thus helped set the stage for the American Revolution and the emergence of democratic government.

Puritans who settled in New England valued religious devotion, hard work, and obedience to strict rules regulating daily life. They also valued education. In 1642 the Massachusetts legislature required parents and ministers to teach all children to read so that they could understand the Bible. Five years later, the legislature ordered towns with at least 50 families to establish an elementary school and those with 100 families or more to set up secondary schools. Soon afterward, other New England colonies adopted similar legislation.

Life in the Middle Colonies

The Middle Colonies attracted groups of non-English immigrants. These included Scots-Irish and Germans, many of whom immigrated to Pennsylvania because of the colony's religious toleration and brought important skills, training, and experiences. The rise of trade caused several Northern ports—including Boston, New York City, and Philadelphia—to grow into cities. In these cities a new society with **distinct** social classes developed.

At the top of the social structure were wealthy merchants who controlled the city's trade. These rich merchants composed a tiny minority, but they patterned themselves after the British upper class. They wore elegant imported clothing and rode through the streets in fancy carriages. Skilled artisans and their families made up nearly half of the urban population. Artisans were skilled workers such as carpenters, smiths, glassmakers, coopers, bakers, masons, and shoemakers. Alongside the artisans in social status were innkeepers and retailers who owned their own businesses.

At the bottom of urban colonial society were people without skills or property. Many of these people were employed at the harbor, where they loaded and serviced ships. Others worked as servants. These people made up about 30 percent of urban society. Below them in status were indentured servants and enslaved Africans. Relatively few enslaved people lived in the North. Those who did usually lived in cities, where they made up between 10 and 20 percent of the population. They too served as laborers and servants for the city's wealthier inhabitants.

town meeting a gathering of free men in a New England town to elect leaders, which developed into the local town government

distinct separate, apart, or different from others

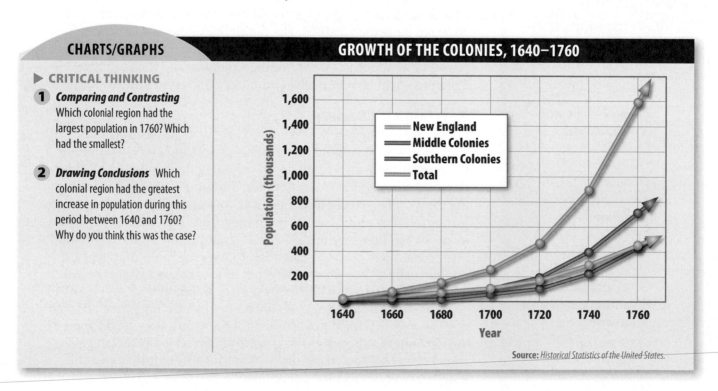

CHARTS/GRAPHS

▶ **CRITICAL THINKING**

1 *Comparing and Contrasting* Which colonial region had the largest population in 1760? Which had the smallest?

2 *Drawing Conclusions* Which colonial region had the greatest increase in population during this period between 1640 and 1760? Why do you think this was the case?

GROWTH OF THE COLONIES, 1640–1760

New England
Middle Colonies
Southern Colonies
Total

Population (thousands): 1,600, 1,400, 1,200, 1,000, 800, 600, 400, 200

Year: 1640, 1660, 1680, 1700, 1720, 1740, 1760

Source: *Historical Statistics of the United States.*

Southern Society

Although many immigrants to the Southern Colonies hoped to become wealthy, very few succeeded. The plantation system created a society with distinct social classes. Wealthy planters led very different lives from small farmers in the middle and enslaved Africans at the bottom. The majority of landowners in the colonial South were small farmers living inland. These "backcountry" farmers worked small plots of land, lived in tiny houses, and largely practiced subsistence farming, producing only enough to feed their families. Landless tenant farmers made up another large group in the South. Tenant farmers led difficult lives but had higher social status than indentured servants. Indentured servants had higher social status than enslaved Africans who worked on the plantations.

Indentured Servants In early colonial days, there was plenty of land, but not enough workers to tend the crop. England had the opposite problem. The English enclosure movement had forced many farmers off their land. Many of them left England to become **indentured servants** in the colonies. Indentured servants were not enslaved, but neither were they free. The person who bought a servant's contract promised to provide food, clothing, and shelter to the servant until the indenture expired. In return, the servant agreed to work for the owner of the contract for a specific number of years. Under the Virginia headright system, every indentured servant transported to America earned the landowner another 50 acres of land.

The Growth of Enslaved Labor In 1676, after Virginia's governor refused to protect backcountry farmers from attacks by Native Americans, planter Nathaniel Bacon organized his own militia to do the fighting. He then marched his force against the capital, Jamestown, which they burned to the ground. Bacon's Rebellion ended shortly afterward when Bacon became ill and died. The rebellion, however, had lasting consequences. It convinced many wealthy planters that land should be made available to backcountry farmers and led to an increased reliance on enslaved labor.

Planters began to switch to enslaved African labor for several reasons. Unlike indentured servants, enslaved workers did not have to be freed and would never demand their own land, making them a more **reliable** labor source. In addition, when cheap land became available in the 1680s in other colonies, fewer English settlers were willing to become indentured servants.

At the same time, the English government adopted policies that encouraged slavery. English law limited trade between the colonies and other countries. Before the 1670s, if colonists wanted to acquire enslaved Africans, they had to

This painting shows tobacco farming in colonial Virginia. Tobacco was key to the economy of the Southern Colonies.

▶ **CRITICAL THINKING**
Determining Cause and Effect Why were tobacco plantations often located near rivers?

indentured servant an individual who contracts to work for a colonist for a specified number of years in exchange for transportation to the colonies, food, clothing, and shelter

reliable dependable; giving the same results on successive trials

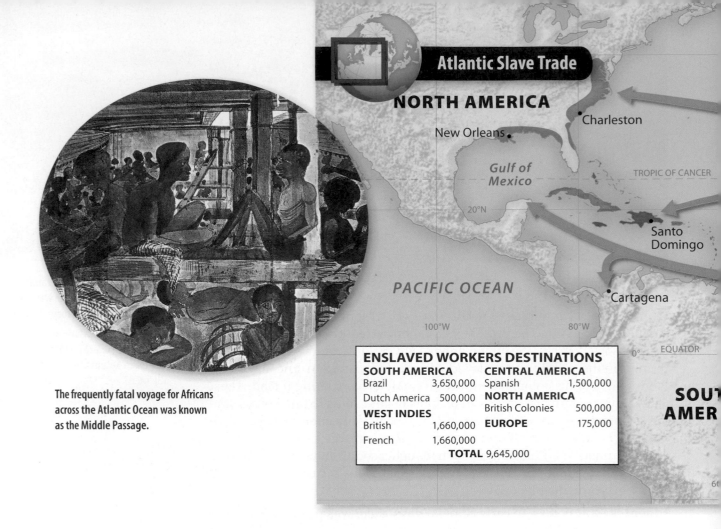

NORTH AMERICA

• Charleston

New Orleans •

*Gulf of
Mexico*

TROPIC OF CANCER

20°N

PACIFIC OCEAN

• Santo
Domingo

• Cartagena

100°W   80°W

EQUATOR
0°

SOUT
AMER

The frequently fatal voyage for Africans
across the Atlantic Ocean was known
as the Middle Passage.

ENSLAVED WORKERS DESTINATIONS			
SOUTH AMERICA		**CENTRAL AMERICA**	
Brazil	3,650,000	Spanish	1,500,000
Dutch America	500,000	**NORTH AMERICA**	
WEST INDIES		British Colonies	500,000
British	1,660,000	**EUROPE**	175,000
French	1,660,000		
		TOTAL 9,645,000	

buy them from the Dutch or Portuguese, which was difficult to arrange.
In 1672 King Charles II granted a charter to the Royal African Company to
engage in the slave trade. This made it easier to acquire enslaved people.
Planters also discovered another advantage to slavery; because enslaved
Africans, unlike indentured servants, were considered property, planters
could use them as collateral to borrow money and expand their plantations.

☑ **PROGRESS CHECK**

Examining How did slavery grow in the colonies?

The Colonial Economies

GUIDING QUESTION *How did the economies of the New England, Middle, and Southern Colonies differ?*

In the early colonial era, settlers lacked money to invest in local industry.
As a result, they had to import most manufactured goods from England.
Unfortunately, they produced few goods that England wanted in return.
Instead of trading directly with England, colonial merchants developed
systems of **triangular trade** involving a three-way exchange of goods.

Economic Relationships

The first part of the triangular trade system started with New England
merchants who shipped fish, lumber, and meat to sugar planters in the
Caribbean. In return for these goods, they received bills of exchange—credit
slips from English merchants—or molasses, which they brought home to
turn into rum. New England merchants would then trade the bills to

triangular trade
a three-way trade route for
exchanging goods between
America, Europe, and Africa

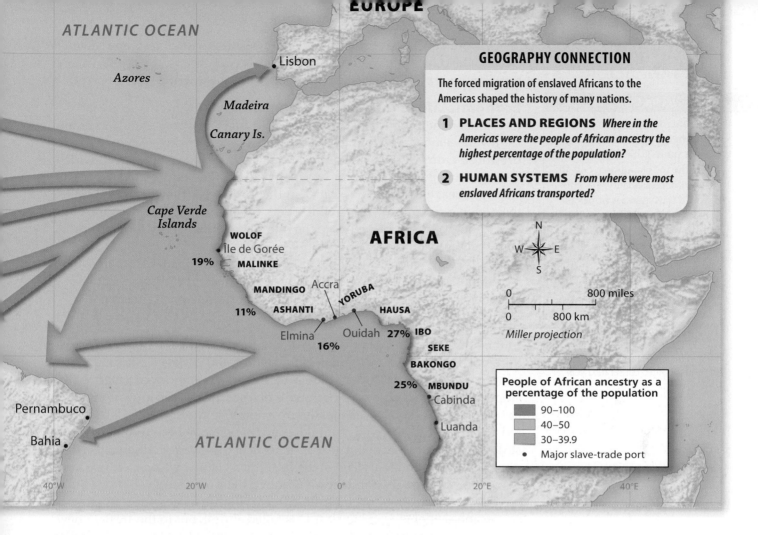

ATLANTIC OCEAN

Lisbon

Azores

Madeira

Canary Is.

Cape Verde Islands

WOLOF

Île de Gorée

19%   MALINKE

MANDINGO   Accra

11%   ASHANTI   YORUBA

Elmina   Ouidah   27%   IBO

16%   SEKE

BAKONGO

25%   MBUNDU

Cabinda

Luanda

AFRICA

HAUSA

Pernambuco

Bahia

ATLANTIC OCEAN

40°W   20°W   0°   20°E   40°E

GEOGRAPHY CONNECTION

The forced migration of enslaved Africans to the Americas shaped the history of many nations.

1 PLACES AND REGIONS *Where in the Americas were the people of African ancestry the highest percentage of the population?*

2 HUMAN SYSTEMS *From where were most enslaved Africans transported?*

0   800 miles

0   800 km

Miller projection

People of African ancestry as a percentage of the population

- 90–100
- 40–50
- 30–39.9
- • Major slave-trade port

English merchants for hardware, linens, and other English goods. The second part of the three-way trade involved the transport of finished goods such as guns and rum from New England to West Africa. In return, they received enslaved Africans. The last part of the trade system was the shipping of enslaved Africans to the Caribbean. The demand for enslaved labor on plantations fueled the triangular trade system.

Trade with the Caribbean sugar plantations made many New England merchants rich. With their new wealth, they built factories to refine raw sugar and distilleries to turn molasses into rum. They also traded with the Southern Colonies, exchanging fish, rum, and grain for rice, tobacco, and indigo.

New England Economy

New England colonists tended to cultivate crops in small farms. The main crop was corn, but farmers also grew other grains and vegetables, tended apple orchards, and raised dairy cattle, sheep, and pigs.

More than any other industry, fishing and whaling brought prosperity to New England. Nearby lay the Grand Banks, a shallow area in the Atlantic Ocean that teemed with cod, mackerel, halibut, and herring. Colonists found markets for their fish in the colonies, southern Europe, and the Caribbean. Whale blubber was used to make candles and lamp oil, and whale bones were used to fashion buttons, combs, and other items.

New England also developed a thriving lumber industry. Maine and New Hampshire had many waterfalls near the coast to power sawmills. Lumber was used for furniture, buildings, and products such as barrels, which were used to ship and store almost everything in the colonial era.

❝Wrote my father a long letter about his plantation affairs . . . on the pains I have taken to bring the indigo, ginger, cotton, lucerne, and casada to perfection. I would have greater hopes of the indigo, if I could have the seed earlier next year from the West Indies, than of any of the other things I have tried.❞

—Eliza Lucas, quoted in
Life of General Thomas Pinckney, 1895

DBQ *DRAWING CONCLUSIONS*
Why did Eliza Lucas ask her father to send the "seed earlier next year"?

Shipbuilding also became an important business. With forests and sawmills close to the coast, ships could be built quickly and cheaply. By the 1770s, one out of every three English ships had been built in America.

Economic Life in the Middle Colonies

Colonists in the Middle Colonies—Pennsylvania, New York, New Jersey, and Delaware—benefited from fertile soil and a long growing season. Farmers produced crops of rye, oats, barley, potatoes, and especially wheat, which became an important cash crop. As merchants in the Middle Colonies began selling wheat and flour to colonies in the Caribbean, they benefited from the region's geography. Three wide rivers—the Hudson, the Delaware, and the Susquehanna—ran deep into the interior, making it easy for farmers to ship their crops to the coast.

In the early and mid-1700s, the demand for wheat soared, thanks to population growth in Europe resulting from a decline of disease. Between 1720 and 1770, wheat prices nearly doubled, bringing great prosperity.

Southern Colonies

In the South, wealthy planters stood on society's top rung and led very different lives from small farmers in the middle and enslaved Africans at the bottom. What linked all groups, however, was an economy based on growing crops for export. Tobacco was the South's first successful crop grown primarily to be sold at market. It was mostly grown in Virginia and Maryland. As indentured servants arrived in Virginia and Maryland, tobacco production rose steadily. Unfortunately, about 40 to 60 percent of the indentured servants who came to Virginia and Maryland in the 1600s died before earning their freedom. Few who survived their indenture acquired their own land.

In South Carolina, meanwhile, after trying unsuccessfully to grow sugarcane, settlers turned to rice. This failed at first, but in the 1690s, a new variety was introduced, and planters imported enslaved Africans to cultivate it. West Africans had grown rice for centuries and knew how to raise and harvest it. Rice became a major cash crop in South Carolina and Georgia.

Planters had also tried another crop, indigo, without much success. Indigo was used to make blue dye for cloth. It was rare and in high demand, and anyone who could grow it could make a large profit. In the early 1740s, a 17-year-old named Eliza Lucas discovered that indigo needed high ground and sandy soil, not the wetlands that suited rice. Indigo quickly became another important cash crop.

✓ **PROGRESS CHECK**

Summarizing How did farmers in the Middle Colonies and the Southern Colonies benefit from the geography of their regions?

LESSON 4 REVIEW

Reviewing Vocabulary
1. *Describing* Describe the significance of: town meeting, indentured servant, and triangular trade.

Using Your Notes
2. *Comparing* Review the notes you completed for the lesson to compare the economic similarities between the New England Colonies and the Middle Colonies.

Answering Guiding Questions
3. *Analyzing* How did the three colonial regions reflect geographic and social differences?

4. *Examining* How did the economies of the New England, Middle, and Southern Colonies differ?

Writing Activity
5. EXPOSITORY Take on the role of a New England Puritan. Write a letter to a cousin in England explaining a typical day.

networks

There's More Online!

- ☑ **BIOGRAPHY** John Locke
- ☑ **BIOGRAPHY** Phyllis Wheatley
- ☑ **VIDEO** Governance and New Ideas
- ☑ **INTERACTIVE SELF-CHECK QUIZ**

Reading HELPDESK

Content Vocabulary

- mercantilism
- pietism
- rationalism
- revival

Academic Vocabulary

- contract
- widespread

TAKING NOTES: *Cause and Effect*

ACTIVITY Complete a graphic organizer similar to the one below by identifying the effects on the colonies caused by the Navigation Acts, the Enlightenment, and the Great Awakening.

Cause	Main point	Effect on colonists
Navigation Acts		
The Enlightenment		
The Great Awakening		

LESSON 5
Governance and New Ideas

ESSENTIAL QUESTIONS • *How did the movement of people, goods, and ideas cause social changes over time?* • *How were the colonies affected by global conflicts?* • *How did the colonies develop identities independent of Great Britain?*

IT MATTERS BECAUSE

The ideas of the Enlightenment and the Great Awakening were the foundation of the colonists' quest for independence from England and for the formation of a representative democracy.

The Imperial System

GUIDING QUESTION *How did the Navigation Acts affect colonial economies?*

The British imperial system was based on the principle that one of the colonies' most important functions was to provide wealth to the home country. This imperial system was a closed system designed to keep competition out.

Mercantilism

Mercantilism is an economic theory about the world economy. Mercantilists believed that to become wealthy, a country must acquire gold and silver. A country could do this by selling more goods to other countries than it bought from them. This would cause more gold and silver to flow into the country than flowed out to pay for products from other countries. Mercantilists also argued that a country should be self-sufficient in raw materials. If it had to buy raw materials from another country, gold and silver would flow out to pay for them. Thus, to be self-sufficient, a country needed colonies where raw materials were available. The home country would then buy raw materials from its colonies and sell them manufactured goods in return.

Mercantilism provided some benefits to colonies. It gave them a reliable market for some of their raw materials and an eager supplier of manufactured goods they needed. Mercantilism also had drawbacks, however. It prevented colonies from selling goods to other nations, even if they could get a better price. Furthermore, if a colony produced nothing the home country needed, it could not acquire gold or silver to buy manufactured goods.

Fotostock

The Navigation Acts

When Charles II assumed the throne in 1660, he and his advisers were determined to generate wealth for England in America. They established policies based on mercantilist ideas. Beginning in 1660, the king asked Parliament to pass a series of Navigation Acts that imposed restrictions on colonial trade. These acts required that all goods shipped to and from the colonies be carried on English ships (including those built in the colonies), and listed specific products that could be sold only to England or other English colonies. Many of these goods—including sugar, tobacco, cotton, wool, and indigo—were the major products that earned money for the American colonies. Anger at the Navigation Acts encouraged colonists to break the new laws. New England merchants began smuggling goods to Europe, the Caribbean, and Africa.

Dominion of New England

In 1685 King James II assumed the throne and took decisive action to end the smuggling. The colonial charters of some colonies had already been revoked, and in 1685 Massachusetts, New Hampshire, and Maine were merged into a new royal province called the Dominion of New England. The Dominion was to be governed by an English governor-general appointed by the king. The following year, Plymouth, Rhode Island and Connecticut were added to the Dominion, and by 1688, New York and New Jersey had been added as well.

King James II appointed Sir Edmund Andros to be the Dominion's first governor-general. Andros became very unpopular because he levied new taxes and rigorously enforced the Navigation Acts. Equally disturbing to Puritans were Andros's efforts to undermine their congregations. For example, he declared that only marriages performed in Anglican churches were legal.

☑ PROGRESS CHECK

Analyzing What was the impact of the Navigation Acts on the economy of the colonies?

mercantilism the theory that a state's power depends on its wealth

This image shows a thriving English port. England's wealth and power increased as a result of trade with its colonies.

▶ **CRITICAL THINKING**
Drawing Conclusions Why would colonists be angered by the system of trade established by the British?

The Glorious Revolution

GUIDING QUESTION *How did the Glorious Revolution affect the English colonies?*

While Andros was angering New England colonists, the people of England were growing suspicious of their new king, James II. James offended many English people by disregarding Parliament, revoking town charters, prosecuting Anglican bishops, and practicing Catholicism.

News of the birth of James's son in 1688 triggered a crisis. Opponents of James had been content to wait until he died, because they expected his Protestant daughter Mary to succeed him. The son, however, was now first in line for the throne and would be raised Catholic. To prevent a Catholic dynasty, Parliament invited Mary and her Dutch husband, William of Orange, to claim the throne. James abdicated in what became known as the Glorious Revolution.

Soon afterward, the colonists ousted Governor-General Andros. William and Mary permitted Rhode Island and Connecticut to resume their previous forms of government, but in 1691 they merged Massachusetts Bay, Plymouth, and Maine into the new royal colony of Massachusetts. The colony was headed by a governor appointed by the king, and the colonists were allowed to elect an assembly.

Before assuming the throne, William and Mary had to swear their acceptance of the English Bill of Rights. This document, written in 1689, said monarchs could not suspend Parliament's laws or create their own courts, nor could they impose taxes or raise an army without Parliament's consent. The English Bill of Rights also guaranteed freedom of speech within Parliament, banned excessive bail and cruel and unusual punishments, and guaranteed every English subject the right to an impartial jury in legal cases. The ideas in this document would later help shape the United States Bill of Rights.

✓ PROGRESS CHECK

Summarizing What were the key effects of the Glorious Revolution on the English colonies?

The Enlightenment and the Great Awakening

GUIDING QUESTION *What effects did the Enlightenment and the Great Awakening have on colonial society?*

During the 1700s, the English colonies came under the influence of the Enlightenment and the Great Awakening. The former championed human reason while the latter stressed a new personal relationship with God.

Enlightenment Thinkers

Enlightenment thinkers came to believe that natural laws applied to social, political, and economic relationships, and that people could figure out these natural laws if they employed reason. This emphasis on logic and reasoning was known as **rationalism.**

One of the most influential Enlightenment writers was the political philosopher John Locke. His writings reflected lessons learned from the Glorious Revolution, that there were times when revolution against the king could be justified. Locke's **contract** theory of government and natural rights profoundly influenced the thinking of future American political leaders. During this period of turmoil Locke published *Two Treatises of Government.* In that work, Locke attempted to use reason to discover and

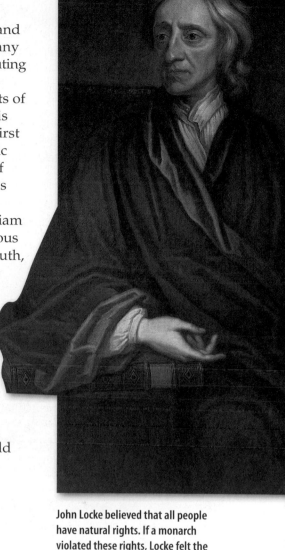

John Locke believed that all people have natural rights. If a monarch violated these rights, Locke felt the people had a right to overthrow the monarch.

▶ CRITICAL THINKING
Predicting Consequences How do you think John Locke would have reacted to the way King James II treated Parliament?

rationalism philosophy that emphasizes the role of logic and reason in gaining knowledge

contract a binding legal document between two parties

PHOTO: DEA PICTURE LIBRARY/De Agostini Picture Library/Getty Images

The Trial of John Peter Zenger

In 1733 John Peter Zenger began printing the *New York Weekly Journal,* a newspaper highly critical of New York governor William Cosby. Unable to identify the anonymous writers and publisher, Cosby ordered Zenger's arrest for printing libel. The jury found Zenger not guilty. In doing so, the jury engaged in "jury nullification." Zenger was clearly guilty—but the jury, in effect, decided the law was wrong and refused to convict Zenger.

In his summation to the jury, Zenger's attorney, Andrew Hamilton, compared free speech and free press to freedom of religion and noted that liberty depends upon the ability to publish criticisms of the government:

❝. . . [W]e well know that it is not two centuries ago that a man would have been burnt as an heretic, for owning such opinions in matters of religion as are publicly wrote and printed at this day. . . . I think it is pretty clear that in New York a man may make very free with his God, but he must take special care what he says of his governor. It is agreed upon by all men, that this is a reign of liberty; and while men keep within the bounds of truth, I hope they may with safety both speak and write their sentiments of the conduct of men in power. I mean of that part of their conduct only, which affects the liberty or property of the people under their administration; were this to be denied, then the next step may make them slaves; For what notions can be entertained of slavery, beyond that of suffering the greatest injuries and oppressions without the liberty of complaining; or if they do, to be destroyed, body and estate, for so doing?❞

—from *A Brief Narrative of the Case and Trial of John Peter Zenger*

DBQ Document Based Questions

1 *Interpreting* What point is Hamilton making when he says that "a man may make very free with his God, but he must take special care what he says of his governor"?

2 *Identifying Central Issues* What does Hamilton say will happen if people are not allowed to express their opinions about those in the government?

explain the natural laws that applied to politics and society and why people created government to safeguard those natural laws:

PRIMARY SOURCE

❝123. If man in the state of nature be so free . . . why will he part with his freedom? . . . [T]he enjoyment of the property he has in this state is very unsafe, very unsecure. This makes him willing . . . to join in society with others . . . for the mutual *preservation* of their lives, liberties and estates. . . .

192. For no government can have a right to obedience from a people who have not freely consented to it; which they can never be supposed to do, till . . . they are put in a full state of liberty to choose their government. . . .❞

—from *Two Treatises of Government*

Equally important was Locke's *An Essay Concerning Human Understanding,* in which he argued that people's minds were blank slates that could be shaped by society and education, making people better. These ideas, that all people have rights and that society can be improved, became core American beliefs.

Jean-Jacques Rousseau carried Locke's ideas further. In *The Social Contract,* he argued that a government should be formed by the consent of the people, who would then make their own laws. Another influential writer was Baron de Montesquieu. In *The Spirit of Laws,* Montesquieu suggested that there were three types of political power—executive, legislative, and judicial. These powers should be separated into different branches to protect people's liberty:

PRIMARY SOURCE

❝In order to have this liberty, it is necessary the government be so constituted as one man need not be afraid of another.

When the legislative and executive powers are united in the same body of magistrates, there can be no liberty....

Again, there is no liberty, if the judiciary power be not separated from the legislative and executive. Were it joined with the legislative, the life and liberty of the subject would be exposed to arbitrary control; for the judge would be then the legislator. Were it joined to the executive power, the judge might behave with violence and oppression.❞

—from *The Spirit of Laws*

Jonathan Edwards was a preacher known for his fiery sermons, most notably his "Sinners in the Hands of an Angry God."

▶ **CRITICAL THINKING**
Drawing Conclusions How do you think people were affected after hearing one of Edwards's emotional sermons?

Religion

While some Americans turned away from a religious worldview, others renewed their Christian faith. Many Americans embraced a European religious movement called **pietism,** which stressed an individual's piety (devoutness) and an emotional union with God. Throughout the colonies, ministers held religious **revivals**—large public meetings for preaching and prayer. This **widespread** resurgence of increased religious fervor became known as the Great Awakening.

In 1734 a Massachusetts preacher named Jonathan Edwards helped launch the Great Awakening. In powerful, terrifying sermons, he argued that a person had to repent and convert. His emotional, as opposed to rational, style of preaching was typical of the fervor of the Great Awakening. George Whitefield, an Anglican minister from England, also attracted and inspired many of his listeners to a more religious life.

The Great Awakening peaked around 1740. Those who embraced the new ideas—including Baptists, some Presbyterians and Congregationalists, and a new group called Methodists—won many converts, while churches that held on their traditional styles often lost members.

The Enlightenment and the Great Awakening had different origins, but both profoundly affected colonial society. The Enlightenment provided arguments against British rule. The Great Awakening served to undermine allegiance to traditional authority.

pietism movement in the 1700s that stressed an individual's piety and an emotional union with God

revival large public meeting for preaching and prayer

widespread having influence on or affecting a large group; widely diffused or prevalent

✔ **PROGRESS CHECK**

Determining Cause and Effect Why did the Great Awakening cause division in established churches?

LESSON 5 REVIEW

Reviewing Vocabulary
1. *Explaining* What is rationalism, and how does it relate to the Enlightenment?

Using Your Notes
2. *Comparing* Use your notes to write a short paragraph that compares the effects of the Navigation Acts, the Enlightenment, and the Great Awakening on the colonists. What main impact seems common to all three?

Answering Guiding Questions
3. *Drawing Conclusions* How did the Navigation Acts affect colonial economies?

4. *Identifying Cause and Effect* How did the Glorious Revolution affect the English colonies?

5. *Evaluating* What effects did the Enlightenment and the Great Awakening have on colonial society?

Writing Activity
6. PERSUASIVE Write an argument in favor of the Navigation Acts. Assume that your purpose is to convince the colonists to accept the Navigation Acts and remain obedient subjects of the British crown.

Directions: On a separate sheet of paper, answer the questions below. Make sure you read carefully and answer all parts to the question.

Lesson Review

Lesson 1

1 *Explaining* What was the agricultural revolution?

2 *Analyzing* How did different cultures establish themselves in North America?

Lesson 2

3 *Identifying Central Issues* What motive drove Christopher Columbus when his ships arrived in the Bahamas?

4 *Explaining* Why did Pope Alexander VI establish a line of demarcation in 1493?

Lesson 3

5 *Identifying Cause and Effect* What effect did the Protestant Reformation have on England?

6 *Evaluating* What was the importance of tobacco in the early colonial economy?

Lesson 4

7 *Explaining* What prompted the ports of Boston, New York City, and Philadelphia to grow into cities?

8 *Making Connections* How did the triangular trade system affect the colonial economies?

Lesson 5

9 *Identifying Cause and Effect* What was the impact and influence of *Two Treatises of Government*?

10 *Explaining* What was the Dominion of New England?

21st Century Skills

11 **IDENTIFYING CAUSE AND EFFECT** What caused Spain to explore and colonize the Americas? What was one effect of that exploration?

12 **ECONOMICS** How did unemployment and an increase in population contribute to the establishment of English colonies in America?

Exploring the Essential Questions

13 *Gathering Information* Create a world map that shows the colonies, New Spain, Great Britain, the Netherlands, France, Spain, and Africa. Write a caption over each region that states the effect each area had on the Americas or the colonies. For the colonies, write a caption that tells how each developed its own identity away from Great Britain.

DBQ Document-Based Questions

Use the document to answer the following questions.

The excerpt below is from Jean-Jacques Rousseau's *The Social Contract*.

PRIMARY SOURCE

"Man is born free; and everywhere he is in chains. One thinks himself the master of others, and still remains a greater slave than they. . . . But, as men cannot engender new forces, but only unite and direct existing ones, they have no other means of preserving themselves than . . . [with] a sum of forces great enough to overcome the resistance. . . . The problem is to find a form of association which will defend and protect with the whole common force the person and goods of each associate, and in which each, while uniting himself with all, may still obey himself alone, and remain as free as before. . . . [T]his act of association creates a moral and collective body."

—from *The Social Contract*

14 *Analyzing Primary Sources* According to the excerpt, what benefits does a group enjoy over individuals?

15 *Identifying Perspectives* If you were a colonist who just arrived in the royal colony of Massachusetts, would you be concerned about the excerpt above or pleased by it? Support your answer with reasoning.

Extended-Response Question

16 **EXPOSITORY** Write a three-paragraph essay that analyzes the motivations of European exploration in the Americas. Your essay should include the following factors: economics, religion, politics, and social class.

Need Extra Help?

If You've Missed Question	1	2	3	4	5	6	7	8	9	10	11	12	13	14	15	16
Go to page(s)	4	4	13	13	16	17	24	26	31	30	13	17	12	34	34	10

The American Revolution

1754–1783

ESSENTIAL QUESTION • *Why do people rebel?*

netw rks

There's More Online about the causes and
events of the American Revolution.

CHAPTER 2

Lesson 1
*The Colonies Fight
for Their Rights*

Lesson 2
The Revolution Begins

Lesson 3
The War for Independence

Lesson 4
*The War Changes
American Society*

The Story Matters...

The American Revolution was a
turning point in world history. At its
core, it was a struggle for individual
rights and self-determination. By
rebelling against their British colonial
protector, the colonists defiantly set
out on a new course for independence.

As the head of the Continental Army,
George Washington faced the
daunting task of defeating the
powerful British army. After years of
bitter fighting, Washington and the
colonists eventually prevailed,
ushering in the birth of a new and
independent nation.

◄ George Washington was both a military
and political leader. He served as
commander of the Continental Army
and presided over the writing of the
Constitution. Washington would go on
to serve two terms as the first president
of the United States.

PHOTO: Francis G. Mayer/CORBIS

The French and Indian War was part of a larger global conflict between France and Britain known as the Seven Years' War. The British victory in the French and Indian War came at a high cost. Britain had large debts to repay and it had more territory to govern and control. Britain imposed new restrictions and taxes on its American colonies to pay for the costs of governing and protecting the colonies. Colonists were angered by these changes, and tensions between Britain and the colonies increased.

Step Into the Place

Read the quotes and look at the information presented on the map.

 How do the opinions addressed in these quotes reflect the differing British and colonial views in the aftermath of the French and Indian War?

PRIMARY SOURCE

❝We have not yet recovered from a War undertaken solely for their Protection . . . and . . . no Time was ever so seasonable for claiming their assistance. The Distribution is too unequal, of Benefits only to the Colonies, and all of the Burdens upon the Mother Country.❞

—Thomas Whately, from *Considerations Upon This Trade and Finances of the Kingdom*, 1763

PRIMARY SOURCE

❝We are told to be quiet when we see that very money which is torn from us by lawless force made use of still further to oppose us, to feed and pamper a set of infamous wretches who swarm like the locusts of Egypt.❞

—Samuel Adams, 1765

PHOTOS: left page The Granger Collection, New York; right page Geoffrey Clements/Fine Art/CORBIS

Step Into the Time

Choose an event from the time line and write a paragraph explaining how that event demonstrated a struggle for individual rights.

U.S. PRESIDENTS

UNITED STATES

WORLD

1745

1755

1754 French and Indian War begins

1748 Montesquieu's *The Spirit of Laws* is published

1751 Chinese invade Tibet and control succession to throne

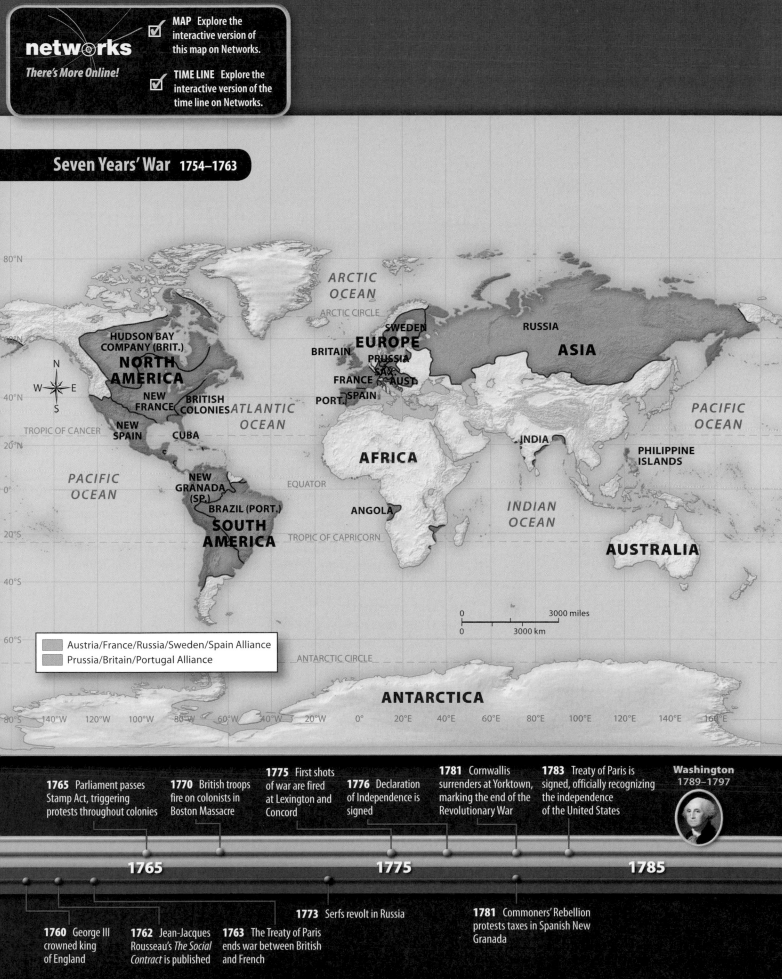

Seven Years' War 1754–1763

ARCTIC OCEAN

ARCTIC CIRCLE

HUDSON BAY COMPANY (BRIT.)

NORTH AMERICA

NEW FRANCE

BRITISH COLONIES

NEW SPAIN

CUBA

ATLANTIC OCEAN

TROPIC OF CANCER

PACIFIC OCEAN

EQUATOR

NEW GRANADA (SP.)

BRAZIL (PORT.)

SOUTH AMERICA

TROPIC OF CAPRICORN

SWEDEN

EUROPE

BRITAIN

PRUSSIA

SAX.

FRANCE

AUST.

PORT.

SPAIN

RUSSIA

ASIA

AFRICA

ANGOLA

INDIA

PACIFIC OCEAN

PHILIPPINE ISLANDS

INDIAN OCEAN

AUSTRALIA

N W E S

0 3000 miles
0 3000 km

ANTARCTIC CIRCLE

Austria/France/Russia/Sweden/Spain Alliance
Prussia/Britain/Portugal Alliance

ANTARCTICA

80°S 140°W 120°W 100°W 80°W 60°W 40°W 20°W 0° 20°E 40°E 60°E 80°E 100°E 120°E 140°E 160°E

1765 Parliament passes Stamp Act, triggering protests throughout colonies

1770 British troops fire on colonists in Boston Massacre

1775 First shots of war are fired at Lexington and Concord

1776 Declaration of Independence is signed

1781 Cornwallis surrenders at Yorktown, marking the end of the Revolutionary War

1783 Treaty of Paris is signed, officially recognizing the independence of the United States

Washington 1789–1797

1765   1775   1785

1760 George III crowned king of England

1762 Jean-Jacques Rousseau's *The Social Contract* is published

1763 The Treaty of Paris ends war between British and French

1773 Serfs revolt in Russia

1781 Commoners' Rebellion protests taxes in Spanish New Granada

networks
There's More Online!

☑ **BIOGRAPHY** Samuel Adams

☑ **IMAGE** The Death of General Braddock

☑ **VIDEO** The Colonies Fight for Their Rights

☑ **INTERACTIVE SELF-CHECK QUIZ**

LESSON 1
The Colonies Fight for Their Rights

ESSENTIAL QUESTION • *Why do people rebel?*

Reading **HELP**DESK

Content Vocabulary
• customs duty
• inflation
• nonimportation agreement
• writ of assistance

Academic Vocabulary
• **dominance** • **substitute**

TAKING NOTES: *Organizing*

ACTIVITY Complete a graphic organizer similar to the one below by listing the causes of the French and Indian War.

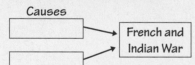

Causes → French and Indian War

IT MATTERS BECAUSE
In the mid-1700s, Britain and France fought a war for control of North America. Britain emerged from the conflict victorious. After the war, Parliament's attempts to raise revenue from the colonies met with resistance and protests.

The French and Indian War

GUIDING QUESTION *How did the French and Indian War affect the colonies?*

The French and English had been vying for **dominance** in Europe since the late 1600s, fighting three major wars between 1689 and 1748. Most of the fighting took place in Europe, but whenever France and England were at war, their colonies went to war as well. In 1754 a fourth struggle began.

The First Skirmish

In the 1740s, the British and French both became interested in the Ohio River valley. Using the Ohio River and the Mississippi River, the French could travel from the St. Lawrence River Valley to Louisiana. British fur traders and land speculators, who bought land to sell for profit, were also interested in the valley.

The French built a chain of forts from Lake Ontario to the Ohio River. In response, the British governor of Virginia asked George Washington, a young militia officer, to expel the French.

As Washington's troops marched toward the Ohio River in the spring of 1754, they encountered a small French force. After a brief battle, Washington retreated a short distance and built a stockade named Fort Necessity. A little over a month later, a large French force arrived and forced Washington to surrender. Meanwhile, the fighting between France and Britain expanded into a world war.

The Albany Conference

Even before the fighting started, Britain asked its colonies to prepare for war and to negotiate an alliance with the Iroquois. The Iroquois controlled western New York—land the French passed through to reach the Ohio River. In 1754 colonial delegates met with Iroquois leaders in Albany, New York.

At the Albany Conference, the Iroquois refused an alliance with the British but did offer halfhearted support. The conference also issued the Albany Plan of Union, a proposal developed by a committee led by Benjamin Franklin. The Plan of Union proposed that the colonies form a federal government. Although the colonies rejected the plan, it showed that some colonial leaders were thinking about joining together for the common defense.

dominance being in a state or position of command or control over all others

The British Triumph

In 1755 British general Edward Braddock arrived in Virginia with 1,400 British troops. After linking up with 450 Virginia militia troops, Braddock appointed Lieutenant Colonel George Washington his aide. Braddock began marching west, intending to attack Fort Duquesne, a French fort. Seven miles from the fort, French and Native American forces ambushed the British, and Braddock was killed. Washington rallied the men and organized a retreat.

The successful ambush emboldened the Delaware people who began attacking British settlers in western Pennsylvania. For the next two years, the French and Indian War, as it was called in the colonies, raged along the frontier.

Gradually, the British fleet cut off supplies and reinforcements from France. The Iroquois, realizing the British would probably win the war, pressured the Delaware to end their attacks. With their Native American allies giving up, the French were badly outnumbered. The British seized Quebec and took control of New France. The war ended in 1763 with the Treaty of Paris, which virtually eliminated French power in North America.

✔ **PROGRESS CHECK**

Summarizing What were the main effects of the French and Indian War on the colonies?

PHOTO: PoodlesRock/Corbis Art/CORBIS

GEOGRAPHY CONNECTION

The French and Indian War established British control of North America. The French and Indian War was part of a global conflict that became known as the Seven Years' War.

1 **THE WORLD IN SPATIAL TERMS** *From what port did the British fleet sail to begin their attack on Quebec?*

2 **PHYSICAL SYSTEMS** *Why do you think all the battles occurred along rivers, lakes, and the coast?*

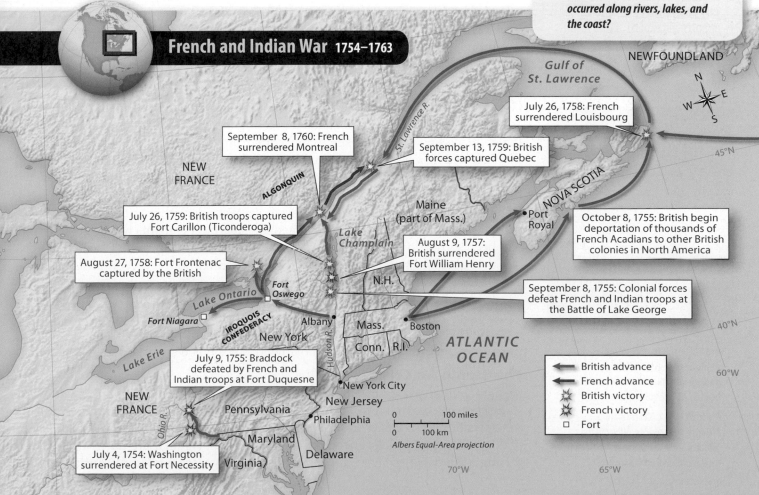

French and Indian War 1754–1763

July 26, 1758: French surrendered Louisbourg

September 8, 1760: French surrendered Montreal

September 13, 1759: British forces captured Quebec

July 26, 1759: British troops captured Fort Carillon (Ticonderoga)

August 9, 1757: British surrendered Fort William Henry

October 8, 1755: British begin deportation of thousands of French Acadians to other British colonies in North America

August 27, 1758: Fort Frontenac captured by the British

September 8, 1755: Colonial forces defeat French and Indian troops at the Battle of Lake George

July 9, 1755: Braddock defeated by French and Indian troops at Fort Duquesne

July 4, 1754: Washington surrendered at Fort Necessity

NEWFOUNDLAND

Gulf of St. Lawrence

St. Lawrence R.

NEW FRANCE

ALGONQUIN

Maine (part of Mass.)

NOVA SCOTIA

Port Royal

Lake Champlain

N.H.

Fort Oswego

Lake Ontario

Fort Niagara

IROQUOIS CONFEDERACY

Albany

Mass.

Boston

Conn. R.I.

Hudson R.

ATLANTIC OCEAN

Lake Erie

New York

NEW FRANCE

Ohio R.

Pennsylvania

Philadelphia

New York City

New Jersey

Maryland

Delaware

Virginia

0   100 miles
0   100 km
Albers Equal-Area projection

← British advance
← French advance
✴ British victory
✴ French victory
□ Fort

45°N

40°N

60°W

65°W

70°W

The Right to Tax

❝The single question is, whether the parliament can legally impose duties to be paid *by the people of these colonies only,* FOR THE SOLE PURPOSE OF RAISING A REVENUE, *on commodities which she obliges us to take from her alone;* or, in other words, whether the parliament can legally take money out of our pockets, without our consent.❞

—John Dickinson, "Letters From a Farmer in Pennsylvania, to the Inhabitants of the British Colonies," *Pennsylvania Gazette,* December 10, 1767

DBQ **EXPLORING ISSUES** Do you think the British parliament had the right to impose duties on the colonists? Why?

customs duty a tax on imports and exports

inflation the loss of value of money

In an attempt to lower Britain's war debt, George Grenville supported policies that placed the financial burden on the colonies.

▶ **CRITICAL THINKING**
Making Inferences Why did the colonists believe the Sugar Act violated their traditional English rights?

Growing Discontent

GUIDING QUESTION *What actions by Great Britain angered the American colonists after the French and Indian War?*

Great Britain's victory in 1763 left the country deeply in debt. It had to pay not only the cost of the war but also the cost of governing and defending its new territories. Many new policies that the British government adopted to solve its financial problems were unpopular in the colonies.

The Proclamation of 1763

In the spring of 1763, Pontiac, chief of the Ottawa people, decided to go to war against the British. He united several Native American groups and they attacked forts along the frontier and burned down several towns. They did so because settlers had been moving into western Pennsylvania in defiance of a treaty. British leaders did not want to bear the cost of another war.

In early October, King George III issued the Proclamation of 1763. The proclamation drew a north-south line along the Appalachian Mountains. Colonists could not settle west of that line without permission. This enraged many farmers and land speculators, who wanted access to the land.

Customs Reform

In 1763 George Grenville became prime minister and the first lord of the Treasury. Grenville had to find a way to reduce Britain's debt and pay for the 10,000 British troops now stationed in North America.

Grenville knew that merchants were smuggling many goods into and out of the colonies without paying **customs duties,** taxes on imports and exports. He convinced Parliament to pass a law allowing smugglers to be tried at a new vice-admiralty court in Nova Scotia. Unlike colonial courts, where the juries were often sympathetic to smugglers, vice-admiralty courts were run by naval officers. These courts had no juries and did not follow British common law because Admiralty cases involved property not people. Colonists objected, arguing that these courts denied their rights as British citizens.

The Sugar Act and the Currency Act

Grenville also introduced the American Revenue Act of 1764, better known as the Sugar Act. The act raised tax rates on imports of raw sugar and molasses. It also placed new taxes on silk, wine, coffee, pimento, and indigo.

Colonial merchants complained that the Sugar Act hurt trade. Many were also furious that the act violated traditional English rights. Under the act, the property of merchants accused of smuggling was presumed illegal until its legality was proven. The act let officials seize goods without due process—proper court procedures—and prevented lawsuits by merchants whose goods had been seized. In colonial cities, pamphlets were circulated against the Sugar Act that gave rise to the expression: "No taxation without representation." This reflected the colonists' lack of representation in Parliament.

To slow **inflation,** Parliament also passed the Currency Act of 1764. This act banned the use of paper money in the colonies because it tended to lose value quickly. The act angered colonists who used paper money to repay loans. Since the money lost value after it was borrowed, the loans were easier to repay.

The Stamp Act Crisis

Parliament then passed the Stamp Act which taxed most printed materials. The stamp tax was the first direct tax levied on the colonists. As word of the Stamp Act spread in the colonies in the spring of 1765, a huge debate began. A flood of editorials, pamphlets, speeches, and resolutions against the tax swept through the colonies. The Virginia House of Burgesses passed resolutions

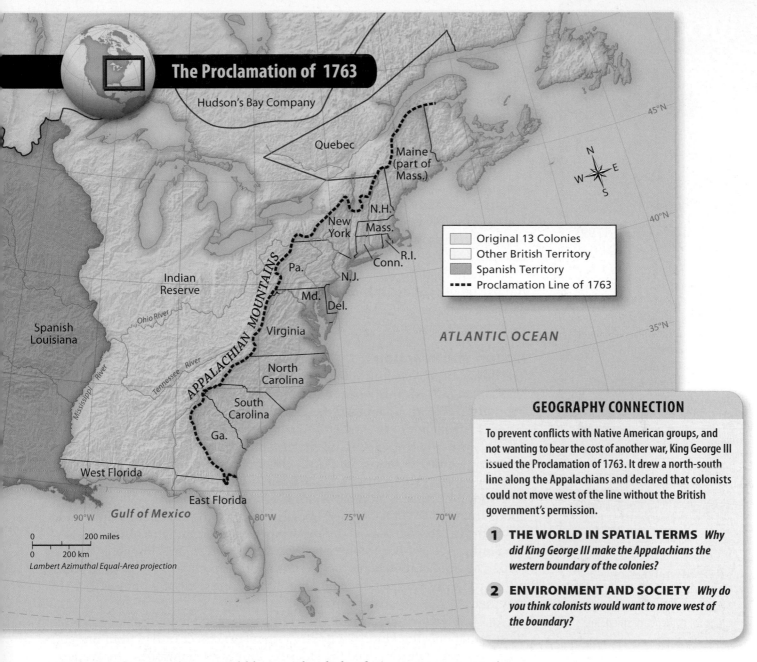

The Proclamation of 1763

Hudson's Bay Company

Quebec

Maine (part of Mass.)

N.H.
New York
Mass.
Conn.
R.I.

Pa.
N.J.
Md.
Del.

Indian Reserve

Ohio River

Spanish Louisiana

Virginia

APPALACHIAN MOUNTAINS

Tennessee River

Mississippi River

North Carolina

South Carolina

Ga.

West Florida

East Florida

90°W   Gulf of Mexico   80°W   75°W   70°W

45°N
40°N
35°N

ATLANTIC OCEAN

Legend
- Original 13 Colonies
- Other British Territory
- Spanish Territory
- **····** Proclamation Line of 1763

0   200 miles
0   200 km
Lambert Azimuthal Equal-Area projection

GEOGRAPHY CONNECTION

To prevent conflicts with Native American groups, and not wanting to bear the cost of another war, King George III issued the Proclamation of 1763. It drew a north-south line along the Appalachians and declared that colonists could not move west of the line without the British government's permission.

1 **THE WORLD IN SPATIAL TERMS** *Why did King George III make the Appalachians the western boundary of the colonies?*

2 **ENVIRONMENT AND SOCIETY** *Why do you think colonists would want to move west of the boundary?*

declaring that Virginians could be taxed only by their own representatives. Other colonial assemblies passed similar resolutions. By summer, a group called the Sons of Liberty was organizing demonstrations and intimidating stamp distributors.

In October 1765, representatives from nine colonies met for what became known as the Stamp Act Congress. They issued a declaration which argued that because taxation depended upon representation, only the colonists' political representatives, and not Parliament, had the right to tax them.

When the Stamp Act went into effect on November 1, 1765, the colonists ignored it. Instead, they began boycotting all British goods. People **substituted** sage and sassafras for imported tea. In New York, 200 merchants signed a **nonimportation agreement,** pledging not to buy any British goods until Parliament repealed the Stamp Act. Pressured by these protests, Parliament did repeal it in 1766, but also affirmed its authority to make laws for the colonies.

substitute to put or use in the place of another

nonimportation agreement a pledge by merchants not to buy imported goods from a particular source

☑ **PROGRESS CHECK**

Evaluating Why did the Stamp Act anger colonists more than previous taxes?

Patrick Henry (1736–1799)

From 1765 to 1775, Patrick Henry's criticisms of British policies spurred colonial discontent. Throughout his public career, Henry championed individual rights and the interests of ordinary Americans. He opposed tyranny by government, whether the government of Great Britain or the new government proposed by the U.S. Constitution. In his famous speech of March 1775, he declared, "Give me liberty or give me death!"

▶ **CRITICAL THINKING**
Analyzing Primary Sources How could Patrick Henry's quotation relate to the Townshend Acts?

writ of assistance
a search warrant enabling customs officers to enter any location to look for evidence of smuggling

The Townshend Acts

GUIDING QUESTION *How did the colonists begin resisting British policies?*

During the Stamp Act crisis, Britain's financial problems worsened. Protests in Britain forced Parliament to lower property taxes there, yet the government still had to pay for its troops in America. In 1767 Charles Townshend, now chancellor of the Exchequer, introduced new regulations and taxes. These came to be called the Townshend Acts.

One of the Townshend Acts was the Revenue Act of 1767. This act put new customs duties on glass, lead, paper, paint, and tea imported by the colonies. Violators of the Revenue Act had to face trial in vice-admiralty courts. The Townshend Acts, like the Sugar Act, also allowed officials to seize private property under certain circumstances without following due process.

To help customs officers arrest smugglers, the Revenue Act legalized the use of **writs of assistance.** The writs were general search warrants that enabled customs officers to enter any location during the day to look for evidence of smuggling.

Action and Reaction

The Townshend Acts infuriated many colonists. In defiance of the acts, the Massachusetts assembly began organizing resistance against Britain. In February 1768, Sam Adams and the Massachusetts assembly drafted a "circular letter" criticizing the Townshend Acts to send to the other colonies. British officials ordered the Massachusetts assembly to withdraw the letter. The assembly refused. Furious, the British government ordered the Massachusetts assembly dissolved. In August 1768, the merchants of Boston and New York responded by signing nonimportation agreements, vowing not to import goods from Britain. Philadelphia's merchants joined the boycott in March 1769.

Sam Adams also played an important role in organizing resistance to the Stamp Act and the Townshend Acts in Boston. Adams forged an anti-British alliance of merchants, lawyers, and other members of the social elite with artisans, shopkeepers, and common laborers, all of whom worked together to protest British tax policies.

In May 1769, Virginia's House of Burgesses passed the Virginia Resolves, stating that only the House could tax Virginians. Under orders from Britain, Virginia's governor dissolved the House of Burgesses. In response, the leaders of the House of Burgesses—including George Washington, Patrick Henry, and Thomas Jefferson—immediately called the members to a convention. This convention then passed a nonimportation law, blocking the sale of British goods in Virginia.

The growing dispute between colonists and British authorities centered on the extent of Parliament's power over the colonies, particularly the power to levy taxes. In a 1774 essay, the British writer Samuel Johnson expressed Britain's view of the proper relationship between the colonists and the British government: "He that accepts protection, stipulates [agrees to] obedience. We have always protected the Americans; we may, therefore, subject them to government."

The Boston Massacre

In Boston, riots sparked by the Townshend duties led customs officials to demand additional protection in June 1768. As a result, four additional British regiments arrived in 1768. Bostonians referred to the British troops stationed there as "lobster backs" because of the red coats they wore. Crowds

This illustration of the Boston Massacre by Paul Revere depicts the colonists' protest of the Townshend Acts and the clash with British troops.

▶ CRITICAL THINKING

Interpreting Significance Why were nonimportation agreements used in response to the Townshend Acts?

PHOTO: Library of Congress

constantly heckled and harassed the troops. On March 5, 1770, a crowd of colonists began taunting and throwing snowballs at a British soldier guarding a customs house. His call for help brought Captain Thomas Preston and a squad of soldiers.

In the midst of the tumult, the troops began firing into the crowd. According to accounts, the first colonist to die was a man of African and Native American descent known as both Michael Johnson and Crispus Attucks. When the smoke cleared, three people lay dead, two more would die later, and six others were wounded. The shootings became known as the Boston Massacre. Colonial newspapers portrayed the British as tyrants who were willing to kill people who stood up for their rights.

News of the Boston Massacre raced like lightning across the colonies. It might have set off a revolution then and there, but only a few weeks later, news arrived that the British had repealed almost all of the Townshend Acts. Parliament kept one tax—a tax on tea—to uphold its right to tax the colonies. At the same time, it allowed the colonial assemblies to resume meeting. Peace and stability returned to the colonies, but only temporarily.

✓ **PROGRESS CHECK**

Examining How did the Virginia Resolves show opposition to British policies?

Connections to TODAY

Right to Protest

Americans have a long tradition of exercising freedom of speech and assembly to protest. When the British increased taxes and instituted restrictive acts, many colonists publicly voiced their displeasure. Just as the colonists did hundreds of years ago, we still have the right to protest things we disagree with or find unjust.

LESSON 1 REVIEW

Reviewing Vocabulary
1. *Explaining* Why do you think the writs of assistance legalized by the Revenue Act angered the colonists?

Using Your Notes
2. *Identifying* Use your notes to write a short paragraph that identifies the main factors that led to the French and Indian War.

Answering the Guiding Questions
3. *Analyzing* How did the French and Indian War affect the colonies?

4. *Summarizing* What actions by Great Britain angered the American colonists after the French and Indian War?

5. *Describing* How did the colonists begin resisting British policies?

Writing Activity
6. **PERSUASIVE** Suppose that you are a member of the Sons of Liberty. Write a pamphlet explaining what your group does and urging other colonists to join.

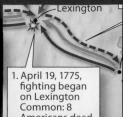

Lexington

1. April 19, 1775, fighting began on Lexington Common: 8 Americans dead

networks

There's More Online!

- ☑ **BIOGRAPHY** George Rogers Clark
- ☑ **BIOGRAPHY** Thomas Paine
- ☑ **GRAPHIC NOVEL** From Revolution to Declaration
- ☑ **IMAGE** Battle of Lexington
- ☑ **PRIMARY SOURCE** The Declaration of Independence
- ☑ **VIDEO** The Revolution Begins
- ☑ **INTERACTIVE SELF-CHECK QUIZ**

LESSON 2
The Revolution Begins

ESSENTIAL QUESTION • *Why do people rebel?*

Reading HELPDESK

Content Vocabulary
- committee of correspondence
- minuteman

Academic Vocabulary
- enforce
- submit

TAKING NOTES: *Organizing*

ACTIVITY Use the major headings of the lesson to create an outline similar to the one below, with information about the rising tensions between the colonies and Britain.

The Revolution Begins
I. Massachusetts Defies Britain
    A.
    B.
    C.
    D.
II.

IT MATTERS BECAUSE

After years of escalating tensions, a revolt against British rule began in the colonies in the 1770s. The colonists established a new government for themselves and organized militias to combat what they saw as British tyranny.

Massachusetts Defies Britain

GUIDING QUESTION *What caused the colonies to begin their revolution against Great Britain?*

Despite the tragedy of the Boston Massacre, the British decision to repeal the Townshend Acts had appeared to end another crisis in colonial relations. Then, in the spring of 1772, Britain introduced several policies that again ignited the flames of rebellion in the colonies. This time the fire could not be put out.

The *Gaspee* Affair

After Britain repealed the Townshend Acts, trade with the American colonies resumed, and so did smuggling. To intercept smugglers, the British sent customs ships to patrol North American waters. One such ship was the *Gaspee*. In June 1772, when the *Gaspee* ran aground, some 150 colonists seized and burned the ship.

The British sent a commission to investigate and gave it the power to take suspects to Britain for trial. Colonists believed this violated their right to a trial by a jury of their peers. After the Virginia House of Burgesses received a letter in March 1773 from Rhode Island asking for help, one of its members, Thomas Jefferson, suggested that each colony create a **committee of correspondence** to communicate with the other colonies about British activities. These committees of correspondence helped unify the colonies and shape public opinion. They also helped colonial leaders coordinate their plans.

The Boston Tea Party

In May 1773, Britain's Parliament helped the British East India Company out of debt by passing the Tea Act of 1773. Prior to the Tea Act, colonial merchants had been smuggling in cheaper Dutch tea. As a result, the British East India Company had more than 17 million pounds of tea that it needed to sell quickly.

The Tea Act reduced the tax on tea shipped to the colonies from the British East India Company, but maintained the Townshend duty. This made more colonists willing to buy British tea, and smuggling decreased. The Tea Act enraged colonial merchants, who feared it was a step by the British to squeeze them out of business. It also angered colonists, who did not want to pay the tax.

In October 1773, the East India Company shipped 1,253 chests of tea to Boston, New York, Philadelphia, and Charles Towne. The committees of correspondence decided that the tea must not be unloaded. On December 16, 1773, the night before officials planned to bring the tea ashore, a group of about 150 men secretly gathered at the Boston dock. One of the men was George Hewes, a struggling Boston shoemaker who had grown to despise the British. He gladly joined the other volunteers as they prepared to sneak aboard several British ships anchored in Boston Harbor and destroy the tea stored on board:

PRIMARY SOURCE

❝They divided us into three parties, for the purpose of boarding the three ships which contained the tea. . . . We then were ordered by our commander to open the hatches and take out all the chests of tea and throw them overboard. . . .❞

—quoted in *The Spirit of 'Seventy-Six: The Story of the American Revolution as Told by Participants*

Crowds on the shore cheered as the men dumped 342 chests of tea into Boston Harbor. A witness later testified that Sam Adams and John Hancock were among those who boarded the ships. The raid later came to be called the Boston Tea Party.

The Coercive Acts

The Boston Tea Party was the last straw for the British. In the spring of 1774, Parliament passed four new laws that came to be known as the Coercive Acts. These laws were intended to punish Massachusetts and put an end to colonial challenges to British authority.

The first act was the Boston Port Act. It shut down Boston's port until the city paid for the tea that had been destroyed. The second act was the Massachusetts Government Act. It required all council members, judges, and sheriffs in Massachusetts to be appointed by the governor instead of being elected. Town meetings could only be held with the governor's permission.

committee of correspondence
committee organized in each colony to communicate with and unify the colonies

This lithograph, titled *The Destruction of Tea at Boston Harbor,* was created by engravers Currier and Ives in 1846. The engravers depicted the scene in daylight—most likely to make the image clearer—although it happened at night.

▶ **CRITICAL THINKING**
Interpreting Significance What was the significance of the Boston Tea Party as a demonstration of protest?

WHAT WERE THE COERCIVE ACTS?

Britain responded to the Boston Tea Party with four acts intended to punish Massachusetts and reassert British authority.

▶ **CRITICAL THINKING**

1 *Explaining* What was the purpose of the Boston Port Act?

2 *Drawing Conclusions* Why would the British want to control town meetings?

1.	**Boston Port Act** • Closed the port of Boston until Massachusetts paid for the tea
2.	**Massachusetts Government Act** • No town meeting could be held without the governor's consent • Required all sheriffs, council members, and judges to be appointed by the governor
3.	**Administration of Justice Act** • Allowed trials of British soldiers and officials to be transferred to Britain to protect them from American juries
4.	**Quartering Act** • Required local officials to lodge British troops at the scene of a disturbance; in private homes, if necessary

enforce to urge or carry out using force

The third act, the Administration of Justice Act, allowed the governor to transfer trials of British soldiers and officials to Britain to protect them from American juries. The final act was a new Quartering Act. It required local officials to provide lodging for British soldiers. To **enforce** the acts, the British sent more troops to New England and appointed General Thomas Gage the governor of Massachusetts.

In July 1774, a month after the last Coercive Act had become law, the British introduced the Quebec Act. The Quebec Act stated that a governor and council appointed by the king would run Quebec. It also extended Quebec's boundaries to include much of what is today Ohio, Illinois, Michigan, Indiana, and Wisconsin. If colonists moved west, they would live in territory where they had no elected assembly. The Coercive Acts and the Quebec Act together became known as the Intolerable Acts.

The First Continental Congress

In May 1774, the Virginia House of Burgesses called for a day of fasting to protest the arrival of British troops in Boston. When Virginia's governor dissolved the House, the burgesses went to a nearby tavern. In a resolution, they urged the colonies to suspend trade with Britain and to send delegates to a colonial congress to discuss more action. Similar appeals were made in New York and Rhode Island.

On September 5, 1774, 55 colonial delegates met in Philadelphia for the First Continental Congress. The delegates represented 12 of Britain's North American colonies. (Florida, Georgia, Nova Scotia, and Quebec did not attend.) Some delegates believed compromise with Britain was still possible; others believed the time had come to fight.

The Congress issued the Declaration of Rights and Grievances, which expressed loyalty to the king, but also condemned the Coercive Acts. Days later, the delegates approved a plan to form committees to enforce a boycott of British goods. The delegates agreed to hold a second Continental Congress in May 1775 if the crisis had not been resolved.

☑ **PROGRESS CHECK**

Analyzing How did the Tea Act spark colonists to revolt against Great Britain?

The Revolution Begins

GUIDING QUESTION *How did the battles at Lexington and Concord shape the American Revolution?*

In October 1774, members of the suspended Massachusetts assembly defied the British and organized the Massachusetts Provincial Congress. They formed the Committee of Safety and chose John Hancock to lead it, giving him the power to call up the militia.

A full-scale rebellion was now underway. Militias began to drill and practice shooting. The town of Concord created a special unit of men trained and ready to "stand at a minute's warning in case of alarm." They became known as the **minutemen.** Through the summer and fall of 1774, British control of the colonies weakened as colonists created provincial congresses and militias raided military depots for ammunition.

minutemen companies of civilian soldiers who boasted they were ready to fight at a minute's notice

Loyalists and Patriots

Although many colonists did not agree with Parliament's policies, they were still loyal to the king and to Britain and believed that British law should be upheld. Americans who supported the British side in the conflict were known as Loyalists or Tories. Many Loyalists were government officials, Anglican ministers, or merchants and landowners. Some farmers remained loyal because they regarded the king as their protector against the merchants who controlled the local governments.

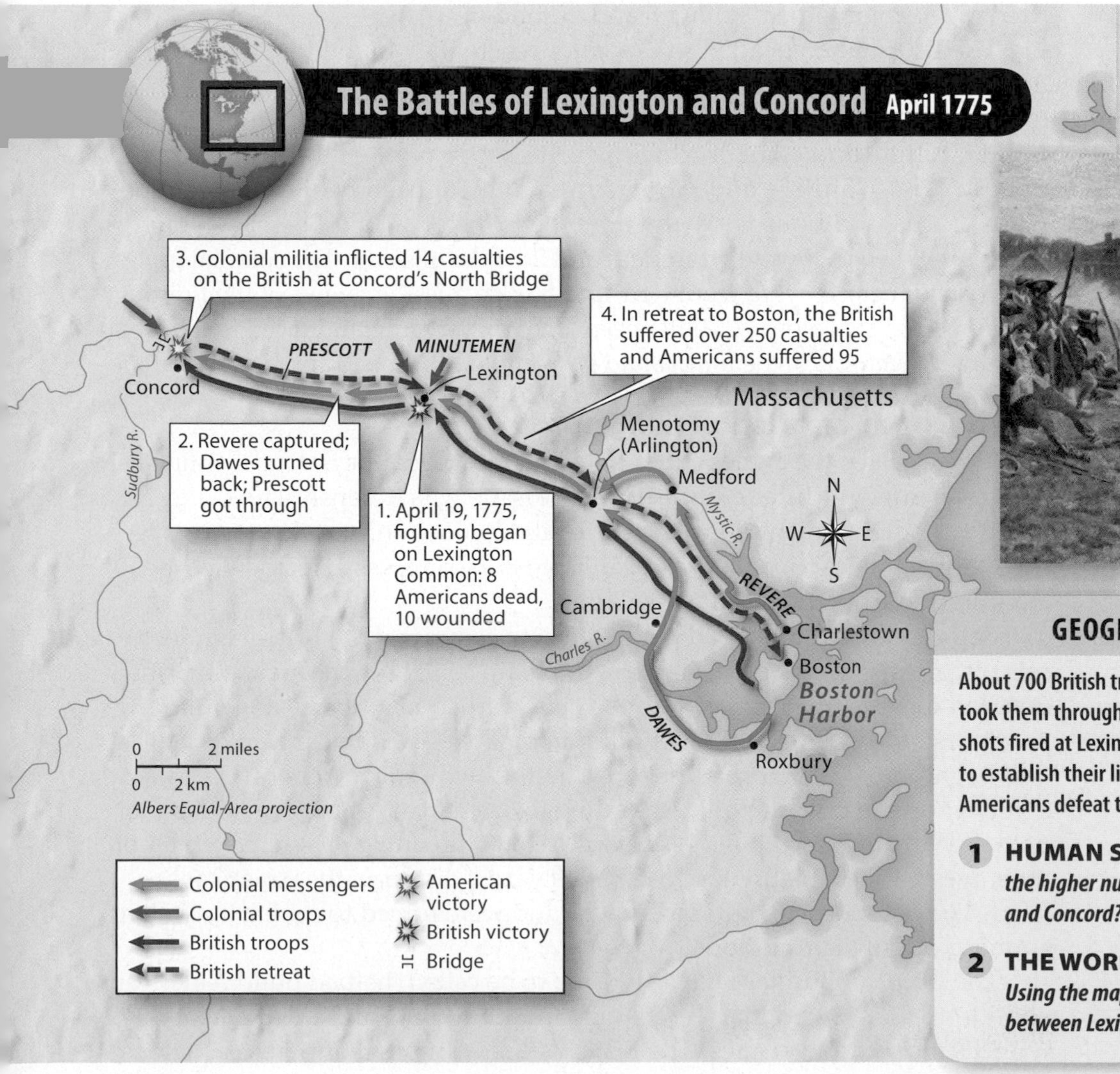
The Battles of Lexington and Concord April 1775
3. Colonial militia inflicted 14 casualties on the British at Concord's North Bridge
4. In retreat to Boston, the British suffered over 250 casualties and Americans suffered 95
PRESCOTT
MINUTEMEN
Concord
Lexington
Massachusetts
2. Revere captured; Dawes turned back; Prescott got through
Sudbury R.
Menotomy (Arlington)
Medford
Mystic R.
1. April 19, 1775, fighting began on Lexington Common: 8 Americans dead, 10 wounded
N
W
E
S
REVERE
Cambridge
Charlestown
Charles R.
Boston
Boston Harbor
DAWES
Roxbury
0 2 miles
0 2 km
Albers Equal-Area projection
Colonial messengers
Colonial troops
British troops
British retreat
American victory
British victory
Bridge

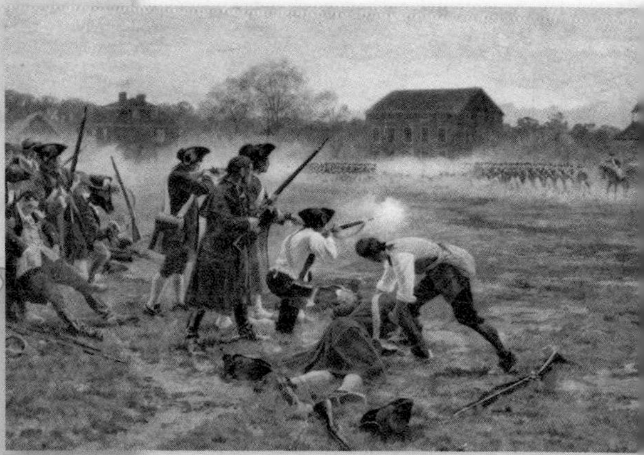

GEOGRAPHY CONNECTION

About 700 British troops set out for Concord on a road that took them through the town of Lexington. From the first shots fired at Lexington (image, above), the will to fight to establish their liberties and independence helped the Americans defeat the British.

1. **HUMAN SYSTEMS** *Which side suffered the higher number of casualties at Lexington and Concord?*
2. **THE WORLD IN SPATIAL TERMS** *Using the map legend, estimate the distance between Lexington and Boston.*

Those who believed that the British had become tyrants were known as Patriots or Whigs. Patriots were artisans, farmers, merchants, planters, lawyers, and urban workers. They were strong in New England and Virginia, while most Loyalists lived in Georgia, the Carolinas, and New York. Patriot groups enforced the boycott of British goods, sometimes by tarring and feathering Loyalists. Loyalists fought back, but there were not as many of them and they were not well organized.

Lexington and Concord

In April 1775, the British government risked armed conflict by ordering General Gage to arrest the Massachusetts Provincial Congress. Gage did not know where the Congress was sitting, so he decided to seize the militia's supply depot at Concord instead. On April 18, about 700 British troops set out for Concord on a road that took them through the town of Lexington.

Patriot leaders heard about the plan and sent Paul Revere and William Dawes to sound the alarm. The two men raced to Lexington and warned people that the British were coming. A third man, Dr. Samuel Prescott, joined them as they headed for Concord. A British patrol stopped Revere and Dawes, but Prescott got through in time to warn Concord.

On April 19, British troops arrived in Lexington and spotted some 70 minutemen lined up on the village green. The British marched onto the field and ordered them to disperse. The minutemen had begun to back away when a shot was fired; no one is sure by whom. The British soldiers then fired at the minutemen, killing 8 and wounding 10.

The British then headed to Concord, where they found that most of the military supplies had been removed by the colonial militia. When they tried to cross the North Bridge on the far side of town, they ran into some 400 colonial militia. A fight broke out, forcing the British to retreat. As the British headed back to Boston, militia and farmers fired at them from behind trees, stone walls, barns, and houses. By the time the British reached Boston, 73 men had been killed, 174 were wounded, and 26 were missing. The colonial forces had lost 49 men, 41 were wounded, and 5 were missing. News of the fighting spread across the colonies. Militia from all over New England raced to the area to help. By May 1775, the militia had surrounded Boston, trapping the British.

The Second Continental Congress

Three weeks after the battles at Lexington and Concord, the Second Continental Congress met in Philadelphia. The first issue was defense. The Congress voted to "adopt" the militia army surrounding Boston, and they named it the Continental Army. On June 15, 1775, the Congress selected George Washington to command the new army.

Before Washington could get to his new command the British landed reinforcements in Boston. Determined to gain control of the area, the British decided to seize the hills north of the city. Warned in advance, the militia acted first. On June 16, 1775, they dug in on Breed's Hill near Bunker Hill and began building a fort at the top. The following day, General Gage sent 2,200 troops to take the hill. According to legend, an American commander named William Prescott told his troops, "Don't fire until you see the whites of their eyes!" When the British closed at 40 yards' distance, the Americans fired. They stopped two British attacks and were forced to retreat only after running out of ammunition.

The Battle of Bunker Hill, as it came to be called, helped build American confidence. It showed that the colonial militia could stand up to one of the world's most feared armies. The British suffered more than 1,000 casualties

British troops retreated from a confident colonial militia at the Battle of Bunker Hill.

▶ **CRITICAL THINKING**
Determining Cause and Effect What is the relationship between the Battles of Lexington and Concord and the Battle of Bunker Hill?

in the fighting. Shortly afterward, General Gage resigned and was replaced by General William Howe. The situation became a stalemate with the British troops encircled by colonial militia.

✓ **PROGRESS CHECK**

Interpreting Why was the Battle of Bunker Hill significant to the American cause?

The Decision to Declare Independence

GUIDING QUESTION *How did written statements help define the Revolution?*

Despite the onset of fighting, many colonists in the summer of 1775 were not prepared to break away from Great Britain. Most members of the Second Continental Congress wanted the right to govern themselves, but they did not want to break with the British Empire. By 1776 opinions had changed. Frustrated by Britain's refusal to compromise, many Patriot leaders began to call for independence.

Efforts at Peace

In July 1775, as the siege of Boston continued, the Continental Congress sent a document known as the Olive Branch Petition to King George III. Written primarily by John Dickinson, the petition stated that the colonies were still loyal to the king and asked him to call off hostilities until the situation could be negotiated peacefully.

When the Olive Branch Petition arrived in London in August 1775, the king refused to look at it. Instead he issued the Proclamation for Suppressing Rebellion and Sedition, declaring that the colonists were now in "open and avowed rebellion." The proclamation called on all loyal British subjects in the colonies to "bring the traitors to justice."

When the Continental Congress authorized an attack on British troops based in Quebec, relations with the British were further strained. The delegates hoped the attack would convince the French in Quebec to rebel and join in fighting the British. The American forces captured the city of Montreal, but the French did not rebel.

With no compromise with Britain likely, the Continental Congress began to act like an independent government. It sent people to negotiate with the Native Americans and established a postal system, a Continental Navy, and a Marine Corps. By March 1776, the Continental Navy had raided the Bahamas and had begun seizing British merchant ships.

The Fighting Spreads

As the Revolution began, Governor Dunmore of Virginia organized two Loyalist armies to assist British troops in Virginia, one composed of white Loyalists, the other of enslaved Africans. Dunmore proclaimed that Africans enslaved by rebels would be freed if they fought for the Loyalists. The announcement convinced many Southern planters that the colonies had to declare independence. Otherwise, they might lose their labor force. They increased their efforts to raise a large Patriot army.

In December 1775, the Patriot troops attacked and defeated Dunmore's forces near Norfolk, Virginia. Months later the British pulled their soldiers out of Virginia, leaving the Patriots in control. In North Carolina, Patriot troops dispersed Loyalists at the Battle of Moore's Creek Bridge in February 1776. The British then decided to seize Charles Towne, South Carolina, but the city militia thwarted their attack.

POLITICAL CARTOONS

AMERICAN RESISTANCE

In this 1779 British cartoon, a horse named "America" throws its rider, King George III.

▶ **CRITICAL THINKING**

1 *Identifying Central Issues* Why did Americans wish to rid themselves of King George as their leader?

2 *Drawing Conclusions* What is the cartoon's artist saying about the outcome of the American Revolution?

THE HORSE AMERICA, throwing his Master

While fighting raged in the South, Washington ordered his troops to capture the hills south of Boston. After the Americans seized the hills by surprise and surrounded Boston, the British navy evacuated the British troops, leaving the Patriots in control.

Despite their defeats, it was clear that the British were not backing down. In December 1775, Parliament passed the Prohibitory Act, shutting down trade with the colonies and ordering a naval blockade. The British also began recruiting mercenaries, or soldiers for hire, from Germany.

Common Sense and Independence

As the war dragged on, more and more Patriots began to think that the time had come to declare independence, although they feared that most colonists were still loyal to the king. In January 1776 public opinion began to change when Thomas Paine published a persuasive pamphlet called *Common Sense*. Until *Common Sense* appeared, nearly everyone viewed Parliament, not the king, as the enemy. In *Common Sense,* Paine attacked King George III. Parliament, he wrote, did nothing without the king's support. Paine argued that monarchies had been set up by seizing power from the people. King George III was a tyrant, and it was time for the colonists to declare independence:

Thomas Paine appealed to many colonists by using direct and clear language to suggest independence from Britain.

▶ **CRITICAL THINKING**
Drawing Inferences How could Thomas Paine's use of language have increased the appeal of *Common Sense*?

PRIMARY SOURCE

❝Every thing that is right or reasonable pleads for separation. The blood of the slain, the weeping voice of nature cries, 'TIS TIME TO PART. . . .

. . . Every spot of the old world is over-run with oppression. Freedom hath been hunted round the globe. Asia and Africa have long expelled her,—Europe regards her like a stranger, and England hath given her warning to depart. O receive the fugitive, and prepare in time an asylum for mankind.❞

—from *Common Sense*, 1776

Within three months, *Common Sense* had sold 100,000 copies. George Washington noted that "*Common Sense* is working a powerful change in the minds of men." One by one, the provincial congresses and legislatures told their representatives at the Continental Congress to vote for independence.

In early July, a committee **submitted** a document that Thomas Jefferson had drafted on independence. On July 4, 1776, the Continental Congress issued this Declaration of Independence. The colonies had now become the United States of America. The American Revolution had begun.

submit to put forward for consideration or judgment

✓ **PROGRESS CHECK**

Analyzing How did Thomas Paine help persuade colonists to declare independence?

PHOTO: Library of Congress

LESSON 2 REVIEW

Reviewing Vocabulary

1. ***Explaining*** Explain how the committees of correspondence helped unite the colonies against the British.

2. ***Describing*** Write about two instances where the colonists did not submit to the British.

Using Your Notes

3. ***Organizing*** Use your notes to indicate ways in which colonists defied Britain after the repeal of the Townshend Acts.

Answering the Guiding Questions

4. ***Summarizing*** What caused the colonies to begin their revolution against Great Britain?

5. ***Describing*** How did the battles at Lexington and Concord shape the American Revolution?

6. ***Making Generalizations*** How did written statements help define the Revolution?

Writing Activity

7. **DESCRIPTIVE** Suppose that you were a participant in the Boston Tea Party. Write a diary entry describing the event.

THE DECLARATION
of INDEPENDENCE

Words are spelled as originally written.

In Congress, July 4, 1776. The unanimous Declaration of the thirteen united States of America,

[Preamble]

What It Means

The Preamble The Declaration of Independence has four parts. The Preamble explains why the Continental Congress drew up the Declaration.

When in the Course of human events, it becomes necessary for one people to dissolve the political bands which have connected them with another, and to assume among the Powers of the earth, the separate and equal station to which the Laws of Nature and of Nature's God entitle them, a decent respect to the opinions of mankind requires that they should declare the causes which **impel** them to the separation.

impel: force

[Declaration of Natural Rights]

What It Means

Natural Rights The second part, the Declaration of Natural Rights, states that people have certain basic rights and that government should protect those rights. John Locke's ideas strongly influenced this part. In 1690 Locke wrote that government was based on the consent of the people and that people had the right to rebel if the government did not uphold their right to life, liberty, and property.

We hold these truths to be self-evident, that all men are created equal, that they are **endowed** by their Creator with certain unalienable Rights, that among these are Life, Liberty, and the pursuit of Happiness.

That to secure these rights, Governments are instituted among Men, deriving their just powers from the consent of the governed,

That whenever any Form of Government becomes destructive of these ends, it is the Right of the People to alter or to abolish it, and to institute new Government, laying its foundation on such principles and organizing its powers in such form, as to them shall seem most likely to effect their Safety and Happiness. Prudence, indeed, will dictate that Governments long established should not be changed for light and transient causes; and accordingly all experience hath shown, that mankind are more disposed to suffer, while

endowed: provided

evils are sufferable, than to right themselves by abolishing the forms to which they are accustomed. But when a long train of abuses and usurpations, pursuing invariably the same Object evinces a design to reduce them under absolute **Despotism**, it is their right, it is their duty, to throw off such Government, and to provide new Guards for their future security.

[List of Grievances]

Such has been the patient sufferance of these Colonies; and such is now the necessity which constrains them to alter their former Systems of Government. The history of the present King of Great Britain is a history of repeated injuries and **usurpations**, all having in direct object the establishment of an absolute Tyranny over these States. To prove this, let Facts be submitted to a candid world.

He has refused his Assent to Laws, the most wholesome and necessary for the public good.

He has forbidden his Governors to pass Laws of immediate and pressing importance, unless suspended in their operation till his Assent should be obtained; and when so suspended, he has utterly neglected to attend to them.

He has refused to pass other Laws for the accommodation of large districts of people, unless those people would **relinquish** the right of Representation in the Legislature, a right **inestimable** to them and formidable to tyrants only.

He has called together legislative bodies at places unusual, uncomfortable, and distant from the depository of their

despotism: unlimited power

What It Means

List of Grievances The third part of the Declaration is a list of the colonists' complaints against the British government. Notice that King George III is singled out for blame.

usurpations: unjust uses of power

relinquish: give up
inestimable: priceless

▼ *Declaration of Independence* by John Trumbull depicts the presentation of the Declaration of Independence to John Hancock (seated right), president of the Continental Congress.

annihilation: destruction

convulsions: violent disturbances

Naturalization of Foreigners: process by which foreign-born persons become citizens

tenure: term

quartering: lodging

render: make

Public Records, for the sole purpose of fatiguing them into compliance with his measures.

He has dissolved Representative Houses repeatedly, for opposing with manly firmness his invasions on the rights of the people.

He has refused for a long time, after such dissolutions, to cause others to be elected; whereby the Legislative Powers, incapable of **Annihilation**, have returned to the People at large for their exercise; the State remaining in the mean time exposed to all the dangers of invasion from without, and **convulsions** within.

He has endeavoured to prevent the population of these States; for that purpose obstructing the Laws for **Naturalization of Foreigners;** refusing to pass others to encourage their migrations hither, and raising the conditions of new Appropriations of Lands.

He has obstructed the Administration of Justice, by refusing his Assent to Laws for establishing Judiciary Powers.

He has made Judges dependent on his Will alone, for the **tenure** of their offices, and the amount and payment of their salaries.

He has erected a multitude of New Offices, and sent hither swarms of Officers to harass our people, and eat out their substance.

He has kept among us, in times of peace, Standing Armies without the Consent of our legislature.

He has affected to render the Military independent of and superior to the Civil Power.

He has combined with others to subject us to a jurisdiction foreign to our constitution, and unacknowledged by our laws; giving his Assent to their acts of pretended legislation:

For **quartering** large bodies of troops among us:

For protecting them, by a mock Trial, from Punishment for any Murders which they should commit on the Inhabitants of these States:

For cutting off our Trade with all parts of the world:

For imposing taxes on us without our Consent:

For depriving us in many cases, of the benefits of Trial by Jury:

For transporting us beyond Seas to be tried for pretended offences:

For abolishing the free System of English Laws in a neighbouring Province, establishing therein an Arbitrary government, and enlarging its Boundaries so as to **render** it at once an example and fit instrument for introducing the same absolute rule into these Colonies:

For taking away our Charters, abolishing our most valuable Laws, and altering fundamentally the Forms of our Governments:

For suspending our own Legislature, and declaring themselves invested with Power to legislate for us in all cases whatsoever.

He has **abdicated** Government here, by declaring us out of his Protection and waging War against us.

He has plundered our seas, ravaged our Coasts, burnt our towns, and destroyed the lives of our people.

He is at this time transporting large armies of foreign mercenaries to compleat the works of death, desolation and tyranny, already begun with circumstances of Cruelty & **perfidy** scarcely paralleled in the most barbarous ages, and totally unworthy the Head of a civilized nation.

He has constrained our fellow Citizens taken Captive on the high Seas to bear Arms against their Country, to become the executioners of their friends and Brethren, or to fall themselves by their Hands.

He has excited domestic **insurrections** amongst us, and has endeavoured to bring on the inhabitants of our frontiers, the merciless Indian Savages, whose known rule of warfare, is an undistinguished destruction of all ages, sexes and conditions.

In every stage of these Oppressions We have **Petitioned for Redress** in the most humble terms: Our repeated Petitions have been answered only by repeated injury. A Prince, whose character is thus marked by every act which may define a Tyrant, is unfit to be the ruler of a free People.

Nor have We been wanting in attention to our British brethren. We have warned them from time to time of attempts by their legislature to extend an **unwarrantable jurisdiction** over us. We have reminded them of the circumstances of our emigration and settlement here. We have appealed to their native justice and magnanimity, and we have conjured them by the ties of our common kindred to disavow these usurpations, which, would inevitably interrupt our connections and correspondence. They too have been deaf to the voice of justice and of **consanguinity**. We must, therefore, acquiesce in the necessity, which denounces our Separation, and hold them, as we hold the rest of mankind, Enemies in War, in Peace Friends.

[Resolution of Independence by the United States]

We, therefore, the Representatives of the united States of America, in General Congress, Assembled, appealing to the Supreme Judge of the world for the **rectitude** of our intentions, do, in the Name, and by Authority of the good People of these Colonies, solemnly publish and declare,

abdicated: given up

perfidy: violation of trust

insurrections: rebellions

petitioned for redress: asked formally for a correction of wrongs

unwarrantable jurisdiction: unjustified authority

consanguinity: originating from the same ancestor

What It Means

Resolution of Independence The final section declares that the colonies are "Free and Independent States" with the full power to make war, to form alliances, and to trade with other countries.

rectitude: rightness

That these United Colonies are, and of Right ought to be Free and Independent States; that they are Absolved from all Allegiance to the British Crown, and that all political connection between them and the State of Great Britain, is and ought to be totally dissolved; and that as Free and Independent States, they have full Power to levy War, conclude Peace, contract Alliances, establish Commerce, and to do all other Acts and Things which Independent States may of right do.

And for the support of this Declaration, with a firm reliance on the Protection of Divine Providence, we mutually pledge to each other our Lives, our Fortunes and our sacred Honor.

What It Means

Signers of the Declaration The signers, as representatives of the American people, declared the colonies independent from Great Britain. Most members signed the document on August 2, 1776.

John Hancock
  President from
    Massachusetts

Georgia
Button Gwinnett
Lyman Hall
George Walton

North Carolina
William Hooper
Joseph Hewes
John Penn

South Carolina
Edward Rutledge
Thomas Heyward, Jr.
Thomas Lynch, Jr.
Arthur Middleton

Maryland
Samuel Chase
William Paca
Thomas Stone
Charles Carroll
  of Carrollton

Virginia
George Wythe
Richard Henry Lee
Thomas Jefferson
Benjamin Harrison
Thomas Nelson, Jr.
Francis Lightfoot Lee
Carter Braxton

Pennsylvania
Robert Morris
Benjamin Rush
Benjamin Franklin
John Morton
George Clymer
James Smith
George Taylor
James Wilson
George Ross

Delaware
Caesar Rodney
George Read
Thomas McKean

New York
William Floyd
Philip Livingston
Francis Lewis
Lewis Morris

New Jersey
Richard Stockton
John Witherspoon
Francis Hopkinson
John Hart
Abraham Clark

New Hampshire
Josiah Bartlett
William Whipple
Matthew Thornton

Massachusetts
Samuel Adams
John Adams
Robert Treat Paine
Elbridge Gerry

Rhode Island
Stephen Hopkins
William Ellery

Connecticut
Samuel Huntington
William Williams
Oliver Wolcott
Roger Sherman

networks

There's More Online!

- ☑ **BIOGRAPHY** Marquis de Lafayette
- ☑ **IMAGE** Treaty of Paris
- ☑ **VIDEO** The War for Independence
- ☑ **INTERACTIVE SELF-CHECK QUIZ**

Reading **HELP**DESK

Content Vocabulary
- guerrilla warfare
- morale

Academic Vocabulary
- equip
- objective

TAKING NOTES: *Sequencing*

ACTIVITY Complete a time line similar to the one below to record the major battles of the American Revolution and their outcomes.

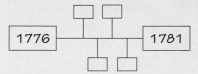

1776   1781

LESSON 3
The War for Independence

ESSENTIAL QUESTION • *Why do people rebel?*

IT MATTERS BECAUSE

The Continental Army experienced several setbacks while fighting against the British military in a war that lasted many years. Eventually, the Americans, with the help of the French and other nations, were able to foil the British war strategy and win independence.

The Opposing Sides

GUIDING QUESTION *How did the opposing sides of the Revolutionary War compare with each other?*

On the day that the Continental Congress voted for independence, the British began landing troops in New York Harbor. By mid-August, they had assembled some 32,000 men under the command of General William Howe. British officials did not expect the rebellion to last long. The British troops, called "redcoats" because of their uniforms, were disciplined, well trained, and well **equipped.**

Compared to the British troops, the Continental Army was inexperienced and poorly equipped. Throughout the war, it struggled to keep its recruits and pay their wages. Although more than 230,000 men served in the Continental Army at various times, it rarely numbered more than 20,000 at any one time. Many soldiers deserted or refused to reenlist when their terms were up. Others left their posts and returned to their farms at planting or harvest time.

Paying for the war was equally difficult. Lacking the power to tax, the Continental Congress issued paper money. These "Continentals" were not backed by gold or silver and became almost worthless very quickly. Fortunately, Robert Morris, a wealthy Pennsylvania merchant and banker, personally pledged large amounts of money for the war effort. Morris also set up an efficient method of buying rations and uniforms, arranged for foreign loans, and convinced the Congress to create the Bank of North America to finance the military.

The Continental Army was not the only force the British had to worry about. British troops also had to fight the local militias. The militias were poorly trained, but they fought differently.

equip to furnish with provisions; to make ready for action

guerrilla warfare a hit-and-run technique used in fighting a war; fighting by small bands of warriors using tactics such as sudden ambushes

They did not always line up for battle. They hid behind trees and walls and ambushed British troops and supply wagons, then they disappeared. This kind of fighting is called **guerrilla warfare,** and it is very difficult to defeat.

Another problem for the British was that they were not united at home. Many merchants and members of Parliament opposed the war. The British had to win quickly and cheaply; otherwise, opinions in Parliament would shift against the war. The United States did not have to defeat Britain—it simply had to survive until the British became tired of paying for the war.

The European balance of power also hampered the British. The French, Dutch, and Spanish were all eager to exploit Britain's problems. As a result, Britain had to station much of its military elsewhere in the world to defend its empire. The European balance of power also meant that the Patriots might be able to find allies against the British.

All of these factors meant that the British needed to win quickly. To do so, they had to convince the rebellious American colonists that their cause was hopeless. At the same time, the British had to make it safe to surrender. If the Patriots thought they would be hanged for treason, they would never surrender.

General Howe's strategy, therefore, had two parts. First, he sent a large number of troops to capture New York City. This would separate New England from the South and demonstrate to Americans that they could not win. The second part of Howe's strategy was diplomatic. He invited delegates from the Continental Congress to a peace conference. Howe promised that rebels who laid down their arms and swore loyalty to the king would be pardoned. When the Americans realized that Howe had no authority to negotiate a compromise, they refused to talk further.

☑ **PROGRESS CHECK**

Identifying What disadvantages did British troops have when fighting colonial militia?

CHARTS/GRAPHS

THE OPPOSING SIDES

At the time of the American Revolution, the British military was among the most powerful forces in the world. The ragtag colonial forces did not seem to have a chance, yet perseverance and the desire for freedom tipped the scales in the colonists' favor.

▶ **CRITICAL THINKING**

1 ***Comparing and Contrasting*** How were the colonial and British armies' approaches to warfare similar? How were they different?

2 ***Analyzing Information*** How did other advantages help the colonists in the war?

COLONIAL

Advantages
- Fighting on home ground
- Good decisions by generals
- Fighting for rights and freedoms
- French alliance providing loans, naval support, and troops
- Time: the longer the war dragged on, the more likely the British were to give up

Disadvantages
- Untrained soldiers
- Food and ammunition shortages
- Weak and divided central government

BRITISH

Advantages
- Well-trained, well-supplied army and navy
- Wealthy nation with substantial resources
- Strong central government

Disadvantages
- Fighting in unfamiliar, hostile territory
- Fighting far from Britain
- Many troops were mercenaries, many indifferent to the cause
- Halfhearted support at home

Battles in the North

GUIDING QUESTION *How did the colonial army keep itself in the war during difficult early years, and what was the turning point of the war?*

Although the British had sent a huge force to seize New York City, the Congress asked Washington to try to defend it. To do so, Washington moved much of his army to Long Island. British troops attacked them in the summer of 1776. Many American soldiers fled, and some 1,500 were wounded or killed. The British captured New York City and used it as their headquarters for the rest of the war. Washington moved most of his remaining troops from Manhattan Island to White Plains, New York.

Around this time, Washington sent volunteer Captain Nathan Hale to spy on the British. Although Hale was disguised, he was caught by the British and hanged. Brave until the end and based on tradition, Hale's last words were: "I only regret that I have but one life to lose for my country."

Crossing the Delaware

At the Battle of White Plains in October 1776, the British surprised Washington by heading toward Philadelphia—where the Continental Congress was meeting—instead of going to White Plains. Washington's troops moved quickly to get there ahead of the British.

As both armies headed toward Philadelphia, the British stopped their advance and dispersed into winter camps in New Jersey. At this point, Washington tried something daring—a winter attack. In the 1700s, armies did not usually fight in the winter because of the weather and scarce food supplies. On December 25, 1776, Washington led some 2,400 men across the Delaware River and attacked a camp at Trenton in the middle of a sleet storm. They killed or captured almost 1,000 Hessian mercenaries there. Several days later, Washington's forces scattered three British regiments near Princeton.

Philadelphia Falls

In early 1777, British general John Burgoyne, based in Quebec, developed a plan to isolate New England. Unfortunately for the British, they did not coordinate the plan. Burgoyne began marching south from Montreal on June 17, 1777, and General Howe did not move his 15,000 troops until July 23, when they traveled by ship to Maryland and attacked Philadelphia. Howe defeated Washington at the Battle of Brandywine Creek and captured Philadelphia, but the Continental Congress escaped and no Loyalist uprising occurred.

Howe also failed to destroy the Continental Army, which set up its winter camp at Valley Forge. Joining Washington at Valley Forge were two European military officers, the Marquis de Lafayette from France and Baron Friedrich von Steuben from Prussia. These officers helped Washington improve discipline and boost **morale,** or feeling of confidence, among the weary troops despite the camp's harsh conditions. Bitter cold and food shortages killed more than 2,000 men.

The Battle of Saratoga

In June 1777, General Burgoyne and about 9,500 troops marched from Quebec into New York. Another 900 troops under the command of Colonel Barry St. Leger headed down the St. Lawrence to the eastern end of Lake Ontario. There, they joined more than 1,000 allied Iroquois warriors and headed east toward Albany.

PHOTO: PoodlesRock/Fine Art/CORBIS

Analyzing PRIMARY SOURCES

Thomas Paine on the War for Independence

❝These are the times that try men's souls. The summer-soldier and the sun-shine patriot will, in this crisis, shrink from the service of their country; but he that stands it *now*, deserves the thanks of man and woman.❞

—Thomas Paine, *The American Crisis*

DBQ **SYNTHESIZING** What does Paine mean when he states that the "summer-soldier and sun-shine patriot" will shrink from service?

morale a feeling of confidence or enthusiasm

British general John Burgoyne surrendered to American general Horatio Gates at Saratoga on October 17, 1777.

▶ **CRITICAL THINKING**
Predicting Consequences What do you think were the consequences of the surrender by British general John Burgoyne?

The War for Independence 1776–1777

Quebec

Nova Scotia

Maine (part of Mass.)

Montreal

BURGOYNE 1777

St. Lawrence R.

ST. LEGER, 1777

N.H.

Oct. 17, 1777: Burgoyne surrendered at Saratoga

Ft. Ticonderoga July 6, 1777

Saratoga

Bennington Aug. 16, 1777

Boston

GENERAL HOWE, MARCH 17, 1776

Oriskany Aug. 6, 1777

Albany

Bemis Heights Oct. 7, 1777

Mass.

ATLANTIC OCEAN

Kingston

Conn.

R.I.

Sept. 1776: British captured New York City

N.Y.

Fort Montgomery □

40°N

New York City

Penn.

Princeton

N.J.

Brooklyn Heights Aug. 27, 1776

GENERAL HOWE, 1776

Germantown Oct. 4, 1777

Brandywine Creek Sept. 11, 1777

Trenton

Philadelphia

Dec. 1776, Jan. 1777: Americans attacked British at Trenton and Princeton

Md.

Del.

Sept. 1777: Howe captured Philadelphia

Virginia

Chesapeake Bay

GENERAL HOWE, 1777

75°W

0   100 miles
0   100 km
Albers Equal-Area projection

American forces
British forces
American victory
British victory
□ Fort

GEOGRAPHY CONNECTION

In March 1777, General John Burgoyne proposed a three-pronged attack to isolate New England from the other American states. The three forces would meet near Albany and then march east, but they did not coordinate the plan.

1 PLACES AND REGIONS *What are two colonial victories that occurred in New Jersey?*

2 HUMAN SYSTEMS *How did General Howe make his attack on America?*

At first, Burgoyne's troops easily seized Fort Ticonderoga. The Congress fired that region's commander and replaced him with General Horatio Gates. Meanwhile, the British and Iroquois forces were driven back by American troops led by General Benedict Arnold.

Burgoyne's march slowed to a crawl when American troops cut off their food supply. In desperation, Burgoyne retreated to Saratoga, where he was quickly surrounded by an American army. On October 17, 1777, he surrendered to General Gates. More than 5,000 British soldiers were taken prisoner. The victory improved American morale. Benjamin Franklin and others were sent to France in September 1776 to ask for troops. The French had not been willing to risk war until they believed the Americans could win. Because of the victory at Saratoga, the French were convinced.

On February 6, 1778, the United States signed two treaties. France became the first country to recognize the United States as an independent nation. The second treaty allied the United States and France. By June 1778, Britain and France were at war.

The War in the West

Not all the fighting in the Revolutionary War took place in the East. In 1778 Patriot George Rogers Clark took 175 troops down the Ohio River and captured several towns. By February 1779, the British had surrendered, giving the Americans control of the region.

In July 1778, Chief Joseph Brant, also known as Thayendanegea, joined the British with four Iroquois nations and attacked western Pennsylvania. The following summer, they were defeated by American troops. These battles destroyed the power of the Iroquois people. Farther south, the Cherokee suffered a similar fate after they attacked settlers in Virginia and North Carolina. Militia units retaliated by setting fire to set fire to hundreds of Cherokee towns.

The War at Sea
Americans fought the British at sea as well as on land. Instead of attacking the British fleet directly, American warships attacked British merchant ships. By the war's end, millions of dollars of cargo had been seized, seriously harming Britain's trade and economy.

Perhaps the most famous naval battle of the war involved the American naval officer John Paul Jones. Jones attacked the British warship *Serapis*, but the heavier guns of the British ship nearly sank Jones's ship. When the British commander called on Jones to surrender, Jones replied, "I have not yet begun to fight!" The battle lasted more than three hours before the British surrendered.

☑ PROGRESS CHECK

Summarizing How was the first treaty with France a turning point for the United States?

Battles in the South

GUIDING QUESTION *How did the Revolutionary War end?*

After the British defeat at Saratoga, General Howe resigned. He was replaced by Sir Henry Clinton, who ordered the British troops in Philadelphia to abandon the city and return to New York City. Clinton wanted to gather all his forces in one place before beginning a new campaign. Washington ordered his forces at Valley Forge to intercept the British. The two sides met at the Battle of Monmouth—the last major battle in the North. Neither side won, but for the first time American troops were able to stand up against the British in a conventional battle. After Clinton reached New York, he began a campaign in the South, where the British had the strongest Loyalist support. The British hoped to keep the South, even if they lost the North.

The Struggle in the Carolinas
In December 1778, some 3,500 British troops captured Savannah, Georgia. They seized control of Georgia's backcountry and returned the British royal governor to power. The next **objective** was to capture Charles Town, South Carolina—the largest city in the South. Clinton attacked Charles Town, his forces quickly surrounding the city, trapping the American forces inside. On May 12, 1780, the Americans surrendered. About 5,500 Americans were taken prisoner, the greatest American defeat in the war.

After capturing Charles Town, Clinton returned to New York, leaving General Charles Cornwallis in command. The Continental Congress then sent General Horatio Gates to defend the South Carolina backcountry. His attempt to destroy a British supply base at Camden, South Carolina, failed.

The Battle of Kings Mountain
After the Battle of Camden, the British began subduing the Carolina backcountry. Two British cavalry officers, Banastre Tarleton and Patrick Ferguson, led many of the Loyalist forces in the region. These troops became known for their brutality. Enraged at Ferguson's tactics, the "overmountain" men, as they were known, put together a militia. They intercepted Ferguson at Kings Mountain on October 7, 1780, and destroyed his army. By late 1781, the British controlled very little of the South.

According to tradition, Mary Hays, known as "Molly Pitcher," carried water to the troops during the Battle of Monmouth and helped fire a cannon after the crew was killed.

▶ **CRITICAL THINKING**
Drawing Conclusions Why might there be differing accounts of Molly Pitcher's actions during battle?

objective strategic position to be attained or a purpose to be achieved by a military operation

PHOTO: Fraunces Tavern® Museum, New York City

The British surrender at Yorktown. John Trumbull was not present at the surrender, but did his best to depict true likenesses of those he knew personally, such as George Washington, shown on horseback in the background.

▶ **CRITICAL THINKING**
Determining Cause and Effect What events led to the British surrender at the end of the war?

The Battle of Yorktown

In the spring of 1781, Cornwallis marched into Virginia. There he joined forces with Benedict Arnold, a former American general who had changed sides to fight for the British. The British gave him command of British troops and ordered him to Virginia.

After Arnold joined Cornwallis, the British began to conquer Virginia. Then, a large American force led by General Anthony Wayne arrived. Outnumbered and too far inland, Cornwallis retreated to the coastal town of Yorktown to protect his supplies and to maintain communications by sea.

Cornwallis's retreat created an opportunity. Washington decided to march on New York City with 6,000 French troops. As the troops headed to New York, Washington learned that Admiral de Grasse and his French fleet were sailing north from the Caribbean to the Chesapeake Bay. Washington canceled the attack on New York City. Instead, he and the French general Rochambeau headed to Yorktown. Rochambeau's fleet cut off the flow of supplies to Cornwallis and prevented him from escaping by sea.

On September 28, 1781, American and French forces surrounded Yorktown and began to bombard it. On October 14, Washington's aide, Alexander Hamilton, led an attack that captured key British defenses. Three days later, Cornwallis began negotiations to surrender, and on October 19, 1781, some 8,000 British soldiers laid down their weapons.

The Treaty of Paris

In March 1782, Parliament voted to begin peace negotiations. John Adams, Benjamin Franklin, and John Jay conducted most of the negotiations for the United States. On September 3, 1783, three treaties were signed—between Britain and the United States and between Britain and France and Spain.

In the final settlement, known as the Treaty of Paris, Britain recognized the United States of America as an independent nation, with the Mississippi River as its western border. Britain gave Florida back to Spain, and France received colonies in Africa and the Caribbean. On November 24, 1783, the last British troops left New York City. The American Revolution was over. A new nation was born.

☑ **PROGRESS CHECK**

Sequencing How was the war won at Yorktown?

PHOTO: The Granger Collection, New York

LESSON 3 REVIEW

Reviewing Vocabulary
1. *Describing* How would a British soldier describe the guerrilla warfare tactics used by the colonists?

2. *Discussing* In the present day, what might be ways to boost the morale of American troops?

Using Your Notes
3. *Identifying* Use your notes to identify the key battles of the American Revolution and the result of these battles.

Answering the Guiding Questions
4. *Comparing and Contrasting* How did the opposing sides of the Revolutionary War compare with each other?

5. *Determining Cause and Effect* How did the colonial army keep itself in the war during difficult early years, and what was the turning point of the war?

6. *Summarizing* How did the Revolutionary War end?

Writing Activity
7. **PERSUASIVE** Suppose that you are a colonial leader during the American Revolution. Write a letter to convince the ruler of a European nation to support the Americans in the war.

networks

There's More Online!

- ☑ **BIOGRAPHY** Abigail Adams
- ☑ **IMAGE** Noah Webster's *American Spelling Book*
- ☑ **VIDEO** The War Changes American Society
- ☑ **INTERACTIVE SELF-CHECK QUIZ**

LESSON 4
The War Changes American Society

ESSENTIAL QUESTION · *Why do people rebel?*

Reading HELPDESK

Content Vocabulary

- republic
- emancipation
- manumission

Academic Vocabulary

- contradiction
- revolutionary

TAKING NOTES: *Organizing*

ACTIVITY As you read, complete a graphic organizer similar to the one below by listing the features of the U.S. political system set up after the Revolution.

Features of New U.S. Political System

IT MATTERS BECAUSE

The American Revolution changed society in a variety of ways. New forms of government encouraged new political ideas. Additionally, many of those who had been loyal to Britain left; this strengthened the development of a new, American cultural identity.

New Political Ideas

GUIDING QUESTION *What new political ideas defined the American republic?*

When American leaders declared independence and founded the United States, they were aware that they were creating something new. By breaking away from the king, they had established a **republic.** A republic is a form of government in which power resides with a body of citizens who make laws for the whole. Elected officials exercise that power but are responsible to the citizens and must govern according to laws or a constitution.

In an ideal republic, all citizens are equal under the law, regardless of their wealth or social class. These ideas contradicted traditional practices that restricted the rights of many people on the basis of their race, class, or gender. Despite these **contradictions,** republican ideas began to change American society after the war.

New State Constitutions

Events before the Revolution led many Americans to believe that each state's constitution should be written down and that it should limit the government's power over the people. At the same time, many, including John Adams, worried that democracy could endanger a republican government and lead to tyranny. When Adams used the word *democracy,* he meant a society where the majority rules. He and other founders feared that in a pure democracy, minority groups would not have their rights protected. For example, the poor might vote to take everything away from the rich. Adams argued that government needed "checks and balances" to prevent any group in society from becoming strong enough to take away the rights of the minority.

republic form of government in which power resides in a body of citizens entitled to vote

contradiction a situation in which inherent factors, actions, or propositions are inconsistent or contrary to one another

Adams favored separation of powers; he believed the executive, legislative, and judicial branches should be independent of one another. He also argued that the legislature should have two houses: a senate to represent people of property and an assembly to protect the rights of the common people. His ideas influenced several of the new state constitutions drafted during the Revolution.

Many states also attached a list of rights to their constitutions. This began in 1776 when George Mason drafted Virginia's Declaration of Rights, which guaranteed Virginians freedom of speech and religion as well as the right to bear arms and the right to trial by jury. It also barred the state from searching homes without a warrant or taking property without proper court proceedings.

Voting Rights Expand

The Revolution led to an expansion of voting rights in most of the states. The experience of fighting alongside people of every social class and region increased Americans' belief in equality and weakened feelings of deference toward the upper class.

As a result, most of the new state constitutions made it easier for men to get the right to vote. Many states let any white male who paid taxes vote, whether or not he owned property. In most states, people still had to own a certain amount of property to hold elective office, but the practice of giving veterans land grants as payment for military service increased the number of people eligible to hold office.

Freedom of Religion

The Revolution also led to changes in the relationship between church and state. Many of the Revolution's leaders feared "ecclesiastical tyranny"—the power of a church, backed by the government, to make people worship in a certain way.

In Virginia, Baptists led a movement to abolish taxes collected to support the Anglican Church. Thomas Jefferson wrote the Virginia Statute for Religious Freedom, which was enacted in 1786. The statute declared:

PRIMARY SOURCE

❝[N]o man shall be compelled to . . . support any religious worship, place or ministry . . . nor shall otherwise suffer on account of his religious opinions or belief; but that all men shall be free to profess . . . their opinions in matters of religion.❞

—from the Virginia Statute for Religious Freedom

The statute also declared that Virginia no longer had an official church and that the state could not collect taxes for churches.

✓ PROGRESS CHECK

Examining What freedoms did the Virginia Declaration of Rights guarantee, reflecting new ideas about individual rights?

The War and American Society

GUIDING QUESTION *How did life change for women, African Americans, Native Americans, and Loyalists after the war?*

Alert to the contradictions between slavery and the affirmation of natural rights in the Declaration of Independence, the Pennsylvania legislature passed a gradual emancipation act in 1780. In the next 21 years, all of the Northern states put slavery on the road to extinction, turning the Mason-Dixon line into a symbolic divide between free and slave states. While the American ideals of equality and liberty did not yet apply to women and enslaved people in the South, both groups did find their lives changed by the Revolution, as did Loyalists who had supported Britain.

George Mason was the principal author of the Virginia Declaration of Rights. Mason's ideas were widely copied, and other states adopted similar declarations of rights to protect citizens.

▶ CRITICAL THINKING
Interpreting Significance Why did other states find it important to draft a declaration of rights?

Women at War

Women played a vital role in the Revolutionary War, contributing on both the home front and the battlefront. With their husbands, brothers, and sons at war, some women took over running family farms. Others traveled with the army—cooking, washing, and nursing the wounded. Women also served as spies and couriers; a few even joined the fighting.

After the war, as Americans thought about what their **revolutionary** ideals implied, women made some advances. They could more easily get a divorce and gained more access to education. Many schools for girls were founded, and more women learned to read.

African Americans

Thousands of enslaved African Americans obtained their freedom during the Revolution. Many planters freed enslaved people who agreed to fight the British, and General Washington let African Americans join the Continental Army. He also urged state militias to admit African Americans and to offer freedom to all who served.

After the Revolution, many Americans realized that enslaving people did not fit in with the new ideals of liberty and equality. Opposition to slavery had been growing steadily even before the Revolution, especially in the North. After the war began, **emancipation,** or freedom from enslavement, became a major issue. Many Northern states took steps to end slavery, often by passing laws that freed enslaved people when they reached a certain age. Ending slavery in the North was thus a gradual process that took several decades.

With a new Massachusetts constitution that said that all people were free and equal, some African Americans sued to win their freedom. Quock Walker, an enslaved person who had been assaulted by the man who claimed to own him, believed that the law was on his side. Massachusetts chief justice William Cushing agreed and found in his favor.

revolutionary constituting or bringing about a major or fundamental change

emancipation the act or process of freeing enslaved persons

Dinah Morris was one of the first enslaved people in the North granted her freedom during the American Revolution.

▶ CRITICAL THINKING
Making Generalizations Why would life continue to be difficult for African Americans even after being granted their freedom?

PRIMARY SOURCE

❝Our [state] Constitution . . . sets out with declaring that all men are born free and equal—and that every subject is entitled to liberty and to have it guarded by the laws, as well as life and property—and in short is totally repugnant to the idea of [people] being born slaves. This being the case, I think the idea of slavery is inconsistent with our own conduct and Constitution.❞

—Chief Justice William Cushing,
Massachusetts court ruling, 1783

Discrimination against African Americans did not disappear with emancipation, however. African Americans were often only able to get only low-level jobs such as digging, carrying, or sweeping. Free African Americans also faced voting restrictions, segregation, or kidnapping and transportation to the South, where they would again be enslaved. Despite the hardships, freedom offered the possibility of choices and opportunities.

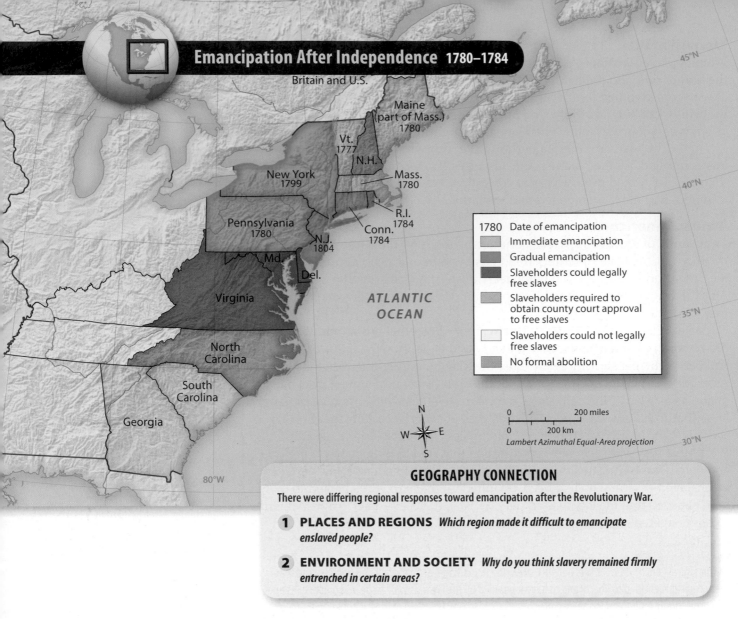

Britain and U.S.

Maine
(part of Mass.)
1780

Vt.
1777

N.H.

Mass.
1780

New York
1799

R.I.
1784

Pennsylvania
1780

Conn.
1784

N.J.
1804

Md.

Del.

Virginia

ATLANTIC
OCEAN

North
Carolina

South
Carolina

Georgia

1780	Date of emancipation
	Immediate emancipation
	Gradual emancipation
	Slaveholders could legally free slaves
	Slaveholders required to obtain county court approval to free slaves
	Slaveholders could not legally free slaves
	No formal abolition

0   200 miles

0   200 km

Lambert Azimuthal Equal-Area projection

GEOGRAPHY CONNECTION

There were differing regional responses toward emancipation after the Revolutionary War.

1 **PLACES AND REGIONS** *Which region made it difficult to emancipate enslaved people?*

2 **ENVIRONMENT AND SOCIETY** *Why do you think slavery remained firmly entrenched in certain areas?*

Once free, many African Americans moved to Northern cities to find jobs. Some found opportunities to begin a new life in occupations from which they had previously been barred, such as artists and ministers.

The story was quite different in the South, which relied on enslaved labor to sustain its agricultural economy. Southern leaders showed little interest in ending slavery. Only Virginia took steps toward ending the institution. In 1782 the state passed a law encouraging **manumission,** or the voluntary freeing of enslaved people, especially for those who had fought in the Revolution. Through this law, about 10,000 enslaved people obtained their freedom, but the vast majority remained in bondage.

manumission the voluntary freeing of enslaved persons

Native Americans

The Revolution did not help most Native Americans. By aligning with the British against colonists, the Iroquois Confederacy was weakened after the war and member groups fought against each other. Few Native Americans on either side of the conflict were recognized for their contributions.

The Loyalists Flee

Many women, many Native Americans, and a great number of African Americans found their lives little changed as a result of the Revolution. For many Loyalists, however, the end of the war changed everything.

Because of their support for the British during the war, Loyalists often found themselves shunned by former friends and neighbors, and state governments sometimes seized their property.

Unwilling to live under the new government about 100,000 Loyalists left the United States. Most moved to British North America, particularly Nova Scotia, New Brunswick, and the region near Niagara Falls, which was then part of Quebec. In 1791 Britain made the region near Niagara Falls a separate colony called Upper Canada. Today it is the province of Ontario.

An American Culture Emerges

In the United States, victory over the British united Americans and created powerful nationalist feelings. The Revolution War helped this process in two ways. First, Americans in all states had a common enemy. Soldiers from all over the country had fought side by side in each other's states. Second, the war gave rise to a common folklore. Stories of the Revolution and its heroes encouraged Americans to see themselves as belonging to the same group.

American Painters The Revolution also inspired American painters, including John Trumbull and Charles Willson Peale. Their work contributed to an American identity. Trumbull served in the Continental Army as an aide to Washington. He is best known for his depiction of important events in the Revolution. Peale was a soldier who survived the winter at Valley Forge. He is best known for his portraits of Washington and other Patriot leaders.

Changes in Education As they started a new nation, American leaders considered an educated public to be critical to the republic's success. Several state constitutions provided for government-funded universities. At the same time, elementary schools instituted an American-centered style of teaching. Tossing out British textbooks, they taught republican ideas and the history of the struggle for independence.

Noah Webster was one of the educators who believed that Americans needed to develop their own educational system based on their own culture. He is most famous for his 1828 *American Dictionary of the English Language,* in which he set out to standardize American English and underscore its differences from British English.

As Americans began to build a national identity separate from Britain's, leaders of the United States turned their attention to the creation of a new government. They wanted to promote the ideals and beliefs that the colonists had fought so hard to secure.

In addition to compiling a dictionary that has become the standard of American English, Noah Webster also created *The American Spelling Book,* which became the basic textbook in early nineteenth-century America.

▶ **CRITICAL THINKING**
Making Inferences Why do you think Webster created a textbook that emphasized American English?

☑ **PROGRESS CHECK**

Making Connections How did the ideals of the American Revolution affect the treatment and status of different groups in American society?

LESSON 4 REVIEW

Reviewing Vocabulary
1. *Explaining* Explain why laws encouraging manumission were different from complete emancipation.

Using Your Notes
2. *Identifying* Use your notes to identify the changes brought about by the new U.S. political system.

Answering the Guiding Questions
3. *Describing* What new political ideas defined the American republic?

4. *Analyzing* How did life change for women, African Americans, Native Americans, and Loyalists after the war?

Writing Activity
5. EXPOSITORY Suppose that you are on a committee to write a new state constitution. List the freedoms you want protected in that constitution, and explain why you feel it is important to guarantee each one.

Directions: On a separate sheet of paper, answer the questions below. Make sure you read carefully and answer all parts of the question.

Lesson Review

Lesson 1

1 *Making Connections* What did the Albany Plan of Union show about how the colonies might respond in a time of struggle?

2 *Analyzing* What was the impact of the French and Indian War on the relationship between Britain and the American colonies?

Lesson 2

3 *Determining Cause and Effect* What was the significance of the Boston Tea Party and the Coercive Acts in driving the colonists toward independence?

4 *Drawing Inferences* How might Loyalists have responded to Thomas Paine's *Common Sense* pamphlet?

Lesson 3

5 *Summarizing* What were the strengths and weaknesses of the British army and the American troops?

6 *Predicting Consequences* If the American troops had lost the Battle of Saratoga, would the outcome of the Revolutionary War have been the same?

Lesson 4

7 *Drawing Inferences* What was the importance of Virginia's Declaration of Rights and what was the Declaration designed to protect?

8 *Determining Cause and Effect* How did life change for women during and after the American Revolution?

21st Century Skills

9 **IDENTIFYING CAUSE AND EFFECT** How did the colonies respond to the restrictions of the Stamp Act and what was the effect of their response?

10 **CITIZENSHIP** How did the end of the American Revolution create a new feeling of nationalism?

Exploring the Essential Question

11 *Determining Cause and Effect* Create an illustrated cause and effect chart that depicts four acts of rebellion that occurred between 1772 and 1795. Charts can include photos, sketched images, and maps. After your chart is complete, write a brief summary about why people rebel.

DBQ Document-Based Question

Use the document to answer the following questions.

In 1766 Benjamin Franklin testified before Parliament about the colonists' reaction to the Stamp Act:

PRIMARY SOURCE

"**Q.** Don't you know that the money [tax] arising from the stamps was all to be laid out in America?

A. I know it is appropriated by the act to the American service; but it will be spent in the conquered Colonies where the soldiers are, not in the colonies that pay it. . . .

Q. Do you think it right that America should be protected by this country and pay no part of the expence?

A. That is not the case. The Colonies raised, cloathed, and payed, during the last war, near 25000 men, and spent many millions.

Q. Were you not reimbursed by [P]arliament?

A. We were only reimbursed what, in your opinion, we had advanced beyond our proportion, or beyond what might reasonably be expected from us; and it was a very small part of what we spent. Pennsylvania, in particular, disbursed about 500,000 Pounds, and the reimbursements, in the whole, did not exceed 60,000 Pounds. "

—from Benjamin Franklin's testimony before Parliament, 1766

12 *Analyzing* Why does Franklin say that the tax is unfair?

Extended-Response Question

13 *Comparing and Contrasting* After the American Revolution, a new culture emerged in the United States. Write an expository essay that compares and contrasts American culture before and after the Revolution in these areas: government, society, the arts, and education.

Need Extra Help?

If You've Missed Question	**1**	**2**	**3**	**4**	**5**	**6**	**7**	**8**	**9**	**10**	**11**	**12**	**13**
Go to page	39	40	44	51	57	59	64	65	40	67	44	68	38

Creating a Constitution

1781–1789

ESSENTIAL QUESTION · *What gives a government authority?*

The Story Matters...

The end of the Revolutionary War marked the start of a different kind of battle: one to create a national government that was strong and effective but would not deprive the states or the people of their rights and independence. Cooling the hot debates over a new constitution at the Pennsylvania State House in 1787 was the steady resolve, hard work, and keen intelligence of Virginia delegate James Madison.

◄ Man With a Plan: Quiet, scholarly James Madison is often called the Father of the Constitution. His Virginia Plan became the blueprint for a government that could fairly represent every state, regardless of size. His careful notes of the closed sessions remain our most significant historical record of what really happened that momentous summer of 1787.

PHOTO: American School/Bridgeman Art Library/Getty Images

CHAPTER 3

Place and Time: United States 1781–1793

In the sweltering Philadelphia summer of 1787, the 55 delegates to the Constitutional Convention clashed and compromised in proceedings that were closed to the public. Despite the heat, humidity, disagreements, and close quarters, the delegates persevered until September 17, 1787, when a draft of a remarkable document was ready to take to the states.

Step Into the Place

Read the quotes and look at the information presented on the map.

 How do the opinions expressed in the quotes help shape the new government?

PRIMARY SOURCE

"In a single republic . . . usurpations are guarded against by a division of the government into distinct and separate departments. In the compound republic of America, the power surrendered by the people, is first divided between two distinct governments, and then the portion allotted to each, subdivided among distinct and separate departments. Hence a double security arises to the rights of the people. The different governments will controul [control] each other, at the same time that each will be controuled [controlled] by itself."

— James Madison, from *The Federalist,* No. 51, 1788

PRIMARY SOURCE

"*What concerns all, should be considered by all*; and individuals may injure a whole society, by not declaring their sentiments. It is therefore not only their right, but their duty, to declare them. . . . Before this tribunal of *the people*, let every one freely speak, what he really thinks, but with so sincere a reverence for the cause he ventures to discuss, as to use the utmost caution, lest he should lead any into errors, upon a point of such sacred concern as the public happiness."

—John Dickinson, from *Letters of Fabius,* 1788

Step Into the Time

Choose an event from the time line and write a description of how that event relates to the spirit of freedom and democracy of the new United States.

March 1781 The Articles of Confederation are ratified by the states

September 1783 Treaty of Paris ends the American Revolutionary War

U.S. PRESIDENTS

UNITED STATES

WORLD

1781   1783   1785

1783 Latin American soldier and statesman Simón Bolívar is born

1784 American ships begin trading with China at the port of Canton

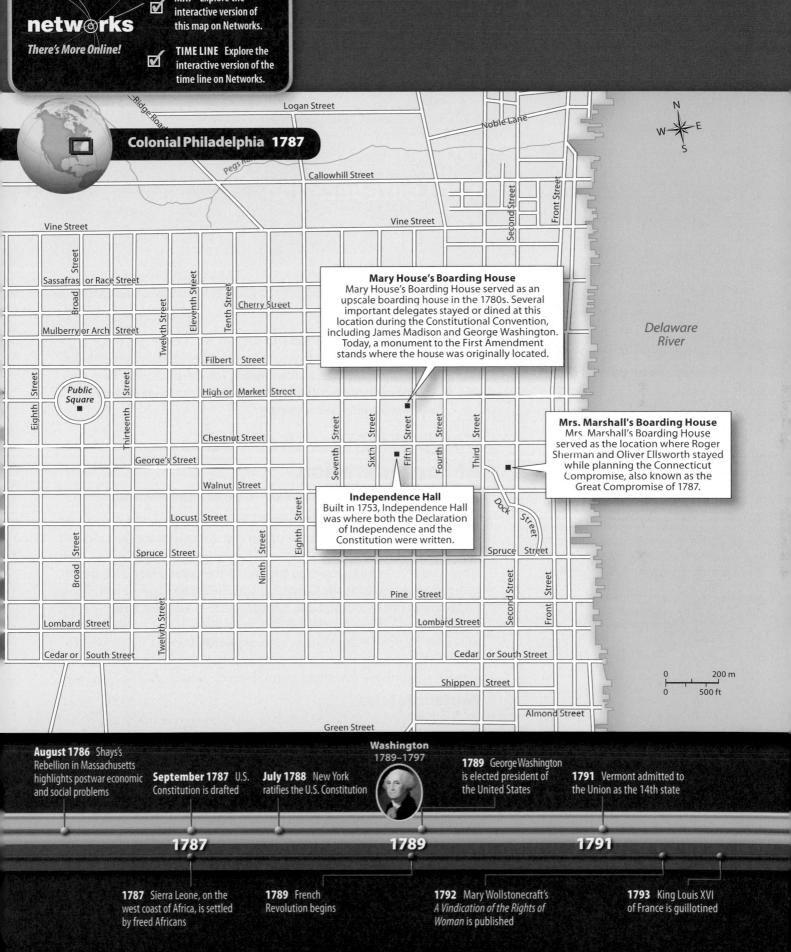

networks
There's More Online!

☑ **MAP** Explore the interactive version of this map on Networks.

☑ **TIME LINE** Explore the interactive version of the time line on Networks.

Colonial Philadelphia 1787

Logan Street

Noble Lane

Ridge Road

Pegs Run

Callowhill Street

Vine Street

Vine Street

Sassafras or Race Street

Broad Street

Mulberry or Arch Street

Eleventh Street

Twelfth Street

Cherry Street

Tenth Street

Filbert Street

Eighth Street

Public Square

Tenth Street

Thirteenth

High or Market Street

George's Street

Chestnut Street

Seventh Street

Sixth Street

Fifth Street

Fourth Street

Third Street

Walnut Street

Locust Street

Eighth Street

Broad Street

Spruce Street

Ninth Street

Dock Street

Spruce Street

Second Street

Front Street

Second Street

Front Street

Pine Street

Lombard Street

Lombard Street

Twelfth Street

Cedar or South Street

Cedar or South Street

Shippen Street

Almond Street

Green Street

Delaware River

Mary House's Boarding House
Mary House's Boarding House served as an upscale boarding house in the 1780s. Several important delegates stayed or dined at this location during the Constitutional Convention, including James Madison and George Washington. Today, a monument to the First Amendment stands where the house was originally located.

Mrs. Marshall's Boarding House
Mrs. Marshall's Boarding House served as the location where Roger Sherman and Oliver Ellsworth stayed while planning the Connecticut Compromise, also known as the Great Compromise of 1787.

Independence Hall
Built in 1753, Independence Hall was where both the Declaration of Independence and the Constitution were written.

0   200 m

0   500 ft

August 1786 Shays's Rebellion in Massachusetts highlights postwar economic and social problems

September 1787 U.S. Constitution is drafted

July 1788 New York ratifies the U.S. Constitution

Washington 1789–1797

1789 George Washington is elected president of the United States

1791 Vermont admitted to the Union as the 14th state

1787

1789

1791

1787 Sierra Leone, on the west coast of Africa, is settled by freed Africans

1789 French Revolution begins

1792 Mary Wollstonecraft's *A Vindication of the Rights of Woman* is published

1793 King Louis XVI of France is guillotined

networks

There's More Online!

☑ **CHART/GRAPH** Imports from Britain

☑ **MAP** British Forts

☑ **VIDEO** The Confederation

☑ **INTERACTIVE SELF-CHECK QUIZ**

LESSON 1
The Confederation

Reading **HELP**DESK

Content Vocabulary
• duty   • recession

Academic Vocabulary
• explicit   • occupy

NOTE TAKING: *Organizing*

ACTIVITY As you read, complete a graphic organizer similar to the one below by listing the achievements of the Congress.

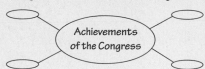

Achievements of the Congress

ESSENTIAL QUESTION • *What gives a government authority?*

IT MATTERS BECAUSE
The Articles of Confederation were the first national constitution of the United States. Written during the Revolutionary War, the Articles of Confederation created a weak national government, which proved to be ineffective.

Congress Under the Articles of Confederation

GUIDING QUESTION *How did government operate under the Articles of Confederation?*

In November 1777 the Continental Congress adopted the Articles of Confederation, a plan for a loose union of the states under the authority of the Congress. Under the Articles of Confederation, once a year, each state would select a delegation to send to the capital city. This group, generally referred to as the Congress, was the entire government. There were no executive and judicial branches. The Congress had the right to declare war, raise armies, and sign treaties. It did not have the power to impose taxes. It was also **explicitly** denied the power to regulate trade. Instead, those powers were held by the states. The lack of power to impose taxes and regulate trade weakened the Congress.

Western Policies

Without the power to tax or regulate trade, the government depended on state contributions for funding. The Congress also raised money by selling land west of the Appalachian Mountains.

To make it easier for settlers to buy land, the Land Ordinance of 1785 arranged the land into townships. Each township was divided into 36 sections. In 1787 the Congress passed the Northwest Ordinance, which created the Northwest Territory, the area north of the Ohio River and east of the Mississippi River. This area could eventually be divided into several territories. When the population of a territory reached 60,000, the territory could apply for admission as a state. The Northwest Ordinance also protected civil liberties and banned slavery in the new territory. This meant that as the nation expanded, it would be divided between Southern slaveholding states and Northern free states.

Success in Trade

In addition to organizing western settlement, the Congress tried to promote trade with other nations, including Holland, Prussia, and Sweden, through new treaties. A previous commercial treaty with France also permitted American merchants to sell goods to French colonies in the Caribbean. These new treaties helped offset the restrictions on trade with British colonies in the Caribbean. By 1790, the trade of the United States was greater than the trade of the American colonies before the Revolution.

☑ **PROGRESS CHECK**

Explaining Why did the Congress need to enact the Land Ordinance of 1785 and the Northwest Ordinance?

The Congress Falters

GUIDING QUESTION *What challenges did the new government face?*

The Congress's trade treaties and its system of settling the West were two of its major achievements. Other problems were not so easily solved.

Problems With Trade

During the boycotts of the 1760s and the Revolutionary War, American artisans and manufacturers had prospered by making goods that people had previously bought from the British. After the war, British merchants flooded the United States with inexpensive British goods, driving many American artisans out of business.

explicit fully revealed or expressed and leaving no question as to meaning

---

GEOGRAPHY CONNECTION

The Northwest Ordinance established a process for creating new states and admitting them to the Union "on an equal footing with the original States in all respects."

1 THE WORLD IN SPATIAL TERMS *What was the area of a township in the Northwest Territory?*

2 HUMAN SYSTEMS *How did the Land Ordinance of 1785 help promote public education?*

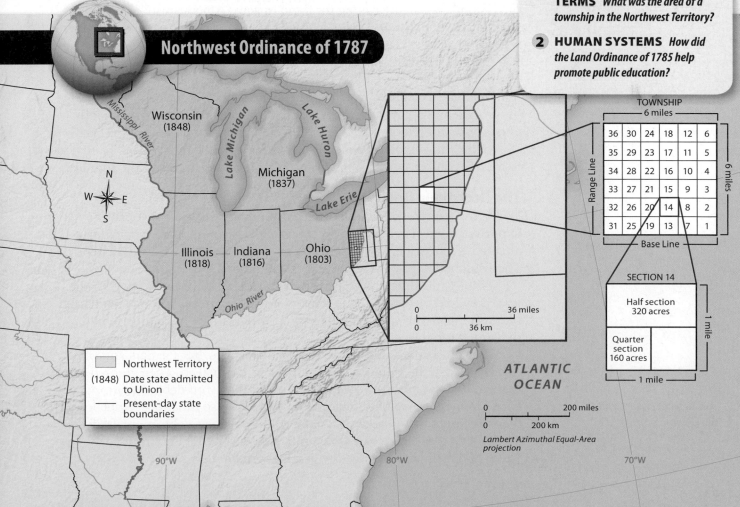

Northwest Ordinance of 1787

Wisconsin (1848)

Lake Michigan
Lake Huron
Lake Erie

Michigan (1837)

Mississippi River

Illinois (1818)
Indiana (1816)
Ohio (1803)

Ohio River

N
W E
S

Northwest Territory
(1848) Date state admitted to Union
Present-day state boundaries

0   36 miles
0   36 km

ATLANTIC OCEAN

0   200 miles
0   200 km

Lambert Azimuthal Equal-Area projection

90°W   80°W   70°W

TOWNSHIP
6 miles

36	30	24	18	12	6
35	29	23	17	11	5
34	28	22	16	10	4
33	27	21	15	9	3
32	26	20	14	8	2
31	25	19	13	7	1

Range Line
6 miles
Base Line

SECTION 14

Half section 320 acres

Quarter section 160 acres

1 mile
1 mile

Rebels occupy a courthouse in western Massachusetts to prevent the courts from taking their property for unpaid debts during Shays's Rebellion.

▶ CRITICAL THINKING

Making Generalizations What does this painting of Shays's Rebellion illustrate about the challenges the government faced under the Articles of Confederation?

duty a tax on imports

occupy to take control or possession of a location

George Washington explained the predicament in a letter he wrote to the French minister: "[W]e cannot manufacture fine articles so cheaply as we can import them, and must, while we continue an agricultural people, be supplied from some quarter. . . . Under the present rigorous restrictions, it is thought that trade is unprofitable for us, and will decay or be disused as soon as other avenues of receiving our produce shall be gradually opened."

Many states restricted British imports, but they did not all impose the same **duties,** or taxes, on foreign goods. The British took their goods to the states with the lowest taxes. From there they moved those products to the other states. The states tried to prevent the British from exploiting the different trade laws by levying tariffs on British goods that crossed state lines. The Congress could not address the problem because it had no power to regulate commerce. Each state was beginning to act independently, which threatened the unity of the new nation.

Problems With Diplomacy

Before the war, many American merchants and planters had borrowed money from British lenders. As part of the Treaty of Paris, which ended the Revolutionary War, the United States had agreed that the states would let the British lenders sue in American courts to recover their debts. Many states made this process difficult, however, and the courts often sided with the American debtors. In addition, states refused to return to Loyalists their property confiscated during the war.

In retaliation, British forces continued to **occupy** frontier posts despite a provision in the treaty calling for them to leave American soil. The Congress had no power to impose taxes to raise the money for a financial settlement with Britain, or to raise an army to enforce the treaty.

American dealings with Spain also showed the weaknesses of the Articles of Confederation. The United States wanted to claim land in North America that Spain also claimed. Due to a dispute over the border between the state of Georgia and Spanish territory, Spain forbade Americans to deposit their goods on Spanish territory at the mouth of the Mississippi River. This effectively closed the Mississippi to frontier farmers, who used the river to ship their goods to market. The Congress's limited power prevented a diplomatic solution.

The Economic Crisis

While the Congress struggled with diplomatic issues, the country was experiencing a severe economic **recession.** Farmers were particularly affected. Farm prices had fallen, and many farmers were deeply in debt. They still had to pay their mortgages and other debts.

At the same time, the war had left many states in debt. To pay for the war, they had issued bonds to borrow money from wealthy merchants and planters. With the war over, their creditors wanted the bonds to be redeemed for gold or silver.

The states could raise taxes to pay their debts, but farmers and other debtors urged the states to issue paper money instead. They wanted to make the paper money available to farmers to pay off debts and mortgages. Paper money was not backed by gold and silver, so inflation—a decline in the value of money—began. Debtors could pay their debts more easily with money that was losing value. Lenders, however, would not receive the true value of the amount that was originally borrowed.

recession an economic slowdown

Between 1785 and 1787, seven states issued paper money. In Rhode Island, paper money became so worthless that merchants refused to accept it. After a mob rioted against the merchants, the state assembly passed a law forcing merchants to accept the paper money or be arrested and fined. This demonstrated to many American leaders that unless a government was properly designed, the people could use the power of government to steal from the wealthy.

Shays's Rebellion

The property owners' fears seemed justified when an uprising known as Shays's Rebellion erupted in Massachusetts in 1786. The conflict was triggered when the government of Massachusetts decided to raise taxes instead of issuing paper money to pay off its debts. The taxes fell most heavily on poor farmers, particularly poor farmers in the western part of the state. As the recession grew worse, many found it impossible to pay their taxes as well as their mortgages and other debts. Those who could not pay often faced the loss of their farms.

Angry at the state legislature's indifference to their plight, in late August 1786, angry farmers in western Massachusetts rebelled. They closed down several county courthouses to block farm foreclosures and then marched to the state supreme court. Daniel Shays, a bankrupt farmer and a former captain in the Continental Army, emerged as one of the leaders of the rebellion.

In January 1787, Shays and about 1,200 farmers headed to a state arsenal intending to seize weapons before marching on Boston. In response, the governor sent a force under General Benjamin Lincoln to defend the arsenal. Before Lincoln arrived, Shays attacked, and the militia defending the arsenal opened fire. Four farmers died. The next day, Lincoln's troops arrived and ended the rebellion. The fears the rebellion had raised, however, were harder to disperse.

People with greater income and social status saw Shays's Rebellion, as well as inflation and an unstable currency, as signs that the republic was at risk. They feared that as states became more responsive to poor people, they would take property from the wealthy and weaken property rights. People began to argue for a stronger central government. The Confederation's failure to deal with these issues, as well as the problems with trade and diplomacy, only added fuel to their argument.

☑ **PROGRESS CHECK**

Summarizing What concerns of the people did the government face after Shays's Rebellion?

LESSON 1 REVIEW

Reviewing Vocabulary
1. *Identifying Cause and Effect* What effect did duties on British goods have on trade between states?

Using Your Notes
2. *Summarizing* Use your notes to identify the accomplishments of the U.S. government under the Articles of Confederation.

Answering the Guiding Questions
3. *Explaining* How did government operate under the Articles of Confederation?

4. *Categorizing* What challenges did the new government face?

Writing Activity
5. **PERSONAL** Take on the role of a newspaper publisher during the time of the Congress. Write an editorial expressing your opinion of Shays's Rebellion, the actions taken by farmers who owed heavy debts due to the recession, and suggest how the government might handle such situations better in the future.

PHOTOS: (l to r)The Granger Collection, New York, Stock Montage/Archive Photos/Getty Images, Corbis/PunchStock

networks

There's More Online!

☑ **CHART/GRAPH** Structure of the Constitution

☑ **GRAPHIC ORGANIZER** Comparing the Two Plans

☑ **VIDEO** A New Constitution

☑ **INTERACTIVE SELF-CHECK QUIZ**

Reading HELPDESK

Content Vocabulary

- **popular sovereignty**
- **federalism**
- **separation of powers**
- **checks and balances**
- **veto**
- **amendment**

Academic Vocabulary

- **financier**

TAKING NOTES: Summarizing

ACTIVITY As you read about the Constitution, use the major headings of this lesson to fill in an outline similar to the one below.

> A New Constitution
> I. The Constitutional Convention
>   A.
>   B.
> II.
>   A.
>   B.

LESSON 2
A New Constitution

ESSENTIAL QUESTION • *What gives a government authority?*

IT MATTERS BECAUSE

In 1787 the delegates to the Constitutional Convention intended to revise the Articles of Confederation. Instead, they began drafting a constitution for a new national government. The delegates negotiated many difficult compromises before agreeing on the framework for the new federal system.

The Constitutional Convention

GUIDING QUESTION *Who attended the Constitutional Convention, and what problems did they face?*

The political and economic problems facing the United States in 1787 led many American leaders to two conclusions: the nation would not survive without a strong central government, and the Articles of Confederation had to be revised or replaced. People who supported a stronger central government became known as "nationalists." Influential nationalists included Benjamin Franklin, George Washington, John Adams, James Madison, and the **financier** Robert Morris.

One of the most influential nationalists was James Madison. He was a member of the Virginia legislature and head of its commerce committee. Madison was well aware of Virginia's trade problems with the other American states and with Britain. He firmly believed that a stronger national government was needed.

In 1786 Madison convinced Virginia's legislature to call a convention of all the states to discuss trade and taxation problems. Representatives from the states were to meet in Annapolis, Maryland. When the convention began, however, delegates from only five states were present, too few to reach a final decision on the problems facing the states. The delegates did discuss the weakness of the Articles of Confederation and expressed interest in modifying them.

Another important nationalist, New York delegate Alexander Hamilton, recommended that the Congress itself call for a convention. Members of the Congress were initially reluctant to do so, but news of Shays's Rebellion changed many minds. In February 1787, Congress called for a convention of the states "for the sole purpose of revising the Articles of Confederation."

Every state except Rhode Island sent delegates to what became known as the Constitutional Convention. In May 1787, the delegates took their places in the Pennsylvania State House in Philadelphia. They knew they faced a daunting task: to balance the rights of the states with the need for a stronger national government.

The Framers

The 55 delegates who attended the convention included some of the most distinguished leaders in the country. The majority were attorneys, and most of the others were planters and merchants. Most had experience in colonial, state, or national government. Seven had served as state governors. Thirty-nine had been members of the Congress. Eight had signed the Declaration of Independence.

The delegates chose George Washington of Virginia, hero of the American Revolution, as presiding officer. At 81, Benjamin Franklin of Pennsylvania was the oldest delegate. Other notable delegates included New York's Alexander Hamilton and Connecticut's Roger Sherman. The scholarly James Madison took careful notes on the debates. The meetings were closed to the public to help ensure honest and open discussion free from outside political pressures.

The Virginia Plan

The Virginia delegation brought a detailed plan—mostly the work of James Madison—for a new national government. The Virginia Plan recommended scrapping the Articles of Confederation and creating a new national government with the power to make laws binding upon the states and to raise money through taxes.

The Virginia Plan proposed that the government be divided into legislative, executive, and judicial branches, and that the legislature, or Congress, be divided into two houses. The voters in each state would elect members of the first house. Members of the second house would be nominated by the state governments, but actually elected by the first house.

In both houses, the number of representatives for each state would reflect that state's population. The Virginia Plan would benefit states with large populations like Virginia, New York, and Massachusetts, giving them more votes than states with smaller populations.

The Virginia Plan drew sharp reactions. The delegates accepted the idea of dividing the government into three branches, but the smaller states strongly opposed any changes that would base representation on population.

financier one who deals with finance and investment on a large scale

Analyzing
PRIMARY SOURCES

James Madison's Virginia Plan

"Conceiving that an individual independence of the States is utterly irreconcilable . . . I have sought for some middle ground, which may at once support a due supremacy of the national authority, and not exclude the local authorities wherever they can be subordinately useful. . . . I would propose next that in addition to the present federal powers, the national Government should be armed with positive and compleat [complete] authority in all cases which require uniformity; such as the regulation of trade, including the right of taxing both exports and imports, the fixing the terms and forms of naturalization, etc. etc."

—from a letter to George Washington, April 16, 1787

DBQ *INFERRING* What evidence in Madison's letter to Washington demonstrates that the Virginia Plan was a compromise?

Delegates at the Constitutional Convention in Philadelphia, 1787

▶ **CRITICAL THINKING**
Making Inferences Why do you think Benjamin Franklin is pictured in the middle of this painting?

**Roger Sherman
(1721–1793)**

Roger Sherman, delegate to the Constitutional Convention for Connecticut, was also an attorney and judge highly respected for his knowledge and integrity. His proposal of the Great Compromise, or the Connecticut Compromise, assured that the interests of both small states and large states would be represented in the new government. As a result of this compromise, the Senate and the House of Representatives make up the legislative branch of the federal government.

▶ **CRITICAL THINKING**
Drawing Inferences Why do you think Sherman is not as well known as some other Framers?

They feared that the larger states would outvote them. William Paterson, a New Jersey delegate, offered a counterproposal that came to be called the New Jersey Plan. The plan modified the Articles of Confederation instead of abandoning them. It called for Congress to have a single house in which each state was equally represented and gave Congress the power to raise taxes and regulate trade.

The delegates had to choose only one plan for further negotiation. After debating on June 19, the convention voted to proceed with the Virginia Plan. Thus, the convention delegates decided to go beyond their original purpose of revising the Articles of Confederation and instead create a new constitution.

✓ **PROGRESS CHECK**

Explaining Why did some delegates object to the Virginia Plan?

A Union Built on Compromise

GUIDING QUESTION *What compromises were made to create the new constitutional government?*

After the convention voted for the Virginia Plan, tempers flared as delegates from the small states insisted that each state have equal representation. In July 1787 the convention appointed a committee to work out a compromise.

The Connecticut Compromise

The compromise the committee worked out was based on a proposal from Roger Sherman of Connecticut. Called the Connecticut Compromise, or the Great Compromise, it proposed that in one house of Congress—the House of Representatives—representation would be based on population. In the other house—the Senate—the states would have equal representation. Voters would elect the representatives, but the state legislatures would choose the senators.

Compromise Over Slavery

The committee also proposed that each state could elect one member to the House of Representatives for every 40,000 people. Southern delegates wanted to count enslaved people. Northern delegates objected because enslaved people could not vote. They also suggested that if enslaved people were counted for representation, they should be counted for taxation too. In the end, a solution referred to as the Three-Fifths Compromise was worked out. Every five enslaved persons would count as three free persons to determine both representation and taxes.

The dispute over how to count enslaved people was not the only issue dividing the North and the South. Southerners feared that a strong national government might impose taxes on the export of farm products or ban the importation of enslaved Africans. The Southern delegates insisted that the new constitution forbid interference with the slave trade and limit Congress's power to regulate trade. Yet Northern delegates knew that Northern merchants and artisans needed a government capable of controlling imports.

Eventually, delegates agreed that the new Congress could not tax exports. They also decided that it could not ban the slave trade until 1808 or impose high taxes on the importation of enslaved people. On September 20, 39 of the delegates signed the new Constitution and sent it to Congress. Eight days later, the Constitution was sent to the states for approval. Nine of the thirteen states had to ratify the Constitution for it to take effect.

✓ **PROGRESS CHECK**

Explaining What compromises were made in the process of creating the new government? What concerns did they address?

A Framework for Limited Government

GUIDING QUESTION *How was the new government structured?*

The new Constitution was based on the idea of **popular sovereignty,** or rule by the people. Rather than a direct democracy, it created a system of government in which elected officials represented the voice of the people. The new Constitution also established **federalism,** a system that divided power between the federal, or national, government and state governments.

Checks and Balances

The new Constitution provided for a **separation of powers** among the three branches of the federal government. The two houses of Congress would compose the law-making, or legislative, branch. The executive branch, headed by a president, would implement and enforce the laws passed by Congress. The judicial branch would hear cases involving those laws. No one serving in one branch could serve in another branch at the same time.

In addition to separating the powers of the government, the delegates to the convention created a system of **checks and balances** to prevent any one branch from becoming too powerful. Within this system, each branch would have some ability to limit the power of the other branches.

popular sovereignty government subject to the will of the people

federalism political system in which power is divided between the national and state governments

separation of powers government principle in which power is divided among different branches

checks and balances a system in which each branch of government has the ability to limit the power of the other branches to prevent any one branch from becoming too powerful

COMPARING CONSTITUTIONS

The Articles of Confederation		The Federal Constitution
One—the Congress	**How Many Houses in the Legislature?**	Two—the House of Representatives and the Senate
Members of Congress appointed annually by state legislatures	**How Are Delegates Chosen?**	Representatives elected every two years by voters; senators originally chosen by state legislatures for a six-year term (today voters elect senators)
No separate executive branch; members of the Congress elect a president annually; government departments are run by committees created by the Congress	**How Is Executive Power Exercised?**	Separate executive branch; president elected every four years by Electoral College; president conducts policy, selects officers to run government departments, appoints ambassadors and judges
Judicial matters left to the states and local courts; the Congress acts as a court for disputes between states	**How Is Judicial Power Exercised?**	Separate judicial branch with a Supreme Court and lower courts created by Congress; judges appointed by the president but confirmed by the Senate
Only states can levy taxes	**What Taxes Can Be Levied?**	Federal government can levy taxes
The Congress regulates foreign trade but has no power to regulate interstate trade	**Can Trade Be Regulated?**	Federal government regulates both interstate and foreign commerce

CHARTS/GRAPHS

The weaknesses of the Articles of Confederation led to its replacement by a new federal Constitution.

▶ **CRITICAL THINKING**

1 **Comparing and Contrasting** How is the election of members of the House of Representatives different from the election of members of the Congress under the Articles of Confederation?

2 **Evaluating** How did the Constitution solve the problems experienced under the Articles with interstate and foreign trade?

Analyzing PRIMARY SOURCES

Thomas Jefferson on Separation of Powers

❝My idea is that we should be made one nation in every case concerning foreign affairs, and separate ones in whatever is merely domestic; that the Federal government should be organized into Legislative, Executive and Judiciary, as are the State governments, and some peaceable means of enforcement devised for the Federal head over the States.❞

—from a letter to the Honorable J. Blair, August 13, 1787

DBQ *ANALYZING PRIMARY SOURCES* In what areas did Jefferson think the states should act individually?

veto the power of the chief executive to reject laws passed by the legislature

amendment a change to the Constitution

The Pennsylvania State House (now known as Independence Hall) was the meeting place of the Continental Congress and the Constitutional Convention.

Under the Constitution, the president—as head of the executive branch—was given far-reaching powers. The president would be commander in chief of the armed forces. The president could also propose legislation, appoint judges, put down rebellions, and **veto,** or reject, acts of Congress.

Although the president could veto acts of Congress, the legislative branch would have the power to override a presidential veto with a two-thirds vote in both houses. The Senate would have to approve or reject presidential appointments to the executive branch, as well as any treaties with foreign nations. Congress could even impeach, or formally accuse of misconduct, and remove the president or other high officials from office.

Members of the judicial branch would hear all cases arising under federal law and the Constitution. The powers of the judiciary would be balanced by the other two branches. The president would have the power to nominate members of the judiciary, but the Senate would have to confirm such nominations. Finally, Congress would have the power to remove federal judges and Supreme Court justices.

Amending the Constitution

The delegates in Philadelphia recognized that the Constitution might need to be amended, or changed over time. To ensure that this was possible, they created a clear system for making **amendments,** or changes to the Constitution. To prevent the Constitution from being changed constantly, the delegates made the process difficult.

The delegates created a two-step process for amending the Constitution—proposal and ratification. An amendment could be proposed by a vote of two-thirds of the members of both houses of Congress. Alternatively, two-thirds of the states could call a constitutional convention to propose new amendments. To become effective, the proposed amendment then had to be ratified by three-fourths of the state legislatures or by conventions in three-fourths of the states.

The success of the Philadelphia Convention in creating a government that reflected the country's many different viewpoints was, in Washington's words, "little short of a miracle." The convention, John Adams declared, was "the single greatest effort of national deliberation that the world has ever seen."

☑ **PROGRESS CHECK**

Explaining How is the power of government divided under the system of federalism?

LESSON 2 REVIEW

Reviewing Vocabulary
1. *Making Connections* Explain the connection between the president's veto power and the system of checks and balances the delegates to the Constitutional Convention created.

Using Your Notes
2. *Sequencing* Using the information from your outline, explain the steps delegates took to create a Constitution that would reflect the needs and points of view of all the states.

Answering the Guiding Questions
3. *Summarizing* Who attended the Constitutional Convention, and what problems did they face?

4. *Describing* What compromises were made to create the new constitutional government?

5. *Explaining* How was the new government structured?

Writing Activity
6. **DESCRIPTIVE** Take on the role of a delegate to the Constitutional Convention. Write a journal entry describing the arguments from each side, as well as your own opinions on them, prior to the Connecticut Compromise and the Three-Fifths Compromise.

Reading HELPDESK

Content Vocabulary

• **bill of rights**

Academic Vocabulary

• **framework**
• **specific**

TAKING NOTES: *Organizing*

ACTIVITY As you read, complete a graphic organizer similar to the one below by listing the sources of support and goals of the Federalists and Anti-Federalists.

	Federalists	Anti-Federalists
Sources of Support		
Goals		

LESSON 3
Ratifying the Constitution

ESSENTIAL QUESTION • *What gives a government authority?*

IT MATTERS BECAUSE

The delegates to the Constitutional Convention had finished their work. They had created the framework for a new government. Then came the toughest test of the new Constitution: winning approval from nine of the thirteen states. In the race toward ratification, there would be more debates, more arguments, some brilliant persuasive writing, and finally, an addition of ten amendments that would guarantee critical rights and freedoms to all citizens.

A Great Debate

GUIDING QUESTION *Why was there a debate over accepting the Constitution, and what were the opposing sides of the debate?*

As soon as the Constitutional Convention in Philadelphia ended, delegates rushed home to begin the campaign for ratification. Each state would hold a convention to vote on the new Constitution. Nine states had to vote for the Constitution to put it into effect. As Americans learned about the new plan of government, they began to argue over whether it should be ratified.

Federalists

Supporters of the Constitution called themselves Federalists. The name was chosen with care. It emphasized that the Constitution would create a federal system. Federalists believed that power should be divided between a central government and state governments. They hoped the name would remind Americans who feared a central government that the states would retain many of their powers.

Some Federalists were large landowners who wanted the property protection a strong central government could provide. Supporters also included merchants and artisans living in large coastal cities. The inability of the Congress to regulate trade had hit these citizens hard. They believed that an effective federal government that could impose taxes on foreign goods would help their businesses.

James Madison (1751–1836)

Although many individuals contributed to the framing of the U.S. Constitution, the master builder was James Madison. He believed that power should be divided among the national government, state governments, and the people. In 1808 he was elected the fourth president of the United States.

▶ **CRITICAL THINKING**
Identifying Were Madison's ideas those of a Federalist or Anti-Federalist? Why?

framework a set of guidelines to be followed

Many farmers who lived near the coast or along rivers that led to the coast also supported the Constitution, as did farmers who shipped goods across state borders. These farmers depended on trade for their livelihood and wanted a strong central government that could regulate trade consistently.

Anti-Federalists

Opponents of the Constitution were called Anti-Federalists—a misleading name, as they were not against federalism. They accepted the need for a national government, but the real issue for them was whether the national government or the state governments would be supreme. Prominent Anti-Federalists included John Hancock, Patrick Henry, Richard Henry Lee of Virginia, and George Clinton, governor of New York. Two members of the Constitutional Convention, Edmund Randolph and George Mason, became Anti-Federalists because they believed the new Constitution should have included a bill of rights. Samuel Adams agreed. He opposed the Constitution because he believed it endangered the independence of the states.

Many Anti-Federalists were western farmers living far from the coast. They considered themselves self-sufficient and were suspicious of the wealthy and powerful. Many were also deeply in debt and suspected that the new Constitution was simply a way for wealthy creditors to get rid of paper money and foreclose on their farms.

The Federalist

Although many influential leaders were Anti-Federalists, their campaign was a negative one. They complained that the Constitution failed to protect basic rights, but they offered no alternative. In contrast, the Federalists presented a definite program to meet the nation's problems. The Federalists were better organized and offered a very convincing case in their speeches, pamphlets, and debates in state conventions. Many newspapers also supported the Federalists.

The Federalists' arguments for ratification were summarized in *The Federalist*—a collection of 85 essays written by James Madison, Alexander Hamilton, and John Jay. Under the joint pen name of "Publius," the three men published most of the essays in New York newspapers in late 1787 and early 1788 before collecting them in *The Federalist*. The essays explained the new **framework** of government created by the Constitution and why it was needed. Even today, judges, lawyers, lawmakers, and historians rely upon *The Federalist* essays to help them interpret the Constitution.

✓ **PROGRESS CHECK**

Summarizing What was the main issue of debate between the Federalists and the Anti-Federalists over the Constitution?

Battle for Ratification

GUIDING QUESTION *What occurred during the ratification process, and how was ratification completed?*

As the ratifying conventions began to gather, the Federalists knew that they had clear majorities in some states. The vote was going to be much closer in others, however, including the large and important states of Massachusetts, Virginia, and New York.

The first state conventions for ratification took place in December 1787 and January 1788. Although Delaware, Pennsylvania, New Jersey, Georgia, and Connecticut all quickly ratified the Constitution, the most important battles still lay ahead.

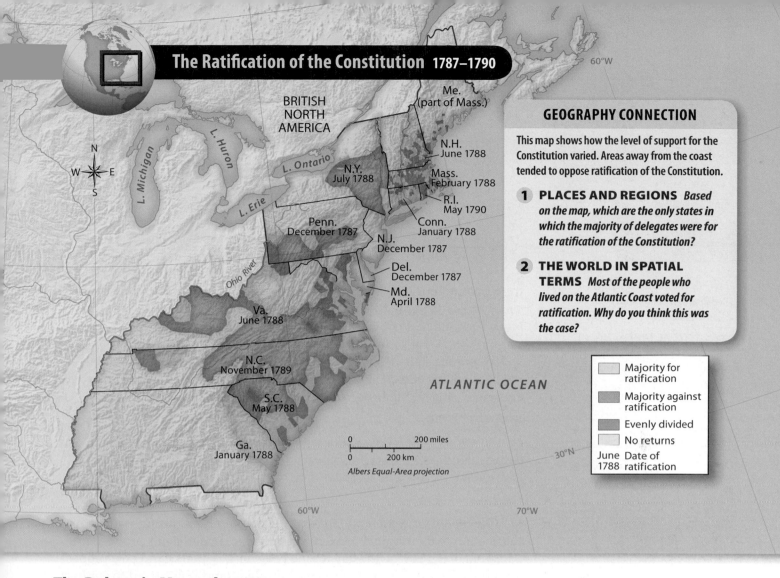

The Ratification of the Constitution 1787–1790

BRITISH NORTH AMERICA

Me. (part of Mass.)

N.H. June 1788

N.Y. July 1788

Mass. February 1788

R.I. May 1790

Penn. December 1787

Conn. January 1788

N.J. December 1787

Del. December 1787

Md. April 1788

Va. June 1788

N.C. November 1789

S.C. May 1788

Ga. January 1788

ATLANTIC OCEAN

L. Michigan
L. Huron
L. Ontario
L. Erie
Ohio River

N W E S

0   200 miles
0   200 km
Albers Equal-Area projection

60°W

70°W

30°N

GEOGRAPHY CONNECTION

This map shows how the level of support for the Constitution varied. Areas away from the coast tended to oppose ratification of the Constitution.

1 **PLACES AND REGIONS** *Based on the map, which are the only states in which the majority of delegates were for the ratification of the Constitution?*

2 **THE WORLD IN SPATIAL TERMS** *Most of the people who lived on the Atlantic Coast voted for ratification. Why do you think this was the case?*

Majority for ratification
Majority against ratification
Evenly divided
No returns
June 1788 Date of ratification

The Debate in Massachusetts

In Massachusetts, Anti-Federalists held a clear majority when the convention met in January 1788. Among them were John Hancock and Samuel Adams, who both had signed the Declaration of Independence. Adams refused to support the new Constitution unless Federalists could give him a guarantee "that the said Constitution be never construed to authorize Congress to infringe the just liberty of the Press, or the rights of Conscience; or to prevent the people of the United States . . . from keeping their own arms; . . . or to subject the people to unreasonable searches and seizures of their persons, papers, or possessions."

Federalists moved quickly to meet Adams's objections to the Constitution. **Specifically,** Federalists promised to attach a **bill of rights**—guarantees of fundamental individual rights—to the Constitution once it was ratified, although they contended it was not necessary:

❝I go further, and affirm that bills of rights, in the sense and to the extent in which they are contended for, are not only unnecessary in the proposed Constitution, but would even be dangerous. They would contain various exceptions to powers not granted; and, on this very account, would afford a colorable [seemingly valid] pretext to claim more than were granted. For why declare that things shall not be done which there is no power to do?❞

—Alexander Hamilton, from *The Federalist*, No. 84, 1788

specific related to a particular individual, situation, relation, or effect

bill of rights a summary of fundamental rights and privileges guaranteed to a people against violation by the state

On July 26, 1788, New Yorkers celebrated the ratification of the Constitution.

▶ **CRITICAL THINKING**

Drawing Conclusions Why do you think a float in this parade was named for Hamilton?

Federalists also promised to support an amendment that would reserve for the states all powers not specifically granted to the federal government. These concessions helped persuade Samuel Adams to vote for ratification. John Hancock and his supporters were won over by hints that local Federalists would support him for president of the United States. In the final vote, 187 members voted for the Constitution, while 168 voted against it.

The Debate in Virginia

By the end of June 1788, Maryland, South Carolina, and New Hampshire had ratified the Constitution. The Federalists had reached the minimum number of states required to put the new Constitution into effect, but Virginia and New York still had not ratified. Many saw the support of these two large, populous states as crucial to the new government's success.

In Virginia, Patrick Henry, Richard Henry Lee, George Mason, and other Anti-Federalists argued strongly against ratification. George Mason raised an argument similar to the one Sam Adams had made in Massachusetts:

PRIMARY SOURCE

❝...[T]he State Legislatures have no Security for the Powers now presumed to remain to them; or the People for their Rights. There is no Declaration of any kind for preserving the Liberty of the Press, the [trial] by Jury in civil [cases]; nor against the Danger of standing [armies] in time of Peace.❞
—from "Objections to the new Constitution of Government," 1787

George Washington and James Madison presented the arguments for ratification to the Virginia convention. In the end, Madison's promise to add a bill of rights won the day for the Federalists. Upon hearing the proposal for a bill of rights, Virginia governor Edmund Randolph agreed to support the new Constitution. Randolph had attended the Constitutional Convention but had refused to sign the final document, worried that it lacked sufficient protections of the people's rights. His decision to change sides convinced others to change their votes as well. The Virginia convention voted narrowly for the new Constitution, 89 in favor and 79 against.

New York Votes To Ratify

In New York, the majority of the convention members, including Governor George Clinton, were Anti-Federalists. The Federalists, led by Alexander Hamilton and John Jay, managed to delay the final vote until news arrived that New Hampshire and Virginia had both voted for the Constitution. The new federal government was now in effect and had the support of influential Virginians. If New York refused to ratify, it would be in a very awkward position. It would have to operate independently of all of the surrounding states.

Soon after ratification by New Hampshire and Virginia, delegates from New York City warned that the city would secede from the state of New York if the new Constitution were not ratified. These arguments were effective. The vote was very close—30 to 27—but the Federalists won.

Ratification

By July 1788, all the states except Rhode Island and North Carolina had ratified the Constitution. The new government could be launched without their ratification votes.

In mid-September 1788, the Congress set up a timetable for the election of the new government. It chose March 4, 1789, as the date for the first meeting of the new Congress.

The two states that had held out finally ratified the Constitution after the new government was in place. North Carolina waited until a bill of rights had actually been proposed, then voted to ratify the Constitution in November 1789. Rhode Island, still nervous about losing its independence, did not ratify the Constitution until May 1790, and even then the vote was very close—34 to 32.

The United States now had a new government, but no one knew if the new Constitution would work any better than the Articles of Confederation had. With both anticipation and nervousness, the American people waited for their new government to begin. Many expressed great confidence when George Washington was elected unanimously by the Electoral College to be the first president under the new Constitution.

The Bill of Rights

One of the most important acts of the new Congress was the introduction of a series of amendments that came to be known as the Bill of Rights. During the campaign to ratify the Constitution, the Federalists had promised to add such amendments. James Madison, one of the leaders in Congress, made the passage of a bill of rights top priority. He hoped it would demonstrate the good faith of federal leaders and build support for the new government.

In drafting the Bill of Rights, Madison relied heavily on the Virginia Declaration of Rights that George Mason prepared in 1776 and the Virginia Statute for Religious Freedom that Thomas Jefferson wrote in 1777. In late September 1789, Congress agreed on 12 constitutional amendments. They were then sent to the states for ratification, but only ten were approved. These ten went into effect and are generally referred to as the Bill of Rights. The first eight protect the rights of individuals against actions of the federal government. The last two set limits on the powers of the new national government. The Ninth Amendment states that the people have other rights not listed. The Tenth Amendment states that any powers not specifically given to the federal government are reserved to the states or to the people.

✓ **PROGRESS CHECK**

Analyzing What key concession made by the Federalists gave them enough support for the Constitution to be ratified?

LESSON 3 REVIEW

Reviewing Vocabulary
1. *Explaining* Why was a bill of rights so important to some Anti-Federalists?

Using Your Notes
2. *Comparing and Contrasting* Use the notes you completed during the lesson to write a paragraph that identifies the differences between the Federalists and the Anti-Federalists.

Answering the Guiding Questions
3. *Explaining* Why was there a debate over accepting the Constitution, and what were the opposing sides of the debate?

4. *Summarizing* What occurred during the ratification process, and how was ratification completed?

Writing Activity
5. **PERSUASIVE** Assume the role of a Federalist or an Anti-Federalist at a state ratifying convention. Write a speech in which you try to convince your audience to either accept or reject the new Constitution.

Directions: On a separate sheet of paper, answer the questions below. Make sure you read carefully and answer all parts to the question.

Lesson Review

Lesson 1

① *Explaining* In what ways was the Congress under the Articles of Confederation successful in achieving its goals?

② *Evaluating* What were the weaknesses of the Articles of Confederation, and how did those weaknesses affect the new republic?

Lesson 2

③ *Analyzing* How did the Virginia Plan influence the final Constitution?

④ *Identifying Central Issues* What conflict was resolved by the Connecticut Compromise?

Lesson 3

⑤ *Summarizing* How did Federalists win over many Anti-Federalists in order to obtain ratification?

⑥ *Making Connections* What role did *The Federalist* play in the debate over the Constitution?

21st Century Skills

⑦ **CIVIC LITERACY** What concerns did Shays's Rebellion raise about the ability of the Articles of Confederation to govern?

⑧ **LEADERSHIP AND RESPONSIBILITY** How were the Framers of the Constitution able to address conflict and resolve tensions when composing the new Constitution?

⑨ **CRITICAL THINKING AND PROBLEM SOLVING** In what ways did the new Constitution resolve the weaknesses of the Articles of Confederation?

⑩ **FINANCIAL, ECONOMIC, BUSINESS, AND ENTREPRENEURIAL LITERACY** In what ways were the Articles of Confederation an economic failure?

⑪ **INFORMATION LITERACY** How did the Framers of the Constitution prevent any one branch of the federal government from becoming too powerful?

Exploring the Essential Question

⑫ *Comparing and Contrasting* Make a comparison chart of the primary weaknesses of the Articles of Confederation and how they were addressed by the new Constitution using the information from the chapter. After your chart is complete, write a brief summary about what gives a government authority.

DBQ Document-Based Questions

Use the document to answer the following questions.

In this excerpt from a textbook he wrote, the Reverend Jedidiah Morse discusses the defects of the Articles of Confederation.

PRIMARY SOURCE

❝[The Articles of Confederation] were framed during the rage of war, when a principle of common safety supplied the place of a coercive power in government; . . .

When resolutions were passed in Congress, there was no power to compel obedience. . . . Had one state been invaded by its neighbour, the Union was not constitutionally bound to assist in repelling the invasion, and supporting the constitution of the invaded state. . . .❞

—from *The American Geography, or a View of the Present Situation of the United States of America,* 1794

⑬ *Summarizing* What defects in the Articles of Confederation does Morse mention?

⑭ *Analyzing* Why does Morse think that the Articles of Confederation were effective during the American Revolution but not afterward?

Extended-Response Question

⑮ *Contrasting* Contrast the arguments of the Federalists for a strong centralized government with the arguments of Anti-Federalists. Use specific political, economic, and foreign policy events that took place after the American Revolution in your response.

Need Extra Help?

If You've Missed Question	①	②	③	④	⑤	⑥	⑦	⑧	⑨	⑩	⑪	⑫	⑬	⑭	⑮
Go to page	72	72	77	78	83	82	75	77	79	73	79	79	86	86	81

The CONSTITUTION HANDBOOK

Reading **HELP**DESK

Content Vocabulary

- **popular sovereignty**
- **federalism**
- **enumerated powers**
- **reserved powers**
- **concurrent powers**
- **impeach**
- **bill**
- **cabinet**
- **judicial review**
- **due process**

Academic Vocabulary

- **grant**
- **responsive**

TAKING NOTES: *Organizing*

ACTIVITY As you read about the Constitution, use the major headings of the handbook to fill in an outline like the one below.

I. Major Principles
  A.
  B.
  C.
  D.
  E.
  F.

IT MATTERS BECAUSE

The Constitution is the most important document of the United States. It serves as the framework of national government and the source of American citizens' basic rights. To preserve self-government, all citizens need to understand their rights and responsibilities.

Major Principles

GUIDING QUESTION *How does the Constitution lay the framework for individual rights and a balanced representative government?*

The principles outlined in the Constitution were the Framers' solution to the complex problems of a representative government. The Constitution rests on seven major principles of government: (1) **popular sovereignty,** (2) republicanism, (3) limited government, (4) **federalism,** (5) separation of powers, (6) checks and balances, and (7) individual rights.

Popular Sovereignty and Republicanism

The opening words of the Constitution, "We the people," reinforce the idea of popular sovereignty, or "authority of the people." In the Constitution, the people consent to be governed and specify the powers and rules by which they shall be governed.

The Articles of Confederation's government had few powers, and it was unable to cope with the many challenges facing the nation. The new federal government had greater powers, but it also had specific limitations. A system of interlocking responsibilities kept any one branch of government from becoming too powerful.

Voters are sovereign, that is, they have ultimate authority in a republican system. They elect representatives and give them the responsibility to make laws and run the government. For most Americans today, the terms *republic* and *representative democracy* mean the same thing: a system of limited government in which the people are the final source of authority.

A replica of the U.S. Constitution

▶ **CRITICAL THINKING**

Drawing Conclusions Why do you think the first three words of the Constitution were written in such a large size?

popular sovereignty authority of the people

federalism political system in which power is divided between the national and state governments

grant to award or give as law

enumerated powers powers listed in the Constitution as belonging to the federal government

reserved powers powers retained by the states

concurrent powers powers shared by the state and federal governments

Limited Government

Although the Framers agreed that the nation needed a stronger central authority, they feared misuse of power. They wanted to prevent the government from using its power to give one group special advantages or to deprive another group of its rights. By creating a limited government, they restricted the government's authority to specific powers **granted** by the people.

The delegates to the Constitutional Convention were very specific about the powers granted to the new government. Their decision to provide a written outline of the government's structure also served to show what they intended. Articles I, II and III of the Constitution describe the powers of the federal government and the limits on those powers. Other limits are set forth in the Bill of Rights, which guarantees certain rights to the people.

Federalism

In establishing a strong central government, the Framers did not deprive states of all authority. The states gave up some powers to the national government but retained others. This principle of shared power is called federalism. The federal system allows the people of each state to deal with their needs in their own way, but at the same time, it lets the states act together to deal with matters that affect all Americans.

The Constitution defines three types of government powers. Certain powers belong only to the federal government. These **enumerated powers** include the power to coin money, regulate interstate and foreign trade, maintain the armed forces, and create federal courts (Article I, Section 8).

The second kind of powers are those retained by the states, known as **reserved powers,** including the power to establish schools, set marriage and divorce laws, and regulate trade within the state. Although reserved powers are not specifically listed in the Constitution, the Tenth Amendment says that all powers not granted to the federal government "are reserved to the States."

The third set of powers defined by the Constitution is **concurrent powers**—powers the state and federal governments share. They include the right to raise taxes, borrow money, provide for public welfare, and administer criminal justice. Conflicts between state law and federal law must be settled in a federal court. The Constitution declares that it is "the supreme Law of the Land."

PHOTO: Comstock/PunchStock

Separation of Powers

To prevent any single group or institution in government from gaining too much authority, the Framers divided the federal government into three branches: legislative, executive, and judicial. Each branch has its own functions and powers. The legislative branch, Congress, makes the laws. The executive branch, headed by the president, carries out the laws. The judicial branch, consisting of the Supreme Court and other federal courts, interprets and applies the laws.

In addition to giving separate responsibility to separate branches, the membership of each branch is chosen in different ways. The president nominates federal judges, and the Senate confirms the appointments. People vote for members of Congress. Voters cast ballots for president, but the method of election is indirect. On Election Day the votes in each state are counted. Whatever candidate receives a majority receives that state's electoral votes, which total the number of senators and representatives the state has in Congress. Electors from all states meet to formally elect a president. A candidate must win a majority of votes in the Electoral College to win.

Checks and Balances

The Framers who wrote the Constitution deliberately created a system of checks and balances in which each branch of government can check, or limit, the power of the other branches. This system helps balance the power of the three branches and prevents any one branch from becoming too powerful. For example, imagine that Congress passes a law. The president can reject the law by vetoing it. However, Congress can override, or reverse, the president's veto if two-thirds of the members of both the Senate and the House of Representatives vote again to approve the law.

CHARTS/GRAPHS

The Framers deliberately created a system of checks and balances to limit the power of each branch of government.

▶ CRITICAL THINKING

1. **Analyzing Information** How can the president help control the judiciary?

2. **Drawing Conclusions** Why is it important that the legislative branch can override a presidential veto?

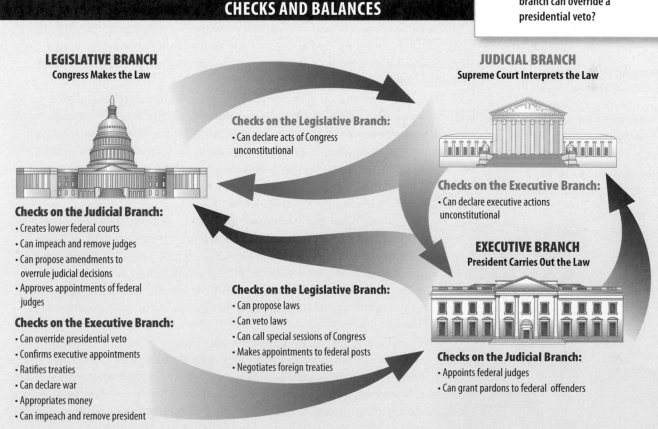

CHECKS AND BALANCES

LEGISLATIVE BRANCH
Congress Makes the Law

JUDICIAL BRANCH
Supreme Court Interprets the Law

Checks on the Legislative Branch:
• Can declare acts of Congress unconstitutional

Checks on the Executive Branch:
• Can declare executive actions unconstitutional

EXECUTIVE BRANCH
President Carries Out the Law

Checks on the Judicial Branch:
• Creates lower federal courts
• Can impeach and remove judges
• Can propose amendments to overrule judicial decisions
• Approves appointments of federal judges

Checks on the Executive Branch:
• Can override presidential veto
• Confirms executive appointments
• Ratifies treaties
• Can declare war
• Appropriates money
• Can impeach and remove president

Checks on the Legislative Branch:
• Can propose laws
• Can veto laws
• Can call special sessions of Congress
• Makes appointments to federal posts
• Negotiates foreign treaties

Checks on the Judicial Branch:
• Appoints federal judges
• Can grant pardons to federal offenders

Individual Rights

In 1791 the states ratified 10 amendments to the Constitution to protect certain basic rights, including freedom of speech, religion, and the right to a trial by jury. Congress approved these 10 amendments and referred to them as the Bill of Rights. Over the years, 17 more amendments have been added to the Constitution. Some give additional rights to American citizens and some modify how the government works. Included among them are amendments that abolish slavery, guarantee voting rights, authorize an income tax, and set a two-term limit on the presidency.

☑ **PROGRESS CHECK**

Explaining Describe some of the principles outlined in the Constitution that help ensure individual rights and a balanced representative government.

The Legislative Branch

GUIDING QUESTION *How is the legislative branch organized, and what are its functions?*

The legislative branch includes the two houses of Congress: the Senate and the House of Representatives. Congress has two primary roles: to make the nation's laws and to decide how to spend federal funds.

The government cannot spend any money unless Congress appropriates, or sets aside, funds. All tax and spending bills must originate in the House of Representatives and be approved in both the House and the Senate before moving to the president to be signed.

Congress also monitors the executive branch and investigates possible abuses of power. The House of Representatives can **impeach,** or bring formal charges against, any federal official it suspects of wrongdoing or misconduct. If an official is impeached, the Senate acts as a court and tries the accused official. Officials who are found guilty may be removed from office.

The Senate has certain additional powers. Two-thirds of the Senate must ratify treaties made by the president. The Senate must also confirm presidential appointments of federal officials such as department heads, ambassadors, and federal judges.

All members of Congress have the responsibility to represent their constituents, the people of their home states and districts. As a constituent, you can expect your senators and representative to promote national and state interests. Congress members introduce thousands of **bills**—proposed laws—every year. Because individual members of Congress cannot possibly study all these bills carefully, both houses form committees of selected members to evaluate proposed legislation.

Standing committees are permanent committees in both the House and the Senate that specialize in a particular topic, such as agriculture, commerce, or veterans' affairs. These committees are usually divided into subcommittees that focus on a particular aspect of an issue. The House and the Senate also form temporary select committees to deal with issues requiring special attention. These committees meet only until they complete their task.

Occasionally the House and the Senate form joint committees with members from both houses. These committees meet to consider specific issues. One type of joint committee, a conference committee, has a special function. If the House and the Senate pass different versions of the same bill, a conference committee meets to work out a compromise bill acceptable to both houses.

impeach to bring formal charges against a federal official

bill a proposed law

In 2010 John Boehner of Ohio became the 61st Speaker of the House. All members of Congress have the responsibility to represent their constituents.

▶ **CRITICAL THINKING**

Identifying Central Issues Why is important that members of Congress represent their constituents?

HOW A BILL BECOMES LAW

1. A legislator introduces a bill in the House or Senate, where it is referred to a committee for review.

2. After review, the committee decides whether to shelve it or to send it back to the House or Senate with or without revisions.

3. The House or Senate then debates the bill, making revisions if desired. If the bill is passed, it is sent to the other house.

4. If the House and Senate pass different versions of the bill, the houses must meet in a conference committee to decide on a compromise version.

5. The compromise bill is then sent to both houses.

6. If both houses pass the bill, it is sent to the president to sign.

7. If the president signs the bill, it becomes law.

8. The president may veto the bill, but if two-thirds of the House and Senate vote to approve it, it becomes law without the president's approval.

CHARTS/GRAPHS

The legislative process is complex. It begins when a member of Congress introduces a bill. That bill then works its way to the president who either signs the bill into law or vetoes it.

▶ **CRITICAL THINKING**

1 *Analyzing Information*
What is the role of a conference committee?

2 *Identifying Central Issues*
How can a bill become law without the approval of the president?

Once a committee in either house of Congress approves a bill, it is sent to the full Senate or House for debate. After debate the bill may be passed, rejected, or returned to the committee for further changes. When both houses pass a bill, it goes to the president. If the president approves the bill and signs it, the bill becomes law. If the president vetoes the bill, it does not become law unless Congress takes it up again and votes to override the veto.

☑ **PROGRESS CHECK**

Describing Describe the organization and functions of the legislative branch.

The Executive Branch

GUIDING QUESTION *How does the president carry out laws that Congress passes?*

The executive branch of government includes the president, the vice president, and various executive offices, departments, and agencies. The executive branch executes, or carries out, the laws that Congress passes.

The President's Roles

The president plays a number of different roles in government. These roles include serving as the nation's chief executive, chief diplomat, commander in chief of the military, chief of state, and legislative leader.

Chief Executive As chief executive, the president is responsible for carrying out the nation's laws.

Chief Diplomat As chief diplomat, the president directs foreign policy, appoints ambassadors, and negotiates treaties with other nations.

Commander in Chief As commander in chief of the armed forces, the president can give orders to the military and direct its operations. The president cannot declare war; only Congress holds this power. The president can send troops to other parts of the world for up to 60 days but must notify Congress when doing so. The troops may remain longer only if Congress gives its approval or declares war.

Chief of State As chief of state, the president is symbolically the representative of all Americans. The president fulfills this role when receiving foreign ambassadors or heads of state, visiting foreign nations, or honoring Americans.

Legislative Leader The president serves as a legislative leader by proposing laws to Congress and working to see that they are passed. In the annual State of the Union address to the American people, the president presents his goals for legislation in the upcoming year.

President Barack Obama signs a bill into law. As chief executive, the president is responsible for carrying out the laws of the nation.

▶ **CRITICAL THINKING**

Making Generalizations Why is it important that the president carries out the laws of the nation?

cabinet a group of advisers to the president

The Executive at Work

Many executive offices, departments, and independent agencies help the president carry out and enforce the nation's laws. The Executive Office of the President (EOP) is made up of individuals and agencies that directly assist the president. Presidents rely on the EOP for advice and for gathering information needed for decision making.

The executive branch has 15 executive departments, each responsible for a different area of government. For example, the Department of State carries out foreign policy, and the Department of the Treasury manages the nation's finances. The department heads have the title of secretary, and are members of the president's **cabinet.** The cabinet helps the president set policies and make decisions.

☑ **PROGRESS CHECK**

Explaining What functions does the president fulfill as Legislative Leader?

The Judicial Branch

GUIDING QUESTION *How does the judicial branch function to review and evaluate laws and interpret the Constitution?*

Article III of the Constitution calls for the creation of a Supreme Court and "such inferior [lower] courts as Congress may from time to time ordain and establish." The federal courts of the judicial branch review and evaluate laws and interpret the Constitution in making their decisions.

District and Appellate Courts

United States district courts are the lowest level of the federal court system. These courts consider criminal and civil cases that come under federal authority, such as kidnapping, federal tax evasion, claims against the federal government, and cases involving constitutional rights, such as free speech. There are 94 district courts, with at least one in every state.

The appellate courts, or courts of appeal, consider district court decisions in which the losing side has asked for a review of the verdict. If an appeals court disagrees with the lower court's decision, it can overturn the verdict or order a retrial. There are 14 appeals courts: one for each of 12 federal districts, one military appeals court, and an appellate court for the federal circuit.

The Supreme Court

The Supreme Court is the final authority in the federal court system. It consists of a chief justice and eight associate justices. Most of the Court's cases come from appeals of lower court decisions. Only cases involving foreign diplomats or disputes between states can begin in the Supreme Court.

Supreme Court Independence The president appoints the Court's justices for life, and the Senate confirms the appointments. The public has no input. The Framers hoped that by appointing judges, they would be free to evaluate the law with no concern for pleasing voters.

Judicial Review The role of the judicial branch is not described in detail in the Constitution, but the role of the courts has grown as powers implied in the Constitution have been put into practice. In 1803 Chief Justice John Marshall expanded the power of the Supreme Court by striking down an act of Congress in the case of *Marbury* v. *Madison*. Although not mentioned in the Constitution, judicial review has become a major power of the judicial branch. **Judicial review** gives the Supreme Court the ultimate authority to interpret the meaning of the Constitution.

judicial review the process by which the Supreme Court has the final authority to interpret the Constitution

☑ **PROGRESS CHECK**

Analyzing How does the judicial branch evaluate laws and interpret the Constitution?

CHARTS/GRAPHS

The judicial branch consists of a system of federal courts that reviews and evaluates laws and interprets the Constitution.

▶ **CRITICAL THINKING**

1 *Analyzing Information* How many routes to the U.S. Supreme Court are shown in the chart?

2 *Drawing Conclusions* Why might the Supreme Court review only decisions made by a small number of lower courts?

THE FEDERAL COURT SYSTEM

U.S. Supreme Court

Front row, left to right, Justices Clarence Thomas, Antonin Scalia, Chief Justice John Roberts, Anthony Kennedy, and Ruth Bader Ginsburg; back row, left to right, Justices Sonia Sotomayor, Stephen Breyer, Samuel Alito, Elena Kagan

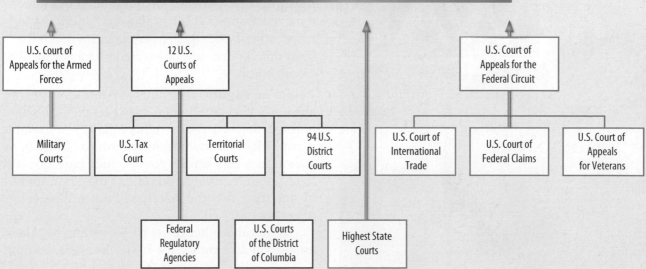

U.S. Court of Appeals for the Armed Forces	12 U.S. Courts of Appeals				U.S. Court of Appeals for the Federal Circuit	
Military Courts	U.S. Tax Court	Territorial Courts	94 U.S. District Courts	U.S. Court of International Trade	U.S. Court of Federal Claims	U.S. Court of Appeals for Veterans
	Federal Regulatory Agencies	U.S. Courts of the District of Columbia	Highest State Courts			

Rights and Responsibilities

GUIDING QUESTION *What are the protections and freedoms the Constitution and the Bill of Rights provide Americans?*

All citizens of the United States have certain basic rights, but they also have specific responsibilities. Living in a system of self-government means ultimately that every citizen is partly responsible for how society is governed and for the actions the government takes on his or her behalf.

The Rights of Americans

The rights of Americans fall into three broad categories: to be protected from unfair actions of the government, to receive equal treatment under the law, and to retain certain basic freedoms.

Protection From Unfair Actions Parts of the Constitution and the Bill of Rights protect all Americans from unfair treatment by the government or the law. Among these rights are the right to a lawyer when accused of a crime and the right to a trial by jury when charged with a crime. In addition, the Fourth Amendment protects us from unreasonable searches and seizures. This provision requires police to have a court order before searching a person's home for criminal evidence. To obtain this, the police must have a very strong reason to suspect someone of a crime.

Equal Treatment All Americans, regardless of race, religion, or political beliefs, have the right to be treated the same under the law. The Fifth Amendment states that no person shall "be deprived of life, liberty, or property, without due process of law." **Due process** means that the government must follow procedures established by law and guaranteed by the Constitution, treating all people equally. The Fourteenth Amendment requires every state to grant its citizens "equal protection of the laws."

Basic Freedoms The First Amendment describes our basic freedoms— freedom of speech, freedom of religion, freedom of the press, freedom of assembly, and the right to petition. In a democracy, power rests in the hands of the people. Therefore, citizens in a democratic society must be able to exchange ideas freely. The First Amendment allows citizens to criticize the government, in speech or in the press, without fear of punishment.

In addition, the Ninth Amendment states that the rights of Americans are not limited to those in the Constitution. This has allowed Americans to assert other basic rights over the years that have been upheld in court, or assured by amending the Constitution.

Limits on Rights The rights of Americans are not absolute. They are limited based on the principle of respecting everyone's rights equally. For example, many cities and towns require groups to obtain a permit to march on city streets. Such laws do limit free speech, but they also protect the community by ensuring that the march will not endanger other people.

In this and other cases, the government balances an individual's rights, the rights of others, and the

due process the following of procedures established by law

The First Amendment of the Constitution guarantees basic freedoms, such as the freedom of assembly.

▶ **CRITICAL THINKING**

Making Inferences Why do you think basic freedoms are just as important today as they were when the Framers wrote the Constitution?

PHOTO: Jim West/Alamy

PROPOSAL

Amendment proposed by a vote of two-thirds of both houses of Congress

or

Amendment proposed by a national convention requested by two-thirds of states

RATIFICATION

After approval by three-fourths of state legislatures

or

After approval by three-fourths of state ratifying conventions

New amendment to the Constitution

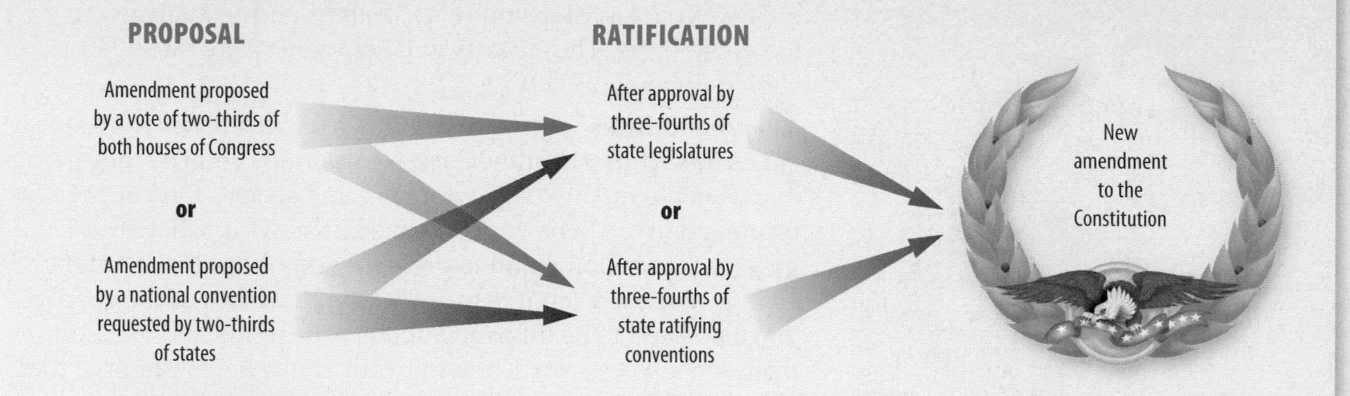

CHARTS/GRAPHS

Article V of the Constitution enables Congress and the states to amend, or change, the Constitution.

▶ **CRITICAL THINKING**

1 *Analyzing Information* What role do the states play in the amendment process?

2 *Analyzing Information* How many approvals by state legislatures are required for an amendment to the Constitution?

community's health and safety. Most Americans are willing to accept some limitations on their rights to gain these protections as long as the restrictions are reasonable and apply equally to all. A law banning all marches would violate the First Amendment rights of free speech and assembly and be unacceptable. Similarly, a law preventing only certain groups from marching would be unfair because it would not apply equally to everyone.

Citizens' Responsibilities

Citizens in a democratic society have both duties and responsibilities. Duties are actions required by law. Responsibilities are voluntary actions. Fulfilling duties and responsibilities ensures good government and protects rights.

Duties One basic duty of all Americans is to obey the law. Laws serve three important functions. They help maintain order; they protect the health, safety, and property of all citizens; and they make it possible for people to live together peacefully. If you believe a law is wrong, you can work through your representatives to change it.

Americans also have a duty to pay taxes. The government uses tax money to defend the nation, to build roads and bridges, and to assist people in need. Americans often benefit from services provided by the government. Another duty of citizens is to defend the nation. All males aged 18 and older must register with the government in case the nation needs to call on them for military service. Military service is not automatic, but a war could make it necessary.

The Constitution guarantees all Americans the right to a trial by a jury of their equals. For this reason, you may be called to jury duty when you reach the age of 18. Having a large group of jurors on hand is necessary to guarantee the right to a fair and speedy trial. You also have a duty to serve as a trial witness if called to do so.

ROCK THE VOTE

Registration drives encourage others to exercise their responsibility to vote.

▶ **CRITICAL THINKING**

Making Inferences How might an increase in young voters make an impact on an election?

responsive open and quick to take action

Most states require you to attend school until a certain age. School is where you gain the knowledge and skills needed to be a good citizen. In school you learn to think more clearly, to express your opinions more accurately, and to analyze the ideas of others. These skills will help you make informed choices when you vote.

Responsibilities The responsibilities of citizens are not as clear-cut as their duties, but they are as important because they help maintain the quality of government and society. One important responsibility is to be well informed. Knowing what your government is doing and expressing your thoughts about its actions helps to keep it **responsive** to the wishes of the people. You also need to be informed about your rights and to assert them when necessary. Knowing your rights helps preserve them. Other responsibilities include accepting responsibility for your actions, and supporting your family.

To enjoy your rights to the fullest, you must be prepared to respect the rights of others. Respecting the rights of others also means respecting the rights of people with whom you disagree. Respecting and accepting others regardless of race, religion, beliefs, or other differences is essential in a democracy.

Vote, Vote, Vote! Perhaps the most important responsibility of American citizens is to vote when they reach the age of 18. Voting allows you to participate in government and to guide its direction. When you vote for people to represent you in government, you will be exercising your right of self-government. If you disapprove of the job your representatives are doing, it will be your responsibility to help elect other people in the next election. You can also let your representatives know what you think about issues through letters, telephone calls, and petitions and by taking part in public meetings or political rallies.

☑ **PROGRESS CHECK**

Describing What are the rights and responsibilities of an American citizen?

CONSTITUTION HANDBOOK REVIEW

Reviewing Vocabulary
1. *Analyzing* Explain the significance of popular sovereignty to the Constitution.

Using Your Notes
2. *Identifying* Use the notes you completed during the lesson to identify the major principles of the Constitution.

Answering the Guiding Questions
3. *Summarizing* How does the Constitution lay the framework for individual rights and a balanced representative government?

4. *Explaining* How is the legislative branch organized, and what are its functions?

5. *Listing* How does the president carry out laws that Congress passes?

6. *Defining* How does the judicial branch function to review and evaluate laws and interpret the Constitution?

7. *Describing* What are the protections and freedoms the Constitution and the Bill of Rights provide Americans?

Writing Activity
8. **PERSUASIVE** Write a short paragraph taking a pro or con position on the following question: Should communities permit rallies by unpopular groups, such as the KKK, even though such rallies may upset some members of the community or could possibly incite violence?

THE CONSTITUTION
of the UNITED STATES

The Constitution of the United States is a truly remarkable document. It was one of the first written constitutions in modern history. The entire text of the Constitution and its amendments follow. For easier study, those passages that have been set aside or changed by the adoption of amendments are printed in blue. Also included are explanatory notes that will help clarify the meaning of important ideas presented in the Constitution.

The Preamble introduces the Constitution and sets forth the general purposes for which the government was established. The Preamble also declares that the power of the government comes from the people.

The printed text of the document shows the spelling and punctuation of the parchment original.

Article I.
The Legislative Branch

The Constitution contains seven divisions called articles. Each article covers a general topic. For example, Articles I, II, and III create the three branches of the national government—the legislative, executive, and judicial branches. Most of the articles are divided into sections.

Section 1. Congress

Lawmaking The power to make laws is given to a Congress made up of two chambers to represent different interests: the Senate to represent the states and the House to be more responsive to the people's will.

Section 2. House of Representatives

Division of Representatives Among the States The number of representatives from each state is based on the size of the state's population. Each state is entitled to at least one representative. The Constitution states that each state may specify who can vote, but the Fifteenth, Nineteenth, Twenty-fourth, and Twenty-sixth Amendments have established guidelines that all states must follow regarding the right to vote. *What are the qualifications for members of the House of Representatives?*

Vocabulary

preamble: *introduction*
constitution: *principles and laws of a nation*
enumeration: *census or population count*
impeachment: *bringing charges against an official*

Preamble

We the People of the United States, in Order to form a more perfect Union, establish Justice, insure domestic Tranquility, provide for the common defence, promote the general Welfare, and secure the Blessings of Liberty to ourselves and our Posterity, do ordain and establish this **Constitution** for the United States of America.

Article I

Section 1

All legislative Powers herein granted shall be vested in a Congress of the United States, which shall consist of a Senate and House of Representatives.

Section 2

[1.] The House of Representatives shall be composed of Members chosen every second Year by the People of the several States, and the Electors in each State shall have the Qualifications requisite for Electors of the most numerous Branch of the State Legislature.

[2.] No person shall be a Representative who shall not have attained the Age of twenty five Years, and been seven Years a Citizen of the United States, and who shall not, when elected, be an Inhabitant of that State in which he shall be chosen.

[3.] Representatives and direct Taxes shall be apportioned among the several States which may be included within this Union, according to their respective Numbers, which shall be determined by adding to the whole Number of free Persons, including those bound to Service for a Term of Years, and excluding Indians not taxed, three fifths of all other Persons. The actual **Enumeration** shall be made within three Years after the first Meeting of the Congress of the United States, and within every subsequent Term of ten Years, in such Manner as they shall by Law direct. The Number of Representatives shall not exceed one for every thirty Thousand, but each State shall have at Least one Representative; and until such enumeration shall be made, the State of New Hampshire shall be entitled to chuse three; Massachusetts eight, Rhode-Island and Providence Plantations one, Connecticut five, New-York six, New Jersey four, Pennsylvania eight, Delaware one, Maryland six, Virginia ten, North Carolina five, South Carolina five, and Georgia three.

[4.] When vacancies happen in the Representation from any State, the Executive Authority thereof shall issue Writs of Election to fill such Vacancies.

[5.] The House of Representatives shall chuse their Speaker and other Officers; and shall have the sole Power of **Impeachment**.

Section 3

[1.] The Senate of the United States shall be composed of two Senators from each State, chosen by the Legislature thereof, for six Years; and each Senator shall have one Vote.

[2.] Immediately after they shall be assembled in Consequence of the first Election, they shall be divided as equally as may be into three Classes. The Seats of the Senators of the first Class shall be vacated at the Expiration of the second Year, of the second Class at the Expiration of the fourth Year, and of the third Class at the Expiration of the sixth Year, so that one third may be chosen every second Year; and if Vacancies happen by Resignation, or otherwise, during the Recess of the Legislature of any State, the Executive thereof may make temporary Appointments until the next Meeting of the Legislature, which shall then fill such Vacancies.

[3.] No Person shall be a Senator who shall not have attained to the Age of thirty Years, and been nine Years a Citizen of the United States, and who shall not, when elected, be an Inhabitant of that State for which he shall be chosen.

[4.] The Vice President of the United States shall be President of the Senate, but shall have no Vote, unless they be equally divided.

[5.] The Senate shall chuse their other Officers, and also a **President pro tempore**, in the Absence of the Vice President, or when he shall exercise the Office of the President of the United States.

[6.] The Senate shall have the sole Power to try all Impeachments. When sitting for that Purpose, they shall be on Oath or Affirmation. When the President of the United States is tried, the Chief Justice shall preside: And no Person shall be convicted without the Concurrence of two thirds of the Members present.

[7.] Judgment in Cases of Impeachment shall not extend further than to removal from Office, and disqualification to hold and enjoy any Office of honor, Trust or Profit under the United States: but the Party convicted shall nevertheless be liable and subject to Indictment, Trial, Judgment and Punishment, according to Law.

Section 4

[1.] The Times, Places and Manner of holding Elections for Senators and Representatives, shall be prescribed in each State by the Legislature thereof; but the Congress may at any time by Law make or alter such Regulations, except as to the Places of chusing Senators.

[2.] The Congress shall assemble at least once in every Year, and such Meeting shall be on the first Monday in December, unless they shall by Law appoint a different Day.

Section 3. The Senate

Voting Procedure Originally, senators were chosen by the legislators of their own states. The Seventeenth Amendment changed this, so that senators are now elected by their state's people. There are 100 senators, 2 from each state.

What Might Have Been

Electing Senators South Carolina delegate Charles Pinckney suggested during the Convention that the members of the Senate come from four equally proportioned districts within the United States and that the legislature elect the executive every seven years.

Section 3. The Senate

Trial of Impeachments One of Congress's powers is the power to impeach—to accuse government officials of wrongdoing, put them on trial, and, if necessary, remove them from office. The House decides if the offense is impeachable. The Senate acts as a jury, and when the president is impeached, the Chief Justice of the United States serves as the judge. A two-thirds vote of the members present is needed to convict impeached officials. *What punishment can the Senate give if an impeached official is convicted?*

Vocabulary

president pro tempore: *presiding officer of the Senate who serves when the vice president is absent*

Vocabulary

quorum: *minimum number of members that must be present to conduct sessions*

adjourn: *to suspend a session*

concurrence: *agreement*

emoluments: *salaries*

revenue: *income raised by government*

bill: *draft of a proposed law*

Section 6. Privileges and Restrictions

Pay and Privileges To strengthen the federal government, the Founders set congressional salaries to be paid by the United States Treasury rather than by members' respective states. Originally, members were paid $6 per day. In 2011, all members of Congress received a base salary of $174,000.

Section 7. Passing Laws

Revenue Bill All tax laws must originate in the House of Representatives. This ensures that the branch of Congress that is elected by the people every two years has the major role in determining taxes.

Section 5

[1.] Each House shall be the Judge of the Elections, Returns and Qualifications of its own Members, and a Majority of each shall constitute a **Quorum** to do Business; but a smaller Number may **adjourn** from day to day, and may be authorized to compel the Attendance of absent Members, in such Manner, and under such Penalties as each House may provide.

[2.] Each House may determine the Rules of its Proceedings, punish its Members for disorderly Behaviour, and, with the **Concurrence** of two thirds, expel a Member.

[3.] Each House shall keep a Journal of its Proceedings, and from time to time publish the same, excepting such Parts as may in their Judgment require Secrecy; and the Yeas and Nays of the Members of either House on any question shall, at the Desire of one fifth of those Present, be entered on the Journal.

[4.] Neither House, during the Session of Congress, shall, without the Consent of the other, adjourn for more than three days, nor to any other Place than that in which the two Houses shall be sitting.

Section 6

[1.] The Senators and Representatives shall receive a Compensation for their Services, to be ascertained by Law, and paid out of the Treasury of the United States. They shall in all Cases, except Treason, Felony and Breach of the Peace, be privileged from Arrest during their Attendance at the Session of their respective Houses, and in going to and returning from the same; and for any Speech or Debate in either House, they shall not be questioned in any other Place.

[2.] No Senator or Representative shall, during the Time for which he was elected, be appointed to any civil Office under the Authority of the United States, which shall have been created, or the **Emoluments** whereof shall have been encreased during such time; and no Person holding any Office under the United States, shall be a Member of either House during his Continuance in Office.

Section 7

[1.] All Bills for raising **Revenue** shall originate in the House of Representatives; but the Senate may propose or concur with Amendments as on other **Bills**.

[2.] Every Bill which shall have passed the House of Representatives and the Senate, shall, before it become a Law, be presented to the President of the United States; If he approve he shall sign it, but if not he shall return it, with his Objections to that House in which it shall have originated, who shall enter the Objections at large on their Journal, and proceed to reconsider it. If after such Reconsideration two thirds of that House shall agree to pass the Bill, it shall be sent, together with the Objections, to the other House, by which it shall likewise be reconsidered, and if approved by two thirds of that House, it shall become a Law. But in all such Cases the Votes of both Houses shall be determined by yeas and Nays, and the Names of the Persons voting for and against the Bill shall be entered on the Journal of each House respectively. If any Bill shall not be returned by the President within ten Days (Sundays excepted) after it shall have been presented to him, the Same shall be a Law, in like Manner as if he had signed it, unless the Congress by their Adjournment prevent its Return, in which Case it shall not be a Law.

[3.] Every Order, **Resolution**, or Vote to which the Concurrence of the Senate and House of Representatives may be necessary (except on a question of Adjournment) shall be presented to the President of the United States; and before the Same shall take Effect, shall be approved by him, or being disapproved by him, shall be repassed by two thirds of the Senate and House of Representatives, according to the Rules and Limitations prescribed in the Case of a Bill.

Section 8

[1.] The Congress shall have the Power to lay and collect Taxes, Duties, Imposts and Excises, to pay the Debts and provide for the common Defence and general Welfare of the United States; but all Duties, Imposts and Excises shall be uniform throughout the United States;

[2.] To borrow Money on the credit of the United States;

[3.] To regulate Commerce with foreign Nations, and among the several States, and with the Indian Tribes;

[4.] To establish an uniform Rule of **Naturalization**, and uniform Laws on the subject of Bankruptcies throughout the United States;

[5.] To coin Money, regulate the Value thereof, and of foreign Coin, and fix the Standard of Weights and Measures;

[6.] To provide for the Punishment of counterfeiting the Securities and current Coin of the United States;

[7.] To establish Post Offices and post Roads;

[8.] To promote the Progress of Science and useful Arts, by securing for limited Times to Authors and Inventors the exclusive Right to their respective Writings and Discoveries;

[9.] To constitute Tribunals inferior to the supreme Court;

[10.] To define and punish Piracies and Felonies committed on the high Seas, and Offences against the Law of Nations;

[11.] To declare War, grant Letters of Marque and Reprisal, and make Rules concerning Captures on Land and Water;

[12.] To raise and support Armies, but no Appropriation of Money to that Use shall be for a longer Term than two Years;

[13.] To provide and maintain a Navy;

[14.] To make Rules for the Government and Regulation of the land and naval Forces;

Section 7. Passing Laws

How Bills Become Laws A bill may become a law only by passing both houses of Congress and being signed by the president. The president can check Congress by rejecting—vetoing—its legislation. *How can Congress override the president's veto?*

Section 8. Powers Granted to Congress

Powers of Congress Expressed powers are those powers directly stated in the Constitution. Most of the expressed powers of Congress are listed in Article I, Section 8. These powers are also called enumerated powers because they are numbered 1–18. *Which clause gives Congress the power to declare war?*

Vocabulary

resolution: *legislature's formal expression of opinion*

naturalization: *procedure by which a citizen of a foreign nation becomes a citizen of the United States*

Section 8. Powers Granted to Congress

Elastic Clause The final enumerated power is often called the "elastic clause." This clause gives Congress the right to make all laws "necessary and proper" to carry out the powers expressed in the other clauses of Article I. It is called the elastic clause because it lets Congress "stretch" its powers to meet situations the Founders could never have anticipated.

What does the phrase "necessary and proper" in the elastic clause mean? Almost from the beginning, this phrase was a subject of dispute. The issue was whether a strict or a broad interpretation of the Constitution should be applied. The dispute was first addressed in 1819, in the case of *McCulloch* v. *Maryland*, when the Supreme Court ruled in favor of a broad interpretation. The Court stated that the elastic clause allowed Congress to use its powers in any way that was not specifically prohibited by the Constitution.

Section 9. Powers Denied to the Federal Government

Original Rights A writ of habeas corpus issued by a judge requires a law official to bring a prisoner to court and show cause for holding the prisoner. A bill of attainder is a bill that punishes a person without a jury trial. An "ex post facto" law is one that makes an act a crime after the act has been committed. *What does the Constitution say about bills of attainder?*

[15.] To provide for calling forth the Militia to execute the Laws of the Union, suppress Insurrections and repel Invasions;

[16.] To provide for organizing, arming, and disciplining, the Militia, and for governing such Part of them as may be employed in the Service of the United States, reserving to the States respectively, the Appointment of the Officers, and the Authority of training the Militia according to the discipline prescribed by Congress;

[17.] To exercise exclusive Legislation in all Cases whatsoever, over such District (not exceeding ten Miles square) as may, by Cession of particular States, and the Acceptance of Congress, become the Seat of Government of the United States, and to exercise like Authority over all Places purchased by the Consent of the Legislature of the State in which the Same shall be, for the Erection of Forts, Magazines, Arsenals, dock-Yards, and other needful Buildings; And

[18.] To make all Laws which shall be necessary and proper for carrying into Execution the foregoing Powers, and all other Powers vested by this Constitution in the Government of the United States, or in any Department or Officer thereof.

Section 9

[1.] The Migration or Importation of such Persons as any of the States now existing shall think proper to admit, shall not be prohibited by the Congress prior to the Year one thousand eight hundred and eight, but a Tax or duty may be imposed on such Importation, not exceeding ten dollars for each Person.

[2.] The Privilege of the Writ of Habeas Corpus shall not be suspended, unless when in Cases of Rebellion or Invasion the public Safety may require it.

[3.] No Bill of Attainder or ex post facto Law shall be passed.

[4.] No Capitation, or other direct, Tax shall be laid, unless in Proportion to the Census or Enumeration herein before directed to be taken.

[5.] No Tax or Duty shall be laid on Articles exported from any State.

[6.] No Preference shall be given by any Regulation of Commerce or Revenue to the Ports of one State over those of another: nor shall Vessels bound to, or from, one State, be obliged to enter, clear, or pay Duties in another.

[7.] No Money shall be drawn from the Treasury, but in Consequence of Appropriations made by Law; and a regular Statement and Account of the Receipts and Expenditures of all public Money shall be published from time to time.

[8.] No Title of Nobility shall be granted by the United States: And no Person holding any Office of Profit or Trust under them, shall, without the Consent of the Congress, accept of any present, Emolument, Office, or Title, of any kind whatever, from any King, Prince, or foreign State.

Section 10

[1.] No State shall enter into any Treaty, Alliance, or Confederation; grant Letters of Marque and Reprisal; coin Money; emit Bills of Credit; make any Thing but gold and silver Coin a Tender in Payment of Debts; pass any Bill of Attainder, ex post facto Law, or Law impairing the Obligation of Contracts, or grant any Title of Nobility.

[2.] No State shall, without the Consent of the Congress, lay any Imposts or Duties on Imports or Exports, except what may be absolutely necessary for executing its inspection Laws: and the net Produce of all Duties and Imposts, laid by any State on Imports and Exports, shall be for the Use of the Treasury of the United States; and all such Laws shall be subject to the Revision and Controul of the Congress.

[3.] No State shall, without the Consent of Congress, lay any Duty of Tonnage, keep Troops, or Ships of War in time of Peace, enter into any Agreement or Compact with another State, or with a foreign Power, or engage in War, unless actually invaded, or in such imminent Danger as will not admit of delay.

Article II

Section 1

[1.] The executive Power shall be vested in a President of the United States of America. He shall hold his Office during the Term of four Years, and, together with the Vice President, chosen for the same Term, be elected, as follows.

[2.] Each State shall appoint, in such Manner as the Legislature thereof may direct, a Number of Electors, equal to the whole Number of Senators and Representatives to which the State may be entitled in the Congress: but no Senator or Representative, or Person holding an Office of Trust or Profit under the United States, shall be appointed an Elector.

[3.] The Electors shall meet in their respective States, and vote by Ballot for two Persons, of whom one at least shall not be an Inhabitant of the same State with themselves. And they shall make a List of all the Persons voted for, and of the Number of Votes for each; which List they shall sign and certify, and transmit sealed to the Seat of the Government of the United States, directed to the President of the Senate. The President of the Senate shall, in the Presence of the Senate and House of Representatives, open all the Certificates, and the Votes shall then be counted. The Person having the greatest Number of Votes shall be the President, if such Number be a Majority of the whole Number of Electors appointed; and if there be more than one who have such Majority, and have an equal Number of Votes, then the House of Representatives shall immediately chuse by Ballot one of them for President; and if no person have a Majority, then from the five highest on the List the said House

Section 1. President and Vice President

Qualifications The president must be a citizen of the United States by birth, at least 35 years of age, and a resident of the United States for 14 years.

Section 1. President and Vice President

Vacancies If the president dies, resigns, is removed from office by impeachment, or is unable to carry out the duties of the office, the vice president becomes president. (see Amendment XXV)

Section 1. President and Vice President

Salary Originally, the president's salary was $25,000 per year. The president's current salary is $400,000 plus a $50,000 nontaxable expense account per year. The president also receives living accommodations in two residences—the White House and Camp David.

Section 2. Powers of the President

Cabinet Mention of "the principal officer in each of the executive departments" is the only suggestion of the president's cabinet to be found in the Constitution. The cabinet is an advisory body, and its power depends on the president. Section 2, Clause 1 also makes the president the head of the armed forces. This established the principle of civilian control of the military.

shall in like Manner chuse the President. But in chusing the President, the Votes shall be taken by States, the Representation from each State having one Vote; A quorum for this Purpose shall consist of a Member or Members from two thirds of the States, and a Majority of all the States shall be necessary to a Choice. In every Case, after the Choice of the President, the Person having the greatest Number of Votes of the Electors shall be the Vice President. But if there should remain two or more who have equal Votes, the Senate shall chuse from them by Ballot the Vice President.

[4.] The Congress may determine the Time of chusing the Electors, and the Day on which they shall give their Votes; which Day shall be the same throughout the United States.

[5.] No Person except a natural born Citizen, or a Citizen of the United States, at the time of the Adoption of this Constitution, shall be eligible to the Office of President; neither shall any Person be eligible to that Office who shall not have attained to the Age of thirty five Years, and been fourteen Years a Resident within the United States.

[6.] In Case of the Removal of the President from Office, or of his Death, Resignation, or Inability to discharge the Powers and Duties of the said Office, the Same shall devolve on the Vice President, and the Congress may by Law provide for the Case of Removal, Death, Resignation or Inability, both of the President and Vice President, declaring what Officer shall then act as President, and such Officer shall act accordingly, until the Disability be removed, or a President shall be elected.

[7.] The President shall, at stated Times, receive for his Services, a Compensation, which shall neither be encreased nor diminished during the Period for which he shall have been elected, and he shall not receive within that Period any other Emolument from the United States, or any of them.

[8.] Before he enter on the Execution of his Office, he shall take the following Oath or Affirmation:—"I do solemnly swear (or affirm) that I will faithfully execute the Office of President of the United States, and will to the best of my Ability, preserve, protect and defend the Constitution of the United States."

Section 2

[1.] The President shall be Commander in Chief of the Army and Navy of the United States, and of the Militia of the several States, when called into the actual Service of the United States; he may require the Opinion, in writing, of the principal Officer in each of the executive Departments, upon any Subject relating to the Duties of their respective Offices, and he shall have Power to grant Reprieves and Pardons for Offences against the United States, except in Cases of Impeachment.

[2.] He shall have Power, by and with the Advice and Consent of the Senate, to make Treaties, provided two thirds of the Senators present concur; and he shall nominate, and by and with the Advice and Consent of the Senate, shall appoint Ambassadors, other public Ministers and Consuls, Judges of the supreme Court, and all other Officers of the United States, whose Appointments are not herein otherwise provided for, and which shall be established by Law: but the Congress may by Law vest the Appointment of such inferior Officers, as they think proper, in the President alone, in the Courts of Law, or in the Heads of Departments.

[3.] The President shall have Power to fill up all Vacancies that may happen during the Recess of the Senate, by granting Commissions which shall expire at the End of their next Session.

Section 3

He shall from time to time give to the Congress Information of the State of the Union, and recommend to their Consideration such Measures as he shall judge necessary and expedient; he may, on extraordinary Occasions, convene both Houses, or either of them, and in Case of Disagreement between them, with Respect to the Time of Adjournment, he may adjourn them to such Time as he shall think proper; he shall receive Ambassadors and other public Ministers; he shall take Care that the Laws be faithfully executed, and shall Commission all the Officers of the United States.

Section 4

The President, Vice President and all civil Officers of the United States, shall be removed from Office on Impeachment for, and Conviction of, Treason, Bribery, or other high Crimes and Misdemeanors.

Article III

Section 1

The judicial Power of the United States, shall be vested in one supreme Court, and in such inferior Courts as the Congress may from time to time ordain and establish. The Judges, both of the supreme and inferior Courts, shall hold their Offices during good Behaviour, and shall, at stated Times, receive for their Services, a Compensation, which shall not be diminished during their Continuance in Office.

Section 2

[1.] The judicial Power shall extend to all Cases, in Law and Equity, arising under this Constitution, the Laws of the United States, and Treaties made, or which shall be made, under their Authority;—to all Cases affecting Ambassadors, other public Ministers and Consuls;—to all Cases of admiralty and maritime Jurisdiction;—to Controversies to which the United States shall be a Party;—to Controversies

Section 2. Powers of the President

Treaties The president is responsible for the conduct of relations with foreign countries. *What role does the Senate have in approving treaties?*

Section 3. Powers of the President

Executive Orders An important presidential power is the ability to issue executive orders. An executive order is a rule or command the president issues that has the force of law. Only Congress can make laws under the Constitution, but executive orders are considered part of the president's duty to "take care that the laws be faithfully executed." This power is often used during emergencies. Over time, the scope of executive orders has expanded. Decisions by federal agencies and departments are also considered to be executive orders.

Section 4. Impeachment

Reasons for Removal From Office This section states the reasons for which the president and vice president may be impeached and removed from office. Only Andrew Johnson and Bill Clinton have been impeached by the House. Richard Nixon resigned before the House could vote on possible impeachment.

Article III. The Judicial Branch

The term *judicial* refers to courts. The Constitution set up only the Supreme Court but provided for the establishment of other federal courts. The judiciary of the United States has two different systems of courts. One system consists of the federal courts, whose powers derive from the Constitution and federal laws. The other includes the courts of each of the 50 states, whose powers derive from state constitutions and laws.

Section 2. Jurisdiction

General Jurisdiction Federal courts deal mostly with "statute law," or laws passed by Congress, treaties, and cases involving the Constitution itself.

Section 2. Jurisdiction

The Supreme Court A court with "original jurisdiction" has the authority to be the first court to hear a case. The Supreme Court generally has "appellate jurisdiction" in that it mostly hears cases appealed from lower courts.

Section 2. Jurisdiction

Jury Trial Except in cases of impeachment, anyone accused of a crime has the right to a trial by jury. The trial must be held in the state where the crime was committed. Jury trial guarantees were strengthened in the Sixth, Seventh, Eighth, and Ninth Amendments.

Vocabulary

original jurisdiction: *authority to be the first court to hear a case*

appellate jurisdiction: *authority to hear cases appealed from lower courts*

treason: *violation of the allegiance owed by a person to his or her own country, for example, by aiding an enemy*

Article IV. Relations Among the States

Article IV explains the relationship of the states to one another and to the national government. This article requires each state to give citizens of other states the same rights as its own citizens, addresses the admission of new states, and guarantees that the national government will protect the states.

Section 1. Official Acts

Recognition by States This provision ensures that each state recognizes the laws, court decisions, and records of all other states. For example, a marriage license issued by one state must be accepted by all states.

between two or more States;—between a State and Citizens of another State;—between Citizens of different States,—between Citizens of the same State claiming Lands under Grants of different States, and between a State, or the Citizens thereof, and foreign States, Citizens or Subjects.

[2.] In all Cases affecting Ambassadors, other public Ministers and Consuls, and those in which a State shall be Party, the supreme Court shall have **original Jurisdiction**. In all the other Cases before mentioned, the supreme Court shall have **appellate Jurisdiction**, both as to Law and Fact, with such Exceptions, and under such Regulations as the Congress shall make.

[3.] The Trial of all Crimes, except in Cases of Impeachment, shall be by Jury; and such Trial shall be held in the State where the said Crimes shall have been committed; but when not committed within any State, the Trial shall be at such Place or Places as the Congress may by Law have directed.

Section 3

[1.] Treason against the United States, shall consist only in levying War against them, or in adhering to their Enemies, giving them Aid and Comfort. No Person shall be convicted of Treason unless on the Testimony of two Witnesses to the same overt Act, or on Confession in open Court.

[2.] The Congress shall have Power to declare the Punishment of Treason, but no Attainder of Treason shall work Corruption of Blood, or Forfeiture except during the Life of the Person attainted.

Article IV

Section 1

Full Faith and Credit shall be given in each State to the public Acts, Records, and judicial Proceedings of every other State. And the Congress may by general Laws prescribe the Manner in which such Acts, Records and Proceedings shall be proved, and the Effect thereof.

Section 2

[1.] The Citizens of each State shall be entitled to all Privileges and Immunities of Citizens in the several States.

[2.] A Person charged in any State with **Treason**, Felony, or other Crime, who shall flee from Justice, and be found in another State, shall on Demand of the executive Authority of the State from which he fled, be delivered up, to be removed to the State having Jurisdiction of the Crime.

[3.] No Person held to Service of Labour in one State, under the Laws thereof, escaping into another, shall, in Consequence of any Law or Regulation therein, be discharged from such Service or Labour, but shall be delivered up on Claim of the Party to whom such Service or Labour may be due.

Section 3

[1.] New States may be admitted by the Congress into this Union; but no new State shall be formed or erected within the Jurisdiction of any other State; nor any State be formed by the Junction of two or more States, or Parts of States, without the Consent of the Legislatures of the States concerned as well as of the Congress.

[2.] The Congress shall have Power to dispose of and make all needful Rules and Regulations respecting the Territory or other Property belonging to the United States; and nothing in this Constitution shall be so construed as to Prejudice any Claims of the United States, or of any particular State.

Section 4

The United States shall guarantee to every State in this Union a Republican Form of Government, and shall protect each of them against Invasion; and on Application of the Legislature, or of the Executive (when the Legislature cannot be convened) against domestic Violence.

Article V

The Congress, whenever two thirds of both Houses shall deem it necessary, shall propose **Amendments** to this Constitution, or, on the Application of the Legislatures of two thirds of the several States, shall call a Convention for proposing Amendments, which, in either Case, shall be valid to all Intents and Purposes, as Part of this Constitution, when ratified by the Legislatures of three fourths of the several States, or by Conventions in three fourths thereof, as the one or the other Mode of **Ratification** may be proposed by the Congress; Provided that no Amendment which may be made prior to the Year One thousand eight hundred and eight shall in any Manner affect the first and fourth Clauses in the Ninth Section of the first Article; and that no State, without its Consent, shall be deprived of its equal Suffrage in the Senate.

Article VI

[1.] All Debts contracted and Engagements entered into, before the Adoption of this Constitution, shall be as valid against the United States under this Constitution, as under the Confederation.

[2.] This Constitution, and the Laws of the United States which shall be made in Pursuance thereof; and all Treaties made, or which shall be made, under the Authority of the United States, shall be the supreme Law of the Land; and the Judges in every State shall be bound thereby, any Thing in the Constitution or Laws of any State to the Contrary notwithstanding.

[3.] The Senators and Representatives before mentioned, and the Members of the several State Legislatures, and all executive and judicial Officers, both of the United States and of the several States, shall be bound by Oath or Affirmation,

Section 3. New States and Territories

New States Congress has the power to admit new states. It also determines the basic guidelines for applying for statehood. Two states, Maine and West Virginia, were created within the boundaries of another state. In the case of West Virginia, President Lincoln recognized the West Virginia government as the legal government of Virginia during the Civil War. This allowed West Virginia to secede from Virginia without obtaining approval from the Virginia legislature.

Article V. The Amendment Process

Article V explains how the Constitution can be amended, or changed. All of the 27 amendments were proposed by a two-thirds vote of both houses of Congress. Only the Twenty-first Amendment was ratified by constitutional conventions of the states. All other amendments have been ratified by state legislatures. *What is an amendment?*

Vocabulary

amendment: *a change to the Constitution*
ratification: *process by which an amendment is approved*

Article VI. Constitutional Supremacy

Article VI contains the "supremacy clause." This clause establishes that the Constitution, laws passed by Congress, and treaties of the United States "shall be the supreme Law of the Land." The "supremacy clause" recognizes the Constitution and federal laws as supreme when in conflict with those of the states.

to support this Constitution; but no religious Test shall ever be required as a Qualification to any Office or public Trust under the United States.

Article VII

The Ratification of the Conventions of nine States, shall be sufficient for the Establishment of this Constitution between the States so ratifying the Same.

Done in Convention by the Unanimous Consent of the States present the Seventeenth Day of September in the Year of our Lord one thousand seven hundred and Eighty seven and of the Independence of the United States of America the Twelfth. In witness whereof We have hereunto subscribed our Names,

Article VII. Ratification

Article VII addresses ratification and states that, unlike the Articles of Confederation, which required approval of all thirteen states for adoption, the Constitution would take effect after it was ratified by nine states.

Signers

George Washington,
President and Deputy from Virginia

New Hampshire
John Langdon
Nicholas Gilman

Massachusetts
Nathaniel Gorham
Rufus King

Connecticut
William Samuel Johnson
Roger Sherman

New York
Alexander Hamilton

New Jersey
William Livingston
David Brearley
William Paterson
Jonathan Dayton

Pennsylvania
Benjamin Franklin
Thomas Mifflin
Robert Morris
George Clymer
Thomas FitzSimons
Jared Ingersoll
James Wilson
Gouverneur Morris

Delaware
George Read
Gunning Bedford, Jr.
John Dickinson
Richard Bassett
Jacob Broom

Maryland
James McHenry
Daniel of St. Thomas Jenifer
Daniel Carroll

Virginia
John Blair
James Madison, Jr.

North Carolina
William Blount
Richard Dobbs Spaight
Hugh Williamson

South Carolina
John Rutledge
Charles Cotesworth Pinckney
Charles Pinckney
Pierce Butler

Georgia
William Few
Abraham Baldwin

Attest: William Jackson, Secretary

The Amendments

This part of the Constitution consists of changes and additions. The Constitution has been amended 27 times throughout the nation's history.

Amendment I

Congress shall make no law respecting an establishment of religion, or prohibiting the free exercise thereof; or abridging the freedom of speech, or of the press; or the right of the people peaceably to assemble, and to petition the Government for a redress of grievances.

Amendment II

A well regulated Militia, being necessary to the security of a free State, the right of the people to keep and bear Arms, shall not be infringed.

Amendment III

No Soldier shall, in time of peace be **quartered** in any house, without the consent of the Owner, nor in time of war, but in a manner to be prescribed by law.

Amendment IV

The right of the people to be secure in their persons, houses, papers, and effects, against unreasonable searches and seizures, shall not be violated, and no **Warrants** shall issue, but upon probable cause, supported by Oath or affirmation, and particularly describing the place, to be searched, and the persons or things to be seized.

Amendment V

No person shall be held to answer for a capital, or otherwise infamous crime, unless on a presentment or indictment of a Grand Jury, except in cases arising in the land or naval forces, or in the Militia, when in actual service in time of War or public danger; nor shall any person be subject for the same offence to be twice put in jeopardy of life or limb; nor shall be compelled in any criminal case to be a witness against himself, nor be deprived of life, liberty, or property, without due process of law; nor shall private property be taken for public use without just compensation.

Amendment VI

In all criminal prosecutions, the accused shall enjoy the right to a speedy and public trial, by an impartial jury of the State and district wherein the crime shall have been committed, which district shall have been previously ascertained by law, and to be informed of the nature and cause of the accusation; to be confronted with the witnesses against him; to have compulsory process for obtaining Witnesses in his favor, and to have the assistance of counsel for his defence.

Amendment VII

In Suits at common law, where the value in controversy shall exceed twenty dollars, the right of trial by jury shall be preserved, and no fact tried by a jury, shall be otherwise reexamined in any Court of the United States, than according to the rules of **common law**.

The Bill of Rights

The first 10 amendments are known as the Bill of Rights (1791). These amendments limit the powers of the federal government. The First Amendment protects the civil liberties of individuals in the United States. The amendment freedoms are not absolute, however. They are limited by the rights of other individuals. *What freedoms does the First Amendment protect?*

Vocabulary

quarter: *to provide living accommodations*
warrant: *document that gives police particular rights or powers*

Amendment 5

Rights of the Accused This amendment contains protections for people accused of crimes. One of the protections is that government may not deprive any person of life, liberty, or property without due process of law. This means that the government must follow proper constitutional procedures in trials and in other actions it takes against individuals. *According to Amendment V, what is the function of a grand jury?*

Amendment 6

Right to Speedy and Fair Trial A basic protection is the right to a speedy, public trial. The jury must hear witnesses and evidence on both sides before deciding the guilt or innocence of a person charged with a crime. This amendment also provides that legal counsel must be provided to a defendant. In 1963, in *Gideon* v. *Wainwright*, the Supreme Court ruled that if a defendant cannot afford a lawyer, the government must provide one to defend him or her. *Why is the right to a "speedy" trial important?*

Vocabulary

common law: *law established by previous court decisions*

Amendment 9

Powers Reserved to the People
This amendment prevents government from claiming that the only rights people have are those listed in the Bill of Rights.

Amendment 10

Powers Reserved to the States
This amendment protects the states and the people from the federal government. It establishes that powers not given to the national government and not denied to the states by the Constitution belong to the states or to the people. These are checks on the "necessary and proper" power of the federal government, which is provided for in Article I, Section 8, Clause 18.

Amendment 11

Suits Against the States The Eleventh Amendment (1795) provides that a lawsuit brought by a citizen of the United States or a foreign nation against a state must be tried in a state court, not in a federal court. The Supreme Court had ruled in *Chisholm* v. *Georgia* (1793) that a federal court could try a lawsuit brought by citizens of South Carolina against a citizen of Georgia.

Vocabulary

bail: *money that an accused person provides to the court as a guarantee that he or she will be present for a trial*
majority: *more than half*

Amendment 12

Election of President and Vice President The Twelfth Amendment (1804) corrects a problem that had arisen in the method of electing the president and vice president, which is described in Article II, Section 1, Clause 3. This amendment provides for the Electoral College to use separate ballots in voting for president and vice president. *If no candidate receives a majority of the electoral votes, who elects the president?*

Amendment VIII

Excessive **bail** shall not be required, nor excessive fines imposed, nor cruel and unusual punishments inflicted.

Amendment IX

The enumeration in the Constitution, of certain rights, shall not be construed to deny or disparage others retained by the people.

Amendment X

The powers not delegated to the United States by the Constitution, nor prohibited by it to the States, are reserved to the States respectively, or to the people.

Amendment XI

The Judicial power of the United States shall not be construed to extend to any suit in law or equity, commenced or prosecuted against one of the United States by Citizens of another State, or by Citizens or Subjects of any Foreign State.

Amendment XII

The electors shall meet in their respective states and vote by ballot for President and Vice-President, one of whom, at least, shall not be an inhabitant of the same state with themselves; they shall name in their ballots the person voted for as President, and in distinct ballots the person voted for as Vice-President, and they shall make distinct lists of all persons voted for as President, and of all persons voted for as Vice-President, and of the number of votes for each, which lists they shall sign and certify, and transmit sealed to the seat of the government of the United States, directed to the President of the Senate;—The President of the Senate shall, in the presence of the Senate and House of Representatives, open all the certificates and the votes shall then be counted;—The person having the greatest number of votes for President, shall be the President, if such number be a **majority** of the whole number of Electors appointed; and if no person have such majority, then from the persons having the highest numbers not exceeding three on the list of those voted for as President, the House of Representatives shall choose immediately, by ballot, the President. But in choosing the President, the votes shall be taken by states, the representation from each state having one vote; a quorum for this purpose shall consist of a member or members from two-thirds of the states, and a majority of all the states shall be necessary to a choice. And if the House of Representatives shall not choose a President whenever the right of choice shall devolve upon them, before the fourth day of March next following, then the Vice-President shall act as President, as in the case of the death or other constitutional disability of the President. The person having the greatest number of votes as Vice-President, shall be the Vice-President, if such number be a majority of the whole number of Electors appointed, and if no person have a majority, then from the two highest numbers on the list, the Senate shall choose the Vice-President; a quorum for the purpose shall consist of two-thirds of the whole number of Senators, and a majority of the whole number shall be necessary to a choice. But no person constitutionally ineligible to the office of President shall be eligible to that of Vice-President of the United States.

Amendment XIII

Section 1

Neither slavery nor involuntary servitude, except as a punishment for crime whereof the party shall have been duly convicted, shall exist within the United States, or any place subject to their jurisdiction.

Section 2

Congress shall have power to enforce this article by appropriate legislation.

Amendment XIV

Section 1

All persons born or naturalized in the United States, and subject to the jurisdiction thereof, are citizens of the United States and of the State wherein they reside. No State shall make or enforce any law which shall **abridge** the privileges or immunities of citizens of the United States; nor shall any State deprive any person of life, liberty, or property, without due process of law; nor deny to any person within its jurisdiction the equal protection of the laws.

Section 2

Representatives shall be apportioned among the several States according to their respective numbers, counting the whole number of persons in each State, excluding Indians not taxed. But when the right to vote at any election for the choice of electors for President and Vice President of the United States, Representatives in Congress, the Executive and Judicial officers of a State, or the members of the Legislature thereof, is denied to any of the male inhabitants of such State, being twenty-one years of age, and citizens of the United States, or in any way abridged, except for participation in rebellion, or other crime, the basis of representation therein shall be reduced in the proportion which the number of such male citizens shall bear to the whole number of male citizens twenty-one years of age in such State.

Section 3

No person shall be a Senator or Representative in Congress, or elector of President and Vice President, or hold any office, civil or military, under the United States, or under any State, who, having previously taken an oath, as a member of Congress, or as an officer of the United States, or as a member of any State legislature, or as an executive or judicial officer of any State, to support the Constitution of the United States, shall

Amendment 13

Abolition of Slavery Amendments Thirteen (1865), Fourteen, and Fifteen often are called the Civil War or Reconstruction amendments. The Thirteenth Amendment outlaws slavery.

Amendment 14

Rights of Citizens The Fourteenth Amendment (1868) originally was intended to protect the legal rights of the freed slaves. Its interpretation has been extended to protect the rights of citizenship in general by prohibiting a state from depriving any person of life, liberty, or property without "due process of law." In addition, it states that all citizens have the right to equal protection of the laws in all states.

Vocabulary

abridge: *to reduce*

Amendment 14. Section 2

Representation in Congress This section reduced the number of members a state had in the House of Representatives if it denied its citizens the right to vote. Later civil rights laws and the Twenty-fourth Amendment guaranteed the vote to African Americans.

Amendment 14. Section 3

Penalty for Engaging in Insurrection The leaders of the Confederacy were barred from state or federal offices unless Congress agreed to remove this ban. By the end of Reconstruction, all but a few Confederate leaders were allowed to return to public service.

Amendment 14. Section 4

Public Debt The public debt acquired by the federal government during the Civil War was valid and could not be questioned by the South. However, the debts of the Confederacy were declared to be illegal. *Could former slaveholders collect payment for the loss of their slaves?*

Amendment 15

Voting Rights The Fifteenth Amendment (1870) prohibits the government from denying a person's right to vote on the basis of race. Despite the law, many states denied African Americans the right to vote by such means as poll taxes, literacy tests, and white primaries.

Amendment 16

Income Tax The origins of the Sixteenth Amendment (1913) date back to 1895, when the Supreme Court declared a federal income tax unconstitutional. To overturn this decision, this amendment authorizes an income tax that is levied on a direct basis.

Vocabulary

insurrection: *rebellion against the government*
apportionment: *distribution of seats in House based on population*
vacancy: *an office or position that is unfilled or unoccupied*

Amendment 17

Direct Election of Senators The Seventeenth Amendment (1913) states that the people, instead of state legislatures, elect United States senators. *How many years are in a Senate term?*

---

have engaged in insurrection or rebellion against the same, or given aid or comfort to the enemies thereof. But Congress may by a vote of two-thirds of each House, remove such disability.

Section 4

The validity of the public debt of the United States, authorized by law, including debts incurred for payment of pensions and bounties for service in suppressing **insurrection** or rebellion, shall not be questioned. But neither the United States nor any State shall assume or pay any debt or obligation incurred in aid of insurrection or rebellion against the United States, or any claim for the loss or emancipation of any slave; but all such debts, obligations and claims shall be held illegal and void.

Section 5

The Congress shall have power to enforce, by appropriate legislation, the provisions of this article.

Amendment XV

Section 1

The right of citizens of the United States to vote shall not be denied or abridged by the United States or by any State on account of race, color, or previous condition of servitude.

Section 2

The Congress shall have power to enforce this article by appropriate legislation.

Amendment XVI

The Congress shall have power to lay and collect taxes on incomes, from whatever source derived, without **apportionment** among the several States and without regard to any census or enumeration.

Amendment XVII

Section 1

The Senate of the United States shall be composed of two Senators from each State, elected by the people thereof, for six years; and each Senator shall have one vote. The electors in each State shall have the qualifications requisite for electors of the most numerous branch of the State legislatures.

Section 2

When **vacancies** happen in the representation of any State in the Senate, the executive authority of such State shall issue writs of election to fill such vacancies: *Provided*, That the legislature of any State may empower the executive thereof to make temporary appointments until the people fill the vacancies by election as the legislature may direct.

Section 3

This amendment shall not be so construed as to affect the election or term of any Senator chosen before it becomes valid as part of the Constitution.

Amendment XVIII

Section 1
After one year from ratification of this article, the manufacture, sale, or transportation of intoxicating liquors within, the importation thereof into, or the exportation thereof from the United States and all territory subject to the jurisdiction thereof for beverage purposes is hereby prohibited.

Section 2
The Congress and the several States shall have concurrent power to enforce this article by appropriate legislation.

Section 3
This article shall be inoperative unless it shall have been ratified as an amendment to the Constitution by the legislatures of the several States, as provided in the Constitution, within seven years from the date of the submission hereof to the States by the Congress.

Amendment XIX

Section 1
The right of citizens of the United States to vote shall not be denied or abridged by the United States or by any State on account of sex.

Section 2
Congress shall have power by appropriate legislation to enforce the provisions of this article.

Amendment XX

Section 1
The terms of the President and Vice President shall end at noon on the 20th day of January, and the terms of the Senators and Representatives at noon on the 3d day of January, of the years in which such terms would have ended if this article had not been ratified; and the terms of their successors shall then begin.

Section 2
The Congress shall assemble at least once in every year, and such meeting shall begin at noon on the 3rd day of January, unless they shall by law appoint a different day.

Section 3
If, at the time fixed for the beginning of the term of the President, the **President elect** shall have died, the Vice President elect shall become President. If a President shall not have been chosen before the time fixed for the beginning of his term, or if the President elect shall have failed to qualify, then the Vice President elect shall act as President until a President shall have qualified; and the Congress may by law

Amendment 18
Prohibition The Eighteenth Amendment (1919) prohibited the production, sale, or transportation of alcoholic beverages in the United States. Prohibition proved to be difficult to enforce. This amendment was later repealed by the Twenty-first Amendment.

Amendment 19
Woman Suffrage The Nineteenth Amendment (1920) guaranteed women the right to vote. By then women had already won the right to vote in many state elections, but the amendment made their right to vote in all state and national elections constitutional.

Amendment 20
"Lame-Duck" The Twentieth Amendment (1933) sets new dates for Congress to begin its term and for the inauguration of the president and vice president. Under the original Constitution, elected officials who retired or who had been defeated remained in office for several months. For the outgoing president, this period ran from November until March. Such outgoing officials, referred to as "lame ducks," could accomplish little. *What date was chosen as Inauguration Day?*

Vocabulary
president elect: *individual who is elected president but has not yet begun serving his or her term*

provide for the case wherein neither a President elect nor a Vice President elect shall have qualified, declaring who shall then act as President, or the manner in which one who is to act shall be selected, and such person shall act accordingly until a President or Vice President shall have qualified.

Section 4

The Congress may by law provide for the case of the death of any of the persons from whom the House of Representatives may choose a President whenever the right of choice shall have devolved upon them, and for the case of the death of any of the persons from whom the Senate may choose a Vice President whenever the right of choice shall have devolved upon them.

Section 5

Section 1 and 2 shall take effect on the 15th day of October following the ratification of this article.

Section 6

This article shall be inoperative unless it shall have been ratified as an amendment to the Constitution by the legislatures of three-fourths of the several States within seven years from the date of its submission.

Amendment XXI

Section 1

The eighteenth article of amendment to the Constitution of the United States is hereby repealed.

Section 2

The transportation or importation into any State, Territory, or possession of the United States for delivery or use therein of intoxicating liquors, in violation of the laws thereof, is hereby prohibited.

Section 3

This article shall be inoperative unless it shall have been ratified as an amendment to the Constitution by conventions in the several States, as provided in the Constitution, within seven years from the date of the submission hereof to the States by the Congress.

Amendment XXII

Section 1

No person shall be elected to the office of the President more than twice, and no person who had held the office of President, or acted as President, for more than two years of a term to which some other person was elected President shall be elected to the office of the President more than once. But this Article shall not apply to any person holding the office of President when this Article was proposed by the Congress, and shall not prevent any person who may be holding the office of President, or acting as President, during the term within which this Article becomes operative from holding the office of President or acting as President during the remainder of such term.

Section 2

This article shall be inoperative unless it shall have been ratified as an amendment to the Constitution by the legislatures of three-fourths of the several States within seven years from the date of its submission to the States by the Congress.

Amendment XXIII

Section 1

The District constituting the seat of Government of the United States shall appoint in such manner as the Congress may direct:

A number of electors of President and Vice President equal to the whole number of Senators and Representatives in Congress to which the District would be entitled if it were a State, but in no event more than the least populous State; they shall be in addition to those appointed by the States, but they shall be considered, for the purposes of the election of President and Vice President, to be electors appointed by a State; and they shall meet in the District and perform such duties as provided by the twelfth article of amendment.

Section 2

The Congress shall have power to enforce this article by appropriate legislation.

Amendment XXIV

Section 1

The right of citizens of the United States to vote in any primary or other election for President or Vice President, for electors for President or Vice President, or for Senator or Representative in Congress, shall not be denied or abridged by the United States or any State by reason of failure to pay any poll tax or other tax.

Section 2

The Congress shall have power to enforce this article by appropriate legislation.

Amendment XXV

Section 1

In case of the removal of the President from office or his death or resignation, the Vice President shall become President.

Section 2

Whenever there is a vacancy in the office of the Vice President, the President shall nominate a Vice President who shall take the office upon confirmation by a majority vote of both Houses of Congress.

Amendment 23

D.C. Electors The Twenty-third Amendment (1961) allows citizens living in Washington, D.C., to vote for president and vice president, a right previously denied residents of the nation's capital. The District of Columbia now has three presidential electors, the number to which it would be entitled if it were a state.

Amendment 24

Abolition of the Poll Tax
The Twenty-fourth Amendment (1964) prohibits poll taxes in federal elections. Prior to the passage of this amendment, some states had used such taxes to keep low-income African Americans from voting. In 1966 the Supreme Court banned poll taxes in state elections as well.

Amendment 25

Presidential Disability and Succession The Twenty-fifth Amendment (1967) established a process for the vice president to take over leadership of the nation when a president is disabled. It also set procedures for filling a vacancy in the office of vice president.

This amendment was used in 1973, when Vice President Spiro Agnew resigned from office after being charged with accepting bribes. President Richard Nixon then appointed Gerald R. Ford as vice president in accordance with the provisions of the Twenty-fifth Amendment. A year later, President Nixon resigned during the Watergate scandal, and Ford became president. President Ford then had to fill the vice presidency, which he had left vacant upon assuming the presidency. He named Nelson A. Rockefeller as vice president. Thus, individuals who had not been elected held both the presidency and the vice presidency. *Whom does the president inform if he or she cannot carry out the duties of the office?*

Amendment 26

Voting Age of 18 The Twenty-sixth Amendment (1971) lowered the voting age in both federal and state elections to 18.

Amendment 27

Congressional Salary Restraints The Twenty-seventh Amendment (1992) makes congressional pay raises effective during the term following their passage. James Madison offered the amendment in 1789, but it was never adopted. In 1982 Gregory Watson, then a student at the University of Texas, discovered the forgotten amendment while doing research for a school paper. Watson made the amendment's passage his crusade.

Section 3

Whenever the President transmits to the President pro tempore of the Senate and the Speaker of the House of Representatives his written declaration that he is unable to discharge the powers and duties of his office, and until he transmits to them a written declaration to the contrary, such powers and duties shall be discharged by the Vice President as Acting President.

Section 4

Whenever the Vice President and a majority of either the principal officers of the executive departments or of such other body as Congress may by law provide, transmit to the President pro tempore of the Senate and the Speaker of the House of Representatives their written declaration that the President is unable to discharge the powers and duties of his office, the Vice President shall immediately assume the power and duties of the office of Acting President.

Thereafter, when the President transmits to the President pro tempore of the Senate and the Speaker of the House of Representatives his written declaration that no inability exists, he shall resume the powers and duties of his office unless the Vice President and a majority of either the principal officers of the executive department or of such other body as Congress may by law provide, transmit within four days to the President pro tempore of the Senate and the Speaker of the House of Representatives their written declaration that the President is unable to discharge the powers and duties of his office. Thereupon Congress shall decide the issue, assembling within forty-eight hours for that purpose if not in session. If the Congress, within twenty-one days after receipt of the latter written declaration, or, if Congress is not in session, within twenty-one days after Congress is required to assemble, determines by two-thirds vote of both Houses that the President is unable to discharge the powers and duties of his office, the Vice President shall continue to discharge the same as Acting President; otherwise, the President shall resume the power and duties of his office.

Amendment XXVI

Section 1

The right of citizens of the United States, who are eighteen years of age or older, to vote shall not be denied or abridged by the United States or by any State on account of age.

Section 2

The Congress shall have power to enforce this article by appropriate legislation.

Amendment XXVII

No law, varying the compensation for the services of Senators and Representatives, shall take effect, until an election of representatives shall have intervened.

Federalists and Republicans

1789–1816

ESSENTIAL QUESTION • *Why do people form political parties?*

◄ Alexander Hamilton, born and raised in the British West Indies, played a key role in the establishment of the U.S. government. He was killed in a duel in 1804.

networks

There's More Online about how America's first political parties were formed.

CHAPTER 4

Lesson 1
Washington and Congress

Lesson 2
Partisan Politics

Lesson 3
Jefferson in Office

Lesson 4
The War of 1812

The Story Matters...

In 1789 Alexander Hamilton became the first secretary of the Department of the Treasury. It was a critical job, and Hamilton had to ensure that the new government had enough money to run the country. He supported taxing imports, honoring all debts remaining from the Revolutionary War, establishing a national bank, and imposing a tax on whiskey. The different reactions to Hamilton's ideas shaped the emerging political parties of the Federalists and the Democratic-Republicans.

Place and Time: United States 1789–1815

Of all the remarkable accomplishments of Thomas Jefferson's presidency, the purchase of the Louisiana Territory is one of the most historically significant. By acquiring this vast territory from France, Jefferson more than doubled the size of the United States and gave the nation control of the entire Mississippi River. This territorial expansion made it possible for eager Americans to move farther west.

Step Into the Place

Read the quotes and look at the information presented on the map.

DBQ **What can be learned about the region west of the Mississippi River from these quotes? Why does Jefferson say it is better that the opposite bank "should be settled by our own brethren"?**

PRIMARY SOURCE

❝I know that the acquisition of Louisiana has been disapproved by some from a candid apprehension [fear] that the enlargement of our territory would endanger its union. . . . The larger our association, the less will it be shaken by local passions; and in any view is it not better that the opposite bank of the Mississippi should be settled by our own brethren and children than by strangers of another family?❞

—Thomas Jefferson, from his Second Inaugural Address, March 4, 1805

PRIMARY SOURCE

❝The planes [plains] appeared covered with Spectators viewing the White men and the articles which we had, our party [weak] and much reduced in flesh as well as Strength. . . . [W]e attempted to have Some talk with those people but Could not for the want of an Interpreter thro' [through] which we Could Speake [speak], we were Compelled to converse altogether by Signs. — I got the Twisted hare to draw the river from his Camp down which he did with great [cheerfulness] on a white Elk Skin. . . . [A]t the falls he places Establishments of white people . . . and informs that great numbers of Indians reside on all those [forks] as well as the main river.❞

—William Clark, from *The Journals of Lewis & Clark Expedition*, Vol. 5
Sunday, September 22, 1805

Step Into the Time

Choose an event from the time line and write a paragraph that predicts the social impact that event might have on the United States.

Washington
1789–1797

J. Adams
1797–1801

U.S. PRESIDENTS

UNITED STATES

WORLD

1789 Washington becomes president

1794 Jay's Treaty is signed

1790

1795

1789 French Revolution begins

1791 French constitution limits power of monarchy

1798 Quasi-War between France and the United States begins

networks
There's More Online!

☑ **MAP** Explore the interactive version of this map on Networks.

☑ **TIME LINE** Explore the interactive version of the time line on Networks.

The Louisiana Purchase

← Lewis and Clark's expedition
← Zebulon Pike's expedition
☐ United States, 1803

BRITISH TERRITORY

Ft. Clatsop, winter quarters 1805–1806

OREGON TERRITORY

Columbia R.

Snake R.

Lewis

Clark

Ft. Mandan, winter quarters 1804–1805

Missouri R.

LOUISIANA PURCHASE

SPANISH TERRITORY

Pikes Peak

Santa Fe

Colorado R.

Arkansas R.

Rio Grande

Red R.

Brazos R.

Chihuahua

Natchitoches

New Orleans

Maine

Vt.

N.H.

New York

Mass.

R.I.

Penn.

Conn.

N.J.

Ohio

Md. Del.

Indiana Territory

Ohio R.

St. Louis

Virginia

Kentucky

Tennessee

North Carolina

South Carolina

Mississippi Territory

Georgia

ATLANTIC OCEAN

Spanish Florida

Gulf of Mexico

PACIFIC OCEAN

0   200 miles
0   200 km

Lambert Azimuthal Equal-Area projection

50°N

30°N

110°W   100°W   90°W   80°W

Jefferson 1801–1809

1803 Louisiana Purchase doubles size of the nation

1804 Lewis and Clark begin to explore the Louisiana Purchase

Madison 1809–1817

1811 Battle of Tippecanoe breaks up Tecumseh's confederacy

1812 United States declares war on Britain

December 15, 1814 Hartford Convention meets

December 24, 1814 Treaty of Ghent is signed

1800   **1805**   **1810**   **1815**

1804 Napoleon becomes emperor of France

1805 British navy wins Battle of Trafalgar

1812 Napoleon invades, then retreats from Russia

1815 Congress of Vienna ends Napoleonic Wars

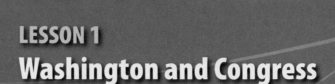

LESSON 1
Washington and Congress

PHOTOS: (l to r) The Granger Collection, New York, The Granger Collection, New York, The Granger Collection, New York, Library of Congress

Reading **HELP**DESK

Content Vocabulary

- cabinet • agrarianism
- bond
- speculator
- enumerated powers
- implied powers

Academic Vocabulary

- revenue • creditor

TAKING NOTES: *Organizing*

ACTIVITY As you read, complete a graphic organizer similar to the one below to record details about Hamilton's and Madison's ideas for financing the government.

Hamilton's Plan	Madison's Response	Result

ESSENTIAL QUESTION • *Why do people form political parties?*

It Matters Because

President Washington and the First Congress had to decide how to make the new government function effectively. The conflicting philosophies of Thomas Jefferson and Alexander Hamilton became the basis for two new political parties.

Creating a New Government

GUIDING QUESTION *What challenges did the United States face in organizing its new financial system?*

The Philadelphia Convention had given the nation a new Constitution. George Washington's task, and the task facing the newly elected Congress, was to take the words of the Constitution and turn them into an effective government for the United States. To get the government up and running, the president needed a bureaucracy to handle different responsibilities. In 1789 Congress created the Department of State, the Department of the Treasury, the Department of War, and the Office of the Attorney General.

To manage these departments, Washington wanted individuals who were "disposed to measure matters by a Continental scale," instead of thinking only of their own states. He chose Thomas Jefferson as secretary of state, Alexander Hamilton as secretary of the treasury, General Henry Knox as secretary of war, and Edmund Randolph as attorney general. Washington regularly met with these men to ask for their advice. The department heads came to be known as the **cabinet,** a group of advisers to the president.

Congress also established the federal judiciary. The Judiciary Act of 1789 created 13 district courts and three courts of appeal, in addition to the Supreme Court established by the Constitution. With the Senate's consent, Washington appointed the federal judges and selected John Jay to become the first chief justice.

Financing the Government

The most pressing need for the new government was a source of **revenue,** or income to pay for the nation's expenses and massive war debts. Without funds, the government could not operate. James

Madison, one of the leaders in Congress, and Hamilton responded to this need with different plans for financing the government.

The Tariff of 1789 Madison's plan was to tax imports. After much discussion, Congress passed the Tariff Act of 1789, which set tax rates on certain imported items. Congress also passed the Tonnage Act, levying a tax per ton of cargo on ships entering the United States, with foreign ships taxed at a higher rate.

Hamilton's Financial Program Hamilton supported these measures, but he believed the government also needed the ability to borrow money. To fund the Revolutionary War, the Congress under the Articles of Confederation had issued **bonds**—paper notes promising to repay money with interest after a certain length of time. By 1789, the United States owed roughly $40 million to American citizens and another $11.7 million to foreign lenders. Few believed the bonds would be repaid in full, and many had been sold at a fraction of their face value. Hamilton asked Congress to redeem the bonds at full value.

Hamilton believed that if the United States accepted these debts at full value, then wealthy **creditors**, bankers, and merchants who owned the bonds would have enough confidence in the federal government's financial stability to lend it money in the future. Hamilton had described the importance of debt several years earlier: "A national debt if it is not excessive will be to us a national blessing; it will be a powerful cement of our union. It will also create a necessity for keeping up taxation . . . which without being oppressive, will be a spur to industry. . . ."

Opposition to Hamilton's Plan Led by Madison, critics argued that Hamilton's plan was unfair to the original purchasers who, fearing they would never be repaid, had sold their bonds at a low price. They were outraged that **speculators,** most from the North, who had bought the bonds at those low prices would now benefit. Hamilton's plan to assume the states' debts also worried Madison and other Southerners in Congress. The Southern states, with the exception of South Carolina, had nearly paid off their war debts.

The debate raged for months. In July 1790, Hamilton, Madison, and Jefferson reached a compromise. Southerners voted for Hamilton's plan, and in return, the nation's capital would, in ten years time, relocate to an area on the Potomac River that would be called the District of Columbia. Southerners believed that having the capital in the South would keep the federal government responsive to their region's interests.

The Bank of the United States

With his system of public credit finally in place, Hamilton asked Congress to create a national bank to manage the nation's debts and issue bank notes— paper money. The notes would serve as a national currency and promote trade, encourage investment, and promote economic growth.

Southerners opposed the plan. Madison argued that Congress could not establish a bank because it was not among the federal government's **enumerated powers,** or powers specifically listed in the Constitution.

Hamilton disagreed, noting that Article I, Section 8, of the Constitution gave the federal government the power "to make all laws which shall be necessary and proper" to execute its responsibilities. The "necessary and proper" clause created **implied powers**—powers not listed in the Constitution but necessary for the government to do its job. In 1791 Congress created the Bank of the United States with a 20-year charter.

cabinet a group of advisers to the president

revenue the income of a government from all sources, used to pay for a nation's expenses

bond a note issued by the government that promises to pay off a loan with interest

creditor one to whom a debt is owed

speculator a person who risks money in hopes of a financial profit

enumerated powers powers listed in the Constitution as belonging to the federal government

implied powers powers not specifically listed in the Constitution but claimed by the federal government

The government's use of federal troops against civilians during the Whiskey Rebellion worried many people.

▶ **CRITICAL THINKING**
Making Generalizations Why do you think the tax imposed on the manufacture of whiskey led to a rebellion?

This 1798 cartoon shows the fight in Congress between Federalist Roger Griswold (holding the cane) and Democratic-Republican Matthew Lyon (holding fireplace tongs).

This cartoon is critical of Thomas Jefferson, showing him as willing to sacrifice U.S. neutrality on the French "Altar to Gallic Despotism."

POLITICAL CARTOONS

These political cartoons demonstrate the friction that existed between the political parties during the late 1700s.

▶ **CRITICAL THINKING**

1 *Identifying Central Issues* How does the cartoon on the left represent the artist's opinion of Congress?

2 *Making Inferences* In the cartoon on the right, why do you think the artist shows Jefferson kneeling at the altar?

The Whiskey Rebellion

Hamilton also believed the government had the right to impose taxes. In 1791 Congress imposed an excise tax on the manufacture of whiskey. The new tax enraged western farmers who distilled their grain into whiskey before sending it to market. The Whiskey Rebellion erupted in 1794 in western Pennsylvania. Farmers terrorized tax collectors, stopped court proceedings, and robbed the mail. Later that year, Washington led about 13,000 troops to crush the rebellion. The rebels dispersed without a fight.

✔ **PROGRESS CHECK**

Summarizing What challenges were involved in organizing the federal financial system?

The Rise of Political Parties

GUIDING QUESTION *What defined the two emerging political parties during this time?*

During Washington's first term in office, the debate over Hamilton's financial program divided Congress into factions based on their views of the federal government's role. These factions became the nation's first political parties. Hamilton's supporters called themselves Federalists. His opponents, led by Madison and Jefferson, took the name Democratic-Republicans, although most people at the time referred to them as Republicans.

The Democratic-Republicans later became known as the Democrats. The party known today as the Republican Party is a different party that was founded in 1854. The Federalist Party does not exist today.

Hamilton and the Federalists

Hamilton favored a strong national government. He believed that democracy was dangerous to liberty. "The people are turbulent and changing; they seldom judge or determine right," he had written in 1787. This distrust led him to favor putting government into the hands of the "rich, well-born, and able." Hamilton favored policies that supported manufacturing and trade since he believed they were the basis of national wealth and power.

Jefferson and the Republicans

Although James Madison led the opposition to Hamilton's programs in Congress, Thomas Jefferson emerged as the leader of the Democratic-Republicans. Jefferson believed that the strength of the United States was its independent farmers. His ideas are sometimes referred to as **agrarianism**. Jefferson argued that owning land enabled people to be independent. As long as most people owned land, they would fight to preserve the Republic.

Jefferson feared that too much emphasis on commerce would lead to a society sharply divided between the rich, who owned everything, and the poor, who worked for wages. Jefferson also believed that the wealthy would corrupt the government and threaten the rights and liberties of ordinary people.

agrarianism the philosophy that agriculture and land ownership are the backbone of the economy

Jefferson believed that an economy based on agriculture and widespread land ownership would cultivate an independent and virtuous citizenry.

▶ **CRITICAL THINKING**
Identifying Central Issues How did the Federalists and the Republicans differ in their views of the strength of the United States?

PRIMARY SOURCE

❝Dependence begets subservience and venality [openness to bribery], suffocates the germ of virtue. . . . While we have land to labour . . . let us never wish to see our citizens occupied at a work-bench, or twirling a distaff. . . .[L]et our work-shops remain in Europe. It is better to carry provisions and materials to workmen there than bring them to the provisions and materials, and with them their manners and principles.❞

—Thomas Jefferson, from *Notes on the State of Virginia*

In general, Democratic-Republicans supported agriculture over commerce and trade. Over time, they became the party that stood for the rights of states against the power of the federal government.

The development of America's first two political parties divided the country regionally. The rural South and West tended to support the Republicans, while the more urban Northeast tended to support the Federalists. Although these parties emerged during the dispute over Hamilton's programs, events in Europe would deepen the divisions between them and create new crises for the young nation.

✓ **PROGRESS CHECK**

Drawing Conclusions How was the rise of political parties in the United States related to the financial challenges facing the nation?

PHOTO: Library of Congress

LESSON 1 REVIEW

Reviewing Vocabulary

1. ***Explaining*** Explain the difference between enumerated powers and implied powers.

Using Your Notes

2. ***Comparing and Contrasting*** Review the notes you completed through the lesson. Then write a paragraph that analyzes the ways Madison and Hamilton differed in their approaches to building national revenue and how this contributed to the rise of political parties.

Answering Guiding Questions

3. ***Evaluating*** What challenges did the United States face in organizing its new financial system?

4. ***Drawing Conclusions*** What defined the two emerging political parties during this time?

Writing Activity

5. **PERSONAL** Thomas Jefferson wrote, "While we have land to labour . . . let us never wish to see our citizens occupied at a work-bench, or twirling a distaff." Write a one-page response in which you share your position on whether or not agrarianism is truly the best basis for a strong economy and democracy.

networks

There's More Online!

☑ **BIOGRAPHY** John Adams

☑ **BIOGRAPHY** Aaron Burr

☑ **IMAGE** Election Banner

☑ **VIDEO** Partisan Politics

☑ **INTERACTIVE SELF-CHECK QUIZ**

LESSON 2
Partisan Politics

ESSENTIAL QUESTION · *Why do people form political parties?*

Reading HELPDESK

Content Vocabulary

- **most-favored nation**
- **alien**
- **sedition**
- **interposition**
- **nullification**

Academic Vocabulary

- **radical** • **neutral**

TAKING NOTES: *Organizing*

ACTIVITY As you read, complete a graphic organizer similar to the one below by listing the provisions of treaties made by the United States.

Treaty	Provisions
Jay's Treaty	
Pinckney's Treaty	
Convention of 1800	

IT MATTERS BECAUSE

Although Washington wanted to remain neutral in the ongoing war between France and Britain, staying out of the conflict was not easy. With the election of 1800, the United States underwent its first transfer of political power, from the Federalist Party to the Democratic-Republican Party.

Trade and Western Expansion

GUIDING QUESTION *How did Washington negotiate problems with foreign countries?*

Shortly after George Washington was inaugurated in 1789, the French Revolution began in Europe. At first, most Americans sympathized with the revolutionaries, who seemed to be fighting for the same rights Americans had won a few years earlier. By the spring of 1793, however, a new group of French **radicals,** those whose political views and practices were considered extreme, had seized control. They executed thousands of people, including the king and queen. Many Federalists, shocked by the violence and chaos, opposed the French revolutionaries. Despite the bloodshed, many Republicans supported the revolutionaries, because they seemed to be fighting for liberty.

When France declared war on Britain, President Washington found himself in a difficult position. The United States traded with both Britain and France. Yet the Treaty of 1778 with France required the United States to help defend France's colonies in the Caribbean. Washington wanted the United States to remain **neutral,** not aligning with either side. In April 1793, Washington declared the United States to be "friendly and impartial" toward both warring powers.

Jay's Treaty and Pinckney's Treaty

Despite Washington's declaration, the British began intercepting all ships carrying goods to French ports, including hundreds of American ships. At the same time, reports appeared that the British, operating out of forts they still occupied on American territory, were inciting Native Americans to attack western settlers. Together, these events pushed Congress to the brink of war in 1794.

Determined to avoid war, Washington sent John Jay to Britain to seek a solution. Britain agreed to a treaty but drove a hard bargain. Jay was forced to agree that Britain had the right to seize cargoes bound for French ports. The British then agreed to give up their forts on American territory and granted the United States **most-favored nation** status. Republicans attacked the treaty, accusing the Federalists of being pro-British. Washington reluctantly signed the treaty, avoided war, and protected the fragile American economy.

Jay's Treaty helped the United States win concessions from Spain, which still controlled Florida and territory west of the Mississippi River. In 1795 Spain joined France in its war against Britain. Fearing that the United States would join forces with Britain to seize Spain's North American holdings, Spain offered to negotiate all outstanding issues with the United States. In 1795 the Spanish signed the Treaty of San Lorenzo, or Pinckney's Treaty, granting the United States the right to navigate the Mississippi and deposit goods at New Orleans.

Westward Expansion

In the 1780s, Americans began to settle in the area between the Appalachians and the Mississippi River. A Native American chief of the Miami named Little Turtle led Native American resistance to American settlement in the region. In late 1790 and again in 1791, Little Turtle's forces defeated U.S. troops. After these disasters, Washington sent General Anthony Wayne to stop the Native American attacks. In August 1794, Wayne's forces defeated the Native American forces, led by the Shawnee chief Blue Jacket, at the Battle of Fallen Timbers.

radical one whose political views, practices, or policies are considered extreme

neutral not aligned with any political or ideological group

most-favored nation a policy between countries ensuring fair trading practices

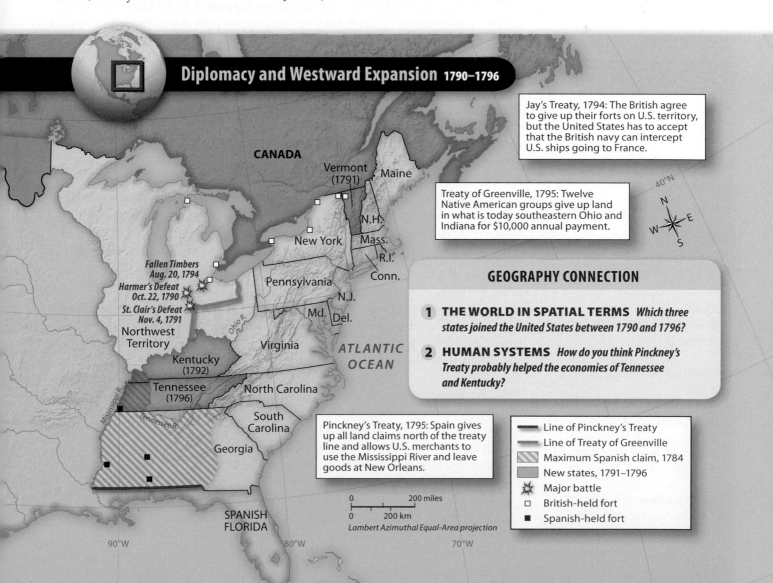

Diplomacy and Westward Expansion 1790–1796

Jay's Treaty, 1794: The British agree to give up their forts on U.S. territory, but the United States has to accept that the British navy can intercept U.S. ships going to France.

Treaty of Greenville, 1795: Twelve Native American groups give up land in what is today southeastern Ohio and Indiana for $10,000 annual payment.

Pinckney's Treaty, 1795: Spain gives up all land claims north of the treaty line and allows U.S. merchants to use the Mississippi River and leave goods at New Orleans.

CANADA

Vermont (1791)
Maine
N.H.
New York
Mass.
R.I.
Conn.
Pennsylvania
N.J.
Md. Del.
Virginia
Kentucky (1792)
Tennessee (1796)
North Carolina
South Carolina
Georgia
Northwest Territory

Fallen Timbers Aug. 20, 1794
Harmer's Defeat Oct. 22, 1790
St. Clair's Defeat Nov. 4, 1791

Ohio R.
Mississippi R.
Tennessee R.

ATLANTIC OCEAN

SPANISH FLORIDA

GEOGRAPHY CONNECTION

1 **THE WORLD IN SPATIAL TERMS** *Which three states joined the United States between 1790 and 1796?*

2 **HUMAN SYSTEMS** *How do you think Pinckney's Treaty probably helped the economies of Tennessee and Kentucky?*

Line of Pinckney's Treaty
Line of Treaty of Greenville
Maximum Spanish claim, 1784
New states, 1791–1796
Major battle
British-held fort
Spanish-held fort

0   200 miles
0   200 km
Lambert Azimuthal Equal-Area projection

90°W   80°W   70°W   40°N

❝It is our true policy to steer clear of permanent alliances with any portion of the foreign world. . . . Taking care to keep ourselves . . . on a respectable defensive posture, we may safely trust to temporary alliances for extraordinary emergencies.❞

—President George Washington, from his Farewell Address, September 17, 1796

DBQ *PREDICTING CONSEQUENCES*
What do you think might happen if the United States did enter into a permanent alliance with another nation?

Wayne's victory dealt a decisive blow to Native American resistance in the Northwest Territory. In August 1795, 12 Native American nations signed the Treaty of Greenville. They agreed to give up part of southern Ohio and Indiana in exchange for a yearly payment of $9,500 from the federal government. After the treaty was signed, the flow of settlers to the region rapidly increased. By 1803, Ohio had enough settlers to become a state.

✔ **PROGRESS CHECK**
Summarizing How did Washington negotiate conflict with Britain?

The War Between the Parties

GUIDING QUESTION *What disagreements characterized the battles between the first political parties in the United States?*

When Washington decided in 1796 to step down as president after two terms, the United States held its first openly contested election. The Federalists rallied around John Adams for president, while the Republicans nominated Thomas Jefferson. John Adams edged out Jefferson 71 to 68 in the Electoral College and became the second president of the United States.

The Quasi-War With France

Enraged by Jay's Treaty, the French began seizing goods from American ships headed to Britain. France's actions led many Federalists to call for war. Adams sent Charles Pinckney, Elbridge Gerry, and John Marshall to Paris to negotiate with the French government. After weeks of waiting, three agents of the French government approached the Americans and asked for a bribe of $250,000 and a loan of $12 million just to start talks. John Marshall later recalled the demand for a bribe, "Mr. X again returned to the subject of money; said he, Gentlemen, . . . it is expected that you will offer money . . . what is your answer? We replied, it is no; no; not a sixpence." This inspired the Federalist slogan: "Millions for defense but not one cent for tribute."

When President Adams informed Congress, he referred to the French agents as X, Y, and Z. Newspapers referred to the incident as the XYZ Affair. Irate Americans called for war. In June 1798, Congress suspended trade with France. The two nations were soon fighting an undeclared war at sea, known as the Quasi-War. Eventually, the two countries signed the Convention of 1800, which released the United States from the Treaty of 1778 and brought the Quasi-War to an end.

The Alien and Sedition Acts

At the height of public anger at France in 1798, the Federalists pushed four laws through Congress, known as the Alien and Sedition Acts. The first three laws were aimed at **aliens**—people living in the country who were not citizens. The first extended the number of years that immigrants had to wait before they could become citizens from 5 to 14 years. The next two laws gave the president the power to deport without trial any alien deemed dangerous to the nation. The fourth law tried to prevent **sedition,** or incitement to rebellion. This law made it illegal to criticize the federal government or any government official, depriving citizens of their basic right to free speech.

In 1798 and 1799, the Republican-controlled legislatures of Kentucky and Virginia passed resolutions, anonymously written by Jefferson and Madison, that criticized the Alien and Sedition Acts. The Virginia Resolutions introduced the theory of **interposition.** They argued that if the federal government did something unconstitutional, the state could interpose between the federal government and the people and stop the illegal action. The Kentucky Resolutions advanced the theory of **nullification.** According to this theory,

alien a person living in a country who is not a citizen of that country

sedition incitement to rebellion

interposition theory that a state should be able to intervene between the federal government and the people to stop an illegal action

nullification theory that states have the right to declare a federal law invalid if the federal government passed an unconstitutional law, the states had the right to nullify the law, or declare it invalid.

The Election of 1800

John Adams faced a tough battle for reelection in 1800. The Alien and Sedition Acts had angered many people, as had new taxes on houses, land, and enslaved people. The Republican nominees, Thomas Jefferson for president and Aaron Burr for vice president, opposed the taxes and the national bank.

The election revealed a flaw in the system for selecting the president. The Constitution does not let citizens choose presidents directly. Each state chooses electors—the same number as it has senators and representatives. This group, known as the Electoral College, then votes for the president. Under the original terms of the Constitution, each elector in the Electoral College voted for two people, normally one for the presidential candidate and another for the vice-presidential candidate. To avoid a tie between Jefferson and Burr, the Republicans intended for one elector to refrain from voting for Burr, but when the votes were counted, Jefferson and Burr each had 73. Since no candidate had a majority, the Federalist-controlled House of Representatives had to choose the president.

Many Federalists despised Jefferson, but Alexander Hamilton convinced his followers to support Jefferson. In February 1801, one Federalist cast a blank ballot so that Jefferson received more votes than Burr and became president.

The election of 1800 was an important turning point in American history. At the time, the Federalists controlled the army, the presidency, and Congress. They could have refused to step down and overthrown the Constitution. Instead, they respected the people's right to choose the president. The election of 1800 demonstrated that power in the United States could be peacefully transferred despite strong disagreements between the parties.

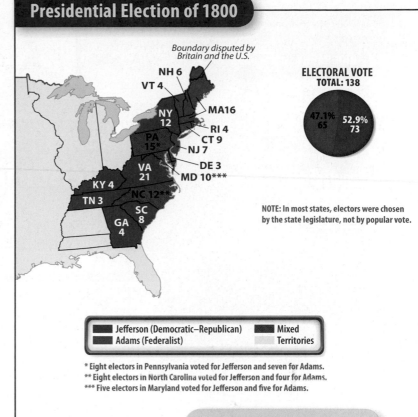

Presidential Election of 1800

Boundary disputed by Britain and the U.S.

NH 6
VT 4
NY 12
MA 16
RI 4
PA 15*
CT 9
NJ 7
VA 21
DE 3
MD 10***
KY 4
NC 12**
TN 3
SC 8
GA 4

ELECTORAL VOTE
TOTAL: 138

47.1% 65
52.9% 73

NOTE: In most states, electors were chosen by the state legislature, not by popular vote.

■ Jefferson (Democratic–Republican)   ■ Mixed
■ Adams (Federalist)   ■ Territories

* Eight electors in Pennsylvania voted for Jefferson and seven for Adams.
** Eight electors in North Carolina voted for Jefferson and four for Adams.
*** Five electors in Maryland voted for Jefferson and five for Adams.

GEOGRAPHY CONNECTION

The election of 1800 was the first transfer of power between parties under the federal Constitution.

1 PLACES AND REGIONS
Why do you think more states supported Jefferson than Adams?

2 HUMAN SYSTEMS *What was the significance of having the president elected by the Electoral College instead of by popular vote?*

☑ **PROGRESS CHECK**

Summarizing How did the Alien and Sedition Acts reflect growing political tensions?

LESSON 2 REVIEW

Reviewing Vocabulary

1. *Describing* Describe what the terms *interposition* and *nullification* mean and how the terms differ from each other.

Using Your Notes

2. *Making Connections* Review the notes that you completed through the lesson. What did the various treaties signed in the first few years of the United States say about the country?

Answering Guiding Questions

3. *Drawing Conclusions* How did Washington negotiate problems with foreign countries?

4. *Evaluating* What disagreements characterized the battles between the first political parties in the United States?

Writing Activity

5. PERSUASIVE Write a short essay in favor of the Alien and Sedition Acts.

networks

There's More Online!

- ☑ **BIOGRAPHY** John Marshall
- ☑ **BIOGRAPHY** Lewis and Clark
- ☑ **BIOGRAPHY** Sacagawea
- ☑ **IMAGE** Hamilton-Burr Duel
- ☑ **MAP** The Louisiana Purchase
- ☑ **PRIMARY SOURCE** "Ograbme" Political Cartoon
- ☑ **VIDEO** Jefferson in Office
- ☑ **INTERACTIVE SELF-CHECK QUIZ**

LOUISIANA PURCHASE

Reading **HELP**DESK

Content Vocabulary

- judicial review
- embargo

Academic Vocabulary

- license

TAKING NOTES: *Cause and Effect*

ACTIVITY As you read, complete a graphic organizer similar to the one below by listing causes and effects of the historical events listed.

CAUSE	EVENT	EFFECT
	The Louisiana Purchase	
	Lewis and Clark Expedition	
	Marbury v. Madison	
	Embargo of 1807	

LESSON 3
Jefferson in Office

ESSENTIAL QUESTION · *Why do people form political parties?*

IT MATTERS BECAUSE

President Jefferson worked to limit the scope of the federal government. He purchased the Louisiana Territory, and tried to keep the United States out of European conflicts. The Supreme Court established the power of judicial review.

Jefferson's Administration

GUIDING QUESTION *What changes occurred in the United States during Jefferson's administration?*

Thomas Jefferson privately referred to his election as the "Revolution of 1800." He believed that Washington and Adams had acted too much like royalty, and he tried to create a less formal style for the presidency. Despite these changes, he did not overturn all of the Federalists' policies. Instead he sought to integrate Republican ideas into the policies that the Federalists had already put in place. A strong believer in small government, Jefferson hoped to limit federal power. He began paying off the federal debt, cut government spending, and did away with the hated whiskey tax. Instead of a standing army, he planned to rely on local militia. Jefferson chose Albert Gallatin to be secretary of the treasury. Gallatin, like Hamilton before him, worked to solidify the structure and procedures of the Department of the Treasury.

The Louisiana Purchase

One of Jefferson's strongest beliefs was that a republic could survive only if most of the people owned land. This led him to support the idea of expanding the country farther west.

In 1800 French leader Napoleon Bonaparte convinced Spain to give Louisiana back to France in exchange for helping Spain take control of part of Italy. Napoleon's deal worried Jefferson, because it gave France control of the lower Mississippi and the port of New Orleans. Jefferson ordered his ambassador to France to try to block the deal or gain concessions for the United States. By 1803, Napoleon had begun making plans to conquer Europe and was short on funds. He offered to sell all of the Louisiana Territory, as well as New Orleans, to the United States. The ambassador immediately accepted.

On April 30, 1803, the United States bought Louisiana from France for $11.25 million. It also agreed to take on French debts of about $3.75 million owed to American citizens, making the total cost about $15 million. The Senate easily approved the Louisiana Purchase, which more than doubled the size of the United States and gave the nation control of the entire Mississippi River.

Lewis and Clark Jefferson chose Meriwether Lewis and William Clark to lead an expedition into the Louisiana Territory to find a route to the Pacific Ocean. In May 1804, the "Corps of Discovery" headed west up the Missouri River. Along the way they met Sacagawea, a Shoshone woman who became their guide and interpreter. The expedition found a path through the Rocky Mountains and eventually traced the Columbia River to the Pacific Ocean. The expedition also gave the United States a claim to the Oregon Territory.

The Pike Expedition In 1805 Zebulon Pike mapped much of the upper Mississippi River, and in 1806 he headed west to find the headwaters of the Arkansas River. He traveled to Colorado, where he charted the mountain now known as Pikes Peak. His account of this trip gave Americans their first detailed descriptions of the Great Plains and the Rocky Mountains.

The Essex Junto The Louisiana Purchase alarmed New England Federalists. They worried about losing influence in national affairs through the addition of new states. A small group of Federalists known as the Essex Junto drafted a plan to remove New England from the Union. They persuaded Vice President Aaron Burr to run for governor of New York in 1804. During the campaign, Alexander Hamilton called Burr "a dangerous man, and one who ought not to be trusted with the reins of government." Offended, Burr challenged him to a duel. When the two met, Burr shot and killed Hamilton. Burr was later accused of plotting to create his own country in the West. He was charged with treason but acquitted.

GEOGRAPHY CONNECTION

The Lewis and Clark expedition found a route from Missouri through the Rocky Mountains to the Pacific Ocean.

1 **PHYSICAL SYSTEMS**
How did the geography of the route followed by the Corps of Discovery make movement difficult for the explorers?

2 **PLACES AND REGIONS**
How did the Louisiana Purchase change the size of the United States?

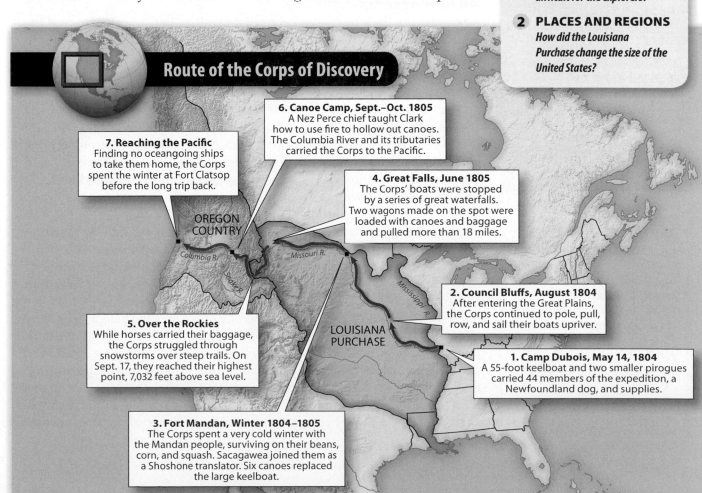

Route of the Corps of Discovery

6. Canoe Camp, Sept.–Oct. 1805
A Nez Perce chief taught Clark how to use fire to hollow out canoes. The Columbia River and its tributaries carried the Corps to the Pacific.

7. Reaching the Pacific
Finding no oceangoing ships to take them home, the Corps spent the winter at Fort Clatsop before the long trip back.

4. Great Falls, June 1805
The Corps' boats were stopped by a series of great waterfalls. Two wagons made on the spot were loaded with canoes and baggage and pulled more than 18 miles.

OREGON COUNTRY

Columbia R.

Snake R.

Missouri R.

Mississippi R.

2. Council Bluffs, August 1804
After entering the Great Plains, the Corps continued to pole, pull, row, and sail their boats upriver.

5. Over the Rockies
While horses carried their baggage, the Corps struggled through snowstorms over steep trails. On Sept. 17, they reached their highest point, 7,032 feet above sea level.

LOUISIANA PURCHASE

1. Camp Dubois, May 14, 1804
A 55-foot keelboat and two smaller pirogues carried 44 members of the expedition, a Newfoundland dog, and supplies.

3. Fort Mandan, Winter 1804–1805
The Corps spent a very cold winter with the Mandan people, surviving on their beans, corn, and squash. Sacagawea joined them as a Shoshone translator. Six canoes replaced the large keelboat.

MARBURY v. *MADISON*, 1803

Background of the Case

William Marbury had been appointed a justice of the peace shortly before President John Adams left office. Adams had signed Marbury's appointment, but the documents had not been delivered when Adams left office. The new secretary of state, James Madison, was supposed to deliver the documents, but President Jefferson told him to hold them, hoping Marbury would quit and allow Jefferson to appoint someone else. Marbury then asked the Supreme Court to issue a court order telling Madison to deliver the documents.

Chief Justice John Marshall

How the Court Ruled

Marbury based his request for a court order on the Judiciary Act of 1789, which said that requests for federal court orders go directly to the Supreme Court. In *Marbury* v. *Madison*, the Supreme Court decided that part of the Judiciary Act was unconstitutional and thus invalid. The Constitution specifies which cases can go directly to the Supreme Court, and court orders are not mentioned. The decision established the Court's power to declare laws unconstitutional and invalid.

▶ **CRITICAL THINKING**

❶ *Identifying* What important responsibility did the decision in *Marbury* v. *Madison* establish as a duty of the Supreme Court?

❷ *Describing* Under this new authority, the Supreme Court worked with the other branches of government according to what system of limitation?

---

judicial review power of the Supreme Court to determine whether laws of Congress are constitutional and to strike down those that are not

Analyzing PRIMARY SOURCES

Marbury v. *Madison*

❝ . . . [I]f both the law and the [C]onstitution apply to a particular case, so that the court must either decide that case conformable to the law, disregarding the [C]onstitution; or conformably to the [C]onstitution, disregarding the law; the court must determine which of these conflicting rules governs the case. This is of the very essence of judicial duty. ❞

—Chief Justice John Marshall

DBQ *ANALYZING INFORMATION*
Why is it important to exercise judicial duty?

An Independent Judiciary

At the end of their term, the Federalist majority in Congress enacted the Judiciary Act of 1801, creating 16 new federal judgeships. President John Adams then appointed Federalists to these positions. Republicans in Congress were not pleased. One of Congress's first acts after Jefferson took office was to repeal the Judiciary Act of 1801.

Republican leaders believed that the impeachment power was one of the checks and balances in the Constitution and tried to remove other Federalists from the judiciary. Congress could impeach and remove judges for arbitrary or unfair decisions, not just for criminal behavior. In 1804 the House impeached Supreme Court justice Samuel Chase. The Senate, however, refused to convict him. Many senators did not think he was guilty of any misdeeds that would justify his removal according to the Constitution. The impeachment of Justice Chase established that judges could be removed only for criminal behavior, not simply because Congress disagreed with their decisions.

The most important judicial appointment President Adams had made before leaving office was the choice of John Marshall as chief justice of the United States. He was more responsible than any other justice for making the Supreme Court into a powerful, independent branch of the federal government.

Marshall increased the power of the Supreme Court in 1803 with the decision in *Marbury* v. *Madison*. In this case, the Supreme Court ruled part of the Judiciary Act of 1789 to be unconstitutional. The decision marked the first time the Supreme Court asserted the power of **judicial review.** Although the Supreme Court would not strike down another federal law until the case of *Dred Scott* v. *Sandford* 54 years later, the power to do so had been established.

✓ **PROGRESS CHECK**

Explaining Why did President Jefferson decide to purchase the Louisiana Territory?

Rising International Tensions

GUIDING QUESTION *How did Jefferson avoid being involved in the war between France and Great Britain?*

Jefferson also had to contend with pirate raids against American ships in the Mediterranean. During his second term, he had to focus his efforts on keeping the United States out of the war between Britain and France.

The Barbary Pirates

For years, the Barbary States on the North African coast—Morocco, Algiers, Tunis, and Tripoli—had menaced Mediterranean shipping. European nations paid "tribute" to these countries to guarantee that their ships would not be disturbed. Jefferson refused to continue such payments. In 1801 Tripoli declared war on the United States. Jefferson sent a naval squadron into the Mediterranean in what was the United States's first foreign military conflict. The conflict dragged on and off for years until the tribute payments ended in 1815. Still, the United States had demonstrated independence.

Economic Warfare

In 1806, while again at war with France, Britain declared that ships going to Europe needed British **licenses** and would be searched for illegal goods. Napoleon declared that merchants who obeyed the British system would have their goods confiscated when they reached Europe. No matter whose commands they honored, American merchants would lose their goods.

Impressment The British navy was short of recruits because of low pay and terrible shipboard conditions. British sailors often deserted to American vessels. Britain tried to solve this problem by impressment, a legalized form of kidnapping that forced people into military service. Britain often stopped American ships to search for deserters, often taking American sailors. In June 1807, the British warship *Leopard* stopped the American ship USS *Chesapeake*. When the *Chesapeake's* captain refused to comply, the *Leopard* opened fire and killed three Americans. The British then seized four American sailors.

The Embargo of 1807 The attack on the *Chesapeake* enraged the public, and American newspapers clamored for war. Instead of going to war, Jefferson asked Congress to pass the Embargo Act of 1807, halting all trade between the United States and Europe. The **embargo** wound up hurting the United States more than France or Great Britain. Realizing the embargo was not working, Congress repealed it in 1809, shortly before Jefferson left office.

☑ **PROGRESS CHECK**

Examining Why did Jefferson have Congress pass the Embargo Act?

license permission or freedom to act

embargo a government ban on trade with other countries

The British warship *Leopard* fires on the *Chesapeake* off the coast of Virginia.

▶ **CRITICAL THINKING**
Drawing Conclusions Why do you think the American public was angered by the attack on the *Chesapeake*?

LESSON 3 REVIEW

Reviewing Vocabulary
1. *Defining* What is an embargo?

Using Your Notes
2. *Cause and Effect* Use your notes to write a short paragraph that identifies the cause and effect of each event listed.

Answering Guiding Questions
3. *Evaluating* What changes occurred in the United States during Jefferson's administration?

4. *Drawing Conclusions* How did Jefferson avoid being involved in the war between France and Great Britain?

Writing Activity
5. EXPOSITORY How did *Marbury* v. *Madison* affect the power of the Supreme Court, and how did the decision align with the Constitution? Write a paragraph to explain your answer.

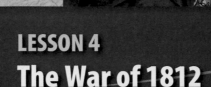
LESSON 4
The War of 1812

Reading HELPDESK

Content Vocabulary

• nationalism

Academic Vocabulary

• overseas • enable

TAKING NOTES: *Organizing*

ACTIVITY Complete a graphic organizer similar to the one below by listing the causes of the War of 1812.

EVENT	CAUSES
War of 1812	

ESSENTIAL QUESTION • *Why do people form political parties?*

IT MATTERS BECAUSE

Trade restrictions and the belief that the British encouraged Native American attacks on Americans led to the War of 1812, the second major clash between the United States and Britain in North America. Although neither side won a clear victory, the war gave Americans a strong sense of national pride.

The Decision for War

GUIDING QUESTION *What led the United States into the War of 1812?*

After Thomas Jefferson announced that he would not run again for president in 1808, the Republican Party nominated James Madison. The Federalists nominated Charles Pinckney. Madison won the election easily. He assumed office at a time when tensions between the United States and Britain were rising. It would fall to Madison to decide whether or not to lead the United States into its first full-scale war since the Revolution.

Economic Pressures

Like Jefferson, Madison wanted to avoid war. To force the British to stop seizing American ships, he asked Congress to pass the Non-Intercourse Act. This act forbade trade with France and Britain but authorized the president to reopen trade with whichever country removed its trade restrictions first.

In May 1810, Congress took a different approach with a plan drafted by Nathaniel Macon of North Carolina. The plan, called Macon's Bill Number Two, reopened trade with both Britain and France but stated that if either nation dropped its restrictions on trade, the United States would stop importing goods from the other nation. Soon afterward, Napoleon announced that France would no longer restrict American trade but still allowed for the seizure of American ships. When Britain refused to drop its trade restrictions, Congress passed a nonimportation act against Britain. In June 1812, Britain finally ended all restrictions, but it was too late. Soon after, the British learned that the United States had declared war.

PHOTOS: (l to r)Tecumseh (1768-1813) (oil on canvas), American School, (19th century)/Private Collection/Peter Newark American Pictures/The Bridgeman Art Library, Anne S.K. Brown Military Collection, Brown University Library, Library of Congress/The Bridgeman Art Library, Library of Congress

The War Hawks

Most members of Congress who wanted war came from the South and the West. Named the War Hawks by their opponents, they believed the nation's reputation was in danger if the United States did not go to war to stop the British from seizing American sailors. Americans in the South and the West had other reasons for wanting to go to war. British trade restrictions had hurt Southern planters and Western farmers, who earned much of their income by shipping crops **overseas.** Western farmers also accused the British in Canada of arming Native Americans and encouraging them to attack American settlements.

Tecumseh and Tippecanoe

Although Western settlers blamed the British for their problems with the Native Americans, it was the increasing demands of speculators and settlers that sparked Native American resistance. Tecumseh, a Shawnee leader, wanted Native Americans to unite to protect their lands. While Tecumseh worked for political union, his brother Tenskwatawa ("the Prophet") called for the spiritual rebirth of Native American cultures. He and his followers lived at Prophetstown on the Tippecanoe River in Indiana.

Aware that Tecumseh's movement was gaining strength, William Henry Harrison, governor of the Indiana Territory, prepared to stamp it out. In November 1811, after learning that Tecumseh had gone south to recruit more followers, he gathered a force and marched toward Prophetstown. Tenskwatawa sent fighters to intercept Harrison and his troops near the Tippecanoe River. The ensuing Battle of Tippecanoe resulted in about 150 casualties on both sides, but the Americans claimed it as a victory. The clash shattered Native American confidence in the Prophet. Many, including Tecumseh, fled to Canada.

Tecumseh's flight to Canada and the British-made rifles his forces had been using seemed to be evidence of British support. Many Western farmers argued that war with Britain would **enable** the United States to seize Canada

overseas situated, originating in, or relating to lands beyond the sea

enable to make possible, practical, or easy

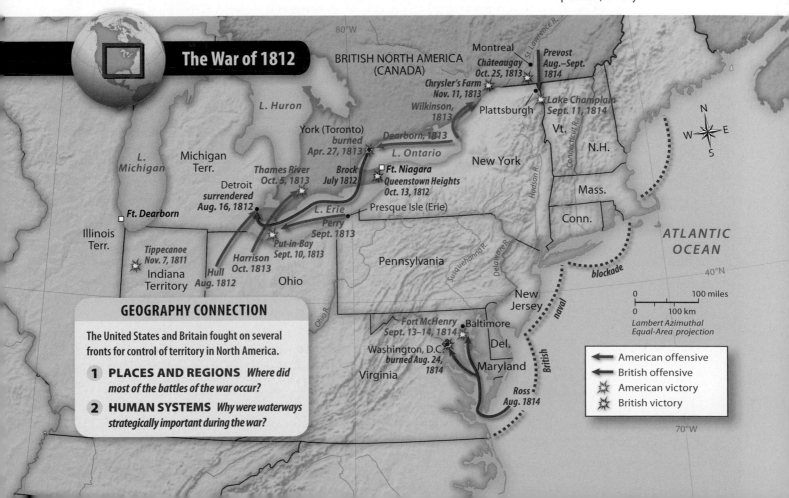

The War of 1812

BRITISH NORTH AMERICA (CANADA)

Montreal
Châteaugay Oct. 25, 1813
Prevost Aug.–Sept. 1814
Chrysler's Farm Nov. 11, 1813
Wilkinson, 1813
Lake Champlain Sept. 11, 1814
Plattsburgh
L. Huron
York (Toronto) burned Apr. 27, 1813
Dearborn, 1813
L. Ontario
Vt.
N.H.
L. Michigan
Michigan Terr.
Thames River Oct. 5, 1813
Brock July 1812
Ft. Niagara Queenstown Heights Oct. 13, 1812
New York
Detroit surrendered Aug. 16, 1812
L. Erie
Presque Isle (Erie)
Mass.
Ft. Dearborn
Perry Sept. 1813
Put-in-Bay Sept. 10, 1813
Conn.
ATLANTIC OCEAN
Illinois Terr.
Tippecanoe Nov. 7, 1811
Harrison Oct. 1813
Pennsylvania
blockade
40°N
Indiana Territory
Hull Aug. 1812
Ohio
New Jersey
naval
0   100 miles
0   100 km
Lambert Azimuthal Equal-Area projection

Fort McHenry Sept. 13–14, 1814
Baltimore
Del.
British
Washington, D.C. burned Aug. 24, 1814
Maryland
Virginia
Ross Aug. 1814

GEOGRAPHY CONNECTION

The United States and Britain fought on several fronts for control of territory in North America.

1 **PLACES AND REGIONS** *Where did most of the battles of the war occur?*

2 **HUMAN SYSTEMS** *Why were waterways strategically important during the war?*

➤ American offensive
➤ British offensive
✷ American victory
✷ British victory

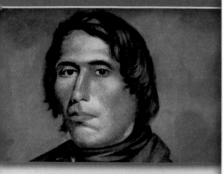

Tecumseh (1768–1813)

Tecumseh grew up in the Ohio River valley and fought in several conflicts with settlers. In leading the Native American resistance against the United States, Tecumseh believed that all Native Americans were one group and urged his people to reject the idea of owning land individually. Tecumseh tried to unite many Native American groups against the steady flow of American settlers into their territories. Tecumseh was killed during the Battle of the Thames. After his death, his confederacy collapsed.

▶ **CRITICAL THINKING**
Summarizing What were Tecumseh's feelings about the Native American way of life?

and end Native American attacks. In June 1812, President Madison gave in to the pressure and asked Congress to declare war. The vote in Congress split along regional lines. The South and the West generally voted for war; the Northeast did not.

☑ **PROGRESS CHECK**

Identifying What key factors led to the U.S. decision to declare war on Britain?

The Invasion of Canada

GUIDING QUESTION *Was the decision for war a popular one for Americans?*

Although the Republican-led Congress had called for war, the nation was not ready to fight. The army had fewer than 7,000 troops and little equipment. The navy had only 16 ships. Americans were deeply divided over the war. Many people in New York and New England called it "Mr. Madison's War," implying that it did not deserve the nation's support.

Paying for the war also posed a problem. The year before, the charter that authorized the Bank of the United States had expired. This made it difficult for the government to borrow money because most private bankers, located in the Northeast, opposed the war and would not lend money to the government. Despite this, President Madison ordered the military to invade Canada and later rechartered the bank.

Three Strikes Against Canada

American military leaders planned to attack Canada from three directions—from Detroit, from Niagara Falls, and up the Hudson River valley toward Montreal. All three attacks failed. The British navy on Lake Erie moved troops to Detroit and forced the American commander, General William Hull, to surrender. The British then shifted their troops to the Niagara peninsula, where they took up positions on Queenstown Heights, along the river. From there, they easily drove off some 600 American troops who had landed on the Canadian side of the river. The American force would have been larger, except that the New York militia refused to cross the river, arguing that the terms of their service did not require them to leave the country. The third American attack fared no better than the first two. General Henry Dearborn, marching up the Hudson River toward Montreal, called off the attack after militia troops again refused to cross the border.

Perry's Victory on Lake Erie

The following year, the United States had more success after Commodore Oliver Perry arranged for the construction of a fleet on the coast of Lake Erie in Ohio. On September 10, 1813, Perry's fleet attacked the British fleet. After a grueling four-hour battle, the British surrendered.

After Perry's victory gave the Americans control of Lake Erie, he notified General Harrison: "Dear general—We have met the enemy—and they are ours. Two ships, two brigs, one schooner, and one sloop. Yours, with great respect and esteem." The victory also enabled Harrison to recover Detroit and march into Canada, where he defeated a combined force of British troops and Native Americans at the Battle of the Thames River.

British troops and Canadian militia, however, stopped the American attack from the east at the Battle of Stony Creek, and Harrison retreated to Detroit. By the end of 1813, the United States still had not conquered any territory in Canada.

☑ **PROGRESS CHECK**

Explaining Why did many Americans call the War of 1812 "Mr. Madison's War"?

The War Ends

GUIDING QUESTION *What was the outcome of the War of 1812?*

In 1814 Napoleon's empire collapsed. With the war against France over, the British were now able to send more of their military to deal with the United States.

British Attack Washington, D.C., and Baltimore

In August 1814, a British fleet sailed into Chesapeake Bay and landed troops within marching distance of Washington, D.C. The British easily dispersed the poorly trained militia defending the capital and entered the city unopposed. Madison and other government officials fled. The British set fire to the White House and the Capitol.

Baltimore, however, was ready for the British. The city militia inflicted heavy casualties on the British troops that went ashore. After bombarding Fort McHenry, the British abandoned their attack. Francis Scott Key, a young lawyer held aboard a British ship during the shelling, was elated to see the American flag still flying above the fort at dawn. On the back of a letter, he scribbled a poem about the battle that would later become the national anthem of the United States: "The Star-Spangled Banner."

Events in New England and New Orleans

In December 1814, Federalists from New England met in Hartford, Connecticut, to discuss what they could do independently of the United States. Members of the Essex Junto urged New England to secede, but moderate delegates refused to support such extreme action. Instead, the Hartford Convention called for constitutional amendments designed to increase the region's political power.

That same month, a British fleet with some 7,500 men landed near New Orleans. The American commander, General Andrew Jackson, had not yet received the news that negotiators had signed the Treaty of Ghent on December 24. On January 8, 1815, Jackson led the American troops to a decisive victory in the Battle of New Orleans. He became a national hero. As **nationalism** surged, the Federalists at the Hartford Convention appeared unpatriotic and they never recovered nationally. The War of 1812 increased the nation's prestige overseas and generated a new spirit of patriotism and national unity.

✓ **PROGRESS CHECK**

Examining What were the effects of the Battle of New Orleans?

This engraving depicts the triumph of Andrew Jackson (on horseback at right) over the British at the Battle of New Orleans.

▶ **CRITICAL THINKING**
Drawing Conclusions How could the victory in the Battle of New Orleans have helped Jackson's political ambitions?

nationalism loyalty and devotion to a nation

LESSON 4 REVIEW

Reviewing Vocabulary
1. *Summarizing* What is nationalism, and what event inspired nationalism in many Americans?

Using Your Notes
2. *Understanding Relationships* Use your notes to write a short paragraph that explains the causes of the War of 1812 and how they affected the United States.

Answering Guiding Questions
3. *Evaluating* What led the United States into the War of 1812?

4. *Drawing Conclusions* Was the decision for war a popular one for Americans?

5. *Analyzing* What was the outcome of the War of 1812?

Writing Activity
6. **EXPOSITORY** Write a short essay that explains Tecumseh's goals and the consequences of his organization of Native Americans.

Directions: On a separate sheet of paper, answer the questions below. Make sure you read carefully and answer all parts to the question.

Lesson Review

Lesson 1

1 *Identifying* What were two sources of revenue for the new federal government?

2 *Naming* What were the first two major political parties that emerged in the United States?

Lesson 2

3 *Summarizing* What right was granted the United States through Pinckney's Treaty?

4 *Analyzing* Why was the presidential election of 1800 a major turning point in American political history?

Lesson 3

5 *Explaining* In *Marbury* v. *Madison*, what power was asserted by the Supreme Court? How is that power defined?

6 *Examining* Why did Thomas Jefferson have Congress pass the Embargo Act, and what was its effect on the United States?

Lesson 4

7 *Analyzing* Why did Western farmers argue for war with Britain?

8 *Evaluating* How did the War of 1812 affect national politics?

21st Century Skills

9 **IDENTIFYING CAUSE AND EFFECT** What were some of the causes for the War of 1812?

10 **GEOGRAPHY SKILLS** What were the eastern and western boundaries of the Louisiana Purchase?

11 **IDENTIFYING PERSPECTIVES AND DIFFERING INTERPRETATIONS** How did the Republicans feel about Jay's Treaty?

12 **PROBLEM SOLVING** What were some of the problems the Lewis and Clark expedition faced, and how were they solved?

13 **ECONOMICS** What prompted France to sell the Louisiana Territory to the United States?

Exploring the Essential Question

14 *Drawing Conclusions* Write an essay that identifies the reasons political parties were formed in the United States. Your essay should also explain which political party would better lead the country at a time of international crisis: the Federalists or the Democratic-Republicans.

DBQ Document-Based Question

Analyze the cartoon to answer the following question.

In this cartoon French leaders harass a woman symbolizing the United States.

PRIMARY SOURCE

15 *Analyzing* In response to what historic event was this cartoon created? How do you know?

Extended-Response Question

16 *Evaluating* Suppose you were a small farmer of English descent living in 1800 in South Carolina. Write a narrative essay that describes which political party you plan to join and why. Be sure to explain how your choice relates to your economic interests.

Need Extra Help?

If You've Missed Question	**1**	**2**	**3**	**4**	**5**	**6**	**7**	**8**	**9**	**10**	**11**	**12**	**13**	**14**	**15**	**16**
Go to page	121	122	125	127	130	131	133	135	132	129	125	129	128	122	126	122

Growth and Division

1816–1832

ESSENTIAL QUESTIONS • *How did the nation's economy help shape its politics?* • *How did the economic differences between the North and the South cause tension?*

networks

There's More Online about the growth of the United States in the 1800s.

CHAPTER 5

The Story Matters...

The geographic and economic growth of the United States in the 1800s led to conflict. Settlers showed little respect for Native Americans' rights as they pushed groups, such as the Seminole, off land they had occupied for hundreds of years. In the South, the success of cotton farming locked the region into an economy dependent on enslaved labor. Whether or not to allow slavery to expand into newly formed states became a topic of fierce debate.

◀ Seminole leader Osceola led a valiant attempt to stop the removal of the Seminole from Florida. Osceola was seized and imprisoned at Fort Moultrie in South Carolina, where he died in 1838.

PHOTO: Superstock/Getty Images

137

After the War of 1812, a strong sense of national pride swept the United States. Industrialization was beginning to transform the North, leading to bigger cities, while little industry developed in the South. Innovations in transportation changed the ways people traveled and the ways goods were transported. They also increased the speed with which people and goods moved, which helped link regions of the country more closely. Nevertheless, sectionalism and political tensions grew between the North and the South.

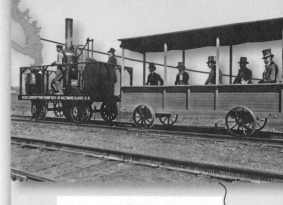

Step Into the Place

Read the quote and look at the information presented on the map.

DBQ **What do the quote and the information on the map indicate about U.S. industry in the 1800s?**

Train:
The *Tom Thumb* was the first American locomotive. Railroads reduced travel times, allowing people and goods to move quickly from city to city and helping to encourage settlement in the West.

PRIMARY SOURCE

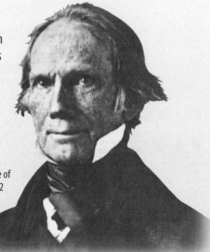

66 This transformation of the condition of the country from gloom and distress to brightness and prosperity, has been mainly the work of American legislation, fostering American industry, instead of allowing it to be controlled by foreign legislation, cherishing foreign industry. 99

—Senator Henry Clay, from a speech "In Defence of the American System," February 1832

Wagon:
People could travel more quickly due to an increased number of roads and improved road quality. Many people traveled west on these roads using Conestoga wagons.

PHOTOS: left page (cl)The Granger Collection, New York, (tr) Underwood & Underwood/Bettmann/CORBIS, (cr) The Landis Valley Museum, (bl, br)detail/White House Collection/The White House Historical Association; right page detail/White House Collection/The White House Historical Association

Step Into the Time

Choose a world event from the time line and write a paragraph explaining the connections between that event and events in the United States during the time period.

Madison
1809–1817

Monroe
1817–1825

1819 Spain cedes Florida to the United States

1820 Henry Clay guides the Missouri Compromise through Congress

1823 Monroe Doctrine declared

U.S. PRESIDENTS			
UNITED STATES			
WORLD	**1817**	**1819**	**1821**	**1823**

March 1821 Greece declares independence from the Ottoman Empire

September 1821 Mexican independence recognized by Spain

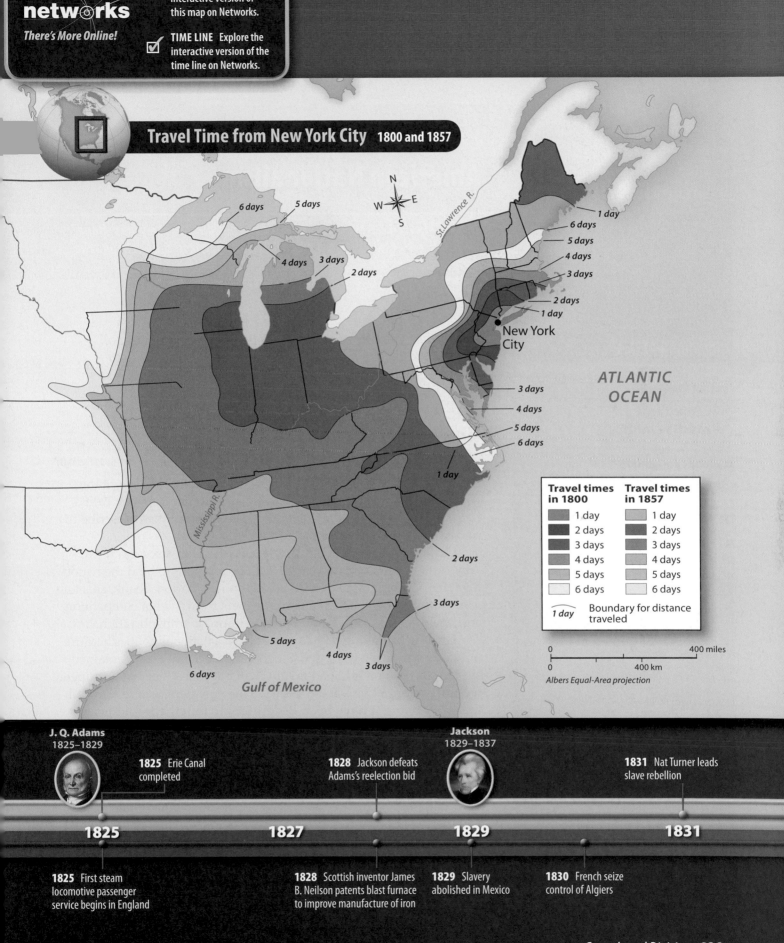

☑ **MAP** Explore the interactive version of this map on Networks.

☑ **TIME LINE** Explore the interactive version of the time line on Networks.

networks
There's More Online!

Travel Time from New York City 1800 and 1857

6 days
5 days
4 days
3 days
2 days

St. Lawrence R.

1 day
6 days
5 days
4 days
3 days
2 days
1 day

New York City

ATLANTIC OCEAN

3 days
4 days
5 days
6 days

1 day

Mississippi R.

2 days

3 days

5 days
4 days
3 days

6 days

Gulf of Mexico

Travel times in 1800	Travel times in 1857
1 day	1 day
2 days	2 days
3 days	3 days
4 days	4 days
5 days	5 days
6 days	6 days

⌒ 1 day Boundary for distance traveled

0   400 miles
0   400 km
Albers Equal-Area projection

J. Q. Adams
1825–1829

1825 Erie Canal completed

1828 Jackson defeats Adams's reelection bid

Jackson
1829–1837

1831 Nat Turner leads slave rebellion

1825   **1827**   **1829**   **1831**

1825 First steam locomotive passenger service begins in England

1828 Scottish inventor James B. Neilson patents blast furnace to improve manufacture of iron

1829 Slavery abolished in Mexico

1830 French seize control of Algiers

networks

There's More Online!

☑ **BIOGRAPHY** Osceola

☑ **MAP** National Road

☑ **MAP** Nationalism and Diplomacy

☑ **PRIMARY SOURCE** Excerpts from *McCulloch v. Maryland*

☑ **VIDEO** American Nationalism

☑ **INTERACTIVE SELF-CHECK QUIZ**

Reading **HELP**DESK

Content Vocabulary
• revenue tariff
• protective tariff

Academic Vocabulary
• interpret • finalize

TAKING NOTES: *Organizing*

ACTIVITY As you read about the growth of the United States, complete a graphic organizer similar to the one below by listing actions that strengthened the federal government after the War of 1812.

LESSON 1
American Nationalism

ESSENTIAL QUESTIONS • *How did the nation's economy help shape its politics?* • *How did the economic differences between the North and the South cause tension?*

IT MATTERS BECAUSE

After the War of 1812, the federal government began building the national road, defended its authority to regulate interstate commerce, and declared the Western Hemisphere off-limits for future colonization.

Economic Nationalism

GUIDING QUESTION *How would you characterize the United States during the Era of Good Feelings?*

After the War of 1812, a strong sense of national pride swept the United States. The *Columbian Centinel,* a Boston newspaper, called this time the "Era of Good Feelings." The name came to describe the period of James Monroe's presidency.

During the last two years of James Madison's second term, American leaders proposed an ambitious program to bind the nation together. The program included creating a new national bank, enacting a tariff protecting American manufacturers from foreign competition, and building new canals and roads to improve transportation.

Partisan infighting had largely ended in national politics because only one political party—the Democratic-Republicans—remained strong. The War of 1812 had taught Republican leaders that a stronger federal government was necessary. This new perspective allowed many who might have been Federalists to join the Republicans instead. James Monroe won the presidency in 1816 with 83 percent of the electoral vote. The Federalist Party then faded away.

The Second Bank

Republicans had traditionally opposed the idea of a national bank. They had blocked the charter renewal of the First Bank of the United States in 1811 and offered nothing in its place. The results were disastrous. With no national bank to regulate currency, prices rose rapidly during the War of 1812. When the government borrowed money to pay for the war, it had to pay high interest rates on the loans.

These problems led many Republicans to change their minds about a national bank. In 1816 Representative John C. Calhoun of

PHOTOS: The Granger Collection, New York

South Carolina introduced a bill proposing the Second Bank of the United States. With the support of Representative Henry Clay of Kentucky, it passed that same year. The bank had the power to issue notes that would serve as a national currency and to control state banks.

Tariffs and Transportation

Protection of manufacturers was another part of the Republican program. After the War of 1812, inexpensive British goods threatened to put American manufacturers out of business. Congress responded with the Tariff of 1816. Unlike earlier **revenue tariffs,** which provided income for the federal government, this was a **protective tariff** that raised the prices of imports to nurture growing American manufacturers.

Republicans also wanted to improve the transportation system. In 1816 Calhoun sponsored a federal internal improvement plan, but President Madison vetoed it, arguing that spending money to improve transportation was not expressly granted in the Constitution. Nevertheless, road and canal construction soon began, with private businesses and state and local governments funding much of the work.

revenue tariff a tax on imports for the purpose of raising money

protective tariff a tax on imports designed to protect American manufacturers

☑ **PROGRESS CHECK**

Explaining Why did many Republicans change their minds about a national bank?

Judicial Nationalism

GUIDING QUESTION *How did the Marshall Court strengthen the national government?*

Between 1816 and 1824, the Supreme Court under Chief Justice John Marshall issued several rulings that helped unify the nation after the war. These decisions established the dominance of the national government over the states.

Martin v. Hunter's Lessee

In 1816 the Court decided in *Martin* v. *Hunter's Lessee* that it had authority to hear all appeals of state court decisions in cases involving federal statutes and treaties. In this case, Denny Martin, a British subject, had tried to sell land in Virginia he had inherited from his uncle, a Loyalist. State law held

GEOGRAPHY CONNECTION

In 1806 Congress funded the surveying of a major east-west highway. By the 1820s, the National Road was a heavily traveled route.

1 **THE WORLD IN SPATIAL TERMS** *Where did the national road begin and end?*

2 **HUMAN SYSTEMS** *How might the construction of the road have led to changes in the land around it?*

Building the National Road 1811–1838

National Road
1820 boundary

CANADA

Michigan Territory

Lake Michigan

Lake Erie

New York

Pennsylvania

Ohio

Illinois

Indiana

Wheeling
Columbus
Richmond
Springfield
Zanesville
Indianapolis
Uniontown
Cumberland

Terre Haute

Effingham
Vandalia

St. Louis

Kentucky

Virginia

Maryland

District of Columbia

Wabash River
Ohio River
Potomac River
Mississippi River

100 miles
100 km
Albers Equal-Area projection

that no "enemy" could inherit land, but the Court ruled that Virginia's law conflicted with Jay's Treaty, which stated that land belonging to Loyalists before the war was still theirs. The decision helped establish the Supreme Court as the nation's court of final appeal.

McCulloch v. Maryland

This 1819 case concerned Maryland's attempt to tax the Second Bank of the United States. First, the Court addressed the authority of the federal government to create a national bank, deciding that the Constitution did grant this power under the "necessary and proper" clause. Marshall observed that the Constitution gave the federal government the power to collect taxes, to borrow money, to regulate commerce, and to raise armies and navies. He concluded that the Constitution's "necessary and proper" clause allowed the federal government to create a bank.

Marshall then argued that the federal government was "supreme in its own sphere of action." This meant that a state government could not interfere with an agency of the federal government operating within the state's borders. Taxing the national bank was a form of interference and, thus, unconstitutional.

Gibbons v. Ogden

This 1824 case involved a company that had been granted a monopoly by the state of New York to control all steamboat traffic on New York waters. When the company tried to expand into New Jersey, the case went to court. The Supreme Court declared the monopoly unconstitutional, **interpreting** federal controls over interstate commerce granted by the Constitution to include all trade along the coast or on waterways dividing the states. This ensured

interpret to explain the meaning of complex material

🏛 ANALYZING SUPREME COURT CASES

McCULLOCH v. *MARYLAND*, 1819

Background to the Case

In 1816 President James Madison and Congress worked to establish the Second Bank of the United States. Two years later, the state of Maryland passed legislation imposing a tax on the Second Bank. The cashier at the Second Bank's branch in Baltimore, Maryland, James McCulloch, refused to pay the tax, and the matter went to the Supreme Court.

How the Court Ruled

In a unanimous decision the Court found that, under the "necessary and proper" clause, the federal government did have the unenumerated power to establish a national bank and that, while the states had the power to tax, they could not interfere with instruments of the federal government, and the tax was construed to be interference. This established the supremacy of the federal government over the governments of the states.

The Second Bank of the United States was located in Philadelphia. In McCulloch v. Maryland, *the Supreme Court ruled that the federal government had the right to establish a national bank and that the states could not tax it or otherwise interfere in any federal enterprise.*

▶ **CRITICAL THINKING**

❶ ***Identifying Central Issues*** What two questions did the *McCulloch* v. *Maryland* ruling address?

❷ ***Interpreting Significance*** What effect did the decision have on the power of the federal government?

PHOTO: The Granger Collection, New York

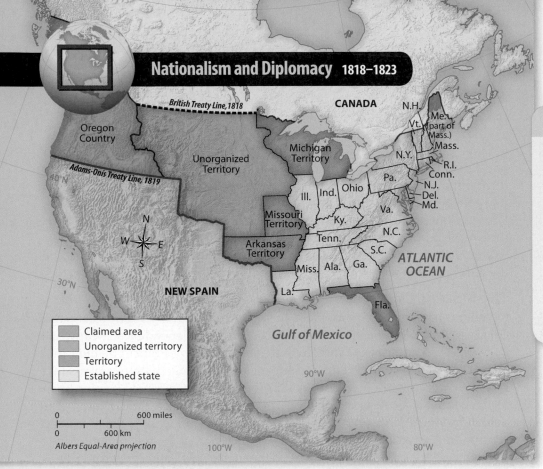

Nationalism and Diplomacy 1818–1823

British Treaty Line, 1818

CANADA

Oregon Country

Unorganized Territory

Adams-Onis Treaty Line, 1819

40°N

Michigan Territory

N.H.
Me. (part of Mass.)
Vt.
Mass.
N.Y.
R.I.
Conn.
Pa.
N.J.
Ohio
Del.
Md.
Va.
Ky.
N.C.
Tenn.
S.C.
Ga.

Ill.
Ind.

Missouri Territory

30°N

NEW SPAIN

Arkansas Territory

Miss.
Ala.
La.
Fla.

ATLANTIC OCEAN

Claimed area
Unorganized territory
Territory
Established state

Gulf of Mexico

90°W

80°W

0   600 miles
0   600 km
Albers Equal-Area projection

100°W

GEOGRAPHY CONNECTION

A surge of national pride after the War of 1812 led the United States to expand.

1 PLACES AND REGIONS
In what parts of the country did "Unorganized territory" lie?

2 ENVIRONMENT AND SOCIETY *Where would you expect most of the U.S. population to live during this era?*

precedence of federal law over state law in interstate transportation and later allowed for federally-controlled internal improvement projects.

All these cases strengthened the federal government at the expense of the states. They helped make the "necessary and proper" clause and the interstate commerce clause major vehicles for expanding federal power.

✓ **PROGRESS CHECK**

Identifying How did the ruling in *Gibbons* v. *Ogden* expand federal power over the states?

Nationalist Diplomacy

GUIDING QUESTION *How would you describe U.S. diplomacy during the Era of Good Feelings?*

The wave of nationalism within Congress and among voters also influenced the nation's foreign affairs. Led by President Monroe, the United States expanded its borders and asserted itself internationally.

Jackson Invades Florida

Spanish-held Florida was a source of anger and frustration for Southerners. Many runaway enslaved people fled there, knowing that Americans had no authority to capture them in Spanish territory. Similarly, many of the Creek had retreated to Florida as American settlers seized their lands. These groups united with other Native Americans and adopted the name *Seminole*, meaning "runaway." The Seminoles in Spanish Florida and Americans in Georgia staged raids against each other. As tensions heightened, Seminole leader Kinache warned an American general to stay out of Florida:

PRIMARY SOURCE

❝You charge me with killing your people, stealing your cattle, and burning your houses. It is I that have cause to complain of the Americans. . . . I shall use force to stop any armed Americans from passing my towns or my lands.❞
—from the *Niles Register*, December 12, 1818

The Monroe Doctrine

66 [T]he occasion has been judged proper for asserting . . . that the American continents . . . are henceforth not to be considered as subjects for future colonization by any European powers. . . .

. . . With the movements in this hemisphere, we are, of necessity, more immediately connected. . . . With the existing colonies . . . of any European power, we have not interfered, and shall not interfere. But, with the governments who have declared their independence, and maintained it, . . . we could not view any interposition for the purpose of oppressing them, or controlling, in any other manner, their destiny, by any European power, in any other light than as the manifestation of an unfriendly disposition towards the United States. 99

—from President Monroe's message to Congress, December 2, 1823

DBQ *ANALYZING PRIMARY SOURCES* What does the Monroe Doctrine prohibit?

finalize to put in finished form

The warning was ignored. In late 1817, John C. Calhoun, now secretary of war, ordered General Andrew Jackson into Florida to stop the Seminole raids. After destroying several Seminole villages, Jackson disobeyed orders and seized the Spanish settlements of St. Marks and Pensacola, and removed the Spanish governor of Florida from power.

Furious, Spanish officials demanded that Jackson be punished. Secretary of State John Quincy Adams, however, defended Jackson, arguing that Spain had failed to keep order in Florida, and used the incident to pressure Spain during the ongoing border negotiations. Occupied with problems throughout its Latin American empire, Spain gave in and ceded all of Florida to the United States in the Adams-Onís Treaty of 1819. The treaty also **finalized** the western border of the Louisiana Purchase, which now lay along the Sabine, Red, and Arkansas Rivers to the Rocky Mountains and then followed the 42nd parallel west to the Pacific Ocean.

The Monroe Doctrine

Rebellions had begun to erupt in Spain's colonies in 1809. By 1824, all of Spain's colonies on the American mainland had declared independence. Meanwhile, Britain, Austria, Prussia, and Russia (later joined by France) formed the Quadruple Alliance in an effort to suppress anti-monarchy movements in Europe. Over Britain's objection, in 1823 the Alliance considered helping Spain regain control of its overseas colonies. Britain and the United States made a great deal of money trading with Latin America and did not want Spain to reassert control. In August 1823, British officials suggested that the two nations issue a joint statement supporting the independence of the new Latin American nations.

At the same time, Russia's presence in North America was growing. Russia claimed Alaska, and in 1821 announced that its empire extended south into the Oregon Country between Russian Alaska and the western United States.

Secretary of State Adams urged Monroe to avoid working with the British when dealing with Spain and Russia. He did not want the United States to be regarded as Britain's junior partner. Monroe agreed, and in 1823, without consulting the British, he declared the American continents were "henceforth not to be considered as subjects for future colonization by any European powers."

The president's proclamation, later called the Monroe Doctrine, marked the beginning of a long-term American policy of trying to prevent European powers from interfering in Latin American political affairs. The Monroe Doctrine also upheld Washington's policy of avoiding entanglements in European power struggles.

☑ **PROGRESS CHECK**

Describing How did the United States acquire Florida?

LESSON 1 REVIEW

Reviewing Vocabulary

1. *Comparing and Contrasting* What are the similarities and differences between revenue tariffs and protective tariffs?

Using Your Notes

2. *Summarizing* Use your notes to describe ways that the federal government gained power in this period.

Answering the Guiding Questions

3. *Expressing* How would you characterize the United States during the Era of Good Feelings?

4. *Explaining* How did the Marshall Court strengthen the national government?

5. *Making Generalizations* How would you describe U.S. diplomacy during the Era of Good Feelings?

Writing Activity

6. EXPOSITORY Write a short essay explaining "economic nationalism" and describing why the United States adopted this approach after the War of 1812.

Reading **HELP**DESK

Content Vocabulary

- **free enterprise system**
- **interchangeable parts**
- **labor union**
- **strike**

Academic Vocabulary

- **transportation**
- **extraction**

TAKING NOTES: *Organizing*

ACTIVITY As you read about early industry in the United States, complete a graphic organizer similar to the one below by listing the major milestones in transportation and industrialization that occurred in the early 1800s.

Transportation	Industrialization

LESSON 2
Early Industry

ESSENTIAL QUESTIONS · *How did the nation's economy help shape its politics?* · *How did the economic differences between the North and the South cause tension?*

IT MATTERS BECAUSE

A revolution in transportation and industry led to dramatic social and economic changes. Early industrialization also led to the growth of Northern towns and cities.

A Revolution in Transportation

GUIDING QUESTION *Why did improved transportation help the nation's economy?*

In the summer of 1817, workers began building a canal across rural upstate New York to connect the Hudson River at Albany to Lake Erie at Buffalo. The new Erie Canal would span a colossal 363 miles (584 km). Building the canal was difficult and dangerous, but the canal workers completed the immense project in 1825. The Erie Canal was a striking example of a revolution in **transportation** that swept through the Northern states in the early 1800s. This revolution led to dramatic social and economic changes.

Roads and Turnpikes

As early as 1806, the nation took the first steps toward a transportation revolution when Congress authorized the surveying of a major east-west highway, the National Road. Construction started in 1811, and by 1818, the roadway reached from the Potomac River at Cumberland, Maryland, to Wheeling, Virginia (now West Virginia), on the Ohio River. The National Road turned out to be the only great federally-funded transportation project of its time, however. Madison and his successors did not believe that the federal government had the power to fund roads and other "internal improvements." Instead, states, localities, and private businesses constructed roads. New York alone had some 4,000 miles (6,400 km) of toll roads by 1821.

Steamboats and Canals

Rivers offered a faster, cheaper, and more efficient way to move goods than did roads, which were often little more than wide paths. A barge could hold many wagonloads of grain or coal. Loaded boats and barges, however, could usually travel only downstream, as moving against the current with heavy cargoes proved difficult.

transportation method of travel from one place to another

The steamboat changed all that. In 1807 Robert Fulton and Robert R. Livingston stunned the nation when their *Clermont* chugged 150 miles up the Hudson River from New York City to Albany in just 32 hours. The steamboat made river travel more reliable and upstream travel easier. By 1850 over 700 steamboats, also called riverboats, traveled along the nation's waterways. The growth of river travel and the construction of thousands of miles of canals increased trade and stimulated new economic growth.

The "Iron Horse"

Another mode of transportation—the railroad—also developed in the early 1800s. In 1830 the locomotive *Tom Thumb* pulled the nation's first load of train passengers down 13 miles of track at a then-astounding 10 miles per hour. Trains traveled much faster than stagecoaches or wagons and could go anywhere track was laid. More than any other form of transportation, trains helped settle the West and stimulate trade.

Between 1830 and 1861, the nation laid more than 30,000 miles of railroad track, boosting the demand for coal, which was used in the production of iron for the rails. Coal **extraction** shot up by nearly 20 million tons.

extraction the act or process of drawing or pulling something out

✓ **PROGRESS CHECK**

Identifying Cause and Effect How did steamboats improve transportation?

GEOGRAPHY CONNECTION

In a little over 50 years, the transportation revolution changed the nature of travel in the United States.

1 HUMAN SYSTEMS *How did goods carried on the Erie Canal reach destinations such as Boston or Pittsburgh?*

2 PHYSICAL SYSTEMS *In general, what direction do most roads run? What direction do most canals run?*

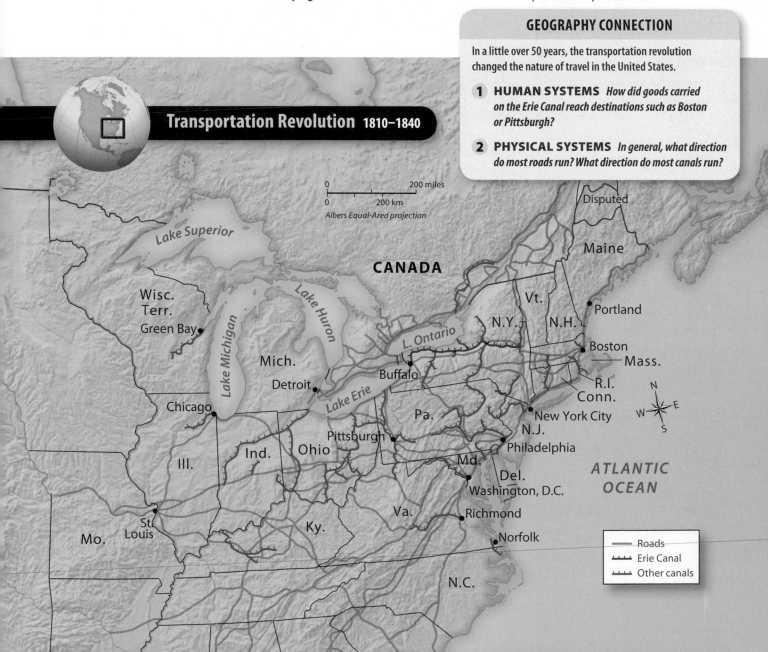

Transportation Revolution 1810–1840

	Roads
	Erie Canal
	Other canals

A New System of Production

GUIDING QUESTION *How did the Industrial Revolution change the economy and way of life?*

Along with dramatic changes in transportation, a revolution occurred in business and industry. The Industrial Revolution, which began in Great Britain in the mid-1700s, consisted of several basic developments. Manufacturing shifted from hand tools to large, complex machines. Skilled artisans gave way to unskilled workers, and factories replaced home-based workshops.

Industry developed quickly in the United States for several reasons. The American **free enterprise system,** in which individuals could make money and decide how to use it without strict government controls, encouraged innovation. Such conditions fostered competition and entrepreneurial creativity. The Constitution had also removed internal trade barriers, which provided a wider market for business. Many states also helped industrialization with laws that let companies become corporations and raise money by issuing stock. These laws limited investor liability, encouraging investment and stimulating economic growth.

The first movements toward full industrialization began in the Northeast, where many streams and rivers could provide textile mills with waterpower. Entrepreneur Francis C. Lowell began opening a series of mills in northeastern Massachusetts in 1814, introducing mass production of cotton cloth to the United States. By 1840, dozens of textile mills had been built in the Northeast. Industrialists also applied factory techniques to producing lumber, shoes, leather, wagons, and other products.

Technological Advances

A wave of inventions and technological innovations further spurred industrial growth. Eli Whitney, the inventor of the cotton gin, popularized the concept of **interchangeable parts**, transforming gun-making from a one-by-one process into a factory process. Using this process, machines made large quantities of identical pieces that workers assembled into finished goods.

Communications improved as well. Samuel Morse invented the telegraph and developed Morse code for sending messages. By 1844, the first long-distance telegraph line connected Washington, D.C., and Baltimore. Spurred by the demands of journalism and other businesses that needed quick, reliable long-distance communication, more than 50,000 miles of telegraph wire connected most parts of the country by 1860.

The Rise of Large Cities

Industrialization drew rural people to towns in search of factory jobs with higher wages. The population of many cities doubled or tripled. New York City was the nation's largest city in the 1820s. Its growing importance as a business center also increased its financial network. This led to the expansion of the city's financial district on Wall Street and the New York Stock Exchange.

Workers Begin to Organize

The industrial boom created a new kind of laborer, the factory worker, whose ranks swelled to 1.3 million by 1860. As factories grew in size, workers faced longer hours, lower pay, and more unsafe working conditions. Hoping to help improve wages and working conditions, some workers began to join **labor unions.** Most unions were local and focused on a single trade, such as printing or shoemaking. They pushed for similar changes, however, including higher wages or a shorter, 10-hour workday.

This is one of the thousands of young women who worked at the textile mills in Lowell, Massachusetts, in the early 1800s. "Mill girls" lived in crowded dorms next to the mills and were closely monitored by their employers at all times. During their free time, some mill girls read books from local lending libraries or attended public lectures or church-sponsored events.

▶ **CRITICAL THINKING**
Analyzing Primary Sources What do details in this photograph tell you about the young woman's workday?

free enterprise system
market economy in which privately owned businesses have the freedom to operate for a profit with limited government intervention

interchangeable parts
uniform pieces that can be made in large quantities to replace other identical pieces

labor union an organization of workers formed for the purpose of advancing its members' interests

PHOTO: American Textile History Museum, Lowell, MA

The growth of cities led to change and reform of American society.

▶ **CRITICAL THINKING**

1 *Analyzing Primary Sources*
What is the overall tone of the painting?

2 *Making Generalizations*
Based on the chart, how would you describe wealth distribution in Northern cities during this period?

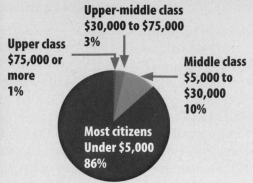

Upper-middle class
$30,000 to $75,000
3%

Upper class
$75,000 or more
1%

Middle class
$5,000 to $30,000
10%

Most citizens
Under $5,000
86%

The County Election by George Caleb Bingham shows how festive and inclusive elections had become by the 1850s. He created the work to celebrate the democratic principles of the Whig Party.

Source: *The American Historical Review* 1971

In 1833 most people in the Northeast were farmers who made a moderate or low income.

During this time, unions had little success. Most employers refused to recognize or bargain with them. Unions also had little power or money to support **strikes,** or work stoppages, to achieve their goals. The courts saw unions as unlawful conspiracies that limited free enterprise. In an 1835 case involving a union's demand that its workers be paid at least one dollar to make a pair of shoes, a New York court declared:

strike work stoppage by workers to force an employer to meet demands

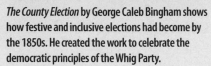

PRIMARY SOURCE

❝Competition is the life of trade. If the defendants cannot make coarse boots for less than $1 per pair, let them refuse to do so; but let them not directly or indirectly undertake to say that others shall not do the same work for a less price.❞

—from *The People* v. *Fisher,* 1835

Unions did make some gains, however. In 1840 President Martin Van Buren reduced the workday for federal employees to 10 hours. Two years later, in *Commonwealth* v. *Hunt,* the Massachusetts Supreme Court ruled that union strikes were legal.

☑ **PROGRESS CHECK**

Explaining Why did industrialization begin in the Northeast?

Life in the North

GUIDING QUESTION *How did the northern United States change during this time?*

Most of the cities in the North were still relatively small before the Civil War, compared to the expansion that would come later. They had, however, begun to suffer some of the negative results of growth: crime, overcrowding, and public health problems. Immigration from Europe also added to the growing population and its problems.

The population growth in urban centers provided many challenges to city leaders. To combat rising crime and frequent labor riots, many cities established police departments. Fire, which had long been a concern in crowded conditions when many structures were still made of wood, was also a major urban danger. Volunteer or loosely organized fire departments that had existed since colonial times were professionalized during this period.

Sanitation was another major challenge. As the urban poor crowded into cities, garbage and human waste overwhelmed inadequate sanitation systems. Diseases such as cholera and typhoid broke out in crowded areas.

These epidemics eventually led to improvements in municipal sanitation, with New York City leading the way.

Men of all social classes worked outside the home. Many poor women worked as domestic servants or factory workers or took in work that could be done in the home, such as laundry or sewing. Middle-class women who were not part of a family business were expected to remain at home to create an orderly, nurturing environment. In towns, women found that bakeries, butcher shops, clothiers, and candle shops offered goods that women once had to labor long hours to produce at home. Institutions of higher education were not available to women until the 1830s, and even then few women had the prior education or resources to attend college.

Public education was limited, but according to the 1840 census, nearly 80 percent of the total population was literate, including over 90 percent of the white population. Most young people learned from family members, church schools, or private schools and tutors if they could afford them. Some well-to-do young men attended college.

Northern cities became havens for runaway enslaved people as well as free African Americans, but most African Americans remained poor. Many African American women worked as laundresses and domestic servants. Many African American men found work in New England's shipping industry as sailors or dockworkers. In cities with larger African American populations, such as New York and Philadelphia, a small African American middle class emerged, including carpenters, shoemakers, schoolteachers, and ministers.

Even though industry and cities expanded in the Northeast during the first half of the nineteenth century, agriculture remained the country's leading economic activity. On most farms, the entire family shared the work. Fields had to be planted, tended, and plowed. Cows, pigs, and chickens had to be cared for. In the winter months, men and boys made repairs and cut wood for the fire while women spun thread into yarn and wove cloth for clothing. Until the last decades of the century, farming employed more people and produced more wealth than any other kind of work.

Northern farmers produced enough to sell their surplus in the growing cities and towns. The farmers' labors not only helped feed the population but also nourished the region's economy. As parts of the North began concentrating on manufacturing, the South continued to tie its fortunes to agriculture—and to the institution of slavery.

☑ **PROGRESS CHECK**

Comparing Why was farming more important in the South than in the North?

Analyzing PRIMARY SOURCES

Agriculture in the North

❝As far as the eye can stretch in the distance, nothing but corn and wheat fields are to be seen; and on some points of the Scioto Valley [in Ohio], as high as a thousand acres of corn may be seen in adjoining fields, belonging to some eight or ten different proprietors.❞

—from *The Cultivator,* September 1851

DBQ *ANALYZING PRIMARY SOURCES* Based on this source, what did most people living in the Scioto Valley do for a living at this time?

LESSON 2 REVIEW

Reviewing Vocabulary

1. *Determining Cause and Effect* How did the free enterprise system fuel industrialization?

2. *Identifying* What advances did labor unions make during this time?

Using Your Notes

3. *Making Connections* Review the notes that you completed during the lesson, and then use them to describe the relationship between industrialization and transportation.

Answering the Guiding Questions

4. *Explaining* Why did improved transportation help the nation's economy?

5. *Summarizing* How did the Industrial Revolution change the economy and way of life?

6. *Making Generalizations* How did the northern United States change during this time?

Writing Activity

7. **DESCRIPTIVE** Write a short descriptive essay on what city life was like in this period. Be sure to include descriptive words and phrases.

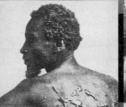

netw⊚rks
There's More Online!

☑ **BIOGRAPHY** Nat Turner

☑ **BIOGRAPHY** Eli Whitney

☑ **CHART/GRAPH** Cotton Production

☑ **IMAGE** Escaped Slave Reward Poster

☑ **MAP** Cotton Production and the Enslaved Population

☑ **VIDEO** The Land of Cotton

☑ **INTERACTIVE SELF-CHECK QUIZ**

Reading **HELP**DESK

Content Vocabulary

- cotton gin
- yeoman farmer
- task system

Academic Vocabulary

- annual
- ambiguous

TAKING NOTES: *Organizing*

ACTIVITY As you read about the South in the early to mid-1800s, complete a graphic organizer similar to the one below by listing the main categories of Southern society.

Southern Society

Highest _____

_____

_____

Lowest _____

LESSON 3
The Land of Cotton

ESSENTIAL QUESTIONS · *How did the nation's economy help shape its politics?* · *How did the economic differences between the North and the South cause tension?*

IT MATTERS BECAUSE

The economy of the South was based on the production of tobacco, rice, cotton, and other cash crops for export. Southern society had a distinct class system made up of the planter elite, yeoman farmers, and enslaved people.

The Southern Economy

GUIDING QUESTION *How did the Southern economy become dependent upon cotton and slavery?*

The South thrived on the production of several major cash crops. In the upper Southern states—Maryland, Virginia, Kentucky, and Tennessee—farmers grew tobacco. Rice paddies dominated the coastal regions of South Carolina and Georgia. In Louisiana and parts of eastern Texas, fields of sugarcane stretched for miles. No crop, however, played a greater role in the South's fortunes than did cotton. It was grown in a wide belt stretching from inland South Carolina, west through Georgia, Alabama, and Mississippi, and into eastern Texas.

During a visit to the South in 1793, young New Englander Eli Whitney noticed that removing cotton seeds by hand from the fluffy bolls was so tedious that it took a worker an entire day to separate a pound of cotton lint. In only 10 days, Whitney built a simple **cotton gin**—*gin* being short for *engine*—that quickly and efficiently combed the seeds out of cotton bolls.

The invention of the cotton gin happened at the same time that textile mills were expanding in Europe. Mills in England and France clamored for all the cotton they could get. In 1792, the South produced about 6,000 bales of cotton. By 1801, **annual** production had reached 100,000 bales.

Cotton Becomes King

Cotton soon dominated the region. By the late 1840s, Southerners were producing more than 2 million bales of cotton annually, and in 1860 production reached almost 4 million bales. In that year, Southern cotton sold for a total of $192 million—more than half the value of all U.S. exports. Southerners began saying, "Cotton is King."

The cotton gin also strengthened the institution of slavery. The spread of cotton plantations across the Deep South made the demand for slave labor skyrocket. Congress had outlawed the foreign slave trade in 1808, but a high birthrate among enslaved women—encouraged by slaveholders eager to sell new laborers at high prices—meant that the enslaved population kept growing. Between 1820 and 1850, the number of people born into slavery in the South rose from about 1.5 million to nearly 4 million.

Industry Lags

Although the South became prosperous from agriculture, it did not industrialize as quickly as the North. For the most part, the South remained a rural region, with only three large cities: Baltimore, Charleston, and New Orleans.

The South did have some industry, including coal, iron, salt, and copper mines, along with ironworks and textile mills. The region still relied heavily on imported goods, however, which worried some. In 1860 manufacturing in the South accounted for only 16 percent of the nation's total. Most Southerners were content to rely on agriculture.

☑ **PROGRESS CHECK**

Making Inferences Why was the South slow to industrialize?

Society in the South

GUIDING QUESTION *What words best describe Southern society in the early nineteenth century?*

The South's economy resulted in a society with a rigid and clearly defined class structure. At the top of Southern society was the planter elite, who owned the larger plantations. The 1850 census showed that in a Southern white population of just over 6 million, a total of 347,725 families were slaveholders.

cotton gin a machine that removed seeds from cotton fiber

annual occurring or happening every year

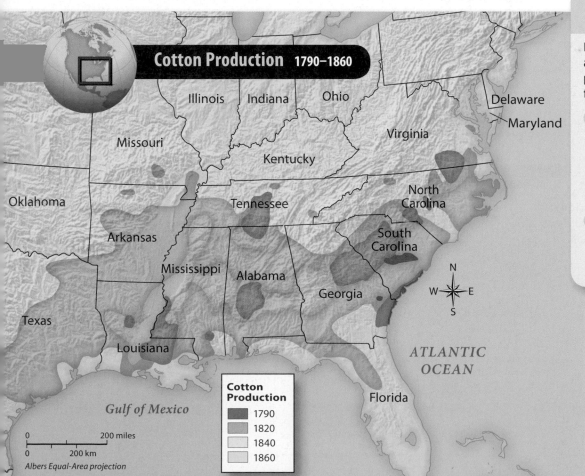

Cotton Production 1790–1860

Cotton Production
- 1790
- 1820
- 1840
- 1860

0   200 miles
0   200 km
Albers Equal-Area projection

GEOGRAPHY CONNECTION

In 1790 cotton was grown in only a few pockets of the South. Cotton production spread quickly in the following decades.

1 PLACES AND REGIONS
Through what region did cotton production spread most widely between 1820 and 1840?

2 HUMAN SYSTEMS
What assumption can you make about cotton prices after 1840?

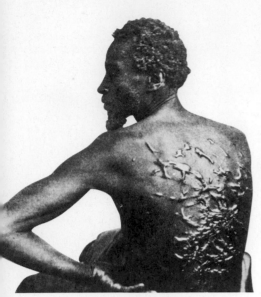

This man, named Gordon, escaped from his slaveholder in Mississippi during the Civil War. Here, he shows the scars he received from a brutal whipping earlier in his life.

▶ **CRITICAL THINKING**

Analyzing Primary Sources What does this photograph indicate about the treatment of enslaved persons?

yeoman farmer a person who owns and cultivates a small farm

Of this number, around 38,000 were planters, defined as those who held 20 or more enslaved people. Although wealthy planters made up a tiny group, they dominated the region's economy and its political system.

Ordinary farmers—often called **yeoman farmers**—and their families made up the vast majority of the white population. In his novel *Adventures of Huckleberry Finn,* author Mark Twain gives his impressions of a typical small Southern farm before the Civil War:

PRIMARY SOURCE

❝A rail fence around a two-acre yard . . . big double log-house for the white folks—hewed logs, with the chinks stopped up with mud or mortar . . . outside of the fence a garden . . . then the cotton fields begins, and after the fields the woods.❞

—from *Adventures of Huckleberry Finn,* 1884

A small urban class of lawyers, doctors, merchants, and other professionals also existed. Agriculture's influence was so great, however, that even many of them invested in or owned farms.

Near the bottom of the social ladder were the white, rural poor, made up mostly of families living on land too barren for successful farming. This group scratched a meager existence from hunting and fishing, vegetable gardening, and raising a few half-wild hogs and chickens. At the bottom of society were African Americans. In 1850 nearly 3.6 million African Americans lived in the South—about 37 percent of the total population of the South.

☑ **PROGRESS CHECK**

Identifying What group dominated the South economically and politically?

Slavery

GUIDING QUESTION *How did enslaved African Americans cope with their working conditions?*

Rice and cotton plantations, as well as tobacco farms, depended on enslaved labor. The vast majority of enslaved African Americans toiled in the South's fields. Some, however, worked in factories or as skilled workers. Others became house servants.

Enslaved people had few legal rights. State slave codes forbade enslaved people from owning property or leaving a slaveholder's premises without

CHARTS/GRAPHS · **SLAVERY IN THE SOUTH**

Most Southern slaveholders did not have as many enslaved workers as shown in this 1860 photograph.

▶ **CRITICAL THINKING**

1 *Analyzing Primary Sources* What can you say about the lives of enslaved people from this photograph?

2 *Making Generalizations* What do the percentages shown on this circle graph say about the prevalence of slaveholding in the South?

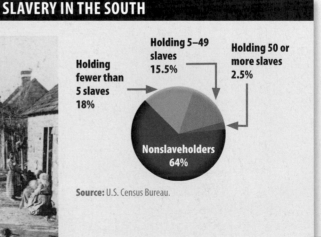

Holding fewer than 5 slaves 18%

Holding 5–49 slaves 15.5%

Holding 50 or more slaves 2.5%

Nonslaveholders 64%

Source: U.S. Census Bureau.

permission. They could not bring a lawsuit or sign a contract. They could not possess firearms or testify in court against a white person. Laws banned them from learning to read and write. Society viewed enslaved persons as property.

Plantation Life

On farms and small plantations that held few enslaved people, the **task system** was used to organize enslaved labor. Under this system, workers were given a specific set of jobs to accomplish every day. After completing their tasks, they were allowed to spend the remainder of the day as they chose. Some enslaved people earned money through their skill as artisans. Others cultivated personal gardens or hunted for extra food.

As cotton production became more common and slavery more widespread, slaveholders with large plantations adopted the gang system of labor. Under this system, enslaved people worked in groups that labored from sunup to sundown—plowing, planting, cultivating, or picking, depending on the season.

A driver acted as the director of a work gang. Often these individuals were enslaved people themselves, chosen for their loyalty or willingness to cooperate. They ensured that the workers labored continuously. No matter which system was used, slavery was a degrading experience. The abolitionist Frederick Douglass recalled how life as an enslaved person affected him:

PRIMARY SOURCE

❝My natural elasticity was crushed, my intellect languished, the disposition to read departed, the cheerful spark that lingered about my eye died; the dark night of slavery closed in upon me; and behold a man transformed into a brute!❞❞

—from *Narrative of the Life of Frederick Douglass*, 1845

Enslaved Women and Children

Enslaved African American women worked long, hard days in the fields or in the plantation house, where they served as maids, nannies, or cooks. These jobs carried great responsibilities and constant demands, along with the scrutiny of the master or mistress of the house. On larger plantations, older women cared for the babies of other women in nurseries while the mothers worked. Where family relationships were allowed, they also cooked and cared for their own families. Children of enslaved parents might be allowed to play, often with the plantation owner's own children, but as soon as they were able, they were given chores. Most enslaved children were prevented from getting an education, although some learned to read.

Free African Americans

Some 250,000 free African Americans lived in the South by the time of the Civil War, the majority of whom lived in rural areas. Some had earned their freedom through service in the American Revolution, and others were the half-white children of slaveholders who had freed them. Still others had managed to purchase freedom for themselves and their families.

Free African Americans had an **ambiguous** position in Southern society. In cities such as Charleston and New Orleans, some were successful enough to become slaveholders themselves. In other places, they had to obtain licenses to preach or to own firearms.

Some 226,000 free African Americans lived outside the South, where slavery had been outlawed. They, too, faced discrimination. Nevertheless, free African Americans could organize their own churches, publish newspapers, and earn (and keep) money from the jobs they held.

BIOGRAPHY

Frederick Douglass (1818?–1895)

Born into slavery, Frederick Douglass worked as a field hand and a house servant. Though some states made it illegal to teach an enslaved person to read, Douglass learned to read while living in Baltimore. Seeking freedom, he fled and changed his name to elude slave hunters. Douglass then became an eloquent spokesperson for the abolitionist movement. His autobiography, which described his experiences as an enslaved person, became an American literary classic. Douglass also founded and edited an antislavery newspaper and was the first African American to hold high ranking office in the federal government.

▶ **CRITICAL THINKING**
Drawing Inferences How was education important to Douglass's life?

task system a method of organizing enslaved labor in which workers were given a specific set of jobs to accomplish every day, after which they were allowed to spend their time as they chose

ambiguous undefined; uncertain

Thinking Like a
HISTORIAN

Coping With Enslavement

African Americans dealt with the horrors of slavery in a variety of ways. From language to music to religion, they developed a culture that provided them with a sense of mutual support.

African American Culture Songs were important to many enslaved people. Field workers often used songs to pass the long workdays. Some songs were more provocative than most planters knew, using subtle language and meanings to lament the singers' bondage and to express a continuing hope for freedom.

Songs also played a key role in African American religion. By the early 1800s, many African Americans were Christians. The religious services enslaved people held often centered on praying about their dreams of freedom or a better life in the next world.

Resistance and Rebellion Many enslaved people found ways to oppose the lives forced on them. Some quietly staged work slowdowns. Others broke tools or set fire to houses and barns. Still others risked beatings or mutilations to run away. Some turned on their slaveholders and killed them. On occasion, enslaved people also plotted uprisings.

Many Southerners feared the possibility of uprisings, but they rarely occurred. The first major slave uprising in the United States was plotted in 1800. Organized by an enslaved man named Gabriel Prosser, the resisters made their own weapons and ammunition. They planned to capture Richmond and kill all whites living there, except for French people, Methodists, and Quakers—groups whom Prosser felt were against slavery—and elderly women and children. The plot, however, was exposed, and Governor James Monroe sent out the state militia. Prosser and other leaders were eventually captured, tried, and executed.

In 1822 Denmark Vesey, a free African American in Charleston, South Carolina, was accused of planning an armed revolt to free enslaved people. Whether Vesey actually planned an uprising is still debated. When the authorities learned of the plot, Vesey was tried, convicted, and hanged.

A group of African Americans in Virginia did carry out an armed uprising during the early hours of August 22, 1831. Leading the attack was Nat Turner, an enslaved minister who believed God had chosen him to bring his people out of bondage. Turner and his followers killed more than 50 white men, women, and children before state and local troops put down the uprising. After his capture, Turner was tried and convicted. Six days later he was hanged.

✓ **PROGRESS CHECK**

Drawing Conclusions What was life like for enslaved people in the 1800s?

LESSON 3 REVIEW

Reviewing Vocabulary
1. *Explaining* What was the purpose of the cotton gin?

Using Your Notes
2. *Contrasting* Use your notes to describe the differences between the three types of farmers in the South during this era.

Answering the Guiding Questions
3. *Determining Cause and Effect* How did the Southern economy become dependent upon cotton and slavery?

4. *Describing* What words best describe Southern society in the early nineteenth century?

5. *Synthesizing* How did enslaved African Americans cope with their working conditions?

Writing Activity
6. EXPOSITORY Suppose that you are a European visitor to the South in 1830. Write a newspaper article explaining your impressions of life in this region.

netw⊙rks

There's More Online!

☑ **BIOGRAPHY** John Quincy Adams

☑ **BIOGRAPHY** Henry Clay

☑ **BIOGRAPHY** Andrew Jackson

☑ **MAP** Presidential Election of 1828

☑ **VIDEO** Growing Sectionalism

☑ **INTERACTIVE SELF-CHECK QUIZ**

Reading **HELP**DESK

Content Vocabulary

- **favorite sons**
- **corrupt bargain**
- **mudslinging**

Academic Vocabulary

- **controversy**
- **ignorance**

TAKING NOTES: *Organizing*

ACTIVITY As you read about growing sectionalism in the United States, complete a graphic organizer similar to the one below by listing the divisive issues of the 1820s.

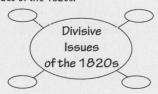

Divisive Issues of the 1820s

LESSON 4
Growing Sectionalism

ESSENTIAL QUESTIONS · *How did the nation's economy help shape its politics?* · *How did the economic differences between the North and the South cause tension?*

IT MATTERS BECAUSE

Sectional disputes over slavery and its westward expansion eroded the spirit of nationalism that swept the nation after the War of 1812. The one-party political system, dominated by the Democratic-Republicans, began to unravel in the 1820s.

The Missouri Compromise

GUIDING QUESTION *What was the goal of the Missouri Compromise?*

In 1819 controversy erupted over Missouri's application for admission to the Union as a slave state. At the time, the Union consisted of 11 free and 11 slave states. While Northerners already had a majority in the House of Representatives, to admit Missouri as a slave state would upset the balance of power in the Senate. It would also mean extending slavery into the northern part of the Louisiana Purchase. Many Northerners objected to Missouri's entering the Union as a slave state.

Acting for slavery's opponents, Congressman James Tallmadge, Jr., of New York proposed a resolution that prohibited slaveholders from bringing new slaves into Missouri. The resolution also called for all enslaved children currently living in Missouri to be freed at age 25. The House accepted the proposal, but the Senate rejected it. Most senators and members of the House of Representatives from the South voted against the ban, while most from the North voted in favor of it.

Finally, a solution emerged when Maine, which for decades had been part of Massachusetts, requested admission to the Union as a separate state. The Senate decided to combine Maine's request with Missouri's, and it voted to admit Maine as a free state and Missouri as a slave state. This solution preserved the balance in the Senate. Senator Jesse Thomas of Illinois then proposed an amendment that would prohibit slavery in the Louisiana Purchase territory north of Missouri's southern border. This would allow slavery to expand into Arkansas territory south of Missouri, but it would keep it out of the rest of the Louisiana Purchase. By a very close vote, carefully managed by Henry Clay of Kentucky, the House accepted what became known as the Missouri Compromise.

PHOTO: The Granger Collection, New York

Free state/territory

Closed to slavery by the Missouri Compromise

Slave state/territory

Opened to slavery by the Missouri Compromise

0   400 miles

0   400 km
Albers Equal-Area projection

CANADA

PACIFIC OCEAN

NEW SPAIN

Unorganized Territory

Michigan Territory

Vt. N.H. Maine free state in 1820

N.Y. Mass. R.I. Conn.

Pa. N.J. Del. Md.

Ill. Ind. Ohio

Mo. Admitted as slave state in 1821

Va.

Ky.

Missouri Compromise Line 36°30'N

Tenn.

N.C.

Arkansas Terr.

S.C.

Miss. Ala. Ga.

La.

ATLANTIC OCEAN

Fla. Terr

Gulf of Mexico

110°W   100°W   90°W   80°W

40°N

30°N

GEOGRAPHY CONNECTION

The Missouri Compromise temporarily calmed the debate over the expansion of slavery by maintaining a balance between free states and slave states.

1 PLACES AND REGIONS *Which state came into the Union as a slave state, and which came in as a free state?*

2 HUMAN SYSTEMS *Based on the map, what prediction can be made about the future number of slave states and free states?*

Once the issue was settled, however, a new problem developed. Pro-slavery members of the Missouri constitutional convention added a clause to the proposed state constitution banning free African Americans from entering the state. This new **controversy** threatened final approval of Missouri's admission to the Union. Senator Clay engineered a solution by getting the Missouri legislature to state that they would not honor the spirit of the clause's wording.

The Compromise merely postponed the debate over the future of slavery. As John Quincy Adams wrote, "I take it for granted that the present question is a mere preamble—a title-page to a great tragic volume. . . . The President thinks this question will be winked away by a compromise. But so do not I. Much am I mistaken if it is not destined to survive his political and individual life and mine."

☑ **PROGRESS CHECK**

Explaining What were the terms of the Missouri Compromise?

The Elections of 1824 and 1828

GUIDING QUESTION *What did the presidential elections of 1824 and 1828 indicate about the United States?*

Politics reflected the sectional tensions of the day. The Democratic-Republican Party had supporters throughout the nation. The presidential campaigns of 1824 and 1828, however, showed how deeply the party was divided along regional lines.

Four candidates ran for president in 1824. All were Republicans. All were **"favorite sons,"** men who enjoyed the support of leaders from their own state and region. William Crawford of Georgia ran on the principles of states'

controversy a prolonged public dispute

favorite sons politicians who enjoy the support of leaders from their own state and region

rights and strict interpretation of the Constitution. Kentucky's Henry Clay favored the American System—the national bank, the protective tariff to encourage American industry, and nationwide internal improvements. John Quincy Adams of New England favored internal improvements but was less enthusiastic about tariffs. Andrew Jackson of Tennessee emphasized his leadership qualities and military heroism.

On Election Day, Jackson won the most popular votes, but no candidate won a majority in the Electoral College. Following constitutional procedure, the election went to the House of Representatives, which would select the president from the three candidates who had received the most electoral votes. Clay, who had placed fourth, was eliminated. As Speaker of the House, however, Clay had tremendous influence. On a snowy February 9, 1825, Clay threw his support behind Adams, who won the House election easily.

When Adams later appointed Clay secretary of state, Jackson's supporters accused Adams and Clay of striking a **"corrupt bargain."** Adams and Clay denied any wrongdoing, but the incident split the party. Jackson's supporters began referring to themselves as Democrats, while Clay and his supporters formed a new party, the National Republicans.

In his first message to Congress, John Quincy Adams announced an ambitious program of nationalist legislation, including a national university, astronomical observatories, and scientific research. His proposals struck many legislators as a return to Federalist ideas, and opponents in Congress argued that it was a waste of taxpayers' money.

In the end, Congress granted the president funds for improving rivers and harbors and for extending the National Road westward, but this was far less than Adams had wanted. The repeated rebuffs Adams suffered in Congress set the stage for his defeat in 1828.

The election of 1828 pitted John Quincy Adams against Andrew Jackson. Jackson fought to achieve a victory that his supporters believed had been unjustly denied him in 1824. Both candidates engaged in **mudslinging,** criticizing each other's personalities and morals. Adams called his opponent "incompetent both by his **ignorance** and by the fury of his passions." Jackson attacked Adams as an out-of-touch aristocrat and revived the alleged "corrupt bargain" between Adams and Clay.

When the results came in, Jackson had 56 percent of the popular vote and 178 of the 261 electoral votes, a clear victory. Many of the voters who supported Jackson were from the West and the South, rural and small-town men who saw Jackson as the candidate most likely to represent their interests.

☑ **PROGRESS CHECK**

Making Inferences Why was Jackson especially eager to win the election of 1828?

---

corrupt bargain an improper or unlawful agreement between politicians

Analyzing
PRIMARY SOURCES

Henry Clay's American System

66The object of the bill . . . is to create this home market, and to lay the foundations of a genuine American policy. . . . Are we doomed to behold our industry languish and decay, yet more and more? But there is a remedy, and that remedy consists in modifying our foreign policy, and in adopting a genuine AMERICAN SYSTEM. We must naturalize the arts in our country; and we must naturalize them by the only means which the wisdom of nations has yet discovered to be effectual; by adequate protection against the otherwise overwhelming influence of foreigners.99

—Henry Clay, from a speech before Congress, March 1824

DBQ ***ANALYZING PRIMARY SOURCES*** Why does Clay believe the American System is necessary?

mudslinging attempt to ruin an opponent's reputation with insults

ignorance the state of being uneducated, uninformed, or unaware

---

LESSON 4 REVIEW

Reviewing Vocabulary

1. ***Drawing Conclusions*** What does the fact that the 1824 presidential election fielded "favorite sons" from four regions suggest about sectionalism in the United States?

Using Your Notes

2. ***Making Generalizations*** Use your notes to write a few sentences describing the tensions beginning to divide Americans during this time.

Answering the Guiding Questions

3. ***Explaining*** What was the goal of the Missouri Compromise?

4. ***Inferring*** What did the presidential elections of 1824 and 1828 indicate about the United States?

Writing Activity

5. **EXPOSITORY** Write a short essay describing how sectionalism contributed to the tensions between Jackson and his supporters and Adams and his supporters during the 1824 and 1828 elections.

Directions: On a separate sheet of paper, answer the questions below. Make sure you read carefully and answer all parts to the question.

Lesson Review

Lesson 1

1 *Interpreting Significance* Why did the United States need a protective tariff after the War of 1812?

2 *Making Generalizations* Describe the Supreme Court's general interpretation of the Constitution under Chief Justice John Marshall.

Lesson 2

3 *Identifying Cause and Effect* How did railroads help boost industrialization?

4 *Identifying Perspectives* Why did business owners refuse to recognize labor unions?

Lesson 3

5 *Identifying Cause and Effect* How did the invention of the cotton gin lead to an increased demand for enslaved labor?

6 *Describing* Describe the class structure of the South that existed by the middle of the 1800s.

Lesson 4

7 *Identifying Central Issues* What argument was used to support the accusation of a "corrupt bargain" between John Quincy Adams and Henry Clay?

8 *Drawing Conclusions* Why did Andrew Jackson win the election of 1828?

21st Century Skills

9 UNDERSTANDING RELATIONSHIPS AMONG EVENTS How did Jackson's invasion of Spanish-held Florida lead to establishing the borders of the Louisiana Purchase?

10 IDENTIFYING CAUSE AND EFFECT In the 1850s, what urban problems were made worse by overcrowding?

11 CREATE AND ANALYZE ARGUMENTS AND DRAW CONCLUSIONS How did the laws related to the rights of enslaved people make life even more difficult for them?

12 EXPLAINING CONTINUITY AND CHANGE How did the Missouri Compromise postpone a national debate about slavery?

Exploring the Essential Questions

13 *Analyzing Information* Make an informative poster titled *Differences Between the North and the South.* Use text, graphs, and illustrations to identify the economic differences between the two regions, and how the differences created political tension between them.

DBQ Document-Based Questions

Use the document to answer the following questions.

An 1828 presidential election campaign poster for Andrew Jackson focuses on the accusations of a "corrupt bargain" between John Quincy Adams and Henry Clay during the 1824 presidential election.

14 *Analyzing Visuals* Why do you think the person who designed this poster used different sizes of type?

15 *Drawing Conclusions* Lines 4–5 of the poster say, "He who could not barter nor bargain for the presidency!" How are these lines important to the overall message of the poster?

PRIMARY SOURCE

Jackson Forever!

Extended-Response Question

16 *Making Connections* During the time period between 1816–1832, what helped unify the people of the United States, bringing them closer together? What events or issues caused tensions and divisions between people?

Need Extra Help?

If You've Missed Question	1	2	3	4	5	6	7	8	9	10	11	12	13	14	15	16
Go to page	141	141	146	147	150	151	157	157	144	148	152	155	145	158	158	140

The Spirit of Reform

1828–1845

netw⊙rks

There's More Online about reform movements and social changes in the United States in the decades before the Civil War.

CHAPTER 6

The Story Matters...

During the mid-nineteenth century, increasing tensions arose between the North and the South. Southerners strove to protect their agricultural economy and way of life even as abolitionists such as Harriet Beecher Stowe railed against the institution of slavery. Northerners saw her antislavery novel *Uncle Tom's Cabin* as an indictment of the institution of slavery, while slaveholders saw it as slander.

◄ Harriet Beecher Stowe came from a family of reformers. Their efforts to achieve change in areas ranging from abolition to religious freedom reflected the spirit of their time.

PHOTO: The Granger Collection, New York

Place and Time: United States 1828–1848

During the early to mid-1800s, reformers worked to change American society. Among the causes reformers embraced were efforts to expand voting rights, improve care for people with mental illness, reform prisons, stop the abuse of alcohol, achieve greater rights for women, and end slavery. Many reformers were inspired by a revival of religious fervor that swept the nation. Known as the Second Great Awakening, this era of religious intensity led to a movement to revive people's commitment to religion.

Step Into the Place

Read the quotes and look at the information presented on the map.

 How would you characterize the goals and the reach of the Second Great Awakening?

PRIMARY SOURCE

"Let the truth take hold upon your conscience—throw down your rebellious weapons—give up your refuges of lies. . . . Another moment's delay, and it may be too late for ever. The Spirit of God may depart from you—the offer of life may be made no more, and this one more slighted offer of mercy may close up your account, and seal you over to all the horrors of eternal death."
—Charles G. Finney, from *Sermons on Important Subjects,* 1836

PRIMARY SOURCE

"For as unseemly as it may appear now-a-days for a woman to preach, it should be remembered that nothing is impossible with God. And why should it be thought impossible, heterodox, or improper for a woman to preach? [S]eeing the Saviour died for the woman as well as for the man.

If the man may preach, because the Saviour died for him, why not the woman? [S]eeing he died for her also. Is he not a whole Saviour, instead of a half one?"
—Jarena Lee, from *Religious Experience and Journal of Mrs. Jarena Lee,* 1849

Step Into the Time

Choose an event from the time line and write a paragraph predicting the general social, political, and economic consequences that event might have on reform in the United States.

U.S. PRESIDENTS

UNITED STATES

WORLD

1825

1830

1828 North-South rift develops over "Tariff of Abominations"

Jackson 1829–1837

1830 Mormon religion officially organizes

1832 Democrats hold their first presidential nominating convention

1829 Mexico abolishes slavery

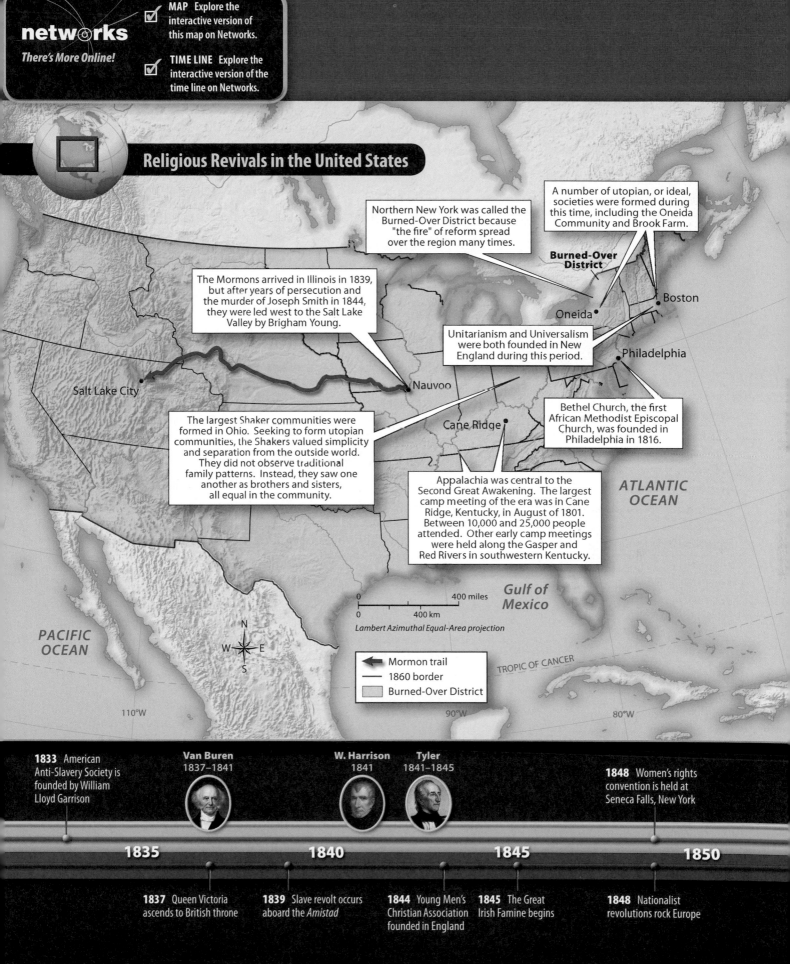

Religious Revivals in the United States

Northern New York was called the Burned-Over District because "the fire" of reform spread over the region many times.

A number of utopian, or ideal, societies were formed during this time, including the Oneida Community and Brook Farm.

Burned-Over District

The Mormons arrived in Illinois in 1839, but after years of persecution and the murder of Joseph Smith in 1844, they were led west to the Salt Lake Valley by Brigham Young.

Unitarianism and Universalism were both founded in New England during this period.

Bethel Church, the first African Methodist Episcopal Church, was founded in Philadelphia in 1816.

The largest Shaker communities were formed in Ohio. Seeking to form utopian communities, the Shakers valued simplicity and separation from the outside world. They did not observe traditional family patterns. Instead, they saw one another as brothers and sisters, all equal in the community.

Appalachia was central to the Second Great Awakening. The largest camp meeting of the era was in Cane Ridge, Kentucky, in August of 1801. Between 10,000 and 25,000 people attended. Other early camp meetings were held along the Gasper and Red Rivers in southwestern Kentucky.

Salt Lake City

Nauvoo

Cane Ridge

Oneida

Boston

Philadelphia

ATLANTIC OCEAN

PACIFIC OCEAN

Gulf of Mexico

0   400 miles
0   400 km
Lambert Azimuthal Equal-Area projection

N W E S

TROPIC OF CANCER

← Mormon trail
— 1860 border
▢ Burned-Over District

110°W   90°W   80°W

1833 American Anti-Slavery Society is founded by William Lloyd Garrison

Van Buren 1837–1841

W. Harrison 1841

Tyler 1841–1845

1848 Women's rights convention is held at Seneca Falls, New York

1835   1840   1845   1850

1837 Queen Victoria ascends to British throne

1839 Slave revolt occurs aboard the *Amistad*

1844 Young Men's Christian Association founded in England

1845 The Great Irish Famine begins

1848 Nationalist revolutions rock Europe

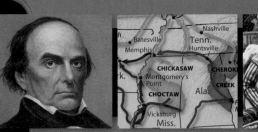

networks

There's More Online!

- ☑ **IMAGE** Andrew Jackson Campaign Poster
- ☑ **IMAGE** Andrew Jackson Speaking
- ☑ **IMAGE** Trail of Tears
- ☑ **VIDEO** Jacksonian America
- ☑ **INTERACTIVE SELF-CHECK QUIZ**

Reading **HELP**DESK

Content Vocabulary
- **suffrage**
- **spoils system**
- **caucus system**
- **secede**

Academic Vocabulary
- **evident**
- **exposure**

TAKING NOTES: *Organizing*

ACTIVITY As you read about the growth of the United States, complete a graphic organizer similar to the one below by listing the positions of Jackson and Calhoun during the nullification crisis.

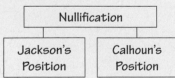

Nullification	
Jackson's Position	Calhoun's Position

LESSON 1
Jacksonian America

ESSENTIAL QUESTIONS · *Can average citizens change society?*
· *How did reforms of this era increase tensions between North and South?*

IT MATTERS BECAUSE

Andrew Jackson was elected president with popular support. He stood for federal authority, tried to relocate Native Americans, and undermined the Bank of the United States. The Whig Party emerged to oppose him.

A New Era in Politics

GUIDING QUESTION *Why was this time period considered a new era in politics?*

On his inauguration day, President Andrew Jackson broke tradition by inviting the public to his reception. Margaret Bayard Smith, who was one of the thousands of Americans attending the White House gala in 1829, later wrote:

PRIMARY SOURCE

❝[A] rabble . . . [were] scrambling, fighting, romping. . . . The President, after having been *literally* nearly pressed to death . . . by the people in their eagerness to shake hands with Old Hickory, had retreated through the back way. . . . Ladies and gentlemen, only had been expected . . . not the people en masse. But it was the People's day, and the People's President and the People would rule.❞

—from *Forty Years of Washington Society*, 1906

The scene at the gala reflected a new era in politics. Beginning in the early 1800s and continuing through the presidency of Andrew Jackson, ordinary citizens had become a greater political force.

In the early 1800s, elections became more democratic as many states lowered or eliminated property ownership as a voting qualification. As a result, the number of eligible voters, still mostly white men, grew significantly. In addition, with the growth of cities and towns, the percentage of working people who did not own property increased. These people paid taxes and had an interest in the political affairs of their communities. They wanted a greater voice in electing those who represented them. Additionally, the selection of presidential electors became more democratic as more states allowed voters, rather than the state legislature, to choose electors.

The expansion of **suffrage**—the right to vote—was **evident** in the turnout for the presidential election of 1828. In 1824 approximately

PHOTOS: (l to r) iStock Montage/Archive Photos/Getty Images, SuperStock/SuperStock, Bettmann/CORBIS, Library of Congress

355,000 American citizens had voted for president. Four years later, more than 1.1 million citizens cast a ballot in the presidential election.

Jackson benefited from the large number of new voters, many of whom lived on the frontiers of the West and the South. Many of the citizens who voted for the first time in 1828 saw in Jackson a man whose origins were little different from their own and whose achievements they greatly admired.

Jackson believed that the majority should rule in a democracy and that ordinary citizens should play a role in government. These beliefs led Jackson to support the **spoils system**—the common practice of giving people government jobs on the basis of party loyalty. He was the first president to fire a large number of federal employees in order to appoint his own supporters. He considered the spoils system democratic because it ended the permanent, nonelected office-holding class.

The method for choosing presidential candidates also changed. Before the 1830s, political parties used the **caucus system** to select candidates. The members of a party who served in Congress, known as the party caucus, met to choose the party's nominee for president. Many people, however, believed that the caucus system restricted nominations to the elite and well-connected. They replaced the caucus with a national nominating convention, at which delegates from the states gathered to choose the party's presidential nominee.

✓ **PROGRESS CHECK**

Identifying What were two changes that made the voting system more democratic?

The Nullification Crisis

GUIDING QUESTION *What were the issues that led to the nullification crisis?*

Jackson had not been in office long before he had to focus on a national crisis. It centered on South Carolina, but it also highlighted the growing rift between the nation's Northern and Southern regions.

The Debate Over Nullification

In the early 1800s, South Carolina's economy began to decline. Many of the state's residents blamed this situation on the nation's tariffs. Because it had few industries, South Carolina imported manufactured goods from England. Tariffs made these imports extremely expensive. After the passage of the so-called Tariff of Abominations in 1828, South Carolinians stopped short of threatening to **secede,** or withdraw, from the Union.

The growing turmoil troubled John C. Calhoun, the nation's vice president and a South Carolinian. Calhoun put forth the idea of nullification, saying that states had the right to nullify, or declare invalid, a federal law. The issue boiled over in early 1830, when Senators Robert Hayne and Daniel Webster confronted each other in a debate on the floor of the Senate. Webster defended the Union, while Hayne championed states' rights. Webster stated that liberty depended on the strength of the Union: "I have not accustomed myself to hang over the precipice of disunion, to see whether, with my short sight, I can fathom the depth of the abyss below. . . . Liberty *and* Union, now and forever, one and inseparable!"

Jackson Defends the Union

Congress passed another tariff law in 1832. At Jackson's request, it cut tariffs significantly, but South Carolinians were not satisfied. In November 1832, a special state convention adopted an ordinance of nullification declaring the tariffs of 1828 and 1832 to be unconstitutional.

Jackson considered the nullification ordinance an act of treason, and he sent a warship to Charleston. In 1833 Congress passed the Force Bill, authorizing the president to use the military to enforce acts of Congress.

PHOTO: Stock Montage/Archive Photos/Getty Images

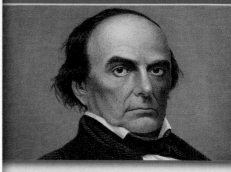

BIOGRAPHY

Daniel Webster (1782–1852)

Daniel Webster served in Congress as a representative from New Hampshire and Massachusetts before serving as a senator from Massachusetts. As an attorney, Webster argued many cases before the Supreme Court, including *McCulloch* v. *Maryland*, in which the Court upheld his arguments that strengthened the federal government. During the 1830 Senate debates with Robert Hayne, Webster argued against the idea that states could nullify a federal law.

▶ **CRITICAL THINKING**
Drawing Conclusions Why would Webster be considered a nationalist?

suffrage the right to vote

evident obvious, clear

spoils system the practice of handing out government jobs to supporters; replacing government employees with the winning candidate's supporters

caucus system a system in which members of a political party meet to choose their party's candidate for president or decide policy

secede to leave or withdraw

As tensions rose, Senator Henry Clay pushed through Congress a bill that would lower the nation's tariffs gradually until 1842. In response, South Carolina repealed its nullification of the tariff law. Both sides claimed victory, and the issue was laid to rest, at least temporarily.

☑ **PROGRESS CHECK**

Analyzing Why were the tariffs so strongly opposed in South Carolina?

Policies Toward Native Americans

GUIDING QUESTION *How did the lives of Native Americans change under the Jackson administration?*

Andrew Jackson's commitment to extending democracy did not benefit everyone. His attitude toward Native Americans reflected the views of many Westerners at that time. Jackson had fought the Creek and Seminole people in Georgia and Florida, and in his Inaugural Address he declared his intention to move all Native Americans to the Great Plains.

Many Americans believed that the Great Plains was a wasteland that would never be settled. They thought that if they moved Native Americans to that region, the nation's conflict with them would be over. In 1830 Jackson pushed through Congress the Indian Removal Act, which provided money for relocating Native Americans. Most Native Americans eventually gave in and resettled on the Great Plains, but not the Cherokee of Georgia. The Cherokee had adopted a written language, drawn up a written constitution modeled on the U.S. Constitution, and sent many of their children to schools established by white missionaries.

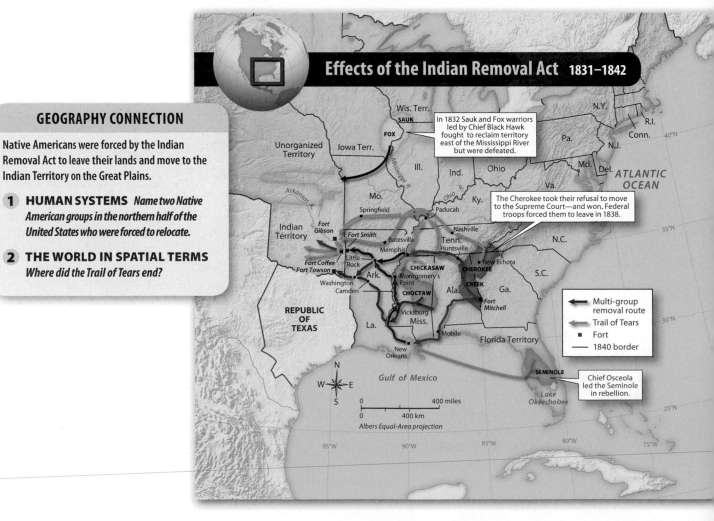

GEOGRAPHY CONNECTION

Native Americans were forced by the Indian Removal Act to leave their lands and move to the Indian Territory on the Great Plains.

1 **HUMAN SYSTEMS** *Name two Native American groups in the northern half of the United States who were forced to relocate.*

2 **THE WORLD IN SPATIAL TERMS** *Where did the Trail of Tears end?*

Effects of the Indian Removal Act 1831–1842

In 1832 Sauk and Fox warriors led by Chief Black Hawk fought to reclaim territory east of the Mississippi River but were defeated.

The Cherokee took their refusal to move to the Supreme Court—and won. Federal troops forced them to leave in 1838.

Chief Osceola led the Seminole in rebellion.

← Multi-group removal route
← Trail of Tears
■ Fort
— 1840 border

The Cherokee sued the state of Georgia in order to challenge the state's attempt to take their lands. Their case, *Cherokee Nation* v. *Georgia,* eventually reached the Supreme Court. In 1832 Chief Justice John Marshall stated the Georgia law did not apply to the Cherokee because they were a sovereign nation. Jackson disagreed. "Marshall has made his decision," the president reportedly said, "now let him enforce it."

Most Cherokee resisted the government's offers of Western land. In 1838 Jackson's successor, Martin Van Buren, sent in the army to force the remaining Cherokee from their homes and march them to what is now Oklahoma. About 2,000 Cherokee died in camps while waiting for the relocation to begin, and some 2,000 others died of starvation, disease, and **exposure** on the journey, which became known as the Trail of Tears. By 1838, most Native Americans living east of the Mississippi had been moved to reservations.

exposure the condition of being unprotected, especially from severe weather

✓ **PROGRESS CHECK**

Explaining What was the Trail of Tears?

Jackson Battles the National Bank

GUIDING QUESTION *Why was Jackson against the Second Bank of the United States, and how did his opposition to it shape the country?*

One of the biggest controversies of Jackson's presidency was his campaign against the Second Bank of the United States. Jackson regarded the Bank as a monopoly that benefited the wealthy elite. At the time, most paper money was issued by private state banks as bank notes that could be redeemed for gold or silver coins. Often, however, the banks issued more paper money than they could redeem in gold or silver. This eased the availability of credit, but it also risked causing inflation. To prevent the state banks from lending too much money, the Bank of the United States regularly collected bank notes and asked state banks to redeem them for gold and silver. This action forced state banks to be careful about how much money they lent, and it also limited inflation.

Many Western settlers, who needed easy credit to run their farms, were unhappy with the Bank's policies, which took notes out of circulation. Also, despite *McCulloch* v. *Maryland,* Jackson believed the bank was unconstitutional. Jackson's congressional opponents tried to make the Bank an issue in the 1832 presidential election by introducing a bill to extend its charter for another 20 years. Congress passed the bill, but Jackson vetoed it.

JACKSON BATTLES THE BANK   **POLITICAL CARTOONS**

Jackson holds up an order removing federal deposits from the Bank. The men scurrying to safety are newspaper publishers, bankers, and other Bank supporters.

President Jackson's efforts to unseat the Second Bank of the United States in the early 1830s became nationally known.

▶ **CRITICAL THINKING**

1 *Analyzing Primary Sources* How is the cartoon pro-Jackson?

2 *Interpreting Significance* What does the Bank's collapsing symbolize?

The Whigs never expected John Tyler of Virginia to become president. He went on to oppose much of the Whig legislation in Congress.

▶ **CRITICAL THINKING**
Interpreting Significance What was significant about Tyler becoming president?

After Jackson won reelection in 1832, he believed the people wished him to destroy the Bank at once. He removed federal deposits from the Bank and placed them in state banks, greatly weakening the Bank. It was a major political victory for Jackson, but critics later charged that destroying the Bank contributed significantly to the financial woes that plagued the country in the years ahead.

By the mid-1830s, a new party had emerged to oppose Jackson. Named for an English party that sought to limit the king's power, the Whigs advocated a stronger federal government and support for industrial development.

Martin Van Buren

The Whigs were united in opposing Jackson, but they were unable to settle on a leader. Helped by Jackson's popularity, Democrat Martin Van Buren won the 1836 presidential election. He had little time to savor his victory, however. During the Panic of 1837—a crippling economic crisis—many banks and businesses failed, thousands of farmers lost their land, and unemployment soared. A firm believer in his party's philosophy of a limited federal government, Van Buren did little to ease the crisis.

"Tippecanoe and Tyler Too"

The Whigs looked forward to ousting the Democrats in the presidential election of 1840. They nominated General William Henry Harrison, hero of the Battle of Tippecanoe. John Tyler, a Southerner and former Democrat, was the vice-presidential candidate. Adopting the campaign slogan "Tippecanoe and Tyler too," the Whigs blamed Van Buren for the economic depression.

The strategy worked. Harrison won a decisive victory, and on March 4, 1841, delivered his inauguration speech. The weather that day was bitterly cold, but Harrison insisted on delivering his nearly two-hour address without a hat or coat. He came down with pneumonia and died on April 4, thereby serving the shortest term of any American president. Vice President John Tyler then became president. This was a shock to Whig leaders as Tyler actually opposed many Whig policies and had been put on the ballot mainly to attract Southern voters. Their fears were realized when Tyler blocked Whig legislation.

Foreign relations occupied the country's attention during much of Tyler's administration, especially relations with Britain. Disputes over the border between Maine and Canada, and other issues, resulted in the 1842 Webster-Ashburton Treaty, which established the border between the United States and Canada from Maine to Minnesota.

✅ **PROGRESS CHECK**
Explaining What was the Panic of 1837?

LESSON 1 REVIEW

Reviewing Vocabulary
1. *Identifying* How were presidential candidates selected under the caucus system?
2. *Defining* What is a synonym for *secede*?

Using Your Notes
3. *Contrasting* Use your notes to identify how Jackson and Calhoun viewed the rights of the Union differently.

Answering the Guiding Questions
4. *Interpreting* Why was this time period considered a new era in politics?

5. *Identifying* What were the issues that led to the nullification crisis?
6. *Stating* How did the lives of Native Americans change under the Jackson administration?
7. *Making Generalizations* Why was Jackson against the Second Bank of the United States, and how did his opposition to it shape the country?

Writing Activity
8. **PERSONAL** Historians disagree about Jackson's legacy. What do you think? Write a short essay in which you describe your own thoughts and opinions about Jackson's actions while in office.

Reading **HELP**DESK

Content Vocabulary

- **nativism**
- **utopia**
- **romanticism**
- **transcendentalism**

Academic Vocabulary

- **predominantly**
- **philosopher**

TAKING NOTES: *Organizing*

ACTIVITY As you read about the growth of the United States, complete a graphic organizer similar to the one below by listing the beliefs of religious groups during the Second Great Awakening.

Religious Groups	Beliefs

PHOTOS: (l to r) FPG/Taxi/Getty Images, FPG/Taxi/Getty Images, Bettmann/CORBIS

LESSON 2
A Changing Culture

ESSENTIAL QUESTIONS • *Can average citizens change society?*
• *How did reforms of this era increase tensions between North and South?*

IT MATTERS BECAUSE

Between 1815 and 1860, over 5 million immigrants arrived in the United States. Most found opportunity, but some found discrimination and prejudice. During the 1820s and 1830s, a new religious movement began to emerge.

The New Wave of Immigrants

GUIDING QUESTION *Why did many German and Irish immigrants travel to the United States in the mid-1800s?*

In June 1850, Daniel Guiney decided to leave his impoverished town in Ireland and move to the United States. After settling in Buffalo, New York, Guiney wrote home about the land where he now resided:

PRIMARY SOURCE

❝We arrived here about five o'clock in the afternoon of yesterday, fourteen of us together, where we were received with the greatest kindness and respectability. . . . When we came to the house we could not state to you how we were treated. We had potatoes, meat, butter, bread, and tea for dinner. . . . If you were to see Denis Reen when Daniel Danihy dressed him with clothes suitable for this country, you would think him to be a boss or steward, so that we have scarcely words to state to you how happy we felt at present.❞

—quoted in *Out of Ireland*, from a letter dated August 9, 1850

Guiney was just one of the millions of immigrants who came in search of a better life in the mid-1800s. Between 1815 and 1860, the United States experienced a massive influx of immigrants, mostly from Europe. Many had fled violence and political turmoil at home, while others sought to escape starvation and poverty. Although immigrants provided a large source of labor for American industries, many citizens feared the influence of so many foreigners.

Germans and Irish Arrive

The largest wave of immigrants, almost 2 million, came from Ireland. The Irish were fleeing a devastating famine that began in 1845 when a fungus destroyed much of the nation's crop of potatoes—a staple in the Irish diet. Tens of thousands of people died of starvation.

The Spirit of Reform **167**

Pushed by political turmoil and famine, many German and Irish immigrants flocked to the United States during the mid-1800s.

▶ **CRITICAL THINKING**

1 *Analyzing Information* In what year did Irish immigration to the United States peak? Why might it have declined afterward?

2 *Analyzing Information* In what year did German immigration to the United States peak? What was the largest number of German immigrants in a single year?

Source: *Historical Statistics of the United States: Colonial Times to 1970.*

Most Irish immigrants arrived with no money and few skills. They generally settled in Northeastern cities and worked as unskilled laborers and servants.

Germans were the second-largest group of immigrants to arrive. At the time, Germany was divided into many states. In 1848 revolutionaries tried to impose reforms but failed. The ensuing violence and repression convinced many Germans to emigrate. By 1860, over 1 million had arrived in the United States. Most had enough money to buy land in Ohio and Pennsylvania, where they became farmers or went into business.

Nativism

nativism hostility toward immigrants

predominantly being most frequent or common

Many immigrants encountered discrimination in the United States. The arrival of immigrants from other cultures with different languages and religions produced feelings of **nativism,** or hostility toward foreigners. Also, in the 1800s, many Americans were anti-Catholic. The arrival of **predominantly** Catholic Irish immigrants led to the rise of nativist groups that pledged never to vote for a Catholic and pushed for laws banning immigrants and Catholics from holding office. In July 1854, the American Party formed. Membership was secret, and members questioned about it answered, "I know nothing." The Know-Nothings, as the party became known, built a large following in the 1850s.

☑ **PROGRESS CHECK**

Identifying How did the increase in immigration during the mid-1800s benefit American industries?

A Religious Revival

GUIDING QUESTION *What was the overall message of the Second Great Awakening, and how did it affect American society?*

While immigrants added to the diversity of society, Americans were transforming society in other ways. Traditional Protestantism experienced a dramatic revival, and new forms of worship emerged.

The Second Great Awakening

In the early 1800s, many church leaders worked to revive Americans' commitment to religion in what came to be called the Second Great Awakening. Leaders of various Protestant denominations held camp meetings that attracted thousands of followers for several days of song, prayer, and emotional outpourings of faith. The movement urged individuals to readmit God into their daily lives. Ministers preached that all people—not just a chosen few—could attain grace through faith.

Presbyterian minister Charles Grandison Finney preached that each person contained within himself or herself the capacity for spiritual rebirth and salvation. Finney helped found modern revivalism. His camp meetings were carefully planned to create as much emotion as possible. He compared his methods to those used by politicians and salespeople, and he used emotion to focus people's attention on his message. Finney began preaching in upstate New York, launching a series of revivals in towns along the Erie Canal, and then moved into the Northeast. He warned against using politics to change society. He believed that if Christian ideas reformed people from within, society would become better, but if people remained selfish and immoral, political reforms would not make any difference.

New Religious Groups

A number of new religious groups emerged during the Second Great Awakening. Many Americans were looking for spiritual answers but chose to look to new religious ideas rather than return to traditional Protestant beliefs. Two groups that grew rapidly during the 1830s were the Unitarians and Universalists. Unitarians reject the idea that Jesus was the son of God, arguing instead that he was a great teacher. Their name comes from the belief that God is a unity, rather than a trinity of Father, Son, and Holy Spirit. Universalists reject the idea of hell, believing that God intends to save everyone.

Another group that began during this period was the Church of Jesus Christ of Latter-day Saints, whose followers are commonly known as Mormons. Joseph Smith began preaching Mormon ideas in 1830 after claiming to have been called to restore the Christian church to its original form. Smith published *The Book of Mormon* in that year, saying it was a translation of words that he had received from an angel. Smith made thousands of converts. After enduring harassment in Ohio, Missouri, and elsewhere, the Mormons moved to Commerce, Illinois, in 1839. They bought the town and renamed it Nauvoo. Mormons prospered in the Midwest, but persecution continued. In 1844 local residents murdered Smith. Brigham Young then became the leader of the Church, and the Mormons left Illinois for what would later become the Utah Territory, where they settled permanently.

Utopian Communities

Some Americans in the 1830s concluded that society had corrupted human nature. They decided that the solution was to separate from society and form a **utopia,** or ideal society. Cooperative living and the absence of private property characterized these communities. Perhaps the best known were Brook Farm in Massachusetts and the Oneida Community in upstate New York.

One utopian religious group, the Shakers, believed in social and spiritual equality for all members. The number of Shakers peaked at about 6,000 members before their numbers began to decline. Since they did not believe in marrying or having children, the group could only expand by making converts.

☑ **PROGRESS CHECK**

Identifying What was the goal of forming a utopian society?

Connections to TODAY

Utopian Communities

Utopian living has never fallen completely out of favor in the United States. From time to time, new utopian communities emerge. Beginning in the 1960s, counterculture movements created utopian communes, many in northern California and upstate New York. These were not religious utopias, but politically and ecologically motivated farming communities that attempted to be completely self-sufficient and renounced material consumerism.

utopia a community based on a vision of a perfect society sought by reformers

Emotional sermons, such as the one shown here, were a main feature of the Second Great Awakening, which spread across the nation at outdoor camp meetings.

▶ **CRITICAL THINKING**
Analyzing Primary Sources What does this painting show about the Second Great Awakening?

Cultural Renaissance

GUIDING QUESTION *How did writings of this time reflect American society?*

❝I went to the woods because I wished to live deliberately, to front only the essential facts of life. . . . I wanted to live deep and suck out all the marrow of life, to live so sturdily and Spartan-like . . . and reduce [life] to its lowest terms, and, if it proved to be mean . . . publish its meanness to the world; or if it were sublime, to know it by experience, and be able to give a true account of it in my next excursion.**❞**

—Henry David Thoreau, from *Walden, or, Life in the Woods*, 1854

DBQ *ANALYZING PRIMARY SOURCES* How does this excerpt reflect the idea of romanticism?

philosopher person who seeks wisdom or enlightenment

romanticism a literary, artistic, and philosophical movement in the late 1700s and early 1800s emphasizing the imagination, the emotions, and the individual above society

transcendentalism a philosophy stressing the relationship between human beings and nature, spiritual things over material things, and the importance of the individual conscience

The optimism of the Second Great Awakening influenced **philosophers** and writers. Many leading thinkers adopted the tenets of **romanticism,** a movement that advocated the supremacy of feeling, spirituality, the individual, and nature. A notable expression of American romanticism came from the transcendentalists. **Transcendentalism** urged people to transcend, or overcome, the limits of their minds and let their souls reach out to embrace the beauty of the universe.

American Writers Emerge

The most influential transcendentalist was Ralph Waldo Emerson. In his 1836 essay "Nature," Emerson wrote that those who wanted fulfillment should try to commune with nature. Emerson influenced other writers, including Margaret Fuller and Henry David Thoreau. Thoreau wrote *Walden,* a philosophical journal recounting his experiences, emotions, and thoughts during his two-year stay in a handmade cabin at Walden Pond near Concord, Massachusetts.

Uniquely American fiction writers included Washington Irving, famous for writing "The Legend of Sleepy Hollow" (1819), and James Fenimore Cooper, who romanticized Native Americans and frontier explorers in his *Leatherstocking Tales*, including *The Last of the Mohicans* (1826). Nathaniel Hawthorne, of New England, wrote short stories and novels. His novel *The Scarlet Letter* (1850), set in Puritan society, explored the persecution and psychological suffering that may result from sin. Herman Melville wrote the great novel *Moby-Dick* (1851). Poet and short story writer Edgar Allan Poe achieved fame as a writer of terror and mystery stories. Important poets of the era included Walt Whitman, who published *Leaves of Grass* in 1855, and Emily Dickinson, who wrote unconventional, deeply personal poems.

The Penny Press

As more Americans learned to read and gained the right to vote, publishers began producing inexpensive newspapers, known as penny papers, which provided reports of fires, crimes, marriages, gossip, politics, local news, and other content people wanted. General interest magazines directed at a more specialized readership also emerged around this time. In 1830 Louis A. Godey founded *Godey's Lady's Book*, a magazine for women. *The Atlantic Monthly* catered to the well educated, while *Harper's Weekly* published everything from book reviews to news reports.

☑ PROGRESS CHECK

Explaining How are transcendentalism and romanticism related?

LESSON 2 REVIEW

Reviewing Vocabulary
1. *Defining* What is nativism?

2. *Identifying* What features of mid-nineteenth-century life did transcendentalism reject?

Using Your Notes
3. *Describing* Use your notes to describe the new American religious groups that arose during the Second Great Awakening.

Answering the Guiding Questions
4. *Determining Cause and Effect* Why did many German and Irish immigrants travel to the United States in the mid-1800s?

5. *Summarizing* What was the overall message of the Second Great Awakening, and how did it affect American society?

6. *Making Generalizations* How did writings of this time reflect American society?

Writing Activity
7. EXPOSITORY Write a short essay to explain how the writers of this era were uniquely American in nature.

Reading **HELP**DESK

Content Vocabulary

- **benevolent society**
- **temperance**
- **penitentiary**

Academic Vocabulary

- **institution**
- **imposition**

TAKING NOTES: *Outlining*

ACTIVITY As you read about the growth of the United States, use the major headings in the lesson to create an outline similar to the one below about American reform efforts in the first half of the nineteenth century.

```
        Reforming Society
 I. The Reform Spirit
     A.
     B.
     C.
     D.
 II.
```

LESSON 3
Reforming Society

ESSENTIAL QUESTIONS • *Can average citizens change society?*
• *How did reforms of this era increase tensions between North and South?*

IT MATTERS BECAUSE

The Second Great Awakening created an environment for social change. Spurred on by this religious revival, as well as a heightened belief in the power of individuals to improve society, reform movements arose.

The Reform Spirit

GUIDING QUESTION *What motivated reformers to tackle society's problems?*

In 1841 a clergyman asked schoolteacher Dorothea Dix to lead a Sunday school class at a local prison. What Dix saw there appalled her. Mentally ill persons lay neglected in dirty, unheated rooms. Putting aside her teaching career, she began a crusade to improve conditions for the mentally ill and to provide them with the facilities and treatment they needed.

In 1843 Dix composed a letter to the Massachusetts legislature. She called for a new approach to mental illness based on greater levels of care and respect. She related the story of a mentally ill woman who had been severely mistreated for several years and was considered a "raging maniac." Dix explained that the woman had been taken in by a local couple who treated her kindly and with respect. She wrote, "Go there now, and you will find her 'clothed,' and though not perfectly in her 'right mind,' so far restored as to be a safe and comfortable inmate." Largely through Dix's efforts, more than a dozen states enacted prison reforms that created special **institutions,** often referred to as asylums, for the mentally ill.

The reform movements of the mid-1800s stemmed in large part from the revival of religious fervor. Revivalists preached the power of individuals to improve themselves and the world. Lyman Beecher, a prominent minister, insisted that true reform could take place only through "the voluntary energies of the nation itself." Under the guidance of Beecher and other religious leaders, associations known as **benevolent societies** sprang up in cities and towns across the country. At first, they focused on spreading the word of God and attempting to convert nonbelievers. Soon, however, they sought to combat a number of social problems.

This photo shows the Beecher family in the mid-1800s. Patriarch Lyman Beecher (center, seated), one of the nation's best-known ministers, preached salvation and social reform. His daughter Catharine was a leader in education reform and worked to increase women's access to higher education. His daughter Isabella founded the Connecticut Woman Suffrage Association. His daughter Harriet was the abolitionist author of the famous novel *Uncle Tom's Cabin*. Three sons—Henry Ward, Edward, and Charles—were ministers and important abolitionists.

▶ CRITICAL THINKING

Making Generalizations How did the Beecher family reflect the social concerns of the 1800s?

institution an established organization or corporation

benevolent society an association focusing on spreading the word of God and combating social problems

temperance moderation in or abstinence from consuming alcohol

imposition something established or brought about as if by force

penitentiary prison whose purpose is to reform prisoners

One striking feature of the reform effort was the overwhelming presence of women. One reason was that many unmarried women with uncertain futures discovered in religion a foundation on which to build their lives. As more women turned to the church, many also joined religious-based reform groups. These reform groups targeted aspects of society including drunkenness, prisons, and education.

The Temperance Movement

Many reformers argued that no behavior caused more crime, disorder, and poverty than the abuse of alcohol. While not everyone agreed, no one doubted that heavy alcohol consumption was widespread in the early 1800s. Members of groups advocating **temperance,** or moderation in the consumption of alcohol, began preaching the evils of alcohol and persuading heavy drinkers to give up liquor. In 1833 several of the groups united to form the American Temperance Union.

Temperance societies also pushed for laws prohibiting the sale of liquor. In 1851 Maine passed the first state prohibition law, an example followed by a dozen other states by 1855. Other states passed "local option" laws, which allowed towns and villages to prohibit liquor sales within their boundaries.

Prison Reform

Some reformers focused on providing better facilities for prisoners, the insane, and the poor. Many states replaced their overcrowded prisons with facilities aimed at rehabilitating prisoners rather than simply locking them away. By the beginning of the Civil War, most states had established public mental institutions to keep the mentally ill out of the prison system.

Prison officials imposed rigid discipline to rid criminals of the "laxness" they believed had led them astray. Solitary confinement and the **imposition** of silence on work crews were meant to give prisoners the chance to meditate and think about their wrongdoing. The name of these prisons, **penitentiaries,** expressed the idea that they were places where prisoners would achieve penitence, or remorse.

Educational Reform

In the early 1800s, many reformers worked to establish a system of public education—government-funded schools open to all citizens. The increase in the number of voters in the 1820s and 1830s and the arrival of millions of new immigrants convinced many people of the need for public education. Most American leaders and social reformers believed that a democratic republic could survive only if the electorate were well educated.

Horace Mann was a leader of the movement for public education. As president of the Massachusetts Senate, Mann helped create a state board of education in 1837. He then left the state senate to serve as secretary of the new board. During his 12 years in this role, he doubled teachers' salaries, opened 50 new high schools, and established training schools for teachers. Massachusetts quickly became a model for other states. As he wrote in one report, Mann was convinced the nation needed public education:

❝[T]he establishment of a republican government, without well-appointed and efficient means for the universal education of the people, is the most rash and fool-hardy experiment ever tried by man. . . . It may be an easy thing to make a republic; but it is a very laborious thing to make republicans; and woe to the republic that rests upon no better foundations than ignorance, selfishness, and passion!❞

— from "Annual Report of the Massachusetts Board of Education," 1848

In 1852 Massachusetts passed the first mandatory school attendance law. New York passed a similar measure the next year. Reformers focused on creating elementary schools. These would teach all children the basics of reading, writing, and arithmetic, and instill a work ethic. These schools were open to all, supported by local and state taxes and tuition.

By the 1850s, tax-supported elementary schools had gained widespread support in the Northeastern states. They had also begun to spread to the rest of the country. Rural areas responded more slowly because children were needed to help with planting and harvesting for large portions of the year. Reformer Calvin Wiley took the lead in North Carolina. In 1839 North Carolina began providing aid to local communities that established taxpayer-funded schools.

Women's Education

When officials talked about educating voters, they had men in mind. Women were still not allowed to vote in the early 1800s. Nonetheless, women reformers, such as Catharine Beecher, seized the opportunity to push for more educational opportunities for girls and women.

Emma Willard, who founded a girls' school in Vermont in 1814, was another educational pioneer. Her school covered the usual subjects for young women, such as cooking and etiquette, but it also taught academic subjects such as history, math, and literature, which were rarely taught to women. In 1837 Mary Lyon opened Mount Holyoke Female Seminary in Massachusetts, the first institution of higher education for women.

In 1849 new opportunities for higher education enabled Elizabeth Blackwell to become the first woman to earn a medical degree. In 1857 she founded the New York Infirmary for Women and Children— a hospital staffed entirely by women.

✔ PROGRESS CHECK

Identifying Cause and Effect What behaviors did the temperance movement hope to eliminate?

Reformers in the 1800s pushed for more education for women. The Emerson School for Girls in Boston was an early example of a girls' school.

▶ CRITICAL THINKING

Making Connections How does the classroom depicted below compare with your educational experience?

The Early Women's Movement

GUIDING QUESTION *How do you think the lives of women changed from the colonial period to the mid-1800s?*

In the early 1800s, the Industrial Revolution began to change the economic roles of men and women. In the 1700s, most economic activity took place in or near the home because most Americans lived and worked in a rural farm setting. Although husbands and wives had distinct chores, maintaining the farm was the main focus of their efforts. By the mid-1800s, these circumstances had started to change, especially in the Northeastern states. The development of factories and other work centers separated the home from the workplace. Men often left home to go to work, while women tended the house and children. This development led to the emergence of the first women's movement.

"True Womanhood"

As the nature of work changed, many Americans began to divide life into two spheres of activity—the home and the workplace. Many believed the home to be the proper sphere for women. This was partly because the outside world was seen as corrupt and dangerous, and partly because of popular ideas about the family.

The Christian revivalism of the 1820s and 1830s greatly influenced the American family. For many parents, raising children was a solemn responsibility. They were preparing young people for a disciplined Christian life. Women often were viewed as more moral and charitable than men, and they were expected to be models of piety and virtue to their households.

The idea that women should be homemakers and take responsibility for developing their children's characters evolved into a set of ideas known as "true womanhood." In 1841 Catharine Beecher, a daughter of minister and reformer Lyman Beecher, wrote a book called *A Treatise on Domestic Economy*. The popular volume argued that women could find fulfillment at home and gave instruction on child care, cooking, and health matters.

Women Seek Greater Rights

Many women did not believe the ideas of true womanhood were limiting. Instead, the new ideas implied that wives were now partners with their husbands and in some ways were morally superior to them. Women were held up as the conscience of the home and society.

This mid-nineteenth century lithograph shows a romanticized view of family life. During this era women were often viewed as morally superior to men, yet kept under the political and legal control of men.

▶ **CRITICAL THINKING**

Analyzing Information Why did the idea of "true womanhood" seem to some women to offer greater equality?

PHOTO: SuperStock/Getty Images

The idea that women had an important role to play in building a virtuous home was soon extended to making society more virtuous. As women became involved in the moral crusades of the era, some began to argue that they needed greater political rights to promote their ideas.

One advocate of this idea was Margaret Fuller. Fuller argued that every woman had the right and the capability to form her own spiritual relationship. She believed that if men and women were treated equally, it would end injustice in society.

In 1848 Lucretia Mott and Elizabeth Cady Stanton, two women active in the antislavery movement, organized the Seneca Falls Convention. This gathering of women reformers marked the beginning of an organized women's movement. The convention issued a "Declaration of Sentiments and Resolutions."

Susan B. Anthony (left) and Elizabeth Cady Stanton (right) were two of the most prominent advocates for woman suffrage. Stanton helped organize the Seneca Falls Convention.

▶ **CRITICAL THINKING**
Drawing Conclusions Why might reformers for women's rights often have been abolitionists as well?

PRIMARY SOURCE

❝ We hold these truths to be self-evident: that all men and women are created equal; that they are endowed by their Creator with certain inalienable rights. . . .

Resolved, That woman is man's equal—was intended to be so by the Creator, and the highest good of the race demands that she should be recognized as such. . . .

Resolved, That it is the duty of women of this country to secure to themselves their sacred right to the elective franchise. . . .

Resolved, therefore, That, being invested by the Creator with the same capabilities, and the same consciousness of responsibility for their exercise, it is demonstrably the right and duty of woman, equally with man, to promote every righteous cause by every righteous means . . . both in private and in public, by writing and by speaking, by any instrumentalities proper to be used, and in any assemblies proper to be held. . . . ❞

—from The Declaration of Sentiments and Resolutions, July 1848

The proposal to focus on the right to vote shocked many of the women present. Nonetheless, the Seneca Falls Convention is considered by many to be the unofficial beginning of the struggle for women's voting rights.

Throughout the 1850s, women continued to organize conventions to gain greater rights for themselves. The conventions met with some success. By 1865, for example, 29 states had passed laws that allowed wives to hold property in their own names. Above all, these conventions paved the way for a stronger women's movement to emerge after the Civil War.

✓ **PROGRESS CHECK**

Summarizing What developments sparked the first women's movement?

LESSON 3 REVIEW

Reviewing Vocabulary

1. *Explaining* What was the goal of the temperance movement?

2. *Contrasting* How was a penitentiary different from earlier prisons?

3. *Describing* Use your notes to describe the different goals of the social reform movements that arose during this time.

Answering the Guiding Questions

4. *Determining Cause and Effect* What motivated reformers to tackle society's problems?

5. *Hypothesizing* How do you think the lives of women changed from the colonial period to the mid-1800s?

Writing Activity

6. PERSUASIVE Suppose that you are a reformer of this time writing a letter to a state legislator. Persuade that person to support your desired reform by giving reasons and specific examples.

networks

There's More Online!

☑ **BIOGRAPHY** William Lloyd Garrison

☑ **BIOGRAPHY** Sojourner Truth

☑ **IMAGE** American Anti-Slavery Society

☑ **MAP** Emancipation in the United States

☑ **VIDEO** The Abolitionist Movement

☑ **INTERACTIVE SELF-CHECK QUIZ**

Reading **HELP**DESK

Content Vocabulary

• gradualism • abolition
• emancipation

Academic Vocabulary

• compensate
• demonstration

TAKING NOTES: *Organizing*

ACTIVITY As you read, complete a graphic organizer similar to the one below by recording the early events of the abolitionist movement.

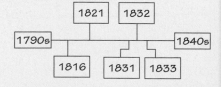

LESSON 4
The Abolitionist Movement

ESSENTIAL QUESTIONS • *Can average citizens change society?*
• *How did reforms of this era increase tensions between North and South?*

IT MATTERS BECAUSE
The issue of slavery was far from being resolved in the United States. In the 1830s and 1840s, slavery became a hotly debated topic as calls for abolition were published throughout the land.

The New Abolitionists

GUIDING QUESTION *What different methods of ending slavery were debated during this time?*

In the 1830s a growing number of Americans had begun to demand an immediate end to slavery in the South. Of all the reform movements that began in the early 1800s, the movement to end slavery was the most divisive. By pitting North against South, it polarized the nation and helped bring about the Civil War.

Early Opposition to Slavery

From the earliest days of the Republic, many Americans had opposed slavery. Some of the nation's founders knew that a nation based on the principles of liberty and equality would have difficulty remaining true to its ideals if it continued to enslave human beings.

Gradualism Early antislavery societies generally supported an approach known as **gradualism,** or the belief that slavery had to be ended gradually. First, they would stop traders from bringing any more enslaved people into the country. Then they would phase out slavery in the North and the Upper South before finally ending slavery in the Lower South. Some people in favor of gradualism felt that slaveholders should be **compensated** for their loss. Supporters of gradualism believed it would give the South's economy time to adjust to the loss of enslaved labor.

Colonization Few people in antislavery societies believed that ending slavery would end racism in the United States. Many thought that the best solution was to send African Americans to their ancestral homelands in Africa. In December 1816, antislavery reformers founded the American Colonization Society (ACS) to move African Americans to Africa. By 1821, the ACS had acquired land in West Africa. The following year, free African Americans began boarding ships to take them to Africa, where they established a colony that later became the nation of Liberia.

Colonization was never a realistic solution to racism. Moving roughly 1.5 million African Americans from the United States to Africa was nearly impossible. Furthermore, most African Americans regarded the United States as their home and did not want to move to another continent. Only about 15,000 African Americans moved to Africa between 1821 and 1860.

Abolitionism

Gradualism and colonization remained the main goals of antislavery groups until the 1830s. Then a new idea, **abolition,** began to gain ground. Abolitionists argued that enslaved African Americans should be freed immediately, without gradual measures or compensation to slaveholders. The first well-known advocate of abolition was a free African American from North Carolina named David Walker, who advocated violence and rebellion as the only way to end slavery. Although Walker's ideas were influential, the rapid development of a large, national abolitionist movement in the 1830s was largely due to the efforts of William Lloyd Garrison.

William Lloyd Garrison After working for a Quaker publisher of a Baltimore antislavery newspaper, Garrison moved to Boston in 1831. He founded and edited the antislavery newspaper the *Liberator*. The paper's style was anything but moderate, as Garrison wrote caustic attacks on slavery and called for an immediate end to it. To those who objected to his fiery language, Garrison responded that the time for moderation was over:

❝I am aware, that many object to the severity of my language; but is there not cause for severity? I *will be* as harsh as truth, and as uncompromising as justice. On this subject, I do not wish to think, or speak, or write, with moderation. No! no! Tell a man whose house is on fire, to give a moderate alarm; tell him to moderately rescue his wife from the hands of the ravisher; tell the mother to gradually extricate her babe from the fire into which it has fallen;—but urge me not to use moderation in a cause like the present. I am in earnest— I will not equivocate—I will not excuse—I will not retreat a single inch—AND I WILL BE HEARD.❞
—from the *Liberator,* January 1, 1831

In Garrison's opinion, the situation was clear: slavery was immoral and slaveholders were evil. The only option was immediate and complete **emancipation**—the freeing of all enslaved people.

In 1833 abolitionists founded the American Anti-Slavery Society, and Garrison became one of its key leaders. By 1838, there were more than 1,350 chapters and more than 250,000 members. Garrison and Theodore Weld recruited and trained many abolitionists for the American Anti-Slavery Society. Arthur and Lewis Tappan, two devout and wealthy brothers from New York City, helped to finance the movement.

Other Abolitionist Leaders Many women were active in the abolitionist movement. Among the earliest were Sarah and Angelina Grimké, South Carolina sisters who moved north to work openly against slavery. Prudence Crandall worked as a teacher and an abolitionist in Connecticut. Lucretia Mott, a women's rights advocate, often spoke out in favor of abolitionism as well.

African American Abolitionists Not surprisingly, free African Americans played a prominent role in the abolitionist movement. Even before Garrison launched his crusade, African Americans had established at least 50 abolitionist societies in the North. African Americans bought copies of the *Liberator* and helped sell copies. Many began writing and speaking out against slavery and taking part in protests and **demonstrations.**

BIOGRAPHIES

**Sarah Grimké (1792–1873)
Angelina Grimké (1805–1879)**
Sarah and Angelina Grimké were born in South Carolina, where their father was a plantation owner. Both sisters witnessed the suffering of enslaved people. They both moved to the North and became outspoken abolitionists. In 1836 Angelina published the pamphlet *An Appeal to the Christian Women of the South,* urging women to fight against slavery. In 1838 Angelina became the first American woman to address a legislative body when she gave a speech on abolition and women's rights to the Massachusetts state legislature. Also in 1838, thousands in Boston attended the sisters' public lectures on women's rights.

▶ **CRITICAL THINKING**
Making Connections What similarities do you think the Grimké sisters saw in abolition and women's rights?

gradualism the theory that slavery should be ended gradually

compensate to make payment for a loss or injury

abolition the immediate ending of slavery

emancipation the act or process of freeing enslaved persons

demonstration an outward expression or display

Frederick Douglass was one of the most prominent African Americans in the abolitionist movement. In 1838 Douglass had escaped from slavery in Maryland by posing as a free African American sailor. Douglass wrote his autobiography in 1845. He also published his own antislavery newspaper, the *North Star,* and became a powerful public speaker for the abolitionist cause:

PRIMARY SOURCE

❝What, to the American slave, is your 4th of July? I answer: a day that reveals to him, more than all other days in the year, the gross injustice and cruelty to which he is the constant victim. To him, your celebration is a sham; your boasted liberty, an unholy license; your national greatness, swelling vanity; your sounds of rejoicing are empty and heartless; . . . a thin veil to cover up crimes which would disgrace a nation of savages.❞

—Frederick Douglass, from a speech delivered in Rochester, New York, July 5, 1852

Another important African American abolitionist was Sojourner Truth. She gained freedom in 1827 when New York freed all remaining enslaved people in the state. Her antislavery speeches drew huge crowds, thanks to her folksy wit and strong message. Truth once said, "I have had five children and never could take any one of [them] up and say, '[M]y child' or '[M]y children,' unless it was when no one could see me. . . . I was forty years a slave, but I did not know how dear to me was my posterity."

✓ **PROGRESS CHECK**

Comparing and Contrasting How did gradualism differ from abolitionism?

The Response to Abolitionism

GUIDING QUESTION *Why was abolitionism not a popular movement in the North or the South?*

Abolitionism was a powerful force, and it provoked a powerful response. In the North, citizens looked upon the abolitionist movement with views ranging from strong support to indifference to opposition. In the South, many residents feared that their entire way of life was under attack. They rushed to defend the institution of slavery, which they saw as the key to the region's economy.

Reaction in the North

While many Northerners disapproved of slavery, some opposed abolitionism even more. They viewed the movement as a threat to the existing social system. Some whites, including many prominent businesspeople, warned it would lead to war between the North and the South. Others feared it might create an influx of freed African Americans in the North, overwhelming the labor and housing markets. Many in the North also did not want to severely damage the Southern economy, which supplied Northern textile mills with cotton.

Given this opposition, it was not surprising that mobs in Northern cities attacked abolitionists. A mob in Boston stoned and almost hanged Garrison. Lewis Tappan's home was sacked by a New York mob in 1834. In 1837 abolitionist publisher Reverend Elijah P. Lovejoy was killed trying to protect his printing press. Yet Northerners also resented Southern slave-catchers, and Northern states passed personal liberty laws restricting slave recapture.

Reaction in the South

To most Southerners, slavery was vital to Southern life. While the North was building factories, the South remained agricultural, tied to cotton and the enslaved people who

Born into slavery, Sojourner Truth experienced lies and abuse at the hands of slaveholders. After gaining her freedom, she gave many speeches promoting both abolitionism and women's rights.

▶ **CRITICAL THINKING**

Making Inferences How do you think Sojourner Truth's life experiences influenced her work as an abolitionist?

178

This illustration shows pro-slavery forces raiding a post office in Charleston, South Carolina, and destroying abolitionist materials, including copies of the *Liberator*. The reward poster refers to Arthur Tappan, president of the American Anti-Slavery Society.

▶ **CRITICAL THINKING**

1 *Inferring* Why would people destroy abolitionist materials?

2 *Analyzing Visuals* How does this illustration convey the seriousness of the tension over slavery?

harvested it. Southerners responded to criticisms of slavery by defending the institution. South Carolina's governor called it a "national benefit." Thomas Dew, a leading Southern academic, claimed that most enslaved people had no desire for freedom because of their close relationship with their slaveholders.

In 1831, eight months after Garrison first printed the *Liberator*, Nat Turner, an enslaved man who was a preacher, led a revolt that killed more than 50 Virginians. Many Southerners thought newspapers like the *Liberator* sparked the rebellion. They demanded the suppression of abolitionist material as a condition for remaining in the Union. In 1836, under pressure from Southern politicians, the House of Representatives passed a gag rule providing that all abolitionist petitions be shelved without debate.

Few people accepted the idea that slavery should be ended immediately. The abolitionist movement, however, became a constant and powerful reminder of how deeply slavery was dividing the nation.

✓ **PROGRESS CHECK**

Explaining How did abolitionism threaten the economy of the South?

PHOTO: Bettmann/CORBIS

LESSON 4 REVIEW

Reviewing Vocabulary

1. *Defining* What was gradualism?

2. *Explaining* What did abolitionists strive to achieve?

Using Your Notes

3. *Analyzing* Use your notes to write a short paragraph that explains why publishing was important to the abolitionists.

Answering the Guiding Questions

4. *Comparing and Contrasting* What different methods of ending slavery were debated during this time?

5. *Identifying Perspectives* Why was abolitionism not a popular movement in the North or the South?

Writing Activity

6. EXPOSITORY Write a short essay explaining the problems that abolitionists confronted.

Directions: On a separate sheet of paper, answer the questions below. Make sure you read carefully and answer all parts to the question.

Lesson Review

Lesson 1

1 *Interpreting Significance* How did the expansion of voting rights contribute to Andrew Jackson's victory in the 1828 presidential election?

2 *Identifying Perspectives* Why would South Carolina threaten to secede over new federal tariffs?

Lesson 2

3 *Identifying Cause and Effect* Why did the arrival of Irish and German immigrants lead to feelings of nativism?

4 *Identifying Central Issues* What did utopian communities hope to achieve?

Lesson 3

5 *Explaining* What was the temperance movement, and what was one method for achieving its supporters' key goal?

6 *Constructing Arguments* Why did educational reformers believe that education was important in a democratic republic?

Lesson 4

7 *Identifying Central Issues* What was the main idea behind gradualism?

8 *Comparing* How were Angelina Grimké and Sojourner Truth similar?

21st Century Skills

9 **CREATE AND ANALYZE ARGUMENTS AND DRAW CONCLUSIONS** Why do you think the federal government forced Native Americans to relocate?

10 **PROBLEM SOLVING** Why do you think colonization plans did not solve the increasing tensions about slavery?

Exploring the Essential Questions

11 *Analyzing* Write an oral presentation explaining how people in the early to mid-1800s tried to reform American society. Include how these reform attempts affected the relationship between the North and the South.

DBQ Document-Based Questions

Use the documents to answer the following questions.

The first excerpt is from an article in the *N.Y. Courier & Enquirer*, April 11, 1835, and the second excerpt is from a letter from William Lloyd Garrison to a fellow abolitionist.

PRIMARY SOURCE

❝[D]o you . . . feel this disregard for the constitution of your country? Are you ready to do an act that . . . must plunge this great nation into confusion and disaster, and then stand with impious lips to charge the calamity upon your God! We trust not—we will not suffer ourselves to entertain so foul a suspicion of our countrymen.❞

—"Shall the Government be Preserved, or the Abolitionists Have Their Will"

❝Henceforth, when the American oppressor attempts to convince us that the slaves are his property, by pointing us to the color of their skin and texture of their hair, by showing us how large a sum he had paid for their bodies and their souls, by proving that they were bequeathed to him by some defunct predecessor, we will kindle at the insult, and tell him that nothing will satisfy us but A BILL OF SALE FROM THE ALMIGHTY!❞

—William Lloyd Garrison, letter to Oliver Johnson, February 10, 1836

12 *Analyzing Primary Sources* In the Garrison excerpt, who is the "American oppressor," and why do you think Garrison used that name?

13 *Evaluating Counter Arguments* How do you think Garrison would respond to the first excerpt's claim that abolition would bring about "confusion and disaster"?

Extended-Response Question

14 *Synthesizing* Write a brief essay explaining how political, economic, and social changes affected society during this era. Why did changes generate strong feelings?

Need Extra Help?

If You've Missed Question	1	2	3	4	5	6	7	8	9	10	11	12	13	14
Go to page	162	163	167	169	172	172	176	177	164	176	168	180	180	162

Manifest Destiny

1820–1848

ESSENTIAL QUESTIONS • *Why did people want to move west in the 1800s?* • *How did westward migration affect the relationship between the United States and other countries and peoples during this time?*

The Story Matters...

Beginning in the 1820s, Americans began moving in large numbers west across the Great Plains. They headed south to Texas and west to Oregon, Utah, and California. By 1848, the United States had acquired much of the Southwest from Mexico and divided the Oregon Territory with Great Britain.

Just before Mexican independence, Spain began allowing foreigners to settle in the Texas territory. After 15 years, Texas won independence from Mexico.

◄ Stephen F. Austin devoted his life to establishing Texas as an independent nation. His dying words were reported to be "The independence of Texas is recognized!"

PHOTO: The Granger Collection, New York

CHAPTER 7

Place and Time: United States 1821–1848

By 1820, settlers were streaming across the Appalachian Mountains and pushing the frontier westward to the Mississippi River and beyond. In the years that followed, restless Americans continued to seek new opportunities farther west. They followed overland trails across the Great Plains to the Oregon Country and California. To many, the United States seemed destined to expand across the entire continent, carrying the ideals of freedom to new lands. In 1845 magazine editor John Louis O'Sullivan called this America's "Manifest Destiny."

Step Into the Place

Read the quote and look at the information presented on the map.

 How does the quote reflect the concept of Manifest Destiny, and how does the map reflect progress toward fulfilling it?

PRIMARY SOURCE

" [O]ur national birth was the beginning of a new history. . . . [W]e are the nation of progress, of individual freedom, of universal enfranchisement. . . .

We must onward to the fulfilment of our mission—to . . . freedom of conscience, freedom of person, freedom of trade and business pursuits, universality of freedom and equality. This is our high destiny. . . . For this blessed mission to the nations of the world . . . has America been chosen; and her high example shall smite unto death the tyranny of kings, hierarchs, and oligarchs. . . . "

—John Louis O'Sullivan, from "The Great Nation of Futurity,"
The United States Magazine, and Democratic Review,
November 1839

Step Into the Time

Choose an event from the time line and write a paragraph predicting the general social, political, or economic consequences that event might have on the westward migration.

U.S. PRESIDENTS

Monroe 1817–1825

J. Q. Adams 1825–1829

Jackson 1829–1837

December 1823 Monroe Doctrine asserts U.S. authority in the Western Hemisphere

1834 U.S. Congress approves Indian Territory in the Great Plains

UNITED STATES

WORLD

1820

1825

1830

September 1821 Spain recognizes Mexico's independence

1823 United Provinces of Central America gain independence from Mexico

1824 Formerly enslaved Americans in Africa name their territory Liberia

October 1824 Mexico's first president, Guadalupe Victoria, takes office

1830 Mexico declares that no more Americans may settle in Texas

MAP Explore the interactive version of this map on Networks.

TIME LINE Explore the interactive version of the time line on Networks.

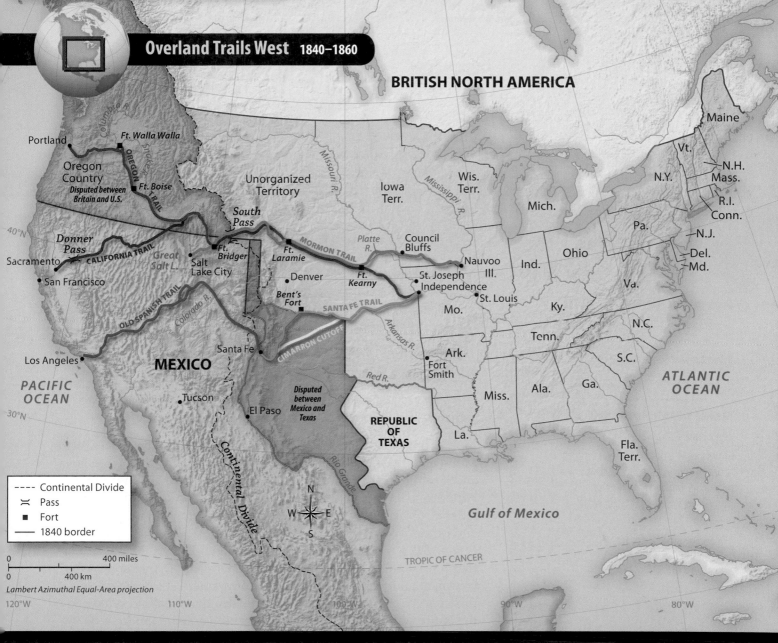

Overland Trails West 1840–1860

BRITISH NORTH AMERICA

Maine

Vt.

N.H.

N.Y.

Mass.

R.I.

Conn.

Pa.

N.J.

Del.

Md.

Portland

Ft. Walla Walla

Oregon Country
Disputed between Britain and U.S.

Ft. Boise

Unorganized Territory

Wis. Terr.

Iowa Terr.

Mich.

Ohio

Ind.

South Pass

Donner Pass

Sacramento

San Francisco

Great Salt L.

Ft. Bridger

Salt Lake City

Ft. Laramie

Denver

Ft. Kearny

Council Bluffs

Nauvoo
Ill.

St. Joseph

Independence

St. Louis

Mo.

Va.

Ky.

N.C.

Tenn.

Ark.

S.C.

Bent's Fort

Los Angeles

MEXICO

Tucson

El Paso

Santa Fe

Disputed between Mexico and Texas

Fort Smith

REPUBLIC OF TEXAS

Miss.

Ala.

Ga.

La.

Fla. Terr.

PACIFIC OCEAN

ATLANTIC OCEAN

Gulf of Mexico

Rio Grande

Red R.

Arkansas R.

Colorado R.

Platte R.

Missouri R.

Mississippi R.

Snake R.

Columbia R.

CALIFORNIA TRAIL

OREGON TRAIL

OLD SPANISH TRAIL

MORMON TRAIL

SANTA FE TRAIL

CIMARRON CUTOFF

Continental Divide

40°N

30°N

TROPIC OF CANCER

- - - Continental Divide
✕ Pass
■ Fort
— 1840 border

0 — 400 miles
0 — 400 km
Lambert Azimuthal Equal-Area projection

120°W   110°W   100°W   90°W   80°W

N W E S

Van Buren 1837–1841

1836 Texas wins independence from Mexico

April 4, 1841 William H. Harrison becomes first president to die in office

W. Harrison 1841

1843 "Great Migration" heads west on the Oregon Trail

Tyler 1841–1845

March 1845 Congress votes to annex the Republic of Texas

1846 Mormons begin their trek from Illinois to Salt Lake Valley

Polk 1845–1849

February 2, 1848 Treaty of Guadalupe Hidalgo ends the war with Mexico

1835   **1840**   **1845**   **1850**

January 1833 Santa Anna is elected president of Mexico

August 1833 Slavery is abolished in the British Empire

1841 Civil war begins in Peru

1845 Great Irish Famine begins

May 1846 U.S. war with Mexico begins

June 15, 1846 Britain and the United States divide Oregon Territory

1848 Revolutions for independence occur throughout Europe

netw◉rks

There's More Online!

☑ **BIOGRAPHY** Kit Carson

☑ **BIOGRAPHY** Brigham Young

☑ **GRAPHIC NOVEL** "Westward Ho!"

☑ **VIDEO** The Western Pioneers

☑ **INTERACTIVE SELF-CHECK QUIZ**

LESSON 1
The Western Pioneers

ESSENTIAL QUESTIONS • *Why did people want to move west in the 1800s?* • *How did westward migration affect the relationship between the United States and other countries and peoples during this time?*

PHOTOS: (l to r) iStock Montage/Archive Photos/Getty Images, Christie's Images/CORBIS, Typical pioneer's covered wagon (b/w photo), American Photographer, (19th century) / Private Collection / Peter Newark American Pictures / The Bridgeman Art Library

Reading **HELP**DESK

Content Vocabulary
- **squatter**
- **overlander**

Academic Vocabulary
- **guarantee**
- **convert**

TAKING NOTES: *Organizing*

ACTIVITY As you read about the growth of the United States, complete a graphic organizer similar to the one below, listing the reasons that Americans emigrated to the West.

> Reasons Americans Went West

IT MATTERS BECAUSE

In the 1840s, Americans made the grueling trek to the frontier of the Midwest and the rich lands of the Oregon Country. New farming equipment eased the clearing and cultivating of new land, encouraging settlement of the Midwest.

Settling New Lands

GUIDING QUESTION *How did the idea of Manifest Destiny and new agricultural equipment encourage western settlement?*

In 1800, only about 387,000 white settlers lived west of the Appalachian Mountains. By 1820, that population had risen to more than 2.4 million, and it continued to grow rapidly. By the time of the Civil War, more Americans lived west of the Appalachians than lived along the Atlantic Coast. Some Americans headed west for religious reasons, and others to own their own farms.

In 1845 a magazine editor named John Louis O'Sullivan declared that it was the "manifest destiny" of Americans "to overspread the continent allotted by Providence." Many Americans believed in this concept of Manifest Destiny—the idea that God had bestowed the entire continent to the Americans and wanted them to settle the western lands.

Farming New Lands

Early pioneers became known as **squatters** because they settled on lands they did not own. The federal government intended to survey the land and then sell large parcels to real estate companies, but squatters wanted to buy the land they occupied directly from the federal government.

Bowing to public pressure, Congress passed the Preemption Act of 1830. This law protected squatters by **guaranteeing** them the right to claim land before it was surveyed and the right to buy up to 160 acres at the government's minimum price of $1.25 per acre.

Plows and Reapers

A few decades earlier, farmers had only wooden plows to break up the grass cover and roots of Midwestern sod. Plowing became easier after 1819, when Jethro Wood patented an iron-bladed plow, and also in 1837, when John Deere engineered a plow with steel blades. Midwestern agriculture also received a boost from the mechanical reaper, which Cyrus McCormick patented in 1834. For centuries farmers had cut grain by hand, using a sickle or a scythe—exhausting and time-consuming work. With a McCormick reaper pulled by horses or mules, farmers could harvest far more grain with far less effort.

Settling the Pacific Coast

The United States, Britain, and Native Americans all laid claim to the Oregon Country, which included present-day Oregon, Washington, and British Columbia. In 1818 Britain and the United States had agreed to occupy the land jointly. In the 1830s, American missionaries began arriving in Oregon to **convert** Native Americans. These missionaries spread the word about Oregon and persuaded others to come to the lush Willamette Valley.

✔ PROGRESS CHECK

Identifying How did actions by the federal government make it easier for settlers to move west during this time?

squatter someone who settles on public land under government regulation with the hope of acquiring title to the land

guarantee to assure or promise to secure against default

convert to bring over from one belief, view, or party to another

overlander someone who travels overland to the West

Westward Migration

GUIDING QUESTIONS *Why did many settlers travel west? What was the trip west like for these individuals and groups?*

Much of the western terrain was difficult to travel through. A small number of mountain men made their living by trapping beaver and selling the furs. At the same time, they gained a thorough knowledge of the territory and the local Native Americans. By the 1840s, these men had carved out several East-to-West trails that helped settlers travel. The most popular route was the Oregon Trail. Others included the California Trail and the Santa Fe Trail.

Emigrants made the journey in groups of covered wagons called wagon trains. Before starting out, they assembled outside a frontier town. Early wagon trains hired mountain men to guide them. Later, most of the travelers—known as **overlanders**—used guidebooks to find their own way.

The typical trip west took five to six months, with wagon trains progressing about 15 miles (24 km) per day. Generally, men drove the wagons, hunted game, and cared for the animals, while women looked after the children, cooked meals, cleaned the camp, and washed clothes. As Elizabeth Smith Geer recounted, the trip was exhausting and difficult:

PRIMARY SOURCE

❝I carry my babe and lead, or rather carry, another through snow, mud, and water, almost to my knees. It is the worst road. . . . [T]here was not one dry thread on one of us—not even my babe. . . . I have not told you half we suffered. I am not adequate to the task.❞

—quoted in *Women's Diaries of the Westward Journey*, 1982

Native Americans

Although travelers feared attacks by Native Americans, these were rare. By one estimate, 362 emigrants died due to Native American attacks between 1840 and 1860, while emigrants killed 462 Native Americans in the same period. Native Americans often gave emigrants

Entitled *American Progress*, this famous painting of the idea of Manifest Destiny depicts America as a woman leading the country into the West. She carries a book, which represents American enlightenment, and is laying a telegraph wire.

▶ **CRITICAL THINKING**
Analyzing Primary Sources What symbolizes progress in the painting? Why is the left portion of the painting darker than the right?

Settlers often traveled long distances in covered wagons, enduring difficulties and danger to reach the West.

▶ **CRITICAL THINKING**
Analyzing Primary Sources What do you think was the greatest danger facing travelers on the overland trails?

food and helpful information about routes, edible plants, and sources of water. Overlanders also renewed their provisions by trading other goods with Native Americans, sometimes using horses as currency.

As overland traffic increased, Native Americans on the Great Plains became concerned and angry over the threat pioneers posed to their way of life. The Sioux, Cheyenne, Arapaho, and other groups relied on buffalo for food, shelter, clothing, tools, and countless other necessities of everyday life. Now they feared that the age-old wanderings of the buffalo herds would be disrupted.

Hoping to ensure peace, the federal government negotiated the Treaty of Fort Laramie in 1851. The United States promised eight Native American groups that specific territories of the Great Plains would belong to them as long as they allowed settlers to pass through peacefully. The government also agreed to make payments to the groups. Not all Native Americans approved of the treaty, however. The Sioux chief Black Hawk spoke out against it, saying:

PRIMARY SOURCE

❝You have split my lands and I don't like it. . . . These lands once belonged to the Kiowas and Crows, but we whipped these nations out of them, and in this we did what the white men do when they want the lands of the Indians.❞

—quoted in *America: A Narrative History,* 2007

The Mormon Migration

Unlike those bound for the West in search of land, the Mormons followed a deeply rooted American tradition—the quest for religious freedom. The Mormons, however, had to seek that freedom by leaving the Eastern states, instead of coming to them.

In 1844 a mob murdered the Mormon leader Joseph Smith. Two years later, the church's new leader, Brigham Young, took his people west to escape further persecution. Several thousand Mormons forged their way along a path that became known as the Mormon Trail. It served as a valuable route into the western United States. In 1847 the Mormons stopped at the Great Salt Lake in what is now Utah. Undeterred by the wildness of the area, they claimed the land they called "Deseret."

✓ **PROGRESS CHECK**

Describing How did Native American groups react to Americans' increased westward migration?

PHOTO: Typical pioneer's covered wagon (b/w photo), American Photographer, (19th century) / Private Collection / Peter Newark American Pictures / The Bridgeman Art Library

LESSON 1 REVIEW

Reviewing Vocabulary
1. *Stating* How did squatters get their land?

Using Your Notes
2. *Determining Cause and Effect* Use the notes you completed during the lesson to explain why many Americans traveled west during this era.

Answering the Guiding Questions
3. *Making Connections* How did the idea of Manifest Destiny and new agricultural equipment encourage western settlement?

4. *Summarizing* Why did many settlers travel west? What was the trip west like for these individuals and groups?

Writing Activity
5. DESCRIPTIVE Suppose that you are emigrating from the East to a frontier farm in the West. Write a journal entry describing a day in your journey.

LESSON 2
The Hispanic Southwest

ESSENTIAL QUESTIONS • *Why did people want to move west in the 1800s?* • *How did westward migration affect the relationship between the United States and other countries and peoples during this time?*

Reading **HELP**DESK

Content Vocabulary
• secularize   • vaquero
• mestizo

Academic Vocabulary
• civil   • ultimately

TAKING NOTES: *Organizing*

ACTIVITY As you read about Americans and the Hispanic Southwest, use a graphic organizer similar to the one below to list features of each Mexican territory after Mexico gained independence.

Territory	Features
California	
New Mexico	
Texas	

IT MATTERS BECAUSE
After Mexico won its independence from Spain in 1821, the Mexican government neglected its far northern territories. American influence there grew as more Americans settled in the region.

Mexican Independence and the Borderlands

GUIDING QUESTION *How did life change for many Mexicans living in the northern territories after gaining independence from Spain?*

In 1821, after more than a decade of fighting, Mexico won its independence from Spain. During the decades that followed, Mexico experienced great turmoil and political chaos. As the young Mexican republic struggled to establish a stable national government, it neglected its northern borderlands, which included California, New Mexico, and Texas.

The Mexican frontier was threatened on several fronts. The region was sparsely populated by Native Americans and Hispanic settlers. Settlements in Texas and New Mexico faced attacks by Apaches, Comanches, and other Native American groups. The region was also threatened by the westward expansion of the United States and the southward expansion of Russian settlements along the Pacific Coast from Alaska. The frontier presidios, or forts, became weak and left frontier settlers vulnerable to attack.

By the time Mexico became independent, the mission system used by Spain to spread Christianity and Spanish culture had nearly collapsed. Missions controlled vast tracts of land on which grazed cattle, sheep, and horses. Native Americans tended the livestock and did other work at the missions under conditions of near slavery. In 1834 the Mexican government **secularized**—or transferred from religious control to **civil** control— the missions and then transferred the land to private ownership. Most of the land ended up in the hands of cattle ranchers, who relied on Native Americans for labor.

Spanish missions were self-sufficient, fortified, religious communities established to convert Native Americans to Catholicism and incorporate them into Spanish society.

▶ **CRITICAL THINKING**
Interpreting Significance What was the most dominant feature of a mission complex? How is that significant?

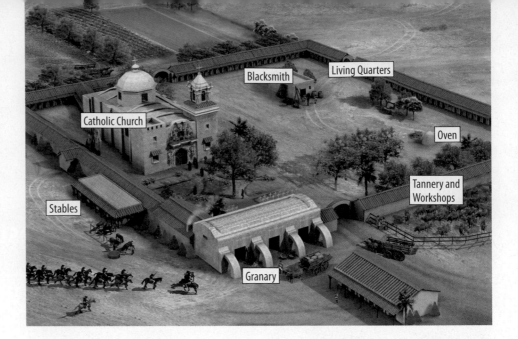

secularize to transfer the use, possession, or control of something from church to civil authority

civil of or relating to citizens

mestizo a person of mixed blood or ancestry

vaqueros men on horseback who herded cattle on haciendas

ART: Marcell Lavedet

California

Secularization of the missions had a tremendous impact on life in California because it freed up land for cattle ranching, which became the mainstay of the economy. Rancheros, or ranchers, owned sprawling tracts of land. These predominantly white "Spanish Dons" and their families constituted less than 10 percent of California's population but dominated California society.

Beneath these elites was a class of **mestizos** (persons of mixed European and Native American ancestry). Some of this middle class worked as **vaqueros** (cowboys), but many were skilled craftspeople.

At the bottom of society were Native Americans. Their situation improved little after independence. Although freed from the missions, they were often exploited by the new class of rancheros. Many escaped to live among the independent Native Americans on the edges of the California frontier.

In the California territory, men played a powerful role in the family, and only men could vote or hold elective office. Yet women, especially upper-class women, had rights and privileges as well. Unlike American women of the era, Hispanic women retained control over their own property after marriage and could seek legal redress in the courts.

New Mexico

As in California, Mexican independence brought little immediate change to New Mexico (which included present-day Arizona). Although New Mexico had a larger Hispanic population (approximately 44,000 in 1827), it remained largely rural. Sheep ranching thrived in New Mexico's dry climate. Large ranches were established south of Santa Fe in the Rio Grande Valley. Throughout the region, corn, peppers, and potatoes were staple crops. The local Pueblo people had raised corn for centuries.

In the 1820s, when the Navajo and Apache launched a series of attacks on New Mexico, the Mexican government was unable to provide protection. This fed a growing dissatisfaction with the national government. Finally, in 1837, Pueblo people and Hispanic settlers north of Santa Fe launched a rebellion and killed the unpopular territorial governor and 16 other government officials.

✔ **PROGRESS CHECK**

Explaining What were the differences and similarities between life for Native Americans before and after Mexican independence?

Americans Arrive in the Borderlands

GUIDING QUESTION *How did American influence increase after Mexican independence?*

After Mexican independence in 1821, American influence in the borderlands grew. A few Americans settled in California before Mexican independence, and immigration increased afterward. Trade with the United States increased significantly once Mexico was no longer part of Spain's empire. Traders from the United States, Russia, and other countries arrived in California ports to exchange manufactured goods for sea otter and seal skins and the hides and tallow derived from cattle.

In 1839, hoping to attract more settlers, Juan Bautista Alvarado, the governor of California, granted 50,000 acres in the Sacramento Valley to John Sutter. There, Sutter built a trading post and cattle ranch. "Sutter's Fort" was often the first stopping point for Americans reaching California. As more Americans arrived, the differences between California and southern Mexico increased. This fueled political tensions between frontier leaders and the Mexican national government. The American population, however, was still relatively small. Only about 700 Americans lived in California in 1845.

During the colonial period, New Mexicans received most manufactured goods from traders who came north from the Mexican state of Chihuahua. This began to change in 1821, the year of Mexican independence, when an American trader named William Becknell arrived in Santa Fe. He opened the Santa Fe Trail, which became a major trade route connecting Santa Fe with Independence, Missouri. Caravan wagons brought American manufactured goods to New Mexico and exchanged them for silver, mules, and furs. As trade increased, a small American population settled in Santa Fe.

East of New Mexico, Texas had long served as a buffer territory between the United States and the rest of Mexico. Texas was a sparsely populated region where settlers faced recurring raids by the Comanche and Apache. Most of the 3,000 or so Spanish-speaking Tejanos were concentrated in the towns of San Antonio and Goliad (then called La Bahía). Just before Mexican independence, Spain began allowing foreigners to settle in Texas. Mexico continued this policy, and Americans soon began to flood into that territory.

The decision to invite Americans to settle in Texas led **ultimately** to a revolt against Mexican rule and independence for Texas. California and New Mexico remained Mexican territory for 25 years after Mexican independence. Texas—where Americans soon vastly outnumbered Tejanos—broke away from Mexico after 15 years.

✔ **PROGRESS CHECK**

Making Inferences How did trade increase the influence of foreigners in the borderlands?

Analyzing PRIMARY SOURCES

Foreign Traders in California

❝In Monterey there are a number of English and Americans (English or 'Ingles' all are called who speak the English language) who have married Californians, become united to the Catholic church, and acquired considerable property. Having more industry, frugality, and enterprise than the natives, they soon get nearly all the trade into their hands. They usually keep shops, in which they retail the goods purchased in larger quantities from our vessels, and also send a good deal into the interior, taking hides in pay, which they again barter with our vessels.❞

—Richard Henry Dana, from *Two Years Before the Mast,* 1842

DBQ *IDENTIFYING BIAS* What does the writer, an American sailor, say that shows bias, or prejudice, against native Californians?

ultimately in the end, finally, or eventually

LESSON 2 REVIEW

Reviewing Vocabulary

1. ***Speculating*** Which group in California probably had more political power after independence, mestizos or rancheros? Explain.

2. ***Making Generalizations*** Were Native Americans in California better off before or after Mexico secularized the missions?

Using Your Notes

3. ***Summarizing*** Review the notes you completed during the lesson and write a paragraph about the impact Mexican independence had on California, New Mexico, and Texas.

Answering the Guiding Questions

4. ***Interpreting*** How did life change for many Mexicans living in the northern territories after gaining independence from Spain?

5. ***Summarizing*** How did American influence increase after Mexican independence?

Writing Activity

6. **EXPOSITORY** Describe how the lives of Native Americans changed and did not change in the northern Mexican territories during this time.

networks

There's More Online!

☑ **BIOGRAPHY** Antonio López de Santa Anna

☑ **BIOGRAPHY** Sam Houston

☑ **CHART/GRAPH** Texans vs. Mexicans

☑ **IMAGE** The Alamo

☑ **IMAGE** Battle of San Jacinto

☑ **MAP** American Settlement of Texas

☑ **VIDEO** Independence for Texas

☑ **INTERACTIVE SELF-CHECK QUIZ**

Reading **HELP**DESK

Content Vocabulary
- *empresario*
- *convention*
- *annexation*

Academic Vocabulary
- *reinforcement*

TAKING NOTES: *Organizing*

ACTIVITY As you read, complete a graphic organizer similar to the one below by filling in the major battles of the Texas war for independence and the outcome of each battle.

Major Battle	Outcome

LESSON 3
Independence for Texas

ESSENTIAL QUESTIONS · *Why did people want to move west in the 1800s?* · *How did westward migration affect the relationship between the United States and other countries and peoples during this time?*

IT MATTERS BECAUSE

Mexico encouraged Americans to settle in Texas, but Americans did not assimilate as the Mexican government had hoped. The struggle over control of the territory resulted in rebellion and, finally, independence for Texas.

Opening Texas to Americans

GUIDING QUESTION *How did the growing Americanization of Texas affect the Americans' relationship with the Mexican government?*

In July 1821, Stephen F. Austin set off from Louisiana for Texas. He went to carry out the plan his father, Moses Austin, had made with the Spanish government to bring 300 American families to settle in Texas. Moses died before he could fulfill his part of the agreement. On his deathbed, he asked Stephen to take his place in Texas.

When Austin settled in Texas, it was not a wild and empty land. Spanish-speaking Tejanos had established settlements in the southern portion of the region, and the land to the north was the territory of the Apache, Comanche, and other Native American groups. In 1824 Texas was joined with Coahuila to become part of the Mexican state of Coahuila y Texas.

Unable to persuade its own citizens to settle on this frontier, Mexico allowed foreigners to settle there. Between 1823 and 1825, Mexico passed three colonization laws, which offered cheap land to nearly anyone willing to come. The last law granted immigrants a 10-year exemption from paying taxes, but required that they become Mexican citizens and convert to Roman Catholicism.

Empresarios and Settlers

Under the National Colonization Act, Mexico gave *empresarios,* a Spanish word meaning "agents" or "contractors," large grants of Texas land. In exchange, the *empresarios* promised to fill the land with a certain number of settlers and govern the colonies they established. Stephen Austin was the most successful *empresario*. By the mid-1830s, Austin had persuaded some 1,500 American families to immigrate.

Americanizing Texas

Americans in Texas initially accepted Mexican citizenship, but many did not accept Mexican customs or Roman Catholicism. Many Mexicans, in turn, distrusted the settlers because of their American lifestyle and rejection of Mexican ways. One Mexican general foresaw future troubles with the Americans in Texas:

PRIMARY SOURCE

❝The Americans from the north have taken possession of practically all the eastern part of Texas, in most cases without the permission of the authorities. . . .

. . . [In San Felipe de Austin, the] population is nearly two hundred persons, of which only ten are Mexicans, for the balance are all Americans from the North with an occasional European. . . . Beyond the village . . . are scattered the families brought by Stephen Austin, which today number more than two thousand persons. . . . [T]he spark that will start the conflagration that will deprive us of Texas, will start from this colony.❞

—José María Sánchez, from "A Trip to Texas in 1828,"
The Southwestern Historical Quarterly, 1926

In 1826 Benjamin Edwards, brother of *empresario* Haden Edwards, led a rebellion against Mexican authority. He declared that American settlements in Texas now constituted the independent nation of Fredonia. He gained few followers, however. When threatened by Mexican troops and militia from Stephen Austin's colony, the rebels dispersed.

Although most settlers ignored Edwards's call for revolution, the Mexican government feared it signaled an American plot to acquire Texas. In 1830 Mexico closed its borders to further immigration by Americans and banned the importation of enslaved labor as well. Mexico also taxed goods imported from foreign countries, hoping to discourage trade with the United States.

These laws infuriated the settlers. Without immigration their settlements could not grow. The import tax meant higher prices for goods they were accustomed to purchasing from the United States. Perhaps worst of all, the Mexican government was making rules for them. They saw no reason to obey a government they hardly considered their own.

☑ **PROGRESS CHECK**

Explaining What caused the American presence in Texas to grow so quickly?

empresario a person who arranged for the settlement of Texas in the early 1800s

American Settlement of Texas 1820s

Texas
Other Mexican states
— International boundary
— Mexico state boundary
--- Empresario boundary
Burnet (1826) Empresario name and date land granted

Nuevo Mexico
UNITED STATES
Cameron (1828)
Wavell (1826)
Unassigned
Texas
Filisola (1831)
Cameron (1827)
MEXICO
Austin & Williams (1825)
Burnet (1826)
Nacogdoches
Woodbury & Company (1826)
Austin (1824)
Vehlein (1828)
Zavala (1829)
Milam (1826)
Austin (1825)
DeWitt (1825)
San Felipe de Austin
Anahuac
San Antonio
Gonzales
De Leon (1824)
Victoria
McMullen & McGloin (1828)
Goliad
Coahuila
San Patricio
Power & Hewetson (1826)
Gulf of Mexico
Tamaulipas

0   200 miles
0   200 km
Albers Equal-Area projection

GEOGRAPHY CONNECTION

In the 1820s, American settlers looking for land and new opportunities flocked to the Mexican state of Texas.

1 **THE WORLD IN SPATIAL TERMS** *Along what river was San Felipe de Austin founded?*

2 **THE WORLD IN SPATIAL TERMS** *What other Mexican states bordered Texas?*

Texas Goes to War

GUIDING QUESTION *How was the Texas war for independence similar to the American Revolution? How was it different?*

With tensions simmering, Texas settlers met at **conventions** in the Texas town of San Felipe in 1832 and 1833. At the first, Stephen Austin was chosen the convention's president. This convention asked Mexico to reopen Texas to American immigrants and to ease taxes on imports. The second convention sought to make Texas a separate state from Coahuila, and it agreed on a constitution. Austin was sent to negotiate with the Mexican government.

In the fall of 1833, negotiations stalled. Austin sent a letter to Tejano leaders suggesting that Texas start peacefully organizing its own state government. Then he visited Mexican president Antonio López de Santa Anna and convinced him to agree to several demands. On his way home, Austin was arrested. Mexican officials had intercepted his letter to the Tejanos. Suspected of trying to incite a rebellion, Austin was imprisoned in Mexico City, without trial. Soon afterward, President Santa Anna declared himself dictator. Austin was released from prison in July 1835. Seeing that further negotiation with Santa Anna was pointless, Austin urged Texans to organize an army.

The Early Battles

The Mexican army had serious problems. Continuing political instability in Mexico City had denied the army sound leadership, training, and support. Against this handicapped force, the Texan army enjoyed its first taste of victory at the military post of Gonzales, about 70 miles to the east of San Antonio. There, Mexican soldiers ordered the Texans to surrender their arms. The rebels refused and, having no orders to attack, the Mexicans retreated to San Antonio. The Texans followed and laid siege to the city. In December 1835, the rebels, numbering between 300 and 400, drove the much larger Mexican force out of San Antonio.

On March 2, 1836, Texas declared its independence from Mexico. Shortly thereafter, the Texans drafted a new constitution that drew heavily from the U.S. Constitution and specifically protected slavery.

The Alamo

Few of the Texas rebels had any military training and at first had no leader. Finally, a former governor of Tennessee and proven military leader named Sam Houston took command. In the meantime, Santa Anna organized a force of several thousand to put down the rebellion.

PHOTO: Randy Faris/Flirt/CORBIS

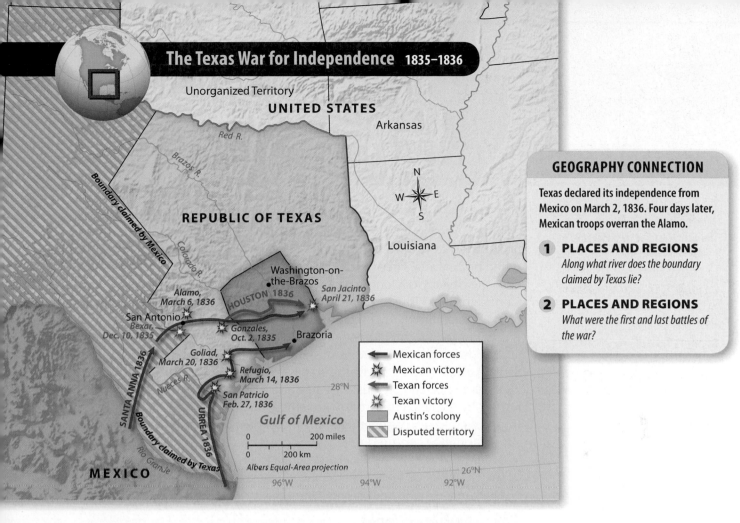

The Texas War for Independence 1835–1836

Unorganized Territory

UNITED STATES

Arkansas

Red R.

Brazos R.

REPUBLIC OF TEXAS

Boundary claimed by Mexico

Colorado R.

Louisiana

Washington-on-
the-Brazos

HOUSTON 1836

Alamo,
March 6, 1836

San Jacinto
April 21, 1836

San Antonio
Bexar,
Dec. 10, 1835

Gonzales,
Oct. 2, 1835

Brazoria

Goliad,
March 20, 1836

SANTA ANNA 1836

Refugio,
March 14, 1836

Nueces R.

28°N

San Patricio
Feb. 27, 1836

URREA 1836

Gulf of Mexico

Boundary claimed by Texas

Rio Grande

MEXICO

0   200 miles

0   200 km

Albers Equal-Area projection

96°W   94°W   92°W   26°N

→ Mexican forces
✳ Mexican victory
← Texan forces
✳ Texan victory
▨ Austin's colony
▨ Disputed territory

GEOGRAPHY CONNECTION

Texas declared its independence from Mexico on March 2, 1836. Four days later, Mexican troops overran the Alamo.

1 PLACES AND REGIONS
Along what river does the boundary claimed by Texas lie?

2 PLACES AND REGIONS
What were the first and last battles of the war?

When Mexican forces arrived at San Antonio in February 1836, they found more than 180 Texas rebels holed up in an abandoned Catholic mission called the Alamo. Under the command of Lieutenant Colonel William B. Travis, the small force in the Alamo sought to delay Santa Anna and give Houston's army more time to prepare. On February 24, Travis dispatched a courier from the mission with a plea for help:

PRIMARY SOURCE

❝I am besieged with a thousand or more of the Mexicans under Santa Anna. . . . I shall never surrender or retreat. Then, I call on you in the name of Liberty, of patriotism, and everything dear to the American character, to come to our aid with all dispatch. . . . I am determined to sustain myself as long as possible and die like a soldier who never forgets what is due his own honor and that of his country. VICTORY OR DEATH.❞
—quoted in *Lone Star: A History of Texas and Texans*, 1983

The call for **reinforcements** almost went unanswered. About 33 settlers, most from Gonzales, decided to join the fight and made it into the Alamo. The Texans held off Santa Anna's besieging army for 13 days. It was during the standoff that the new Texas government formally declared independence. On March 6, 1836, Santa Anna's army stormed the Alamo. The Texans fought off their attackers for several hours before being overrun. The defenders of the Alamo had bought Houston's army nearly two extra weeks to organize.

reinforcement additional assistance, material, or support to strengthen an existing situation

Goliad

Two weeks later, the Mexican army overwhelmed Texan troops led by James W. Fannin at Goliad, a town southeast of San Antonio near the Gulf Coast. Fannin and his men surrendered, hoping that the Mexicans would disarm them and expel them from Texas. Though the Mexican field general at Goliad wrote to Santa Anna requesting clemency, Santa Anna demanded execution.

The Battle of San Jacinto was a decisive victory for Texan forces. The victory assured the independence of Texas and ended the war.

▶ **CRITICAL THINKING**
Inferring What aspect of the Battle of San Jacinto suggests that the Texans wanted revenge for earlier losses?

At dawn on March 27, 1836, a firing squad executed over 300 men. The losses at the Alamo and Goliad devastated Texans but also united them in support of their new country.

The Battle of San Jacinto

With the Texan army in disarray, Sam Houston desperately needed more time to recruit fresh volunteers and to train the soldiers who remained. Rather than fight, he chose to retreat, heading east toward Louisiana.

Houston was biding his time. Up against a larger, more disciplined army, he decided to wait for Santa Anna to make a mistake. It came on April 21, when both armies were encamped along the San Jacinto River near what is now the city of Houston. Santa Anna no longer saw the Texan army as a threat. Confident that Houston would wait until the next day to launch an attack, Santa Anna allowed his men to sleep in the afternoon.

Eager for a fight, Houston's soldiers convinced the officers to launch an afternoon assault. Shielded from sight by a hill, Houston's troops crept up on Santa Anna's sleeping soldiers and charged. Yelling "Remember the Alamo" and "Remember Goliad," Houston's men attacked the Mexican soldiers with guns, knives, and clubs. Hundreds were killed, and more than 700 of Santa Anna's troops were taken prisoner. The Texans suffered only 9 killed and 34 wounded.

Among the captured men was Santa Anna himself. Houston forced him to order his army out of Texas and sign a treaty recognizing the independence of the Republic of Texas. The Mexican Congress refused to accept the treaty but was unwilling to launch another military campaign. Texas had won the war.

The Republic of Texas

annexation the incorporation of a territory within the domain of a country

In September 1836, the newly independent republic called its citizens to the polls. They elected Sam Houston as their first president and voted in favor of **annexation**, or becoming part of the United States. Given that Americans had enthusiastically supported the war, most Texans assumed the United States would want to annex the republic. Many Northern members of Congress, however, opposed admitting Texas as a slave state.

President Andrew Jackson did not want to increase tensions between North and South or risk a war with Mexico, which continued to claim ownership of Texas. Jackson made no move toward annexation, although on his last day in office, he did sign a resolution officially recognizing the independence of Texas.

☑ **PROGRESS CHECK**

Explaining What was the role of volunteer soldiers in the Texas war for independence?

LESSON 3 REVIEW

Reviewing Vocabulary

1. *Determining Importance* How did the *empresarios* influence Texas settlement?

2. *Drawing Conclusions* Why would Texans vote to be annexed by the United States after fighting so hard for their independence?

Using Your Notes

3. *Summarizing* Use the notes you completed during the lesson and write a short paragraph describing how the Texas war for independence was won.

Answering the Guiding Questions

4. *Interpreting* How did the growing Americanization of Texas affect the Americans' relationship with the Mexican government?

5. *Summarizing* How was the Texas war for independence similar to the American Revolution? How was it different?

Writing Activity

6. DESCRIPTIVE Describe the Battle of the Alamo and the Battle of San Jacinto, using descriptive words for the motivations of the Texans in each battle and the results.

netw⦿rks

There's More Online!

- ☑ **BIOGRAPHY** Winfield Scott
- ☑ **MAP** Presidential Election of 1844
- ☑ **MAP** Boundaries of the U.S. and Mexico, 1844 and 1848
- ☑ **PRIMARY SOURCE** Polk's Victory Political Cartoon
- ☑ **VIDEO** The War With Mexico
- ☑ **INTERACTIVE SELF-CHECK QUIZ**

Reading **HELP**DESK

Content Vocabulary
- envoy
- cede

Academic Vocabulary
- resolution
- secure

TAKING NOTES: *Organizing*

ACTIVITY As you read about the war with Mexico, use the major headings of the lesson to complete the outline started below.

> The War With Mexico
> I. The Lingering Question of Texas
> A.
> B.
> C.

LESSON 4
The War With Mexico

ESSENTIAL QUESTIONS · *Why did people want to move west in the 1800s?* · *How did westward migration affect the relationship between the United States and other countries and peoples during this time?*

IT MATTERS BECAUSE

By 1844, control of Oregon and the annexation of Texas had become major political issues. After the annexation of Texas, the border between the United States and Mexico was in dispute. The United States declared war on Mexico and took Mexico's northern territories.

The Lingering Question of Texas

GUIDING QUESTION *Why were some Americans against the idea of annexing Texas?*

The dispute over Texas between the United States and Mexico began in 1803, when the United States claimed Texas as part of the Louisiana Purchase. The Adams-Onís Treaty of 1819 ended that claim, but the idea of acquiring Mexican territory still had strong popular support.

Tensions increased during the administration of John Tyler, who hoped to bring Texas into the Union. Since Texas had a large population of Southerners who had taken slaves into Texas, Texans were certain to support slavery. Antislavery leaders in Congress therefore opposed Texas's annexation. Moreover, Mexico had never recognized the independence of Texas and still considered it Mexican territory.

In early 1844, President Tyler brought the matter of Texas before the Senate. He blundered, however, by including in the supporting documents a letter written by Secretary of State John C. Calhoun that contained a fierce defense of slavery. Outraged Northerners pointed to the letter as evidence that annexation was nothing but a pro-slavery plot. The Senate voted 35 to 16 against annexation. Tyler's failed maneuver destroyed his chances for reelection.

The Election of 1844

The presidential election of 1844 pitted Whig senator Henry Clay against Democrat James K. Polk, a former member of Congress and governor of Tennessee. Polk promised to annex not only Texas but also the contested Oregon Territory. In addition, he vowed to buy California from Mexico. This appealed to Northerners and Southerners because it expanded the country while maintaining the delicate balance between free and slave states.

ELECTORAL VOTE
TOTAL: 275

38.2%
105   61.8%
170

POPULAR VOTE
TOTAL: 2,700,861

2.31%
62,300

48.14%
1,300,097

49.56%
1,338,464

■ Polk (Democratic)   ▨ Territories
■ Clay (Whig)   ▨ Claimed areas
■ Birney (Liberty)   ▨ Other countries

GEOGRAPHY CONNECTION

In the presidential election of 1844, the popular vote was fairly close, but Democrat James K. Polk won the electoral vote by a large margin.

1 THE WORLD IN SPATIAL TERMS *Which states did Clay win in the 1844 election?*

2 HUMAN SYSTEMS *Why are no election results shown for the territories?*

The Democrats' unity on annexation caused Clay to backpedal and say that he, too, supported the annexation of Texas. This so angered antislavery segment of the Whig Party that they decided to back the small Liberty Party, which supported abolition. With the Whig vote split, Polk won the election.

The Oregon Question

Polk took a strong stance on what came to be known as the Oregon Question. Despite British claims to Oregon, which had been established in the Convention of 1818, Polk and the Democrats held that the United States had a "clear and unquestionable" right to all of the Oregon Country, including part of the region north of the 49th parallel that is today British Columbia. Their rallying cry, "Fifty-four Forty or Fight," declared that the United States should control all of Oregon below the line of 54°40′ north latitude.

Despite such slogans, few Americans wanted to fight the British to gain control of Oregon. In June 1846, the two nations negotiated the Oregon Treaty. In this agreement, the United States received all of Oregon south of 49° north latitude and west of the Rocky Mountains, except for the southern tip of Vancouver Island. In exchange, the British were guaranteed navigation rights on the Columbia River.

The Annexation of Texas

resolution a formal expression of opinion, will, or intent voted by an official body or assembly

Even before Polk took office, outgoing president Tyler pushed an annexation **resolution** through Congress in February 1845, and Texas joined the Union that year. As predicted, Mexico was outraged and broke diplomatic relations with the U. S. government. Matters worsened when the two countries disputed the location of Texas's southwestern border. Mexico said it was at the Nueces River. Texans, and then the United States, claimed the Rio Grande, about 150 miles (240 km) farther west and south, as the boundary, covering more territory than the Mexican claim.

envoy a person delegated to represent one country to another

Polk's intentions in California added to the growing strife with Mexico. In November 1845, he sent John Slidell as a special **envoy,** or representative, to Mexico City to try to purchase the territory. Mexico's president, José Joaquín Herrera, refused to meet with Slidell.

☑ **PROGRESS CHECK**

Explaining What did the slogan "Fifty-four Forty or Fight" refer to?

The War With Mexico

GUIDING QUESTION *Was the war with Mexico justified?*

Herrera's snub ended any realistic chance of a diplomatic solution. Polk ordered troops led by General Zachary Taylor to cross the Nueces River—in Mexico's view, an invasion of its territory. Polk hoped that Mexico would fire the first shot so he could win popular support for a war. On May 9, 1846, news of an attack on Taylor's men reached Polk. In an address to Congress, Polk declared that the United States was at war "by the act of Mexico herself." On May 13, Congress voted overwhelmingly in favor of war.

Calling All Volunteers

Polk and his advisers developed a three-pronged military strategy to capture Santa Fe, New Mexico, to the north and California to the west, and advance to Mexico City to force Mexico to surrender. To implement the ambitious plan, Congress authorized the president to call for 50,000 volunteers.

ANALYZING PRIMARY SOURCES

Should the United States Go to War with Mexico?

Although many Americans supported war with Mexico for personal or political gain or because they subscribed to the principle of Manifest Destiny, many were against it. Debates raged between citizens, in newspapers, and in Congress over President Polk's motives and the tactics he had used to force a declaration of war against America's southern neighbor. While Polk insisted that Mexico had been the aggressor, many thought that the United States had purposely incited the war to gain more land or, as Frederick Douglass believed, to extend slavery into new territory.

❝Upon the pretext that Texas, a nation as independent as [Mexico], thought proper to unite its destinies with our own, [Mexico] has affected to believe that we have severed her rightful territory, and, in official proclamations and manifestoes, has repeatedly threatened to make war upon us, for the purpose of reconquering Texas. In the meantime, we have tried every effort at reconciliation. . . . But now, after reiterated menaces, Mexico has passed the boundary of the United States, has invaded our territory, and shed American blood upon the American soil. . . .

As war exists, and, notwithstanding all our efforts to avoid it, exists by the act of Mexico herself, we are called upon, by every consideration of duty and patriotism, to vindicate, with decision, the honor, the rights, and the interests of our country.❞

—President James K. Polk, from
The Congressional Globe, May 11, 1846

❝The war . . . was [begun] with no higher or holier motive than that of upholding and propagating slavery. In 1829 Mexico . . . had declared the entire abolition of slavery in her territories. The consequence was a decrease in the value of slaves in the border states of America. . . . What was the desperate purpose of the United States? . . . [T]hey stirred up a revolt against Mexico in Texas, which . . . was ultimately severed from the mother country. Their next step was kindly to recognise the independence of Texas, and in 1844 it was annexed to the Union. An army of men was sent to protect the Texians . . . and the Mexicans firing at the invaders, the United States at once recognised a war.❞

—abolitionist Frederick Douglass, from a speech delivered in Bristol, England, April 1, 1847

DBQ Document Based Questions

❶ *Summarizing* According to President Polk, what was the U.S. attitude toward war with Mexico before Mexican forces attacked?

❷ *Identifying* What reasons does Polk give for declaring war on Mexico?

❸ *Summarizing* According to Frederick Douglass, what steps did the United States take to incite the war?

❹ *Identifying* What does Douglass say is the true reason for the war with Mexico?

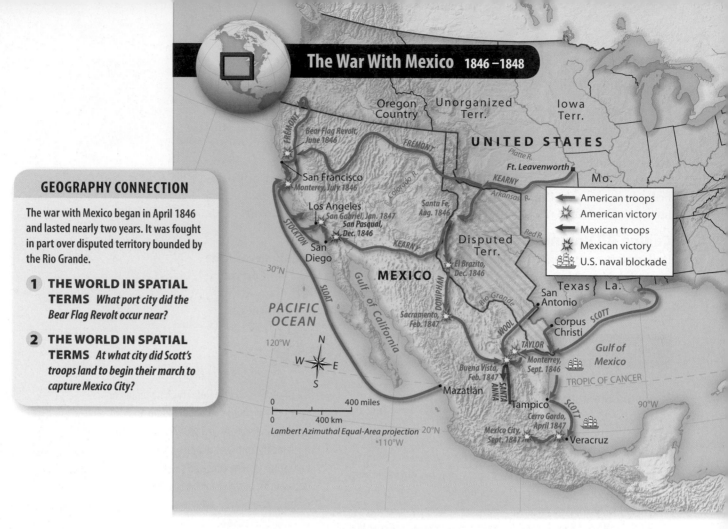

GEOGRAPHY CONNECTION

The war with Mexico began in April 1846 and lasted nearly two years. It was fought in part over disputed territory bounded by the Rio Grande.

1 **THE WORLD IN SPATIAL TERMS** *What port city did the Bear Flag Revolt occur near?*

2 **THE WORLD IN SPATIAL TERMS** *At what city did Scott's troops land to begin their march to capture Mexico City?*

Some 73,000 answered the call. Undisciplined and unruly, the volunteers proved to be less than ideal soldiers. One officer bemoaned that the green recruits constantly demanded his attention:

PRIMARY SOURCE

❝[O]ne wanted me to read a letter just received, another wanted me to write one for him, another wanted me to send his money home, another wanted me to keep it for him . . . one complained that his uniform was too large, another that *his* was too small.❞

—from *Memoirs of a Maryland Volunteer,* June 15, 1846

The Fighting Begins

In early May, several days before Polk signed the declaration of war, Taylor's troops defeated Mexican forces, first at Palo Alto and then at Resaca de la Palma. Taylor then moved south, defeating Mexican forces at Matamoros. By late September, he had marched about 200 miles (322 km) west from the coast of the Gulf of Mexico and captured Monterrey.

In the meantime, Colonel Stephen W. Kearny led troops from Fort Leavenworth, west of Missouri, toward Santa Fe. The march through the dry countryside was brutal, but when Kearny's men reached the city in August, the Mexican force there had already fled. With Santa Fe **secured,** Kearny led a small U.S. force into California.

Before Kearny arrived, and even before war with Mexico was officially declared, settlers in northern California led by American general John C. Frémont had begun an uprising. The official Mexican presence in the territory had never been strong, and the settlers had little trouble overcoming it. On June 14, 1846, they declared California independent of Mexico and renamed

secure to make free from risk of loss

the region the Bear Flag Republic. A few weeks later, the Bear Flag Republic came to an end when American naval forces arrived and took possession of California for the United States.

To Mexico City

Despite having lost vast territories, Mexico's leaders refused to surrender. Polk decided to force things to a conclusion by sending soldiers on ships to the Mexican port of Veracruz. From there they would march west and capture the Mexican capital, Mexico City.

Polk placed General Winfield Scott in command of this campaign. In March 1847, Scott's force landed near Veracruz, which his forces took 20 days later. Having taken control of this strategic port, the American troops then headed for Mexico City, fighting vicious and bloody battles with Mexican forces along the way. For two days they stormed Chapultepec Castle, which guarded the city, and finally entered Mexico City on September 14. American forces were in control of the capital and went on to establish a formal occupation of Mexico.

The Peace Treaty

After the fall of Mexico City, Mexico's leaders could no longer hold out. On February 2, 1848, Mexican leaders signed the Treaty of Guadalupe Hidalgo. In the agreement, Mexico **ceded,** or gave up, some 500,000 square miles (1,295,000 sq. km) of territory to the United States. This land is now the states of California, Utah, and Nevada as well as parts of New Mexico, Arizona, Colorado, and Wyoming. Mexico also accepted the Rio Grande as the southern border of Texas. In exchange, the United States paid Mexico $15 million and agreed to take over $3.25 million in debts Mexico owed to American citizens.

With Oregon and the former Mexican territories now under the American flag, the dream of Manifest Destiny was finally realized: the United States now stretched from ocean to ocean. Valuable ports on the West Coast opened up new markets to the Pacific nations of Asia. The question of whether the new lands should allow slavery, however, would soon lead the country into a bloody civil war. The experience that soldiers such as Robert E. Lee and Ulysses S. Grant gained during the war with Mexico would soon be used to lead Americans in battle against one another.

✔ **PROGRESS CHECK**

Explaining How did the war with Mexico extend beyond the dispute over the location of Texas's southwestern border?

General Winfield Scott leads American forces into Mexico City in September 1847.

▶ CRITICAL THINKING

Drawing Inferences What was the value of capturing Mexico City?

cede to give up by treaty

LESSON 4 REVIEW

Reviewing Vocabulary

1. *Determining Importance* Why did Mexico agree to cede so much territory to the United States?

2. *Speculating* Why do you think Mexico's president refused to meet with the special U.S. envoy sent to talk about purchasing California?

Using Your Notes

3. *Summarizing* Use the notes you completed during the lesson to write a short paragraph summarizing the war with Mexico.

Answering the Guiding Questions

4. *Interpreting* Why were some Americans against the idea of annexing Texas?

5. *Drawing Conclusions* Was the war with Mexico justified?

Writing Activity

6. **EXPOSITORY** Suppose that you are James K. Polk, the Democratic candidate for president in 1844. Write a speech in which you explain your platform.

Directions: On a separate sheet of paper, answer the questions below. Make sure you read carefully and answer all parts to the question.

Lesson Review

Lesson 1

1 *Making Generalizations* What sent overlanders west into unknown territory?

2 *Interpreting Significance* How did the westward migration affect Native Americans?

Lesson 2

3 *Determining Cause and Effect* How did secularizing the missions affect life in California?

4 *Identifying Central Issues* How was the 1837 rebellion in Santa Fe an example of the weakness of civil authority in Mexican territory?

Lesson 3

5 *Comparing and Contrasting* What was Stephen F. Austin's role as an *empresario,* and how did he renounce that role?

6 *Identifying Central Issues* What was the purpose of the conventions held in Texas in 1832 and 1833?

Lesson 4

7 *Determining Cause and Effect* What was the effect of President James Polk's promise to annex Texas, contest the Oregon Territory, and buy California?

8 *Determining Cause and Effect* What motivated President Polk to order troops to cross the Nueces River into Mexican territory?

21st Century Skills

9 **IDENTIFYING PERSPECTIVES AND DIFFERING INTERPRETATIONS** How did Native Americans treat emigrants at first, and how did their perspective change as overland traffic increased?

10 **DRAWING CONCLUSIONS** Why were there still so few Americans in California in 1845?

11 **UNDERSTANDING RELATIONSHIPS AMONG EVENTS** How did the Frémont rebellion in California likely affect the outcome of the war with Mexico?

Exploring the Essential Questions

12 *Determining Cause and Effect* Create a cause-and-effect diagram that identifies the causes of westward migration in the 1800s, as well the effects the migration had on the relationship between the United States and other countries and other people.

DBQ Document-Based Questions

Use the image to answer the following questions.

Lewis Cass of Michigan was the Democratic candidate for president in 1848. This political cartoon depicts Cass as the inheritor of President Polk's aggressive policies.

PRIMARY SOURCE

13 *Analyzing Primary Sources* Cass is saying "New Mexico, California, Chihuahua, Zacatecas, MEXICO, Peru, Yucatan, Cuba"—what does this mean?

14 *Drawing Conclusions* Why is the sword Cass holds labeled "Manifest Destiny"?

Extended-Response Question

15 *Comparing and Contrasting* What were the similarities and differences between the Texas war for independence and the war with Mexico?

Need Extra Help?

If You've Missed Question	1	2	3	4	5	6	7	8	9	10	11	12	13	14	15
Go to page	185	185	187	188	190	192	195	196	185	189	198	184	200	200	192

Sectional Conflict Intensifies

1848–1861

networks
There's More Online about the sectional conflict between the North and the South.

CHAPTER 8

ESSENTIAL QUESTION • *Was the Civil War inevitable?*

Lesson 1
Slavery and Western Expansion

Lesson 2
The Crisis Deepens

Lesson 3
The Union Dissolves

The Story Matters...

The United States was not yet 100 years old when it faced its greatest challenge: a sectional rift between the North and the South that previous compromises could not resolve. Despite the efforts of many who desired to preserve the Union, the young nation was thrown into turmoil by a bloody and terrible war.

◄ Harriet Tubman, herself once enslaved, helped thousands of people escape from slavery in the South through her work as a conductor on the Underground Railroad. The Underground Railroad was a network of escape routes that stretched from the Southern states' border to freedom in the North and in Canada.

PHOTO: American School/The Bridgeman Art Library/Getty Images

From the days of the Constitutional Convention until the late 1840s, people in the North and the South had made compromises to keep the nation united. These compromises did not end the practice of slavery, however, so abolitionists used the Underground Railroad network to secretly aid enslaved people who attempted to escape to freedom.

Step Into the Place

Read the quote and look at the information presented on the map.

 What dangers were faced by enslaved people who escaped and by the people who helped them, such as Levi Coffin and Harriet Tubman?

PRIMARY SOURCE

66 We knew not what night or what hour of the night we would be roused from slumber by a gentle rap at the door. . . . Outside in the cold or rain, there would be a two-horse wagon loaded with fugitives, perhaps the greater part of them women and children. I would invite them, in a low tone, to come in, and they would follow me into the darkened house without a word, for we knew not who might be watching and listening. 99

—from *Reminiscences of Levi Coffin: The Reputed President of the Underground Railroad*, 1880

PHOTOS: left page (t)North Wind Picture Archives/Alamy, (bl to br)detail/White House Collection/The White House Historical Association; right page (tl)The Granger Collection, New York, (bl to br) detail/White House Collection/The White House Historical Association

Step Into the Time

Choose an event from the time line and write a paragraph predicting the general social, political, and economic consequences that event may have had on the national discussion of slavery.

U.S. PRESIDENTS

UNITED STATES

WORLD

Polk 1845–1849

1848 War with Mexico ends

1849 Harriet Tubman escapes from slavery

Taylor 1849–1850

Fillmore 1850–1853

1850 Compromise of 1850 is adopted in an attempt to ease sectional tensions

1848

1850

1848 Revolutions occur in Vienna, Warsaw, Venice, Rome, Paris, and Milan

1851 Taiping Rebellion begins in China

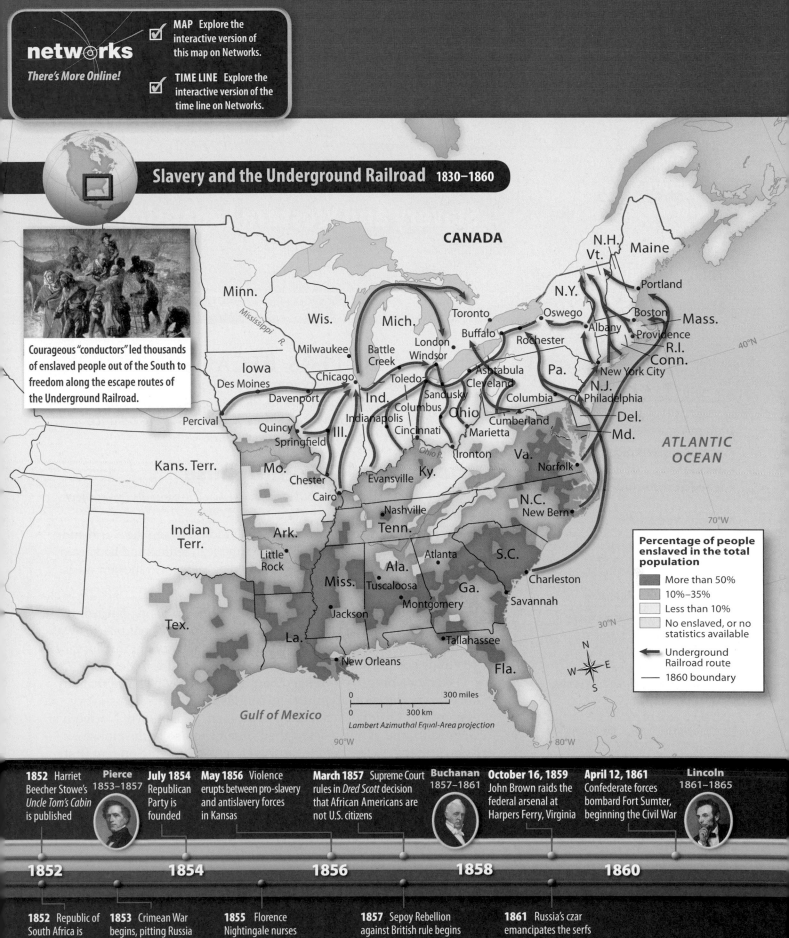

networks
There's More Online!

☑ MAP Explore the interactive version of this map on Networks.

☑ TIME LINE Explore the interactive version of the time line on Networks.

Slavery and the Underground Railroad 1830–1860

Courageous "conductors" led thousands of enslaved people out of the South to freedom along the escape routes of the Underground Railroad.

CANADA

N.H.
Vt. Maine
Minn.
Wis. Mich.
Milwaukee
Iowa
Des Moines
Toronto
Portland
N.Y.
Oswego Boston
Buffalo Albany Providence Mass.
Rochester R.I.
Conn.
Battle Creek London Windsor
Chicago Toledo Ashtabula Pa. New York City
Sandusky Cleveland N.J.
Ind. Columbus Columbia Philadelphia
Indianapolis Ohio Del.
Springfield Cincinnati Cumberland Md.
Quincy Marietta
Davenport
Percival
Kans. Terr.
Mo. Ohio R. Ironton Va. ATLANTIC
Chester Evansville Ky. Norfolk OCEAN
Cairo
Nashville N.C.
Indian Terr. Ark. Tenn. New Bern
Little Rock Atlanta S.C.
Ala.
Miss. Tuscaloosa Ga. Charleston
Jackson Montgomery Savannah
Tex.
La. Tallahassee
New Orleans Fla.
Gulf of Mexico

Mississippi R.

40°N
70°W
30°N
80°W
90°W

Percentage of people enslaved in the total population

- More than 50%
- 10%–35%
- Less than 10%
- No enslaved, or no statistics available
- ← Underground Railroad route
- — 1860 boundary

0   300 miles
0   300 km
Lambert Azimuthal Equal-Area projection

N
W E
S

1852 Harriet Beecher Stowe's *Uncle Tom's Cabin* is published

Pierce 1853–1857

July 1854 Republican Party is founded

May 1856 Violence erupts between pro-slavery and antislavery forces in Kansas

March 1857 Supreme Court rules in *Dred Scott* decision that African Americans are not U.S. citizens

Buchanan 1857–1861

October 16, 1859 John Brown raids the federal arsenal at Harpers Ferry, Virginia

April 12, 1861 Confederate forces bombard Fort Sumter, beginning the Civil War

Lincoln 1861–1865

1852 | **1854** | **1856** | **1858** | **1860**

1852 Republic of South Africa is established

1853 Crimean War begins, pitting Russia against Britain and Turkey

1855 Florence Nightingale nurses wounded soldiers in Crimea

1857 Sepoy Rebellion against British rule begins in India

1861 Russia's czar emancipates the serfs

networks

There's More Online!

☑ **BIOGRAPHY** John C. Calhoun

☑ **BIOGRAPHY** Harriet Beecher Stowe

☑ **BIOGRAPHY** Harriet Tubman

☑ **BIOGRAPHY** Daniel Webster

☑ **IMAGE** Underground Railroad

☑ **VIDEO** Slavery and Western Expansion

☑ **INTERACTIVE SELF-CHECK QUIZ**

Reading HELPDESK

Content Vocabulary

- **popular sovereignty**
- **secession**
- **transcontinental railroad**

Academic Vocabulary

- **survival**
- **perception**

TAKING NOTES: *Categorizing*

ACTIVITY As you read about slavery and western expansion, complete a graphic organizer similar to the one below by pairing the presidential candidates of 1848 with their positions on slavery in the West.

Candidate	Position

LESSON 1
Slavery and Western Expansion

ESSENTIAL QUESTION · *Was the Civil War inevitable?*

IT MATTERS BECAUSE

The spread of slavery into new territory became the overriding political issue of the 1850s. Admitting new slave states or new free states would upset the balance of power in the national government.

The Search for Compromise

GUIDING QUESTION *Did the North or the South achieve more of its goals in the Compromise of 1850? Why?*

The war with Mexico greatly increased tension between the North and the South. It had opened new lands to American settlers and had again raised the issue of whether slavery should be allowed in the new areas.

The Wilmot Proviso

In August 1846, Representative David Wilmot, a Democrat from Pennsylvania, proposed an addition to a war appropriations bill. Known as the Wilmot Proviso, the bill stated "neither slavery nor involuntary servitude shall ever exist" in any territory gained from Mexico.

Wilmot's proposal outraged Southerners. They believed that any antislavery decision about the territories would threaten slavery everywhere. Over fierce Southern opposition, a coalition of Northern Democrats and Whigs passed the Wilmot Proviso in the House of Representatives. The Senate, however, refused to vote on it at first. South Carolina senator John C. Calhoun prepared a series of resolutions to counter the Wilmot Proviso. He argued that because the states collectively owned the territories, Congress had no right to ban slavery there. Calhoun warned that "political revolution, anarchy, [and] civil war" would surely erupt if the North failed to heed Southern concerns. The Calhoun Resolutions never came to a vote, but they showed the growing anger of many Southerners.

Popular Sovereignty

The issue of slavery's expansion divided the nation along sectional lines. Many moderates began searching for a way to spare Congress from having to wrestle with the issue of slavery in the territories.

That's you Dad! more "FREE SOIL." We'll rat'em out yet. Long life to Davy Wilmot.

Free-Soil Democrats were nicknamed "Barn Burners," after the legendary Dutch farmer who burned down his barn to kill all the rats. They opposed Lewis Cass for president and supported the Wilmot Proviso.

▶ CRITICAL THINKING

1 *Analyzing Primary Sources* What is the main idea of this cartoon?

2 *Identifying Central Issues* Is the cartoon supporting free soil or popular sovereignty? How do you know?

Michigan senator Lewis Cass proposed that the citizens of each new territory should decide whether to permit slavery, an idea that came to be called **popular sovereignty.** This idea appealed to many in Congress. Many Northerners supported the idea, believing Northerners would settle most of the new territory and then ban slavery there.

The Free-Soil Party Emerges As the 1848 election approached, the Whigs chose a war hero, Zachary Taylor, to run for president. The Whigs in the North were divided, however. One group of Northern Whigs, known as Conscience Whigs, opposed slavery. They objected to Taylor because they believed he wanted to expand slavery westward. The decision to nominate Taylor led many Conscience Whigs to quit the party. They joined with antislavery Democrats from New York who were frustrated that their party had nominated Lewis Cass instead of Martin Van Buren. These two groups then joined members of the abolitionist Liberty Party to form the Free-Soil Party, which opposed slavery in the "free soil" of Western territories. The Free-Soil Party's slogan summed up their views: "Free Soil, Free Speech, Free Labor, and Free Men."

As a result, candidates from three parties campaigned for the presidency in 1848. Democrat Lewis Cass supported popular sovereignty, although this support was not mentioned in the South. His promise to veto the Wilmot Proviso, should Congress pass it, however, was often reported. Former president Martin Van Buren ran for the Free-Soil Party. General Zachary Taylor, a Whig, avoided the whole issue of slavery in the territories. On Election Day, the Free-Soilers split the Democratic vote in New York. As a result, Taylor won the state and enough electoral votes to win the election.

The Forty-Niners Head to California In 1848 gold was discovered in the foothills of the Sierra Nevada in California. By the end of 1849, more than 80,000 "Forty-Niners" had arrived to look for gold. The rise in California's population enabled it to apply for statehood. Congress had to decide whether it would be a free state or slave state. Although President Taylor was a slaveholder, he did not think slavery's **survival** depended on its expansion westward. He believed that the way to avoid a fight in Congress was to have Californians make their own decision about slavery. With Taylor's encouragement, California applied for admission as a free state in late 1849.

popular sovereignty the idea that people living in a territory had the right to decide by voting whether to allow slavery

survival the continuation of life or existence

As word of the discovery of gold in the Sierra Nevada spread around the world, people rushed to California hoping to strike it rich.

▶ CRITICAL THINKING
Drawing Conclusions How did the sudden influx of residents affect the California territory's status?

PHOTO: The Granger Collection, New York

The Great Debate Begins

If California became a free state, the slaveholding states would be in the minority in the Senate. Southerners feared that this might result in limits on slavery and states' rights. A few Southern leaders began to talk openly of **secession**—of taking their states out of the Union.

Clay's Proposal In early 1850, Senator Henry Clay of Kentucky tried to find a compromise that would enable California to join the Union. He proposed eight resolutions, listed in pairs, offering concessions to both sides. The first pair allowed California to enter as a free state, but the rest of the territory obtained from Mexico would have no restrictions on slavery. The second pair settled the boundary between New Mexico and Texas in favor of New Mexico. Texas would be compensated by having the federal government take on its debts. This would be good for the many Southerners who held Texas bonds.

Clay's third pair of resolutions outlawed the slave trade in the District of Columbia, but slavery itself would still be legal. The final pair of resolutions prohibited Congress from interfering with the interstate slave trade and called on Congress to pass a stronger fugitive slave act. These concessions were intended to reassure the South that after California joined the Union, the North would not use its control of the Senate to abolish slavery. Clay's proposals triggered a massive debate and would need the approval of Senator John C. Calhoun, a defender of the South's rights.

Calhoun's Response Calhoun believed that Northern agitation against slavery threatened to destroy the South. He demanded its equal rights in the territories, the return of fugitive slaves, and a guarantee of a balance of power between the sections. Otherwise, secession was the only honorable solution.

The Compromise of 1850

At first, Congress did not pass Clay's bill, in part because President Taylor opposed it. Then, Taylor died unexpectedly and was succeeded by Vice President Millard Fillmore, who supported the compromise.

Thirty-seven-year-old Stephen A. Douglas of Illinois took charge to resolve the crisis. He divided the large compromise initiative into several smaller bills. In this format, senators could abstain or vote against whatever parts they disliked while supporting the rest. By fall, Congress had passed all the parts of the original proposal. President Fillmore also had signed them into law.

✔ **PROGRESS CHECK**

Summarizing How did the California gold rush affect the issue of slavery?

Analyzing PRIMARY SOURCES

Webster on Secession

"I wish to speak to-day, not as a Massachusetts man, nor as a northern man, but as an American. . . . I speak to-day for the preservation of the Union. 'Hear me for my cause'. . . . There can be no such thing as a peaceable secession. Peaceable secession is an utter impossibility. . . . I see as plainly as I see the sun in heaven what that disruption itself must produce; I see that it must produce war, and such a war as I will not describe."

—Daniel Webster, from *Appendix to the Congressional Globe*, May 7, 1850

DBQ **DRAWING INFERENCES**

Why do you think Webster says that he "will not describe" the war?

This painting depicts Henry Clay, Daniel Webster, John Calhoun, and others debating the slavery issue and California's entry into the Union.

▶ **CRITICAL THINKING**
Drawing Inferences Why do you think Clay wanted to offer something to both sides of the slavery debate?

The Fugitive Slave Act

GUIDING QUESTION *Under what circumstances, if any, do you believe citizens should disobey a law?*

Henry Clay had conceived of the Fugitive Slave Act of 1850 to benefit slaveholders. It actually hurt the Southern cause, however, by creating hostility toward slavery among Northerners who had been indifferent.

Northern Resistance

Under the Fugitive Slave Act, any African American could be accused of being a runaway and captured. The accused then would be brought before a federal commissioner. Unable to testify, the accused had no way to prove his or her case. A sworn statement asserting that the captive had escaped or testimony from white witnesses was all a court needed to order the person sent south. Furthermore, commissioners had an incentive to rule in favor of the slaveholder. They received a $10 fee if they sided with the slaveholder, but only $5 if the decision went the other way. A person who refused to assist slave catchers capture fugitives could be jailed.

Newspaper accounts of the unjust seizure of African Americans fueled the fire. Many Northerners were angered by such seizures and by the requirement that ordinary citizens help capture runaways. This provision drove many into action. Frederick Douglass emphasized this part of the law in his speeches. He asked the audience if they would turn a runaway over to the "pursuing bloodhounds." "No!" the crowd roared.

The Underground Railroad

Although the Fugitive Slave Act included heavy penalties for helping a runaway, whites and free African Americans continued their work with the Underground Railroad. This informal system helped thousands of people escape slavery. Members, called "conductors," transported runaways in secret and saw them to freedom in the Northern states or in Canada.

The most famous "conductor" was Harriet Tubman, herself a runaway. She risked many trips to the South, even after slaveholders offered a large reward for her capture. A Quaker abolitionist, Levi Coffin, became the most famous "stationmaster." It is estimated that he and his wife, Catherine, sheltered and protected some 3,300 African Americans during their escape to freedom.

Uncle Tom's Cabin

Harriet Beecher Stowe had seen slavery firsthand when she lived in Cincinnati, Ohio. A letter from her sister Isabella describing slave catchers dragging off African Americans led her to write *Uncle Tom's Cabin*. "Now Hattie," Isabella wrote, "if I could use a pen as you can, I would write something that would make this whole nation feel what an accursed thing slavery is."

After running as a newspaper serial, *Uncle Tom's Cabin* came out as a book in 1852. The book changed Northern **perceptions** of African Americans and slavery. Theatrical dramatizations of the novel reached an even wider audience than the novel, which eventually sold millions of copies. Southerners tried unsuccessfully to have the novel banned. They attacked its portrayal of slavery, accusing Stowe of writing "distortions" and "falsehoods." The book's dramatic impact on public opinion added to the sectional tensions leading up to the Civil War.

✔ **PROGRESS CHECK**

Examining What was an unintended consequence of the Fugitive Slave Act?

The Fugitive Slave Act allowed slave catchers to seize African Americans they accused of having escaped slavery.

▶ **CRITICAL THINKING**
Drawing Inferences What effect would the actions of the slave catchers have had on Northerners' opinions of slaveholders?

perception comprehension or understanding influenced by observation, interpretation, and attitude

The Kansas-Nebraska Act

GUIDING QUESTION *Why did Kansas become a battleground between pro-slavery and antislavery groups?*

The opening of Oregon to settlement and the admission of California to the Union convinced Americans that a **transcontinental railroad** should be built to connect the West Coast to the rest of the country. The railroad would promote settlement and growth in the territories along the route.

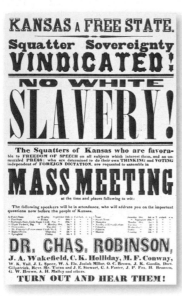

transcontinental railroad
a railway system extending across the continent

Debating the Route of the Transcontinental Railroad

The choice of the railroad's eastern starting point became a new issue in the sectional conflict. Two proposed routes were a northern route from Chicago and a southern route from New Orleans.

The southern route ran through a small section of northern Mexico. Secretary of War Jefferson Davis, a supporter of the South's interests, convinced President Franklin Pierce to buy this land. Pierce sent James Gadsden to Mexico to pay $10 million for a 30,000-square-mile strip of land that became known as the Gadsden Purchase.

Senator Stephen A. Douglas of Illinois supported the northern route. He knew that the route required Congress to organize the unsettled lands west of Missouri and Iowa. He proposed a bill to name the lands the territory of Nebraska. Southern senators said that if he wanted Nebraska organized, the Missouri Compromise must be repealed.

Repealing the Missouri Compromise

Douglas wanted to open the northern Great Plains to settlement. He devised a bill that proposed to undo the Missouri Compromise and allow slavery in the region. He also proposed dividing the region into two territories: Nebraska in the north, adjacent to the free state of Iowa, and Kansas in the south, west of the slave state of Missouri. This looked like Nebraska was intended to be free territory, while Kansas was intended for slavery. Douglas's bill outraged Northern Democrats, Whigs, Free-Soilers, and antislavery Democrats. Despite this opposition, the Kansas-Nebraska Act was passed in May 1854.

"Bleeding Kansas"

Kansas became the first battleground between those favoring the extension of slavery and those opposing it. Since eastern Kansas offered the same climate and rich soil as the slave state of Missouri, settlers moving there from Missouri were likely to bring enslaved persons with them. Northerners hurried into the territory in hopes of creating an antislavery majority. They could count on the support of the New England Emigrant Aid Company, which recruited and outfitted antislavery settlers bound for Kansas. With supplies and rifles, antislavery Northerners headed to the new territory.

Pro-slavery senator David Atchison of Missouri responded by calling on men from his state to go to Kansas. In 1855 thousands of Missourians—called "border ruffians" in the press—voted illegally in Kansas, helping to elect a pro-slavery legislature. Antislavery settlers then held a convention in Topeka and drafted their own constitution that banned slavery. By early 1856, Kansas had two territorial governments.

On May 21, 1856, border ruffians attacked the town of Lawrence, a stronghold of antislavery settlers. The attackers wrecked newspaper presses, plundered shops and homes, and burned a hotel and the home of the elected free-state governor. "Bleeding Kansas," as newspapers dubbed the territory, became the scene of a territorial civil war between pro-slavery and antislavery settlers. By the end of 1856, about 200 people had died in the fighting and some $2 million worth of property had been destroyed.

This poster advertises a series of meetings to rally support for keeping slavery out of Kansas. Some leaders of the "free soil" movement argued that if African American slavery were allowed to continue to spread, the enslavement of white laborers, or "white slavery," would be next.

▶ **CRITICAL THINKING**

Drawing Inferences What does the poster mean by "squatter sovereignty"?

During negotiations over the Kansas-Nebraska Act, Representative Preston Brooks beat Senator Charles Sumner with his cane for criticizing Brooks's cousin, Senator Andrew Butler. While many Northerners were outraged by the incident, Southerners voiced their approval by sending canes to Brooks.

▶ **CRITICAL THINKING**

1 *Analyzing Primary Sources* Which side do you think the cartoonist favored—the North or the South? Explain your response.

2 *Drawing Conclusions* How might reactions to this incident be different in the North and in the South?

The Caning of Charles Sumner

Meanwhile, the Senate hotly debated the future of the Western territories. On May 22, 1856, Massachusetts senator Charles Sumner, a fiery abolitionist, gave a speech accusing pro-slavery senators of forcing Kansas into the ranks of slave states. He singled out Senator Andrew P. Butler of South Carolina, saying Butler had "chosen a mistress . . . the harlot, Slavery."

Several days later, Butler's second cousin, Representative Preston Brooks, approached Sumner at his desk in the Senate chamber. He shouted that Sumner's speech had been "a libel on South Carolina, and Mr. Butler, who is a relative of mine," and then raised a gold-handled cane and beat Sumner savagely, leaving the senator severely injured and bleeding on the floor.

Many Southerners considered Brooks to be a hero. Shocked by the attack and outraged by the flood of Southern support for Brooks, Northerners strengthened their determination to resist the "barbarism of slavery." One New York clergyman confided in his journal that "no way is left for the North, but to strike back, or be slaves."

✓ **PROGRESS CHECK**

Describing Why did Stephen A. Douglas propose repealing the Missouri Compromise?

PHOTO: Bettmann/CORBIS

LESSON 1 REVIEW

Reviewing Vocabulary

1. *Analyzing* Why was secession discussed in the debate about California entering the Union?

2. *Paraphrasing* In your own words, define popular sovereignty.

Using Your Notes

3. *Summarizing* Review your notes and write a paragraph about the presidential candidates in 1848 and their stance on issues of the time.

Answering the Guiding Questions

4. *Comparing and Contrasting* Did the North or the South achieve more of its goals in the Compromise of 1850? Why?

5. *Analyzing Ethical Issues* Under what circumstances, if any, do you believe citizens should disobey a law?

6. *Explaining* Why did Kansas become a battleground between pro-slavery and antislavery groups?

Writing Activity

7. PERSUASIVE Take on the role of a reporter for a Northern or Southern newspaper in 1846. Write an article that explains the Wilmot Proviso and provide a regional perspective of the reporter you have chosen.

networks

There's More Online!

☑ **BIOGRAPHY** John Brown

☑ **MAP** Presidential Election of 1856

☑ **MAP** United States, 1819–1854

☑ **PRIMARY SOURCE** Excerpts from *Dred Scott v. Sandford*

☑ **VIDEO** The Crisis Deepens

☑ **INTERACTIVE SELF-CHECK QUIZ**

LESSON 2
The Crisis Deepens

ESSENTIAL QUESTION · *Was the Civil War inevitable?*

Reading **HELP**DESK

Content Vocabulary
- **referendum**
- **insurrection**

Academic Vocabulary
- **correspondence**
- **formulate**

TAKING NOTES: *Categorizing*

ACTIVITY As you read about the North-South split, complete a graphic organizer like the one below to categorize events as executive, legislative, judicial, or nongovernmental.

Executive	
Legislative	
Judicial	
Nongovernmental	

IT MATTERS BECAUSE

The controversy over slavery accelerated the breakdown of the major political parties and the formation of new ones. Friction intensified until the North and the South became unable to compromise any further.

Political Realignments of the 1850s

GUIDING QUESTION *What events led to the creation of the Republican Party?*

The Kansas-Nebraska Act finally split the Whig Party between the pro-slavery Southern Whigs and the antislavery Northern Whigs. Every Northern Whig in Congress had voted against the bill, while most Southern Whigs had voted for it. "We Whigs of the North," wrote one member from Connecticut, "are unalterably determined never to have even the slightest political **correspondence** or connexion" with the Southern Whigs.

Anger over the Kansas-Nebraska Act convinced former Whigs, members of the Free-Soil Party, and a few antislavery Democrats to work together during the congressional elections of 1854. This coalition adopted the name "Republican" for the new party.

New Parties Arise

In July 1854 the Republican Party was officially organized. Although Republicans did not agree on whether slavery should be abolished in the Southern states, they did agree that it had to be kept out of the territories. Many Northern voters seemed to agree, and the Republicans and other antislavery parties made great strides in the 1854 elections.

At the same time, Northern anger against the Democrats enabled the American Party—also known as the Know-Nothings—to make gains, particularly in the Northeast. The nativist Know-Nothings opposed immigration, especially of Catholics. Prejudice and fear of immigrants helped the American Party win many seats in Congress and state legislatures in 1854. Soon, however, the Know-Nothings suffered the same fate as the Whigs and split along sectional lines. Before long, the Republican Party absorbed many Northern Know-Nothings.

The Election of 1856

To gain wide support in the 1856 campaign, Republicans nominated John C. Frémont, a famous Western explorer. Frémont had spoken in favor of Kansas becoming a free state. He had little political experience but also no embarrassing record to defend.

The Democrats nominated James Buchanan. He had served in Congress for over 20 years and had been the American ambassador to Russia and then to Great Britain. Buchanan was in Britain during the debate over the Kansas-Nebraska Act and had not taken a stand on the issue. His record in Congress, however, showed that he believed the best way to save the Union was to make concessions to the South.

The American Party tried to reunite its Northern and Southern members at its convention, but most of the Northern delegates walked out when the party refused to call for the repeal of the Kansas-Nebraska Act. Hoping to attract the vote of former Whigs, the remaining delegates then chose former president Millard Fillmore to represent the American Party.

The national campaign was really two separate contests: Buchanan against Frémont in the North, and Buchanan against Fillmore in the South. Buchanan had solid support in the South and needed only his home state of Pennsylvania and one other state to win the presidency. Democrats campaigned on the idea that only Buchanan could save the Union and that the election of Frémont would cause the South to secede. When the votes were counted, Buchanan had won.

The *Dred Scott* Decision

In his March 1857 Inaugural Address, James Buchanan suggested that the nation let the Supreme Court decide the question of slavery in the territories. Most people who listened to the address did not know that Buchanan had been in contact with members of the Supreme Court and therefore knew that an important ruling on this issue was imminent.

Many Southern members of Congress had quietly pressured the Supreme Court justices to issue a ruling on slavery in the territories. They expected the Southern majority on the Court to rule in favor of the South's position. They were not disappointed. Two days after the inauguration, the Court released its opinion in the case of *Dred Scott* v. *Sandford*.

Dred Scott was an enslaved man whose Missouri slaveholder had taken him to live in free territory and then returned with Scott to Missouri. Assisted by abolitionists, Scott sued to end his slavery, arguing that the time he had spent in free territory meant that he was free. Scott's case went all the way to the Supreme Court.

On March 6, 1857, Chief Justice Roger B. Taney delivered the majority opinion in the case. Taney ruled against Scott because, he claimed, African Americans were not citizens and therefore could not sue in the courts. Taney then addressed the Missouri Compromise's ban on slavery in territory north of Missouri's southern border:

This election campaign poster from 1856 shows John C. Frémont and William L. Dayton, the first Republican Party candidates for president and vice president.

▶ **CRITICAL THINKING**
Analyzing Primary Sources How does the poster portray the Republican Party?

correspondence a close resemblance or connection

Chief Justice Roger B. Taney wrote the majority opinion in the *Dred Scott* v. *Sandford* case. The Court's decision declared Congress could not ban slavery in the territories.

▶ **CRITICAL THINKING**
Interpreting Significance What was the effect of the Court's decision on the growing sectional crisis? Explain.

PRIMARY SOURCE

❝[I]t is the opinion of the court that the act of Congress which prohibited a citizen from holding and owning [enslaved persons] in the territory of the United States north of the line therein mentioned, is not warranted by the Constitution and is therefore void.❞

—from *Dred Scott* v. *Sandford*, 1857

Instead of removing the issue of slavery in the territories from politics, the *Dred Scott* decision itself became a political issue that further intensified the sectional conflict. The Supreme Court had said that the federal government could not prohibit slavery in the territories. Free soil, one of the basic ideas uniting Republicans, was unconstitutional.

Southerners cheered the decision, but Republicans condemned it and claimed it was not binding. They argued that it was an *obiter dictum,* an incidental opinion not called for by the circumstances of the case. Many African Americans publicly declared contempt for any government that could produce such an edict. Among them was Philadelphia activist Robert Purvis, who declared in 1857:

PRIMARY SOURCE

❝Mr. Chairman, look at the facts—here, in a country with a sublimity of impudence that knows no parallel, setting itself up before the world as a *free country, a land of liberty!, 'the land of the free,* and the *home of the brave,'* the *'freest country in all the world!'* . . . and yet here are millions of men and women groaning under a bondage the like of which the world has never seen—bought and sold, whipped, manacled, killed all the day long.❞

—quoted in *Witness for Freedom,* 1993

☑ **PROGRESS CHECK**

Explaining What laws, political developments, and court decisions contributed to the split between the North and the South during this time?

🏛 ANALYZING SUPREME COURT CASES

DRED SCOTT v. *SANDFORD,* 1857

Background of the Case

Between 1833 and 1843, enslaved African American Dred Scott and his wife Harriet had lived in the free state of Illinois and in the part of the Louisiana Territory that was considered free under the Missouri Compromise. When he was returned to Missouri, Scott sued his slaveholder, based on the idea that he was free because he had lived in free areas, and won. That decision was reversed by the Missouri Supreme Court and Scott's case went to the U.S. Supreme Court.

How the Court Ruled

The 7-2 decision enraged many Northerners and delighted many in the South. In his lengthy opinion for the Court, Chief Justice Roger B. Taney ruled that African Americans—enslaved or free—were not citizens of the United States. Thus, Scott had no rights under the Constitution and no right to sue in federal court. Further, Taney decreed that Congress did not have the authority to ban slavery in the territories. Thus, the Missouri Compromise was unconstitutional.

Chief Justice Roger B. Taney delivered the Supreme Court's ruling in the **Dred Scott** *case. The decision made Scott and his family a topic for the nation's press.*

▶ **CRITICAL THINKING**

❶ *Identifying Central Issues* Why was the Missouri Compromise declared unconstitutional?

❷ *Interpreting Significance* Why was the decision in *Dred Scott* v. *Sandford* so significant?

PHOTO: Library of Congress

The Emergence of Abraham Lincoln

GUIDING QUESTION *How did Lincoln and the Republican Party benefit from the Lincoln-Douglas debates?*

After losing in 1856, Republicans needed a strong candidate to compete in the 1860 presidential election. They also knew that Senator Stephen Douglas of Illinois was a rising star in the Democratic Party and a Northerner whom the South might trust with the presidency in order to stop a Republican victory. To win, Republicans needed a candidate who could defeat Douglas in his home state of Illinois. They also needed Douglas to take unpopular positions on the issues under consideration.

Kansas's Constitution

Douglas began to lose popularity in the South due to events in Kansas. Hoping to end the troubles there, President Buchanan urged the territory to apply for statehood. The pro-slavery legislature scheduled an election for delegates to a constitutional convention, but antislavery Kansans boycotted it, claiming it was rigged. The resulting constitution, drafted in the town of Lecompton in 1857, legalized slavery in the territory.

Each side then held its own **referendum** on the Lecompton constitution. Antislavery forces voted it down and pro-slavery forces approved it. Buchanan accepted the pro-slavery vote and asked Congress to admit Kansas as a slave state. The Senate quickly voted to accept the constitution, but the House blocked it. Southern leaders were stunned when even Stephen Douglas refused to support them. Many had thought he understood the South's concerns.

Southern leaders in Congress agreed to allow Kansas to hold another constitutional referendum. They expected to win because rejecting the constitution would delay statehood for at least two more years. However, Kansans overwhelmingly rejected the Lecompton constitution. They did not want slavery in their state. Kansas did not become a state until 1861.

Lincoln and Douglas

In 1858 Illinois Republicans chose Abraham Lincoln to run for the U.S. Senate against Douglas, the Democratic incumbent. Lincoln launched his campaign with a memorable speech, in which he declared:

PRIMARY SOURCE

❝'A house divided against itself cannot stand.' I believe this government cannot endure, permanently half *slave* and half *free*. I do not expect the Union to be *dissolved*—I do not expect the house to *fall*—but I *do* expect it will cease to be divided. It will become *all* one thing, or *all* the other.❞
—from a speech delivered at Springfield, Illinois, June 16, 1858

The nationally prominent Douglas regularly drew large crowds on the campaign trail. Seeking to overcome Douglas's fame, Lincoln proposed a series of debates between the candidates, which would expose him to larger audiences than he could attract on his own. Douglas accepted.

Although not an abolitionist, Lincoln believed slavery to be morally wrong and opposed its spread into the territories. Douglas, by contrast, supported popular sovereignty. During a debate in Freeport, Illinois, Lincoln asked Douglas if the people of a territory could legally exclude slavery before achieving statehood. If Douglas said yes, he would appear to be opposing the *Dred Scott* ruling, which would cost him Southern support. If he said no, it would make it seem as if he had abandoned popular sovereignty, the principle on which he had built his following in the North.

Douglas tried to avoid the dilemma, **formulating** an answer that became known as the Freeport Doctrine. He said that he accepted the *Dred Scott* ruling.

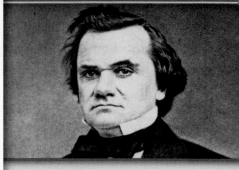

BIOGRAPHY

Stephen Douglas (1813–1861)

As a young man of 20, Stephen Douglas went to Illinois, where he rose quickly in politics. Nicknamed "The Little Giant" due to his short stature and solid build, he was a hard worker who had a way with words. During the 1858 debates in the Senate race against Abraham Lincoln, he set forth the "Freeport Doctrine." Although popular sovereignty had been struck down as unconstitutional, Douglas argued that territories could keep slavery out by passing local laws that were unsupportive of slavery. In 1860 he lost to Lincoln in the presidential race, but Douglas continued to work to protect the Union until his early death in 1861.

▶ **CRITICAL THINKING**
Making Inferences How do you think Douglas views the role of local government?

referendum the practice of letting voters accept or reject measures proposed by the legislature

formulate to prepare or devise according to a systematized statement or formula

He added, however, that people could still keep slavery out by refusing to pass the laws needed to regulate and enforce it. His response angered Southerners.

Lincoln attacked Douglas's claim that he "cared not" whether Kansans voted for or against slavery, declaring:

PRIMARY SOURCE

❝Has any thing ever threatened the existence of this Union save and except this very institution of Slavery? What is it that we hold most dear amongst us? Our own liberty and prosperity. What has ever threatened our liberty and prosperity save and except this institution of Slavery? If this is true, how do you propose to improve the condition of things by enlarging Slavery—by spreading it out and making it bigger? . . . That is no proper way of treating what you regard a wrong.❞

—from a speech delivered at Alton, Illinois, October 15, 1858

During the 1858 Senate campaign, Lincoln and Douglas met several times to debate issues. This image shows them in Charleston, Illinois.

▶ **CRITICAL THINKING**
Drawing Conclusions What did Lincoln gain from participating in the debates?

Although Douglas won the Senate election, Lincoln used the debates to make clear the principles of the Republican Party. He stepped onto the national stage as a man of eloquence and insight.

✓ **PROGRESS CHECK**

Examining What were the positions of Stephen Douglas and Abraham Lincoln on slavery in the territories?

John Brown's Raid

GUIDING QUESTION *How was John Brown's revolt similar to or different from a previous time in American history when citizens revolted against an unfair government?*

In 1859 a fervent abolitionist, John Brown, took direct action against slavery. He had developed a plan to seize the federal arsenal at Harpers Ferry, Virginia (today in West Virginia), free and arm the enslaved people in the area, and begin an **insurrection** against slaveholders.

On the night of October 16, 1859, Brown and 18 followers seized the arsenal. Soon, however, they were facing a contingent of U.S. Marines. Less than 36 hours after it had begun, Brown's attempt to start a slave insurrection ended with his capture. A Virginia court sentenced him to death. In his last words to the court, Brown repented nothing:

insurrection an act of rebellion against the established government

PRIMARY SOURCE

❝I believe that to have interfered as I have done, as I have always freely admitted I have done, in behalf of [God's] despised poor, was not wrong, but right. Now, if it is deemed necessary that I should forfeit my life for the furtherance of the ends of justice, and mingle my blood . . . with the blood of millions in this slave country whose rights are disregarded by wicked, cruel and unjust enactments—I submit: so let it be done.❞

—from *The Life and Letters of Captain John Brown*, 1861

On December 2, the day of his execution, Brown handed one of his jailers a prophetic note: "I, John Brown, am now quite certain that the crimes of this guilty land will never be purged away but with blood. I had, as I now think, vainly flattered myself that without very much bloodshed it might be done."

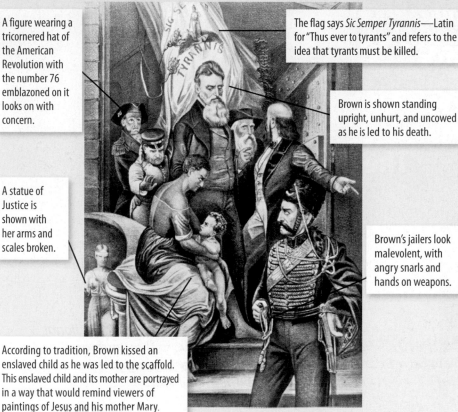

A figure wearing a tricornered hat of the American Revolution with the number 76 emblazoned on it looks on with concern.

The flag says *Sic Semper Tyrannis*—Latin for "Thus ever to tyrants" and refers to the idea that tyrants must be killed.

Brown is shown standing upright, unhurt, and uncowed as he is led to his death.

A statue of Justice is shown with her arms and scales broken.

Brown's jailers look malevolent, with angry snarls and hands on weapons.

According to tradition, Brown kissed an enslaved child as he was led to the scaffold. This enslaved child and its mother are portrayed in a way that would remind viewers of paintings of Jesus and his mother Mary.

Printed in the North in 1863, in the middle of the Civil War, this lithograph image depicts John Brown being led to his execution. The symbols in the image show how John Brown had become a martyr to many Northerners.

▶ **CRITICAL THINKING**

1 *Identifying Central Issues*
How is John Brown depicted in this image?

2 *Drawing Conclusions*
Why do you think that the statue of Justice is depicted as broken?

Many Northerners viewed Brown as a martyr for a noble cause. The execution, Henry David Thoreau predicted, would strengthen abolitionist feeling in the North. "He is not Old Brown any longer," Thoreau declared, "he is an angel of light."

For most Southerners, however, Brown's raid offered all the proof they needed that Northerners were actively plotting the murder of slaveholders. "Defend yourselves!" cried Georgia senator Robert Toombs. "The enemy is at your door."

☑ **PROGRESS CHECK**

Evaluating In what ways might a Northerner and a Southerner view John Brown's raid differently?

LESSON 2 REVIEW

Reviewing Vocabulary

1. *Identifying Cause and Effect* What might cause an insurrection?

2. *Defining* Who votes in a referendum?

Using Your Notes

3. *Summarizing* Use your notes to write a short paragraph explaining the events that increased the North-South split.

Answering the Guiding Questions

4. *Identifying* What events led to the creation of the Republican Party?

5. *Describing* How did Lincoln and the Republican Party benefit from the Lincoln-Douglas debates?

6. *Comparing and Contrasting* How was John Brown's revolt similar to or different from a previous time in American history when citizens revolted against an unfair government?

Writing Activity

7. **EXPOSITORY** Suppose that you have just read the Supreme Court's ruling in the *Dred Scott* case. Write a letter to the editor explaining your reaction to the decision and its effect on the issue of slavery.

networks

There's More Online!

☑ **BIOGRAPHY** Jefferson Davis

☑ **BIOGRAPHY** Abraham Lincoln

☑ **MAP** Presidential Election of 1860

☑ **VIDEO** The Union Dissolves

☑ **INTERACTIVE SELF-CHECK QUIZ**

LESSON 3
The Union Dissolves

ESSENTIAL QUESTION · *Was the Civil War inevitable?*

Reading **HELP**DESK

Content Vocabulary
• martial law

Academic Vocabulary
• commitment
• impose

TAKING NOTES: *Outlining*

ACTIVITY As you read, use the major headings of this lesson to outline the events that led to the U.S. Civil War.

```
        The Union Dissolves
I. The Election of 1860
   A.
   B.
   C.
   D.
II.
```

IT MATTERS BECAUSE

All efforts at compromise failed to end the sectional differences over slavery between the North and the South. The outcome of the 1860 election triggered a showdown and the first shots of the Civil War.

The Election of 1860

GUIDING QUESTION *How did the South react to the election of a Republican president?*

John Brown's raid on Harpers Ferry was a turning point for the South. Southerners were worried by the idea that Northerners would try to arm enslaved people and encourage them to rebel. Although Republican leaders quickly denounced Brown's raid, many Southerners blamed Republicans and Brown because they both opposed slavery. As one Atlanta newspaper noted: "We regard every man in our midst an enemy to the institutions of the South who does not boldly declare that he believes African slavery to be a social, moral, and political blessing."

The Democrats Split

In April 1860, with the South in an uproar, Democrats held their convention in Charleston, South Carolina, to choose their nominee for president. The debate over slavery in the territories finally tore apart the Democratic Party. Northern delegates wanted to support popular sovereignty, while Southern delegates wanted the party to uphold the *Dred Scott* decision. They also wanted to endorse a federal slave code for the territories. Stephen A. Douglas was not able to get the votes needed to be nominated for president, but neither was anyone else.

In June 1860, the Democrats met again. Douglas's supporters in the South had organized delegations to ensure his nomination. The original Southern delegations objected to this and walked out. The remaining Democrats then chose Douglas to run for president.

The Southern Democrats who had walked out organized their own convention. They nominated the current vice president,

PHOTO: Library of Congress

John C. Breckinridge of Kentucky. Breckinridge supported the *Dred Scott* decision and agreed to endorse a federal slave code for the territories.

This split improved the Republicans' chances to win the election. Some Southerners may have intended this, hoping that a Republican win would convince Southern states to secede. Others, including many former Whigs, feared for the Union. They created the Constitutional Union Party, and campaigned on a position of upholding both the Constitution and the Union.

Lincoln Is Elected

With no chance of winning electoral votes in the South, the Republican candidate had to win nearly all of the North. To better their chances, the Republicans passed over Senator William Seward of New York, whom some regarded as an extremist. Instead, they nominated Abraham Lincoln, whose debates with Douglas had made him very popular in the North.

During the campaign, Republicans tried to convince voters they were more than just an antislavery party. They reaffirmed the right of Southern states to preserve slavery within their borders. Republicans also supported higher tariffs, a new homestead law, and the transcontinental railroad.

It was the threat to slavery, however, that angered many Southerners. Yet, with Democratic votes split between Douglas and Breckinridge, Lincoln won the election anyway. The survival of Southern society and culture seemed to be at stake. For many Southerners, there was no choice now but to secede.

Secession Begins

The dissolution of the Union began with South Carolina. By February 1, 1861, six more states in the Lower South—Mississippi, Florida, Alabama, Georgia, Louisiana, and Texas—had voted to secede. Meanwhile, Congress tried to find a compromise to save the Union. Ignoring those efforts, the secessionists seized all federal property in their states, including arsenals and forts. Only Fort Sumter in Charleston Harbor, Fort Pickens in Pensacola Harbor, and a few islands off the coast of Florida remained out of their control.

In an attempt to reach a compromise, Senator John J. Crittenden of Kentucky proposed several constitutional amendments. One would guarantee slavery where it already existed. Another would reinstate the Missouri Compromise line, extending it to the border of California.

GEOGRAPHY CONNECTION

The slavery issue split the Democratic Party, and the election of 1860 became a four-way race.

1 PLACES AND REGIONS
How does the map show that Lincoln was a sectional candidate?

2 THE USES OF GEOGRAPHY
How did the split in the Democratic Party help Lincoln win the election?

Presidential Election of 1860

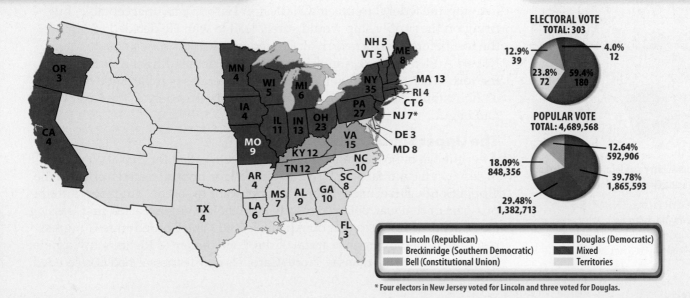

ELECTORAL VOTE
TOTAL: 303

12.9% 39
4.0% 12
23.8% 72
59.4% 180

POPULAR VOTE
TOTAL: 4,689,568

12.64% 592,906
18.09% 848,356
39.78% 1,865,593
29.48% 1,382,713

Lincoln (Republican)
Breckinridge (Southern Democratic)
Bell (Constitutional Union)
Douglas (Democratic)
Mixed
Territories

* Four electors in New Jersey voted for Lincoln and three voted for Douglas.

OR 3 · CA 4 · MN 4 · WI 5 · MI 6 · IA 4 · IL 11 · IN 13 · OH 23 · MO 9 · KY 12 · TN 12 · AR 4 · MS 7 · AL 9 · GA 10 · LA 6 · TX 4 · FL 3 · SC 8 · NC 10 · VA 15 · MD 8 · DE 3 · NJ 7* · PA 27 · NY 35 · CT 6 · RI 4 · MA 13 · ME 8 · NH 5 · VT 5

Some historians argue that most secessionists believed in the constitutionality of their actions. They contend that secessionists believed they represented traditional rights and interpretation of the relationship between the states and the national government. Slavery may have been the fundamental issue that divided the North and the South, but many Southerners felt that the North had violated the compact embodied by the Constitution. Secession may have amounted to a defensive counterrevolution against Republican hostilities toward the South's interests. Under this way of thinking, when the South lost the war, states' rights lost with it.

commitment an agreement or pledge to do something in the future

Fort Sumter was located in the harbor outside Charleston, South Carolina.

▶ **CRITICAL THINKING**
Drawing Inferences What advantage would the North have if it were able to defend and keep Fort Sumter?

This would prohibit slavery north of the line and would protect slavery south of it. Lincoln asked congressional Republicans to stand firm, and Crittenden's Compromise did not pass. Virginia then held a peace conference. None of the secessionist states attended. The plan they developed was defeated in Congress.

Founding the Confederacy

In February 1861, the seceding states met in Montgomery, Alabama. They declared themselves to be a new nation—the Confederate States of America, or the Confederacy, as it became known. They drafted a constitution based largely on the U.S. Constitution, but with some important changes. It declared that each state was independent and guaranteed slavery in Confederate territory. It banned protective tariffs and the international importation of slaves. It also limited the presidency to a single six-year term. The delegates chose Jefferson Davis, a former senator from Mississippi, as president.

☑ **PROGRESS CHECK**

Identifying How did the split of the Democratic Party affect the outcome of the election of 1860?

The Civil War Begins

GUIDING QUESTION *Do you think it is ever appropriate for the government to declare martial law?*

In his Inaugural Address on March 4, 1861, Lincoln spoke directly to the seceding states. He repeated his **commitment** not to interfere with slavery where it existed. Yet he insisted that "the Union of these States is perpetual." Lincoln did not threaten the seceded states, but he said he intended to "hold, occupy, and possess" federal property in those states. Lincoln also encouraged reconciliation:

PRIMARY SOURCE

❝In *your* hands, my dissatisfied countrymen, and not in *mine* is the momentous issue of civil war. The government will not assail *you*. You can have no conflict, without yourselves being the aggressors. . . .
. . . We are not enemies, but friends. We must not be enemies. Though passion may have strained, it must not break our bonds of affection.❞

—from Lincoln's First Inaugural Address, March 4, 1861

Fort Sumter Falls

In April, Lincoln announced that he would send a ship to resupply Fort Sumter. Confederate president Jefferson Davis faced a difficult decision. Leaving the federal troops in Charleston Harbor was unacceptable, but firing on the supply ship would surely lead to war. He decided to capture the fort before the ship's arrival. Confederate leaders sent a note to Major Robert Anderson, Fort Sumter's commander, demanding the surrender of the fort. When they were refused, the Confederates bombarded the fort for 33 hours until Anderson and his men finally surrendered. The Civil War had begun.

The Upper South Secedes

After the fall of Fort Sumter, President Lincoln called for 75,000 volunteers to serve in the military for 90 days. The call for troops created a crisis in the Upper South. Here, many people did not want to secede, but faced with the prospect of civil war, believed they had no choice. Virginia acted first, passing an Ordinance of Secession on April 17, 1861. The Confederate Congress responded by moving the capital of the Confederacy to Richmond, Virginia. By early June 1861, Arkansas, North Carolina, and Tennessee had also seceded.

Hanging On to the Border States

With the Upper South states having seceded, Lincoln was determined to keep the slaveholding border states in the Union. Delaware seemed safe, but Lincoln worried about Kentucky, Missouri, and Maryland. Virginia's secession had placed a Confederate state across the Potomac River from the nation's capital. If Maryland seceded, Washington, D.C., would be surrounded by Confederate territory. To prevent Maryland from seceding, Lincoln **imposed martial law** in Baltimore, where angry mobs had already attacked federal troops. Under martial law, the military takes control of an area and replaces civilian authorities, and it suspends certain civil rights.

Kentucky stayed neutral until September 1861, when Confederate forces occupied part of the state. The invasion angered many Kentucky legislators, who now voted to fight the Confederacy. This decision led other Kentuckians who supported the Confederacy to create a rival government and secede.

Missouri worried Lincoln, too. Although many Missourians sympathized strongly with the Confederacy, its convention voted overwhelmingly against secession. A struggle then broke out between pro-Unionist forces and a pro-Confederate militia led by Governor Claiborne F. Jackson. In the end, Missouri stayed with the Union with the support of federal forces.

From the beginning of the Civil War, Lincoln had been willing to take political, even constitutional, risks to preserve the Union. Now the issue of its preservation shifted to the battlefield.

☑ **PROGRESS CHECK**

Identifying What action did Lincoln take to prevent Maryland's secession?

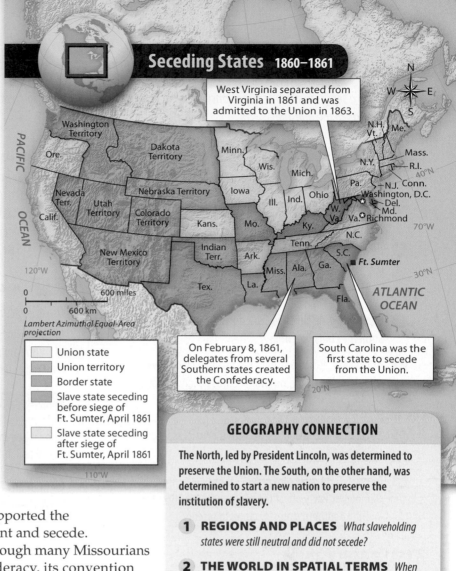

Seceding States 1860–1861

West Virginia separated from Virginia in 1861 and was admitted to the Union in 1863.

On February 8, 1861, delegates from several Southern states created the Confederacy.

South Carolina was the first state to secede from the Union.

■ Ft. Sumter

Legend:
- Union state
- Union territory
- Border state
- Slave state seceding before siege of Ft. Sumter, April 1861
- Slave state seceding after siege of Ft. Sumter, April 1861

0 — 600 miles
0 — 600 km
Lambert Azimuthal Equal-Area projection

GEOGRAPHY CONNECTION

The North, led by President Lincoln, was determined to preserve the Union. The South, on the other hand, was determined to start a new nation to preserve the institution of slavery.

1 REGIONS AND PLACES *What slaveholding states were still neutral and did not secede?*

2 THE WORLD IN SPATIAL TERMS *When Virginia seceded, why might President Lincoln be worried that Maryland might also secede?*

impose to establish authority by force

martial law the law administered by military forces that is invoked by a government in an emergency

---

LESSON 3 REVIEW

Reviewing Vocabulary

1. *Defining* How does martial law help control an area?

Using Your Notes

2. *Summarizing* Use your notes to write a short paragraph about the events that led to the Civil War.

Answering the Guiding Questions

3. *Describing* How did the South react to the election of a Republican president?

4. *Analyzing* Do you think it is ever appropriate for the government to declare martial law?

Writing Activity

5. PERSUASIVE Suppose that you are an adviser to President Lincoln and you have just heard about the attack on Fort Sumter in South Carolina. Write a brief report for the president, advising him on what steps to take next.

Directions: On a separate sheet of paper, answer the questions below. Make sure you read carefully and answer all parts to the question.

Lesson Review

Lesson 1

1 *Identifying Cause and Effect* What was a result of the Fugitive Slave Act?

2 *Analyzing* Why did some Northerners support popular sovereignty?

Lesson 2

3 *Explaining* In the *Dred Scott* decision, what did the Supreme Court determine?

4 *Analyzing* What was John Brown's raid, and how did it signal that peaceful compromise was no longer possible?

Lesson 3

5 *Listing* Which seven states were the first to secede from the Union?

6 *Identifying Cause and Effect* How did the split of the Democratic Party affect the outcome of the 1860 election and the Southern states' decision to secede?

21st Century Skills

7 **IDENTIFYING RELATIONSHIPS AMONG EVENTS** What was the unintended impact of the Fugitive Slave Act?

8 **EXPLAINING CONTINUITY AND CHANGE** How were the Republican Party and the Free-Soil Party related?

9 **IDENTIFYING CAUSE AND EFFECT** What was the cause of the caning of Senator Charles Sumner?

10 **IDENTIFYING PERSPECTIVES AND DIFFERING INTERPRETATIONS** Contrast how Southerners and Northerners felt about John Brown's raid on Harpers Ferry.

Exploring the Essential Question

11 *Speculating* Create a time line showing the events that led to the Civil War and identify how the events affected the divide between the North and the South. Then write a paragraph explaining whether or not the Civil War could have been avoided.

DBQ Document-Based Questions

Use the document to answer the following questions.

In 1850 many Southern politicians, such as Senator John C. Calhoun of South Carolina, were opposed to limits on slavery and also were opposed to limits on states' rights.

PRIMARY SOURCE

❝[T]he equilibrium between [the North and the South] . . . as it stood when the constitution was ratified and the Government put into action, has been destroyed. . . . [O]ne section has the exclusive power of controlling the Government, which leaves the other without any adequate means of protecting itself against its encroachment and oppression.❞

—John C. Calhoun, from a speech in the Senate, March 4, 1850

12 *Analyzing Primary Sources* What is the "equilibrium" to which Calhoun refers?

13 *Hypothesizing* If a Southerner in 1850 had agreed with Calhoun's message in this speech, what do you think that person would have said about secession?

Extended-Response Question

14 *Making Connections* Write a short essay explaining how the sectional conflict over slavery reflected a tension between states' rights and the authority of the federal government. What was the result of this tension?

Need Extra Help?

If You've Missed Question	**1**	**2**	**3**	**4**	**5**	**6**	**7**	**8**	**9**	**10**	**11**	**12**	**13**	**14**
Go to page	207	205	211	214	217	216	207	210	209	214	204	220	220	204

The Civil War

1861–1865

ESSENTIAL QUESTIONS · *Can the nation's union of states be broken?*
· *Should war be conducted against both military and civilian populations?*

networks

There's More Online about the
American Civil War.

The Story Matters...

The Civil War was in many respects
the first modern war. Both sides
fielded large armies equipped with
mass-produced weapons. Railroads
and the telegraph ensured rapid
troop movements and faster
communications. Hundreds of
thousands of soldiers were killed as
a result of these changes.

◄ President Abraham Lincoln faced
many challenges in his effort to
preserve the Union. As a result of his
determination and commitment to
the best ideals of the nation, Lincoln
is counted as one of the nation's
greatest presidents.

PHOTO: CORBIS

221

The Civil War began with each side confident in its ability to quickly dominate its opponent. Both sides were soon proven wrong. The war was long, bloody, and devastatingly costly in terms of lives lost. The Confederacy's loss at Gettysburg marked a turning point in the war that the South could not later overcome.

Step Into the Place

Read the quotes and look at the information presented on the map.

 How does the following quote express President Lincoln's attitude about the sacrifices many soldiers made during the course of the Civil War?

PRIMARY SOURCE

❝Four score and seven years ago our fathers brought forth on this continent, a new nation, conceived in Liberty, and dedicated to the proposition that all men are created equal.

Now we are engaged in a great civil war, testing whether that nation, or any nation so conceived and so dedicated, can long endure. We are met on a great battle-field of that war. We have come to dedicate a portion of that field, as a final resting place for those who here gave their lives that that nation might live. It is altogether fitting and proper that we should do this.

But, in a larger sense, we can not dedicate—we can not consecrate—we can not hallow—this ground. The brave men, living and dead, who struggled here, have consecrated it, far above our poor power to add or detract. The world will little note nor long remember what we say here, but it can never forget what they did here. It is for us the living, rather, to be dedicated here to the unfinished work which they who fought here have thus far so nobly advanced. It is rather for us to be here dedicated to the great task remaining before us—that from these honored dead we take increased devotion to that cause for which they gave the last full measure of devotion—that we here highly resolve that these dead shall not have died in vain—that this nation, under God, shall have a new birth of freedom—and that government of the people, by the people, for the people, shall not perish from the earth.❞

—President Abraham Lincoln, the Gettysburg Address, November 19, 1863

Step Into the Time

Choose an event from the time line and write a paragraph predicting the general social, political, and economic consequences that event might have on the Civil War.

U.S. PRESIDENTS

UNITED STATES

WORLD

1859   1860   1861

1859 John Brown leads raid on federal arsenal at Harpers Ferry, Virginia

April 12, 1861 Fort Sumter attacked

July 21, 1861 First Battle of Bull Run

Lincoln 1861–1865

February 19, 1861 Russian serfs emancipated by Czar Alexander II

March 17, 1861 Italy declares independence

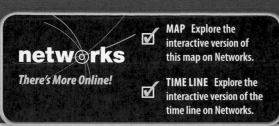
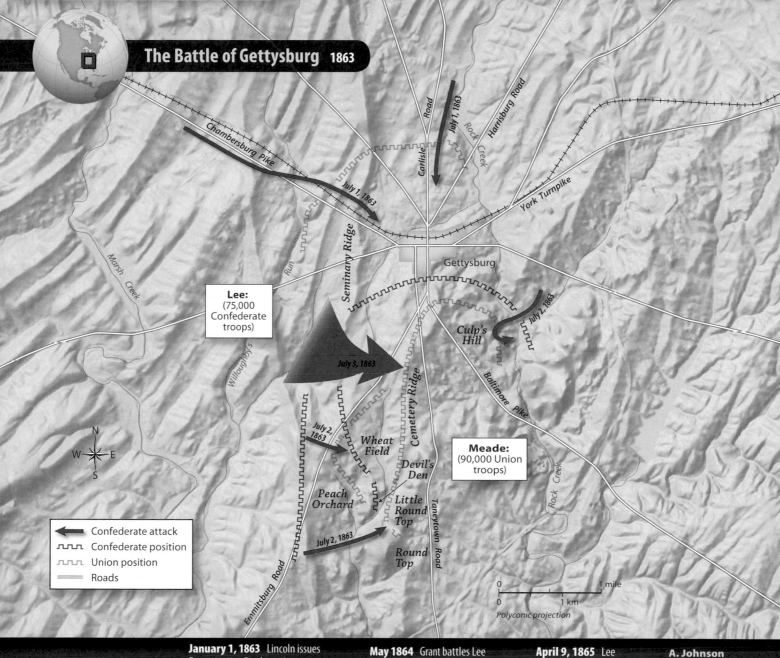

The Battle of Gettysburg 1863

Lee: (75,000 Confederate troops)

Meade: (90,000 Union troops)

Chambersburg Pike

Marsh Creek

Seminary Ridge

Willoughby's Run

Carlisle Road

July 1, 1863

Rock Creek

Harrisburg Road

York Turnpike

Gettysburg

July 2, 1863

Culp's Hill

Baltimore Pike

Rock Creek

July 3, 1863

Cemetery Ridge

Wheat Field

Devil's Den

Peach Orchard

Little Round Top

Round Top

Taneytown Road

Emmitsburg Road

N W E S

→ Confederate attack

⊓⊔ Confederate position

⊓⊔ Union position

══ Roads

0   1 mile
0   1 km
Polyconic projection

September 17, 1862
Battle of Antietam halts Lee's invasion of the North

January 1, 1863 Lincoln issues Emancipation Proclamation

July 1–3, 1863 Battle of Gettysburg

July 4, 1863 Surrender of Vicksburg

May 1864 Grant battles Lee in Virginia

September 1864 Atlanta falls and Sherman begins March to the Sea

April 9, 1865 Lee surrenders to Grant

April 14, 1865 Lincoln is assassinated

A. Johnson
1865–1869

1862   **1863**   **1864**   **1865**

1862 British firm builds Confederate warship *Alabama,* which begins sinking Union ships

June 10, 1863 French troops occupy Mexico City

March 21, 1864 USS *Hendrick Hudson* sinks blockade runner *Wild Pigeon* near Havana, Cuba

September 28, 1864 Karl Marx founds International Workingmen's Association to promote socialism

networks

There's More Online!

☑ **GRAPHIC NOVEL** Fort Sumter's Last Stand

☑ **IMAGE** Confederate Soldiers

☑ **SLIDE SHOW** Civil War Technology

☑ **VIDEO** The Opposing Sides

☑ **INTERACTIVE SELF-CHECK QUIZ**

LESSON 1
The Opposing Sides

ESSENTIAL QUESTIONS · *Can the nation's union of states be broken?*
· *Should war be conducted against both military and civilian populations?*

Reading **HELP**DESK

Content Vocabulary

- **greenback**
- **conscription**
- **habeas corpus**
- **attrition**

Academic Vocabulary

- **sufficient** • **implement**

TAKING NOTES: *Organizing*

ACTIVITY Use the major headings of this lesson to create an outline that records the advantages and disadvantages of the North and the South at the start of the Civil War.

The Opposing Sides
I. Choosing Sides
A.
B.
C.
D.
E.

IT MATTERS BECAUSE

At the start of the Civil War, the North and the South each had distinct advantages and disadvantages. Both sides expected the conflict to end quickly. Instead, the Civil War became a long, bloody, and bitter struggle in which neither side won an easy triumph.

Choosing Sides

GUIDING QUESTION *What were the advantages and disadvantages for the North and the South at the start of the war?*

When the Civil War began, hundreds of military officers had to choose whether to support the Union or the Confederacy. Eventually, 313 officers, or about one-third of the total, resigned to join the Confederacy.

The Opposing Sides

In 1860 the United States had eight military colleges, and seven of them were in the South. These colleges provided the Confederacy with a large number of trained officers to lead its armies. The North had a strong naval tradition. More than three-fourths of the United States Navy's officers came from the North. Perhaps even more important, most of the navy's warships and all but two of the nation's shipyards remained under Union control.

The North also had several economic advantages over the South. The North had a larger population, giving it an advantage in raising an army and in supporting the war effort. In addition, in 1860 the North produced almost 90 percent of total manufacturing output, including iron vital for manufacturing weapons and equipment. The North also had more railroad lines to enable the movement of armies and supplies.

Financing the War

Both the North and the South had to raise money for the war. The North controlled the national treasury and could expect continued revenue from tariffs. Concern about the North's ability to win the

PHOTOS: (l to r)Andrew J. Russell/Medford Historical Society Collection/CORBIS, Bettmann/CORBIS, Library of Congress, Library of Congress

war, however, caused many people to withdraw gold and silver from the banks. Without gold and silver, the banks could not buy government bonds, and without the gold and silver, the government could not pay its suppliers and troops. To solve this problem, Congress passed the Legal Tender Act in February 1862. This act created a national currency and allowed the government to issue paper money. These paper bills came to be known as **greenbacks** because of their color.

In contrast to the Union, the Confederacy's financial situation was poor. Most Southern planters were in debt and unable to buy bonds. The best hope for the South to raise money was by taxing trade. Shortly after the war began, however, the Union navy blockaded Southern ports, which reduced trade and revenue. The Confederacy then imposed new taxes, but many Southerners refused to pay. Lacking **sufficient** money, the Confederacy was forced to print paper money to pay its bills. This caused rapid inflation in the South. By the end of the war, the South had experienced 9,000 percent inflation, compared to only 80 percent in the North.

Party Politics in the North

As the Civil War began, President Abraham Lincoln had to contend with divisions within his own party. Many members of the Republican Party were abolitionists. Lincoln's goal, however, was to preserve the Union, even if it meant allowing slavery to continue.

The president also had to contend with the Democrats. One faction, known as the War Democrats, supported a war to restore the Union but opposed ending slavery. Another faction, known as the Peace Democrats, opposed the war and called for reuniting the states through negotiation rather than force.

One major disagreement between Republicans and Democrats concerned the use of **conscription,** or forcing people into military service. In 1862 Congress passed a militia law requiring states to use conscription if they could not recruit enough volunteers. Many Democrats opposed the law, and riots erupted in several strongly Democratic districts.

To enforce the militia law, Lincoln suspended writs of **habeas corpus,** a person's right not to be imprisoned unless charged with a crime and given a trial. A writ of habeas corpus is a court order that requires the government either to charge an imprisoned person with a crime or let the person go free. When writs of habeas corpus are suspended, a person can be imprisoned indefinitely without trial. In this case, Lincoln suspended the writ for anyone who openly supported the rebels or encouraged others to resist the militia draft.

greenback a piece of U.S. paper money first issued by the North during the Civil War

sufficient enough, adequate

conscription requiring people to enter military service

habeas corpus a legal order for an inquiry to determine whether a person has been lawfully imprisoned

Soldiers of the 110th Pennsylvania Infantry Regiment. Union troops were generally better equipped than Confederate forces.

▶ **CRITICAL THINKING**
Making Generalizations What advantages might troops have by being better equipped than opposing troops?

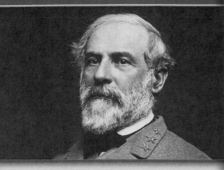

Robert E. Lee (1807–1870)

The son of a distinguished—though not wealthy—Virginia family, Robert E. Lee was raised in the socially exclusive world of the aristocratic South. Offered command of Union troops at the beginning of the Civil War, Lee refused, unable to oppose his fellow Virginians. As a general of the Confederacy, Lee was a hero to Southerners during the war. He felt a responsibility to set an example of Southern honor in defeat. His swearing of renewed allegiance to the United States after the war inspired thousands of former Confederate soldiers to do the same. Later, as president of Washington College in Virginia (later renamed Washington and Lee), Lee encouraged his students to put the war behind them and to behave as responsible citizens.

▶ **CRITICAL THINKING**
Summarizing How did Lee work to heal the wounds of the Civil War?

Weak Southern Government

Although the South had no organized opposition party, President Jefferson Davis still faced many problems. The Confederate constitution emphasized states' rights and limited the central government's power. This commitment to states' rights often interfered with Davis's ability to conduct the war. Although many Southern leaders supported the war, some opposed Jefferson Davis when he supported conscription and established martial law early in 1862.

The Diplomatic Challenge

The outbreak of the Civil War put the major governments of Europe in a difficult position. The United States did not want the Europeans interfering in the war and expected them to respect the North's blockade of Southern ports. Confederate leaders wanted the exact opposite. They wanted the Europeans, particularly the British, to recognize the Confederate States of America as an independent nation and to provide military assistance to the South. Southern leaders knew that British and French textile factories depended on Southern cotton. To pressure these nations, many Southern planters voluntarily agreed to stop selling cotton to them until they recognized the Confederacy.

The British and French met informally with Confederate representatives in May 1861. The French promised to recognize the Confederacy if the British did so as well. British leaders, however, were not ready to risk war with the United States. Until the Confederacy won decisive victories on the battlefield and proved it would survive and eventually win the war, the British would not risk recognizing it. The Confederacy sent negotiators to Europe on its behalf, but they were unable to gain the support the South wanted.

☑ **PROGRESS CHECK**

Explaining How were the political challenges that the North and the South faced after the Civil War began different?

The First Modern War

GUIDING QUESTION *Why is the Civil War considered to be the first modern war?*

Unlike most of the wars fought in Europe during the previous two centuries, the Civil War was not fought by small, disciplined armies with limited goals. It involved huge armies, made up mostly of civilian volunteers who required vast quantities of supplies and equipment.

Military Technology

By the 1850s, French and American inventors had developed a new, inexpensive conoidal—or cone-shaped—bullet for rifles. Rifles firing conoidal bullets were accurate at much greater ranges. This meant that troops would be fired on

---

POLITICAL CARTOONS | **THE PENDING CONFLICT**

▶ **CRITICAL THINKING**

1 *Making Inferences* Do you think the cartoon was created by a Northerner or a Southerner? Why?

2 *Predicting Consequences* How would British and French support have helped the South to overcome the North's advantages in the war?

This cartoon depicts the "Union" fighting "Secession." Union's feet are entangled by a copperhead snake, representing Democrats who opposed the war, and his arms are bound by the Constitution. Secession tramples the flag, and holds a club labeled "Pirate Alabama"—referring to a Southern warship the British let the South build in Britain. Behind the fighters are two men—one representing France and the other Britain. The British figure is handing clubs to Secession to help him beat Union.

several more times while charging enemy lines. Defenders were able to inflict very high casualties on attacking forces from the protection of trenches and barricades. High casualties meant that armies had to keep replacing soldiers. **Attrition,** the wearing down of one side by the other through exhaustion of soldiers and resources, played a critical role as the war dragged on. The North, with its large population, could replace its troops much more easily than the South.

Military Strategies

Early in the war, Jefferson Davis imagined a struggle similar to the Revolutionary War. His generals would pick their battles carefully, attacking and retreating when necessary and avoiding large battles that might risk heavy losses. Davis believed that if the South waged a defensive war of attrition in this manner, it would force the Union to spend its resources until it became tired of the war and agreed to negotiate. The idea of a defensive war of attrition, however, outraged many Southerners. Believing themselves superior fighters, they scorned the idea of defensive warfare. "The idea of waiting for blows, instead of inflicting them, is altogether unsuited to the genius of our people," boasted the *Richmond Examiner* in 1861. Southern disdain for remaining on the defensive meant that Southern troops often went on the offensive, charging enemy lines and suffering very high casualties.

Early in the war, the general in chief of the United States, Winfield Scott, proposed a strategy for defeating the South. Scott suggested that the Union blockade Confederate ports and send gunboats down the Mississippi to divide the Confederacy. The South, thus separated, would gradually run out of resources and surrender. The plan would take time, Scott admitted, but it would defeat the South with the least amount of bloodshed. Northern newspapers referred to the strategy as the Anaconda Plan, after the snake that slowly strangles its prey to death.

Opponents argued that a rapid and massive invasion of the South would bring victory more quickly. Although Lincoln agreed to **implement** Scott's suggestions and imposed a blockade of Southern ports, he hoped that a quick victory over the Southern forces massing in Virginia might discredit the secessionists and bring an end to the crisis.

✓ PROGRESS CHECK

Describing Why were many Southerners opposed to fighting a war of attrition?

The Anaconda Plan

- Blockade Southern ports on the Atlantic
- Isolate the Confederacy from European aid and trade
- Cut off flow of supplies, equipment, money, food and cotton
- Exhaust Southern resources, forcing surrender
- Control the Mississippi with Union gunboats
- Divide the eastern part of the Confederacy from the western part
- Capture New Orleans, Vicksburg, and Memphis
- Cut off shipping to and from interior

Many Northerners thought it would take too long to achieve victory with the Anaconda Plan.

▶ CRITICAL THINKING
Drawing Inferences How would the Anaconda Plan avoid bloodshed?

attrition the act of wearing down by constant harassment or attack

implement to put into action; to carry out

LESSON 1 REVIEW

Reviewing Vocabulary

1. *Identifying* Why might the use of conscription have been negatively viewed?

2. *Explaining* How would the overall population of each side affect the rate of attrition?

Using Your Notes

3. *Explaining* Use your notes to explain how the belief in states' rights hampered the Confederate government during the war.

Answering the Guiding Questions

4. *Analyzing* What were the advantages and disadvantages for the North and the South at the start of the war?

5. *Inferring* Why is the Civil War considered to be the first modern war?

Writing Activity

6. DESCRIPTIVE Suppose that you are living in one of the border states at the beginning of the Civil War. Write a letter to a relative explaining why you are planning to join either the Union or the Confederate army.

networks

There's More Online!

- ☑ **BIOGRAPHY** Thomas "Stonewall" Jackson
- ☑ **BIOGRAPHY** George McClellan
- ☑ **IMAGE** Ironclad Battleship
- ☑ **MAP** War in the West
- ☑ **MAP** War in the East
- ☑ **VIDEO** The Early Stages
- ☑ **INTERACTIVE SELF-CHECK QUIZ**

Reading **HELP**DESK

Content Vocabulary

- bounty
- blockade runner

Academic Vocabulary

- assemble • crucial

TAKING NOTES: *Organizing*

ACTIVITY As you read, use a graphic organizer like the one below to record the results of the early Civil War battles.

Battle	Results
First Battle of Bull Run	
Battle of Shiloh	
Battle of Murfreesboro	
Seven Days' Battles	
Second Battle of Bull Run	

LESSON 2
The Early Stages

ESSENTIAL QUESTIONS • *Can the nation's union of states be broken?*
• *Should war be conducted against both military and civilian populations?*

IT MATTERS BECAUSE

Despite their careful strategizing, both sides experienced setbacks and casualties early in the Civil War. By issuing the Emancipation Proclamation, Lincoln put ending slavery at the heart of the Union war effort.

Mobilizing the Troops

GUIDING QUESTIONS *Why was it necessary for both sides to resort to conscription?*

In the first months of the Civil War, President Lincoln faced pressure to strike quickly against the South. Confederate troops were gathering 25 miles (40 km) south of Washington, D.C., along the Bull Run River near Manassas Junction. Lincoln approved an assault on these forces, hoping that a Union victory would lead to a quick end to the conflict. Instead, Confederate forces routed the Union troops, forcing them to retreat in a panic.

The Union defeat at the First Battle of Bull Run made it clear that the North would need a large, well-trained army to defeat the South. Lincoln had originally called for 75,000 men to serve for three months. The day after Bull Run, he signed another bill for the enlistment of 500,000 men for three years.

Enlistment levels were high at first, but as the war dragged on, a lack of volunteers forced both sides to use conscription. The South introduced conscription in April 1862 for all white men between the ages of 18 and 35. This draft exempted certain people, including key government workers and teachers. After 1862, it exempted planters who held at least 20 enslaved African Americans.

The North tried to encourage enlistment by offering a **bounty**— bonus money—to men who promised to serve three years. Congress passed the Militia Act in July 1862, giving Lincoln the authority to call state militias, which included drafted troops, into federal service. Finally, after these measures failed to meet military needs, Congress introduced a national draft in 1863 to raise the necessary troops.

☑ **PROGRESS CHECK**

Summarizing What was the significance of the First Battle of Bull Run?

The Naval War

GUIDING QUESTION *How successful was the Union's naval blockade of Southern ports?*

In April 1861, President Lincoln proclaimed a blockade of all Confederate ports. By the spring of 1862, the Union navy had sealed off every major Southern harbor along the Atlantic coast, except for Charleston, South Carolina, and Wilmington, North Carolina. Lincoln intended to hurt the South's economy as much as possible by cutting its trade with the world.

The Blockade

Although the Union blockade became increasingly effective over time, Union vessels were thinly spread. They found it difficult to stop all of the **blockade runners**—small, fast smuggling vessels. Blockade runners allowed the South to ship at least some of its cotton to Europe in exchange for needed supplies. The amount of material that made it through the blockade, however, was much less than the amount that had been shipped before the war.

Confederate ships, including the famous warships *Alabama* and *Florida,* worked out of foreign ports to attack Northern merchant ships at sea. These attacks strained U.S. relations with Britain, where the ships had been built. Union leaders did not think that Britain should have allowed construction of the ships. They demanded payment for the losses the Union suffered.

Farragut Seizes New Orleans

In February 1862, David G. Farragut took command of a Union force comprised of 42 warships and 15,000 soldiers led by General Benjamin Butler. A military veteran, Farragut became a hero for his actions at the battle for New Orleans. In early April, his fleet began bombarding Confederate forts on the lower Mississippi River. When the attack failed to destroy the forts, Farragut made a daring decision to head upriver, past the forts in single file, exposing themselves to attack. The forts opened fire, while Confederate gunboats tried to ram the fleet, and tugboats placed flaming rafts in front of Union ships. Remarkably, all but four of Farragut's ships survived the battle and continued upriver.

On April 25, 1862, Farragut arrived at New Orleans. Six days later, General Butler's troops took control of the city. The South's largest city, and a center of the cotton trade, was now in Union hands.

☑ PROGRESS CHECK

Evaluating Why was the Union seizure of New Orleans important? Explain.

bounty money given as a reward, such as to encourage enlistment in the army

blockade runner ship that runs through a blockade, usually to smuggle goods through a protected area

PHOTO: Library of Congress

The Civil War witnessed the first use of ships covered by iron plates, known as ironclads. In March 1862, the *Virginia,* an ironclad warship, battled the Union's newly built ironclad, the *Monitor.* Though the ships battled for hours, neither was able to sink the other.

▶ **CRITICAL THINKING**

Identifying Central Issues How was the naval war important to the overall war effort?

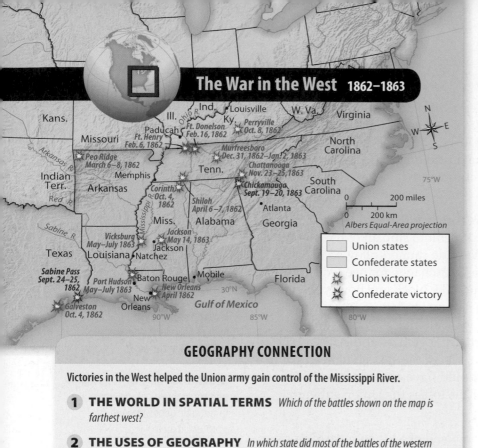

The War in the West

GUIDING QUESTION *Why was the Battle of Shiloh important for the war in the West?*

In February 1862, Union general Ulysses S. Grant began a campaign to seize control of the Cumberland River and the Tennessee River. Grant soon had Kentucky and most of western Tennessee under Union control. This provided the Union with a river route deep into the Confederacy.

Shiloh

Next, Grant led his troops up the Tennessee River to attack Corinth, Mississippi. Seizing Corinth would cut the Confederacy's only rail line connecting Mississippi and western Tennessee. Confederate forces launched a surprise attack on Grant's troops on April 6, 1862, near a church named Shiloh.

Although the Union troops were forced back, Grant rushed around the battlefield and managed to **assemble** a defensive line. The next morning, knowing reinforcements were coming, Grant went on the offensive. He surprised the Confederates, forcing a retreat. The Battle of Shiloh stunned people in both the North and the South. Twenty thousand troops were killed or wounded, more than in any other battle up to that point.

Murfreesboro

Confederate troops evacuated and quickly moved east by railroad to Chattanooga, Tennessee. Here, they were placed under the command of General Braxton Bragg. Bragg took his troops into Kentucky, hoping the Union armies would follow, but his invasion failed. Union troops led by General Don Carlos Buell stopped Bragg's forces at the Battle of Perryville. Lincoln then ordered Buell to seize Chattanooga.

Frustrated at Buell's slow advance, Lincoln fired him and put General William Rosecrans in command. As Rosecrans's forces headed south, Bragg's forces attacked them west of the Stones River near Murfreesboro. Although the Union lines fell back before the onslaught, they did not break, and the battle ended without a victor. Four days later, with Union reinforcements arriving from Nashville, Bragg decided to retreat.

☑ **PROGRESS CHECK**

Evaluating Why was the Union's campaign to control the Cumberland and Tennessee Rivers successful?

GEOGRAPHY CONNECTION

Victories in the West helped the Union army gain control of the Mississippi River.

1 **THE WORLD IN SPATIAL TERMS** *Which of the battles shown on the map is farthest west?*

2 **THE USES OF GEOGRAPHY** *In which state did most of the battles of the western front of the war occur?*

assemble to bring together in a certain place for a particular purpose

The warship *Essex* helped Admiral David G. Farragut establish Union control over the Mississippi River.

▶ **CRITICAL THINKING**

Making Inferences Why would the *Essex* have been an effective tool in helping to control the Mississippi River?

PHOTO: Bettmann/CORBIS

The War in the East

GUIDING QUESTION *Why was the Battle of Antietam a crucial victory for the Union?*

While troops were struggling for control of Tennessee and the Mississippi River, Union general George B. McClellan waged another major campaign. That was the campaign in the east to capture Richmond, Virginia.

The Peninsula Campaign

It took McClellan 30 days to capture Yorktown, giving the Confederates time to move into position near Richmond. Then, as he advanced toward Richmond, he allowed the Chickahominy River to divide his forces. Southern troops then attacked and inflicted heavy casualties.

In late June 1862, Confederate general Robert E. Lee began a series of attacks on McClellan's army that became known as the Seven Days' Battles. Lee did not win a decisive victory. Nevertheless, he inflicted heavy casualties and forced McClellan to retreat. Over McClellan's protests, Lincoln ordered him to withdraw and bring his troops back to Washington.

As McClellan's troops withdrew, Lee decided to attack the Union forces defending Washington. The maneuvers by the two sides led to another battle at Bull Run—the site of the first major battle of the war. Again, the South forced the North to retreat, leaving Confederate forces only 20 miles (32 km) from Washington. Soon after, word came that Lee's forces had crossed into Maryland and begun an invasion of the North.

The Battle of Antietam

General Lee and Jefferson Davis both believed that a successful invasion might convince the North to accept Southern independence. They also thought that a victory on Northern soil would help the South win recognition from the British and help the Peace Democrats in the upcoming midterm elections. Heading north, Lee could also feed his troops from Northern farms.

When he learned that McClellan had been sent after him, Lee ordered his troops to congregate near Sharpsburg, Maryland. Meanwhile, McClellan's troops took positions along Antietam (an•TEE•tuhm) Creek, east of Lee.

PHOTO: Library of Congress

The War in the East 1862–1863

Fortification
Union victory
Confederate victory
Indecisive battle

Pennsylvania
Gettysburg July 1–3, 1863
Antietam September 17, 1862
West Virginia
Frederick
Maryland
Washington, D.C.
Delaware
New Jersey
40°N
74°W
Shenandoah R.
Potomac R.
Manassas Junction
Second Bull Run August 29–30, 1862
Chancellorsville May 1–4, 1863
Fredericksburg December 13, 1862
Chesapeake Bay
38°N
Seven Days June 25–July 1, 1862
York R.
Richmond
Virginia
James R.
Yorktown
Hampton Roads, March 8–9, 1862
Ft. Monroe

0   80 miles
0   80 km
Albers Equal-Area projection

N W E S

GEOGRAPHY CONNECTION

Despite Confederate victories in the East, Lee's unsuccessful invasion of the North proved costly as the British decided not to intervene.

1 **THE WORLD IN SPATIAL TERMS** *Which battles shown above took place outside Virginia's borders?*

2 **PLACES AND REGIONS** *Approximately how far apart were the two capital cities of Richmond and Washington, D.C.?*

The soldiers of the Union army sit above their encampment at Cumberland Landing during the Peninsula Campaign.

▶ **CRITICAL THINKING**
Drawing Conclusions How did the Peninsula Campaign contribute to the Confederate invasion of the North?

Lincoln reads the Emancipation Proclamation to members of his cabinet. Left of Lincoln are Secretary of War Edwin M. Stanton (seated) and Secretary of the Treasury Salmon P. Chase. In front of the table sits Secretary of State William Seward.

▶ CRITICAL THINKING
Analyzing Information How did the Emancipation Proclamation change the war?

crucial something considered important or essential

On September 17, 1862, McClellan ordered his troops to attack. The Battle of Antietam, the bloodiest one-day battle in American history, ended with nearly 6,000 men killed and some 17,000 wounded. Lee then retreated to Virginia.

The Battle of Antietam was a **crucial** Union victory. The British government had been ready to intervene as a mediator if Lee's invasion had succeeded. The British once again decided to wait and see how the war progressed.

The Emancipation Proclamation

The victory at Antietam also set the stage for Lincoln to end slavery in the South. Although most Democrats opposed any move to end slavery, Republicans were divided on the issue. Lincoln had at first described the conflict simply as a war to preserve the Union. A year later, however, many Northerners—including Lincoln—began to conclude that slavery had to end. Representative George Julian, a Republican from Indiana, summed up the argument for freeing enslaved people in an important speech:

PRIMARY SOURCE

❝[W]hen I say that this rebellion has its source and life in slavery, I only repeat a simple truism. . . . The mere suppression of the rebellion will be an empty mockery of our sufferings and sacrifices, if slavery shall be spared to canker the heart of the nation anew, and repeat its diabolical deeds.❞

—from *The Congressional Globe,* January 14, 1862

As Lee's forces marched toward Antietam, Lincoln said that if the Union could drive those forces from Northern soil, he would issue a proclamation ending slavery.

On September 22, 1862, Lincoln kept his promise. He publicly announced that he would issue the Emancipation Proclamation freeing all enslaved persons in states still in rebellion after January 1, 1863. In this proclamation, Lincoln declared "that all persons held as slaves within said designated States . . . are, and henceforward shall be free; and that the Executive Government of the United States . . . will recognize and maintain the freedom of said persons." The Proclamation freed enslaved African Americans only in states at war with the Union. Yet, by its very existence, it transformed the conflict from a war to preserve the Union to a war of liberation.

✓ **PROGRESS CHECK**

Examining Why did President Lincoln issue the Emancipation Proclamation?

LESSON 2 REVIEW

Reviewing Vocabulary
1. *Determining Cause and Effect* Why did the Union offer a bounty to those who enlisted?

Using Your Notes
2. *Explaining* Use your notes to explain why the early battles of the war were inconclusive.

Answering the Guiding Questions
3. *Identifying Cause and Effect* Why was it necessary for both sides to resort to conscription?

4. *Assessing* How successful was the Union's naval blockade of Southern ports?

5. *Making Connections* Why was the Battle of Shiloh important for the war in the West?

6. *Identifying* Why was the Battle of Antietam a crucial victory for the Union?

Writing Activity
7. PERSUASIVE Suppose that you are asked to advise President Lincoln about issuing the Emancipation Proclamation. Write a short paper in which you advise him on whether to issue it and explain the reasons for your position.

networks

There's More Online!

- ☑ **BIOGRAPHY** Elizabeth Blackwell
- ☑ **BIOGRAPHY** Julia Ward Howe
- ☑ **IMAGE** Women Working in Munitions Factory
- ☑ **SLIDE SHOW** Nursing During the Civil War
- ☑ **VIDEO** Life During the War
- ☑ **INTERACTIVE SELF-CHECK QUIZ**

Reading HELPDESK

Content Vocabulary

- **hardtack**
- **prisoner of war**

Academic Vocabulary

- **denial** • **supplement**

TAKING NOTES: *Organizing*

ACTIVITY Use the following graphic organizer to list the contributions that women made during the Civil War.

Women's Contributions to the Civil War

LESSON 3

Life During the War

ESSENTIAL QUESTIONS • *Can the nation's union of states be broken?*
• *Should war be conducted against both military and civilian populations?*

IT MATTERS BECAUSE

The economic hardships of the war damaged the morale of Southerners, but the North enjoyed an economic boom. Life for soldiers was difficult, with limited medical treatment and horrific conditions in prison camps.

The Wartime Economies

GUIDING QUESTION *How did the Northern and Southern economies differ during the Civil War?*

Both the North and the South struggled to keep their economies running, but the South suffered more from inflation and shortages. The North responded more quickly to the demands of the war.

By the end of 1862, the South's economy had begun to suffer. The collapse of its transportation system, the blockade of Southern ports, and the presence of Union troops in several important farming regions led to severe food shortages during the winter of 1862–1863. Hearing of the hardships faced by their families, many soldiers deserted and returned home. In the spring of 1863, food shortages led to riots. Mobs of armed women raided shops for food in several communities. In the Confederate capital, Richmond, several hundred women broke into shops, yelling, "Bread! Bread!" and then began to loot the stores for food, clothing, shoes, and other goods.

In contrast, the North experienced an economic boom. Its growing industries supplied troops with uniforms, munitions, and other necessities. The expanded use of mechanized reapers and mowers made farming possible with fewer workers, many of whom were women. Women also took the place of men in various industries.

The North, however, also experienced mob violence. In 1863 riots broke out over the Union's new conscription law that made all healthy males aged 20 to 45 eligible for military service. However, if a man could find a replacement or pay a $300 fee, he did not have to serve. The most infamous of the draft riots occurred in New York City.

☑ **PROGRESS CHECK**

Explaining What hardships did Southerners face at home?

African Americans in the Military

GUIDING QUESTION *Why did many African Americans enlist in the Union forces, and how might this have helped to challenge racial prejudices?*

The Emancipation Proclamation officially permitted African Americans to enlist in the Union army and navy. Almost immediately, thousands of African Americans rushed to join the military. Frederick Douglass's two sons, Charles and Lewis, were among them. Douglass approved of his sons' decision. He believed that serving in the military would help African Americans overcome racial prejudices:

PRIMARY SOURCE

❝Once let the black man get upon his person the brass letters, U.S.; let him get an eagle on his button, and a musket on his shoulder and bullets in his pocket, and there is no power on earth which can deny that he has earned the right to citizenship.❞

—Frederick Douglass, from a speech delivered July 6, 1863

About 180,000 African Americans served in the Union army during the Civil War, roughly 10 percent of the army's total soldiers. As many as 18,000 African Americans served in the Union navy.

Among the first African American regiments officially organized in the North was the 54th Massachusetts Infantry Regiment. The regiment fought valiantly at Fort Wagner near Charleston Harbor in July 1863. During that battle, nearly half of its soldiers were killed or wounded. After the war ended, a Northern newspaper editorial declared that the heroism of the 54th Massachusetts Regiment forever answered the question of whether African Americans could make good soldiers:

PRIMARY SOURCE

❝It is not too much to say that if this Massachusetts Fifty-fourth had faltered when its trial came, two hundred thousand [African American] troops for whom it was a pioneer would never have been put into the field, or would not have been put in for another year, which would have been equivalent to protracting the war into 1866. But it did not falter. It made Fort Wagner such a name to [African Americans] as Bunker Hill has been for ninety years to white Yankees.❞

—from the *New York Tribune*, September 8, 1865

African American servicemen, such as the members of the Fourth Colored Regiment, fought bravely for the Union. African Americans made up about 10 percent of the Union army.

▶ **CRITICAL THINKING**

Analyzing Information How did African American troops contribute to the success of the Union in the Civil War?

✔ **PROGRESS CHECK**

Analyzing Why was it crucial that the 54th Massachusetts did not falter in battle?

PHOTO: William Horace Smith/Bettmann/CORBIS

Military Life

GUIDING QUESTION *What was life like for soldiers in the field and the women who aided the war effort?*

Early in the war, Union general Irvin McDowell's troops stopped to pick berries and foolishly wasted water from their canteens to wash them. "They were not used to denying themselves much. They were not used to journeys on foot," McDowell later reflected. Self-**denial** and long marches would prove to be only the first of the harsh realities of the war.

The Soldiers in the Field

Union and Confederate soldiers suffered many hardships during the long periods between battles. Some Southern soldiers had no shoes and had to sleep without blankets. For the Union soldier, meals often consisted of **hardtack** (a hard biscuit made of wheat flour), potatoes, and beans, flavored at times with dried salt pork. Confederate bread was usually made of cornmeal. When possible, soldiers **supplemented** their diet with fruit or vegetables taken or bought from farms they passed.

Battlefield Medicine

When Americans went to war in 1861, most were not prepared for the horrors of battle. The Civil War produced huge numbers of casualties, and doctors struggled to tend to the wounded. In the mid-1800s, doctors had little understanding of infection and germs. They used the same unsterilized instruments on patient after patient. As a result, infection spread quickly in field hospitals. Doctors often amputated limbs to prevent gangrene and other infections from spreading throughout the body.

Disease was one of the greatest threats facing Civil War soldiers. Some regiments lost half their men to illness before even going into battle. Crowded together in camps, drinking from unsanitary water supplies, many soldiers became sick. Smallpox, dysentery, typhoid, and pneumonia killed thousands.

Women Serve as Nurses

Women helped the war effort by managing family farms and businesses. They made contributions on the battlefield by serving as nurses to the wounded. Before the war, most army nurses were men. During the Civil War, women took on many of the nursing tasks in army hospitals.

In 1861 Elizabeth Blackwell, the first female physician in the United States, started the nation's first training program for nurses. Her work led to the creation of the United States Sanitary Commission, an organization that provided medical assistance and supplies to army camps and hospitals. Many women volunteered to care for wounded soldiers and raised money to send medical supplies to army camps.

PHOTO: Library of Congress

Analyzing
PRIMARY SOURCES

Field Hospital Conditions

❝As a wounded man was lifted on the table, often shrieking with pain . . . the surgeon quickly examined the wound and resolved upon cutting off the wounded limb. Some ether was administered. . . . The surgeon snatched his knife from between his teeth, where it had been while his hands were busy, wiped it rapidly once or twice across his blood-stained apron, and the cutting began. The operation accomplished, the surgeon would look around with a deep sigh, and then—'Next!'❞

—quoted in *The Civil War: An Illustrated History*

DBQ **ANALYZING PRIMARY SOURCES** What does this excerpt indicate about doctors' work during the Civil War?

denial refusal to satisfy a request or desire

hardtack a hard biscuit made of wheat flour

supplement to add to

Soldiers wounded at the Battle of the Wilderness in 1864 rest at a hospital in Fredericksburg, Virginia.

▶ **CRITICAL THINKING**
Analyzing Primary Sources What does the photo show about the conditions in Civil War field hospitals?

Clara Barton (1821–1912)

Clara Barton was working in the U.S. Patent Office in Washington, D.C., when the Civil War began. With her organizational drive, she quickly saw the need for a way to distribute medical and other supplies to wounded soldiers. Barton's relief operation proved effective, and she received permission to personally travel with the medical ambulances out into the battlefields.

▶ **CRITICAL THINKING**

Drawing Conclusions Based on what Barton accomplished, what kind of person was she?

prisoner of war a person captured in war, especially a member of the military

Not all women helping at the front lines were members of the Sanitary Commission. Clara Barton left her job in a patent office to nurse soldiers on the battlefield. She fed the sick, bandaged the wounded, and even dug out bullets.

Although Southern women were encouraged to stay at home and make bandages and other supplies, many founded small hospitals. Some even braved the horrors of the battlefield. Kate Cumming served as a nurse following the Battle of Shiloh. In her diary, she vividly described a makeshift hospital:

PRIMARY SOURCE

❝[N]othing that I had ever heard or read had given me the faintest idea of the horrors witnessed here. . . . The men are lying all over the house. . . . The foul air from this mass of human beings at first made me giddy and sick, but I soon got over it.❞

—from *A Journal of Hospital Life in the Confederate Army of Tennessee,* 1866

The Civil War was a turning point for the nursing profession in the United States. The courage and energy shown by the women also helped break down the belief that women were weaker than men.

Military Prisons

The horrors of the battlefield and danger of disease were not the only hardships endured by soldiers during the Civil War. **Prisoners of war**—soldiers captured by the enemy in battle—also suffered terribly during the conflict.

Early in the war, the Union and the Confederacy held formal prisoner exchanges. After Lincoln issued the Emancipation Proclamation, however, the Confederacy announced that it would not exchange freed African Americans for Southern white prisoners. Instead, it would either re-enslave or execute all African American troops captured in battle.

In response to the Confederacy's treatment of African American troops, Lincoln stopped all prisoner exchanges. Both the North and the South thus found themselves with large and growing numbers of prisoners of war. Taking care of them proved difficult, especially in the South. While conditions were bad in Northern prisons, food shortages kept the South from even feeding prisoners adequately.

The most infamous Confederate prison, Andersonville in Georgia, had no shade or shelter. Exposure, overcrowding, lack of food, and disease killed more than 100 men per day during the sweltering summer of 1864. In all, some 13,000 of the 45,000 prisoners sent to Andersonville died there. After the war, Henry Wirz, Andersonville's commandant, became the only person executed for war crimes committed during the Civil War.

✔ **PROGRESS CHECK**

Stating How did the roles of women change during the war?

PHOTO: Royalty-Free/CORBIS

LESSON 3 REVIEW

Reviewing Vocabulary

1. ***Defining*** What purpose did hardtack serve?

Using Your Notes

2. ***Summarizing*** Use your notes to summarize how women contributed to the Civil War effort.

Answering the Guiding Questions

3. ***Contrasting*** How did the Northern and Southern economies differ during the Civil War?

4. ***Inferring*** Why did many African Americans enlist in the Union forces, and how might this have helped to challenge racial prejudices?

5. ***Describing*** What was life like for soldiers in the field and the women who aided the war effort?

Writing Activity

6. **DESCRIPTIVE** Suppose that you are a nurse on one of the battlefields during the Civil War. Write a journal entry describing the conditions of the soldiers and your reaction to the situation.

networks

There's More Online!

- ☑ **BIOGRAPHY** Mathew Brady
- ☑ **IMAGE** Ironclads at Vicksburg
- ☑ **MAP** Grant Closes in on Vicksburg
- ☑ **VIDEO** The Turning Point
- ☑ **INTERACTIVE SELF-CHECK QUIZ**

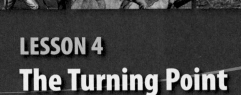

LESSON 4
The Turning Point

ESSENTIAL QUESTIONS · *Can the nation's union of states be broken?*
· *Should war be conducted against both military and civilian populations?*

Reading **HELP**DESK

Content Vocabulary
- forage
- siege

Academic Vocabulary
- encounter
- promote

TAKING NOTES: *Organizing*

ACTIVITY Use a graphic organizer similar to the one below to record the results of the battles that shaped the Union victory.

Battle	Results
Vicksburg	
Chancellorsville	
Gettysburg	
Chickamauga Creek	
Missionary Ridge	

IT MATTERS BECAUSE
For a while, the North floundered under a series of generals who were overly cautious or intimidated by the reputation of General Robert E. Lee. The tide of the war began to turn after the North won pivotal victories at Vicksburg and Gettysburg.

Vicksburg Falls

GUIDING QUESTION *Why was Vicksburg an important victory for the Union forces?*

In April 1862, Admiral David G. Farragut captured New Orleans and secured control of the Mississippi River delta for the Union. Later that year, General Ulysses S. Grant seized control as far south as Memphis after his victory at Shiloh. There remained, however, one major Confederate stronghold on the river—Vicksburg, Mississippi. "Vicksburg is the key," Lincoln said. "The war can never be brought to a close until that key is in our pocket." If Grant could take Vicksburg, the Confederacy would be cut in two.

Grierson's Raid
The city of Vicksburg was on the east bank of the Mississippi River. Grant decided to march his troops south around the city on the west bank, then cross to the east bank and attack from the south. To distract the Confederates while he carried out this maneuver, Grant ordered Colonel Benjamin Grierson to take 1,700 cavalry troops on a raid through Mississippi. Grierson's forces traveled 600 miles (965 km), tearing up railroads, burning depots, and fighting skirmishes.

The Siege of Vicksburg
After returning to the east bank of the Mississippi River, Grant embarked on a march east, ordering his troops to live off the country. **Foraging** as they marched, Grant's troops headed east, marching 180 miles (290 km) in 17 days, fighting five battles, and inflicting 7,200 casualties on the Confederates. The march ended by driving the Confederate forces back into their defenses at Vicksburg.

In May 1863, Grant launched two assaults on Vicksburg, but the city's defenders repulsed both attacks. Grant decided that the only way to take the city was to put it under **siege.** The siege of Vicksburg lasted for six weeks, with Confederate troops and the city's residents facing near starvation. On July 4, 1863, the Confederate commander at Vicksburg surrendered. The Union victory had cut the Confederacy in two.

✔ **PROGRESS CHECK**

Analyzing Why did Grant order a raid through Mississippi, and was it successful?

During the siege of Vicksburg, Union troops dug an elaborate network of "approach trenches" along their lines, allowing them to get close to the Confederate fortifications. In the meantime, gunboats bombarded the city. The city was unable to receive food and other supplies and surrendered on July 4, 1863.

▶ **CRITICAL THINKING**

Analyzing How did the Union work to break down the defenses at Vicksburg?

•

forage to search or raid for food

siege a military blockade of a city or fortified place to force it to surrender

The Road to Gettysburg

GUIDING QUESTION *Why was the Battle of Gettysburg a turning point in the war?*

Shortly after General McClellan's victory at Antietam, Lincoln became frustrated with him. At Antietam, McClellan might have made a greater effort to destroy Lee's army, but he let it slip away. He then moved so slowly after the battle that Lee was able to recover and block McClellan's advance on Richmond. On November 7, 1862, Lincoln fired McClellan and gave command of the army to General Ambrose Burnside.

Lincoln wanted a general who was not intimidated by Lee's reputation. He urged Burnside to push south into Virginia and destroy Lee's army. Lincoln did not know that the turning point in the east would come not in Virginia but to the north, in Pennsylvania.

Fredericksburg and Chancellorsville

On December 13, 1862, Burnside ordered a series of assaults against Lee's troops entrenched in the hills south of Fredericksburg, Virginia. The Union troops suffered over 12,000 casualties, more than twice the loss suffered by the Confederates. Distressed by the defeat and faced with complaints about Burnside from other officers, Lincoln replaced him with General Joseph Hooker.

General Hooker devised a plan to get at Lee's troops on the hills near Fredericksburg. First, he left a large part of his army at Fredericksburg to keep Lee's troops from moving. He then took the rest of the army west to circle around behind Lee's troops and attack from the rear. Realizing what was happening, Lee also divided his forces. He left a small force at Fredericksburg and headed west with most of his troops to stop Hooker.

On May 2, 1863, Lee's troops attacked Hooker's forces in dense woods known as the Wilderness near Chancellorsville, Virginia. Although outnumbered two to one, Lee aggressively divided his forces and repeatedly defeated the Union troops. On May 5, Hooker decided to retreat.

The Battle of Gettysburg

Having weakened the Union forces at Chancellorsville, Lee decided to invade the North again. In June 1863, he marched into Pennsylvania where his troops seized livestock, food, and clothing. After Hooker failed to stop Lee, Lincoln removed him from command and appointed General George Meade as his replacement. Meade immediately headed north to intercept Lee.

At the end of June, as Lee's army foraged in the Pennsylvania countryside, some of his troops headed into the town of Gettysburg, hoping to seize a supply of shoes. When they arrived near the town, however, they **encountered** Union cavalry. On July 1, 1863, the Confederates pushed the Union troops out of the town, into the hills to the south. At the same time, the main forces of both armies hurried to the scene of the fighting.

encounter to come upon face-to-face as an enemy or adversary

The Union line stretched from Culp's Hill and Cemetery Hill in the north, and south along Cemetery Ridge to another hill called Little Round Top. The Union forces controlled the high ground and were deployed in such a way that troops could easily be moved from one part of the line to another, depending on where the enemy attacked.

On July 2, Lee tried to seize Little Round Top. Controlling that hill would have allowed his artillery to fire down the length of the Union line. After savage fighting, his attack was repulsed. Lee believed the Union had shifted so many troops south to hold Little Round Top that it had left its line on Cemetery Ridge vulnerable to attack.

The following day, he ordered nearly 15,000 men under the command of General George E. Pickett and General A. P. Hill to undertake a massive assault. The attack came to be known as Pickett's Charge. A mile-wide line of Confederate troops marched across open farmland toward Union positions on Cemetery Ridge. Union artillery ripped holes in the Confederate line as it advanced. When the Confederates neared the crest of the ridge, Union troops, protected by trenches and barricades, unleashed volley after volley. The Union soldiers drove the Confederates back, inflicting some 7,000 casualties in less than half an hour of fighting.

The Aftermath

Fewer than 5,000 Confederate troops made it up Cemetery Ridge, and Union troops quickly overwhelmed those who did. Lee then quickly rallied his troops and began a retreat to Virginia on a rainy July 4. Confederate forces soon became trapped between a swollen Potomac River and pursuing Union troops, but General Meade, with his army depleted by the battle, decided not to attack the defenses put up by the retreating Confederate forces.

At Gettysburg, approximately 28,000 Confederate forces were killed or wounded. This amounted to over one-third of Lee's entire force. The Union army suffered about 23,000 casualties, but could better afford the losses.

On July 3, 1863, during Pickett's Charge, Confederate soldiers charged up Cemetery Ridge into cannon fire. The Confederates suffered a great number of casualties. Soon after the attack failed, General Lee ordered Southern forces to withdraw.

More than 50,000 Americans were killed or wounded during the Battle of Gettysburg. Photos such as this one (inset) by Mathew Brady brought home the grim realities of war.

▶ **CRITICAL THINKING**
Identifying Cause and Effect What was the result of Pickett's Charge?

Gettysburg proved to be the turning point of the war. The Union's victory strengthened the Republicans politically and ensured that Britain would not recognize the Confederacy. For the rest of the war, Lee's forces fought on the defensive, slowly giving ground to the Union army.

✓ PROGRESS CHECK

Summarizing How did the Battle of Gettysburg affect Confederate forces?

Battle for Tennessee

GUIDING QUESTION *How did General Grant earn Lincoln's trust in guiding the Union forces?*

After the Union's major victories at Vicksburg and Gettysburg, fierce fighting erupted in Tennessee near Chattanooga. Chattanooga was a vital railroad junction. Both sides knew that if the Union forces captured Chattanooga, they would control a major railroad running south to Atlanta.

Chickamauga Creek

During the summer of 1863, Union general William Rosecrans outmaneuvered Confederate general Braxton Bragg. In early September, Rosecrans forced Confederate troops to evacuate Chattanooga without a fight. Bragg did not retreat far, however. When Rosecrans advanced into Georgia, Bragg launched an assault against him at Chickamauga Creek on September 19, 1863. Bragg soon smashed through part of the Union defenses, and Rosecrans ordered his troops to fall back to Chattanooga, where he found himself almost completely surrounded by Bragg's forces.

The Battle of Chattanooga

In an effort to save the Union troops in Chattanooga, Lincoln sent some of Meade's forces to help Rosecrans. Dozens of trains were assembled, and 11 days later, 20,000 troops arrived after traveling more than 1,200 miles (1,930 km).

In 1863 Confederate troops attacked Union troops at Chickamauga Creek near Chattanooga, Tennessee.

▶ CRITICAL THINKING

Making Inferences Why do you think the control of the railroad in Chattanooga was important during the Civil War?

PHOTO: Buyenlarge/Archive Photos/Getty Images

Lincoln also decided to reorganize the military leadership in the West, and he placed Grant in overall command. Grant then hurried to Chattanooga to take charge of the coming battle. In late November, he ordered his troops to attack Confederate positions on Lookout Mountain. Charging uphill through swirling fog, the Union forces quickly drove the Confederate troops off the mountain.

Confederate soldiers retreating from Lookout Mountain hurried to join other Confederate forces at Missionary Ridge east of Chattanooga. The Confederates were outnumbered, but they awaited an attack by Union troops, secure on a high rugged position just as the Union troops had been at Cemetery Ridge near Gettysburg.

Grant did not intend to storm Missionary Ridge. He believed that an all-out assault would be suicidal. Instead, he ordered General William Tecumseh Sherman to attack Confederate positions on the north end of the ridge. When Sherman failed to break through, Grant ordered 23,000 men under General George Thomas to launch a limited attack against the Confederates in front of Missionary Ridge as a diversion.

To Grant's astonishment, Thomas's troops overran the Confederate trenches and charged up the steep slope of Missionary Ridge itself. "They shouted 'Chickamauga,'" one Union soldier remembered, "as though the word itself were a weapon." The rapid charge scattered the surprised Confederates, who retreated in panic, leaving Missionary Ridge—and Chattanooga—to the Union army.

Grant Becomes General in Chief

By the spring of 1864, Grant had accomplished two crucial objectives for the Union. His capture of Vicksburg had given the Union control of the Mississippi River, while his victory at Chattanooga had secured eastern Tennessee and cleared the way for an invasion of Georgia.

Lincoln rewarded Grant by appointing him general in chief of the Union forces and **promoting** him to lieutenant general, a rank no one had held since George Washington. Grant then headed east to join the Army of the Potomac, leaving Sherman in command of the western Union forces. When the president met Grant in March 1864, he told him, "I wish to express in this way my entire satisfaction with what you have done. . . . The particulars of your plan I neither know nor seek to know." The president had finally found a general he trusted to win the war.

☑ **PROGRESS CHECK**

Analyzing Why was Chattanooga a critical location to control?

PHOTO: M Price/Hulton-Deutsch Collection/CORBIS

promote to advance in station, rank, or honor

LESSON 4 REVIEW

Reviewing Vocabulary
1. *Explaining* Explain why Grant used a siege as a way to take the city of Vicksburg.

Using Your Notes
2. *Contrasting* Use your notes to write a paragraph contrasting the battle at Chickamauga Creek with the battle at Gettysburg.

Answering the Guiding Questions
3. *Making Inferences* Why was Vicksburg an important victory for the Union forces?

4. *Analyzing* Why was the Battle of Gettysburg a turning point in the war?

5. *Making Connections* How did General Grant earn Lincoln's trust in guiding the Union forces?

Writing Activity
6. **DESCRIPTIVE** Take on the role of a Confederate soldier at Missionary Ridge. Write a letter to your family describing the battle and your feelings about its result.

networks

There's More Online!

- ☑ **BIOGRAPHY** William T. Sherman
- ☑ **IMAGE** Sherman's Destruction
- ☑ **MAP** Sherman's March to the Sea
- ☑ **VIDEO** The War Ends
- ☑ **INTERACTIVE SELF-CHECK QUIZ**

LESSON 5
The War Ends

ESSENTIAL QUESTIONS • *Can the nation's union of states be broken?*
• *Should war be conducted against both military and civilian populations?*

Content Vocabulary
- pillage
- mandate

Academic Vocabulary
- subordinate
- structure

TAKING NOTES: *Organizing*

ACTIVITY Use a graphic organizer similar to the one below to record the final battles of the Civil War and their result.

IT MATTERS BECAUSE

After four bloody years of fighting, Union forces began to wear down the Confederate army. As the war neared its conclusion, however, the assassination of President Lincoln left the nation with many questions about how to reunite the Union.

Grant Versus Lee

GUIDING QUESTION *How did military strategies change during the war's final year?*

In the spring of 1864, the most successful general of the Union army faced the most renowned Confederate commander. Ulysses S. Grant put his most trusted **subordinate,** William Tecumseh Sherman, in charge of operations in the West. He then headed to Washington, D.C., to take command of the Union troops facing Robert E. Lee.

From the Wilderness to Cold Harbor

The first battle of Grant's campaign erupted in May in the Wilderness, a densely forested area near Fredericksburg, Virginia. Intense fighting lasted two days, continuing even after the woods caught fire. Despite suffering heavy casualties, Grant attacked again near Spotsylvania Courthouse. The two armies battled for 11 days, often in bloody hand-to-hand combat.

Unlike past campaigns, in which several weeks of reinforcing and resupplying followed battles, warfare now continued without pause. Savage combat, advances and retreats, and the digging of defensive trenches filled most days and nights.

Unable to break Lee's lines at Spotsylvania, Grant headed toward Cold Harbor, a strategic crossroads northeast of Richmond. Grant decided to launch an all-out assault at Cold Harbor. The attack cost his army 7,000 casualties, compared to 1,500 for Confederate forces.

The Siege of Petersburg

Stopped by Lee at Cold Harbor in June, Grant ordered General Philip Sheridan to stage a cavalry raid north and west of Richmond. While Sheridan's troops distracted Lee, Grant headed southeast, crossed the

James River, and then turned west toward Petersburg. Capturing Petersburg would cut an important railroad line into Richmond.

When the first Union troops reached the outskirts of Petersburg, they paused. The city was defended by miles of barricades 20 feet (7 m) thick. In front of the Confederate trenches were ditches up to 15 feet (4.6 m) deep. Carefully positioned cannons supported Confederate lines. The strength of the defenses that the Confederates had erected at Petersburg intimidated the Union troops, who were already exhausted. Realizing a full-scale frontal assault would be suicidal, Grant ordered his troops to put the city under siege.

subordinate one who is under the authority of a superior

☑ PROGRESS CHECK

Summarizing What strategies did the Confederates use to defend Petersburg?

The Union Advances

GUIDING QUESTION *Do you think armies should treat civilians differently from soldiers during a war?*

While Grant fought Lee, General Sherman marched his army from Chattanooga toward Atlanta, and the Union navy prepared to seal the last major port on the Gulf of Mexico east of the Mississippi—Mobile, Alabama.

Farragut Attacks Mobile

On August 5, 1864, Admiral Farragut took 18 ships past the three Confederate forts defending Mobile Bay. As the fleet headed into the bay, a mine—which in the 1860s was called a torpedo—blew up a Union ship. The explosion brought the fleet to a halt, right in front of a fort's guns. "Damn the torpedoes! Full speed ahead!" cried Farragut, whose ship led the way through the minefield.

GEOGRAPHY CONNECTION

After a series of battles between their forces, Lee eventually surrendered to Grant.

1 **HUMAN SYSTEMS** *How long did the final contest between Grant and Lee take, from the Battle of the Wilderness to the surrender at Appomattox Courthouse?*

2 **THE WORLD IN SPATIAL TERMS** *Based on the positions of the armies on the map, why do you think Lee chose to surrender at Appomattox Courthouse?*

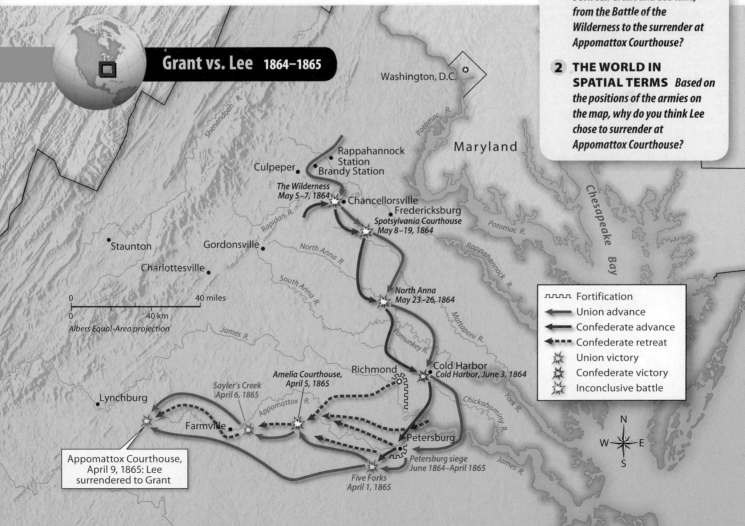

Grant vs. Lee 1864–1865

Washington, D.C.

Shenandoah R.

Potomac R.

Maryland

Culpeper • Rappahannock Station • Brandy Station

The Wilderness May 5–7, 1864 — Chancellorsville • Fredericksburg

Spotsylvania Courthouse May 8–19, 1864

Rapidan R.

Staunton • Gordonsville •

Charlottesville •

North Anna R.

South Anna R.

Potomac R.

Rappahannock R.

Chesapeake Bay

0 — 40 miles
0 — 40 km
Albers Equal-Area projection

James R.

North Anna May 23–26, 1864

Pamunkey R.

Mattaponi R.

Lynchburg •

Sayler's Creek April 6, 1865

Amelia Courthouse, April 5, 1865

Richmond

Appomattox R.

Cold Harbor Cold Harbor, June 3, 1864

Chickahominy R.

York R.

Farmville •

Petersburg

Petersburg siege June 1864–April 1865

James R.

Appomattox Courthouse, April 9, 1865: Lee surrendered to Grant

Five Forks April 1, 1865

🔲🔲🔲 Fortification
⬅ Union advance
⬅ Confederate advance
◀--- Confederate retreat
✦ Union victory
✦ Confederate victory
✦ Inconclusive battle

N
W—E
S

Analyzing SUPREME COURT CASES

Ex Parte Milligan

In 1864 Lambdin P. Milligan was arrested for conspiracy by the Union general in charge of Indiana. Milligan was tried in a military court, found guilty, and sentenced to hang. Lawyers for Milligan sought a writ of habeas corpus, believing the military trial was unconstitutional. The Supreme Court ruled in his favor. If civilian courts are open, it is unconstitutional to try a civilian in a military court. Milligan was freed.

DBQ **SPECULATING** What difference did it make that the military trial took place in Indiana and not somewhere in the South?

structure something that is composed or arranged into a unified whole, as a building or edifice

pillage to loot or plunder

mandate authorization to act given to a representative

The war devastated the South and left several major cities, including Richmond (below), in ruins.

▶ **CRITICAL THINKING**
Predicting Consequences How do you think the damage caused by the war affected the South in the years to come?

After getting past the Confederate forts, Farragut's ships destroyed a Confederate fleet defending Mobile Bay. Although Farragut did not capture Mobile, he did seal off the bay. Blockade runners moving goods in and out of the Deep South could no longer use any port east of Texas.

Sherman's March to the Sea

In late August 1864, Sherman sent his troops south around Atlanta to cut the roads and railways leading into the city. After occupying Atlanta, Sherman proposed to march across Georgia. He ordered all civilians to leave Atlanta. To end the war, he believed, he had no choice but to "make old and young, rich and poor, feel the hard hand of war." Sherman then ordered his troops to destroy everything of military value, including mills, factories, railroads, and warehouses. The fires intended to destroy these **structures** quickly spread, burning down large portions of the city.

On November 15, 1864, Sherman began his March to the Sea. His troops cut a path of destruction through Georgia that was, in places, 60 miles (97 km) wide. They ransacked houses, burned crops, and killed cattle. By December 21, 1864, they had reached the coast and seized the city of Savannah. After reaching the sea, Sherman turned his troops north and headed into South Carolina. As the troops marched north, they **pillaged** and burned many towns, including Columbia, the state capital. Sherman's march demoralized Southerners.

☑ **PROGRESS CHECK**
Identifying Cause and Effect What effect did the capture of Mobile have on the South?

The South Surrenders

GUIDING QUESTION *What do you think life was like in the South at the conclusion of the Civil War?*

When Sherman and Grant began their campaigns in the spring of 1864, Lincoln knew that his own reelection depended on their success. He did not know, however, that the war was nearly over. Only a few months later, the Confederacy was on the verge of collapse.

The Election of 1864

To challenge Lincoln in 1864, the Democrats nominated General George B. McClellan. Knowing the country was growing weary of the war, McClellan pledged to negotiate a cease-fire if the Confederacy agreed to rejoin the Union as part of the negotiations. However, the capture of Atlanta came just in time to revitalize Northern support for the war and for Lincoln, who won reelection with 55 percent of the popular vote. Lincoln viewed his reelection as a **mandate** to end slavery permanently by amending the Constitution. On January 31, 1865, the Thirteenth Amendment, banning slavery in the United States, narrowly passed the House of Representatives and was sent to the states for ratification.

Surrender

On April 1, 1865, Union troops led by Sheridan cut the last railroad line into Petersburg at the Battle of Five Forks. The following night, Lee's troops withdrew from their positions near the city and raced west. Lee's desperate attempt to escape Grant's forces failed when Sheridan's cavalry got ahead of Lee's troops and blocked the road at Appomattox Courthouse. When

his troops failed to break through, Lee sadly observed, "[T]here is nothing left for me to do but go and see General Grant, and I would rather die a thousand deaths." With his battered troops surrounded and outnumbered, Lee surrendered to Grant at Appomattox Courthouse on April 9, 1865.

Grant's generous terms of surrender guaranteed that the United States would not prosecute Confederate soldiers for treason. When Grant agreed to let Confederate soldiers take their horses home "to put in a crop to carry themselves and their families through the next winter," Lee thanked him, adding that the kindness would "do much toward conciliating our people."

Lincoln's Assassination

With the war over, Lincoln described his plan to restore the Southern states to the Union. In the speech, he mentioned including African Americans in Southern state governments. One listener, the actor John Wilkes Booth, sneered to a friend, "That is the last speech he will ever make."

The president's advisers repeatedly warned him not to appear unescorted in public. Nevertheless, on the evening of April 14, 1865, Lincoln went to Ford's Theatre with his wife to see a play. During the third act, Booth slipped quietly behind him and shot the president in the back of the head. Lincoln's death shocked the nation.

Aftermath of the Civil War

The North's victory in the Civil War strengthened the power of the federal government over the states. It also transformed American society by finally ending the enslavement of millions of African Americans. At the same time, it left the South socially and economically devastated. Following the war, many questions remained unresolved. Americans from the North and the South tried to answer these questions in the years following the Civil War—an era known as Reconstruction.

✓ **PROGRESS CHECK**

Explaining What effect did the Union's victory in the war have on the federal government?

LESSON 5 REVIEW

Reviewing Vocabulary

1. *Explaining* Explain why Lincoln believed that his reelection was a mandate to end slavery.

Using Your Notes

2. *Identifying Cause and Effect* Use your notes on the battles at the end of the Civil War to explain the effect of Farragut's blockade of Mobile Bay.

Answering the Guiding Questions

3. *Analyzing* How did military strategies change during the war's final year?

4. *Analyzing Ethical Issues* Do you think armies should treat civilians differently from soldiers during a war?

5. *Making Connections* What do you think life was like in the South at the conclusion of the Civil War?

Writing Activity

6. **DESCRIPTIVE** Take on the role of a newspaper reporter living in Georgia during Sherman's march. Write a brief article describing the Union's actions and their effects on the people of Georgia.

Directions: On a separate sheet of paper, answer the questions below. Make sure you read carefully and answer all parts to the question.

Lesson Review

Lesson 1

1 *Identifying Cause and Effect* What effect did a weak central government have on the Confederacy during the Civil War?

2 *Analyzing* Why did people support the Anaconda Plan?

Lesson 2

3 *Identifying Cause and Effect* How did the Emancipation Proclamation change the way people viewed the Civil War?

4 *Assessing* What was one result of the Battle of Antietam?

Lesson 3

5 *Explaining* What roles did women play during the Civil War?

6 *Analyzing* Why did Frederick Douglass believe that African Americans should serve in the Union military?

Lesson 4

7 *Drawing Conclusions* Why was the Battle of Gettysburg such a significant loss for the South?

8 *Identifying Cause and Effect* Why did President Lincoln make Ulysses S. Grant the general in chief of the Union forces?

Lesson 5

9 *Evaluating* Why did Sherman decide to destroy everything of military value during his March to the Sea?

10 *Exploring Issues* How did the Civil War change the South socially and economically?

21st Century Skills

11 **PROBLEM SOLVING** What strategy did General Ulysses S. Grant use to capture the city of Vicksburg?

12 **EXPLAINING CONTINUITY AND CHANGE** By 1864, when Grant faced Lee near Spotsylvania Courthouse, how had the nature of the war changed?

Exploring the Essential Questions

13 *Defending* Write the text for a short debate that argues the question of whether the nation's union of states had been broken during the Civil War. Include an argument as to whether war should be conducted against both military and civilian populations.

DBQ Document-Based Questions

Use the document to answer the following questions.

Before the Civil War, Robert E. Lee was a respected officer in the United States Army. When Lee learned that his home state of Virginia had voted in 1861 to secede from the Union, he had to choose whether to fight for the Union or the Confederacy.

PRIMARY SOURCE

❝My Dear Sister:

. . . With all my devotion to the Union, and the feeling of loyalty and duty of an American citizen, I have not been able to make up my mind to raise my hand against my relatives, my children, my home. I have, therefore, resigned my commission in the army, and save in defense of my native State . . . I hope I may never be called upon to draw my sword. I know you will blame me; but you must think as kindly of me as you can. . . .❞

—from *Personal Reminiscences, Anecdotes, and Letters of General Robert E. Lee,* 1875

14 *Analyzing Primary Sources* Why did Robert E. Lee think it was necessary to resign from the U.S. Army at the start of the war?

15 *Identifying Perspectives* If a person in 1861 had agreed with the message in Lee's letter, would that person have been eager to fight in the Civil War? Why?

Extended-Response Question

16 *Making Connections* Write an essay describing two key issues that severely divided the country during the Civil War. Explain how the war illustrated the passion that Americans felt about those particular issues. Be sure to include an introduction and at least three paragraphs using details to support your views.

Need Extra Help?

If You've Missed Question	**1**	**2**	**3**	**4**	**5**	**6**	**7**	**8**	**9**	**10**	**11**	**12**	**13**	**14**	**15**	**16**
Go to page	225	227	232	231	235	234	238	241	244	245	237	242	224	246	246	224

Reconstruction

1865–1877

ESSENTIAL QUESTIONS · *How do nations recover from war?*
· *Was Reconstruction a success or a failure?*

The Story Matters...

The Civil War preserved the Union and brought an end to slavery, but left many issues unsettled. The federal government next had to decide under what conditions the secessionist states would be fully restored to the Union. Reconstruction was an era of intense political conflicts over the future of the South and the rights of the formerly enslaved.

◄ Senator Charles Sumner (left) of Massachusetts joined Representative Thaddeus Stevens of Pennsylvania to introduce Radical Republican reforms that would grant civil rights to African Americans, prevent former Confederate leaders from regaining political power, and transform the South's customs and institutions.

PHOTO: The Granger Collection, New York

Reconstruction was an era in which African Americans gained more than just their freedom. Constitutional amendments granted citizenship rights to African Americans and voting rights to African American men. Such gains, however, did not end poverty—a problem that affected both African Americans and whites in the South. In the place of the plantation system, sharecropping emerged. Sharecroppers worked and lived on land rented from white landowners, but the system usually left the sharecroppers indebted to the landowners and thus tied to the land. The sharecropping system kept generations of African American and white Southerners in poverty.

As Reconstruction came to an end, even the political rights of African Americans were stripped away. Hiram Rhodes Revels of Mississippi was the first African American to serve in the U.S. Senate, where he spoke up for the rights of African Americans. In the excerpt below, Revels explains how the gains made by African Americans during Reconstruction were eroded.

Step Into the Place

Read the quote and look at the information presented on the map.

DBQ According to Hiram Rhodes Revels, how has the enslavement of African Americans continued since Reconstruction?

PRIMARY SOURCE

"Since reconstruction, the masses of my people have been, as it were, enslaved in mind by unprincipled adventurers, who, caring nothing for country, were willing to stoop to anything no matter how infamous, to secure power to themselves, and perpetuate it.... My people have been told by these schemers, when men have been placed on the ticket who were notoriously corrupt and dishonest, that they must vote for them.... The bitterness and hate created by the late civil strife has, in my opinion, been obliterated in this state, except perhaps in some localities, and would have long since been entirely obliterated, were it not for some unprincipled men who would keep alive the bitterness of the past."

—Hiram Rhodes Revels, from a letter to President Ulysses S. Grant, November 6, 1875

Step Into the Time

Choose an event from the time line and write a paragraph predicting the general social, political, or economic consequence that event might have on Reconstruction.

A. Johnson 1865–1869

Grant 1869–1877

March 3, 1865 Freedmen's Bureau is founded

April 15, 1865 Lincoln dies

1866 Congress passes the Fourteenth Amendment

1867 Radical Republicans take control of Congress

U.S. PRESIDENTS

UNITED STATES

WORLD

1865

1867

1869

1866 Spain abolishes Cuban slave trade

1867 International Anti-Slavery Conference held in Paris

1868 Australia adopts law regulating Pacific Islander labor trade

1869 Paraguay abolishes slavery

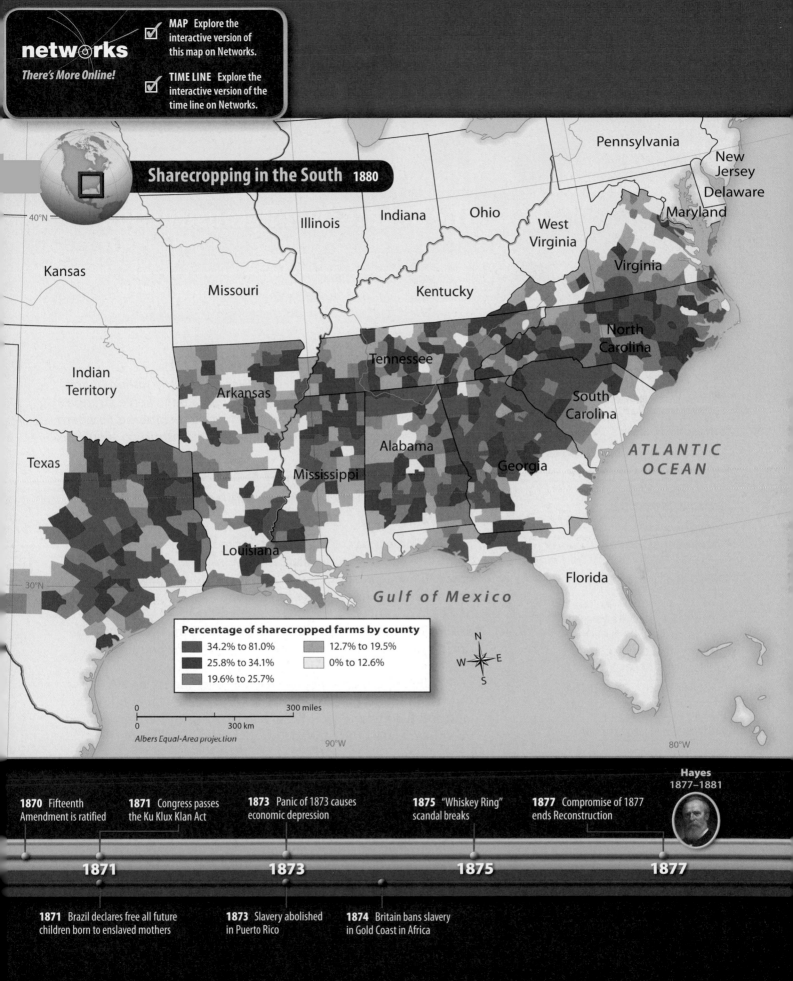

Sharecropping in the South 1880

Percentage of sharecropped farms by county

- 34.2% to 81.0%
- 25.8% to 34.1%
- 19.6% to 25.7%
- 12.7% to 19.5%
- 0% to 12.6%

300 miles

300 km

Albers Equal-Area projection

networks
There's More Online!

☑ **MAP** Explore the interactive version of this map on Networks.

☑ **TIME LINE** Explore the interactive version of the time line on Networks.

Hayes
1877–1881

1870 Fifteenth Amendment is ratified

1871 Congress passes the Ku Klux Klan Act

1873 Panic of 1873 causes economic depression

1875 "Whiskey Ring" scandal breaks

1877 Compromise of 1877 ends Reconstruction

1871   **1873**   **1875**   **1877**

1871 Brazil declares free all future children born to enslaved mothers

1873 Slavery abolished in Puerto Rico

1874 Britain bans slavery in Gold Coast in Africa

Reconstruction **249**

networks

There's More Online!

☑ **BIOGRAPHY** Thaddeus Stevens

☑ **BIOGRAPHY** Charles Sumner

☑ **VIDEO** The Debate Over Reconstruction

☑ **INTERACTIVE SELF-CHECK QUIZ**

LESSON 1

The Debate Over Reconstruction

ESSENTIAL QUESTIONS · *How do nations recover from war?*
· *Was Reconstruction a success or a failure?*

Reading **HELP**DESK

Content Vocabulary

- **amnesty**
- **pocket veto**
- **black codes**
- **impeach**

Academic Vocabulary

- **requirement**
- **precedent**

TAKING NOTES: *Organizing*

ACTIVITY As you read about Reconstruction, complete a graphic organizer similar to the one below by explaining how each listed piece of legislation affected African Americans.

Legislation	Effect
black codes	
Civil Rights Act of 1866	
Fourteenth Amendment	
Fifteenth Amendment	

IT MATTERS BECAUSE

In the months after the Civil War ended, the nation began to rebuild and reunite. Almost immediately, fierce struggles began over how long it should take to restore the Southern states to the Union and how punitive Reconstruction should be.

The Reconstruction Battle Begins

GUIDING QUESTION *How did the Radical Republicans' Reconstruction plan differ from President Lincoln's plan?*

By 1865, large areas of the former Confederacy lay in ruins. The South's economy was in a state of collapse. The value of land had fallen. Confederate money was worthless. Roughly two-thirds of the transportation system no longer functioned. Dozens of bridges had been destroyed, and miles of railroad track were useless. Most dramatically of all, the emancipation of African Americans had thrown the economic system into chaos. Until the South adjusted to this new reality, it could not maintain its agricultural output.

While some Southerners were bitter over the Union's military victory, for others the most important struggle was rebuilding their land and their lives. Meanwhile, the president and Congress faced the difficult task of Reconstruction, or rebuilding after the war.

Lincoln's Plan

In December 1863, President Lincoln offered a general **amnesty,** or pardon, to all Southerners who took an oath of loyalty to the United States and accepted the Union's proclamations concerning slavery. When 10 percent of a state's voters in the 1860 presidential election had taken this oath, they could organize a new state government. Certain people, such as former Confederate government officials and military officers, could not take the oath or be pardoned. In March 1865, in his Second Inaugural Address, President Lincoln spoke of ending the war "[w]ith malice toward none, with charity for all." President Lincoln wanted a moderate policy to reconcile the South with the Union instead of punishing it for treason.

The Radical Republicans

The more radical Republicans in Congress quickly resisted Lincoln's plan. Led by Representative Thaddeus Stevens of Pennsylvania and Senator Charles Sumner of Massachusetts, the radicals did not want to reconcile with the South. They wanted, in Stevens's words, to "revolutionize Southern institutions, habits, and manners."

The Radical Republicans, as they became known, had three main goals. First, they wanted to prevent the leaders of the Confederacy from returning to power after the war. Second, they wanted the Republican Party to become a powerful political force in the South. Third, they wanted the federal government to help African Americans achieve political equality by guaranteeing their right to vote in the South.

Republicans knew that once the Southern states were restored to the Union, the South would gain about 15 seats in the House of Representatives. Before the Civil War, the number of Southern seats in the House was based on the Three-Fifths Compromise in the Constitution. According to this compromise, only three-fifths of the enslaved population counted toward representation. The abolition of slavery entitled the South to more representatives in Congress. This would endanger Republican control of Congress unless Republicans could find a way to protect the voting rights of African Americans.

Many of the Radical Republicans had been abolitionists before the Civil War and had pushed Lincoln to make emancipation a goal of the war. They knew that giving African American men in the South the right to vote would help their party win elections. Most believed in a right to political equality for all men, regardless of race.

The Wade-Davis Bill

Caught between Lincoln and the Radical Republicans were a large number of moderate Republicans. The moderates thought Lincoln was being too lenient, but that the radicals went too far in their support for African Americans.

By the summer of 1864, the moderates and the radicals had agreed on an alternative to Lincoln's plan for Reconstruction. They introduced it in Congress as the Wade-Davis Bill. This bill required the majority of the adult white males in a former Confederate state to take an oath of allegiance to the Union. The state could then hold a constitutional convention to create a new state government. Each state's convention would then have to do three things. It would have to abolish slavery, reject all debts the state had acquired as part of the Confederacy, and deprive all former Confederate government officials and military officers of the right to vote or hold office.

Although Congress passed the Wade-Davis Bill, Lincoln blocked it with a **pocket veto**—that is, he let the session of Congress expire without signing the bill. He thought that imposing a harsh peace would be counterproductive. The president wanted "no persecution, no bloody work."

☑ **PROGRESS CHECK**

Explaining What part of President Lincoln's plan for Reconstruction did the Radical Republicans reject?

Freedmen's Bureau

GUIDING QUESTION *How did the Freedmen's Bureau help formerly enslaved African Americans?*

After considering different approaches to restoring the Southern states to the Union, Lincoln decided that harsh terms would only alienate many whites in the South. The devastation of the war and the collapse of the economy had left hundreds of thousands of people unemployed, homeless, and hungry.

PHOTOS: (l)Library of Congress, (r)Historical/CORBIS

Analyzing
PRIMARY SOURCES

Senator Henry Wilson on the Rights of a Man

❝[Congress] must see to it that the man made free by the Constitution . . . is a freeman indeed; that he can go where he pleases, work when and for whom he pleases; . . . that he can go into the schools and educate himself and his children; that the rights and guarantees of the good old common law are his, and that he walks the earth, proud and erect in the conscious dignity of a free man.❞

—from *The Congressional Globe*, December 21, 1865

DBQ *MAKING INFERENCES*
What might prevent freed African Americans from being truly free despite Reconstruction legislation?

amnesty the act of granting a pardon to a large group of people

pocket veto the president's indirect veto of a bill by letting a session of Congress expire without signing the bill

After the war, Senator Sumner (left) and Representative Stevens (right) offered a plan for Reconstruction. Called Radical Reconstruction, it called for protecting the civil rights of African Americans.

▶ **CRITICAL THINKING**
Analyzing Information Why were the views of Sumner and Stevens considered "radical"?

The Freedmen's Bureau was established to help formerly enslaved people make new lives for themselves. The Bureau provided food, clothing, and medical care and helped African Americans find work and get an education.

▶ CRITICAL THINKING
Identifying Central Issues What might have happened if the Freedmen's Bureau had not been established?

At the same time, thousands of freed African Americans—now known as freedmen—needed help and protection.

To help the freedmen feed themselves, Union general William T. Sherman reserved all abandoned plantation land within 30 miles of the coast from Charleston, South Carolina, to Jacksonville, Florida, for the use of freed African Americans. Over the next few months, Union troops settled more than 40,000 African Americans on roughly half a million acres of land in South Carolina and Georgia.

The refugee crisis prompted Congress to establish the Bureau of Refugees, Freedmen, and Abandoned Lands—better known as the Freedmen's Bureau. The Bureau's mission was to feed and clothe war refugees in the South using surplus army supplies. Between 1865 and 1870, the Bureau issued some 22 million rations and helped prevent mass starvation in the South.

The Bureau also helped formerly enslaved people find work on plantations. It negotiated labor contracts with planters, specifying the amount of pay workers would receive and the number of hours they had to work. It also set up special courts to deal with grievances between workers and planters.

Although many Northerners applauded the Bureau's efforts, some felt that freed African Americans should receive "forty acres and a mule" to support themselves. These people urged the government to seize Confederate land and give it to the freedmen. To others, however, taking land and giving it to freedmen seemed to violate individual property rights. Ultimately, Congress refused to support land confiscation.

Although the Freedmen's Bureau failed to provide African Americans with land to make a fresh start, it did make an important contribution in the field of education. The Bureau worked closely with Northern charities to educate formerly enslaved African Americans. It provided buildings for schools, paid teachers, and helped establish colleges for training African American teachers.

✓ PROGRESS CHECK

Explaining What was the first task of the Freedmen's Bureau?

Schools funded by the Freedmen's Bureau led to a dramatic increase in literacy among African Americans. By 1870, more than 4,000 new schools had been established.

▶ CRITICAL THINKING
Drawing Inferences Why do you think education was a priority for formerly enslaved people?

PHOTOS: (t)Bettmann/CORBIS, (b)detail/Cook Collection/Valentine Richmond History Center

Johnson Takes Office

GUIDING QUESTION *Why were congressional Republicans angry with Johnson's Reconstruction plan?*

After Lincoln's assassination, Vice President Andrew Johnson, a Southern Democrat before the war, became president. Like Lincoln, Johnson believed that a moderate policy was best to bring the seceded states back into the Union and to win Southern loyalty.

Johnson's Plan

In the summer of 1865, Johnson initiated what he called his restoration program. He offered to pardon all former citizens of the Confederacy who took an oath of loyalty to the Union and to return their property. He excluded from the pardon former Confederate officers and officials, as well as any Confederate citizen with property worth more than $20,000. Under another program, each former Confederate state had to call a constitutional convention to revoke its ordinance of secession, ratify the Thirteenth Amendment, and reject all Civil War debts.

Under these provisions, Johnson began granting pardons to thousands of Southerners. When Congress met in December 1865, many members were angry to see that Southern voters had elected former Confederate leaders. Congress refused to seat the representatives of the former Confederate states.

Black Codes

The new Southern state legislatures passed a series of laws known as **black codes,** which severely limited African Americans' rights. The black codes varied between states but seemed intended to keep African Americans in a condition similar to slavery. The black codes angered many Northerners.

☑ **PROGRESS CHECK**

Explaining What immediate outcome resulted from Johnson's Reconstruction plan?

Radical Republicans Take Control

GUIDING QUESTION *What methods did the Radical Republicans use to prevent President Johnson's interference with their Reconstruction plan?*

Political developments convinced many moderate Republicans to join the Radicals. In late 1865, House and Senate Republicans created the Joint Committee on Reconstruction to develop their own program.

The Fourteenth Amendment

To override the black codes, Congress passed the Civil Rights Act of 1866, granting citizenship to all persons born in the United States except Native Americans. The act allowed African Americans to own property and be treated equally in court. The Republicans also introduced the Fourteenth Amendment to the Constitution, granting citizenship to all persons born or naturalized in the United States. It also prohibited states from depriving any person of life, liberty, or property "without due process of law," and denying any person "equal protection of the laws." Increasing violence in the South swayed moderates, and Congress passed the amendment in June.

Johnson attacked the amendment and made it the major issue of the 1866 midterm elections. He hoped that voters would reject the Radical Republicans and elect a congressional majority supportive of his plan. As the election campaign got under way, however, more violence erupted in the South. The Republicans won a roughly 3-to-1 majority in Congress. The Fourteenth Amendment was ratified in 1868.

Connections to
TODAY

The Fourteenth Amendment

The Fourteenth Amendment granted citizenship and equal rights to African Americans after the Civil War and prevented the denial of "life, liberty, or property, without due process of law." Over time, courts interpreted the amendment so that due process was not just limited to procedural considerations. Even if proper procedures are followed, the essential principles on which a person was denied life, liberty, or property might violate the spirit of due process. The Fourteenth Amendment has been cited in court rulings to protect First Amendment rights, which states must guarantee. These include the freedom of religion, the freedom of speech, the freedom of the press, the right to assembly, and the right to petition.

black codes laws passed in the South just after the Civil War aimed at controlling freedmen and enabling plantation owners to exploit African American workers

---

Military Districts and Commanders

1	General John Schofield
2	General Daniel Sickles
3	General John Pope
4	General Edward Ord
5	General Philip Sheridan
1868	Date of readmission to Union

Colorado Territory

New Mexico Territory

MEXICO

Indian Territory

Arkansas 1868

Texas 1870

Louisiana 1868

Mississippi 1870

Alabama 1868

Georgia 1870

Tennessee 1866 (not part of a military district)

North Carolina 1868

South Carolina 1868

Virginia 1870

West Virginia

Kentucky

Florida 1868

Pennsylvania

New Jersey

Md. Delaware

Illinois Indiana Ohio

ATLANTIC OCEAN

Gulf of Mexico

40°N

90°W

0   300 miles
0   300 km
Albers Equal-Area projection

N W E S

What are the Provisions of the Reconstruction Amendments?

The Thirteenth Amendment (1865)
- Slavery is illegal.

The Fourteenth Amendment (1868)
- All people born or naturalized in the United States are citizens (Native Americans were excluded).
- The states may not deny anyone the equal protection of the laws.
- Leaders of the Confederacy cannot serve in the U.S. government or military without a two-thirds vote by Congress.

The Fifteenth Amendment (1870)
- The rights of citizens to vote shall not be denied on account of race, color, or previous condition of servitude.

GEOGRAPHY CONNECTION

Military reconstruction divided the former Confederacy into military districts to protect the rights of freedmen and to ensure order.

1 **THE WORLD IN SPATIAL TERMS** *Which former Confederate state was not part of a military district?*

2 **ENVIRONMENT AND SOCIETY** *What generalization can you make about the location of Southern states and when they were readmitted to the Union?*

requirement a necessity or condition that must be met

impeach to formally charge a public official with misconduct in office

precedent an earlier occurrence of something that may serve as a model for similar occurrences in the future

Military Reconstruction

In March 1867, congressional Republicans passed the Military Reconstruction Act, essentially wiping out Johnson's programs. The act divided the former Confederacy—except for Tennessee, which had ratified the Fourteenth Amendment in 1866—into five military districts. A Union general was in charge of each district.

In the meantime, each former Confederate state had to hold another constitutional convention. Their new constitutions had to give the right to vote to all adult male citizens, regardless of race. After a state had ratified its new constitution, it had to ratify the Fourteenth Amendment before it could elect members to Congress. With military officers supervising voter registration, the Southern states began holding elections and organizing constitutional conventions. By the end of 1868, six former Confederate states—North Carolina, South Carolina, Florida, Alabama, Louisiana, and Arkansas—had met all the **requirements** and were readmitted to the Union.

The Republicans knew that President Johnson could refuse to enforce the laws they passed. They also knew, however, that Secretary of War Edwin M. Stanton agreed with their program and would enforce it. Furthermore, they trusted General Ulysses S. Grant to support their policies. To prevent Johnson from bypassing Grant or firing Stanton, Congress passed the Command of the Army Act and the Tenure of Office Act. The first required all orders from the president to go through the headquarters of the general of the army—Grant's headquarters. The second required the Senate to approve the removal of any government official whose appointment had required the Senate's consent.

Determined to challenge the Tenure of Office Act, Johnson fired Stanton on February 21, 1868. Three days later, the House of Representatives voted to **impeach** Johnson, meaning that they charged him with "high crimes and misdemeanors" in office. The main charge against Johnson was that he had broken the law by refusing to uphold the Tenure of Office Act.

As provided in the Constitution, the Senate put the president on trial. If two-thirds of the senators found the president guilty, he would be removed from office. On May 16, 1868, the Senate voted 35 to 19 that Johnson was guilty—one vote short of conviction. Dissenting senators believed that it would set a dangerous **precedent** to impeach a president simply because he did not agree with congressional policies. William Crook, the president's bodyguard, described what happened when the votes were counted: "The Radical Senators [were enraged]; all over the house people began to stir. . . . [T]here was a wild outburst, chiefly groans of anger and disappointment . . ."

Although Johnson remained in office, he finished his term quietly and did not run for reelection in 1868. The Republicans nominated General Grant to run for president. During the campaign, ongoing violence in the South convinced many that the Southern states could not be trusted to reorganize their governments without military supervision. Grant won five of the Deep South states—Tennessee, Alabama, South Carolina, North Carolina, and Florida—and most of the Northern states. The Republicans kept large majorities in both houses of Congress.

With their majority secure and a trusted president in office, Republicans moved to expand their Reconstruction program. Realizing the importance of African American voters, Congress passed the Fifteenth Amendment to the Constitution. This amendment declared that the right to vote "shall not be denied . . . on account of race, color, or previous condition of servitude." By March 1870, enough states had ratified the amendment to make it part of the Constitution.

Radical Reconstruction had a dramatic impact on the South, particularly in the short term. It changed Southern politics by bringing hundreds of thousands of African Americans into the political process for the first time. This, in turn, angered many white Southerners, who responded by fighting back against the federal government's policies.

✓ **PROGRESS CHECK**

Explaining Why did the Radical Republicans force Southern states to hold new constitutional conventions?

PHOTO: Bettmann/CORBIS

BIOGRAPHY

Andrew Johnson (1808–1875)

Born into poverty in North Carolina, Andrew Johnson apprenticed as a tailor as a boy and eventually opened his own tailor shop in Tennessee. He became a skilled public speaker, often defending small farmers and states' rights. Johnson went on to serve in both houses of Congress and supported legislation that would benefit the poor. After Tennessee seceded from the Union in 1861, Johnson remained in the Senate, refusing to join the Confederacy. In the North, he was viewed as a hero but was deemed a traitor by most Southerners. In 1864 Republicans nominated Johnson, a Southerner and a Democrat, for vice president.

▶ **CRITICAL THINKING**
Drawing Inferences How do you think Johnson's past influenced his Reconstruction plan?

LESSON 1 REVIEW

Reviewing Vocabulary

1. *Drawing Conclusions* Why did Southern states pass black codes?

2. *Identifying Central Issues* Why was Johnson impeached?

Using Your Notes

3. *Summarizing* Review the notes you completed during the lesson and describe how each piece of legislation affected African Americans.

Answering the Guiding Questions

4. *Comparing and Contrasting* How did the Radical Republicans' Reconstruction plan differ from President Lincoln's plan?

5. *Summarizing* How did the Freedmen's Bureau help formerly enslaved African Americans?

6. *Interpreting* Why were congressional Republicans angry with Johnson's Reconstruction plan?

7. *Summarizing* What methods did the Radical Republicans use to prevent Johnson's interference with their Reconstruction plan?

Writing Activity

8. NARRATIVE Write a short narrative explaining your opinion of Johnson's Reconstruction plan. What was Reconstruction meant to do? If he had had more time to implement his plan, would it have met that goal, or was his plan hopelessly flawed?

networks

There's More Online!

- ☑ **BIOGRAPHY** Blanche K. Bruce
- ☑ **BIOGRAPHY** Hiram Revels
- ☑ **CHART/GRAPH** African American Colleges and Universities
- ☑ **IMAGE** Emancipation Celebration
- ☑ **VIDEO** Republican Rule
- ☑ **INTERACTIVE SELF-CHECK QUIZ**

Reading **HELP**DESK

Content Vocabulary

- carpetbagger
- scalawag
- graft

Academic Vocabulary

- **commissioner**
- **comprehensive**

TAKING NOTES: *Organizing*

ACTIVITY As you read, complete a graphic organizer similar to the one below by identifying how African Americans helped govern the South during Reconstruction.

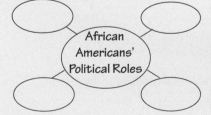

African Americans' Political Roles

LESSON 2
Republican Rule

ESSENTIAL QUESTIONS · *How do nations recover from war?*
· *Was Reconstruction a success or a failure?*

IT MATTERS BECAUSE

Under the Republican-controlled Congress, the South began to rebuild. African Americans gained some new opportunities, particularly in politics, while some white Southerners organized to resist these changes.

Republican Rule in the South

GUIDING QUESTION *How did African Americans participate in politics during Reconstruction?*

By late 1870, the Republican Party was in power in the South and introducing major reforms. Most white Southerners believed that the Union Army had forced the new Republican governments on them.

Carpetbaggers and Scalawags

As Reconstruction began, some Northerners moved to the South. Many were eventually elected to positions in the South's new state governments. Southerners, particularly Democratic Party supporters, referred to these newcomers as **carpetbaggers** because some came with suitcases made of carpet fabric. Many local residents viewed the Northerners as intruders seeking to exploit the South.

Some carpetbaggers did seek to take advantage of the war-torn region, and corruption plagued parts of the South. Others, however, hoped to find greater opportunities than those that existed for them in the North or the West. Some simply wanted to help. Many Northern schoolteachers, for example, moved south to help educate whites and African Americans.

While many Southerners despised carpetbaggers, they also disliked white Southerners who worked with the Republicans and supported Reconstruction. They called these people **scalawags**—an old Scots-Irish term for weak, underfed, worthless animals.

The scalawags were a diverse group. Some were former Whigs who had grudgingly joined the Democratic Party before the war. Many were owners of small farms who did not want the wealthy planters to regain power. Still others were business people who favored Republican plans for developing the South's economy.

African Americans in Politics

The Fifteenth Amendment allowed many freedmen to take part in governing the South. At first the leadership of the African American community came from people who had been educated before the war. These included artisans, shopkeepers, and ministers. Many had lived in the North and fought in the Union Army. Aided by the Republican Party, these leaders delivered speeches to formerly enslaved people, drawing them into politics. Within a few years, many African Americans went from being enslaved laborers to legislators and administrators. They were working in nearly all levels of government, from mayor to police chief to school **commissioner** to the state legislature, and even to Congress.

Republican Reforms

With formerly enslaved men making such political gains, many Southerners claimed that "Black Republicanism" ruled the South. Such claims, however, were greatly exaggerated. No African American was ever elected governor. In South Carolina, African Americans did gain control of the legislature but were able to hold power for only one term.

The Republican Party took power in the South because it had the support of a large number of white Southerners. Poor white farmers, who resented the planters and the Democratic Party that dominated the South before the Civil War, often joined with African American voters to elect Republicans.

The newly elected Republican governments instituted a number of reforms. They repealed the black codes and made many more state offices elective. They established state hospitals and rebuilt roads, railways, and bridges. They also established a system of public schools.

Although many Republicans wanted to help the South, others were corrupt. **Graft,** or gaining money illegally through politics, was common in the South. It was also common in the North at the time, but it gave Democrats another issue that would help them regain power in the 1870s.

✓ PROGRESS CHECK

Explaining Why did some Northerners move to the South, and how were they received?

African American Communities

GUIDING QUESTION *What role did churches and schools play in the lives of African Americans during and after Reconstruction?*

In addition to entering politics, African Americans worked to improve their lives in other ways during Reconstruction. Many tried to set up their own thriving communities and to gain an education.

African American Churches

Churches often became the center of African American communities. They housed schools and hosted social events and political gatherings. In rural areas, church picnics, festivals, and other activities provided residents with many of their recreational and social opportunities. In many communities, churches acted as unofficial courts. They promoted social values, settled disputes, and disciplined individuals for improper behavior.

A Desire to Learn

Once freed, many African Americans immediately sought an education. In the first years of Reconstruction, the Freedmen's Bureau, with the help of Northern charities, established schools for African Americans across the South.

This sketch from 1868 shows African Americans campaigning. In the sketch, women and children are present, suggesting that the entire community valued politics and was interested in political issues, even though only adult males could vote.

▶ CRITICAL THINKING
Identifying Central Issues Why do you think African Americans were so enthusiastic about participating in politics?

carpetbagger name given to Northerners who moved to the South after the Civil War and supported the Republicans

scalawag name given to Southerners who supported the Republicans and Reconstruction of the South

commissioner the officer in charge of a department or bureau of the public service

graft the acquisition of money in dishonest ways, as in bribing a politician

Due to the establishment of several African American colleges and universities during Reconstruction, African Americans had more educational opportunities.

▶ **CRITICAL THINKING**

1 *Identifying Central Issues* What is the purpose of teaching students to respect labor and to work with skilled hands?

2 *Interpreting Significance* Why do you think many of the schools began with a religious purpose or affiliation?

African American Colleges and Universities	
Name of Institution	**Description**
Atlanta University	Georgia, founded in 1865 with funds from the American Missionary Association and the Freedmen's Bureau; now Clark Atlanta University
Fisk University	Tennessee, founded in 1866 and named in honor of General Clinton B. Fisk of the Tennessee Freedmen's Bureau, who let the school use former Union Army barracks as a campus
Morehouse College	Georgia, founded in 1867 as the Augusta Institute; one of the four founders was a formerly enslaved man, the Reverend Richard C. Coulter
Hampton Institute	Virginia, founded as a trade and agricultural school in 1868; originally a makeshift school set up in 1861 for enslaved people fleeing to Union Army camps; Mary Peake, a free African American who broke the law against educating enslaved people, was its first organizer

comprehensive covering widely and completely

By 1870, some 4,000 schools and 9,000 teachers—roughly half of them African American—taught some 200,000 formerly enslaved people of all ages. In the 1870s, Reconstruction governments built a **comprehensive** public school system in the South. By 1876, about 40 percent of all African American children (roughly 600,000 students) attended school.

Several African American academies were established. These academies grew into a network of African American colleges and universities. The founder of the Hampton Institute expressed the founding mission of that educational institution:

PRIMARY SOURCE

❝The thing to be done was clear: to train selected [African American] youth who should go out and teach and lead their people, first by example, by getting land and homes; to give them not a dollar that they could earn for themselves; to teach respect for labor, to replace stupid drudgery with skilled hands; and, to these ends, to build up an industrial system, for the sake not only of self-support and intelligent labor, but also for the sake of character.❞

—Samuel Armstrong, from a speech opening the Hampton Normal and Agricultural Institute, April 1, 1868

☑ **PROGRESS CHECK**

Identifying Why was developing a network of African American schools so important for the goals of Reconstruction?

Southern Resistance

GUIDING QUESTION *How did the federal government react to the Southern resistance groups that developed during Reconstruction?*

At the same time as these changes were taking place, African Americans faced intense resentment from many Southern whites. Many Southerners also despised the "Black Republican" governments, which they believed Northerners had forced upon them.

Unable to strike openly at the Republicans running their states, some Southerners organized secret societies to terrorize African Americans and white supporters of Reconstruction. The largest of these groups was the Ku

Klux Klan. Started in 1866 by former Confederate soldiers in Pulaski, Tennessee, the Klan grew rapidly throughout the South. Its goal was to drive out Northern reformers and politicians and to keep African Americans from voting or exercising their civil rights in any way. By doing this, members of the Klan hoped to regain control of the South for white people and the Democratic Party.

Hooded, white-robed Klan members rode in bands at night, terrorizing supporters of the Republican governments. They broke up Republican meetings; drove Freedmen's Bureau officials out of their communities; burned African American homes, schools, and churches; and attempted to keep African Americans and white Republicans from voting.

Some Republicans and African Americans formed their own militia groups and fought back. As the violence perpetrated by both sides increased, one group of African Americans sent a petition to Congress asking for help:

PRIMARY SOURCE

❝We believe you are not familiar with the description of the Ku Klux Klan's riding nightly over the country, going from county to county, and in the county towns spreading terror wherever they go by robbing, whipping, ravishing, and killing our people without provocation, compelling colored people to break the ice and bathe in the chilly waters of the Kentucky River. . . . We pray you will take some steps to remedy these evils.❞
—from a petition to Congress, March 25, 1871

The Ku Klux Klan's activities outraged President Ulysses S. Grant and congressional Republicans. In 1870 and 1871, Congress passed three Enforcement Acts to combat the acts of violence in the South. The first act made it a federal crime to interfere with a citizen's right to vote. The second put federal elections under the supervision of federal marshals. The third act, also known as the Ku Klux Klan Act, outlawed the activities of the Klan. Local authorities and federal agents, acting under the Enforcement Acts, arrested more than 3,000 Klan members throughout the South. Southern juries, however, convicted only about 600. Fewer served any time in prison.

✓ **PROGRESS CHECK**

Explaining Why was the federal government unable to destroy the Ku Klux Klan during Reconstruction?

Members of the Klan dressed in white hoods and robes, at first to symbolize the spirits of fallen Confederate soldiers.

▶ **CRITICAL THINKING**
Drawing Inferences Why do you think these Klan members wanted their picture taken in their hoods and robes?

LESSON 2 REVIEW

Reviewing Vocabulary

1. *Explaining* Why did many Southerners resent Northerners who came South to implement Reconstruction, calling them carpetbaggers?

2. *Making Generalizations* Why did many Southerners hate other Southerners who supported Reconstruction, calling them scalawags?

Using Your Notes

3. *Identifying* Use the notes you completed during the lesson to identify how African Americans helped govern the South during Reconstruction.

Answering the Guiding Questions

4. *Making Generalizations* How did African Americans participate in politics during Reconstruction?

5. *Summarizing* What role did churches and schools play in the lives of African Americans during and after Reconstruction?

6. *Synthesizing* How did the federal government react to the Southern resistance groups that developed during Reconstruction?

Writing Activity

7. **EXPOSITORY** Describe how the lives of African Americans changed and did not change in the South during this time.

networks

There's More Online!

- ☑ **BIOGRAPHY** Horace Greeley
- ☑ **IMAGE** Agricultural Work
- ☑ **VIDEO** Reconstruction Collapses
- ☑ **INTERACTIVE SELF-CHECK QUIZ**

LESSON 3
Reconstruction Collapses

ESSENTIAL QUESTIONS · *How do nations recover from war?*
· *Was Reconstruction a success or a failure?*

Reading **HELP**DESK

Content Vocabulary

- "sin tax" · debt peonage
- tenant farmer
- sharecropper
- crop lien

Academic Vocabulary

- outcome
- circumstance

TAKING NOTES: *Organizing*

ACTIVITY As you read the lesson, complete an outline similar to the one below by listing the major events of the Grant administration and the end of Reconstruction.

> I. The Grant Administration
> A.
> B.
> II.
> A.

IT MATTERS BECAUSE

As Reconstruction came to an end in the late 1870s, the gains made by African Americans after the Civil War were steadily eroded by Southern whites as they reclaimed control of state legislatures. In the meantime, Southerners were developing strategies for a rebirth of the region's economy.

The Grant Administration

GUIDING QUESTION *How did political and economic issues during the Grant administration weaken Reconstruction?*

As commander of the Union forces, Ulysses S. Grant had led the North to victory in the Civil War. His reputation then won him the presidency in the election of 1868. Unfortunately, he had little political experience. His belief that the president's role was to carry out the laws and leave the development of policy to Congress left him weak and ineffective. Eventually, his lack of experience helped divide the Republican Party and undermine public support for Reconstruction.

The Republican Split

During Grant's first term in office, the Republican-controlled Congress continued to enforce Reconstruction and to expand its economic programs. They kept tariffs high, tightened banking regulations, and increased federal spending on infrastructure. Taxes on alcohol and tobacco, nicknamed **"sin taxes"** and introduced as emergency measures during the war, were kept in place.

Democrats attacked these Republican economic policies. They argued that wealthy Americans had too much influence in Grant's administration. Some Republicans, known as Liberal Republicans, agreed. They tried to prevent Grant's renomination in 1872. When that failed, they split the Republican Party by nominating their own candidate, publisher Horace Greeley. To attract Southern support, the Liberal Republicans promised to pardon nearly all former Confederates and to remove Union troops from the South. Then, believing that only a united effort would defeat Grant, the Democratic Party also

PHOTOS: (l to r)Bettmann/CORBIS, Historical/CORBIS, Library of Congress nominated Greeley. Despite the split in his own party and Greeley's passionate campaigning, Grant easily won reelection.

In Grant's second term, a series of scandals hurt his administration. Grant's secretary of war, William Belknap, had accepted bribes from merchants at Western army posts and resigned to avoid impeachment. In 1875 the Whiskey Ring scandal broke. Government officials and distillers in St. Louis, Missouri, had filed false tax reports, cheating the government out of millions of dollars. Reportedly, Grant's private secretary, Orville E. Babcock, was involved, but this was never proven.

The Panic of 1873

In addition to the political scandals of Grant's second term, the nation endured a severe economic crisis. The turmoil started in 1873 when bad investments forced the powerful banking firm of Jay Cooke and Company into bankruptcy. A wave of fear known as the Panic of 1873 quickly spread. Dozens of smaller banks closed, and the stock market plummeted. Thousands of businesses shut down, and unemployment soared. The administration scandals and the deepening economic depression hurt the Republicans politically. In the 1874 midterm elections, the Democrats won control of the House of Representatives and made gains in the Senate.

☑ **PROGRESS CHECK**

Explaining How was the Republican Party hurt by Grant's administration?

Reconstruction Ends

GUIDING QUESTION *Why was the Compromise of 1877 considered the end of Reconstruction?*

The rising power of the Democrats made enforcing Reconstruction more difficult. At the same time, many Northerners became more concerned with their own economic problems than with conditions in the South.

"Redeeming" the South

In the 1870s, Southern Democrats had worked to regain control of their state and local governments from Republicans. Southern terrorist groups, such as the Ku Klux Klan and the Knights of the White Camellia, intimidated African American and white Republican voters, while some Democrats resorted to various forms of election fraud, such as stuffing ballot boxes and stealing ballot boxes in Republican precincts. Southern Democrats also called on all whites to help "redeem"—or save—the South from "Black Republican" rule.

By appealing to white racism and defining elections as a struggle between whites and African Americans, Democrats were able to win back the support of white owners of small farms who had supported Republicans. By 1876, the Democrats had taken control of all Southern state legislatures except those of Louisiana, South Carolina, and Florida. In those states, the large number of African American voters, protected by Union troops, were able to keep the Republicans in power.

The Compromise of 1877

With Grant's reputation damaged by scandals, the Republicans decided not to nominate him for a third term in 1876. Instead, they nominated Rutherford B. Hayes, a former governor of Ohio. Many Americans regarded Hayes as a moral man untainted by scandal or corruption. Hayes wanted to end Radical Reconstruction.

"WHISKEY RING"

POLITICAL CARTOONS

This cartoon shows the Grant administration looking for those guilty of fraud in a whiskey barrel, which symbolizes the Whiskey Ring.

▶ **CRITICAL THINKING**

1 *Analyzing Visuals* How far does the cartoonist suggest that the corruption in government has spread?

2 *Drawing Inferences* The poster states: "I beg to repeat that these frauds on the government shall be probed to the very BOTTOM." What is the message intended by pairing that statement with this image?

"sin tax" federal tax on alcohol and tobacco

PHOTO: Bettmann/CORBIS

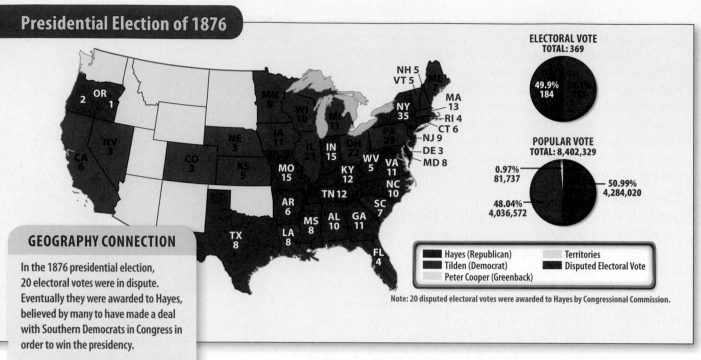

ELECTORAL VOTE
TOTAL: 369

49.9%
184

POPULAR VOTE
TOTAL: 8,402,329

0.97%
81,737

50.99%
4,284,020

48.04%
4,036,572

■ Hayes (Republican)   Territories
■ Tilden (Democrat)   ■ Disputed Electoral Vote
■ Peter Cooper (Greenback)

Note: 20 disputed electoral votes were awarded to Hayes by Congressional Commission.

GEOGRAPHY CONNECTION

In the 1876 presidential election, 20 electoral votes were in dispute. Eventually they were awarded to Hayes, believed by many to have made a deal with Southern Democrats in Congress in order to win the presidency.

1 PLACES AND REGIONS *Which candidate was more popular with voters in the Western states?*

2 HUMAN SYSTEMS *How does the map show that a divide still existed in the United States?*

Analyzing PRIMARY SOURCES

A Call for Unity

❝Let me assure my countrymen of the Southern States that it is my earnest desire to regard and promote their truest interests, the interests of the white and of the colored people, both and equally, and to put forth my best efforts in behalf of a civil policy which will forever wipe out . . . the color line, and the distinction between North and South, to the end that we may have, not merely a united North or a united South, but a united country.❞

—Rutherford B. Hayes, from his Inaugural Address, March 5, 1877

DBQ *IDENTIFYING CENTRAL ISSUES* What does Hayes suggest is the main problem in the United States as he takes office?

The Democrats responded by nominating Samuel Tilden, a wealthy corporate lawyer and former governor of New York who had tried to end the corruption in New York City's government. On Election Day, Tilden clearly won 184 electoral votes, 1 short of a majority. Hayes clearly won 165 electoral votes, leaving 20 votes in dispute. Nineteen of the votes were in the three Southern states Republicans still controlled: Louisiana, South Carolina, and Florida. There had been so much election fraud on both sides that no one could tell which candidate had won.

To resolve the situation, Congress appointed a 15-person commission made up of 8 Republicans and 7 Democrats, which voted along party lines to give all the disputed votes to Hayes. The commission's recommendations, however, were not binding if either house of Congress rejected them. After much debate, several Southern Democrats joined with Republicans in the House and voted to accept the commission's findings. This gave the election to Hayes. Some people believed Hayes could not have won without the support of Southern Democrats, and they concluded that a deal had been made. The **outcome** of the election has been called the Compromise of 1877.

Historians are not sure if a deal actually was made and, if so, what its exact terms were. The Compromise of 1877 reportedly included a promise by the Republicans to pull federal troops out of the South if Hayes were elected. That is, in fact, what happened within a month of Hayes taking office. It is also true that the nation was tired of the politics of Reconstruction and that even Republican leaders were ready to end it. Indeed, President Grant pulled troops out of Florida even before Hayes took office, so it is possible that no deal was actually made.

In his inaugural speech, President Hayes stated that the United States was ready to be fully reunited. In April 1877, he pulled federal troops out of the South. Without soldiers to support them, the last Republican governments in South Carolina and Louisiana collapsed. The Democrats had "redeemed" the South. Reconstruction was over.

✔ **PROGRESS CHECK**

Explaining What led to the end of Reconstruction?

A "New South" Arises

GUIDING QUESTION *How did the South's postwar economy force many African Americans into difficult circumstances?*

Some Southern leaders called for the creation of a "New South"—a phrase coined by Henry W. Grady, editor of the *Atlanta Constitution.* This meant developing a strong industrial economy in the South.

Powerful white Southerners and Northern financiers did bring great economic changes to parts of the South. By 1890, thousands of miles of railroad track crisscrossed the South, and a thriving iron and steel industry developed around Birmingham, Alabama. Tobacco processing became big business, and numerous cotton mills appeared. Despite its industrial growth, however, the South remained largely agrarian. Only a small percentage of the labor force worked in manufacturing.

The collapse of Reconstruction ended African Americans' hopes of being granted their own land in the South. Instead, many returned to plantations owned by whites, where they either worked for wages or became **tenant farmers,** paying rent for the land they farmed. Most tenant farmers eventually became **sharecroppers.** Sharecroppers did not pay their rent in cash. Instead, they paid a share of their crops—often as much as one-half to two-thirds.

Many sharecroppers also needed more seed and supplies than their landlords could provide. As a result, country stores sold them supplies on credit—often at interest rates as high as 40 percent. To ensure sharecroppers paid their debts, laws allowed merchants to put liens on their crops. These **crop liens** meant that the merchants could take crops to cover the debts.

The crop-lien system and high interest rates led many sharecroppers into a financial condition called **debt peonage.** Debt peonage trapped sharecroppers on the land because they could not make enough money to pay off their debts and leave, nor could they declare bankruptcy. Failure to pay off debts led to legal problems. The Civil War had ended slavery, but the failure of Reconstruction trapped many African Americans in economic **circumstances** that severely limited their new freedom.

✓ **PROGRESS CHECK**

Explaining Why did the South remain agrarian despite its efforts to industrialize?

The industry of the "New South" was still driven by agriculture. The workers shown here are processing tobacco in a Richmond tobacco factory in 1899.

outcome something that follows as a result or consequence

tenant farmer a farmer who works land owned by another and pays rent either in cash or crops

sharecropper a farmer who works land for an owner who provides equipment and seed and receives a share of the crop

crop lien an obligation placed on a farmer to repay a debt with crops

debt peonage the condition of sharecroppers who could not pay off their debts and, therefore, could not leave the property they worked

circumstance a condition or situation

PHOTOS: Historical/CORBIS

LESSON 3 REVIEW

Reviewing Vocabulary

1. *Identifying Central Issues* Why was the life of a sharecropper difficult?

2. *Defining* How did crop liens trap sharecroppers?

Using Your Notes

3. *Summarizing* Use the notes you completed during the lesson to write a short paragraph describing the problems that led to the end of Reconstruction.

Answering the Guiding Questions

4. *Analyzing Cause and Effect* How did political and economic issues during the Grant administration weaken Reconstruction?

5. *Making Inferences* Why was the Compromise of 1877 considered the end of Reconstruction?

6. *Analyzing* How did the South's postwar economy force many African Americans into difficult circumstances?

Writing Activity

7. DESCRIPTIVE Did Reconstruction create good job opportunities? Write an essay in which you describe the job options for whites and African Americans in the "New South" during Reconstruction.

Directions: On a separate sheet of paper, answer the questions below. Make sure you read carefully and answer all parts to the question.

Lesson Review

Lesson 1

1 *Making Inferences* Why do you think President Lincoln offered an amnesty to most Southerners, but he did not offer it to former Confederate officials or military officers?

2 *Identifying Cause and Effect* Why did Congress move to impeach President Johnson?

Lesson 2

3 *Analyzing* In addition to being a place for worship, why was the church an important part of the African American community?

4 *Explaining* What were the goals of the Ku Klux Klan?

Lesson 3

5 *Identifying Central Issues* What was the main issue of the "Whiskey Ring" scandal of 1875?

6 *Making Inferences* How did sharecroppers fall into debt peonage?

21st Century Skills

7 **IDENTIFYING PERSPECTIVES AND DIFFERING INTERPRETATIONS** How was the Radical Republicans' view of the South different from President Lincoln's?

8 **COMPARE AND CONTRAST** During Reconstruction, how did the lives of freed African Americans change under the black codes?

9 **EXPLAINING CONTINUITY AND CHANGE** During Reconstruction, how did access to education change for African Americans in the South?

10 **UNDERSTANDING RELATIONSHIPS AMONG EVENTS** How did the outcome of the presidential election of 1876 lead to the Compromise of 1877?

Exploring the Essential Questions

11 *Identifying Central Issues* Write a script for an educational television program that demonstrates how the United States tried to recover from the Civil War during Reconstruction. In the script identify your point of view as to whether Reconstruction was a success or a failure.

DBQ Document-Based Questions

Use the image to answer the following questions.

This 1872 lithograph depicts African Americans elected to Congress. Senator Hiram R. Revels of Mississippi is on the far left. The other men are members of the House of Representatives elected from Alabama, Florida, Georgia, and South Carolina.

PRIMARY SOURCE

12 *Synthesizing* How are these African American elected officials depicted in this lithograph?

13 *Analyzing Perspectives* Why would different people in the South have had contrasting opinions about this lithograph?

Extended-Response Question

14 *Analyzing Ethical Issues* Write an essay analyzing the ways that racism and the idea of racial equality were both factors during the events of Reconstruction. Include an introduction and at least three supporting paragraphs in your essay.

Need Extra Help?

If You've Missed Question	1	2	3	4	5	6	7	8	9	10	11	12	13	14
Go to page	250	255	257	259	261	263	250	253	257	262	250	264	264	250

Settling the West

1865–1890

ESSENTIAL QUESTION • *Why would people take on the challenges of life in the West?*

◄ Sitting Bull (1831–1890)

PHOTO: The Granger Collection, New York

The Story Matters...

After the Civil War, Americans continued migrating to the western frontier. Their lives were filled with hardships. But this movement west created more hardships for the Native Americans, which dramatically altered their way of life.

Sitting Bull, a leader of the Sioux, steadfastly defended his people against forces trying to strip them of their homes, their culture, and their very existence.

Place and Time: United States 1860–1900

Miners, ranchers, and farmers led the way to the expansion of the western territories. Homesteading allowed settlers to claim acres of land to cultivate and build new lives. With the building of railroads to connect the western states to the East, the population quickly grew. For centuries this land was home to many groups of Native Americans. The settling of the West altered their way of life forever.

Step Into the Place

Read the quotes and look at the information presented on the map.

 How does the first quote compare to the information and feelings expressed in the second quote from the document?

PRIMARY SOURCE

❝My heart is full of sorrow that so many were killed on each side, but when they compel us to fight, we must fight. . . . Tonight we shall mourn for our dead, and for those brave white men lying up yonder on the hillside.❞

—Sitting Bull, after the Battle of the Little Bighorn, 1876

PRIMARY SOURCE

❝The Seventh [Infantry] can handle anything it meets.❞

—General George A. Custer while declining reinforcements for the Battle of the Little Bighorn

❝. . . It is the opinion at headquarters among those who are most familiar with the situation, that Custer struck Sitting Bull's main camp. . . . Custer dropped squarely into the midst of no less than ten thousand red devils and was literally torn to pieces. The movement made by Custer is censured to some extent at military headquarters in this city. . . .❞

—as reported in the *New York Times*, July 7, 1876

Step Into the Time

Choose an event from the time line and write a paragraph predicting the general social, political, and economic consequences that event might have on settling the West.

U.S. PRESIDENTS				A. Johnson 1865–1869		Grant 1869–1877
UNITED STATES						
WORLD	1860				1870	

1862 Homestead Act makes cheap land available to settlers

1864 Sand Creek Massacre takes place

1867 Chisholm Trail cattle drive begins

1868 Sioux move to Black Hills reservation

1866 French explore the Mekong River

1873 British raise their flag at Port Moresby in New Guinea

1876 Belgium founds International Association for the Exploration and Civilization of Africa

The Battle of the Little Bighorn, 1876

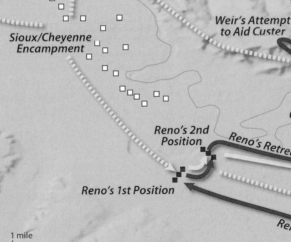

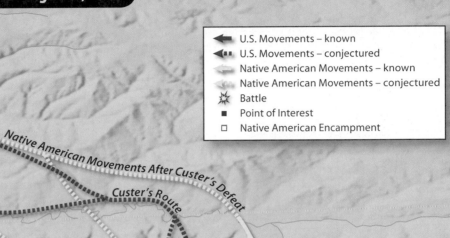

	U.S. Movements – known
	U.S. Movements – conjectured
	Native American Movements – known
	Native American Movements – conjectured
✳	Battle
■	Point of Interest
□	Native American Encampment

The Last Stand

Calhoun Hill

Little Bighorn River

Native American Movements After Custer's Defeat

Custer's Route

Sioux/Cheyenne Encampment

Weir's Attempt to Aid Custer

Custer's Advance

Benteen's Advance

Retreat Crossing

Reno's 2nd Position

Reno's Retreat

Entrenchment

Little Bighorn River

Reno's 1st Position

Reno's Advance

Reno Creek

Reno Ford

N W E S

0 — 1 mile
0 — 1 km

GCS WGS 1984 projection

Hayes 1877–1881	**Garfield** 1881	**Arthur** 1881–1885	**Cleveland** 1885–1889	**1887** Dawes Act passed **1889** Oklahoma Land Rush takes place	**B. Harrison** 1889–1893	**Cleveland** 1893–1897	**McKinley** 1897–1901

1880   **1890**   **1900**

1884 Fifteen nations meet at Berlin West Africa Conference to set rules for the colonization of Central Africa

1886 Gold is discovered in South Africa

1889 Boer War begins between Afrikaners and British in southern Africa

1891 Russia begins Trans-Siberian railway

Settling the West **267**

Reading HELPDESK

Content Vocabulary

- vigilance committee
- hydraulic mining
- open range
- hacienda
- barrios

Academic Vocabulary

- extract
- adapt
- prior

TAKING NOTES: *Organizing*

ACTIVITY As you read, complete a graphic organizer like the one below listing the locations of mining booms and the discoveries made there.

Mining Booms & Discoveries

LESSON 1
Miners and Ranchers

ESSENTIAL QUESTION · *Why would people take on the challenges of life in the West?*

IT MATTERS BECAUSE

The migration of miners and ranchers to western territories resulted in populations large enough to qualify for statehood. People mined for gold, silver, and lead or shipped longhorn cattle to the East.

Growth of the Mining Industry

GUIDING QUESTION *How did mineral discoveries shape the settlement of the West?*

Mining played an important role in the settling of the American West. Demand for minerals rose dramatically after the Civil War as the United States changed from a farming nation to an industrial nation. Mining also led to the building of railroads to connect the mines to factories back east.

Boomtowns

In 1859 a prospector named Henry Comstock staked a claim near Virginia City, Nevada. When others found a rich source nearby, Comstock claimed he owned the land and quickly struck a deal to share the fortune. He later sold his claim for thousands of dollars, not realizing that the sticky, blue-gray clay that made mining in the area difficult was nearly pure silver ore worth millions.

News of the Comstock Lode, as the strike came to be called, brought a flood of prospectors to Virginia City. So many people arrived that, in 1864, Nevada was admitted as the thirty-sixth state in the Union. This occurred many times in the American West. News of a mineral strike would start a stampede of prospectors. Almost overnight, tiny frontier towns were transformed into small cities. Virginia City, for example, grew from a town of a few hundred people to nearly 30,000 in just a few months. It had an opera house, shops with furniture and fashions from Europe, several newspapers, and a six-story hotel.

These quickly growing towns were called boomtowns. The term *boom* refers to a time of rapid economic growth. Boomtowns were rowdy places. Prospectors fought over claims, and thieves haunted the streets and trails. Often, "law and order" was enforced by **vigilance committees**—self-appointed volunteers who would track down and punish wrongdoers. In some cases, they responded with their own form of justice, but most people respected the law and tried to deal firmly but fairly with the accused.

Eventually, the mines that supported the boomtown economy would be used up. A few boomtowns were able to survive when the mines closed, but many of them did not. Instead, these boomtowns went "bust"—a term borrowed from card games in which players lost all of their money. In Virginia City, for example, the silver mines were exhausted by the 1880s, and most residents moved on; only about 500 people remained by 1930. Other towns were completely abandoned and became ghost towns.

Mining Leads to Statehood

After gold was discovered in 1858 in Colorado near Pikes Peak, miners rushed to the area, declaring "Pikes Peak or Bust." Many panned for gold without success and headed home, complaining of a "Pikes Peak hoax." In truth, the Colorado mountains contained plenty of gold and silver, although much of it was hidden beneath the surface and hard to **extract.** Deep deposits of lead mixed with silver were found at Leadville in the 1870s. News of the strike attracted as many as 1,000 newcomers a week, making Leadville one of the West's most famous boomtowns. This bonanza spurred the building of railroads through the Rocky Mountains and transformed Denver, the supply point for the mining areas, into the second-largest city in the West, after San Francisco.

vigilance committee
group of ordinary citizens who organize to find criminals and bring them to justice

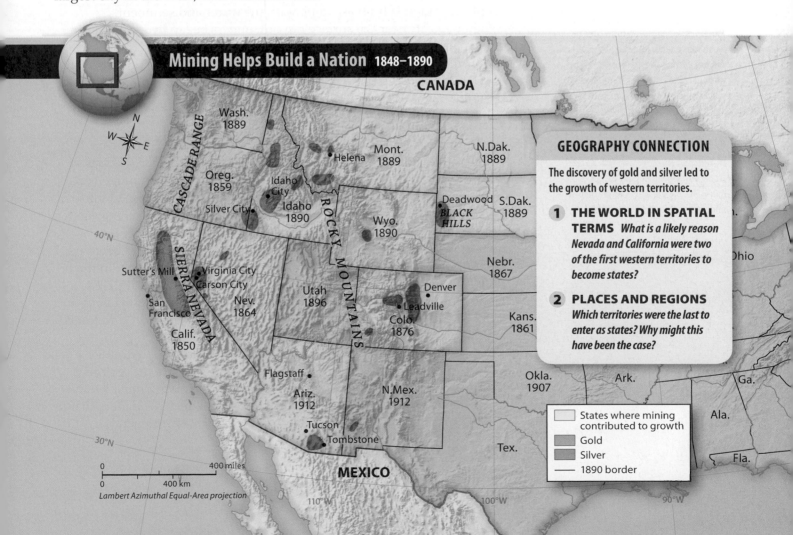

Mining Helps Build a Nation 1848–1890

CANADA

Wash. 1889

Oreg. 1859

CASCADE RANGE

Helena

Mont. 1889

N.Dak. 1889

Idaho City

Silver City

Idaho 1890

ROCKY MOUNTAINS

Wyo. 1890

Deadwood
BLACK HILLS

S.Dak. 1889

40°N

SIERRA NEVADA

Sutter's Mill

Virginia City

Carson City

San Francisco

Nev. 1864

Utah 1896

Denver

Leadville

Colo. 1876

Nebr. 1867

Kans. 1861

Ohio

Calif. 1850

Flagstaff

Ariz. 1912

N.Mex. 1912

Okla. 1907

Ark.

Ga.

Ala.

30°N

Tucson

Tombstone

Tex.

Fla.

0   400 miles

0   400 km

Lambert Azimuthal Equal-Area projection

MEXICO

110°W

100°W

90°W

GEOGRAPHY CONNECTION

The discovery of gold and silver led to the growth of western territories.

1 THE WORLD IN SPATIAL TERMS *What is a likely reason Nevada and California were two of the first western territories to become states?*

2 PLACES AND REGIONS *Which territories were the last to enter as states? Why might this have been the case?*

States where mining contributed to growth
Gold
Silver
— 1890 border

extract to remove by force

The discovery of gold in the Black Hills of the Dakota Territory and copper in Montana drew miners to the region in the 1870s. When the railroads were completed, many farmers and ranchers settled the area. In 1889 Congress admitted three new states: North Dakota, South Dakota, and Montana.

In the Southwest, the Arizona Territory followed a similar pattern. Miners had already begun moving to Arizona in the 1860s and 1870s to work one of the nation's largest copper deposits. When silver was found at the town of Tombstone in 1877, it set off a boom that attracted a huge wave of prospectors to the territory.

The boom lasted about 30 years, and during that time Tombstone became famous for its lawlessness. Marshal Wyatt Earp and his brothers gained their reputations during the famous gunfight at the O.K. Corral there in 1881. Although Arizona did not grow as quickly as Colorado, Nevada, or Montana, by 1912 it had enough people to apply for statehood, as did the neighboring territory of New Mexico.

Mining Technology

Extracting minerals from the rugged mountains of the American West required ingenuity and patience. Early prospectors extracted shallow deposits of ore in a process called placer mining, using simple tools like picks, shovels, and pans.

hydraulic mining method of mining by which water is sprayed at a very high pressure against a hill or mountain, washing away large quantities of dirt, gravel, and rock and exposing the minerals beneath the surface

Other prospectors used sluice mining to search riverbeds more quickly than the panning method. A sluice diverted the current of a river into trenches. The water was directed to a box with metal "riffle" bars that caused heavier minerals to settle to the bottom of the box. A screen at the end kept the minerals from escaping with the water and sediment.

When deposits near the surface ran out, miners began **hydraulic mining** to remove large quantities of earth and process it for minerals. Miners sprayed water at very high pressure against the hill or mountain they were mining. The water pressure washed away the dirt, gravel, and rock and exposed the minerals beneath the surface.

Changes to the Land

Hydraulic mining began in the Sierra Nevada mountains in California. It effectively removed large quantities of minerals and generated millions of dollars in gold. Unfortunately, it also had a devastating effect on the local environment. Millions of tons of silt, sand, and gravel were washed into local rivers. This sediment raised the riverbed. As a result, the rivers began overflowing their banks, causing major floods that wrecked fences, destroyed orchards, and deposited rocks and gravel on what had been good farm soil, destroying thousands of acres of rich farmland. In the 1880s, farmers fought back by suing the mining companies. In 1884 federal judge Lorenzo Sawyer ruled in favor of the farmers. He declared hydraulic mining a "public and private nuisance" and issued an injunction stopping the practice.

Congress eventually passed a law in 1893 allowing hydraulic mining if the mining company created a place to store the sediment. By then, most mining companies had moved to quartz mining—the kind of mining familiar to people today—in which deep mine shafts are dug, and miners go underground to extract the minerals.

Miners used high-pressure water to wash loose earth into ditches. The ditches carried the water and earth into riffle boxes that agitated the water, causing the silver or gold to settle out. The leftover debris, called tailings or "slickens," was then washed into a nearby stream.

▶ **CRITICAL THINKING**
Determining Cause and Effect How might this mining practice have helped miners in their search for minerals?

☑ **PROGRESS CHECK**

Explaining What role did mining play in the development of the American West?

Ranching and Cattle Drives

GUIDING QUESTION *Why was cattle ranching an important business for the Great Plains?*

The lure of the Great Plains brought other Americans west to herd cattle. The Texas longhorn, a cattle breed descended from Spanish cattle introduced two centuries earlier, was well **adapted** to this region and flourished on scarce water and tough prairie grasses. By 1865, some 5 million roamed the Texas grasslands. Another boon to cattle ranching was the **open range,** a vast area of grassland that the federal government owned. Here, ranchers could graze their herds free of charge and unrestricted by private property.

Cowboys drove millions of cattle north from Texas to the railroads in Kansas and points beyond.

▶ **CRITICAL THINKING**

Making Generalizations What effect did the increased ability to move cattle to different parts of the country have on the cattle industry?

adapt to change in order to meet the demands of a certain environment or circumstance

open range vast areas of grassland owned by the federal government

prior before or previous

The Long Drive Begins

Prior to the Civil War, ranchers had little incentive to round up the longhorns and move them to market. Beef prices were low, and moving cattle to eastern markets was not practical. But during the war, eastern cattle had been slaughtered in huge numbers to feed the armies of the Union and the Confederacy. After the war, beef prices soared. Also, by this time, railroads had reached the Great Plains, heading to towns in Kansas and Missouri. Ranchers and livestock dealers realized that if they could move their cattle to the railroad, the longhorns could be sold for a huge profit and shipped east to market.

In 1866 ranchers rounded up about 260,000 longhorns and drove them to Sedalia, Missouri—the first "long drive." Other cattle trails soon opened, including the route to Abilene, Kansas, as the railroads expanded in the West. Cowboys from major ranches went north with the herds, which could number anywhere from 2,000 to 5,000 cattle.

The End of the Open Range

Before long, sheep herders moved their flocks onto the range and farmers came in, breaking up the land for their crops. Eventually, hundreds of square miles of fields were fenced cheaply and easily with a new invention—barbed wire. The fences blocked the cattle trails. The cattle industry faced other struggles. Prices plunged in the mid-1880s, and many ranchers went bankrupt. The harsh winter of 1886–1887 buried the Plains in deep snow. Many cattle froze or starved to death.

Although it survived these terrible blows, the cattle industry was changed forever. The era of the open range ended, and cowboys became ranch hands. From then on, herds were raised on fenced-in ranches.

 **PROGRESS CHECK**

Analyzing Describe the reasons for the growth of the cattle industry on the Great Plains.

Settling the Hispanic Southwest

GUIDING QUESTION *What was the relationship like between Hispanics in the Southwest and new settlers?*

For centuries, much of what is today the American Southwest belonged to Spain's empire. After Mexico won its independence, the region became the northern territories of the Republic of Mexico. When the United States defeated Mexico in 1848, it acquired this vast region. According to the Treaty of Guadalupe Hidalgo, which ended the war, the region's residents retained their property rights and could become American citizens.

Landowners and Newcomers

In California, the Spanish mission system had collapsed by the early 1800s. In its place, a society dominated by a landholding elite had emerged. These landowners owned vast **haciendas**—ranches that covered thousands of acres. The heavy influx of "Forty-Niners" during the California gold rush of 1849, however, changed this society dramatically. California's population grew from about from 14,000 to around 100,000 in less than two years. Suddenly, Hispanic Californians were vastly outnumbered.

Some Hispanic Californians welcomed the newcomers and the economic growth that resulted. Others distrusted the English-speaking prospectors, who tried to exclude them from the mines. When California achieved statehood in 1850, Hispanics served in many state and local offices. Increasingly, however, the original Hispanic population found its status diminished, and Hispanics were often relegated to lower-paying and less desirable jobs.

As they had done with Native Americans, settlers from the East clashed with Mexican Americans over land. Across the region, many Hispanics lost their land to the new settlers. Mexican American claims to the land often dated back to Spanish land grants. These grants were hundreds of years old and defined the boundaries of property in vague terms. When more than one person claimed ownership of a property, American courts frequently held that the old land grants were insufficient proof of ownership. This allowed others to stake claim to the property. In some instances, outright fraud was used to take land illegally from Mexican Americans.

The cattle boom of the 1870s and 1880s had a tremendous impact on Hispanics in the Southwest, where many had long worked as vaqueros (the Spanish word for "cowboys"). Spanish vaqueros had a long history of sharing their techniques for managing cattle. They shared methods of branding with Florida cattlemen as far back in history as when Florida was a Spanish colony. This interaction with American cowboys enriched the English language with such Spanish words as *lariat, lasso,* and *stampede.*

hacienda a huge ranch

In the mid-19th century, most Hispanics in the Southwest lived on large haciendas where they worked in the fields or helped tend cattle.

▶ **CRITICAL THINKING**
Identifying Central Issues How might the change from being the majority to becoming the minority have affected Hispanics in the Southwest?

Clashes and Compromises in the Southwest

With the increasing demand for beef in the eastern United States, English-speaking ranchers wanted to expand their herds and claimed large tracts of land of Mexican origin. In some cases, the Hispanic population fought back. In New Mexico, residents of the town of Las Vegas were outraged when English-speaking ranchers tried to fence in land that had long been used by the community to graze livestock. In 1889 a group of Hispanic New Mexicans calling themselves *Las Gorras Blancas* ("The White Caps") raided ranches owned by English speakers, tore down their fences, and burned their barns and houses. Attempts were made to call in federal troops to stop the raids, but the president refused to send them. The raids finally ended in 1891.

Despite the influx of English-speaking settlers, Hispanics in New Mexico remained more influential in public affairs than did their counterparts in California and Texas. Hispanics remained the majority, both in population and in the territorial legislature. In addition, a Hispanic frequently served as New Mexico's territorial delegate to Congress.

As more railroads were built in the 1880s and 1890s, the population of the Southwest continued to swell. The region attracted not only Americans and European immigrants from the East but also immigrants from Mexico. Mexican immigrants worked mainly in agriculture and on the railroads. In the growing cities of the Southwest—such as El Paso, Albuquerque, and Los Angeles—Hispanics settled in neighborhoods called **barrios.** These neighborhoods had Spanish-speaking businesses and Spanish-language newspapers, and they helped keep Hispanic cultural and religious traditions alive. As native Californian Mariano Guadalupe Vallejo explained in 1890:

A fancily dressed vaquero, known as a *charro*, poses for a photo in 1890.

▶ **CRITICAL THINKING**
Making Generalizations Based on the appearance of the vaquero, what generalizations can be made about the man?

barrios Spanish-speaking neighborhoods in a town or city

PRIMARY SOURCE

❝No class of American citizens is more loyal than the Spanish Californians, but we shall always be especially proud . . . to honor the founders of our ancient families, and the saints and heroes of our history since the days when Father Junipero planted the cross at Monterey.❞

—quoted in *Foreigners in Their Native Land*

✔ **PROGRESS CHECK**

Describing How did vaqueros contribute to the cattle industry in the West?

LESSON 1 REVIEW

Reviewing Vocabulary
1. *Analyzing* What was the significance of barrios to Hispanic culture in the West?

Using Your Notes
2. *Listing* Review the notes that you completed throughout the lesson and list the discoveries that attracted prospectors and settlers to the boomtowns of the American West.

Answering the Guiding Questions
3. *Determining Cause and Effect* How did mineral discoveries shape the settlement of the West?

4. *Summarizing* Why was cattle ranching an important business for the Great Plains?

5. *Analyzing* What was the relationship like between Hispanics in the Southwest and new settlers?

Writing Activity
6. **PERSUASIVE** Suppose that you are a farmer near Nevada City, California, in the 1880s. Write a letter explaining why hydraulic mining endangers your livelihood and therefore should be banned.

networks

There's More Online!

☑ **IMAGE** Farming in the West

☑ **IMAGE** Sod House

☑ **VIDEO** Farming the Plains

☑ **INTERACTIVE SELF-CHECK QUIZ**

LESSON 2
Farming the Plains

ESSENTIAL QUESTION · *Why would people take on the challenges of life in the West?*

Reading **HELP**DESK

Content Vocabulary

- **homestead**
- **dry farming**
- **sodbuster**
- **bonanza farm**

Academic Vocabulary

- **prospective** · **innovation**

TAKING NOTES: *Organizing*

ACTIVITY As you read about the settlement of the Great Plains, complete a graphic organizer similar to the one below by listing the ways the government encouraged settlement.

Assistance
in Settling
Great Plains

IT MATTERS BECAUSE

The Homestead Act encouraged settlers to move to the Great Plains. Although life was difficult, settlers discovered that they could grow wheat using new technologies. By 1890, the land had been settled and cultivated, and there was no longer a true frontier in the United States.

The Beginnings of Settlement

GUIDING QUESTION *What encouraged settlers to move west to the Great Plains?*

The Great Plains is a vast region of prairie roughly west of the Mississippi River and east of the Rocky Mountains in the United States and Canada. Although the population of the Great Plains grew steadily after the Civil War, the settlers faced many challenges. Summer temperatures could top 100°F. Prairie fires were a frequent danger. Sometimes swarms of grasshoppers destroyed crops. Winter brought terrible blizzards and extreme cold. A settler who experienced the fierce winters wrote in her diary on March 12, 1884:

PRIMARY SOURCE

❝Nobody can describe a blizzard. There is one kind in which the snow sticks all over everything, and another that is colder, in which the snow drives with terrible force, the sun shining above it. This is the Dakota boomer's exhilarating weather!❞

—from *The Checked Years: A Bonanza Farm Diary, 1884–1888*

In this dry grassland, trees grew naturally only along rivers and streams. Without trees to use as timber, many settlers cut chunks of sod, densely packed soil held together by grass roots, to build their homes. To obtain water, they had to drill wells more than 100 feet deep and operate the pump by hand. Land once thought to be worthless was eventually transformed into America's wheat belt. Major Stephen Long, who explored the region with an army expedition in 1819, called it the "Great American Desert":

❝[I]t is almost wholly unfit for cultivation, and of course uninhabitable by a people depending upon agriculture for their subsistence. . . . [T]he scarcity of wood and water, almost uniformly prevalent, will prove an insuperable obstacle in the way of settling the country.❞

—quoted in *An Account of an Expedition from Pittsburgh to the Rocky Mountains, Performed in the Years 1819, 1820*

During the late 1800s, the construction and development of the railroads stimulated growth. Railroad companies sold land along the rail lines at low prices and provided credit to **prospective** settlers. Pamphlets and posters spread the news across Europe and America that cheap land could be claimed by anyone willing to move.

In 1862 the government encouraged settlement on the Great Plains by passing the Homestead Act. For a small registration fee, an individual could file for a **homestead**—a tract of public land available for settlement. A homesteader could claim up to 160 acres of land and receive title to it after living there for five years. With their property rights assured and the railroads providing lumber and supplies, more settlers moved to the Plains.

✓ **PROGRESS CHECK**

Analyzing What developments of the late 1800s attracted settlers to endure the hardships of the Great Plains?

The Wheat Belt

GUIDING QUESTION *What new methods and technologies revolutionized agriculture and made it practical to cultivate the Plains?*

New farming methods and inventions in the nineteenth century improved agriculture. The Morrill Land-Grant College Act of 1862 provided each state 30,000 acres to sell for monies to fund existing colleges or to create new ones that focused on agriculture and the mechanical arts.

One new farming method, called **dry farming,** was to plant seeds deep in the ground, where there was enough moisture for them to grow. By the 1860s, Plains farmers were using steel plows, threshing machines, seed drills, and reapers. These new machines made dry farming possible. Still, soil on the Plains could blow away during a dry season. Many **sodbusters,** as those who plowed the Plains were called, eventually lost their homesteads through the combined effects of drought, wind erosion, and overuse of the land.

Large landholders could buy mechanical reapers and steam tractors that made it easier to harvest a large crop. Threshing machines knocked kernels loose from the stalks. Mechanical binders tied the stalks into bundles for collection. These **innovations** were well suited for harvesting wheat, a crop that could endure the dry conditions of the Plains.

During the 1880s, many farmers from the states of the old Northwest Territory moved to the Great Plains to take advantage of the inexpensive land and new technology. The Wheat Belt began at the eastern edge of the Great Plains and covered much of the Dakotas and parts of Nebraska and Kansas. The new machines allowed a family to bring in a substantial harvest on a wheat farm of several hundred acres. Some wheat farms covered up to 65,000 acres. These were called **bonanza farms** because they yielded big profits. Like mine owners, bonanza farmers formed companies, invested in property and equipment, and hired laborers as needed.

prospective to be likely to, or have intentions to, perform an act

homestead a piece of U.S. public land acquired by living on it and cultivating it

dry farming a way of farming dry land in which seeds are planted deep in the ground where there is some moisture

sodbuster a name given to Great Plains farmers

innovation a new idea or method

Technology helped make it possible to farm the vast open grasslands of America. Here, horse-drawn farm equipment is used to gather hay in the 1880s.

▶ **CRITICAL THINKING**
Determining Cause and Effect
How did technology help facilitate the settlement of the Great Plains?

bonanza farm a large, highly profitable wheat farm

Farmers Fall on Hard Times

The bountiful harvests in the Wheat Belt helped the United States become the world's leading exporter of wheat by the 1880s. Then things began to go wrong. A severe drought struck the Plains in the late 1880s, destroying crops and turning the soil to dust. In addition, competition from other wheat-producing nations increased. By the 1890s, a glut of wheat on the world market caused prices to drop.

Some farmers tried to make it through these difficult times by mortgaging their land—that is, they borrowed money from a bank based on the value of their land. If they failed to meet their mortgage payments, they forfeited the land to the bank. Some who lost their land continued to work it as tenant farmers, renting the land from its new owners. By 1900, tenants cultivated about one-third of the farms on the Plains.

Closing the Frontier

On April 22, 1889, the government opened one of the last large territories for settlement. Within hours, thousands of people raced to stake claims in an event known as the Oklahoma Land Rush. The next year, the Census Bureau reported that there was no longer a true frontier left in America. In reality, there was still a lot of unoccupied land, and new settlement continued into the 1900s, but the "closing of the frontier" marked the end of an era. It worried many people, including historian Frederick Jackson Turner. Turner believed that the frontier had provided a "safety-valve of social discontent." It was a place where Americans could always make a fresh start.

Most settlers did indeed make a fresh start, adapting to the difficult environment of the Plains. Water from their deep wells enabled them to plant trees and gardens. Railroads brought lumber and brick to replace sod as a building material, coal for fuel, and manufactured goods from the East, such as clothes and household goods. Small-scale farmers rarely became wealthy, but they could be self-sufficient. Typical homesteaders raised cattle, chickens, and a few crops. The real story of the West was about ordinary people who settled down and built homes and communities through great effort.

☑ **PROGRESS CHECK**

Identifying How did new technologies help improve settlers' ability to cultivate larger, more profitable farms?

LESSON 2 REVIEW

Reviewing Vocabulary
1. *Explaining* Why were some settlers on the Great Plains called homesteaders?

Using Your Notes
2. *Drawing Conclusions* Use your notes to explain why you think the government and the railroads used special policies to attract settlement in the Great Plains.

Answering the Guiding Questions
3. *Identifying Cause and Effect* What encouraged settlers to move west to the Great Plains?

4. *Summarizing* What new methods and technologies revolutionized agriculture and made it practical to cultivate the Plains?

Writing About History
5. **PERSONAL** Write an essay expressing your opinion about whether the "closing of the frontier" described by historian Frederick Jackson Turner was good or bad for the country.

Reading **HELP**DESK

Content Vocabulary

- nomad
- annuity
- assimilate
- allotment

Academic Vocabulary

- relocate
- ensure
- approximately

TAKING NOTES: *Sequencing*

ACTIVITY As you read about Native Americans during the late 1800s, complete a time line like the one below to record the clashes between Native Americans and the U.S. government and the results of each.

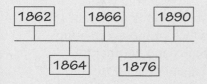

| 1862 | 1866 | 1890 |

| 1864 | 1876 |

LESSON 3
Native Americans

ESSENTIAL QUESTION · *Why would people take on the challenges of life in the West?*

IT MATTERS BECAUSE

As miners, ranchers, and farmers entered Native American lands on the Great Plains, clashes grew more common. Conflicts continued as the government tried to force Native Americans onto reservations and pressured them to assimilate into the culture of the United States.

Struggles of the Plains Indians

GUIDING QUESTION *How did westward migration change the Plains Indians' way of life?*

For centuries the Great Plains were home to many groups of Native Americans. Some lived in farming and hunting communities, but many were **nomads** who roamed the land following their main source of food—the buffalo. The Plains Indian nations were divided into bands, ranging from a few dozen to several hundred people, who lived in extended family groups and respected nature.

The settlers who migrated to the Plains deprived these Native Americans of their hunting grounds, broke treaties that guaranteed them land, and often forced them to **relocate.** Native Americans resisted by attacking settlers' property and occasionally going to war with them.

The Dakota Sioux Uprising

In 1862 the Dakota people (part of the Sioux) had a conflict with the settlers in Minnesota. The Sioux had agreed to live on a reservation in exchange for **annuities** that frequently never reached them. At the time, many Dakota lived in poverty and faced starvation. When local traders refused to provide food on credit, the Dakota protested by launching a rebellion that killed hundreds of settlers.

A military tribunal sentenced more than 300 Dakota to death after the uprising. After reviewing the evidence, however, President Lincoln reduced the number condemned to death to 38. Others fled the reservation when federal troops arrived and became exiles in a region that bore their name—the Dakota Territory.

Native Americans are attacked by U.S. troops at Sand Creek.

▶ **CRITICAL THINKING**
Drawing Inferences Why do you think obtaining peace between Native Americans and settlers was so difficult?

nomad a person who continually moves from place to place, usually in search of food

relocate to move to a new place

annuity money paid by contract at regular intervals

ensure to guarantee or make certain

Red Cloud's War

The Dakota Territory was home to another group of Sioux, the Lakota, nomads who had won control of their hunting grounds from other Native Americans. Their chiefs were Red Cloud, Crazy Horse, and Sitting Bull. In December 1866, the U.S. Army was building forts along the Bozeman Trail, the path to the Montana gold mines. Crazy Horse tricked the fort's commander into sending Captain William Fetterman and about 80 soldiers out to pursue what they thought was a small raiding party.

Hundreds of waiting warriors wiped out the unit, an event that became known as Fetterman's Massacre, marking the start of "Red Cloud's War." The Sioux continued to resist any military presence in the region, and in 1868 the army abandoned its posts along the trail.

Sand Creek Massacre

In Colorado, tensions began to rise in the 1860s between miners entering the territory in search of silver and gold and the Cheyenne and Arapaho who already lived there. As the number of settlers increased, bands of Native Americans began raiding wagon trains and ranches. By the summer of 1864, dozens of homes had been burned and an estimated 200 settlers killed. The governor persuaded the Native Americans to surrender at Fort Lyon, where he promised food and protection. Those who failed to report would be subject to attack.

Although a number of Native Americans surrendered, many others did not. In November 1864, Chief Black Kettle brought several hundred Cheyenne to the fort to negotiate a peace deal. Fort Lyon's commander, Major Scott Anthony, allowed the chief to make camp at nearby Sand Creek while he awaited orders. Shortly afterward, Colonel John Chivington of the Colorado Volunteers attacked Black Kettle's camp, even though the Cheyenne were there to negotiate.

What actually happened at Sand Creek is unclear. Some witnesses stated that Black Kettle had been flying both an American flag and a white flag of truce, which Chivington ignored. Others reported that the American troops fired on the unsuspecting Native Americans and then brutally murdered hundreds of women and children. Still others described a savage battle in which both sides fought ferociously for two days. Few soldiers died, but the number of Native Americans reported killed varied from 69 to 600. The truth of what happened at Sand Creek is still debated.

A Doomed Plan for Peace

As conflicts escalated with Native Americans, Congress took action. In 1867 Congress formed an Indian Peace Commission, which proposed creating two large reservations on the Plains, one for the Sioux and another for Native Americans of the southern Plains. Federal agents would run the reservations, and the army would deal with any groups that refused to report or remain there.

The Indian Peace Commission's plan was doomed to failure. Although negotiators pressured Native American leaders into signing treaties, they could not **ensure** that those leaders or their followers would abide by them. Nor could anyone prevent settlers from violating their terms. The Native Americans who did move to reservations faced many of the same conditions that drove the Dakota Sioux to violence—poverty, despair, and the corrupt practices of American traders.

✔ **PROGRESS CHECK**

Explaining How did the arrival of new settlers affect the Plains Indians?

The Last Native American Wars

GUIDING QUESTION *Were Native Americans justified in leaving the reservations and refusing further relocation by the government?*

By the 1870s, many Native Americans on the southern Plains had left the reservations in disgust. They preferred hunting buffalo on the open plains. The buffalo were rapidly disappearing, however. Professional buffalo hunters had invaded the area, seeking hides for markets in the East. Other hunters killed for sport, leaving carcasses to rot. When herds of buffalo blocked rail traffic, the railroad companies killed them and fed the meat to workers. The army, determined to force Native Americans onto reservations, encouraged buffalo killing. By 1889, very few buffalo remained.

Battle of the Little Bighorn

In 1876 prospectors overran the Lakota Sioux reservation in the Dakota Territory to mine gold in the Black Hills. The Lakota saw no reason to abide by a treaty that settlers were violating, so many left the reservation to hunt near the Bighorn Mountains in southeastern Montana. The government responded by sending an expedition accompanied by Lieutenant Colonel George A. Custer and the Seventh Cavalry. Custer underestimated the fighting capabilities of the Lakota and the Cheyenne. On June 25, 1876, ignoring orders, and acting on his own initiative, he launched a three-pronged attack in broad daylight on one of the largest groups of Native American warriors ever assembled on the Great Plains.

GEOGRAPHY CONNECTION

Native Americans fought hard to maintain their land and way of life, but over time, they agreed to move to reservations in different areas of the country to save their people.

1 PLACES AND REGIONS *In what region of the United States did a majority of battles occur between the settlers and the Native Americans during this time period?*

2 HUMAN SYSTEMS *From what state to what state did the Nez Perce travel in 1877? Through what other states did they pass?*

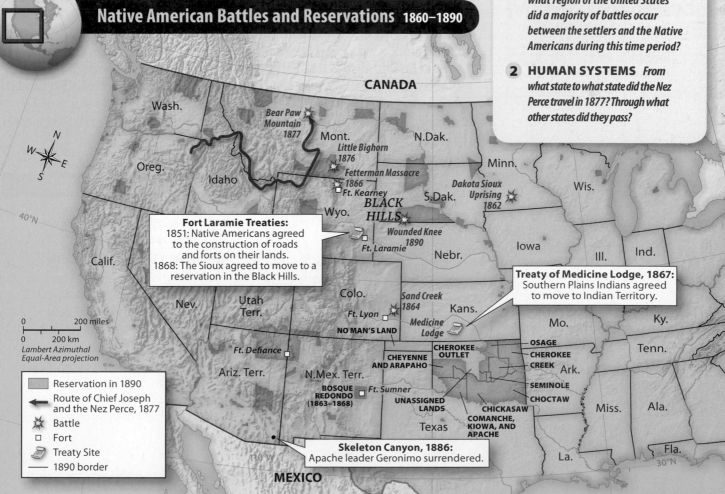

Native American Battles and Reservations 1860–1890

Fort Laramie Treaties:
1851: Native Americans agreed to the construction of roads and forts on their lands.
1868: The Sioux agreed to move to a reservation in the Black Hills.

Treaty of Medicine Lodge, 1867: Southern Plains Indians agreed to move to Indian Territory.

Skeleton Canyon, 1886: Apache leader Geronimo surrendered.

CANADA

Wash. · Bear Paw Mountain 1877 · Mont. · N.Dak. · Oreg. · Idaho · Little Bighorn 1876 · Fetterman Massacre 1866 · Ft. Kearney · Minn. · Wis. · Dakota Sioux Uprising 1862 · BLACK HILLS · S.Dak. · Wyo. · Wounded Knee 1890 · Ft. Laramie · Iowa · Ill. · Ind. · Nebr. · Calif. · Nev. · Utah Terr. · Colo. · Sand Creek 1864 · Ft. Lyon · Kans. · Mo. · Ky. · NO MAN'S LAND · Medicine Lodge · Tenn. · Ft. Defiance · Ariz. Terr. · N.Mex. Terr. · CHEYENNE AND ARAPAHO · CHEROKEE OUTLET · OSAGE · CHEROKEE · CREEK · Ark. · BOSQUE REDONDO (1863–1868) · Ft. Sumner · UNASSIGNED LANDS · SEMINOLE · CHOCTAW · Miss. · Ala. · Texas · CHICKASAW · COMANCHE, KIOWA, AND APACHE · La. · Fla. · MEXICO

40°N · 110°W · 30°N

0   200 miles
0   200 km
Lambert Azimuthal Equal-Area projection

Reservation in 1890
Route of Chief Joseph and the Nez Perce, 1877
Battle
Fort
Treaty Site
1890 border

George Custer (1839–1876)

George Custer graduated at the bottom of his West Point class, but through heroism during the Civil War, he became a general at age 23. The Cheyenne called him "Yellow Hair" because he wore his curly blond hair to his shoulders. President Grant removed Custer from his post for testifying about corruption in the Bureau of Indian Affairs, but he was soon reinstated—a decision that cost him his life and those of his troops.

▶ **CRITICAL THINKING**

Drawing Inferences Why do you think Custer was removed from his command for testifying against the Bureau of Indian Affairs?

The Native American forces first repulsed a cavalry charge from the south. Then they turned on Custer and his more than 200 soldiers, killing them all. One Lakota recalled the scene later: "[T]he soldiers were piled one on top of another, dead, and here and there an Indian among the soldiers."

Newspaper accounts portraying Custer as a victim of a massacre produced a public outcry in the East, and the army stepped up its campaign against Native Americans on the Plains. Sitting Bull fled with his followers to Canada, but the other Lakota were forced to return to the reservation and give up the Black Hills.

Flight of the Nez Perce

Farther west, the Nez Perce people, led by Chief Joseph, refused to be moved to a smaller reservation in Idaho in 1877. When the army came to relocate them, they fled their homes and embarked on a journey of more than 1,300 miles. Finally, in October 1877, Chief Joseph acknowledged that the struggle was over:

PRIMARY SOURCE

❝Our chiefs are killed. . . . The little children are freezing to death. My people . . . have no blankets, no food. . . . Hear me, my chiefs; I am tired; my heart is sick and sad. From where the sun now stands I will fight no more forever.❞

—from his speech of surrender to the U.S. Army, 1877

Chief Joseph and his followers were then exiled to Oklahoma.

Tragedy at Wounded Knee

Native American resistance came to a final, tragic end on the Lakota Sioux reservation in 1890. Defying government orders, the Lakota continued to perform the Ghost Dance, a ritual that celebrated a hoped-for day of reckoning when settlers would disappear, the buffalo would return, and Native Americans would be reunited with their dead ancestors.

Federal authorities had banned the ceremony, fearing it would lead to violence. They blamed the latest defiance on Sitting Bull, who had returned from Canada, and sent police to arrest the chief. Sitting Bull's supporters tried to stop the arrest. In the exchange of gunfire that followed, Sitting Bull was killed.

POLITICAL CARTOONS

CARL SCHURZ INVESTIGATING THE BUREAU OF INDIAN AFFAIRS

This cartoon from 1878 shows Secretary of the Interior Carl Schurz investigating the Indian "bureau."

▶ **CRITICAL THINKING**

1 ***Analyzing*** According to the cartoon, why was the Bureau of Indian Affairs unable to help Native Americans?

2 ***Drawing Inferences*** Why do you think Schurz did not want the War Department to regain control of Indian affairs?

Due to a cumbersome system of handling the administration of Indian laws, the agents of the Bureau of Indian Affairs (BIA) had many opportunities for personal enrichment and an invitation for large-scale corruption. Secretary of the Interior Carl Schurz attempted to cleanse the BIA of corruption and prevent the War Department from regaining management of Indian affairs.

A group of Ghost Dancers then fled the reservation, and the army went after them. On December 29, 1890, a deadly battle ensued at Wounded Knee Creek in South Dakota, taking the lives of 25 U.S. soldiers and **approximately** 200 Lakota men, women, and children.

approximately an estimate of a figure that is close to the actual figure

The Dawes Act

Some Americans had long opposed the mistreatment of Native Americans. In her 1881 book *A Century of Dishonor,* Helen Hunt Jackson detailed the years of broken promises and injustices. Her descriptions of events such as the Sand Creek Massacre sparked new debate on the issue. Some Americans believed the solution was to encourage Native Americans to **assimilate** into American society as landowners and citizens.

assimilate to absorb a group into the culture of another population

In 1887 Congress passed the Dawes Act, which altered the reservation system by dividing reservation land into **allotments** for farming or ranching. Under the act, 160 acres were allotted to each head of household, 80 acres to each single adult, and 40 acres to each child. Any land remaining after allotments would be sold to American settlers, with the proceeds going into a trust for Native Americans. Citizenship would be granted to Native Americans who stayed on their allotments for 25 years.

allotment a plot of land assigned to an individual or a family for a specified use

The Dawes Act failed to achieve its goals. Some Native Americans succeeded as farmers or ranchers, but many had little training or enthusiasm for either pursuit. Like homesteaders, they often found their allotments too small to be profitable, so they leased them. In addition, some Native American groups had grown attached to their reservations and hated to see them transformed into homesteads to be shared with settlers. Few stayed long enough to qualify for citizenship.

In the end, the assimilation policy proved a dismal failure. No legislation could provide a satisfactory solution to the Native American issue, because there was no entirely satisfactory solution to be had. Native Americans on the Plains were doomed because they were dependent on buffalo for food, clothing, fuel, and shelter. When the herds were wiped out, they had no way to sustain their way of life. Few adopted the lifestyles of American settlers in place of their traditional cultures.

In 1924 Congress passed the Citizenship Act, granting all Native Americans citizenship. In 1934 the Indian Reorganization Act reversed the Dawes Act's policy of assimilation. It restored some reservation lands, gave Native Americans control over those lands, and permitted them to elect their own governments.

☑ **PROGRESS CHECK**

Cause and Effect What effect did Helen Hunt Jackson's book *A Century of Dishonor* have?

LESSON 3 REVIEW

Reviewing Vocabulary

1. *Making Connections* What is an annuity? What was the connection between annuities and the Dakota Sioux Uprising of 1862?

Using Your Notes

2. *Making Generalizations* Review the notes that you completed throughout the lesson to write a generalization about the result of the battles between Native Americans and the United States government.

Answering the Guiding Questions

3. *Summarizing* How did westward migration change the Plains Indians' way of life?

4. *Defending* Were Native Americans justified in leaving the reservations and refusing further relocation by the government?

Writing About History

5. DESCRIPTIVE Assume the role of a Plains Indian who has been granted an allotment under the Dawes Act. Write a journal entry describing how you feel and how the change has affected your life.

Directions: On a separate sheet of paper, answer the questions below. Make sure you read carefully and answer all parts to the question.

Lesson Review

Lesson 1

1 *Drawing Conclusions* What led to the sudden emigration to the West, and what effect did this migration have on the United States?

2 *Naming* What major agricultural enterprise became vital to the settlement of the southern Great Plains? Why was it important?

3 *Assessing* What did Native Americans and Mexican Americans have in common with settlers from the East?

Lesson 2

4 *Identifying* What factors helped to encourage settlement of the Great Plains?

5 *Analyzing* What methods revolutionized agriculture? How did farming technology and innovations contribute to the formation of the Wheat Belt?

Lesson 3

6 *Explaining* What factors caused conflicts between new settlers to the West and Native Americans?

7 *Describing* What provisions did the Dawes Act make for Native Americans who remained on reservations?

8 *Evaluating* What were the consequences of the Dawes Act?

21st Century Skills

9 **IDENTIFYING CAUSE AND EFFECT** How were Hispanics in California affected by the gold rush?

10 **GEOGRAPHY SKILLS** What territory did the Wheat Belt encompass?

11 **UNDERSTANDING RELATIONSHIPS AMONG EVENTS** Why did the Dakota Sioux launch a major uprising in Minnesota?

12 **PROBLEM SOLVING** What problems did sodbusters encounter when farming the Great Plains? How did some sodbusters overcome these problems?

13 **ECONOMICS** What happened to boomtowns once the mines that supported them were used up?

Exploring the Essential Question

14 *Discussing* Write an essay in which you describe the hardships of and advantages to emigrating west during the nineteenth century.

DBQ Document-Based Questions

Use the image to answer the following questions.

This engraving from 1889 depicts the Oklahoma Land Rush.

15 *Naming* What is the significance of the title of this engraving, *The Rush for the Promised Land: Over the Border to Oklahoma*?

16 *Analyzing Visuals* What impression does this image give about the settlers who are rushing into the vast frontier to the "Promised Land"?

Extended-Response Question

17 *Analysis* If you were a settler moving to a new community in the Great Plains, would you stay and make a new life for yourself or would you leave? Write a descriptive essay that supports the reasons for your decision.

Need Extra Help?

If You've Missed Question	1	2	3	4	5	6	7	8	9	10	11	12	13	14	15	16	17
Go to page	268	271	272	274	275	277	281	281	272	275	277	275	269	274	274	282	275

Industrialization

1865–1901

ESSENTIAL QUESTION • *How did the United States become an industrialized society after the Civil War?*

◀ Andrew Carnegie devoted his full attention to the steel industry in the 1870s.

PHOTO: The Granger Collection, New York

The Story Matters...

Andrew Carnegie founded Carnegie Steel, one of the new businesses that fueled the Industrial Revolution in the United States. He became a multimillionaire, his company employed tens of thousands of workers, and his steel built the skyscrapers, bridges, and railroads that made the United States the world's leading industrial nation. Carnegie and other big-business leaders provided the leadership for an industrial society.

American business and industry grew rapidly after the Civil War ended. Natural resources and a large labor force contributed to industry's growth. Inventions, such as the telephone and the lightbulb, spurred economic development. Railroads accelerated the nation's industrialization and linked the country together. Corporations could produce goods more efficiently. With industrialization came the benefits of new products versus the struggles of low wages, long hours, and difficult working conditions. All of these things changed the way people lived and worked.

Step Into the Place

Look at the information presented on the map to identify the regions affected by the building of the transcontinental railroad.

DBQ How could an increase in the number of railroad lines across the West contribute to the economic growth of the United States?

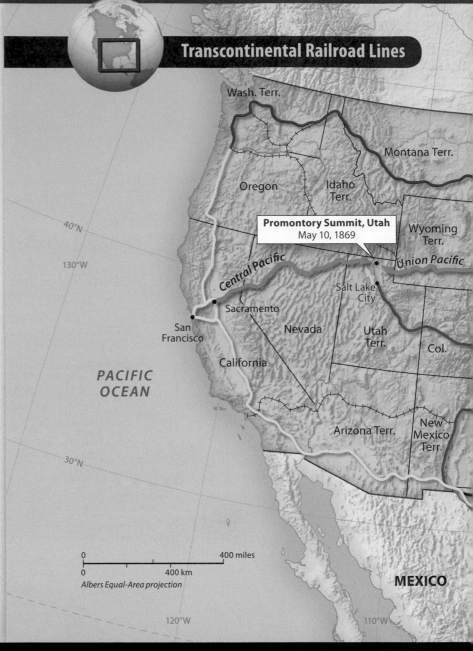

Transcontinental Railroad Lines

Wash. Terr.

Montana Terr.

Oregon

Idaho Terr.

40°N

Promontory Summit, Utah
May 10, 1869

Wyoming Terr.

130°W

Union Pacific

Central Pacific

Salt Lake City

Sacramento

San Francisco

Nevada

Utah Terr.

Col.

California

PACIFIC OCEAN

Arizona Terr.

New Mexico Terr.

30°N

| 0 | 400 miles |
| 0 | 400 km |

Albers Equal-Area projection

MEXICO

120°W   110°W

Step Into the Time

Choose an event from the time line and write a paragraph reflecting on how that event is representative of the changing times during the late 1800s.

U.S. PRESIDENTS

UNITED STATES

WORLD

1865   1875   1880

1876 Alexander Graham Bell invents telephone

Hayes 1877–1881

Garfield 1881

1882 Standard Oil forms trust

1869 Dmitry Mendeleyev creates periodic table of elements

1873 Jules Verne's *Around the World in 80 Days* is published

1876 Nikolaus Otto builds first practical gasoline engine

1880 John Milne develops seismograph

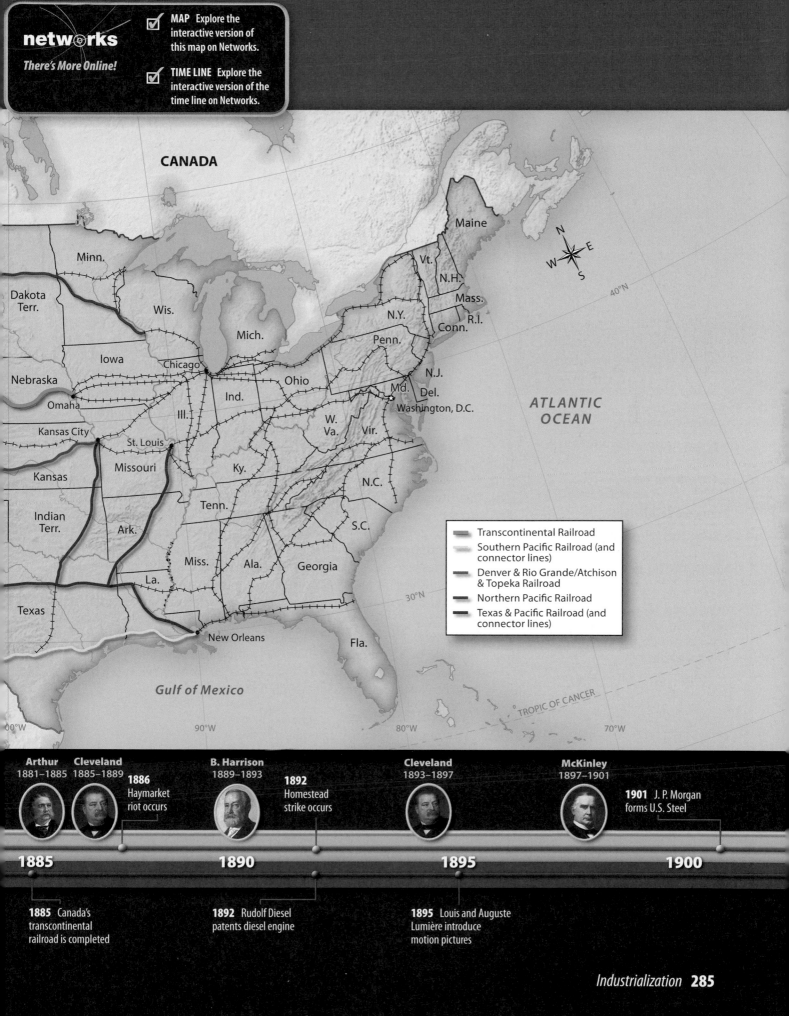

networks

There's More Online!

☑ **MAP** Explore the interactive version of this map on Networks.

☑ **TIME LINE** Explore the interactive version of the time line on Networks.

CANADA

Maine

Minn.

Dakota Terr.

Wis.

Mich.

Vt.

N.H.

Mass.

N.Y.

Conn.

R.I.

Iowa

Chicago

Ohio

Penn.

N.J.

Nebraska

Ind.

Md.

Del.

Washington, D.C.

Omaha

Ill.

W. Va.

Vir.

ATLANTIC OCEAN

40°N

Kansas City

St. Louis

Kansas

Missouri

Ky.

N.C.

Indian Terr.

Ark.

Tenn.

S.C.

Texas

Miss.

Ala.

Georgia

La.

30°N

New Orleans

Fla.

TROPIC OF CANCER

Gulf of Mexico

100°W

90°W

80°W

70°W

▬▬	Transcontinental Railroad
▬▬	Southern Pacific Railroad (and connector lines)
▬▬	Denver & Rio Grande/Atchison & Topeka Railroad
▬▬	Northern Pacific Railroad
▬▬	Texas & Pacific Railroad (and connector lines)

Arthur 1881–1885

Cleveland 1885–1889

1886 Haymarket riot occurs

B. Harrison 1889–1893

1892 Homestead strike occurs

Cleveland 1893–1897

McKinley 1897–1901

1901 J. P. Morgan forms U.S. Steel

1885

1890

1895

1900

1885 Canada's transcontinental railroad is completed

1892 Rudolf Diesel patents diesel engine

1895 Louis and Auguste Lumière introduce motion pictures

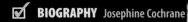

networks

There's More Online!

☑ **BIOGRAPHY** Josephine Cochrane

☑ **BIOGRAPHY** Lewis Latimer

☑ **BIOGRAPHY** Orville and Wilbur Wright

☑ **VIDEO** Rise of Industry

☑ **INTERACTIVE SELF-CHECK QUIZ**

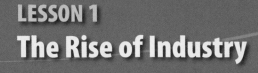

LESSON 1
The Rise of Industry

ESSENTIAL QUESTION · *How did the United States become an industrialized society after the Civil War?*

Reading HELPDESK

Content Vocabulary

• **gross national product**
• **laissez-faire**
• **entrepreneur**

Academic Vocabulary

• **resource**   • **practice**

TAKING NOTES: *Organizing*

ACTIVITY As you read about the changes industrialization brought to the United States, complete the graphic organizer shown below with the causes of industrialization.

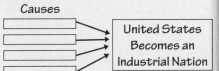

Causes

United States Becomes an Industrial Nation

IT MATTERS BECAUSE

American business and industry grew rapidly after the end of the Civil War. Industrialization changed the way people lived and worked.

The United States Industrializes

GUIDING QUESTION *Why was the United States successful at industrialization?*

Although the First Industrial Revolution reached the United States in the early 1800s, most Americans still lived on farms when the Civil War began in 1861. After the war, industry rapidly expanded, and millions of Americans left their farms to work in mines and factories as part of the Second Industrial Revolution.

Building on the advances of the First Industrial Revolution, the Second Industrial Revolution was characterized by an increase in technology. This was primarily due to advances in electrification after 1890. By the late 1800s, the United States was the world's leading industrial nation. Its **gross national product** (GNP)—the total value of all goods and services that a country produces during a year—was growing faster than it ever had before.

Natural Resources

An abundance of raw materials was one reason for the nation's industrial success. The United States had vast natural **resources,** including timber, coal, iron, and copper. This meant that American companies could obtain resources cheaply and did not have to import them from other countries. Many of these resources were located in the American West. The settlement of the West helped accelerate industrialization, as did the transcontinental railroad. Railroads took settlers and miners to the West and carried resources back to the East.

At the same time, people began using a new resource: petroleum. Even before the automotive age, petroleum was in high demand because it could be turned into kerosene. The American oil industry was built on the demand for kerosene, a fuel used in lanterns and stoves. The industry began in western Pennsylvania, where residents had long noticed oil bubbling to the surface of area springs and streams. In 1859 Edwin Drake drilled the first oil well near Titusville, Pennsylvania, and by 1900, oil fields had been drilled from Pennsylvania to Texas. A rise in oil production led to economic expansion.

A Large Workforce

The human resources available to American industry were as important as natural resources in enabling the nation to industrialize rapidly. Between 1860 and 1910, the population of the United States nearly tripled. This population growth provided industry with an abundant workforce and created greater demand for consumer goods.

Population growth stemmed from two sources—large families and a flood of immigrants. Because of better living conditions, more children survived and grew to adulthood. Social and economic conditions in parts of Europe and China convinced many people to immigrate to the United States in search of a better life. Some were seeking to escape oppressive governments and religious persecution. Between 1870 and 1910, more than 17 million immigrants arrived in the United States. Norwegian immigrant Andreas Ueland arrived in 1871:

PRIMARY SOURCE

❝Father died in January, 1870. That changed abruptly my whole aspect of life. An older brother was to have the farm after Mother; what was I to do? . . . There was left the choice to stay home and wait for something to turn up, go out as a laborer or to learn a trade, or to sea, or to America!❞

—from *Recollections of an Immigrant*

✔ **PROGRESS CHECK**

Summarizing What were two significant factors in the growth of U.S. industry?

gross national product
the total value of goods and services produced by a country during a year

resources materials used in the production process, such as money, people, land, wood, or steel

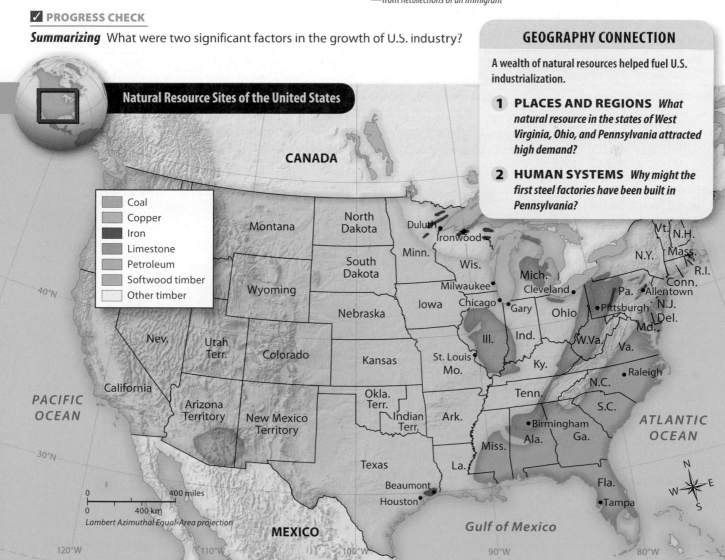

GEOGRAPHY CONNECTION

A wealth of natural resources helped fuel U.S. industrialization.

1 **PLACES AND REGIONS** *What natural resource in the states of West Virginia, Ohio, and Pennsylvania attracted high demand?*

2 **HUMAN SYSTEMS** *Why might the first steel factories have been built in Pennsylvania?*

Natural Resource Sites of the United States

Coal
Copper
Iron
Limestone
Petroleum
Softwood timber
Other timber

CANADA

Montana
North Dakota
Duluth
Ironwood
Minn.
Wis.
Mich.
Vt.
N.H.
N.Y.
Mass.
R.I.
South Dakota
Milwaukee
Cleveland
Pa.
Allentown
Conn.
Wyoming
Iowa
Chicago
Gary
Ohio
Pittsburgh
N.J.
Del.
Nebraska
Ill.
Ind.
W.Va.
Va.
Md.
Nev.
Utah Terr.
Colorado
Kansas
St. Louis
Mo.
Ky.
California
Arizona Territory
New Mexico Territory
Okla. Terr.
Indian Terr.
Ark.
Tenn.
N.C.
Raleigh
S.C.
PACIFIC OCEAN
Birmingham
Ala.
Ga.
ATLANTIC OCEAN
Miss.
Texas
La.
Beaumont
Houston
Fla.
Tampa
Gulf of Mexico
MEXICO

40°N
30°N
120°W
110°W
100°W
90°W
80°W

0   400 miles
0   400 km
Lambert Azimuthal Equal-Area projection

N E S W

New Inventions

GUIDING QUESTION *What invention from this period has had the most impact on your daily life?*

❝He then sketched for me an instrument that he thought would [transmit speech], and we discussed the possibility of constructing one. I did not make it; it was altogether too costly and the chances of its working too uncertain, to impress his financial backers . . . who were insisting that the wisest thing for Bell to do was to perfect the harmonic telegraph; then he would have money and leisure enough to build air castles like the telephone.❞

—Thomas A. Watson, from "Recollections of the Birth and Babyhood of the Telephone," 1913

DBQ *MAKING INFERENCES*
What can you infer about the difficulties that inventors faced during the late 1800s?

New inventions and technology were also important to industrialization. Technologies and inventions eased transportation and communication. They also encouraged new industries, which in turn produced more wealth and jobs.

Perhaps the leading pioneer in new technology was Thomas Alva Edison. His laboratory at Menlo Park, New Jersey was the forerunner of the modern research laboratory. Edison first achieved international fame in 1877 with the invention of the phonograph. Two years later, he perfected the electric generator and the lightbulb. Inventor Lewis Latimer developed the carbon filament that made the incandescent bulb more durable and longer-lasting. Edison's laboratory went on to invent or improve several other major devices, including the battery and the motion picture.

Cyrus Field laid a telegraph cable across the Atlantic Ocean in 1866, enabling faster communication between the United States and Europe. In 1874 Scottish immigrant Alexander Graham Bell began experimenting with ways to transmit sound via an electrical current. In 1876 he succeeded in inventing the telephone, revolutionizing communications.

Engineer and industrialist George Westinghouse invented an air-brake system for railroads, and an alternating current (AC) system to distribute electricity using transformers and generators. He founded the Westinghouse Electric Company, which was the first to use hydroelectric power.

Technology changed the way that people lived. After the Civil War, Thaddeus Lowe invented the ice machine, the basis of the refrigerator. In 1877 Gustavus Swift shipped the first refrigerated load of meat. In 1882 an Edison company started supplying electric power to New York City. Four years later, Josephine Cochrane developed the automatic dishwasher.

POLITICAL CARTOONS — GOVERNMENT AND THE ECONOMY

These two political cartoons address tariffs and protectionism in the United States in the late 1800s.

The cartoon on the left depicts a flood of European goods damaging the demand for products made at American factories. The cartoon on the right shows a shopper being pulled between paying extra money to trusts (monopolies) to buy domestic goods and extra money (duties) to buy foreign goods.

▶ **CRITICAL THINKING**

1 *Interpreting* What event is shown as leading to the destruction of American factories?

2 *Analyzing* What argument does the cartoon on the right make about free trade?

The gate is labeled "Protection." The flood is labeled "European Pauper Manufactures."

This cartoon is entitled "The Consumer Consumed."

Changes also took place in the clothing industry. The Northrop automatic loom allowed cloth to be made more quickly. Power-driven sewing machines and cloth cutters, as well as machines for producing shoes, meant that clothing and shoe production moved from small shops to large factories.

☑ **PROGRESS CHECK**

Evaluating Which invention do you think has had the most lasting influence?

Free Enterprise

GUIDING QUESTION *How did laissez-faire economics promote industrialization?*

Laissez-faire (LEH•SAY•FAYR) economics helped the country industrialize. Supporters of laissez-faire believe that government should not interfere in the economy other than to protect property rights and maintain peace. They believe that government regulation of the economy increases costs and eventually hurts society more than it helps. An economic system with little or no government regulation is known as a free enterprise system.

Laissez-faire relies on supply and demand to regulate wages and prices. Supporters believe that competition promotes efficiency and wealth. They advocate low taxes and limited government debt to ensure that private individuals make most of the decisions about spending the nation's wealth. The United States **practiced** a mixture of laissez-faire economics by keeping taxes low while promoting private investment. The government also built transportation networks that supported economic growth.

The prospect of making money in manufacturing and transportation attracted **entrepreneurs,** people who risk their capital to organize and run businesses. Northern entrepreneurs traditionally supported high tariffs to protect their businesses from foreign competition. They also supported federal subsidies for companies building roads, canals, and railroads. Southern leaders were against subsidies and favored low tariffs to promote trade and to keep the cost of imported goods low.

During the Civil War, Congress greatly increased tariff rates on imports, causing other countries to raise their tariffs on U.S. goods. This hurt American companies trying to sell goods abroad. Tariffs were later lowered as American companies became larger and more competitive. The United States benefited from being one of the largest free-trade areas in the world. Supporters of laissez-faire contend this contributed to the nation's economic growth.

☑ **PROGRESS CHECK**

Assessing How did laissez-faire economics encourage businesses to industrialize?

laissez-faire a policy that government should interfere as little as possible in the nation's economy

practice to do something repeatedly so it becomes the standard

entrepreneur one who organizes, manages, and assumes the risks of a business or enterprise

---

LESSON 1 REVIEW

Reviewing Vocabulary

1. *Defining* What does gross national product measure? Create a line graph of the nation's Gross National Product over the last five years.

Using Your Notes

2. *Defending* Use your notes to identify what you think was the most important cause of American industrialization. Then write a sentence or two identifying your choice and defending its importance.

Answering Guiding Questions

3. *Evaluating* Why was the United States successful at industrialization?

4. *Making Connections* What invention from this period has had the most impact on your daily life?

5. *Analyzing Cause and Effect* How did laissez-faire economics promote industrialization?

Writing Activity

6. PERSONAL Industrialization changed nearly every aspect of American life. Consider whether these changes have been generally positive or generally negative. Write a paragraph in which you express your thoughts and feelings about the pros and cons of widespread industrialization.

networks

There's More Online!

☑ **BIOGRAPHY** Jay Gould

☑ **BIOGRAPHY** Leland Stanford

☑ **VIDEO** Railroads

☑ **INTERACTIVE SELF-CHECK QUIZ**

Reading **HELP**DESK

Content Vocabulary

• time zone • land grant

Academic Vocabulary

• integrate • investor

TAKING NOTES: *Organizing*

ACTIVITY As you read about the development of a nationwide rail network, complete a graphic organizer similar to the one below to list the effects of this network on the nation.

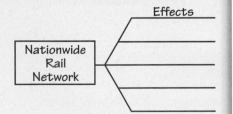

Effects

Nationwide Rail Network

LESSON 2
The Railroads

ESSENTIAL QUESTION • *How did the United States become an industrialized society after the Civil War?*

IT MATTERS BECAUSE

Major railroads, including the transcontinental railroad, were constructed rapidly after the Civil War ended. Railroads required major capital investment and government land grants. The potential profits led to some corruption as well.

Linking the Nation

GUIDING QUESTION *How did the transcontinental railroad transform the West?*

In 1865 the United States had about 35,000 miles of railroad track, almost all of it east of the Mississippi River. After the Civil War, railroad construction expanded dramatically. By 1900, the United States had more than 200,000 miles of track.

The Transcontinental Railroad

The railroad boom began in 1862 with the Pacific Railway Act. This act gave two corporations—the Union Pacific and the Central Pacific—permission to build a transcontinental railroad. It also offered each company land along its right-of-way.

Under the direction of engineer Grenville Dodge, a former Union general, the Union Pacific Railroad began pushing westward from Omaha, Nebraska, in 1865. The laborers faced blizzards in the mountains, scorching heat in the desert, and, sometimes, angry Native Americans. Labor, money, and engineering problems plagued the supervisors of the project. As Dodge observed:

PRIMARY SOURCE

❝[E]verything—rails, ties, bridging, fastenings, all railway supplies, fuel for locomotives and trains, and supplies for men and animals on the entire work, had to be transported from the Missouri River.❞

—from *How We Built the Union Pacific Railway*, 1910

The railroad workers of the Union Pacific included Civil War veterans, newly recruited Irish immigrants, frustrated miners and farmers, cooks, adventurers, and ex-convicts. At the height of the project, the Union Pacific employed about 10,000 workers.

PHOTOS: (l to r) Philip Gendreau/Bettmann/CORBIS, MPI/Archive Photos/Getty Images, Bettmann/CORBIS, Library of Congress

The Central Pacific Railroad began as the dream of engineer Theodore Judah. He sold stock in his fledgling Central Pacific Railroad Company to four Sacramento merchants: Leland Stanford, Charley Crocker, Mark Hopkins, and Collis P. Huntington. These "Big Four" eventually made huge fortunes. Stanford became governor of California, served as a U.S. senator, and founded Stanford University.

Because of a shortage of labor in California, the Central Pacific Railroad hired about 10,000 workers from China. It paid them about $1 a day. All the equipment—rails, cars, locomotives, and machinery—was shipped from the eastern United States. The equipment suppliers traveled either around Cape Horn at the tip of South America or over the Isthmus of Panama in Central America.

Workers completed the transcontinental railroad in only four years, despite the physical challenges. Each mile of track required 400 rails, and each rail took 10 spikes. The Central Pacific, starting from the west, laid a total of 688 miles of track. The Union Pacific laid 1,086 miles. On May 10, 1869, hundreds of spectators gathered at Promontory Summit, Utah. They watched dignitaries hammer five gold and silver spikes into the final rails that would join the Union Pacific and Central Pacific. Engineer Grenville Dodge was at the ceremony:

PRIMARY SOURCE

66 The two trains pulled up facing each other, each crowded with workmen. . . . The officers and invited guests formed on each side of the track. . . . Prayer was offered; a number of spikes were driven in the two adjoining rails . . . and thus the two roads were wedded into one great trunk line from the Atlantic to the Pacific. 99

— from *How We Built the Union Pacific Railway*, 1910

After Leland Stanford hammered in the last spike, telegraph operators sent the news across the nation. Cannons blasted in New York City, Chicago held a parade, and Philadelphia citizens rang the Liberty Bell.

Railroads Spur Growth

The transcontinental railroad was the first of many lines that began crisscrossing the nation after the Civil War. By linking the nation, railroads increased the markets for many products, spurring industrial growth. Railroad companies also stimulated the economy by spending huge amounts of money on steel, coal, timber, and other materials.

Large rail companies consolidated hundreds of small, unconnected railroads to create large, **integrated** railroad systems. Southern states particularly benefited from improved transportation, as railroads spurred

integrate to combine two previously separate things

The Union Pacific and Central Pacific lines met in Utah. Ceremonial gold and silver spikes were driven into the track, joining the two lines.

▶ **CRITICAL THINKING**
Predicting Consequences How might the completion of the transcontinental railroad change American life?

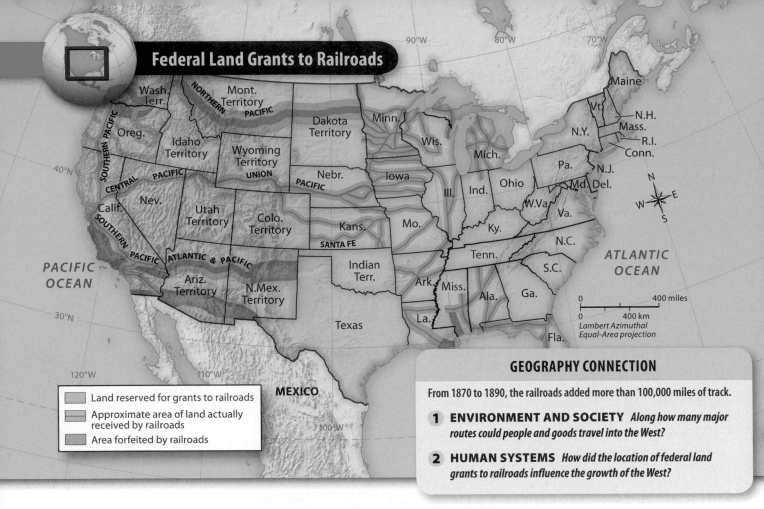

Federal Land Grants to Railroads

GEOGRAPHY CONNECTION

From 1870 to 1890, the railroads added more than 100,000 miles of track.

1 **ENVIRONMENT AND SOCIETY** *Along how many major routes could people and goods travel into the West?*

2 **HUMAN SYSTEMS** *How did the location of federal land grants to railroads influence the growth of the West?*

Land reserved for grants to railroads

Approximate area of land actually received by railroads

Area forfeited by railroads

---

the growth of new industries such as the Florida tourist trade. As rail systems grew, increased efficiency helped freight prices drop by over half between 1860 and 1900.

The railroads even unified the nation's clocks. Before the 1880s, each community set its own clocks, creating multiple local time zones. This interfered with train scheduling and passenger safety. These issues spurred the American Railway Association to divide the country into four **time zones** in 1883.

✔ **PROGRESS CHECK**

Explaining How did the transcontinental railroad help unite the nation?

Robber Barons

GUIDING QUESTION *How did government grants to build railroads result in large-scale corruption?*

Most private **investors** could not raise the money needed to build railroads. As a result, the federal government gave **land grants** to many railroad companies. Companies sold the land to raise money for construction. In time, the great wealth accumulated by many railroad entrepreneurs, such as Cornelius Vanderbilt and Jay Gould, led to accusations of swindling investors and taxpayers and bribing officials. Bribery did occur, partly because the government helped fund railroads. To get more grants, some investors began bribing members of Congress.

The Crédit Mobilier Scandal

Corruption in the railroad industry became public in 1872 with the Crédit Mobilier scandal. Crédit Mobilier was a construction company set up by several stockholders of the Union Pacific Railroad, including Oakes Ames, a member of Congress. Acting for both the Union Pacific and Crédit Mobilier, the investors signed overpriced contracts with themselves. Because the same investors controlled both companies, Union Pacific paid the inflated bills. It was almost bankrupt by the time it was completed. To convince Congress to give the railroad more grants, Ames sold other members of Congress shares at a price well below their market value.

During the election campaign of 1872, a letter appeared in the *New York Sun* listing members of Congress who bought shares. The scandal led to an investigation that implicated several politicians, including Representative James A. Garfield, who later became president, and sitting Vice President Schuyler Colfax. Neither criminal nor civil charges were filed against anyone involved with Crédit Mobilier, however. Nor did the scandal affect the outcome of the elections.

The Great Northern Railroad

Not all railroad men were robber barons, a term used to describe industrialists who grew wealthy unethically. James J. Hill built and operated the Great Northern Railroad, from Wisconsin and Minnesota to Washington in the west, without any federal land grants or subsidies. Hill identified goods that were in demand in China so that his railroad could ship these goods to Washington, for delivery in Asia. This way, his railroad efficiently hauled goods both east and west, instead of simply sending goods east and coming back empty like other railroads. The Great Northern became the most successful transcontinental railroad and one of the few railroads of the time that was not eventually forced into bankruptcy.

☑ **PROGRESS CHECK**

Explaining Why did robber barons bribe people in Congress?

PHOTO: Bettmann/CORBIS

JAY GOULD: ROBBER BARON

Railroad owners became condemned as robber barons as the American public increasingly began to suspect them of bribery, cheating, and swindling.

POLITICAL CARTOONS

Jay Gould bowls on Wall Street with balls labeled "Trickery" and "False Reports." The pins are labeled "Banker," "Inexperienced Investor," "Small Operator," and "Stock Broker."

▶ **CRITICAL THINKING**

1 *Analyzing Primary Sources* What does this political cartoon suggest about attitudes toward Jay Gould?

2 *Predicting Consequences* What is a likely outcome of the actions of robber barons on the people represented by the bowling pins?

time zone a geographic region in which the same standard time is kept

investor one who puts money into a company in order to gain a future financial reward

land grant a grant of land by the federal government, especially for roads, railroads, or agricultural colleges

---

LESSON 2 REVIEW

Reviewing Vocabulary

1. *Explaining* Why did the government give land grants to railroad companies?

2. *Problem Solving* What problem did establishing time zones solve?

Using Your Notes

3. *Identifying Cause and Effect* Review your notes and write a brief explanation of how the growth of railroads helped American businesses expand.

Answering the Guiding Questions

4. *Analyzing Information* How did the transcontinental railroad transform the West?

5. *Drawing Conclusions* How did government grants to build railroads result in large-scale corruption?

Writing Activity

6. EXPOSITORY Between 1860 and 1890, the amount of railroad track in the United States increased dramatically. How would you expect the growth of the railroad to influence settlement patterns?

Reading **HELP**DESK

Content Vocabulary

- corporation
- economies of scale
- **monopoly** • **trust**
- **holding company**

Academic Vocabulary

- **distribution**
- **consumer**

TAKING NOTES: *Organizing*

ACTIVITY As you read about the rise of corporations in the United States, use the following graphic organizer to identify the steps big businesses took to weaken or eliminate competition.

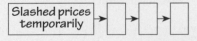

LESSON 3
Big Business

IT MATTERS BECAUSE

Following the Civil War, large corporations developed that could consolidate business functions and produce goods more efficiently. Retailers began using new techniques to attract consumers.

The Rise of Big Business

GUIDING QUESTION *What advantages do large corporations have over small businesses?*

By 1900, big business dominated the economy, operating vast complexes of factories and **distribution** facilities. The **corporation,** an organization owned by many people but treated by law as though it were a person, made big business possible. Stockholders own corporations through shares of ownership called stock. Selling stock allows a corporation to raise money while spreading out the financial risk.

Before the 1830s, few corporations existed because entrepreneurs had to convince state legislatures to issue them charters. In the 1830s, however, states began allowing companies to become corporations and issue stock without a charter from the legislature.

With the money raised from selling stock, corporations could invest in new technologies, hire large workforces, and purchase machines. This greatly increased their efficiency. They achieved **economies of scale,** in which the cost of manufacturing is decreased by producing goods quickly in large quantities.

All businesses have fixed costs and operating costs. *Fixed costs* are costs a company pays even if it is not operating (loans, mortgages, and taxes). *Operating costs* are incurred when running a company (wages, shipping costs, buying raw materials). Small manufacturers usually had low fixed costs but high operating costs. If sales dropped, it was cheaper to shut down temporarily. Big manufacturers, however, had the high fixed costs of building and maintaining a factory, while operating costs were low. Operating costs, such as wages, were such a small part of total costs that it made sense to continue operating, even in a recession.

In these circumstances, big corporations had several advantages. They could produce more goods at a lower cost and could stay open in bad economic times by cutting prices to increase sales. Rebates from the railroads further lowered their operating costs. Eventually, small businesses that could not compete with large corporations were forced out of business.

☑ PROGRESS CHECK

Explaining How do economies of scale affect corporations?

Consolidating Industry

GUIDING QUESTION *What new business strategies allowed businesses to weaken or eliminate competition?*

Falling prices benefited **consumers** but cut into manufacturers' profits. Many companies organized pools or other arrangements to keep prices at a certain level. Pools interfered with competition and property rights. Companies that formed pools had no legal protection and could not enforce their agreements in court. Pools generally did not last long, as one member inevitably cut prices to steal market share from the others.

Andrew Carnegie and Steel

The remarkable life of Andrew Carnegie illustrates the rise of big business in the United States. A Scottish immigrant, Carnegie went to work at age 12 in a textile factory. He worked his way up to become secretary to Thomas Scott, a superintendent of the Pennsylvania Railroad. When Scott was promoted, Carnegie became the new superintendent.

Carnegie bought shares in iron mills and factories that made sleeping cars and railroad locomotives, as well as a company that built railroad bridges. By his early 30s, he quit his job to concentrate on his investments. In 1875 Carnegie opened a steel mill near Pittsburgh. He began using the Bessemer process to make high-quality steel quickly and cheaply. He often boasted about how cheaply he could produce steel:

distribution the act or process of being given out or disbursed to clients, consumers, or members of a group

corporation an organization that is authorized by law to carry on an activity but treated as though it were a single person

economies of scale the reduction in the cost of a good brought about especially by increased production at a given facility

consumer a person who buys what is produced by an economy

TYPES OF BUSINESS ORGANIZATIONS			CHARTS/GRAPHS
	Sole Proprietorship	**Partnership**	**Corporation**
Who owns the business?	One owner who often manages the business	Two or more owners who usually manage the business	Shareholders, whether private or public Managers are hired
How is money raised?	Uses savings of owner Borrows from creditors	Invests savings from limited partners Borrows from creditors	Sells stock Borrows from creditors
Advantages	Ease of setup Nominal cost	Shared responsibility by each partner	Exists as a separate entity Limited liability
Disadvantages	Owner is personally liable for all debts Commingling of personal and business property and funds Cannot raise capital by selling an interest in the business	Owners are personally liable for obligations and debts Requires more legal and accounting services Partners may disagree on the management of the company	Must adhere to the principles that govern a corporation

▶ **CRITICAL THINKING**

1 *Drawing Inferences* Comparing proprietorships and corporations, why do you think both still exist today?

2 *Making Generalizations* Based on the chart, what generalizations can you make about why a corporation might have a competitive advantage over a sole proprietorship?

VERTICAL INTEGRATION AND HORIZONTAL INTEGRATION

Vertical integration and horizontal integration helped consolidate industry.

▶ **CRITICAL THINKING**

1 *Analyzing Information*
How does a large company benefit when it buys its competitors?

2 *Identifying Central Issues*
Why did business owners want to vertically integrate their companies?

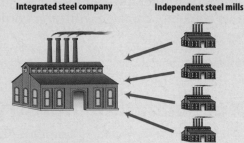

Vertical Integration

Integrated steel company

↑

Steel mill

↑

Shipping facilities

↑

Iron mine   Limestone quarry   Coal mine

Vertical integration occurs when a company owns all parts of the industrial process.

Horizontal Integration

Integrated steel company   Independent steel mills

Horizontal integration occurs when a company grows by buying its competitors.

PRIMARY SOURCE

❝Two pounds of ironstone . . . one pound and a half of coal, mined, manufactured into coke . . . one-half pound of lime, . . . [and] a small amount of manganese ore, . . . these four pounds of materials manufactured into one pound of steel, for which the consumer pays one cent.❞

—from *Triumphant Democracy*, 1893

Carnegie also began the vertical integration of the steel industry. Instead of paying companies for coal, lime, and iron, Carnegie's steel company bought coal mines, limestone quarries, and iron ore fields. Vertical integration saved money and enabled many companies to expand.

Rockefeller and Standard Oil

Business leaders such as John D. Rockefeller also pushed for horizontal integration. Rockefeller's Standard Oil began buying out competitors. By 1880, it controlled about 90 percent of the U.S. oil refining industry, a near **monopoly.** Rockefeller was so successful that the *New York Times* declared that he "had accumulated close to $1,500,000,000 . . . probably the greatest amount of wealth that any private citizen had ever been able to accumulate by his own efforts."

New Business Organizations

Many Americans feared monopolies. They believed that a monopoly could charge whatever it wanted for its products. In the late 1800s, many states tried to stop horizontal integration and the rise of monopolies by making it illegal for one company to own stock in another company. Companies, however, soon discovered ways around the laws.

Trusts In 1882 Standard Oil formed the first **trust.** A trust is a legal arrangement that allows one person to manage another person's property. The person who manages that property is called a trustee. Instead of buying a company outright, Standard Oil had stockholders of that company give their stock to Standard Oil trustees in exchange for shares in the trust and its profits. The trustees could control a group of companies as if they were one large, merged company.

monopoly total control of a type of industry by one person or one company

trust a combination of firms or corporations formed by a legal agreement, especially to reduce competition

Holding Companies A new general incorporation law in 1889 allowed corporations to own stock in other businesses without special legislative permission. Many companies used the law to create **holding companies.** A holding company does not produce anything itself but owns the stock of companies that do produce goods. The holding company manages its companies, effectively merging them into one.

Investment Banking Investment bankers began to help put new holding companies together. Perhaps the most successful investment banker was J. P. Morgan. He specialized in helping companies sell large blocks of stock to investment bankers at a discount. The bankers would then sell the stock for a profit. In the mid-1890s, investment bankers became interested in selling stock in holding companies. In 1901 J. P. Morgan bought out Andrew Carnegie and merged Carnegie Steel with other large steel companies into an enormous holding company. It was called the United States Steel Corporation, or U.S. Steel.

holding company
a company whose primary business is owning a controlling share of stock in other companies

Selling the Product

The creation of giant manufacturing companies in the United States pushed retailers to expand in size as well. The vast array of products that American industries produced led retailers to look for new ways to attract consumers. N. W. Ayer and Son, the first advertising company, began creating large illustrated ads instead of relying on the old small print line ads previously used in newspapers. By 1900, retailers were spending over $90 million a year on advertising in newspapers and magazines.

Advertising attracted readers to the newest retail business, the department store. In 1877 advertisements billed John Wanamaker's new Philadelphia department store, the Grand Depot, as the "largest space in the world devoted to retail selling on a single floor." When it opened, only a handful of department stores existed in the United States. Soon hundreds sprang up, providing a huge selection of products in one large building.

Chain stores, a group of retail outlets owned by the same company, first appeared in the mid-1800s. In contrast to department stores, chain stores such as Woolworth's focused on offering low prices.

To reach the millions of people who lived in rural areas, retailers began issuing mail-order catalogs. Two of the largest mail-order retailers were Montgomery Ward and Sears, Roebuck and Co. Their huge catalogs were widely distributed through the mail. They used attractive illustrations and appealing descriptions to advertise thousands of items for sale.

☑ **PROGRESS CHECK**

Summarizing What makes monopolies disadvantageous for the consumer?

LESSON 3 REVIEW

Reviewing Vocabulary

1. *Summarizing* How did corporations use vertical and horizontal integration to grow?

2. *Explaining* How did trusts and holding companies create unofficial monopolies?

Using Your Notes

3. *Making Connections* Review the notes you completed throughout the lesson to identify a way that a corporation today could use similar tactics to weaken its competition.

Answering the Guiding Questions

4. *Evaluating* What advantages do large corporations have over small businesses?

5. *Synthesizing* What new business strategies allowed businesses to weaken or eliminate competition?

Writing Activity

6. EXPOSITORY Industrialization introduced many new ideas about how businesses could be formed and operated. Write a one-page essay explaining how these new ways of organizing businesses led to the establishment of corporate monopolies.

networks

There's More Online!

☑ **BIOGRAPHY** Eugene Debs

☑ **BIOGRAPHY** Samuel Gompers

☑ **BIOGRAPHY** "Mother Jones"

☑ **CHART/GRAPH** Comparing Major Strikes

☑ **PRIMARY SOURCE** Communist Party Manifesto

☑ **VIDEO** Unions

☑ **INTERACTIVE SELF-CHECK QUIZ**

Reading **HELP**DESK

Content Vocabulary

• deflation • closed shop
• industrial union
• lockout
• arbitration
• injunction

Academic Vocabulary

• restraint • constitute

TAKING NOTES: *Sequencing*

ACTIVITY As you read about the increase of labor unions in the late 1800s, complete a time line similar to the one below by filling in the year of each incident of labor unrest discussed and the results of each incident.

| 1877 | | | |

LESSON 4
Unions

ESSENTIAL QUESTION • *How did the United States become an industrialized society after the Civil War?*

IT MATTERS BECAUSE

Workers tried to form unions in the 1800s, hoping to improve wages, hours, and working conditions. Business leaders worked with some trade unions but generally opposed industrial unions. Strikes during this era sometimes led to violence, which hurt the unions' image and slowed their growth.

Working in the United States

GUIDING QUESTION *Why did workers try to form unions in the late 1800s?*

Life for workers in the industrial United States was difficult. Many workers performed dull, repetitive tasks in dangerous, unhealthy working conditions. Workers breathed in lint, dust, and toxic fumes. Heavy machines lacking safety devices led to injuries. Despite these conditions, industrialism led to a dramatic rise in the standard of living. The average worker's wages rose by 50 percent between 1860 and 1890. Nevertheless, the uneven division of income between the wealthy and the working class caused resentment among workers. In 1900 the average industrial worker made 22¢ per hour and worked 59 hours per week.

Deflation, or a rise in the value of money, added to tensions. Between 1865 and 1897, deflation caused prices to fall, which increased the buying power of workers' wages. Although companies cut wages regularly in the late 1800s, prices fell even faster, so that wages were actually still going up in buying power. Workers, however, resented getting less money. Eventually, many concluded that they needed a union to bargain for higher wages and better working conditions.

Early Unions

There were two basic types of industrial workers in the United States in the 1800s—craft workers and common laborers. Craft workers, such as machinists, iron molders, stonecutters, shoemakers, and printers, had special skills and training. They received higher wages and had more control over their time. Common laborers had few skills and received lower wages.

PHOTOS: (l to r) Historical/CORBIS, Library of Congress, Historical/CORBIS, The Granger Collection, New York

In the 1830s, as industrialization began to spread, craft workers began to form trade unions. By 1873, there were 30 national trade unions in the United States. Among the largest and most successful were the Iron Molders' International Union, the International Typographical Union, and the Knights of St. Crispin—the shoemakers' union.

Opposition to Unions

Employers often had to negotiate with trade unions because the unions represented workers whose skills they needed. Employers, however, generally viewed unions as conspiracies that interfered with property rights. Business leaders particularly opposed **industrial unions,** which united all the workers in a particular industry.

Companies used several techniques to stop workers from forming unions. They required workers to take oaths or sign contracts promising not to join a union. They hired detectives to identify union organizers. Workers who tried to organize a union or strike were fired and placed on a blacklist—a list of "troublemakers"—so that no company would hire them. Companies used **"lockouts"** to break up existing unions. They locked workers out of the property and refused to pay them. If the union called a strike, employers would hire replacements, or strikebreakers.

Efforts to break unions often succeeded because there were no laws giving workers the right to form unions or requiring owners to negotiate with them. Courts frequently ruled that strikes were "conspiracies in restraint of trade," for which labor leaders might be fined or jailed.

Unions also suffered from the perception that they were un-American. In the 1800s, the ideas of Karl Marx, called Marxism, became very influential in Europe. Marx argued that the basic force shaping capitalist society was the class struggle between workers and owners. He believed that workers would eventually revolt, seize control of the factories, and overthrow the government. Eventually, Marx thought, the state would disappear, leaving a communist society where classes did not exist.

While many labor supporters agreed with Marx, a few supported anarchism. Anarchists believe that society does not need any government. In the late 1800s, anarchists assassinated government officials and set off bombs across Europe, hoping to begin a revolution.

deflation a decline in the volume of available money or credit that results in lower prices, and therefore increases the buying power of money

industrial union an organization of common laborers and craft workers in a particular industry

lockout a company tool to fight union demands by refusing to allow employees to enter its facilities to work

restraint the act of limiting, restricting, or keeping under control

ANNUAL NONFARM EARNINGS

Earnings (dollars) vs. Year (1865–1900)

Real wages
Not adjusted for inflation

Source: *Historical Statistics of the United States: Colonial Times to 1970*

PHOTO: Historical/CORBIS

CHARTS/GRAPHS

In the late 1800s, industrial workers toiled in dangerous, unhealthy conditions. Bad working conditions eventually led workers to seek to organize unions, hoping to improve their situations.

▶ CRITICAL THINKING

1 *Comparing and Contrasting* How did changes in real wages and wages that were not adjusted for deflation differ?

2 *Drawing Conclusions* Why do you think workers wanted to organize?

During the same period, tens of thousands of European immigrants headed to America. Anti-immigrant feelings were already strong in the United States and, as people began to associate immigrant workers with radical ideas, they became suspicious of unions. These fears, and concerns for law and order, often led officials to use the courts, the police, and even the army to crush strikes and break up unions.

☑ **PROGRESS CHECK**

Identifying Cause and Effect How did working conditions encourage workers to form unions in the late 1800s?

Struggling to Organize

GUIDING QUESTION *What made it difficult for union workers to create large industrial unions?*

Although workers attempted on many occasions to create large industrial unions, they rarely succeeded. In many cases, the confrontations with owners and the government led to violence and bloodshed. In 1869 William Sylvis, president of the National Labor Union, wrote to Karl Marx in support of his work and to express his own beliefs:

PRIMARY SOURCE

❝[M]onied power is fast eating up the substance of the people. We have made war upon it, and we mean to win it. If we can we will win through the ballot box; if not, we will resort to sterner means. A little blood-letting is sometimes necessary in desperate cases.❞

—quoted in *History of Labour in the United States,* 1921

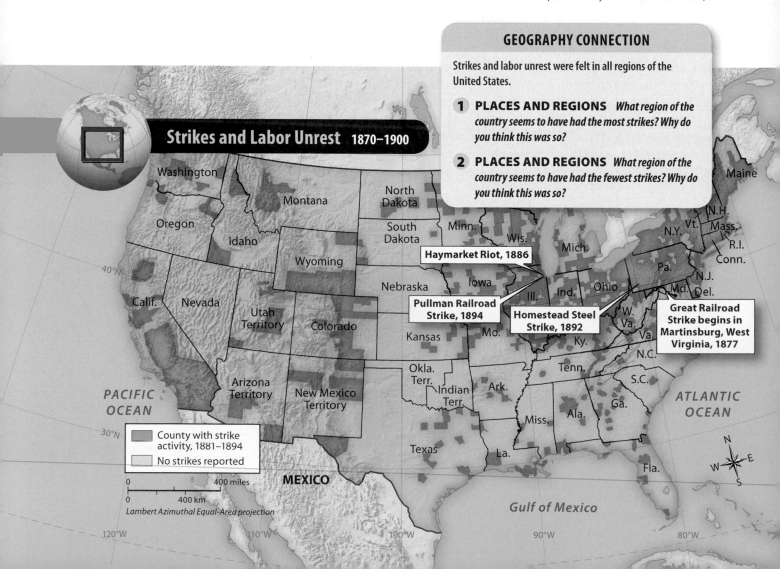

GEOGRAPHY CONNECTION

Strikes and labor unrest were felt in all regions of the United States.

1 **PLACES AND REGIONS** *What region of the country seems to have had the most strikes? Why do you think this was so?*

2 **PLACES AND REGIONS** *What region of the country seems to have had the fewest strikes? Why do you think this was so?*

Strikes and Labor Unrest 1870–1900

Haymarket Riot, 1886

Pullman Railroad Strike, 1894

Homestead Steel Strike, 1892

Great Railroad Strike begins in Martinsburg, West Virginia, 1877

County with strike activity, 1881–1894

No strikes reported

0   400 miles
0   400 km
Lambert Azimuthal Equal-Area projection

PACIFIC OCEAN

ATLANTIC OCEAN

MEXICO

Gulf of Mexico

The Great Railroad Strike

The Panic of 1873 was a severe recession that struck the American economy and forced many companies to cut wages. The economy had still not recovered when, in July 1877, the Baltimore and Ohio Railroad announced it was cutting wages for the third time. In Martinsburg, West Virginia, workers walked off the job and blocked the tracks.

As word spread, railroad workers across the country walked off the job. The strike eventually involved some 80,000 railroad workers and affected two-thirds of the nation's railways. Angry strikers smashed equipment, tore up tracks, and blocked rail service in New York City, Baltimore, Pittsburgh, St. Louis, and Chicago. The governors of several states called out their militias. In many places, gun battles erupted between the militia and the strikers.

Declaring a state of "insurrection," President Rutherford B. Hayes sent federal troops to Martinsburg, Baltimore, Pittsburgh, and elsewhere. It took 12 bloody days for police, state militias, and federal troops to restore order. By the time the strike collapsed, more than 100 people lay dead, and over $10 million in railroad property had been destroyed. The violence of this strike alarmed many Americans and pointed to the need for more peaceful means to settle labor disputes.

The Knights of Labor

The Knights of Labor, founded in 1869, took a different approach to labor issues. Its leader, Terence Powderly, opposed strikes in favor of boycotts and **arbitration,** in which a third party helps workers and employers reach an agreement. In *Thirty Years of Labor*, Powderly argued that disputes were best settled by "a tribunal where the interests, not alone of the employer and his workmen would be considered, but . . . which would carefully investigate the cause of the strike and the effect of the stoppage of work by one branch of industry upon all others." Unlike other unions, the Knights welcomed women and African Americans. They called for an eight-hour workday, equal pay for women, no child labor, and worker-owned factories.

The Haymarket Riot In 1886 supporters of the eight-hour workday called for a nationwide strike on May 1. On May 3, Chicago police intervening in a fight on a picket line opened fire on the strikers, killing four. The next day, about 3,000 people gathered to protest the shootings in Chicago's Haymarket Square. Someone threw a bomb, police opened fire, and workers shot back, injuring about 170 people and killing 10 policemen. Eight men were arrested for the bombing. Though evidence against them was weak, public anger resulted in eight convictions. Four were executed.

Union critics used the Haymarket riot to claim that dangerous radicals dominated the unions. One of the men arrested was a member of the Knights of Labor. The blow to the Knights' reputation along with lost strikes led to a decline in their membership and influence.

The Homestead and Pullman Strikes

In the summer of 1892, another labor dispute led to bloodshed. A steel mill owned by Andrew Carnegie in Homestead, Pennsylvania, was managed by Henry Clay Frick, an anti-union business partner. Frick proposed cutting wages by 20 percent. He then locked out employees (who were members of the Amalgamated Association of Iron, Steel, and Tin Workers) and had the Pinkerton Detective Agency bring in replacements. When the Pinkertons and strikebreakers approached the plant, the strikers resisted. Over the next

In 1894 a former quarry foreman named Jacob Coxey organized unemployed workers and began a march on Washington to demand jobs on public works projects. The marchers were known as "Coxey's Army."

▶ **CRITICAL THINKING**
Analyzing Primary Sources What does this photograph indicate about workers' interest in organizing to achieve their goals?

arbitration settling a dispute by agreeing to accept the decision of an impartial outsider

14 hours, Pinkertons and strikers clashed, leaving several dead and dozens injured. The governor of Pennsylvania sent in the militia to protect the strikebreakers, and four months later, the strike collapsed.

In 1894 the Pullman Palace Car Company slashed workers' wages without lowering rents and prices in the company town. American Railway Union (ARU) workers refused to handle Pullman cars, and railroads ground to a near halt. Railroad managers arranged to have U.S. mail cars attached to the Pullman cars, and President Cleveland sent in federal troops to keep the mail running. A federal court then issued an **injunction,** or formal order, to halt the boycott. Both the strike and the ARU collapsed. The Supreme Court later upheld the right to issue such an injunction. This gave business a powerful tool for dealing with labor unrest.

✔ **PROGRESS CHECK**

Identifying Central Issues How did major strikes prevent large industrial unions from maintaining power and influence?

New Unions Emerge

GUIDING QUESTION *How were the new industrial unions different from the older trade unions?*

Although workers often shared the same complaints about wages and working hours, unions took different approaches to how they tried to improve workers' lives. Trade unions remained the most common type of labor organization, but unskilled workers were not represented by trade unions. New types of unions emerged to support these workers.

The Rise of the AFL

The American Federation of Labor (AFL) was the dominant labor organization of the late 1800s. In 1886 leaders of several national trade unions created the AFL. It focused on promoting the interests of skilled workers.

Samuel Gompers was the first president of the AFL, a position he held almost continuously until 1924. While other unions became involved in politics, Gompers tried to concentrate on "pure and simple" unionism, focusing on wages, working hours, and working conditions. He was willing to use strikes to create change but preferred to negotiate.

The AFL had three main goals. First, it tried to convince companies to recognize unions and agree to collective bargaining. Second, it pushed for **closed shops,** meaning that companies could hire only union members. Third, it promoted an eight-hour workday.

By 1900, the AFL was the biggest union in the country with more than 500,000 members. Still, at that time, the AFL represented less than 15 percent of all nonfarm workers. Most AFL members were white men, because the unions discriminated against African Americans, and only a few would admit women.

The IWW

In 1905 a group of labor radicals, many of them socialists, created the Industrial Workers of the World (IWW). Nicknamed "the Wobblies," the IWW wanted to organize all workers according to industry, without making distinctions between skilled and unskilled workers. The IWW endorsed using strikes and declared: "The working class and the employing class have nothing in common."

The IWW believed all workers should be organized into "One Big Union." In particular, the IWW tried to organize the unskilled workers who were ignored by most unions.

Samuel Gompers concentrated his efforts on improving working conditions and believed that a just society was built on a fair labor policy.

▶ **CRITICAL THINKING**
Drawing Conclusions How do you think Gompers would view a society that did not allow labor unions?

In 1912 the IWW led a successful strike of 25,000 textile workers in Lawrence, Massachusetts, to protest wage cuts. The companies reversed the wage cuts after 10 weeks. The Lawrence strike was the Wobblies' greatest victory. Most IWW strikes failed. The IWW never gained a large membership, in part because its radical philosophy and controversial strikes led many to condemn the organization.

Women and Organized Labor

After the Civil War, the number of female wage earners began to increase. By 1900, women made up more than 18 percent of the labor force. The types of jobs women did outside the home reflected society's ideas about what **constituted** "women's work." About one-third of women wage earners worked as domestic servants. Another third worked as teachers, nurses, sales clerks, and office clerical workers. The remaining third were industrial workers, often in the garment industry or food-processing plants.

Women were paid less than men even when they performed the same jobs. It was assumed that a woman had a man helping support her, and that a man needed higher wages in order to support a family. Most unions excluded women.

One of the most famous labor leaders of the era was Mary Harris Jones, also known as "Mother Jones." Jones worked as a labor organizer for the Knights of Labor before helping organize mine workers. Her public speaking abilities made her a very successful organizer, leading John D. Rockefeller to dub her "the most dangerous woman in America."

In 1900 Jewish and Italian immigrants who worked in the clothing business in New York City founded the International Ladies' Garment Workers Union (ILGWU), which represented female and male workers in the women's clothing industry. Membership expanded rapidly, and in 1909 a strike of some 30,000 garment workers won the ILGWU recognition in the industry, better wages, and benefits for employees.

In 1903 Mary Kenney O'Sullivan and Leonora O'Reilly decided to establish a separate union for women. With the help of Jane Addams and Lillian Wald, they established the Women's Trade Union League (WTUL), which pushed for an eight-hour workday, a minimum wage, an end to evening work for women, and the abolition of child labor.

By the beginning of the twentieth century, many women had entered the workforce. Some were industrial workers in clothing or food-processing factories.

▶ CRITICAL THINKING
Formulating Questions What is one question that you could ask to begin researching women in the industrial workforce?

constitute to compose, make up, or form

✔ **PROGRESS CHECK**

Explaining Why did women need to form their own trade unions?

LESSON 4 REVIEW

Reviewing Vocabulary

1. *Contrasting* What is the difference between a closed shop and a lockout?

2. *Paraphrasing* What is another word or phrase for an injunction?

Using Your Notes

3. *Comparing* Use your notes from the lesson to identify some common features of incidents of labor unrest.

Answering the Guiding Questions

4. *Drawing Conclusions* Why did workers try to form unions in the late 1800s?

5. *Making Generalizations* What made it difficult for union workers to create large industrial unions?

6. *Contrasting* How were the new industrial unions different from the older trade unions?

Writing Activity

7. PERSUASIVE Suppose that you are a union leader. Write a letter to a factory owner in which you try to persuade him or her to make changes in wages or other work policies on behalf of the factory's workers. Be sure to be specific about your requests and the reasons why they are necessary.

Directions: On a separate sheet of paper, answer the questions below. Make sure you read carefully and answer all parts to the question.

Lesson Review

Lesson 1

1 *Identifying Central Issues* Why do supporters of laissez-faire economics not favor government regulation?

2 *Determining Cause and Effect* What role did immigration play in the Second Industrial Revolution?

Lesson 2

3 *Identifying Central Issues* What kinds of business practices caused some railroad owners to be accused of being "robber barons"?

4 *Drawing Conclusions* What gave the railroads the power to reshape American society, even so far as telling Americans what time it was?

Lesson 3

5 *Evaluating* How do big businesses benefit from economies of scale?

6 *Explaining* What was Standard Oil's purpose for forming a trust?

Lesson 4

7 *Determining Cause and Effect* How did deflation play a role in the rise of unions?

8 *Making Inferences* Why do you think companies felt that unions were "conspiracies that interfered with property rights"?

21st Century Skills

9 TIME, CHRONOLOGY, AND SEQUENCING What led to the formation of the first women's unions?

10 UNDERSTANDING RELATIONSHIPS AMONG EVENTS What goal did the major strikes of the period have in common?

11 IDENTIFYING/EXPLAINING CONTINUITY & CHANGE How did the flood of new inventions during this time not only change the way people lived but also contribute to the industrialization of the United States?

Exploring the Essential Question

12 *Analyzing* Write an oral presentation explaining the factors that contributed to the United States becoming an industrialized society after the Civil War.

DBQ Document-Based Questions

Use the quote to answer the following questions.

Andrew Carnegie published an article on wealth and how it should be used in society. In the article, he describes industrial society's inequalities, but insists that there is no other way.

PRIMARY SOURCE

❝*We assemble thousands of operatives in the factory, in the mine, and in the counting-house, of whom the employer can know little or nothing, and to whom the employer is little better than a myth. Rigid castes are formed, and, as usual, mutual ignorance breeds mutual distrust. The price which society pays for the law of competition, like the price it pays for cheap comforts and luxuries, is great; but the advantages of this law are also greater still than its cost—for it is to this law that we owe our wonderful material development, which brings improved conditions in its train. But, whether the law be benign or not, we must say of it: It is here; we cannot evade it; no substitutes for it have been found; and while the law may be sometimes hard for the individual, it is best for the race, because it ensures the survival of the fittest in every department.*❞

—Andrew Carnegie, from "The Gospel of Wealth," 1901

13 *Identifying Central Issues* What problems does Carnegie associate with industrialization and the workers?

14 *Drawing Inferences* Using what you know about laissez-faire, economies of scale, and unions, explain how this situation between workers and employers is the result of competition.

Extended-Response Question

15 *Drawing Conclusions* Write an expository essay explaining three ways retailers—companies that sell products directly to consumers—responded to growing industrialization.

Need Extra Help?

If You've Missed Question	1	2	3	4	5	6	7	8	9	10	11	12	13	14	15
Go to page	289	287	292	291	294	296	298	299	303	300	288	286	304	289	297

Urban America

1865–1896

ESSENTIAL QUESTIONS • *Why do people migrate?* • *How is urban life different from rural life?*

The Story Matters...

European and Asian immigrants arrived in the United States in great numbers during the late 1800s. Providing cheap labor, they made rapid industrial growth possible. They also helped populate the growing cities. As jobs in urban areas became more plentiful, many Americans moved from farms and small towns to cities. Read the chapter to learn how the events of the late nineteenth century shaped the United States as it is today.

◄ For many European immigrants, the Statue of Liberty was their first glimpse of America. The Statue of Liberty often represented the hopes and dreams of people looking for a better life.

PHOTO: PhotoLink/Photodisc/Getty Images

CHAPTER 13

Place and Time: United States 1865–1896

Drawn to cities by jobs available in America's growing industries, the urban population of the United States grew from around 10 million in 1870 to more than 30 million by the turn of the century. Immigrants from Europe, Africa, Asia, Canada, Mexico, and South America began looking for better work and a higher standard of living. Rural Americans also began moving to the cities. Industrialization led to urbanization, new political parties, new art and literature, and different ideas about government's role in society. Industrialization brought changes to society, including new social classes and increased segregation for African Americans. New philosophies and movements sprang up to respond to all of these changes.

Step Into the Place

Look at the information presented on the map.

DBQ **Why might the levels of immigration between "old" and "new" immigrants from Europe be roughly equal?**

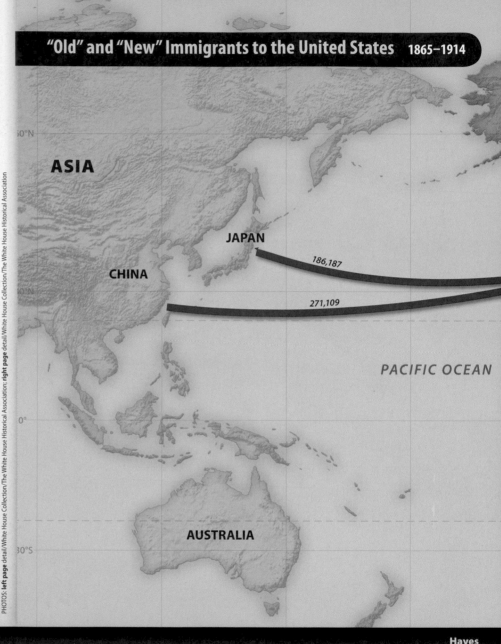

"Old" and "New" Immigrants to the United States 1865–1914

ASIA

JAPAN

186,187

CHINA

271,109

PACIFIC OCEAN

AUSTRALIA

50°N

30°N

0°

30°S

PHOTOS: **left page** detail/White House Collection/The White House Historical Association; **right page** detail/White House Collection/The White House Historical Association

Step Into the Time

Choose an event from the time line and write a paragraph about how that event might have affected the movement of people to the United States during the late 1800s.

Hayes
1877–1881

1860s First Japanese immigrants arrive in California

1870 Fifteenth Amendment ratified

1874 Farmers' Alliance founded

U.S. PRESIDENTS

UNITED STATES

1870

WORLD

1875

1871 Britain legalizes labor unions

1872 Ballot Act makes voting secret in Britain

1875 Work begins in France on Statue of Liberty

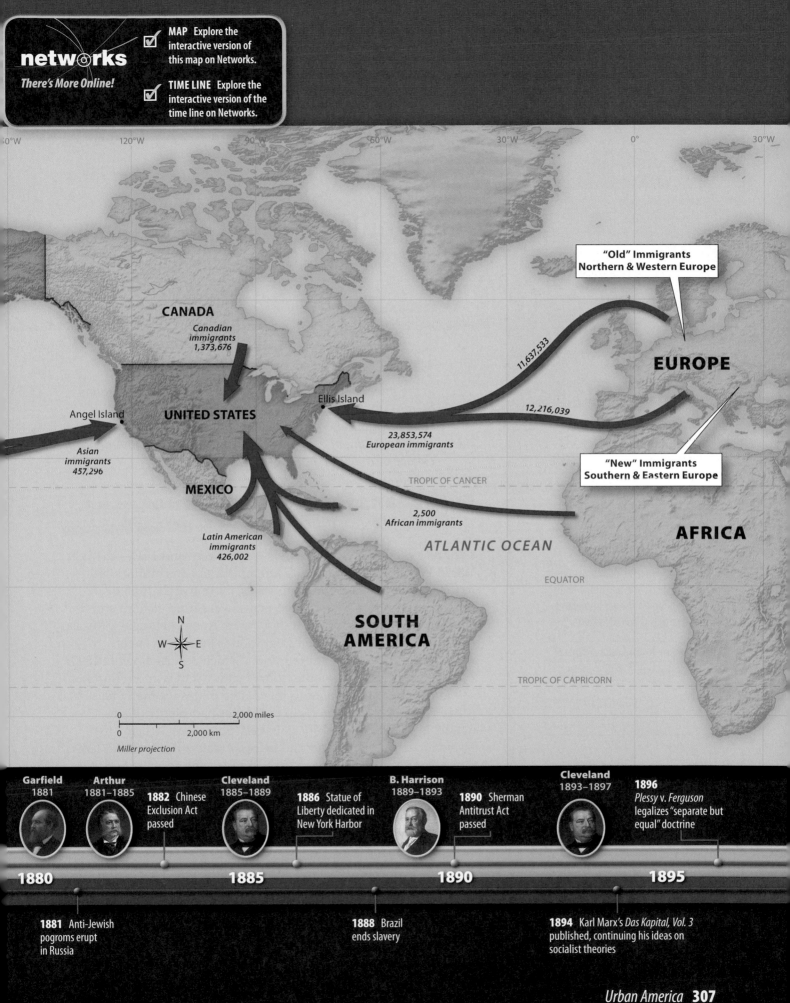

networks
There's More Online!

☑ MAP Explore the interactive version of this map on Networks.

☑ TIME LINE Explore the interactive version of the time line on Networks.

"Old" Immigrants
Northern & Western Europe

"New" Immigrants
Southern & Eastern Europe

EUROPE

AFRICA

CANADA

Canadian immigrants
1,373,676

Ellis Island

UNITED STATES

Angel Island

Asian immigrants
457,296

MEXICO

Latin American immigrants
426,002

11,637,533

12,216,039

23,853,574
European immigrants

TROPIC OF CANCER

2,500
African immigrants

ATLANTIC OCEAN

EQUATOR

SOUTH AMERICA

TROPIC OF CAPRICORN

N W E S

0   2,000 miles
0   2,000 km

Miller projection

Garfield
1881

Arthur
1881–1885

1882 Chinese Exclusion Act passed

Cleveland
1885–1889

1886 Statue of Liberty dedicated in New York Harbor

B. Harrison
1889–1893

1890 Sherman Antitrust Act passed

Cleveland
1893–1897

1896 *Plessy* v. *Ferguson* legalizes "separate but equal" doctrine

1880

1885

1890

1895

1881 Anti-Jewish pogroms erupt in Russia

1888 Brazil ends slavery

1894 Karl Marx's *Das Kapital, Vol. 3* published, continuing his ideas on socialist theories

networks
There's More Online!

☑ **CHART/GRAPH** Immigration Restrictions

☑ **IMAGE** Nativism Political Cartoon

☑ **VIDEO** Immigration

☑ **INTERACTIVE SELF-CHECK QUIZ**

LESSON 1
Immigration

ESSENTIAL QUESTIONS • *Why do people migrate?* • *How is urban life different from rural life?*

Reading **HELP**DESK

Content Vocabulary
• nativism

Academic Vocabulary
• immigrant   • ethnic

TAKING NOTES: *Categorizing*

ACTIVITY As you read, fill out a graphic organizer similar to the one below with the reasons people left their homelands to immigrate to the United States.

Reasons for Immigrating to U.S.	
Push Factors	Pull Factors

IT MATTERS BECAUSE

In the late nineteenth century, a major wave of immigration began. Most immigrants settled in cities, where distinctive ethnic neighborhoods emerged. Some Americans, however, feared that the new immigrants would not adapt to American culture or might be harmful to American society.

Europeans Flood Into America

GUIDING QUESTION *How did European immigrants of the late 1800s change American society?*

Between 1865—the year the Civil War ended—and 1914—the year World War I began—nearly 25 million Europeans immigrated to the United States. By the late 1890s, more than half of all **immigrants** entering the United States were from eastern and southern Europe, including Italy, Greece, Austria-Hungary, Russia, and Serbia. This period of immigration is known as "new" immigration. The "old" immigration, which occurred before 1890, had been primarily of people from northern and western Europe.

Europeans immigrated to the United States for many reasons. Many came because American industries had plenty of jobs available or they offered special skills. Some Greeks came to Florida to dive for sponges and helped create a thriving and large Greek community in Tarpon City. Europe's industrial cities, however, also offered plenty of jobs, so economic factors do not entirely explain why people migrated. Many other immigrants came to the United States in the hope of finding better jobs that would let them escape poverty and the restrictions of social class in Europe. Some moved to avoid forced military service, which in some nations lasted for many years. In some cases, as in Italy, high food prices encouraged people to leave. In Poland and Russia, population pressure caused emigration. Others, especially Jews living in Russia and the Austro-Hungarian Empire, fled to escape religious persecution. Many of the new immigrants lacked the resources to buy land, so they settled in American cities and worked mainly in unskilled jobs.

PHOTOS: (l to r) Michael Maslan Historic Photographs/Historical/CORBIS, Library of Congress, The Granger Collection, New York

The Atlantic Voyage

The voyage to the United States was often very difficult. Most immigrants booked passage in steerage, the cheapest accommodations on a steamship. Edward Steiner, an Iowa clergyman who posed as an immigrant in order to write a book on immigration, described the miserable quarters:

PRIMARY SOURCE

❝[T]here is neither breathing space below nor deck room above, and the 900 steerage passengers . . . are positively packed like cattle. . . . The stenches become unbearable. . . . The food, which is miserable, is dealt out of huge kettles into the dinner pails provided by the steamship company. When it is distributed, the stronger push and crowd, so that meals are anything but orderly procedures.❞

—from *On the Trail of the Immigrant,* 1906

Immigrants migrated to the United States from all across Europe seeking an opportunity to better their lives.

▶ **CRITICAL THINKING**

Drawing Conclusions Why do you think most immigrants came to the cities?

Ellis Island

Most immigrants passed through Ellis Island, a tiny island in New York Harbor. A medical examiner who worked there later described how "hour after hour, ship load after ship load . . . the stream of human beings with its kaleidoscopic variations was . . . hurried through Ellis Island by the equivalent of 'step lively' in every language of the earth." About 12 million immigrants passed through Ellis Island between 1892 and 1954.

Diverse Cities

By the 1890s, immigrants made up a large percentage of the population of major cities, including New York, Chicago, Milwaukee, and Detroit. Immigrants lived in neighborhoods that were often separated into **ethnic** groups, such as "Little Italy" or the Jewish "Lower East Side" in New York City. There they spoke their native languages and re-created the churches, synagogues, clubs, and newspapers of their homelands. This wave of immigrants changed the face and size of America's cities and its workforce.

immigrant one who enters and becomes established in a country other than that of his or her original nationality

ethnic relating to large groups of people classed according to common racial, national, tribal, religious, linguistic, or cultural origin or background

✓ **PROGRESS CHECK**

Explaining How did Edward Steiner describe the immigrant experience of traveling to the United States?

WHY DID PEOPLE EMIGRATE?

CHARTS/GRAPHS

Immigrants (thousands) vs Year

Legend:
- From northern and western Europe
- From southern and eastern Europe
- From the Americas
- From Asia

Y-axis: 0, 200, 400, 600, 800, 1,000
X-axis: 1865 1870, 1880, 1890, 1900, 1910 1914

Source: *Historical Statistics of the United States.*

Push Factors
- Farm poverty and worker uncertainty
- Wars and compulsory military service
- Political tyranny
- Religious oppression
- Population pressure

Pull Factors
- Plenty of land and plenty of work
- Higher standard of living
- Democratic political system
- Opportunity for social advancement

Push factors and pull factors impacted U. S. immigration.

1 Which two areas had the lowest immigration rates to the United States during the 1865–1914 period?

2 Which area accounted for the highest emigration to the United States before 1890?

PHOTO: Michael Maslan Historic Photographs/Historical/CORBIS

Many Chinese came to America to escape poverty and civil war. Some helped build railroads. Others set up small businesses. These children were photographed in San Francisco's Chinatown around 1900.

Asian Immigration

GUIDING QUESTION *How were the experiences of Asian immigrants different from those of European immigrants?*

In the mid-1800s, China had a growing population combined with severe unemployment, poverty, and famine. In 1850 the Taiping Rebellion caused such suffering that thousands of Chinese left for the United States. In the early 1860s, Chinese workers emigrated in larger numbers to work on the Central Pacific Railroad. Chinese immigrants settled mainly in western cities, where they worked as laborers, servants, skilled tradespeople, or merchants. Because native-born Americans discriminated against them, some Chinese opened their own businesses.

Japanese also began migrating to the United States. Although some came earlier, the number of Japanese immigrants soared upward between 1900 and 1910. As Japan industrialized, economic problems caused many Japanese to leave their homeland for new economic opportunities.

Until 1910, Asian immigrants arriving in San Francisco first stopped at a two-story shed at the wharf. In January 1910, California opened a barracks on Angel Island for Asian immigrants. Most were young men in their teens or twenties, who nervously awaited the results of their immigration hearings. The wait could last for months.

☑ **PROGRESS CHECK**

Making Generalizations How did the experiences of immigrating to the United States compare for Chinese and Europeans?

Nativism Resurges

GUIDING QUESTION *Why did nativists oppose immigration?*

Eventually, the wave of immigration led to increased feelings of **nativism** for many Americans. Nativism is an extreme dislike of immigrants by native-born people. It had surfaced during the heavy wave of Irish immigration in the 1840s and 1850s. By the late 1800s it was focused mainly on Asians, Jews, and eastern Europeans.

Nativists opposed immigration for many reasons. Some feared that the influx of Catholics from countries such as Ireland, Italy, and Poland would swamp the mostly Protestant United States. Many labor unions argued that immigrants undermined American workers because they would work for low wages and accept jobs as strikebreakers.

nativism hostility toward immigrants by native-born people

Backlash Against Catholics

Nativism led to the founding of a group called the American Protective Association. Founded by Henry Bowers in 1887, its members initially vowed not to hire or vote for Irish Catholics and later all Catholic immigrants. These immigrants, usually illiterate and working at the lowest-paying jobs, suffered from this type of discrimination.

Restrictions on Asian Immigration

In the West, anti-Chinese sentiment sometimes led to racial violence. Denis Kearney, an Irish immigrant, organized the Workingman's Party of California in the 1870s to fight Chinese immigration. The party won seats in California's legislature and pushed to stop Chinese immigration.

In 1882 Congress passed the Chinese Exclusion Act. The law barred Chinese immigration for 10 years and prevented the Chinese already in the

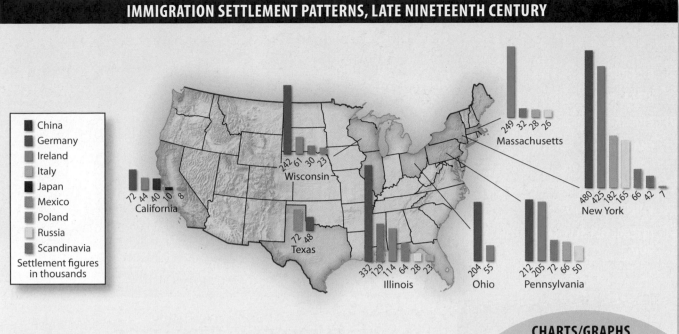

China
Germany
Ireland
Italy
Japan
Mexico
Poland
Russia
Scandinavia

Settlement figures in thousands

California 72 44 40 10 8

Wisconsin 242 61 30 23

Massachusetts 249 32 28 26

New York 480 425 182 165 66 42 7

Texas 72 48

Illinois 332 129 114 64 28 23

Ohio 204 55

Pennsylvania 212 205 72 66 50

CHARTS/GRAPHS

This graph shows where different immigrant groups settled in the United States.

▶ **CRITICAL THINKING**

1 *Analyzing Information*
How would you contrast the immigration settlement patterns in Texas and Ohio?

2 Create a bar graph showing the three largest immigrant groups in your state in the last five years.

country from becoming citizens. The Chinese in the United States organized letter-writing campaigns, but their efforts failed. Congress made the law permanent in 1902, but it was repealed in 1943.

In October 1906, the San Francisco Board of Education ordered "all Chinese, Japanese, and Korean children" to attend the racially segregated "Oriental School" in response to rising Japanese immigration. This caused an international incident, as Japan took offense at the insulting treatment of its people.

In response, President Theodore Roosevelt proposed a limit on Japanese immigration if the school board would rescind its segregation order. After Roosevelt negotiated an agreement with Japan, the San Francisco school board revoked its segregation order. This deal became known as the "Gentlemen's Agreement" because it was not a formal treaty and depended on the leaders of both countries to uphold the agreement.

✓ **PROGRESS CHECK**

Explaining How did President Roosevelt respond to Japan's protests about the treatment of Japanese students?

LESSON 1 REVIEW

Reviewing Vocabulary

1. *Explaining* What is nativism, and why did some Americans dislike immigrants?

Using Your Notes

2. *Categorizing* Use your notes on the reasons for immigrating to explain the push and pull factors for one of the immigrant groups discussed in the lesson.

Answering the Guiding Questions

3. *Interpreting* How did European immigrants of the late 1800s change American society?

4. *Comparing and Contrasting* How were the experiences of Asian immigrants different from those of European immigrants?

5. *Analyzing* Why did some Americans oppose immigration?

Writing Activity

6. **DESCRIPTIVE** Suppose that you are an immigrant who has arrived in the United States in the 1800s. Choose a country to be from and write a letter to a relative in your home country describing why you decided to move to America and what you found when you arrived.

networks

There's More Online!

☑ **BIOGRAPHY** George Plunkitt

☑ **BIOGRAPHY** Jacob Riis

☑ **BIOGRAPHY** William Tweed

☑ **CHART/GRAPH** Rising Urban Populations

☑ **IMAGE** Jacob Riis Photographs

☑ **VIDEO** Urbanization

☑ **INTERACTIVE SELF-CHECK QUIZ**

LESSON 2
Urbanization

ESSENTIAL QUESTIONS · *Why do people migrate?* · *How is urban life different from rural life?*

Reading HELPDESK

Content Vocabulary

- skyscraper
- tenement
- political machine
- party boss
- graft

Academic Vocabulary

- incentive
- trigger

TAKING NOTES: *Organizing*

ACTIVITY As you read, use the following graphic organizer to identify the problems the nation's cities faced.

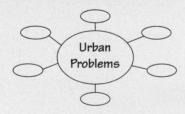

Urban Problems

IT MATTERS BECAUSE

Native-born Americans and immigrants were drawn to cities by the jobs available in America's growing industries. The new, modern cities developed skyscrapers, public transportation systems, and neighborhoods divided by social class. In many cities, political machines controlled city government.

Americans Migrate to the Cities

GUIDING QUESTION *How do you think life in big cities was different from life on farms and in small towns?*

After the Civil War, the urban population of the United States exploded. New York City, which had more than 800,000 inhabitants in 1860, grew to almost 3.5 million by 1900. During the same period, Chicago swelled from some 109,000 residents to more than 1.6 million. The United States had only 131 cities with populations of 2,500 or more residents in 1840; by 1900, there were more than 1,700 such urban areas.

Most newly arrived immigrants as well as rural Americans, moved to U.S. cities during this time. Cities offered more and better-paying jobs, electricity, modern plumbing, and entertainment.

As city populations grew, the rising value of land provided an **incentive** to try new strategies of urban development. Some businessmen built upward rather than outward. Tall, steel frame buildings called **skyscrapers** began to appear. Other businessmen, such as industrialist Hamilton Disston, transformed and reshaped the landscape. Disston drained parts of the Florida Everglades to create more land to build and grow upon. Disston purchased about 4 million acres of land in the state and set off a land boom in Florida that resulted in the formation of many cities such as Kissimmee and Gulfport and encouraged rapid urbanization around St. Petersburg.

To move people around cities quickly, various kinds of mass transit developed. At first, almost all cities relied on the horsecar, a railroad car pulled by horses. In 1890 horsecars moved about 70 percent of urban traffic in the United States. More than 20 cities, beginning with San Francisco in 1873, installed cable cars, which were pulled along tracks by underground cables. Then, in 1887, engineer Frank J. Sprague developed the electric trolley car. The country's first electric trolley line opened the following year in Richmond, Virginia.

In the largest cities, congestion became a severe problem. Chicago responded by building an elevated railroad, while Boston, followed by New York, built the first subway systems.

✓ **PROGRESS CHECK**

Summarizing What attracted people to cities in the 1800s?

Separation by Class

GUIDING QUESTION *How did the living conditions of the urban working class differ from those of other social classes?*

In the growing cities, the upper, middle, and working classes lived in separate and distinct parts of town. The boundaries between neighborhoods can still be seen in many American cities today.

During the last half of the 1800s, the wealthiest families established fashionable districts in the heart of a city. As their homes grew larger, wealthy women increasingly relied on more servants, such as cooks, maids, butlers, nannies, and chauffeurs, and spent a great deal of money on social activities. In an age in which many New Yorkers lived on $500 a year, socialite Cornelia Sherman Martin spent $360,000 on a dance.

American industrialization expanded the middle class, which included doctors, lawyers, engineers, managers, social workers, architects, and teachers. Many middle-class people moved away from the central city to escape the crime and pollution and to be able to afford larger homes. Some used new commuter rail lines to move to "streetcar suburbs."

In the late 1800s, wealthier families had at least one live-in servant. This gave the woman of the house more time to pursue activities outside the home, including "women's clubs." At first these clubs focused on social and educational activities, but over time "club women" became active in charitable and reform activities. In Chicago, for example, the Women's Club helped establish juvenile courts and exposed the terrible conditions at the Cook County Insane Asylum.

Few families in the urban working class could hope to own a home. Most spent their lives in crowded **tenements,** or multifamily apartment buildings. The first tenement in the United States was built in 1839. In New York City, three out of four residents squeezed into dark and crowded tenements. To supplement the average industrial worker's annual income

Before the mid-1800s, few buildings exceeded four or five stories. To make wooden and stone buildings taller required thick lower walls. This changed when steel companies began mass-producing cheap steel girders and steel cable.

▶ **CRITICAL THINKING**
Predicting Consequences What long-term effects do you think new building technologies had on cities?

incentive something that motivates a person into action

skyscraper a very tall building

tenement multifamily apartments, usually dark, crowded, and barely meeting minimum living standards

In the late 1800s, large numbers of people from farms and small towns, as well as immigrants, settled in cities.

▶ **CRITICAL THINKING**
Identifying Central Issues Why were so many people drawn to cities during this era?

PHOTO: Lewis Wickes Hine/Historical/CORBIS

Most working-class families lived in apartments, often only a single room in size. They had no servants, and typically husbands and wives both had to work.

▶ **CRITICAL THINKING**
Drawing Conclusions How effective was urban society at meeting the needs of the working class?

of $445, many families rented precious space to a boarder. Zalmen Yoffeh, a journalist, lived in a New York tenement as a child. He recalled his family's everyday struggle:

PRIMARY SOURCE

❝With . . . one dollar a day [our mother] fed and clothed an ever-growing family. She took in boarders. Sometimes this helped; at other times it added to the burden of living. Boarders were often out of work and penniless; how could one turn a hungry man out? She made all our clothes. She walked blocks to reach a place where meat was a penny cheaper, where bread was a half cent less. She collected boxes and old wood to burn in the stove.❞
—from "The Passing of the East Side," *Menorah Journal*, 1929

Within the working class, some people were better off than others. For example, white native-born men earned higher wages than African American men, immigrants, and women. One economist estimated that 64 percent of working-class families began to rely on more than one wage earner. In some cases, the whole family worked, including the children. The dangerous working conditions faced by child workers, and the fact that they were not in school, alarmed many reformers.

A growing number of women took jobs outside the home. White native-born women were better educated than other women. Thus, many found jobs as teachers, clerks, or secretaries. Many women, however, were domestic servants, with immigrant women filling these jobs in the North and African American women doing such work in the South. Domestic servants endured long hours, low wages, and social isolation.

✓ **PROGRESS CHECK**

Explaining What was working life like for working-class families?

Urban Problems

GUIDING QUESTION *What types of problems developed due to the rapid growth of urban areas?*

City living posed the risks of crime, violence, fire, disease, and pollution. The rapid growth of cities made these problems worse and complicated the ability of urban governments to respond to these problems.

Crime was a growing problem in American cities. Minor criminals, such as pickpockets, swindlers, and thieves, thrived in crowded urban living conditions. Major crimes multiplied as well. From 1880 to 1900, the murder rate jumped sharply from 25 per million people to more than 100 per million people.

Disease and pollution posed even bigger threats. Improper sewage disposal contaminated city drinking water and **triggered** epidemics of typhoid fever and cholera. Though flush toilets and sewer systems existed in the 1870s, pollution remained a severe problem as horse manure was left in the streets, smoke belched from chimneys, and soot and ash accumulated from coal and wood fires.

The **political machine,** an informal political group designed to gain and keep power, came about partly because cities had grown much faster than their governments. New city dwellers needed jobs, housing, food, heat, and police protection. In exchange for votes, political machines and the **party bosses** who ran them eagerly provided these necessities. George Plunkitt, one of New York's most powerful bosses, explained the benefit of political machines: "I can always get a job for a deservin' man. . . . I know every big employer in the district and in the whole city, for that matter, and they ain't in the habit of sayin' no to me when I ask them for a job."

trigger to cause an action that causes a greater reaction

political machine an organization linked to a political party that often controlled local government

party boss the person in control of a political machine

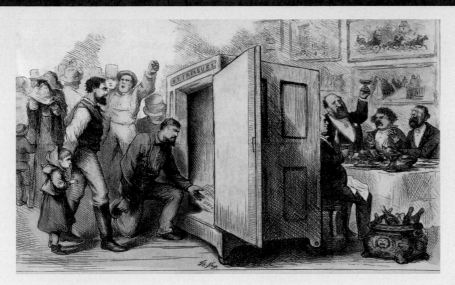

Critics of political machines said that they took bribes and gave contracts to friends, robbing cities of resources. In this image, workers in New York find the city treasury empty, while behind the scenes, Boss Tweed and other city politicians enjoy a sumptuous feast.

▶ **CRITICAL THINKING**

1 *Drawing Inferences* What point is the artist trying to make?

2 *Predicting Consequences* What problems could develop in cities as a result of the fraud of political machines?

The party bosses also controlled the city's finances. Many machine politicians grew rich as the result of fraud or **graft,** gaining money or power illegally. Outright fraud occurred when party bosses accepted bribes from contractors who were supposed to compete fairly to win contracts to build streets, sewers, and buildings. Corrupt bosses also sold permits to their friends to operate public utilities, such as railroads, waterworks, and power systems. Tammany Hall, the New York City Democratic political machine, was the most infamous such organization. William "Boss" Tweed was its leader during the 1860s and 1870s. Tweed's corruptness led to a prison sentence in 1874.

City machines often controlled all the city services, including the police department. In St. Louis, the "boss" never feared arrest when he called out to his supporters at the police-supervised voting booth, "Are there any more repeaters out here that want to vote again?"

Opponents of political machines, such as cartoonist Thomas Nast, blasted corrupt bosses. Defenders argued that political machines provided necessary services and helped assimilate new city dwellers.

graft the acquisition of money in dishonest ways, as in bribing a politician

✓ **PROGRESS CHECK**

Identifying Why were political machines so influential in cities?

LESSON 2 REVIEW

Reviewing Vocabulary

1. *Explaining* Explain why tenements were a difficult place to live for the urban working class.

Using Your Notes

2. *Summarizing* Use your notes on urban problems to explain why life in cities could be so difficult.

Answering the Guiding Questions

3. *Interpreting* How do you think life in big cities was different from life on farms and in small towns?

4. *Comparing and Contrasting* How did the living conditions of the urban working class differ from those of other social classes?

5. *Making Connections* What types of problems developed due to the rapid growth of urban areas?

Writing Activity

6. PERSUASIVE Take on the role of an urban planner in a major city in the late 1800s. Write a letter to members of the city government listing specific reasons for the importance of setting aside city land for parks and recreational areas.

networks

There's More Online!

☑ **BIOGRAPHY** Jane Addams

☑ **BIOGRAPHY** Mark Twain

☑ **IMAGES** Thomas Eakins Paintings

☑ **VIDEO** Social Darwinism and Social Reform

☑ **INTERACTIVE SELF-CHECK QUIZ**

LESSON 3
Social Darwinism and Social Reform

Reading **HELP**DESK

Content Vocabulary

- **individualism**
- **Social Darwinism**
- **philanthropy**
- **settlement house**
- **Americanization**

Academic Vocabulary

- **evolution**   • **publish**

TAKING NOTES: *Categorizing*

ACTIVITY As you read, complete a graphic organizer similar to the one below by filling in the main idea of each of the theories and movements listed.

Theory or Movement	Main Idea
Social Darwinism	
Laissez-Faire	
Gospel of Wealth	
Realism	

ESSENTIAL QUESTIONS • *Why do people migrate?* • *How is urban life different from rural life?*

IT MATTERS BECAUSE

The industrialization of the United States led to new art and literature and new ideas about government's role in society. Social Darwinists believed society developed through "survival of the fittest." Other Americans thought steps needed to be taken to help the less fortunate.

Gilded Age Ideas

GUIDING QUESTION *What was the main idea of Social Darwinism, and how did it compare with the idea of individualism?*

In 1873 Mark Twain and Charles Warner wrote a novel entitled *The Gilded Age: A Tale of Today*. Historians later adopted the term and applied it to the era in American history that began about 1870 and ended around 1900. The era was in many ways a time of marvels. Amazing new inventions led to rapid industrial growth. Cities grew in size and people thronged the crowded streets. Wealthy entrepreneurs built spectacular mansions. Skyscrapers reached to the sky, and electric lights banished the darkness.

By calling this era the Gilded Age, Twain and Warner were sounding an alarm. Something is gilded if it is covered with gold on the outside but made of cheaper material inside. A gilded age might appear to sparkle, but critics pointed to corruption, poverty, crime, and great disparities in wealth between the rich and the poor.

Whether the era was golden or merely gilded, it was certainly a time of great cultural activity. Industrialism and urbanization altered the way Americans looked at themselves and their society, and these changes gave rise to new values, new art, and new entertainment.

The Idea of Individualism

One of the strongest beliefs of the era—and one that remains strong today—was the idea of **individualism.** Many Americans firmly believed that no matter how humble their origins, Americans could rise in society and go as far as their talents and commitment would take them. No one expressed the idea of individualism better than

Horatio Alger, who wrote more than 100 "rags-to-riches" novels. In his books, a poor person goes to the big city and, through a combination of hard work and luck, becomes successful. Even though such dramatic jumps upward in social standing were not commonplace, Alger's popular books convinced many young people that no matter how many obstacles they faced, success was possible.

Social Darwinism

Another powerful idea of the era was **Social Darwinism.** This philosophy, loosely derived from Charles Darwin's theories, strongly reinforced the idea of individualism.

Herbert Spencer British philosopher Herbert Spencer applied Darwin's theory of **evolution** and natural selection to human society. In his 1859 book *On the Origin of Species by Means of Natural Selection,* Darwin argued that plant and animal life had evolved over millions of years by a process he called natural selection. In this process, those species that cannot adapt to the environment in which they live gradually die out, while those that do adapt, thrive, and live on.

Spencer used this theory to argue that human society also evolved through competition and natural selection. He said that society became better because only the fittest people survived. Spencer and others, such as American scholar William Graham Sumner, became known as Social Darwinists and their ideas as Social Darwinism. "Survival of the fittest" became the catchphrase of their philosophy.

Some industrial leaders used Social Darwinism to justify their support of laissez-faire capitalism. This economic doctrine opposed any government programs that interfered with business.

Darwinism and the Church Many devout Christians found Darwin's conclusions offensive. They rejected the theory of evolution because they believed it contradicted the Bible's account of creation. Some clergy, however, concluded that evolution might have been God's way of creating the world. One of the most famous ministers of the era, Henry Ward Beecher, called himself a "Christian evolutionist."

Carnegie's Gospel of Wealth Andrew Carnegie advocated a gentler version of Social Darwinism that he called the Gospel of Wealth. This philosophy held that wealthy Americans should engage in **philanthropy,** using their fortunes to create the conditions that would help people help themselves. Building schools and hospitals, for example, was better than giving handouts to the poor. Carnegie funded the creation of public libraries in cities across the nation.

PRIMARY SOURCE

❝In bestowing charity, the main consideration should be to help those who will help themselves; to provide part of the means by which those who desire to improve may do so; to give those who desire to rise the aids by which they may rise; to assist, but rarely or never to do all. Neither the individual nor the race is improved by almsgiving. Those worthy of assistance, except in rare cases, seldom require assistance. The really valuable men of the race never do, except in cases of accident or sudden change. . . . He is the only true reformer who is as careful and as anxious not to aid the unworthy as he is to aid the worthy, and, perhaps, even more so, for in almsgiving more injury is probably done by rewarding vice than by relieving virtue. . . .❞

—Andrew Carnegie, from *The Gospel of Wealth and Other Timely Essays,* 1886

✓ PROGRESS CHECK

Summarizing How did Horatio Alger's books demonstrate the idea of individualism?

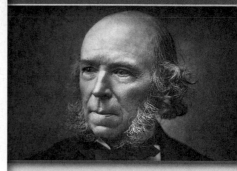
individualism the belief that no matter what a person's background is, he or she can still become successful through effort

Social Darwinism a philosophy based on Charles Darwin's theories of evolution and natural selection, asserting that humans have developed through competition and natural selection with only the strongest surviving

evolution the scientific theory that humans and other forms of life have evolved over time

philanthropy providing money to support humanitarian or social goals

The Rebirth of Reform

GUIDING QUESTION *What methods and philosophies were developed for helping the urban poor?*

The tremendous changes that industrialism and urbanization brought triggered a debate over how best to address society's problems. Some Americans embraced the ideas of individualism and Social Darwinism. Others disagreed, arguing that society's problems could be fixed only if Americans and their government began to take a more active role in regulating the economy and helping those in need.

Challenging Social Darwinism

In 1880 journalist Henry George published *Progress and Poverty,* a discussion of the American economy that quickly became a national best seller. George observed, "The present century has been marked by a prodigious increase in wealth-producing power." This should, he asserted, have made poverty "a thing of the past." Instead, he claimed, the "gulf between the employed and the employer is growing wider; social contrasts are becoming sharper." In other words, laissez-faire economics was making society worse—not better.

Most economists now argue that George's analysis was flawed. Industrialism did make some Americans very wealthy, but it also improved the standard of living for most others as well. At the time, however, Americans in the midst of poverty did not see improvement. George's ideas spurred reformers to challenge Social Darwinism.

Lester Frank Ward In 1883 Lester Frank Ward published *Dynamic Sociology,* in which he argued that humans were different from animals because they had the ability to make plans to produce the future outcomes they desired. Ward's ideas came to be known as Reform Darwinism. People, he insisted, had succeeded in the world because of their ability to cooperate. Government, he argued, could regulate the economy, cure poverty, and promote education more efficiently than competition in the marketplace could.

Looking Backward Writer Edward Bellamy promoted another alternative to Social Darwinism and laissez-faire economics. In 1888 he published *Looking Backward,* a novel about a man who falls asleep in 1887 and awakens in the year 2000 to find that the nation has become a perfect society with no crime, poverty, or politics. In this fictional society, the government owns all industry and shares the wealth equally with all Americans. Bellamy's ideas were essentially a form of socialism.

Naturalism in Literature Criticism of industrial society also appeared in literature in a new style of writing known as naturalism. Naturalists challenged the idea of Social Darwinism by suggesting that some people failed in life simply because they were caught up in circumstances they could not control.

Among the most prominent naturalist writers were Stephen Crane, Jack London, and Theodore Dreiser. Stephen Crane's novel *Maggie, A Girl of the Streets* (1893) told the story of a girl's descent into prostitution and death. Jack London's tales of the Alaskan wilderness demonstrated the power of nature over civilization. Theodore Dreiser's novels, such as *Sister Carrie* (1900), painted a world where people sinned without punishment and where the pursuit of wealth and power often destroyed their character.

A young newsboy sells papers on a street corner in 1910.

318

After visiting a settlement house in London, England, Jane Addams decided to open Hull House in 1889 to assist poor immigrants in Chicago. Addams wrote books about her experience at Hull House, giving an example to others throughout the nation.

▶ **CRITICAL THINKING**
Drawing Conclusions Based on her involvement with Hull House, how would you describe Jane Addams as a person?

Helping the Urban Poor

The plight of the urban poor prompted some reformers to find new ways to help. The Social Gospel movement worked to better conditions in cities according to the biblical ideals of charity and justice. Washington Gladden, a minister, was an early advocate who popularized the movement in writings such as *Applied Christianity* (1887). Walter Rauschenbusch, a Baptist minister from New York, became the leading voice in the Social Gospel movement. The Church, he argued, must "demand protection for the moral safety of the people." The Social Gospel movement inspired many churches to build gyms, provide social programs and child care, and help the poor.

The Salvation Army and the Young Men's Christian Association (YMCA) also combined faith and an interest in reform. The Salvation Army offered practical aid and religious counseling to the urban poor. The YMCA tried to help industrial workers and the urban poor by organizing Bible studies, citizenship training, and group activities. The YMCA also provided low-cost boarding houses for young men. The head of the Chicago YMCA, Dwight L. Moody, was a gifted preacher whose revival meetings drew thousands of people. Moody rejected both the Social Gospel movement and Social Darwinism. He believed the way to help the poor was not by providing them with services but by redeeming their souls and reforming their character.

The **settlement house** movement began as an offshoot of the Social Gospel movement. In the late 1800s, idealistic reformers—including many college-educated women—established settlement houses in poor, often heavily immigrant neighborhoods. The reformers lived in these settlement houses, which were community centers offering everything from medical care and English classes to kindergartens and recreational programs. Jane Addams opened Hull House in Chicago in 1889. Jewish reformer Lillian Wald founded the Henry Street Settlement in New York City. Both women were a powerful force in social work and the settlement house movement.

settlement house an institution located in a poor neighborhood that provided numerous community services such as medical care, child care, libraries, and classes in English

Public Education

As the United States became increasingly industrialized and urbanized, it needed more trained and educated workers. The number of public schools increased dramatically after the Civil War. The number of children attending school rose from 7,562,000 in 1870 to 15,503,000 in 1900. Public schools were often crucial to the success of immigrant children. At school they were taught English and learned about American history and culture, a process known as **Americanization.**

Schools also tried to instill discipline. Grammar schools divided students into grades and drilled them in punctuality, neatness, and efficiency—necessary habits for the workplace. Vocational education in high schools taught skills required in specific trades. However, children in cities had greater access to education than those in rural areas. Many African Americans also faced education inequalities. Some started their own schools, following the example of Booker T. Washington, who founded the Tuskegee Institute in 1881.

Americanization the process of acquiring or causing a person to acquire American traits and characteristics

✓ PROGRESS CHECK

Explaining Why were public schools important to the success of immigrant children?

A Changing Culture

GUIDING QUESTION *Why do you think artists and writers started portraying America more realistically?*

The late 1800s was a period of great cultural change for writers and artists. It was also a time when many urban Americans took advantage of new forms of entertainment.

Realism

A new movement in art and literature called realism began in the 1800s. Just as Darwin tried to explain the natural world scientifically, artists and writers tried to portray the world realistically. Perhaps the best-known American realist painter was Thomas Eakins. He painted men rowing, athletes playing baseball, and surgeons and scientists in action.

Writers also attempted to capture the world as they saw it. In several novels, William Dean Howells presented realistic descriptions of American life. For example, his novel *The Rise of Silas Lapham* (1885) described the attempts of a self-made man to enter Boston society. Also an influential literary critic, Howells was the first to declare Mark Twain an incomparable American genius. Twain, whose real name was Samuel Clemens, **published** his masterpiece, *Adventures of Huckleberry Finn*, in 1884. In this novel, the title character and his friend Jim, who has escaped from slavery, float down the Mississippi River on a raft. Twain wrote in local dialect with a lively sense of humor:

publish to make a document available to the general public

PRIMARY SOURCE

❝'Say, who is you? Whar is you? Dog my cats ef I didn' hear sumf'n. Well, I know what I's gwyne to do: I's gwyne to set down here and listen tell I hears it agin.'

So he set down on the ground betwixt me and Tom. He leaned his back up against a tree, and stretched his legs out till one of them most touched one of mine. My nose begun to itch. It itched till the tears come into my eyes. But I dasn't scratch. Then it begun to itch on the inside. Next I got to itching underneath. I didn't know how I was going to set still. This miserableness went on as much as six or seven minutes; but it seemed a sight longer than that.❞

—from *Adventures of Huckleberry Finn,* 1884

Popular Culture

Popular culture changed considerably in the late 1800s. Industrialization improved the standard of living for many people, enabling them to spend money on entertainment and recreation. Increasingly, urban Americans divided their lives into separate units—that of work and that of home. People began "going out" to public entertainment.

In cities, saloons often outnumbered groceries. As a place for social gathering, saloons played a major role in the lives of male workers. Saloons offered drinks, free toilets, water for horses, and free newspapers for customers. They even offered the first "free lunch": salty food that made patrons thirsty and eager to drink more. Saloons also served as political centers, and saloonkeepers were often key figures in political machines.

Working-class families and single adults could find entertainment at new amusement parks such as New York City's Coney Island. Amusements such as water slides and railroad rides cost only a nickel or dime. People also began watching professional sports. Formed in 1869, the first professional baseball team was the Cincinnati Red Stockings. In 1903 the first official World Series was played between the Boston Americans and the Pittsburgh Pirates. Football gained in popularity and by the late 1800s had spread to public colleges.

As work became less strenuous, many people looked for activities involving physical exercise. Tennis, golf, and croquet became popular. In 1891 James Naismith, athletic director for a college in Massachusetts, invented a new indoor game called basketball.

People also enjoyed comic theater and music. Adapted from French theater, vaudeville took on an American flavor in the early 1880s with its hodgepodge of animal acts, singers, comedians, acrobats, and dancers. Like vaudeville, ragtime music echoed the hectic pace of city life. Its syncopated rhythms grew out of the music of riverside honky-tonks, saloon pianists, and banjo players, using the patterns of African American music. Scott Joplin, one of the most important African American ragtime composers, became known as the King of Ragtime. He wrote his most famous piece, "The Maple Leaf Rag," in 1899.

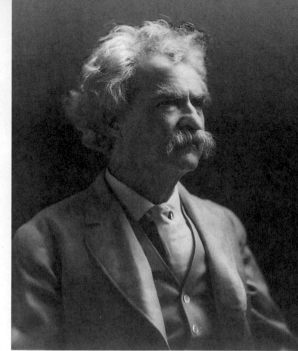

With his book *Adventures of Huckleberry Finn,* Mark Twain had written a true American novel. The setting, subject, characters, and style were clearly American.

▶ **CRITICAL THINKING**
Making Inferences Why did Mark Twain write *Adventures of Huckleberry Finn* using local dialect?

PHOTO: Library of Congress

✓ **PROGRESS CHECK**

Analyzing Why was it possible to pursue more leisure activities and popular entertainment during this time period?

LESSON 3 REVIEW

Reviewing Vocabulary
1. *Explaining* Explain the significance of philanthropy, and identify the reason for its growth during the late 1800s.

Using Your Notes
2. *Defining* Use your notes on the theories and movements of the Gilded Age to explain its defining characteristics.

Answering the Guiding Questions
3. *Comparing* What was the main idea of Social Darwinism, and how did it compare with the idea of individualism?

4. *Summarizing* What methods and philosophies were developed for helping the urban poor?

5. *Making Connections* Why do you think artists and writers started portraying America more realistically?

Writing Activity
6. DESCRIPTIVE Suppose that you are a newspaper editor in the late 1800s. Write an editorial in which you support or oppose the philosophy of Social Darwinism.

netw⊚rks

There's More Online!

- ☑ **BIOGRAPHY** William Jennings Bryan
- ☑ **CHART/GRAPH** Political Parties
- ☑ **MAP** Presidential Election of 1896
- ☑ **VIDEO** Politics of the Gilded Age
- ☑ **INTERACTIVE SELF-CHECK QUIZ**

LESSON 4
Politics of the Gilded Age

ESSENTIAL QUESTIONS • *Why do people migrate?* • *How is urban life different from rural life?*

Reading **HELP**DESK

Content Vocabulary

- **populism**
- **deflation**
- **greenbacks**
- **cooperatives**
- **inflation**
- **graduated income tax**

Academic Vocabulary

- **currency**
- **bond**
- **strategy**

TAKING NOTES: *Organizing*

ACTIVITY As you read about the emergence of populism in the 1890s, use the major headings of the lesson to create an outline similar to the one below.

Politics of the Gilded Age
I. Politics in Washington
A.
B.
C.
II.
A.
B.

IT MATTERS BECAUSE

In the late 1800s, the two major political parties were closely competitive, and issues such as tariffs and business regulations were hotly debated. Meanwhile, farmers facing falling crop prices and deflation tried to overcome their problems by forming organizations. In the 1890s, many farmers joined the Populist Party.

Politics in Washington

GUIDING QUESTION *Why was civil service reform needed?*

After President James A. Garfield was elected in 1880, many of his supporters tried to claim the "spoils of office"—the government jobs that are handed out following an election victory. President Garfield did not believe in the spoils system. After repeated rejections, one of these job seekers reasoned that he would have a better chance for a job if Vice President Chester A. Arthur were president. This man shot President Garfield on July 2, 1881. Weeks later, Garfield died from his wounds.

Civil Service Reforms

For many, Garfield's assassination highlighted the need to reform the political system. Under the spoils system, elected politicians extended patronage, rewarding their supporters by giving them government jobs. Many Americans believed the patronage system made the government inefficient and corrupt, and support was building for the reform of civil service.

When Rutherford B. Hayes became president in 1877, he tried to end patronage by firing officials who had been given jobs because of their support of the party and replacing them with reformers. His actions split the Republican Party between "Stalwarts" (who supported patronage), "Halfbreeds" (who backed some reform), and reformers. No reforms were passed. In 1880 the Republicans nominated James Garfield, a "Halfbreed," for president and Chester A. Arthur, a "Stalwart," for vice president.

PHOTOS: (l to r) The Granger Collection, New York; Image provided courtesy of Paul A. Hubanks, Hulton Archive/Archive Photos/Getty Images, The Granger Collection, New York

Despite the feud over patronage, the Republicans managed to win the election, only to have Garfield assassinated a few months later.

Garfield's assassination turned public opinion against the spoils system. In 1883 Congress passed the Pendleton Act, requiring that some jobs be filled by competitive written exams, rather than by patronage. This marked the beginning of professional civil service—a system where most government workers are given jobs based on qualifications rather than on political affiliation. Only about 10 percent of federal jobs were made civil service positions in 1883, but the percentage increased over time.

The Election of 1884

In 1884 the Democrats nominated Grover Cleveland, the governor of New York, for president. Cleveland was a reformer with a reputation for honesty. The Republicans nominated James G. Blaine, a former Speaker of the House rumored to have accepted bribes. Some Republicans were so unhappy with Blaine that they supported Cleveland. They became known as "Mugwumps," from an Algonquian word meaning "great chief."

Cleveland narrowly won the election, and then he faced supporters who expected him to reward them with jobs. Mugwumps, on the other hand, expected him to increase the number of jobs under the civil service system. Cleveland chose a middle course and angered both sides. Soon, however, economic issues replaced the patronage reform debate.

The power of large corporations concerned Americans. Small businesses and farmers had become particularly angry at the railroads. While large corporations could negotiate rebates and lower rates because of the volume of goods they shipped, others were forced to pay much higher rates. Eventually many states passed laws regulating railroad rates. In 1886 the Supreme Court ruled in the case of *Wabash, St. Louis, and Pacific Railway* v. *Illinois* that only the federal government could regulate interstate commerce. Public pressure forced Congress to act, and in 1887 Cleveland signed the Interstate Commerce Act. This was the first federal law to regulate interstate commerce.

Tariffs were another economic issue. Many Democrats thought that Congress should cut tariffs because they raised the price of imported goods. High tariffs also forced other nations to respond in kind, making it difficult for farmers to export surpluses. In December 1887 President Cleveland proposed lowering tariffs. The Democratic House passed moderate tariff reductions, but the Republican Senate rejected the bill.

Republicans Regain Power

In 1888 the Republicans and their presidential candidate, Benjamin Harrison, received large campaign contributions from industrialists who benefited from high tariffs. Cleveland and the Democrats campaigned against high tariff rates. In one of the closest presidential elections in American history, Harrison lost the popular vote but won the electoral vote, giving Republicans control of the White House.

The party passed legislation to address points of national concern. In 1890 Representative William McKinley pushed through a bill that cut some taxes and tariff rates but increased rates on other goods. The McKinley Tariff, intended to protect American industry from foreign competition, instead

POLITICAL DEBATES OF THE GILDED AGE

POLITICAL CARTOONS

Senator George H. Pendleton is congratulated for his civil service bill. An overflowing trash bin suggests that reform is impossible.

▶ **CRITICAL THINKING**

1. Did the artist who drew the cartoon favor civil service reform? How does he indicate his opinion?
2. How might the passage of civil service reform change how government works?

helped trigger a steep rise in the price of all goods. In 1890 Congress also passed the Sherman Antitrust Act to curb the power of the large business combinations known as trusts. The act prohibited any "combination . . . or conspiracy, in restraint of trade or commerce among the several States."

☑ **PROGRESS CHECK**

Summarizing What actions did Congress take to reform the civil service? Why were these steps necessary?

Unrest in Rural America

GUIDING QUESTION *What kinds of problems did farmers face?*

Populism was a movement to increase farmers' political power and work for legislation in their interest. An economic crisis following the Civil War led farmers to join the Populist movement. New technology enabled farmers to produce more crops, but increased supply caused prices to fall. High tariffs also made it hard for farmers to sell their goods overseas. In addition, mortgages with large banks and rail shipping costs that continued to increase made the farmers' difficulties worse.

The Money Supply

Some farmers thought adjusting the money supply would solve their problems. During the Civil War, the government had expanded the money supply by issuing millions of dollars in **greenbacks,** paper **currency** that could not be exchanged for gold or silver coins. The increased money supply without an increase in goods for sale caused **inflation,** or a decline in the value of money. As the paper money lost value, the prices of goods soared.

After the Civil War ended, the United States had three types of currency in circulation—greenbacks, gold and silver coins, and national banknotes backed by government **bonds.** To get inflation under control, the federal government stopped printing greenbacks and began paying off its bonds. In 1873 Congress also decided to stop making silver into coins. These decisions meant that the money supply was insufficient for the country's growing economy. As the economy expanded, **deflation**—an increase in the value of money and a decrease in prices—began.

Deflation hit farmers especially hard. Falling prices meant that they sold their crops for less and then had to borrow money for seed and other supplies to plant their next crops. With money in short supply, interest rates began to rise, increasing the amount farmers owed. Rising interest rates also made mortgages more expensive, and despite their lower income, farmers had to make the same mortgage payments to the banks.

The Grange Takes Action

In 1866 the Department of Agriculture sent Oliver H. Kelley to tour the rural South and report on farmers' conditions. Realizing that farmers were isolated, Kelley founded the first national farm organization, the Patrons of Husbandry, in 1867. It became known as the Grange.

In 1873 the nation plunged into a severe recession, and farm income fell sharply. Grangers responded by pressuring states to regulate railroad and warehouse rates. To reduce harmful competition among farmers, the Grangers also tried creating organizations called **cooperatives** in which member farmers worked together to increase prices and lower costs. None of the **strategies** improved farmers' economic conditions.

populism a political movement founded in the 1890s representing mainly farmers that favored free coinage of silver and government control of railroads and other large industries

greenback a unit of paper currency first issued by the federal government during the Civil War

currency paper money used as a medium of exchange

inflation an ongoing increase in prices and decrease in the value of money

bond a note issued by the government that promises to pay off a loan with interest

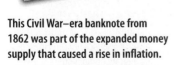

This Civil War–era banknote from 1862 was part of the expanded money supply that caused a rise in inflation.

▶ **CRITICAL THINKING**

Making Inferences Why would an increase in the amount of paper currency cause it to lose value?

PHOTO: Image provided courtesy of Paul A. Hubanks

The Farmers' Alliance

As the Grange began to fall apart, a new organization, known as the Farmers' Alliance, began to form. By 1890, the Alliance had between 1.5 and 3 million members. When Charles W. Macune became the leader of the Alliance, he announced a plan to organize very large cooperatives, which he called exchanges. The exchanges failed because they overextended themselves, or because wholesalers, railroad owners, and bankers made it difficult for them to stay in business. They also failed because they were still too small to affect world prices for farm products.

✔ **PROGRESS CHECK**

Explaining What measures did the nation take after the Civil War to improve its economic situation? What was the result?

The Rise of Populism

GUIDING QUESTION *What were the goals of the People's Party?*

By 1890, many people in the Alliance were dissatisfied. They felt that only through politics could they achieve their goals. However, many Alliance members had become distrustful of both the Republican and Democratic Parties. They believed that both parties favored industry and banks over farmers. From 1888 to 1892, regional Alliance groups met to discuss how to proceed. Some Alliance leaders, especially in the Midwest, wanted to form a new political party and push for political reforms. Most Southern leaders did not want to weaken the power of the Democratic Party in the South. They suggested that the Alliance produce a list of demands and promise to vote for candidates who supported those demands.

In July 1892, more than 1,000 delegates met in Omaha, Nebraska, to form the People's Party. The party held its first national convention and nominated James B. Weaver to run for president. The Omaha convention's platform called for a return to unlimited coinage of silver. It also called for federal ownership of railroads and a **graduated income tax.**

Populists also adopted proposals that were designed to appeal to organized labor. Ideas such as an eight-hour workday and immigration restrictions were put forth as appealing options. In the end, however, populism held little appeal to urban voters, who continued their traditional party allegiances. Many workers continued to vote for the Democrats, whose candidate, Grover Cleveland, won the election.

✔ **PROGRESS CHECK**

Summarizing Why did Southern Alliance groups resist the idea of a national People's Party?

deflation an ongoing decrease in prices and an increase in the value of money

cooperative a store where farmers buy products from each other; an enterprise owned and operated by those who use its services

strategy a plan or method for achieving a goal

graduated income tax a tax based on the net income of an individual or business and which taxes different income levels at different rates

FORMATION OF THE PEOPLE'S PARTY

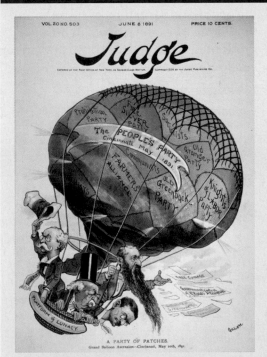

VOL. 20 NO. 503   JUNE 6 1891   PRICE 10 CENTS.

Judge

A PARTY OF PATCHES.
Grand Balloon Ascension—Cincinnati, May 20th, 1891.

POLITICAL CARTOONS

The People's Party is shown as a patchwork of assorted movements and philosophies supporting a "Platform of Lunacy."

▶ **CRITICAL THINKING**
1 Why do you think the People's Party platform is portrayed as one of lunacy?
2 How does the patchwork balloon represent the artist's point of view?

The Election of 1896

GUIDING QUESTION *Why did the Populists support the Democratic candidate—William Jennings Bryan—in 1896?*

As the election of 1896 approached, leaders of the People's Party decided to make the free coinage of silver the focus of their campaign and to hold their convention after the Republican and Democratic conventions. They believed, correctly, that the Republicans would endorse a gold standard. They also expected the Democrats to nominate Grover Cleveland, even though Cleveland favored a gold standard. The People's Party hoped that when it endorsed silver, pro-silver Democrats would choose the Populists.

Unfortunately, their strategy failed. William Jennings Bryan made an impassioned pro-silver speech at the convention and won the nomination.

PRIMARY SOURCE

❝Having behind us the producing masses of this nation and the world supported by the commercial interests, the laboring interests and the toilers everywhere, we will answer their demand for a gold standard by saying to them: You shall not press down upon the brow of labor this crown of thorns; you shall not crucify mankind upon a cross of gold.❞

—from a speech at the Democratic National Convention, 1896

The Populists faced a difficult choice: endorse Bryan and risk undermining their identity as a party, or nominate their own candidate and risk splitting the silver vote. They chose to support Bryan.

The Republicans appealed to workers with the promise that McKinley would provide a "full dinner pail." Also most business leaders supported the Republicans, convinced that unlimited silver coinage would ruin the country. Many employers warned workers that if Bryan won, businesses would fail and unemployment would rise further. McKinley's reputation as a moderate on labor issues and as tolerant toward ethnic groups helped improve the Republican Party's image with urban workers and immigrants. When the votes were counted, McKinley had won with a decisive victory.

The Populist Party declined after 1896. The Populists' efforts to ease the economic hardships of farmers and to regulate big business failed. Only long after the party's demise were Populist proposals such as a graduated income tax and further governmental regulation of the economy achieved.

✔ **PROGRESS CHECK**

Evaluating Why did the Republicans win the election of 1896?

LESSON 4 REVIEW

Reviewing Vocabulary
1. *Explaining* Explain the significance of: populism, greenbacks, inflation, deflation.

Using Your Notes
2. *Comparing and Contrasting* Use your notes to explain how the Farmers' Alliance contributed to the rise of a new political party.

Answering the Guiding Questions
3. *Cause and Effect* Why was civil service reform needed?

4. *Describing* What kinds of problems did farmers face?

5. *Summarizing* What were the goals of the People's Party?

6. *Making Connections* Why did the Populists support the Democratic candidate—William Jennings Bryan—in 1896?

Writing Activity
7. **PERSUASIVE** Suppose that you support the Populist Party and that you have been asked to write copy for a campaign poster. Include a slogan and text that provides reasons for people to support the Populists.

networks

There's More Online!

☑ **BIOGRAPHY** W.E.B. Du Bois

☑ **BIOGRAPHY** Booker T. Washington

☑ **VIDEO** The Rise of Segregation

☑ **INTERACTIVE SELF-CHECK QUIZ**

Reading **HELP**DESK

Content Vocabulary
- poll tax
- segregation
- Jim Crow laws
- lynch

Academic Vocabulary
- discrimination

TAKING NOTES: *Organizing*

ACTIVITY Use a graphic organizer similar to the following to list the ways that states disenfranchised African Americans and legalized discrimination.

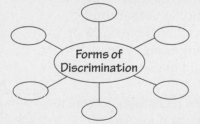

Forms of Discrimination

LESSON 5
The Rise of Segregation

IT MATTERS BECAUSE

After Reconstruction ended, Southern states began passing laws that weakened the rights of African Americans by introducing segregation and denying voting rights. African American leaders struggled to protect civil rights and improve their quality of life.

Resistance and Repression

GUIDING QUESTION *How did African Americans resist racism and try to improve their way of life following Reconstruction?*

After Reconstruction, many African Americans in the rural South lived in poverty. Most were sharecroppers, landless farmers who gave their landlords a large portion of their crops as rent. Sharecropping usually left farmers in chronic debt. Many eventually left farming and sought jobs in Southern towns or headed west to claim homesteads.

In the mid-1870s, Benjamin "Pap" Singleton became convinced that African Americans would never be given a chance to get ahead in the South. He began urging African Americans to move west, specifically to Kansas, and form their own independent communities. His ideas soon set in motion a mass migration. In less than two months, approximately 6,000 African Americans left their homes in the rural South and headed to Kansas. The newspapers called it "an Exodus," like the ancient Jews' escape from Egyptian bondage referred to in the Bible. The migrants themselves came to be known as "Exodusters." The first Exodusters, many possessing little more than hope and the clothes on their backs, arrived in Kansas in the spring of 1879.

While some African Americans fled the South, others joined poor white farmers who had created the Farmers' Alliance. Alliance leaders urged African Americans to form a similar organization. In 1886 African American farmers established the Colored Farmers' National Alliance, which numbered about 1.2 million members by 1890.

In 1879 an estimated 6,000 to 15,000 African Americans known as Exodusters left the rural South and headed to Kansas.

▶ **CRITICAL THINKING**
Examining Why did the Exodusters migrate to Kansas?

poll tax a tax of a fixed amount per person that had to be paid before the person could vote

When the Populist Party formed in 1891, many African American farmers joined the new organization. This posed a major challenge to the Democratic Party in the South. If poor whites joined African Americans in voting for the Populists, the coalition might be unbeatable. To win back the poor white vote, Democratic leaders began appealing to racism. In addition, election officials began using various methods to make it harder and harder for African Americans to vote. As one Democratic leader in the South told a reporter, "Some of our people, some editors especially, deny that [African Americans] are hindered from voting; but what is the good of lying? They are interfered with, and we are obliged to do it, and we may as well tell the truth."

☑ **PROGRESS CHECK**

Summarizing What did the Democratic Party do to prevent the Populists from gaining too much power?

Imposing Segregation

GUIDING QUESTION *What laws did Southern states pass to impose segregation and deny African Americans their voting rights?*

After Reconstruction ended in 1877, the rights of African Americans were gradually undermined. Attempts to unify whites and African Americans failed. Instead, a movement to diminish the civil rights of African Americans gained momentum as the century ended.

Taking Away the Vote
The Fifteenth Amendment prohibits states from denying citizens the right to vote on the basis of "race, color, or previous condition of servitude." However, it does not bar states from denying the right to vote on other grounds. In the late 1800s, Southern states began imposing restrictions. Though they did not mention race, they were meant to make it hard or impossible for African Americans to vote.

In 1890 Mississippi began requiring all citizens registering to vote to pay a **poll tax** of $2, a sum beyond the means of most poor African Americans or poor whites. Mississippi also instituted a literacy test, requiring voters to read and understand the state constitution. Few African Americans born after the Civil War had been able to attend school, and those who had grown up under slavery were largely illiterate. Even those who knew how to read often failed the test because officials deliberately picked passages that few people could understand. Other Southern states adopted similar restrictions. The number of African Americans registered to vote in Southern states fell drastically between 1890 and 1900.

Election officials were far less strict in applying the poll tax and literacy requirements to whites, but the number of white voters also fell significantly. To let more whites vote, Louisiana introduced the "grandfather clause." This allowed any man to vote if he had an ancestor who could vote in 1867. This provision, adopted in several Southern states, exempted most whites from voting restrictions.

Legalizing Segregation

African Americans in the North were often discriminated against, but **segregation,** or the separation of the races, was different in the South. Southern states passed laws that rigidly enforced **discrimination.** These laws became known as **Jim Crow laws.**

In 1883 the Supreme Court set the stage for legalized segregation when it overturned the Civil Rights Act of 1875. That law had prohibited keeping people out of public places on the basis of race and barred racial discrimination in selecting jurors. The Supreme Court, however, ruled that the Fourteenth Amendment provided only that "no state" could deny citizens equal protection under the law. Private organizations, such as hotels, theaters, and railroads, were free to practice segregation.

Encouraged by the Supreme Court's ruling and by the decline of congressional support for civil rights, Southern states passed a series of laws establishing racial segregation in virtually all public places. Southern whites and African Americans could no longer ride together in the same railroad cars or even drink from the same water fountains.

In 1892 an African American named Homer Plessy challenged a Louisiana law that forced him to ride in a separate railroad car from whites.

segregation the separation or isolation of a race, class, or group

discrimination different treatment or preference on a basis other than individual merit

Jim Crow laws statutes enacted to enforce segregation

🏛 ANALYZING SUPREME COURT CASES

PLESSY v. *FERGUSON,* 1896

Background to the Case

When Homer Adolph Plessy, a light-skinned man who was one-eighth African American, took a seat in the whites-only section of an East Louisiana Railway train and refused to move, he was arrested. Convicted of breaking a Louisiana law enacted in 1890, Plessy appealed his case to the Louisiana Supreme Court, then to the United States Supreme Court. The incident was planned in advance to test the statute to emphasize the folly of the law.

A conductor orders an African American off a whites-only train car in Philadelphia, Pennsylvania.

How the Court Ruled

The Court upheld the right of states to make laws that sustained segregation. The majority of justices wanted to distinguish between political rights guaranteed by the Fourteenth and Fifteenth Amendments and social rights. Although the words *separate but equal* do not appear in the Court's responses, the ruling of the Court allowed for the separation of the races in public facilities. This phrase came to describe a condition that persisted until 1954.

▶ CRITICAL THINKING

❶ *Identifying Central Issues* Why did the words *separate but equal* become associated with the Supreme Court ruling against Homer Plessy?

❷ *Making Generalizations* How do you interpret the fact that it took the Supreme Court until 1954 to change the *Plessy* v. *Ferguson* ruling?

Ida B. Wells (1862–1931)

Born in Holly Springs, Mississippi, Ida B. Wells is best known for her strong criticism of lynching, which she called "our country's national crime." Wells's political and reform activities included other issues such as segregation and women's suffrage. In 1913 she marched with an integrated group of suffragists in Washington, D.C. Wells married Chicago lawyer and editor Ferdinand L. Barnett in 1895. In 1910 she formed the Negro Fellowship League. She and her husband moved to an all-white Chicago neighborhood to challenge restrictive housing agreements.

▶ **CRITICAL THINKING**
Describing How did Ida B. Wells try to stop the practice of lynching?

lynch to execute, by hanging, without lawful approval

He was arrested for riding in a "whites-only" car. In 1896 the Supreme Court, in *Plessy* v. *Ferguson*, upheld the Louisiana law and the doctrine of "separate but equal" facilities for African Americans. The ruling established the legal basis for discrimination in the South for more than 50 years. While public facilities for African Americans in the South were always separate, they were far from equal.

☑ **PROGRESS CHECK**

Summarizing What was the purpose of the "grandfather clause"?

The African American Response

GUIDING QUESTION *How did African American community leaders respond to legalized segregation?*

Historian Rayford Logan characterized the last decade of the nineteenth century and the opening of the twentieth century as the nadir, or low point, of African American status in American society. The African American community responded to violence and discrimination in several ways. Ida B. Wells, Mary Church Terrell, Booker T. Washington, and W.E.B. Du Bois each used different approaches to address these issues.

Ida B. Wells

In the late 1800s, mob violence increased in the United States, particularly in the South. Between 1890 and 1899, there was an average of 154 people **lynched**—executed, by hanging, without a legal trial—each year.

In 1892 Ida B. Wells, a fiery young African American woman from Tennessee, launched a fearless crusade against lynching. After a mob drove Wells out of town, she settled in Chicago and continued her campaign. In 1895 she published a book denouncing mob violence and demanding "a fair trial by law for those accused of crime, and punishment by law after honest conviction." Although Congress rejected an antilynching bill, the number of lynchings decreased significantly in the 1900s, due in part to the efforts of activists such as Wells.

Mary Church Terrell

One lynching victim had been a close friend of Mary Church Terrell, a college-educated woman who had been born during the Civil War. This death, and President Benjamin Harrison's refusal to publicly condemn lynching, started Terrell on her lifelong battle against lynching, racism, and sexism. Terrell worked with woman suffrage workers such as Jane Addams and Susan B. Anthony. She helped found the National Association for the Advancement of Colored People. She also formed the Women Wage Earner's Association, which assisted African American nurses, waitresses, and domestic workers.

Terrell led a boycott against department stores in Washington, D.C., that refused to serve African Americans. In an address to the National American Woman Suffrage Association, Terrell said, "With courage, born of success achieved in the past, with a keen sense of the responsibility which we shall continue to assume, we look forward to a future large with promise and hope. Seeking no favors because of our color, nor patronage because of our needs, we knock at the bar of justice, asking an equal chance."

Calls for Compromise

One of the most famous African Americans of the late nineteenth century was the influential educator Booker T. Washington. He proposed that African Americans concentrate on achieving economic goals rather than political ones. In 1895 Washington summed up his views in a speech before a mostly white audience in Atlanta. Known as the Atlanta Compromise, the speech urged African Americans to postpone the fight for civil rights and instead concentrate on preparing themselves educationally and vocationally for full equality.

PRIMARY SOURCE

❝The wisest among my race understand that the agitation of questions of social equality is the extremest folly, and that progress in the enjoyment of all the privileges that will come to us must be the result of severe and constant struggle rather than of artificial forcing. . . . It is important and right that all privileges of the law be ours, but it is vastly more important that we be prepared for the exercises of these privileges. The opportunity to earn a dollar in a factory just now is worth infinitely more than the opportunity to spend a dollar in an opera-house.❞

—Booker T. Washington, from *Up From Slavery*, 1901

With the help of Booker T. Washington, Tuskegee Institute was founded in 1881 to teach African Americans trades and agricultural skills. In this image, students are working in the Tuskegee Institute print shop.

▶ **CRITICAL THINKING**
Drawing Conclusions What do you think was Booker T. Washington's economic goal for establishing the Tuskegee Institute?

Du Bois Rejects Compromise

The Atlanta Compromise speech provoked a strong challenge from W.E.B. Du Bois, the leader of a new generation of African American activists. In his 1903 book *The Souls of Black Folk,* Du Bois explained why he saw no advantage in giving up civil rights, even temporarily. He was particularly concerned with protecting and exercising voting rights. "Negroes must insist continually, in season and out of season," he wrote, "that voting is necessary to proper manhood, that color discrimination is barbarism." In the years that followed, many African Americans worked to win the vote and end discrimination. The struggle, however, would prove to be a long one.

✓ **PROGRESS CHECK**

Describing What was the nature of the compromise urged by Booker T. Washington in the Atlanta Compromise speech?

LESSON 5 REVIEW

Reviewing Vocabulary
1. *Explaining* Explain the importance of Jim Crow laws and how these laws contributed to segregation.

Using Your Notes
2. *Describing* Use your notes on the forms of discrimination to describe the conditions in which many African Americans in the South lived after Reconstruction.

Answering the Guiding Questions
3. *Identifying Cause and Effect* How did African Americans resist racism and try to improve their way of life following Reconstruction?

4. *Identifying* What laws did Southern states pass to impose segregation and deny African Americans their voting rights?

5. *Differentiating* What are the different ways African American community leaders responded to legalized segregation?

Writing Activity
6. EXPOSITORY Imagine that you are living in the 1890s. Write a letter to the editor of the local newspaper explaining your view of the Supreme Court ruling in *Plessy* v. *Ferguson*.

Directions: On a separate sheet of paper, answer the questions below. Make sure you read carefully and answer all parts to the question.

Lesson Review

Lesson 1

1 *Identifying* In the late nineteenth century many native-born Americans, as well as labor unions, opposed immigration. What were their concerns?

2 *Summarizing* What caused European and Chinese immigrants to migrate to the United States in the late nineteenth century?

Lesson 2

3 *Making Connections* What factors caused the nation's cities to grow in population at the end of the nineteenth century?

4 *Explaining* How did political machines come about, and what effect did they have in a city?

Lesson 3

5 *Naming* Which philosophy was a gentler version of Social Darwinism, and what was its intention?

6 *Defining* What is the main idea of individualism?

Lesson 4

7 *Analyzing* Why was deflation hard on farmers, but inflation was not?

8 *Identifying Central Issues* What were the goals of the People's Party? How did urban workers vote in the 1892 elections and why?

Lesson 5

9 *Assessing* What was the ruling in the *Plessy* v. *Ferguson* case, and what was its impact in the South?

10 *Examining* How did African American leaders respond to legalized segregation?

21st Century Skills

11 **COMPARE AND CONTRAST** How were the experiences of European and Asian immigrants different?

12 **ECONOMICS** In what ways was life different depending upon the social class to which a person belonged?

13 **IDENTIFYING CAUSE AND EFFECT** What events instigated the Populist movement?

Exploring the Essential Question

14 *Exploring Issues* Draw a map with detailed caption boxes. The map should either explain why people migrated in the late 1800s or describe how urban life was different from rural life.

DBQ Document-Based Question

Use the document to answer the following question. This 1882 excerpt is from a business newspaper and addresses the effects of immigration on the nation.

PRIMARY SOURCE

66 *[The immigrant] adds . . . to the immediate prosperity and success of certain lines of business. [O]cean steamers . . . get very large returns in carrying passengers of this description. . . .*

. . . These immigrants not only produce largely, . . . but, having wants which they cannot supply themselves, create a demand for outside supplies. . . . Thus it is that the Eastern manufacturer finds the call upon him for his wares and goods growing more urgent all the time. . . . 99

— from *Commercial and Financial Chronicle*

15 *Specifying* According to the editorial, what effect did immigration have on the nation's economy?

Extended-Response Question

16 *Identifying Central Issues* Write an expository essay that identifies how urbanization influenced social and political life during this time period. The essay should contain an introduction and at least two paragraphs.

Need Extra Help?

If You've Missed Question	**1**	**2**	**3**	**4**	**5**	**6**	**7**	**8**	**9**	**10**	**11**	**12**	**13**	**14**	**15**	**16**
Go to page	310	308	312	314	317	316	324	325	329	330	309	313	325	312	332	312

Becoming a World Power

1872–1917

ESSENTIAL QUESTION • *How are empires built?*

netw⊙rks

There's More Online about how the United States became a world power.

CHAPTER 14

The Story Matters...

International economic and military competition convinced the United States that it must become a world power, on par with Britain and Spain. By acquiring new lands before and after the Spanish-American War, the United States became more prominent, but it also took on new responsibilities. In the late 1800s, the United States increased its trade and military presence in East Asia and Latin America. By the early 1900s, it had created an American empire.

◄ Matthew Calbraith Perry, commodore of the U.S. Navy, negotiated the opening of Japan to the West with the Treaty of Kanagawa in 1854.

PHOTO: The Granger Collection, New York

Place and Time: United States 1872–1917

U.S. economists, politicians, and other leaders recognized that economic growth could only come through expansion into foreign markets. With that in mind, the United States embarked on a path toward imperialism that included colonization and the acquisition of new territory. One strategic acquisition was the Panama Canal. After agreeing to pay for the rights to the project and the land around it, President Roosevelt pushed for the canal's completion. William Gorgas, a U.S. Army surgeon, helped control a major obstacle facing the construction of the Panama Canal: disease.

Step Into the Place

Read the quotes and look at the information presented on the map.

 What challenges did the construction of the Panama Canal pose?

PRIMARY SOURCE

❝No single great material work which remains to be undertaken on this continent is as of such consequence to the American people as the building of a canal across the isthmus connecting North and South America.❞

—Theodore Roosevelt, from a speech to Congress, 1901

PRIMARY SOURCE

❝The route of the Panama Canal lay through a low, swampy country . . . where . . . yellow fever and malaria prevailed to an alarming extent. . . .

We appreciated that, if the Americans were subject to this disease to any considerable extent, we should have great difficulty in keeping them at Panama . . . and if we could afford to pay sufficiently high wages to induce them to stay, Congress, in all probability, would not sanction the continuance of the work, if we lost from yellow fever fifteen or sixteen hundred Americans every year.❞

—William C. Gorgas, from *Sanitation in Panama*, 1915

Step Into the Time

Choose an event from the time line and write a paragraph predicting the general social, political, or economic consequences that might occur as a result of U.S. expansionism.

U.S. PRESIDENTS

UNITED STATES

WORLD

 Grant 1869–1877

1878 U.S. signs treaty with Samoa to use the harbor of Pago Pago

 Hayes 1877–1881

 Garfield 1881

Arthur 1881–1885

 **Cleveland** 1885–1889

1872   1877   1882   1887

1874 Britain annexes Fiji Islands

1882 Germany, Austria, and Italy form Triple Alliance

1889 First Pan-American conference is held

networks
There's More Online!

- **MAP** Explore the interactive version of this map on Networks.
- **TIME LINE** Explore the interactive version of the time line on Networks.

The Panama Canal

Caribbean Sea
Canal Zone
Canal route
Locks
10°N
9°N
80°W
79°W
81°W
W
E
S
Cacique
Portobelo
El Porvenir
Gulf of San Blas
San Blas
Colón
Cristobal
Gatun Locks
Gatún
Palmas Bellas
Miguel de la Borda
Lake Gatún
Panamá
Chepo
Gamboa
Pedro Miguel Locks
Colón
Arenosa
Miraflores Locks
Panamá
Pueblo Nuevo
La Chorrera
Capira
Panamá Bay
Calovébora
La Pintada
Chame
Santa Fé
Penonomé
Veraguas
Coclé
San Carlos
Isla Pedro González
San Miguel
Antón
Río Hato
Gulf of Panamá
Isla del Rey
Cañazas
Natá
Isla San José
San Francisco
Aguadulce
Parita Bay
PACIFIC OCEAN
0 20 miles
0 20 km
Albers Equal Area Conic projection
10°N
COSTA RICA
Caribbean Sea
N
W
E
S
PANAMA
8°N
COLOMBIA
0 50 miles
0 50 km
PACIFIC OCEAN
83°W
80°W
78°W

B. Harrison 1889–1893

1893 Americans overthrow Queen Liliuokalani of Hawaii

Cleveland 1893–1897

1898 USS *Maine* explodes in Havana Harbor

McKinley 1897–1901

T. Roosevelt 1901–1909

1904 Senate approves treaty leasing the Panama Canal

Taft 1909–1913

1892 | 1897 | 1902 | 1907 | 1912 | 1917

1894 Sino-Japanese War breaks out

1899 John Hay sends Open Door notes

1900 Boxer Rebellion begins in China

1904 Russo-Japanese War begins

netw⊙rks

There's More Online!

☑ **BIOGRAPHY** Sanford B. Dole

☑ **BIOGRAPHY** Queen Liliuokalani

☑ **BIOGRAPHY** Matthew Perry

☑ **CHART/GRAPH** U.S. Foreign Investments

☑ **VIDEO** The Imperlialist Vision

☑ **INTERACTIVE SELF-CHECK QUIZ**

Reading HELPDESK

Content Vocabulary

- **imperialism**
- **protectorate**
- **Pan-Americanism**

Academic Vocabulary

- **expansion** - **conference**

TAKING NOTES: *Organizing*

ACTIVITY As you read about the development of the United States as a world power, use the major headings of the lesson to create an outline for the lesson similar to the one below.

The Imperialist Vision
I. Building Support for Imperialism
   A.
   B.
   C.
II.
   A.
   B.

LESSON 1
The Imperialist Vision

ESSENTIAL QUESTION · *How are empires built?*

IT MATTERS BECAUSE

During the late 1800s, the desire to find new markets, increase trade, and build a powerful navy caused the United States to become more involved in international affairs.

Building Support for Imperialism

GUIDING QUESTION *Why did the United States assert itself as a world power?*

Following the Civil War, most Americans showed little interest in expanding their nation's territory outside the United States. Instead, they focused on reconstructing the South, settling the West, and building up industry. In the 1880s, economic and military competition from Europe and a growing feeling of cultural superiority convinced many Americans that the United States should become a world power.

A Desire for New Markets

Many European nations were expanding overseas, a development called the New Imperialism. **Imperialism** is the economic and political domination of a strong nation over weaker ones. European nations expanded their power overseas for many reasons. They needed to import raw materials for manufacturing. High tariffs in industrialized nations—intended to protect domestic industries— reduced trade, forcing companies to look for new markets overseas. Investment opportunities had also slowed in Western Europe, so Europeans began looking overseas for places to invest their capital.

To protect their investments, European nations began exerting control over territories, making some into colonies and others into **protectorates.** In a protectorate, the imperial power protected local rulers against rebellions and invasion. In return, rulers usually had to accept Europeans' advice on how to govern their countries.

As the United States industrialized, many Americans noticed the **expansion** of European power overseas and took an interest in the new imperialism. Many concluded that the nation needed new overseas markets to keep its economy strong.

A Feeling of Superiority

Certain key ideas encouraged Americans to support the nation's expansion overseas. Historian John Fiske argued that English-speaking nations had superior character, ideas, and systems of government. Many Americans linked his ideas, known as Anglo-Saxonism, with the idea of Manifest Destiny. These Americans believed the nation was destined to expand overseas to spread its civilization to others.

PRIMARY SOURCE

❝The work which the English race began when it colonized North America is destined to go on until every land . . . that is not already the seat of an old civilization shall become English in its language, in its religion, in political habits and traditions, and to a predominant extent in the blood of its people.❞

—John Fiske, from "Manifest Destiny," *Harper's Magazine*, 1885

Building a Modern Navy

As these ideas gained support, the United States became more assertive in foreign affairs. In 1888 the country risked war to prevent Germany from taking control of Samoa. The crisis ended peacefully. However, it led some Americans to believe that the United States would be shut out of foreign markets if it did not build up its navy and acquire bases overseas.

U.S. naval officer Captain Alfred T. Mahan helped build public support for the idea that a nation needed large fleets of ships to trade with the world and a large navy to defend the right to trade with other countries. With the support of influential government officials, proponents of these ideas convinced Congress to authorize the construction of a large navy.

☑ **PROGRESS CHECK**

Summarizing Why did Americans' attitudes toward overseas expansion change?

imperialism the actions used by one nation to exercise political or economic control over a smaller or weaker nation

protectorate a country that is technically independent but is actually under the control of another country

expansion the act or process of increasing or enlarging the extent, number, volume, or scope

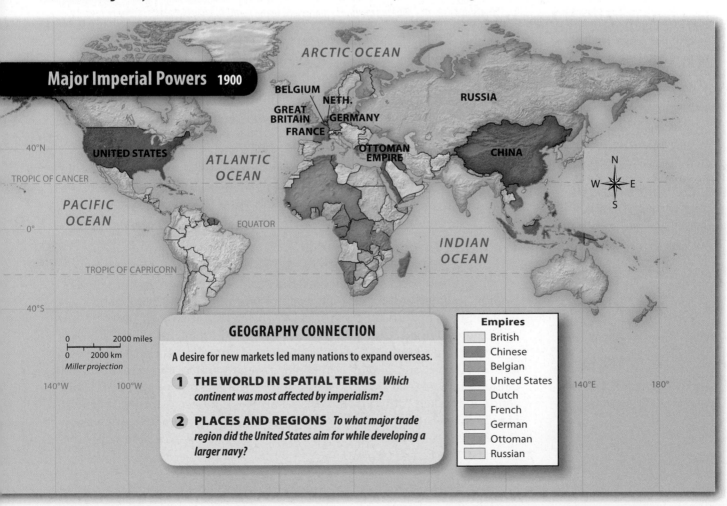

Major Imperial Powers 1900

GEOGRAPHY CONNECTION

A desire for new markets led many nations to expand overseas.

1 THE WORLD IN SPATIAL TERMS *Which continent was most affected by imperialism?*

2 PLACES AND REGIONS *To what major trade region did the United States aim for while developing a larger navy?*

Empires
- British
- Chinese
- Belgian
- United States
- Dutch
- French
- German
- Ottoman
- Russian

0   2000 miles
0   2000 km
Miller projection

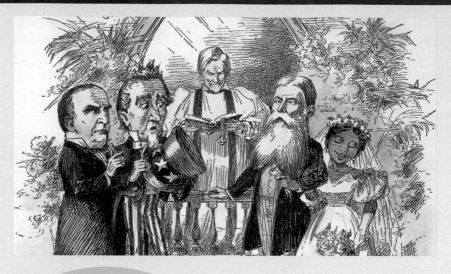

POLITICAL CARTOONS

In the wedding depicted in this cartoon, President McKinley is Uncle Sam's best man and Sanford B. Dole gives away the bride, who represents Hawaii.

▶ **CRITICAL THINKING**
Interpreting Significance How does the artist of this cartoon portray America's annexation of Hawaii?

Analyzing PRIMARY SOURCES

Mahan on Military Bases

❝To provide resting places for them [warships], where they can coal and repair, would be one of the first duties of a government proposing to itself the development of the power of the nation at sea.❞

—Alfred Thayer Mahan, from *The Influence of Sea Power Upon History,* 1890

DBQ *IDENTIFYING CENTRAL ISSUES* Why do you think establishing "resting places" is a key issue for developing naval power?

American Expansion in the Pacific

GUIDING QUESTION *Why did the United States look to the Pacific for new markets?*

From the earliest days of the Republic, Americans had expanded their nation by moving westward. When looking overseas for new markets, the United States naturally looked to the Pacific.

Perry Opens Japan

In 1852 President Millard Fillmore ordered Commodore Matthew C. Perry to negotiate a trade treaty with Japan. In 1853 warships under Perry's command entered Edo Bay (now Tokyo Bay). Japan's rulers, fearing the influence of Western ideas, had limited contact with the West. After seeing the warships, however, the Japanese realized they were not powerful enough to resist modern weapons. In 1854, Japan signed the Treaty of Kanagawa, giving the United States trading rights at two Japanese ports.

Annexing Samoa and Hawaii

As trade with Asia grew, the United States needed ports for its ships to refuel and resupply as they crossed the Pacific. Pago Pago, in the Samoan Islands, had one of the finest harbors in the South Pacific. In 1878 the United States negotiated permission to open a base there. An 1899 agreement divided Samoa between Germany and the United States.

More important was Hawaii. Americans found that sugarcane grew well in Hawaii, and planters established sugar plantations there. In 1875 the United States signed a treaty exempting Hawaiian sugar from tariffs. This action was taken to aid Hawaii during an economic recession and prevent Hawaii from turning to Britain or France for help. When the treaty was up for renewal, the United States insisted Hawaii grant it exclusive rights to a naval base at Pearl Harbor.

In 1887 sugar planters forced Hawaii's king to accept a constitution limiting his power. The planters wanted Hawaii to become part of the United States. After ascending the throne in 1891, Queen Liliuokalani tried to reassert the Hawaiian monarchy's power, but the planters, supported by U.S. sailors, overthrew the monarchy in 1893. The United States annexed Hawaii in 1898.

☑ PROGRESS CHECK

Explaining How did the search for new overseas markets push the United States to become a world power?

Diplomacy in Latin America

GUIDING QUESTION *How did the United States attempt to strengthen its ties and influence with the nations of Latin America?*

In the 1800s, the United States also sought to build influence in Latin America. The United States bought raw materials from Latin America, but Latin America bought most of its manufactured goods from Europe. Many Americans wanted to increase the sale of goods in Latin America and to show that the United States was the dominant power in the region. Secretary of State James G. Blaine advocated **Pan-Americanism,** the idea that the United States and Latin American nations should work together. He suggested that the United States invite the Latin American nations to a **conference** in Washington, D.C.

Blaine had two goals for the Pan-American conference of 1889. The first was to create a customs union requiring all nations of the Western Hemisphere to reduce tariffs against each other and treat each other equally in trade. Blaine hoped this would turn the Latin Americans away from European products. The second was to create a system for nations of the Western Hemisphere to work out disputes peacefully, while also keeping Europeans from meddling in American affairs.

Latin American delegates rejected both ideas. They did, however, agree to create the Commercial Bureau of the American Republics, promoting cooperation among nations of the Western Hemisphere. Today that organization is known as the Organization of American States (OAS).

☑ PROGRESS CHECK

Drawing Conclusions How would increasing trade with Latin America strengthen U.S. dominance in the region?

Organization of American States

This is the logo for the OAS, the world's oldest regional organization.

▶ **CRITICAL THINKING**
Drawing Conclusions How does the OAS logo represent the idea of Pan-Americanism?

Pan-Americanism
the idea that the United States and Latin American nations should work together

conference a meeting of two or more persons for discussing matters of common concern

---

LESSON 1 REVIEW

Reviewing Vocabulary
1. *Explaining* How did Anglo-Saxonism help foster American imperialism?

Using Your Notes
2. *Listing* Review the notes you completed during the lesson to list the factors that led the United States to realize an imperialist vision in the 1890s.

Answering the Guiding Questions
3. *Analyzing* Why did the United States assert itself as a world power?

4. *Summarizing* Why did the United States look to the Pacific for new markets?

5. *Describing* How did the United States attempt to strengthen its ties and influence with the nations of Latin America?

Writing Activity
6. **PERSUASIVE** Suppose that you are living in the United States in the 1890s. Write a letter to the president persuading him to support or oppose an imperialist policy for the United States.

networks

There's More Online!

- ☑ **BIOGRAPHY** Emilio Aguinaldo
- ☑ **BIOGRAPHY** William Randolph Hearst
- ☑ **BIOGRAPHY** Joseph Pulitzer
- ☑ **CHART/GRAPH** Spanish-American War Deaths
- ☑ **IMAGE** Guerilla Fighters
- ☑ **IMAGE** Yellow Journalism
- ☑ **MAP** Distance Between the U.S. and the Philippines
- ☑ **VIDEO** The Spanish-American War
- ☑ **INTERACTIVE SELF-CHECK QUIZ**

Reading **HELP**DESK

Content Vocabulary

- yellow journalism
- autonomy • jingoism

Academic Vocabulary

- intervene • volunteer

TAKING NOTES: *Organizing*

ACTIVITY As you read about the Spanish-American War, complete a graphic organizer like the one below by listing the circumstances that contributed to war with Spain.

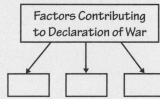

Factors Contributing to Declaration of War

LESSON 2
The Spanish-American War

ESSENTIAL QUESTION • *How are empires built?*

IT MATTERS BECAUSE

During the Spanish-American War, the United States defeated Spanish troops in Cuba and the Philippines. Afterward, the United States annexed the Philippines and became an imperial power.

The Coming of War

GUIDING QUESTION *Why was the United States willing to go to war with Spain over Cuba?*

By 1898, Cuba and Puerto Rico were two of Spain's last remaining colonies in the Western Hemisphere. Cubans had periodically revolted against Spanish rule, and many Americans regarded the Spanish as tyrants. Ultimately, the United States issued a declaration of war against Spain. Although the fighting lasted only a few months, the war dramatically altered the position of the United States on the world stage.

The Cuban Rebellion Begins

Cuba was one of Spain's oldest colonies in the Americas. Its sugarcane plantations generated considerable wealth for Spain and produced nearly one-third of the world's sugar in the mid-1800s. Until Spain abolished slavery in 1886, about one-third of the Cuban population was enslaved and forced to work for wealthy landowners on the plantations.

In 1868 Cuban rebels declared independence and launched a guerrilla war against Spanish authorities. Lacking internal support, the rebellion collapsed a decade later. Many Cuban rebels then fled to the United States, including their leader, José Martí.

By the early 1890s, the United States and Cuba had become closely linked economically. Cuba exported much of its sugar to the United States, and Americans had invested approximately $50 million in Cuba's sugar plantations, mines, and railroads. These economic ties created a crisis in 1894, when the United States imposed a new tariff on sugar that devastated Cuba's economy. With Cuba in financial distress, the Cuban rebels launched a new rebellion in February 1895. Martí died during the fighting, but the rebels seized control of eastern Cuba, declared independence, and formally established the Republic of Cuba in September 1895.

America Supports Cuba

When the uprising began, President Grover Cleveland declared the United States neutral. However, stories of Spanish atrocities in two of the nation's major newspapers, the *New York Journal* and the *New York World,* swayed many Americans in the rebels' favor. This sensationalist reporting, in which writers exaggerated or made up stories to attract readers, became known as **yellow journalism.** Although some stories were invented, Cubans indeed suffered horribly.

The Spanish sent nearly 200,000 troops to the island to put down the rebellion and appointed General Valeriano Weyler as governor. The rebels' raids destroyed a considerable amount of property, some belonging to Americans. The rebels hoped that the destruction of American property would lead to American intervention in the war. To prevent villagers from helping the rebels, Weyler herded hundreds of thousands of rural men, women, and children into "reconcentration camps," where tens of thousands died of starvation and disease.

Calls for War

In 1897 Republican William McKinley became president of the United States. In September 1897, he asked Spain whether the United States could help negotiate an end to the conflict, so that the United States would not have to **intervene** in the war. Spain removed Weyler from office and offered the Cubans **autonomy,** but only if Cuba remained part of the Spanish Empire. The rebels refused to negotiate.

Spain's concessions enraged many Spanish loyalists in Cuba. In January 1898, the loyalists rioted in Havana. McKinley sent the battleship USS *Maine* to Havana to protect Americans living there. On February 9, 1898, the *New York Journal* printed a letter written by the Spanish ambassador to the United States, describing McKinley as "weak." The United States erupted in fury over the insult.

Then, on February 15, 1898, the *Maine* exploded in Havana Harbor. To this day, no one is sure why the *Maine* exploded. Many Americans believed the Spanish did it. "Remember the *Maine*!" became the rallying cry for those demanding a declaration of war against Spain.

McKinley faced tremendous pressure to go to war. Within the Republican Party, **jingoism** —aggressive nationalism—was very strong. On April 11, 1898, McKinley asked Congress to authorize the use of force.

yellow journalism type of sensational, biased, and often false reporting for the sake of attracting readers

intervene to get involved in the affairs of another

autonomy the quality of or state of being self-governing

President McKinley sent the battleship *Maine* to Cuba to help Americans evacuate. When the ship exploded, an enraged nation blamed Spain, although the explosion may have originated within the ship. "Remember the *Maine*!" became the battle cry for war.

▶ **CRITICAL THINKING**
Analyzing What do you think contributed to American sympathy with the Cubans?

On April 19, Congress proclaimed Cuba independent, demanded that Spain withdraw from the island, and authorized the president to use armed force. On April 24, Spain declared war on the United States.

☑ **PROGRESS CHECK**

Examining What events led to the war with Spain in 1898?

A War on Two Fronts

GUIDING QUESTION *How was the Spanish-American War different from earlier U.S. wars?*

The U.S. Navy was ready for war with Spain. The navy blockaded Cuba, and Commodore George Dewey, commander of the American naval squadron based in Hong Kong, was ordered to attack the Spanish fleet based in the Philippines, then a Spanish colony. American naval planners wanted to prevent the Spanish fleet from sailing east to attack the United States.

The Battle of Manila Bay

On May 1, 1898, the American ships in Dewey's squadron entered Manila Bay in the Philippines. They quickly destroyed the outdated and outgunned Spanish fleet.

Dewey's quick victory surprised McKinley. Hastily, the army assembled 20,000 troops to sail from San Francisco to the Philippines. On the way, the Americans also seized the island of Guam, another Spanish possession.

While waiting for the American troops to arrive, Dewey contacted Emilio Aguinaldo, a Filipino revolutionary leader who had staged an unsuccessful uprising against the Spanish in 1896. Now, while Aguinaldo and his rebels took control of most of the islands, American troops seized the Philippine capital of Manila.

American Forces in Cuba

The Spanish in Cuba were not prepared for war. Their soldiers were weak and sick, and their warships were old with untrained crews. If the United States could defeat the Spanish fleet, Spain would not be able to supply its troops in Cuba. Eventually, Spain would have to surrender.

The U.S. Army was not prepared for war, either. The army had recruited **volunteers** but lacked proper resources to train and equip them. One volunteer cavalry unit was a rough mix of cowboys, miners, and law officers known as the "Rough Riders."

Between June 22 and 24, some 17,000 U.S. troops had landed east of Santiago, Cuba. The Spanish fleet, well protected by powerful shore-based guns, occupied Santiago Harbor. Americans wanted to capture those guns to drive the Spanish fleet out of the harbor and into battle with the American fleet waiting nearby. The Rough Riders accompanied the army as it advanced. Colonel Theodore Roosevelt was second in command.

On July 1, American troops attacked a village near Santiago and the San Juan Heights. The Rough Riders and the all African American 9th and 10th Cavalry Regiments attacked and held Kettle Hill, then assisted in the capture of San Juan Hill.

In Santiago the Spanish commander panicked and ordered the Spanish fleet to flee the harbor. On July 3, American warships attacked them, destroying every Spanish vessel. Later, the Spanish in Santiago surrendered, leaving American troops to occupy nearby Puerto Rico.

☑ PROGRESS CHECK

Summarizing On what two fronts was the Spanish-American War fought?

jingoism extreme nationalism marked by aggressive foreign policy

volunteer person who joins the military by choice

Rough Rider and future president Theodore Roosevelt

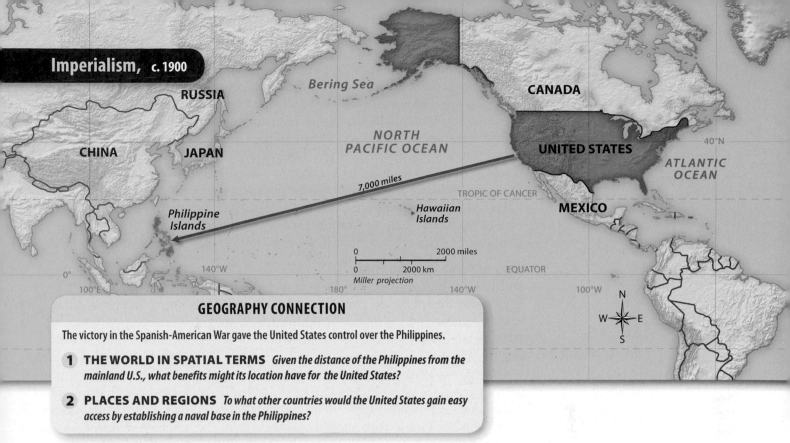

GEOGRAPHY CONNECTION

The victory in the Spanish-American War gave the United States control over the Philippines.

1 THE WORLD IN SPATIAL TERMS *Given the distance of the Philippines from the mainland U.S., what benefits might its location have for the United States?*

2 PLACES AND REGIONS *To what other countries would the United States gain easy access by establishing a naval base in the Philippines?*

An American Empire

GUIDING QUESTION *How did the United States develop an overseas empire?*

As American and Spanish leaders met to discuss the terms for a peace treaty, Americans debated what to do about their newly acquired lands. Cuba would receive its independence as promised, and Spain had agreed to the U.S. annexation of Guam and Puerto Rico. The big question was what to do with the Philippines. The United States faced a difficult choice—remain true to its republican ideals or become an imperial power that ruled a foreign country without the consent of its people. The issue sparked an intense political debate.

The Debate Over Annexation

Many people emphasized the economic and military benefits of taking the Philippines. It would provide the United States with another Pacific naval base, a stopover on the way to China, and a large market for American goods. Other supporters believed America had a duty to help "less civilized" peoples. "Surely this Spanish war has not been a grab for the empire," commented a New England minister, "but a heroic effort [to] free the oppressed and to teach millions of ignorant, debased human beings thus freed how to live."

Other Americans argued that the cost of an empire far outweighed the economic benefits it provided. Some worried that competition from cheap Filipino labor would drive down American wages. Still others believed imperialism violated American principles. President McKinley ultimately decided to annex the islands.

On December 10, 1898, the United States and Spain signed the Treaty of Paris, under which Cuba became independent. Also, the United States acquired Puerto Rico and Guam and paid Spain $20 million for the Philippines. After an intense debate, the Senate approved the treaty in February 1899. The United States had become an imperial power.

The Platt Amendment

Although the United States had promised to grant Cuba its independence, conditions were attached to the new Cuban constitution. The Platt Amendment, submitted by Senator Orville Platt, specified the following: (1) Cuba could not make any treaty with another nation that would weaken its independence; (2) Cuba had to allow the United States to buy or lease naval stations in Cuba; (3) Cuba's debts had to be kept low to prevent foreign countries from landing troops to enforce payment; and (4) the United States would have the right to intervene to protect Cuban independence and keep order. Reluctantly, the Cubans added the amendment to their constitution. The Platt Amendment, which effectively made Cuba an American protectorate, remained in effect until its repeal in 1934.

Governing Puerto Rico

In 1900 Congress passed the Foraker Act, establishing a civil government for Puerto Rico. The law provided for an elected legislature, and a governor and executive council that were appointed by the president. Supreme Court rulings later held that Puerto Ricans were not American citizens and so did not have rights of citizens.

Congress gradually allowed Puerto Ricans greater self-government. In 1917 it granted Puerto Ricans U.S. citizenship. Thirty years later, Puerto Ricans were allowed to elect their own governor. A debate eventually began over whether Puerto Rico should become a state, become independent, or continue as a self-governing commonwealth of the United States. The debate over Puerto Rico's status continues today.

ANALYZING PRIMARY SOURCES

The Annexation Debate

Americans were divided over whether the United States should give the Filipinos their independence or become an imperial power by annexing the Philippines.

Albert J. Beveridge
United States Senator

PRIMARY SOURCE

❝The Opposition tells us that we ought not to govern a people without their consent. I answer, The rule of liberty that all just government derives its authority from the consent of the governed, applies only to those who are capable of self-government. We govern the Indians without their consent, we govern our territories without their consent, we govern our children without their consent.... Would not the people of the Philippines prefer the just, humane, civilizing government of this Republic to the savage, bloody rule of pillage and extortion from which we have rescued them?❞

—from *The Meaning of the Times*

PRIMARY SOURCE

❝A harbor and coaling station in the Philippines would answer every trade and military necessity and such a concession could have been secured at any time without difficulty. It is not necessary to own people in order to trade with them. We carry on trade today with every part of the world, and our commerce has expanded more rapidly than the commerce of any European empire.

... Imperialism finds no warrant in the Bible. The command 'Go ye into all the world and preach the gospel to every creature' has no Gatling gun attachment....❞

— from *Speeches of William Jennings Bryan*

William Jennings Bryan
Presidential Candidate

DBQ Document Based Questions

① ***Making Inferences*** According to Albert Beveridge, why is annexation of the Philippines an honorable course of action?

② ***Analyzing*** What are William Jennings Bryan's two main criticisms of imperialism?

Many people debated the decision to annex the Philippines, arguing over costs and benefits of the new empire.

President McKinley raises the American flag over the Philippines while William Jennings Bryan tries to chop it down.

▶ **CRITICAL THINKING**

1 *Identifying Central Issues* Based on the cartoon, what do you think McKinley is trying to accomplish?

2 *Drawing Conclusions* How do the actions of McKinley in the cartoon represent his feelings about U.S. imperialism?

Rebellion in the Philippines

In 1899 the United States met resistance in the Philippines when Emilio Aguinaldo ordered his troops to attack the American soldiers who had been sent there. The conflict continued for almost three years. To fight the Filipino guerrillas, the U.S. military established reconcentration camps to separate Filipino guerrillas from civilians. Thousands died from disease and starvation. Many U.S. soldiers died fighting the guerrillas.

While American troops fought the guerrillas, the first U.S. civilian governor of the islands, William Howard Taft, tried to win over the Filipinos by improving education, transportation, and health care. These reforms slowly reduced Filipino hostility.

In March 1901, American troops captured Aguinaldo. On July 4, 1902, the United States declared the war over. Gradually the Filipinos gained more control over their government. By the mid-1930s, they elected their own congress and president. In 1946 they gained full independence from the United States.

✓ **PROGRESS CHECK**

Explaining What did the United States do to expand its territorial interests?

LESSON 2 REVIEW

Reviewing Vocabulary

1. *Describing* Describe the level of autonomy that Cuba obtained after the Spanish-American War.

2. *Identifying Central Issues* Identify two results of the United States's intervening in the revolution in Cuba.

Using Your Notes

3. *Finding the Main Idea* Review the notes that you completed during the lesson to identify what all the events had in common.

Answering the Guiding Questions

4. *Explaining* Why was the United States willing to go to war with Spain over Cuba?

5. *Contrasting* How was the Spanish-American War different from earlier U.S. wars?

6. *Analyzing* How did the United States develop an overseas empire?

Writing Activity

7. DESCRIPTIVE Suppose that you are a Filipino living during the time of the U.S. annexation of the Philippine Islands. Write a journal entry in which you describe your feelings about American control of the islands.

networks

There's More Online!

- ☑ **BIOGRAPHY** John Hay
- ☑ **BIOGRAPHY** Theodore Roosevelt
- ☑ **BIOGRAPHY** Pancho Villa
- ☑ **VIDEO** New American Diplomacy
- ☑ **INTERACTIVE SELF-CHECK QUIZ**

LESSON 3
New American Diplomacy

Reading **HELP**DESK

Content Vocabulary
- sphere of influence
- Open Door policy
- dollar diplomacy
- guerrilla

Academic Vocabulary
- access
- tension

TAKING NOTES: *Organizing*

ACTIVITY Complete a graphic organizer similar to the one below to list reasons the United States wanted a canal through Central America.

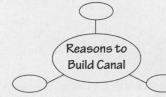

Reasons to Build Canal

ESSENTIAL QUESTION • *How are empires built?*

IT MATTERS BECAUSE

The United States's influence continued to expand into foreign countries. President Theodore Roosevelt mediated disputes in Asia and Latin America and acquired the Panama Canal Zone. Presidents Taft and Wilson increased U.S. trade and influence in Latin America.

American Diplomacy in Asia

GUIDING QUESTION *Why did the United States want to eliminate spheres of influence in China?*

In 1899 the United States was a major power in Asia, with naval bases all across the Pacific. Operating from those bases, the United States Navy—by then the world's third-largest navy—could exert American power anywhere in East Asia. The nation's main interest in Asia, however, was not conquest but commerce. Between 1895 and 1900, U.S. exports to China quadrupled. Although China bought only about two percent of U.S. exports, the vast Chinese markets excited American business leaders, especially those in the textile, oil, and steel industries.

The Open Door Policy

In 1894 war erupted between China and Japan over Korea, which was a client state dependent upon China. Western observers were astonished when Japan easily defeated China's massive military. The war showed that Japan had mastered Western technology and that China was weaker than anyone had thought. In the peace treaty, China recognized Korea's independence and gave Japan territory in Manchuria.

The Russians were concerned about Japan's rising power. They did not want Japan to acquire the territory in Manchuria because it bordered Russia. Backed by France and Germany, Russia forced Japan to return the Manchurian territory it had acquired. Then, in 1898, Russia demanded China lease the territory to Russia instead.

Leasing meant the territory would still belong to China, even though a foreign government would maintain overall control. Soon

Germany, France, and Britain also demanded "leaseholds" in China. Each leasehold became the center of a country's **sphere of influence,** an area where a foreign nation controlled economic development.

U.S. politicians and businessmen worried about these events. President McKinley and Secretary of State John Hay both supported what they called an **Open Door policy,** which would allow all countries to trade with China.

In 1899 Hay asked countries with leaseholds in China not to discriminate against other nations wanting to do business in their sphere of influence. Each nation responded by saying it accepted the Open Door policy but would not follow it unless all the others agreed. Once Hay had received assurances from all of the nations with leaseholds, he declared that the United States expected the other powers to uphold the policy.

The Boxer Rebellion

While foreign countries debated **access** to China's market, secret Chinese societies organized to fight foreign control and influence. One group, the Society of Righteous and Harmonious Fists, was known to Westerners as the Boxers. In 1900 this group decided to destroy both the "foreign devils" and their Chinese Christian converts, whom they believed were corrupting Chinese society.

In what came to be called the Boxer Rebellion, the Boxers and some Chinese troops attacked foreign embassies in Peking (now Beijing) and Tientsin (now Tianjin), killing more than 200 foreigners, including many Christian missionaries. After the German ambassador to China was killed, eight nations—Germany, Austria-Hungary, Britain, France, Italy, Japan, Russia, and the United States—intervened. A large multinational force rescued the foreigners and ended the rebellion.

During the crisis, Secretary of State John Hay worked with British diplomats to persuade the other powers not to partition China. In a second set of Open Door notes, Hay convinced the participating powers to accept compensation from China for damages caused by the rebellion. After some discussion, the powers agreed not to break up China into European-controlled colonies. The United States retained access to China's lucrative trade in tea, spices, and silk and gained a larger market for its own goods.

☑ **PROGRESS CHECK**

Making Inferences What was the importance of the Open Door policy to the United States?

sphere of influence
section of a country where a foreign nation enjoys special rights and powers

Open Door policy a policy that allowed each foreign nation in China to trade freely in the other nations' spheres of influence

access freedom or ability to obtain or make use of

International soldiers pose in Tientsin (now Tianjin) after rescuing their besieged delegations during the Boxer Rebellion. The American is second from the left.

▶ **CRITICAL THINKING**
Drawing Conclusions Why were the Boxers and other secret Chinese societies organized?

PHOTO: ullstein bild/The Granger Collection, New York

Roosevelt and Taft's Diplomacy

GUIDING QUESTION *Was President Roosevelt correct in his belief that a strong military presence promoted global peace?*

President McKinley was reelected in 1900, but his second term was cut short by an assassin's bullet. After McKinley's death in September 1901, Vice President Theodore Roosevelt assumed the presidency. Roosevelt favored increasing U.S. power. He also accepted some of Anglo-Saxonism's ideas. He believed that the United States had a duty to shape the "less civilized" corners of the Earth.

Balancing Power in East Asia

President Roosevelt supported the Open Door policy in China and worked to prevent any nation from controlling trade there. To that end, he helped negotiate a resolution to a war between Japan and Russia that had begun in 1904. At a 1905 peace conference, Roosevelt helped to mediate Russia's recognition of Japan's territorial gains. He also persuaded Japan to stop seeking further territory.

In the years after the treaty, relations between the United States and Japan steadily grew worse. As the two nations vied for greater influence in Asia, they pledged to respect each other's territorial possessions, uphold the Open Door policy, and support China's independence.

The Panama Canal

Roosevelt believed that displaying U.S. power to the world would deter nations from fighting. He expressed this belief with a West African saying, "Speak softly and carry a big stick." His "big stick" policy was evident in the U.S. acquisition and construction of the Panama Canal. He and others believed that having a canal through Central America was vital to U.S. power in the world and would save time and money for commercial and military shipping. In 1889, a French company abandoned its efforts to build a canal in Panama. In 1902 Congress authorized the U.S. purchase of the French company's assets and the construction of a canal.

Panama was a province of Colombia at that time. In 1903 the United States offered Colombia a large sum of money and yearly rent for the right to build the canal and to control a narrow strip of land on either side of it. When Colombia refused, **tension** increased between Colombia and Panamanians who opposed Colombian rule. Worried that the United States might back out of its offer, the French company met with Panamanian officials and decided to make a deal with the United States. In November 1903, with U.S. warships looming offshore, Panama revolted against Colombia. Within days, the United States recognized Panama's independence, and the two nations signed a treaty allowing the canal to be built, ensuring the canal stayed in Panama.

PHOTO: Bettmann/CORBIS

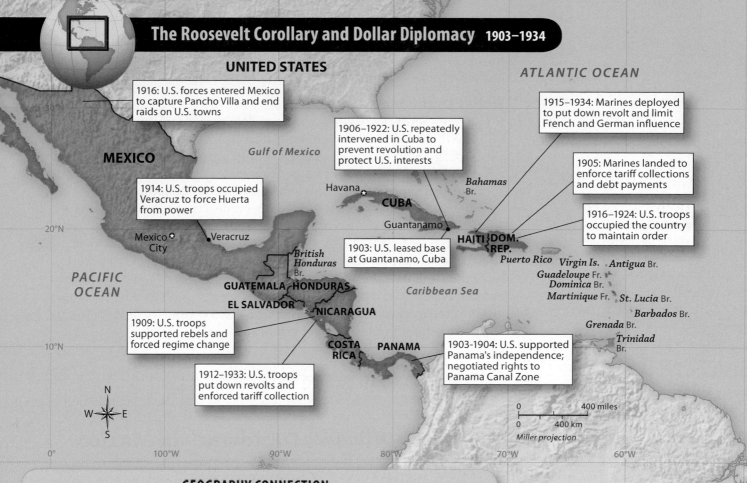

The Roosevelt Corollary and Dollar Diplomacy 1903–1934

UNITED STATES

ATLANTIC OCEAN

1916: U.S. forces entered Mexico to capture Pancho Villa and end raids on U.S. towns

1906–1922: U.S. repeatedly intervened in Cuba to prevent revolution and protect U.S. interests

1915–1934: Marines deployed to put down revolt and limit French and German influence

1905: Marines landed to enforce tariff collections and debt payments

1916–1924: U.S. troops occupied the country to maintain order

MEXICO

Gulf of Mexico

Havana

CUBA

Bahamas Br.

1914: U.S. troops occupied Veracruz to force Huerta from power

Guantanamo

Mexico City

Veracruz

1903: U.S. leased base at Guantanamo, Cuba

HAITI DOM. REP.

Puerto Rico   Virgin Is.   Antigua Br.

British Honduras Br.

Guadeloupe Fr.
Dominica Br.
Martinique Fr.   St. Lucia Br.

PACIFIC OCEAN

GUATEMALA HONDURAS

Caribbean Sea

Barbados Br.

EL SALVADOR

NICARAGUA

Grenada Br.

1909: U.S. troops supported rebels and forced regime change

COSTA RICA

PANAMA

Trinidad Br.

1912–1933: U.S. troops put down revolts and enforced tariff collection

1903-1904: U.S. supported Panama's independence; negotiated rights to Panama Canal Zone

N W E S

0   400 miles
0   400 km
Miller projection

0°   100°W   90°W   80°W   70°W   60°W

GEOGRAPHY CONNECTION

The United States became increasingly involved in the affairs of Latin America.

1 **HUMAN SYSTEMS** *What are the main reasons the United States intervened in Latin American states?*

2 **PLACES AND REGIONS** *Where did the United States invest the most money in Latin America? Why do you think this happened?*

During the construction, malaria and yellow fever, transmitted by mosquitoes, sickened workers and slowed their progress. By inspecting and controlling all potential breeding places, Surgeon General of the U.S. Army William Crawford Gorgas helped maintain a Canal Zone in which mosquitoes could not live. His efforts minimized disease and allowed workers to continue the building of the canal.

The Roosevelt Corollary

By the early 1900s, American officials had become concerned about large debts that Latin American nations owed European banks. In 1902, after Venezuela defaulted on its debts, Britain, Germany, and Italy blockaded Venezuelan ports. The crisis was resolved peacefully after the United States pressed both sides to reach an agreement. Roosevelt then gave an address to Congress in which he stated what came to be known as the Roosevelt Corollary to the Monroe Doctrine. It stated that the United States would intervene in Latin American affairs when necessary to maintain economic and political stability in the Western Hemisphere.

The goal of the Roosevelt Corollary was to prevent European powers from using the debt problems of Latin America to justify intervening in the region. The United States first applied the Roosevelt Corollary in the Dominican Republic, which had fallen behind on its debt payments to European nations. In 1905 the United States began collecting customs tariffs in the Dominican Republic, using the Marine Corps as its agent.

Dollar Diplomacy

Roosevelt's successor, William Howard Taft, placed less emphasis on military force and more on economic development. Taft believed that supporting Latin American industry would increase trade and profits for American businesses and lift Latin America countries out of poverty and social disorder. His policy came to be called **dollar diplomacy.**

To give Europeans less reason to intervene in Latin American affairs, Taft's administration worked to replace European loans with loans from American banks. In 1911 American bankers began making loans to Nicaragua to support its shaky government. The next year, civil unrest forced Nicaragua's president to ask for greater assistance. U.S. marines entered Nicaragua, replaced the customs collector with an American agent, and formed a committee to control the customs commissions. U.S. troops supported the government and customs until 1933.

> **dollar diplomacy** a policy of joining the business interests of a country with its diplomatic interests abroad

☑ **PROGRESS CHECK**

Explaining Why was it important for the United States to influence Latin American nations?

Woodrow Wilson's Diplomacy in Mexico

GUIDING QUESTION *How did "moral diplomacy" shape President Wilson's foreign policy?*

"It would be the irony of fate," said Woodrow Wilson just before he was inaugurated in 1913, "if my administration had to deal chiefly with foreign affairs." Wilson had written books on state government, Congress, and George Washington, as well as a history of the nation. His experience and interest were in domestic policy. He was a university professor before entering politics and was a committed progressive. Foreign affairs, however, absorbed much of Wilson's time and energy as president.

Wilson opposed imperialism. He believed that democracy was essential to a nation's stability and prosperity. He wanted the United States to promote democracy to create a world free of revolution and war. He hoped the United States would lead by moral example, but his first international crisis thwarted that hope.

The Mexican Revolution

For more than 30 years, Porfirio Díaz ruled Mexico as a dictator. During Díaz's reign, Mexico became much more industrialized, but foreign investors owned and financed the new railroads and factories that were built. Most Mexican citizens remained poor and landless. In 1910 discontent erupted into revolution. Francisco Madero, a reformer who seemed to support democracy, constitutional government, and land reform, led the revolution. Madero, however, proved to be an unskilled administrator. Worried about Madero's plans for land reform, conservative forces plotted against him. In 1913 General Victoriano Huerta seized power, and Madero was murdered.

Huerta's brutality repulsed Wilson, who refused to recognize the new government. Instead, Wilson announced a new policy. To win U.S. recognition, groups that seized power in Latin America would have to establish a government based on law, not on force. Wilson believed that, without U.S. support, Huerta soon would be overthrown. Meanwhile, Wilson ordered the navy to intercept arms shipments to Huerta's government. He also permitted Americans to arm Huerta's opponents.

Wilson Sends Troops Into Mexico

In April 1914, American sailors visiting the Mexican city of Tampico were arrested after entering a restricted area. Although they were quickly released, their American commander demanded an apology. The Mexicans refused. Wilson saw the refusal as an opportunity to overthrow Huerta. He asked Congress to authorize the use of force, and shortly after Congress passed the resolution, he learned that a German ship was unloading weapons at the Mexican port of Veracruz. Wilson immediately ordered American warships to Veracruz, where U.S. marines forcibly seized the city.

Although the president expected the Mexican people to welcome his action, anti-American riots broke out. Wilson then accepted international mediation to settle the dispute. Venustiano Carranza, whose forces had acquired arms from the United States, became Mexico's president.

Mexican forces opposed to Carranza were not appeased, and they conducted raids into the United States, hoping to force Wilson to intervene. In March 1916, Pancho Villa (VEE•yuh) and a group of **guerrillas**—armed fighters who carry out surprise attacks—burned the town of Columbus, New Mexico, killing 17 Americans. Wilson responded by sending about 5,800 troops under General John J. Pershing across the border to find and capture Villa. The expedition dragged on with no success. Wilson's growing concern over the war raging in Europe finally caused him to recall Pershing's troops in 1917.

Wilson's Mexican policy damaged U.S. foreign relations. The British ridiculed the president's attempt to "shoot" the Mexicans into self-government. Latin Americans regarded his "moral imperialism" as no improvement over Theodore Roosevelt's "big stick" diplomacy. In fact, Wilson followed Roosevelt's example in the Caribbean. In 1914 he negotiated exclusive rights for naval bases and a canal with Nicaragua. In 1915 he sent marines into Haiti to put down a rebellion. The marines remained there until 1934. In 1916 he sent troops into the Dominican Republic to preserve order and to set up a government he hoped would be more stable and democratic than the current regime.

☑ **PROGRESS CHECK**

Examining Why did President Wilson's "moral diplomacy" not accomplish its intended purpose?

BIOGRAPHY

General John J. Pershing 1860–1948

During the Spanish-American War, General John J. Pershing earned the praise of his superior officers, one of whom said that Pershing was "the coolest and bravest man I ever saw under fire." Pershing was made commander of the expedition into Mexico to capture Pancho Villa. Though the mission failed, it made Pershing a respected public figure.

▶ **CRITICAL THINKING**

Predicting After the failed expedition to capture Villa, what was the next military conflict in which General Pershing commanded troops?

guerrillas armed fighters who carry out surprise attacks

LESSON 3 REVIEW

Reviewing Vocabulary

1. *Explaining* How did the Open Door policy help prevent any one nation from monopolizing trade with China?

Using Your Notes

2. *Identifying* Use your notes to identify major reasons that the United States wanted to build a canal through Central America.

Answering the Guiding Questions

3. *Analyzing* Why did the United States want to eliminate spheres of influence in China?

4. *Evaluating* Was President Roosevelt correct in his belief that a strong military presence promoted global peace?

5. *Comparing and Contrasting* How did "moral diplomacy" shape President Wilson's foreign policy?

Writing Activity

6. **EXPOSITORY** Suppose that you are a Mexican citizen during Wilson's presidency. Write a radio news broadcast expressing your feelings about American actions in Mexico.

Directions: On a separate sheet of paper, answer the questions below. Make sure you read carefully and answer all parts to the question.

Lesson Review

Lesson 1

1 *Identifying* Why did the United States support sugar planters in their attempt to overthrow Queen Liliuokalani?

2 *Explaining* Why did James G. Blaine convene the Pan-American conference in 1889?

Lesson 2

3 *Summarizing* What were the main results of the United States victory in the Spanish-American War?

4 *Evaluating* How did Filipinos feel about the U.S. government after the Spanish-American War?

Lesson 3

5 *Identifying* Why did the United States decide to build a canal through Panama? How did Roosevelt assist Panama in becoming independent?

6 *Analyzing* How did the Roosevelt Corollary and dollar diplomacy affect U.S. relations with other countries?

21st Century Skills

7 **IDENTIFYING PERSPECTIVE AND DIFFERING INTERPRETATIONS** After helping the United States defeat Spain during the Spanish-American War, how did Filipinos react to the news that the United States would annex their nation?

8 **GEOGRAPHY SKILLS** What role did Hawaii play in the expansion of American trade to the countries of East Asia?

9 **DECISION MAKING** Describe the opposing sides in the U.S. decision to annex the Philippines.

10 **ECONOMICS** How was the United States economy affected by the 1898 Treaty of Paris, the Open Door policy, and dollar diplomacy?

Exploring the Essential Question

11 *Determining Cause and Effect* Create a cause-and-effect diagram that identifies the causes of American imperialism and the effects they had on the emergence of the United States as a world power.

DBQ Document-Based Questions

Use the document to answer the following questions.

Carl Schurz, the leader of the liberal wing of the Republican Party, opposed American expansion abroad. In the following excerpt, Schurz attacks the arguments for taking over the Philippine Islands:

PRIMARY SOURCE

❝ Many imperialists admit that our trade with the Philippines themselves will not nearly be worth its cost; but they say that we must have the Philippines as a foothold . . . for the expansion of our trade on the Asiatic continent, especially in China. Admitting this . . . I ask what kind of a foothold we should really need. . . . And now I ask further, whether we could not easily have had these things if we had, instead of making war upon the Filipinos, favored the independence of the islands. Everybody knows that we could. We might have those things now for the mere asking if we stopped the war and came to a friendly understanding with the Filipinos tomorrow. . . . ❞

—quoted in *The Policy of Imperialism*

12 What does Schurz believe is necessary to establish a foothold in trade with Asia?

13 What action does Schurz suggest the United States could have taken to obtain trade with Asia?

Extended Response Question

14 Discuss U.S. foreign policy during the late 1800s and early 1900s. How were the various countries and regions of the world changed by the policies of the United States? Write an expository essay that includes an introduction, several paragraphs, and a conclusion that supports your position.

Need Extra Help?

If You've Missed Question	1	2	3	4	5	6	7	8	9	10	11	12	13	14
Go to page	338	339	344	345	348	349	345	338	343	343	336	352	352	338

The Progressive Movement

1890–1920

ESSENTIAL QUESTION • *Can politics fix social problems?*

netw⬤rks

There's More Online about the Progressive movement and the changes it made.

CHAPTER 15

The Story Matters...

Today we assume that our foods and medicines are safe, but in the 1800s, that was not so. Through the efforts of the progressives, who wanted to improve life for all Americans, changes were made that not only safeguarded food and medicine, but also gave women the right to vote, improved working conditions, and conserved the nation's natural places.

◀ Alice Paul, a Quaker social worker, fought militantly for woman suffrage, enduring several incarcerations for her efforts to win women the right to vote.

PHOTO: The Granger Collection, New York

Industrialization changed American society. Cities were crowded, working conditions were often poor, and the political system was unresponsive. These conditions gave rise to the Progressive movement. Led by journalists, clergy, social workers, and other concerned citizens, the Progressive movement campaigned for both political and social reforms.

Step Into the Place

Read the quotes and look at the information presented on the map.

 As the United States became an industrialized nation, how did the government address the rapid exploitation of public lands and natural resources?

PRIMARY SOURCE

"We have become great because of the lavish use of our resources and we have just reason to be proud of our growth. But the time has come to inquire seriously what will happen when our forests are gone, when the coal, the iron, the oil and the gas are exhausted, when the soils shall have been still further impoverished and washed into the streams, polluting the rivers, denuding the fields and obstructing navigation."

—President Theodore Roosevelt, from a speech delivered at the Conference on the Conservation of the Nation's Resources, 1908

PRIMARY SOURCE

"The first principle of conservation is development, the use of the natural resources now existing on this continent for the benefit of the people who live here now. There may be just as much waste in neglecting the development and use of certain natural resources as there is in their destruction. . . .

Conservation stands emphatically for the development and use of water-power now, without delay. It stands for the immediate construction of navigable waterways . . . as assistants to the railroads. . . .

In addition . . . natural resources must be developed and preserved for the benefit of the many, and not merely for the profit of the few."

— Gifford Pinchot, Chief of U.S. Forest Service, from *The Fight for Conservation*, 1910

Step Into the Time

Choose an event from the time line and write a paragraph that suggests how the event might have impacted social reform.

1889 Jane Addams opens Hull House in Chicago

| | B. Harrison 1889–1893 | Cleveland 1893–1897 | McKinley 1897–1901 | T. Roosevelt 1901–1909 |

U.S. PRESIDENTS

UNITED STATES

WORLD

1890   1895   1900

1884 Toynbee Hall, the first settlement house, is established in London

1891 Australian Woman Suffrage League founded in Sydney

1893 New Zealand becomes the first nation to grant suffrage to women

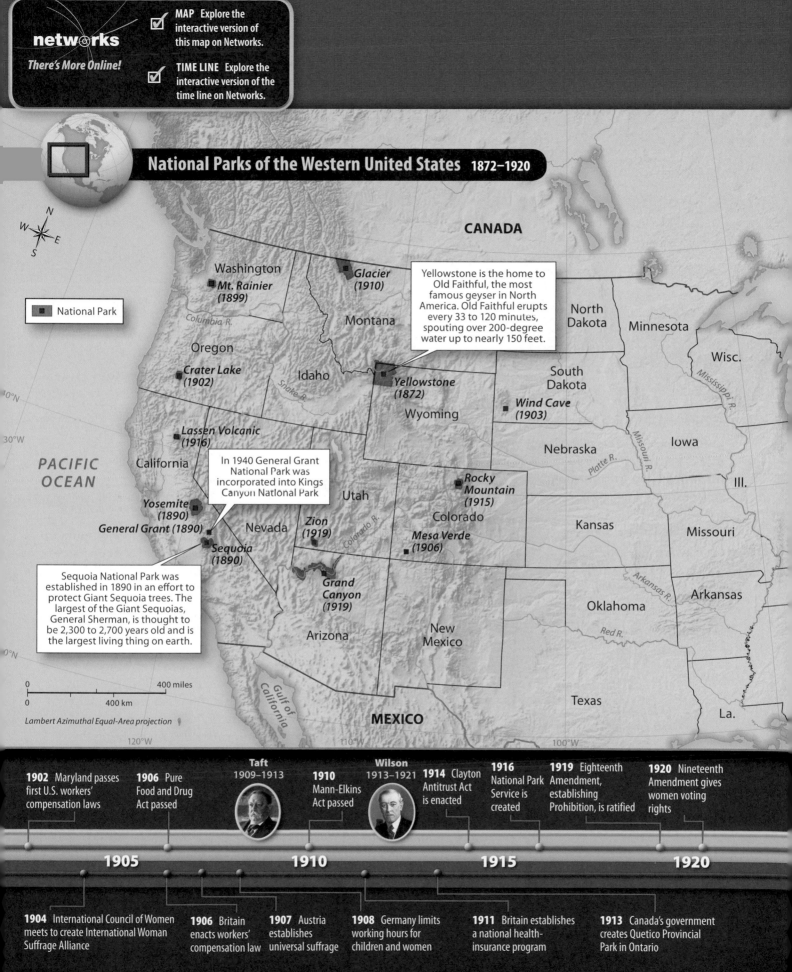

networks

There's More Online!

☑ **MAP** Explore the interactive version of this map on Networks.

☑ **TIME LINE** Explore the interactive version of the time line on Networks.

National Parks of the Western United States 1872–1920

CANADA

Washington
Mt. Rainier (1899)

Glacier (1910)

Montana

Columbia R.

Oregon

Crater Lake (1902)

Idaho

Snake R.

Yellowstone (1872)

Wyoming

Yellowstone is the home to Old Faithful, the most famous geyser in North America. Old Faithful erupts every 33 to 120 minutes, spouting over 200-degree water up to nearly 150 feet.

North Dakota

Minnesota

Wisc.

Mississippi R.

South Dakota

Wind Cave (1903)

■ National Park

40°N

Lassen Volcanic (1916)

30°W

California

In 1940 General Grant National Park was incorporated into Kings Canyon National Park

Utah

Nebraska

Missouri R.

Platte R.

Iowa

Ill.

PACIFIC OCEAN

Yosemite (1890)

General Grant (1890)

Sequoia (1890)

Nevada

Zion (1919)

Colorado R.

Rocky Mountain (1915)

Colorado

Mesa Verde (1906)

Kansas

Missouri

Sequoia National Park was established in 1890 in an effort to protect Giant Sequoia trees. The largest of the Giant Sequoias, General Sherman, is thought to be 2,300 to 2,700 years old and is the largest living thing on earth.

Grand Canyon (1919)

Arkansas R.

Arkansas

Oklahoma

Red R.

0°N

Arizona

New Mexico

Gulf of California

Texas

La.

0   400 miles

0   400 km

Lambert Azimuthal Equal-Area projection

MEXICO

120°W   110°W   100°W

Taft 1909–1913

Wilson 1913–1921

1902 Maryland passes first U.S. workers' compensation laws

1906 Pure Food and Drug Act passed

1910 Mann-Elkins Act passed

1914 Clayton Antitrust Act is enacted

1916 National Park Service is created

1919 Eighteenth Amendment, establishing Prohibition, is ratified

1920 Nineteenth Amendment gives women voting rights

1905   **1910**   **1915**   **1920**

1904 International Council of Women meets to create International Woman Suffrage Alliance

1906 Britain enacts workers' compensation law

1907 Austria establishes universal suffrage

1908 Germany limits working hours for children and women

1911 Britain establishes a national health-insurance program

1913 Canada's government creates Quetico Provincial Park in Ontario

Reading **HELP**DESK

Content Vocabulary

- muckraker
- direct primary
- initiative
- referendum
- recall
- suffrage
- prohibition

Academic Vocabulary

- legislation
- advocate

TAKING NOTES: *Organizing*

ACTIVITY As you read about the beginnings of progressivism, complete a graphic organizer similar to the one below by filling in the beliefs of progressives.

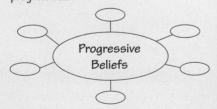

Progressive Beliefs

LESSON 1
The Roots of Progressivism

ESSENTIAL QUESTION • *Can politics fix social problems?*

IT MATTERS BECAUSE

The Progressive Era was a time when many Americans tried to improve their society. They tried to make government honest, efficient, and more democratic. The movement for woman suffrage gained more support, as did efforts to limit child labor and reduce alcohol abuse.

The Rise of Progressivism

GUIDING QUESTION *Who were progressives, and what did they believe caused social problems?*

Progressivism was a collection of different ideas and activities, not a tightly organized political movement with a specific set of goals. Rather, it was a series of responses to problems in American society that had emerged from the growth of industry. Progressives had many different ideas about how to fix the problems they saw in American society.

Who Were the Progressives?

Progressivism was partly a reaction against laissez-faire economics and its emphasis on an unregulated market. Progressives generally believed that industrialization and urbanization had created many social problems. After seeing the poverty of the working class and the filth and crime of urban society, reformers began doubting the free market's ability to address those problems.

Progressives belonged to both major political parties. Most were urban, educated, middle-class Americans. Among their leaders were journalists, social workers, educators, politicians, and members of the clergy. Most agreed that government should take a more active role in solving society's problems. At the same time, they doubted that the government in its present form could fix those problems. They concluded that government had to be fixed before it could be used to fix other problems.

One reason progressives thought they could improve society was their strong faith in science and technology. The application of scientific knowledge had produced the lightbulb, the telephone,

PHOTOS: (l to r)Bettmann/CORBIS, Library of Congress, Keystone/Hulton Archive/Getty Images, Library of Congress

and the automobile. It had built skyscrapers and railroads. Science and technology had benefited people; thus, progressives believed using scientific principles could also produce solutions for society.

The Muckrakers

Among the first people to articulate progressive ideas was a group of crusading journalists who investigated social conditions and political corruption. President Theodore Roosevelt nicknamed these writers **"muckrakers"** because of what he perceived as their obsession with scandal and corruption. Widely circulated, cheap newspapers and magazines helped spread the muckrakers' ideas.

Muckrakers uncovered corruption in many areas. Some, such as Ida Tarbell and Charles Edward Russell, concentrated on exposing the unfair practices of large corporations. Other muckrakers targeted government and social problems. Lincoln Steffens reported on vote stealing and other corrupt political practices of political machines.

Still other muckrakers concentrated on social problems. In his influential book *How the Other Half Lives* (1890), Jacob Riis published photographs and descriptions of the poverty, disease, and crime that afflicted many immigrant neighborhoods in New York City. By raising awareness of these problems, the muckrakers stimulated calls for reform.

muckraker a journalist who uncovers abuses and corruption in a society

✓ **PROGRESS CHECK**

Stating What groups of people made up the Progressive movement?

Reforming Government

GUIDING QUESTION *How did progressives hope to make government more efficient and responsive to citizens?*

Progressivism included a wide range of reform activities. Different issues led to different approaches, and some progressives even took opposing positions on how to address some problems. They condemned government corruption but did not always agree on the best way to fix the problem.

Progressive photographer Jacob Riis captured the poverty, disease, and crime common in many of New York City's immigrant neighborhoods.

▶ **CRITICAL THINKING**
Determining Cause and Effect What did progressives believe caused the social problems that Riis photographed?

direct primary a vote held by all members of a political party to decide their candidate for public office

initiative the right of citizens to place a measure or issue before the voters or the legislature for approval

legislation a proposed law to be voted on by a governing body

referendum the practice of letting voters accept or reject measures proposed by the legislature

recall the right that enables voters to remove unsatisfactory elected officials from office

Making Government Efficient

One group of progressives drew its ideas for increasing government efficiency from business. Theories of business efficiency first became popular in the 1890s. Books such as Frederick W. Taylor's *The Principles of Scientific Management* (1911) described how a company could increase efficiency by managing time, breaking tasks down into small parts, and using standardized tools—a scientific approach to business that some progressives wanted to extend to government.

Progressives saw corruption and inefficiency in city government. Many municipal leaders traditionally chose political supporters and friends to run city departments, even though these people often knew little about managing city services.

Progressives supported proposals to reform city government. One, a commission plan, divided city government into several departments, with each one under an expert commissioner's control. A second, a council-manager system, employed a city manager who was hired by the city council. In both systems, experts play a major role in managing the city. Galveston, Texas, adopted the commission system in 1901. In other cities, political machines were weakened by having officials elected city-wide instead of by neighborhoods.

Democratic Reforms

Another group of progressives focused on making government more democratic and more responsive to citizens. Many believed that the key to improving government was to make elected officials more responsive and accountable to voters.

Wisconsin became a "laboratory of democracy" under the leadership of its governor, Robert M. La Follette, who attacked the way political parties ran their conventions. Party bosses controlled the selection of convention delegates and the nomination of candidates. La Follette pressured the state legislature to pass a law requiring parties to hold a **direct primary,** in which all party members could vote for a candidate to run in the general election.

The direct primary soon spread to other states. Other progressives also pushed for additional reforms: the initiative, the referendum, and the recall. The **initiative** permitted a group of citizens to introduce **legislation** and required the legislature to vote on the legislation. The **referendum** allowed citizens to vote on proposed laws directly, without going to the legislature. Both of these measures empowered public interest groups to speed change. The **recall** provided voters an option to demand a special election to remove an elected official from office before his or her term had expired.

Progressives also targeted the U.S. Senate. The U.S. Constitution originally directed each state legislature to elect two senators. Political machines and business interests often influenced these elections. Some senators, once elected, repaid their supporters with federal contracts and jobs. To counter corruption in the Senate, reformers called for the direct election of senators by voters. In 1912 Congress passed a direct-election amendment. In 1913 the amendment was ratified and became the Seventeenth Amendment to the Constitution. Although direct election was meant to end corruption, it also removed one of the state legislatures' checks on federal power.

✔ **PROGRESS CHECK**

Summarizing How did progressives hope to solve problems through political reform?

In 1900 the political machine running Galveston, Texas, failed to help the city recover from a devastating hurricane, so local business leaders convinced the state to allow them to take control.

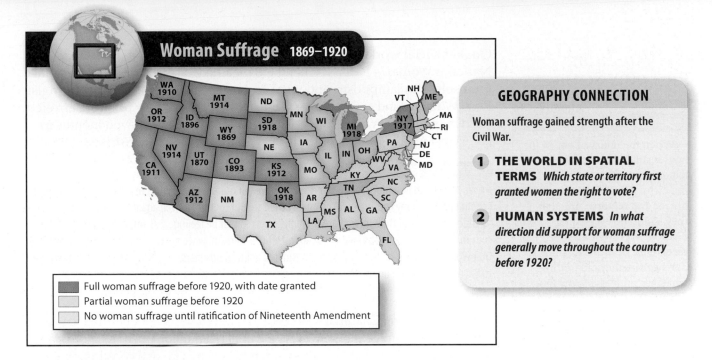

Woman Suffrage 1869–1920

GEOGRAPHY CONNECTION

Woman suffrage gained strength after the Civil War.

1 **THE WORLD IN SPATIAL TERMS** *Which state or territory first granted women the right to vote?*

2 **HUMAN SYSTEMS** *In what direction did support for woman suffrage generally move throughout the country before 1920?*

Full woman suffrage before 1920, with date granted
Partial woman suffrage before 1920
No woman suffrage until ratification of Nineteenth Amendment

Woman Suffrage

GUIDING QUESTION *Why did the progressives support the woman suffrage movement?*

At the first women's rights convention in Seneca Falls, New York, in 1848, Elizabeth Cady Stanton convinced the delegates that winning **suffrage**—the right to vote—should be a priority. Decades later, this right still had not been gained. It became a major goal for female progressives.

suffrage the right to vote

Early Challenges

The woman suffrage movement started slowly. Suffragists were threatened and called unfeminine and immoral. Many of the movement's supporters were abolitionists as well, and in the years before the Civil War, ending slavery took priority over women's voting rights.

After the Civil War, Congress introduced the Fourteenth and Fifteenth Amendments to grant citizenship to African Americans and voting rights to African American men. Leaders of the woman suffrage movement wanted these amendments to give women the right to vote as well. They were disappointed when established politicians refused.

The debate over these two amendments split the movement into two groups: the New York City–based National Woman Suffrage Association, founded by Stanton and Susan B. Anthony in 1869, and the Boston-based American Woman Suffrage Association, led by Lucy Stone and Julia Ward Howe. The first group wanted to focus on passing a constitutional amendment. The second believed that the best strategy was convincing state governments to grant women the right to vote first. This split weakened the suffrage movement. By 1900, only Wyoming, Idaho, Utah, and Colorado had granted women full voting rights.

Building Support

In 1890 the two groups united to form the National American Woman Suffrage Association (NAWSA). The movement still faced the challenge of convincing women to become politically active. As the Progressive movement gained momentum, however, many women realized that they needed the vote to promote reforms and pass labor laws. Women began lobbying lawmakers, organizing marches, and delivering speeches.

❝When the injury of one of the boys resulted in his death, we felt quite sure that the owners of the factory would share our horror and remorse, and that they would do everything possible to prevent the recurrence of such a tragedy. To our surprise they did nothing whatever, and I made my first acquaintance then with those pathetic documents signed by the parents of working children, that they will make no claim for damages resulting from 'carelessness'.❞

—from *Twenty Years at Hull House*, 1910

DBQ **DRAWING INFERENCES**

Based on this excerpt, what insight does Addams's description offer about the progressives' view of child labor and the conditions in factories?

Quaker social worker and former NAWSA member Alice Paul founded the National Woman's Party. Its members picketed, blocked sidewalks, chained themselves to lampposts, and went on hunger strikes if arrested. Suffragist Rose Winslow and several other women, including Alice Paul, were arrested for picketing the White House. After being sentenced to seven months in jail, Winslow and other women prisoners went on a hunger strike.

PRIMARY SOURCE

❝We have been in solitary for five weeks. . . . I have felt quite feeble the last few days—faint, so that I could hardly get my hair brushed, my arms ached so. But today I am well again. . . . [Alice Paul] dreaded forcible feeding frightfully, and I hate to think how she must be feeling. . . . I am really all right. If this continues very long perhaps I won't be. All the officers here know we are making this hunger strike [so] that women fighting for liberty may be considered political prisoners. . . . [W]e don't want women ever to have to do this over again.❞

—Rose Winslow, quoted in *Jailed for Freedom*, 1920

In 1915 Carrie Chapman Catt became NAWSA's leader and tried to mobilize the suffrage movement in one final nationwide push. As more states granted women the right to vote, Congress began to favor a constitutional amendment. In 1918 the House of Representatives passed a woman suffrage amendment. In the Senate, however, the amendment failed by two votes.

During the midterm elections of 1918, Catt used NAWSA's resources to defeat two antisuffrage senators. In 1919 the Senate passed the amendment by slightly more than the two-thirds vote needed. On August 26, 1920, after three-fourths of the states had ratified it, the Nineteenth Amendment guaranteeing women the right to vote went into effect.

✓ **PROGRESS CHECK**

Identifying Cause and Effect What progressive goals did suffragists believe they could achieve if women had the right to vote?

Reforming Society

GUIDING QUESTION *What problems did social-welfare progressives attempt to reform?*

While many progressives focused on reforming the political system, others focused on social problems, such as crime, illiteracy, alcohol abuse, child labor, and the health and safety of Americans. These social-welfare progressives created charities to help the poor and disadvantaged. They also pushed for new laws they hoped would fix social problems.

Many progressives focused on fixing social-welfare problems, such as child labor.

▶ **CRITICAL THINKING**

Drawing Conclusions Why do you think progressives made their fight against child labor a key issue?

Child Labor

Probably the most emotional progressive issue was the campaign against child labor. Children had always worked on family farms, but mines and factories presented more dangerous and unhealthy working conditions. Muckraker John Spargo's 1906 book, *The Bitter Cry of the Children,* presented detailed evidence of child labor conditions. It told of coal mines that hired thousands of 9- or 10-year-old "breaker boys" to pick slag out of coal, paying them 60 cents for a 10-hour day. It described how the work bent their backs permanently and often crippled their hands. Reports like these convinced states to pass laws that set a minimum age for employment and established other limits on child labor, such as maximum hours children could work. At the same time, many states began passing compulsory education laws, requiring young children to be in school instead of at work.

Health and Safety Codes

Many adult workers also labored in difficult conditions. Factories, coal mines, and railroads were particularly dangerous. When workers were injured or killed on the job, they and their families received little or no compensation. Progressives joined union leaders to pressure states for workers' compensation laws. These laws established insurance funds that employers financed. Workers injured in accidents received payments from the funds.

In two cases, *Lochner* v. *New York* (1905) and *Muller* v. *Oregon* (1908), the U.S. Supreme Court addressed government's authority to regulate business to protect workers. In the *Lochner* case, the Court ruled that a New York law forbidding bakers to work more than 10 hours a day was unconstitutional, saying the state did not have the right to interfere with the liberty of employers and employees. In the *Muller* case, which involved women working in laundries in Oregon, however, the Court upheld the state's right to limit hours. The different judgments were based on gender differences. The Court stated that healthy mothers were the state's concern and, therefore, the limits on women's working hours did not violate their Fourteenth Amendment rights.

On March 25, 1911, a tragedy occurred in New York City that led to new reforms. A fire on the top floors of the Triangle Shirtwaist Company caused nearly 150 of the factory's 500 workers to lose their lives. The disaster illustrated that fire precautions and inspections were inadequate. In response, New York created a Factory Investigating Commission and soon passed new laws that reformed the labor code.

Some progressives also favored zoning laws as a method of protecting the public. These laws divided a town or city into zones for commercial, residential, or other development, thereby regulating how land and buildings could be used. Building codes set minimum standards for light, air, room size, and sanitation and required buildings to have fire escapes. Health codes required restaurants and other facilities to maintain clean environments for their patrons.

The Prohibition Movement

Many progressives blamed alcohol for many of society's problems. Settlement-house workers knew that wages were often spent on alcohol and that drunkenness often led to physical abuse and illness. Some employers believed drinking hurt workers' efficiency. From these concerns emerged the temperance movement, which **advocated** that people stop, or at least moderate, their alcohol consumption.

Women were important leaders of the temperance movement. In 1874 a group of women formed the Woman's Christian Temperance Union

BIOGRAPHY

Florence Kelley
(1859–1932)

Progressive Florence Kelley dedicated her life to campaigning for reforms. While working at Chicago's Hull House in the 1890s, she conducted research that encouraged the passage of the first law banning children younger than 14 from factory work. Later, she contributed to the foundation of the United States Children's Bureau to protect children. Her research on the effects of long workdays on women's health contributed to the Supreme Court's decision in *Muller* v. *Oregon*.

▶ **CRITICAL THINKING**
Making Generalizations In what areas did Florence Kelley's actions contribute to significant reform?

advocate to propose a certain position or viewpoint

The temperance movement gained a key victory in 1917 when Congress passed the Eighteenth Amendment. Prohibition went into effect in 1920, after the amendment was ratified.

▶ **CRITICAL THINKING**
Summarizing Why did the temperance movement push for the prohibition of alcoholic beverages?

prohibition laws banning the manufacture, transportation, and sale of alcoholic beverages

(WCTU). By 1911, the WCTU had nearly 250,000 members. As the WCTU's second president, Frances Willard served for nearly 20 years and championed rights for women, including equal pay and suffrage. In 1893 evangelical Protestant ministers formed another group, the Anti-Saloon League. When the temperance movement began, it concentrated on reducing alcohol consumption. Later it pressed for **prohibition**—laws banning the manufacture, transportation, and sale of alcoholic beverages.

Progressives Versus Big Business

Many progressives agreed that big business needed regulation. Some believed the government should break up big companies to restore competition. This led to the passage of the Sherman Antitrust Act in 1890. Others argued that big business was the most efficient way to organize the economy. They pushed for government to regulate big companies and prevent them from abusing their power. The Interstate Commerce Commission (ICC), created in 1887 to regulate the railroads, was an early example of this kind of thinking.

Some activists even went so far as to advocate socialism—the idea that the government should own and operate industry for the community. They wanted the government to buy up large companies, especially industries that affected everyone, such as railroads and utilities. At its peak, socialism had some national support. Eugene V. Debs, the former leader of the American Railway Union, won nearly a million votes as the American Socialist Party candidate for president in 1912. Most progressives and most Americans, however, believed in the superiority of the American system of free enterprise.

✓ **PROGRESS CHECK**
Explaining How did progressives seek to improve working conditions?

LESSON 1 REVIEW

Reviewing Vocabulary
1. *Drawing Conclusions* What was the primary goal of Progressive Era muckrakers?

2. *Determining Cause and Effect* Why did women's organizations work for the passage of prohibition?

Using Your Notes
3. *Organizing* Use your notes to write a statement summarizing progressive beliefs.

Answering the Guiding Questions
4. *Identifying Central Issues* Who were progressives, and what did they believe caused social problems?

5. *Summarizing* How did progressives hope to make government more efficient and responsive to citizens?

6. *Monitoring* Why did the progressives support the woman suffrage movement?

7. *Identifying* What problems did social-welfare progressives attempt to reform?

Writing Activity
8. **PERSUASIVE** Suppose that you are one of the progressives who wanted to bring about change to municipal government. Prepare a persuasive speech that you could deliver to convince people to support your call for reform.

networks

There's More Online!

- ☑ **BIOGRAPHY** Upton Sinclair
- ☑ **BIOGRAPHY** Gifford Pinchot
- ☑ **VIDEO** Roosevelt and Taft
- ☑ **INTERACTIVE SELF-CHECK QUIZ**

LESSON 2
Roosevelt and Taft

ESSENTIAL QUESTION · *Can politics fix social problems?*

Reading **HELP**DESK

Content Vocabulary

- **Social Darwinism**
- **arbitration**
- **insubordination**

Academic Vocabulary

- **regulate**
- **environmental**

TAKING NOTES: *Outlining*

ACTIVITY As you read about the Roosevelt and Taft administrations, use the headings from the lesson to create an outline similar to the one below.

Roosevelt and Taft
I. Roosevelt Revives the Presidency
  A.
  B.
  C.
II.

IT MATTERS BECAUSE

Energetic and strong-willed, Theodore Roosevelt extended the federal government's ability to conserve natural resources and to curb the power of big business. His successor, William Howard Taft, was less popular with progressives.

Roosevelt Revives the Presidency

GUIDING QUESTION *How much do you think a president's personal beliefs should shape national policy?*

Theodore Roosevelt became president at age 42—the youngest person ever to take the office. In international affairs, he believed in **Social Darwinism,** which held that nations were in competition and only the strongest would survive. Domestically, however, he was a committed progressive. He believed that government should balance the needs of competing groups in American society on behalf of the public interest. His reform programs soon became known as the Square Deal.

Roosevelt Takes on the Trusts

Roosevelt thought that trusts and other large business organizations were efficient and part of the reason for the prosperity of the United States. Yet he also felt that the monopoly power of some trusts hurt the public interest. He wanted to ensure that trusts did not abuse their power.

His first target was J. P. Morgan's railroad holding company, Northern Securities. The company planned an exchange of stock that would merge existing railroad systems, creating a monopoly on railroad traffic in the Northwest. Farmers and business owners feared that without railroad competition, shipping rates would rise and reduce their profits. In 1902 Roosevelt ordered the attorney general to sue Northern Securities under the Sherman Antitrust Act. The suit charged Northern Securities with restraint of trade.

Wealthy, powerful businessmen, including John D. Rockefeller (top right) and J. P. Morgan (right) tower over Theodore Roosevelt, who stands on Wall Street, carrying a sword labeled "Public Service."

▶ **CRITICAL THINKING**

1 *Analyzing* What do the giants in the political cartoon represent?

2 *Inferring* What point does the cartoon make by picturing Roosevelt as tiny in relation to the giants?

Social Darwinism
a philosophy, based on Charles Darwin's theories of evolution and natural selection, stating that humans have developed through competition and natural selection with only the strongest surviving

The suit puzzled J. P. Morgan, who asked what could be done to fix the problem. Unmoved, Roosevelt proceeded with the case. In 1904, in *Northern Securities* v. *United States,* the Supreme Court ruled that Morgan's firm had violated the Sherman Antitrust Act. Roosevelt was hailed as a "trustbuster," and his popularity with the public grew.

The Coal Strike of 1902

As president, Roosevelt believed that it was his job to keep society operating efficiently by helping settle conflicts between different groups and their interests. In the fall of 1902, he put this belief into practice. He worked to help resolve a coal strike between mine owners and nearly 150,000 members of the United Mine Workers (UMW). The UMW wanted increased pay, reduced hours, and union recognition. If the strike had dragged on, the nation would have faced a coal shortage that could have shut down factories and left many homes unheated.

arbitration settling a dispute by agreeing to accept the decision of an impartial outsider

Roosevelt urged the UMW and the mine owners to accept **arbitration**—a settlement negotiated by an outside party. The union agreed to arbitration. The mine owners refused, however, until Roosevelt threatened to order the army to run the mines. By intervening in the dispute, he took the first step toward establishing the federal government as an honest broker between powerful groups in society.

Regulating Big Business

regulate to control or direct with rules

Despite his lawsuit against Northern Securities and his role in the coal strike, Roosevelt believed that most trusts benefited the economy. He held that breaking up the trusts would do more harm than good. Instead, he proposed to create a federal agency to investigate corporations and publicize the findings. Roosevelt believed the most effective way to prevent big business from abusing its power was to keep the public informed.

environmental relating to the environment; the complex system of plants, animals, water, and soil

In 1903 Roosevelt convinced Congress to create the Department of Commerce and Labor. The following year, this department began investigating U.S. Steel, a gigantic holding company that had been created in 1901. Worried about a possible antitrust lawsuit, the company's leaders met privately with Roosevelt. They offered to open their files for examination. In exchange, the Department of Commerce and Labor would privately tell the company about any problems and allow them to fix the problems quietly. Roosevelt accepted this "gentlemen's agreement," as he called it, and soon made similar deals with other companies. These deals gave him the ability to **regulate** big business without having to sacrifice economic efficiency by breaking up the trusts.

In keeping with his belief in regulation, Roosevelt pushed the Hepburn Act through Congress in 1906. The act was intended to strengthen the Interstate Commerce Commission (ICC) by giving it the power to set railroad rates. At first, railroad companies were suspicious of the ICC. However, the railroads eventually realized they could work with the commission to set rates and regulations that limited competition and prevented new competitors from entering the industry. By 1920, the ICC had begun setting rates at levels intended to ensure the industry's profits.

By 1905, consumer protection had become a national issue. Journalists and others reported on questionable and potentially dangerous practices of the manufacturers of patent medicines. They revealed that many of these medicines contained unknown ingredients and that the manufacturers made unproven health claims. For similar reasons, food preparation businesses came under scrutiny. In 1906 Upton Sinclair published a novel, *The Jungle*, based on his close observations of the slaughterhouses of Chicago. The appalling conditions in the meatpacking industry, as described by Sinclair, enraged consumers. The government responded by passing the Meat Inspection Act and the Pure Food and Drug Act on the same day in 1906. It helped businesses by enlarging consumer confidence in their products.

✔ PROGRESS CHECK

Analyzing What were Theodore Roosevelt's beliefs about big business, and how did he act on those beliefs during the early 1900s?

Conservation

GUIDING QUESTION *Why did President Roosevelt support conservation?*

Of all his progressive actions, Roosevelt may be best remembered for his efforts in the area of **environmental** conservation. Roosevelt realized that the nation's bountiful natural resources were being used up at an alarming rate. He urged Americans to conserve those resources.

Roosevelt was an enthusiastic outdoorsman, and he valued the country's minerals, animals, and rugged terrain. He cautioned against unregulated use of public lands and argued that conservation should be the guiding principle in managing the United States's natural resources.

In his 1907 annual message to Congress, Roosevelt said: "[T]o waste, to destroy our natural resources, to skin and exhaust the land instead of using it so as to increase its usefulness, will result in undermining in the days of our children the very prosperity which we ought by right to hand down to them amplified and developed."

Western Land Development

Roosevelt quickly applied his philosophy in the dry Western states, where farmers and city dwellers competed for scarce water. In 1902 Roosevelt supported passage of the Newlands Reclamation Act.

Analyzing PRIMARY SOURCES

Upton Sinclair on the Meatpacking Industry

❝[T]here would come all the way back from Europe old sausage that had been rejected, and that was [moldy] and white—it would be dosed with borax and glycerine, and dumped into the hoppers, and made over again for home consumption. . . . There would be meat stored in great piles in rooms; and the water from leaky roofs would drip over it, and thousands of rats would race about [upon] it.❞

—from *The Jungle*, 1906

DBQ **DRAWING INFERENCES**
Based on this excerpt, how would you describe the attitude of slaughterhouse owners in Sinclair's time?

American naturalist John Muir looks out over Yosemite. Muir believed in preserving wilderness areas and successfully lobbied for the creation of Yosemite National Park.

**Gifford Pinchot
(1865–1946)**

Connecticut native Gifford Pinchot studied forestry at schools in Europe before becoming head of the U.S. Forest Service. As head, he helped develop the forest service system and was influential in the conservation movement, which he enthusiastically supported. He advocated wise use of natural resources and their stewardship by the federal government, believing that business would not sufficiently protect America's natural resources.

▶ **CRITICAL THINKING**

Making Generalizations How might Pinchot's study of forestry have helped him in his work with the U.S. Forest Service?

This act authorized the use of federal funds from public land sales to pay for irrigation and land development projects. The federal government thus began transforming the West's landscape and economy on a large scale.

Gifford Pinchot

Roosevelt also backed efforts to save the nation's forests. He supported careful management of the timber resources of the West. He appointed his close friend Gifford Pinchot to head the United States Forest Service, established in 1905.

As progressives, Roosevelt and Pinchot both believed that trained experts in forestry and resource management should manage the nation's forests. These professional managers would apply the same scientific standards to the landscape that others were applying to managing cities and industry. Roosevelt and Pinchot rejected the laissez-faire argument that the best way to preserve public land was to sell it to lumber companies, who would carefully conserve it because it was the source of their profits. With the president's support, Pinchot's department drew up regulations to control lumbering on federal lands. Roosevelt also added more than 100 million acres to the protected national forests and established five new national parks and 51 federal wildlife reservations.

Roosevelt's Legacy

President Theodore Roosevelt changed the role of the federal government and the nature of the presidency. He used his power in the White House to present his views, calling it his "bully pulpit." Increasingly, Americans began looking to the federal government to solve the nation's economic and social problems.

Under Roosevelt, the power of the executive branch of government had dramatically increased. The Interstate Commerce Commission, through the Hepburn Act, could set rates. The Department of Commerce and Labor could monitor business. And the attorney general could rapidly bring antitrust lawsuits under the Expedition Act. In addition, Roosevelt's concern for the environment and for protection of the wild areas of the United States helped develop a national parks system that preceded the establishment of the National Park Service in 1916.

☑ **PROGRESS CHECK**

Examining What were President Roosevelt's views on conservation, and how did he act on those views?

Taft's Reforms

GUIDING QUESTION *How did President Taft's beliefs differ from the progressives' beliefs?*

Roosevelt believed William Howard Taft, his secretary of war, was the ideal person to continue his policies. Taft easily secured the Republican nomination and won the election of 1908. The Democratic candidate, William Jennings Bryan, lost for a third time.

PHOTO: The Granger Collection, New York

The Payne-Aldrich Tariff

Like many progressives, Taft believed high tariffs limited competition, hurt consumers, and protected trusts. Roosevelt had warned him to stay away from tariff reform because it would divide the Republican Party. Nevertheless, Taft called Congress into special session to lower tariff rates. The tariff debate did, indeed, divide the Republican Party into two groups: the progressives, who favored tariff reduction, and conservative Republicans, who wanted to maintain high tariffs. As negotiations dragged on, Taft's support for tariff reductions waned. Finally, he signed into law the Payne-Aldrich Tariff, which hardly cut tariffs at all and actually raised them on some goods.

Progressives felt outraged by Taft's decision. "I knew the fire had gone out of [the progressive movement]," recalled Gifford Pinchot, after Roosevelt left office. "Its leader was gone, and in his place [was] a man whose fundamental desire was to keep out of trouble."

Ballinger Versus Pinchot

In 1909 Taft further angered progressives by replacing Roosevelt's secretary of the interior, James R. Garfield, with Richard A. Ballinger. Garfield was an aggressive conservationist; Ballinger was a conservative corporate lawyer. Once in office, Ballinger tried to open nearly a million acres of public lands to private development. Ballinger expressed his disgust with the "excitement" for conservation:

insubordination
disobedience to authority

> **PRIMARY SOURCE**
>
> ❝[M]any people have been led to believe that conservation holds the secret of our National well-being. The demagogue, the fanatic, the sentimentalist, the faddist are crusading under the banner of conservation mainly because it is popular, and holds the attention of the hour.❞
>
> —quoted in the *New York Times*, August 13, 1910

Gifford Pinchot accused Ballinger of planning to give valuable public lands in Alaska to a private business group for his own profit. Taft's attorney general investigated the charges and decided they were unfounded. Not satisfied, Pinchot went to the press and asked Congress to investigate. Taft fired Pinchot for **insubordination,** or disobedience to authority. The congressional investigation cleared Ballinger.

This page from the *Los Angeles Times*, January 9, 1910, highlights the controversy between progressive Gifford Pinchot and Taft's secretary of the interior, Richard Ballinger. Pinchot leaked a story to the press alleging that Ballinger turned over public lands for personal profit.

▶ **CRITICAL THINKING**
Determining Cause and Effect Why do you think Pinchot made accusations against Ballinger?

PHOTO: Picture Research Consultants & Archives

Part I—Telegraph Sheet—12 Pages

LOS ANGELES Times

MINIMUM TEMPERATURES: LOS ANGELES, 45; Boston, 20; New York, 16; Washington, 16; Pittsburgh, 8; Cincinnati, 6; Chicago, 18; Kansas City, 26; St. Paul, —4; Jacksonville, 86.

SUNDAY MORNING, JANUARY 9, 1910.

On All News Stands, Trains and Streets, 5 CENTS.

BELLIGERENT.

PINCHOT DEFIANT.

Urges Friends to Fight.

Tells Former Subordinates That Battle Has Just Begun.

THE MAN WHO STARTED ALL THE RUMPUS.

BRITAIN BOILING.

PRESS IS ABLAZE.

British Election Hottest in History.

Despite Invective Margin Between Victory and Defeat Is Narrow.

At a Georgia cotton mill in 1909, two boys keep a spinning machine running by repairing broken thread and replacing bobbins as they are filled.

▶ **CRITICAL THINKING**
Predicting Consequences What might happen if one of these boys slips?

By the second half of Taft's term of office, many Americans had come to believe that he had betrayed the Square Deal. Popular indignation was so great that the congressional elections of 1910 resulted in a sweeping Democratic victory. Democrats took the majority in the House, and Democrats and progressive Republicans gained control of the Senate from conservative Republicans.

Taft's Achievements

Despite his political problems, Taft also had several successes. Although Roosevelt was nicknamed the "trustbuster," Taft actually brought twice as many antitrust cases in four years as his predecessor had in seven. In other areas, Taft also pursued progressive policies. In 1912 he established the Children's Bureau. This agency investigated and publicized the problems of child labor. The agency still exists today, and deals with issues such as child abuse prevention, adoption, and foster care.

The Ballinger-Pinchot controversy aside, Taft was a dedicated conservationist, and his achievements in this area equal or surpass those of Roosevelt. In 1910 Taft set up the Bureau of Mines to monitor the activities of mining companies, expand national forests, and protect waterpower sites from private development. The bureau helped make possible many new technologies in the field of mining.

After Taft took office in 1909, Roosevelt left the country for a long voyage to Africa and Europe. He did not return to the United States until June 1910. Although disturbed by stories of Taft's "betrayal" of his progressivism, Roosevelt refused to criticize the president. He soon became impatient. In 1907, while president, Roosevelt had approved the purchase of the Tennessee Coal and Iron Company by U.S. Steel. In October 1911, Taft declared that the deal violated the Sherman Antitrust Act. Roosevelt believed Taft's focus on breaking up trusts was destroying the system of cooperation and regulation that he had set up with big business. In November 1911, Roosevelt publicly criticized Taft for this decision.

After Roosevelt broke with Taft, it was only a matter of time before progressives convinced Roosevelt to reenter politics. In late February 1912, Roosevelt announced he would enter the presidential campaign of 1912 and attempt to replace Taft as the Republican nominee for president.

☑ **PROGRESS CHECK**

Evaluating Which of Taft's actions most harmed his standing among progressives?

PHOTO: Library of Congress

LESSON 2 REVIEW

Reviewing Vocabulary

1. *Explaining* Why did President Taft fire Gifford Pinchot for insubordination?

Using Your Notes

2. *Identifying* Use your notes to identify ways in which Taft helped conservation efforts and child labor problems.

Answering the Guiding Questions

3. *Evaluating* How much do you think a president's personal beliefs should shape national policy?

4. *Analyzing* Why did President Roosevelt support conservation?

5. *Examining* How did President Taft's beliefs differ from the progressives' beliefs?

Writing Activity

6. **EXPOSITORY** Who did more to support the conservation of natural resources: President Roosevelt or President Taft? Write an essay in which you express your opinion and support it with specific examples.

networks

There's More Online!

- ☑ **BIOGRAPHY** Louis D. Brandeis
- ☑ **MAP** The Federal Reserve
- ☑ **VIDEO** The Wilson Years
- ☑ **INTERACTIVE SELF-CHECK QUIZ**

Reading **HELP**DESK

Content Vocabulary
- income tax
- unfair trade practices

Academic Vocabulary
- academic
- unconstitutional

TAKING NOTES: *Outlining*

ACTIVITY As you read about progressivism during the Wilson administration, complete a chart similar to the one below by listing Wilson's progressive economic and social reforms.

Economic Reforms	Social Reforms

LESSON 3
The Wilson Years

ESSENTIAL QUESTION • *Can politics fix social problems?*

IT MATTERS BECAUSE

Woodrow Wilson, a progressive Democrat, won the election of 1912. While in office, he supported lower tariffs, more regulation of business, and the creation of the Federal Reserve System.

The Election of 1912

GUIDING QUESTION *How was the election of 1912 different from previous presidential elections?*

The 1912 presidential campaign featured a current president, a former president, and an **academic** who had entered politics only two years earlier. The election's outcome determined the path of the Progressive movement.

Picking the Candidates

Believing that President William Howard Taft had failed to live up to progressive ideals, Theodore Roosevelt informed seven state governors that he was willing to accept the Republican nomination. "My hat is in the ring!" he declared. "The fight is on."

The struggle for control of the Republican Party reached its climax at the national convention in Chicago in June 1912. Conservatives rallied behind Taft. Most progressives supported Roosevelt. When it became clear that Taft's delegates controlled the nomination, Roosevelt decided to leave the party and campaign as an independent.

Declaring himself "fit as a bull moose," Roosevelt became the presidential candidate for the newly formed Progressive Party, which quickly became known as the Bull Moose Party. Because Taft had alienated so many groups, the election of 1912 became a contest between two progressives: Roosevelt and the Democratic candidate Woodrow Wilson.

After a university teaching career that culminated in his becoming the president of Princeton University, Woodrow Wilson entered politics as a firm progressive. As the governor of New Jersey, he pushed through many progressive reforms.

The Progressive Movement **369**

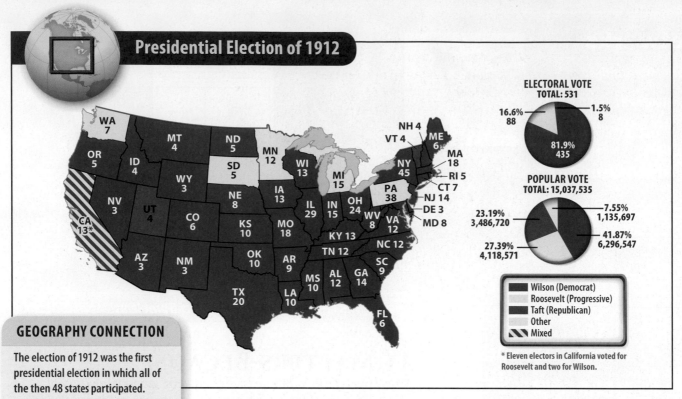

ELECTORAL VOTE
TOTAL: 531

16.6% 88
1.5% 8
81.9% 435

POPULAR VOTE
TOTAL: 15,037,535

23.19% 3,486,720
7.55% 1,135,697
27.39% 4,118,571
41.87% 6,296,547

■ Wilson (Democrat)
▨ Roosevelt (Progressive)
■ Taft (Republican)
▨ Other
▨ Mixed

* Eleven electors in California voted for Roosevelt and two for Wilson.

GEOGRAPHY CONNECTION

The election of 1912 was the first presidential election in which all of the then 48 states participated.

1 THE WORLD IN SPATIAL TERMS
In which two states did Taft win electoral votes?

2 PLACES AND REGIONS
In what region did Roosevelt have the most electoral support?

He introduced the direct primary, established utility regulatory boards, and allowed cities to adopt the commissioner form of government. In less than two years, New Jersey became a model of progressive reform.

Wilson Versus Roosevelt

The election of 1912 was a contest between two progressives with different approaches to reform. Roosevelt accepted large trusts as a fact of life and set out to create proposals to increase regulation. He favored laws to protect women and children in the labor force and supported workers' compensation for those injured on the job. Roosevelt called his program the New Nationalism.

Wilson countered with what he called the New Freedom. He criticized Roosevelt's New Nationalism for supporting "regulated monopoly." Wilson argued that Roosevelt's approach gave the federal government too much power in the economy and did nothing to restore competition. Wilson believed that freedom outweighed efficiency.

As expected, Roosevelt and Taft split the Republican voters. Wilson won the Electoral College with 435 votes. He won the election even though he received less than 42 percent of the popular vote. For the first time since Grover Cleveland's election in 1892, a Democrat was elected president.

✓ PROGRESS CHECK

Summarizing How did having three nominees running for president make the election of 1912 different from others?

Wilson's Reforms

GUIDING QUESTION *How did Wilson earn the respect of progressives?*

As the new Chief Executive, Wilson lost no time in embarking on his program of progressive reform. During his eight years as president, Wilson demonstrated his executive power as he crafted reforms affecting tariffs, the banking system, trusts, and workers' rights.

Reforming Tariffs

Five weeks after taking office, Wilson appeared before Congress, the first president to do so since John Adams. He had come to present his bill to reduce tariffs. Wilson personally lobbied members of Congress to support the tariff reduction bill. Not even Roosevelt had taken such an active role in promoting legislation.

In 1913 Congress passed the Underwood Tariff, and Wilson signed it into law. This law reduced the average tariff on imported goods to about 30 percent of the value of the goods and provided for levying the first federal graduated **income tax**—a direct tax on people's earnings. *Graduated* refers to the percentage of a person's income that is taxed. A person with a large income would pay more income tax than a person with a small income. The Sixteenth Amendment, also passed in 1913, had given the federal government the power to levy such a tax on income.

Reforming the Banks

The United States had not had a central bank since the 1830s. Periodic economic depressions that had occurred after that time had destroyed numerous small banks, wiping out many of their customers' life savings.

To restore public confidence in the banking system, Wilson supported a federal reserve system. Banks would have to keep part of their deposits in one of 12 reserve banks, providing a cushion against unexpected financial losses. The Federal Reserve Act of 1913 created the regional reserve banks, supervised by a Board of Governors appointed by the president. The Board could set the interest rates the reserve banks charged other banks, thereby indirectly controlling the nation's interest rates and the amount of money in circulation. This act became one of the most significant pieces of legislation in American history.

Antitrust Action

During his campaign, Wilson had promised to restore competition to the economy by breaking up monopolies. After the election, he realized that Roosevelt had been right: big businesses were more efficient and unlikely to be replaced by smaller, more competitive firms. Wilson decided against pursuing the monopolies. Progressives in Congress, however, continued to demand action against big business. In 1914, at Wilson's request, Congress created the Federal Trade Commission (FTC) to monitor American business. The FTC had the power to investigate companies and issue "cease and desist" orders against those it found to be engaging in **unfair trade practices,** or practices that hurt competition. If a business disagreed with its rulings, it could take the FTC to court.

Wilson did not want the FTC to break up big business. Instead, it was to work toward limiting unfair trade practices. He deliberately appointed conservative business leaders as the FTC's first commissioners. Unsatisfied by Wilson's approach, progressives in Congress responded by passing the Clayton Antitrust Act in 1914. The act outlawed certain practices that restricted competition such as price discrimination, or charging different customers different prices. The passing of the Clayton Antitrust Act corrected deficiencies in the Sherman Antitrust Act of 1890.

Before the law passed, labor unions lobbied Congress to exempt unions. As a result, the Clayton Antitrust Act stated that its provisions did not apply to labor organizations or agricultural organizations. When the bill became law, Samuel Gompers, the head of the American Federation of Labor, called the act the workers' "Magna Carta" because it gave unions the right to exist.

academic a person associated with higher learning at a scholarly institution

income tax a tax based on the net income of a person or business

Analyzing PRIMARY SOURCES

Wilson's New Freedom

❝I am perfectly willing that [a business] should beat any competitor by fair means. . . . But there must be no squeezing out the beginner . . . no secret arrangements against him. All the fair competition you choose, but no unfair competition of any kind . . .❞

—from *The New Freedom,* 1918

DBQ *MAKING INFERENCES*
What can you infer about Wilson's belief in free enterprise?

unfair trade practices trading practices that derive a gain at the expense of competition

African American leaders such as W.E.B. Du Bois worked to end racial discrimination, communicating through publications including the NAACP's journal, *The Crisis*.

▶ **CRITICAL THINKING**

Making Connections What are ways that people today work to reduce discrimination?

unconstitutional not in accordance with or authorized by the constitution of a state or society

Regulating Big Business

In 1916 Wilson signed the first federal law regulating child labor. The Keating-Owen Child Labor Act prohibited the employment of children under the age of 14 in factories producing goods for interstate commerce. Although the Supreme Court declared the law **unconstitutional** in 1918, Wilson's effort helped his reputation among progressives. He also supported the Adamson Act, which established the eight-hour workday for railroad workers, and the Federal Farm Loan Act, which helped provide low-interest loans to farmers.

☑ **PROGRESS CHECK**

Drawing Conclusions Why was the Federal Reserve Act so important?

Progressivism's Legacies and Limits

GUIDING QUESTION *What do you believe were progressivism's most important success and biggest failure?*

During his presidency, Wilson built upon Roosevelt's foundation. He expanded both the federal government and the power of the president.

New Roles for Government

Progressivism made important changes in the political life of the United States. Before this era, most Americans did not expect the government to pass laws protecting workers or regulating big business. In fact, many courts had previously ruled the passage of such laws unconstitutional. By the end of the Progressive Era, however, both legal and public opinion had shifted. Increasingly, Americans expected the government, particularly the federal government, to play a more active role in regulating the economy and solving social problems.

The Limits of Progressivism

The most conspicuous limit to progressivism was its failure to address racial and religious discrimination. African Americans themselves, however, were absorbing the reform spirit, which fueled their long-standing desire for advancement. In 1905 W.E.B. Du Bois and 28 other African American leaders met at Niagara Falls to demand full rights for African Americans. There they launched what became known as the Niagara Movement.

Du Bois and other African American leaders believed that voting rights were essential to end lynching and racial discrimination. "The power of the ballot we need in sheer self-defense," Du Bois said, "else what shall save us from a second slavery? Freedom too, the long-sought we still seek,—the freedom of life and limb, the freedom to work and think, the freedom to love and aspire. Work, culture, liberty,—all these we need, not singly, but together."

In 1908 race riots in Springfield, Illinois, shocked many people, including Mary White Ovington, a settlement house worker. She had been studying African Americans in New York, determined to do something to improve their situation. Other progressives, including Jane Addams of Hull House and muckrakers Ida Wells-Barnett and Lincoln Steffens, joined Ovington in calling for change. Capitalizing on Springfield as Abraham Lincoln's hometown and on the centennial of his birthday on February 12, 1909, they organized a national conference in Springfield to take stock of the progress in emancipation. At a second conference the following year, the National Association for the Advancement of Colored People (NAACP) was born. Through Du Bois, the members learned of the Niagara Movement, and the two groups eventually merged.

African Americans were not the only minority group facing discrimination. Jewish people also lived in fear of mob violence. In 1913 Leo Frank, a Jew being tried in Atlanta for a murder that the facts proved he did not commit, was sentenced to death. Although his sentence was changed to life imprisonment, a mob lynched him two years later.

In this context, lawyer Sigmund Livingston started the Anti-Defamation League (ADL) to combat stereotypes and discrimination. According to its 1913 charter, the ADL's "ultimate purpose [was] to secure justice and fair treatment to all citizens alike and to put an end forever to unjust and unfair discrimination against and ridicule of any sect or body of citizens." The ADL worked to remove negative portrayals of Jews in movies, in print, and on stage. For example, the League protested a World War I army manual that claimed Jews were likely to pretend to be sick to escape work or battle. When the ADL complained, President Wilson had the manual recalled.

☑ PROGRESS CHECK

Constructing Arguments What do you think were progressivism's most important success and biggest failure?

LESSON 3 REVIEW

Reviewing Vocabulary

1. Defining The Federal Trade Commission had the power to investigate companies engaging in what actions that unfairly limited competition?

Using Your Notes

2. Comparing and Contrasting Review the notes that you completed during the lesson to write a statement comparing and contrasting Wilson's economic and social reforms.

Answering the Guiding Questions

3. Contrasting How was the election of 1912 different from previous presidential elections?

4. Monitoring How did Wilson earn the respect of progressives?

5. Evaluating What do you believe were progressivism's most important success and biggest failure?

Writing Activity

6. EXPOSITORY During the Progressive Era, nongovernmental organizations such as the NAACP and the ADL worked to gain rights and end discrimination for minority groups. Explain what steps these groups took to correct injustices in American life.

Directions: On a separate sheet of paper, answer the questions below. Make sure you read carefully and answer all parts to the question.

Lesson Review

Lesson 1

1 *Describing* What were the goals of progressives, and how did they hope to achieve these goals?

2 *Making Generalizations* How did progressives believe that the reforms they proposed to municipal government would improve society?

3 *Analyzing Cause and Effect* What combination of events encouraged middle-class and working-class women to increasingly support the woman suffrage movement during the Progressive Era?

Lesson 2

4 *Sequencing* What steps did Theodore Roosevelt take to rein in big business?

5 *Defending* What arguments might a conservationist use to justify President Roosevelt's expansion of the power of the federal government?

6 *Comparing* Explain two political ideals shared by President Roosevelt and President Taft.

Lesson 3

7 *Contrasting* On what progressive political issue did Roosevelt and Wilson most differ during their 1912 presidential campaigns?

8 *Making Connections* How does President Wilson's Federal Reserve Act of 1913 continue to affect Americans today?

9 *Analyzing* How did progressivism live up to its ideals, and how did it fail?

21st Century Skills

10 **TIME, CHRONOLOGY, AND SEQUENCING** What developments in American society encouraged reformers to seek change that led to the Progressive movement?

11 **COMPARE AND CONTRAST** What were two ways that President Taft broke with the policies and ideals of President Roosevelt?

12 **IDENTIFYING CAUSE AND EFFECT** What factor had the most influence on the outcome of the presidential election of 1912?

13 **ECONOMICS** How did the reforms of President Wilson affect the practices of big business?

Exploring the Essential Question

14 *Identifying Central Issues* Make an informative poster that identifies how progressives tried to fix society's problems. Your poster should include charts, illustrations, graphs, or lists to support your information.

DBQ Document-Based Questions

Analyze the photo to answer the following questions.

PRIMARY SOURCE

In 1903 President Roosevelt visited John Muir in Yosemite Valley. Muir's focus was to express the need for the Yosemite Valley to be managed by the United States government.

15 *Analyzing* How do you think President Roosevelt's passion to protect the environment is reflected in this image?

16 *Making Inferences* How did this event most likely affect Roosevelt's conservation policies?

Extended-Response Question

17 *Identifying Central Issues* Write an essay that identifies how the actions and policies of Presidents Roosevelt, Taft, and Wilson supported the goals and ideals of progressivism. Your essay should include an introduction, at least two supporting paragraphs, and a conclusion.

Need Extra Help?

If You've Missed Question	1	2	3	4	5	6	7	8	9	10	11	12	13	14	15	16	17
Go to page	356	358	359	363	365	366	370	371	372	356	367	370	370	361	374	374	363

PHOTO: Library of Congress

World War I and Its Aftermath

1914–1920

ESSENTIAL QUESTION • *Why do nations go to war?*

PHOTO: Underwood & Underwood/Bettmann/CORBIS

◀ General John J. Pershing commanded the American Expeditionary Force in several successful battles against the Central Powers during World War I.

networks

There's More Online about the involvement of the United States in World War I.

CHAPTER 16

The Story Matters...

When war began between European nations in 1914, the United States tried to remain neutral, but attacks on U.S. ships eventually caused the United States to enter the war.

To successfully fight the war, the U.S. government used progressive ideas to manage the economy, build a large military, and shape public opinion. America's involvement in the war effort had a profound impact on American society for years to come.

Political conflicts in Europe sparked the beginning of World War I. The United States attempted to keep its long-standing policy to remain neutral in Europe's wars until events eroded U.S. neutrality and finally led to the nation's involvement. World War I was the first time in U.S. history that the United States sent troops to fight in Europe. After the war, the United States suffered economic uncertainty and social tensions as many Americans became anti-immigrant, anticommunist, and antiunion.

Step Into the Place

Read the quotes and look at the information presented on the map.

 How do the concerns addressed in the quotes reflect conflicting opinions about the United States becoming involved in World War I?

PRIMARY SOURCE

"We have been neutral not only because it was the fixed and traditional policy of the United States to stand aloof from the politics of Europe and because we had had no part either of action or of policy in the influences which brought on the present war, but also because it was manifestly our duty to prevent, if it were possible, the indefinite extension of the fires of hate and desolation kindled by that terrible conflict and seek to serve mankind by reserving our strength and our resources for the anxious and difficult days of restoration and healing which must follow. . . ."

—President Woodrow Wilson, *Wilson Accepts His Renomination*, speech delivered at Long Branch, New Jersey, September 2, 1916

PRIMARY SOURCE

"It is to be expected that nations will continue to arm in defense of their respective interests, as they are conceived, and nothing will avail to diminish this burden save some practical guaranty of international order. We, in this country, can, and should, maintain our fortunate freedom from entanglements with interests and policies, which do not concern us. But there is no national isolation in the world of the twentieth century."

—Charles Evans Hughes, quoted in *The Official Report of the Proceedings of the Sixteenth Republican National Convention,* June 1916

PHOTOS: (tl tr)Library of Congress, (b)detail/White House Collection/The White House Historical Association

Step Into the Time

Choose an event from the time line and write a paragraph describing the general social, political, or economic effect the event might have for World War I and its aftermath.

Wilson
1913–1921

U.S. PRESIDENTS

UNITED STATES

WORLD

1914   1915   1916

May 7, 1915 German submarine sinks the *Lusitania*

June 28, 1914 Franz Ferdinand assassinated

February 21, 1916 Battle of Verdun

July 1, 1916 Battle of the Somme begins

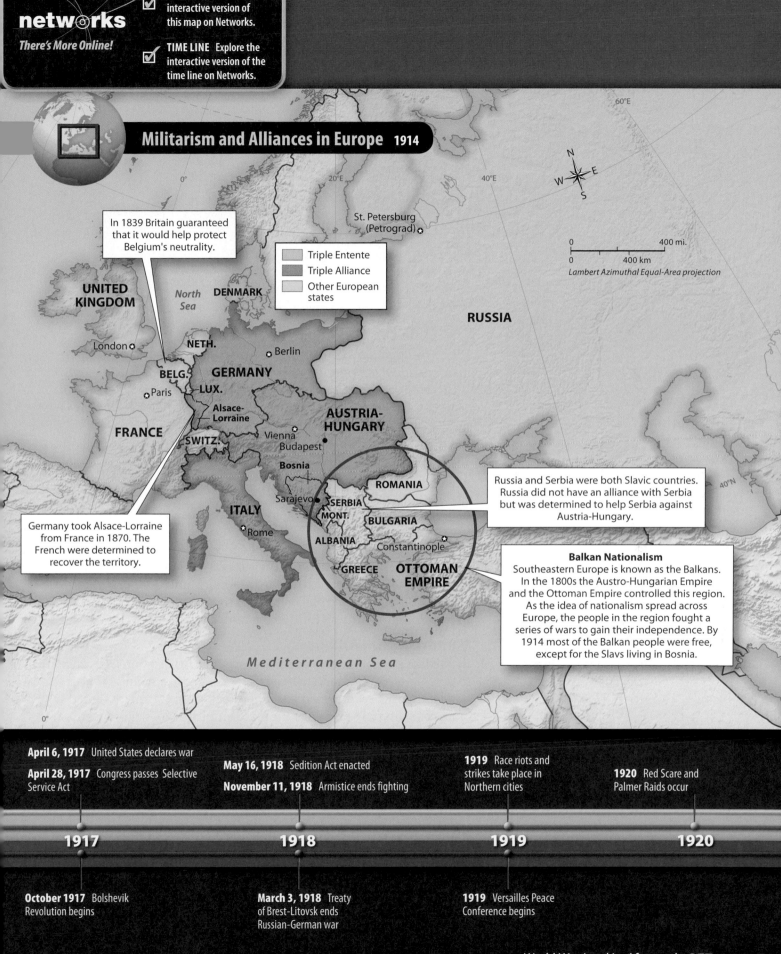

Militarism and Alliances in Europe 1914

In 1839 Britain guaranteed that it would help protect Belgium's neutrality.

Triple Entente
Triple Alliance
Other European states

0 — 400 mi.
0 — 400 km
Lambert Azimuthal Equal-Area projection

UNITED KINGDOM

North Sea

DENMARK

St. Petersburg (Petrograd)

RUSSIA

London

NETH.

Berlin

BELG.

GERMANY

Paris

LUX.

Alsace-Lorraine

FRANCE

Vienna

AUSTRIA-HUNGARY

Budapest

SWITZ.

Bosnia

Germany took Alsace-Lorraine from France in 1870. The French were determined to recover the territory.

Sarajevo

SERBIA

ROMANIA

MONT.

BULGARIA

ITALY

Rome

ALBANIA

Constantinople

Russia and Serbia were both Slavic countries. Russia did not have an alliance with Serbia but was determined to help Serbia against Austria-Hungary.

GREECE

OTTOMAN EMPIRE

Balkan Nationalism
Southeastern Europe is known as the Balkans. In the 1800s the Austro-Hungarian Empire and the Ottoman Empire controlled this region. As the idea of nationalism spread across Europe, the people in the region fought a series of wars to gain their independence. By 1914 most of the Balkan people were free, except for the Slavs living in Bosnia.

Mediterranean Sea

April 6, 1917 United States declares war

April 28, 1917 Congress passes Selective Service Act

May 16, 1918 Sedition Act enacted

November 11, 1918 Armistice ends fighting

1919 Race riots and strikes take place in Northern cities

1920 Red Scare and Palmer Raids occur

1917

1918

1919

1920

October 1917 Bolshevik Revolution begins

March 3, 1918 Treaty of Brest-Litovsk ends Russian-German war

1919 Versailles Peace Conference begins

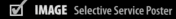

netw⊚rks

There's More Online!

☑ **IMAGE** Selective Service Poster

☑ **MAP** Presidential Election of 1916

☑ **VIDEO** The United States Enters World War I

☑ **INTERACTIVE SELF-CHECK QUIZ**

Reading **HELP**DESK

Content Vocabulary

• militarism
• nationalism
• propaganda
• contraband

Academic Vocabulary

• emphasis   • erode

TAKING NOTES: *Organizing*

ACTIVITY As you read, identify the factors that contributed to World War I by completing a graphic organizer similar to the one below.

Factors Contributing to World War I

LESSON 1

The United States Enters World War I

ESSENTIAL QUESTION • Why do nations go to war?

IT MATTERS BECAUSE

Through the late 1800s and early 1900s, imperialism, shifting national boundaries, old alliances, and nationalist sentiments among European nations set the stage for World War I. Attacks on U.S. ships and American support for the Allies eventually caused the United States to enter the war.

World War I Begins

GUIDING QUESTION *What political circumstances in Europe led to World War I?*

In 1914 tensions were building among European nations, stemming from events that dated to the 1860s. In 1864, while Americans fought the Civil War, the German kingdom of Prussia launched the first of a series of wars to unite the various German states into one nation. By 1871, Prussia had united Germany and established the German Empire, which became one of the most powerful nations in the world, transforming European politics.

Militarism and Alliances

In 1870, as part of its plan to unify Germany, Prussia forced France to give up territory along the German border. As a result, France and Germany became enemies. To protect itself, Germany signed alliances with Italy and with the huge empire of Austria-Hungary, which controlled much of southeastern Europe. This became known as the Triple Alliance.

The new alliance alarmed Russian leaders, who feared that Germany intended to expand eastward. In addition, Russia and Austria-Hungary were competing for influence in southeastern Europe. A common interest in opposing Germany and Austria-Hungary led Russia and France to sign the Franco-Russian Alliance in 1894. Under the alliance, the two nations promised to come to each other's aid in a war against the Triple Alliance.

Such alliances fostered **militarism**—the strong buildup of armed forces to intimidate and threaten other nations. Over time, German militarism led Britain to become involved in the alliance system. Britain's policy was to try to prevent one nation from controlling all of Europe. By the late 1800s, Germany had clearly become Europe's strongest nation.

In 1898 Germany began building a large modern navy. The buildup threatened the British, who rushed to build warships. By the early 1900s, Britain and Germany were engaged in an arms race. The race convinced Britain to build closer ties with France and Russia. The British refused to sign a formal alliance, so the relationship became known as an entente cordiale, or friendly understanding. Britain, France, and Russia became known as the Triple Entente.

Imperialism and Nationalism

By the late 1800s, **nationalism,** or a feeling of intense pride in one's homeland, had become a powerful idea in Europe. Nationalists place primary **emphasis** on promoting their homeland's culture and interests. They believe in the right of self-determination—the idea that those who share a national identity should have their own country and government. In the 1800s, nationalism led to a crisis in the Balkan region of southeastern Europe.

In the 1700s and 1800s, imperialism—the ruling or controlling of other peoples or nations through annexation, military conquest, or economic domination—was how European powers built empires. For years the Ottoman Empire and the Austro-Hungarian Empire had ruled the Balkans. But as nationalism spread in the late 1800s and early 1900s, national groups such as the South Slavs—Serbs, Bosnians, Croats, and Slovenes—began to press for independence. The Serbs, who were the first to gain independence, formed a nation called Serbia between the two empires. Serbia believed that its mission was to unite the South Slavs.

Russia supported the Serbs, but Austria-Hungary worked to limit Serbia's growth. In 1908 Austria-Hungary annexed Bosnia, which had belonged to the Ottoman Empire, outraging the Serbs. The annexation demonstrated that Austria-Hungary had no intention of letting the Slavic people in its empire become independent.

An Assassination Brings War

In June 1914, Archduke Franz Ferdinand, heir to the Austro-Hungarian throne, visited the Bosnian capital of Sarajevo. As he and his wife rode through the city, Bosnian revolutionary Gavrilo Princip rushed their car and shot them dead. The assassination occurred with the knowledge of Serbian officials who hoped to start a war that would damage Austria-Hungary.

Austria-Hungary decided the time had come to crush Serbia in order to prevent Slavic nationalism from undermining its empire. Knowing an attack on Serbia might trigger a war with Russia, the Austrians asked their German allies for support. Austria-Hungary then issued an ultimatum to the Serbian government. The Serbs counted on Russia to back them up, and the Russians, in turn, counted on France.

On July 28, Austria-Hungary declared war on Serbia. Russia immediately mobilized its army, including troops stationed on the German border. Within days Germany declared war on Russia and France. World War I had begun.

Germany immediately launched a massive invasion of France, hoping to knock the French out of the war, so it

militarism a policy of aggressive military preparedness

nationalism loyalty and devotion to a nation

emphasis a special importance given to an object or idea

The assassination of Archduke Franz Ferdinand in late June 1914 spurred Austria-Hungary to declare war on Serbia, beginning World War I.

▶ **CRITICAL THINKING**

Identifying Central Issues How did the conflict between the policy of imperialism and the principle of nationalism lead to war between Austria-Hungary and Serbia?

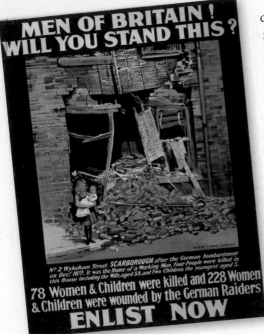

MEN OF BRITAIN !
WILL YOU STAND THIS ?

Nº 2 Wykeham Street, SCARBOROUGH after the German bombardment on Dec. 16th. It was the Home of a Working Man. Four People were killed in this House including the Wife aged 58, and Two Children, the youngest aged 5.

78 Women & Children were killed and 228 Women & Children were wounded by the German Raiders

ENLIST NOW

During World War I, both Britain and Germany produced propaganda posters. German propaganda was mostly anti-Russian and did not appeal to Americans, however, while British propaganda did.

▶ CRITICAL THINKING
Analyzing Primary Sources What message does this poster want to convince the viewer to believe?

propaganda the spreading of ideas about an institution or individual for the purpose of influencing opinion

Thinking Like a
HISTORIAN

Determining Cause and Effect

Propaganda is a powerful force to influence opinion. In wartime, propaganda can be used to convince people to take sides or participate for a particular cause or reason. As a historian, how much do you think the British propaganda swayed the United States to support the Allies in World War I, or were other reasons, such as business, more of a deciding factor?

could turn its attention east to Russia. But the German plan required forces to advance through Belgium. The British government, which had signed an earlier treaty with Belgium guaranteeing the country's neutrality, declared war on Germany when German troops crossed the Belgian frontier.

Those fighting for the Triple Entente were called the Allies. Italy joined them in 1915 after being promised control of Austro-Hungarian territory after the war. What remained of the Triple Alliance—Germany and Austria-Hungary—joined with the Ottoman Empire and Bulgaria to form the Central Powers. Germany quickly conquered much of France, but Russia was a fierce opponent to the east. When Russia invaded Germany, the Germans were forced to move some troops eastward to thwart the attack. The Western Front became a bloody stalemate along hundreds of miles of trenches, with British and French forces on one side and German forces on the other.

☑ **PROGRESS CHECK**

Evaluating How did the complex web of European alliances contribute to the outbreak of World War I?

The United States Declares War

GUIDING QUESTION *What events motivated the United States to join the war?*

When the war began, President Wilson immediately declared the United States to be neutral. Despite his plea, many Americans took sides. American public opinion generally favored the Allied cause, although many German Americans and Irish Americans were hostile to Britain.

Americans Take Sides

For more than two years, the United States officially remained neutral. During this time a great debate began over whether the United States should prepare for war. Some believed that preparing for war was the best way to stay out of the conflict. Others, including Jane Addams, founded organizations urging the president not to build up the military. Many government officials, however, were decidedly pro-British, though Secretary of State William Jennings Bryan favored neutrality. In addition, many American military leaders believed that an Allied victory was the only way to preserve the international balance of power.

British officials worked diligently to win American support. One method they used was **propaganda,** or information designed to influence opinion. The British cut the transatlantic telegraph cable from Europe to the United States so most war news would be based on British reports. The American ambassador to Britain endorsed many of these reports, and American public opinion swayed in favor of the Allies.

Companies in the United States also had strong ties to the Allies, and many American banks invested heavily in an Allied victory. By 1917, American loans to the Allies totaled over $2 billion. Although other banks, particularly in the Midwest where pro-German feelings were strongest, lent some $27 million to Germany, the country's prosperity was intertwined with the Allies. If the Allies won, the investments would be paid back; if not, the money might never be repaid.

Moving Toward War

A series of events gradually **eroded** American neutrality and drew the United States into the war. Shortly after the war began, the British blockaded German ports. They forced neutral merchant ships sailing to Europe to land at British ports to be inspected for **contraband,** or goods prohibited from shipment to Germany and its allies. Although the U.S. government protested Britain's decision, the German response angered Americans even more. In February 1915, the Germans announced that they would use submarines called U-boats to sink without warning any ship they found in the waters around Britain. This decision went against an international treaty signed by Germany that banned attacks on civilian ships without warning.

On May 7, 1915, a U-boat sank the British passenger ship *Lusitania*, killing over 1,000 passengers—including 128 Americans. The attack gave credibility to British propaganda and changed American attitudes about the war. Wilson tried to defuse the crisis by sending official protests to Germany insisting that it stop endangering noncombatants. But in March 1916, a U-boat torpedoed a French passenger ship. Wilson threatened to break off diplomatic relations with Germany, but then decided to issue one last warning demanding that the German government abandon its methods or risk war with the United States.

erode to wear away at something until it disappears

contraband goods whose importation, exportation, or possession is illegal

ANALYZING PRIMARY SOURCES

Should the United States Stay Neutral in World War I?

Despite President Wilson's pronouncement that Americans should remain neutral in thought as well as action, many were deeply divided about whether the United States should remain neutral in World War I. Voices spoke out loudly on both sides of the issues.

——— YES ———

66Germany is not moving against this country. She has not been guilty of any aggression against us. She has taken the lives of a few of our citizens, because they got in the way when she was prosecuting a war against another nation and fighting to preserve her existence. If the German Government should make aggressive warfare against the United States you would not need any exhortation in the Senate of the United States to arouse the patriotism of the American people. You would not be holding open your enlisting stations without getting any soldiers.99

—from the *Congressional Record,* March 4, 1917

John Works, Civil War veteran and U.S. senator

——— NO ———

66I have come to the conclusion that the German Government is utterly hostile to all nations with democratic institutions because those who compose it see in democracy a menace to absolutism and the defeat of the German ambition for world domination. . . .

. . . Germany must not be permitted to win this war and to break even, though to prevent it this country is forced to take an active part. This ultimate necessity must be constantly in our minds in all our controversies with the belligerents. American public opinion must be prepared for the time, which may come, when we will have to cast aside our neutrality and become one of the champions of democracy.99

—from *War Memoirs of Robert Lansing,* July 11, 1915

Robert Lansing, Secretary of State

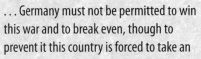

DBQ Document Based Questions

❶ *Summarizing* When does Senator Works believe war against Germany would be justified?

❷ *Identifying Central Issues* Based on these sources, on what issue were most people divided in the neutrality debate?

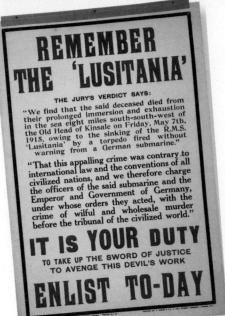

REMEMBER
THE 'LUSITANIA'

THE JURY'S VERDICT SAYS:
"We find that the said deceased died from
their prolonged immersion and exhaustion
in the sea eight miles south-south-west of
the Old Head of Kinsale on Friday, May 7th,
1915, owing to the sinking of the R.M.S.
'Lusitania' by a torpedo fired without
warning from a German submarine."

"That this appalling crime was contrary to
international law and the conventions of all
civilized nations, and we therefore charge
the officers of the said submarine and the
Emperor and Government of Germany,
under whose orders they acted, with the
crime of wilful and wholesale murder
before the tribunal of the civilized world."

IT IS YOUR DUTY
TO TAKE UP THE SWORD OF JUSTICE
TO AVENGE THIS DEVIL'S WORK

ENLIST TO-DAY

The sinking of the *Lusitania* angered
many Americans and proved to be a
turning point in the war.

▶ **CRITICAL THINKING**
Determining Cause and Effect What
were two long-term effects of the sinking
of the *Lusitania*?

Germany did not want to strengthen the Allies by drawing the
United States into the war. It promised with certain conditions to sink
no more merchant ships without warning. This pledge met the foreign
policy goals of both Germany and President Wilson by delaying the
entry of the United States into the war. President Wilson's efforts
played an important part in his reelection bid in 1916. His campaign
slogan, "He kept us out of war," helped the "peace" candidate win a
narrow victory.

The United States Declares War

Events, however, soon brought the country to the brink of war. In
January 1917, German official Arthur Zimmermann sent a telegram to
the German ambassador in Mexico promising Mexico the return of its
"lost territory in Texas, New Mexico, and Arizona" if it allied with
Germany. British intelligence intercepted the Zimmermann telegram,
and it ran in American newspapers. Furious, many Americans
concluded that war with Germany was necessary.

Then, on February 1, 1917, Germany resumed unrestricted
submarine warfare. German military leaders believed that they could starve
Britain into submission if U-boats began sinking all ships on sight. They did
not believe that the United States could raise an army and transport it to
Europe in time if it decided to enter the war. Between February 3 and
March 21, U-boats sank six American ships. Roused to action, President
Wilson asked Congress to declare war on Germany on April 2, 1917:

PRIMARY SOURCE

❝It is a fearful thing to lead this great peaceful people into war. . . . But the right is more precious than
peace, and we shall fight for the things which we have always carried nearest to our hearts—for
democracy, for the right of those who submit to authority to have a voice in their own governments, for
the rights and liberties of small nations. . . .❞

—quoted in the *Congressional Record*, 1917

Within days the Senate and the House had voted for the resolution, and
Wilson signed it. The United States was at war. Even so, 50 representatives
and 6 senators had voted against declaring war.

✓ **PROGRESS CHECK**

Summarizing How did Germany's use of unrestricted submarine warfare bring the
United States into World War I?

LESSON 1 REVIEW

Reviewing Vocabulary
1. ***Explaining*** Explain how militarism contributed to the beginning
   of World War I.

2. ***Monitoring*** How did British propaganda influence American
   public opinion?

Using Your Notes
3. ***Comparing and Contrasting*** Use your notes to write a short
   essay comparing and contrasting the factors that caused European
   nations and the United States to become involved in World War I.

Answering Guiding Questions
4. ***Identifying Cause and Effect*** What political circumstances in
   Europe led to World War I?

5. ***Summarizing*** What events motivated the United States to join
   the war?

Writing Activity
6. **EXPOSITORY** Suppose you are an American survivor of the
   sinking of the *Lusitania*. Write a letter to President Wilson about
   what you think he should do.

LESSON 2
The Home Front

ESSENTIAL QUESTION · *Why do nations go to war?*

Reading **HELP**DESK

Content Vocabulary
- **victory garden**
- **espionage**

Academic Vocabulary
- **migrate** • **draft**

TAKING NOTES: *Organizing*

ACTIVITY As you read, use the major headings of this lesson to create an outline similar to the one below.

> The Home Front
> I. Organizing the Economy
>   A.
>   B.
>   C.
> II.
>   A.
>   B.

IT MATTERS BECAUSE
To fight World War I, the U.S. government used progressive ideas and new government agencies to mobilize the population and organize the economy.

Organizing the Economy

GUIDING QUESTION *What did Congress do to prepare the economy for war?*

When the United States entered the war in April 1917, progressives controlled the federal government. Their ideas about planning and management shaped how the government organized the war effort.

Wartime Agencies

As part of the war effort, Congress created new agencies staffed by business executives, managers, and government officials to coordinate mobilization and ensure the efficient use of national resources. These agencies emphasized cooperation between big business and government.

The War Industries Board (WIB) coordinated the production of war materials. Early problems convinced President Wilson to expand the Board's powers. The WIB told manufacturers what they could produce, allocated raw materials, ordered new factory construction, and sometimes set prices.

The Food Administration, run by Herbert Hoover, was responsible for increasing food production while reducing civilian consumption. The agency encouraged families to conserve food and grow their own vegetables in **victory gardens.** "Eat more corn, oats and rye products—fish and poultry—fruits, vegetables and potatoes, baked, boiled and broiled foods. . . . Eat less wheat, meat, sugar and fats to save for the army and our allies," urged Food Administration posters.

The Fuel Administration managed use of coal and oil. To conserve energy, it introduced daylight saving time, shortened workweeks for civilian goods factories, and encouraged Heatless Mondays.

victory garden a garden planted by civilians during war to raise vegetables for home use, leaving more of other foods for the troops

By the end of the war, the United States had spent about $32 billion. To fund the war effort, Congress raised income tax rates, placed new taxes on corporate profits, imposed an extra tax on the profits of arms factories, and borrowed over $20 billion through the sale of Liberty Bonds and Victory Bonds. Americans who bought bonds were lending money to the government to be repaid with interest in a specified number of years.

Mobilizing the Workforce

The war effort also required the cooperation of workers. To prevent strikes from disrupting the war effort, the government established the National War Labor Board (NWLB) in April 1918. The NWLB often pressured industry to improve wages, adopt an eight-hour workday, and allow unions the right to organize and bargain collectively. In exchange, labor leaders agreed not to disrupt war production with strikes or other disturbances. As a result, membership in unions increased by over one million between 1917 and 1919.

With so many men in the military, employers were willing to hire women for jobs traditionally held by men. Some 1 million women joined the workforce for the first time, and another 8 million switched to better industrial jobs. Women worked in factories, shipyards, and railroad yards and served as police officers, mail carriers, and train engineers. When the war ended, however, most women returned to their previous jobs or stopped working. Yet the changes demonstrated that women were capable of holding jobs that many had believed only men could do.

Desperate for workers, Henry Ford sent agents to the South to recruit African Americans. Other companies quickly followed suit. Promises of high wages and plentiful work convinced between 300,000 and 500,000 African Americans to move north. This massive population movement became known as the Great Migration. The racial makeup of such cities as Chicago, New York, Cleveland, and Detroit changed greatly. Eventually, so did politics in the Northern cities, where African Americans were able to vote.

migrate to move from one location to another

The war also encouraged other groups to **migrate.** Between 1917 and 1920, more than 100,000 Mexicans migrated into the Southwest, providing

---

CHARTS/GRAPHS

PAYING FOR WORLD WAR I

To pay for the war, the U.S. government raised taxes and issued bonds. The government printed posters, organized parades, and asked movie stars to help promote war bonds. Here, actor Douglas Fairbanks urges Americans to buy Liberty Bonds at a rally in New York City in 1918.

▶ **CRITICAL THINKING**

1 *Drawing Inferences* What can you infer about government finances by the disparity between the amount of revenue raised through loans versus taxation?

2 *Predicting Consequences* What consequence might result from the way the war was paid for?

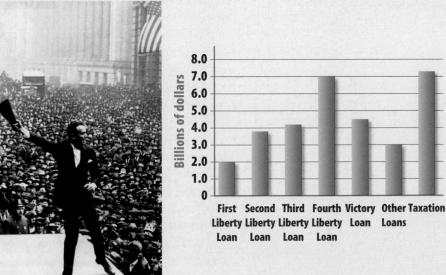

PHOTO: Bettmann/CORBIS

labor for farmers and ranchers. Mexican Americans also found new opportunities in factory jobs in Chicago, St. Louis, Omaha, and other American cities. Like other immigrant groups before them, they faced hostility and discrimination. Mexican Americans tended to settle in separate neighborhoods, called barrios, where they could support one another.

Shaping Public Opinion

Progressives did not think that organizing the economy was enough to ensure the success of the war effort. They also believed the government needed to shape public opinion. Soon after Congress declared war, Wilson created the Committee on Public Information (CPI) to "sell" the war to the American people. Headed by journalist George Creel, the CPI recruited advertising executives, artists, authors, songwriters, entertainers, public speakers, and motion picture companies to help sway public opinion in favor of the war.

The CPI distributed pamphlets and arranged for thousands of "four-minute speeches" to be delivered at movie theaters and other public places. Some 75,000 speakers, known as Four-Minute Men, urged audiences to support the war in various ways, from buying war bonds to reporting draft dodgers to the authorities. Nongovernmental groups also helped raise awareness and funds for the war. For example, the American Jewish Joint Distribution Committee raised $63 million in relief funds. The Jewish Welfare Board set up centers at home and abroad for Jewish servicemen.

In addition to using propaganda, the government passed legislation to limit opposition to the war and to fight **espionage,** or spying to acquire government information. The Espionage Act of 1917 made it illegal to aid the enemy, give false reports, or interfere with the war effort. The Sedition Act of 1918 made it illegal to speak against the war publicly. In practice, it allowed officials to prosecute anyone who criticized the government. These two laws led to more than 2,000 convictions.

Despite protests, the constitutionality of the Espionage and Sedition Acts was upheld in court. In *Schenck* v. *United States* (1919), Justice Oliver Wendell Holmes wrote the unanimous opinion of the Court:

PRIMARY SOURCE

66 The question . . . is whether the words used are . . . of such a nature as to create a clear and present danger that they will bring about the substantive evils that Congress has a right to prevent. . . . When a nation is at war many things that might be said in time of peace are such a hindrance to its effort that their utterance will not be endured so long as men fight. 99

—from *United States Supreme Court Reports,* 1920

Wartime fears led to attacks on German Americans, labor activists, socialists, and pacifists. Ads urged Americans to monitor their fellow citizens. Some German Americans hid ties to their culture to avoid suspicion or abuse. Individuals and businesses changed their names, and many German-language newspapers ceased publication.

✓ **PROGRESS CHECK**

Explaining What were some new agencies that Congress established to help manage the wartime economy?

Eugene V. Debs, leader of the American Socialist Party, was arrested and sentenced to 10 years in prison under the Espionage Act for giving an antiwar speech in Canton, Ohio.

▶ **CRITICAL THINKING**
Interpreting Significance What did the sentencing of Debs and others show about wartime freedom?

espionage spying, especially to gain government secrets

Building the Military

GUIDING QUESTION *How were progressive ideals used in preparing the military for war?*

Progressives did not abandon their ideas when it came to building up the military. Instead, they applied those ideas to develop a new system for recruiting a large army.

Volunteers and Conscripts

When the United States entered the war in 1917, the army and the National Guard together had slightly more than 200,000 troops. Many men quickly volunteered, but many more were still needed.

Many progressives believed that forced military service was a violation of democratic and republican principles. Believing a **draft** was necessary, however, Congress, with Wilson's support, created a new system called selective service.

draft to select a person at random for mandatory military service

Instead of having the military run the draft from Washington, D.C., the Selective Service Act of 1917 required all men between 21 and 30 to register for the draft. A lottery randomly determined the order in which they were called before a local draft board in charge of selecting or exempting people from military service. The thousands of local boards were the heart of the system. The members of the draft boards were civilians from local communities. Progressives believed local people, understanding community needs, would know which men to draft and would do a far better job than a centralized government bureaucracy. Eventually, about 2.8 million Americans were drafted.

Not all American soldiers were drafted. Approximately 2 million men volunteered for military service. Some had heard stories of German atrocities and wanted to fight back. Others believed democracy was at stake. Many believed they had a duty to respond to their nation's call.

Although the horrors of war soon became apparent to the American troops, their morale remained high, helping to ensure victory. More than 50,000 Americans died in combat, and over 200,000 were wounded. Another 60,000 soldiers died from disease, mostly from the influenza epidemic of 1918 and 1919. The flu epidemic was not limited to the battlefield. It spread around the world and made more than a quarter of all Americans sick. The disease killed an estimated 25 to 50 million people worldwide, including more than 500,000 Americans.

PHOTO: Library of Congress

The U.S. Army kept many African American soldiers from combat, assigning them to work as cooks, laborers, and laundrymen. The 369th Regiment, however, was assigned to the French Army and spent 191 days in the frontline trenches. The entire regiment was awarded the French Croix de Guerre for gallantry in combat.

▶ **CRITICAL THINKING**

Comparing and Contrasting Why do you think the experiences of the 369th Regiment differed from those of other African American soldiers during World War I?

Of the nearly 400,000 African Americans who were drafted, about 42,000 served overseas as combat troops. African American soldiers encountered discrimination and prejudice in the army, where they served in racially segregated units, almost always under the supervision of white officers. Despite these challenges, many African American soldiers fought with distinction. For example, the African American 92nd and 93rd Infantry Divisions fought in bitter battles along the Western Front. Many of the soldiers in those divisions won praise from the French commander, Marshal Philippe Pétain, and the United States commander, General John Pershing.

An estimated 12,000 Native Americans and about 20,000 Puerto Ricans served in the armed forces. Thousands of Mexican Americans also served in the war, volunteering for service more than any other minority group in the United States. Some Asian immigrants fought on the side of the United States even before they were citizens. Though they faced discrimination, many Asians served in the U.S. Army with distinction, being granted citizenship in recognition of their contributions.

Women Join the Military

World War I was the first war in which women officially served in the armed forces, although they served only in noncombat positions. As the military prepared for war in 1917, it faced a severe shortage of clerical workers because so many men were assigned to active duty. Early in 1917, the navy authorized the enlistment of women to meet its clerical needs.

Women serving in the navy wore a standard uniform and were assigned the rank of yeoman. By the end of the war, more than 11,000 women had served in the navy. Although most performed clerical duties, others served as radio operators, electricians, pharmacists, chemists, and photographers. Unlike the navy, the army refused to enlist women. Instead, it began hiring women as temporary employees to fill clerical jobs. The only women to actually serve in the army were in the Army Nurse Corps.

Women had served as nurses in both the army and the navy since the early 1900s, but as auxiliaries. They were not assigned ranks and were not technically enlisted in the army or navy. More than 20,000 nurses served in the Army Nurse Corps during the war, including more than 10,000 overseas.

☑ PROGRESS CHECK

Synthesizing How did progressive ideas influence the roles of women during World War I?

Connections to TODAY

Women in the Military

Although women's roles in the military during World War I were limited, their entry into service paved the way for many advances. Today, about 5 percent of general officers in the U.S. Army, including the Army Reserve and the Army National Guard, are women. In 2008 Ann E. Dunwoody became the first female four-star general in army history.

LESSON 2 REVIEW

Reviewing Vocabulary

1. Explaining How did victory gardens help civilians contribute to the war effort?

Using Your Notes

2. Summarizing Use the notes you completed during the lesson to write a short summary of how World War I affected life on the home front.

Answering Guiding Questions

3. Making Generalizations What did Congress do to prepare the economy for war?

4. Synthesizing How were progressive ideals used in preparing the military for war?

Writing Activity

5. NARRATIVE Suppose that you are a woman entering the workforce for the first time during World War I. Write a letter to a friend in which you explain why you have decided to go to work and what type of job you are doing. Share your feelings about your new job.

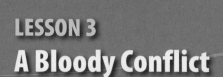

netw⦿rks

There's More Online!

☑ **BIOGRAPHY** Henry Cabot Lodge

☑ **BIOGRAPHY** John Pershing

☑ **BIOGRAPHY** Eddie Rickenbacker

☑ **CHART/GRAPH** Military v. Civilian Dead

☑ **IMAGE** Trench Warfare

☑ **SLIDE SHOW** World War I Technology

☑ **VIDEO** A Bloody Conflict

☑ **INTERACTIVE SELF-CHECK QUIZ**

Reading **HELP**DESK

Content Vocabulary

- **convoy**
- **armistice**
- **national self-determination**
- **reparations**

Academic Vocabulary

- **network** • **resolve**
- **adequately**

TAKING NOTES: *Organizing*

ACTIVITY As you read, complete a graphic organizer similar to the one below by listing the kinds of warfare and technology used in the fighting.

Warfare and Technology Used in World War I

LESSON 3
A Bloody Conflict

ESSENTIAL QUESTION · *Why do nations go to war?*

IT MATTERS BECAUSE

New technology caused both sides to lose millions of lives during World War I. The arrival of American troops helped the Allies win, but the peace treaty set the stage for another war to come.

Combat in World War I

GUIDING QUESTION *How did new technologies increase the number of casualties compared with previous wars?*

By the spring of 1917, World War I had devastated Europe. Old-fashioned strategies and new technologies resulted in terrible destruction. Many Americans believed, however, that their troops would make a difference and quickly bring the war to an end.

Trench Warfare

Early offensives demonstrated that warfare had changed. Powerful artillery guns placed far behind the front lines hurled huge explosive shells onto the battlefield. More people were killed by artillery fire than by any other weapon. As one American noted in his diary:

PRIMARY SOURCE

❝Many dead Germans along the road. One heap on a manure pile. . . . Devastation everywhere. Our barrage has rooted up the entire territory like a plowed field. Dead horses galore, many of them have a hind quarter cut off—the [Germans] need food. Dead men here and there.❞

—quoted in *The American Spirit*, November 3, 1918

To protect themselves from artillery, troops began digging trenches. On the Western Front—where German troops fought French, British, and Belgian forces—the troops dug a **network** of trenches that stretched from the English Channel to the Swiss border. Both sides used barbed wire and a new weapon, the machine gun, to guard against the enemy. Attacks usually began with a massive artillery barrage. Soldiers then raced across the rough landscape toward enemy trenches. Troops used any weapon available to kill the enemy. The new style of fighting, which both sides eventually utilized, resulted in the loss of hundreds of thousands of men and a stalemate on the Western Front. Offensive and defensive moves by the Allies and the Germans failed to be particularly successful.

New Technology

Breaking through enemy lines required new technologies. The Germans first used poison gas in 1915, and the Allies soon followed. Gas caused vomiting, blindness, and suffocation. Both sides developed gas masks to counter fumes. In 1916 the British introduced the armored tank, which could crush barbed wire and cross trenches. But there were still too few of the slow, unreliable machines to revolutionize warfare.

World War I also marked the first use of aircraft in war. Early in the war, the Germans used giant rigid balloons called zeppelins to drop bombs on British warships in the North Sea. At first, airplanes were used to spy on enemy troops and ships. Then the Allies equipped them with machine guns and rockets to attack the German zeppelin fleet. Other aircraft carried small bombs to drop on enemy lines. As technology advanced, airplanes shot down other airplanes in battles known as dogfights. But early military aircraft were difficult to fly and easy to destroy. A combat pilot had an average life expectancy of about two weeks.

✓ **PROGRESS CHECK**

Describing What new technologies were introduced in World War I, and how did they impact the war?

To protect against poison gas attacks, troops carried gas masks similar to these masks worn by American soldiers in 1917.

network an interconnected system

The War in the Trenches

From Ypres on France's coast, down through Somme, Marne, and Verdun, Allied forces held off German advances.

North Sea
Baltic Sea
UNITED KINGDOM
London
NETH.
Ypres
BELG.
Somme
Paris
Marne
Verdun
Western Front
FRANCE
SWITZ.
GERMANY
Berlin
Tannenberg
RUSSIA
Eastern Front
Vienna
Budapest
AUSTRIA-HUNGARY
Italian Front
Isonzo
Trieste
ITALY
Rome
MONTENEGRO
Sarajevo
SERBIA
ALBANIA
ROMANIA
BULGARIA
Constantinople
Black Sea
GREECE
OTTOMAN EMPIRE
Gallipoli
40°N

GEOGRAPHY CONNECTION

Troops on both sides of the conflict dug an extensive network of trenches to protect themselves from artillery fire and enemy attacks.

1 **THE WORLD IN SPATIAL TERMS** *Along which borders did the line of trench warfare stretch?*

2 **PLACES AND REGIONS** *How do you think the Central Powers' war efforts were affected by fighting the war in the west and in the east?*

Allied Powers
Central Powers
Neutral Powers
— Line of trench warfare, 1914–1916
✶ Allied victory
✶ Central Powers victory

0   400 miles
0   400 km
Lambert Azimuthal Equal-Area projection

Mediterranean Sea

0°   20°E   40°E

The Americans Arrive

GUIDING QUESTION *Why was the arrival of U.S. forces so important to the war effort?*

Nearly two million American troops marched into the bloody stalemate in the Western Front. Although the American "doughboys" were inexperienced, they were fresh and eager to fight. As the Americans began to arrive, many in Germany concluded that the war was lost.

Winning the War at Sea

American admiral William S. Sims proposed that merchant ships and troop transports travel in groups called **convoys.** Small, maneuverable warships called destroyers protected convoys across the Atlantic. If a ship was sunk, other ships in the convoy could rescue survivors. Convoys greatly reduced shipping losses and ensured that American troops arrived safely in time to help the Allies on the Western Front.

Russia Leaves the War

In March 1917, riots broke out in Russia. Czar Nicholas II, the leader of the Russian Empire, abdicated his throne, and the Russian Revolution began. A temporary government took command whose leaders wanted Russia to stay in the war. However, the government was unable to deal **adequately** with the problems afflicting the nation, so Vladimir Lenin's Bolshevik Party seized power and established a Communist government in November 1917.

Germany's military fortunes improved with the Bolshevik takeover. Lenin pulled Russia out of the war to concentrate on establishing a Communist state. He explained:

PRIMARY SOURCE

❝ [I]t is necessary with particular thoroughness, persistence and patience to . . . prove without overthrowing capital it is impossible to end the war by a truly democratic peace.❞

—from *The April Theses,* 1917

Lenin agreed to the Treaty of Brest-Litovsk with Germany on March 3, 1918. Under this treaty, Russia gave up the Ukraine, its Polish and Baltic territories, and Finland. With the Eastern Front settled, Germany could concentrate its forces in the west.

convoy a group that travels with something, such as a ship, to protect it

adequately sufficiently; completed to its minimum requirements

Air battles first occurred during World War I. These early planes, however, were hard to fly and easy to destroy during dogfights.

▶ **CRITICAL THINKING**
Making Generalizations How did the use of aircraft change battle during World War I?

Americans Enter Combat

At the time World War I began, many Americans believed they owed the French a debt for their help in the American Revolution. General John J. Pershing, commander of the American Expeditionary Force (AEF), arrived in Paris on July 4, 1917. British and French commanders wanted to integrate American troops into their armies. Pershing refused, and eventually only one unit, the 93rd Infantry Division—an African American unit—was transferred to the French.

Germany's Last Offensive On March 21, 1918, the Germans launched a massive gas attack and artillery bombardment along the Western Front. Strengthened by reinforcements from the Russian front, the Germans pushed deep into Allied lines. By early June, they were less than 40 miles (64 km) from Paris. In late May, as the

PHOTO: Stapleton Collection/Historical Picture Library/CORBIS offensive continued, the Americans launched their first major attack, quickly capturing the village of Cantigny. On June 1, American and French troops blocked the German drive on Paris at the town of Château-Thierry. On July 15, the Germans launched one last massive attack in an attempt to take Paris, but American and French troops held their ground.

The Battle of the Argonne Forest With the German drive stalled, French marshal Ferdinand Foch, supreme commander of the Allied forces, ordered massive counterattacks. In mid-September American troops drove back German forces at the battle of Saint-Mihiel. On September 26, 1918, the most massive offensive for the American Expeditionary Force was launched in the region between the Meuse River and the Argonne Forest. Although the Germans inflicted heavy casualties, their positions slowly fell to the advancing American troops. By early November, the Americans had opened a hole on the eastern flank of the German lines. All across the Western Front, the Germans began to retreat.

The War Ends

Meanwhile, a revolution had engulfed Austria-Hungary. In October 1918, Poland, Hungary, and Czechoslovakia declared independence. By early November, the governments of the Austro-Hungarian Empire and the Ottoman Empire had surrendered to the Allies.

In late October, sailors in Kiel, the main base of the German fleet, mutinied. Within days, groups of workers and soldiers seized power in other German towns. The German emperor stepped down, and on November 9, Germany became a republic. Two days later, the government signed an **armistice**—an agreement to stop fighting. On November 11, 1918, the fighting stopped.

☑ **PROGRESS CHECK**

Identifying Cause and Effect How did the arrival of American troops affect German attitudes about the war?

A Flawed Peace

GUIDING QUESTION *Why did President Wilson's ideas for peace negotiations differ from those of French premier Clemenceau and British prime minister Lloyd George?*

Although the fighting had stopped, World War I was not over. In January 1919, delegates from 27 countries traveled to the peace conference at the Palace of Versailles, near Paris. The treaty with Germany that resulted came to be called the Treaty of Versailles. The conference also negotiated the Treaty of Saint-Germain, ending the war with Austria-Hungary. Negotiations on the Treaty of Versailles lasted five months. The most important participants were the so-called "Big Four": President Wilson of the United States, British prime minister David Lloyd George, French premier Georges Clemenceau, and Italian prime minister Vittorio Orlando. Russian representatives were not invited to the conference because Allied leaders refused to recognize Lenin's government as legitimate.

The Fourteen Points

President Wilson arrived in Paris in 1919 with a peace plan known as the Fourteen Points. It was based on "the principle of justice to all peoples and nationalities." In the first five points, Wilson proposed to eliminate the causes of the war through free trade, freedom of the seas, disarmament, an impartial adjustment of colonial claims, and open diplomacy.

BIOGRAPHY

Alvin York (1887–1964)
Alvin York grew up poor in the mountains of Tennessee. After being drafted, he tried to avoid military service as a conscientious objector due to his pacifist Christian beliefs. York later became convinced that he could fight for a just cause. During the Battle of the Argonne Forest, German machine guns on a fortified hill fired on York's platoon and killed nine men. York took command and charged the machine guns. He went on to kill several Germans, capture the machine guns, and take 132 prisoners. For his actions, he received the Medal of Honor and the French Croix de Guerre.

▶ **CRITICAL THINKING**
Describing How did York contribute to the American victory at the Argonne?

armistice a temporary agreement to end fighting

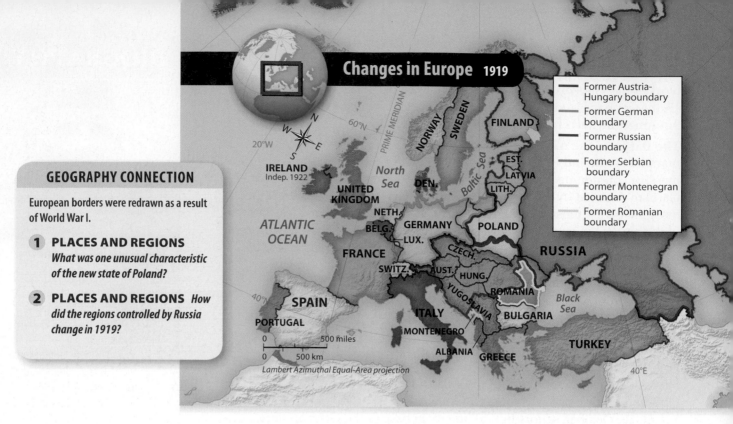

Changes in Europe 1919

Legend:
— Former Austria-Hungary boundary
— Former German boundary
— Former Russian boundary
— Former Serbian boundary
— Former Montenegran boundary
— Former Romanian boundary

Lambert Azimuthal Equal-Area projection

GEOGRAPHY CONNECTION

European borders were redrawn as a result of World War I.

1 **PLACES AND REGIONS** *What was one unusual characteristic of the new state of Poland?*

2 **PLACES AND REGIONS** *How did the regions controlled by Russia change in 1919?*

The next eight points addressed the right of **national self-determination,** the idea that the borders of countries should be based on ethnicity and national identity. Supporters of this idea believed that when borders are not based on national identity, nations are more likely to go to war to **resolve** border disputes. This principle also meant that no nation should keep territory taken from another nation. This required the Central Powers to evacuate all invaded countries and Germany to restore the French territory of Alsace-Lorraine, taken in 1871.

The fourteenth point called for the creation of a League of Nations. The League's members would help preserve peace by pledging to respect and protect each other's territory and political independence. Wilson was willing to give up his other goals in exchange for support for the League.

The Treaty of Versailles

Wilson's popularity in Europe put him in a strong negotiating position. The peace conference decided to use the Fourteen Points as the basis for negotiations. But not everyone was impressed by Wilson's ideas. Premier Clemenceau of France and British prime minister Lloyd George wanted to punish the Germans for the suffering they had inflicted on the rest of Europe. Additionally, Britain refused to give up its sizable naval advantage by agreeing to Wilson's call for freedom of the seas.

The Treaty of Versailles, reluctantly signed by Germany on June 28, 1919, included many terms designed to punish and weaken Germany. Germany's armed forces were greatly reduced and its troops were not allowed west of the Rhine River. The treaty also specifically blamed "the aggression of Germany" for the war. This allowed the Allies to demand that Germany pay **reparations**—monetary compensation for all of the war damages it had caused. A commission decided that Germany owed the Allies about $33 billion. This sum far exceeded what Germany could pay all at once and was intended to keep its economy weak for a long time.

Wilson had somewhat better success in promoting national self-determination. The Austro-Hungarian Empire, the Russian Empire, the

national self-determination the free choice by the people of a nation of their own future political status

resolve to come to an agreement

reparations payment by the losing country in a war to the winner for the damages caused by the war

German Empire, and the Ottoman Empire were dismantled, and new nations created. In general, the majority of people in each new country were from one ethnic group. But both Poland and Czechoslovakia were given territory where the majority of the people were German, and Germany was split in two in order to give Poland access to the Baltic Sea. This arrangement helped set the stage for a new series of crises in the 1930s.

The Treaty of Versailles ignored freedom of the seas, free trade, and Wilson's goal of a fair settlement of colonial claims. No colonial people in Asia or Africa received independence. France and Britain took over colonial areas in Africa and the Middle East, and Japan assumed responsibility for colonies in East Asia. The treaty did, however, call for the creation of a League of Nations. League members promised to reduce armaments, to submit all disputes that endangered the peace to arbitration, and to aid any member who was threatened with aggression.

The Belgian town of Ypres (shown above) was the site of some of the heaviest fighting of World War I. The war devastated Europe's people and places. The physical scars on the landscape and the millions of casualties affected Europe for years to come.

▶ CRITICAL THINKING
Predicting Consequences How did the damage caused during World War I change Europe in later years?

The U.S. Senate Rejects the Treaty

President Wilson was confident the American people would support the Treaty of Versailles. But he had badly underestimated opposition to the League of Nations in the Senate. One group of senators, nicknamed the "Irreconcilables," assailed the League as the kind of "entangling alliance" that the Founders had warned against. A larger group of senators known as the "Reservationists" agreed to ratify the treaty if it was amended to say that any military action by the United States required the approval of Congress. Wilson refused, fearing the change would undermine the League's effectiveness.

Wilson decided to take his case directly to the American people. Starting in September 1919, he traveled some 8,000 miles and made more than 30 major speeches in three weeks. Soon afterward he suffered a stroke. Although bedridden, Wilson still refused to compromise on the treaty.

The Senate voted in November 1919 and in March 1920, but both times it refused to give its consent to the treaty. After Wilson left office in 1921, the United States negotiated separate peace treaties with each of the Central Powers. The League of Nations took shape without the United States.

✔ PROGRESS CHECK

Comparing and Contrasting How did Wilson's perspective on the best outcome of the peace process differ from those of European leaders?

PHOTO: Hulton Archive/Getty Images

LESSON 3 REVIEW

Reviewing Vocabulary
1. *Contrasting* What is the difference between an armistice and a treaty?

2. *Applying* How did ideas of national self-determination influence the Treaty of Versailles?

Using Your Notes
3. *Explaining* Review the notes you completed during the lesson and then write a paragraph explaining how new technology changed warfare during World War I.

Answering Guiding Questions
4. *Identifying Cause and Effect* How did new technologies increase the number of casualties compared with previous wars?

5. *Drawing Conclusions* Why was the arrival of American forces so important to the war effort?

6. *Identifying Perspectives* Why did President Wilson's ideas for peace negotiations differ from those of French premier Clemenceau and British prime minister Lloyd George?

Writing Activity
7. **EXPOSITORY** Write a brief essay that explains the reasons the U.S. Senate refused to give its consent to the Treaty of Versailles.

networks

There's More Online!

☑ **BIOGRAPHY** J. Edgar Hoover

☑ **BIOGRAPHY** A. Mitchell Palmer

☑ **IMAGE** Palmer Raid

☑ **MAP** Presidential Election of 1920

☑ **VIDEO** The War's Impact

☑ **INTERACTIVE SELF-CHECK QUIZ**

LESSON 4
The War's Impact

Reading **HELP**DESK

Content Vocabulary
• cost of living • deport
• general strike

Academic Vocabulary
• widespread • authorities

TAKING NOTES: *Organizing*

ACTIVITY As you read, complete a graphic organizer similar to the one below to list the effects of the end of World War I on the U.S. economy.

Effects of End of World War I on Economy →
- [ ]
- [ ]
- [ ]

ESSENTIAL QUESTION • *Why do nations go to war?*

IT MATTERS BECAUSE
America's victory overseas led to turmoil at home. The end of the wartime economy led to a depression and fears of communism, as strikes, riots, and bombings took place.

An Economy in Turmoil

GUIDING QUESTION *Why did many workers participate in strikes following the war?*

After the war ended, government agencies removed their controls from the economy. People raced to buy goods that had been rationed, while businesses raised prices they had been forced to keep low. The result was rapid inflation that greatly increased the **cost of living**—the cost of food, clothing, shelter, and other essentials. With orders for war materials evaporating, factories laid off workers. Returning soldiers found that jobs were scarce.

Inflation Leads to Strikes

While workers wanted higher wages to keep up with inflation, companies resisted because inflation was also driving up their operating costs. During the war, union membership had increased greatly. Business leaders, however, were determined to break the power of the unions. By the end of 1919, more than 3,600 strikes involving more than four million workers had taken place.

The Seattle General Strike In Seattle, some 35,000 shipyard workers walked off the job demanding higher wages and shorter hours. Other unions in Seattle soon organized a **general strike**—a strike that involves all workers in a community—of more than 60,000 people that paralyzed the city for five days. The strikers returned to work without making any gains, but their actions worried many Americans because the general strike was a common tactic of Communists and some radical groups in Europe.

The Boston Police Strike One of the most famous strikes of 1919 occurred in Boston, where roughly 75 percent of the police force walked off the job. Riots and looting forced Governor Calvin

Coolidge to call in the National Guard. When the strikers tried to return to work, the police commissioner instead fired them. Despite protests, Coolidge agreed that the men should be fired, declaring: "There is no right to strike against the public safety by anybody, anywhere, anytime." Coolidge's response earned him **widespread** public support and convinced the Republicans to make him their vice-presidential candidate in 1920.

The Steel Strike Soon after the police strike, an estimated 350,000 steelworkers went on strike for higher pay, shorter hours, and recognition of their union. U.S. Steel refused to talk to union leaders and set out to break the union. It blamed the strike on foreign radicals and called for loyal Americans to return to work. Meanwhile, the company hired African American and Mexican workers as replacements. Clashes between company guards and strikers were frequent. In Gary, Indiana, a riot left 18 strikers dead. The strike collapsed in 1920, setting back the union cause in the steel industry for more than a decade.

Racial Unrest

Postwar economic turmoil also contributed to widespread racial unrest. Many African Americans had moved north during the war to take factory jobs. As people began to be laid off and returning soldiers found it hard to find work and affordable housing, many blamed African Americans for taking their jobs. Frustration and racism combined to produce violence.

In the summer of 1919, 25 race riots broke out across the nation. The riots began in July, when a mob of angry whites burned shops and homes in an African American neighborhood in Longview, Texas. A week later in Washington, D.C., gangs of African Americans and whites fought each other for four days before troops got the riots under control.

The worst violence occurred in Chicago. On a hot July day, African Americans went to a whites-only beach. Both sides began throwing stones, and an African American teenager drowned as a result. A full-scale riot then erupted. Angry African Americans attacked white neighborhoods while whites attacked African American neighborhoods. The riot lasted for almost two weeks until the government sent in the National Guard to impose order. By the time the rioting ended, 38 people had been killed—15 white and 23 African American—and more than 500 had been injured.

cost of living the cost of purchasing goods and services essential for survival

general strike a strike involving all the workers in a particular geographic location

widespread widely diffused or prevalent

Some strikes became so violent and out of control that the federal government was forced to call in the National Guard to impose order. Here, troops get rioting under control during the Boston Police Strike of 1919.

▶ **CRITICAL THINKING**
Analyzing Information Why do you think the government reacted against strikes so strongly in 1919?

PHOTO: Underwood & Underwood/Bettmann/CORBIS

The race riots of 1919 disillusioned some African Americans who felt their wartime contributions had been for nothing. For others, however, the wartime struggle for democracy encouraged them to fight for their rights at home. For the first time, African Americans organized and fought back. The NAACP experienced a surge in membership after the war, and in 1919 it launched a new campaign for a federal law against lynching.

✓ PROGRESS CHECK

Identifying Cause and Effect Why did the number of strikes increase after the war?

The Red Scare

GUIDING QUESTION *Do you agree or disagree with A. Mitchell Palmer's efforts to prevent a "radical" revolution in the United States?*

Since the late 1800s, many Americans had accused immigrants of importing socialist and communist ideas and had blamed them for labor unrest and violence. Events in Russia seemed to justify fears of a Communist revolution. The strikes of 1919 fueled fears that Communists, or "reds," might seize power, leading to a nationwide panic known as the Red Scare. Many people were particularly concerned about workers using strikes to start a revolution.

The Palmer Raids

In April the postal service intercepted more than 30 parcels containing homemade bombs addressed to prominent Americans. The next month, a parade in Cleveland to protest the jailing of American Socialist Party leader Eugene Debs turned into a series of riots. Two people were killed and another 40 were injured. In June eight bombs in eight cities exploded within minutes of one another, suggesting a nationwide conspiracy.

One of these bombs damaged the home of United States attorney general A. Mitchell Palmer. Palmer took action, establishing a special division within the Justice Department, the General Intelligence Division, which eventually became the Federal Bureau of Investigation (FBI). Although evidence pointed to no single group, Palmer's agents targeted the foreign-born. On November 7, 1919, Palmer ordered a series of raids on offices of the Union of Russian Workers in 12 cities. Less than seven weeks later, a transport ship left New York for Russia carrying 249 immigrants who had been **deported,** or expelled from the country.

deport to expel an individual from the country

In September 1920, a bomb made of 100 pounds of dynamite and 500 pounds of steel fragments exploded in New York City, killing 38 people and injuring 100 others.

▶ CRITICAL THINKING
Analyzing Primary Sources
What effect do you think the event depicted below had on public attitudes toward political radicals?

In January 1920, Palmer ordered another series of raids on the headquarters of various radical organizations. Nearly 6,000 people were arrested. Palmer's raids continued until the spring of 1920, and **authorities** detained thousands of suspects. Palmer's agents often ignored the civil liberties of suspects. Officers entered homes and offices without search warrants. Some suspects were jailed indefinitely and were not allowed to talk to their attorneys. Many of the nearly 600 immigrants who were deported never had a court hearing. Palmer defended his actions:

authorities those who have control over determining and enforcing what is right or wrong

PRIMARY SOURCE

66Like a prairie-fire, the blaze of revolution was sweeping over every American institution of law and order a year ago. It was eating its way into the homes of the American workmen . . . leaping into the belfry of the school bell, crawling into the sacred corners of American homes . . . burning up the foundations of society.99

—from "The Case Against the 'Reds,'" *Forum*, 1920

For a while, Palmer was regarded as a national hero. But his raids failed to turn up any hard evidence of revolutionary conspiracy. The Red Scare, however, greatly influenced people's attitudes during the 1920s. The New York state legislature expelled five members of the Socialist Party in January 1920, and within a few months, nearly 30 states passed sedition laws making it illegal to join groups advocating revolution. Many linked radicalism with immigrants, which led to calls to limit immigration.

The Election of 1920

Economic problems, labor unrest, racial tensions, and the fresh memories of World War I created a general sense of disillusionment in the United States. During the 1920 campaign, Ohio governor James M. Cox and his running mate, Assistant Secretary of the Navy Franklin D. Roosevelt, ran on a platform of progressive ideals. President Wilson tried to convince the Democrats to make the campaign a referendum on the Treaty of Versailles and the League of Nations. The Republican candidate, Warren G. Harding, called for a return to "normalcy," arguing that the country needed to return to the days before the Progressive Era reforms. Harding won the election by a landslide. Many Americans hoped to put racial, labor, and economic troubles behind them and build a more prosperous and stable society.

✓ **PROGRESS CHECK**

Constructing Arguments Do you think that the events of 1919 justified Palmer's actions? Why or why not?

Analyzing
PRIMARY SOURCES

Warren G. Harding on a Return to Normalcy

66[Our] present need is not heroics, but healing; not nostrums, but normalcy; not revolution, but [bold] restoration; not agitation, but adjustment; not surgery, but serenity; not the dramatic, but the dispassionate; . . . not submergence in internationality, but sustainment in triumphant nationality.99

—from a speech given May 14, 1920

DBQ *MAKING GENERALIZATIONS* What feelings did Harding hope to promote in this speech?

Reviewing Vocabulary

1. Defining What types of costs are included in the cost of living?

2. Stating What happens to a person who is deported?

Using Your Notes

3. Explaining Use the notes you completed during the lesson to write a paragraph explaining the effects of the end of World War I on the U.S. economy.

Answering Guiding Questions

4. Identifying Cause and Effect Why did many workers participate in strikes following the war?

5. Identifying Central Issues Do you agree or disagree with A. Mitchell Palmer's efforts to prevent a "radical" revolution in the United States?

Writing Activity

6. PERSUASIVE Radical, labor, and racial unrest increased after World War I, and the federal government responded strongly. The National Guard was sent in to break up strikes and riots, and government agents detained and deported thousands of immigrants and radicals. Do you sympathize with those reacting against society, or with the government? Write a short persuasive speech explaining your position and offering reasons to support it.

Directions: On a separate sheet of paper, answer the questions below. Make sure you read carefully and answer all parts to the question.

Lesson Review

Lesson 1

1 *Explaining* Why did the majority of Americans sympathize with the Allies, even before the United States entered the war?

2 *Identifying Cause and Effect* What events triggered the U.S. entry into World War I?

Lesson 2

3 *Making Generalizations* What were the contributions of women and African Americans on the home front during the war?

4 *Drawing Inferences* How did government efforts to ensure public support for the war effort lead to restrictions on civil liberties?

Lesson 3

5 *Defending* What facts support the statement that technology made World War I the first modern war?

6 *Interpreting Significance* What impact did the arrival of American troops have on the course of the war?

Lesson 4

7 *Drawing Conclusions* What circumstances caused economic and racial unrest in 1919?

8 *Identifying Perspectives* Why did many Americans come to fear Communists and other radicals after the end of World War I?

21st Century Skills

9 **RESEARCH SKILLS** Search the Internet to find a propaganda poster from World War I. Write a paragraph explaining what makes it propaganda and the message it intends to convey.

10 **PROBLEM SOLVING** How did Congress ensure that the United States would have enough troops to serve in World War I?

11 **IDENTIFYING CAUSE AND EFFECT** How did the different technologies of World War I lead to the deaths of so many soldiers?

12 **TIME, CHRONOLOGY, AND SEQUENCING** What events led up to the Red Scare?

Exploring the Essential Question

13 *Synthesizing* Write a brief essay discussing the motivations of each of the following countries in taking part in World War I: Germany, Austria-Hungary, the Balkan states, France, Russia, Italy, Britain, and the United States. What major themes emerge as to why nations go to war?

DBQ Document-Based Questions

Use the cartoon to answer the following questions.

14 *Interpreting* Henry Cabot Lodge was the chairman of the Foreign Relations Committee. Use this cartoon to interpret why the artist shows him helping the Treaty of Versailles out of the "operating room" of the Foreign Relations Committee.

15 *Constructing Arguments* Do you think President Wilson was right not to compromise on the Treaty of Versailles? Why or why not?

Extended-Response Question

16 *Constructing Arguments* After World War I, the United States refused to ratify the Treaty of Versailles despite the efforts of Woodrow Wilson to convince Americans that ratification would help ensure an enduring peace. Write a persuasive essay that either supports or opposes the ratification of the Treaty of Versailles. Your essay should include an introduction, at least two paragraphs, and a conclusion.

Need Extra Help?

If You've Missed Question	1	2	3	4	5	6	7	8	9	10	11	12	13	14	15	16
Go to page	380	381	384	385	388	390	394	396	380	386	388	394	378	391	391	392

The Jazz Age

1921–1929

ESSENTIAL QUESTIONS • *How was social and economic life different in the early twentieth century from that of the late nineteenth century?* • *How has the cultural identity of the United States changed over time?*

netw‿rks

There's More Online about the Jazz Age and the early twentieth century.

CHAPTER 17

The Story Matters...

American culture changed in the 1920s, although not everyone approved. Young people adopted new styles of dress, listened to new kinds of music, and had more independence than earlier generations.

African American artists and entertainers of the Harlem Renaissance reached a wide audience, helping overcome racial barriers in American society.

◄ The works of legendary jazz singer and trumpet player Louis Armstrong are still widely played in many areas of contemporary culture. His improvised melodies influence jazz and other American music to this day.

PHOTO: John Springer Collection/CORBIS

Place and Time: United States 1920–1930

After the suffering of World War I, Americans were ready to enjoy life and eager to buy new goods that had not been available during the war. The new technology of the assembly line made the automobile much more affordable and spurred economic growth. The growing African American population in the North sparked new trends in literature, music, and art, and made African Americans a powerful political voice. Yet some people believed traditional society and morality were under attack, causing nativism and racism to increase in the 1920s.

Step Into the Place

Read the quotes and look at the information presented on the map.

 How do the following quote and the information in the map show how technology changed life in the 1920s?

PRIMARY SOURCE

66 Every piece of work in the shop moves; it may move on hooks on overhead chains going to assembly in the exact order in which the parts are required; it may travel on a moving platform, or it may go by gravity, but the point is that there is no lifting or trucking of anything other than materials. . . . No workman has anything to do with moving or lifting anything. 99

—Henry Ford describing his assembly line, from *My Life and Work*, 1922

PHOTOS: **left page:** (tr)/Library of Congress, (bl br)detail/White House Historical Association; **right page** detail/White House Collection/The White House Historical Association

Step Into the Time

Choose an event from the time line and write a paragraph about how that event might have influenced the identity of the United States.

U.S. PRESIDENTS

Harding 1921–1923

Coolidge 1923–1929

UNITED STATES

1920 Prohibition begins

1922 Claude McKay's *Harlem Shadows* is published

1920

1922

WORLD

1921 Chinese Communist Party founded

1922 James Joyce's *Ulysses* is published

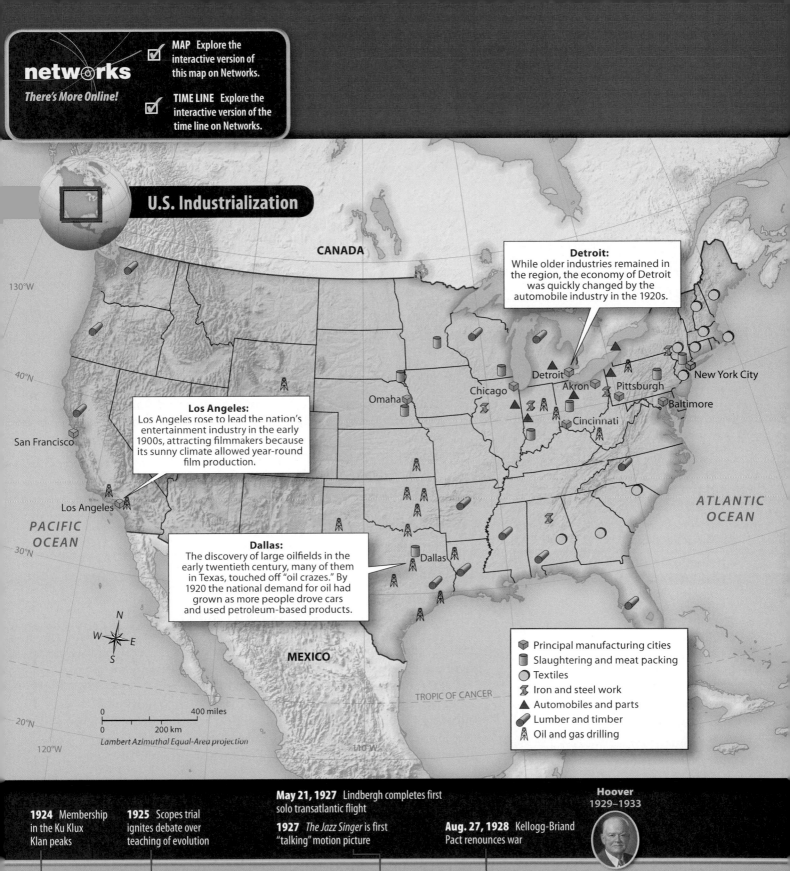

networks
There's More Online!

☑ **MAP** Explore the interactive version of this map on Networks.

☑ **TIME LINE** Explore the interactive version of the time line on Networks.

U.S. Industrialization

CANADA

130°W

40°N

Detroit:
While older industries remained in the region, the economy of Detroit was quickly changed by the automobile industry in the 1920s.

Detroit

New York City

Akron

Pittsburgh

Chicago

Baltimore

Omaha

Cincinnati

Los Angeles:
Los Angeles rose to lead the nation's entertainment industry in the early 1900s, attracting filmmakers because its sunny climate allowed year-round film production.

San Francisco

Los Angeles

ATLANTIC OCEAN

PACIFIC OCEAN

30°N

Dallas:
The discovery of large oilfields in the early twentieth century, many of them in Texas, touched off "oil crazes." By 1920 the national demand for oil had grown as more people drove cars and used petroleum-based products.

Dallas

N
W—E
S

MEXICO

TROPIC OF CANCER

| 0 | 400 miles |
| 0 | 200 km |

Lambert Azimuthal Equal-Area projection

20°N

120°W

110°W

- ⬡ Principal manufacturing cities
- ⬓ Slaughtering and meat packing
- ◯ Textiles
- ⚒ Iron and steel work
- ▲ Automobiles and parts
- ⬗ Lumber and timber
- ⛏ Oil and gas drilling

May 21, 1927 Lindbergh completes first solo transatlantic flight

Hoover
1929–1933

1924 Membership in the Ku Klux Klan peaks

1925 Scopes trial ignites debate over teaching of evolution

1927 *The Jazz Singer* is first "talking" motion picture

Aug. 27, 1928 Kellogg-Briand Pact renounces war

1924

1926

1928

1930

1924 Soviet leader Vladimir Lenin dies

1926 British inventor John Logie Baird demonstrates early version of television

1927 German scientist Werner Heisenberg announces the uncertainty principle

1929 National Revolutionary Party (PRI) founded in Mexico

networks

There's More Online!

☑ **BIOGRAPHY** Calvin Coolidge

☑ **BIOGRAPHY** Warren G. Harding

☑ **BIOGRAPHY** Charles Evans Hughes

☑ **CHART/GRAPH** Unemployment

☑ **CHART/GRAPH** U.S. Budget

☑ **VIDEO** The Politics of the 1920s

☑ **INTERACTIVE SELF-CHECK QUIZ**

Reading **HELP**DESK

Content Vocabulary

• **supply-side economics**
• **cooperative individualism**
• **isolationism**

Academic Vocabulary

• **investigation**
• **revelation**

TAKING NOTES: *Organizing*

ACTIVITY As you read about Presidents Harding and Coolidge, create an outline similar to the one below to list features and accomplishments of their administrations.

> The Politics of the 1920s
> I. The Harding Administration
>   A.
>   B.
> II.
> III.
>   A.
>   B.

LESSON 1
The Politics of the 1920s

ESSENTIAL QUESTIONS · *How was social and economic life different in the early twentieth century from that of the late nineteenth century?* · *How has the cultural identity of the United States changed over time?*

IT MATTERS BECAUSE

Warren G. Harding's administration suffered from corruption and scandals. This damaged Americans' faith in their government. Harding's successor, Calvin Coolidge, worked to restore confidence, to promote a healthy U.S. economy, and to facilitate peace and restore economic stability abroad.

The Harding Administration

GUIDING QUESTION *How was Harding's effort to return to "normalcy" prevented by political scandals?*

Born in 1865 in Corsica, Ohio, Warren G. Harding began his career in Ohio state politics. In 1898 voters elected Harding to the Ohio General Assembly, where he fit in comfortably with the powerful Ohio Republican political machine. In 1903 he was elected lieutenant governor. He became a U.S. senator in 1914. After serving one term, Harding ran for and won the presidency in 1920.

In his campaign, Harding promised "a return to normalcy" following the war. His genial manner endeared him to the nation. People applauded the easygoing atmosphere of the Harding administration replacing the reform and war fervor of President Wilson's last years.

Teapot Dome and Other Scandals

Harding made several notable appointments to the cabinet. These included former Supreme Court justice Charles Evans Hughes as secretary of state, former Food Administrator Herbert Hoover as secretary of commerce, and business tycoon Andrew Mellon as secretary of the treasury. Many of his other appointments, however, were disastrous. He gave cabinet posts and other high-level jobs to friends and political allies from Ohio. Harding felt comfortable among his old friends, known as the Ohio Gang. Alice Roosevelt Longworth, daughter of President Theodore Roosevelt, described a typical evening in Harding's White House study:

"The air [would be] heavy with tobacco smoke, trays with bottles containing every imaginable brand of whiskey . . . cards and poker chips at hand—a general atmosphere of waistcoat unbuttoned, feet on desk, and spittoons alongside."

—from *Crowded Hours*, 1933

Several of these men used their influential posts for their own gain. Colonel Charles R. Forbes, an Ohio acquaintance of Harding's, sold scarce medical supplies from veterans' hospitals and kept the money for himself. He cost the public about $250 million.

In June 1923, while traveling from Alaska to California, Harding became ill with what was probably a heart attack. He died in San Francisco on August 2, shortly before the news of the Forbes scandal broke. Early the next morning, the vice president, Calvin Coolidge, took the oath of office and became president.

The most famous scandal, known as Teapot Dome, began in early 1922. Harding's secretary of the interior, Albert B. Fall, secretly allowed private interests to lease lands containing U.S. Navy oil reserves at Teapot Dome, Wyoming, and Elk Hills, California. In return, Fall received bribes from these private interests totaling more than $300,000. After the *Wall Street Journal* broke the story, the Senate launched an **investigation** that took most of the 1920s to complete. In 1929 Secretary Fall became the first cabinet secretary to go to prison.

Attorney general Harry Daugherty was investigated for accepting bribes from a German agent seeking to buy a German-owned company that had been seized by the U.S. government during World War I. Daugherty refused to open Justice Department files to a congressional committee. He also refused to testify under oath, claiming immunity, or freedom from prosecution, on the grounds that he had had confidential dealings with President Harding. Daugherty was later dismissed by President Coolidge.

"Silent Cal" Takes Over

Calvin Coolidge was very different from Harding. A critic joked that Coolidge could be "silent in five languages." Coolidge quickly distanced himself from the Harding administration. However, he asked the most capable cabinet members—Hughes, Mellon, and Hoover—to remain.

Analyzing PRIMARY SOURCES

Coolidge and Prosperity

"After all, the chief business of the American people is business. They are profoundly concerned with producing, buying, selling, investing and prospering in the world. . . . In all experience, the accumulation of wealth means the multiplication of schools, the increase of knowledge, the dissemination of intelligence, the encouragement of science, the broadening of outlook, the expansion of liberties, the widening of culture."

—Calvin Coolidge, from a speech to newspaper editors, quoted in the *New York Times*, January 18, 1925

DBQ *DRAWING CONCLUSIONS*
Why did Coolidge think that "the accumulation of wealth" was so important?

CORRUPTION IN GOVERNMENT

MILL END REMNANT SALE
A Whole Lot of Junk, such as Moral Responsibility, Honor, Ethics, etc., to be practically given away.
A Triumph of Merchandising!

WELCOME GHOULS

EXTRAORDINARY SALE! Capitol, Army, Navy, White House, etc., Remarkable Values at only **19¢** each Thursday Only No phone or Mail Orders

Sight Seeing Tours Ruins of Washington

AMERICAN INSTITUTIONS CABINET MEMBERS LAWYERS, ETC. BOUGHT, SOLD & QUOTED.

POLITICAL CARTOONS

"Bargain Day in Washington" shows the U.S. Capitol, the Washington Monument, the army, the White House, and the navy as having been "sold" to the highest bidder.

▶ **CRITICAL THINKING**

1 *Comparing and Contrasting* What similarity does the cartoon suggest between the White House and the U.S. Capitol?

2 *Analyzing Information* What does the cartoon imply about corruption in the federal government?

Coolidge believed that prosperity rested on business leadership and that government should interfere with business and industry as little as possible.

In the year following Harding's death and the **revelations** of the scandals, Coolidge avoided crises and adopted policies intended to keep the nation prosperous. He easily won the Republican nomination for president in 1924. The Republicans promised the American people that the policies that had brought prosperity would continue. Coolidge won the election easily.

☑ **PROGRESS CHECK**

Comparing How did the Coolidge administration differ from the Harding administration?

Policies of Prosperity

GUIDING QUESTION *What government policies helped the economy recover from the postwar recession?*

Andrew Mellon, a successful banker and industrialist, was secretary of the treasury under President Harding and the chief architect of economic policy. When Mellon took office, he had three major goals: to balance the budget, to reduce the government's debt, and to cut taxes. Mellon argued that if taxes were lower, businesses and some consumers would spend and invest their extra money. This would cause the economy to grow, and Americans would earn more money. The government then would collect more in taxes. This idea is known today as **supply-side economics.**

At Mellon's urging, Congress dramatically reduced tax rates. By 1928, Congress had reduced the income tax rate most Americans paid to 0.5 percent, down from 4 percent. They cut the rate for the wealthiest Americans to 25 percent, down from 73 percent. The federal budget fell from $6.4 billion to less than $3 billion in seven years.

Secretary of Commerce Herbert Hoover also sought to promote economic growth. He tried to balance government regulation with his philosophy of **cooperative individualism.** This idea involved encouraging businesses to form trade associations that would voluntarily share information with the federal government. Hoover believed this system would reduce costs and promote economic efficiency.

☑ **PROGRESS CHECK**

Summarizing What strategies helped promote economic growth and recovery after World War I?

Trade and Arms Control

GUIDING QUESTION *Do you think it is possible to abolish war?*

Before World War I, the United States was a debtor nation. By the end of the war, wartime allies owed the United States more than $10 billion in war debts. By the 1920s, the United States was the dominant economic power in the world. Under Secretary of State Charles Evans Hughes, the nation tried to use its economic power to promote peace and stability.

The Myth of Isolationism

Most Americans, tired of being entangled in the politics of Europe, favored **isolationism.** This is the idea that the United States will be safer and more prosperous if it stays out of world affairs. To many, it appeared that the United States had become isolationist. It had not ratified the Treaty of Versailles and had not joined the League of Nations. But in fact, the United States was too powerful and too interconnected with other countries economically to be truly isolationist. Instead of relying on armed force and the collective security

revelation an act of revealing to view or making known

supply-side economics an economic theory that lower taxes will boost the economy as businesses and individuals invest their money, thereby creating higher tax revenue

cooperative individualism President Hoover's policy of encouraging manufacturers and distributors to form their own organizations and volunteer information to the federal government in an effort to stimulate the economy

isolationism a national policy of avoiding involvement in world affairs

of the League of Nations, the United States tried to promote peace by using economic policies and arms control agreements.

The Dawes Plan

America's former allies, Britain and France, had difficulty making the payments on their immense war debts. Meanwhile, Germany was trying to make huge cash payments to these nations as punishment for starting the war—payments that were crippling the German economy.

To address this problem, in 1924 American diplomat Charles G. Dawes negotiated an agreement with France, Britain, and Germany. American banks would make loans to Germany to help it to make reparations payments. In exchange, Britain and France would accept less in reparations and pay back more on their war debts to the United States.

The Washington Conference

Despite their debts, the major powers were involved in a costly postwar naval arms race. In 1921 the United States invited representatives from eight major countries—Britain, France, Italy, China, Japan, Belgium, the Netherlands, and Portugal—to Washington, D.C., to discuss disarmament. Secretary of State Charles Evans Hughes proposed a 10-year halt on the construction of new warships. The result was the Five-Power Naval Limitation Treaty between Britain, France, Italy, Japan, and the United States. But the conference also angered the Japanese because their navy was required to be smaller than those of the United States and Britain.

The Kellogg-Briand Pact

The Washington Conference inspired U.S. secretary of state Frank Kellogg and French foreign minister Aristide Briand to propose a treaty to outlaw war altogether. On August 27, 1928, the United States and 14 other nations signed the Kellogg-Briand Pact. All signing nations agreed to abandon war and to settle all disputes by peaceful means.

The London Naval Treaties

From January to April 1930, five nations met in London to extend the Washington Conference. The United States, Britain, France, Italy, and Japan agreed on ratios for war ships, halting the arms race through 1936. In 1934 Japan announced it would not extend the treaty past 1936, so the five nations met again in December 1935. The United States, Britain, and France again signed the treaty. Japan and Italy declined to sign the treaty.

✔ **PROGRESS CHECK**

Identifying What initiatives did the United States take in the 1920s to help ensure economic stability and peace in Europe?

PHOTO: Library of Congress

U.S. secretary of state Frank Kellogg is remembered today for promoting the Kellogg-Briand Pact, a treaty to outlaw war.

▶ **CRITICAL THINKING**
Predicting Consequences What might happen today if the United States and other nations followed the key idea of the Kellogg-Briand Pact?

LESSON 1 REVIEW

Reviewing Vocabulary
1. *Specifying* What were some ways in which the United States showed signs of isolationism after World War I?

Using Your Notes
2. *Comparing* Name one important way in which the Harding and Coolidge administrations were alike in terms of political appointments.

Answering the Guiding Questions
3. *Drawing Conclusions* How was Harding's effort to return to "normalcy" prevented by political scandals?

4. *Cause and Effect* What government policies helped the economy recover from the postwar recession?

5. *Analyzing* Do you think it is possible to abolish war?

Writing About History
6. **PERSUASIVE** Suppose that you are a farmer or business owner in the 1920s. Write a letter to your representatives in Congress about why tax cuts are a good or bad idea.

networks

There's More Online!

☑ **BIOGRAPHY** Henry Ford

☑ **BIOGRAPHY** Charles Lindbergh

☑ **CHART/GRAPH**
Average Hourly Earnings

☑ **IMAGE** Consumer Products

☑ **IMAGE** Radio Technicians

☑ **MAP** Lindbergh's Flight

☑ **SLIDE SHOW** The Car
Changes America

☑ **VIDEO** A Growing Economy

☑ **INTERACTIVE SELF-CHECK
QUIZ**

Reading **HELP**DESK

Content Vocabulary

• **mass production** • **Model T**
• **assembly line**

Academic Vocabulary

• **disposable** • **credit**

TAKING NOTES: *Organizing*

ACTIVITY As you read about the booming era of the 1920s, complete a graphic organizer like the one below to analyze the causes of growth and prosperity.

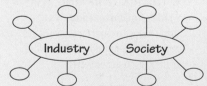

406

LESSON 2
A Growing Economy

ESSENTIAL QUESTIONS • *How was social and economic life different in the early twentieth century from that of the late nineteenth century?* • *How has the cultural identity of the United States changed over time?*

IT MATTERS BECAUSE

In the 1920s, widespread ownership of automobiles, radios, and other innovations changed how Americans lived. The Coolidge administration tried to promote stability in international affairs and encouraged business growth.

The Rise of New Industries

GUIDING QUESTION *How did new industries change the lives of Americans in the 1920s?*

By the 1920s, the automobile had become part of American life. A 1925 survey conducted in Muncie, Indiana, found that 21 out of 26 families who owned cars did not have bathtubs with running water. As one farm wife explained, "You can't ride to town in a bathtub."

Increased automobile ownership was just one example of Americans' rising standard of living. Real per capita earnings soared 22 percent between 1923 and 1929 even as work hours decreased. In 1923 U.S. Steel cut its daily work shift from 12 hours to 8 hours. In 1926 Henry Ford cut the workweek for his employees from six days to five, and farm machinery company International Harvester instituted an annual two-week paid vacation for employees. **Mass production,** or large-scale manufacturing done with machinery, made these changes possible by increasing supply and reducing costs. Workers made more and the goods they bought cost less.

Ford, the Assembly Line, and the Model T

The moving **assembly line** divided operations into simple tasks and cut unnecessary motion to a minimum. In 1913 automaker Henry Ford installed the first moving assembly line at a plant in Highland Park, Michigan. By the following year, workers were building an automobile every 93 minutes. By 1925, a Ford car was rolling off the line every 10 seconds.

Ford's assembly line product, the **Model T,** demonstrated the economic concept of elasticity, or how sensitive product demand is to price. In 1908, the Model T's first year, the car sold for $850. In 1914 mass production reduced the price to $490. Ford also increased his

PHOTOS: (l to r)Topham/The Image Works, The Granger Collection, New York, Library of Congress, Science & Society Picture Library/SSPL/Getty Images, Hulton Archive/Getty Images

workers' wages in 1914 to $5 a day—doubling their pay—and reduced the workday to eight-hour shifts. He took these dramatic steps to win workers' loyalty and to undercut union organizers. By 1924, Model Ts were selling for $295, and Ford sold millions of them.

PRIMARY SOURCE

❝There is one rule for the industrialist and that is: Make the best quality of goods possible at the lowest cost possible paying the highest wages possible.❞

—Henry Ford, quoted in *Mass Production, the Stock Market Crash, and the Great Depression*, 1996

Ford's mass-production methods opened the door for new companies to manufacture cars. By the mid-1920s, General Motors and Chrysler competed successfully with Ford. The auto industry also spurred growth in the production of steel, petroleum, rubber, plate glass, nickel, and lead.

Cars revolutionized American life. They eased the isolation of rural families and let more people live farther from work. A new kind of worker, the auto commuter, appeared. Other forms of urban transportation, such as the trolley, became less popular.

The popularity of the automobile led to an increase in American industries that produced materials needed to build cars.

▶ **CRITICAL THINKING**
Determining Cause and Effect How was the rubber industry affected by the invention of the car?

Consumer Products

In response to rising **disposable** income, many other new goods came on the market. Americans bought such innovations as electric razors, facial tissues, frozen foods, and home hair color. Mouthwash, deodorants, cosmetics, and perfumes became popular products.

Companies created many new products for the home. As indoor plumbing became more common, Americans' concern for hygiene led to the development of numerous household cleaning products. New appliances advertised as labor-savers—such as electric irons, vacuum cleaners, washing machines, and refrigerators—changed the way people cleaned their homes and clothing and prepared meals.

Birth of the Airline Industry

After the Wright brothers' first successful flight in 1903, the aviation industry began developing. Leading the way was American inventor Glenn Curtiss, who invented ailerons—surfaces attached to wings that could be tilted to steer the plane. Ailerons made it possible to build rigid wings and much larger aircraft. The federal government began to support the airline industry. In 1918 the postmaster general introduced the world's first airmail service.

In 1925 Congress passed the Kelly Act, authorizing postal officials to hire private airplane operators to carry mail. The Air Commerce Act of 1926 provided federal aid to build airports. The transatlantic solo flight of former airmail pilot Charles Lindbergh in 1927 banished doubt about the potential of aircraft. By 1928, 48 airlines were serving 355 American cities.

The Radio Industry

In 1913 American engineer Edwin Armstrong invented a special circuit that made it practical to transmit sound via long-range radio. The radio industry began a few years later. In November 1920, the Westinghouse Company broadcast the news of Harding's landslide election victory from station KDKA in Pittsburgh—one of the first public broadcasts in history. That success persuaded Westinghouse to open other stations.

mass production the production of large quantities of goods using machinery and often an assembly line

assembly line a production system with machines and workers arranged so that each person performs an assigned task again and again as the item passes before him or her

Model T automobile built by the Ford Motor Company from 1908 until 1927

disposable remaining to a person after deduction of taxes and living expenses

PHOTO: Topham/The Image Works

Radio technicians prepare for the first NBC radio show, which was broadcast in 1926. Radio networks helped create a national community as people across the country could listen to the same political speeches, music, sports, news, and entertainment programs.

▶ **CRITICAL THINKING**

Drawing Inferences How might the growing nationwide availability of radio programs have affected Americans' sense of their culture?

In 1926 the National Broadcasting Company (NBC) set up a network of stations to broadcast daily radio programs. By 1927, almost 700 stations dotted the country. Sales of radio equipment grew from $10.6 million in 1921 to $411 million in 1929, by which time more than 12 million radios were in use across the country.

In 1928 the Columbia Broadcasting System (CBS) assembled a coast-to-coast network of stations to rival NBC. The two networks sold advertising time and hired musicians, actors, and comedians from vaudeville, movies, and the nightclub circuit to appear on their shows. Americans experienced the first presidential election campaign to use radio in 1928, when the radio networks sold more than $1 million in advertising time to the Republican and Democratic Parties.

☑ **PROGRESS CHECK**

Analyzing How did the new industries such as the automobile and radio change the way people lived?

The Consumer Society

GUIDING QUESTION *How did attitudes toward credit and consumerism change in the 1920s?*

Higher wages and shorter workdays resulted in a decade-long buying spree that kept the economy booming. Shifting from traditional attitudes of thrift and prudence, Americans in the 1920s enthusiastically accepted their new role as consumers.

Easy Consumer Credit

One notable aspect of the economic boom was the growth of individual borrowing. **Credit** had been available before the 1920s, but most Americans had considered debt shameful. Now attitudes toward debt started changing, as people began believing in their ability to pay their debts over time. Many listened to the sales pitch "Buy now and pay in easy installments," and began to accumulate debt. Americans bought 75 percent of their radios and 60 percent of their automobiles on the installment plan. Some started buying on credit at a rate exceeding their income.

credit an amount or sum of money placed at a person's disposal by a bank on condition that it will be repaid with interest

Mass Advertising

When Otto Rohwedder developed a commercial bread slicer in 1928, he faced a problem common to inventions: the invention—sliced bread—was something no one knew they needed. To attract consumers, manufacturers turned to advertising, another booming industry in the 1920s.

Advertisers linked products with qualities associated with the modern era, such as progress, convenience, leisure, success, and style. Advertisers also preyed on consumers' fears and anxieties, such as insecurities about one's status or weight. For example, a 1923 advertisement for face cream read: "These premature lines are only the troubles of a skin allowed to be too dry. . . . The society woman keeps her skin smooth and fresh season in and season out."

The Managerial Revolution

By the early 1920s, many industries had already created modern organizational structures. Companies were split into divisions with functions such as sales, marketing, and accounting. Managers were hired to run these divisions, freeing executives and owners from the day-to-day running of the companies. The large numbers of new managers helped expand the middle class, adding to the nation's prosperity. These new developments in business organization generated more business profit, which improved the nation's standard of living.

PRIMARY SOURCE

❝[I]t is not only by technical skill that modern civilization is sustained. It depends to a large degree on accumulated and invested capital. . . . Civilization and profits go hand in hand.❞

—Calvin Coolidge, quoted in the *New York Times*, November 28, 1920

Advertisements in the 1920s enticed buyers with new technology, endorsements, money-back guarantees, and quick credit approval.

▶ **CRITICAL THINKING**

1 *Drawing Conclusions* Why did manufacturers offer money back when paid for at time of purchase?

2 *Predicting Consequences* What was the danger of buying products on credit?

Uneven Prosperity

Not all Americans shared in the economic boom. For example, thousands of African Americans who held factory jobs during World War I were replaced by returning servicemen. Native Americans, though granted citizenship in 1924, were often isolated on reservations where there was little productive work. Also, many immigrants had difficulty finding work. Most were farmers and factory workers with pitifully low wages. Many people in the Deep South were also left out of the economic boom as the traditional agricultural economic base there eroded after the war.

☑ **PROGRESS CHECK**

Explaining How did changing attitudes about credit affect people's daily lives?

The Farm Crisis

GUIDING QUESTION *Why did farmers miss out on the prosperity of the 1920s?*

American farmers did not share in the prosperity of the 1920s. On average, they earned less than one-third of the income of other American workers. Technological advances in fertilizers, seed varieties, and farm machinery allowed them to produce more, but higher yields without an increase in demand meant that they received lower prices. Between 1920 and 1921, corn and wheat prices declined considerably. Costs for improved farming technology, meanwhile, continued to increase.

Although many people benefited from the economic boom of the 1920s, several groups did not share in the general prosperity. For many African Americans, such as this family in rural Georgia, the 1920s were a time of poverty.

▶ **CRITICAL THINKING**
Comparing and Contrasting
In the 1920s, how was the life of a factory worker who lived in a big city different from the life of a farmer living in a rural area?

PHOTO: Hulton Archive/Getty Images

Many factors contributed to this "quiet depression" in American agriculture. During the war, the government had urged farmers to produce more to meet the great need for food in Europe. Many farmers borrowed heavily to buy new land and new machinery to raise more crops. Sales were strong, prices were high, and farmers prospered. After the war, however, European farm output rose, and the debt-ridden countries of Europe had little money to spend on American farm products. In addition, Congress passed the Fordney-McCumber Act in 1922, making matters worse by raising tariffs dramatically. This dampened the American market for foreign goods and sparked a reaction in foreign markets against buying American agricultural products.

Congress tried to pass legislation to help farmers sell their surpluses, but President Coolidge vetoed the bills. He argued that with money flowing to farmers under the proposed law, they would be encouraged to produce even greater surpluses. Agriculture remained in recession throughout the 1920s.

☑ **PROGRESS CHECK**

Synthesizing What factors led to the growing economic crisis in farming?

LESSON 2 REVIEW

Reviewing Vocabulary
1. ***Explaining*** How did the assembly line help make cars affordable for more Americans?

Using Your Notes
2. ***Hypothesizing*** Review your notes on the economic growth of the 1920s. How might the economy of the 1920s have been different without the advertising industry?

Answering the Guiding Questions
3. ***Summarizing*** How did new industries change the lives of Americans in the 1920s?

4. ***Synthesizing*** How did attitudes toward credit and consumerism change in the 1920s?

5. ***Identifying Cause and Effect*** Why did farmers miss out on the prosperity of the 1920s?

Writing Activity
6. **PERSUASIVE** Think about the advantages of buying an automobile for rural families of the 1920s. Then write an advertisement for a Model T aimed at a farm family of the era.

networks

There's More Online!

☑ **BIOGRAPHY** Clarence Darrow

☑ **BIOGRAPHY** Sacco & Vanzetti

☑ **BIOGRAPHY** Margaret Sanger

☑ **BIOGRAPHY** John Scopes

☑ **VIDEO** A Clash of Values

☑ **INTERACTIVE SELF-CHECK QUIZ**

Reading **HELP**DESK

Content Vocabulary

• **nativism**   • **creationism**
• **anarchist**   • **speakeasy**
• **evolution**

Academic Vocabulary

• **source**   • **deny**

TAKING NOTES: *Organizing*

ACTIVITY As you read about Americans' reactions to immigrants during the 1920s, complete a graphic organizer similar to the one below by filling in the causes and effects of anti-immigrant prejudices.

Anti-Immigrant
Prejudices

LESSON 3
A Clash of Values

ESSENTIAL QUESTIONS · *How was social and economic life different in the early twentieth century from that of the late nineteenth century?* · *How has the cultural identity of the United States changed over time?*

IT MATTERS BECAUSE
The 1920s are often called the Roaring Twenties because to many the decade seemed to be one long party. Many urban Americans celebrated the new "modern" culture. However, many rural Americans believed traditional society was under attack. Nativism and racism increased, women sought to break free of traditional roles, and supporters of the new morality clashed with those who supported more traditional values.

Nativism and Immigration Policies

GUIDING QUESTION *Why did nativism strengthen during the 1920s, and how did the government deal with the tensions?*

The 1920s was a time of economic growth, but it was also a time of turmoil. An economic recession, an influx of immigrants, and cultural tensions combined to create an atmosphere of disillusionment and intolerance. The fear and prejudice many felt toward Germans and Communists during and after World War I expanded to include all immigrants. This triggered a general rise in racism and **nativism**—a belief that one's native land needs to be protected against immigrants.

During World War I, immigration to the United States had dropped sharply. By 1921, however, it had returned to prewar levels, with the majority of immigrants coming from southern and eastern Europe. Many Americans blamed the bombings, strikes, and recession of the postwar years on immigrants. Many believed immigrants were taking jobs that would otherwise have gone to soldiers returning home from the war.

The Sacco-Vanzetti Case
The Sacco-Vanzetti case reflected the prejudices and fears of the era. On April 15, 1920, two men robbed and murdered two employees of a shoe factory in Massachusetts. Police subsequently arrested two Italian immigrants, Nicola Sacco and Bartolomeo Vanzetti, for the crime.

European Immigration, 1900–1924

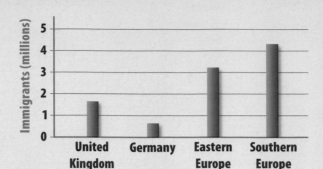

Source: *Historical Statistics of the United States: Millenial to Edition*

Nicola Sacco and Bartolomeo Vanzetti were anarchists who were convicted of murdering two men during a 1920 armed robbery.

The case created a furor when newspapers revealed that the two men were **anarchists,** or people who oppose all forms of government. They also reported that Sacco owned a gun similar to the murder weapon and that the bullets used in the murders matched those in Sacco's gun. The evidence was questionable, but the fact that the accused men were anarchists and foreigners led many people to assume they were guilty, including the jury. On July 14, 1921, Sacco and Vanzetti were found guilty and sentenced to death. After six years of appeals, Sacco and Vanzetti were executed on August 23, 1927.

PRIMARY SOURCE

❝I might have died, unmarked, unknown, a failure. Now we are not a failure. This is our career and our triumph.❞

— Bartolomeo Vanzetti before his execution, *The Letters of Sacco and Vanzetti,* 2007

nativism hostility toward immigrants

anarchist a person who believes that there should be no government

source the point at which something is provided

Return of the Ku Klux Klan

The group that most wanted to restrict immigration was the Ku Klux Klan, or KKK. The old KKK began in the South after the Civil War and used threats and violence to intimidate newly freed African Americans. The new Klan also targeted Catholics, Jews, immigrants, and other groups said to be "un-American." William J. Simmons founded the new Ku Klux Klan in 1915, with a pledge to preserve America's white, Protestant civilization. With the help of professional promoters to sell Klan memberships, more and more people joined. By 1924, membership was close to 4 million as it spread beyond the South into the North and West.

Klan membership began to decline in the late 1920s, mainly due to scandals and power struggles among its leaders. In addition, new restrictions on immigration deprived the Klan of one of its major issues.

Analyzing
PRIMARY SOURCES

Ku Klux Klan Poster

DBQ *MAKING INFERENCES*
In what way can the message in this Klan poster be construed as nativism?

National Origins Act

American immigration policies became more restrictive in response to nativist groups like the KKK. Even some business leaders, who had favored immigration as a **source** of cheap labor, now saw the new immigrants as radicals. In 1921 President Harding signed the Emergency Quota Act, which restricted annual admission to the United States by ethnic group. In 1924 the National Origins Act made immigration restriction a permanent policy. The law set quotas at 2 percent of each national group represented in the U.S. Census of 1890—long before the heavy wave of immigration from southern and eastern Europe. As a result, new quotas deliberately favored immigrants from northwestern Europe.

Increasing Mexican Immigration

Employers still needed immigrants, a source of cheap labor, for agriculture, mining, and railroad work. Mexican immigrants could fill this need because the National Origins Act exempted natives of the Western Hemisphere from the quotas. Large numbers of Mexican immigrants had already begun moving to the United States due to the Newlands Reclamation Act of 1902. The act funded irrigation projects in the Southwest and led to the creation of large farms that needed thousands of workers. By the end of the 1920s, nearly 700,000 Mexicans had migrated to the United States.

☑ PROGRESS CHECK

Contrasting How did the National Origins Act help deal with the tensions created by nativism?

A Clash of Cultures

GUIDING QUESTION *Why do you think some Americans feared the "new morality"?*

Groups that wanted to restrict immigration also wanted to preserve what they considered to be traditional values. They feared that a "new morality" was taking over. This trend glorified youth and personal freedom and brought big changes—particularly to the status of women.

Changes for Women

Having won the right to vote in 1920, many women sought to break free from traditional roles. Women who attended college often found support to pursue careers. Many working-class women took jobs because they needed the wages, but work was also a way to break away from parental authority and establish financial independence. Romance, pleasure, and friendship became linked to successful marriages. Sigmund Freud's theories also affected people's ideas about relationships, especially his theories about human sexuality. Women's fashions changed during the 1920s: women "bobbed," or shortened, their hair and wore flesh-colored silk stockings. Some women, known as flappers, smoked cigarettes, drank prohibited liquor, and wore makeup and sleeveless dresses with short skirts.

Many professional women made major contributions in science, medicine, law, and literature. In medicine, Florence Sabin's research led to a dramatic drop in death rates from tuberculosis. Public-health nurse Margaret Sanger believed that families could improve their standard of living by limiting the number of children they had. She founded the American Birth Control League in 1921 to promote knowledge about birth control. During the 1920s and 1930s, the use of birth control increased dramatically, particularly in the middle class.

Religious Fundamentalism

While many Americans embraced the new morality, others did not welcome these changes and feared that the country was losing its traditional values. Many joined a religious movement known as Fundamentalism.

Fundamentalists believed the Bible was literally true and without error. They rejected Charles Darwin's theory of **evolution,** which said that all life forms had developed from lower forms of life over millions of years. Instead, they embraced **creationism**—the belief that God created the world as described in the Bible.

evolution the scientific theory that humans and other forms of life have evolved over time

creationism the belief that God created the world and everything in it, usually in the way described in the Bible

During the 1920s, fashions changed for women who wanted the glamorous look of movie stars.

▶ CRITICAL THINKING
Analyzing Visuals How do you think this woman portrays the attitude and "new morality" of the 1920s?

Prohibition led to the creation of a special federal bureau charged with stopping the sale of illegal alcohol. In this photo, a federal agent cracks open barrels of illegal rum to prevent it from being sold.

▶ **CRITICAL THINKING**

Analyzing Primary Sources The Volstead Act greatly increased federal police powers. What elements of this photo convey a sense of power?

deny to declare untrue

speakeasy a place where alcoholic beverages are sold illegally

In 1925 Tennessee outlawed any teaching that **denied** "the story of the Divine Creation of man as taught in the Bible," or taught that "man descended from a lower order of animals." The American Civil Liberties Union (ACLU) advertised for a teacher willing to be arrested for teaching evolution. John T. Scopes, a biology teacher in Dayton, Tennessee, volunteered. At Scopes's trial, William Jennings Bryan, a three-time presidential candidate, was the prosecutor representing the creationists. Clarence Darrow, one of the country's most celebrated trial lawyers, defended Scopes. Scopes was found guilty and fined $100, although the conviction was later overturned on a technicality. The trial had been broadcast over the radio, and Darrow's blistering cross-examination of Bryan hurt the Fundamentalist cause.

PRIMARY SOURCE

❝You can only protect your liberties in this world by protecting the other man's freedom. You can only be free if I am free.❞

—Clarence Darrow, address to the court in *People* v. *Lloyd,* 1920

Prohibition

The movement to ban alcohol sales grew stronger in the early 1900s. When the Eighteenth Amendment went into effect in January 1920, the Volstead Act gave the U.S. Treasury Department the power to enforce Prohibition, marking a dramatic increase in federal police powers.

In the 1920s, Treasury Department agents made more than 540,000 arrests, but Americans still ignored the law. People flocked to secret bars called **speakeasies** to purchase alcohol. Liquor also was readily available in rural areas through bootlegging—the illegal production and distribution of alcohol. Huge profits could be made smuggling liquor from Canada and the Caribbean. Organized crime became big business, and gangsters used their money to corrupt local politicians. Al Capone, one of the most successful and well-known gangsters of the era, had many police officers, judges, and other officials on his payroll.

The battle to repeal Prohibition began almost as soon as the Eighteenth Amendment was ratified. The Twenty-first Amendment, ratified in 1933, repealed the Eighteenth Amendment. Though diseases and some social problems were reduced, Prohibition did not improve society as dramatically as its supporters had hoped.

✓ **PROGRESS CHECK**

Identifying What political, social, and economic contributions did women make to American society in the 1920s?

PHOTO: Library of Congress/Archive Photos/Getty Images

LESSON 3 REVIEW

Reviewing Vocabulary

1. *Explaining* Why were Sacco and Vanzetti considered anarchists, and how did that affect the result of their trial?

Using Your Notes

2. *Making Connections* Use your notes from this lesson to write a statement that makes a connection between the causes of nativism and the rise of the Ku Klux Klan.

Answering the Guiding Questions

3. *Identifying Cause and Effect* Why did nativism strengthen during the 1920s, and how did the government deal with the tensions?

4. *Drawing Conclusions* Why do you think some Americans feared the "new morality"?

Writing About History

5. PERSUASIVE Suppose it is the 1920s. Write a letter to your senator to persuade him to support Prohibition or its repeal.

networks

There's More Online!

☑ **BIOGRAPHY** F. Scott & Zelda Fitzgerald

☑ **BIOGRAPHY** Willa Cather

☑ **SLIDE SHOW** Artists and Entertainers

☑ **VIDEO** Cultural Innovations

☑ **INTERACTIVE SELF-CHECK QUIZ**

LESSON 4
Cultural Innovations

ESSENTIAL QUESTIONS · *How was social and economic life different in the early twentieth century from that of the late nineteenth century?* · *How has the cultural identity of the United States changed over time?*

Reading **HELP**DESK

Content Vocabulary
• bohemian • mass media

Academic Vocabulary
• diverse • unify

TAKING NOTES: *Organizing*

ACTIVITY As you read about the 1920s, complete a graphic organizer like the one below by filling in the main characteristics of art, literature, and popular culture of the era.

Cultural Movement	Main Characteristics
Art	
Literature	
Popular Culture	

IT MATTERS BECAUSE

The 1920s was an era of great artistic innovation and enormous change in popular culture. Artists and writers experimented with new techniques. Broadcast radio introduced the latest trends in music and entertainment. Motion pictures became a major leisure-time activity, and Americans began to fall in love with sports such as baseball and boxing.

Art and Literature

GUIDING QUESTION *How did many artists and writers of the time describe the 1920s?*

During the 1920s, American artists and writers challenged traditional ideas as they searched for meaning in the modern world. Many artists, writers, and intellectuals flocked to Manhattan's Greenwich Village and Chicago's South Side. The artistic and unconventional, or **bohemian,** lifestyle of these places allowed artists, musicians, and writers greater freedom of expression.

Modern American Art

European art movements greatly influenced the modernists of American art. Perhaps most striking was the **diverse** range of artistic styles, each attempting to express the individual, modern experience. American painter John Marin drew on the urban dynamics of New York City for inspiration:

PRIMARY SOURCE

❝[T]he whole city is alive; buildings, people, all are alive; and the more they move me the more I feel them to be alive.

It is this 'moving of me' that I try to express, so that I may recall the spell I have been under and behold the expression of the different emotions that have been called into being.❞
—from *Camera Work*, No. 42–43, April–July, 1913

Painter Charles Sheeler applied the influences of photography and the geometric forms of Cubism to urban and rural American landscapes. Edward Hopper revived the visual accuracy of realism.

His paintings conveyed a modern sense of disenchantment and isolation in haunting scenes. Georgia O'Keeffe's landscapes and flowers were admired in many museums throughout her long life and are still admired today.

Poets and Writers

Writers of the 1920s varied greatly in their styles and subject matter. Illinois poet and writer Carl Sandburg used common speech to glorify the Midwest. So did the novels of Pulitzer Prize winner Willa Cather, such as *The Song of the Lark*. Sinclair Lewis poked fun at small-town life in *Main Street*. Edith Wharton criticized upper-class ignorance and pretensions in her Pulitzer Prize–winning novel *The Age of Innocence*. In Greenwich Village, another Pulitzer Prize winner, Edna St. Vincent Millay, wrote about women's inner lives.

Several poets influenced poetic style and subject matter. Some—such as Amy Lowell, Ezra Pound, and William Carlos Williams—used clear, concise images to express moments in time. Others, such as T. S. Eliot, criticized what they saw as a loss of spirituality in modern life.

Among playwrights, Eugene O'Neill was probably the most innovative. His plays, filled with bold artistry and modern themes, portrayed realistic characters and situations, offering a modern vision of life that often touched on the tragic. *Long Day's Journey Into Night* is a memorable example.

Some American writers, disillusioned by World War I and the emerging consumer society, moved to Paris, a center of artistic activity. American experimental writer Gertrude Stein dubbed them a "Lost Generation." Her Paris apartment became a home away from home for many writers. Among them was Ernest Hemingway, who wrote moving novels about war and its aftermath, such as *A Farewell to Arms*. Another visitor was F. Scott Fitzgerald. He criticized society's superficiality in *The Great Gatsby,* in which colorful characters—some modeled after his wife Zelda, who was a dancer, painter, and novelist—chased futile dreams:

PRIMARY SOURCE

❝They were careless people, Tom and Daisy—they smashed up things and creatures and then retreated back into their money or their vast carelessness, or whatever it was that kept them together, and let other people clean up the mess they had made.❞

—from *The Great Gatsby*, 1925

☑ **PROGRESS CHECK**

Describing Why did many artists, poets, playwrights, and novelists move to Paris in the 1920s?

Popular Culture

GUIDING QUESTION *Why did many Americans have more time for entertainment, and how did they spend their time?*

The economic prosperity and new technology of the 1920s provided many Americans with more spending money and leisure time. Millions of Americans eagerly watched sports and enjoyed music, theater, and other forms of popular entertainment.

Movies and Radio Shows

During the era of silent films, theaters hired piano players to provide music during the feature, while subtitles explained the plot. Audiences gathered to see such stars as Mary Pickford, Charlie Chaplin, Douglas Fairbanks, Sr.,

bohemian unconventional; not bound by the rules of society

diverse being different from one another

and Rudolph Valentino. In 1927 the golden age of Hollywood began with the first "talking" picture, *The Jazz Singer*.

Famous songwriter Irving Berlin worked in New York City's Tin Pan Alley, where composers wrote popular music. Berlin's famous songs include "Puttin' on the Ritz" and "White Christmas." Radio broadcasts offered everything from classical music to comedy. In the popular show *Amos 'n' Andy*, the troubles of two African American characters (portrayed by white actors) captured the nation's attention.

The **mass media**—radio, movies, newspapers, and magazines aimed at a broad audience—did more than just entertain. They also fostered a sense of shared experience that helped **unify** the nation.

Sports

Sports such as baseball and boxing reached new heights of popularity in the 1920s, thanks to motion pictures and radio. Baseball star Babe Ruth became a national hero, famous for hitting hundreds of home runs. Fans also idolized boxer Jack Dempsey, who was world heavyweight champion from 1919 until 1926, when he lost the title to Gene Tunney. When Dempsey attempted to win back the title in 1927, one store sold $90,000 worth of radios in the two weeks before the event.

Newspaper coverage helped build enthusiasm for college football. One of the most famous players of the 1920s was Red Grange of the University of Illinois. He was known as the "Galloping Ghost" because of his speed and ability to evade the opposing team. The triumphs of Bobby Jones, the best golfer of the decade, and tennis players Bill Tilden and Helen Wills also thrilled sports fans. When swimmer Gertrude Ederle shattered records by swimming the English Channel in a little over 14 hours in 1927, Americans were enchanted.

☑ **PROGRESS CHECK**

Explaining Why did new national pastimes emerge during the 1920s, and what were some of the most popular new ways for Americans to spend their leisure time?

Part of what made the 1920s feel new and modern was the rise of mass culture. Movies, which were very popular in the 1920s, brought Americans together in a shared experience.

▶ **CRITICAL THINKING**
Compare and Contrast How does seeing a movie today compare and contrast with what you observe in the photograph of early moviegoers?

mass media medium of communication (such as television and radio) intended to reach a wide audience

unify to bring together with similar goals or ideas

PHOTO: Culver Pictures, Inc./SuperStock

LESSON 4 REVIEW

Vocabulary Review
1. *Comparing* How is today's mass media similar to that of the 1920s?

Using Your Notes
2. *Drawing Conclusions* Review the notes that you completed during the lesson. Why do you think the art and literature of the 1920s had such a diverse range of styles?

Answering the Guiding Questions
3. *Synthesizing* How did many artists and writers of the time describe the 1920s?

4. *Summarizing* Why did many Americans have more time for entertainment, and how did they spend their time?

Writing Activity
5. PERSONAL Imagine that you are a teenager of the 1920s and your parents have just purchased your family's first radio. Write about something you are excited to be able to listen to.

LESSON 5
African American Culture and Politics

ESSENTIAL QUESTIONS • *How was social and economic life different in the early twentieth century from that of the late nineteenth century?* • *How has the cultural identity of the United States changed over time?*

Reading **HELP**DESK

Content Vocabulary
• **jazz**   • **blues**

Academic Vocabulary
• **symbolize**   • **ongoing**
• **impact**

TAKING NOTES: *Organizing*

ACTIVITY As you read about the African American experience in the 1920s, complete a graphic organizer similar to the one below by filling in the causes and effects of the Harlem Renaissance.

Causes   Effects
        Harlem
      Renaissance

IT MATTERS BECAUSE

The Harlem Renaissance was a creative era for African American artists. It sparked new trends in literature, music, and art. The growing African American population in the North meant an increasing number of African Americans had political power to continue the struggle for civil rights.

The Harlem Renaissance

GUIDING QUESTION *What does the Harlem Renaissance reveal about African American culture in the 1920s?*

During World War I and the 1920s, hundreds of thousands of African Americans joined the Great Migration from the rural South to industrial cities in the North. Populations swelled in large Northern cities. Nightclubs and music filled these cities, particularly the New York City neighborhood of Harlem. Artistic development, racial pride, and political organization combined in a flowering of African American arts. This became known as the Harlem Renaissance.

The Writers

Claude McKay was the first important writer of the Harlem Renaissance. In his 1922 poetry collection, *Harlem Shadows*, McKay expressed a proud defiance and bitter contempt of racism. These were two major characteristics of Harlem Renaissance writing.

> **PRIMARY SOURCE**
>
> ❝O kinsmen! we must meet the common foe!
> Though far outnumbered let us show us brave,
> And for their thousand blows deal one deathblow!
> What though before us lies the open grave?
> Like men we'll face the murderous, cowardly pack,
> Pressed to the wall, dying, but fighting back!❞
>
> —from "If We Must Die", in *African American Literature*

Langston Hughes was a prolific, original, and versatile writer. He became a leading voice of the African American experience in America. Zora Neale Hurston wrote some of the first major stories featuring African American women as central characters. Other notable writers of the Harlem Renaissance include Countee Cullen, Alain Locke, and Dorothy West.

Jazz, Blues, and the Theater

New Orleans native Louis Armstrong moved to Chicago in 1922. There he introduced an early form of **jazz,** a musical style influenced by Dixieland and ragtime, with syncopated rhythms and improvisational elements. In Chicago, Armstrong broke away from the New Orleans tradition of group playing by performing highly imaginative solos on the cornet and trumpet.

Composer, pianist, and bandleader Edward "Duke" Ellington also had a special sound, a blend of improvisation and orchestration using different combinations of instruments. Like many other African American entertainers, Ellington got his start at the Cotton Club, the most famous nightclub in Harlem (but one that served only white customers). Years later, Ellington reflected on the music of the era by saying, "Everything, and I repeat, everything had to swing. And that was just it, those cats really had it; they had that soul. And you know you can't just play some of this music without soul. Soul is very important."

Bessie Smith seemed to **symbolize** soul. She became known as the Empress of the Blues. Smith sang of unfulfilled love, poverty, and oppression—the classic themes of the **blues,** a soulful style of music that evolved from African American spirituals.

Theater also flourished during the Harlem Renaissance. *Shuffle Along,* the first musical written, produced, and performed by African Americans, made its Broadway debut in 1921. The show's success helped launch a number of careers, including those of Florence Mills and Paul Robeson. Robeson received wide acclaim for his performance in the title role of Eugene O'Neill's *Emperor Jones.* He also gained fame four years later for his work in the musical *Show Boat.* Robeson often appeared at the famous Apollo Theater in Harlem.

Josephine Baker transformed a childhood knack for flamboyance into a career as a well-known singer and dancer on Broadway. She later moved to Paris and launched an international career.

☑ **PROGRESS CHECK**

Making Generalizations What does the work of writers and performers of the Harlem Renaissance show about African American culture of the 1920s?

PHOTO: Frank Driggs Collection/Archive Photos/Getty Images

jazz American style of music that developed from ragtime and blues and that uses syncopated rhythms and improvisation

symbolize to represent, express, or identify by a symbol

blues style of music evolving from African American spirituals and noted for its melancholy sound

Along with the Apollo Theater, the Cotton Club was one of the famous clubs in Harlem. Many performers launched careers by appearing on its stage.

▶ **CRITICAL THINKING**
Making Generalizations How did Harlem nightclubs like the Cotton Club help promote African American performing arts?

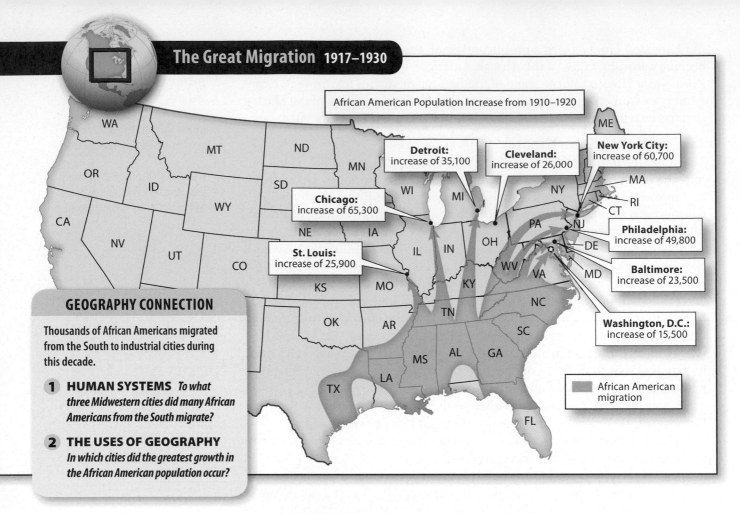

African American Population Increase from 1910–1920

Detroit: increase of 35,100

Cleveland: increase of 26,000

New York City: increase of 60,700

Chicago: increase of 65,300

Philadelphia: increase of 49,800

St. Louis: increase of 25,900

Baltimore: increase of 23,500

Washington, D.C.: increase of 15,500

African American migration

GEOGRAPHY CONNECTION

Thousands of African Americans migrated from the South to industrial cities during this decade.

1 HUMAN SYSTEMS *To what three Midwestern cities did many African Americans from the South migrate?*

2 THE USES OF GEOGRAPHY *In which cities did the greatest growth in the African American population occur?*

African Americans and 1920s Politics

GUIDING QUESTION *How did African American leaders differ in their approaches to political actions during this decade?*

In 1919 approximately 1,300 African American veterans of World War I marched through Manhattan to Harlem. W.E.B. Du Bois captured their sense of pride and defiance in a speech:

PRIMARY SOURCE

❝We *return*. We *return from fighting*. We *return fighting*. Make way for Democracy! We saved it in France, and by the Great Jehovah, we will save it in the United States of America, or know the reason why.❞
—from *The Crisis*, May 1919

Growing Political Power in the North

World War I set the stage for African Americans to reenter American politics. The Great Migration of African Americans to the North had a significant **impact** as well. As their numbers grew in city neighborhoods, African Americans became an influential voting bloc. In 1928 African American voters in Chicago helped elect Oscar DePriest. He was the first African American representative in Congress from a Northern state.

The NAACP Battles Injustice

The National Association for the Advancement of Colored People (NAACP) battled hard against segregation and discrimination against African Americans. Its efforts focused primarily on lobbying public officials and working through the court system. The NAACP's persistent protests against the horrors of lynching led to the passage of antilynching legislation

impact a lasting impression upon an individual or group

in the House of Representatives in 1922. The Senate defeated the bill, but the NAACP's **ongoing** protests kept the issue in the news. This probably helped reduce the number of lynchings that took place.

ongoing being in process; continuing

In 1930 the NAACP joined with labor unions to launch a highly organized national campaign against the nomination of Judge John J. Parker to the U.S. Supreme Court. The North Carolina judge allegedly was racist and antilabor. By a narrow margin, the Senate refused to confirm Parker's nomination. This proved that African Americans had become a powerful political force.

Black Nationalism and Marcus Garvey

While the NAACP fought for integration and improvement in the economic and political position of African Americans, other groups began to emphasize black nationalism and black pride. Some began calling for African Americans to separate from white society.

A dynamic leader from Jamaica, Marcus Garvey captured the imagination of millions of African Americans with his "Negro Nationalism." Garvey founded the Universal Negro Improvement Association (UNIA), aimed at promoting black pride and unity. He was inspired by Booker T. Washington's call for self-reliance. The central message of Garvey's Harlem-based movement was that African Americans could gain economic and political power by educating themselves. Garvey also advocated separation and independence from whites. In 1920 he told his followers they would never find justice or freedom in America. He proposed leading them to Africa.

The emerging African American middle class and intellectuals distanced themselves from Garvey and his push for racial separation. The FBI saw UNIA as a dangerous catalyst for African American uprisings. Garvey also alienated key figures in the Harlem Renaissance by calling them "weak-kneed and cringing . . . [flatterers of] the white man." Convicted of mail fraud in 1923, he served time in prison. In 1927 President Coolidge used Garvey's immigrant status to have him deported to Jamaica.

Despite Garvey's failure to keep his movement alive, he instilled millions of African Americans with a sense of pride in their heritage and inspired hope for the future. These feelings reemerged strongly in the 1950s and played a vital role in the civil rights movement of the 1960s.

☑ **PROGRESS CHECK**

Summarizing What differing steps did African Americans take to achieve political goals during the 1920s?

Marcus Garvey's "back to Africa" movement gave pride and hope to millions of African Americans.

▶ **CRITICAL THINKING**
Comparing and Contrasting How did Marcus Garvey's approach to political action differ from that of the NAACP?

PHOTO: Hulton Archive/Archive Photos/Getty Images

LESSON 5 REVIEW

Reviewing Vocabulary
1. *Drawing Conclusions* Why do you think the blues emerged as a main musical form of the Harlem Renaissance?

Using Your Notes
2. *Synthesizing* Review the notes that you completed during the lesson to determine how the Harlem Renaissance reflected the growing cultural and political power of African Americans.

Answering the Guiding Questions
3. *Explaining* What does the Harlem Renaissance reveal about African American culture in the 1920s?

4. *Contrasting* How did African American leaders differ in their approaches to political actions during this decade?

Writing Activity
5. **DESCRIPTIVE** Suppose that you witnessed African American men back from World War I marching through New York City and heard the beginnings of W.E.B. Du Bois's speech. Write a paragraph describing the event, including the ideas and attitudes the event conveyed.

Directions: On a separate sheet of paper, answer the questions below. Make sure you read carefully and answer all parts to the question.

Lesson Review

Lesson 1

1 *Identifying* Describe two major scandals that plagued the Harding administration.

2 *Assessing* How did the United States promote world peace and stability?

Lesson 2

3 *Analyzing* How did new industrial innovations such as assembly lines and mass production affect the American worker and the American consumer?

4 *Evaluating* What factors contributed to the "quiet depression" among farmers in the 1920s?

Lesson 3

5 *Analyzing Ethical Issues* How did the Sacco-Vanzetti case exemplify the rise of nativism in the United States?

6 *Describing* How did women's roles change during the 1920s?

Lesson 4

7 *Making Connections* How did many writers in the 1920s react to the changing American culture?

8 *Explaining* What effect did mass media such as radios and newspapers have on the American public?

Lesson 5

9 *Synthesizing* How did the Harlem Renaissance help change perceptions of African Americans?

10 *Identifying Cause and Effect* What effects did the Great Migration have on African Americans' political power?

21st Century Skills

11 *Identifying Cause and Effect* Why was there a general rise in nativism in the 1920s?

12 *Economics* What was Calvin Coolidge's primary economic philosophy?

13 *Compare and Contrast* How did the financial state of farmers contrast with the financial state of manufacturing?

14 *Identifying Perspectives and Differing Interpretations* What groups in America did not profit from the growing prosperity of the 1920s? Why?

Exploring the Essential Question

15 *Drawing Conclusions* Write a one-act play that shows how the culture of the United States changed in the 1920s.

DBQ Document-Based Questions

Use the political cartoon to answer the following questions.

16 *Summarizing* What incident is depicted in the cartoon? How do you know?

17 *Making Generalizations* Why do you think the artist named this cartoon the "White House Highway"?

Extended-Response Question

18 *Expository* Write an essay that explains why you agree or disagree with Coolidge's approach to the role business played in the economic and cultural boom of the 1920s.

Need Extra Help?

If You've Missed Question	1	2	3	4	5	6	7	8	9	10	11	12	13	14	15	16	17	18
Go to page	402	405	406	409	411	413	415	417	418	420	411	404	409	409	408	422	422	404

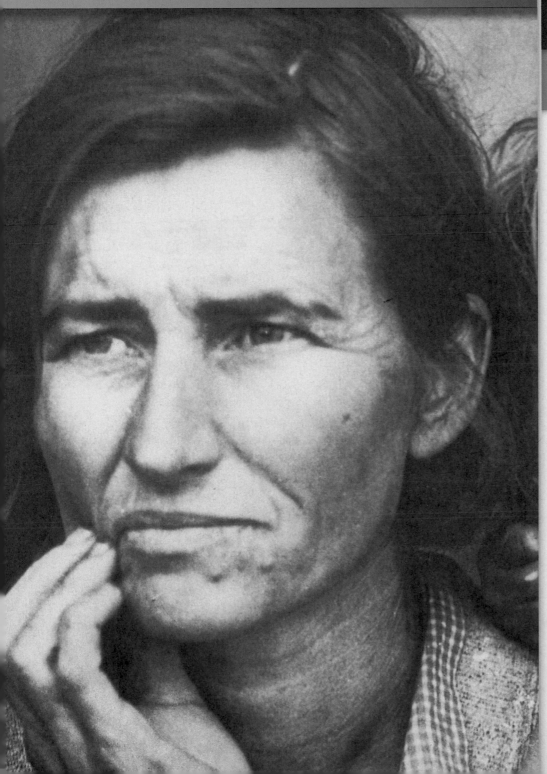

The Great Depression Begins

1929–1932

ESSENTIAL QUESTIONS • *What causes changes in the economy over time?*
• *How do depressions affect societies?*

netw⊚rks

There's More Online about the Great Depression and its effects on society.

CHAPTER 18

The Story Matters...

During the prosperous 1920s, optimism drove stock prices to new highs, but risky investment practices set the stage for a crash. Sensing danger, investors sold their holdings, causing the market to lose billions of dollars and the nation's banks to collapse.

Companies went out of business, millions of Americans were unemployed, and families could not buy food. When a terrible drought struck the Great Plains, farmers were unable to grow crops, leading to even more devastation.

◄ A destitute mother and other workers' families were stranded after the pea crop they were to harvest failed. The government sent 20,000 pounds of food to help the stranded workers at the farm in California.

PHOTO: Dorothea Lange/Bettmann/CORBIS

423

When the stock market crashed in October 1929, the extreme optimism of the 1920s turned to the profound despair of the Great Depression. By the early 1930s, more Americans were demanding the government's help. Veterans grew frustrated and began to march to Capitol Hill to demand the immediate payment of a promised bonus. Wearing ragged military uniforms and singing old war songs, this "Bonus Army" traveled the highways and railroads to Washington, D.C., to protest their plight. By July 1932, more than 15,000 unemployed veterans, each asking the government for early payment of cash bonuses due to be paid in 1945, converged on the nation's capital.

Step Into the Place

Read the quotes and look at the information presented on the map.

DBQ How do the following quotes reflect the ways people helped one another during the Great Depression?

PRIMARY SOURCE

"The conductor'd want to find out how many guys were in the yard, so he would know how many empty boxcars to put onto the train. Of course, the railroad companies didn't know this, but these conductors, out of their sympathy, would put two or three empty boxcars in the train, so these bonus marchers could crawl into them and ride comfortable into Washington."

—Jim Sheridan, a traveler with the Bonus Army in 1932, quoted in *An American Epic*

PRIMARY SOURCE

"With American flags flying before them, sixteen truckloads of war veterans came to the end of a transcontinental hitch-hike today with the avowed purpose of remaining in Washington until Congress pays their bonus in full.

Weather-beaten, travel-strained and dog-tired, the former soldiers—330 from the Pacific Coast—crossed the District line in trucks supplied by Maryland and found a hot stew, bread, milk and coffee awaiting them."

—from the *New York Times*, May 30, 1932

PHOTOS: **left page** (tl)Underwood & Underwood/Historical/CORBIS, (tr)Underwood/Historical/CORBIS, (b)detail/White House Historical Association; **right page** detail/White House Collection/The White House Historical Association; ;TEXT: "Weary Bonus Army Reaches Capital by Truck; Police Demand Congress Care for Hundreds," by The Associated Press. Published May 30, 1932.

Step Into the Time

Choose an event from the time line and write a paragraph describing the general social, political, or economic consequences that event had on the Great Depression.

U.S. PRESIDENTS

Hoover
1929–1933

November 1928 Herbert Hoover is elected president

1929 Wall Street crashes on October 24 ("Black Thursday") and October 29 ("Black Tuesday")

UNITED STATES

WORLD

1928

1929

1928 First Five-Year Plan to industrialize the Soviet Union begins

1929 Young Plan reduces war reparations for Germany

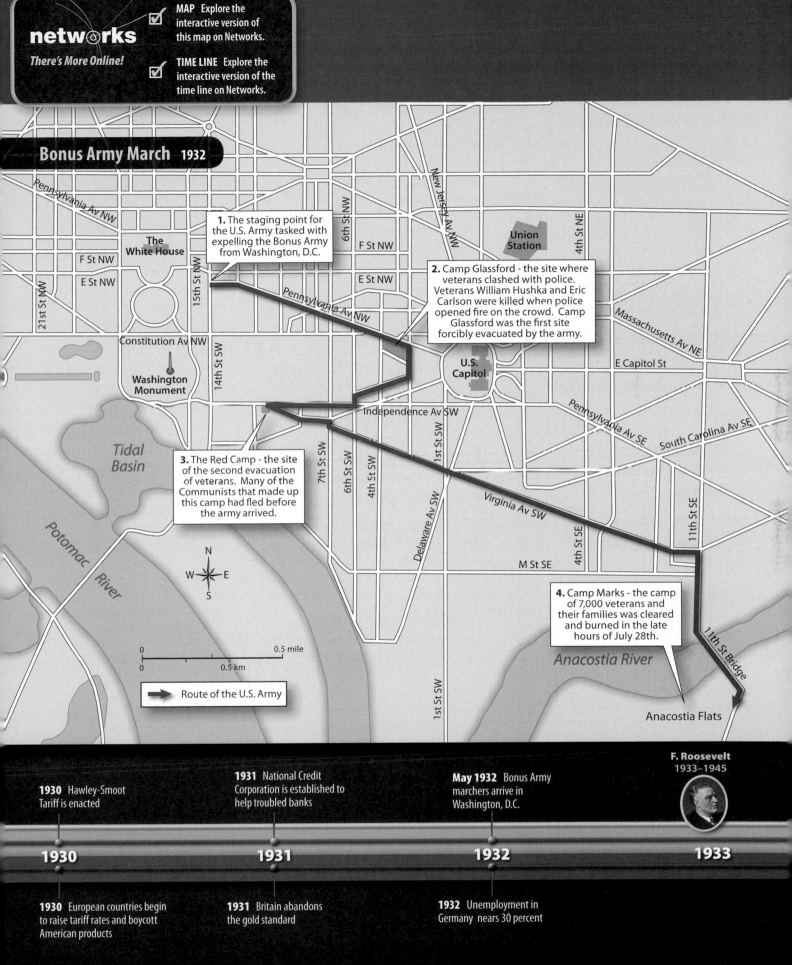

networks
There's More Online!

☑ MAP Explore the interactive version of this map on Networks.

☑ TIME LINE Explore the interactive version of the time line on Networks.

Bonus Army March 1932

1. The staging point for the U.S. Army tasked with expelling the Bonus Army from Washington, D.C.

2. Camp Glassford - the site where veterans clashed with police. Veterans William Hushka and Eric Carlson were killed when police opened fire on the crowd. Camp Glassford was the first site forcibly evacuated by the army.

3. The Red Camp - the site of the second evacuation of veterans. Many of the Communists that made up this camp had fled before the army arrived.

4. Camp Marks - the camp of 7,000 veterans and their families was cleared and burned in the late hours of July 28th.

Pennsylvania Av NW

The White House

F St NW
E St NW
21st St NW
15th St NW
14th St SW

Constitution Av NW

Washington Monument

Tidal Basin

Potomac River

6th St NW
F St NW
E St NW

Pennsylvania Av NW

New Jersey Av NW

Union Station

4th St NE

Massachusetts Av NE

E Capitol St

U.S. Capitol

Independence Av SW

Pennsylvania Av SE

South Carolina Av SE

7th St SW
6th St SW
4th St SW
1st St SW
Delaware Av SW
Virginia Av SW

4th St SE
11th St SE

M St SE

N
W   E
S

0   0.5 mile
0   0.5 km

Anacostia River

11th St Bridge

Anacostia Flats

1st St SW

→ Route of the U.S. Army

1930 Hawley-Smoot Tariff is enacted

1931 National Credit Corporation is established to help troubled banks

May 1932 Bonus Army marchers arrive in Washington, D.C.

F. Roosevelt 1933–1945

1930

1931

1932

1933

1930 European countries begin to raise tariff rates and boycott American products

1931 Britain abandons the gold standard

1932 Unemployment in Germany nears 30 percent

networks

There's More Online!

☑ **BIOGRAPHY** Herbert Hoover

☑ **BIOGRAPHY** Alfred E. Smith

☑ **CHART/GRAPH** Income and Spending

☑ **CHART/GRAPH** Unemployment

☑ **CHART/GRAPH** Value of Exports

☑ **IMAGE** Car for Sale

☑ **VIDEO** Causes of the Great Depression

☑ **INTERACTIVE SELF-CHECK QUIZ**

Reading **HELP**DESK

Content Vocabulary
- stock market
- bull market
- speculation
- margin
- margin call
- bank run
- installment

Academic Vocabulary
- collapse
- invest
- sum

TAKING NOTES: *Organizing*

ACTIVITY As you read the lesson, complete a graphic organizer similar to the one below to list the causes of the Depression.

Causes

Great Depression

LESSON 1
The Causes of the Great Depression

ESSENTIAL QUESTIONS • *What causes changes in the economy over time?* • *How do depressions affect societies?*

IT MATTERS BECAUSE

Although the 1920s were prosperous, speculation in the stock market, risky lending policies, overproduction, and uneven income distribution eventually undermined the economy and led to the Great Depression.

The Long Bull Market

GUIDING QUESTION *What economic choices caused the economy to become unstable in the late 1920s?*

The economic **collapse** that began in 1929 seemed unimaginable months before. In the 1928 election, both presidential candidates painted a rosy picture of the future. Republican presidential nominee Herbert Hoover declared, "We are nearer to the final triumph over poverty than ever before in the history of any land."

The Election of 1928

For the presidential election of 1928, the Democrats chose Alfred E. Smith, governor of New York. Smith was the first Roman Catholic to win a major party's presidential nomination. He faced a tough challenger, as Herbert Hoover was secretary of commerce and former head of the Food Administration.

Smith's religious beliefs became a campaign issue. Some Protestants claimed the Catholic Church financed Smith's campaign and would have inappropriate influence on American politics. The attacks embarrassed Hoover, a Quaker, and he tried to quash them, but the charges damaged Smith's candidacy.

The prosperity of the 1920s—for which the Republicans took full credit—was a bigger challenge to Smith's candidacy. Hoover won in a landslide. On March 4, 1929, an estimated 50,000 onlookers stood in the rain to listen to Hoover's Inaugural Address. "I have no fears for the future of our country," proclaimed Hoover. "It is bright with hope."

The Stock Market Soars

The optimism that swept Hoover into office also drove stock prices to new highs. Sometimes the **stock market** has a long period of rising stock prices, or a **bull market.** The bull market of the 1920s convinced many to **invest** in stocks. By 1929, approximately 10 percent of American households owned stocks.

Before the late 1920s, stock prices generally reflected their true values. In the late 1920s, however, many investors failed to consider a company's earnings and profits. Buyers engaged in **speculation,** or betting the market would continue to climb, thus enabling them to sell stock and make money quickly.

Many investors bought stocks on **margin,** making only a small cash down payment (as low as 10 percent of the price). With $1,000, an investor could buy a **sum** of $10,000 worth of stock. The remaining $9,000 came as an interest-bearing loan from the stockbroker. Quick profits were possible if stock prices kept rising, but problems came when prices began to fall. To protect a loan, a broker could issue a **margin call,** demanding the investor repay the loan at once.

☑ **PROGRESS CHECK**

Summarizing What investment decisions destabilized the economy during the 1920s?

The Great Crash

GUIDING QUESTION *How did the stock market crash trigger a chain of events that led to the Depression?*

The bull market lasted only as long as investors continued putting new money into it. In September 1929, the market peaked. Prices then began an uneven downward slide. As investors decided the boom was over, they sold more stock, causing prices to decline even further.

The Stock Market Crash

On Monday, October 21, 1929, the comedian Groucho Marx was awakened by a telephone call from his broker. "You'd better get down here with some cash to cover your margin," the broker said. The stock market had plunged. The dazed comedian had to pay back the money he had borrowed to buy stocks, which were now selling for far less than he had paid for them. Other brokers made similar margin calls. Customers put stocks up for sale at a frenzied pace, driving the market into a tailspin.

On October 24, a day that came to be called Black Thursday, the market plummeted further. Marx was wiped out. His earnings from plays and films were gone, and he was deeply in debt. His son recalled his visit to the

collapse a sudden loss of force, value, or effect

stock market a system for buying and selling stocks in corporations

bull market a long period of rising stock prices

invest to put money into a company in order to gain a future financial reward

speculation act of buying stocks at great risk with the anticipation that the prices will rise

margin buying a stock by paying only a fraction of the stock price and borrowing the rest

sum a specified amount of money

margin call demand by a broker that investors pay back loans made for stocks purchased on margin

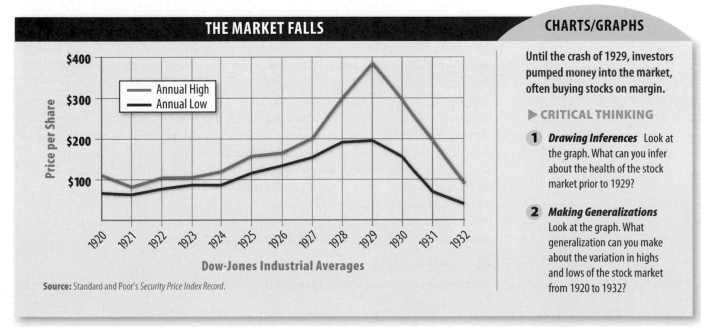

THE MARKET FALLS

Price per Share

$400
$300
$200
$100

— Annual High
— Annual Low

1920 1921 1922 1923 1924 1925 1926 1927 1928 1929 1930 1931 1932

Dow-Jones Industrial Averages

Source: Standard and Poor's *Security Price Index Record.*

CHARTS/GRAPHS

Until the crash of 1929, investors pumped money into the market, often buying stocks on margin.

▶ **CRITICAL THINKING**

1 ***Drawing Inferences*** Look at the graph. What can you infer about the health of the stock market prior to 1929?

2 ***Making Generalizations*** Look at the graph. What generalization can you make about the variation in highs and lows of the stock market from 1920 to 1932?

Mayhem erupted on Wall Street after the stock market crashed.

▶ **CRITICAL THINKING**
Identifying Central Issues What investment practices most destabilized the stock market?

brokerage firm, as Groucho spotted his broker:

PRIMARY SOURCE

❝He was sitting in front of the now-stilled ticker-tape machine, with his head buried in his hands. Ticker tape was strewn around him on the floor, and the place . . . looked as if it hadn't been swept out in a week. [Groucho] tapped [him] on the shoulder, [and said] 'Aren't you the fellow who said nothing could go wrong—that we were in a world market?' 'I guess I made a mistake,' said Mr. Green. 'No, I'm the one who made a mistake,' said [Groucho]. 'I listened to you.'❞

—from *Life with Groucho,* 1954

The following week, on October 29, a day that was later dubbed Black Tuesday, prices took the steepest dive yet. That day, more than 16 million shares of stock were sold, and the value of the industrial index (a measure of the value of leading industrial companies) dropped by 10 percent. By mid-November, the market price of stocks had dropped by more than one-third. Some $30 billion was lost, a sum roughly equal to the total wages Americans earned in 1929. Although the stock market crash was not the major cause of the Depression, it undermined the economy's ability to overcome other weaknesses.

Banks Begin to Close

The market crash weakened the nation's banks in two ways. First, by 1929, banks had lent billions to stock speculators. Second, many banks had invested depositors' money in the stock market, hoping for high returns. When stock values collapsed, banks lost money on their investments, and speculators defaulted on their loans. Having suffered serious losses, many banks cut back drastically on loans. With less credit available, consumers and businesses were not able to borrow as much money, sending the economy into a recession.

Some banks could not absorb the losses they suffered and had to close. The government did not insure bank deposits, so if a bank failed, customers, including even those who did not invest in the stock market, lost their savings. As a growing number of banks closed in 1929 and 1930, a severe crisis of confidence in the banking system further destabilized the economy.

News of bank failures worried Americans. Some depositors made runs on banks, thus causing the banks to fail. A **bank run** takes place when many depositors decide to withdraw their money at the same time, usually out of fear that the bank will collapse. Most banks make a profit by lending money received from depositors and collecting interest on the loans. The bank keeps only a fraction of depositors' money in reserve. Usually, that reserve is enough to meet the bank's needs. If too many people withdraw their money, however, the bank will collapse. By 1932, about one in four banks in the United States had gone out of business.

✓ **PROGRESS CHECK**

Determining Cause and Effect How did the failure of the stock market contribute to a larger economic decline?

The Roots of the Great Depression

GUIDING QUESTION *What were the underlying conditions that led to the collapse of the U.S. economy?*

The stock market crash played a major role in putting the economy into a recession. Yet the crash would not have led to a long-lasting depression if other forces had not been at work. The roots of the Great Depression were deeply entangled in the economy of the 1920s.

The Uneven Distribution of Income

Overproduction was a factor leading to the onset of the Great Depression. More efficient machinery increased the production capacity of factories and farms. Most Americans did not earn enough to buy up the goods they helped produce. Manufacturing output per person-hour rose 32 percent, but the average worker's wage increased only 8 percent. In 1929 the top 5 percent of all American households earned 30 percent of the nation's income. In contrast, about two-thirds of families earned less than $2,500 a year, leaving them with little disposable income.

Farmers, in particular, did not share in the prosperity of the 1920s, as many had gone into debt to buy land or equipment during World War I, when demand for their products was high. When prices fell, they tried to produce even more to pay their debts, taxes, and living expenses. Prices dropped so low that many farmers went bankrupt and lost their farms.

During the 1920s, many Americans had purchased high-cost items, such as refrigerators and cars, on the **installment** plan. Purchasers could make small down payments and pay the remainder of the item's price in monthly installments. Paying off such debts eventually forced some buyers to stop making new purchases. Because of the decrease in demand for their products, manufacturers in turn cut production and laid off employees.

The slowdown in retail sales reverberated throughout the economy. When radio sales slumped, for example, orders for copper wire, wood cabinets, and glass radio tubes slowed. Montana copper miners, Minnesota lumberjacks, and Ohio glassworkers lost jobs. Jobless workers cut purchases, further reducing sales. This put even more Americans out of work.

bank run persistent and heavy demands by a bank's depositors, creditors, or customers to withdraw money

installment regular periodic payment made to pay off the cost of an item when buying it on credit

CHARTS/GRAPHS

▶ CRITICAL THINKING

1 *Identifying Central Issues* What basic economic principle underlay the cause of the Great Depression?

2 *Analyzing Information* What effect did the decline in automobile sales have on related industries?

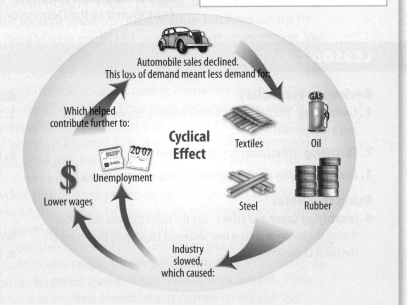

CAUSES OF THE GREAT DEPRESSION

What Caused the Economy to Collapse?

Low Interest Rates
Federal Reserve kept interest rates low; companies borrowed money and expanded more than necessary.

Overproduction
Companies made more goods than could be sold.

Uneven Distribution of Wealth
Not everyone who wanted consumer goods could afford them.

High Tariffs
Tariffs restricted foreign demand for American goods.

Falling Demand
With too many goods unsold, production was cut back and employees were laid off.

Stock Market Speculation
Low interest rates encouraged borrowing money to speculate, endangering bank solvency.

Automobile sales declined. This loss of demand meant less demand for:

Textiles
Oil
Steel
Rubber

Cyclical Effect

Industry slowed, which caused:

Unemployment

Lower wages

Which helped contribute further to:

CHAPTER 19

Place and Time: United States 1931–1941

Franklin D. Roosevelt and his administration had a monumental task in 1933. The Great Depression had affected millions of Americans. People began to demand help from the federal government. Promising a "New Deal" for the American people, President Roosevelt took immediate steps to put people back to work, strengthen the economy, and establish a safety net for the nation. Roosevelt's critics challenged his plan because never before had the federal government intervened so directly in the economy.

Step Into the Place

Read the quotes and look at the information presented on the map.

DBQ **What different perspectives do these excerpts reveal about the role of government in the economy?**

PRIMARY SOURCE

❝So, first of all, let me assert my firm belief that the only thing we have to fear is fear itself—nameless, unreasoning, unjustified terror which paralyzes needed efforts to convert retreat into advance. . . .

Our greatest primary task is to put people to work. This is no unsolvable problem if we face it wisely and courageously. It can be accomplished in part by direct recruiting by the Government itself, treating the task as we would treat the emergency of a war, but at the same time, through this employment, accomplishing greatly needed projects to stimulate and reorganize the use of our natural resources.❞

—President Franklin D. Roosevelt, from his first Inaugural Address, March 4, 1933

PRIMARY SOURCE

❝Now what would I have my party do? I would have them re-declare the principles that they put forth in that 1932 platform [reduce the size of government, balance the federal budget]. . . .

Just get the platform of the Democratic party and get the platform of the Socialist party and . . . make your mind up to pick up the platform that more nearly squares with the record, and you will have your hand on the Socialist platform.

[I]t is all right with me, if they want to disguise themselves as Karl Marx or Lenin or any of the rest of that bunch, but I won't stand for their allowing them to march under the banner of Jackson or Cleveland.❞

—Alfred E. Smith, former Democratic presidential candidate, from a speech delivered January 25, 1936

PHOTOS: (tl)The Granger Collection, New York, (tr)Library of Congress, (bl br)detail/White House Collection/The White House Historical Association

Step Into the Time

Choose an event from the time line and write a paragraph describing how that event might have influenced Roosevelt's New Deal policies.

U.S. PRESIDENTS	**Hoover** 1929–1933	**F. Roosevelt** 1933–1945
UNITED STATES	1933 Unemployment peaks at 24.9%	1934 Securities and Exchange Commission is created
WORLD	1931	1933

January 1933 Hitler becomes German chancellor during economic turmoil

1933 World Economic Conference fails to reduce tariffs

1934 Britain passes the Unemployment Assistance Act

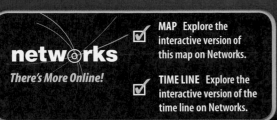
Public Works Projects of the New Deal

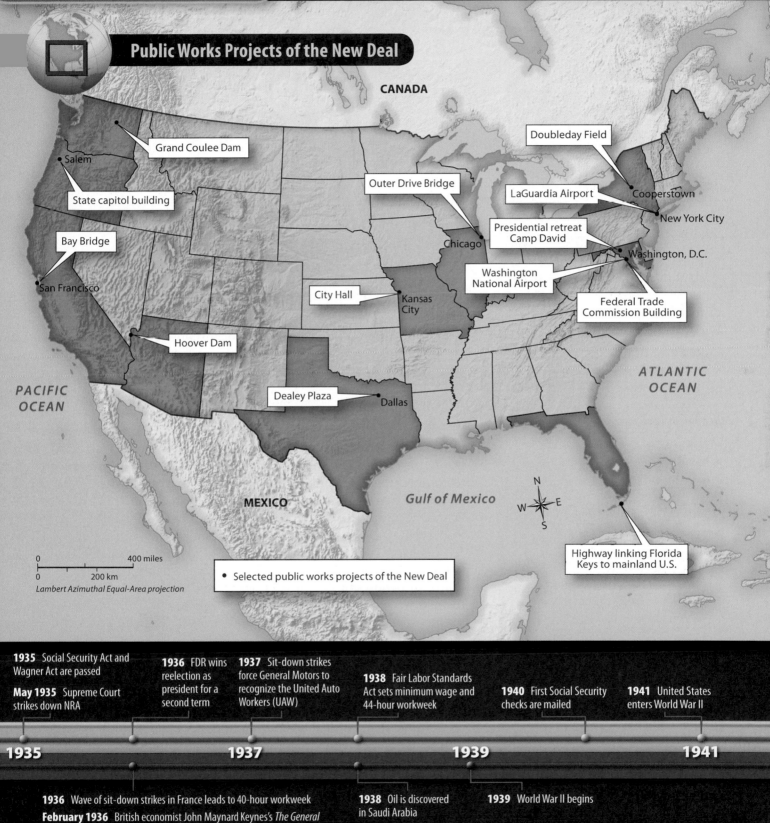

CANADA

Grand Coulee Dam

Salem

State capitol building

Bay Bridge

San Francisco

Hoover Dam

Outer Drive Bridge

Chicago

City Hall

Kansas City

Dealey Plaza

Dallas

PACIFIC OCEAN

Doubleday Field

Cooperstown

LaGuardia Airport

New York City

Presidential retreat Camp David

Washington, D.C.

Washington National Airport

Federal Trade Commission Building

ATLANTIC OCEAN

MEXICO

Gulf of Mexico

N
W · E
S

Highway linking Florida Keys to mainland U.S.

0 ——— 400 miles
0 ——— 200 km
Lambert Azimuthal Equal-Area projection

• Selected public works projects of the New Deal

1935 Social Security Act and Wagner Act are passed

May 1935 Supreme Court strikes down NRA

1936 FDR wins reelection as president for a second term

1937 Sit-down strikes force General Motors to recognize the United Auto Workers (UAW)

1938 Fair Labor Standards Act sets minimum wage and 44-hour workweek

1940 First Social Security checks are mailed

1941 United States enters World War II

1935

1937

1939

1941

1936 Wave of sit-down strikes in France leads to 40-hour workweek

February 1936 British economist John Maynard Keynes's *The General Theory of Employment, Interest, and Money* is published

1938 Oil is discovered in Saudi Arabia

1939 World War II begins

Reading HELPDESK

Content Vocabulary

- polio
- gold standard
- bank holiday
- fireside chats

Academic Vocabulary

- apparent
- ideology
- fundamental

TAKING NOTES: *Sequencing*

ACTIVITY As you read about Roosevelt's first three months in office, complete a time line to record the major problems he addressed during this time.

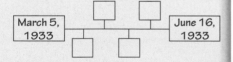

LESSON 1
The First New Deal

ESSENTIAL QUESTIONS • *Can government fix the economy?*
• *Is government responsible for the economic well-being of its citizens?*

IT MATTERS BECAUSE

Franklin Delano Roosevelt was elected president in 1932, following his promise of a "New Deal" for Americans. In his first hundred days in office, he introduced a flood of legislation designed to rescue banks, industry, and agriculture and provide jobs for the unemployed.

Roosevelt's Rise to Power

GUIDING QUESTION *What qualities make an effective leader?*

A distant cousin of Theodore Roosevelt, Franklin Delano Roosevelt grew up in Hyde Park, New York. In his youth, Franklin learned to hunt, ride horses, and sail; he also developed a lifelong commitment to conservation and a love of rural areas in the United States. Roosevelt was educated at Harvard and then at Columbia Law School. While at Harvard, he became friends with Theodore Roosevelt's niece Eleanor, whom he later married.

Intensely competitive, Roosevelt liked to be in control. He also liked being around people. His charming personality, deep rich voice, and wide smile expressed confidence and optimism. In short, his personality seemed made for a life in politics.

Roosevelt began his political career in 1910 when he was elected to the New York State Senate. He earned a reputation as a progressive reformer. Three years later, he became assistant secretary of the navy in the Wilson administration. In 1920 his reputation (and famous surname) helped him win the vice-presidential nomination on the unsuccessful Democratic ticket.

After losing the election, Roosevelt temporarily withdrew from politics. The next year, he caught the dreaded paralyzing disease **polio.** Although there was no cure, Roosevelt refused to give in. He began a vigorous exercise program to restore muscle control. With heavy steel braces on his legs, he was able to seem to walk short distances by leaning on a cane and someone's arm and swinging his legs forward from his hips.

While recovering from polio, Roosevelt depended on his wife and his aide Louis Howe to keep his name prominent in the New York Democratic Party. Eleanor Roosevelt became an effective public speaker, and her efforts kept her husband's political career alive.

By the mid-1920s, Roosevelt was again active in the Democratic Party. In 1928 he ran for governor of New York. He campaigned hard to show that his illness had not slowed him down, and he narrowly won the election. Two years later, he was reelected in a landslide. As governor, Roosevelt oversaw the creation of the first state relief agency to aid the unemployed.

Roosevelt's popularity in New York paved the way for his presidential nomination in 1932. Americans saw in him an energy and optimism that gave them hope despite the tough economic times. After Roosevelt became president, his serenity and confidence amazed people. When one aide commented on his attitude, Roosevelt replied, "If you had spent two years in bed trying to wiggle your big toe, after that anything else would seem easy."

In mid-June 1932, when the country was deep in the Depression, Republicans gathered in Chicago and nominated Herbert Hoover to run for a second term as president. Later that month, the Democrats also held their national convention in Chicago. When Roosevelt won the nomination, he broke with tradition by flying to Chicago to accept it in person. His speech set the tone for his campaign:

PRIMARY SOURCE

❝Let it be from now on the task of our Party to break foolish traditions. . . . [I]t is inevitable that the main issue of this campaign should revolve about . . . a depression so deep that it is without precedent. . . . Republican leaders not only have failed in material things, they have failed in national vision, because in disaster they have held out no hope. . . . I pledge you, I pledge myself, to a new deal for the American people.❞

—speech delivered to the Democratic National Convention, July 2, 1932

From that point forward, Roosevelt's policies for ending the Depression became known as the New Deal. Roosevelt's confidence that he could make things better contrasted sharply with Herbert Hoover's **apparent** failure to do anything effective. On Election Day, Roosevelt won in a landslide, winning the electoral vote in all but six states.

✓ **PROGRESS CHECK**

Interpreting What characteristics did Roosevelt have that made him popular with Americans?

polio abbreviated term for poliomyelitis, an acute infectious disease affecting the skeletal muscles, often resulting in permanent disability and deformity

apparent appearing to be fact as far as can be understood

Franklin Roosevelt delivers his first Inaugural Address.

▶ **CRITICAL THINKING**

Interpreting Significance Why was it important that Franklin Roosevelt inspired optimism among so many Americans?

The Hundred Days

GUIDING QUESTION *Why are the first hundred days so important for a president?*

Roosevelt won the presidency in November 1932, but the situation grew worse between the election and his inauguration. Unemployment continued to rise and bank runs increased. People feared that Roosevelt would abandon the **gold standard** and reduce the value of the dollar to fight the Depression. Under the gold standard, one ounce of gold equaled a set number of dollars. To reduce the value of the dollar, the United States would have to stop exchanging dollars for gold. Many Americans and foreign investors with deposits in American banks decided to take their money out of the banks and convert it to gold before it lost its value.

Across the nation, people stood in long lines with paper bags and suitcases, waiting to withdraw their money from banks. By March 1933, more than 4,000 banks had collapsed, wiping out nine million savings accounts. In 38 states, governors declared **bank holidays**—closing the remaining banks before bank runs could put them out of business.

By the day of Roosevelt's inauguration, most of the nation's banks were closed. One in four workers was unemployed. Roosevelt knew he had to restore the nation's confidence. "First of all," he declared in his Inaugural Address, "let me assert my firm belief that the only thing we have to fear is fear itself. . . . This nation asks for action, and action now!"

The New Deal Begins

Roosevelt and his advisers came into office bursting with ideas about how to end the Depression. Roosevelt had no clear agenda, nor did he have a strong political **ideology.** He argued, "The country needs bold, persistent experimentation. . . . Above all, try something."

The new president sent bill after bill to Congress. Between March 9 and June 16, 1933—which came to be called the Hundred Days—Congress passed 15 major acts to resolve the economic crisis. These programs made up what would be called the First New Deal.

A Divided Administration

Although he alone made the final decision about what policies and programs to pursue, Roosevelt depended on his advisers for new ideas. He deliberately chose advisers who disagreed with one another because he wanted to hear many different points of view.

One influential group of President Roosevelt's advisers supported the belief that if the government agencies worked with businesses to regulate wages, prices, and production, they could lift the economy out of the Depression. A second group of advisers, who distrusted big business and felt business leaders had caused the Depression, wanted government planners to run key parts of the economy. A third group of advisers supported former president Woodrow Wilson's "New Freedom" philosophy. They wanted Roosevelt to break up big companies and allow competition to set wages, prices, and production levels. This group of advisers also thought that the government should impose regulations to keep economic competition fair.

✓ **PROGRESS CHECK**

Summarizing What were the key accomplishments during Roosevelt's first hundred days in office?

---

gold standard a monetary standard in which one ounce of gold equals a set number of dollars

bank holiday closing of banks during the Great Depression to avoid bank runs

ideology a system of thought that is held by an individual, group, or culture

Banks and Debt Relief

GUIDING QUESTION *Why did Roosevelt broadcast "fireside chats"?*

Roosevelt knew that very few of the new programs would work as long as the nation's banks remained closed. Before he did anything else, he had to restore people's confidence in the banking system. Within a week of his taking office, the Emergency Banking Relief Act was passed. The new law required federal examiners to survey the nation's banks and issue Treasury Department licenses to those that were financially sound.

On March 12, Roosevelt addressed the nation by radio. Sixty million people listened to this first of many "**fireside chats.**" He said, "I assure you that it is safer to keep your money in a reopened bank than under the mattress." When banks opened on March 13, deposits far outweighed withdrawals. The banking crisis was over.

The FDIC and SEC

Many of Roosevelt's advisers wanted to go further, pushing for new regulations for banks and the stock market. Roosevelt agreed, and supported the Securities Act of 1933 and the Glass-Steagall Banking Act. The Securities Act required companies that sold stocks and bonds to provide complete and truthful information to investors. The Securities and Exchange Commission (SEC) was created to regulate the stock market and stop fraud. The Glass-Steagall Act separated commercial banking from investment banking. Commercial banks handle everyday transactions and could no longer risk depositors' money through stock speculation. The act also created the Federal Deposit Insurance Corporation (FDIC) to provide government insurance for bank deposits. The creation of the FDIC increased public confidence in the banking system.

Mortgage and Debt Relief

Terrified of losing their homes and farms, many Americans cut back on spending to make sure they could pay their mortgages. Roosevelt responded by introducing policies to help Americans with their debts. For example, the Home Owners' Loan Corporation bought the mortgages of home owners who were behind in their payments. It then restructured the loans with longer repayment terms and lower interest rates.

The Farm Credit Administration (FCA) helped farmers refinance their mortgages. These loans saved millions of farms from foreclosure. Although the FCA may have slowed economic recovery by making less money available to lend to more efficient businesses, it did help many desperate and impoverished people hold onto their land.

✓ **PROGRESS CHECK**

Summarizing How did the government restore confidence in the banking system?

Farms and Industry

GUIDING QUESTION *How did New Deal legislation try to stabilize agriculture and industry?*

Many of Roosevelt's advisers believed that both farmers and businesses were suffering because prices were too low and production too high. To help the nation's farmers, Congress passed the Agricultural Adjustment Act. The act was based on a simple idea—that prices for farm goods were low because farmers grew too much food. Under this act, the government's Agricultural Adjustment Administration (AAA) would pay farmers not to raise

BIOGRAPHY

Eleanor Roosevelt (1884–1962)

Eleanor Roosevelt transformed the role of First Lady. She traveled, toured factories and coal mines, and met with workers, then told her husband what people were thinking. She was a strong supporter of civil rights and urged him to stop discrimination in New Deal programs. After President Roosevelt's death, she was appointed a delegate to the United Nations in 1946, where she helped draft the Universal Declaration of Human Rights.

▶ **CRITICAL THINKING**
Predicting Consequences How might Franklin Roosevelt's political career have been different if Eleanor had not been his wife?

fireside chats radio broadcasts made by Roosevelt to the American people to explain his initiatives

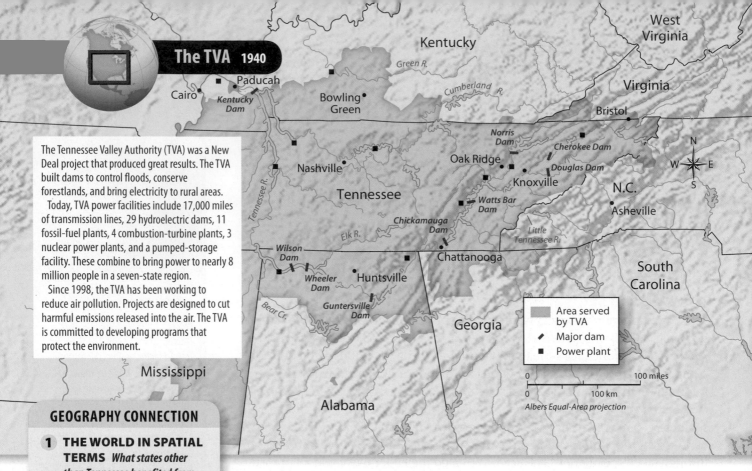

The TVA 1940

The Tennessee Valley Authority (TVA) was a New Deal project that produced great results. The TVA built dams to control floods, conserve forestlands, and bring electricity to rural areas.

Today, TVA power facilities include 17,000 miles of transmission lines, 29 hydroelectric dams, 11 fossil-fuel plants, 4 combustion-turbine plants, 3 nuclear power plants, and a pumped-storage facility. These combine to bring power to nearly 8 million people in a seven-state region.

Since 1998, the TVA has been working to reduce air pollution. Projects are designed to cut harmful emissions released into the air. The TVA is committed to developing programs that protect the environment.

Area served by TVA

◆ Major dam

■ Power plant

0   100 miles
0   100 km
Albers Equal-Area projection

GEOGRAPHY CONNECTION

1 THE WORLD IN SPATIAL TERMS *What states other than Tennessee benefited from the TVA projects?*

2 PLACES AND REGIONS *Why do you think the majority of the projects were located in eastern Tennessee?*

certain livestock, grow certain crops, and produce dairy products. Over the next two years, farmers withdrew millions more acres from cultivation and received more than $1 billion in support payments. The program met its goal, although raising food prices in a depression drew harsh criticism. Also, not all farmers benefited. Thousands of tenant farmers, many of them African Americans, lost their jobs and homes when landlords took their fields out of production.

The government turned its attention to manufacturing in June 1933, with the National Industrial Recovery Act (NIRA). Once passed, this law authorized the National Recovery Administration (NRA), to suspend antitrust laws and allowed business, labor, and government to cooperate with rules, or codes of fair competition, for each industry. Codes set prices, established minimum wages, shortened workers' hours to create more jobs, permitted unionization, and helped businesses develop industry-wide rules of fair competition. The NRA revived a few industries, but the codes were difficult to administer. Employers disliked that the NRA allowed workers to form unions. They also argued that paying minimum wages forced them to raise prices. After the NRA was instituted, industrial production fell. The NRA was declared unconstitutional in 1935.

✓ **PROGRESS CHECK**

Examining How was the Agricultural Adjustment Act intended to stabilize the agricultural industry?

Relief Programs

GUIDING QUESTION *How did New Deal programs differ from President Hoover's attempts to combat the Depression?*

Many of President Roosevelt's advisers emphasized tinkering with prices and providing debt relief to solve the Depression. Others maintained that the Depression's **fundamental** cause was low consumption. They thought

fundamental being of central importance

getting money into the hands of needy individuals would be the fastest remedy. Because neither Roosevelt nor his advisers wanted to give money to the unemployed, they supported work programs for the unemployed.

The CCC

The most highly praised New Deal work relief program was the Civilian Conservation Corps (CCC). The CCC offered unemployed young men 18–25 years old the opportunity to work under the direction of the forestry service planting trees, fighting forest fires, and building reservoirs. To prevent a repeat of the Dust Bowl, the workers planted a line of more than 200 million trees, known as a Shelter Belt, from north Texas to North Dakota.

The young men lived in camps near their work areas and earned $30 a month, $25 of which was sent directly to their families. The average CCC worker returned home after six to twelve months, better nourished and with greater self-respect. CCC programs also taught more than 40,000 of their recruits to read and write. By the time the CCC closed down in 1942, it had put 3 million young men to work outdoors—including 80,000 Native Americans, who helped reclaim land they had once owned. After a second Bonus Army march on Washington in 1933, Roosevelt added some 250,000 veterans to the CCC as well.

FERA and the PWA

A few weeks after authorizing the CCC, Congress established the Federal Emergency Relief Administration (FERA). Roosevelt chose Harry Hopkins, a former social worker, to run FERA. Initially, it did not create projects for the unemployed. Instead, it gave money to state and local agencies to fund their relief projects.

After meeting with Roosevelt to discuss his new job, Hopkins took the next two hours to spend $5 million on relief projects. When critics charged that some of the projects did not make sense in the long run, Hopkins replied, "People don't eat in the long run—they eat every day."

In June 1933, Congress authorized another relief agency, the Public Works Administration (PWA). One-third of the nation's unemployed were in the construction industry. To put them back to work, the PWA began building highways, dams, schools, and other government facilities.

The PWA awarded contracts to construction companies. By insisting that contractors not discriminate against African Americans, the agency broke down some of the racial barriers in the construction trades.

The CWA

By the fall of 1933, neither FERA nor the PWA had reduced unemployment significantly, and Hopkins realized that unless the federal government acted quickly, a huge number of unemployed citizens would be in severe distress once winter began. After Hopkins explained the situation, President Roosevelt authorized him to set up the Civil Works Administration (CWA).

Hiring workers directly, the CWA employed 4 million people, including 300,000 women. The agency built or improved 1,000 airports, 500,000 miles of roads, 40,000 school buildings, and 3,500 playgrounds and parks. The program spent nearly $1 billion in just five months. Although the CWA helped many people get through the winter, President Roosevelt was alarmed by how quickly the agency was spending money. He did not want Americans to get used to the federal government providing them with jobs. Warning that the Civil Works Administration would "become a habit with the country,"

This poster for the Civilian Conservation Corps (CCC) expresses the optimism of the New Deal.

▶ **CRITICAL THINKING**

Drawing Conclusions How did the CCC provide opportunities for work, play, study, and health?

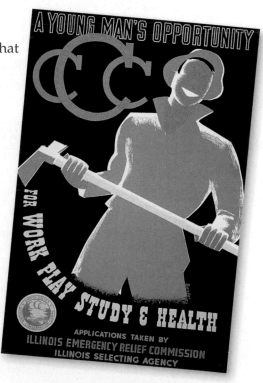

This political cartoon from 1933 depicts the efforts made by President Roosevelt to end the Great Depression with his New Deal.

President Roosevelt tries to "prime" the economic pump using taxpayer dollars to get the economy going again.

▶ **CRITICAL THINKING**

1 *Analyzing Primary Sources* How does the artist feel about the New Deal?

2 *Interpreting Significance* What symbols are used to convey the artist's message?

Connections to
TODAY

Emergency Economic Stabilization Act

Government relief programs and legislation to help banks and other financial institutions are still enacted today. In 2008 the Emergency Economic Stabilization Act became law. It provided up to $700 billion to the secretary of the treasury to buy mortgages and other troubled assets from the country's banks "to promote financial market stability."

Roosevelt insisted that it be shut down the following spring. Hopkins summarized what the CWA had accomplished:

PRIMARY SOURCE

❝Long after the workers of CWA are dead and gone and these hard times are forgotten, their effort will be remembered by permanent useful works in every county of every state.❞

—from *Spending to Save: The Complete Story of Relief,* 1936

Success of the First New Deal

During his first year in office, Roosevelt convinced Congress to pass an astonishing array of legislation. The First New Deal did not restore prosperity, but it reflected Roosevelt's zeal for action and his willingness to experiment. Banks were reopened, many more people retained their homes and farms, and more people were employed. Perhaps the most important result of the First New Deal was a change in the spirit of the American people. Roosevelt's actions had inspired hope and restored Americans' faith in their nation.

✓ **PROGRESS CHECK**

Identifying How did the relief programs help combat the Depression?

Reviewing Vocabulary

1. *Defining* How did polio affect President Roosevelt's character and physical abilities?

2. *Explaining* What did people fear would happen if the nation went off the gold standard?

Using Your Notes

3. *Summarizing* Use the notes you completed during the lesson to write a short paragraph summarizing how Roosevelt addressed the major problems during his first three months in office.

Answering the Guiding Questions

4. *Identifying* What qualities make an effective leader?

5. *Making Inferences* Why are the first hundred days so important for a president?

6. *Describing* Why did Roosevelt broadcast "fireside chats"?

7. *Analyzing* How did New Deal legislation try to stabilize agriculture and industry?

8. *Contrasting* How did New Deal programs differ from President Hoover's attempts to combat the Depression?

Writing Activity

9. PERSONAL If you were an adviser to President Roosevelt, what ideas would you suggest to end the Depression? Provide an explanation of why your ideas would work.

Reading HELPDESK

Content Vocabulary
- deficit spending
- binding arbitration
- sit-down strike

Academic Vocabulary
- benefit
- finance
- thereby

TAKING NOTES: *Organizing*

ACTIVITY As you read about President Roosevelt's Second New Deal, complete a graphic organizer similar to the one below by filling in his main legislative successes during this period.

Legislation	Provisions

LESSON 2
The Second New Deal

ESSENTIAL QUESTIONS • *Can government fix the economy?*
• *Is government responsible for the economic well-being of its citizens?*

IT MATTERS BECAUSE

Criticism of the New Deal led President Roosevelt to introduce new legislation in 1935. These laws created the Works Progress Administration, the National Labor Relations Board, and the Social Security Administration.

Launching the Second New Deal

GUIDING QUESTION *Why did President Roosevelt decide to introduce new legislation to fight the Depression?*

President Roosevelt was tremendously popular during his first two years in office, but opposition to his policies began to grow. New Deal programs had created more than 2 million new jobs. More than 10 million workers remained unemployed, however, and the nation's total income was about half of what it had been in 1929.

Criticism From Right and Left

Roosevelt faced hostility from both the political right and the left. The right wing had long believed that the New Deal regulated business too tightly. Opponents thought that it gave the federal government too much power over the states. By late 1934, the right wing increased its opposition as Roosevelt started **deficit spending,** abandoning a balanced budget and borrowing money to pay for his programs. Many business leaders became alarmed at the growing deficit.

Some on the left, however, believed that the New Deal had not gone far enough. They wanted even more economic intervention to shift wealth from the rich to middle-income and poor Americans. One outspoken critic was Huey Long. As governor of Louisiana, Long had championed the poor. He improved schools, colleges, and hospitals, and built roads and bridges. These **benefits** made him popular, and he built a powerful but corrupt political machine. In 1930 Long was elected to the U.S. Senate. In 1934 he established the Share Our Wealth Society to "pull down these huge piles of gold until there shall be a real job, not a little old sow-belly, black-eyed pea job but a real spending money, beef-steak and gravy. . . Ford in the garage . . . red, white, and blue job for every man." Long planned to run for president in 1936.

Roosevelt and the New Deal **449**

Roosevelt also faced a challenge from Catholic priest and popular radio host Father Charles Coughlin. Once an ardent New Deal supporter, the Detroit resident had grown impatient with its moderate reforms. He called for inflating the currency and nationalizing the banking system. In 1934 he organized the National Union for Social Justice, which some Democrats feared would become a new political party.

A third challenge came from California physician Francis Townsend. He proposed that the federal government pay citizens over age 60 a pension of $200 a month. Recipients would have to retire and spend the entire check each month. Townsend believed that the plan would increase spending and free up jobs for the unemployed. His proposal attracted millions of supporters, especially older Americans, who mobilized as a political force for the first time. Together, the three men had supporters around the country. Roosevelt faced the possibility of a coalition that would prevent his reelection.

The WPA

In 1935 Roosevelt launched a series of programs, now known as the Second New Deal, to generate greater economic recovery. Among these new programs was the Works Progress Administration (WPA), the New Deal's largest public works program. Between 1935 and 1941, the WPA employed 8.5 million workers and spent $11 billion to construct about 650,000 miles of roadways, 125,000 public buildings, 853 airports, more than 124,000 bridges, and more than 8,000 parks. One WPA program, called Federal Number One, **financed** artists, musicians, theater people, and writers. Artists created murals and sculptures for public buildings; musicians set up orchestras and smaller musical groups; playwrights, actors, and directors wrote and staged plays; and writers recorded the stories of those who had once been enslaved and others whose voices had not often been heard.

The Supreme Court's Role

In May 1935, in *Schechter Poultry Corporation* v. *United States,* the Supreme Court struck down the authority of the National Recovery Administration. The Schechter brothers had been convicted of violating the NRA's poultry code. The Court ruled that the Constitution did not allow Congress to delegate its legislative powers to the executive branch, and therefore the NRA's codes were unconstitutional. Roosevelt worried that the ruling suggested the Supreme Court could strike down the rest of the New Deal.

Roosevelt knew he needed a new series of programs to keep voters' support. He called congressional leaders to a White House conference and thundered that Congress could not go home until it passed his new bills. That summer, Congress passed Roosevelt's programs.

✓ **PROGRESS CHECK**

Synthesizing What factors encouraged Roosevelt to introduce the Second New Deal?

deficit spending
government practice of spending borrowed money rather than raising taxes, usually in an attempt to boost the economy

benefit something that promotes well-being or is a useful aid

finance to provide money for a project

Some, including Dr. Francis Townsend, criticized the New Deal for not going far enough to relieve the economic troubles of poor and middle-class Americans.

▶ **CRITICAL THINKING**
Comparing and Contrasting
How did the political left's criticisms of the New Deal differ from those of the political right?

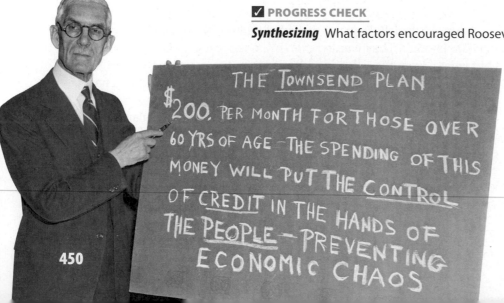

THE TOWNSEND PLAN
$200. PER MONTH FOR THOSE OVER 60 YRS OF AGE — THE SPENDING OF THIS MONEY WILL PUT THE CONTROL OF CREDIT IN THE HANDS OF THE PEOPLE — PREVENTING ECONOMIC CHAOS

Reforms for Workers and Senior Citizens

GUIDING QUESTION *How did the Wagner Act and the Social Security Act affect Americans?*

When the Supreme Court struck down the NRA, it also invalidated the section of the NIRA that gave workers the right to organize. Democrats knew that the working-class vote was key to winning reelection in 1936. They also believed that unions could help end the Depression because high union wages would give workers more money to spend, **thereby** boosting the economy. Opponents disagreed, arguing that high wages forced companies to charge higher prices and hire fewer people. Despite these concerns, Congress pushed ahead with new labor legislation.

The Wagner Act

In July 1935, Congress passed the National Labor Relations Act, also called the Wagner Act. This act guaranteed workers the right to unionize and bargain collectively. It also established the National Labor Relations Board (NLRB), which organized factory elections by secret ballot to determine whether workers wanted a union. The NLRB could also investigate employers' actions and stop unfair practices. The Wagner Act also set up a process called **binding arbitration,** whereby dissatisfied union members took their complaints to a neutral party who would listen to both sides and decide on the issues.

The Wagner Act led to a burst of labor activity. In 1935 John L. Lewis, leader of the United Mine Workers, helped form the Committee for Industrial Organization (CIO), which set out to organize unions that included all workers, skilled and unskilled, in a particular industry. First, it focused on the automobile and steel industries, two of the largest industries in which workers were not yet unionized. Organizers used new tactics to get employers to recognize the unions. For example, during **sit-down strikes,** employees stopped work inside the factory and refused to leave. This technique prevented management from sending in replacement workers. It was a common CIO tactic for several years.

In late December 1936, the United Auto Workers (UAW), a CIO union, began a sit-down strike at General Motor's plant in Flint, Michigan. Family, friends, and others passed food and other provisions to them through windows. Violence broke out when police launched a tear gas assault on strikers, wounding 13, but the strike held. On February 11, 1937, General Motors recognized the UAW as its employees' sole bargaining agent. The UAW became one of the most powerful unions in the United States.

U.S. Steel, the nation's largest steel producer and a long-standing opponent of unionizing, decided it did not want to repeat GM's experience. In March 1937, the company recognized the CIO's steelworkers union. Smaller steel producers did not follow suit and suffered bitter strikes. By 1941, however, the steelworkers union had won contracts throughout the industry.

PHOTO: Bettmann/CORBIS

Analyzing
PRIMARY SOURCES

The GM Strike

❝Beds were made up on the floor of each car, the seats being removed if necessary. . . . I could not see—and I looked for it carefully—the slightest damage done anywhere to the General Motors Corporation. The nearly completed car bodies, for example, were as clean as they would be in the salesroom, their glass and metal shining.❞

—Bruce Bliven, from "Sitting Down in Flint," *The New Republic,* January 27, 1937

DBQ *DRAWING CONCLUSIONS*
How do the strikers seem to have acted during the strike?

thereby because of that

binding arbitration
process in which a neutral party hears arguments from two opposing sides and makes a decision that both must accept

sit-down strike
method of boycotting work by sitting down at work and refusing to leave the establishment

---

Sit-down strikers at the GM Fisher body plant in Flint, Michigan, took over the plant in late December 1936. Their action led to a national strike that lasted until February 11, 1937.

▶ **CRITICAL THINKING**
Analyzing Primary Sources What did the atmosphere within the GM Fisher plant seem to be during the strike?

The Social Security Act provided small incomes to millions of Americans who were unable to work through no fault of their own.

▶ **CRITICAL THINKING**
Predicting Consequences How might Social Security have changed Americans' sense of personal economic security?

In the late 1930s, employees in other industries worked hard to gain union recognition from their employers. Union membership tripled from roughly 3 million in 1933 to about 9 million in 1939. In 1938 the CIO changed its name to the Congress of Industrial Organizations and became a federation of industrial unions.

Social Security

After passing the Wagner Act, Congress began work on one of the United States's most important pieces of legislation. This was the Social Security Act, which provided some financial security for older Americans, unemployed workers, and others. Roosevelt and his advisers viewed the bill primarily as an insurance measure. Workers earned the right to receive benefits because they paid special taxes to the federal government, just as they paid premiums in buying a life insurance policy. The legislation also provided modest welfare payments to others in need, including people with disabilities and poor mothers with dependent children.

Some critics did not like the fact that the money came from payroll taxes imposed on workers and employers, but to Roosevelt these taxes were crucial:

PRIMARY SOURCE

❝We put those payroll contributions there so as to give the contributors a legal, moral, and political right to collect their pensions and their unemployment benefits. With those taxes in there, no . . . politician can ever scrap my social security program.❞

—quoted in "Memorandum on Conference with FDR Concerning Social Security Taxation," 1941

What Roosevelt did not anticipate was that Congress would later borrow from the Social Security fund to pay for other programs without raising payroll taxes.

The core of Social Security was the monthly retirement benefit, which people collected when they stopped working at age 65. Unemployment insurance supplied a temporary income to workers who had lost their jobs. Although Social Security helped many people, at first it left out many of the neediest Americans, such as farm and domestic workers. About 65 percent of all African American workers in the 1930s fell into these two categories. Nevertheless, Social Security established the principle that the federal government should be responsible for those who, through no fault of their own, were unable to work.

✓ **PROGRESS CHECK**

Evaluating What were some benefits of the Wagner Act and the Social Security Act for the American public?

LESSON 2 REVIEW

Vocabulary Review
1. *Defining* What happens when the federal government starts a policy of deficit spending?

2. *Explaining* What was one unique feature of sit-down strikes?

Using Your Notes
3. *Summarizing* Review the notes that you completed during the lesson, and then summarize the provisions of Roosevelt's major legislation of the Second New Deal.

Answering the Guiding Questions
4. *Identifying Cause and Effect* Why did President Roosevelt decide to introduce new legislation to fight the Depression?

5. *Analyzing* How did the Wagner Act and the Social Security Act affect Americans?

Writing Activity
6. **PERSUASIVE** Choose a person or group who criticized the New Deal. Write an editorial to the local newspaper expressing why readers should be in support of or opposition to that viewpoint.

networks

There's More Online!

☑ **BIOGRAPHY** Mary McLeod Bethune

☑ **CHART/GRAPH** Monthly Unemployment Rate

☑ **GRAPHIC ORGANIZER** New Deal Coalition

☑ **GRAPHIC ORGANIZER** Relief, Reform, Recovery

☑ **IMAGE** Court Packing Reaction

☑ **VIDEO** The New Deal Coalition

☑ **INTERACTIVE SELF-CHECK QUIZ**

Reading **HELP**DESK

Content Vocabulary

• court-packing
• broker state
• safety net

Academic Vocabulary

• recovery • mediate

TAKING NOTES: *Outlining*

ACTIVITY As you read, create an outline similar to the one below.

> The New Deal Coalition
> I. Roosevelt's Second Term
>   A.
>   B.
>   C.
> II.
>   A.
>   B.

LESSON 3
The New Deal Coalition

ESSENTIAL QUESTIONS • *Can government fix the economy?*
• *Is government responsible for the economic well-being of its citizens?*

IT MATTERS BECAUSE

President Roosevelt was reelected in a landslide in 1936. Early in his second term, however, his court-packing plan and a new recession hurt him politically. The Fair Labor Standards Act, the last significant piece of New Deal legislation, provided new protections for workers.

Roosevelt's Second Term

GUIDING QUESTION *Why do you think Roosevelt easily won reelection?*

In 1936 millions of voters owed their jobs, mortgages, and bank accounts to the New Deal. Many African Americans, who had reliably voted Republican since Reconstruction, switched their allegiance to the Democratic Party. Women and African Americans had made modest gains, thanks to the support of Eleanor Roosevelt, who toured the country and recounted her experiences to her husband. She persuaded him to address some of their problems in his New Deal programs. A Democratic Party coalition emerged, including not just the white South but also African Americans, farmers, workers, immigrants, women, progressives, and intellectuals.

The Election of 1936

The Republicans nominated Kansas governor Alfred Landon as their presidential challenger. He wanted to "free the spirit of American enterprise," but could not convince most voters change was needed. Roosevelt won more than 60 percent of the popular vote.

The Court-Packing Plan

Although the New Deal was popular, the Supreme Court saw things differently. In January 1936, it declared the Agricultural Adjustment Act unconstitutional. Cases pending on Social Security and the Wagner Act meant that the Court might strike down other New Deal programs.

Roosevelt was furious. After his reelection, he tried to change the Court's political balance. He sent Congress a bill that would increase the number of justices and allow the president to appoint an additional

court-packing the act of a leader to change the political balance of power in a nation's judiciary system by appointing judges who will rule in favor of his or her policies

justice if a sitting justice who had served 10 years did not retire within six months of reaching age 70. The bill, if passed, would have allowed Roosevelt to appoint up to six new justices.

The **court-packing** plan, as it was called, was a major political mistake. Many Southern Democrats feared new justices would overturn segregation. African American leaders worried future justices might oppose civil rights. Many Americans thought the plan gave the president too much power. The Court appeared to back down, narrowly upholding the constitutionality of both the Wagner Act and the Social Security Act. Soon after, a conservative justice's resignation allowed Roosevelt to appoint a justice who supported the New Deal.

Although the bill was quietly killed and Roosevelt achieved his goal of changing the Court's view of the New Deal, the court-packing plan hurt his reputation. Moreover, it caused conservative Democrats to work with Republicans to block any further New Deal proposals.

The Recession of 1937

recovery an economic upturn, as after a depression

Roosevelt's problems continued. In early 1937, the economy seemed to be on the verge of **recovery.** Industrial output was almost back to pre-Depression levels, and many people believed the worst was over. Concerned about rising debt, Roosevelt ordered the WPA and the PWA to be cut significantly. Unfortunately, he cut spending just as the first Social Security payroll taxes took $2 billion out of the economy. By the end of 1937, about 2 million people were out of work.

A debate over the value of government spending arose within the administration. The leaders of the WPA and the PWA cited a new economic theory called Keynesianism (KAYN • zee • uh • nih • zuhm), which held that government should spend heavily in a recession to jump-start the economy.

PRIMARY SOURCE

❝But this *long run* is a misleading guide to current affairs. *In the long run* we are all dead. Economists set themselves too easy, too useless a task if in tempestuous seasons they can only tell us that when the storm is long past the ocean is flat again.❞

—John Maynard Keynes, from *A Tract on Monetary Reform*, 1923

At first, Roosevelt was reluctant to begin deficit spending again. Some critics believed the recession proved the public was becoming too dependent on government spending. But in early 1938, with no recovery in sight, Roosevelt asked Congress for $3.75 billion for the PWA, the WPA, and other programs.

✓ **PROGRESS CHECK**

Analyzing Cause and Effect What factors helped Roosevelt win a landslide victory in 1936?

The New Deal Ends

GUIDING QUESTION *What impact has New Deal legislation had on federal and state governments?*

In his second Inaugural Address, Roosevelt had pointed out that despite the nation's progress in climbing out of the Depression, many Americans were still poor:

PRIMARY SOURCE

❝I see one-third of a nation ill-housed, ill-clad, ill-nourished. . . . The test of our progress is not whether we add more to the abundance of those who have much; it is whether we provide enough for those who have too little.❞

—from *The Public Papers and Addresses of Franklin D. Roosevelt: The Constitution Prevails*, 1937

Mary McLeod Bethune, shown with Eleanor Roosevelt, became the first African American woman to head a federal agency.

▶ **CRITICAL THINKING**
Comparing and Contrasting What mood does the photograph convey?

The Last New Deal Reforms

One of the president's goals for his second term was to provide better housing for the nation's poor. Eleanor Roosevelt, who had toured poverty-stricken Appalachia and the rural South, strongly urged the president to do something. Roosevelt responded with the passage of the National Housing Act, which established the United States Housing Authority. This organization received $500 million to subsidize loans to builders willing to construct low-cost housing.

Roosevelt also sought to help the nation's tenant farmers. About 150,000 white and 195,000 African American tenant farmers were expelled from farms when landlords took their land out of production under the AAA. To stop this trend, Congress created the Farm Security Administration to give loans to tenants so they could purchase farms.

The last major piece of New Deal reform was the Fair Labor Standards Act, which abolished child labor, limited the workweek to 44 hours for most workers, and set the first federal minimum wage at 25 cents an hour. The recession of 1937 enabled Republicans to win seats in Congress in the midterm elections of 1938. Together with conservative Southern Democrats, they began blocking further New Deal legislation. By 1939, the New Deal era had come to an end.

The New Deal's Legacy

The New Deal did not end the Depression, but it did give many Americans a stronger sense of security and stability. As a whole, the New Deal tended to balance competing economic interests. Supreme Court decisions in 1937 and 1942 further increased federal power over the economy and allowed it to **mediate** between competing groups.

In taking on this mediating role, the New Deal established what some have called the **broker state,** in which the government works out conflicts among different interests. This broker role has continued under the administrations of both parties ever since. The New Deal also brought about a new public attitude toward government. Roosevelt's programs had succeeded in creating a **safety net**—safeguards and relief programs that protected people against economic disaster. Throughout the hard times of the Depression, most Americans maintained a surprising degree of confidence in the American system.

Another legacy of the New Deal is a continuing debate over how much government should intervene in the economy. Critics have argued that the New Deal made the federal government too powerful.

mediate to attempt to resolve conflict between hostile people and groups

broker state role of government to work out conflicts among competing interest groups

safety net something that provides security against misfortune; specifically, government relief programs intended to protect against economic disaster

☑ **PROGRESS CHECK**

Evaluating How did the New Deal change how government worked?

LESSON 3 REVIEW

Reviewing Vocabulary

1. *Stating* What was Roosevelt's court-packing plan?

2. *Defining* What is a broker state?

3. *Explaining* How does a safety net work?

Using Your Notes

4. *Summarizing* Review the notes that you completed during the lesson. What were the key events of the final years of the New Deal?

Answering the Guiding Questions

5. *Synthesizing* Why do you think Roosevelt easily won reelection?

6. *Evaluating* What impact has New Deal legislation had on federal and state governments?

Writing Activity

7. **PERSONAL** Do you think that Roosevelt's solution to the 1937 recession was the best one? Write a short essay in which you give your opinions about Roosevelt's actions and describe your own ideas about ways that could have eased the crisis.

Directions: On a separate sheet of paper, answer the questions below. Make sure you read carefully and answer all parts to the question.

Lesson Review

Lesson 1

1 *Identifying Central Issues* What were the Hundred Days?

2 *Interpreting* What was the initial response to Roosevelt's fireside chats?

Lesson 2

3 *Identifying Cause and Effect* Why was the Wagner Act enacted?

4 *Drawing Conclusions* What was the significance of the Social Security Act?

Lesson 3

5 *Assessing* Why was the court-packing plan such a mistake for Roosevelt?

6 *Analyzing* Which groups were a part of the New Deal coalition?

21st Century Skills

7 **COMPARE AND CONTRAST** Tell how the political right and the left differed in their objections to the New Deal.

8 **EXPLAINING CONTINUITY AND CHANGE** Why did African Americans shift away from their long tradition of supporting the Republican Party?

9 **TIME, CHRONOLOGY, AND SEQUENCING** Why was Roosevelt's cutback of the WPA and PWA premature?

Exploring the Essential Questions

10 *Analyzing Ethical Issues* Write a short story set in 1939. The story should include details about how the government tried to fix the economy and help people in the 1930s. Have two of the story's characters debate this question: "Is government responsible for the economic well-being of its citizens?"

DBQ Document-Based Questions

Use the document to answer the following questions.

PRIMARY SOURCE

❝ This trip to the mining areas was my first contact with the work being done by the Quakers. I liked the idea of trying to put people to work to help themselves. The men were started on projects and taught to use their abilities to develop new skills. The women were encouraged to revive any household arts they might once have known but which they had neglected in the drab life of the mining village.

This was only the first of many trips into the mining districts but it was the one that started the homestead idea [placing people in communities with homes farms, and jobs]. . . . It was all experimental work, but it was designed to get people off relief, to put them to work building their own homes and to give them enough land to start growing food. ❞

—from *The Autobiography of Eleanor Roosevelt*, 1937

11 *Drawing Conclusions* Why did Eleanor Roosevelt like the Quaker project?

12 *Making Connections* Based on this excerpt, what are the benefits that she saw in the homestead idea?

Extended-Response Question

13 *Simulating* Review the various New Deal programs discussed in the chapter. Select one that you think could be used or adapted to a current situation. Explain what group or groups it would help and how it would do so.

Need Extra Help?

If You've Missed Question	**1**	**2**	**3**	**4**	**5**	**6**	**7**	**8**	**9**	**10**	**11**	**12**	**13**
Go to page	444	445	451	451	453	453	449	453	454	444	456	456	445

A World in Flames

1931–1941

ESSENTIAL QUESTIONS • *Could World War II have been prevented?*
• *Why do some people fail to respond to injustice while others try to prevent injustice?*

The Story Matters...

After Japanese forces attacked American forces at Pearl Harbor on December 7, 1941, thousands of men and women volunteered to serve in the U.S. military. With the U.S. declaration of war, American soldiers were thrown into a fight to the death between fascism and democracy.

◄ U.S. Navy serviceman Dorie Miller was a cook on the USS *West Virginia* docked at Pearl Harbor, Hawaii, on December 7, 1941. He heroically took over an antiaircraft gun when his commanding officer was fatally wounded. He later won the Navy Cross for his courageous actions during the battle. On November 25, 1944, Miller was officially listed as "presumed dead" a year after his escort cruiser was torpedoed in the Pacific.

PHOTO: Library of Congress

After the experience of World War I, many Americans and Europeans did not want to be involved in such a war ever again. Many Americans believed that some European nations would always be fighting one another and there was no reason for the United States to step in. As another war brewed overseas during the 1930s, Americans were torn between ignoring it and using their influence to maintain peace. When war finally erupted, the nation remained supportive of its traditional allies, if reluctant to enter the fray itself. After the conflict reached U.S. soil, however, Americans devoted themselves to victory.

Step Into the Place

Read the quotes and look at the information presented on the map.

 How are these two quotes similar in their description of the Japanese attack on Pearl Harbor and the outbreak of war?

PRIMARY SOURCE

66 We saw a lot of planes diving down and we thought that the army air force was practicing again. We didn't know what it was. . . . [T]wo planes came over us and they were so low that you could see the pilots in the plane. They dropped bombs on each side of us, but missed. Then we saw the big red ball, which signified they were Japanese planes. Well then we knew we were at war. 99

—Will Lehner, a sailor aboard the USS *Ward* during the attack on Pearl Harbor, from an interview, 2004

PRIMARY SOURCE

66 Yesterday, December 7, 1941—a date which will live in infamy—the United States of America was suddenly and deliberately attacked by naval and air forces of the Empire of Japan. . . . No matter how long it may take us to overcome this premeditated invasion, the American people in their righteous might will win through to absolute victory. . . . I ask that the Congress declare that since the unprovoked and dastardly attack by Japan on Sunday, December 7, 1941, a state of war has existed between the United States and the Japanese Empire. 99

—President Franklin D. Roosevelt, from his speech to Congress, December 8, 1941

PHOTOS: (tl)MPI/Archive Photos/Getty Images, (tr)Official U.S. Navy Photograph, now in the collections of the National Archives, (b)detail/ White House Collection/The White House Historical Association

Step Into the Time

Choose an event from the time line and describe how the event reflects the state of the world leading up to 1941.

U.S. PRESIDENTS

UNITED STATES

WORLD

F. Roosevelt 1933–1945

1934 Nye Committee holds hearings on causes of World War I

1931

1933

1931 Japan invades Manchuria

1933 Hitler becomes chancellor of Germany

1934 Hitler denounces Treaty of Versailles

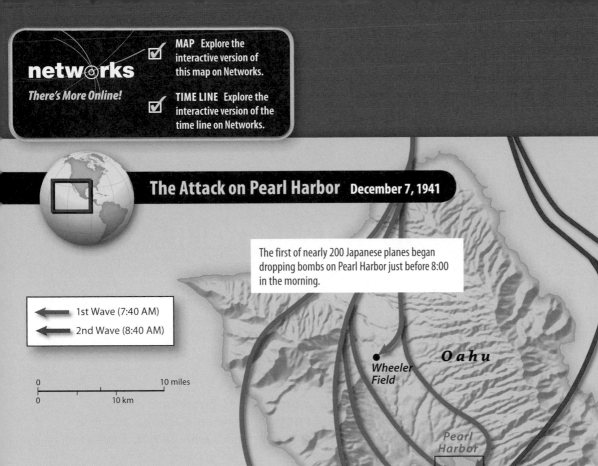

The Attack on Pearl Harbor December 7, 1941

networks
There's More Online!

☑ **MAP** Explore the interactive version of this map on Networks.

☑ **TIME LINE** Explore the interactive version of the time line on Networks.

The first of nearly 200 Japanese planes began dropping bombs on Pearl Harbor just before 8:00 in the morning.

← 1st Wave (7:40 AM)
← 2nd Wave (8:40 AM)

0   10 miles
0   10 km

Oahu

● *Wheeler Field*

↘ *Kaneohe Naval Air Station*

Pearl Harbor

● *Hickam Field*

● Honolulu

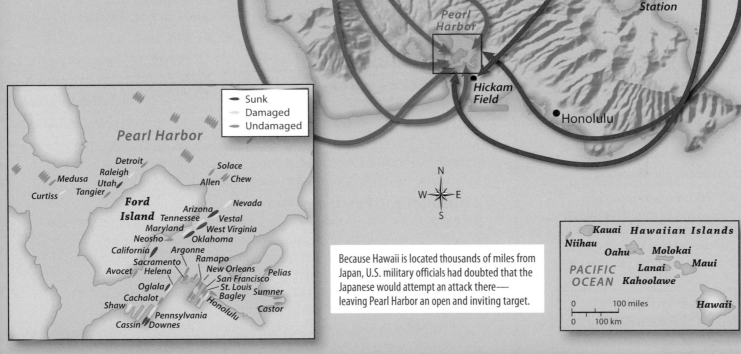

Pearl Harbor

- — Sunk
- — Damaged
- — Undamaged

Detroit
Raleigh
Medusa   Utah
Tangier
Curtiss

Solace
Allen   Chew

Ford Island

Nevada
Arizona
Tennessee   Vestal
Maryland   West Virginia
Neosho   Oklahoma
California   Argonne
Sacramento   Ramapo
Avocet   Helena   New Orleans
Oglala   San Francisco   Pelias
Cachalot   St. Louis
Shaw   Bagley   Sumner
Honolulu   Castor
Cassin   Downes
Pennsylvania

N
W ✦ E
S

Because Hawaii is located thousands of miles from Japan, U.S. military officials had doubted that the Japanese would attempt an attack there—leaving Pearl Harbor an open and inviting target.

Kauai **Hawaiian Islands**
Niihau   *Oahu*   *Molokai*
PACIFIC OCEAN   *Lanai*   *Maui*
Kahoolawe

0   100 miles
0   100 km   *Hawaii*

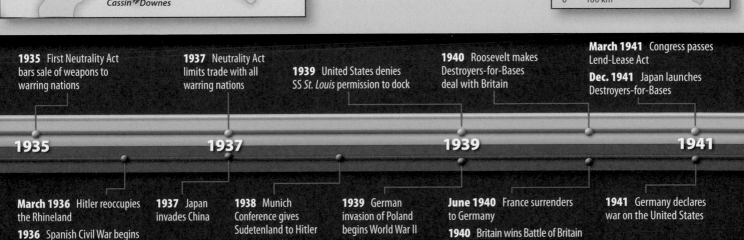

1935 First Neutrality Act bars sale of weapons to warring nations

1937 Neutrality Act limits trade with all warring nations

1939 United States denies SS *St. Louis* permission to dock

1940 Roosevelt makes Destroyers-for-Bases deal with Britain

March 1941 Congress passes Lend-Lease Act

Dec. 1941 Japan launches Destroyers-for-Bases

1935   **1937**   **1939**   **1941**

March 1936 Hitler reoccupies the Rhineland
1936 Spanish Civil War begins

1937 Japan invades China

1938 Munich Conference gives Sudetenland to Hitler

1939 German invasion of Poland begins World War II

June 1940 France surrenders to Germany
1940 Britain wins Battle of Britain

1941 Germany declares war on the United States

A World in Flames **459**

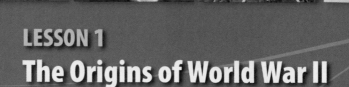

Reading **HELP**DESK

Content Vocabulary

- fascism
- appeasement
- collective

Academic Vocabulary

- exploit
- command
- dominate

TAKING NOTES: *Organizing*

ACTIVITY As you read about the events in Europe and Asia after World War I, complete a graphic organizer similar to the one below, using the major headings of the lesson to create an outline.

> The Origins of World War II
> I. The Rise of Dictators
>   A.
>   B.
>   C.
>   D.
> II.

LESSON 1
The Origins of World War II

ESSENTIAL QUESTIONS · *Could World War II have been prevented?* · *Why do some people not respond to injustice while others try to prevent injustice?*

IT MATTERS BECAUSE

In the years following World War I, aggressive and expansionist governments took power in Europe and Asia. Meanwhile, most Americans did not want to get involved in another foreign war.

The Rise of Dictators

GUIDING QUESTION *What economic and political conditions following World War I encouraged dictatorships?*

The Treaty of Versailles, along with the economic depression that followed, contributed to the rise of antidemocratic governments in both Europe and Asia. These antidemocratic states would eventually break the peace agreement that ended World War I.

Mussolini and Fascism in Italy

One of Europe's first dictatorships arose in Italy. In 1919 Benito Mussolini founded Italy's Fascist movement. **Fascism** was an aggressive nationalistic movement that considered the nation more important than the individual. Fascists believed that order in society and national greatness came through a dictator who led a strong government and built an empire.

Fascism was also strongly anticommunist. After the Russian Revolution, many Europeans feared that Communists, allied with labor unions, were trying to bring down their governments. Mussolini **exploited** these fears by portraying fascism as a bulwark against communism, protecting private property and the middle class. He pledged to return Italy to the glories of the Roman Empire.

Backed by the Blackshirts, a Fascist militia, Mussolini threatened to march on Rome in 1922, claiming he was defending Italy against a communist revolution. Liberal members of the Italian parliament insisted that the king declare martial law. When he refused, the cabinet resigned. Conservative advisers then persuaded the king to appoint Mussolini as the premier. Once in office, Mussolini—who took the title of Il Duce, or "The Leader"—embarked on an ambitious program of bringing order to Italy.

Stalin Takes Over the Soviet Union

After the Russian Revolution, the Communist Party, led by Vladimir Lenin, created the Union of Soviet Socialist Republics (USSR) in 1922. The Communists instituted one-party rule, suppressed individual liberties, and punished opponents.

After Lenin died in 1924, Joseph Stalin came to power. By 1926, Stalin was the new Soviet dictator. He began a massive effort to industrialize his country using Five-Year Plans. Steel production increased, but industrial wages declined by 43 percent from 1928 to 1940. Family farms were combined and turned into **collectives,** or government-owned farms. Peasants who resisted by killing livestock or hoarding crops faced show trials or death from starvation. As many as 10 million peasants died in famines during 1932 and 1933. Stalin also sought to expand Soviet influence beyond its borders, proclaiming, "[W]orld dictatorship can be established only when the victory of socialism has been achieved in certain countries or groups of countries . . . [growing into] a World Union of Soviet Socialist Republics uniting the whole of mankind. . . ."

Stalin tolerated no opposition, targeting political enemies along with artists and intellectuals. He used concentration camps, which held nearly 2 million people by 1935. Prisoners were used as slave labor. Between 15 and 20 million people died under Stalin's rule, which lasted until his death in 1953.

Hitler and Nazi Germany

Adolf Hitler was a fervent nationalist who hated both the victorious Allies and the German government that had accepted their peace terms ending World War I. He became the leader of the National Socialist German Workers' Party, or Nazi Party. The Nazis were one of many political parties that arose out of postwar Germany's political and economic chaos. The party called for Germany to expand its territory and to reject the terms of the Treaty of Versailles. It also was anti-Semitic. In November 1923, the Nazis tried to seize power by marching on city hall in Munich, Germany. The plan failed, the Nazi Party was banned for a time, and Hitler was arrested.

While in prison, Hitler wrote *Mein Kampf* ("My Struggle"), in which he claimed that Germans, particularly blond, blue-eyed Germans, belonged to a "master race" called Aryans. He argued that the Slavic peoples of Eastern Europe belonged to an inferior race, which Germans should enslave. Hitler's racism was strongest, however, toward Jews. Hitler blamed the Jews for many of the world's problems, especially for Germany's defeat in World War I.

After his release, Hitler changed his tactics. He focused on getting Nazis elected to the Reichstag, the lower house of the German parliament. When the Depression struck Germany, many desperate Germans began to vote for radical parties, including the Nazis and Communists. By 1932, the Nazis were the largest party in the Reichstag. The following year, the German president appointed Hitler as chancellor.

After taking office, Hitler called for new elections. Storm troopers, as the Nazi paramilitary units were called, began intimidating voters. After the election, the Reichstag, **dominated** by the Nazis and other right-wing parties, voted to give Hitler dictatorial powers. In 1934 Hitler became president, which gave him control of the army. He then gave himself the new title of Der Führer, or "The Leader."

fascism a political system headed by a dictator that calls for extreme nationalism and often racism and no tolerance of opposition

exploit to take unfair advantage of

collective a farm, especially in Communist countries, formed from many small holdings collected into a single unit for joint operation under governmental supervision

dominate to be in a state or position of command or control over all others

command to be in control of, to have full power

Mussolini (left), Hitler (center), and Stalin (right) rose to power during times of political and economic instability.

▶ CRITICAL THINKING
Drawing Inferences Why would political and economic instability lead to a rise of dictatorships?

Hideki Tōjō became prime minister of Japan in 1941 and supported an aggressive military policy.

▶ **CRITICAL THINKING**
Predicting Consequences What might be a result of Tōjō's aggressive leadership?

Militarists Control Japan

In Japan, as in Germany, difficult economic times helped undermine the political system. Japanese industries had to import nearly all of the resources they needed to produce goods. When the Depression struck, other countries raised their tariffs, making things worse. Many Japanese military officers blamed the country's problems on corrupt politicians. They believed that Japan was destined to dominate East Asia and that straying from traditional beliefs corrupted the country.

The military leaders argued that seizing territory was the only way Japan could get the resources it needed. In September 1931, the Japanese army invaded Manchuria, a resource-rich region of northern China. In October, hoping to avoid conflict with the United States, Emperor Hirohito's prime minister asked Minister of War Hideki Tōjō to withdraw some troops from China. Tōjō refused, threatening to bring down the government. The military was in **command** of the country. The Japanese army swept through China, and in 1937 invaded Nanking (now Nanjing), destroying the city and killing as many as 300,000 of its residents. The incident became known as the "Rape of Nanking." In October 1941, Tōjō took over as prime minister.

☑ **PROGRESS CHECK**

Examining How did postwar conditions contribute to the rise of dictatorships in Europe?

World War II Begins

GUIDING QUESTION *How did European nations try to prevent war?*

In 1935 Hitler began to defy the Treaty of Versailles that had ended World War I. He announced that Germany would build a new air force and begin a military draft that would greatly expand its army—actions in direct violation of the treaty. Rather than enforce the treaty by going to war, European leaders tried to negotiate with Hitler.

Europe's leaders had several reasons for believing—or wanting to believe—that a deal could be reached with Hitler to avoid war. First, they wanted to avoid a repeat of World War I. Second, some thought most of Hitler's demands were reasonable, including his demand that all German-speaking regions be united. Third, many people assumed that the Nazis would want peace once they gained more territory.

The Austrian *Anschluss*

In late 1937, Hitler again called for the unification of all German-speaking people, including those in Austria and Czechoslovakia. He believed that Germany could expand its territory only by force.

In February 1938, Hitler threatened to invade German-speaking Austria unless Austrian Nazis were given important government posts. Austria's chancellor gave in to this demand, but then tried to put the matter of unification with Germany to a democratic vote. Fearing the outcome, Hitler sent troops into Austria in March and announced the *Anschluss,* or unification, of Austria and Germany.

The Munich Crisis

Hitler next announced German claims to the Sudetenland, an area of Czechoslovakia with a large German-speaking population. The Czechs strongly resisted Germany's demands. France threatened to fight if Germany attacked Czechoslovakia, and the Soviet Union also promised aid. Prime Minister Neville Chamberlain pledged Britain's support to France, its ally.

Representatives of Britain, France, Italy, and Germany met in Munich, Germany, to decide Czechoslovakia's fate. At the Munich Conference, on September 29, 1938, Britain and France agreed to Hitler's demands, a policy that came to be known as **appeasement.** In other words, they made concessions and believed that if they gave Hitler what he wanted, they could avoid war. Czechoslovakia had to give up the Sudetenland or fight Germany on its own. When Chamberlain returned home, he stated, "My good friends, for the second time in our history, a British Prime Minister has returned from Germany bringing peace with honor. I believe it is 'peace for our time.' Go home and get a nice quiet sleep."

Appeasement, however, failed to preserve the fragile peace. In March 1939, Germany sent troops into Czechoslovakia and divided the country. Slovakia became independent in name, but it was actually under German control. The Czech lands became a German protectorate.

Hitler Demands Danzig

A month after the Munich Conference, Hitler demanded that the city of Danzig be returned to German control. Danzig was more than 90 percent German, and it had been part of Poland since World War I. Hitler also requested a highway and railroad across the Polish Corridor.

Hitler's new demands convinced Britain and France that war was inevitable. On March 31, 1939, Britain announced that if Poland went to war to defend its territory, Britain and France would come to its aid. This declaration encouraged Poland to refuse Hitler's demands. In May 1939, Hitler ordered the German army to prepare to invade Poland. He also ordered his foreign minister to begin negotiations with the Soviet Union. If Germany was going to fight Britain and France, Hitler did not want to have to fight the Soviets too.

The Nazi-Soviet Pact

When German officials proposed a non-aggression treaty to the Soviets, Stalin agreed. He believed the best way to protect the Soviet Union was to turn the capitalist nations against each other. If the treaty worked, Germany would go to war against Britain and France.

The non-aggression pact, signed by Germany and the Soviet Union on August 23, 1939, shocked the world. Communism and Nazism were supposed to be opposed to each other. Leaders in Britain and France understood, however, that Hitler had made the deal to free himself for war against their countries and Poland. They did not know that the treaty called for the division of Poland between Germany and the Soviet Union.

The Invasion of Poland and the Fall of France

On September 1, 1939, Germany invaded Poland. Two days later, Britain and France declared war on Germany. World War II had begun. The Germans used a new type of warfare called blitzkrieg, or "lightning war." Blitzkrieg used massed tanks, combined with waves of aircraft and paratroopers, to break through and encircle enemy positions. By October 5, 1939, the Germans had defeated the Polish military.

Meanwhile, Western Europe remained quiet. British and French troops in France waited for a German attack. On May 10, 1940, Hitler launched a new blitzkrieg. While German troops parachuted into the Netherlands, tanks rolled into Belgium and Luxembourg. British and French forces raced north into Belgium. The Germans crossed the Ardennes Mountains of Luxembourg and eastern Belgium. German tanks smashed through the French lines and moved west across northern France. The British and French were trapped in Belgium.

PHOTO: Hulton Archive/Getty Images

BIOGRAPHY

Neville Chamberlain (1869–1940)

After serving at top levels of the British government since the end of World War I, Neville Chamberlain became prime minister in 1937. Chamberlain's term was dominated by growing tension with Nazi Germany. He signed the Munich Agreement with Hitler in 1938 as part of an appeasement policy. Wildly popular as the man who avoided another war, Chamberlain quickly fell from favor when Hitler invaded Poland a year later. Chamberlain resigned, and died of cancer just six months later.

▶ **CRITICAL THINKING**
Drawing Conclusions Why did opinions of Chamberlain change so quickly after Hitler invaded Poland?

appeasement giving in to unjust demands in order to avoid all-out conflict

Britain's Neville Chamberlain (third from left), Mussolini (center), and Hitler (third from right) agreed to prevent war at the Munich Conference in 1938. To appease Hitler, representatives at the conference agreed that Czechoslovakia would give up the Sudetenland to Germany. Less than a year later, Germany had occupied all of Czechoslovakia, invaded Poland, and was at war with Britain and France.

▶ **CRITICAL THINKING**
Drawing Conclusions Why do you think that the policy of appeasement failed?

The Miracle at Dunkirk

German troops drove Allied forces toward the English Channel. The port of Dunkirk became the Allies' only way out. As German forces moved in on Dunkirk, Hitler ordered them to stop. Historians think that Hitler was nervous about risking his tank forces. Whatever his reasons, Hitler's orders provided a three-day delay that allowed Allied forces to evacuate. When the evacuation ended on June 4, an estimated 338,000 British and French troops had been saved during the "Miracle at Dunkirk."

Less than three weeks later, on June 22, 1940, France surrendered. To govern the rest of France, Germany set up a puppet government at the town of Vichy and made Marshal Philippe Pétain the leader but gave him no power. French general Charles de Gaulle led the Free French resistance forces from the French colony of Algiers. He worked with Allied leaders and refused to recognize the defeat of France.

Britain Remains Defiant

Hitler expected Britain to negotiate peace after France surrendered. He was mistaken. On June 4, 1940, British prime minister Winston Churchill delivered a defiant speech, vowing that Britain would never surrender:

PRIMARY SOURCE

❝Even though large tracts of Europe and many old and famous States have fallen or may fall into the grip of the Gestapo and all the odious apparatus of Nazi rule, we shall not flag or fail, we shall go on to the end.... [W]e shall defend our island, whatever the cost may be ... we shall never surrender....❞

—Winston Churchill, from his speech to Parliament, June 4, 1940

That same month, Hitler ordered the German air force, the *Luftwaffe,* to begin attacking British ships in the English Channel. Then, in August and September, the *Luftwaffe* battled the British Royal Air Force in what became known as the Battle of Britain. After London was bombed accidentally, Britain retaliated by bombing Berlin. The *Luftwaffe* then began targeting its attacks on London and other cities. Britain's use of radar gave it the advantage. After major losses on both sides, Hitler canceled the planned invasion of Britain. Churchill praised the sacrifices of the pilots who saved Britain, saying, "Never in the field of human conflict was so much owed by so many to so few."

✓ **PROGRESS CHECK**

Evaluating How was Britain able to prevent Germany from invading?

PHOTO: Historical/CORBIS; TEXT: Speech to Parliament, August 20, 1940, Winston Churchill. Reproduced with permission of Curtis Brown, London on behalf of the Estate of Sir Winston Churchill. Copyright © Winston S. Churchill.

LESSON 1 REVIEW

Reviewing Vocabulary

1. *Explaining* How did fascism put Europe on the path to war?

2. *Stating* How was the Soviet collectivization of agriculture an example of a dictatorial government?

Using Your Notes

3. *Summarizing* Use your notes from the lesson to write a paragraph explaining how dictators came to power during this era.

Answering the Guiding Questions

4. *Evaluating* What economic and political conditions following World War I encouraged dictatorships?

5. *Synthesizing* How did European nations try to prevent war?

Writing Activity

6. **EXPOSITORY** Write a short essay explaining why the Nazi-Soviet Non-Aggression Pact was such a surprise to the world.

netw⚙rks

There's More Online!

☑ **BIOGRAPHY** Dorie Miller

☑ **IMAGE** America First Committee

☑ **IMAGE** Isolationists

☑ **IMAGE** U.S.S. *Arizona* Memorial

☑ **VIDEO** From Neutrality to War

☑ **INTERACTIVE SELF-CHECK QUIZ**

LESSON 2
From Neutrality to War

ESSENTIAL QUESTIONS · *Could World War II have been prevented?*
· *Why do some people fail to respond to injustice while others try to prevent injustice?*

Reading **HELP**DESK

Content Vocabulary
- **internationalism**
- **strategic materials**

Academic Vocabulary
- **revise**   · **underestimate**
- **purchase**

TAKING NOTES: *Organizing*

ACTIVITY As you read about U.S. efforts to stay neutral, complete a graphic organizer similar to the one below by identifying events that shifted American involvement in the war.

> Events That Shifted
> American Involvement

IT MATTERS BECAUSE

Although Americans wanted to avoid fighting in another foreign war, they sent aid when their allies were threatened. The attack on Pearl Harbor convinced the United States to declare war.

American Neutrality

GUIDING QUESTIONS *Why did many Americans support isolationism? Why did President Roosevelt support internationalism?*

The rise of dictatorships and militarism in Europe discouraged many Americans. The sacrifices they had made during World War I seemed pointless. In addition, during the Depression, most European nations announced they would no longer repay their war debts to the United States. In response, many Americans once again began supporting isolationism and trying to avoid involvement in international conflicts.

The Nye Committee
Meanwhile, accusations emerged that arms manufacturers had tricked the United States into entering World War I. In 1934 Senator Gerald P. Nye held hearings to investigate these allegations. The Nye Committee report documented the huge profits that arms factories had made during the war and created the impression that these businesses influenced the decision to go to war. Even more Americans turned toward isolationism.

Legislating Neutrality
In response to growing Italian and German aggression in Europe, Congress passed the Neutrality Act of 1935. This legislation—reflecting a response to the Nye report—made it illegal for Americans to sell arms to any country at war. Then, in 1936, a rebellion erupted in Spain that soon became a civil war. Congress responded by passing a second neutrality act, banning the sale of arms to either side in a civil war.

By 1940, many Americans joined Roosevelt in wanting to help Britain and France in their struggle against Hitler. Isolationists, however, still wished to keep the country from directly entering the conflict.

This political cartoon shows Uncle Sam extending a helping hand to Britain but refusing to sell arms to Britain and France.

▶ **CRITICAL THINKING**

1 *Making Inferences* According to the cartoon, why should the United States refuse to sell arms overseas?

2 *Analyzing Primary Sources* What does this cartoon try to persuade the viewer to believe?

Soon after the Spanish Civil War began, Hitler and Mussolini pledged to cooperate on several international issues, and Japan aligned itself with Germany and Italy. Together, the three nations became known as the Axis Powers. As European tensions worsened, Congress passed the Neutrality Act of 1937, continuing the ban on selling arms to warring nations and also requiring them to buy all nonmilitary supplies from the United States on a "cash-and-carry" basis. Countries had to send their own ships to pick up goods and had to pay in cash. Loans were not allowed. Isolationists knew that attacks on American ships had helped bring the country into World War I. They wanted to prevent such attacks that could bring the nation into another European war.

Roosevelt's Internationalism

internationalism
a national policy of actively trading with foreign countries to foster peace and prosperity

Despite the government's stand on neutrality, President Roosevelt supported **internationalism,** the idea that trade between nations creates prosperity and helps prevent war. He warned that the neutrality acts "might drag us into war instead of keeping us out," but he did not veto the bills. When Japan invaded China in July 1937 without declaring war, Roosevelt claimed the Neutrality Act of 1937 did not apply. He authorized the sale of weapons to China, warning that the nation should not let an "epidemic of lawlessness" infect the world:

PRIMARY SOURCE

❝There is no escape through mere isolation or neutrality. . . . When an epidemic of physical disease starts to spread, the community . . . joins in a quarantine of the patients in order to protect the health of the community against the spread of the disease. . . . War is a contagion, whether it be declared or undeclared.❞

—from *The Public Papers and Addresses of Franklin D. Roosevelt*

☑ **PROGRESS CHECK**

Explaining What steps did the supporters of United States isolationism take to ensure that the country remained neutral in an international conflict?

Neutrality Tested

GUIDING QUESTION *How did President Roosevelt assist Britain while maintaining U.S. neutrality?*

Roosevelt wanted to help Britain and France in their struggle and asked Congress to **revise** the neutrality laws to allow the sale of weapons to warring nations. Congress passed the Neutrality Act of 1939 permitting the sale of weapons, but only on a "cash-and-carry" basis.

In the spring of 1940, the United States faced the first test of its neutrality. Britain asked Roosevelt for old American destroyers to replenish its fleet, and the president used a loophole in the cash-only requirement for **purchases.** He sent 50 ships to Britain in exchange for America's use of British bases in the Atlantic. Because the deal did not involve an actual sale, the Neutrality Act did not apply.

Widespread acceptance of the Destroyers-for-Bases deal indicated a change in public opinion. By July 1940, most Americans favored offering limited aid to the Allies, but debate continued over the scope of that aid. The Fight for Freedom Committee wanted the repeal of neutrality laws and stronger actions against Germany. On the other side, the America First Committee opposed any intervention to help the Allies.

After winning reelection in 1940, Roosevelt expanded the nation's role in the war. Speaking to Congress, he listed the Four Freedoms for which both the United States and Britain stood: freedom of speech, freedom of worship, freedom from want, and freedom from fear.

The Lend-Lease Act

By December 1940, Great Britain had run out of funds to fight the war. Roosevelt proposed the Lend-Lease Act, which allowed the United States to lend or lease arms to any country considered "vital to the defense of the United States." Britain could receive weapons, then return them or pay rent for them after the war. Congress passed the Lend-Lease Act by a wide margin. Lend-lease aid eventually went to the Soviet Union as well, when in June 1941, Hitler invaded the Soviet Union. Roosevelt followed Britain's lead in supporting any state fighting the Nazis.

A Hemispheric Defense Zone

The problem of getting American arms and supplies to Britain remained. German submarines in the Atlantic sank hundreds of thousands of tons of cargo each month. The British Navy lacked the ships to stop them.

Because the United States was still officially neutral, Roosevelt could not order the navy to protect British cargo ships. Instead, he developed the idea of a hemispheric defense zone, declaring that the entire western half of the Atlantic was part of the Western Hemisphere and therefore neutral. He then ordered the U.S. Navy to patrol the western Atlantic and reveal the location of German submarines to the British.

The Atlantic Charter

In August 1941, Roosevelt and Churchill met and developed the Atlantic Charter, which committed both nations to a postwar world of democracy, nonaggression, free trade, economic advancement, and freedom of the seas. Churchill later said that FDR "made it clear that he would look for an 'incident' which would justify him in opening hostilities" with Germany.

In early September, a German submarine, or U-boat, fired on an American destroyer that had been radioing the U-boat's position to the British. Roosevelt promptly responded by ordering American ships to follow a "shoot-on-sight" policy toward German submarines. The Germans escalated hostilities the

BIOGRAPHY

Winston Churchill (1874–1965)

British leader Winston Churchill first won election to Parliament in 1900, rising to become head of the British Navy in 1911. In the years leading up to World War II, he spoke out repeatedly against Hitler's aggression and after becoming prime minister committed the nation to intense efforts to defeat Germany. Churchill became known for his public speaking skills and for his tenacious patriotism during the war. His Conservative Party lost power after the war, but Churchill again served as Britain's prime minister from 1951 until his retirement in 1955.

▶ **CRITICAL THINKING**
Drawing Conclusions Why might Roosevelt have particularly wanted to help Churchill?

revise to make changes to an original work

purchase something obtained especially for a price in money or its equivalent

Despite Roosevelt's support for the British and French, many Americans believed that fighting another war overseas was against the nation's interests.

▶ **CRITICAL THINKING**
Predicting Consequences How would you expect isolationists' feelings to change if the United States suffered a direct attack?

following month, targeting two American destroyers. One of them, the *Reuben James,* sank after being torpedoed, killing over 100 sailors. As the end of 1941 drew near, Germany and the United States continued a tense standoff.

☑ **PROGRESS CHECK**

Summarizing What indications were there that public opinion was shifting away from American isolationism?

Japan Attacks Pearl Harbor

GUIDING QUESTION *How did the United States try to slow Japan's advances in the Pacific?*

Despite the growing tensions in Europe, it was the Japanese attack on Pearl Harbor that finally brought the United States into World War II. Ironically, Roosevelt's efforts to help Britain fight Germany resulted in Japan's decision to attack the United States.

America Embargoes Japan

As German submarines sank British ships in the Atlantic, the British began moving warships from Southeast Asia, leaving India and other colonial possessions vulnerable to Japanese attack. To hinder Japanese aggression, Roosevelt began applying economic pressure. Japan depended on the United States for many key materials, including scrap iron, steel, and especially oil. In July 1940, Congress gave the president the power to restrict the sale of **strategic materials**—items important for fighting a war. Roosevelt then blocked the sale of airplane fuel and scrap iron to Japan. Furious, the Japanese signed an alliance with Germany and Italy, becoming a member of the Axis.

In 1941 Roosevelt began sending lend-lease aid to China, hoping to enable the Chinese to tie down the Japanese and prevent them from attacking elsewhere. The strategy failed. By July 1941, Japan had sent military forces into southern Indochina, directly threatening the British Empire. In response, Roosevelt froze all Japanese assets in the United States, reduced the oil shipments to Japan, and sent General Douglas MacArthur to the Philippines to build up American defenses there.

With its war against China in jeopardy because of a lack of resources, the Japanese military planned to attack the resource-rich British and Dutch colonies in Southeast Asia. They also decided to seize the Philippines and to attack the American fleet at Pearl Harbor. Negotiations with the Americans continued, but neither side would back down. In late November 1941, six Japanese aircraft carriers, two battleships, and several other warships set out for Hawaii.

strategic materials
items needed for fighting a war

Surprise Attack

The Japanese government appeared to be continuing negotiations with the United States in good faith. American intelligence, however, had decoded Japanese messages that made it clear that Japan was preparing to go to war against the United States. On November 27, American commanders at the Pearl Harbor naval base received a war warning from Washington D.C., but it did not mention Hawaii as a possible target. Because of its great distance from Japan, officials doubted that Japan would attack Hawaii.

The U.S. military's inability to interpret the information that they were receiving correctly left Pearl Harbor an open target. Japan's surprise attack on December 7, 1941, was devastating. Eight battleships, three cruisers, three destroyers, and four other vessels were sunk or damaged. The attack destroyed over 180 aircraft and killed 2,403 Americans. Another 1,178 were injured.

That night, a gray-faced Roosevelt met with his cabinet, telling them the country faced the most serious crisis since the Civil War. The next day, he asked Congress to declare war:

PRIMARY SOURCE

❝As Commander in Chief of the Army and Navy I have directed that all measures be taken for our defense, that always will our whole nation remember the character of the onslaught against us. . . . With confidence in our armed forces, with the unbounding determination of our people, we will gain the inevitable triumph.❞

—from his speech to Congress, December 8, 1941

The Senate voted 82 to 0 and the House 388 to 1 to declare war on Japan.

Germany Declares War

Hitler had hoped that Japan would attack the United States so that the majority of U.S. forces would be sent to the Pacific front. He expected the United States to enter the European war as incidents between German submarines and the United States mounted in the Atlantic.

Hitler **underestimated** the strategy of the United States, which was to view Germany as the larger threat but fight the Japanese with the U.S. Navy. By helping Japan, he hoped for Japanese support against the Soviet Union after they had defeated the Americans. On December 11, Germany and Italy both declared war on the United States.

✓ **PROGRESS CHECK**

Sequencing What sequence of events led the United States to a declaration of war?

Because American officials did not expect it, the attack on Pearl Harbor was particularly devastating.

▶ **CRITICAL THINKING**
Determining Cause and Effect What was the immediate result of the attack on Pearl Harbor?

underestimate to estimate lower than the real amount or number

PHOTO: Time & Life Pictures/Getty Images

LESSON 2 REVIEW

Reviewing Vocabulary

1. *Contrasting* How does internationalism differ from isolationism?

2. *Explaining* How did restricting the sale of strategic materials hinder Japan's aggression in the Pacific?

Using Your Notes

3. *Identifying Cause and Effect* Use the notes you completed during the lesson to write a paragraph identifying the events that moved the United States from neutrality to war.

Answering the Guiding Questions

4. *Evaluating* Why did many Americans support isolationism? Why did President Roosevelt support internationalism?

5. *Synthesizing* How did President Roosevelt assist Britain while maintaining U.S. neutrality?

6. *Explaining* How did the United States try to slow Japan's advances in the Pacific?

Writing Activity

7. **EXPOSITORY** Write a short essay in which you discuss why the United States had taken action against the Japanese before the attack.

netw⊙rks

There's More Online!

☑ **IMAGE** *Kristallnacht* Destruction

☑ **MAP** Route of the *St. Louis*

☑ **SLIDE SHOW** Nazi Badges

☑ **VIDEO** The Holocaust

☑ **INTERACTIVE SELF-CHECK QUIZ**

LESSON 3
The Holocaust

ESSENTIAL QUESTIONS · *Could World War II have been prevented?*
· *Why do some people not respond to injustice while others try to prevent injustice ?*

PHOTOS: (l to r)Yad Vashem Photo Archives, courtesy of USHMM, Mary Evans Picture Library/Weimer Archive, Yivo Institute for Jewish Research, Mary Evans Picture Library/Weimer Archive, United States Holocaust Memorial Museum, courtesy of Harold Royall

Reading **HELP**DESK

Content Vocabulary

- concentration camp
- extermination camp

Academic Vocabulary

- prohibit
- virtually
- assume

TAKING NOTES: *Organizing*

ACTIVITY As you read about the Holocaust, complete a graphic organizer similar to the one below, by listing examples of Nazi persecution of European Jews.

Examples of Persecution

IT MATTERS BECAUSE

Nazis first acted upon their racist ideology when they imposed restrictions on Jews and stripped them of basic rights. Eventually, Nazi Germany created concentration camps and systematically attempted to kill all European Jews.

Nazi Persecution of the Jews

GUIDING QUESTION *Why did many Jews remain in Nazi Germany and within Axis-controlled areas of Europe?*

During the Holocaust, the Nazis killed nearly 6 million European Jews. The Nazis also killed millions of people from other groups they considered inferior. The Hebrew term for the Holocaust is *Shoah,* meaning "catastrophe," but it is often used specifically to refer to the Nazi campaign to exterminate the Jews during World War II.

The Nuremberg Laws

Although the Nazis persecuted anyone who dared oppose them, as well as the disabled, Gypsies (now known as Roma), homosexuals, and Slavic peoples, they reserved their strongest hatred for the Jews. This loathing went far beyond the European anti-Semitism that was common at the time. In the Middle Ages, Jews had been subjected to discrimination and sometimes to mob violence and expulsions. But in nineteenth- and twentieth-century Western and Central Europe, both the frequency and intensity of anti-Jewish government policies diminished.

After the Nazis took power, however, they quickly moved to deprive German Jews of many established rights. In September 1935, the Nuremberg Laws took citizenship away from Jewish Germans and banned marriage between Jews and other Germans. Two months later, another decree barred Jews from holding public office or voting. Another law compelled Jews with German-sounding names to adopt "Jewish" names. Soon the passports of Jews were marked with a red J to identify them as Jewish.

By the summer of 1936, at least half of Germany's Jews were jobless, having lost the right to work as civil servants, journalists, farmers, and actors. In 1938 the Nazis also banned Jews from practicing law and medicine and from operating businesses. With no source of income, life for Jews became very difficult.

Despite worsening conditions, many Jews chose to remain in Germany during the early years of Nazi rule. Well integrated into German society before this time, they were reluctant to leave and give up the lives they had built there. Many also thought that conditions would surely improve after a time. In fact, conditions soon became worse.

Kristallnacht

On November 7, 1938, a young Jewish refugee named Herschel Grynszpan shot and killed a German diplomat in Paris. Grynszpan's parents and more than 14,000 other Polish Jews had been deported from Germany to Poland, and the distraught young man was seeking revenge for this act and for the persecution of the Jews in general.

In retaliation, an infuriated Hitler ordered his minister of propaganda, Joseph Goebbels, to stage attacks against the Jews that would seem like a spontaneous popular reaction to news of the murder. On the night of November 9, this plan played out in a spree of destruction. In Vienna, a Jewish child named Frederic Morton watched in terror that night as Nazi storm troopers broke into his family's apartment:

PRIMARY SOURCE

66They yanked out every drawer in every one of our chests and cupboards, and tossed each in the air. They let the cutlery jangle across the floor, the clothes scatter, and stepped over the mess to fling the next drawer. Their exuberance was amazing. . . . 'We might be back,' the leader said. On the way out he threw our mother-of-pearl ashtray over his shoulder, like confetti. We did not speak or move or breathe until we heard their boots against the pavement.99

—quoted in *Facing History and Ourselves*

The anti-Jewish violence that erupted throughout Germany and Austria that night came to be called *Kristallnacht,* or "night of broken glass," because broken glass littered the streets afterward. By the following morning, more than 90 Jews were dead, hundreds were badly injured, and thousands more were terrorized. The Nazis had forbidden police to interfere while roving bands of thugs destroyed 7,500 Jewish businesses and hundreds of synagogues.

The lawlessness of *Kristallnacht* continued to persist. Following the initial night of violence, the Gestapo, the government's secret police, arrested about 30,000 Jewish men. The state also confiscated insurance payments owed to Jewish owners of ruined businesses.

On *Kristallnacht,* November 9, 1938, Nazi storm troopers destroyed Jewish property, such as this burned-out synagogue, and terrorized Jewish families across the Third Reich.

▶ **CRITICAL THINKING**

Making Generalizations How do you think publication of the photograph of the synagogue would have affected world opinion toward the Nazis?

After weeks of fierce resistance, Jews in the Warsaw ghetto in Poland are rounded up for deportation to concentration camps in May 1943.

▶ **CRITICAL THINKING**

Predicting Consequences What details in the photograph suggest what might happen when these people reach the concentration camps?

prohibit to make illegal by an authority

assume to take for granted or as true

Jewish Refugees Try to Flee

Kristallnacht and its aftermath marked a significant escalation of Nazi persecution against the Jews. Many Jews, including Frederic Morton's family, decided that it was time to leave and fled to the United States. Between 1933, when Hitler took power, and the start of World War II in 1939, some 250,000 Jews escaped Nazi-controlled Germany. These emigrants included prominent scientists, such as Albert Einstein, and business owners like Otto Frank, who resettled his family in Amsterdam in 1933. Otto's daughter Anne kept a diary of her family's life in hiding after the Nazis overran the Netherlands. The "secret annex," as she called their hiding place, has become a museum.

Limits on Jewish Immigration By 1938, one U.S. consulate in Germany had a backlog of more than 100,000 visa applications from Jews trying to leave for the United States. Following the Nazi *Anschluss,* some 3,000 Austrian Jews applied for U.S. visas each day. Most never received visas to the United States or to the other countries where they applied. As a result, millions of Jews remained trapped in Nazi-dominated Europe.

Several factors limited Jewish immigration to the United States. Nazi orders **prohibited** Jews from taking more than about four dollars out of Germany. U.S. immigration law, however, forbade granting a visa to anyone "likely to become a public charge." Customs officials tended to **assume** that this description applied to Jews, because Germany had forced them to leave behind any wealth. High unemployment rates in the 1930s also made immigration unpopular. Few Americans wanted to raise immigration quotas, even to accommodate European refugees. Others did not want to admit Jews because they held anti-Semitic attitudes. The existing immigration policy allowed only 150,000 immigrants annually, with a fixed quota from each country. The law permitted no exceptions for refugees or victims of persecution.

International Response At an international conference on refugees in 1938, several European countries, the United States, and Latin America stated their regret that they could not take in more of Germany's Jews without raising their immigration quotas. Meanwhile, Nazi propaganda chief Joseph Goebbels announced, "[I]f there is any country that believes it has not enough Jews, I shall gladly turn over to it all our Jews." Hitler also declared himself "ready to put all these criminals at the disposal of these countries . . . even on luxury ships."

As war loomed in 1939, many ships departed from Germany crammed with Jews desperate to escape. Some of their visas, however, had been forged or sold illegally, and Mexico, Paraguay, Argentina, and Costa Rica all denied access to Jews with such documents. So, too, did the United States.

The *St. Louis* Affair On May 27, 1939, the SS *St. Louis* entered the harbor in Havana, Cuba, with 930 Jewish refugees on board. Most of these passengers hoped to go to the United States eventually, but they had certificates improperly issued by Cuba's director of immigration giving them permission to land in Cuba. When the ships arrived in Havana, the

Cuban government refused to let the refugees come ashore. For several days, the ship's captain steered his ship in circles off the coast of Florida, awaiting official permission to dock at a U.S. port. Denied permission, the ship turned back toward Europe, disembarking in France, Holland, Belgium, and Great Britain. Within two years, the first three of these countries fell under Nazi domination. Many of the refugees brought to these countries perished in the Nazis' "final solution."

☑ **PROGRESS CHECK**

Explaining What factors made it difficult for Jewish people to leave Europe?

The Final Solution

GUIDING QUESTION *How did the Nazis try to exterminate Europe's Jewish population?*

On January 20, 1942, Nazi leaders met at the Wannsee Conference to coordinate the "final solution of the Jewish question." Previous "solutions" had included rounding up Jews, Gypsies, Slavs, and others from conquered areas, shooting them, and piling them into mass graves. Another method forced Jews and other "undesirables" into trucks and then piped in exhaust fumes to kill them. These methods, however, had proven too slow and inefficient for the Nazis.

At Wannsee, the Nazis made plans to round up Jews from the vast areas of Nazi-controlled Europe. Jews were taken to detention centers known as **concentration camps.** There, healthy individuals would work as slave laborers until they dropped dead of exhaustion, disease, or malnutrition. Most others, including the elderly, young children, and the infirm (among them laborers who could no longer work) would be sent to **extermination camps,** attached to many of the concentration camps, to be executed in massive gas chambers.

Concentration Camps

The Nazis had established their first concentration camps in 1933 to jail political opponents. After the war began, the Nazis built concentration camps throughout Europe.

concentration camp
a camp where persons are detained or confined

extermination camp
a camp where men, women, and children were sent to be executed

Men, women, and children are packed onto cattle cars for transport to extermination camps.

▶ **CRITICAL THINKING**
Drawing Inferences What does the fact that Jews were transported on cattle cars indicate about Nazi attitudes toward them?

PHOTO: Yad Vashem Photo Archives, courtesy of USHMM

The Holocaust 1939–1945

Legend:
- ■ Concentration camp
- ■ Extermination camp
- ■ Location of *Einsatzgruppen* (paramilitary death squads)
- — International boundary, January 1938

Jewish Losses: 1939–1945

Baltic States	228,000
Belgium	40,000
Bulgaria	14,000
Byelorussian SSR	245,000
Czechoslovakia	155,000
Denmark	500
France	90,000
Germany and Austria	210,000
Greece	54,000
Hungary	450,000
Italy	8,000
Netherlands	195,000
Poland	3,000,000
Romania	300,000
Russian SSR	107,000
Ukrainian SSR	900,000
Yugoslavia	26,000

400 miles / 400 km

Lambert Azimuthal Equal-Area projection

GEOGRAPHY CONNECTION

Nazi concentration camps and extermination camps extended across several countries.

1. **THE WORLD IN SPATIAL TERMS** *Where were most of the extermination camps located?*

2. **PLACES AND REGIONS** *Which three nations had the highest number of Jewish losses?*

As one of the largest concentration camps, Buchenwald had more than 200,000 prisoners working 12-hour shifts as slave laborers in nearby factories. Although Buchenwald had no gas chambers, hundreds of prisoners died there every month from exhaustion and horrible living conditions. As a U.S. Army chaplain wrote in his diary in 1945:

PRIMARY SOURCE

❝One thousand Weimar citizens toured the Buchenwald camp in groups of 100. They saw blackened skeletons and skulls in the ovens of the crematorium. In the yard outside, they saw a heap of white human ashes and bones. . . . Those who were dead were stripped of their clothing and lay naked, many stacked like cordwood waiting to be burned in the crematory. At one time, 5,000 had been stacked on the vacant lot next to the crematory.❞

—from the diary of Captain Luther D. Fletcher, quoted in *World War II: From the Battle Front to the Home Front*

Leon Bass, a young American soldier, saw Buchenwald at the end of the war. A room built to hold 50 people had housed more than 150, with bunk beds built almost to the ceiling. Bass recalled:

PRIMARY SOURCE

❝I looked at a bottom bunk and there I saw one man. He was too weak to get up; he could just barely turn his head. He was skin and bones. He looked like a skeleton; and his eyes were deep set. He didn't utter a sound; he just looked at me with those eyes, and they still haunt me today.❞

—quoted in *Facing History and Ourselves*

Extermination Camps

In late 1941, the Nazis built extermination facilities at the Chelmno and Auschwitz camps in Poland. After the Wannsee Conference, extermination facilities were built at four other camps in Poland. At these camps, including the infamous Treblinka and Auschwitz, Jews were the Nazis' main victims. Auschwitz alone housed about 100,000 people in 300 prison barracks. Its gas chambers, built to kill 2,000 people at a time, could gas 12,000 people in a day. Of the estimated 1,600,000 people who died at Auschwitz, about 1,300,000 were Jews. Most of the others were Poles, Soviet prisoners of war, or Gypsies.

Upon arrival at Auschwitz, healthy prisoners were selected for slave labor. Elderly or disabled people, the sick, and mothers and children went immediately to the gas chambers, after which their bodies were burned in giant crematoriums.

In only a few years, Jewish culture, which had existed in Europe for more than 1,000 years, had been **virtually** obliterated by the Nazis in the lands they conquered. Despite exhaustive debate, there is still great controversy about why and how an event so horrifying as the Holocaust could have occurred. No consensus has been reached, but most historians point to a number of factors: the German people's sense of injury after World War I; severe economic problems; Hitler's control over the German nation; the lack of a strong tradition of representative government in Germany; German fear of Hitler's secret police; and a long history of anti-Jewish prejudice and discrimination in Europe.

☑ **PROGRESS CHECK**

Explaining What was the purpose and outcome of the Wannsee Conference?

American soldiers force German civilians to view bodies after the liberation of the Buchenwald concentration camp.

▶ **CRITICAL THINKING**
Drawing Conclusions Why did American soldiers force German civilians to view the atrocities at the concentration camp?

virtually almost entirely; nearly

PHOTO: United States Holocaust Memorial Museum, courtesy of Harold Royall

---

LESSON 3 REVIEW

Reviewing Vocabulary

1. ***Defining*** What was the purpose of the concentration camps?

2. ***Identifying*** How was the Buchenwald concentration camp different from Treblinka and Auschwitz?

Using Your Notes

3. ***Making Connections*** Review the notes you completed during the lesson, and then identify an anti-Jewish policy or action that should have warned the world that the Nazis needed to be stopped immediately.

Answering the Guiding Questions

4. ***Evaluating*** Why did many Jews remain in Nazi Germany and within Axis-controlled areas of Europe?

5. ***Explaining*** How did the Nazis try to exterminate Europe's Jewish population?

Writing Activity

6. PERSUASIVE Imagine that you are living in the United States during the 1930s. You believe that more Jewish immigrants should be allowed to come into the country. Write a letter to your representative or senator in Congress to express your point of view.

Directions: On a separate sheet of paper, answer the questions below. Make sure you read carefully and answer all parts to the question.

Lesson Review

Lesson 1

1 **Comparing** What did Hitler, Mussolini, and Stalin have in common?

2 **Defining** What did the leaders of Britain and France do at the Munich Conference? Why was the policy known as appeasement?

Lesson 2

3 **Identifying Central Issues** During the early 1930s, why did many Americans have bitter feelings about World War I?

4 **Drawing Conclusions** How did Roosevelt get aid to Britain while keeping the United States technically neutral?

Lesson 3

5 **Evaluating** Why were Jews, Gypsies, and Slavs persecuted by the Nazis?

6 **Explaining** Why did the United States not waive its immigration quotas to let more Jewish refugees into the country?

21st Century Skills

7 **UNDERSTANDING RELATIONSHIPS AMONG EVENTS** How did the Japanese attack on Pearl Harbor lead to Germany's declaration of war on the United States?

8 **COMPARE AND CONTRAST** What were the similarities and differences between the Japanese and German drives to build an empire?

Exploring the Essential Questions

9 **Speculating** Create a time line showing events that led to World War II and U.S. involvement in the war. Then write a paragraph explaining whether or not the war could have been prevented.

DBQ Document-Based Questions

Use the image below to answer the following questions.

On May 22, 1941, cartoonist Theodor Geisel (later to be known as Dr. Seuss) published this political cartoon criticizing U.S. isolationism in the face of the Nazi threat.

PRIMARY SOURCE

"Ho hum! When he's finished pecking down that last tree he'll quite likely be tired."

10 **Analyzing Visuals** What do the trees and each of the two birds represent?

11 **Identifying Central Issues** Using what you know about U.S. isolationism and Roosevelt's internationalism, explain Geisel's message.

12 **Making Inferences** If a reader saw this cartoon in 1941 and agreed with its message, what policies might that person have supported?

Extended-Response Question

13 **Drawing Conclusions** Write an essay explaining how the Holocaust began—how it evolved from ethnic discrimination to the establishment of concentration camps. Discuss the consequences of the "final solution." Your essay should include an introduction and several paragraphs. Support your answer with relevant facts and details.

PHOTO: The Granger Collection, New York

Need Extra Help?

If You've Missed Question	**1**	**2**	**3**	**4**	**5**	**6**	**7**	**8**	**9**	**10**	**11**	**12**	**13**
Go to page	460	463	465	466	470	472	468	460	460	476	465	465	470

America and World War II

1941–1945

ESSENTIAL QUESTION • *What kinds of sacrifices does war require?*

The Story Matters...

During World War II, millions of Americans enlisted in the armed forces, risking their lives in the struggle. On the home front, Americans also helped the war effort by giving up goods needed by the military and by buying war bonds. Read the chapter to learn how Americans sacrificed during World War II in the hopes of achieving a better future.

◄ "Rosie the Riveter" is a fictional character that came to symbolize women in the workforce during World War II. Images such as this one encouraged women to participate in the war effort.

PHOTO: The Granger Collection, New York

477

After Germany invaded Poland, President Roosevelt expanded the army and built up the country's defenses. After the bombing of Pearl Harbor, the United States was at war. The United States increased the defense budget and rapidly increased production of aircraft, ships, and equipment. The nation was now fighting a war that involved Europe, Africa, and the Pacific.

Step Into the Place

Read the quote and look at the information presented on the map.

 How did the scale of World War II influence Roosevelt's feelings about democracy?

PRIMARY SOURCE

❝The preservation of the spirit and faith of the nation does, and will, furnish the highest justification for every sacrifice that we may make in the cause of national defense.

In the face of great perils never before encountered, our strong purpose is to protect and to perpetuate the integrity of democracy.

For this we muster the spirit of America, and the faith of America.

We do not retreat. We are not content to stand still. As Americans, we go forward, in the service of our country....❞

—Franklin D. Roosevelt, Third Inaugural Address, January 20, 1941

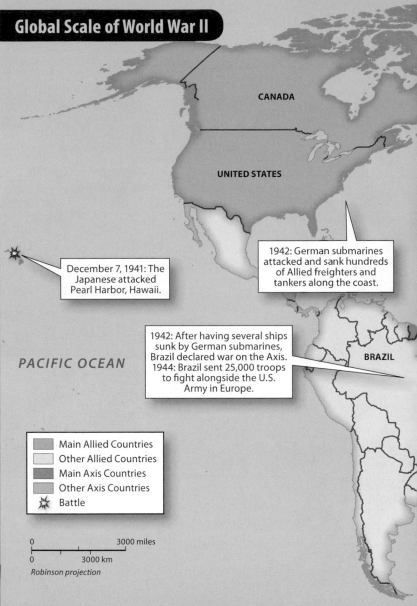

Global Scale of World War II

CANADA

UNITED STATES

December 7, 1941: The Japanese attacked Pearl Harbor, Hawaii.

1942: German submarines attacked and sank hundreds of Allied freighters and tankers along the coast.

1942: After having several ships sunk by German submarines, Brazil declared war on the Axis. 1944: Brazil sent 25,000 troops to fight alongside the U.S. Army in Europe.

BRAZIL

PACIFIC OCEAN

▨	Main Allied Countries
▨	Other Allied Countries
▨	Main Axis Countries
▨	Other Axis Countries
✺	Battle

0   3000 miles

0   3000 km

Robinson projection

Step Into the Time

Choose an event and write a paragraph about how that event may have influenced America and World War II.

F. Roosevelt
1933–1945

U.S. PRESIDENTS

UNITED STATES

WORLD

1941

1942

June 25, 1941 Roosevelt bans discrimination in defense industries

December 8, 1941 United States enters World War II

February 1942 Japanese American relocation ordered

May 1942 Women's Army Auxiliary Corps established

December 7, 1941 Japan attacks Pearl Harbor

May 1942 Japan captures the Philippines

June 1942 United States wins Battle of Midway

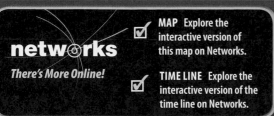
☑ **MAP** Explore the interactive version of this map on Networks.

☑ **TIME LINE** Explore the interactive version of the time line on Networks.

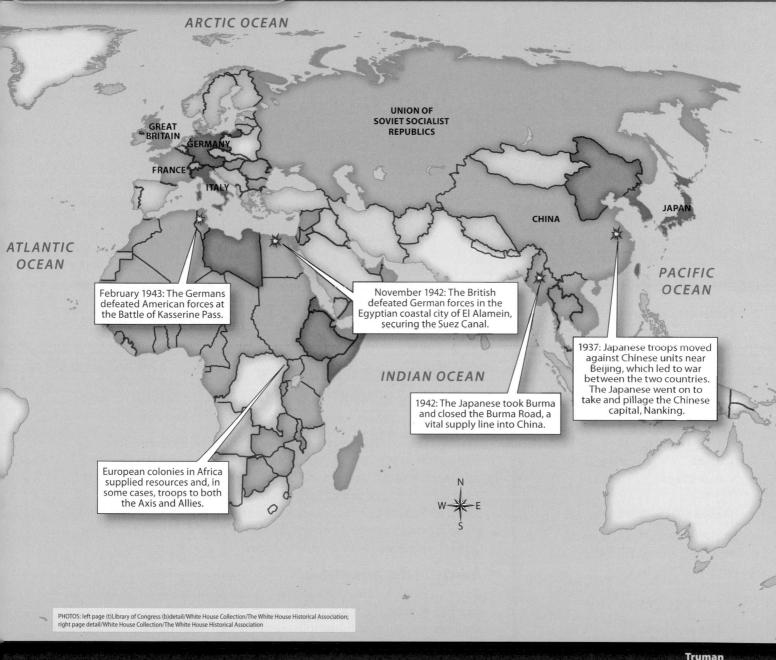

ARCTIC OCEAN

GREAT BRITAIN

GERMANY

FRANCE

ITALY

UNION OF SOVIET SOCIALIST REPUBLICS

CHINA

JAPAN

ATLANTIC OCEAN

PACIFIC OCEAN

INDIAN OCEAN

February 1943: The Germans defeated American forces at the Battle of Kasserine Pass.

November 1942: The British defeated German forces in the Egyptian coastal city of El Alamein, securing the Suez Canal.

1937: Japanese troops moved against Chinese units near Beijing, which led to war between the two countries. The Japanese went on to take and pillage the Chinese capital, Nanking.

1942: The Japanese took Burma and closed the Burma Road, a vital supply line into China.

European colonies in Africa supplied resources and, in some cases, troops to both the Axis and Allies.

N W E S

June 1943 Race riots in Detroit and "zoot suit" riots in Los Angeles

December 1944 Supreme Court rules in *Korematsu* v. *United States* that Japanese American relocation is constitutional

April 1945 Franklin Roosevelt dies in office and Harry S. Truman becomes president

Truman
1945–1953

1943

1944

1945

February 1943 Germans defeated at Stalingrad

July 1943 Allied forces land in Italy

June 6, 1944 Eisenhower leads D-Day invasion

October 1944 MacArthur's forces land in the Philippines

February 1945 U.S. Marines capture Iwo Jima

August 1945 United States drops atomic bombs on Japan

netw⊙rks
There's More Online!

- ☑ **BIOGRAPHY** Oveta Culp Hobby
- ☑ **BIOGRAPHY** Henry Kaiser
- ☑ **BIOGRAPHY** A. Philip Randolph
- ☑ **CHART/GRAPH** Output of Military Products
- ☑ **MAP** Japanese Relocation Camps
- ☑ **MAP** Migration in the United States
- ☑ **SLIDE SHOW** Japanese Internment
- ☑ **SLIDE SHOW** The Real Rosie
- ☑ **VIDEO** Wartime America
- ☑ **INTERACTIVE SELF-CHECK QUIZ**

Reading **HELP**DESK

Content Vocabulary

- **disenfranchised**
- **cost-plus** • **rationing**
- **Sunbelt** • **victory garden**
- **zoot suit**
- **victory suit**

Academic Vocabulary

- **draft** • **justify**
- **coordinate**

TAKING NOTES: *Organizing*

ACTIVITY Use the following graphic organizer to list changes for women and minorities during the war.

	Changes
Women	
African Americans	
Native Americans	
Hispanic Americans	
Japanese Americans	

LESSON 1
Wartime America

PHOTOS: (l to r) Library of Congress, Library of Congress, Bettmann/CORBIS, Library of Congress, National Archives/Time & Life Pictures/Getty Images

ESSENTIAL QUESTION • *What kinds of sacrifices does war require?*

IT MATTERS BECAUSE

After World War I, America returned to isolationism. When the nation entered World War II in 1941, its armed forces ranked nineteenth in might, behind the tiny European nation of Belgium. Three years later, the United States was producing 40 percent of the world's arms.

Building the Military

GUIDING QUESTION *What roles did minorities and women play in the armed forces during World War II?*

Within days of Germany's attack on Poland in 1939, President Roosevelt expanded the army to 227,000 soldiers. Before the spring of 1940, many Americans had opposed a peacetime **draft.** Opinions changed after France surrendered to Germany in June 1940. In September of that year, Congress approved the Selective Training and Service Act—a plan for the first peacetime draft in American history—by a wide margin.

You're in the Army Now

More than 60,000 men enlisted in the month after the attack on Pearl Harbor. At first, the flood of recruits overwhelmed the army's training facilities and equipment supplies. In 1940 the Department of Agriculture had transferred over 350,000 acres to the War Department. New bases such as the Naval Air Station in Jacksonville, Florida, were built, and existing ones such as Eglin Air Force base were expanded. Many recruits lived in tents rather than barracks, carried sticks representing guns, and practiced maneuvers with trucks labeled "TANK."

New recruits were given physical exams and injections against smallpox and typhoid. Then they were issued uniforms, boots, and available equipment, and sent to basic training for eight weeks. Trainees drilled and exercised constantly and learned how to work as a team. Basic training helped break down barriers between soldiers. Recruits came from all over the country, and training together created tight relationships among the troops.

A Segregated Military

Although basic training promoted unity, most recruits did not encounter Americans from every part of society. At the start of the war, the U.S. military was segregated. African Americans were organized into their own units, but white officers generally commanded them. Military leaders typically assigned them to construction and supply units.

Pushing for "Double V" Not all African Americans wanted to support the war. As one African American college student noted: "The Army jim-crows us. . . . Employers and labor unions shut us out. Lynchings continue. We are **disenfranchised** . . . [and] spat upon. What more could Hitler do to us than that?" Nevertheless, most agreed that they should support their country. One leading African American newspaper, the *Pittsburgh Courier,* launched the "Double V" campaign to urge readers to support the war to win a double victory over Hitler's racism abroad and racism at home.

African Americans in Combat Under pressure from African American leaders, President Roosevelt ordered the armed services to recruit African Americans and to put them into combat. He also promoted Colonel Benjamin O. Davis, Sr., the highest-ranking African American officer, to the rank of brigadier general.

In early 1941, the air force created its first African American unit, the 99th Pursuit Squadron. Trained in Tuskegee, Alabama, the pilots became known as the Tuskegee Airmen. Commanded by Lt. Colonel Benjamin O. Davis, Jr., the squadron helped win the Battle of Anzio in Italy. Three other Tuskegee squadrons protected American bombers as they flew to their targets. Known as the 332nd Fighter Group, these squadrons flew 200 such missions without losing a single member to enemy aircraft. Also, the African American 761st Tank Battalion was commended for service during the Battle of the Bulge.

Other Minorities in the Military Although Japanese Americans were not allowed to serve at first, as the war progressed second-generation Japanese Americans served in the 100th Infantry Battalion and the 442nd Regimental Combat Team. Almost half had been in internment camps in the Southwest. Together these units became the most decorated in the history of the United States military. Approximately 500,000 Hispanic Americans served in the armed forces despite racial hostility against them. By the end of the war, 17 Hispanic Americans had received the Congressional Medal of Honor.

About one-third of all able-bodied Native American men aged 18–50 served in the military during the war. More than 400 Navajo marines

draft a system used for choosing people from the population to serve in the military

disenfranchise to deprive of the right to vote

Analyzing
PRIMARY SOURCES

Broadened Perspectives

❝Entrance into the Army in August, 1942, widened my horizons literally as well as experientially: for the first time I travelled beyond a 200 mile radius from Newark. I marveled at the flatness of the prairie in Illinois. . . . Stops at posts in Miami Beach, Florida, and Richmond, Virginia, were my introduction to the American South.❞

—Carl Degler, from *The History Teacher,* vol. 23, 1990

DBQ *ANALYZING PRIMARY SOURCES* Why might entering the army have changed a person's perspective?

U.S. ARMED FORCES, 1939–1946 — CHARTS/GRAPHS

Source: *Historical Statistics of the United States.*

▶ **CRITICAL THINKING**

1 *Comparing and Contrasting* In which years were the armed forces at their highest and lowest levels?

2 *Drawing Conclusions* Between which two years was there the greatest increase in the armed services? What happened during this time period that might account for the increase?

served as "code talkers," relaying critical information and orders over field radios as spoken messages coded in their own language.

Of the half million Jewish Americans who served in the military, approximately 52,000 were decorated for bravery. Because so many European Jews died as a result of the Holocaust, American Jews took on increased leadership in the worldwide Jewish community.

Although the military did not end all segregation during the war, it did integrate military bases in 1943 and steadily expanded the role of African Americans within the armed forces. These successes paved the way for President Truman's decision to fully integrate the military in 1948.

Women Join the Armed Forces

Women also joined the armed forces. The army enlisted them for the first time but barred them from combat. Many army jobs were administrative and clerical. Filling these jobs with women freed more men for combat.

Congress first allowed women in the military in May 1942 by creating the Women's Army Auxiliary Corps (WAAC). It appointed War Department official Oveta Culp Hobby as WAAC's first director. Many women were unhappy that WAAC was not part of the regular army, however. About a year later, the army replaced the WAAC with the Women's Army Corps (WAC), and Hobby became a colonel.

The coast guard, navy, and marines followed suit and set up women's units. Another 68,000 women served as nurses in the army and navy. About 300 women serving as Women Airforce Service Pilots (WASPs) made more than 12,000 flights to deliver planes to the war effort.

☑ **PROGRESS CHECK**

Summarizing How did the status of women and minorities in the armed forces change during the war?

American Economy in Wartime

GUIDING QUESTION *How did the U.S. government mobilize the economy for war?*

Fighting a global war troubled President Roosevelt, but not British prime minister Winston Churchill, who knew that victory depended on industry. He compared the American economy to a gigantic boiler: "Once the fire is lighted under it there is no limit to the power it can generate."

CHARTS/GRAPHS — MOBILIZING INDUSTRY

▶ **CRITICAL THINKING**

1 **Identifying Cause and Effect**
When did tank production begin to drop? Why might this be so?

2 **Predicting Consequences**
How might the changes in industrial production toward the end of the war have affected employment in the late 1940s?

Products (y-axis): 20,000 / 40,000 / 60,000 / 80,000
Year (x-axis): 1941 1942 1943 1944 1945

— Combat aircraft   — Ships   — Tanks

Source: The Big 'L': American Logistics in World War II.

Industrial workers watch as new tanks roll out of the factory.

PHOTO: Bettmann/CORBIS

Converting the Economy

War production increased rapidly after the attack on Pearl Harbor, helped by existing government plans to build thousands of warplanes and a "Two-Ocean" navy. Roosevelt believed that government and business had to work together to prepare for war. He created the National Defense Advisory Committee and asked business leaders to serve on the committee. The president and his advisers believed that giving industry incentives to produce goods quickly was the best way to rapidly mobilize the economy.

Normally, the government asked companies to bid on contracts to produce military equipment, a slow process. Instead, the government signed **cost-plus** contracts, agreeing to pay a company the cost to make a product plus a guaranteed percentage as profit. Under the cost-plus system, the more—and faster—a company produced, the more money it made. Although not cheap, the system got war materials produced quickly and in quantity. Cost-plus convinced many companies to convert to war production, and Congress authorized the Reconstruction Finance Corporation (RFC) to make loans to companies wanting to convert.

American Industry Gets the Job Done

By the fall of 1941, much had already been done to prepare the economy for war, but it was still only partially mobilized. The attack on Pearl Harbor changed everything. By the summer of 1942, almost all major industries and some 200,000 companies had converted to war production. Together they made the nation's wartime "miracle" possible.

Tanks Replace Cars The automobile industry was uniquely suited to mass-producing military goods. Automobile plants began making trucks, jeeps, and tanks. Mass production was critical because the country that could move troops and supplies most quickly usually won the battle.

Automobile factories produced rifles, helmets, artillery, and dozens of other pieces of military equipment along with vehicles. Henry Ford created an assembly line near Detroit for the enormous B-24 "Liberator" bomber. The factory went on to build more than 8,600 aircraft. Overall, the auto industry made nearly one-third of all wartime military equipment.

Building Liberty Ships Ford's remarkable achievement in aircraft production was more than matched by Henry Kaiser's shipyards. German submarines were sinking American cargo ships at a terrifying rate. The United States had to find a way to build cargo ships as quickly as possible. Kaiser's method emphasized speed and results. Instead of building an entire ship in one place from the keel up, parts were prefabricated and brought to the shipyard for assembly.

Kaiser's shipyards built many kinds of ships, but they were best known for basic cargo ships called Liberty ships. When the war began, it took 244 days to build the first Liberty ship. After Kaiser shipyards applied their mass-production techniques, average production time dropped to 41 days. Kaiser's shipyards built 30 percent of all American ships constructed during the war.

As war production grew, controversies between business leaders, government agencies, and the military increased. President Roosevelt created the War Production Board (WPB) to direct priorities and production goals. Later he set up the Office of War Mobilization to settle disputes among the different agencies.

☑ **PROGRESS CHECK**

Explaining How did the government work to quickly prepare the American economy for the war effort?

cost-plus a government contract to pay a manufacturer the cost to produce an item plus a guaranteed percentage

---

Analyzing
PRIMARY SOURCES

The Value of Vehicles

❝The greatest advantage . . . the United States has enjoyed on the ground in the fighting so far [was] . . . the jeep and the two-and-a-half-ton truck. These are the instruments which moved and supplied United States troops in battle, while the German Army . . . depended heavily on animal transport. . . . The United States, profiting from the mass production achievements of its automotive industry . . . had mobility that completely outclassed the enemy.❞

—General George C. Marshall, chief of staff for the U.S. Army, quoted in *Miracle of World War II*

DBQ **MAKING INFERENCES**
Why was U.S. mobility such an important advantage?

During World War II, millions of American women took jobs in wartime factories.

▶ **CRITICAL THINKING**

Making Connections What was the long-term impact of women's wartime participation in the labor force?

Life on the Home Front

GUIDING QUESTION *How did World War II change life for women and minorities in the United States?*

The war dramatically changed American society. Unlike much of Europe and Asia, which experienced devastation, America benefited somewhat from the war. Mobilizing the economy finally ended the Great Depression, creating almost 19 million new jobs and nearly doubling the average family's income. As an Ohio worker noted, "[O]ne of the important things that came out of World War II was the arrival of the working class at a new status level in this society. . . . The war integrated into the mainstream a whole chunk of society that had been living on the edge."

The improvement in the economy did not come without cost. Families had to move to where the defense factories were located. Housing conditions were terrible. The pressures and prejudices of the era led to strikes, race riots, and rising juvenile delinquency. Goods were rationed and taxes were higher. Workers earned more money, but also worked longer hours.

When the war began, American defense factories wanted to hire white men. With so many men in the military, however, there simply were not enough white men to fill all of the jobs. Under pressure to produce, employers began to recruit women and minorities.

Women in Defense Plants

During the Great Depression, many people believed married women should not work outside the home, especially if they took jobs that could go to men trying to support their families. Most working women were young, single, and employed in traditional female jobs such as domestic work or teaching. The wartime labor shortage, however, forced factories to recruit married women for industrial jobs traditionally reserved for men.

Although the government hired nearly 4 million women, primarily for clerical jobs, the women working in the factories captured the public's imagination. The great symbol of the campaign to hire women was "Rosie the Riveter," a character from a popular song by the Four Vagabonds. The lyrics told of Rosie, who worked in a factory while her boyfriend served in the marines. Images of Rosie appeared on posters, in newspapers, and in magazines. Eventually 2.5 million women worked in shipyards, aircraft factories, and other manufacturing plants.

By the end of the war, the number of working women had increased from 12.9 million to 18.8 million. Although most women were laid off or left their jobs voluntarily after the war, their success permanently changed American attitudes about women in the workplace.

African Americans Demand War Work

Factories hired women, but they resisted hiring African Americans. Frustrated by the situation, A. Philip Randolph, the head of the Brotherhood of Sleeping Car Porters—a major union for African American railroad workers—decided to act. He informed President Roosevelt that he was organizing a march on Washington "in the interest of securing jobs . . . in the national defense and . . . integration into the . . . military and naval forces."

On June 25, 1941, Roosevelt issued Executive Order 8802, which stated, "there shall be no discrimination in the employment of workers in defense industries or government because of race, creed, color, or national origin."

To enforce the order, he created the Fair Employment Practices Commission, the first federal civil rights agency since Reconstruction.

Mexican Farmworkers

The wartime economy also benefited Mexicans. In 1942 the federal government arranged for Mexican farmworkers to help harvest crops in the Southwest as part of the Bracero Program, which continued until 1964. More than 200,000 Mexicans came to work during the war. Many also helped build and maintain railroads. Migrant workers thus became important to the Southwest's economic system.

☑ PROGRESS CHECK

Describing What changes did women and minorities experience as a result of economic mobilization?

A Nation on the Move

GUIDING QUESTION *How did the wartime relocation of many Americans affect U.S. government and society?*

The wartime economy created millions of new jobs, leading 15 million Americans to move to find work. The growth of southern California and cities in the Deep South created a new industrial region—the **Sunbelt.** Cities with war industries had to find room for the thousands of arriving workers. Tent cities and parks filled with tiny trailers sprang up. Congress authorized

Sunbelt a new industrial region in southern California and the Deep South that developed during World War II

🏛 ANALYZING SUPREME COURT CASES

KOREMATSU v. *UNITED STATES*, 1944

Background to the Case

During World War II, President Roosevelt's Executive Order 9066 and other legislation gave the military the power to exclude people of Japanese descent from areas that were deemed important to U.S. national defense and security. In 1942 Toyosaburo Korematsu refused to leave San Leandro, California, which had been designated as a "military area" based on Executive Order 9066. Korematsu was found guilty in federal district court of violating Civilian Exclusion Order No. 34. Korematsu petitioned the Supreme Court to review the federal court's decision.

Japanese American women and their children talk together at the Heart of the Mountain Relocation Camp.

How the Court Ruled

In their decision, the majority of the Supreme Court, with three dissenting, found that, although exclusion orders based on race are constitutionally suspect, the government is justified in time of "emergency and peril" to suspend citizens' civil rights. A request for a rehearing of the case in 1945 was denied.

▶ CRITICAL THINKING

❶ *Drawing Conclusions* Why did the Supreme Court find in favor of the government in this case, even though the justices were suspicious of exclusion based on race?

❷ *Constructing Arguments* Under what circumstances, if any, do you think the government should be able to suspend civil liberties of all or specific groups of American citizens?

coordinate to harmonize or bring into common action, movement, or condition

zoot suit men's clothing of extreme cut typically consisting of a thigh-length jacket with wide padded shoulders and baggy, pleated pants with narrow cuffs

victory suit a men's suit with no vest, no cuffs, a short jacket, and narrow lapels, worn during World War II in order to save fabric for the war effort

justify to prove or to show to be just, right, or reasonable

Thinking Like a
HISTORIAN

Distinguishing Fact from Opinion

When *In Defense of Internment: The Case for "Racial Profiling" in World War II and the War on Terror* was published in 2004, many historians were outraged. Author Michelle Malkin supported the decision to put Japanese Americans in internment camps. The Historians' Committee for Fairness said it was "contradicted by several decades of scholarly research." Malkin wrote that Roosevelt had evidence that some spying was taking place on the West Coast, and that Roosevelt was protecting national security.

$150 million for housing in 1940. In 1942 Roosevelt created the National Housing Agency (NHA) to **coordinate** government housing programs.

Racism Leads to Violence

Many African Americans left the South for jobs in war factories in the North and West. However, African Americans often faced suspicion and intolerance. Racial violence erupted in Detroit on Sunday, June 20, 1943. Fighting between white and African American teens triggered a citywide riot that left 25 African Americans and 9 whites dead.

In Los Angeles, the fear of juvenile crime and racism against Mexican Americans became linked in the "zoot suit" riots. Popular with Mexican American teenagers, **zoot suits** had very baggy, pleated pants and an overstuffed, knee-length jacket with wide lapels. Most men, to conserve fabric for the war, wore a **"victory suit"** with no vest, no cuffs, a short jacket, and narrow lapels. In June 1943, after hearing rumors that zoot-suiters had attacked several sailors, some 2,500 soldiers and sailors attacked Mexican American neighborhoods in Los Angeles.

Japanese, German, and Italian American Relocation

When Japan attacked Pearl Harbor, many Americans turned their anger against Japanese immigrants and Japanese Americans. On February 19, 1942, President Roosevelt signed an order allowing the War Department to declare any part of the United States a military zone. He must have felt **justified** four days later when a Japanese submarine surfaced north of Santa Barbara, California, and shelled an oil refinery. Most of the West Coast was declared a military zone, and people of Japanese ancestry were evacuated to 10 internment camps farther inland.

In 1988 President Ronald Reagan apologized to Japanese Americans on behalf of the U.S. government and signed legislation granting $20,000 to each surviving Japanese American who had been interned.

Thousands of people of German and Italian descent also had their freedom restricted. All unnaturalized residents of German and Italian descent aged 14 years or over were deemed enemy aliens and subject to regulations including travel restrictions and the seizure of personal property. More than 5,000 were arrested and sent to live in military internment camps.

✔ **PROGRESS CHECK**

Identifying Cause and Effect How did both voluntary and forced movement during World War II change the United States?

Daily Life in Wartime

GUIDING QUESTION *What steps did the government take to stabilize wages and prices?*

Both wages and prices began to rise quickly during the war because of the high demand for workers and raw materials. Worried about inflation, Roosevelt created the Office of Price Administration and Civilian Supply (OPACS) and the Office of Economic Stabilization (OES) to regulate wages and certain prices. At the end of the war, prices had risen only about half as much as they had during World War I.

While OPACS and OES worked to control inflation, the War Labor Board (WLB) tried to prevent strikes. Most American unions issued a "no strike pledge," instead asking the WLB to mediate wage disputes. By the end of the war, the WLB had helped settle more than 17,000 disputes.

Support and Sacrifices

High demand for raw materials and supplies created shortages. OPACS began **rationing,** or limiting the purchase of, many products to make sure enough were available for military use. Households picked up a book of rationing coupons every month for different kinds of food. When people bought food, they had to have enough coupon points to cover their purchases. Meat, sugar, fats, oils, processed foods, coffee, shoes, and gasoline were all rationed. Driving distances were restricted, and the speed limit was set at 35 miles per hour to save gas and rubber.

Americans also planted gardens in backyards, schoolyards, city parks, and empty lots to produce more food for the war effort. The government encouraged **victory gardens** by praising them in film reels, pamphlets, and official statements. The government organized scrap drives to collect rubber, tin, aluminum, and steel.

The federal government spent more than $300 billion during World War II—more money than it had spent from Washington's administration to the end of Franklin Roosevelt's second term. Congress raised taxes, although not as high as Roosevelt requested due to public opposition to large tax increases. As a result, the extra taxes collected covered only 45 percent of the war's cost. The government issued war bonds—more than $100 billion worth was sold to individuals, banks, and other financial institutions—to make up the difference.

Hollywood Goes to War

In 1942 President Roosevelt created the Office of War Information (OWI). The OWI's role was to improve the public's understanding of the war and to act as a liaison office with the various media. The OWI established detailed guidelines for filmmakers, including a set of questions to be considered before making a movie, such as, "Will this picture help win the war?"

Despite the hardships, the overwhelming majority of Americans believed the war had to be fought. Although the war brought many changes, most Americans united behind one goal—winning the war.

✔ PROGRESS CHECK

Evaluating How did the Office of Price Administration assure there were enough supplies for military use?

Americans donated pots, tires, tin cans, car bumpers, broken radiators, and rusting bicycles to scrap drives held during World War II.

▶ **CRITICAL THINKING**
Drawing Conclusions How did holding scrap drives help the government prevent shortages?

rationing restricting the amount of an item an individual can have due to a limited supply

victory garden garden planted by citizens during war to raise vegetables for home use, leaving more for the troops

---

LESSON 1 REVIEW

Reviewing Vocabulary
1. *Explaining* How did cost-plus contracts help the United States prepare for war?

Using Your Notes
2. *Evaluating* Use the notes that you completed during the lesson to evaluate which groups benefited from the war, and how they did so.

Answering the Guiding Questions
3. *Summarizing* What roles did minorities and women play in the armed forces during World War II?

4. *Analyzing* How did the U.S. government mobilize the economy for war?

5. *Assessing* How did World War II change life for women and minorities in the United States?

6. *Making Connections* How did the wartime relocation of many Americans affect U.S. government and society?

7. *Specifying* What steps did the government take to stabilize wages and prices?

Writing Activity
8. EXPOSITORY Think about what you learned about women and minorities in the workforce during World War I. Write a short essay in which you compare the roles of women and minorities in the workforce during World War I and World War II.

netw⊙rks
There's More Online!

☑ **BIOGRAPHY** Chester Nimitz

☑ **IMAGE** Battle of Tarawa

☑ **IMAGE** Kamikaze Pilots

☑ **PRIMARY SOURCE** Code Breaking

☑ **VIDEO** The War in the Pacific

☑ **INTERACTIVE SELF-CHECK QUIZ**

LESSON 2
The War in the Pacific

ESSENTIAL QUESTION • *What kinds of sacrifices does war require?*

Reading HELPDESK

Content Vocabulary
• amphtrac • kamikaze

Academic Vocabulary
• code

TAKING NOTES: *Organizing*

ACTIVITY Use the following graphic organizer to record the major battles discussed and the victor in each.

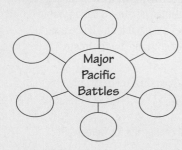

Major Pacific Battles

IT MATTERS BECAUSE

The early battles of the war required changes in strategy from all sides. In the Pacific, the Battle of Midway was a major turning point against the Japanese. After that American victory, Admiral Nimitz and General MacArthur led American forces in a steady advance across the Pacific.

Holding the Line Against Japan

GUIDING QUESTION *Why was the Doolittle Raid important for U.S. forces in the Pacific?*

Admiral Chester Nimitz, the commander of the United States Navy in the Pacific, began planning operations against the Japanese navy. Although the Japanese had badly damaged the American fleet at Pearl Harbor, they had missed the American aircraft carriers, which were at sea on a mission. The United States had several carriers in the Pacific, and Nimitz was determined to use them. In the days just after Pearl Harbor, however, Nimitz could do little to stop Japan's advance into Southeast Asia.

The Fall of the Philippines

A few hours after bombing Pearl Harbor, the Japanese attacked American airfields in the Philippines. Two days later, they landed troops. The American and Filipino forces defending the Philippines were badly outnumbered. Their commander, General Douglas MacArthur, retreated to the Bataan Peninsula. Using the peninsula's rugged terrain, the troops held out for more than three months.

By March, in desperation, the troops ate cavalry horses and mules. The lack of food and supplies, along with diseases such as malaria, scurvy, and dysentery, took their toll. The women of the Army Nurse Corps worked on Bataan in primitive conditions. Patients slept in the open air. One nurse, Rose Meier, reported, "If we needed more room, we got our axes and chopped some bamboo trees down."

Realizing MacArthur's capture would demoralize the American people, President Roosevelt ordered the general to evacuate to Australia. MacArthur promised, "I came through, and I shall return."

On April 9, 1942, the weary defenders of the Bataan Peninsula finally surrendered. Nearly 78,000 prisoners of war were forced to march—sick, exhausted, and starving—65 miles (105 km) to a Japanese prison camp. Almost 10,000 troops died on this march, which was later to be called the Bataan Death March. Private Leon Beck was taken prisoner when Bataan surrendered and took part in the Bataan Death March for 13 days before escaping. He later recalled:

PRIMARY SOURCE

❝They'd halt us in front of these big artesian wells . . . so we could see the water and they wouldn't let us have any. Anyone who would make a break for water would be shot or bayoneted. Then they were left there. Finally, it got so bad further along the road that you never got away from the stench of death. There were bodies laying all along the road in various degrees of decomposition—swollen, burst open, maggots crawling by the thousands. . . .❞

—from *Death March: The Survivors of Bataan,* 1981

Sixty-six women nurses were also captured and sent to the University of Santo Tomas in Manila. They remained there—with 11 navy nurses and some 3,000 Allied civilians—until early in 1945.

Although the troops in the Bataan Peninsula surrendered, a small force held out on the island of Corregidor in Manila Bay. Finally, in May 1942, Corregidor surrendered. The Philippines had fallen to the Japanese.

The Doolittle Raid on Tokyo

Even before the Philippines fell, President Roosevelt was searching for a way to raise the morale of the American people. He wanted to bomb Tokyo, but American planes could reach Tokyo only if an aircraft carrier brought them close enough. However, Japanese ships in the North Pacific prevented carriers from getting near Japan.

In early 1942, a military planner suggested replacing the carrier's usual short-range bombers with long-range B-25 bombers that could attack from farther away. The only problem was that, although B-25s could take off from a carrier, the bombers could not land on its short deck. After attacking Japan, they would have to land in China.

President Roosevelt put Lieutenant Colonel James Doolittle in command of the mission to bomb Tokyo. At the end of March, a crane loaded sixteen B-25s onto the aircraft carrier *Hornet.* The next day, the *Hornet* headed west across the Pacific. On April 18, American bombs fell on Japan for the first time.

Japan Changes Strategy

While Americans rejoiced in the air force's success, Japanese leaders were aghast at the raid. Those bombs could have killed Emperor Hirohito, who was revered as a god. The Doolittle Raid convinced Japanese leaders to change their strategy.

Before the raid, the Japanese navy had disagreed about the next step. The officers in charge of the navy's planning wanted to cut American supply lines to Australia by capturing the south coast of New Guinea. The commander of the fleet, Admiral Yamamoto, wanted to attack Midway Island—the last American base in the North Pacific west of Hawaii. Yamamoto believed that attacking Midway would lure the American fleet into battle and enable his fleet to destroy it.

PHOTO: Library of Congress

General Douglas MacArthur (1880–1964)

General Douglas MacArthur graduated from West Point in 1903. One of his first military assignments was in the Philippines, site of his later World War II defeat and subsequent victory. In 1904 he was appointed aide-de-camp to his father, General Arthur MacArthur, in Japan. Following his World War II success in the Pacific, he was appointed Supreme Commander, Allied Powers (SCAP), in Japan. There he decreased Japan's military and helped reestablish its economy.

▶ **CRITICAL THINKING**
Evaluating What is the significance of MacArthur's early military experience in the Philippines and Japan?

These Navajo code talkers assigned to a Pacific-based marine regiment relay orders using a field radio.

▶ CRITICAL THINKING

Evaluating What advantages did the code talkers provide to American forces?

code a signal or symbol used to represent something that is to be kept secret

The Navajo language is not a written language, and only a small number of people understand it.

▶ CRITICAL THINKING

Drawing Conclusions What was the advantage of having a code that the Japanese could not decipher?

After Doolittle's raid, the Japanese war planners dropped their opposition to Yamamoto's idea. The American fleet had to be destroyed to protect Tokyo from bombing. The attack on New Guinea would still go ahead, but only three aircraft carriers were assigned to the mission. All of the other carriers were ordered to assault Midway.

The Battle of the Coral Sea

The Japanese believed that they could safely proceed with two attacks at once because they thought their operations were secret. What the Japanese did not know was that an American team of **code** breakers based in Hawaii had already broken the Japanese navy's secret code for conducting operations.

In March 1942, decoded Japanese messages alerted the United States to the Japanese attack on New Guinea. In response, Admiral Nimitz sent two carriers, the *Yorktown* and the *Lexington,* to intercept the Japanese in the Coral Sea. There, in early May, carriers from both sides launched all-out airstrikes against each other. Although the Japanese sank the *Lexington* and badly damaged the *Yorktown,* the American attacks prevented the Japanese from landing on New Guinea's south coast and kept the supply lines to Australia open.

The Navajo Code Talkers

When American marines stormed an enemy beach, they used radios to communicate. Using radios, however, meant that the Japanese could intercept and translate the messages. In the midst of the battle, there was no time to use a code-machine. Acting upon the suggestion of Philip Johnston, an engineer who had lived on a Navajo reservation as a child, the marines recruited Navajos to serve as "code talkers."

The Navajo language had no written alphabet and was known only to the Navajo and a few missionaries and anthropologists. The Navajo recruits developed code words, using their own language, that stood for military terms. For example, the Navajo word *jay-sho,* or "buzzard," was code for *bomber; lo-tso,* or "whale," meant *battleship;* and *ni-ma-si,* or "potatoes," stood for *grenades.*

Code talkers proved invaluable in combat. They could relay a message in minutes that would have taken a code-machine operator hours to encipher and transmit. During the Battle of Iwo Jima, code talkers transmitted more than 800 messages during the first 48 hours as the marines struggled to

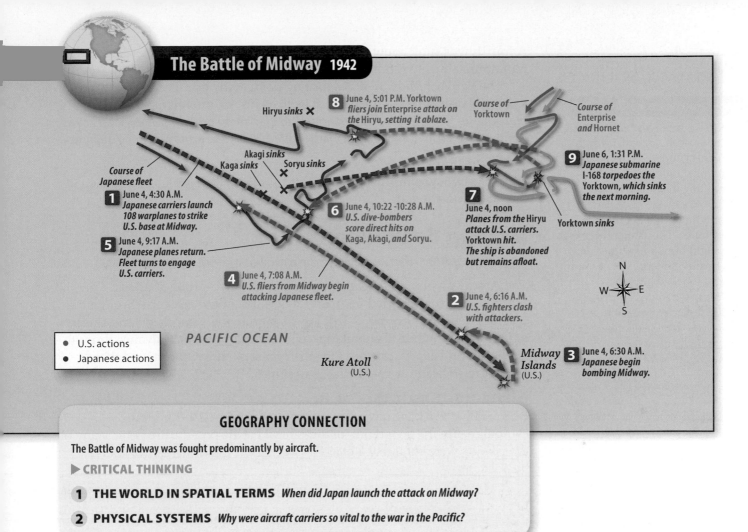

The Battle of Midway 1942

8 June 4, 5:01 P.M. Yorktown *fliers join* Enterprise *attack on the Hiryu, setting it ablaze.*

Hiryu *sinks* ✕

Course of Yorktown

Course of Enterprise and Hornet

9 June 6, 1:31 P.M. *Japanese submarine I-168 torpedoes the* Yorktown, *which sinks the next morning.*

Akagi *sinks*
Kaga *sinks*
Soryu *sinks*

Course of Japanese fleet

1 June 4, 4:30 A.M. *Japanese carriers launch 108 warplanes to strike U.S. base at Midway.*

6 June 4, 10:22 -10:28 A.M. *U.S. dive-bombers score direct hits on* Kaga, Akagi, *and* Soryu.

7 June 4, noon *Planes from the Hiryu attack U.S. carriers.* Yorktown *hit. The ship is abandoned but remains afloat.*

Yorktown *sinks*

5 June 4, 9:17 A.M. *Japanese planes return. Fleet turns to engage U.S. carriers.*

4 June 4, 7:08 A.M. *U.S. fliers from Midway begin attacking Japanese fleet.*

2 June 4, 6:16 A.M. *U.S. fighters clash with attackers.*

N
W · E
S

- U.S. actions
- Japanese actions

PACIFIC OCEAN

Kure Atoll °
(U.S.)

Midway Islands
(U.S.)

3 June 4, 6:30 A.M. *Japanese begin bombing Midway.*

GEOGRAPHY CONNECTION

The Battle of Midway was fought predominantly by aircraft.

▶ **CRITICAL THINKING**

1 **THE WORLD IN SPATIAL TERMS** *When did Japan launch the attack on Midway?*

2 **PHYSICAL SYSTEMS** *Why were aircraft carriers so vital to the war in the Pacific?*

get ashore under intense bombardment. Sworn to secrecy, their mission was not revealed until 1971. In 2001 Congress awarded the code talkers the Congressional Gold Medal for their unique contribution during the war.

☑ **PROGRESS CHECK**

Explaining What did the Doolittle Raid on Tokyo accomplish?

Battle of Midway

GUIDING QUESTION *Why was the Battle of Midway a turning point in the war in the Pacific?*

Back at Pearl Harbor, the code-breaking team now learned of the plan to attack Midway. With so many ships at sea, Admiral Yamamoto transmitted the plans for the Midway attack by radio, using the same code the Americans had already cracked.

Admiral Nimitz had been waiting for the opportunity to ambush the Japanese fleet. He immediately ordered carriers to take up positions near Midway. Unaware that they were heading into an ambush, the Japanese launched their aircraft against Midway on June 4, 1942. The Americans were ready. The Japanese ran into a blizzard of antiaircraft fire, and 38 planes were shot down. As the Japanese prepared a second wave to attack Midway, aircraft from the American carriers *Hornet, Yorktown,* and *Enterprise* then launched a counterattack. The American planes caught the Japanese carriers with fuel, bombs, and aircraft exposed on their flight decks. Within minutes, three Japanese carriers were reduced to burning wrecks.

A fourth was sunk a few hours later, and Admiral Yamamoto ordered his remaining ships to retreat.

The Battle of Midway was a turning point in the war. The Japanese navy lost four large carriers—the heart of its fleet. Just six months after Pearl Harbor, the United States had stopped the Japanese advance. The victory was not without cost, however. The battle killed 362 Americans and 3,057 Japanese.

☑ PROGRESS CHECK

Explaining Why was the United States able to ambush the Japanese at Midway and turn the tide of the war?

Driving Back Japan

GUIDING QUESTIONS *What was the military strategy behind "island-hopping"? Was it successful?*

The American plan to defeat Japan called for a two-pronged attack. The Pacific Fleet, commanded by Admiral Nimitz, would advance through the central Pacific by "hopping" from one island to the next, closer and closer to Japan. Meanwhile, General MacArthur's troops would advance through the Solomon Islands, capture the north coast of New Guinea, and then launch an invasion to retake the Philippines.

Island-Hopping in the Pacific

By the fall of 1943, the navy was ready to launch its island-hopping campaign, but the geography of the central Pacific posed a problem. Many of the islands were coral reef atolls. The water over the coral reef was not

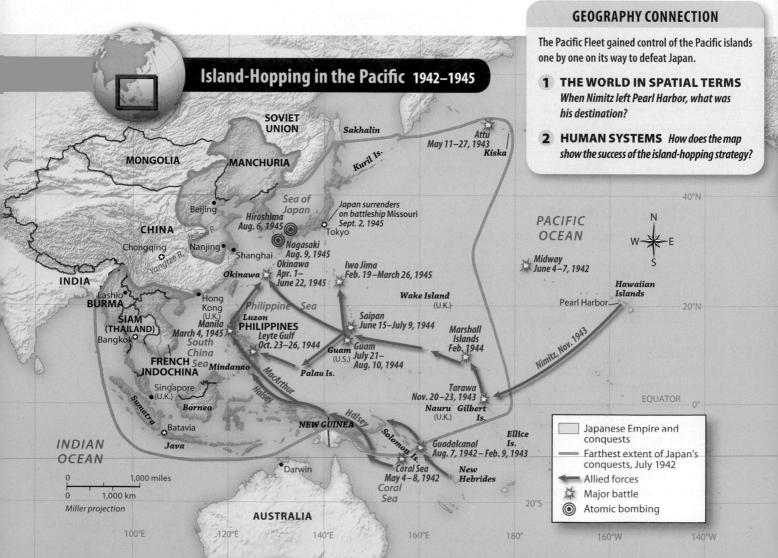

GEOGRAPHY CONNECTION

The Pacific Fleet gained control of the Pacific islands one by one on its way to defeat Japan.

1 THE WORLD IN SPATIAL TERMS *When Nimitz left Pearl Harbor, what was his destination?*

2 HUMAN SYSTEMS *How does the map show the success of the island-hopping strategy?*

Island-Hopping in the Pacific 1942–1945

always deep enough to allow landing craft to get to the shore. If the landing craft ran aground on the reef, the troops would have to wade to the beach. As some 5,000 United States Marines learned at Tarawa Atoll, wading ashore could cause very high casualties. Tarawa, part of the Gilbert Islands, was the navy's first objective. The Japanese base there had to be captured in order to put air bases in the nearby Marshall Islands.

When the landing craft hit the reef, at least 20 ships ran aground. The marines had to plunge into shoulder-high water and wade several hundred yards to the beach. Raked by Japanese fire, only one marine in three made it ashore. Once the marines reached the beach, the battle was still far from over.

Although many troops died wading ashore, one vehicle had been able to cross the reef and deliver its troops onto the beaches. The vehicle was a boat with tank tracks, nicknamed the "Alligator." This amphibious tractor, or **amphtrac,** had been invented in the late 1930s to rescue people in Florida swamps. It had never been used in combat, and the navy decided to buy only 200 of them in 1941. If more had been available at Tarawa, American casualties probably would have been much lower.

More than 1,000 marines died on Tarawa. Photos of bodies lying crumpled next to burning landing craft shocked Americans back home. Many people began to wonder how many lives would be lost in defeating Japan.

The next assault—Kwajalein Atoll in the Marshall Islands—went much more smoothly. This time all of the troops went ashore in amphtracs. Although the Japanese resisted fiercely, the marines captured Kwajalein and nearby Eniwetok with far fewer casualties.

After the Marshall Islands, the navy targeted the Mariana Islands. American military planners wanted to use the Marianas as a base for a new heavy bomber, the B-29 Superfortress. The B-29 could fly farther than any other plane in the world. From airfields in the Marianas, B-29s could bomb Japan. Admiral Nimitz decided to invade three of the Mariana Islands: Saipan, Tinian, and Guam. Despite strong Japanese resistance, American troops captured all three by August 1944. A few months later, B-29s began bombing Japan.

MacArthur Returns

As the forces under Admiral Nimitz hopped across the central Pacific, General Douglas MacArthur's troops began their own campaign in the southwest Pacific. The campaign began by invading Guadalcanal in the Solomon Islands, east of New Guinea, in August 1942. It continued until early 1944, when MacArthur's troops finally captured enough islands to surround the main Japanese base in the region. In response, the Japanese withdrew their ships and aircraft from the base, although they left 100,000 troops behind to hold the island.

Worried that the navy's advance across the central Pacific was leaving him behind, MacArthur ordered his forces to leap nearly 600 miles (966 km) to capture the Japanese base at Hollandia on the north coast of New Guinea. Shortly after securing New Guinea, MacArthur's troops seized the island of Morotai—the last stop before the Philippines.

Other troops fighting in the Pacific included the American Volunteer Group (AVG), known as the Flying Tigers, who helped defend China against Japanese forces.

▶ CRITICAL THINKING
Interpreting Significance How did aircraft help support the troops on the ground?

amphtrac an amphibious tractor used to move troops from ships to shore

To take back the Philippines, the United States assembled an enormous invasion force. In October 1944, over 700 ships carrying more than 160,000 troops sailed for Leyte Gulf in the Philippines. On October 20, the troops began to land on Leyte, an island on the eastern side of the Philippines. A few hours after the invasion began, MacArthur headed to the beach. Upon reaching the shore, he strode to a radio and spoke into the microphone: "People of the Philippines, I have returned. By the grace of Almighty God, our forces stand again on Philippine soil."

To stop the American invasion, the Japanese sent four aircraft carriers toward the Philippines from the north and secretly dispatched another fleet from the west. Believing the Japanese carriers were leading the main attack, most of the American carriers protecting the invasion left Leyte Gulf and headed north to stop them. Seizing their chance, the Japanese warships to the west raced through the Philippine Islands into Leyte Gulf and ambushed the remaining American ships.

The Battle of Leyte Gulf was the largest naval battle in history. It was also the first time that the Japanese used **kamikaze** attacks. *Kamikaze* means "divine wind" in Japanese. It refers to the great storm that destroyed the Mongol fleet during its invasion of Japan in the thirteenth century. Kamikaze pilots would deliberately crash their planes into American ships, killing themselves but also inflicting severe damage. Luckily for the Americans, just as their situation was becoming desperate, the Japanese commander, believing more American ships were on the way, ordered a retreat.

Although the Japanese fleet had retreated, the campaign to recapture the Philippines from the Japanese was long and grueling. More than 80,000 Japanese were killed; fewer than 1,000 surrendered. MacArthur's troops did not capture Manila until March 1945. The battle left the city in ruins and more than 100,000 Filipino civilians dead. The remaining Japanese retreated into the rugged terrain north of Manila; they were still fighting in August 1945 when word came that Japan had surrendered.

kamikaze during World War II, a Japanese suicide pilot whose mission was to crash into his target

Victory in the Battle of Leyte Gulf enables MacArthur to return to the Philippines.

▶ **CRITICAL THINKING**
Analyzing Visuals How does the photo represent the success of the island-hopping strategy?

PHOTO: Digital Stock/CORBIS/Royalty Free

✓ **PROGRESS CHECK**

Describing How did the United States Navy successfully drive back Japanese forces in the Pacific?

LESSON 2 REVIEW

Reviewing Vocabulary

1. *Explaining* Explain how amphtracs helped the marines land more safely on Pacific islands.

Using Your Notes

2. *Explaining* Use your notes on major Pacific battles to explain the causes and effects of the effort to defeat the Japanese in 1942.

Answering the Guiding Questions

3. *Assessing* Why was the Doolittle Raid important for U.S. forces in the Pacific?

4. *Drawing Conclusions* Why was the Battle of Midway a turning point in the war in the Pacific?

5. *Evaluating* What was the military strategy behind "island-hopping"? Was it successful?

Writing Activity

6. **PERSUASIVE** Suppose you are a journalist in 1971 reporting on the government's disclosure about the Navajo code talkers. Write a newspaper article informing Americans how the code talkers assisted the marines at the Battle of Iwo Jima.

networks

There's More Online!

☑ **BIOGRAPHY** Omar Bradley

☑ **BIOGRAPHY** George C. Marshall

☑ **BIOGRAPHY** George Patton

☑ **MAP** The Battle of Stalingrad

☑ **VIDEO** The War in Europe

☑ **INTERACTIVE SELF-CHECK QUIZ**

LESSON 3
The War in Europe

ESSENTIAL QUESTION · *What kinds of sacrifices does war require?*

Reading **HELP**DESK

Content Vocabulary

• periphery
• convoy system

Academic Vocabulary

• target   • intense
• briefly

TAKING NOTES: *Organizing*

ACTIVITY Use the following graphic organizer to record the major battles discussed and when each was fought.

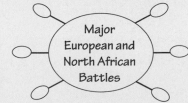

Major European and North African Battles

IT MATTERS BECAUSE

British and American troops won victories over the Axis powers in North Africa and Italy. Next, Allied leaders made plans for an invasion of Europe.

Halting the Germans

GUIDING QUESTION *Why did Churchill and Roosevelt want to attack German-controlled areas in North Africa before areas in Europe?*

Since 1940, U.S. military strategists had discussed with President Roosevelt the pressures of a two-front war. He wanted to get U.S. troops into battle in Europe, but Prime Minister Churchill did not believe the United States and Britain were ready to invade Europe. Instead, the prime minister wanted to attack the **periphery,** or edges, of the German empire. Roosevelt eventually agreed, and in July 1942, he ordered the invasion of Morocco and Algeria—two French territories indirectly under German control.

The Battle for North Africa

Roosevelt decided to invade for two reasons. The invasion would give the army some experience without requiring a lot of troops. It would also help the British troops fight the Germans in Egypt. Most of Britain's empire, including India, Hong Kong, Singapore, Malaya, and Australia, sent supplies to Britain through Egypt's Suez Canal.

German general Erwin Rommel, whose success earned him the nickname "Desert Fox," commanded the "Afrika Korps." After a 12-day battle at the Egyptian coastal city of El Alamein, the British secured the Suez Canal and forced Rommel to retreat in November 1942. Despite this defeat, German forces remained a serious threat in North Africa.

Later that month, American troops commanded by General Dwight D. Eisenhower invaded North Africa. When the Americans advanced into the mountains of western Tunisia, they fought the German army for the first time. At the Battle of Kasserine Pass, the Americans were outmaneuvered and outfought. They suffered roughly 7,000 casualties and lost nearly 200 tanks. Eisenhower fired the general who led the attack and put General George Patton in command. The American and British forces finally pushed the Germans back. On May 13, 1943, the last German troops in North Africa surrendered.

The Battle of the Atlantic

After Germany declared war on the United States, German submarines entered American coastal waters. American cargo ships were easy **targets,** especially at night when the glow from the cities in the night sky silhouetted the vessels. To protect the ships, citizens on the East Coast dimmed their lights every evening and put up special "blackout curtains." If they had to drive at night, they did so with their headlights off.

By August 1942, German submarines had sunk about 360 American ships along the East Coast, including many oil tankers. The loss of so many ships convinced the U.S. Navy to set up a **convoy system** in which cargo ships traveled in groups escorted by warships. The convoy system improved the situation dramatically, making it much more difficult for a submarine to torpedo a cargo ship and escape without being attacked.

The spring of 1942 marked the high point of the German submarine campaign. In May and June alone, more than 1.2 million tons of shipping were sunk. Yet in those same two months, American and British shipyards built more than 1.1 million tons of new shipping. At the same time, American airplanes and warships began to use new technology, including radar, sonar, and depth charges, to locate and attack submarines. As the new technology began to take its toll on German submarines, the Battle of the Atlantic turned in favor of the Allies.

The Battle of Stalingrad

Adolf Hitler was convinced that defeating the Soviet Union depended on destroying the Soviet economy. In May 1942, he ordered his army to capture strategic oil fields, factories, and farmlands in southern Russia and Ukraine. The city of Stalingrad, which controlled the Volga River and was a major railroad junction, was the key to the attack. If the German army captured Stalingrad, they would cut off the Soviets from the resources they needed to stay in the war.

periphery the outer boundary of something

target something or someone fired on or marked for attack

convoy system a system in which merchant ships travel with naval vessels for protection

A British tank successfully navigates a wide ditch in the desert outside a town in North Africa.

▶ **CRITICAL THINKING**

Analyzing Primary Sources How do you think the environment made combat in North Africa challenging?

PHOTO: The Art Archive

When German troops entered Stalingrad in mid-September, Stalin ordered his troops to hold the city at all costs. The Germans were forced to fight from house to house, losing thousands of soldiers in the process. Unlike the Soviets, they were not equipped to fight in the bitter cold. On November 23, Soviet reinforcements arrived and surrounded Stalingrad, trapping almost 250,000 German troops. When the battle ended in February 1943, some 91,000 Germans had surrendered. Only 5,000 of them survived the Soviet prison camps. Each side lost nearly half a million soldiers. The Battle of Stalingrad put the Germans on the defensive.

✔ **PROGRESS CHECK**

Explaining What was Roosevelt's purpose in invading North Africa?

Striking Germany and Italy

GUIDING QUESTION *What were the goals of strategic bombing in Germany and the invasion of Sicily?*

The Allied invasion of North Africa in November 1942 had shown that a large-scale invasion from the sea was possible. The success of the landings convinced Roosevelt to meet again with Churchill to plan the next stage of the war. In January 1943, Roosevelt headed to Casablanca, Morocco, to meet the prime minister.

At the Casablanca Conference, Roosevelt and Churchill agreed to step up the bombing of Germany. The goal of this new campaign was "the progressive destruction of the German military, industrial, and economic system, and the undermining of the morale of the German people." The Allies also agreed to attack the Axis on the island of Sicily. Churchill called Italy the "soft underbelly" of Europe. He was convinced that the Italians would quit the war if the Allies invaded their homeland.

Strategic Bombing

The Allies had been bombing Germany even before the Casablanca Conference. Britain's Royal Air Force had dropped an average of 2,300 tons (2,093 t) of explosives on Germany every month for more than three years. The United States Eighth Army Air Force had dropped an additional 1,500 tons (1,365 t) of bombs during the last six months of 1942. These numbers were small, however, compared to the massive new campaign. Between January 1943 and May 1945, the Royal Air Force and the United States Eighth Army Air Force dropped approximately 53,000 tons (48,230 t) of explosives on Germany every month.

The bombing campaign did not destroy Germany's economy or undermine German morale, but it did cause a severe oil shortage and wrecked the railroad system. It also destroyed so many aircraft factories that Germany's air force could not replace its losses. By the time the Allies landed in France, they had control of the air, ensuring that their troops would not be bombed.

Striking the Soft Underbelly

As the bombing campaign against Germany intensified, plans to invade Sicily also moved ahead. General Dwight D. Eisenhower commanded the invasion, with General Patton and British general Bernard Montgomery

A Soviet gun crew fights against Nazi forces in Stalingrad. Only one day after the Nazis publicly boasted that the city would fall to them, the Red Army turned the tide of the battle.

▶ **CRITICAL THINKING**
Analyzing Imagery How do you think the environment made combat in Stalingrad difficult?

PHOTO: Bettmann/CORBIS

heading the ground forces. The invasion began before dawn on July 10, 1943. Despite bad weather, the Allied troops made it ashore with few casualties. A new amphibious truck delivered supplies and artillery to the soldiers on the beach.

Eight days after the troops came ashore, American tanks smashed through enemy lines and captured the western half of the island. Patton's troops then headed east, while the British attacked from the south. By August 17, the Germans had evacuated the island.

The attack on Sicily created a crisis within the Italian government. The king of Italy, Victor Emmanuel, and a group of Italian generals decided that it was time to depose Mussolini. On July 25, 1943, the king invited the dictator to his palace. "My dear Duce," the king began, "it's no longer any good. Italy has gone to bits. Army morale is at rock bottom. The soldiers don't want to fight anymore. . . . You can certainly be under no illusion as to Italy's feelings with regard to yourself. At this moment, you are the most hated man in Italy." The king then arrested Mussolini, and the new Italian government began negotiating a surrender to the Allies.

Following Italy's surrender, however, German troops seized control of northern Italy, including Rome, and returned Mussolini to power. The Germans then took up positions near the heavily fortified town of Cassino. The terrain near Cassino was steep, barren, and rocky. Rather than

GEOGRAPHY CONNECTION

The war against Germany and Italy was fought on three fronts.

1 THE WORLD IN SPATIAL TERMS *How much west-to-east territory did the Axis control near the end of 1942?*

2 PLACES AND REGIONS *What Allied victories are shown in North Africa?*

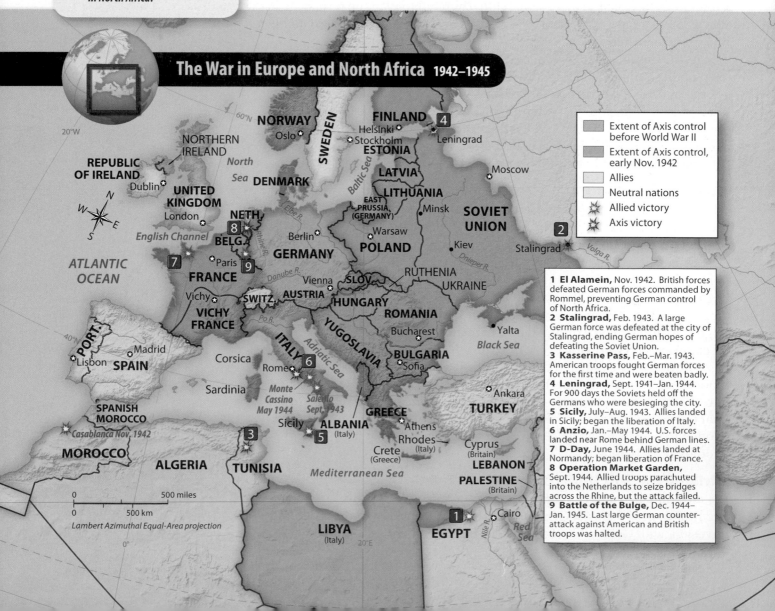

The War in Europe and North Africa 1942–1945

Extent of Axis control before World War II
Extent of Axis control, early Nov. 1942
Allies
Neutral nations
☆ Allied victory
✹ Axis victory

1 El Alamein, Nov. 1942. British forces defeated German forces commanded by Rommel, preventing German control of North Africa.
2 Stalingrad, Feb. 1943. A large German force was defeated at the city of Stalingrad, ending German hopes of defeating the Soviet Union.
3 Kasserine Pass, Feb.–Mar. 1943. American troops fought German forces for the first time and were beaten badly.
4 Leningrad, Sept. 1941–Jan. 1944. For 900 days the Soviets held off the Germans who were besieging the city.
5 Sicily, July–Aug. 1943. Allies landed in Sicily; began the liberation of Italy.
6 Anzio, Jan.–May 1944. U.S. forces landed near Rome behind German lines.
7 D-Day, June 1944. Allies landed at Normandy; began liberation of France.
8 Operation Market Garden, Sept. 1944. Allied troops parachuted into the Netherlands to seize bridges across the Rhine, but the attack failed.
9 Battle of the Bulge, Dec. 1944–Jan. 1945. Last large German counterattack against American and British troops was halted.

attack such difficult terrain, the Allies landed at Anzio, behind German lines. Instead of retreating, however, as the Allies had hoped, the Germans surrounded the Allied troops near Anzio.

It took the Allies five months to break through the German lines at Cassino and Anzio. Finally, in late May 1944, the Germans retreated. Less than two weeks later, the Allies captured Rome. Fighting in Italy continued, however, for another year. The Italian campaign was one of the bloodiest in the war, with more than 300,000 Allied casualties.

The Tehran Conference

Roosevelt wanted to meet with Stalin before the Allies invaded France. In late 1943, Stalin agreed, proposing that Roosevelt and Churchill meet him in Tehran, Iran.

The leaders reached several agreements. Stalin promised to launch a full-scale offensive against the Germans when the Allies invaded France in 1944. Roosevelt and Stalin then agreed to divide Germany after the war so that it would never again threaten world peace. Stalin promised that once Germany was defeated, the Soviet Union would help the United States against Japan. He also accepted Roosevelt's proposal of an international peacekeeping organization after the war. Part of the agreement proclaimed:

PRIMARY SOURCE

❝The common understanding which we have here reached guarantees that victory will be ours. And as to peace—we are sure that our concord will win an enduring Peace. We recognize fully the supreme responsibility . . . to make a peace which will command the goodwill of the overwhelming mass of the peoples of the world and banish the scourge and terror of war for many generations.❞

—from the Tehran Declaration, December 1, 1943

✔ **PROGRESS CHECK**

Evaluating What did Roosevelt and other leaders hope to accomplish by attacking Germany and Italy?

The D-Day Invasion

GUIDING QUESTION *What if D-Day had failed and Germany had defeated the Allies in Europe?*

After the conference in Tehran, Roosevelt headed to Cairo, Egypt, where he and Churchill continued planning an invasion of France to force Germany to again fight the war on two fronts. One major decision still had to be made. The president had to choose the commander for Operation Overlord—the code name for the invasion. Roosevelt selected General Eisenhower.

Planning Operation Overlord

Hitler had fortified the French coast along the English Channel, but he did not know when or where the Allies would land. The Germans believed the landing would be in Pas-de-Calais—the area of France closest to Britain. The Allies encouraged this belief by placing dummy equipment along the coast across from Calais. The real target was farther south, a 60-mile stretch of five beaches along the Normandy coast.

The selection of a site for the largest amphibious landing in history was one of the biggest decisions of World War II. Allied planners considered coastlines from Denmark to Portugal in search of a sheltered location with firm flat beaches within range of friendly fighter planes in England. There also had to be enough roads and paths to move jeeps and trucks off the beaches

BIOGRAPHY

Vernon Baker (1919–2010)
U.S. Army Company C,
370th Regiment, 92nd
Infantry Division

On April 5, 1945, First Lieutenant Vernon Baker and his platoon advanced toward Castle Aghinolfi, a German stronghold in the mountains near Viareggio, Italy. Baker and about 25 others moved ahead of the group, and Baker successfully destroyed an observation post, a dugout, and three machine gun positions. In 1996 his actions earned him a Medal of Honor "for conspicuous gallantry and intrepidity at the risk of his own life above and beyond the call of duty in action on 5 and 6 April 1945." This made Baker one of seven African American World War II veterans to receive belated recognition for their service.

▶ **CRITICAL THINKING**
Drawing Conclusions Why were Baker's actions so important to the assault on Castle Aghinolfi?

and to accommodate the hundreds of thousands of American, Canadian, and British troops set to stream ashore following the invasion. An airfield and a seaport that the Allies could use were also needed. Most important was a reasonable expectation of achieving the element of surprise.

Planners also discussed who should lead France after the invasion. General Eisenhower had informed Charles de Gaulle that the French Resistance forces would assist in the liberation of Paris, but President Roosevelt was not sure he trusted de Gaulle and refused to recognize him as the official French leader.

By the spring of 1944, more than 1.5 million American soldiers, 12,000 airplanes, and 5 million tons (4.6 million t) of equipment had been sent to England. Only setting the invasion date and giving the command to go remained. The invasion had to begin at night to hide the ships crossing the English Channel. The ships had to arrive at low tide so that they could see the beach obstacles. The low tide had to come at dawn so that gunners bombarding the coast could see their targets. Paratroopers, who would be dropped behind enemy lines, needed a moonlit night to see where to land. Perhaps most important of all was good weather. A storm would ground the airplanes, and high waves would swamp landing craft.

Given all these requirements, there were only a few days each month to begin the invasion. The first opportunity was from June 5 to 7, 1944. Eisenhower's planning staff referred to the day any operation began by the letter *D*. The invasion date, therefore, came to be known as D-Day. Heavy cloud cover, strong winds, and high waves made June 5 impossible. The weather was forecast to improve **briefly** a day later. The Channel would still be rough, but the landing ships

briefly for a short time

Allied troops from various parts of the British coast headed for Normandy beaches for the D-Day invasion.

▶ **CRITICAL THINKING**
Identifying Cause and Effect How did the D-Day invasion turn the tide of World War II?

PHOTO: Bettmann/CORBIS

and aircraft could operate. After looking at forecasts one last time, shortly after midnight on June 6, 1944, Eisenhower gave the final order: "OK, we'll go."

The Longest Day

Nearly 7,000 ships carrying more than 100,000 soldiers headed for Normandy's coast. At the same time, 23,000 paratroopers were dropped inland, east and west of the beaches. Allied fighter-bombers raced up and down the coast, hitting bridges, bunkers, and radar sites. At dawn, Allied warships began a tremendous barrage. Thousands of shells rained down on the beaches, code-named "Utah," "Omaha," "Gold," "Sword," and "Juno."

The American landing at Utah Beach went well. The German defenses were weak, and in less than three hours, the troops had captured the beach and moved inland, suffering fewer than 200 casualties. On the eastern flank, the British and Canadian landings also went well. By the end of the day, British and Canadian forces were several miles inland.

Omaha Beach, however, was a different story. Surrounded at both ends by cliffs that rose wall-like from the sea, Omaha Beach was only four miles long. The entire beach overlooked a 150-foot high bluff, and there were only five ravines leading from the beach to the top of the bluff. The Germans had made full use of the geographic advantage the high bluff gave them. They dug trenches and built concrete bunkers for machine guns at the top of the cliffs and positioned them to guard the ravines leading to the beach. Under **intense** German fire, the American assault almost disintegrated.

General Omar Bradley, commander of the American forces landing at Omaha and Utah, began making plans to evacuate. Slowly, however, the American troops began to knock out the German defenses. More landing craft arrived, ramming their way through the obstacles to get to the beach. Nearly 2,500 Americans were either killed or wounded on Omaha, but by early afternoon, Bradley received this message: "Troops formerly pinned down on beaches . . . [are] advancing up heights behind beaches." By the end of the day, nearly 35,000 American troops had landed at Omaha, and another 23,000 had landed at Utah. More than 75,000 British and Canadian troops were on shore as well. The invasion had succeeded.

☑ **PROGRESS CHECK**

Summarizing Why was it so important that all of the conditions be met before Eisenhower could order D-Day to begin? What would have happened if the invasion had failed?

Analyzing
PRIMARY SOURCES

Fighting at Omaha Beach

❝Two hundred yards out, we took a direct hit. . . . Somehow or other, the ramp door opened up . . . and the men in front were being struck by machine gun fire. Everyone started to jump off into the water. . . . The tide was moving us so rapidly. . . . We would grab out at some of those underwater obstructions and mines built on telephone poles and girders, and hang on. We'd take cover, then make a dash through the surf to the next one, fifty feet beyond.❞

—Lieutenant John Bentz Carroll, from *D-Day: Piercing the Atlantic Wall*, 1994

DBQ *MAKING INFERENCES*
Based on this description, what can you infer about the manner of the landing on Omaha Beach?

intense existing in an extreme degree

LESSON 3 REVIEW

Reviewing Vocabulary

1. *Explaining* Explain how using the convoy system helped the United States begin winning the Battle of the Atlantic.

Using Your Notes

2. *Sequencing* Review the notes you completed during the lesson and use them to sequence the major Allied victories.

Answering the Guiding Questions

3. *Analyzing* Why did Churchill and Roosevelt want to attack German-controlled areas in North Africa before areas in Europe?

4. *Determining Cause and Effect* What were the goals of strategic bombing in Germany and the invasion of Sicily?

5. *Speculating* What if D-Day had failed and Germany had defeated the Allies in Europe?

Writing Activity

6. **DESCRIPTIVE** American soldiers invading Normandy on D-Day showed extreme bravery in the face of enormous difficulties. Imagine that you are one of the first soldiers approaching Omaha Beach by water. Write a description of the beach and the atmosphere of the moment. Be sure to include sensory words.

networks

There's More Online!

☑ **IMAGE** Iwo Jima Photograph

☑ **MAP** Japanese Entrenchment on Iwo Jima

☑ **MAP** Axis Expansion and Retreat

☑ **MAP** The Atomic Bomb at Hiroshima

☑ **VIDEO** The War Ends

☑ **INTERACTIVE SELF-CHECK QUIZ**

Reading **HELP**DESK

Content Vocabulary

• hedgerow • napalm

Academic Vocabulary

• despite • nuclear

TAKING NOTES: *Outlining*

ACTIVITY As you read, create an outline of the section similar to the one below, using the major headings as the main points.

The War Ends
I. The Third Reich Collapses
   A.
   B.
II.
   A.
   B.

LESSON 4
The War Ends

ESSENTIAL QUESTION · *What kinds of sacrifices does war require?*

IT MATTERS BECAUSE
Fierce fighting in both Europe and the Pacific during 1945 led to the defeat of the Axis powers. As the war ended, the Allies began war-crimes trials as part of a plan to build a better world.

The Third Reich Collapses

GUIDING QUESTION *Why was the Battle of the Bulge so important to the Allied forces?*

Although D-Day had been a success, it was only the beginning. Surrounding many fields in Normandy were **hedgerows**—dirt walls, several feet thick, covered in shrubbery—built to fence in cattle and crops. They also enabled the Germans to fiercely defend their positions. The battle of the hedgerows ended on July 25, 1944, when 2,500 U.S. bombers blew a hole in the German lines, enabling U.S. tanks to race through the gap.

As the Allies broke out of Normandy, the French Resistance—French civilians who had secretly organized to resist the German occupation—staged a rebellion in Paris. When the Allies liberated Paris on August 25, the streets were filled with French citizens celebrating their victory.

The Battle of the Bulge

As the Allies advanced toward the German border, Hitler decided to stage one last desperate offensive. His goal was to cut off Allied supplies coming through the port of Antwerp, Belgium. The attack began just before dawn on December 16, 1944. Six inches (15 cm) of snow covered the ground, and the weather was bitterly cold. Moving rapidly, the Germans caught the American defenders by surprise. As the German troops raced west, their lines bulged outward, and the attack became known as the Battle of the Bulge.

Eisenhower ordered General Patton to the rescue. Three days later, faster than anyone expected in the midst of a snowstorm, Patton's troops slammed into the German lines. As the weather cleared, Allied aircraft began hitting German fuel depots.

On Christmas Eve, out of fuel and weakened by heavy losses, the German troops driving toward Antwerp were forced to halt. Two days later, Patton's troops broke through to the German line. Fighting continued for three weeks, but the United States had won the Battle of the Bulge. On January 8, the Germans began to withdraw, having suffered more than 100,000 casualties. They had very few resources left to prevent the Allies from entering Germany.

hedgerow an enclosure made of dirt walls covered in shrubbery built to fence in cattle and crops

The War Ends in Europe

While American and British forces fought to liberate France, the Soviets attacked German troops in Russia. By the end of the Battle of the Bulge, the Soviets had driven Hitler's forces out of Russia and across Poland. By February 1945, the Soviets were only 35 miles (56 km) from Germany's capital, Berlin.

Soviet troops crossed Germany's eastern border, while American forces attacked its western border. By the end of February 1945, American troops had reached the Rhine River, Germany's last major line of defense in the west. On March 7, American tanks crossed the Rhine. As German defenses crumbled, American troops raced east to within 70 miles (113 km) of Berlin. On April 16, Soviet troops finally smashed through the German defenses and reached the outskirts of Berlin five days later.

Deep in his Berlin bunker, Adolf Hitler knew the end was near. On April 30, 1945, he committed suicide. On May 7, 1945, Germany accepted the terms for an unconditional surrender. The next day—May 8, 1945—was proclaimed V-E Day, for "Victory in Europe."

American troops march through the snow on January 31, 1945, during the Battle of the Bulge.

▶ **CRITICAL THINKING**
Drawing Inferences Looking at the photo, what can you infer about the conditions during the Battle of the Bulge?

☑ **PROGRESS CHECK**

Explaining Why was the Battle of the Bulge such a disastrous defeat for Germany?

Japan Is Defeated

GUIDING QUESTION *Do you agree or disagree with President Truman's decision to drop the atomic bomb? Explain your reasons.*

Unfortunately, President Roosevelt did not live to see the defeat of Germany. On April 12, 1945, while vacationing in Warm Springs, Georgia, he died of a stroke. His vice president, Harry S. Truman, became president during this difficult time.

The next day, Truman told reporters: "Boys, if you ever pray, pray for me now. . . . When they told me yesterday what had happened, I felt like the moon, the stars, and all the planets had fallen on me." **Despite** his feelings, Truman began at once to make decisions about the war. Although Germany surrendered a few weeks later, the war with Japan continued, and Truman was forced to make some of the most difficult decisions of the war during his first six months in office.

The Battle of Iwo Jima

On November 24, 1944, bombs fell on Tokyo. Above the city flew 80 B-29 Superfortress bombers that had traveled more than 1,500 miles (2,414 km) from new American bases in the Mariana Islands. Many of their bombs missed the targets. By the time the B-29s reached Japan, they did not have enough

despite in spite of

fuel left to fix their navigational errors or to adjust for high winds. The pilots needed an island closer to Japan so the B-29s could refuel. American military planners chose Iwo Jima.

Iwo Jima was perfectly located, roughly halfway between the Marianas and Japan, but its geography was formidable. It had a dormant volcano at its southern tip and rugged terrain with rocky cliffs, jagged ravines, and dozens of caves. Volcanic ash covered the ground. Even worse, the Japanese had built a vast network of concrete bunkers connected by miles of tunnels.

On February 19, 1945, some 60,000 marines landed on Iwo Jima. As the troops leaped from the amphtracs, they sank up to their ankles in the soft ash and were pounded by Japanese artillery. The marines crawled inland, attacking the Japanese bunkers with flamethrowers and explosives. More than 6,800 marines were killed capturing the island. Admiral Nimitz later wrote that, on Iwo Jima, "uncommon valor was a common virtue."

Firebombing Japan

While American engineers prepared airfields on Iwo Jima, General Curtis LeMay, commander of the B-29s based in the Marianas, changed strategy. To help the B-29s hit their targets, he ordered them to drop bombs filled with **napalm**—a type of jellied gasoline. The bombs would not only explode but would also start fires. Even if the B-29s missed their targets, the fires they started would spread to the intended targets.

napalm a type of jellied gasoline

The use of firebombs was very controversial because the fires would also kill civilians; however, LeMay could think of no other way to destroy Japan's war production quickly. Loaded with firebombs, B-29s attacked Tokyo on March 9, 1945. As strong winds fanned the flames, the firestorm grew so intense that it sucked the oxygen out of the air, asphyxiating thousands. As one survivor later recalled:

PRIMARY SOURCE

❝The fires were incredible . . . with flames leaping hundreds of feet into the air. . . . With every passing moment the air became more foul . . . the noise was a continuing crashing roar. . . . Fire-winds filled with burning particles rushed up and down the streets. I watched people . . . running for their lives. . . . The flames raced after them like living things, striking them down. . . . Wherever I turned my eyes, I saw people . . . seeking air to breathe.❞

—quoted in *American Heritage New History of World War II*

The firebombing of Tokyo killed more than 80,000 people and destroyed more than 250,000 buildings. By the end of June 1945, Japan's six key industrial cities had been firebombed. By the end of the war, the B-29s had firebombed 67 Japanese cities.

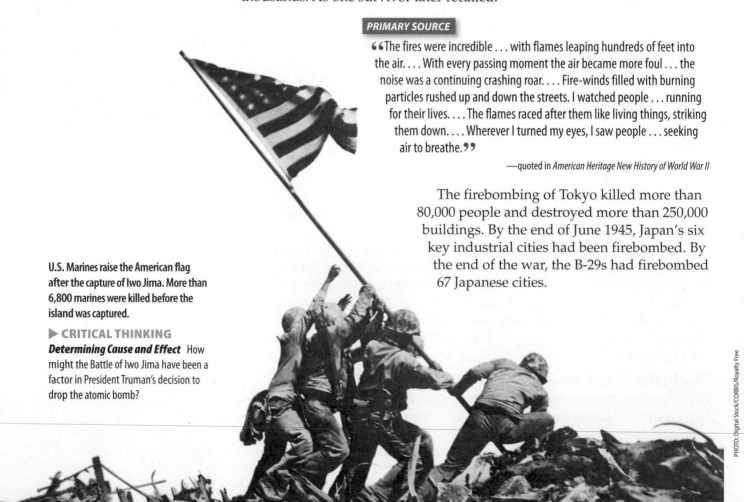

U.S. Marines raise the American flag after the capture of Iwo Jima. More than 6,800 marines were killed before the island was captured.

▶ **CRITICAL THINKING**
Determining Cause and Effect How might the Battle of Iwo Jima have been a factor in President Truman's decision to drop the atomic bomb?

The Invasion of Okinawa

Despite the massive damage that firebombing caused, there were few signs in the spring of 1945 that Japan was ready to quit. Many American officials believed the Japanese would not surrender until Japan had been invaded. To prepare for the invasion, the United States needed a base near Japan to stockpile supplies and build up troops. Iwo Jima was small and still too far away. Military planners chose Okinawa—only 350 miles (563 km) from mainland Japan.

American troops landed on Okinawa on April 1, 1945. Instead of defending the beaches, the Japanese troops took up positions in the island's rugged mountains. To dig the Japanese out of their caves and bunkers, the American troops had to fight their way up steep slopes against constant machine gun and artillery fire. More than 12,000 American soldiers, sailors, and marines died during the fighting, but by June 22, 1945, Okinawa had finally been captured.

The Terms for Surrender

Shortly after the United States captured Okinawa, the Japanese emperor, Hirohito, urged his government to find a way to end the war. The biggest problem was the American demand for unconditional surrender. Many Japanese leaders were willing to surrender, but on one condition: Hirohito had to stay in power.

American officials knew that the fate of Hirohito was the most important issue for the Japanese. Most Americans, however, blamed the emperor for the war and wanted him removed from power. President Truman was reluctant to go against public opinion. Furthermore, he knew the United States was almost ready to test a new weapon that might force Japan to surrender without any conditions. The new weapon was the atomic bomb.

The Manhattan Project

In 1939 Leo Szilard, a Jewish physicist who had fled Nazi persecution, learned that German scientists had split the uranium atom. Szilard had been the first scientist to suggest that splitting the atom might release enormous energy. Worried that the Nazis were working on an atomic bomb, Szilard convinced the world's best-known physicist, Albert Einstein, to sign a letter Szilard had drafted and send it to President Roosevelt. In the letter, Einstein warned that by using uranium, "extremely powerful bombs of a new type may . . . be constructed."

Roosevelt responded by setting up a scientific committee to study the issue. In 1941 the committee met with British scientists who were already working on an atomic bomb. The Americans then convinced Roosevelt to begin a program to build an atomic bomb.

The secret American program to build an atomic bomb was code-named the Manhattan Project and was headed by General Leslie R. Groves. The first breakthrough came in 1942, when Szilard and Enrico Fermi, another physicist, built the world's first **nuclear** reactor at the University of Chicago. Groves then organized a team of engineers and scientists to build an atomic bomb at a secret laboratory in Los Alamos, New Mexico. Physicist J. Robert Oppenheimer led the team. On July 16, 1945, they detonated the world's first atomic bomb in New Mexico.

Hiroshima and Nagasaki

Even before the bomb was tested, American officials began debating how to use it. Admiral William Leahy, chairman of the Joint Chiefs of Staff, opposed using the bomb because it would kill civilians. He believed an economic blockade and conventional bombing would convince Japan to

A key figure of the nuclear age, Enrico Fermi proved a nuclear reaction could be initiated, controlled, and stopped.

▶ **CRITICAL THINKING**
Identifying Central Issues Why was Enrico Fermi's work on nuclear reactions so important?

nuclear relating to the nucleus of an atom

surrender. Secretary of War Henry Stimson wanted to warn the Japanese about the bomb and tell them their emperor could stay in power if they surrendered. Secretary of State James Byrnes, however, wanted to drop the bomb on Japan without any warning.

President Truman later wrote that he "regarded the bomb as a military weapon and never had any doubts that it should be used." His advisers had warned him to expect massive casualties if the United States invaded Japan. Truman believed it was his duty as president to use every weapon available to save American lives.

The Allies threatened Japan with "prompt and utter destruction" if the nation did not surrender, but the Japanese did not reply. Truman then ordered the military to drop the bomb. On August 6, 1945, a B-29 bomber named *Enola Gay* dropped an atomic bomb, code-named "Little Boy," on Hiroshima, an important industrial city.

The bomb destroyed about 63 percent of the city. Between 80,000 and 120,000 people died instantly, and thousands more died later from burns and radiation sickness. Three days later, on August 9, the Soviet Union declared war on Japan. Later that day, the United States dropped another atomic bomb, code-named "Fat Man," on the city of Nagasaki, killing between 35,000 and 74,000 people. Faced with such massive destruction and the shock of the Soviets joining the war, Hirohito ordered his government to surrender. On August 15, 1945—V-J Day—Japan surrendered. The long war was over.

PHOTOS: (l)The Art Archive/Culver Pictures, (r)Myron Davis/Time Life Pictures/Getty Images

ANALYZING PRIMARY SOURCES

People continue to debate whether President Truman's decision to drop atomic bombs on Japan was the best way to end World War II.

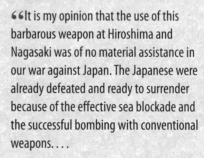

Harry S. Truman
President of the United States

"The world will note that the first atomic bomb was dropped on Hiroshima, a military base.... If Japan does not surrender, bombs will have to be dropped on her war industries and, unfortunately, thousands of civilian lives will be lost....

Having found the bomb we have used it. We have used it against those who attacked us without warning at Pearl Harbor, against those who have starved and beaten and executed American prisoners of war, against those who have abandoned all pretense of obeying international laws of warfare. We have used it in order to shorten the agony of war, in order to save the lives of thousands and thousands of young Americans."

—Harry S. Truman, radio report to the American people, August 9, 1945

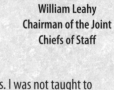

William Leahy
Chairman of the Joint Chiefs of Staff

"It is my opinion that the use of this barbarous weapon at Hiroshima and Nagasaki was of no material assistance in our war against Japan. The Japanese were already defeated and ready to surrender because of the effective sea blockade and the successful bombing with conventional weapons....

The lethal possibilities of atomic warfare in the future are frightening. My own feeling was that in being the first to use it, we had adopted an ethical standard common to the barbarians of the Dark Ages. I was not taught to make war in that fashion, and wars cannot be won by destroying women and children."

—William Leahy, from *I Was There*, 1950

DBQ Document Based Questions

❶ *Explaining* What reasons does Truman offer to justify the use of the atomic bomb?

❷ *Summarizing* Why does Leahy say he was against using the bomb?

The United States dropped an atomic bomb that destroyed the Japanese city of Hiroshima.

▶ **CRITICAL THINKING**
Analyzing Primary Sources What details in the picture illustrate the effect of the atomic bomb?

PHOTO: Bettmann/CORBIS

Putting the Enemy on Trial

In August 1945, the United States, Britain, France, and the Soviet Union created the International Military Tribunal (IMT) to punish German and Japanese leaders for war crimes. The tribunal held trials in Nuremberg, Germany, where Hitler had staged Nazi Party rallies.

Twenty-two German leaders were prosecuted at the Nuremberg Trials. Three were acquitted, 7 were given prison sentences, and 12 were sentenced to death. Trials of lower-ranking leaders continued until April 1949, leading to 24 more executions and 107 prison sentences.

Similar trials were held in Tokyo. The IMT for the Far East charged 25 Japanese leaders with war crimes. The Allies did not indict Hirohito, fearing that any attempt to put the emperor on trial would lead to an uprising. Eighteen Japanese defendants were sentenced to prison. The rest were sentenced to death by hanging.

The trials punished many of the people responsible for World War II and the Holocaust, but they were also part of the American plan for building a better world. As Robert Jackson, chief counsel for the United States at Nuremberg, said in his opening statement to the court: "The wrongs we seek to condemn and punish have been so calculated, so malignant and so devastating, that civilization cannot tolerate their being ignored because it cannot survive their being repeated."

✓ PROGRESS CHECK

Analyzing What arguments did Truman consider when deciding whether to use the atomic bomb?

LESSON 4 REVIEW

Reviewing Vocabulary

1. *Explaining* Explain why napalm bombs are highly destructive.

Using Your Notes

2. *Summarizing* Using the notes you completed during the lesson on factors that led to the end of World War II, explain how the Allies achieved victory in Europe and over Japan.

Answering the Guiding Questions

3. *Analyzing* Why was the Battle of the Bulge so important to the Allied forces?

4. *Defending* Do you agree or disagree with President Truman's decision to drop the atomic bomb? Explain your reasons.

Writing Activity

5. DESCRIPTIVE Suppose that you are in a large U.S. city when news of victory over Japan comes. Describe the celebrations and the mood of the people.

Directions: On a separate sheet of paper, answer the questions below. Make sure you read carefully and answer all parts to the question.

Lesson Review

Lesson 1

1 *Explaining* What economic strategy did Franklin Roosevelt use to convert the U.S. economy to wartime production?

2 *Drawing Conclusions* Why did women serve in noncombat positions in the military and work in factories at home?

Lesson 2

3 *Identifying Cause and Effect* What caused Japan to follow a strategy to destroy the U.S. fleet in the Pacific?

4 *Analyzing* What was the U.S. military goal in the Pacific?

Lesson 3

5 *Specifying* What method did the United States use to prevent huge shipping losses in the Atlantic?

6 *Understanding Historical Interpretation* Why was the invasion of Normandy important?

Lesson 4

7 *Understanding Historical Interpretation* What was the significance of the Battle of the Bulge?

8 *Analyzing Ethical Issues* What arguments did Truman consider when deciding whether to use the atomic bomb?

21st Century Skills

9 **EXPLAINING CONTINUITY AND CHANGE** What kind of discrimination did minorities in the military experience? How did the situation change for some minorities as the war progressed?

10 **IDENTIFYING CAUSE AND EFFECT** Why is the Battle of Midway considered to be one of the turning points in the war?

11 **IDENTIFYING CAUSE AND EFFECT** What conditions had to be met before the Allies would begin the D-Day invasion?

Exploring the Essential Question

12 *Categorizing* Design a booth for a history conference that is titled "Sacrifices Made During World War II." The booth should contain three charts, each listing a different category of sacrifice: Economic, Military/Civilian, and Social. Use text, maps, and illustrations to show the information you would include in this booth.

DBQ Document-Based Question

Use the image to answer the following question.

This poster was published by the War Finance Division of the U.S. Treasury Department in 1944.

13 *Analyzing Visuals* Why did the War Finance Division use the theme of a soldier grasping the American flag for this poster?

PRIMARY SOURCE

To Have and to Hold!

WAR BONDS

Extended-Response Question

14 *Identifying* Write an essay that traces the progress of World War II, making sure to include major events and leaders. In your essay, make note of the war's turning points and the use of the atomic bomb. Discuss major decisions of Franklin D. Roosevelt, Harry S. Truman, Winston Churchill, and Joseph Stalin. Your essay should include an introduction and several paragraphs.

Need Extra Help?

If You've Missed Question	1	2	3	4	5	6	7	8	9	10	11	12	13	14
Go to page	482	482	489	492	496	500	502	506	481	491	499	480	508	480

The Cold War Begins

1945–1960

ESSENTIAL QUESTIONS • *How did the Cold War shape postwar international relations?* • *How did Cold War tensions affect American society?*

◄ Dwight D. Eisenhower, commander of the Allied forces during World War II and army chief of staff under Truman, became president in 1953.

PHOTO: Bettmann/CORBIS

netw⊕rks

There's More Online about the Cold War and its effects on society.

CHAPTER 22

The Story Matters...

The destruction caused by the atomic bomb raised the stakes of military conflict. American concerns about the lack of freedom in countries controlled by the Soviet Union created a growing tension between the two nations. The United States and the Soviet Union would continue in a state of political conflict, military tension, and economic competition for almost 45 years. Conflict broke out in 1950 when Communist North Korea invaded South Korea, expanding the Cold War.

Place and Time: United States 1945–1960

Relations between the Soviet Union and the other Allies soured as the Soviets established Communist governments in Eastern Europe. President Truman authorized billions of dollars of American aid to devastated European nations as well as to the Allies' former enemies, Germany and Japan. Americans grew fearful of the possibility of Communists infiltrating the U.S. government, while others feared an attack with nuclear weapons. By the early 1950s, Americans were looking for someone or something that would make them feel secure.

Step Into the Place

Read the quotes and look at the information presented on the map.

  How do the United States and the Soviet Union each seem to be interpreting the intentions of the other nation?

PRIMARY SOURCE

❝[The] USSR still [believes] in antagonistic capitalist encirclement' with which in the long run there can be no permanent peaceful coexistence.... In summary, we have here a political force committed fanatically to the belief that ... it is desirable and necessary that the internal harmony of our society be disrupted, our traditional way of life be destroyed, the international authority of our state be broken, if Soviet power is to be secure.❞

—George F. Kennan, American diplomat, from "The Long Telegram," February 22, 1946

PRIMARY SOURCE

❝The more the war recedes into the past, the more distinct becomes ... the division of the political forces operating on the international arena into two major camps.... The principal driving force of the imperialist camp is the U.S.A.... The cardinal purpose of the imperialist camp is to strengthen imperialism, to hatch a new imperialist war, to combat socialism and democracy, and to support reactionary and antidemocratic profascist regimes.❞

—Andrey Zhdanov, adviser to Stalin, from *For a Lasting Peace for a People's Democracy*, no. 1, November 1947

Step Into the Time

Choose an event from the time line and write a paragraph about how that event might have influenced American society or international relations.

Truman
1945–1953

U.S. PRESIDENTS

UNITED STATES

WORLD

1945   **1947**   **1949**

1945 Franklin Roosevelt dies

1947 Truman Doctrine declared

1948 Berlin Airlift begins

1949 U.S. and Western European nations form NATO

1950 Senator McCarthy charges U.S. State Department contains Communists

1945 Potsdam Conference discusses terms of surrender and postwar boundaries

1948 Communist coup in Czechoslovakia

1950 North Korea invades South Korea

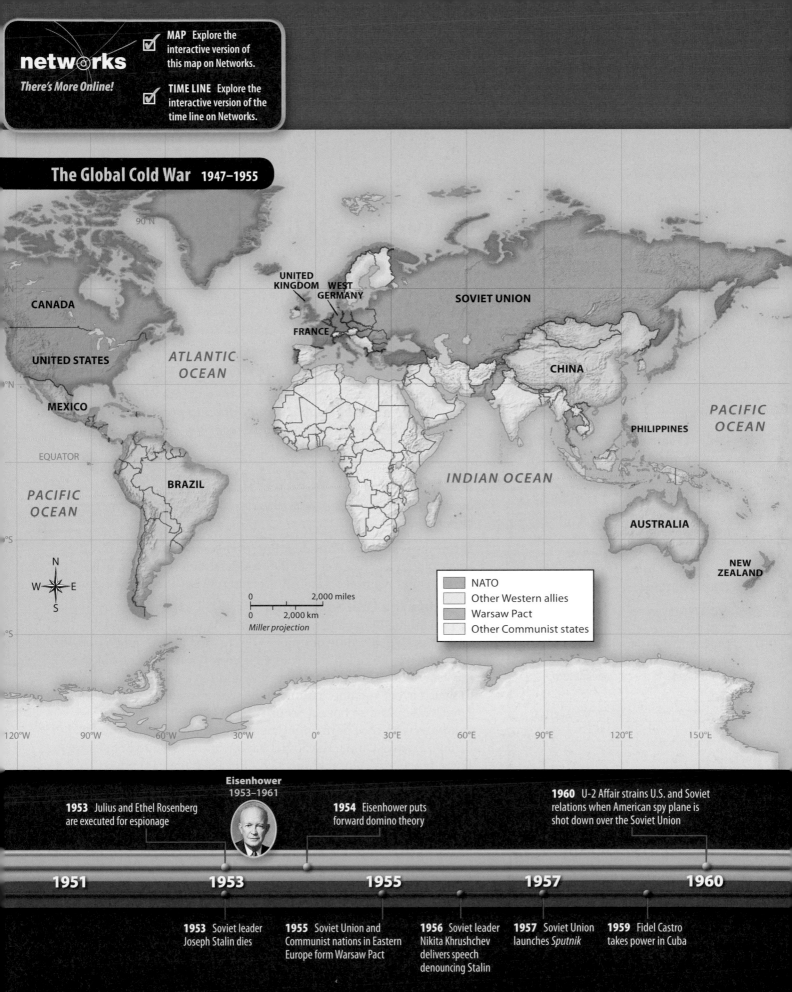

networks
There's More Online!

☑ **MAP** Explore the interactive version of this map on Networks.

☑ **TIME LINE** Explore the interactive version of the time line on Networks.

The Global Cold War 1947–1955

UNITED
KINGDOM   WEST
          GERMANY

FRANCE

SOVIET UNION

CANADA

UNITED STATES

ATLANTIC
OCEAN

MEXICO

CHINA

PACIFIC
OCEAN

EQUATOR

PHILIPPINES

BRAZIL

PACIFIC
OCEAN

INDIAN OCEAN

AUSTRALIA

NEW
ZEALAND

N
W + E
S

0   2,000 miles
0   2,000 km
Miller projection

NATO
Other Western allies
Warsaw Pact
Other Communist states

120°W   90°W   60°W   30°W   0°   30°E   60°E   90°E   120°E   150°E

Eisenhower
1953–1961

1953 Julius and Ethel Rosenberg are executed for espionage

1954 Eisenhower puts forward domino theory

1960 U-2 Affair strains U.S. and Soviet relations when American spy plane is shot down over the Soviet Union

1951   1953   1955   1957   1960

1953 Soviet leader Joseph Stalin dies

1955 Soviet Union and Communist nations in Eastern Europe form Warsaw Pact

1956 Soviet leader Nikita Khrushchev delivers speech denouncing Stalin

1957 Soviet Union launches *Sputnik*

1959 Fidel Castro takes power in Cuba

networks

There's More Online!

- ☑ **BIOGRAPHY** Winston Churchill
- ☑ **BIOGRAPHY** Joseph Stalin
- ☑ **BIOGRAPHY** Harry S. Truman
- ☑ **IMAGE** Postwar Poland
- ☑ **MAP** Divided Berlin
- ☑ **VIDEO** Origins of the Cold War
- ☑ **INTERACTIVE SELF-CHECK QUIZ**

Reading HELPDESK

Content Vocabulary

- **charter**
- **satellite nations**
- **Iron Curtain**

Academic Vocabulary

- **liberate** • **equipment**

TAKING NOTES: *Organizing*

ACTIVITY As you read, complete a graphic organizer similar to the one below by filling in the names of the conferences held during the last days of World War II and the outcomes of each.

Conferences	Outcomes

512

LESSON 1
The Origins of the Cold War

ESSENTIAL QUESTIONS • *How did the Cold War shape postwar international relations?* • *How did Cold War tensions affect American society?*

IT MATTERS BECAUSE

As World War II was coming to an end, the Allied powers set up a peacekeeping organization to prevent future wars. Soon, however, tensions arose over the amount of freedom the Soviets would allow the nations they controlled.

Building a New World

GUIDING QUESTION *How did the conferences at Dumbarton Oaks and Yalta attempt to shape the postwar world?*

Before the war ended, President Roosevelt had wanted to ensure that war would never again engulf the world. He believed that a new international political organization could prevent another world war.

Creating the United Nations

In 1944, at the Dumbarton Oaks estate in Washington, D.C., delegates from 39 countries met to discuss the new organization, which was to be called the United Nations (UN). The delegates at the conference agreed that the UN would have a General Assembly, in which every member nation in the world would have one vote. The UN would also have a Security Council with 11 members. Five countries would be permanent members of the Security Council: Britain, France, China, the Soviet Union, and the United States. These five permanent members would each have veto power.

On April 25, 1945, representatives from 50 countries came to San Francisco to officially organize the United Nations and design its **charter.** The General Assembly was given the power to vote on resolutions and to choose the non-permanent members of the Security Council. The Security Council was responsible for international peace and security. It could ask its members to use military force to uphold a UN resolution.

The Yalta Conference

In February 1945, with the war in Europe nearly over, Roosevelt, Churchill, and Stalin met at Yalta—a Soviet resort on the Black Sea—to plan the postwar world. Several agreements reached at Yalta later played an important role in causing the Cold War.

A key issue discussed at Yalta was Poland. Shortly after the Germans had invaded Poland in 1939, the Polish government fled to Britain. In 1944, however, Soviet troops drove back the Germans and entered Poland. As they **liberated** Poland from German control, the Soviets encouraged Polish Communists to set up a new government. As a result, two governments claimed the right to govern Poland: one Communist and one non-Communist. President Roosevelt and Prime Minister Churchill both argued that the Poles should be free to choose their own government.

Stalin, however, quickly pointed out that every time invaders had entered Russia from the west, they had come through Poland. Eventually, the three leaders compromised. Roosevelt and Churchill agreed to recognize the Polish government set up by the Soviets. Stalin agreed it would include members of the prewar Polish government, and free elections would be held as soon as possible.

The Declaration of Liberated Europe

After reaching a compromise on Poland, the three leaders agreed to issue the Declaration of Liberated Europe. The declaration echoed the Atlantic Charter, asserting "the right of all people to choose the form of government under which they will live." The Allies promised that the people of Europe would be allowed "to create democratic institutions of their own choice" and to create temporary governments that represented "all democratic elements." They pledged "the earliest possible establishment through free elections of governments responsive to the will of the people."

Dividing Germany

The conference then focused on Germany. Roosevelt, Churchill, and Stalin agreed to divide Germany into four zones. Great Britain, the United States, the Soviet Union, and France would each control one zone. The same four countries would also divide the German capital city of Berlin into four zones, even though it was in the Soviet zone.

Although pleased with the decision to divide Germany, Stalin also demanded that Germany pay heavy reparations for the war damages it had caused. An agreement was reached that Germany could pay war reparations with trade goods and products, half of which would go to the Soviet Union.

charter a constitution

liberate to set free

GEOGRAPHY CONNECTION

Germany and its capital Berlin were divided into four zones.

1. **PLACES AND REGIONS** *Which country controlled the smallest region of Germany?*

2. **THE WORLD IN SPATIAL TERMS** *In what zone in the divided Germany was Berlin located?*

The Division of Germany 1945

Allied Occupation Zones, 1945–1949
- American
- British
- French
- Soviet
- Present-day Germany
- Uncertain border

North Sea · Baltic Sea · POLAND · UNITED KINGDOM · NETHERLANDS · BELGIUM · FRANCE · SWITZ. · AUSTRIA · CZECHOSLOVAKIA · Elbe R. · Rhine R. · Danube R. · Berlin · area of inset

0 — 6 mi.
0 — 6 km
West Berlin · East Berlin

0 — 200 miles
0 — 200 km
Lambert Azimuthal Equal-Area projection

equipment the articles or physical resources prepared or furnished for a specific task

The Allies would remove industrial machinery, railroad cars, and other **equipment** from Germany as reparations. Later arguments about reparations greatly increased tensions between the United States and the Soviet Union.

Rising Tensions

The Yalta decisions shaped the expectations of the United States. Two weeks after Yalta, the Soviets pressured the king of Romania into appointing a Communist government. The United States accused the Soviets of violating the Declaration of Liberated Europe. Soon afterward, the Soviets refused to allow more than three non-Communist Poles to serve in the 18-member Polish government. There was also no indication that they intended to hold free elections in Poland as promised. On April 1, President Roosevelt informed the Soviets that their actions in Poland were not acceptable.

Yalta marked a turning point in Soviet-American relations. President Roosevelt had hoped that an Allied victory and the creation of the United Nations would lead to a more peaceful world. Instead, as the war came to an end, the United States and the Soviet Union became increasingly hostile toward each other. The Cold War, an era of confrontation and competition between the nations, lasted from about 1946 to about 1990.

Soviet Concerns

As the war ended, Soviet leaders became concerned about security. They wanted to keep Germany weak and make sure that the countries between Germany and the Soviet Union were under Soviet control. Soviet leaders also believed that communism was a superior economic system that would eventually replace capitalism. They believed that the Soviet Union should encourage communism in other nations. They accepted Lenin's theory that capitalist countries would eventually try to destroy communism. This made them suspicious of capitalist nations.

American Economic Issues

While Soviet leaders focused on securing their borders, American leaders focused on economic problems. They believed that the Great Depression became so severe because nations reduced trade. They also believed that when nations stop trading, they are forced into war to get resources. By 1945, Roosevelt and his advisers were convinced that economic growth through world trade was the key to peace. They also thought that the free enterprise system, with private property rights and limited government intervention in the economy, was the best route to prosperity.

UN Responses to the War

In response to the atrocities of World War II, the United Nations held a General Assembly in December 1946. They passed a resolution that made genocide punishable internationally. The text of the Convention on the Prevention and Punishment of the Crime of Genocide became the first UN human rights treaty. Former First Lady Eleanor Roosevelt chaired a UN Commission on Human Rights in 1948. The international commission drafted the Universal Declaration of Human Rights, which promoted the inherent dignity of every human being and was a commitment to end discrimination.

☑ **PROGRESS CHECK**

Identifying What agreements at the Yalta Conference contributed to the rise of the Cold War?

Left to right: Churchill, Roosevelt, and Stalin. Leaders of the "Big Three" Allied nations met at the Yalta Conference to determine how to organize postwar Europe.

▶ CRITICAL THINKING

Predicting Consequences How might allowing Stalin to influence the political landscape of Eastern Europe affect that region's later foreign policy?

Truman Takes Control

GUIDING QUESTION *Why did the Potsdam Conference further increase tensions between the United States and the Soviet Union?*

Eleven days after confronting the Soviets on Poland, President Roosevelt died and Harry S. Truman became president. Truman was strongly anti-Communist. He believed World War II had begun because Britain had tried to appease Hitler. He did not intend to make that mistake with Stalin. "We must stand up to the Russians," he told Secretary of State Edward Stettinius the day he took office.

Ten days later, Truman did exactly that at a meeting with Soviet foreign minister Molotov. Truman immediately brought up Poland and demanded that Stalin hold free elections as he had promised at Yalta. Molotov took the unexpectedly strong message back to Stalin. The meeting marked an important shift in Soviet-American relations and set the stage for further confrontations.

The Potsdam Conference

In July 1945, with the war against Japan still raging, Truman finally met Stalin at Potsdam, near Berlin. Both men had come to Potsdam to work out a deal on Germany. Truman was now convinced that industry was critical to Germany's survival. Unless its economy was allowed to revive, the rest of Europe would never recover, and the German people might turn to communism out of desperation.

Stalin and his advisers were convinced they needed reparations from Germany. The war had devastated the Soviet economy. Soviet troops had begun stripping their zone in Germany of its machinery and equipment for use back home, but Stalin wanted Germany to pay much more.

At the conference, Truman took a firm stand against heavy reparations. He insisted that Germany's industry had to be allowed to recover. Truman suggested the Soviets take reparations from their zone, while the Allies allowed industry to revive in the other zones. Stalin opposed this idea since the Soviet zone was mostly agricultural. It could not provide all the reparations the Soviets wanted.

To get the Soviets to accept the agreement, Truman offered Stalin a small amount of industrial equipment from the other zones, but required the Soviets to pay for part of it with food shipments. He also offered to accept the new German-Polish border the Soviets had established.

Stalin did not like the proposal. At Potsdam, Truman learned of the successful U.S. atomic bomb tests. He hinted to Stalin that the United States had a new, powerful weapon. Stalin suspected Truman of trying to bully him into a deal. He thought the Americans wanted to limit reparations to keep the Soviets weak.

Despite his suspicions, Stalin had to accept the terms. American and British troops controlled Germany's industrial heartland, and there was no way for the Soviets to get any reparations without cooperating. The Potsdam Conference marked yet another increase in tensions.

The Iron Curtain Descends

Although Truman had won the argument over reparations, he had less success on other issues at Potsdam. The Soviets refused to make stronger commitments to uphold the Declaration of Liberated Europe.

The presence of the Soviet army in Eastern Europe ensured that pro-Soviet Communist governments would eventually be established in the nations of Poland, Romania, Bulgaria, Hungary, and Czechoslovakia.

TEXT: Winston Churchill and the Sinews of Peace Address, March 5, 1946, Westminster College, Fulton, Missouri. Reproduced with permission of Curtis Brown, London on behalf of the Estate of Sir Winston Churchill. Copyright © Winston S. Churchill.

Analyzing
PRIMARY SOURCES

Churchill on the Iron Curtain

❝A shadow has fallen upon the scenes so lately lighted by the Allied victory. . . . From Stettin in the Baltic to Trieste in the Adriatic, an iron curtain has descended across the continent. Behind that line lie all the capitals of the ancient states of Central and Eastern Europe. Warsaw, Berlin, Prague, Vienna, Budapest, Belgrade, Bucharest and Sofia, all these famous cities and the populations around them lie in what I must call the Soviet sphere, and all are subject in one form or another, not only to Soviet influence, but to a very high and, in some cases, increasing measure of control from Moscow.❞

—Winston Churchill, from an address to Westminster College, Fulton, Missouri, March 5, 1946

DBQ *ANALYZING PRIMARY SOURCES* What words and phrases does Churchill use to convey his negative view of what is happening?

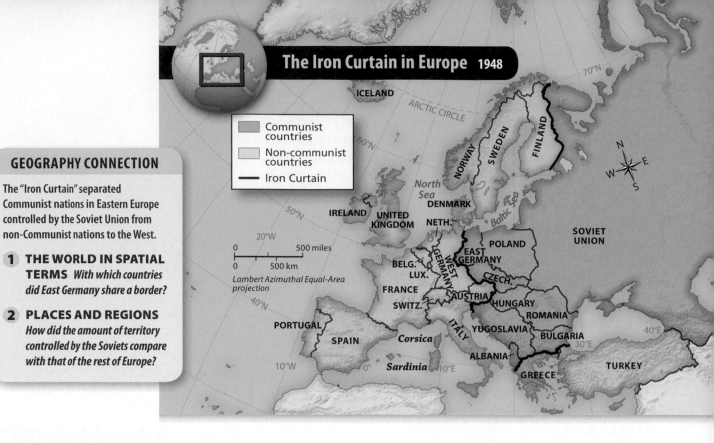

The Iron Curtain in Europe 1948

- Communist countries
- Non-communist countries
- — Iron Curtain

Lambert Azimuthal Equal-Area projection

GEOGRAPHY CONNECTION

The "Iron Curtain" separated Communist nations in Eastern Europe controlled by the Soviet Union from non-Communist nations to the West.

1 THE WORLD IN SPATIAL TERMS *With which countries did East Germany share a border?*

2 PLACES AND REGIONS *How did the amount of territory controlled by the Soviets compare with that of the rest of Europe?*

satellite nations nations politically and economically dominated or controlled by another more powerful country

The Communist countries of Eastern Europe came to be called **satellite nations** because they were controlled by the Soviets, as satellites are tied by gravity to the planets they orbit. Although not under direct Soviet control, these nations had to remain Communist and friendly to the Soviet Union. They also had to follow policies that the Soviets approved.

After watching the Communist takeover in Eastern Europe, the former British prime minister Winston Churchill coined a phrase to describe what had happened. On March 5, 1946, in a speech delivered in Fulton, Missouri, Churchill referred to an "iron curtain" falling across Eastern Europe. The press picked up the term, and for the next 43 years, it described the Communist nations of Eastern Europe and the Soviet Union. With the

Iron Curtain the political and military barrier that isolated Soviet-controlled countries of Eastern Europe after World War II

Iron Curtain separating Eastern Europe from the West, the World War II era had come to an end. The Cold War was about to begin.

✓ PROGRESS CHECK

Determining Cause and Effect How did the Potsdam Conference lead to greater tensions between the Americans and the Soviets?

LESSON 1 REVIEW

Reviewing Vocabulary

1. *Describing* What was the geographic relationship between Soviet satellite nations and the Iron Curtain?

Using Your Notes

2. *Determining Cause and Effect* Use your notes to write a few sentences about the effects of the major conferences of World War II.

Answering the Guiding Questions

3. *Summarizing* How did the conferences at Dumbarton Oaks and Yalta attempt to shape the postwar world?

4. *Explaining* Why did the Potsdam Conference further increase tensions between the United States and the Soviet Union?

Writing Activity

5. PERSONAL Suppose that you were a student who saw Churchill deliver his famous "iron curtain" speech. Write a letter to a friend summarizing Churchill's ideas and giving your own opinions about the rising tensions between the Soviet Union and the West.

networks

There's More Online!

☑ **BIOGRAPHY** Douglas MacArthur

☑ **BIOGRAPHY** Mao Zedong

☑ **IMAGE** Berlin Airlift

☑ **IMAGE** Harry S. Truman

☑ **VIDEO** Early Cold War Years

☑ **VIDEO** MacArthur's Farewell Speech

☑ **INTERACTIVE SELF-CHECK QUIZ**

Reading **HELP**DESK

Content Vocabulary

• **containment**
• **limited war**

Academic Vocabulary

• **insecurity** • **initially**

TAKING NOTES: *Organizing*

ACTIVITY As you read, use a graphic organizer similar to the one below to list early conflicts between the Soviet Union and the United States.

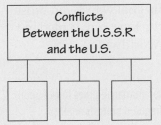

Conflicts Between the U.S.S.R. and the U.S.

LESSON 2
The Early Cold War Years

ESSENTIAL QUESTIONS • *How did the Cold War shape postwar international relations?* • *How did Cold War tensions affect American society?*

IT MATTERS BECAUSE

President Truman worked to contain communism by supporting Greece, Iran, and West Germany. When Communist North Korea invaded South Korea, Truman and the United Nations sent troops to aid South Korea.

Containing Communism

GUIDING QUESTION *What was the policy of containment?*

Despite growing tensions with the Soviet Union, many American officials continued to believe cooperation with the Soviets was possible. In late 1945 the foreign ministers of the former Allies met first in London, then in Moscow, to discuss the future of Europe and Asia. Although both British and American officials pushed for free elections in Eastern Europe, the Soviets refused to budge.

The Long Telegram

Increasingly exasperated by the Soviets' refusal to cooperate, officials at the U.S. State Department asked the American Embassy in Moscow to explain Soviet behavior. On February 22, 1946, diplomat George Kennan responded with what became known as the Long Telegram—a message, thousands of words long, explaining his views of the Soviets. According to Kennan, the Soviets' view of the world came from a traditional "Russian sense of **insecurity**" and fear of the West, intensified by the communist ideas of Lenin and Stalin. Because Communists believed they were in a historical struggle against capitalism, Kennan argued, it was impossible to reach any permanent settlement with them.

Kennan proposed what became basic American policy throughout the Cold War: "a long-term, patient but firm and vigilant **containment** of Russian expansive tendencies." In Kennan's opinion, the Soviet system had major economic and political weaknesses. If the United States could keep the Soviets from expanding their power, it would only be a matter of time before their system would fall apart, beating communism without going to war. The Long Telegram

insecurity the state of not being confident or sure

containment the policy or process of preventing the expansion of a hostile power

circulated widely in Truman's administration and became the basis for the administration's policy of containment—keeping communism within its present territory through diplomatic, economic, and military actions.

Crisis in Iran

While Truman's administration discussed Kennan's ideas, a series of crises erupted during the spring and summer of 1946. These crises seemed to prove that Kennan was right about the Soviets. The first crisis began in Iran.

During World War II, the United States had troops in southern Iran while Soviet troops held northern Iran to secure a supply line from the Persian Gulf. After the war, instead of withdrawing as promised, the Soviet troops remained in northern Iran. Stalin then began demanding access to Iran's oil supplies. To increase the pressure, Soviet troops helped local Communists in northern Iran establish a separate government.

American officials saw these actions as a Soviet push into the Middle East. The secretary of state sent Stalin a strong message demanding that Soviet forces withdraw. At the same time, the battleship USS *Missouri* sailed into the eastern Mediterranean. The pressure seemed to work. Soviet forces withdrew, having been promised a joint Soviet-Iranian oil company, although the Iranian parliament later rejected the plan.

The Truman Doctrine

Frustrated in Iran, Stalin turned northwest to Turkey. There, the straits of the Dardanelles were a vital route from Soviet ports on the Black Sea to the Mediterranean. For centuries Russia had wanted to control this strategic route. In August 1946, Stalin demanded joint control of the Dardanelles with Turkey.

Presidential adviser Dean Acheson saw this move as part of a Soviet plan to control the Middle East. He advised Truman to make a show of force. The president ordered the new aircraft carrier *Franklin D. Roosevelt* to join the *Missouri* in protecting Turkey and the eastern Mediterranean.

Meanwhile, Britain tried to help Greece. In August 1946, Greek Communists launched a guerrilla war against the Greek government. British troops helped fight the guerrillas, but in February 1947, Britain informed the United States that it could no longer afford to help Greece due to Britain's weakened postwar economy.

Shortly after, Truman went before Congress to ask for $400 million to fight Communist aggression in Greece and Turkey. His speech outlined a policy that became known as the Truman Doctrine. Its goal was to aid those who worked to resist being controlled by others. In the long run, it pledged the United States to fight the spread of communism worldwide.

President Truman signs the Foreign Aid Assistance Act, providing aid to Greece and Turkey. The policy of supporting nations resisting Communist pressure became known as the Truman Doctrine.

▶ **CRITICAL THINKING**
Identifying Central Issues What was the main purpose of the Truman Doctrine?

PRIMARY SOURCE

❝The peoples of a number of countries of the world have recently had totalitarian regimes forced upon them against their will. The Government of the United States has made frequent protests against coercion and intimidation, in violation of the Yalta agreement in Poland, Romania, and Bulgaria. At the present moment in world history nearly every nation must choose between alternative ways of life. The choice is too often not a free one. . . . I believe that it must be the policy of the United States to support free peoples who are resisting attempted subjugation by armed minorities or by outside pressures. I believe that we must assist free peoples to work out their own destinies in their own way.❞

—President Truman, from his address to Congress, March 12, 1947

The Marshall Plan

Meanwhile, postwar Western Europe faced grave problems. Economies were ruined, people faced starvation, and political chaos was at hand. In June 1947, Secretary of State George C. Marshall proposed the European

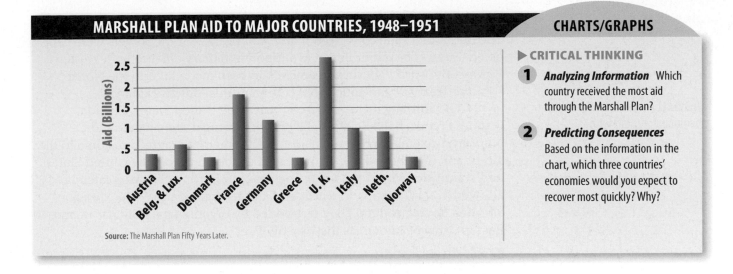

▶ **CRITICAL THINKING**

1 *Analyzing Information* Which country received the most aid through the Marshall Plan?

2 *Predicting Consequences* Based on the information in the chart, which three countries' economies would you expect to recover most quickly? Why?

Source: The Marshall Plan Fifty Years Later.

Recovery Program, or Marshall Plan, which would give European nations American aid to rebuild their economies. Truman saw both the Marshall Plan and the Truman Doctrine as essential for containment. Marshall offered help to all nations planning a recovery program.

Although the Marshall Plan was offered to the Soviet Union and its satellite nations, the Soviets rejected it and developed their own economic program. This action further separated Europe into competing regions. The Marshall Plan pumped billions of dollars in supplies, machinery, and food into Western Europe. The region's recovery weakened the appeal of communism and opened new markets for trade.

In his 1949 Inaugural Address, Truman proposed assistance for underdeveloped countries outside the war zone. The Point Four Program aimed to provide them with "scientific advances and industrial progress" for their improvement and growth. The Department of State administered the program until its merger with other foreign aid programs in 1953.

The Berlin Airlift

Truman and his advisers believed Western Europe's prosperity depended on Germany's recovery. The Soviets, however, still wanted Germany to pay reparations. This dispute brought the nations to the brink of war. By early 1948, American officials had concluded that the Soviets were trying to undermine Germany's economy. In response, the United States, Britain, and France merged their German zones and allowed the Germans to have their own government, creating the Federal Republic of Germany, which became known as West Germany. They also agreed to merge their zones in Berlin and make West Berlin part of West Germany. The Soviet zone became the German Democratic Republic, or East Germany. West Germany was mostly independent but not allowed to have a military.

The creation of West Germany convinced the Soviets they would never get the reparations they wanted. In June 1948, Soviet troops blockaded West Berlin hoping to force the United States to reconsider its decision or abandon West Berlin. Truman sent bombers capable of carrying atomic weapons to bases in Britain. Hoping to avoid war with the Soviets, he ordered the air force to fly supplies into Berlin rather than troops.

The Berlin Airlift began in June 1948 and continued through the spring of 1949, bringing in more than two million tons of supplies to the city. Stalin finally lifted the blockade on May 12, 1949. The airlift symbolized American determination to contain communism and not give in to Soviet demands.

The Creation of NATO

The Berlin blockade convinced many Americans that the Soviets were bent on conquest. The public began to support a military alliance with Western Europe. By April 1949, an agreement had been made to form the North Atlantic Treaty Organization (NATO)—a mutual defense alliance.

NATO **initially** included 12 countries: the United States, Canada, Britain, France, Italy, Belgium, Denmark, Portugal, the Netherlands, Norway, Luxembourg, and Iceland. NATO members agreed to come to the aid of any member who was attacked. For the first time, the United States had committed itself to maintaining peace in Europe. Six years later, NATO allowed West Germany to rearm and join its organization. This decision alarmed Soviet leaders. They responded by organizing a military alliance in Eastern Europe known as the Warsaw Pact.

initially of or relating to the beginning; to start with

☑ **PROGRESS CHECK**

Identifying Central Issues What was the main idea behind containment?

Developments in Asia and the Korean War

GUIDING QUESTION *Why was the Korean War a major turning point in the Cold War?*

The Cold War eventually spread beyond Europe. Conflicts also emerged in Asia, where events in China and Korea brought about a new attitude toward Japan and sent American troops back into battle in Asia less than five years after World War II had ended.

The Chinese Revolution

In China, Communist forces led by Mao Zedong had been struggling against the Nationalist government led by Chiang Kai-shek since the late 1920s. During World War II, the two sides suspended their war to resist Japanese occupation. With the end of World War II, however, civil war broke out again. Although Mao and the Communist forces made great gains, neither side could win nor agree to a compromise.

GEOGRAPHY CONNECTION

NATO was formed as an alliance to defend against an outside attack. In response, the Soviet Union created its own alliance known as the Warsaw Pact.

1 HUMAN SYSTEMS
Which nations are the founding members of NATO?

2 PLACES AND REGIONS *Why was West Germany not a part of the original group of NATO nations?*

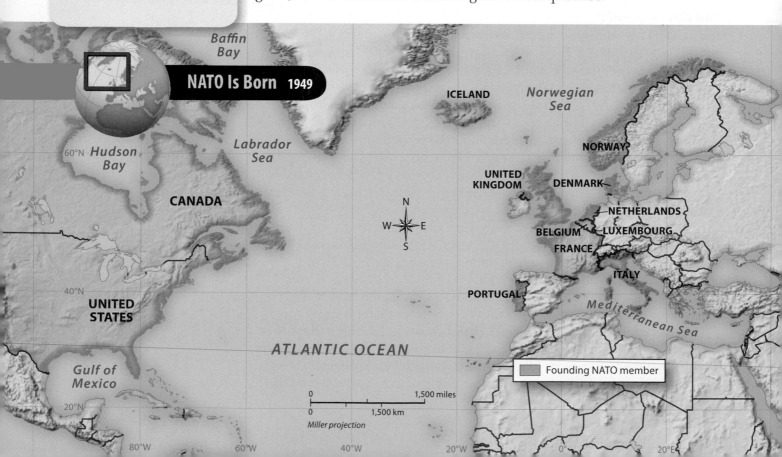

NATO Is Born 1949

Founding NATO member

To prevent a Communist revolution in Asia, the United States sent the Nationalist government $2 billion in aid beginning in the mid-1940s. The Nationalists, however, squandered this advantage through poor military planning and corruption. By 1949 the Communists had captured the Chinese capital of Beijing, while support for the Nationalists declined.

In August 1949, the U.S. State Department discontinued aid to the Chinese Nationalists. The defeated Nationalists then fled to the small island of Formosa (now called Taiwan). The victorious Communists established the People's Republic of China in October 1949.

China's fall to communism shocked Americans. To make matters worse, in September 1949 the Soviet Union announced that it had successfully tested its first atomic weapon. Then, early in 1950, the People's Republic of China and the Soviet Union signed a treaty of friendship and alliance. Many Western leaders feared that China and the Soviet Union would support communist revolutions in other nations.

The United States kept formal diplomatic relations with only the Nationalist Chinese in Taiwan. It used its veto power in the UN Security Council to keep representatives of the new Communist People's Republic of China out of the UN, allowing the Nationalists to retain their seat.

Korea's Border, 1950 and 1953

▶ **CRITICAL THINKING**

Physical Systems What geographical feature forms the border between China and North Korea?

New Policies in Japan

The Chinese revolution brought about a significant change in American policy toward Japan. At the end of World War II, General Douglas MacArthur had taken charge of occupied Japan. His mission was to introduce democracy and keep Japan from threatening war again. Once the United States lost China as its chief ally in Asia, it adopted policies to encourage the rapid recovery of Japan's industrial economy. Just as the United States viewed West Germany as the key to defending all of Europe against communism, it saw Japan as the key to defending Asia.

The Korean War

At the end of World War II, American and Soviet forces entered Korea to disarm the Japanese troops stationed there. The Allies divided Korea at the 38th parallel of latitude. Soviet troops controlled the north, while American troops controlled the south.

As the Cold War began, talks to reunify Korea broke down. A Communist Korean government was organized in the north, while an American-backed government controlled the south. Both governments claimed authority over Korea, and border clashes were common. The Soviets provided military aid to the North Koreans, who quickly built an army. On June 25, 1950, North Korean troops invaded the south, driving back the poorly equipped South Korean forces.

Truman saw the Communist invasion of South Korea as a test of the containment policy and ordered American naval and air power into action. He then called on the United Nations to act. Because the Soviet Union was boycotting the Security Council over its China policy, Truman succeeded. With the pledge of UN troops, he ordered General MacArthur to send American troops from Japan to Korea.

The American and South Korean troops were driven back into a small pocket of territory near the port of Pusan. Inside the "Pusan perimeter," troops stubbornly resisted the North Koreans, buying time for MacArthur to organize reinforcements.

Soldiers of the U.S. 2nd Infantry Division man a machine gun near the Chongchon River in Korea, November 20, 1950.

▶ **CRITICAL THINKING**

Identifying Central Issues What was the objective of the United States during the Korean War?

limited war a war fought with limited commitment of resources to achieve a limited objective, such as containing communism

On September 15, 1950, MacArthur ordered a daring invasion behind enemy lines at the port of Inchon. The Inchon landing took the North Koreans by surprise. Within weeks they were in full retreat back across the 38th parallel. Truman then gave the order to pursue the North Koreans beyond the 38th parallel. MacArthur pushed the North Koreans north to the Yalu River, the border with China.

China Enters the War The Communist People's Republic of China saw the advancing UN troops as a threat and warned them to halt their advance. When warnings were ignored, Chinese forces crossed the Yalu River in November. Hundreds of thousands of Chinese troops flooded across the border, driving the UN forces back across the 38th parallel.

As his troops fell back, an angry MacArthur demanded approval to expand the war against China. He asked for a blockade of Chinese ports, the use of Chiang Kai-shek's Nationalist forces, and the bombing of Chinese cities with atomic weapons.

Truman Fires MacArthur President Truman refused MacArthur's demands because he did not want to expand the war into China or to use the atomic bomb. MacArthur persisted, publicly criticizing the president and arguing that it was a mistake to keep the war limited. "There is no substitute for victory," MacArthur insisted, by which he meant that if the United States was going to go to war, it should use all of its power to win. A limited war was a form of appeasement, he argued, and appeasement "begets new and bloodier war."

Determined to maintain control of policy and show that he commanded the military, an exasperated Truman fired MacArthur for insubordination in April 1951. Later, in private conversation, Truman explained: "I was sorry to have to reach a parting of the way with the big man in Asia, but he asked for it and I had to give it to him."

MacArthur, who remained popular despite being fired, returned home to parades and a hero's welcome. Many Americans criticized the president. Congress and military leaders, however, supported his decision and his Korean strategy. American policy in Asia remained committed to **limited war**—a war fought to achieve a limited objective, such as containing communism. Truman later explained his position:

PRIMARY SOURCE

❝The Kremlin [Soviet Union] is trying, and has been trying for a long time, to drive a wedge between us and the other nations. It wants to see us isolated. It wants to see us distrusted. It wants to see us feared and hated by our allies. Our allies agree with us in the course we are following. They do not believe we should take the initiative to widen the conflict in the Far East. If the United States were to widen the conflict, we might well have to go it alone.❞

—from an address to the Civil Defense Conference, May 7, 1951

Armistice Ends Fighting By mid-1951, UN forces had pushed the Chinese and North Korean forces back across the 38th parallel. The war settled into a series of relatively small battles over hills and other local objectives. In July 1951, peace negotiations began at Panmunjom. As talks continued, the war became increasingly unpopular in the United States. After Dwight D. Eisenhower was elected to the presidency in 1952, the former general traveled to Korea to talk with commanders and their troops. He became determined to bring the war to an end.

PHOTO: Bettmann/CORBIS

NOT A GENERAL'S JOB

POLITICAL CARTOONS

In 1951 President Truman fired General Douglas MacArthur over disagreements about how to conduct the Korean War.

This cartoon suggests that General MacArthur had overstepped his authority in Korea.

▶ **CRITICAL THINKING**

1 *Making Inferences* What does the cartoon imply MacArthur was trying to do in Asia?

2 *Analyzing Primary Sources* Is this cartoon supportive of General MacArthur or critical of him? Explain.

Eisenhower quietly hinted to the Chinese that the United States might use a nuclear attack in Korea. The threat seemed to work. In July 1953, negotiators signed an armistice. The battle line between the two sides in Korea, which was very near the prewar boundary, became the border between North Korea and South Korea. A "demilitarized zone" (DMZ) separated them. American troops are still based in Korea, helping to defend South Korea's border. There has never been a peace treaty to end the war. More than 33,600 American soldiers died in action, and over 20,600 died in accidents or from disease.

Changes in Policy The Korean War marked a turning point in the Cold War. Until 1950, the United States had preferred to use political pressure and economic aid to contain communism. After the Korean War began, the United States embarked on a major military buildup. The war also helped expand the Cold War to Asia. Before 1950, American efforts to contain communism focused on Europe. With the Korean War, the nation became more militarily involved in Asia. By 1954, the United States had signed defense agreements with Japan, South Korea, and Taiwan. The United States also formed the Southeast Asia Treaty Organization (SEATO) in 1954. Aid also began flowing to French forces fighting Communists in Vietnam.

☑ **PROGRESS CHECK**

Analyzing How did the Korean War change the course of the Cold War?

LESSON 2 REVIEW

Reviewing Vocabulary
1. *Defining* What is the defining feature of limited war?

Using Your Notes
2. *Summarizing* Review the notes you completed during the lesson to write a paragraph summarizing the major conflicts between the Soviet Union and the United States during the early years of the Cold War.

Answering the Guiding Questions
3. *Explaining* What was the policy of containment?

4. *Describing* Why was the Korean War a major turning point in the Cold War?

Writing Activity
5. **PERSUASIVE** Write a letter to the editor of a newspaper explaining why you agree or disagree with President Truman's firing of General MacArthur.

netw⦿rks

There's More Online!

☑ **BIOGRAPHY** Alger Hiss

☑ **BIOGRAPHY** Julius & Ethel Rosenberg

☑ **GRAPHIC NOVEL** "Seeking Shelter"

☑ **IMAGE** House Un-American Activities Committee

☑ **PRIMARY SOURCE** Red Scare

☑ **VIDEO** Army-McCarthy Hearings

☑ **VIDEO** Cold War and American Society

☑ **INTERACTIVE SELF-CHECK QUIZ**

Reading HELPDESK

Content Vocabulary

- **subversion**
- **loyalty review program**
- **perjury**
- **censure**
- **fallout**

Academic Vocabulary

- **manipulate** • **convince**

TAKING NOTES: *Outlining*

ACTIVITY As you read, summarize the lesson content by using the major headings to create an outline similar to the one below.

> The Cold War and American Society
> I. A New Red Scare
>   A. The Truman Loyalty Review Program
>   B.
>   C.

LESSON 3
The Cold War and American Society

ESSENTIAL QUESTIONS • *How did the Cold War shape postwar international relations?* • *How did Cold War tensions affect American society?*

IT MATTERS BECAUSE
Fearing subversive activity, the government tried to root out Communists in government, Hollywood, and labor unions, while Americans learned to live with the threat of nuclear attack.

A New Red Scare

GUIDING QUESTION *How did the post–World War II Red Scare compare and contrast with the one that followed World War I?*

During the 1950s, rumors and accusations spawned fears that Communists were trying to take over the world. The Red Scare began in September 1945, when a clerk named Igor Gouzenko walked out of the Soviet Embassy in Ottawa, Canada, and defected. Gouzenko carried documents showing a Soviet effort to infiltrate government agencies in Canada and the United States, with the specific goal of obtaining information about the atomic bomb. The case stunned Americans. It implied that spies had infiltrated the American government. Soon the search for spies escalated into a general fear of Communist **subversion,** or effort to weaken a society and overthrow its government.

The Truman Loyalty Review Program

In early 1947, President Truman established a **loyalty review program** to screen all federal employees. Truman's action seemed to confirm suspicions that Communists had infiltrated the government and so added to fears that communism was sweeping the nation. Between 1947 and 1951, more than six million federal employees were screened for loyalty—a term difficult to define. A person might become a suspect for reading certain books, belonging to various groups, traveling overseas, or seeing certain foreign films. The Federal Bureau of Investigation (FBI) scrutinized some 14,000 people. About 2,000 quit their jobs, many under pressure. Another 212 were fired for "questionable loyalty," despite a lack of actual evidence.

HUAC and Anti-Communist Investigations

FBI director J. Edgar Hoover remained unsatisfied. In 1947 he went before the House Un-American Activities Committee (HUAC). Formed in 1938 to investigate subversive activities in the United States, HUAC had been a minor committee before Hoover's involvement. He urged HUAC to hold public hearings on Communist subversion to expose not just Communists but also "Communist sympathizers" and "fellow travelers." Under Hoover's leadership, the FBI sent agents to infiltrate groups suspected of subversion and wiretapped thousands of telephones.

Hollywood on Trial One of HUAC's first hearings in 1947 focused on the film industry as a cultural force that Communists might **manipulate** to spread their ideas and influence. Future American president Ronald Reagan was head of the Screen Actors Guild at the time and, when called before HUAC, he testified that there were Communists in Hollywood. During the hearings, ten screenwriters, known as the "Hollywood Ten," used their Fifth Amendment right to protect themselves from self-incrimination and refused to testify. The incident led producers to blacklist, or agree not to hire, anyone who was believed to be a Communist or who refused to cooperate with the committee. The blacklist created an atmosphere of distrust and fear.

Alger Hiss In 1948 Whittaker Chambers, a magazine editor and former Communist Party member, told HUAC that several government officials were also former Communists or spies. One official Chambers named was Alger Hiss, a diplomat who had served in Roosevelt's administration, attended the Yalta Conference, and helped organize the United Nations. Hiss sued Chambers for libel, but Chambers testified that, in 1937 and 1938, Hiss had given him secret State Department documents. Hiss denied being either a spy or a member of the Communist Party, and he also denied ever having known Chambers.

The committee was ready to drop the investigation until California representative Richard Nixon **convinced** his colleagues to continue the hearings to determine who had lied. Chambers produced copies of secret documents, along with microfilm that he had hidden in a hollow pumpkin. These "pumpkin papers," Chambers claimed, proved Hiss was lying. A jury agreed and convicted Hiss of **perjury,** or lying under oath.

The Rosenbergs Another spy case centered on accusations that American Communists had sold secrets about the atomic bomb to the Soviets to help them produce a bomb in 1949. In 1950 the hunt for spies led the FBI to arrest Julius and Ethel Rosenberg, a New York couple who were members of the Communist Party. The government charged them with spying for the Soviets.

The Rosenbergs denied the charges but were condemned to death for espionage. Many people believed that they were simply victims caught in the wave of anti-Communist frenzy. Appeals and pleas for clemency failed, however, and the Rosenbergs were executed in June 1953.

Project Venona In 1946 American and British cryptographers, working for a project code-named "Venona," cracked the Soviet Union's spy code, enabling them to read approximately 3,000 messages between Moscow and the United States collected during the Cold War. These messages confirmed extensive Soviet spying and ongoing efforts to steal nuclear secrets. The government did not reveal Project Venona's existence until 1995. The Venona documents provided strong evidence that the Rosenbergs were indeed guilty.

subversion a systematic attempt to overthrow a government by using persons working secretly from within

loyalty review program a policy established by President Truman that authorized the screening of all federal employees to determine their loyalty to the U.S. government

manipulate to operate or arrange manually to achieve a desired effect

convince to bring to belief, consent, or a course of action

perjury lying when one has sworn under oath to tell the truth

Although he had led the effort to develop the atomic bomb, scientist J. Robert Oppenheimer's left-wing views and opposition to the hydrogen bomb led to the suspension of his security clearance and controversial public hearings.

▶ **CRITICAL THINKING**
Drawing Conclusions Why were people suspicious of Oppenheimer?

**Joseph McCarthy
(1908–1957)**

When Wisconsin politician Joseph McCarthy first ran for Senate in 1946, he claimed his opponent was "communistically inclined." His later accusations of Communist subversion made him a national figure. Between 1950 and 1954, McCarthy made headlines for his investigations of government departments and figures, despite his inability to build a solid case against anyone. His often wild accusations became the hallmark of McCarthyism.

▶ **CRITICAL THINKING**
Identifying Central Issues What was the larger threat behind allowing McCarthyism to spread?

The Red Scare Spreads

Many state and local governments, universities, businesses, unions, churches, and private groups also began efforts to find Communists. The University of California required its faculty to take loyalty oaths and fired 157 who refused. Many Catholic groups became anti-Communist and urged members to identify Communists within the Church. The Taft-Hartley Act of 1947 required union leaders to take oaths saying that they were not Communists. Many union leaders did not object. Instead, they launched efforts to purge their own organizations, eventually expelling 11 unions that refused to remove Communist leaders.

✓ **PROGRESS CHECK**

Comparing and Contrasting What was one way that the Red Scare of the 1950s and the Red Scare of the 1920s were similar?

McCarthyism

GUIDING QUESTION *Why did many Americans believe Senator McCarthy's accusations?*

In 1949 the Red Scare intensified as the Soviet Union successfully tested an atomic bomb, and China fell to communism. To many Americans, these events seemed to prove that the United States was losing the Cold War.

In February 1950, little-known senator Joseph R. McCarthy gave a speech to a Republican women's group in West Virginia. Halfway through his speech, McCarthy made a surprising statement when he claimed:

PRIMARY SOURCE

❝While I cannot take the time to name all the men in the State Department who have been named as members of the Communist Party and members of a spy ring, I have here in my hand a list of 205 that were known to the Secretary of State as being members of the Communist Party and who nevertheless are still working and shaping the policy of the State Department.❞

—quoted in *The Fifties*, 1993

The Associated Press sent the statement nationwide. Reporters at an airport asked McCarthy to see his list. McCarthy replied that he would be happy to show it to them, but unfortunately, it was in his bag on the plane. In fact, the list never appeared. McCarthy, however, continued making charges.

McCarthy proclaimed that Communists were a danger at home and abroad. He distributed a booklet accusing Democratic Party leaders of corruption and of protecting Communists. McCarthy often targeted Secretary of State Dean Acheson, calling him incompetent and a tool of Stalin. He also accused George C. Marshall, former army chief of staff and secretary of state, of disloyalty. The prevailing anxiety about communism made many Americans willing to accept McCarthy's claims.

The McCarran Act

In 1950, with McCarthy and others arousing fears of Communist spies, Congress passed the Internal Security Act, also called the McCarran Act. The act made it illegal to attempt to establish a totalitarian government in the United States, and required all Communist-related organizations to publish their records and register with the United States attorney general. Communists could not have passports and, in cases of a national emergency, could be arrested and detained. Unwilling to punish people for their opinions, Truman vetoed the bill, but Congress easily overrode his veto in 1950. Later Supreme Court cases limited the act's scope.

McCarthy's Rise and Fall

In 1953 McCarthy became chairman of the Senate subcommittee on investigations, which forced government officials to testify about alleged Communist influences. Investigations became witch-hunts—searches for disloyalty based on weak evidence and irrational fears. McCarthy's tactic of damaging reputations with vague, unfounded charges became known as McCarthyism.

McCarthy's sensational accusations put him in the headlines, and the press quoted him often and widely. He badgered witnesses and then refused to accept their answers. His tactics left a cloud of suspicion that he and others interpreted as guilt. People were afraid to challenge him.

In 1954 McCarthy began to look for Soviet spies in the United States Army. During weeks of televised hearings, millions of Americans watched McCarthy question and bully officers, harassing them about trivial details and accusing them of misconduct. His popular support began to fade.

Finally, to strike back at the army's lawyer, Joseph Welch, McCarthy brought up the past of a young lawyer in Welch's firm who had been a member of a Communist-front organization while in law school. Welch, who was fully aware of the young man's past, exploded at McCarthy for possibly ruining the young man's career: "Until this moment, I think I never really gauged your cruelty or your recklessness. . . . You have done enough. Have you no sense of decency, sir, at long last? Have you left no sense of decency?"

Spectators cheered. Welch had said what many Americans had been thinking. Later that year, the Senate passed a vote of **censure,** or formal disapproval, against McCarthy. Although he remained in the Senate, McCarthy had lost all influence. He died in 1957.

✔ **PROGRESS CHECK**

Assessing Why were people prepared to accept McCarthy's claims?

Life During the Early Cold War

GUIDING QUESTION *How did fears of nuclear war affect American society?*

The Red Scare and the spread of nuclear weapons had a profound impact on American life in the 1950s. Fears of communism and war affected both ordinary Americans and government leaders.

Facing the Bomb

Americans were shocked when the Soviets successfully tested the more powerful hydrogen bomb, or H-bomb, in 1953. The United States had tested its own H-bomb less than a year earlier. Americans prepared for a surprise

Analyzing
SUPREME COURT CASES

Watkins v. United States, 1957

In 1954 labor organizer John Watkins testified before HUAC. He agreed to discuss his connections with the Communist Party and to identify people who were still members, but refused to talk about those who were no longer members. Watkins received a misdemeanor conviction for refusing to answer questions "pertinent to the question under inquiry." In 1957 he appealed his case to the Supreme Court. In a 6-to-1 decision, the Supreme Court held that the activities of HUAC during its investigations were beyond the scope of the stated aims of the committee, as well as the authority of congressional powers.

▶ **CRITICAL THINKING**
Constructing Arguments What argument would you make in support of John Watkins's position?

Some Americans invested in personal bomb shelters stocked with food, believing it would allow them to survive a bomb blast.

▶ **CRITICAL THINKING**
Interpreting Significance Study the facial expressions of the members of this family. What can you interpret about the likely significance of the bomb shelter for this family?

CANNED FOOD

censure to express a formal disapproval of an action

fallout radioactive particles dispersed by a nuclear explosion

Soviet attack. Schools created bomb shelters and held bomb drills to teach students to "duck-and-cover" to protect themselves from a nuclear bomb blast.

Although "duck-and-cover" might have made people feel safer, it would not have protected them from nuclear radiation. Experts have noted that for every person killed outright by a nuclear blast, four more would die later from **fallout,** the radiation left over after a blast. To protect themselves, some families built backyard fallout shelters.

Popular Culture in the Cold War

As worries about nuclear war and Communist infiltration filled the public imagination, Cold War themes soon appeared in films, plays, television, the titles of dance tunes, and popular fiction. Matt Cvetic, an FBI undercover informant who secretly infiltrated the Communist Party, captivated readers with reports in the *Saturday Evening Post* in 1950. His story was later made into the movie *I Was a Communist for the FBI* (1951). Another film, *Walk East on Beacon* (1952), features the FBI's activities in a spy case. In 1953 Arthur Miller's thinly veiled criticism of the Communist witch-hunts, *The Crucible,* appeared on Broadway. The play remains popular today as a cautionary tale about how hysteria can lead to false accusations.

In 1953 a weekly television series, *I Led Three Lives,* about an undercover FBI counterspy who was also a Communist Party official, debuted. Popular tunes such as "Atomic Boogie" and "Atom Bomb Baby" played on the radio. The next year, author Philip Wylie published *Tomorrow!,* a novel describing the horrific effects of nuclear war on an unprepared American city. Wylie wrote his novel to educate the public about the horrors of atomic war.

One of the most famous and enduring works of this period is John Hersey's nonfiction book *Hiroshima.* Originally published as the August 1946 edition of *The New Yorker* magazine, the book provides six firsthand accounts of the United States dropping the atomic bomb on Hiroshima, Japan. Not only did it make some Americans question the use of the bomb, but *Hiroshima* also underscored the real, personal horrors of a nuclear attack.

At the same time, the country was enjoying postwar prosperity and optimism. That spirit, combined with McCarthyism, fears of Communist infiltration, and the threat of atomic attack, made the early 1950s a time of contrasts. As the 1952 election approached, Americans were looking for someone or something that would make them feel more secure.

☑ **PROGRESS CHECK**

Analyzing How did the Cold War affect popular culture in the 1950s?

Thinking Like a
HISTORIAN

Determining Cause and Effect

The United States experienced two major Red Scares during the twentieth century: one during the 1920s, and one during the 1950s. Both of these scares occurred shortly after a major nation—first Russia, and later China—adopted a Communist form of government. As a historian, find the effect these scares had on American society and determine if they can be related.

LESSON 3 REVIEW

Reviewing Vocabulary

1. *Evaluating* What was the significance of Truman's loyalty review program?

2. *Identifying Cause and Effect* What was the effect of the Senate's vote of censure against McCarthy?

Using Your Notes

3. *Summarizing* Use the notes you completed during the lesson to write a paragraph summarizing how the early years of the Cold War affected American society.

Answering the Guiding Questions

4. *Comparing and Contrasting* How did the post–World War II Red Scare compare and contrast with the one that followed World War I?

5. *Drawing Inferences* Why did many Americans believe Senator McCarthy's accusations?

6. *Describing* How did fears of nuclear war affect American society?

Writing Activity

7. PERSONAL Consider the historical events surrounding the early Cold War era. Were HUAC and Senator McCarthy justified in investigating people who were suspected of being Communists?

LESSON 4
Eisenhower's Cold War Policies

ESSENTIAL QUESTIONS · *How did the Cold War shape postwar international relations?* · *How did Cold War tensions affect American society?*

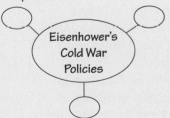
IT MATTERS BECAUSE
President Eisenhower believed developing new technology to deliver nuclear weapons would help prevent war. He also directed the CIA to use covert operations in the struggle to contain communism.

Massive Retaliation

GUIDING QUESTION *How were the policies of massive retaliation and brinkmanship different from previous military policies?*

By the end of 1952, many Americans were ready for a change in leadership. The Cold War had much to do with that attitude. Many people believed that Truman's foreign policy was not working. The Soviet Union had tested an atomic bomb and consolidated its hold on Eastern Europe. China had fallen to communism, and American troops were fighting in Korea.

Tired of the criticism and uncertain he could win, Truman decided not to run again. The Democrats nominated Adlai Stevenson, governor of Illinois. The Republicans chose Dwight D. Eisenhower, the general who had organized the D-Day invasion. Stevenson had little chance against a national hero who had helped win World War II. Americans wanted someone they could trust to lead the nation in the Cold War. Eisenhower won in a landslide.

"More Bang for the Buck"
The Cold War shaped Eisenhower's thinking from the moment he took office. He was convinced that the key to victory was not simply military might but also a strong economy. The United States had to show the world that the free enterprise system could produce a better society than communism. At the same time, economic prosperity would prevent Communists from gaining support in the United States and protect society from subversion.

As a professional soldier, Eisenhower knew the costs associated with large-scale conventional war. Preparing for that kind of warfare, he believed, was too expensive. "We cannot defend the

In 1955 the U.S. Air Force unveiled the huge B-52 bomber, which could fly across continents to drop nuclear bombs. The B-52 is still in use today.

▶ **CRITICAL THINKING**
Analyzing Cause and Effect How did Eisenhower's nuclear strategy lead to the development of new aircraft technology?

massive retaliation a policy of threatening a massive response, including the use of nuclear weapons, against a Communist state trying to seize a peaceful state by force

brinkmanship the practice of pushing a dangerous situation to the limit to force an opponent to back down

nation in a way which will exhaust our economy," the president declared. Instead of maintaining a large and expensive army, the nation "must be prepared to use atomic weapons in all forms." Nuclear weapons, he said, gave "more bang for the buck."

The Korean War had convinced Eisenhower that the United States could not contain communism by fighting a series of small wars. Such wars were unpopular and too expensive. Instead, wars had to be prevented in the first place. The best way to do that seemed to be to threaten to use nuclear weapons. This policy came to be called **massive retaliation.**

The new policy enabled Eisenhower to cut military spending from around $50 billion to about $34 billion by reducing the size of the army, which was expensive to maintain. He then increased the U.S. nuclear arsenal from about 1,000 bombs in 1953 to about 18,000 bombs in 1961.

Brinkmanship

President Eisenhower's willingness to threaten nuclear war to maintain peace worried some people. Critics called this **brinkmanship**—the willingness to go to the brink of war to force the other side to back down—and argued that it was too dangerous. During several crises, however, President Eisenhower felt compelled to threaten nuclear war.

The Taiwan Crisis Shortly after the Korean War ended, a new crisis erupted in Asia. Although Communists had taken power in mainland China, Chinese Nationalists still controlled Taiwan and several small islands along China's coast. In the fall of 1954, China threatened to seize two of the islands. Eisenhower saw Taiwan as part of the "anti-Communist barrier" in Asia that needed to be protected at all costs.

When China began shelling the islands and announced that Taiwan would be liberated, Eisenhower asked Congress to authorize the use of force to defend Taiwan. He then warned that an attack on Taiwan would be resisted by U.S. naval forces and hinted that they would use nuclear weapons to stop an invasion. Soon afterward, China backed down.

The Suez Crisis The following year, a serious crisis erupted in the Middle East. Eisenhower wanted to prevent Arab nations from aligning with the Soviet Union. To build support among Arabs, Secretary of State Dulles offered to help Egypt finance the construction of a dam on the Nile River.

The deal ran into trouble in Congress, however, because Egypt had bought weapons from Communist Czechoslovakia. Dulles was forced to withdraw the offer. A week later, Egyptian troops seized control of the Suez Canal from the Anglo-French company that had controlled it. The Egyptians intended to use the canal's profits to pay for the dam.

In October 1956, British and French troops invaded Egypt. Eisenhower was furious with Britain and France. The situation became even more dangerous when the Soviet Union threatened rocket attacks on Britain and France and offered to send troops to help Egypt. Eisenhower immediately put U.S. nuclear forces on alert, noting, "if those fellows start something, we may have to hit 'em—and, if necessary, with *everything* in the bucket."

Pressured by the United States, the British and French called off the invasion. The Soviet Union had won a major diplomatic victory by supporting Egypt. Soon other Arab nations began accepting Soviet aid.

☑ **PROGRESS CHECK**

Contrasting How did Eisenhower's military policies contrast with those of Truman?

Covert Operations

GUIDING QUESTION *Why did President Eisenhower want to use covert operations to combat the spread of communism?*

President Eisenhower relied on brinkmanship on several occasions, but he knew it could not work in all situations. It could prevent war, but it could not prevent Communists from staging revolutions within countries. To do this, Eisenhower decided to use **covert,** or hidden, operations conducted by the Central Intelligence Agency (CIA).

Many of the CIA's operations took place in **developing nations**—nations with primarily agricultural economies. Many of these countries blamed European imperialism and American capitalism for their problems. Their leaders looked to the Soviet Union as a model of how to industrialize their countries. They often threatened to nationalize, or put under government control, foreign businesses operating in their countries.

One way to stop developing nations from moving into the Communist camp was to provide them with financial aid, as Eisenhower had tried to do in Egypt. In some cases, however, in which the threat of communism seemed stronger, the CIA ran covert operations to overthrow anti-American leaders and replace them with pro-American leaders.

Iran and Guatemala

Two examples of covert operations that achieved American objectives took place in Iran and Guatemala. By 1953 Iranian prime minister Mohammed Mossadegh had nationalized the Anglo-Iranian Oil Company. He seemed ready to make an oil deal with the Soviet Union. The pro-American shah of Iran tried to force Mossadegh out of office but failed and fled into exile. The CIA quickly sent agents to organize street riots and arrange a coup that ousted Mossadegh and returned the shah to power.

The following year, the CIA intervened in Guatemala. In 1950, with Communist support, Jacobo Arbenz Guzmán was elected president of Guatemala. After Arbenz Guzmán assumed office in 1951, his land-reform program took over large estates and plantations, including those of the American-owned United Fruit Company. In May 1954, Communist Czechoslovakia delivered arms to Guatemala. The CIA responded by arming the Guatemalan opposition and training them at secret camps in Nicaragua and Honduras. Shortly after these CIA-trained forces invaded Guatemala, Arbenz Guzmán left office.

Analyzing
PRIMARY SOURCES

Secretary of State Dulles on Brinkmanship

❝You have to take chances for peace, just as you must take chances in war. Some say that we were brought to the verge of war. Of course we were brought to the verge of war. The ability to get to the verge without getting into the war is the necessary art. . . . If you try to run away from it, if you are scared to go to the brink, you are lost. We've had to look it square in the face. . . . We walked to the brink and we looked it in the face. We took strong action.❞

—John Foster Dulles, quoted in *Rise to Globalism*

DBQ **ANALYZING PRIMARY SOURCES** Why did Dulles believe that brinkmanship strengthened U.S. foreign policy?

covert not openly shown or engaged in; secret

developing nation a nation whose economy is primarily agricultural

Trouble in Eastern Europe

Covert operations did not always work as Eisenhower hoped. Stalin died in 1953, and a power struggle began in the Soviet Union. By 1956, Nikita Khrushchev had emerged as the Soviet leader. That year Khrushchev delivered a secret speech to Soviet officials. He attacked Stalin's policies and insisted that there were many ways to build a communist society. Although the speech was secret, the CIA obtained a copy of it and distributed copies of it throughout Eastern Europe and the world.

Many Eastern Europeans had long been frustrated with Communist rule. Hearing Khrushchev's speech further discredited communism. In June 1956, riots erupted in Eastern Europe. By late October, a full-scale uprising had begun in Hungary. Although Khrushchev was willing to tolerate greater freedom in Eastern Europe, he had never meant to **imply** that the Soviets would tolerate an end to communism in the region. Soon after the uprising began, Soviet tanks rolled into the capital of Hungary and crushed the rebellion.

imply to express indirectly

The Eisenhower Doctrine

The United States was not the only nation using covert means to support its foreign policy. President Gamal Abdel Nasser of Egypt had emerged from the Suez crisis as a hero to the Arab people, and by 1957 he had begun working with Jordan and Syria to spread pan-Arabism—the idea that all Arab people should be united into one nation.

Eisenhower and Dulles worried about Nasser's links to the Soviets and feared he was laying the groundwork to take control of the Middle East. In late 1957, Eisenhower asked Congress to authorize the use of military force whenever the president thought it necessary to assist Middle East nations resisting Communist aggression. The policy came to be called the Eisenhower Doctrine. It essentially extended the Truman Doctrine and the policy of containment to the Middle East.

In July 1958, Eisenhower's concerns appeared to be confirmed when left-wing rebels, believed to be backed by Nasser and the Soviets, seized power in Iraq. Fearing his government was next, the president of Lebanon sought help. Eisenhower ordered 5,000 marines to Beirut, the Lebanese capital. Once the situation stabilized, the U.S. forces withdrew.

Soviet leader Nikita Khrushchev rose to power in the mid-1950s, following the death of longtime dictator Joseph Stalin.

▶ **CRITICAL THINKING**
Drawing Conclusions How did covert operations around the world contribute to tensions between the United States and the Soviet Union?

A Spy Plane Is Shot Down

After the Hungarian uprising, Khrushchev reasserted Soviet power and the superiority of communism. Although he had supported "peaceful coexistence" with capitalism, he began accusing the "capitalist countries" of starting a "feverish arms race." In 1957, after the launch of *Sputnik*, Khrushchev boasted, "We will bury capitalism. . . . Your grandchildren will live under communism."

Late the following year, Khrushchev demanded the withdrawal of Allied troops from West Berlin. Secretary of State Dulles rejected Khrushchev's demands. If the Soviets threatened Berlin, Dulles announced, NATO would respond, "if need be by military force." Brinkmanship worked again, and Khrushchev backed down. Eisenhower invited Khrushchev to visit the United States in late 1959. The visit's success led the two leaders to agree to hold a summit in Paris.

PHOTO: Bettmann/CORBIS

Shortly before the summit was to begin in 1960, the Soviet Union shot down an American U-2 spy plane. At first Eisenhower claimed that the aircraft was a weather plane that had strayed off course. Then Khrushchev dramatically produced the pilot, Francis Gary Powers. Eisenhower refused to apologize, saying the flights had protected American security. In **response,** Khrushchev broke up the summit.

In this climate of heightened tension, Eisenhower prepared to leave office. In January 1961, he delivered a farewell address to the nation in which he pointed out that a new relationship had developed between the military establishment and the defense industry. He warned Americans to be on guard against the influence of this **military-industrial complex** in a democracy.

Although he had avoided war and contained communism, Eisenhower was frustrated. He had sent military advisers to South Vietnam to train a South Vietnamese army and also saw Fidel Castro establish a communist regime in Cuba. Eisenhower stated, "I confess that I lay down my official responsibilities in this field with a definite sense of disappointment. As one who has witnessed the horror and the lingering sadness of war . . . I wish I could say tonight that a lasting peace is in sight."

✔ **PROGRESS CHECK**

Identifying Why did Eisenhower direct the CIA to use covert operations?

response something said or done as a reaction

military-industrial complex an informal relationship that some people believe exists between the military and the defense industry to promote greater military spending and influence government policy

The U-2 was America's most sophisticated spy plane. It was able to fly higher than any other plane at the time.

▶ **CRITICAL THINKING**
Drawing Inferences Why was the U-2 used as a spy plane?

PHOTO: NASA

LESSON 4 REVIEW

Reviewing Vocabulary
1. *Explaining* What was the policy of brinkmanship?

2. *Contrasting* How are developing nations primarily different from industrial nations?

Using Your Notes
3. *Evaluating* Use the notes you completed during the lesson to consider Eisenhower's strategies for containing communism. Write a paragraph evaluating whether these strategies were successful. Explain your response.

Answering the Guiding Questions
4. *Contrasting* How were the policies of massive retaliation and brinkmanship different from previous military policies?

5. *Describing* Why did President Eisenhower want to use covert operations to combat the spread of communism?

Writing Activity
6. EXPOSITORY Write a short essay in which you explain Eisenhower's foreign policy goals and practices. Be sure to include details about how these policies influenced historical events.

Directions: On a separate sheet of paper, answer the questions below. Make sure you read carefully and answer all parts to the question.

Lesson Review

Lesson 1

1 *Identifying Central Issues* What decisions were made at Yalta, and what role did they play in the emergence of the Cold War?

2 *Analyzing Information* Why did the Allied victory and the creation of the United Nations not lead to a more peaceful world as President Roosevelt had hoped?

Lesson 2

3 *Identifying Central Issues* What was the policy of containment, and how did it influence U.S. foreign policy?

4 *Determining Cause and Effect* Why was the Korean War a major turning point in the Cold War?

Lesson 3

5 *Interpreting Significance* Following World War II, how did the Red Scare affect the United States?

6 *Drawing Inferences* How did Senator McCarthy's accusations of Communist influence affect domestic life?

Lesson 4

7 *Explaining* What was the role of brinkmanship in Eisenhower's foreign policy? Why was it controversial?

8 *Constructing Arguments* Defend or oppose Eisenhower's use of the CIA for covert operations during the Cold War.

21st Century Skills

9 UNDERSTANDING RELATIONSHIPS AMONG EVENTS How did Cold War fears of nuclear war affect American society?

10 IDENTIFYING PERSPECTIVES AND DIFFERING INTERPRETATIONS Do you think Truman believed that the loyalty review program would calm fears that Communists had infiltrated the government? Why or why not?

Exploring the Essential Questions

11 *Synthesizing* Design a Web site on the Cold War and its effects. On a sheet of paper, describe the Web site and the way you would organize the site's information. Include maps, biographies, and accounts of historic events to show ways Cold War tensions affected American society, and ways the Cold War shaped postwar international relations.

DBQ Document-Based Question

Use the document to answer the following question.

In 1950 Margaret Chase Smith, the only woman in the Senate, was upset by Senator McCarthy's behavior. She had hoped that her colleagues would reprimand him. They failed to do so, and Smith then made her "Declaration of Conscience" speech.

PRIMARY SOURCE

"As a United States Senator, I am not proud of the way in which the Senate has been made a publicity platform for irresponsible sensationalism. I am not proud of the reckless abandon in which unproved charges have been hurled. . . .

As an American, I am shocked at the way Republicans and Democrats alike are playing directly into the Communist design of 'confuse, divide, and conquer'. . . . I want to see our nation recapture the strength and unity it once had when we fought the enemy instead of ourselves."

—from her "Declaration of Conscience" speech to Congress, June 1, 1950

12 *Making Connections* What is the connection between Smith's speech and the dangers of the Red Scare throughout American life?

Extended-Response Question

13 *Analyzing Primary Sources* Write an essay that analyzes the following quote from Joseph Welch: "Until this moment, I think I never really gauged your cruelty or your recklessness. . . . Have you left no sense of decency?" Based on your knowledge of McCarthyism, analyze the relationship between this quote and Joseph McCarthy's career. Support your essay with relevant facts and details.

Need Extra Help?

If You've Missed Question	**1**	**2**	**3**	**4**	**5**	**6**	**7**	**8**	**9**	**10**	**11**	**12**	**13**
Go to page	512	514	517	521	524	526	530	531	525	524	512	534	526

Postwar America

1945–1960

ESSENTIAL QUESTION • *How does prosperity change the way people live?*

◄ Elvis Presley, born poor in Mississippi, rose to fame in the 1950s and became widely known as the "King of Rock 'n' Roll."

PHOTO: Sunset Boulevard/Historical/CORBIS

The Story Matters...

The 1950s was a time of tremendous change in America. New advances in technology planted the seeds of today's computerized world, and developments in medicine saved thousands of lives. A population explosion called the baby boom produced a generation that would change the world. Americans— young and old—also experienced a new genre of music called rock 'n' roll.

After World War II, the United States experienced years of strong economic growth, as well as advances in science, technology, medicine, and transportation. Although the prosperity did not reach everyone, the economic boom meant most Americans enjoyed more prosperity than earlier generations, and a new consumer culture emerged.

Step Into the Place

Look at the information presented on the map to identify where most of the interstate highways were built.

DBQ The creation of the interstate highway system had a tremendous impact on the nation's economy. What were its main effects?

Road Culture Interstate travel encouraged the development of hotels, stores, and restaurants near interstate exits.

The Interstate Highway System

Olympia
Salem
Helena
Boise
Carson City
Sacramento
Salt Lake City
Cheyenne
Denver
Los Angeles
Santa Fe
Phoenix

0   400 miles
0   400 km
Lambert Azimuthal Equal-Area projection

Honolulu

Step Into the Time

Choose an event from the time line and write a paragraph predicting how the event would have made life in America more prosperous than life for earlier generations.

U.S. PRESIDENTS

Truman 1945–1953

UNITED STATES

WORLD

1945   **1947**   **1949**

1944 GI Bill gives financial aid to veterans

1946 ENIAC becomes the first electronic computer

1950 David Riesman publishes *The Lonely Crowd*

1949 George Orwell publishes *Nineteen Eighty-Four*

1950 Octavio Paz publishes *The Labyrinth of Solitude*

networks
There's More Online!

☑ **MAP** Explore the interactive version of this map on Networks.

☑ **TIME LINE** Explore the interactive version of the time line on Networks.

smarck

Pierre ★ St. Paul

Madison

Lansing

Detroit

Chicago

Cleveland

Columbus

Lincoln Des Moines

Springfield

Indianapolis Charleston

St. Louis

Jefferson City

Frankfort

Topeka

Oklahoma City

Little Rock

Nashville

Atlanta

Jackson

Montgomery

Tallahassee

Austin

Baton Rouge

Augusta

Montpelier

Concord

Boston

Albany

Providence

Hartford

New York City

Trenton

Harrisburg

Philadelphia

Baltimore

Dover

Annapolis

Washington, D.C.

Richmond

Raleigh

Columbia

★ State capital
● Top ten city (population, 1950)
— Interstate highway

Commercial Trucking Interstate highways made distribution of goods by transport trucks fast and efficient.

Rise of Suburbs Interstate highways contributed to the growth of suburbs and urban sprawl.

Eisenhower
1953–1961

1951 *I Love Lucy* debuts on television

1955 Salk polio vaccine becomes widely available

1956 Congress passes Federal Highway Act

1958 John Kenneth Galbraith publishes *The Affluent Society*

1959 Lorraine Hansberry's *A Raisin in the Sun* opens on Broadway

1951   **1953**   **1955**   **1957**   **1959**

1953 Soviet Union detonates hydrogen bomb

1957 Six nations found the European Economic Community

1958 People's Republic of China launches Great Leap Forward

1959 St. Lawrence Seaway opens, linking the Great Lakes to the Atlantic Ocean

1960 British rock group adopts the name "The Beatles"

networks

There's More Online!

- ☑ **CHART/GRAPH** New Home Construction
- ☑ **MAP** The Interstate Highway System
- ☑ **VIDEO** Truman and Eisenhower
- ☑ **INTERACTIVE SELF-CHECK QUIZ**

Reading **HELP**DESK

Content Vocabulary
- closed shop
- right-to-work laws
- union shop
- dynamic conservatism

Academic Vocabulary
- legislator   • abandon

TAKING NOTES: *Organizing*

ACTIVITY As you read, complete a graphic organizer like this one by listing characteristics of the postwar economy.

> Characteristics
> of the Postwar Economy

LESSON 1
Truman and Eisenhower

ESSENTIAL QUESTION · *How does prosperity change the way people live?*

IT MATTERS BECAUSE

In the postwar era, Congress limited the power of unions and rejected most of President Truman's plan for a "Fair Deal." When Eisenhower became president, he cut back some government programs but approved billions of dollars for the expansion of the interstate highway system.

Return to a Peacetime Economy

GUIDING QUESTION *What happened when the nation returned to a peacetime economy, and how did government try to ease the transition?*

After the war, many Americans feared the return to a peacetime economy. They worried about unemployment and a recession because military production had stopped and millions of former soldiers needed work. Despite such worries, the economy continued to grow after the war. Increased consumer spending helped ward off a recession. After so many years of economic depression and wartime shortages, Americans rushed out to buy consumer goods.

The Servicemen's Readjustment Act of 1944, popularly called the GI Bill, also boosted the economy. The act provided funds to help veterans establish businesses, buy homes, and attend college. The postwar economy did have problems in the early years after the war. A greater demand for goods led to higher prices. The resulting inflation soon triggered labor unrest. As the cost of living rose, workers in the automobile, steel, electrical, and mining industries went on strike for better pay.

Truman was afraid that the miners' strikes would drastically reduce the nation's energy supply. He ordered the government to take control of the mines. He also pressured mine owners to grant the union most of its demands. Truman even stopped a strike that shut down the nation's railroads by threatening to draft the striking workers into the army.

Labor unrest and high prices prompted many Americans to call for a change. The Republicans seized on these feelings during

PHOTOS: (l to r)Bettmann/CORBIS, Frank Cancellare/Bettmann Premium/CORBIS, Three Lions/Hulton Archive/Getty Images

the 1946 congressional elections, and won control of both houses of Congress for the first time since 1930.

The new conservative Congress quickly set out to limit the power of organized labor. In 1947 **legislators** passed the Taft-Hartley Act, which outlawed the **closed shop,** or the practice of forcing business owners to hire only union members. This law also allowed states to pass **right-to-work laws,** which outlawed **union shops** (shops requiring new workers to join the union). It prohibited featherbedding, or limiting work output in order to create more jobs. It also banned using union money to support political campaigns. Truman, however, vetoed the bill, arguing that it was a mistake:

PRIMARY SOURCE

❝[It would] reverse the basic direction of our national labor policy, inject the Government into private economic affairs on an unprecedented scale, and conflict with important principles of our democratic society. Its provisions would cause more strikes, not fewer.❞

—from a message to the U.S. House of Representatives, June 20, 1947

Despite President Truman's concerns, Congress passed the Taft-Hartley Act in 1947 over his veto. Supporters of the act claimed that the law held irresponsible unions in check. Labor leaders, however, called the act a "slave labor" law, insisting that it erased many of the gains that unions had made since 1933.

✓ **PROGRESS CHECK**

Explaining How did the GI Bill help the nation transition from a wartime economy to a peacetime economy?

Truman's Program

GUIDING QUESTION *How did the Truman administration seek to continue New Deal goals?*

The Democratic Party's loss of control in Congress in the 1946 elections did not dampen President Truman's plans. After taking office, Truman had proposed domestic measures to continue the work of Franklin Roosevelt's New Deal. He worked to push this agenda through Congress.

Truman's Legislative Agenda

Truman's proposals included expanding Social Security benefits and raising the minimum wage. He also proposed public housing and slum clearance, a program to ensure full employment through federal spending and investment, a system of national health insurance, and long-range environmental and public works planning.

In February 1948, Truman also boldly asked Congress to pass a broad civil rights bill. The bill would protect African Americans' right to vote. It would also abolish poll taxes and make lynching a federal crime. He issued an executive order barring discrimination in federal employment and ending segregation in the armed forces. Most of Truman's legislative efforts failed as a coalition of Republicans and conservative Southern Democrats defeated many of his proposals.

legislator one who makes laws as a member of a legislative body for a political unit

closed shop an agreement in which a company agrees to hire only union members

right-to-work law a law making it illegal to require employees to join a union

union shop a business that requires employees to join a union

The GI Bill provided funds for veterans to attend college after the war. By 1947, nearly half of all those attending college were veterans.

▶ **CRITICAL THINKING**
Drawing Inferences Why were so many college students veterans in 1947?

PHOTO: Bettmann/CORBIS

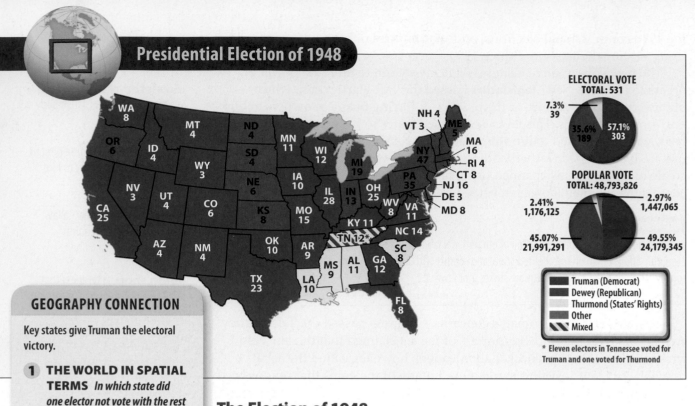

ELECTORAL VOTE
TOTAL: 531

7.3%
39

35.6%
189

57.1%
303

POPULAR VOTE
TOTAL: 48,793,826

2.41%
1,176,125

2.97%
1,447,065

45.07%
21,991,291

49.55%
24,179,345

- ■ Truman (Democrat)
- ■ Dewey (Republican)
- ☐ Thurmond (States' Rights)
- ■ Other
- ⧄ Mixed

* Eleven electors in Tennessee voted for
Truman and one voted for Thurmond

GEOGRAPHY CONNECTION

Key states give Truman the electoral
victory.

1 **THE WORLD IN SPATIAL
TERMS** *In which state did
one elector not vote with the rest
of the state's electors?*

2 **PLACES AND REGIONS**
*In which region did Thurmond
enjoy the most electoral support?*

abandon to withdraw
protection, support, or help

Harry Truman gleefully shows
the incorrect headline
declaring his election defeat.

▶ **CRITICAL THINKING**
*Identifying Central
Issues* What made Truman's
victory such a surprise?

The Election of 1948

As the 1948 presidential election approached, most observers gave Truman
little chance of winning. Some viewed his administration as inept.
In addition, fractures in the Democratic Party seemed to doom his
campaign. Two groups **abandoned** the party at that summer's convention.
A group of Southern Democrats, angry at Truman's support of civil rights,
formed the States' Rights, or Dixiecrat, Party. They nominated South
Carolina governor Strom Thurmond for president. Liberal Democrats who
were frustrated by Truman's ineffective domestic policies and critical of his
anti-Soviet foreign policy formed a new Progressive Party. Henry A.
Wallace was their presidential candidate. Besides these two new
challengers, Truman faced his Republican opponent, New York governor
Thomas Dewey. Dignified and popular, Dewey seemed unbeatable.

Truman remained confident of reelection, however. He traveled more
than 20,000 miles by train and made more than 200 speeches. He attacked
the majority Republican Congress
as "do-nothing, good-for-nothing"
for refusing to enact his legislative
agenda. However, his attacks were
not entirely accurate. The "Do-
Nothing Congress" had passed his
aid program to Greece and Turkey
and the Marshall Plan. Congress
had passed the law that created the
Department of Defense, the
National Security Council, and the
CIA. It had permanently established
the Joint Chiefs of Staff and set up
the air force as an independent
branch of the military. It also had
passed the Twenty-second
Amendment, which limited a

president to two terms in office. But because Congress's actions were in areas that did not affect most Americans directly, Truman's charges began to stick.

Supported by laborers, African Americans, and farmers, Truman won a narrow but stunning victory over Dewey. In addition, the Democratic Party regained control of both houses of Congress.

The Fair Deal

Truman's 1949 State of the Union address repeated his previous domestic agenda. "Every segment of our population and every individual," he declared, "has a right to expect from our Government a fair deal." Whether intentional or not, the president had coined a name—the Fair Deal—to set his program apart from the New Deal.

The 81st Congress did not completely support Truman's Fair Deal. Legislators did raise the legal minimum wage to 75¢ an hour. They increased Social Security benefits by over 75 percent and extended them to 10 million additional people. Congress also passed the National Housing Act of 1949, which provided for the construction of low-income housing and for long-term rent subsidies. Congress refused, however, to pass national health insurance or to provide aid for farmers or schools. Led by conservative Republicans and Dixiecrats, legislators also opposed Truman's civil rights legislation.

✓ PROGRESS CHECK

Making Connections What components of the New Deal did Truman adopt as part of his legislative agenda?

The Eisenhower Years

GUIDING QUESTION *How did Eisenhower's presidency signal a more conservative direction for the government?*

In 1950 the United States went to war in Korea. The war consumed the nation's attention and resources, ending Truman's Fair Deal. By 1952, with the war at a bloody stalemate and his approval rating dropping quickly, Truman decided not to run again.

With no Democratic incumbent to face, Republicans pinned their hopes on a popular World War II hero: Dwight Eisenhower, former commander of the Allied Forces in Europe. The Democrats nominated Illinois governor Adlai Stevenson.

The Republicans adopted the slogan "It's time for a change!" The warm and friendly Eisenhower, known as "Ike," promised to end the war in Korea. "I like Ike" became the Republican rallying cry. Eisenhower won the election in a landslide. The Republicans also gained an eight-seat majority in the House, while the Senate became evenly divided between Democrats and Republicans.

Eisenhower and "Dynamic Conservatism"

President Eisenhower had two favorite phrases. "Middle of the road" described his political beliefs, and **"dynamic conservatism"** meant balancing economic conservatism with activism that would benefit the country. Under the guidance of a cabinet filled with business leaders, Eisenhower ended government price and rent controls. Many conservatives viewed these as unnecessary federal regulations of the economy. Eisenhower's administration believed business growth was vital to the nation. His secretary of defense, the former president of General Motors, declared that "what is good for our country is good for General Motors, and vice versa."

Analyzing
PRIMARY SOURCES

Truman's Fair Deal

❝As we look around the country, many of our shortcomings stand out. . . . Our minimum wages are far too low. . . . Our farmers still face an uncertain future. And too many of them lack the benefits of our modern civilization. Some of our natural resources are still being wasted. We are acutely short of electric power. . . . Five million families are still living in slums and firetraps. . . . Proper medical care is so expensive that it is out of the reach of the great majority of our citizens. Our schools . . . are utterly inadequate. Our democratic ideals are often thwarted by prejudice and intolerance. . . . [E]very individual has a right to expect from our Government a fair deal.❞

—from his State of the Union address, January 5, 1949

DBQ **SUMMARIZING** Why did Truman believe that reforms were needed?

dynamic conservatism
a policy of balancing economic conservatism with some activism in other areas

The expansion of the federal highway system eased commuter traffic.

▶ **CRITICAL THINKING**
Analyzing Information How did the construction of the interstate highway system demonstrate Eisenhower's dynamic conservatism?

To cut federal spending, Eisenhower vetoed a school construction bill and agreed to slash aid to public housing. He also targeted aid to businesses, or what he called "creeping socialism." Shortly after taking office, he abolished the Reconstruction Finance Corporation (RFC), which loaned money to banks, railroads, and other large institutions in financial trouble. Another agency, the Tennessee Valley Authority (TVA), also came under Eisenhower's scrutiny. During his presidency, federal spending for the TVA fell from $185 million to $12 million. Eisenhower also supported some modest tax cuts.

In some areas, Eisenhower took an activist role. He especially pushed for two large government projects. As more Americans owned cars, the need for better roads increased. In 1956 Congress passed the Federal Highway Act, the largest public works program in American history. The act provided for a $25 billion, 10-year project to build more than 40,000 miles (64,400 km) of interstate highways. Congress also authorized the construction of the St. Lawrence Seaway. This project included building a series of locks along the St. Lawrence River that would allow ships to travel from the Great Lakes to the Atlantic Ocean. The three previous administrations had failed to accomplish this feat because of differences with Canada over the waterway.

Extending Social Security

Despite cutting federal spending and attempting to limit the government's role in the economy, President Eisenhower agreed to extend the Social Security system to an additional 10 million people. He also extended unemployment payments to 4 million more citizens. Eisenhower even agreed to raise the minimum wage and to continue to provide some government aid to farmers.

By the time Eisenhower ran for a second term in 1956, the nation had successfully shifted back to a peacetime economy. The battles between liberals and conservatives over whether to continue New Deal policies would continue. In the meantime, most Americans focused their energy on enjoying what had become a decade of tremendous prosperity.

✓ **PROGRESS CHECK**

Explaining What conservative measures did Eisenhower take during his administration?

PHOTO: Three Lions/Hulton Archive/Getty Images

LESSON 1 REVIEW

Reviewing Vocabulary
1. *Contrasting* How does a closed shop differ from a union shop?

2. *Defining* What is meant by the term *dynamic conservatism*?

Using Your Notes
3. *Summarizing* Use the notes you completed to write a paragraph summarizing the state of the U.S. economy after World War II.

Answering the Guiding Questions
4. *Identifying* What happened when the nation returned to a peacetime economy, and how did government try to ease the transition?

5. *Describing* How did the Truman administration seek to continue New Deal goals?

6. *Analyzing* How did Eisenhower's presidency signal a more conservative direction for the government?

Writing Activity
7. **PERSUASIVE** Suppose that you are a member of Congress who heard Truman deliver his speech on the Fair Deal. Write a speech convincing your fellow members of Congress to pass or defeat Truman's Fair Deal measures.

Reading **HELP**DESK

Content Vocabulary

- **baby boom**
- **white-collar job**
- **blue-collar worker**
- **multinational corporation**
- **franchise**
- **rock 'n' roll**
- **generation gap**

Academic Vocabulary

- **phenomenon**
- **conform**

TAKING NOTES: *Sequencing*

ACTIVITY As you read, use a time line to record major events of science, technology, and popular culture during the late 1940s and 1950s.

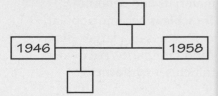

1946   1958

LESSON 2
The Affluent Society

ESSENTIAL QUESTION · *How does prosperity change the way people live?*

IT MATTERS BECAUSE

For many Americans, the 1950s was a time of affluence, with many new technological breakthroughs. In addition, new forms of entertainment created a generational divide between young people and adults.

American Abundance

GUIDING QUESTION *How did the lives of Americans change after World War II?*

The 1950s was a decade of incredible prosperity. Between 1940 and 1955, the average income of U.S. families roughly tripled. People in all income brackets were experiencing a rapid rise in income. In 1958 economist John Kenneth Galbraith published *The Affluent Society,* in which he claimed that the nation's postwar prosperity was a new **phenomenon.** Galbraith suggested that whereas past societies had an "economy of scarcity" with limited economic productivity, the United States had now created an "economy of abundance." New business techniques and technology enabled the production of abundant goods and services. They dramatically raised the U.S. standard of living.

With more disposable income than ever, Americans began spending on new consumer goods. Advertising helped fuel the spending spree. It became the United States's fastest-growing industry. Manufacturers employed new, carefully planned marketing techniques to create consumer demand for their products.

The Growth of Suburbia

Advertisers targeted consumers with money to spend, many of whom lived in new mass-produced suburbs that grew up around cities in the 1950s. Levittown, New York, was one of the earliest of the mass-produced suburbs. It was the brainchild of Bill Levitt, who mass-produced hundreds of simple, similar-looking homes 10 miles east of New York City. Between 1947 and 1951, families rushed to buy the inexpensive homes. Similar suburbs multiplied throughout the nation. The suburban population doubled, while the population of cities rose only 10 percent.

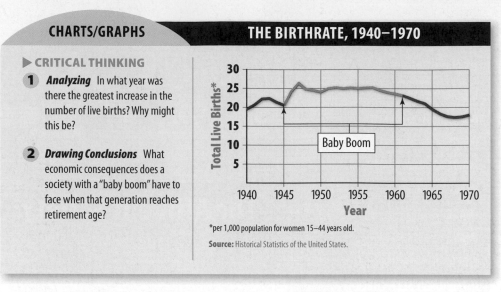

CHARTS/GRAPHS

THE BIRTHRATE, 1940–1970

▶ **CRITICAL THINKING**

1 *Analyzing* In what year was there the greatest increase in the number of live births? Why might this be?

2 *Drawing Conclusions* What economic consequences does a society with a "baby boom" have to face when that generation reaches retirement age?

*per 1,000 population for women 15–44 years old.

Source: Historical Statistics of the United States.

---

phenomenon an event or occurrence that is exceptional or unusual

Reasons for suburban growth varied. Some people wished to escape the crime and congestion of the city. Others believed suburbs offered a better life and were more affordable. The GI Bill and the government's decision to give income tax deductions for mortgage and property tax payments made home ownership more attractive than ever. Between 1940 and 1960, the percentage of Americans who owned their homes rose from about 41 percent to about 61 percent.

The Baby Boom

baby boom a marked rise in birthrate, such as occurred in the United States following World War II

The U.S. birthrate exploded after World War II. From 1945 to 1961, more than 65 million children were born in the United States. At the height of this **baby boom,** a child was born every seven seconds. Many factors contributed to the baby boom. First, young couples who had put off getting married during World War II and the Korean War could finally begin their families. Also, the government encouraged the growth of families by offering generous GI benefits for home purchases. Finally, popular culture celebrated pregnancy, parenthood, and large families.

The Changing Workplace

white-collar job a job in a field not requiring work clothes or protective clothing, such as sales

As the economy grew, ongoing mechanization of farms and factories meant more Americans began working in offices in what came to be called **white-collar jobs.** These employees typically wore a white dress shirt and a tie to work instead of the blue denim work shirts of factory workers and laborers. In 1956 white-collar workers outnumbered **blue-collar workers** for the first time.

blue-collar worker a worker who performs manual labor, particularly work that requires protective clothing

multinational corporation large corporation with overseas investments

Many white-collar employees worked for large corporations. To be more competitive, some corporations expanded overseas. They became **multinational corporations,** locating near raw materials and benefiting from a cheap labor pool. Also during this time **franchises** became popular. In a franchise, a person owns and runs one or more stores of a larger chain. Believing that consumers valued dependability and familiarity, the owners of chain operations often demanded that their franchises **conform** to a uniform look and style.

franchise the right or license to market a company's goods or services in an area, such as a store of a chain operation

conform to change in a way that fits a standard or authority

Many other corporate leaders also expected conformity rather than freethinking. Sociologist David Riesman and others criticized this trend. In his 1950 book *The Lonely Crowd,* Riesman argued that conformity was changing people. He claimed that people used to judge themselves on the basis of their own values and the esteem of their families. But now, he said, "The American is said to be shallower, freer with his money, friendlier, more uncertain of himself and his values, more demanding of approval. . . .

544

[This attitude of] other-direction is becoming the typical character of the 'new' middle class." In his 1956 book *The Organization Man*, William H. Whyte, Jr., attacked the similarity many businesses cultivated in their employees to keep any individual from dominating.

✓ PROGRESS CHECK

Describing How did corporations change the lives of Americans?

Scientific Advances

GUIDING QUESTION *How did technological advances change society?*

As the United States experienced social changes during the postwar era, it also witnessed important scientific advances. During the 1950s, scientists broke new ground in electronics, aviation, and medicine.

Advances in Electronics and Aviation

The electronics industry advanced rapidly after World War II. In 1947 three U.S. physicists developed the transistor, a tiny electric generator that made it possible to create small portable radios.

The computer age also dawned in the postwar era. In 1946 scientists developed one of the nation's earliest computers, ENIAC (Electronic Numerical Integrator and Computer), to make military calculations. Several years later, a newer model, UNIVAC (Universal Automatic Computer), processed business data and started the computer revolution.

Aviation progressed rapidly as well. Aircraft designers used more plastics and light metals, swept-back wings, and new jet engine technology to build planes that could fly farther on the same amount of fuel. These advances made airline travel affordable for more people.

Medical Breakthroughs

Prior to the 1950s, there were few effective treatments for cancer and heart attacks. Medical breakthroughs in the 1950s changed that. The development of radiation treatments and chemotherapy helped many cancer patients survive. Cardiopulmonary resuscitation (CPR), developed in 1950, helped many people survive heart attacks. Doctors also learned to replace worn-out heart valves with artificial valves, and implanted the first pacemakers in 1952.

Tuberculosis and polio had frightened Americans for decades. Tuberculosis patients were isolated in sanatoriums to prevent the spread of this highly contagious lung disease. During the 1950s, a blood test for the disease and new antibiotics helped end fears. In 1956 tuberculosis fell from the list of the top ten fatal diseases.

Polio epidemics typically left their victims dead or paralyzed. Parents frantically tried to protect their children from the disease. Some sent them to the country to avoid excessive contact with others. Public swimming pools and beaches were closed. Parks and playgrounds across the country were deserted. In 1952 a record 58,000 new cases were reported. Finally, research scientist Jonas Salk developed an injectable polio vaccine, which became available to the public in 1955. Researcher Albert Sabin then developed an oral polio vaccine. Safer and more convenient than Salk's vaccine, the Sabin vaccine helped the threat of polio nearly disappear.

✓ PROGRESS CHECK

Evaluating What technological advancements helped treat cancer?

BIOGRAPHY

Dr. Jonas Salk (1914–1995)
Jonas Salk enrolled in college as a prelaw student but soon changed his mind. He switched his major to premed and went on to become a research scientist. Sometimes he made rounds in the overcrowded polio wards of a hospital near his lab, where nurses described their feelings of helpless rage. One nurse said, "I can remember how the staff used to kid Dr. Salk—kidding in earnest—telling him to hurry up and do something." Salk became famous for the polio vaccine he developed in 1952.

▶ CRITICAL THINKING
Analyzing What character traits do you think made Dr. Salk a successful research scientist?

Charitable donations funded the medical research that helped cure or control many childhood diseases.

YOU CAN WALK!!
GIVE TO
POLIO
BUILDING FUND

The New Mass Media

GUIDING QUESTION *How did the new mass media reflect the characteristics of the time?*

Regular television broadcasts had begun in the early 1940s, but there were few stations and sets were expensive. In 1946 no more than 8,000 televisions were in use across the nation. By 1957, though, nearly 40 million sets had been sold, and more than 80 percent of families owned at least one television.

The Rise of Television

Early television programs included comedies, variety shows, and action programs. In 1953 Lucille Ball and her husband, Desi Arnaz, starred in one of the medium's most popular shows ever, a comedy called *I Love Lucy*. One episode attracted an audience of 44 million viewers—more than for the presidential inauguration the following day.

Many early comedy shows, such as those starring Bob Hope and Jack Benny, were adapted from radio programs. Variety shows, such as Ed Sullivan's *Toast of the Town,* provided a mix of comedy, music, dance, and acrobatics. Quiz shows also drew large audiences after the 1955 debut of *The $64,000 Question*. Westerns such as *The Lone Ranger* and *Gunsmoke* grew quickly in popularity. Viewers also enjoyed police shows such as *Dragnet,* featuring Detective Joe Friday. Television news and sports broadcasts grew in popularity as well.

Hollywood Adapts

As television's popularity grew, movies lost viewers. Attendance plunged from 82 million in 1946 to 36 million by 1950. By 1960, one-fifth of the nation's movie theaters had closed. Hollywood used contests, door prizes, and advertising to attract audiences, but failed. Hollywood tried 3-D movies that required the audience to wear special glasses. Viewers quickly tired of the glasses and the films' often-silly plots.

However, Cinemascope—a process that showed movies on large, panoramic screens—finally gave Hollywood something television could not match. Full-color spectacles like *The Robe* and *Around the World in 80 Days* cost a great deal to make, but drew huge audiences and profits.

Radio Draws Them In

Television also forced the radio industry to change. Television made radio comedies, dramas, and soap operas obsolete. Radio stations responded by broadcasting recorded music, news, weather, sports, and talk shows.

Hollywood studios tried to recapture audiences with gimmicks such as contests, door prizes, and even 3-D movies requiring special glasses.

▶ **CRITICAL THINKING**
Making Inferences Why did audiences steadily desert movies during the 1950s?

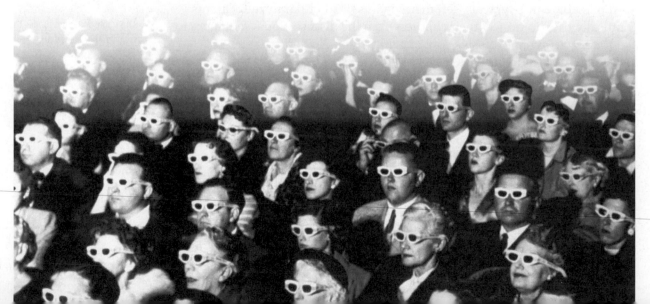

PHOTO: J. R. Eyerman/Time & Life Pictures/Getty Images

Radio had one audience that television could not reach—people traveling in their cars. People commuting from the suburbs, running errands, or traveling on long road trips relied on radio for news and entertainment. As a result, the number of radio stations more than doubled between 1948 and 1957.

✔ **PROGRESS CHECK**

Making Connections Why is television considered part of the new mass media?

New Music and Poetry

GUIDING QUESTIONS *Why did young people in the 1950s develop their own popular culture? Why were the results different from those in previous generations?*

Teens in every generation seek to separate themselves from their parents. In that respect, the 1950s were just like earlier decades, but the results were different for two reasons. First, teens had disposable income that could be spent on entertainment designed specifically for them. Second, the new mass media meant that teens around the country could hear the same music or see the same television shows. The new youth culture became an independent market for the entertainment and advertising industries.

Rock 'n' Roll

In 1951, at a record store in downtown Cleveland, Ohio, radio disc jockey Alan Freed noticed white teenagers buying African American rhythm-and-blues records. Teens also were dancing to the music in the store. Freed convinced his station manager to put the music on the air, and listeners went crazy for it. Soon, white artists began making music that stemmed from these African American sounds, creating a new form of music, **rock 'n' roll.**

With a loud and heavy beat that made it ideal for dancing, and lyrics about themes that appealed to young people, rock 'n' roll became wildly popular. Teens bought recordings from artists such as Buddy Holly, Chuck Berry, and Bill Haley and the Comets. In 1956 teenagers found their first rock 'n' roll hero in music and movie star Elvis Presley. At first, popular television host Ed Sullivan refused to invite Presley to appear on his variety show. He insisted that rock 'n' roll music was not fit for a family-oriented show. After another show featuring Presley upset Sullivan's high ratings, however, he relented.

Presley owed his popularity as much to his moves as to his music, swinging his hips and dancing during his performances in ways that shocked many people. Many adults condemned rock 'n' roll as loud, mindless, and dangerous. The city council of San Antonio, Texas, banned rock 'n' roll from the jukeboxes at public swimming pools.

The rock 'n' roll hits that teens bought in record numbers united them in a world their parents did not share. Thus, in the 1950s, this new music helped to create what became known as the **generation gap,** or the cultural separation between children and their parents.

rock 'n' roll popular music usually played on electronically amplified instruments and characterized by a persistent, heavily accented beat, much repetition of simple phrases, and often country, folk, and blues elements

generation gap a cultural separation between parents and their children

During the 1950s, teens around the nation eagerly bought rock 'n' roll records. The music was popular at dances called hops and even on television programs like *American Bandstand*.

▶ **CRITICAL THINKING**
Predicting Consequences How might the rise of youth culture during the 1950s affect teens of later generations?

The Beat Movement

A group of mostly white writers and artists who called themselves *beats,* or *beatniks,* highlighted a values gap in 1950s America. Beat poets, writers, and artists criticized American culture for its sterility, conformity, and emptiness. In 1956, 29-year-old poet Allen Ginsberg published a long poem titled "Howl" blasting American life. It began, "I saw the best minds of my generation destroyed by madness, starving hysterical naked . . . burning for the ancient heavenly connection to the starry dynamo in the machinery of night." Beat author Jack Kerouac's book *On the Road* (1957), about his freewheeling adventures with a car thief and con artist, shocked some readers. Although the beat movement remained small, it laid the foundations for the widespread youth cultural rebellion of the 1960s.

African American Entertainers

African American entertainers struggled to find acceptance. With a few notable exceptions, television tended to shut out African Americans. In 1956 NBC gave popular African American singer Nat King Cole a 15-minute musical variety show. However, NBC was unable to find a national sponsor for a show hosted by an African American, so it canceled the show two years later.

African American rock 'n' roll singers faced fewer obstacles. Chuck Berry, Little Richard, and Ray Charles all recorded hit songs. The same era also saw the rise of several female African American groups, including the Shirelles and the Ronettes. The music of these early rock 'n' roll artists profoundly influenced popular music around the world. Little Richard and Chuck Berry, for example, inspired the Beatles, whose music swept Britain and the world in the 1960s.

Despite the advances in music and the economic boom of the 1950s, not all Americans were part of the new society. For many minorities and rural poor, the American Dream remained well out of reach.

☑ **PROGRESS CHECK**

Analyzing Cause and Effect What made rock 'n' roll part of the new culture of the 1950s?

Chuck Berry was one of the leading popular music performers of the 1950s.

▶ **CRITICAL THINKING**
Identifying Cause and Effect
How did Berry's popularity influence later generations of musicians?

PHOTO: Michael Ochs Archives/Historical/CORBIS ;TEXT: L. 1-2, 3 (from "burning") -5 from "HOWL" FROM COLLECTED POEMS 1947-1980 by ALLEN GINSBERG. Copyright © 1955 by Allen Ginsberg. Reprinted by permission of HarperCollins Publishers.

LESSON 2 REVIEW

Reviewing Vocabulary
1. *Contrasting* How did white-collar jobs and blue-collar jobs differ?

2. *Defining* What is the generation gap?

Using Your Notes
3. *Explaining* Use the notes you completed during the lesson to write a short paragraph explaining some of the major changes that took place during the 1950s.

Answering the Guiding Questions
4. *Describing* How did the lives of Americans change after World War II?

5. *Analyzing Cause and Effect* How did technological advances change society?

6. *Making Connections* How did the new mass media reflect the characteristics of the time?

7. *Evaluating* Why did young people in the 1950s develop their own popular culture?

Writing Activity
8. **PERSONAL** Think about U.S. youth culture today. Consider how it is similar to and different from the youth culture of the 1950s. Then write a short essay in which you give your opinions about how youth culture can influence society, and whether youth culture is as important as adult culture.

netw⊙rks

There's More Online!

- ☑ **BIOGRAPHY** Ralph Ellison
- ☑ **CHART/GRAPH** Native Americans
- ☑ **CHART/GRAPH** Suburban Dwellers
- ☑ **MAP** Appalachia
- ☑ **VIDEO** Other Side of American Life
- ☑ **INTERACTIVE SELF-CHECK QUIZ**

LESSON 3
The Other Side of American Life

Reading **HELP**DESK

Content Vocabulary

- **poverty line**
- **urban renewal**
- **termination policy**
- **juvenile delinquency**

Academic Vocabulary

- **income**   **entity**

TAKING NOTES: *Organizing*

ACTIVITY As you read , use the major headings of this section to create an outline similar to the one below.

The Other Side of American Life
I. Poverty Amid Prosperity
A.
B.
C.
D.
E.
II.

ESSENTIAL QUESTION · *How does prosperity change the way people live?*

IT MATTERS BECAUSE

During the 1950s, about 20 percent of the American population—particularly people of color and those living in the inner cities and Appalachia—did not share in the general prosperity. Experts also worried about the rise in juvenile delinquency.

Poverty Amid Prosperity

GUIDING QUESTION *Are the people and regions most affected by poverty today the same as in the 1950s?*

The 1950s saw a large expansion of the middle class. At least one in five Americans, or about 30 million people, however, lived below the **poverty line.** This imaginary marker is a figure the government sets to reflect the minimum **income** required to support a family. Many Americans mistakenly thought that the country's prosperity had provided for everyone.

The poor included single mothers and the elderly; minorities such as Puerto Ricans and Mexican immigrants; rural Americans—both African American and white; and inner-city residents, who remained stuck in crowded slums. Many Native Americans endured poverty whether they stayed on reservations or migrated to cities.

The Decline of the Inner City
Poverty was most apparent in the nation's urban centers. As middle-class families moved to the suburbs, they left behind the poor and less educated. Many city centers deteriorated because they no longer received taxes from their former middle-class residents. Cities could no longer provide adequate public transportation, housing, and other services.

When government tried to help inner-city residents, it often made matters worse. **Urban renewal** programs tried to eliminate poverty by tearing down slums and building new high-rises for poor residents. Yet these crowded projects often created an atmosphere of violence. The government also unwittingly created a condition supporting poverty with a rule that evicted residents of public housing as soon as they began earning a higher income.

African Americans

Although more than 3 million African Americans had migrated from the South to Northern cities, long-standing patterns of racial discrimination kept many of them poor. In 1958 African Americans' salaries, on average, were only 51 percent of what whites earned.

In 1959 the play *A Raisin in the Sun,* written by African American author Lorraine Hansberry, opened on Broadway. The play told the story of a working-class African American family struggling against poverty and racism. Hansberry wrote: "The ghettos are killing us; not only our dreams . . . but our very bodies."

Hispanics

Much of the nation's Hispanic population also struggled with poverty. Nearly 5 million Mexicans had come to the United States through the Bracero Program to work on farms and ranches in the Southwest. Braceros were temporary contract workers. Many later returned home, but some 350,000 settled permanently in the United States. They worked long hours, for little pay, in conditions that were often unbearable. The migrant workers' list of grievances included "poor food . . . substandard housing, prejudice and discrimination, physical mistreatment and exposure to pesticides . . . and unsatisfactory earnings," according to one Bracero Program history.

Native Americans

By the middle of the 1900s, Native Americans—who made up less than one percent of the population—were the poorest ethnic group in the nation. After World War II, the United States government launched a program to bring Native Americans into mainstream society. Under the plan, which became known as the **termination policy,** the federal government withdrew all official recognition of the Native American groups as legal **entities** and made them subject to the same laws as white citizens. Another program encouraged Native Americans to relocate from their reservations to cities.

For many Native Americans, relocation was a disaster. For example, in the mid-1950s, the Welfare Council of Minneapolis said of Native American living conditions: "One Indian family of five or six, living in two rooms, will take in relatives and friends who come from the reservations seeking jobs until perhaps fifteen people will be crowded into the space." During the 1950s, Native Americans in Minneapolis could expect to live only 37 years, compared to 68 years for other Minneapolis residents. Benjamin Reifel, a Sioux, described the despair the termination policy produced: "The Indians believed that when the dark clouds of war passed from the skies overhead, their rising tide of expectations, though temporarily stalled, would again reappear. Instead they were threatened by termination. . . . Soaring expectations began to plunge."

Appalachia

The mountainous region of Appalachia, stretching from New York to Georgia, often kept poverty hidden. Coal mining, long the backbone of the Appalachian economy, mechanized in the 1950s, causing soaring unemployment.

poverty line a level of personal or family income below which one is classified as poor by the federal government

income a gain or recurrent benefit usually measured in money derived from capital or labor

urban renewal government programs that attempt to eliminate poverty and revitalize urban areas

termination policy a government policy to bring Native Americans into mainstream society by withdrawing recognition of Native American groups as legal entities

entity something having independent, separate, or self-contained existence

Eight family members lived in this three-room house lined with newspaper in Appalachia in the 1950s.

▶ CRITICAL THINKING
Drawing Conclusions Besides inadequate housing, what other effects did poverty have on people?

Some 1.5 million people left Appalachia to seek a better life in the cities. Appalachia had fewer doctors than the rest of the country, and rates of nutritional deficiency and infant mortality were high. Schooling was considered even worse than in inner-city slums.

juvenile delinquency
antisocial or criminal behavior of young people

☑ **PROGRESS CHECK**

Identifying What are two regions where poverty was most prevalent in the 1950s, and why was their level of prosperity so low?

Juvenile Delinquency

GUIDING QUESTION *What factors were blamed for the rise in juvenile delinquency?*

During the 1950s, many middle-class white Americans found it easy to ignore poverty and racism. Some social problems, however, became impossible to ignore. **Juvenile delinquency**—antisocial or criminal behavior of young people—became one of those problems when the United States saw a 45 percent rise in juvenile crime rates between 1948 and 1953.

Americans disagreed on what had triggered the rise. Experts blamed television, movies, comic books, racism, busy parents, a rising divorce rate, lack of religion, and anxiety over the military draft. Some cultural critics claimed that young people were rebelling against the conformity of their parents. Others blamed a lack of discipline. Bishop Fulton J. Sheen complained that parents had raised bored children who sought new thrills, such as "alcohol, marijuana, even murder." Still others pointed at social causes, blaming teen violence on poverty. Most teens stayed clear of gangs, drugs, and crime. Still, the public stereotyped young people as juvenile delinquents, especially those who had long hair or used street slang.

Concerned about their children, many parents focused on the schools as a possible solution. When baby boomers began entering the school system in the 1950s, enrollments increased by 13 million, and school districts struggled to pay for new buildings and hire more teachers. In 1957 the Soviet Union's launch of *Sputnik I* and *Sputnik II*, the world's first space satellites, caused more panic about education. Many felt that the nation had fallen behind its Cold War enemy. They blamed what they saw as a lack of technical education. Efforts to improve math and science education began. Yet fears about the nation's young people lingered at the end of the decade.

☑ **PROGRESS CHECK**

Evaluating Why do you think schools were a possible solution for juvenile delinquency?

Connections to TODAY

Juvenile Delinquency

Teens are more involved in crime, drugs, and gangs today than they were in the 1950s. There are four times as many juvenile court cases as there were in 1960. In the late 1990s, about 2 million juveniles (ages 10–17) were arrested, mostly for drug-related crimes. Many of these crimes were committed by juveniles in gangs. The number of juvenile cases has dropped in the past decade, but gang crimes are on the rise.

LESSON 3 REVIEW

Reviewing Vocabulary
1. *Defining* If someone is living below the poverty line, what does that mean?

2. *Explaining* Why did some people stereotype certain young people as juvenile delinquents?

Using Your Notes
3. *Making Connections* Use your notes from the lesson to determine what caused some young people to become juvenile delinquents and how society responded with solutions.

Answering the Guiding Questions
4. *Evaluating* Are the people and regions most affected by poverty today the same as in the 1950s?

5. *Identifying* What factors were blamed for the rise in juvenile delinquency?

Writing Activity
6. **PERSONAL** Write about a social problem affecting society today that parallels problems encountered in the 1950s.

Directions: On a separate sheet of paper, answer the questions below. Make sure you read carefully and answer all parts to the question.

Lesson Review

Lesson 1

1 *Explaining* What impact did the Taft-Hartley Act have on organized labor?

2 *Analyzing* How did the GI Bill boost the postwar economy?

Lesson 2

3 *Explaining* Why did economist John Kenneth Galbraith believe that America's postwar economy was a new phenomenon?

4 *Evaluating* Economic prosperity led to new types of arts and entertainment. In what ways did rock 'n' roll contribute to the generation gap?

Lesson 3

5 *Comparing and Contrasting* Explain how the lives of minorities differed from those of white middle-class Americans during the 1950s.

6 *Analyzing* What were some factors that people believed contributed to a rise in juvenile delinquency, and how did they try to solve the problem?

21st Century Skills

7 **ECONOMICS** What factors negatively affected the economy of Appalachia in the 1950s?

8 **UNDERSTANDING RELATIONSHIPS AMONG EVENTS** What conditions in the postwar United States contributed to the baby boom?

9 **PROBLEM SOLVING** In the postwar era, what could the government have done instead of constructing high-rise buildings to improve the inner cities?

10 **IDENTIFYING CAUSE AND EFFECT** How did television change both movies and radio?

Exploring the Essential Question

11 *Gathering Information* Make an informative poster titled "Prosperity in the 1950s." Use text, graphs, and illustrations to show how prosperity impacted the lives of many Americans, and how it did not benefit others.

DBQ Document-Based Questions

Base your answers to questions 12 and 13 on the graph below.

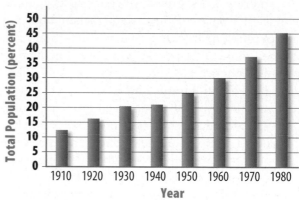

SUBURBAN DWELLERS, 1910–1980

Source: *The First Measured Century.*

12 *Analyzing Visuals* Approximately what percentage of the total population lived in the suburbs in 1910? How long did it take for the percentage of suburban dwellers to double, compared to what it had been in 1910?

13 *Interpreting* Using what you have learned in this chapter what factors contributed to the difference in the percentage of suburban dwellers between 1940 and 1950?

Extended-Response Question

14 *Comparing and Contrasting* Write an expository essay that compares and contrasts the postwar domestic agendas of President Harry Truman and President Dwight Eisenhower. Your essay should include an introduction and at least two paragraphs that explain how their ideas and approaches to domestic issues were similar and different.

Need Extra Help?

If You've Missed Question	**1**	**2**	**3**	**4**	**5**	**6**	**7**	**8**	**9**	**10**	**11**	**12**	**13**	**14**
Go to page	539	538	543	547	550	551	550	544	549	546	543	552	543	538

The New Frontier and the Great Society

1960–1968

ESSENTIAL QUESTIONS • *Can government fix society's problems?*
• *How do you think Presidents Kennedy and Johnson changed American society?*

The Story Matters...

When U.S. intelligence discovered Soviet nuclear missile silos in Cuba, just 90 miles from the United States, the bright New Frontier that President Kennedy had promised Americans seemed very far away. During the 13-day standoff between the United States and the Soviet Union, there was increasing fear that nuclear strikes would occur. The crisis was resolved when President Kennedy helped negotiate both nations away from the brink of nuclear war.

◄ John F. Kennedy won a narrow victory in the 1960 presidential election. During his administration, Kennedy faced both foreign and domestic challenges.

PHOTO: SuperStock/Getty Images

CHAPTER 24

Place and Time: United States 1960–1968

The 1960s began with great optimism in the United States, as President John F. Kennedy seemed ready to lead the way from the fear and accusations of the 1950s to a New Frontier—and to the moon itself. The threat of nuclear war and the assassination of Kennedy could not derail the drive for change. President Lyndon B. Johnson presided over landmark legislation meant to create a Great Society of wealth and equality for all.

Step Into the Place

Read the quotes and look at the information presented on the map.

DBQ **What was Premier Khrushchev referring to when he wrote that "it will be necessary to cut that knot"?**

PRIMARY SOURCE

❝Our goal is not the victory of might, but the vindication of right—not peace at the expense of freedom, but both peace and freedom, here in this hemisphere, and, we hope, around the world. God willing, that goal will be achieved.❞

—President John F. Kennedy, from a speech delivered October 22, 1962

PRIMARY SOURCE

❝If, however, you have not lost your self-control and sensibly conceive what this might lead to, then, Mr. President, we and you ought not now to pull on the ends of the rope in which you have tied the knot of war, because the more the two of us pull, the tighter that knot will be tied. And a moment may come when that knot will be tied so tight that even he who tied it will not have the strength to untie it, and then it will be necessary to cut that knot. . . .❞

—Soviet premier Nikita Khrushchev, from a letter to President Kennedy, October 26, 1962

PHOTOS: left page: (tl)Bettmann/CORBIS, (tr)Hank Walker/Time & Life Pictures/Getty Images, (bl)SuperStock/SuperStock; (br)detail/White House Collection/The White House Historical Association; right page AP Images

Step Into the Time

Choose an event from the time line that you think influenced the relationship between the United States and the Soviet Union. Write a paragraph that predicts the political impact that this event might have had on the two countries.

Kennedy 1961–1963

Oct. 1962 Cuban missile crisis

L. Johnson 1963–1969

March 1961 Peace Corps is created

April 17, 1961 Bay of Pigs invasion

Nov. 1963 Kennedy is assassinated

U.S. PRESIDENTS

UNITED STATES

WORLD

1960   1961   1962   1963

August 1961 Construction of Berlin Wall begins

April 1961 Soviet astronaut Yury Gagarin becomes first person to orbit Earth

1963 Beijing receives grain from the West during a severe famine under Mao's policies

There's More Online!

☑ **MAP** Explore the interactive version of this map on Networks.

☑ **TIME LINE** Explore the interactive version of the time line on Networks.

Cuban Missile Ranges October 1962

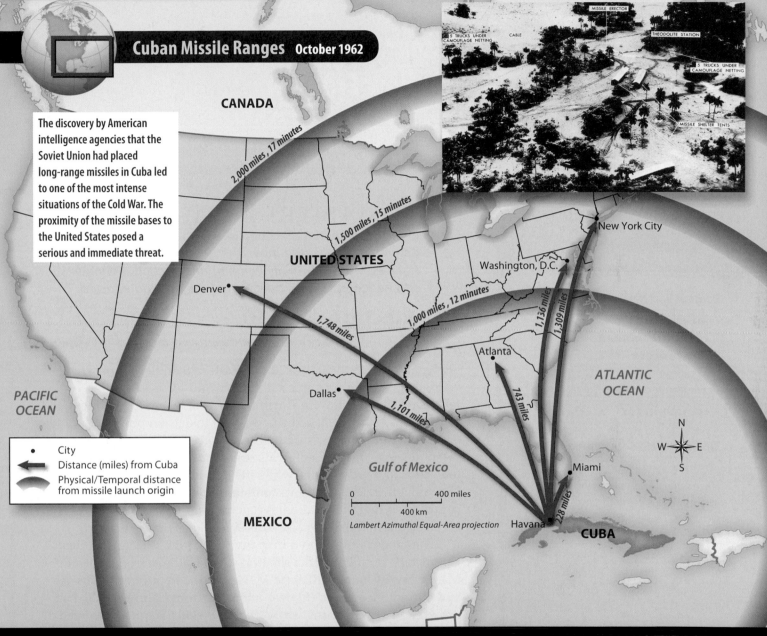

The discovery by American intelligence agencies that the Soviet Union had placed long-range missiles in Cuba led to one of the most intense situations of the Cold War. The proximity of the missile bases to the United States posed a serious and immediate threat.

CANADA

UNITED STATES

2,000 miles, 17 minutes

1,500 miles, 15 minutes

1,000 miles, 12 minutes

Denver

1,748 miles

Dallas

1,101 miles

Atlanta

743 miles

1,136 miles

1,309 miles

New York City

Washington, D.C.

ATLANTIC OCEAN

PACIFIC OCEAN

• City

Distance (miles) from Cuba

Physical/Temporal distance from missile launch origin

Gulf of Mexico

0 — 400 miles
0 — 400 km
Lambert Azimuthal Equal-Area projection

MEXICO

Havana

228 miles

Miami

CUBA

N
W — E
S

MISSILE ERECTOR
5 TRUCKS UNDER CAMOUFLAGE NETTING
CABLE
THEODOLITE STATION
5 TRUCKS UNDER CAMOUFLAGE NETTING
MISSILE SHELTER TENTS

Reading **HELP**DESK

Content Vocabulary

• missile gap
• reapportionment
• due process

Academic Vocabulary

• commentator   • arbitrary

TAKING NOTES: *Categorizing*

ACTIVITY As you read, complete a graphic organizer similar to the one below by listing domestic successes and setbacks of the Kennedy administration.

Successes	Setbacks

LESSON 1
The New Frontier

ESSENTIAL QUESTIONS · *Can government fix society's problems?* · *How do you think Presidents Kennedy and Johnson changed American society?*

IT MATTERS BECAUSE

In the presidential election campaign of 1960, John F. Kennedy promised to move the nation into "the New Frontier." After narrowly winning the election, Kennedy succeeded in getting only part of his agenda enacted.

The Election of 1960

GUIDING QUESTION *How did the election of 1960 change the way candidates ran their campaigns?*

On September 26, 1960, at 9:30 P.M. Eastern Standard Time, an estimated 75 million people sat indoors and focused on their television sets. They were watching the first televised presidential debate. The debate marked a new era of television politics.

During the 1960 presidential race, both parties made substantial use of television. The Democrats spent more than $6 million on television and radio spots, while the Republicans spent more than $7.5 million. Television news **commentator** Eric Sevareid complained that the candidates had become "packaged products." He declared that the "Processed Politician has finally arrived."

The candidates differed in many ways. John F. Kennedy, the Democratic nominee and a senator, was a Catholic from a wealthy Massachusetts family. Richard M. Nixon, the Republican nominee and current vice president, was a Quaker from California. He had grown up in a family that struggled financially. Kennedy seemed outgoing and relaxed. Nixon struck many as formal and stiff.

Although the candidates presented different styles, they differed little on key issues. Both promised to boost the economy, and both portrayed themselves as "Cold Warriors," determined to stop the forces of communism. Kennedy expressed concern about a suspected **"missile gap,"** claiming the United States lagged behind the Soviets in weaponry. Nixon warned that the Democrats' fiscal policies would boost inflation and that only he had the foreign policy experience needed for the nation.

Kennedy's Catholic faith became an issue, just as Al Smith's Catholicism had in 1928. The United States had never had a Catholic president, and many Protestants had concerns about Kennedy.

Kennedy decided to confront this issue openly in a speech: "I believe in an America where the separation of church and state is absolute—where no Catholic prelate would tell the President (should he be a Catholic) how to act and no Protestant minister would tell his parishioners for whom to vote."

The series of four televised debates influenced the election's close outcome. Kennedy won the popular vote by 118,574 out of more than 68 million votes cast, and the Electoral College by 303 votes to 219. Despite his narrow victory, Kennedy captured the imagination of the American public as few presidents had before him. During the campaign, many had been taken with Kennedy's youth and optimism. His Inaugural Address reinforced this impression. In the speech, Kennedy declared that "the torch has been passed to a new generation" and called on citizens to take a more active role in making the nation better. "My fellow Americans," he exclaimed, "ask not what your country can do for you—ask what you can do for your country."

✓ **PROGRESS CHECK**

Explaining How was the presidential election of 1960 different from earlier campaigns?

commentator one who comments, discusses, or reports in an expository manner, especially news on radio or television

missile gap a supposed shortage in the number of nuclear weapons possessed by the United States compared to the number the Soviet Union had

The Kennedy-Nixon debates were the first presidential debates to be televised.

Kennedy Takes Office

GUIDING QUESTION *What were some domestic policies initiated when Kennedy took office?*

Upon entering office, President Kennedy set out to implement a legislative agenda that became known as the New Frontier. He hoped to increase aid to education, provide health insurance to the elderly, and create a Department of Urban Affairs. He would soon find that passing such legislation was no easy task on Capitol Hill. Although the Democrats had majorities in both houses of Congress, Kennedy was unable to push through many of his programs. His narrow victory had not helped many Democrats get elected. Those who did win, therefore, felt that they owed him nothing. In addition, Southern Democrats—a large part of the Democrats in Congress— saw Kennedy's program as too expensive and, together with Republicans, were able to defeat many of Kennedy's proposals.

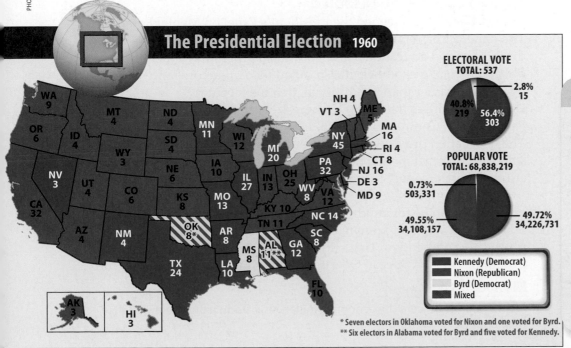

The Presidential Election 1960

ELECTORAL VOTE
TOTAL: 537

2.8% 15
40.8% 219
56.4% 303

POPULAR VOTE
TOTAL: 68,838,219

0.73% 503,331
49.55% 34,108,157
49.72% 34,226,731

Kennedy (Democrat)
Nixon (Republican)
Byrd (Democrat)
Mixed

WA 9, MT 4, ND 4, MN 11, NH 4, VT 3, ME 5, MA 16, NY 45, RI 4, CT 8, NJ 16, DE 3, MD 9, OR 6, ID 4, SD 4, WI 12, MI 20, PA 32, NV 3, UT 4, WY 3, NE 6, IA 10, IL 27, IN 13, OH 25, WV 8, VA 12, CA 32, CO 6, KS 8, MO 13, KY 10, NC 14, AZ 4, NM 4, OK 8*, AR 8, TN 11, SC 8, GA 12, MS 8, AL 11**, TX 24, LA 10, FL 10, AK 3, HI 3

GEOGRAPHY CONNECTION

Senator John F. Kennedy of Massachusetts narrowly defeated Vice President Richard Nixon in the 1960 presidential election.

1 **THE WORLD IN SPATIAL TERMS** *Which states gave one or more electoral votes to Harry Byrd?*

2 **PLACES AND REGIONS** *What region of the nation went most solidly Republican?*

* Seven electors in Oklahoma voted for Nixon and one voted for Byrd.
** Six electors in Alabama voted for Byrd and five voted for Kennedy.

When the Kennedy administration created the Presidential Commission on the Status of Women in 1961, its stated goal was to examine employment policies for women. The reasons for the formation of the commission, however, were not as clear. At the time, the Equal Rights Amendment (ERA) was considered politically dangerous and opposed by some labor leaders. The ERA was stuck in Congress because some thought it was too extreme a step in women's rights. Some believe Kennedy created the commission to address the status of women, appeal to women voters, and avoid the politically-sensitive issue of the ERA. Others believe it was created to pay a political debt to Women's Bureau leader Esther Peterson, a supporter of Kennedy.

Successes and Setbacks

President Kennedy achieved some victories, particularly in improving the economy. Although the economy had soared through much of the 1950s, it had slowed by the end of the decade. To increase economic growth and create jobs, Kennedy advocated deficit spending and investing more funds in defense and space exploration. Such spending did indeed create jobs and stimulate economic growth.

Kennedy also asked businesses to hold down prices and labor leaders to hold down pay increases. The labor unions in the steel industry agreed to reduce their demands for higher wages, but several steel companies raised prices sharply. Kennedy responded by threatening to have the Department of Defense buy cheaper foreign steel. He asked the Justice Department to investigate whether the steel industry was fixing prices. The steel companies backed down and cut their prices, but the victory caused strained relations with the business community.

In addition, the president pushed for tax cuts. When opponents argued that a tax cut would help only the wealthy, Kennedy asserted that lower taxes meant businesses would have more money to expand. This, in turn, would create new jobs and benefit everybody. However, Congress refused to pass the tax cut because of fears that it would cause inflation. Congress also blocked his plans for health insurance for senior citizens and federal aid to education. Congress did agree to Kennedy's request to raise the minimum wage, his proposal for the Area Redevelopment Act, and the Housing Act. These acts helped create jobs and build low-income housing in poor areas.

Expanding Women's Rights

In 1961 Kennedy created the Presidential Commission on the Status of Women. The commission called for federal action against gender discrimination and affirmed the right of women to equally paid employment. The commission proposed the Equal Pay Act, which Kennedy signed in 1963. Kennedy never appointed a woman to his cabinet. A number of women, however, worked in other prominent positions in the administration, including Esther Peterson, assistant secretary of labor and director of the Women's Bureau of the Department of Labor.

A New Focus on the Disabled

In 1961 Kennedy convened the President's Panel on Mental Retardation. The panel's first report called for funding of research into developmental disabilities and educational and vocational programs for people with developmental disabilities. It also called for a greater reliance on residential, rather than institutional, treatment centers.

Responding to the report, Congress enacted the Mental Retardation Facilities and Community Mental Health Centers Construction Act of 1963. This legislation provided grants to build research centers and grants to states to construct mental health centers. It also provided funds to train educational personnel to work with people with developmental disabilities.

In 1962 Eunice Kennedy Shriver, the president's sister, began a day camp at her home for children with developmental disabilities. Camp Shriver, as it was first known, offered people with disabilities a chance to be physically competitive. That effort later grew into the Special Olympics program. The first Special Olympics Games were held in Chicago in 1968.

☑ **PROGRESS CHECK**

Identifying What were the economic initiatives introduced by Kennedy after taking office?

Warren Court Reforms

GUIDING QUESTION *How important are some of the Warren Court rulings for today's society?*

In 1953 Earl Warren, governor of California, became chief justice of the United States. Under Warren's leadership, the Supreme Court issued several rulings that dramatically reshaped American politics and society.

"One Person, One Vote"

Some of the Court's more notable decisions concerned **reapportionment.** By 1960, more Americans resided in urban than in rural areas, but many states' electoral districts did not reflect this shift. In Tennessee, for example, a rural county with only 2,340 voters had one state representative, while an urban county with 133 times more voters had only seven. Thus, rural voters had far more political influence than urban ones. Some Tennessee voters took the matter to court, and their case, *Baker* v. *Carr* (1962), went to the Supreme Court. The Court ruled that federal courts had jurisdiction to hear lawsuits seeking to force states to redraw electoral districts. In *Reynolds* v. *Sims* (1964), the Court ruled that states must reapportion electoral districts along the principle of "one person, one vote," so that all citizens' votes would have equal weight, rather than giving **arbitrary** power to rural voters. The decision shifted political power from rural and often conservative areas to urban areas, where more liberal voters lived. It also boosted the political power of African Americans and Hispanics, who typically lived in cities.

reapportionment
the method states use to draw up political districts based on changes in population

arbitrary existing or coming about seemingly at random or as an unfair or unreasonable act of will

---

📜 ANALYZING SUPREME COURT CASES

BAKER v. *CARR*, 1962
REYNOLDS v. *SIMS*, 1964

Background of the Cases

Although many more Americans were living in urban areas, most states had not redrawn their political districts to reflect this shift. This gave rural voters more political influence than urban voters. In *Baker* v. *Carr*, the Supreme Court ruled on whether federal courts had jurisdiction in lawsuits seeking to force states to redraw their electoral districts. In *Reynolds* v. *Sims*, the Court decided whether uneven electoral districts violated the equal protection clause of the Fourteenth Amendment.

The 1962 Supreme Court. Seated, left to right: Associate Justices Tom Clark and Hugo Black, Chief Justice Earl Warren, Associate Justices William O. Douglas and John Harlan; standing, left to right: Associate Justices Byron White, William Brennan, Potter Stewart, and Arthur Goldberg. Justices Byron White and Arthur Goldberg were appointed by Kennedy.

How the Court Ruled

In *Baker* v. *Carr*, the Supreme Court ruled that federal courts can hear lawsuits seeking to force state authorities to redraw electoral districts. In *Reynolds* v. *Sims*, the Court ruled that the inequality of representation in the Alabama legislature did violate the equal protection clause. These rulings forced states to reapportion their political districts according to the principle of "one person, one vote."

▶ **CRITICAL THINKING**

❶ *Identifying Central Issues* What is the primary problem at issue in the *Reynolds* v. *Sims* case?

❷ *Making Inferences* How do you think reapportionment according to "one person, one vote" changed state politics?

In the Supreme Court case *Miranda v. Arizona*, attorneys argued that Ernesto Miranda (right) had no idea of his legal rights and should have been told that he had the right to a lawyer.

▶ **CRITICAL THINKING**

Drawing Conclusions What can you conclude about what police told suspects before the establishment of Miranda rights?

due process a judicial requirement that laws may not treat individuals unfairly, arbitrarily, or unreasonably, and that courts must follow proper procedures and rules when trying cases

Extending Due Process

The Supreme Court began to use the Fourteenth Amendment to extend the Bill of Rights to the states. Originally, the Bill of Rights applied only to the federal government. Many states had their own bills of rights, but some federal rights did not exist at the state level. The Fourteenth Amendment states that "no state shall . . . deprive any person of life, liberty, or property without due process of law." **Due process** means that the law may not treat individuals unfairly, arbitrarily, or unreasonably.

The Court ruled in several cases that due process meant applying the federal Bill of Rights to the states. In 1961 the Supreme Court ruled in *Mapp* v. *Ohio* that state courts could not consider evidence obtained in violation of the U.S. Constitution. In *Gideon* v. *Wainwright* (1963), the Court ruled that a defendant in a state court had the right to a lawyer, regardless of his or her ability to pay. In *Escobedo* v. *Illinois* (1964), the Court ruled that suspects must be allowed access to a lawyer and informed of their right to remain silent before being questioned. *Miranda* v. *Arizona* (1966) went further, requiring authorities to inform suspects of their right to remain silent; that anything they say can and will be used against them in court; and that they have a right to a lawyer. These warnings are known as Miranda rights.

Prayer and Privacy

The Supreme Court also reaffirmed the separation of church and state. The Court applied the First Amendment to the states in *Engel* v. *Vitale* (1962), ruling that states could not compose official prayers and require those prayers to be recited in public schools. In A*bington School District* v. *Schempp* (1963), it ruled against state-mandated Bible readings in public schools. The Court ruled in *Griswold* v. *Connecticut* (1965) that prohibiting the sale and use of birth control devices violated citizens' constitutional right to privacy. As with most rulings of the Warren Court, some people supported these decisions and others did not. What most people did agree upon, however, was the Court's pivotal role in shaping national policy. These decisions continue to shape the way Americans act and behave today.

☑ **PROGRESS CHECK**

Making Connections Which Warren Court rulings continue to be important today? Why?

PHOTO: Bettmann/CORBIS

LESSON 1 REVIEW

Reviewing Vocabulary

1. *Drawing Conclusions* Why would Americans have worried about a potential "missile gap"?

2. *Explaining* What is the purpose of due process?

Using Your Notes

3. *Making Generalizations* Review the notes that you completed during the lesson. Describe why some parts of the Kennedy administration's agenda were refused by Congress, and why others were passed.

Answering the Guiding Questions

4. *Analyzing* How did the election of 1960 change the way candidates ran their campaigns?

5. *Identifying* What were some domestic policies initiated when Kennedy took office?

6. *Evaluating* How important are some of the Warren Court rulings for today's society?

Writing Activity

7. EXPOSITORY Select one of the Supreme Court rulings from this lesson as a case study. Using the Internet, research additional background information about the case and the long-term impact of the ruling. Then write an essay presenting your findings. Essays should include an introduction, supporting paragraphs, and a conclusion.

networks

There's More Online!

☑ **BIOGRAPHY** Buzz Aldrin

☑ **BIOGRAPHY** Neil Armstrong

☑ **BIOGRAPHY** John Glenn

☑ **IMAGE** The Berlin Wall

☑ **IMAGE** Fidel Castro

☑ **PRIMARY SOURCE** Kennedy's Inaugural Address

☑ **SLIDE SHOW** The Space Program

☑ **VIDEO** JFK and the Cold War

☑ **INTERACTIVE SELF-CHECK QUIZ**

Reading **HELP**DESK

Content Vocabulary

• **flexible response**
• **space race**

Academic Vocabulary

• **conventional** • **remove**
• **institute**

TAKING NOTES: *Sequencing*

ACTIVITY As you read the lesson, complete a graphic organizer similar to the one below to record the major events of the Cold War between 1959 and 1963.

```
        ┌─────┐   ┌─────┐
┌─────┐ │     │   │     │ ┌─────┐
│Jan. │─┤     │   │     ├─│Nov. │
│1959 │ └─────┘   └─────┘ │1963 │
└─────┘   ┌─────┐ ┌─────┐ └─────┘
          │     │ │     │
          └─────┘ └─────┘
```

LESSON 2
JFK and the Cold War

ESSENTIAL QUESTIONS · *Can government fix society's problems?* · *How do you think Presidents Kennedy and Johnson changed American society?*

IT MATTERS BECAUSE

During the Kennedy administration, ongoing tensions with the Soviet Union led to crises over Cuba and West Berlin. To contain communism and stay ahead in technology, President Kennedy created aid programs for developing nations and expanded the space program.

Containing Communism

GUIDING QUESTION *How were President Kennedy's programs to combat communism different from the programs of previous administrations?*

When John F. Kennedy entered the White House in 1961, the Cold War with the Soviet Union dominated all other concerns. He used a range of programs to try to stop the spread of communism. These included a **conventional** weaponry program to give the nation's military more flexibility. The programs also included economic aid to Latin America and the creation of the Peace Corps to help developing nations.

A More Flexible Response

Kennedy took office at a time of growing global instability. Resentment at wealthy Western nations was on the rise in the developing world, often encouraged by the Soviet Union. Kennedy felt that Eisenhower had relied too heavily on nuclear weapons. To allow for a **"flexible response"** to resist Communist movements, the president pushed for a buildup of troops and conventional weapons. He also expanded the Special Forces, an elite army unit used in limited conflicts.

Aid to Other Countries

Kennedy wanted to renew diplomatic focus on Latin America, where governments were often in the hands of the wealthy few and many people lived in extreme poverty. In some countries, these conditions spurred the growth of left-wing movements aimed at overthrowing their governments. In his Inaugural Address, President Kennedy said, "To our sister republics south of our

John F. Kennedy delivered his inaugural speech on January 20, 1961. He spoke of his generation's obligation to defend liberty. Seated at right is incoming Vice President Lyndon Johnson.

▶ **CRITICAL THINKING**
Identifying Central Issues Why do you think that President Kennedy chose to speak of defending liberty during his inaugural speech?

conventional nonnuclear

flexible response the buildup of conventional troops and weapons to allow a nation to fight a limited war without using nuclear weapons

space race the Cold War competition over dominance of space exploration capability

border, we offer a special pledge—to convert our good words into good deeds—in a new alliance for progress. . . ."

When the United States became involved in Latin America, it was usually to help existing governments stay in power and to prevent Communist movements from flourishing. Poor Latin Americans resented this intrusion, just as they resented American corporations, whose presence was seen as a kind of imperialism.

The Alliance for Progress To improve relations between the United States and Latin America, Kennedy proposed the Alliance for Progress, a series of cooperative aid projects with Latin American governments. The Alliance was designed to create a "free and prosperous Latin America" that would be more stable and less likely to support Communist-inspired revolutions.

Over a 10-year period, the United States pledged $20 billion to help Latin American countries establish better schools, housing, health care, and fairer land distribution. The results were mixed. In some countries, the Alliance did promote real reform. In others, local rulers used the money to keep themselves in power.

The Peace Corps Another program aimed at helping developing nations fight poverty was the Peace Corps. This program sent Americans to provide humanitarian services in developing nations. After rigorous training, volunteers spent two years in countries that requested assistance. Among other projects, Peace Corps volunteers built roads, taught English, laid out sewage systems, and trained medical technicians.

The Cold War in Space

In 1961 Yury Gagarin (YUR•ee guh•GAHR•uhn), a Soviet astronaut, became the first person to orbit Earth. Again, as in 1957 with the launch of *Sputnik,* the first satellite, the Soviets had beaten the United States in the **space race.** Kennedy worried that Soviet successes in space might convince the world that communism was better than capitalism. Less than six weeks after the Soviet flight, the president went before Congress and declared: "I believe this Nation should commit itself to achieving the goal, before this decade is out, of landing a man on the Moon." Kennedy's speech set in motion a massive effort to develop the necessary technology. In 1962 John Glenn became the first American to orbit Earth. Six years later, the United States sent three men into orbit in a capsule called *Apollo.* The capsule was launched using the Saturn V, the most powerful rocket ever built. The Saturn V gave both *Apollo* and its lunar module—which astronauts would use to land on the moon—enough velocity to reach the moon.

On July 16, 1969, a Saturn V lifted off in Florida, carrying three American astronauts: Neil Armstrong, Edwin "Buzz" Aldrin, and Michael Collins. On July 20, Armstrong and Aldrin boarded the lunar module, named *Eagle,* and headed down to the moon. Minutes later, Armstrong radioed NASA's flight center in Texas: "Houston . . . the *Eagle* has landed." Armstrong became the first human being to walk on the moon. As he set foot on the lunar surface, he announced: "That's one small step for a man, one giant leap for mankind." The United States had demonstrated its technological superiority over the Soviet Union.

In 1962 John Glenn was the first American to orbit Earth.

▶ **CRITICAL THINKING**
Making Generalizations In addition to being explorers, what other role did the U.S. astronauts play?

institute to initiate or establish

✓ **PROGRESS CHECK**

Analyzing Why do you think the space race was a part of President Kennedy's programs to combat communism?

Crises of the Cold War

GUIDING QUESTIONS *What was the most important foreign policy event of the Kennedy administration? Why was it the most important event?*

President Kennedy's efforts to combat Communist influence in other countries led to some of the most intense crises of the Cold War. At times, these crises left Americans and people in many other nations wondering whether the world would survive.

The Bay of Pigs

The first crisis occurred in Cuba, only 90 miles (145 km) from American shores. There, Fidel Castro had overthrown the corrupt Cuban dictator Fulgencio Batista in 1959. At once, Castro established ties with the Soviet Union, **instituted** drastic land reforms, and seized foreign-owned businesses, many of which were American. Cuba's alliance with the Soviets worried many Americans. Soviet premier Nikita Khrushchev was also expressing his hope to strengthen Cuba's military.

Fearing that the Soviets would use Cuba as a base from which to spread revolution, President Eisenhower had authorized the CIA to secretly train and arm a group of Cuban exiles, known as *La Brigada,* to invade the island. His goal was to set off a popular uprising against Castro. When Kennedy became president, his advisers approved the plan. Kennedy agreed to the operation with some changes. On April 17, 1961, about 1,400 armed Cuban exiles landed at the Bay of Pigs on the south coast of Cuba. The invasion was a disaster. *La Brigada*'s boats ran aground on coral reefs. Then Kennedy canceled their air support to keep the United States's involvement a secret. The expected popular uprising never happened. Within two days, Castro's forces killed or captured almost all the members of *La Brigada.*

The Bay of Pigs was a dark moment for the Kennedy administration. The incident exposed an American plot to overthrow a neighbor's government. The disastrous outcome made the United States look weak and disorganized.

The Berlin Wall Goes Up

In June 1961, Kennedy faced another foreign policy challenge when he met with Soviet premier Nikita Khrushchev in Vienna, Austria. To stop Germans from leaving Communist East Germany for West Berlin, Khrushchev demanded that the Western powers recognize East Germany and withdraw from Berlin. Berlin was a city lying completely within East Germany. Kennedy refused and reaffirmed the West's commitment to West Berlin.

Khrushchev retaliated by building a wall through Berlin, blocking movement between the Soviet sector and the rest of the city. Guards along the wall shot at people who tried to cross from East Berlin to West Berlin. The Berlin Wall stood as a symbol of Cold War divisions.

The Cuban Missile Crisis

During the summer of 1962, American intelligence learned that Soviet technicians and equipment had arrived in Cuba and that military construction was in progress. On October 22, Kennedy announced that the Soviet Union had placed long-range nuclear missiles in Cuba. This location made them a clear threat to the United States.

Kennedy ordered a naval quarantine to stop the delivery of more missiles, and demanded the existing missile sites be dismantled. He warned that if attacked, the United States would respond fully against the Soviet Union. Still, work on the missile sites continued. Nuclear warfare seemed more possible than ever.

Then, after a flurry of secret negotiations, the Soviet Union offered to **remove** the missiles if the United States promised not to invade Cuba. The United States also agreed to remove its missiles from Turkey near the Soviet border.

In reality, neither Kennedy nor Khrushchev wanted nuclear war. "Only lunatics or suicides, who themselves want to perish and to destroy the whole world before they die, could do this," wrote Khrushchev. "We . . . want to live and do not at all want to destroy your country." On October 28, the leaders reached an agreement. The world could breathe again.

remove to take away or change the location of

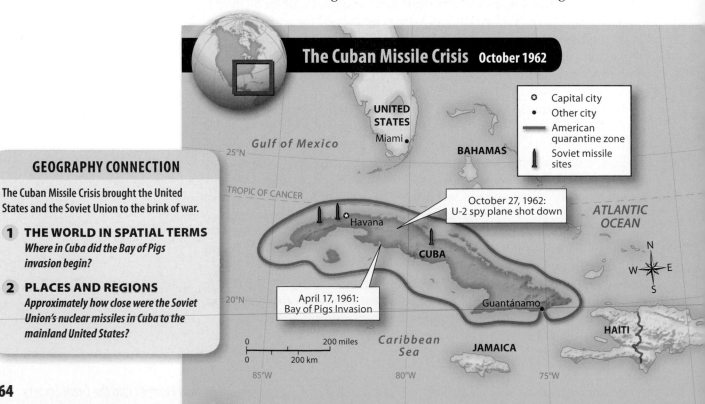

The Cuban Missile Crisis October 1962

GEOGRAPHY CONNECTION

The Cuban Missile Crisis brought the United States and the Soviet Union to the brink of war.

1 **THE WORLD IN SPATIAL TERMS**
Where in Cuba did the Bay of Pigs invasion begin?

2 **PLACES AND REGIONS**
Approximately how close were the Soviet Union's nuclear missiles in Cuba to the mainland United States?

UNITED STATES
Gulf of Mexico
Miami
BAHAMAS
25°N
TROPIC OF CANCER

Capital city
Other city
American quarantine zone
Soviet missile sites

October 27, 1962: U-2 spy plane shot down

ATLANTIC OCEAN

Havana
CUBA

April 17, 1961: Bay of Pigs Invasion

20°N
Guantánamo

HAITI

Caribbean Sea
JAMAICA

0 200 miles
0 200 km

85°W   80°W   75°W

The Cuban missile crisis forced the United States and the Soviet Union to consider the consequences of nuclear war. In August 1963, the two countries agreed to a treaty that banned testing nuclear weapons in the atmosphere. In the long run, however, the missile crisis had consequences. Soviet leadership saw Khrushchev as having agreed to a humiliating retreat, and he fell from power in 1964. The crisis also exposed the Soviets' military inferiority and prompted a dramatic Soviet arms buildup, which the United States matched.

Death of a President

Soon after the Senate ratified the test ban treaty, John F. Kennedy's presidency ended shockingly and tragically. On November 22, 1963, Kennedy and his wife traveled to Texas. As the presidential motorcade rode slowly through the crowded streets of Dallas, gunfire rang out. Someone had shot the president twice. Government officials sped Kennedy to a nearby hospital, where he was pronounced dead moments later.

Lee Harvey Oswald, the man accused of killing Kennedy, appeared to be a confused and embittered Marxist who had spent time in the Soviet Union. He himself was shot to death while in police custody two days after Kennedy's assassination. The bizarre situation led some to speculate that the second gunman, local nightclub owner Jack Ruby, killed Oswald to protect others involved in the crime. In 1964 a national commission headed by Chief Justice Warren concluded that Oswald was the lone assassin. The report of the Warren Commission left some questions unanswered. Theories about a conspiracy to kill the president have persisted, though none has gained wide acceptance.

In the wake of the assassination, the United States and much of the world went into mourning. Kennedy was president for little more than 1,000 days. Yet he made a profound impression on most Americans. Kennedy's successor, Vice President Lyndon Baines Johnson, set out to promote many of the programs that Kennedy left unfinished.

President Kennedy's funeral procession and burial service were broadcast live over all three television networks.

▶ **CRITICAL THINKING**
Predicting Consequences What effect do you think Kennedy's assassination had on how his presidency is remembered?

✓ **PROGRESS CHECK**

Interpreting Significance How do you think the assassination of President Kennedy affected the nation?

PHOTO: Bettmann/CORBIS

LESSON 2 REVIEW

Reviewing Vocabulary

1. *Explaining* How was Kennedy's "flexible response" different from Eisenhower's strategy for containing communism?

2. *Summarizing* Why was the space race so important to the United States?

Using Your Notes

3. *Making Generalizations* Use the notes you completed during the lesson to describe which areas the Kennedy administration succeeded in, and which areas posed setbacks to the president's drive to win the Cold War.

Answering the Guiding Questions

4. *Analyzing* How were President Kennedy's programs to combat communism different from the programs of previous administrations?

5. *Synthesizing* What was the most important foreign policy event of the Kennedy administration? Why was it the most important event?

Writing Activity

6. DESCRIPTIVE Write two to three descriptive paragraphs explaining how President Kennedy's programs affected the world and the American people, both in his leadership and in his death.

netw⊙rks

There's More Online!

☑ **BIOGRAPHY** Barry Goldwater

☑ **BIOGRAPHY** Michael Harrington

☑ **BIOGRAPHY** Robert Weaver

☑ **VIDEO** The Great Society

☑ **INTERACTIVE SELF-CHECK QUIZ**

LESSON 3
The Great Society

ESSENTIAL QUESTIONS · *Can government fix society's problems?* · *How do you think Presidents Kennedy and Johnson changed American society?*

Reading **HELP**DESK

Content Vocabulary

• consensus

Academic Vocabulary

• confine   • subsidy

TAKING NOTES: *Organizing*

ACTIVITY As you read, complete a graphic organizer similar to the one below to list the social and economic programs started during Lyndon Johnson's administration.

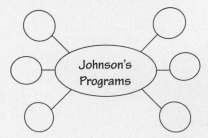

IT MATTERS BECAUSE

Lyndon B. Johnson had decades of experience in Congress and was skilled in getting legislation enacted. When he became president, he moved quickly to push for passage of civil rights and antipoverty bills.

Johnson Takes the Reins

GUIDING QUESTION *How did President Johnson's experience in Congress help him get legislation passed?*

Just hours after President Kennedy had been pronounced dead, Lyndon B. Johnson took the oath of office in the cabin of *Air Force One.* Days later, Johnson appeared before Congress and urged the nation to move forward and build on Kennedy's legacy. "[T]he ideas and ideals which [Kennedy] so nobly represented must and will be translated into effective action," he declared. Although the nation that President Johnson inherited appeared to be booming, not all Americans shared in its prosperity. In his 1962 book *The Other America*, writer Michael Harrington claimed that almost 50 million truly poor Americans lived largely hidden in slums, Appalachia, the Deep South, and Native American reservations. Soon after taking office, Johnson decided to launch an antipoverty crusade.

Johnson's Leadership Style

Lyndon Baines Johnson was born and raised in the "hill country" of central Texas, near the banks of the Pedernales River. Johnson remained a Texan in his heart, and his style posed a striking contrast with Kennedy's. He was a man of impressive stature who spoke directly, convincingly, and even roughly at times. By the time he became president at age 55, Johnson already had 26 years of congressional experience behind him. He earned a reputation as a man who got things done. He did favors, twisted arms, bargained, flattered, and threatened in order to find **consensus,** or general agreement. His ability to build coalitions had made him one of the most effective and powerful leaders in Senate history.

A War on Poverty

Why was Johnson concerned about the poor? He had known hard times growing up, and had seen extreme poverty firsthand in a brief career as a teacher in a low-income area. He also believed that a wealthy, powerful government should try to improve the lives of its citizens. Finally, there was Johnson's ambition. He wanted history to portray him as a great president.

Before his death, Kennedy had plans for an antipoverty program and a civil rights bill. Continuing these efforts seemed logical. Johnson knew that any program linked to the slain president would be popular. In his State of the Union address in 1964, he said: "Unfortunately, many Americans live on the outskirts of hope—some because of their poverty, and some because of their color, and all too many because of both. Our task is to help replace their despair with opportunity. This administration . . . declares unconditional war on poverty in America."

By the summer of 1964, Johnson had convinced Congress to pass the Economic Opportunity Act, which attacked inadequate public services, illiteracy, and unemployment. The act established 10 new programs within a new agency, the Office of Economic Opportunity (OEO). Many of the new programs were directed at young, inner-city Americans.

The Neighborhood Youth Corps provided work-study programs to help the underprivileged earn a high school diploma or college degree. The Job Corps helped unemployed people ages 16–21 acquire job skills. One of the more dramatic programs introduced was VISTA (Volunteers in Service to America), which was essentially a domestic Peace Corps. VISTA put young people with skills and community-minded ideals to work in poor neighborhoods and rural areas to help people overcome poverty. Additional programs included Upward Bound, which offered tutoring to high school students, and a Work Experience Program, which provided day care and other support for those in poor households to enable them to work.

The Election of 1964

Johnson quickly won public approval, but just as quickly had to run for the office he first gained through tragedy. The Republican candidate in the 1964 election was Senator Barry Goldwater of Arizona, known for his strong conservatism. "Extremism in the defense of liberty is no vice. Moderation in the pursuit of justice is no virtue," Goldwater declared when accepting the nomination. Few Americans were ready to embrace Goldwater's message,

consensus general agreement

POVERTY RATE IN AMERICA, 1960–2000

Percentage of population / *Year*

Source: U.S. Census Bureau.

CHARTS/GRAPHS

At left, an unemployed miner and his family posed on the porch of their Kentucky home in 1964.

▶ **CRITICAL THINKING**

1 *Making Generalizations* Based on the data in the chart, what decade had the greatest decrease in the poverty rate? Why do you think this was the case?

2 *Analyzing Information* Based on the data in the chart, how successful was Johnson's War on Poverty?

PHOTOS: John Dominis/Time Life Pictures/Getty Images

WHAT WAS THE GREAT SOCIETY?

Health and Welfare	Education	The War on Poverty	Consumer and Environmental Protection
Medicare (1965) established a comprehensive health insurance program for all senior citizens; financed through the Social Security system.	**Elementary and Secondary Education Act** (1965) targeted aid to students and funded related activities such as adult education and education consulting.	**Office of Economic Opportunity** (1964) oversaw many programs to improve life in inner cities, including Job Corps, an education and job training program for at-risk youth.	**Clean Air Act** (1963) **and Water Quality Act** (1965) supported development of standards and goals for water and air quality.
Medicaid (1965) provided health and medical assistance to low-income families; funded through federal and state governments.	**Higher Education Act** (1965) supported college tuition scholarships, student loans, and work-study programs for low- and middle-income students.	**Housing and Urban Development Act** (1965) established new housing subsidy programs and made federal loans and public housing grants easier to obtain.	**Highway Safety Act** (1966) improved federal, state, and local coordination and created training standards for emergency medical technicians.
Child Nutrition Act (1966) established a school breakfast program and expanded the school lunch and milk programs to improve nutrition.	**Project Head Start** (1965) funded a preschool program for disadvantaged children.	**Demonstration Cities and Metropolitan Development Act** (1966) revitalized urban areas through a variety of social and economic programs.	**Fair Packaging and Labeling Act** (1966) required all consumer products to have true and informative labels.

CHARTS/GRAPHS

▶ **CRITICAL THINKING**

1 *Identifying Central Issues* What was the purpose of the Water Quality Act and Clean Air Act?

2 *Analyzing Information* Which Great Society program do you think had the most effect on American life? Why do you think so?

which seemed too aggressive for a nation nervous about nuclear war. On Election Day, Johnson won in a landslide, gaining more than 61 percent of the popular vote and winning all but six states in the Electoral College.

✓ **PROGRESS CHECK**

Explaining What parts of Johnson's congressional background helped him get his legislation approved?

The Great Society

GUIDING QUESTION *How does Great Society legislation influence current government programs and philosophies?*

After his election, Johnson began working with Congress to create the "Great Society" he had promised during his campaign. His goals reflected the times. The civil rights movement had brought racial inequalities to the forefront, and the strong economy encouraged people to believe that poverty could be reduced. Johnson noted the Great Society's goals during a speech in May 1964, aiming not to **confine** government efforts but to form a society "where the city of man serves not only the needs of the body and the demands of commerce but the desire for beauty and the hunger for community."

Johnson's ambitious vision encompassed more than 60 programs initiated between 1965 and 1968, including Medicare and Medicaid. Medicare had strong support because it was offered to all senior citizens, about half of whom lacked health insurance. Medicare's twin program, Medicaid, financed health care for welfare recipients living below the poverty line. These programs reflected New Deal ideals by entitling categories of Americans to benefits.

Great Society programs also strongly supported education. The Elementary and Secondary Education Act of 1965 granted millions of dollars to public and private schools. Education efforts also extended to preschoolers through Project Head Start, for disadvantaged children who had "never looked at a picture book or scribbled with a crayon."

confine to limit or restrict

During this period, major civil rights goals were also achieved: the Civil Rights Act of 1964 barred discrimination of many kinds and the Voting Rights Act of 1965 protected voters from discriminatory practices. Johnson also urged Congress to act on several pieces of legislation addressing urban issues. One created a new cabinet agency, the Department of Housing and Urban Development, in 1965. Its first secretary, Robert Weaver, was the first African American to serve in the cabinet. A broad-based program informally called "Model Cities" authorized federal **subsidies** to many cities to improve transportation, health care, housing, and policing.

One notable Great Society measure changed the composition of the American population: the Immigration Act of 1965. This act ended the system established in the 1920s that gave preference to northern European immigrants. The new law opened wider the door of the United States to immigrants from all parts of Europe, Asia, and Africa.

The Great Society's Legacy

Great Society programs touched nearly every aspect of American life and improved many lives. In the years since Johnson left office, however, debate has continued over whether the Great Society was truly a success. In many ways, the impact of the Great Society was limited. Some programs did not work as well as hoped. In many cases, the programs grew so quickly they became unmanageable and difficult to evaluate.

Cities, states, and groups eligible for aid began to expect immediate and life-changing benefits. Other Americans opposed the massive growth of federal programs. When Johnson attempted to fund both his grand domestic agenda and the increasingly costly war in Vietnam, the Great Society eventually suffered. Some Great Society initiatives have survived, however, including Medicare and Medicaid, the Department of Transportation, the Department of Housing and Urban Development (HUD), and Project Head Start. Overall, the programs provided some important benefits to poor communities and gave political and administrative experience to minority groups.

An important legacy of the Great Society was the questions it raised. How can the federal government help disadvantaged citizens? How much government help can a society provide without weakening the private sector? How much help can people receive without losing motivation to fight against hardships on their own? Lyndon Johnson took office determined to change the United States in a way few other presidents had attempted. If he fell short, it was perhaps that the goals he set were so high.

☑ **PROGRESS CHECK**

Making Connections What government programs carry on the ideals of the Great Society?

---

subsidy money granted by the government to achieve a specific goal that is beneficial to society

Analyzing
PRIMARY SOURCES

The Challenge of Poverty

❝The walls of the ghettos are not going to topple overnight, nor is it possible to wipe out the heritage of generations of social, economic and educational deprivation by the stroke of a Presidential pen. The war against poverty is a long-range undertaking. It requires staying power as well as a sense of urgency.❞

—*New York Times* editorial,
January 1, 1967

DBQ *USING CONTEXT CLUES*
Based on its use in the passage above, what is the meaning of deprivation?

LESSON 3 REVIEW

Reviewing Vocabulary

1. *Explaining* Why is the ability to build a consensus an important skill for a leader?

Using Your Notes

2. *Categorizing* Use the notes you completed during the lesson to group the programs Johnson created into categories.

Answering the Guiding Questions

3. *Analyzing* How did President Johnson's experience in Congress help him get legislation passed?

4. *Synthesizing* How does Great Society legislation influence current government programs and philosophies?

Writing Activity

5. EXPOSITORY What connections can you make between the ideals of the New Deal and those of the Great Society? Write a short essay in which you analyze efforts to extend New Deal goals through the Great Society, and evaluate the successes and failures of those efforts.

Directions: On a separate sheet of paper, answer the questions below. Make sure you read carefully and answer all parts to the question.

Lesson Review

Lesson 1

1 *Summarizing* In what ways did the rulings of the Supreme Court under Chief Justice Warren benefit American citizens?

2 *Analyzing* Why was President Kennedy unable to achieve all of his New Frontier plans?

Lesson 2

3 *Evaluating* Why did Kennedy want the United States to reach the moon first?

4 *Making Connections* What was the purpose of the Berlin Wall, and what did it come to symbolize?

Lesson 3

5 *Assessing* How did establishing the Medicare program reflect the ideas of the Great Society programs?

6 *Analyzing Issues* What factors motivated President Johnson to try to help Americans living in poverty?

21st Century Skills

7 **UNDERSTANDING RELATIONSHIPS AMONG EVENTS** What fundamental principles were reflected in both the Warren Court reforms and Kennedy's New Frontier?

8 **EXPLAINING CONTINUITY AND CHANGE** What was the purpose behind the Bay of Pigs invasion, and why did it fail?

9 **UNDERSTANDING RELATIONSHIPS AMONG EVENTS** What impact did the construction of the Berlin Wall have on the relationship between the United States and the Soviet Union?

10 **DECISION MAKING** What drove President Johnson's decision to continue the legacy of President Kennedy?

Exploring the Essential Questions

11 *Analyzing Ethical Issues* Write a one-act play that shows how the policies of Presidents Kennedy and Johnson changed American society, including ways that can be seen today. Have characters in the play answer the question: "Can government fix society's problems?"

DBQ Document-Based Questions

Use the cartoon to answer the following questions.

President Johnson's budget is the subject of this 1965 political cartoon.

HERBLOCK'S CARTOON

"Kindly Move Over A Little, Gentlemen"

12 *Analyzing Visuals* What does the boy represent, and why do you think the cartoonist made him so small?

13 *Drawing Inferences* According to the cartoon, what is Johnson trying to do?

Extended-Response Question

14 *Comparing and Contrasting* Write an expository essay that compares, contrasts, and evaluates the New Frontier and the Great Society. Essays should include an introduction, supporting paragraphs, and a conclusion.

Need Extra Help?

If You've Missed Question	**1**	**2**	**3**	**4**	**5**	**6**	**7**	**8**	**9**	**10**	**11**	**12**	**13**	**14**
Go to page	559	557	562	564	568	567	557	563	564	567	557	570	570	557

The Civil Rights Movement

1954–1968

ESSENTIAL QUESTIONS · *Why do you think the civil rights movement made gains in postwar America?* · *What motivates a society to make changes?*

The Story Matters...

The civil rights movement gained momentum rapidly after World War II. Supreme Court rulings, massive protests by civil rights groups, and new federal legislation all combined to make racial segregation illegal in the United States.

◄ Rosa Parks's refusal to give up her seat on a Montgomery, Alabama, bus was the spark that launched the Montgomery bus boycott in 1955.

PHOTO: Bettmann/CORBIS

CHAPTER 25

Place and Time: United States 1954–1968

Rosa Parks made a decision in December 1955 that ignited a movement to end segregation and achieve civil liberties for all Americans. A young pastor by the name of Martin Luther King, Jr., spearheaded efforts to reach these goals. By the mid-1960s, civil rights activists had gained two important pieces of legislation: the Civil Rights Act of 1964 and the Voting Rights Act of 1965.

Step Into the Place

Read the quotes and look at the information presented on the map.

DBQ **Daisy Bates and Orval Faubus both describe the situation in Little Rock, Arkansas, in 1957. How do the two quotes reflect different perspectives?**

PRIMARY SOURCE

❝Suddenly I realized that this calm I had so taken for granted was only the calm before the storm, that this was war, and that as State President of the National Association for the Advancement of Colored People I was in the front-line trenches. Was I ready for war? . . . Who was I really and what did I stand for? . . . [M]y mind ranged over these questions and over the whole course of my life. Toward dawn I knew I had found the answer. I was ready. I drifted off into the sleep of a mind no longer torn by doubt or indecision.❞

—Daisy Bates, from *The Long Shadow of Little Rock: A Memoir*, 1962

PRIMARY SOURCE

❝Malice, envy, hate is deplorable, in any place or in any circumstances, but as President Eisenhower has said himself, you can't change the hearts of people by law. Now, in view of the progress that we have made, all I ask for in this situation, and all I've ever asked for, is some time for the situation to change for it to become acceptable, so that there would not be disorder and violence. . . . So, why should we be so impatient as to want to force it, because force begets force, hate begets hate, malice begets malice. But, if time was given for an adjustment of the attitudes and the feelings of people, then it can be peacefully accomplished, which would be better for all concerned.❞

—Orval Faubus, from an interview with news commentator Mike Wallace, September 15, 1957

Step Into the Time

Choose an event from the time line and write a paragraph describing the general social, political, or economic consequences that event might have had on the civil rights movement.

U.S. PRESIDENTS

UNITED STATES

WORLD

Eisenhower 1953–1961

May 17, 1954 *Brown* v. *Board of Education* ruling is issued

December 1955 Montgomery, Alabama, bus boycott begins

September 1957 Eisenhower sends federal troops to ensure integration of a Little Rock high school

1960 Greensboro sit-in begins

1956

1959

February 1959 European Court of Human Rights holds first session in Strasbourg, France

1960 Nigeria gains independence

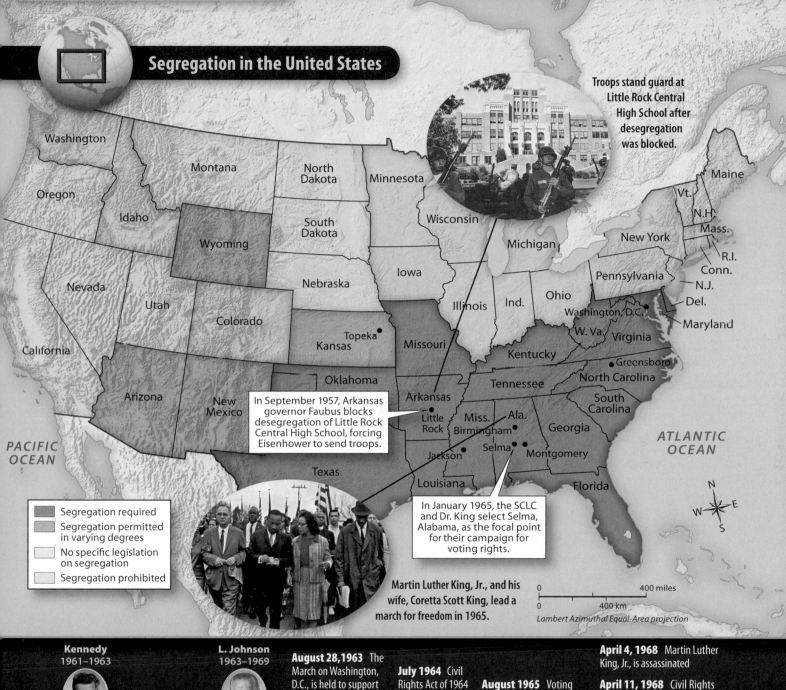

networks

There's More Online!

☑ **MAP** Explore the interactive version of this map on Networks.

☑ **TIME LINE** Explore the interactive version of the time line on Networks.

Segregation in the United States

Washington
Oregon
Montana
Idaho
North Dakota
Minnesota
South Dakota
Wisconsin
Michigan
Maine
Vt.
N.H
Mass.
New York
R.I.
Conn.
N.J.
Pennsylvania
Del.
Wyoming
Iowa
Nebraska
Ohio
Washington, D.C.
Maryland
Nevada
Utah
Illinois
Ind.
W. Va.
Virginia
California
Colorado
Topeka
Kansas
Missouri
Kentucky
Greensboro
Oklahoma
Tennessee
North Carolina
Arizona
New Mexico
Arkansas
Little Rock
Miss.
Ala.
Birmingham
Selma
Montgomery
South Carolina
Georgia
Jackson
Texas
Louisiana
Florida

PACIFIC OCEAN

ATLANTIC OCEAN

Troops stand guard at Little Rock Central High School after desegregation was blocked.

In September 1957, Arkansas governor Faubus blocks desegregation of Little Rock Central High School, forcing Eisenhower to send troops.

In January 1965, the SCLC and Dr. King select Selma, Alabama, as the focal point for their campaign for voting rights.

Martin Luther King, Jr., and his wife, Coretta Scott King, lead a march for freedom in 1965.

Legend
- Segregation required
- Segregation permitted in varying degrees
- No specific legislation on segregation
- Segregation prohibited

0   400 miles
0   400 km

Lambert Azimuthal Equal-Area projection

W-N-E-S

Kennedy 1961–1963

L. Johnson 1963–1969

August 28, 1963 The March on Washington, D.C., is held to support the civil rights bill

July 1964 Civil Rights Act of 1964 passes

August 1965 Voting Rights Act passes

April 4, 1968 Martin Luther King, Jr., is assassinated

April 11, 1968 Civil Rights Act of 1968 is passed

1962   **1965**   **1968**

March 1961 South Africa withdraws from British Commonwealth, adhering to its policy of apartheid

August 1962 Nelson Mandela is arrested in South Africa for stance against apartheid

October 1962 Cuban missile crisis erupts

1964 Tokyo Olympic Games ban South Africa for its apartheid policy

1966 China's Cultural Revolution begins

April 11, 1968 At Mexico Summer Olympics, U.S. sprinters Tommie Smith and John Carlos give black power salute and are suspended from the team

networks

There's More Online!

☑ **BIOGRAPHY** Martin Luther King, Jr.

☑ **BIOGRAPHY** Thurgood Marshall

☑ **BIOGRAPHY** Rosa Parks

☑ **BIOGRAPHY** Linda Brown Thompson

☑ **IMAGE** Montgomery Bus Boycott

☑ **PRIMARY SOURCE** Excerpts from the *Brown* v. *Board of Education* Supreme Court Ruling

☑ **VIDEO** The Movement Begins

☑ **INTERACTIVE SELF-CHECK QUIZ**

Reading **HELP**DESK

Content Vocabulary

• "separate but equal"
• de facto segregation

Academic Vocabulary

• facility

TAKING NOTES: *Organizing*

ACTIVITY As you read, complete a graphic organizer similar to the one below by listing the techniques used to challenge segregation.

Civil Rights Movement

LESSON 1
The Movement Begins

ESSENTIAL QUESTIONS • *Why do you think the civil rights movement made gains in postwar America?* • *What motivates a society to make changes?*

IT MATTERS BECAUSE

After World War II, African Americans and other civil rights supporters challenged segregation in the United States. Their efforts were strongly opposed by Southern segregationists. Eventually, the federal government began to take a firmer stand for civil rights.

The Origins of the Movement

GUIDING QUESTION *What techniques did the civil rights movement use to challenge segregation?*

On December 1, 1955, Rosa Parks left her job as a seamstress in Montgomery, Alabama, and boarded a bus to go home. In 1955, buses in Montgomery reserved seats in the front for whites and seats in the rear for African Americans. Seats in the middle were available to African Americans only if there were few whites on the bus. Parks took a seat just behind the white section, and soon all of the seats on the bus were filled. When the driver noticed a white man standing, he told Parks and three other African Americans in her row to get up so the white man could sit down. When Parks did not move, the driver called the police.

News of Parks's arrest reached the National Association for the Advancement of Colored People (NAACP), which asked Parks whether her case could be used to challenge segregation. Parks replied, "If you think it will mean something to Montgomery and do some good, I'll be happy to go along with it."

Parks's decision would spark a new era in the civil rights movement. The struggle would not be easy. In 1896 the Supreme Court had declared segregation to be constitutional in *Plessy* v. *Ferguson*, which established the **"separate but equal"** doctrine. Laws that segregated African Americans were permitted as long as equal **facilities** were provided. The facilities provided for African Americans, however, were usually of poorer quality than those provided for whites. Areas without laws requiring segregation often had **de facto segregation**—segregation by custom and tradition.

Court Challenges Begin

The civil rights movement had been building for a long time. Since 1909, the NAACP had supported court cases aimed at overturning segregation. Over the years, the NAACP had achieved some victories. In 1935, for example, the Supreme Court ruled in *Norris* v. *Alabama* that exclusion of African Americans from juries violated their rights to equal protection under the law.

New Political Power

African Americans also enjoyed increased political power. Northern politicians increasingly sought their votes and listened to their concerns. During the 1930s, many African Americans benefited from New Deal programs and began supporting the Democratic Party. This gave the party new strength in the North. The northern wing of the party was now able to counter Southern Democrats, who often supported segregation.

The Push for Desegregation

During World War II, African American leaders began to use their political power to help end discrimination in wartime factories. They also increased opportunities for African Americans in the military.

In 1942 James Farmer and George Houser founded the Congress of Racial Equality (CORE) in Chicago. CORE began using sit-ins, a form of protest popularized by union workers in the 1930s, to desegregate restaurants that refused to serve African Americans. Using the sit-in strategy,

"separate but equal"
a doctrine established by the 1896 Supreme Court case *Plessy v. Ferguson* that permitted laws segregating African Americans as long as equal facilities were provided

facility something that is built, installed, or established to serve a particular purpose

de facto segregation segregation by custom and tradition

ANALYZING SUPREME COURT CASES

BROWN v. *BOARD OF EDUCATION* (1954)

Background of the Case

One of the most important Supreme Court cases in American history began in 1952, when the Supreme Court agreed to hear the NAACP's case *Brown* v. *Board of Education of Topeka, Kansas,* and three other cases. They all dealt with the question of whether the principle "separate but equal," established in *Plessy v. Ferguson,* was constitutional with regard to public schools.

How the Court Ruled

In a unanimous decision in 1954, the Court ruled in favor of Linda Brown and the other plaintiffs. In doing so, it overruled *Plessy v. Ferguson*. It rejected the idea that equivalent but separate schools for African American and white students were constitutional. The Court held that racial segregation in public schools violated the Fourteenth Amendment's equal protection clause. Chief Justice Earl Warren summed up the Court's decision, declaring: "[I]n the field of public education, the doctrine of 'separate but equal' has no place. Separate educational facilities are inherently unequal." The Court's rejection of "separate but equal" was a major victory for the civil rights movement. It led to the overturning of laws requiring segregation in other public places.

The children involved in the *Brown* v. *Board of Education* case are shown in this 1953 photograph. They are, from front to back, Vicki Henderson, Donald Henderson, Linda Brown (of the case title), James Emanuel, Nancy Todd, and Katherine Carper. Together, their cases led to the Supreme Court decision that public schools could not be segregated on the basis of race.

▶ CRITICAL THINKING

❶ *Explaining* Why did the Supreme Court find in favor of Linda Brown?

❷ *Examining* Why was the ruling in *Brown* v. *Board of Education* so important?

members of CORE went to segregated restaurants. They sat down and refused to leave. The sit-ins were intended to shame managers into integrating their restaurants. CORE successfully integrated many public facilities in Northern cities, including Chicago, Detroit, Denver, and Syracuse.

Brown v. Board of Education

After World War II, the NAACP continued to challenge segregation in the courts. From 1939 to 1961, the NAACP's chief counsel and director of its Legal Defense and Educational Fund was African American attorney Thurgood Marshall. After the war, Marshall focused his efforts on ending segregation in public schools.

In 1954 the Supreme Court decided to combine several cases and issue a general ruling on segregation in schools. One of the cases involved a young African American girl named Linda Brown, who was denied admission to her neighborhood school in Topeka, Kansas, because of her race. She was told to attend an all-black school across town. With the help of the NAACP, her parents sued the Topeka school board. On May 17, 1954, the Supreme Court ruled unanimously in *Brown v. Board of Education of Topeka, Kansas,* that segregation in public schools was unconstitutional.

Southern Resistance

The *Brown* decision marked a dramatic reversal of the precedent established in the *Plessy* v. *Ferguson* case in 1896. *Brown* v. *Board of Education* applied only to public schools, but the ruling threatened the entire system of segregation. Although it convinced many African Americans that the time had come to challenge segregation, it also angered many white Southerners. Some became even more determined to defend segregation, regardless of what the Supreme Court ruled.

Although some school districts in the Upper South integrated their schools, anger and opposition was a far more common reaction. Senator Harry F. Byrd of Virginia called on Southerners to adopt "massive resistance" against the ruling. Across the South, hundreds of thousands of white Americans joined citizens' councils to pressure their local governments and school boards into defying the Supreme Court. Many states adopted pupil assignment laws, which established elaborate requirements other than race that schools could use to prevent African Americans from attending white schools.

The Supreme Court inadvertently encouraged white resistance when it followed up its decision in *Brown* v. *Board of Education* a year later. The Court ordered school districts to proceed "with all deliberate speed" to end school segregation. The wording was vague enough that many districts were able to keep their schools segregated for many more years.

Massive resistance also appeared in Congress. In 1956 a group of 101 Southern members of Congress signed the "Southern Manifesto." It denounced the Supreme Court's ruling as "a clear abuse of judicial power" and pledged to use "all lawful means" to reverse the decision. Not until 1969 did the Supreme Court order all school systems to desegregate "at once" and operate integrated schools "now and hereafter."

✓ **PROGRESS CHECK**

Examining What two types of segregation were practiced in the South?

Dr. Martin Luther King, Jr., used his position as a minister to preach his message of nonviolent resistance.

▶ **CRITICAL THINKING**
Drawing Conclusions Why do you think Dr. King was effective in getting his message across?

The Civil Rights Movement Begins

GUIDING QUESTION *Why was the Montgomery bus boycott successful?*

In the midst of the uproar over the *Brown* v. *Board of Education* case, Rosa Parks made her decision to challenge segregation of public transportation. Jo Ann Robinson, head of a local group called the Women's Political Council, called on African Americans to boycott Montgomery's buses on the day Rosa Parks appeared in court. The boycott marked the start of a new era of the civil rights movement among African Americans.

The Montgomery Bus Boycott

The Montgomery bus boycott had a successful outcome. Several African American leaders formed the Montgomery Improvement Association to run the boycott and to negotiate with city leaders. They elected a 26-year-old pastor named Martin Luther King, Jr., to lead them.

Dr. King encouraged the people to continue their protest, but cautioned that the protest had to be peaceful:

PRIMARY SOURCE

66 Now let us say that we are not advocating violence. . . . The only weapon that we have in our hands this evening is the weapon of protest. . . . If we were incarcerated behind the iron curtains of a communistic nation—we couldn't do this. If we were trapped in the dungeon of a totalitarian regime— we couldn't do this. But the great glory of American democracy is the right to protest for right. 99

—quoted in *Parting the Waters: America in the King Years,* 1989

King had earned a Ph.D. in theology from Boston University. He believed that the only moral way to end segregation and racism was through nonviolent passive resistance. African Americans, he urged, must say to racists, "[W]e will soon wear you down by our capacity to suffer. And in winning our freedom we will so appeal to your heart and conscience that we will win you in the process."

King's powerful words stirred African Americans in Montgomery to continue their boycott for over a year. In November 1956, the Supreme Court declared Alabama's laws requiring segregation on buses unconstitutional. After the Court's ruling, the Montgomery boycott was ended. Many other cities in the South, however, successfully resisted integrating their public transportation systems for years.

African American Churches

Martin Luther King, Jr., was not the only local minister in the bus boycott. Many of the other leaders were African American ministers. African American churches served as forums for protests and planning meetings and mobilized volunteers.

The Montgomery bus boycott had demonstrated that nonviolent protest could be successful. Dr. King, Reverend Fred Shuttlesworth of Birmingham, Alabama, and other African American ministers and civil rights activists established the Southern Christian Leadership Conference (SCLC) in 1957. The SCLC set out to eliminate segregation and to encourage African Americans to register to vote. Dr. King served as the SCLC's first president. The organization challenged segregation at voting booths and in public transportation, housing, and accommodations.

✔ PROGRESS CHECK

Drawing Conclusions How did the bus boycott create a mass movement for change?

African Americans walk to work during the third month of the Montgomery bus boycott.

▶ CRITICAL THINKING
Determining Cause and Effect
Consider the number of people you see walking in this photograph. Why do you think the bus boycott was effective?

PHOTO: Don Cravens/Time Life Pictures/Getty Images; TEXT: (a) Martin Luther King, Jr., "Address to the Montgomery Improvement Association," December 5, 1955, reprinted in The Papers of Martin Luther King, Jr., vol. 3, ed. Clayborne Carson (Berkeley: University of California Press, 1994), 72. Reprinted by arrangement with The Heirs to the Estate of Martin Luther King Jr., c/o Writers House as agent for the proprietor New York, NY. Copyright 1963 Dr. Martin Luther King, Jr.; copyright renewed 1991 Coretta Scott King; (b) Martin Luther King, Jr., The Papers of Martin Luther King Jr.: Volume IV: Symbol of the Movement, January 1957–December 1958. (Berkeley, University of California Press, 2000) Pg 341. Reprinted by arrangement with The Heirs to the Estate of Martin Luther King Jr., c/o Writers House as agent for the proprietor New York, NY. Copyright 1963 Dr. Martin Luther King Jr; copyright renewed 1991 Coretta Scott King.

Eisenhower Responds

GUIDING QUESTION *How did President Eisenhower respond to the civil rights movement?*

President Eisenhower sympathized with the civil rights movement, yet he feared the possible effect of a court ruling overturning segregation. Following the precedent set by President Truman, he ordered navy shipyards and veterans' hospitals to desegregate. At the same time, Eisenhower disagreed with using protests and court rulings. He believed segregation and racism would end gradually, as values changed. With the nation in the midst of the Cold War, he worried that challenging white Southerners might divide the nation. Publicly, he refused to endorse the *Brown* v. *Board of Education* decision, remarking, "I don't believe you can change the hearts of men with laws or decisions." Regardless, Eisenhower knew he had to uphold the authority of the federal government. As a result, he became the first president since Reconstruction to send troops into the South to protect the rights of African Americans.

Crisis in Little Rock

In September 1957, the school board in Little Rock, Arkansas, was under a federal court order requiring that nine African American students be admitted to Central High. The governor of Arkansas, Orval Faubus, was determined to win reelection. He began to campaign as a defender of white supremacy. He ordered troops from the Arkansas National Guard to prevent the nine students from entering the school. As the National Guard troops surrounded the school, an angry white mob gathered to intimidate students.

Faubus had used the armed forces of a state to oppose the federal government—the first such challenge to the Constitution since the Civil War. Eisenhower knew that he could not allow Faubus to defy the federal government. After a conference between Eisenhower and Faubus proved fruitless, the district court ordered the governor to remove the troops. Instead of ending the crisis, however, Faubus simply left the school to the mob. After the African American students entered the building, angry whites beat at least two African American reporters and broke many windows.

The violence finally convinced President Eisenhower that he had to act. Federal authority had to be upheld. He immediately ordered the U.S. Army to send troops to Little Rock and federalized the Arkansas National Guard. By nightfall, more than 1,000 soldiers of the 101st Airborne Division had arrived. By 5:00 A.M., the troops had encircled the school, bayonets ready. A few hours later, the nine African American students arrived in an army station wagon and walked into the high school. Federal authority had been upheld, but the troops had to stay in Little Rock for the rest of the school year.

Arkansas governor Orval Faubus is shown holding up a paper arguing that the federal government was abusing its power by forcibly integrating Central High.

▶ **CRITICAL THINKING**
Identifying Central Issues Why did President Eisenhower send troops to Little Rock?

New Civil Rights Legislation

In the same year that the Little Rock crisis began, Congress passed the first civil rights law since Reconstruction. The Civil Rights Act of 1957 was intended to protect the right of African Americans to vote. Eisenhower believed firmly in the right to vote, and he viewed it as his responsibility to protect voting rights. He also knew that if he sent a civil rights bill to Congress, conservative Southern Democrats would try to block the

In 1957 Elizabeth Eckford (left center) was one of the "Little Rock Nine," those African American students determined to integrate Central High School in Little Rock.

▶ **CRITICAL THINKING**
Drawing Inferences Why do you think the crowd is shouting at Elizabeth Eckford?

PHOTO: Bettmann/CORBIS

legislation. In 1956 he did send the bill to Congress, hoping not only to split the Democratic Party but also to convince more African Americans to vote Republican.

Several Southern senators did try to stop the Civil Rights Act of 1957. Senate majority leader Democrat Lyndon Johnson, however, put together a compromise that enabled the act to pass. Although its final form was much weaker than originally intended, the act still brought the power of the federal government into the civil rights debate. It created a Civil Rights Division within the Department of Justice and gave it the authority to seek court injunctions against anyone interfering with the right to vote. It also created the United States Commission on Civil Rights to investigate any denial of voting rights. After the bill passed, the SCLC announced a campaign to register 2 million new African American voters.

✓ **PROGRESS CHECK**

Explaining Why did Eisenhower intervene in the Little Rock controversy?

LESSON 1 REVIEW

Reviewing Vocabulary
1. ***Explaining*** Why was the struggle for civil rights more difficult because of the "separate but equal" doctrine established in the *Plessy* v. *Ferguson* case?

Using Your Notes
2. ***Explaining*** Use the notes you completed during the lesson to write a paragraph explaining the different tactics used during civil rights protests and why they were successful.

Answering the Guiding Questions
3. ***Interpreting*** What techniques did the civil rights movement use to challenge segregation?

4. ***Analyzing*** Why was the Montgomery bus boycott successful?

5. ***Summarizing*** How did President Eisenhower respond to the civil rights movement?

Writing Activity
6. **EXPOSITORY** Assume the role of an African American soldier returning from World War II. Write a letter to the editor of a newspaper describing your expectations of civil rights and why you should have those rights.

networks

There's More Online!

- ☑ **BIOGRAPHY** James Meredith
- ☑ **Chart/Graph** Civil Rights Act and Voting Rights Act
- ☑ **IMAGE** Lunch Counter Sit-in
- ☑ **IMAGE** The March on Washington
- ☑ **PRIMARY SOURCE** Excerpt from *Coming of Age in Mississippi*
- ☑ **TIME LINE** Key Events of the Civil Rights Movement
- ☑ **VIDEO** Challenging Segregation
- ☑ **INTERACTIVE SELF-CHECK QUIZ**

Reading HELPDESK

Content Vocabulary
- filibuster • cloture

Academic Vocabulary
- register

TAKING NOTES: *Organizing*

ACTIVITY As you read about the struggle for civil rights, use the following graphic organizer to identify challenges to segregation in the South.

Challenge	Result
Sit-in Movement	
Freedom Riders	

LESSON 2
Challenging Segregation

ESSENTIAL QUESTIONS • *Why do you think the civil rights movement made gains in postwar America?* • *What motivates a society to make changes?*

IT MATTERS BECAUSE

In the early 1960s, the struggle for civil rights intensified. African American citizens and white supporters created organizations that directed protests, targeted inequalities, and attracted the attention of the mass media and the government.

The Sit-in Movement

GUIDING QUESTION *What were the goals of the Student Nonviolent Coordinating Committee?*

In the fall of 1959, four young African Americans—Joseph McNeil, Ezell Blair, Jr., David Richmond, and Franklin McCain—enrolled at North Carolina Agricultural and Technical College, an African American college in Greensboro. The four freshmen often talked about the civil rights movement. In January 1960, McNeil suggested a sit-in. "All of us were afraid," Richmond later recalled. "But we went and did it."

On February 1, 1960, the four friends entered the nearby Woolworth's department store. They purchased school supplies and then sat at the whites-only lunch counter and ordered coffee. When they were refused service, Blair asked, "I beg your pardon, but you just served us at [the checkout] counter. Why can't we be served at the counter here?" The students stayed at the counter until it closed. They then stated that they would sit there daily until they got the same service as white customers. They left the store excited. McNeil recalled, "I just felt I had powers within me, a superhuman strength that would come forward." McCain noted, "I probably felt better that day than I've ever felt in my life."

News of the daring sit-in spread quickly. The following day, 29 African American students arrived at Woolworth's determined to sit at the counter until served. By the end of the week, more than 300 students were taking part. A new mass movement for civil rights had begun. Within two months, sit-ins had spread to 54 cities in nine states. They were staged at segregated stores, restaurants, hotels, and movie theaters. By 1961, sit-ins had been held in more than 100 cities.

The sit-in movement brought large numbers of idealistic and energized college students into the civil rights struggle. Many were discouraged by the slow pace of desegregation. Sit-ins offered them a way to dictate the pace of change.

At first, the leaders of the NAACP and the SCLC were nervous about the sit-in campaign. Those conducting sit-ins were heckled, punched, kicked, beaten with clubs, and burned with cigarettes, hot coffee, and acid. Most did not fight back.

Urged on by former NAACP official and SCLC executive director Ella Baker, students established the Student Nonviolent Coordinating Committee (SNCC) in 1960. African American college students from all across the South made up the majority of SNCC's members. Many whites also joined. SNCC became an important civil rights group.

Volunteer Robert Moses urged the SNCC to start helping rural Southern African Americans, who often faced violence if they tried to **register** to vote. Many SNCC volunteers, including Moses, bravely headed south as part of a voter education project. During a period of registration efforts in 1964 known as Freedom Summer, the Ku Klux Klan brutally murdered three SNCC workers with the complicity of local officials.

SNCC organizer and sharecropper Fannie Lou Hamer was evicted from her farm after registering to vote. Police arrested her in Mississippi as she was returning from a voter registration workshop in 1963. They beat her while she was in jail. She still went on to help organize the Mississippi Freedom Democratic Party and challenged the legality of the state's segregated Democratic Party at the 1964 national convention.

register to file personal information in order to become eligible for an official event

Nonviolent protests, such as this pray-in in Albany, Georgia, in 1962, spread across the nation as the civil rights movement gained momentum.

▶ **CRITICAL THINKING**
Drawing Conclusions What details in this photograph suggest that it was an effective form of protest?

✔ **PROGRESS CHECK**

Making Inferences Why were SNCC organizers willing to put themselves at such personal risk?

The Freedom Riders

GUIDING QUESTION *How did the Kennedy administration's Justice Department help the civil rights movement?*

Despite rulings outlawing segregation in interstate bus service, bus travel remained segregated in much of the South. Alabama was one state in which many bus terminals were still segregated. Alabama's governor, John Patterson, was known to be in favor of segregation. As attorney general of the state, he had banned the NAACP from being active in Alabama, and he had fought the bus boycotts.

In early May 1961, teams of African American and white volunteers who became known as Freedom Riders boarded several southbound interstate buses. Buses were met by angry white mobs in Anniston, Birmingham, and Montgomery, Alabama. The mobs slit bus tires and threw rocks at the windows. In Anniston, someone threw a firebomb into one bus. Fortunately, no one was killed.

In Birmingham, riders emerged from a bus to face a gang of young men armed with baseball bats, chains, and lead pipes. The gang beat the riders viciously. Birmingham public safety commissioner Theophilus Eugene "Bull" Connor claimed that there had been no police at the bus station because it was Mother's Day and he had given many officers the day off.

PHOTO: AP Images

evidence later showed that Connor had told the local Klan to beat the riders until "it looked like a bulldog got a hold of them." The violence made national news, shocking many Americans and drawing the federal government's attention to the plight of African Americans in the South.

Kennedy and Civil Rights

While campaigning for the presidency in 1960, John F. Kennedy had promised to support civil rights. Civil rights leaders such as NAACP executive director Roy Wilkins urged Kennedy to support civil rights legislation after taking office. However, Kennedy knew he needed the support of Southern senators to get other programs through Congress and any new civil rights legislation would anger them.

Kennedy did, however, bring approximately 40 African Americans into high-level government positions. He appointed Thurgood Marshall to a federal judgeship on the Second Circuit Appeals Court in New York. Kennedy also created the Committee on Equal Employment Opportunity (CEEO). He allowed the Justice Department, run by his brother Robert, to actively support the civil rights movement. The department tried to help African Americans register to vote by filing lawsuits across the South.

After the attacks on the Freedom Riders in Montgomery, both Kennedys publicly urged them to have a "cooling off" period. CORE leader James Farmer rejected the idea and announced that the riders would head into Mississippi. To stop the violence, President Kennedy made a deal with Mississippi senator James Eastland. No violence occurred when buses arrived in Jackson, but Kennedy did not protest the riders' arrests.

The cost of bailing the Freedom Riders out of jail used up most of CORE's funds. When Thurgood Marshall learned of the situation, he offered Farmer the use of the NAACP Legal Defense Fund's huge bail-bond account to keep the rides going. When President Kennedy found that the Freedom Riders were still active, he ordered the Interstate Commerce Commission (ICC) to tighten its regulations against segregated bus terminals. Robert Kennedy ordered the Justice Department to take legal action against Southern cities that maintained segregated bus terminals. By late 1962, segregation in interstate bus travel had virtually ended.

Violence in Birmingham

Martin Luther King, Jr., decided in the spring of 1963 to launch demonstrations in Birmingham, Alabama. He knew they would provoke a violent response, but he believed it was the only way to get the president to actively support civil rights. Eight days after the protests began, King was arrested. While in jail, he began writing the "Letter from Birmingham Jail." It was an eloquent defense of nonviolent protest. In his letter, King argued that "there are two types of laws: just and unjust . . . [and] one has a moral responsibility to disobey unjust laws. . . . Any law that uplifts human personality is just. Any law that degrades human personality is unjust. All segregation statutes are unjust because segregation distorts the soul and damages the personality."

After King was released, the protests began to grow again. Public Safety Commissioner Connor responded with force. He ordered police to use clubs, police dogs, and high-pressure fire hoses on the demonstrators.

One powerful demonstration was called the Children's March. On May 2, heroic young people marched in groups from churches to downtown businesses. Many were attacked by police,

A young protester in Birmingham, Alabama, is attacked by police dogs. Millions of Americans watched the graphic violence on televised nightly news.

▶ **CRITICAL THINKING**

Drawing Conclusions In what ways might these violent images have helped the civil rights movement?

PHOTO: Bill Hudson/AP Images; TEXT: Martin Luther King, Jr., "Letter from Birmingham Jail, 16 April 1963. Reprinted by arrangement with The Heirs to the Estate of Martin Luther King, Jr.; c/o Writers House as agent for the proprietor New York, NY. Copyright 1963 Dr. Martin Luther King, Jr; copyright renewed 1991 Coretta Scott King.

and many were arrested. On September 15, 1963, the Ku Klux Klan bombed Birmingham's Sixteenth Street Baptist Church, killing four young girls. News reports of these attacks on children led to greater support for the civil rights movement.

☑ **PROGRESS CHECK**

Constructing Arguments Why do you think there was such a violent reaction to the civil rights movement?

The Civil Rights Act of 1964

GUIDING QUESTION *How did the Civil Rights Act of 1964 allow the federal government to fight racial discrimination?*

Events in Alabama grew more and more tragic. At his inauguration as Alabama's governor, George Wallace had stated, "I draw a line in the dust . . . and I say, Segregation now! Segregation tomorrow! Segregation forever!" On June 11, 1963, federal marshals had to order Wallace to move from where he stood in front of the University of Alabama's admissions office to block two African Americans from enrolling. The next day, a white segregationist murdered civil rights activist Medgar Evers in Mississippi. Evers had been the NAACP's first field secretary, and had focused his efforts on voter registration and boycotts. His death made him a martyr of the civil rights movement. Amid these events, President Kennedy announced a civil rights bill.

The March on Washington

Civil rights leaders kept the pressure on legislators and the president by planning a large-scale march on Washington. On August 28, 1963, more than 250,000 demonstrators, African American and white, gathered near the Lincoln Memorial. They heard speeches and sang songs. Dr. King then delivered a powerful speech calling for freedom and equality for all Americans.

The Bill Becomes Law

Kennedy tried and failed to win passage of civil rights legislation. After his assassination in November 1963, Lyndon Johnson—former leader of the Senate Democrats—became president. He had helped pass the Civil Rights Acts of 1957 and 1960, but had done so by weakening their provisions and by compromising with other Southern senators.

Nevertheless, Johnson worked to get Kennedy's civil rights legislation through Congress. The bill passed the House of Representatives in February 1964. Then it stalled in the Senate for several weeks. Its opponents

Analyzing
PRIMARY SOURCES

"I Have A Dream" Speech

❝I have a dream that one day this nation will rise up and live out the true meaning of its creed: 'We hold these truths to be self-evident, that all men are created equal.' . . .

I have a dream that one day on the red hills of Georgia, the sons of former slaves and the sons of former slave owners will be able to sit down together at the table of brotherhood.

I have a dream that my four little children will one day live in a nation where they will not be judged by the color of their skin but by the content of their character.❞

—Martin Luther King, Jr., from the "Address in Washington," August 28, 1963

DBQ *ANALYZING PRIMARY SOURCES* What is the dream King refers to in his speech?

Martin Luther King, Jr., speaks to the assembled crowd in Washington, D.C.

▶ **CRITICAL THINKING**
Drawing Inferences What details about the March on Washington encouraged more public support for the civil rights movement and put pressure on Congress to act on the civil rights bill?

The Civil Rights Movement **583**

filibuster an attempt to kill a bill by having a group of senators take turns speaking continuously so that a vote cannot take place

cloture a motion that ends debate and calls for an immediate vote

used a **filibuster,** a tactic in which senators speak continuously to prevent a vote. In June the Senate voted for **cloture**—to end debate and take a vote—with a vote of 71 for and 29 against. The Senate then easily passed the bill. On July 2, 1964, Johnson signed the Civil Rights Act of 1964 into law.

The Civil Rights Act of 1964 was the most comprehensive civil rights law Congress had ever enacted. The law made segregation illegal in most places of public accommodation, and it gave citizens of all races and nationalities equal access to public facilities. The law gave the U.S. attorney general more power to bring lawsuits to force school desegregation and required private employers to end discrimination in the workplace. It also established the Equal Employment Opportunity Commission (EEOC) as a permanent federal agency.

✓ **PROGRESS CHECK**

Assessing Did government support for civil rights come from the federal or state level?

The Struggle for Voting Rights

GUIDING QUESTION *Why was the passage of the Voting Rights Act of 1965 a turning point in the civil rights movement?*

Despite the passage of the Civil Rights Act of 1964, voting rights remained an issue. The Twenty-fourth Amendment, ratified in 1964, helped somewhat. It eliminated poll taxes in federal (but not state) elections. Convinced that a new law was needed to protect African American voting rights, Dr. King decided to hold another dramatic protest.

The Selma March

In December 1964, Dr. King received the Nobel Peace Prize in Oslo, Norway, for his work in the civil rights movement. A few weeks later, he announced, "We are not asking, we are demanding the ballot."

In January 1965, the SCLC and Dr. King selected Selma, Alabama, as the focal point for their campaign for voting rights. Although African Americans made up a majority of Selma's population, they made up only 3 percent of registered voters. To prevent African Americans from registering to vote, Sheriff Jim Clark had deputized and armed dozens of white citizens. His posse terrorized African Americans. On one occasion, they even used clubs and cattle prods on them. King's demonstrations in Selma led to the arrest of more than 3,000 African Americans, including schoolchildren, by Sheriff Clark.

CHARTS/GRAPHS

MARCHING FOR FREEDOM, SELMA, 1965

Marchers in Selma, Alabama, hoped to build support for a new voting rights law.

▶ **CRITICAL THINKING**

1 *Identifying Central Issues* How did the Civil Rights Act of 1964 work to end segregation?

2 *Drawing Conclusions* Why do you think counties where less than half of all adults were registered to vote were a focus of the Voting Rights Act of 1965?

The Civil Rights Act of 1964
- Gave the federal government power to prevent racial discrimination and established the Equal Employment Opportunity Commission (EEOC).
- Made segregation illegal in most places of public accommodation.
- Gave the U.S. attorney general more power to bring lawsuits to force school desegregation.
- Required employers to end workplace discrimination.

The Voting Rights Act of 1965
- Authorized the U.S. attorney general to send federal examiners to register qualified voters.
- Suspended discriminatory devices, such as literacy tests, in counties where less than half of all adults were registered to vote.

To keep pressure on the president and Congress to act, Dr. King joined with SNCC activists and organized a "march for freedom" from Selma to the state capitol in Montgomery, a distance of about 50 miles (80 km). On Sunday, March 7, 1965, the march began. The SCLC's Hosea Williams and SNCC's John Lewis led some 600 protesters toward Montgomery.

As the protesters approached the Edmund Pettus Bridge, which led out of Selma, Sheriff Clark ordered them to disperse. Many protesters were beaten in full view of television cameras. This brutal attack, known later as "Bloody Sunday," left 70 marchers hospitalized and another 70 injured.

The nation was stunned as it viewed the shocking footage of law enforcement officers beating peaceful demonstrators. Watching the events from the White House, President Johnson became furious. Eight days later, he appeared before a nationally televised joint session of Congress to propose a new voting rights law.

The Voting Rights Act of 1965

On August 3, 1965, the House of Representatives passed the voting rights bill by a wide margin. The following day, the Senate also passed the bill. The Voting Rights Act of 1965 authorized the U.S. attorney general to send federal examiners to register qualified voters, bypassing local officials who often refused to register African Americans. The law also suspended discriminatory devices, such as literacy tests, in counties where less than half of all adults had been registered to vote.

The results were dramatic. By the end of the year, almost 250,000 African Americans had registered as new voters. The number of African American elected officials in the South also increased. In 1960, for example, no African American from the South held a seat in the U.S. Congress. By 2011, there were 44 African American members of Congress.

The passage of the Voting Rights Act of 1965 marked a turning point in the civil rights movement. The movement had now achieved two major legislative goals. Segregation had been outlawed, and new federal laws were in place to prevent discrimination and protect voting rights. After 1965, the movement began to shift its focus. It turned its attention to the problems of African Americans trapped in poverty and living in ghettos in many of the nation's major cities.

President Johnson signs the Voting Rights Act into law on August 6, 1965.

▶ **CRITICAL THINKING**
Comparing and Contrasting How were the Civil Rights Act of 1964 and the Voting Rights Act of 1965 similar and different?

☑ **PROGRESS CHECK**

Summarizing What was the positive outcome of the brutal response of police to civil rights protests?

PHOTO: AP Images

LESSON 2 REVIEW

Reviewing Vocabulary
1. *Explaining* How did opponents of the Civil Rights Act of 1964 use the filibuster to try to block its passage?

Using Your Notes
2. *Summarizing* Use the notes you completed during the lesson on challenges to segregation to write a paragraph summarizing how the Freedom Riders helped the civil rights movement.

Answering the Guiding Questions
3. *Identifying* What were the goals of the Student Nonviolent Coordinating Committee?

4. *Analyzing* How did the Kennedy administration's Justice Department help the civil rights movement?

5. *Interpreting* How did the Civil Rights Act of 1964 allow the federal government to fight racial discrimination?

6. *Evaluating* Why was the passage of the Voting Rights Act of 1965 a turning point in the civil rights movement?

Writing Activity
7. DESCRIPTIVE Assume the role of a journalist working for a college newspaper in 1960. Write an article for the newspaper describing the sit-in movement, including its participants, goals, and achievements.

networks

There's More Online!

☑ **BIOGRAPHY** Stokely Carmichael

☑ **BIOGRAPHY** Bobby Seale

☑ **BIOGRAPHY** Malcolm X

☑ **IMAGE** Black Power

☑ **PRIMARY SOURCE** Watts Riot

☑ **VIDEO** New Civil Rights Issues

☑ **INTERACTIVE SELF-CHECK QUIZ**

Harlem: July 18–20, 1964

Reading **HELP**DESK

Content Vocabulary
- racism
- black power

Academic Vocabulary
- enforcement

TAKING NOTES: *Organizing*

ACTIVITY As you read, use the following graphic organizer to list major violent events in the civil rights movement and their results.

Event	Result

LESSON 3
New Civil Rights Issues

ESSENTIAL QUESTIONS • *Why do you think the civil rights movement made gains in postwar America?* • *What motivates a society to make changes?*

IT MATTERS BECAUSE

By the mid-1960s, much progress had been made in the area of civil rights. However, leaders of the movement began to understand that merely winning political rights for African Americans would not completely solve their economic problems. African American leaders would continue to try to end economic inequality.

Urban Problems

GUIDING QUESTION *Why did riots break out in dozens of U.S. cities in the late 1960s?*

Despite the passage of civil rights laws in the 1950s and 1960s, **racism** was still common in American society. Changing the law could not change people's attitudes, nor did it end urban poverty.

In 1965 approximately 70 percent of African Americans lived in large cities. Even if African Americans had been allowed to move into white neighborhoods, many were stuck in low-paying jobs with little chance of advancement. In 1960 only 15 percent of African Americans held professional, managerial, or clerical jobs, compared to 44 percent of whites. The average income of African American families was only 55 percent of that of the average income for white families. Almost half of African Americans lived in poverty, with an unemployment rate typically twice that of whites.

Poor neighborhoods in the nation's major cities were overcrowded and dirty, leading to higher rates of illness and infant mortality. Juvenile delinquency rates rose, as did the rate of young people dropping out of school. Complicating matters even more was a rise in the number of single-parent households.

The Watts Riot

Just five days after President Johnson signed the Voting Rights Act, a riot erupted in Watts, an African American neighborhood in Los Angeles. Allegations of police brutality served as the catalyst for this uprising. It lasted for six days and required more than 14,000 members of the National Guard and 1,500 law officers to restore order. Riots broke out in dozens of other American cities between 1964 and 1968. In Detroit, burning, looting, and conflicts with police and the National Guard resulted in 43 deaths and more than 1,000 wounded in 1967. Property loss was estimated at almost $200 million.

racism prejudice or discrimination against a person because of his or her race

The Kerner Commission

In the same year, President Johnson appointed the National Advisory Commission on Civil Disorders—headed by Governor Otto Kerner of Illinois—to study the causes of the urban riots and to make recommendations. The Kerner Commission, as it became known, blamed racism for most inner-city problems. "Our nation is moving toward two societies, one black, one white—separate and unequal," it concluded. The commission recommended the creation of inner-city jobs and the construction of new public housing, but with the spending for the Vietnam War, Johnson never endorsed the recommendations of the commission.

The Shift to Economic Rights

In the mid-1960s, Dr. Martin Luther King, Jr., decided to focus on the economic problems that African Americans faced. To call attention to deplorable housing conditions, Dr. King and his wife Coretta moved into a slum apartment in an African American neighborhood in Chicago. He and the SCLC hoped to improve the economic status of African Americans in poor neighborhoods.

The Chicago Movement, however, made little headway. When Dr. King led a march through the all-white suburb of Marquette Park to demonstrate the need for open housing, he was met by angry white mobs more hostile than those in Birmingham and Selma. Mayor Richard J. Daley met with Dr. King and discussed a new program to clean up the slums. Associations of realtors and bankers also agreed to promote open housing. In theory, mortgages and rental property would be available to everyone, regardless of race. In practice, little changed.

✓ PROGRESS CHECK

Identifying In what way did poverty contribute to the racial divide?

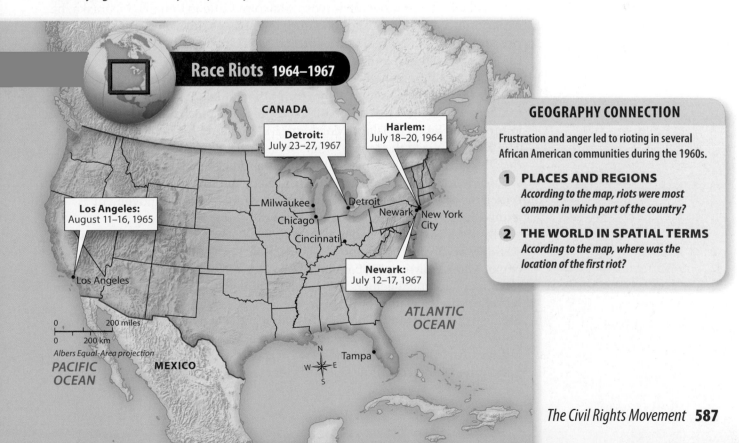

Race Riots 1964–1967

CANADA

Detroit: July 23–27, 1967

Harlem: July 18–20, 1964

Los Angeles: August 11–16, 1965

Milwaukee • Detroit
Chicago • Newark • New York City
Cincinnati •

Newark: July 12–17, 1967

Los Angeles

ATLANTIC OCEAN

0 200 miles
0 200 km
Albers Equal-Area projection

PACIFIC OCEAN

MEXICO

Tampa •

GEOGRAPHY CONNECTION

Frustration and anger led to rioting in several African American communities during the 1960s.

1 PLACES AND REGIONS
According to the map, riots were most common in which part of the country?

2 THE WORLD IN SPATIAL TERMS
According to the map, where was the location of the first riot?

Black Power

GUIDING QUESTION *Why did many young African Americans join the black power movement?*

Dr. King's lack of progress in Chicago seemed to show that nonviolent protests could do little to solve economic problems. After 1965, many African Americans, especially urban young people, began to turn away from King. Some leaders called for more aggressive forms of protest. Some organizations, including CORE and SNCC, believed that African Americans alone should lead their struggle. Many young African Americans called for **black power,** a term that had many meanings. A few, including Robert F. Williams and H. Rap Brown, interpreted black power to mean that physical self-defense was acceptable.

To most, including Stokely Carmichael, the leader of SNCC in 1966, the term meant that African Americans should control the social, political, and economic direction of their struggle:

black power the mobilization of the political and economic power of African Americans, especially to compel respect for their rights and to improve their condition

PRIMARY SOURCE

❝This is the significance of black power as a slogan. For once, black people are going to use the words they want to use—not just the words whites want to hear. . . . The need for psychological equality is the reason why SNCC today believes that blacks must organize in the black community. Only black people can . . . create in the community an aroused and continuing black consciousness.❞

—from "What We Want," the *New York Review of Books,* September 1966

Black power stressed pride in the African American cultural group. It emphasized racial distinctiveness rather than adapting to the dominant culture. African Americans showed pride in their racial heritage by adopting new "Afro" hairstyles and African-style clothing. Many also took African names. Dr. King and some other leaders criticized black power as a philosophy of hopelessness and despair.

Malcolm X

By the early 1960s, a young man named Malcolm X had become a symbol of the black power movement. Born Malcolm Little in Omaha, Nebraska, he experienced a difficult childhood and adolescence. In 1946 he was sent to prison for burglary. Prison transformed Malcolm. He educated himself and played an active role in the prison debate society.

Eventually, he joined the Nation of Islam, commonly known as the Black Muslims. Despite the name, the Nation of Islam is very different from mainstream Islam. The Nation of Islam preached black nationalism. After joining the Nation of Islam, Malcolm Little changed his name to Malcolm X. The X symbolized the family name of his enslaved African ancestors. He declared that his true name had been stolen from him by slavery, and he would no longer use the name white society had given him. Malcolm X's criticisms of white society and the mainstream civil rights movement gained national attention for the Nation of Islam.

By 1964, Malcolm X had broken with the Black Muslims. Discouraged by scandals involving the Nation of Islam's leader, he went to the Muslim holy city of Makkah (Mecca) in Saudi Arabia. After seeing Muslims from many races worshipping together, he no longer promoted separatism. After Malcolm X broke with the Nation of Islam, he continued to criticize the organization. Because of this, organization members shot and killed him in February 1965.

Malcolm X's speeches and ideas influenced a new generation of militant African American leaders who preached black power, black nationalism, and economic self-sufficiency. In 1966 in Oakland, California,

Huey P. Newton and Bobby Seale organized the Black Panthers. Black Panther leaders called for an end to racial oppression and for control of major institutions in the African American community, such as schools, law **enforcement,** housing, and hospitals.

✓ PROGRESS CHECK

Summarizing How did the black power movement lead African Americans away from Dr. King's message of nonviolent disobedience and the goal of integration?

Dr. King Is Assassinated

GUIDING QUESTION *How did Martin Luther King, Jr.'s death affect the civil rights movement?*

In March 1968, Dr. King went to Memphis, Tennessee, to support a strike of African American sanitation workers. At the time, the SCLC had been planning a national "Poor People's Campaign" to promote economic advancement for impoverished Americans. The purpose of this campaign was to lobby the federal government to commit billions of dollars to end poverty and unemployment in the United States. People of all races and nationalities were to converge on Washington, D.C., where they would camp out until both Congress and President Johnson agreed to pass the requested legislation to fund the proposal.

On April 4, 1968, as he stood on his hotel balcony in Memphis, Dr. King was assassinated by a sniper. In a speech the previous night, he had told a gathering at a local church, "I've been to the mountaintop. . . . I've looked over. And I've seen the promised land. I may not get there with you, but I want you to know tonight that we as a people will get to the promised land."

Dr. King's death touched off both national mourning and riots in more than 100 cities, including Washington, D.C. The Reverend Ralph Abernathy, who had served as a trusted assistant to Dr. King for many years, led the Poor People's Campaign in King's absence. However, the demonstration did not achieve any of the major objectives that either King or the SCLC had hoped it would.

In the wake of Dr. King's death, Congress did pass the Civil Rights Act of 1968. The act contained a fair-housing provision outlawing discrimination in housing sales and rentals. Although the civil rights movement generated enormous change and helped transform society, after King's death it lacked the unity of purpose and vision that he had given it.

✓ PROGRESS CHECK

Interpreting Significance In what way was Dr. King's "mountaintop" speech prophetic?

The assassination of Dr. Martin Luther King, Jr., shocked the nation. On April 9, 1968, the country joined in sorrow to mourn his death.

▶ CRITICAL THINKING
Predicting Consequences How do you think the violence that erupted after Dr. King's death affected the civil rights movement?

enforcement the act of urging or carrying out by force

PHOTO: Lynn Pelham/Time & Life Pictures/Getty Images; TEXT: Dr. Martin Luther King, Jr., I've Been tc the Mountaintop delivered April 3, 1968, Mason Temple. Reprinted by arrangement with The Heirs to the Estate of Martin Luther King Jr., c/o Writers House as agent for the proprietor New York, NY. Copyright 1968 Dr. Martin Luther King Jr; copyright re newed 1991 Coretta Scott King

LESSON 3 REVIEW

Reviewing Vocabulary
1. *Explaining* Explain how the findings and recommendations of the Kerner Commission related to racism.

Using Your Notes
2. *Assessing* Use your notes on violent events during the civil rights movement to write a paragraph assessing the result of each event.

Answering the Guiding Questions
3. *Identifying* Why did riots break out in dozens of American cities in the late 1960s?

4. *Analyzing* Why did many young African Americans join the black power movement?

5. *Making Connections* How did Dr. Martin Luther King, Jr.'s death affect the civil rights movement?

Writing Activity
6. EXPOSITORY Assume the role of a reporter in the late 1960s. Suppose that you have interviewed both a follower of Dr. King and a member of the Black Panthers. Write a transcript of each interview.

Directions: On a separate sheet of paper, answer the questions below. Make sure you read carefully and answer all parts to the question.

Lesson Review

Lesson 1

1 *Analyzing Cause and Effect* What instigated the bus boycott in Montgomery, Alabama?

2 *Explaining* What were the goals of the Southern Christian Leadership Conference (SCLC) in 1957?

Lesson 2

3 *Evaluating* What was the significance of the Selma march of 1965?

4 *Explaining* How did the Civil Rights Act of 1964 help African Americans?

Lesson 3

5 *Interpreting* What was the purpose of the Kerner Commission?

6 *Identifying Central Issues* What were some key ideas of black power?

21st Century Skills

7 **CREATE AND ANALYZE ARGUMENTS AND DRAW CONCLUSIONS** Why was *Brown* v. *Board of Education* a significant case?

8 **IDENTIFYING PERSPECTIVES AND DIFFERING INTERPRETATIONS** What were President Eisenhower's opinions on civil rights?

9 **TIME, CHRONOLOGY, AND SEQUENCING** Place the following events in the civil rights movement in chronological order: Civil Rights Act of 1964, sit-ins in Greensboro, Voting Rights Act of 1965, March on Washington, James Meredith enters University of Mississippi, Freedom Riders.

10 **UNDERSTANDING RELATIONSHIPS AMONG EVENTS** How did Malcolm X's speeches and ideas influence a new generation of African American leaders?

Exploring the Essential Questions

11 *Analyzing Ethical Issues* Draw a storyboard for a documentary film about the civil rights movement. The storyboard should describe the gains of the civil rights movement, and the factors that motivated people to make these changes.

DBQ Document-Based Questions

Use the document to answer the following questions.

As he prepared to sign the Civil Rights Act of 1964, President Johnson addressed the American people.

PRIMARY SOURCE

❝ I want to take this occasion to talk to you about what [the Civil Rights Act of 1964] means to every American. . . .

We believe that all men are created equal. Yet many are denied equal treatment. . . .

We believe that all men are entitled to the blessings of liberty. Yet millions are being deprived of those blessings—not because of their own failures, but because of the color of their skin.

The reasons are deeply imbedded in history and tradition and the nature of man. We can understand—without rancor or hatred—how this all happened.

But it cannot continue. Our Constitution, the foundation of our Republic, forbids it. The principles of our freedom forbid it. Morality forbids it. And the law I will sign tonight forbids it. ❞

—from a televised address to the nation, July 2, 1964

12 *Analyzing Primary Sources* According to Johnson, where do the origins of racism come from?

13 *Analyzing Primary Sources* What does Johnson say forbids the continuation of unequal treatment based on race?

Extended-Response Question

14 *Comparing and Contrasting* Select an African American leader who was more militant concerning the problems of racism than Dr. Martin Luther King, Jr. Write an essay comparing and contrasting the two approaches, explaining which was more effective and why.

Need Extra Help?

If You've Missed Question	**1**	**2**	**3**	**4**	**5**	**6**	**7**	**8**	**9**	**10**	**11**	**12**	**13**	**14**
Go to page	574	577	584	583	587	588	575	578	580	588	574	590	590	577

The Vietnam War

1954–1975

ESSENTIAL QUESTIONS • *How does military conflict divide people within cultures?* • *Should citizens support the government during wartime?*

networks

There's More Online about how the Vietnam War changed the United States.

CHAPTER 26

The Story Matters...

Americans had supported their government's war efforts and helped win a decisive victory in World War II. The war in Vietnam, however, was different; people questioned whether the United States should be involved at all. As more Americans came to believe their leaders were not being truthful about the war, the country changed in a profound way.

◀ Hundreds of thousands of young Americans went to Vietnam to fight a war that was different from previous U.S. military conflicts.

PHOTO: Doug Wilson/Historical/CORBIS

Place and Time: Vietnam 1954–1975

The United States wanted to stop the spread of communism after the French defeat by Communist forces in 1954. American involvement in Vietnam would result in eight years of war and the loss of thousands of American lives.

Step Into the Place

Read the quotes and look at the information presented on the map.

DBQ How do these statements by Ho Chi Minh and General William Westmoreland demonstrate the varying beliefs regarding how Vietnam should be controlled?

PRIMARY SOURCE

❝[W]e, members of the Provisional Government of the Democratic Republic of Viet-Nam, solemnly declare to the world that Viet-Nam has the right to be a free and independent country—and in fact it is so already. The entire Vietnamese people are determined to mobilize all their physical and mental strength, to sacrifice their lives and property in order to safeguard their independence and liberty.❞

—Ho Chi Minh, from the *Declaration of Independence of Vietnam*, 1945

PRIMARY SOURCE

❝The objective of the United States government in Vietnam was made clear by the Truman Doctrine of 1947. The Truman Doctrine came after World War II had been concluded, the fighting had stopped, and international arrangements were in disarray. It became very clear that the Soviet Union was going to grab as much real estate as possible in the aftermath of that great war. Thus, the Truman Doctrine said in essence: 'We will not allow a little country to be pushed around and be taken over by the communists. Somebody has to come to their rescue and we will do that. '❞

—General William C. Westmoreland, from *Vietnam in Perspective*, 1987

PHOTOS: left page: (tl)Bettmann/CORBIS, (tr)Dennis Oulds/Hulton Archive/Getty Images, (bl)detail/White House Collection/The White House Historical Association, (br) SuperStock/SuperStock; right page detail/White House Collection/The White House Historical Association

Step Into the Time

Choose an event from the time line and write a paragraph that predicts how the event may have influenced public opinion about involvement in Vietnam.

Eisenhower
1953–1961

Kennedy
1961–1963

1955 U.S. military aid and advisers are sent to South Vietnam

U.S. PRESIDENTS

UNITED STATES

WORLD

1955

1960

1954 France leaves Indochina

1956 Diem refuses to participate in nationwide elections in Vietnam

1958 U.S. troops land in Lebanon

1960 U-2 spy plane is shot down in the Soviet Union

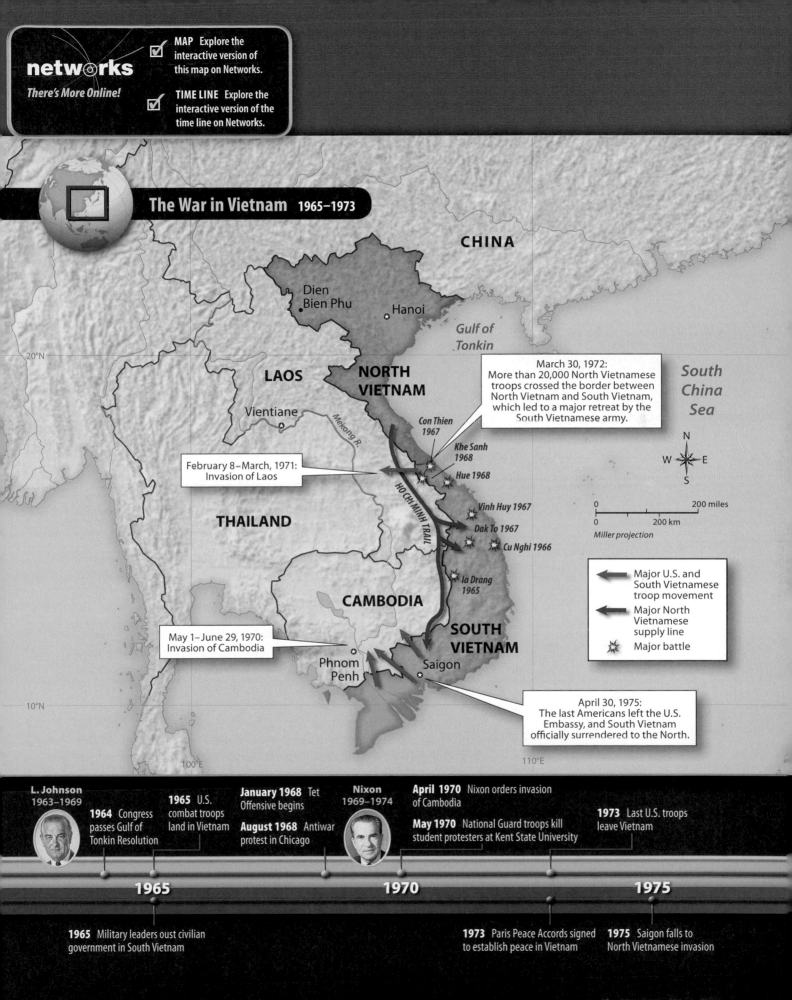

The War in Vietnam 1965–1973

CHINA

Dien Bien Phu

Hanoi

Gulf of Tonkin

20°N

LAOS

NORTH VIETNAM

Vientiane

South China Sea

March 30, 1972: More than 20,000 North Vietnamese troops crossed the border between North Vietnam and South Vietnam, which led to a major retreat by the South Vietnamese army.

Con Thien 1967

Khe Sanh 1968

Mekong R.

February 8–March, 1971: Invasion of Laos

Hue 1968

THAILAND

Vinh Huy 1967

HO CHI MINH TRAIL

Dak To 1967

Cu Nghi 1966

0   200 miles
0   200 km
Miller projection

Ia Drang 1965

CAMBODIA

⬅ Major U.S. and South Vietnamese troop movement

⬅ Major North Vietnamese supply line

✶ Major battle

May 1–June 29, 1970: Invasion of Cambodia

SOUTH VIETNAM

Phnom Penh

Saigon

10°N

100°E

April 30, 1975: The last Americans left the U.S. Embassy, and South Vietnam officially surrendered to the North.

110°E

L. Johnson 1963–1969

1964 Congress passes Gulf of Tonkin Resolution

1965 U.S. combat troops land in Vietnam

January 1968 Tet Offensive begins

August 1968 Antiwar protest in Chicago

Nixon 1969–1974

April 1970 Nixon orders invasion of Cambodia

May 1970 National Guard troops kill student protesters at Kent State University

1973 Last U.S. troops leave Vietnam

1965

1970

1975

1965 Military leaders oust civilian government in South Vietnam

1973 Paris Peace Accords signed to establish peace in Vietnam

1975 Saigon falls to North Vietnamese invasion

netw⊙rks
There's More Online!

☑ **BIOGRAPHY** Ngo Dinh Diem

☑ **BIOGRAPHY** Ho Chi Minh

☑ **IMAGE** Agent Orange

☑ **IMAGE** Soldiers and Helicopter

☑ **VIDEO** Going to War in Vietnam

☑ **INTERACTIVE SELF-CHECK QUIZ**

LESSON 1
Going to War in Vietnam

ESSENTIAL QUESTIONS • *How does military conflict divide people within cultures?* • *Should citizens support the government during wartime?*

Reading HELPDESK

Content Vocabulary
- **domino theory** • **napalm**
- **guerrilla** • **Agent Orange**

Academic Vocabulary
- **strategic** • **traditional**

TAKING NOTES: *Organizing*

ACTIVITY Complete a graphic organizer similar to the one below by providing the reasons the United States aided France in Vietnam.

IT MATTERS BECAUSE
In the late 1940s and early 1950s, most Americans knew little about Indochina, France's colony in Southeast Asia. During the Cold War, however, American officials became concerned that the region might fall to communism.

American Involvement in Vietnam

GUIDING QUESTION *Why did the United States provide military aid to the French in Indochina?*

In 1940 Japan invaded Vietnam, becoming one of a series of foreign nations to rule the Asian country. The Chinese had controlled the region for hundreds of years. Then, from the late 1800s until World War II, the French ruled Vietnam, Laos, and Cambodia—a region then known as French Indochina.

The Growth of Vietnamese Nationalism

By the early 1900s, nationalism had become a powerful force in Vietnam. Several political parties pushed for independence or for reform of French colonial rule. Among the leaders of the nationalist movement was Nguyen That Thanh—better known by his assumed name, Ho Chi Minh. After years in Europe, China, and the Soviet Union, he returned to Southeast Asia. There, he helped found the Indochinese Communist Party in 1930 and worked for independence.

Ho Chi Minh's activities forced him to flee Indochina and spend several years in exile in the Soviet Union and China. In 1941 he returned to Vietnam. By then, Japan had seized control of the country. Ho Chi Minh organized a nationalist group called the Vietminh, which united Communists and non-Communists in the effort to expel the Japanese. Soon afterward, the United States began sending aid to the Vietminh.

America Aids the French

When Japan surrendered to the Allies in 1945, it gave up control of Indochina. Ho Chi Minh quickly declared Vietnam's independence. France had no intention of losing its former colony, however. French troops returned to Vietnam in 1946 and drove the Vietminh into hiding.

The Vietminh fought back against the French-dominated regime and slowly gained control of large areas of the country. As the fighting escalated, France appealed to the United States for help. The request put American officials in a difficult position. The United States opposed colonialism. It had pressured the Dutch to give up their empire in Indonesia and supported the British decision to give India independence in 1947. American officials, however, did not want Vietnam to be Communist.

China's fall to communism and the outbreak of the Korean War helped convince President Truman to aid France. President Eisenhower continued Truman's policy and defended his decision with what became known as the **domino theory**—the idea that if Vietnam fell to communism, the rest of Southeast Asia would follow, like a line of dominoes falling over.

Defeat at Dien Bien Phu

Despite aid from the United States, the French continued to struggle against the Vietminh, who used hit-and-run and ambush tactics. These are the tactics of **guerrillas,** irregular troops who blend into the civilian population and are difficult for regular armies to fight. Rising casualties and a lack of victories made the war unpopular with the French public.

The turning point came in the mountain town of Dien Bien Phu. By seizing the town, the French planned to cut the Vietminh's supply lines and force them into open battle. Soon afterward, a huge Vietminh force surrounded Dien Bien Phu and began bombarding the town. On May 7, 1954, the French forces fell to the Vietminh. The defeat convinced the French to make peace and withdraw from Indochina.

domino theory the belief that if one nation in Asia fell to the Communists, neighboring countries would follow

guerrilla member of an armed band that carries out surprise attacks and sabotage rather than open warfare

GEOGRAPHY CONNECTION

Several factors contributed to American involvement in Vietnam.

1 PLACES AND REGIONS *What aspects of a Communist Vietnam threatened Japan's economy?*

2 THE USES OF GEOGRAPHY *What was the threat to world shipping if Vietnam became a Communist country?*

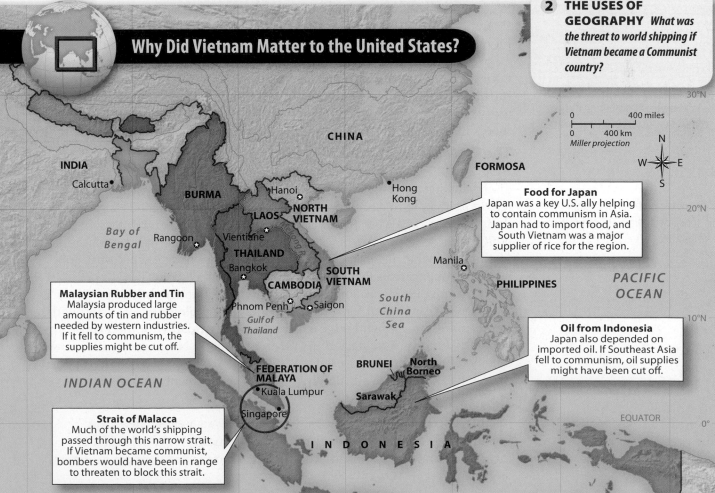

Why Did Vietnam Matter to the United States?

Food for Japan
Japan was a key U.S. ally helping to contain communism in Asia. Japan had to import food, and South Vietnam was a major supplier of rice for the region.

Malaysian Rubber and Tin
Malaysia produced large amounts of tin and rubber needed by western industries. If it fell to communism, the supplies might be cut off.

Oil from Indonesia
Japan also depended on imported oil. If Southeast Asia fell to communism, oil supplies might have been cut off.

Strait of Malacca
Much of the world's shipping passed through this narrow strait. If Vietnam became communist, bombers would have been in range to threaten to block this strait.

Ho Chi Minh, Communist leader of North Vietnam, was determined to reunite Vietnam and began arming Vietcong guerrillas to seize power in South Vietnam.

▶ **CRITICAL THINKING**

Analyzing Information Why did American involvement in Vietnam grow after the Geneva Accords?

strategic important to the conduct or success of a larger plan

traditional set by custom; handed down from one generation to another

Geneva Accords

Negotiations to end the conflict were held in Geneva, Switzerland. The resulting Geneva Accords provided for a temporary division of Vietnam along the 17th parallel. Ho Chi Minh and the Vietminh controlled North Vietnam, and a pro-Western regime led by the fiercely anti-Communist Ngo Dinh Diem (ehn• GOH DIHN deh•EHM) held the South. French troops soon left, and the United States became the principal protector of the new government in South Vietnam.

The accords called for elections to be held in 1956 to reunite the country under a single government. Diem refused to permit the elections, however, fearing Ho Chi Minh would win. Eisenhower approved of Diem's actions and increased American aid to South Vietnam.

✓ **PROGRESS CHECK**

Analyzing Why did the United States protect South Vietnam?

American Involvement Deepens

GUIDING QUESTION *How did American involvement in Vietnam change during the Kennedy and Johnson administrations?*

After Ngo Dinh Diem refused to hold national elections, Ho Chi Minh and the Communists began an armed struggle to reunify the nation. They organized a new guerrilla army of South Vietnamese Communists, which became known as the Vietcong. Eisenhower sent hundreds of military advisers to train South Vietnam's army, but the Vietcong continued to grow more powerful because many Vietnamese opposed Diem's government. By 1961, the Vietcong had established control over much of the countryside.

Kennedy Takes Over

When President Kennedy took office in 1961, he continued to support South Vietnam, believing the country was vital in the battle against communism. From 1961 to late 1963, the number of U.S. military personnel in South Vietnam jumped from about 2,000 to around 15,000. Yet they failed to shore up the floundering Diem regime. For example, the South Vietnamese created special fortified villages known as **strategic** hamlets. They then moved villagers to these hamlets, despite the peasants' resentment at being uprooted from their villages. The program proved to be extremely unpopular.

The Overthrow of Diem

American officials blamed Diem. He made himself even more unpopular by discriminating against Buddhism, one of the country's most widely practiced religions. In the spring of 1963, he banned the **traditional** religious flags for the Buddha's birthday. When Buddhists protested in the streets, Diem's police killed nine people. In response, a Buddhist monk poured gasoline over his robes and set himself on fire, the first of several to do so. Images of their self-destruction horrified Americans as they watched the footage on television news reports.

In August 1963, U.S. ambassador Henry Cabot Lodge arrived in Vietnam. He learned that several Vietnamese generals were plotting to overthrow the unpopular Diem. When Lodge expressed U.S. sympathy for their cause, the generals launched a military coup, seizing power on November 1, 1963. They executed Diem soon after. Despite his unpopularity, Diem had been a respected nationalist. After his death, South Vietnam's government weakened.

Johnson and Vietnam

Just three weeks after Diem's death, Kennedy was assassinated. The presidency— and the growing problem of Vietnam—now belonged to President Lyndon B. Johnson. Although he approached Vietnam cautiously at first, Johnson wanted to keep the country from falling to the Communists. Additionally, some had blamed Democrats when China became Communist in 1949. Should the Democrats "lose" Vietnam, Johnson feared, it might "shatter my Presidency, kill my administration, and damage our democracy."

On August 2, 1964, Johnson announced that North Vietnamese torpedo boats had fired on two U.S. destroyers in the Gulf of Tonkin. Two days later, he reported another attack. Insisting that these were unprovoked, he ordered American aircraft to attack North Vietnamese ships and naval facilities.

Johnson then asked Congress for the authority to defend American forces and allies in Southeast Asia. Congress readily agreed, and on August 7, 1964, it passed the Gulf of Tonkin Resolution. This authorized the president to "take all necessary measures to repel any armed attack against the forces of the United States and to prevent further aggression." Soon after, the Vietcong began to attack bases where American advisers were stationed in South Vietnam. After one particularly damaging attack, Johnson sent American aircraft to bomb North Vietnam.

ANALYZING PRIMARY SOURCES

Should America Fight in Vietnam?

As the war in Vietnam dragged on, Americans became increasingly divided about the nation's role in the conflict. In January 1966, George W. Ball delivered an address to indicate "how we got [into Vietnam] and why we must stay." George F. Kennan, a former ambassador to the Soviet Union, argued that American involvement in Vietnam was "something we would not choose deliberately if the choice were ours to make all over again today."

YES

"[T]he conflict in Viet-Nam is a product of the great shifts and changes triggered by the Second World War.... [T]he Soviet Union under Stalin exploited the confusion to push out the perimeter of its power and influence in an effort to extend the outer limits of Communist domination by force or the threat of force....

George W. Ball
Undersecretary of State

The bloody encounters in [Vietnam] ... are thus in a real sense battles and skirmishes in a continuing war to prevent one Communist power after another from violating internationally recognized boundary lines fixing the outer limits of Communist dominion....

In the long run our hopes for the people of South Viet-Nam reflect our hopes for people everywhere. What we seek is a world living in peace and freedom."

—from a speech delivered January 30, 1966

NO

"Vietnam is not a region of major military-industrial importance.... [E]ven a situation in which South Vietnam was controlled exclusively by the Vietcong ... would not present, in my opinion, dangers great enough to justify our direct military intervention.

George F. Kennan
Former diplomat

And to attempt to crush North Vietnamese strength to a point where Hanoi could no longer give any support for Vietcong political activity in the South would ... have the effect of bringing in Chinese forces at some point....

Our motives are widely misinterpreted; and the spectacle of Americans inflicting grievous injury on the lives of a poor and helpless people ... produces reactions among millions of people throughout the world profoundly detrimental to the image we would like them to hold of this country."

—from testimony before the Senate Foreign Relations Committee, February 10, 1966

DBQ Document Based Questions

1. **Identifying Central Issues** Why does Ball believe that the United States is justified in fighting in Vietnam?

2. **Comparing and Contrasting** What is the fundamental difference between the views of Ball and Kennan?

Both the American public and Johnson's advisers generally supported these actions. Some officials disagreed, however. Undersecretary of State George Ball initially supported involvement in Vietnam, but later turned against it. He warned that if the United States got too involved, it would be difficult to get out. "Once on the tiger's back," he warned, "we cannot be sure of picking the place to dismount."

Other advisers, such as National Security Advisor McGeorge Bundy, believed that success in Vietnam was important to protect American interests and maintain stability in Southeast Asia. In a memo to the president, he argued:

PRIMARY SOURCE

❝The stakes in Vietnam are extremely high. The American investment is very large, and American responsibility is a fact of life which is palpable in the atmosphere of Asia, and even elsewhere. The international prestige of the U.S. and a substantial part of our influence are directly at risk in Vietnam.❞

—quoted in *The Best and the Brightest,* 1972

In March 1965, Johnson again expanded American involvement by ordering a sustained bombing campaign against North Vietnam. That same month, he sent the first U.S. combat troops into Vietnam.

✓ **PROGRESS CHECK**

Describing What event weakened the government of South Vietnam?

A Bloody Stalemate

GUIDING QUESTION *What military tactics were used by the Vietcong, and how did American troops respond?*

By the end of 1965, more than 180,000 U.S. combat troops were fighting in Vietnam. In 1966 that number doubled. The U.S. military entered Vietnam with great confidence. "America seemed omnipotent then," wrote one of the first marines to arrive, Philip Caputo, in his prologue to *A Rumor of War.* "[W]e saw ourselves as the champions of 'a cause that was destined to triumph.'"

Lacking the firepower of the American forces, the Vietcong used ambushes, booby traps, and other guerrilla tactics. These techniques could be greatly destructive. Ronald J. Glasser, an American army doctor, described the devastating effects of one booby trap:

PRIMARY SOURCE

❝Three quarters of the way through the tangle, a trooper brushed against a two-inch vine, and a grenade slung at chest high went off, shattering the right side of his head and body. . . . Nearby troopers took hold of the unconscious soldier and, half carrying, half dragging him, pulled him the rest of the way through the tangle.❞

—quoted in *Vietnam, A History,* 1997

The Vietcong also frustrated American troops by blending in with the general population and then quickly vanishing. "It was a sheer physical impossibility to keep the enemy from slipping away whenever he wished," explained one American general.

"Search and Destroy"

To counter these tactics, American troops tried to find enemy troops, bomb their positions, destroy their supply lines, and force them out into the open

Helicopters allowed U.S. troops to get in and out of jungles and mountainous areas in Vietnam.

▶ **CRITICAL THINKING**
Determining Cause and Effect How did the Vietnamese landscape make troop movements difficult?

PHOTO: MPI/Archive Photos/Getty Images

for combat. American planes dropped **napalm,** a jellied gasoline that explodes on contact. They also used **Agent Orange,** a chemical that strips leaves from trees and shrubs, turning farmland and forest into wasteland.

American military leaders underestimated the Vietcong's strength. They also misjudged the enemy's stamina and the support they had among the South Vietnamese. American generals believed that bombing and killing large numbers of Vietcong would destroy their morale and lead them to surrender. The guerrillas, however, had no intention of surrendering, and they were willing to accept huge losses to achieve their goals.

The Ho Chi Minh Trail

In the Vietcong's war effort, North Vietnamese support was a major factor. Although the Vietcong included many South Vietnamese, North Vietnam provided arms, advisers, and leadership. As Vietcong casualties mounted, North Vietnam began sending North Vietnamese Army units to fight. North Vietnam sent arms and supplies south by way of a network of jungle paths known as the Ho Chi Minh Trail. The trail wound through Cambodia and Laos, bypassing the border between North Vietnam and South Vietnam.

North Vietnam itself received weapons and other support from the Soviet Union and China. Johnson feared directly attacking North Vietnam would bring China into the war, as had happened in Korea. Yet Johnson's limits made winning the war very difficult. Instead of conquering territory, American troops had to fight a war of attrition—defeating enemy forces by wearing them down. This strategy led troops to conduct grisly body counts after battles to determine how many enemy soldiers had been killed. The American military began measuring "progress" in the war by the number of enemy dead.

Bombing from American planes killed many thousands of Vietnamese. American soldiers were also dying in increasing numbers. The notion of a quick and decisive victory grew increasingly remote. As a result, many citizens back home began to question the nation's involvement in the war.

☑ **PROGRESS CHECK**

Explaining What two chemical weapons did the United States use in Vietnam?

PHOTO: Bettmann/CORBIS

Chemicals such as napalm and Agent Orange devastated the landscape of Vietnam.

▶ **CRITICAL THINKING**
Drawing Conclusions How might the use of chemical weapons have encouraged the South Vietnamese populace to support the Vietcong?

napalm a jellied gasoline used for bombs

Agent Orange a chemical defoliant used to clear Vietnamese jungles during the Vietnam War

---

LESSON 1 REVIEW

Reviewing Vocabulary
1. *Explaining* What are guerrilla tactics?
2. *Defining* What was the "domino theory"?

Using Your Notes
3. *Summarizing* Use the notes you completed during the lesson to summarize the reasons the United States aided France in Vietnam.

Answering the Guiding Questions
4. *Evaluating* Why did the United States provide military aid to the French in Indochina?

5. *Describing* How did U.S. involvement in Vietnam change during the Kennedy and Johnson administrations?

6. *Analyzing* What military tactics were used by the Vietcong, and how did U.S. troops respond?

Writing Activity
7. **PERSUASIVE** Take on the role as a member of Congress in 1964. Write a statement supporting or opposing the Gulf of Tonkin Resolution.

networks

There's More Online!

☑ **BIOGRAPHY** Robert F. Kennedy

☑ **BIOGRAPHY** William Westmoreland

☑ **GRAPHIC NOVEL** "The Lottery"

☑ **PRIMARY SOURCE** Vietnam Political Cartoons

☑ **VIDEO** Vietnam Divides the Nation

☑ **INTERACTIVE SELF-CHECK QUIZ**

LESSON 2
Vietnam Divides the Nation

ESSENTIAL QUESTIONS · *How does military conflict divide people within cultures?* · *Should citizens support the government during wartime?*

Reading **HELP**DESK

Content Vocabulary
- credibility gap
- teach-in
- dove
- hawk

Academic Vocabulary
- media
- disproportionate

TAKING NOTES: *Organizing*

ACTIVITY Fill in a graphic organizer similar to the one below, listing reasons for opposition to the Vietnam War.

Reasons for Opposition to Vietnam War

IT MATTERS BECAUSE

As casualties mounted in Vietnam, many Americans began to protest the war. The conflict over the war, increasing violence, and the apparent lack of progress in Vietnam led President Johnson to decide not to run again.

The Antiwar Movement Emerges

GUIDING QUESTION *Why did Americans disagree about the Vietnam War?*

When the first U.S. combat troops arrived in Vietnam in the spring of 1965, about 66 percent of Americans approved of U.S. policy in Vietnam. As the war dragged on, however, public support began to wane. **Media** accounts seemed to contradict government reports. For example, the American commander in South Vietnam, General William Westmoreland, reported that the "enemy's hopes are bankrupt" and "the end begins to come into view." Yet millions of people saw images of American casualties on television in their living rooms each day as Vietnam became the first "television war." For many people, a **credibility gap** had developed—they had a hard time believing what the Johnson administration said about the war.

Congress, which in the Gulf of Tonkin Resolution had granted Johnson a great deal of power to conduct the war, began to seek greater involvement. Beginning in February 1966, the Senate Foreign Relations Committee held "educational" hearings on Vietnam. They called in policy makers and critics to discuss the administration's military strategy.

Teach-ins Begin

In March 1965, a group of faculty members and students at the University of Michigan joined together in a **teach-in.** They discussed the issues surrounding the war and reaffirmed their reasons for opposing it. In May 1965, 122 colleges held a "National Teach-In" by radio for more than 100,000 antiwar demonstrators.

People opposed the war for different reasons. Some saw the conflict as a civil war in which the United States should not

PHOTOS: (l to r)/Arthu~ Rothstein/Historical/CORBIS, Bob Gomel/Time Life Pictures/Getty Images, Bernard Gotfryd/Premium Archive/Getty Images, Dennis Oulds/Hulton Archive/Getty Images

interfere. Others saw South Vietnam as a corrupt dictatorship and believed defending it was immoral.

Anger at the Draft

Thousands of demonstrators held protests against the war. Students for a Democratic Society (SDS) organized a march on Washington, D.C., that drew more than 20,000 people. A rally at the Lincoln Memorial drew tens of thousands of protesters as well.

Many protesters focused on what they saw as an unfair draft system. Until 1969, college students could often defer military service until after graduation. Young people from working-class families unable to afford college were more likely to be drafted. Draftees were most likely to be assigned to combat units, and they commonly made up more than half of casualties. Most who served in Vietnam, however, enlisted voluntarily.

Nevertheless, a **disproportionate** number of working-class and minority youths went to war. Between 1961 and 1966, African Americans constituted about 10 percent of military personnel. Because African Americans were more likely to be assigned to combat units, however, they accounted for almost 20 percent of combat-related deaths. This skewed death rate angered African American leaders. In April 1967, Dr. Martin Luther King, Jr., publicly condemned the conflict: "I speak for the poor of America who are paying the double price of smashed hopes at home and death and corruption in Vietnam. . . . The great initiative in this war is ours. The initiative to stop it must be ours." In response, military officials tried to reduce African American casualties. By war's end, African Americans made up about 12 percent of America's dead.

As the war escalated, an increased draft call put many college students at risk of being drafted. An estimated 500,000 draftees refused to go. Some burned their draft cards, did not show up for induction, or fled the country. From 1965 to 1968, officials prosecuted over 3,000 Americans who refused to serve. In 1969 a lottery system was instituted, so only those with low numbers were subject to the draft. Many draftees argued that if they were old enough to fight, they were old enough to vote. In 1971 the Twenty-sixth Amendment to the Constitution was ratified, giving all citizens age 18 and older the right to vote in all state and federal elections.

Hawks and Doves

In the face of growing opposition to the war, President Johnson remained determined to continue fighting, recognizing the effort as resistance to communism. He assailed his critics in Congress as "selfish men who want to

---

Analyzing
SUPREME COURT CASES

Tinker v. Des Moines

In 1965 students in Des Moines, Iowa, expressed their opposition to the Vietnam War by wearing black armbands to school. The school district then banned the wearing of black armbands and subsequently expelled three students who violated the policy. The students challenged their expulsion as a violation of their First Amendment right to free speech. In 1969 the Supreme Court ruled 7 to 2 in favor of the students, holding that the wearing of black armbands was a form of "symbolic expression" covered by the First Amendment. As long as their symbolic protest was not disruptive, they had a right to express their opinion.

Interpreting Significance How does the *Tinker* decision affect your right to wear a T-shirt supporting a cause you believe in?

CHARTS/GRAPHS

OPPOSITION TO THE VIETNAM WAR

As the Vietnam War progressed, opposition to the conflict generally increased.

▶ **CRITICAL THINKING**

1 *Analyzing Information* During which two years was opposition to the war lowest? What event occurred around that time?

2 *Predicting Consequences* In what year did opposition to the war peak? What consequence might you expect this to have?

Graph: Percentage of People Against U.S. Involvement (y-axis, 10–70) vs. Year (x-axis, 1965–1973). Labeled events: First U.S. combat troops in Vietnam; Tet Offensive; First withdrawal of U.S. troops; Cease-fire signed.

Source: Gallup News Service.

media a means of expression or communication, especially in reference to the agencies of mass communication—newspapers, radio, television, and the Internet

credibility gap lack of trust or believability

teach-in an extended meeting or class held to discuss a social or political issue

disproportionate being out of proportion; lacking in proper relation

dove a person in favor of the United States withdrawing from the Vietnam War

hawk someone who believed the United States should continue its military efforts in Vietnam

Antiwar demonstrators protest in New York City in 1969.

▶ **CRITICAL THINKING**
Analyzing Information What can you learn about war protesters from this photograph?

advance their own interests" and was dismissive of the college protesters. Johnson was not alone in his views. In time, the nation seemed to be divided into two camps. **Doves** wanted the United States to leave Vietnam. **Hawks,** however, wanted the nation to stay and fight. Some saw communism as a threat and challenged the patriotism of the doves. As the two groups debated, the war appeared to take a dramatic turn for the worse.

✓ **PROGRESS CHECK**

Explaining What was the effect of the Vietnam War being a "television war"?

1968: The Pivotal Year

GUIDING QUESTION *Why was 1968 considered the most turbulent year of the 1960s?*

The most turbulent year of the chaotic 1960s was 1968. The year saw a shocking political announcement, two traumatic assassinations, and a political convention held amid strident antiwar demonstrations. First, however, the United States endured a surprise attack in Vietnam.

The Tet Offensive

On January 30, 1968, during Tet, the Vietnamese New Year, the Vietcong and North Vietnamese launched a massive surprise attack. In what was called the Tet Offensive, guerrilla fighters attacked most American airbases in South Vietnam and most of the South's major cities. Vietcong even blasted their way into the American embassy in Saigon.

After about a month of fighting, U.S. and South Vietnamese soldiers repelled the enemy troops, inflicting heavy losses on them. But less tangible damage had been done. The American people were shocked that an enemy supposedly on the verge of defeat could launch such a large-scale attack. The media openly criticized the war. "The American people should be getting ready to accept, if they haven't already, the prospect that the whole Vietnam effort may be doomed," declared the *Wall Street Journal*. Television newscaster Walter Cronkite said that it seemed "more certain than ever that the bloody experience in Vietnam is to end in a stalemate."

Johnson Leaves the Race

Both Johnson and the war had become increasingly unpopular. With the presidential election of 1968 on the horizon, some Democratic politicians made surprising moves. In November 1967, Eugene McCarthy—a little-known liberal senator from Minnesota—declared that he would challenge Johnson for the Democratic presidential nomination. At first, his candidacy was mostly dismissed, but he attracted support from those who opposed the war. In March 1968, McCarthy made a strong showing in the New Hampshire primary, winning more than 40 percent of the vote. Realizing that Johnson was vulnerable, Senator Robert Kennedy, who also opposed the war, quickly entered the race for the Democratic nomination.

With both the country and his own party deeply divided, Johnson appeared on television on March 31, 1968. He announced, "I have concluded that I should not permit the presidency to become involved in the partisan divisions that are developing in this political year. Accordingly, I shall not seek, and I will not accept, the nomination of my party for another term as your President."

PHOTO: Bernard Gotfryd/Premium Archive/Getty Images

A Season of Violence

More shocking events followed Johnson's announcement. On April 4, Dr. Martin Luther King, Jr., was assassinated in Memphis by James Earl Ray. On June 5, Robert Kennedy, who appeared likely to win the Democratic nomination, was gunned down by Sirhan Sirhan, an Arab nationalist.

The violence that seemed to plague the country in 1968 culminated with a chaotic and well-publicized clash between antiwar protesters and police at the Democratic National Convention in Chicago. Thousands of young activists surrounded the convention center to protest the war. Despite these protests, the delegates selected Vice President Hubert Humphrey as the Democratic nominee. Meanwhile, in a park not far from the convention hall, protesters and police began fighting. Demonstrators taunted police with the chant "The whole world is watching!" as the officers tried to force them to disperse. Violence between protesters and police aired on national television.

Nixon Wins the Presidency

At a much more sedate convention, Republicans selected former vice president and 1960 presidential hopeful Richard Nixon as their candidate. A third candidate, Governor George Wallace of Alabama, decided to run in 1968 as an independent. An outspoken segregationist, Wallace sought to attract Americans who felt threatened by the civil rights movement and urban social unrest.

Public opinion polls gave Nixon a wide lead over Humphrey and Wallace. Nixon's campaign promise to unify the nation and restore law and order appealed to Americans who feared their country was spinning out of control. He claimed to represent a silent majority of Americans who sought to maintain law and order but had been overshadowed in recent years by social and political turmoil. He promised that he had a "secret plan" to bring "peace with honor" in Vietnam.

Humphrey's campaign faced significant challenges, but by October 1968, his increasingly antiwar stance and strong campaigning helped turn his numbers around. A week before the election, President Johnson announced that the bombing of North Vietnam had halted and that a cease-fire would follow. These boosts came too late for Humphrey, however. Nixon defeated him by more than 100 electoral votes, although he only won the popular vote by a slim margin of 43 percent to 42 percent.

Protests at the Democratic National Convention in 1968 were nationally televised.

▶ **CRITICAL THINKING**

Drawing Conclusions How might the protests at the convention have affected voters' opinions of Democrats?

✓ **PROGRESS CHECK**

Evaluating Why was the Tet Offensive a turning point in the Vietnam War?

LESSON 2 REVIEW

Reviewing Vocabulary

1. ***Defining*** What was the credibility gap?

2. ***Contrast*** How did doves and hawks differ?

Using Your Notes

3. ***Summarizing*** Use the notes you completed during the lesson to write a paragraph that summarizes the reasons that many people opposed the Vietnam War.

Answering the Guiding Questions

4. ***Identifying*** Why did Americans disagree about the Vietnam War?

5. ***Describing*** Why was 1968 considered the most turbulent year of the 1960s?

Writing Activity

6. **EXPOSITORY** Suppose that you were living in 1968. Write an article for a student newspaper in which you present opposing views about the Vietnam War.

PHOTOS: (l to r)John Filo, Bettmann/CORBIS, Alex Wong/Getty Images News/Getty Images, Steve Northup/Time & Life Pictures/Getty Images

networks

There's More Online!

- ☑ **BIOGRAPHY** Henry Kissinger
- ☑ **BIOGRAPHY** Maya Lin
- ☑ **GRAPHIC NOVEL** "May Day"
- ☑ **PRIMARY SOURCE** Excerpts from *New York Times* v. *United States*
- ☑ **VIDEO** The War Winds Down
- ☑ **INTERACTIVE SELF-CHECK QUIZ**

Reading **HELP**DESK

Content Vocabulary

- linkage
- Vietnamization

Academic Vocabulary

- generation
- unresolved

TAKING NOTES: *Organizing*

ACTIVITY As you read, use the following graphic organizer to list the steps that President Nixon took to end American involvement in Vietnam.

Steps Nixon Took

LESSON 3
The War Winds Down

ESSENTIAL QUESTIONS • *How does military conflict divide people within cultures?* • *Should citizens support the government during wartime?*

IT MATTERS BECAUSE

Shortly after taking office, President Nixon moved to end the nation's involvement in Vietnam. The final years of the conflict yielded more bloodshed and turmoil, as well as growing cynicism.

Nixon Moves to End the War

GUIDING QUESTION *What policies did Nixon employ to end the war?*

As a step toward ending the war, Nixon appointed Henry Kissinger as special assistant for national security affairs. Kissinger embarked upon a policy called **linkage,** or improving relations with the Soviet Union and China, to try to persuade them to reduce their aid to North Vietnam. In August 1969, Kissinger also entered into secret negotiations with North Vietnam's representative, Le Duc Tho.

Meanwhile, Nixon began **Vietnamization.** This process involved the gradual withdrawal of U.S. troops while the South Vietnamese assumed more of the fighting. He announced the withdrawal of 25,000 soldiers on June 8, 1969. At the same time, however, Nixon increased air strikes against North Vietnam and began secretly bombing Vietcong sanctuaries in neighboring Cambodia.

Turmoil at Home Continues

In late 1969, Americans learned that in the spring of 1968 an American platoon under the command of Lieutenant William Calley had massacred unarmed South Vietnamese civilians in the hamlet of My Lai. Most of the victims were old men, women, and children. Calley eventually went to prison for his role in the killings. Jan Barry, a founder of the Vietnam Veterans Against the War, viewed My Lai as a symbol of the dilemma his **generation** faced in the conflict:

PRIMARY SOURCE

❝To kill on military orders and be a criminal, or to refuse to kill and be a criminal is the moral agony of America's Vietnam war generation. It is what has forced upward of sixty thousand young Americans, draft resisters and deserters, to Canada, and created one hundred thousand military deserters a year. . . .❞

—quoted in *Who Spoke Up?: American Protest Against the War in Vietnam, 1963–1975,* 1984

In April 1970, Nixon announced that American troops had invaded Cambodia to destroy Vietcong bases there. Many believed this invasion expanded the war, which it set off many protests. On May 4, Ohio National Guard soldiers armed with tear gas and rifles fired on demonstrators at Kent State University, killing four students. Days later, police killed two student demonstrators at Jackson State College in Mississippi.

An angry Congress began to work to end the president's control of the war. In December 1970, it repealed the Gulf of Tonkin Resolution, which had given the president nearly complete power in directing the conflict.

The following year, a former employee of the Department of Defense, Daniel Ellsberg, leaked what became known as the Pentagon Papers to the *New York Times*. The documents contained details about decisions to expand the war, and confirmed what many Americans had long believed: the government had not been honest with them.

The U.S. invasion of Cambodia led to mass protests and to the tragic killing of four students by National Guard troops at Kent State University in May 1970.

▶ **CRITICAL THINKING**
Determining Cause and Effect How did the invasion of Cambodia lead to the shootings at Kent State University?

The United States Pulls Out

Americans were increasingly ready for the war to end as the presidential election of 1972 approached. Nixon faced Democratic challenger George McGovern, an outspoken critic of the war. Less than a month before the election, however, Kissinger emerged from his secret talks with Le Duc Tho to announce that "peace is at hand." Nixon soundly defeated McGovern.

Soon, Kissinger's peace negotiations broke down over disagreements about the presence of North Vietnamese troops in the South. In December 1972, to force North Vietnam to resume negotiations, the Nixon administration began the most destructive air raids of the war. In what became known as the "Christmas bombings," American B-52s dropped thousands of tons of bombs on North Vietnamese targets for 11 straight days. Then negotiations resumed. On January 27, 1973, the warring sides signed an agreement "ending the war and restoring the peace in Vietnam." The United States promised to withdraw its troops, and both sides agreed to exchange prisoners of war. After almost eight years of war, the nation ended its direct involvement in Vietnam.

linkage policy of improving relations with the Soviet Union and China in hopes of persuading them to cut back their aid to North Vietnam

Vietnamization the process of making South Vietnam assume more of the war effort by slowly withdrawing American troops from Vietnam

generation a group of individuals who were born and who live during the same period of time

The Domino Effect

Peace did not last. In January 1975, Cambodia fell under the control of the Communist group the Khmer Rouge. In March 1975, the North Vietnamese army invaded South Vietnam. Nixon had resigned in August 1974 following Watergate, a scandal that broke as the war was winding down. When the new president, Gerald Ford, asked for funds to aid the South Vietnamese, Congress refused. On April 30, the North Vietnamese captured Saigon, South Vietnam's capital. They then renamed the city Ho Chi Minh City. Laos, another country in the region, was also greatly affected by the Vietnam War. Though Laos was run by a neutral coalition government during most of the war, the constant effects of bombings on the parts of the Ho Chi Minh Trail in Laos destabilized that neutrality. Communists took over in Laos after the fall of Saigon. Thus, the domino effect played out as predicted.

☑ **PROGRESS CHECK**

Sequencing How did the "Christmas bombings" help to put an end to U.S. involvement in the Vietnam War?

The Legacy of Vietnam

GUIDING QUESTION *How was the political and cultural aftermath of the Vietnam War different from previous international conflicts?*

"The lessons of the past in Vietnam," President Ford declared in 1975, "have already been learned—learned by Presidents, learned by Congress, learned by the American people—and we should have our focus on the future." Vietnam had a profound effect on America.

The War's Human Toll

America paid a heavy price for its involvement in Vietnam, far more than the estimated $173 billion in direct costs. Approximately 58,000 young Americans died, and some 300,000 were injured. An estimated 1 million North Vietnamese and South Vietnamese soldiers died, as did millions more civilians. Back home, some soldiers had trouble readjusting. Army Specialist Doug Johnson recalled:

> **PRIMARY SOURCE**
>
> ❝It took a while for me to recognize that I did suffer some psychological problems in trying to deal with my experience in Vietnam. . . . One evening . . . I went to see a movie on post. I don't recall . . . what it was about, but I remember there was a sad part, and that I started crying uncontrollably. It hadn't dawned on me before this episode that I had . . . succeeded in burying my emotions.❞
>
> —quoted in *Touched by the Dragon*, 1998

Because many people considered the war a defeat and wanted to put it behind them, the veterans' sacrifices often went unrecognized. They received relatively few welcome-home parades and celebrations.

🏛 ANALYZING SUPREME COURT CASES

NEW YORK TIMES V. *UNITED STATES*, 1971

Background to the Case

In 1971 Daniel Ellsberg leaked classified documents, known as the Pentagon Papers, to the *New York Times* and the *Washington Post*. When the newspapers attempted to publish these documents, the Nixon administration argued that publication would threaten national security. The case centered on the First Amendment guarantee of a free press.

How the Court Ruled

In a 6-to-3 per curiam opinion—*per curiam* meaning that the decision was issued by the whole Court and not specific justices—the Court found that the Nixon administration had failed to prove that publication of the Pentagon Papers would imperil the nation in any way. The *New York Times* and the *Washington Post* could publish the Pentagon Papers.

Daniel Ellsberg leaked the classified documents known as the Pentagon Papers. The **New York Times** *went to court to battle for its right to print the Pentagon Papers.*

> ▶ **CRITICAL THINKING**
>
> **1** *Drawing Conclusions* Why do you think Daniel Ellsberg leaked the Pentagon Papers to the press?
>
> **2** *Defending* Do you think the government can ever justify media censorship, even based on national security concerns?

The war remained **unresolved** for the American families whose relatives and friends were classified as prisoners of war (POWs) or missing in action (MIA). Despite many official investigations, these families were not convinced that the government had told the truth about POW/MIA policies.

Vietnam remained on the nation's mind nearly a decade later. In 1982 the nation dedicated the Vietnam Veterans Memorial in Washington, D.C., a large black granite wall inscribed with the names of those killed and missing in action in the war.

The War's Impact on the Nation

The war also left a mark on national politics. In 1973 Congress passed the War Powers Act as a way to reestablish some limits on executive power. The act required the president to inform Congress of any commitment of troops abroad within 48 hours, and to withdraw them in 60 to 90 days, unless Congress explicitly approved the troop commitment. No president has recognized this limitation, however, and the courts have tended to avoid the issue.

Nonetheless, every president since the law's passage has asked Congress to authorize the use of military force before committing ground troops to combat. In general, the war shook the nation's confidence and made some begin to question American foreign policies.

On the domestic front, the Vietnam War increased Americans' cynicism about their government. Together with Watergate, Vietnam made many Americans feel that the nation's leaders had misled them.

☑ **PROGRESS CHECK**

Assessing How did the American public treat returning Vietnam veterans?

The Vietnam Veterans Memorial is inscribed with the names of the more than 58,000 people killed or missing in Vietnam.

▶ **CRITICAL THINKING**
Making Generalizations How does the Vietnam Veterans Memorial symbolize U.S. involvement in the war?

unresolved not cleared up; not dealt with successfully

LESSON 3 REVIEW

Reviewing Vocabulary

1. *Defining* What was Vietnamization?

2. *Explaining* What was the goal of the linkage policy?

Using Your Notes

3. *Assessing* Use the notes you completed during the lesson to write a short essay assessing the effectiveness of the various strategies Nixon pursued in Vietnam.

Answering the Guiding Questions

4. *Identifying* What policies did Nixon employ to end the war?

5. *Contrasting* How was the political and cultural aftermath of the Vietnam War different from previous international conflicts?

Writing Activity

6. **PERSONAL** Suppose you are a college student in 1970. Write a journal entry expressing your thoughts and feelings about the events at Kent State University and Jackson State College.

Directions: On a separate sheet of paper, answer the questions below. Make sure you read carefully and answer all parts to the question.

Lesson Review

Lesson 1

1 *Explaining* What military tactics did the Vietminh use in Vietnam?

2 *Analyzing* How did the Gulf of Tonkin Resolution escalate the Vietnam War?

3 *Describing* What was the Ho Chi Minh Trail, and what was its importance in the Vietnam War?

Lesson 2

4 *Identifying Perspectives* Why did many Americans question the fairness of the military draft during the Vietnam War?

5 *Analyzing* In what way did the Vietnam War shape the American presidency in 1968?

Lesson 3

6 *Analyzing* Did the United States successfully protect South Vietnam from communism? Explain your response.

7 *Describing* How did media coverage of the Vietnam War set off a First Amendment debate?

21st Century Skills

8 **IDENTIFYING CAUSE AND EFFECT** How did the Gulf of Tonkin Resolution contribute to U.S. involvement in Vietnam?

9 **UNDERSTANDING RELATIONSHIPS AMONG EVENTS** What was the effect of the "Christmas bombings" of 1972 on the peace negotiations?

10 **COMPARE AND CONTRAST** Explain the difference between Johnson's and Nixon's attitudes toward attacking Cambodia.

11 **IDENTIFYING CAUSE AND EFFECT** How did the Pentagon Papers increase support for the antiwar movement?

Exploring the Essential Questions

12 *Exploring Issues* Create an illustrated time line that identifies key events leading up to, during, and after the Vietnam War. Your time line should reflect how the war affected public opinion about the U.S. government, and how the public was divided during this era. The time line should include visuals such as photos, sketched images, and maps.

DBQ Document-Based Questions

Use the document to answer the following questions.

In the following excerpt, a young man expresses his thoughts about going to war:

PRIMARY SOURCE

❝I read a lot of pacifist literature to determine whether or not I was a conscientious objector. I finally concluded that I wasn't. . . .

The one clear decision I made in 1968 about me and the war was that if I was going to get out of it, I was going to get out in a legal way. I was not going to defraud the system in order to beat the system. I wasn't going to leave the country, because the odds of coming back looked real slim. . . .

With all my terror of going into the Army . . . there was something seductive about it, too. I was seduced by World War II and John Wayne movies. . . . I had been, as we all were, victimized by a romantic, truly uninformed view of war.❞

—quoted in *Nam: The Vietnam War in the Words of the Men and Women Who Fought There,* 1981

13 *Identifying* What options did the young man have regarding the war?

14 *Interpreting* Do you think World War II movies gave him a realistic view of what fighting in Vietnam would be like?

Extended-Response Question

15 *Making Connections* The conflict in Vietnam has been called the first "television war." Americans sitting at home could witness scenes of death and destruction on television. Write an essay about how television has changed the way Americans view war in general, and how television and media coverage could have affected differing opinions about Vietnam.

Need Extra Help?

If You've Missed Question	**1**	**2**	**3**	**4**	**5**	**6**	**7**	**8**	**9**	**10**	**11**	**12**	**13**	**14**	**15**
Go to page	595	597	599	601	602	605	606	597	605	599	605	594	608	608	600

The Politics of Protest

1960–1980

ESSENTIAL QUESTIONS • *What did students, women, and Latinos learn from the civil rights movement and apply to their protest actions?* • *How has society changed for students, women, and Latinos?*

networks

There's More Online about the United States and the politics of protest.

CHAPTER 27

The Story Matters...

The civil rights movement that began in the 1950s inspired other groups in American society to stage protests in the 1960s and 1970s. Students, women, and Latinos all formed organizations and began demanding changes in how American society treated them.

◄ Betty Friedan wrote her 1963 book *The Feminine Mystique* to describe a dissatisfaction many women felt about their social roles. The book also inspired many women to fight for equal rights.

PHOTO: Bettmann/CORBIS

In 1968 Shirley Chisholm became the first African American woman elected to Congress, as a representative for New York. In the House of Representatives, Chisholm supported equality of opportunity for all and the Equal Rights Amendment. Phyllis Schlafly was an attorney who unsuccessfully ran for Congress in 1952. She became a conservative political activist and formed the organization Stop ERA, which campaigned to defeat the Equal Rights Amendment.

Step Into the Place

Read the quotes and look at the information presented on the map.

 How is the focus of Chisholm's argument general and how is Schlafly's specific?

PRIMARY SOURCE

❝Discrimination against women . . . is so widespread that it seems to many persons normal, natural, and right. . . .

. . . It is time we act to assure full equality of opportunity . . . to women.

The argument that this amendment will not solve the problem of sex discrimination is not relevant. . . . Of course laws will not eliminate prejudice from the hearts of human beings. But that is no reason to allow prejudice to continue to be enshrined in our laws.❞

—Representative Shirley Chisholm, from a speech before Congress, August 10, 1970

PRIMARY SOURCE

❝This amendment will absolutely and positively make women subject to the draft. Why any woman would support such a ridiculous and un-American proposal as this is beyond comprehension. . . .

Another bad effect of the Equal Rights Amendment is that it will abolish a woman's right to child support and alimony. . . .

Under present American laws, the man is *always* required to support his wife and each child he has caused to be brought into the world. Why should women abandon these good laws . . . ?❞

—Phyllis Schlafly, from the *Phyllis Schlafly Report*, February 1972

PHOTOS: left page (tl tr)AP Images, (bl br)detail/White House Collection/The White House Historical Association, (c)SuperStock/SuperStock; right page detail/White House Collection/The White House Historical Association

Step Into the Time

Choose an event from the time line and write a paragraph describing how that event might have affected the rights of the people involved.

Eisenhower 1953–1961

Kennedy 1961–1963

1962 César Chávez and Dolores Huerta found National Farm Workers Association

L. Johnson 1963–1969

1966 National Organization for Women founded

U.S. PRESIDENTS

UNITED STATES

WORLD

1960

1965

1961 Construction of Berlin Wall begins

1964 South Africa's Nelson Mandela sentenced to life in prison

1966 Indira Gandhi becomes prime minister of India

ERA Ratification, 1972–1982

CANADA

WA
MT
ND
MN
OR
ID
SD
WI
MI
NH
VT
ME
WY
IA
NY
MA
NV
NE
PA
RI
CA
UT
CO
IL
IN
OH
CT
NJ
KS
MO
WV
VA
DE
MD
AZ
NM
OK
KY
NC
TX
AR
TN
SC
MS
AL
GA
LA
FL

MEXICO

AK

HI

Year Ratified

■	1972	■	1977
■	1973	■	Did not ratify
■	1974	■	Ratified, then rescinded
■	1975		

1968 American Indian Movement founded

Nixon 1969–1974

1970 United Farm Workers wins contract with grape growers

January 1973 *Roe v. Wade* decision on abortion

February 1973 Native Americans clash with FBI at Wounded Knee

Ford 1974–1977

Carter 1977–1981

1970

1975

1980

1967 The Biafran Civil War begins in Nigeria

1968 Soviet Union invades Czechoslovakia

1969 Golda Meir becomes prime minister of Israel

February 1979 Ayatollah Khomeini returns to Iran to lead Islamic republic

May 1979 Margaret Thatcher elected Britain's prime minister

PHOTOS: (l to r)Bettmann/CORBIS, David Fenton/Archive Photos/Getty Images, Vince Streano/Encyclopedia/CORBIS, Bill Ray/Time & Life Pictures/Getty Images, Popperfoto/Getty Images

networks

There's More Online!

☑ **BIOGRAPHY** Bob Dylan

☑ **BIOGRAPHY** Tom Hayden

☑ **BIOGRAPHY** Mario Savio

☑ **PRIMARY SOURCE** Counterculture Political Cartoon

☑ **VIDEO** Students and the Counterculture

☑ **VIDEO** Turning Up the Volume

☑ **INTERACTIVE SELF-CHECK QUIZ**

Reading **HELP**DESK

Content Vocabulary
- **counterculture**
- **hippies** • **communes**

Academic Vocabulary
- **conformity**
- **rationality**

TAKING NOTES: *Organizing*

ACTIVITY As you read about the rise of youth culture and activism, use the major headings of this lesson to create an outline similar to the one below.

Students and the Counterculture

I. The Rise of the Youth Movement

   A.

   B.

II.

   A.

   B.

LESSON 1
Students and the Counterculture

ESSENTIAL QUESTIONS • *What did students, women, and Latinos learn from the civil rights movement and apply to their protest actions?* • *How has society changed for students, women, and Latinos?*

IT MATTERS BECAUSE
The 1960s was one of the most tumultuous decades in American history. The decade also gave birth to a youth movement that challenged the American political system and conventional middle-class values.

The Rise of the Youth Movement

GUIDING QUESTION *How were the protest techniques used by student protesters similar to and different from those of the civil rights movement?*

The roots of the 1960s youth movement stretched back to the 1950s. In the decade after World War II, the country had enjoyed a time of peace and prosperity. Prosperity did not extend to all, however. Some, especially the artists and writers of the beat movement, openly criticized American society. They believed American society had come to value **conformity** over independence and financial gain over spiritual and social advancement. At the same time, the civil rights movement raised serious questions about racism in American society. The nuclear arms race between the United States and the Soviet Union made many of the nation's youth fear for the future. For many young people, the events of the 1950s had called into question the wisdom of their parents and their political leaders.

The youth movement originated with the baby boomers, the huge generation born after World War II. By 1970, 58.2 percent of the American population was under 35 years old. The economic boom of the 1950s meant more families could afford to send their children to college. College life gave young people a sense of freedom and independence. It was on college campuses across the nation that youth protest movements began and reached their peak.

Students for a Democratic Society
Young people were concerned about the injustices they saw in the nation's political and social system. In their view, a small, wealthy elite controlled politics, and wealth was unfairly divided. These young people formed what came to be known as the New Left.

A prominent organization within the New Left was Students for a Democratic Society (SDS). It defined its views in a 1962 declaration known as the Port Huron Statement. Written largely by Tom Hayden, editor of the University of Michigan's student newspaper, the declaration called for an end to apathy and urged citizens to stop accepting a country run by big corporations and big government.

❝ . . . [H]uman degradation, symbolized by the Southern struggle against racial bigotry . . . the Cold War, symbolized by the presence of the Bomb, brought awareness that we ourselves, and our friends, and millions of abstract 'others' . . . might die at any time. . . .

Our work is guided by the sense that we may be the last generation in the experiment with living. ❞

—from the *Port Huron Statement,* 1962

SDS chapters focused on protesting the Vietnam War and other issues, including poverty, campus regulations, nuclear power, and racism.

The Free Speech Movement

Another movement that captured the nation's attention in the 1960s was the free speech movement, led by Mario Savio and others at the University of California at Berkeley. The movement began in the fall of 1964, when the university decided to restrict students' rights to distribute literature and to recruit volunteers for political causes on campus.

Like many college students, those at Berkeley were dissatisfied with practices at their university. Huge classes were divided into sections and taught by graduate students. Many professors claimed they were too busy with research to meet with students. Faceless administrators made rules that were not always easy to obey and imposed punishments for violations. Feeling isolated in this impersonal environment, many Berkeley students rallied to support the free speech movement.

The struggle between Berkeley's students and administrators peaked on December 2, 1964, with a sit-in and powerful speech by Savio. Early the next morning, 600 police officers entered the campus and arrested more than 700 protesters. The arrests set off an even larger protest movement. Within days, a campus-wide strike had stopped classes. Many members of the faculty voiced their support for the free speech movement. In the face of this growing opposition, the administration gave in to the students' demands.

Soon afterward, the Supreme Court upheld students' rights to freedom of speech and assembly on campuses. In a unanimous vote, the Court upheld the section of the Civil Rights Act assuring these rights in places offering public accommodations, which, by definition, included college campuses. The Berkeley revolt became a model for other student protests in the 1960s. The tactics used by the Berkeley protesters were soon being used in college demonstrations across the country.

✔ PROGRESS CHECK

Comparing and Contrasting What techniques did the students on the Berkeley campus use to protest for free speech?

conformity agreement in form, manner, or character

Members of SDS protest the Vietnam War.

▶ CRITICAL THINKING
Identifying Central Issues What are two issues that led to the activism of the members of SDS?

The Counterculture

GUIDING QUESTION *How did the counterculture movement affect the nation?*

While many young Americans in the 1960s sought to reform the system, others rejected it entirely. They tried to create a new lifestyle based on flamboyant dress, rock music, drug use, and communal living. They created what became known as the **counterculture,** and the people were commonly called **"hippies."**

Hippie Culture

Originally, hippies rejected **rationality,** order, and traditional middle-class values. They wanted to build a utopia—a society that was freer, closer to nature, and full of love, tolerance, and cooperation. Many hippies wanted to drop out of society by leaving home. They wanted to live together in **communes**—group living arrangements in which members shared everything and worked together. Much of this was a reaction to the 1950s stereotype of the white-collar "man in the gray flannel suit" who led a constricted and colorless life. Singer-songwriter Bob Dylan expressed the counterculture beliefs through his lyrics:

> **PRIMARY SOURCE**
>
> " Come mothers and fathers throughout the land/and don't criticize what you can't understand/Your sons and your daughters are beyond your command/ Your old road is rapidly agin'/Please get out of the new one if you can't lend your hand/for the times they are a-changin' "
>
> —from "The Times They Are A-Changin'," 1964

The Impact of the Counterculture

After a few years, the counterculture movement began to decline. The fashion and music of the counterculture, however, continued to affect American culture. More individualized dressing, including strands of beads, ragged blue jeans, and long hair for men, became generally accepted. Counterculture musicians made use of folk music and the rhythms of rock 'n' roll. They wrote heartfelt lyrics that expressed the hopes and fears of their generation. Folk singers included Bob Dylan, who became an important voice of the movement, as did singers Joan Baez and Pete Seeger. Rock musicians included Jimi Hendrix, Janis Joplin, and The Who. The music and innovations of these artists continue to influence musicians today.

✓ **PROGRESS CHECK**

Making Connections What kind of society did the counterculture want to build?

Vocabulary

counterculture a culture with values and beliefs different from those of the mainstream

hippies name for young Americans, especially during the 1960s, who rejected the conventions of established society

rationality the quality or state of being agreeable to reason

communes group living arrangements in which members share everything and work together

Members of the counterculture often rejected the expectations of mainstream society.

► **CRITICAL THINKING**
Drawing Inferences How does the style of dress shown express the counterculture's way of thinking?

LESSON 1 REVIEW

Reviewing Vocabulary

1. *Naming* Why were young people who rebelled against mainstream society called the "counterculture"?

2. *Summarizing* What did "conformity" mean to hippies in the 1960s?

Using Your Notes

3. *Making Connections* Use the notes that you completed during the lesson to describe the relationship between student protesters and the hippies.

Answering the Guiding Questions

4. *Comparing and Contrasting* How were the protest techniques used by student protesters similar to and different from those of the civil rights movement?

5. *Synthesizing* How did the counterculture movement affect the nation?

Writing Activity

6. DESCRIPTIVE Suppose that you are a mainstream journalist in the late 1960s. Write a newspaper article about hippies. Describe their hair, clothes, values, and living arrangements.

networks

There's More Online!

☑ **BIOGRAPHY** Shirley Chisholm

☑ **BIOGRAPHY** Betty Friedan

☑ **BIOGRAPHY** Phyllis Schlafly

☑ **CHART/GRAPH** Median Income

☑ **IMAGE** Billie Jean King

☑ **PRIMARY SOURCE** Excerpts from *Roe v. Wade*

☑ **VIDEO** The Feminist Movement

☑ **INTERACTIVE SELF-CHECK QUIZ**

Reading **HELP**DESK

Content Vocabulary

• **feminism**

Academic Vocabulary

• **gender**
• **compatible**

TAKING NOTES: *Organizing*

ACTIVITY As you read about the feminist movement, complete a graphic organizer similar to the one below by listing the main arguments for and against the Equal Rights Amendment (ERA).

Arguments For and Against the ERA	
For ERA	Against ERA

LESSON 2
The Feminist Movement

ESSENTIAL QUESTIONS · *What did students, women, and Latinos learn from the civil rights movement and apply to their protest actions?* · *How has society changed for students, women, and Latinos?*

IT MATTERS BECAUSE

By the 1960s, many women had become dissatisfied with society's perception of women and what their proper roles should be. Some women began to join organizations dedicated to expanding opportunities for women. The Equal Rights Amendment stirred a national debate.

A Renewed Women's Movement

GUIDING QUESTION *What events revitalized the women's movement?*

African Americans and college students were not the only groups seeking to change American society in the 1960s. By the middle of the decade, a new movement had emerged: the feminist, or women's liberation, movement. **Feminism** is the belief that men and women should be equal politically, economically, and socially. The onset of World War II provided women with greater opportunity. After the war, however, many women returned to traditional roles. The new postwar emphasis on establishing families discouraged women from seeking employment.

Despite the popular emphasis on homemaking, the number of women who held jobs outside the home actually increased during the 1950s. Many women went to work to help their families maintain comfortable lifestyles. By 1960, about one-third of all married women were part of the paid workforce. Yet many people continued to believe that women could better serve society by remaining in the home to influence the next generation of men.

Origins of the Movement

By the early 1960s, many women were increasingly resentful of a world where newspaper ads separated jobs by **gender,** banks denied women credit, and female employees often were paid less for the same work. Nearly half of American women worked by the mid-1960s, but three-fourths of these women worked in lower-paying clerical, sales, or factory jobs, or as cleaning women and hospital attendants.

feminism the belief that men and women should be equal politically, economically, and socially

gender term applied to the characteristics of a male or female

One stimulus that invigorated the women's movement was the President's Commission on the Status of Women. Its report highlighted the problems women faced in the workplace and helped create a network of feminist activists who lobbied for women's legislation. In 1963 they won passage of the Equal Pay Act, which in most cases outlawed paying men more than women for the same job.

Many women who had stayed home were also discontent. Betty Friedan tried to describe the reasons for this in her 1963 book *The Feminine Mystique*. Friedan had interviewed women who had graduated with her from Smith College in 1942. She reported that while most had everything they could want in life, they felt unfulfilled. As the book became a best seller, women began reaching out to one another. They poured out their anger and sadness in what came to be known as consciousness-raising sessions. While they talked about their unhappiness, they were also building the base for a nationwide mass movement.

Congress gave the women's movement another boost by including them in the 1964 Civil Rights Act. Title VII of the act outlawed job discrimination not only on the basis of race, color, religion, and national origin, but also on the basis of gender. This provided a strong legal basis for the changes the women's movement later demanded.

But simply having the law on the books was not enough. Even the agency charged with administering the Civil Rights Act—the Equal Employment Opportunity Commission (EEOC)—ruled in 1965 that gender-segregated help-wanted ads were legal.

The Time is NOW

By June 1966, Betty Friedan had returned to an idea that she and other women had been considering—the need for an organization to promote feminist goals. Friedan and others then set out to form the National Organization for Women (NOW). In October 1966 a group of about 30 women and men held the founding conference of NOW.

A group of men and women march together holding signs while participating in a 1976 ERA protest in Pittsburgh, Pennsylvania.

▶ **CRITICAL THINKING**

Drawing Conclusions How might the success of the civil rights movement have encouraged women to organize?

PHOTO: Barbara Freeman/Hulton Archive/Getty Images

"[T]he time has come to confront, with concrete action, the conditions that now prevent women from enjoying the equality of opportunity and freedom of choice which is their right, as individual Americans, and as human beings."

—from *NOW Statement of Purpose*, 1966

The new organization responded to frustrated housewives by demanding greater educational and career opportunities for women. NOW leaders denounced the exclusion of women from certain professions and from most levels of politics. NOW also was against the practice of paying women less than men for equal work. This had been prohibited by the Equal Pay Act, but was still commonplace.

When NOW set out to pass an Equal Rights Amendment to the Constitution, its membership rose to over 200,000. By July 1972, the movement had its own magazine, *Ms.* A key editor of *Ms.* was Gloria Steinem, an author who became one of the movement's leading figures.

✓ **PROGRESS CHECK**

Synthesizing What were two of the forces that helped to bring the women's movement to life in the 1960s?

Successes and Failures

GUIDING QUESTION *What political and economic gains did women make during this time?*

During the late 1960s and early 1970s, the women's movement fought to amend the Constitution and enforce Title VII of the Civil Rights Act. It also worked to repeal laws against abortion and pass legislation against gender discrimination in employment, housing, and education. As a leading voice in the women's movement, Steinem explained the need for such legislation.

"The truth is that all our problems stem from the same sex based myths. We may appear before you as white radicals or the middle-aged middle class or black soul sisters, but we are all sisters in fighting against these outdated myths. Like racial myths, they have been reflected in our laws."

—Gloria Steinem, from testimony before a Senate subcommittee in support of the ERA, May 1970

The Equal Rights Amendment

The women's movement seemed to be off to a strong start when Congress passed the Equal Rights Amendment (ERA) in March 1972. The amendment specified: "Equality of rights under the law shall not be denied or abridged by the United States or by any State on account of sex." To become part of the Constitution, the amendment had to be ratified by 38 states. Many states did so—35 by 1979—but then significant opposition to the amendment began to build.

Opponents argued that it would take away some women's rights. These included the right to alimony in divorce cases and the right to have single-gender colleges. They feared it would eliminate women's exemption from the draft and do away with laws that provided special protection for women in the workforce.

One outspoken opponent was Phyllis Schlafly, organizer of the Stop ERA campaign. By the end of 1979, five states had voted to rescind their approval. Many people had become worried that the amendment would give federal courts too much power to interfere with state laws. Unable to achieve ratification by three-fourths of the states by the deadline set by Congress, the ERA finally failed in 1982.

Feminist and writer Gloria Steinem drew attention to the problems facing women and fought for the ratification of the Equal Rights Amendment.

▶ **CRITICAL THINKING**
Identifying Cause and Effect What was one effect that Gloria Steinem had on the feminist movement?

—*Thinking Like a*—
HISTORIAN

Comparing and Contrasting

The emergence of social movements in the 1960s and 1970s has deep roots in American history. Social movements, historians contend, often share common goals—quality of life issues, political and democratic processes, economic and environmental issues. The significance of the two decades is the concentration of all such issues in a small time span: gender equality at home and at work; political issues and processes; labor and civil rights causes; and environmental and health concerns.

PHOTO: Library of Congress

Tennis great Billie Jean King was a trailblazer in the effort to gain equality for women in sports. In 1972 Title IX banned educational discrimination against women in fields ranging from admissions to extracurricular activities.

▶ **CRITICAL THINKING**

Predicting Consequences What consequence might Title IX have had on girls' involvement in school sports?

Equality in Education

One major achievement of the movement came in the area of education. Kathy Striebel's experience illustrated the discrimination female students often faced in the early 1970s. In 1971 Striebel, a junior high school student in St. Paul, Minnesota, wanted to compete for her school's swim team, but the school did not allow girls to join. Kathy's mother, Charlotte, was a member of the local NOW chapter. Through it, she learned that St. Paul had recently banned gender discrimination in education. She filed a grievance with the city's human rights department, and officials required the school to allow Kathy to swim.

Shortly after joining the team, Kathy beat out one of the boys and earned a spot at a meet. As she stood on the block waiting to swim, the opposing coach declared that she was ineligible because the meet was outside St. Paul and thus beyond the jurisdiction of its laws.

In response, leaders of the women's movement lobbied to ban gender discrimination in education. In 1972 Congress responded by passing a law known collectively as the Educational Amendments. One section, Title IX, prohibited federally funded schools from discriminating against women in nearly all aspects of school operations, from admissions to athletics.

Right to Privacy and *Roe* v. *Wade*

The feminist movement worked to secure the right to make private decisions, including reproductive decisions. A constitutional right to marital privacy was introduced in 1965 when the Supreme Court outlawed state bans on contraceptives for married couples in *Griswold* v. *Connecticut*.

The right to privacy was expanded beyond married couples when activists began challenging laws against abortion. Until 1973, the right to regulate abortion was reserved to the states. The original plan of the Constitution reserved most police power to the states. *Police power* refers to the state's authority to enact laws impinging on personal or property rights in the interest of safety, health, welfare, and morality. Early in the country's history, some abortions were permitted in the early stages of pregnancy. By the mid-1800s, however, states had passed laws prohibiting abortion, except to save the life of the mother. In the late 1960s, some states began adopting more liberal abortion laws. For example, several states allowed abortion if carrying a pregnancy to term might endanger the woman's mental health or if she was a victim of rape or incest.

The big change came with the 1973 Supreme Court decision in *Roe* v. *Wade*. The decision stated that state governments could not regulate abortion during the first three months of pregnancy, a time that was ruled to be within a woman's constitutional right to privacy. During the second three months of pregnancy, states could regulate abortions on the basis of the health of the mother. States could ban abortion in the final three months except in cases of a medical emergency. Those in favor of abortion rights cheered *Roe* v. *Wade* as a victory, but the issue was far from settled politically. The decision gave rise to the right-to-life movement, whose members consider abortion morally wrong and work toward its total ban.

After the *Roe* v. *Wade* ruling, the two sides began an impassioned battle that continues today. In the 1992 case *Planned Parenthood* v. *Casey*, the Supreme Court modified *Roe* v. *Wade*. The Court decided that states could place some restrictions on abortions. For example, doctors could be required to explain the risks and have patients give "informed consent."

PHOTO: Focus On Sport/Getty Images Sport/Getty Images

WOMEN IN THE WORKFORCE

compatible capable of existing in harmony

The number of women in the workforce climbed steadily from the 1950s through the 1990s.

▶ **CRITICAL THINKING**

1 *Comparing and Contrasting*
By how much did the percentage of working women increase between 1950 and 2000?

2 *Making Generalizations*
What general trend do you see in women's participation in the workforce?

Source: *Historical Statistics of the United States: Earliest Times to the Present, Volume 2.*

[bar graph titled "Percentage" vs "Year" showing values for 1950 (~30), 1960 (~35), 1970 (~42), 1980 (~50), 1990 (~57), 2000 (~60)]

Underage girls might now be required to inform their parents before getting an abortion, although the Court did strike down laws requiring women to notify their husbands before having an abortion. It also abandoned the rule that states could ban abortion only in the final trimester. Technology had enabled a fetus to be viable outside the womb much earlier in a pregnancy. States could now restrict abortion based on the viability of the fetus.

The Impact of the Feminist Movement

The women's movement profoundly changed society. Since the 1970s many women have pursued college degrees and careers outside of the home. Many employers now offer options to help women make work life more **compatible** with family life, including flexible hours, on-site child care, and job sharing.

Even with those changes, a significant income gap between men and women still exists. A major reason for the gap is that many working women still hold lower-paying jobs such as bank tellers, administrative assistants, cashiers, schoolteachers, and nurses. Women have made the most dramatic gains in professional jobs since the 1970s. By 2000, women made up more than 40 percent of the nation's graduates receiving medical or law degrees.

☑ **PROGRESS CHECK**

Explaining Why were *Roe* v. *Wade*, Title IX, and the Equal Pay Act cornerstones in the women's rights movement?

More women are working outside the home today in the United States than ever before.

▶ **CRITICAL THINKING**
Making Connections How does the women's movement of the 1960s and 1970s help working women today?

PHOTO: Thomas Barwick/Getty Images

LESSON 2 REVIEW

Reviewing Vocabulary
1. *Explaining* What was the main goal of the feminist movement?

Using Your Notes
2. *Comparing and Contrasting* Review the notes that you completed during the lesson to compare and contrast the arguments for and against the Equal Rights Amendment.

Answering the Guiding Questions
3. *Analyzing Cause and Effect* What events revitalized the women's movement?

4. *Identifying* What political and economic gains did women make during this time?

Writing Activity
5. PERSUASIVE Take a position either for or against the ratification of the Equal Rights Amendment. Then write a newspaper editorial convincing readers to support your position.

networks
There's More Online!

- ☑ **BIOGRAPHY** Henry B. Gonzalez
- ☑ **BIOGRAPHY** Dolores Huerta
- ☑ **MAP** Latino Immigration
- ☑ **SLIDE SHOW** Migrant Workers
- ☑ **VIDEO** Latino Americans Organize
- ☑ **INTERACTIVE SELF-CHECK QUIZ**

LESSON 3
Latino Americans Organize

ESSENTIAL QUESTIONS • *What did students, women, and Latinos learn from the civil rights movement and apply to their protest actions?* • *How has society changed for students, women, and Latinos?*

Reading **HELP**DESK

Content Vocabulary
- repatriation
- bilingualism

Academic Vocabulary
- likewise • adequate

TAKING NOTES: *Sequencing*

ACTIVITY Complete a time line similar to the one below by recording major events in the struggle of Latinos for equal civil and political rights.

1947	1954	1956
1967	1968	1969

IT MATTERS BECAUSE
Most Mexican Americans and Mexican immigrants lived in the Southwest. By the mid-twentieth century, more immigrants arrived from various parts of Latin America. Latinos formed civil rights organizations to challenge discrimination.

Latinos Migrate North

GUIDING QUESTION *Why did many Mexicans migrate to the United States from the early to the mid-1900s, and how did this affect American society?*

Americans of Mexican heritage have lived in what is now the United States since before the founding of the republic. In the twentieth century, Mexican immigration to the United States rose greatly, partly due to the turmoil of the Mexican Revolution that began in 1910. During the 1920s, half a million Mexicans immigrated to the United States through official channels. An unknown number entered the country through other means.

While some persons of Mexican heritage moved to northern states, most remained concentrated in the areas that were once the northern provinces of Mexico. In 1930, 90 percent of ethnic Mexicans in the United States lived in areas of the West and Southwest. As a result of heavy Mexican immigration, the ethnic Mexican population in Texas grew from 71,062 in 1900 to 683,681 in 1930. Southern California, **likewise,** had a large Spanish-speaking population.

Mexicans Face Discrimination

Across the Southwest, most Mexican Americans lived in barrios. Barrios were the product of a combination of the region's history and discrimination against Latinos. Los Angeles was founded as a Spanish town in 1781. A century later when English-speaking settlers arrived, they built around the older Spanish-speaking district. From 1900 to 1930, Mexican immigration increased the ethnic Mexican population of the city from as many as 5,000 to around 150,000. By then, the Spanish-speaking population was segregated in the eastern part of the city. Most lived in dilapidated housing and suffered high rates of infant mortality and disease.

In California and across the Southwest, employment discrimination meant that most ethnic Mexicans could find work only in low-paying jobs. Many worked as agricultural laborers. During the Great Depression, many Mexican Americans faced increased hostility and discrimination as unemployment rates soared. About one-third of the nation's Mexican population returned to Mexico. Some left voluntarily, believing it would be easier to get by in Mexico. Others left as part of the **repatriation**—a series of deportations launched by federal officials. This included not only immigrants but often their American-born children as well.

During World War II, labor shortages in the Southwest led to the creation of the Bracero Program. Under this arrangement, Mexican workers entered into short-term labor contracts, mostly as low-wage farmworkers. Meanwhile, illegal immigration also increased. In 1954 Eisenhower's administration launched a program intended to deport undocumented Latino immigrants. Police swept through barrios seeking undocumented immigrants. As a result, more than 3.7 million Mexicans were deported over the next three years.

The raids were criticized in the United States and in Mexico for intimidating people for simply "looking Mexican." In addition, the program often failed to distinguish between individuals legally in the country—including U.S. citizens—and those who had entered illegally.

Other Latinos Arrive

Although Mexicans remained the largest group of Spanish-speaking newcomers in the 1950s, large numbers of Puerto Ricans arrived as well. American citizens since 1917, Puerto Ricans may move freely within American territory. After World War II, economic troubles prompted more than a million Puerto Ricans to move to the U.S. mainland. The majority settled in New York City, where they faced racial discrimination and high poverty levels.

The nation became home to more than 350,000 Cuban immigrants in the decade after the Cuban Revolution of 1959. Many were professionals and business owners who settled in the Miami, Florida, area. They were typically welcomed as refugees fleeing Communist oppression. By 1970, more than 9 million Latinos lived in the United States.

☑ **PROGRESS CHECK**

Analyzing Cause and Effect What international events encouraged Latinos to move to the United States, and how did this migration affect the nation?

Analyzing PRIMARY SOURCES

Ernesto Galarza on the Importance of the Barrio

❝For the Mexicans the barrio was a colony of refugees. We came to know families from Chihuahua, Sonora, Jalisco, and Durango. . . .

As poor refugees, their first concern was to find a place to sleep, then to eat and find work. In the barrio they were most likely to find all three, for not knowing English, they needed something that was even more urgent than a room, a meal, or a job, and that was information in a language they could understand.❞

—from *Barrio Boy,* 1971

DBQ *DRAWING INFERENCES*
What was the most important benefit that the barrio offered new immigrants?

likewise in the same way; similarly

repatriation being restored or returned to the country of origin, allegiance, or citizenship

---

GROWTH OF LATINO POPULATION IN THE UNITED STATES

CHARTS/GRAPHS

Legend:
- Mexicans
- Puerto Ricans
- Cubans
- Other Latinos
- Total Latinos

(Y-axis: Population (millions), 0 to 36; X-axis: Year, 1910 to 2000)

Source: *Historical Statistics of the United States: Earliest Times to the Present, Volume 1.*

Shown here is a family of Mexican migrant workers who came to the United States as part of the Bracero Program during World War II.

▶ **CRITICAL THINKING**

1 *Analyzing Information* How has the overall Latino population changed since 1950?

2 *Drawing Inferences* Based on the chart, what can you infer about the Latino population in the United States?

Every member of a migrant worker family had to work to survive. Here, Mexican children pick cotton in Texas.

▶ **CRITICAL THINKING**
Drawing Inferences What does this photograph indicate about economic opportunity for migrant farmworkers?

Latinos Organize

GUIDING QUESTION *How was the Latino approach to gaining civil rights similar to and different from the African American civil rights movement?*

Regardless of their citizenship status, people of Mexican heritage were often treated as outsiders by the English-speaking majority. Latinos formed organizations to work for equal rights and fair treatment.

In 1929 a number of Mexican American organizations came together to create the League of United Latin American Citizens (LULAC). The organization's purpose was to fight discrimination against persons of Latin American ancestry. Membership was limited to those of Latin American heritage who were U.S. citizens. LULAC encouraged assimilation into American society and adopted English as its official language.

In *Mendez* v. *Westminster* (1947), a group of Mexican parents won a lawsuit that challenged school segregation in California. Two years after the *Mendez* case, LULAC filed a similar lawsuit that aimed to end the practice of segregating Spanish-speaking children into "Mexican schools" in the state of Texas. During the 1950s, the organization was also a vocal critic of the abuses of deportation authorities. In 1954 the Supreme Court's ruling in *Hernandez* v. *Texas* extended more rights to Latino citizens. The case ended the exclusion of Mexican Americans from juries in Texas.

Another Latino organization, the American GI Forum, was founded to protect the rights of Mexican American veterans. After World War II, Latino veterans were excluded from veterans' organizations. They were also denied medical services by the Veterans Administration.

The GI Forum's first effort to combat racial injustice involved a Mexican American soldier killed during World War II. A funeral home refused to hold his funeral because he was Mexican American. The GI Forum drew national attention to the incident, and the soldier's remains were buried in Arlington National Cemetery. The organization later broadened its scope to challenge discrimination against all Latinos.

☑ **PROGRESS CHECK**

Identifying What were the goals of Latino civil rights organizations?

Protests and Progress

GUIDING QUESTION *How did groups such as the United Farm Workers and* La Raza Unida *promote Latino civil rights?*

As the 1960s began, Latino Americans continued to face prejudice and limited access to **adequate** education, employment, and housing. Encouraged by the African American civil rights movement, Latinos launched a series of campaigns to improve their economic situation and end discrimination.

In the early 1960s, César Chávez and Dolores Huerta organized two groups that fought for farmworkers. In 1965 the groups went on strike in California to demand union recognition, increased wages, and better

adequate sufficient for a specific requirement; completed to its minimum requirements

benefits. When employers resisted, Chávez organized a national boycott of table grapes. Between 14 and 17 million citizens stopped buying grapes, and industry profits tumbled. In 1966 Chávez and Huerta merged their two organizations into the United Farm Workers (UFW). Chávez held a hunger strike in 1968 to support the effort. A UFW spokesman described the impact the hunger strike had on Chávez and the farmworkers: "After twenty-five days, César was carried to a nearby park where the fast ended during a mass with thousands of farmworkers. He had lost thirty-five pounds, but there was no more talk about violence among the farmworkers." The new union kept the boycott going until 1970, when the grape growers finally agreed to raise wages and improve working conditions.

Latino youths also became involved in civil rights. In 1967 college students in San Antonio, Texas, led by José Angel Gutiérrez, founded the Mexican American Youth Organization (MAYO). MAYO organized walkouts and demonstrations to protest discrimination. One Texas walkout led to the creation of bilingual education at a local high school.

MAYO's success and the spread of protests across the West and Southwest convinced Gutiérrez to found a new political party in 1969. It was called *La Raza Unida,* or "the United People." *La Raza Unida* mobilized Mexican American voters with calls for job-training programs and greater access to financial institutions. By the early 1970s, it had elected Latinos to local offices in several cities with large Latino populations. A larger civil rights movement among Mexican Americans, many of whom began calling themselves Chicanos, emerged. The movement fought against discrimination and celebrated ethnic pride.

In the late 1960s, many Latino leaders promoted **bilingualism**—the practice of teaching immigrant students in their own language while they also learned English. Congress supported this movement by passing the Bilingual Education Act in 1968, which directed school districts to set up classes for immigrants in their own language while they were learning English. This became politically controversial. Beginning in the 1980s, an English-only movement began. By the 2000s, more than half of the nation's state legislatures had passed laws or amendments making English the official language of their state.

PHOTO: Arthur Schatz/Time & Life Pictures/Getty Images

✓ **PROGRESS CHECK**

Explaining How did Latinos work for the rights of farmworkers?

BIOGRAPHY

César Chávez (1927–1993)

An Arizona native, labor leader César Chávez grew up a Mexican American migrant farm laborer. He was a community organizer during the 1950s before founding the National Farm Workers Association, a forerunner of the United Farm Workers. A strong supporter of nonviolence, he led peaceful strikes and boycotts that were usually successful. His contributions earned Chávez a Presidential Medal of Freedom the year following his death.

▶ **CRITICAL THINKING**
Drawing Inferences Why might Chávez have cared so much about farm laborers' rights?

bilingualism the practice of teaching immigrant students in their own language

LESSON 3 REVIEW

Reviewing Vocabulary
1. *Defining* What was the repatriation?

2. *Summarizing* How has the bilingualism movement changed over time?

Using Your Notes
3. *Making Generalizations* Review the notes that you completed throughout the lesson, and then describe the successes and setbacks of Latino activists in the twentieth century.

Answering the Guiding Questions
4. *Analyzing Cause and Effect* Why did many Mexicans migrate to the United States from the early to mid-1900s, and how did this affect American society?

5. *Synthesizing* How was the Latino approach to gaining civil rights similar to and different from the African American civil rights movement?

6. *Synthesizing* How did groups such as the United Farm Workers and *La Raza Unida* promote Latino civil rights?

Writing Activity
7. **EXPOSITORY** Write an essay explaining the purpose of the strike against table-grape growers in the 1960s and how strikers planned to achieve their goals.

Directions: On a separate sheet of paper, answer the questions below. Make sure you read carefully and answer all parts to the question.

Lesson Review

Lesson 1

1 *Drawing Inferences* What impact do you think the name "Students for a Democratic Society" had on people?

2 *Identifying Central Issues* What was one key belief that drove many people into the counterculture?

Lesson 2

3 *Evaluating* Why do you think the members of NOW included men (and not just women) in their founding conference?

4 *Comparing* What strategies and techniques did the feminist movement adopt from the civil rights movement?

Lesson 3

5 *Comparing and Contrasting* What are the similarities and differences between LULAC, *La Raza Unida*, and MAYO?

6 *Making Inferences* Why do you think César Chávez and Dolores Huerta merged their unions to form the UFW?

21st Century Skills

7 **EXPLAINING CONTINUITY AND CHANGE** What new movement arose from the *Roe* v. *Wade* decision, and how does that movement influence politics today?

8 **IDENTIFYING CAUSE AND EFFECT** How do you think the Vietnam War affected the youth movement?

9 **UNDERSTANDING RELATIONSHIPS AMONG EVENTS** How might the new Latino activism of the 1960s and 1970s have changed perceptions of Latino immigrants?

Exploring the Essential Questions

10 *Identifying Cause and Effect* Create three cause-and-effect diagrams that show how life had changed for students, women, and Latinos in the United States by the late 1970s (the effects), and the strategies that the different groups used to bring about these changes (the causes).

DBQ Document-Based Questions

Use the photo to answer the following questions.

This photo was published in *Life* magazine in 1965. It shows feminist leader and future cofounder of *Ms.* magazine Gloria Steinem holding a sign with a phrase made popular by the civil rights movement—"We Shall Overcome."

PRIMARY SOURCE

11 *Drawing Conclusions* On Steinem's sign, why is the word "shall" underlined?

12 *Making Connections* How does the message of this photo relate to Title VII of the 1964 Civil Rights Act?

13 *Analyzing Visuals* In this photo, Steinem is seated indoors against a white background. How does this setting affect the message and impact of the photo?

Extended-Response Question

14 *Exploring Issues* Write an expository essay that identifies the factors that triggered the explosion of protests by students, women, and Latinos in the 1960s.

Need Extra Help?

If You've Missed Question	1	2	3	4	5	6	7	8	9	10	11	12	13	14
Go to page	612	614	616	616	622	623	618	612	622	612	624	616	624	612

Politics and Economics

1968–1980

ESSENTIAL QUESTIONS • *How do you think the Nixon administration affected people's attitudes toward government?* • *How does society change the shape of itself over time?*

The Story Matters...

Henry Kissinger and President Nixon reshaped U.S. foreign policy. As President Nixon's national security advisor, Kissinger assisted with diplomatic negotiations with the Soviet Union and the People's Republic of China, building bridges where there had previously been hostility.

◀ Henry Kissinger won the Nobel Peace Prize in 1973 for negotiating the Paris Peace Accords, which aimed to bring about a cease-fire in the Vietnam War and a withdrawal of American forces.

PHOTO: Bettmann/CORBIS

CHAPTER 28

Place and Time: United States 1970–1979

When President Nixon took office, he decided to take a new approach to American relations with the Soviet Union and the People's Republic of China. The United States had been at odds with these Communist countries for decades. Nixon's new approach was one of détente, or easing of tensions, with the two nations. The Cold War was still on, but Nixon believed that only by redefining American foreign policy and forming partnerships with his "opponents" could anything be gained.

Step Into the Place

Read the quote and look at the information presented on the map.

 How do the quote and the information on the map confirm President Nixon's role in establishing relations with China?

PRIMARY SOURCE

❝Now, with regard to the situation we now face, what is it that brings China and the U.S. together? For example, we have differences on Taiwan, not in my opinion so significant over the long run but difficult in the short run. We have differences over Southeast Asia. We have different attitudes toward Japan. We have different attitudes toward Korea. Now we say, and most of our rather naive American press buys this line, that the new relationship between China and America is due to the fact we have a basic friendship between our peoples.❞

—President Richard Nixon, from a meeting with Chinese leader Zhou Enlai, February 22, 1972

PHOTOS: left page (t)Bettmann Premium/ CORBIS, (b) detail/White House Collection/ The White House Historical Association; right page detail/White House Collection/The White House Historical Association

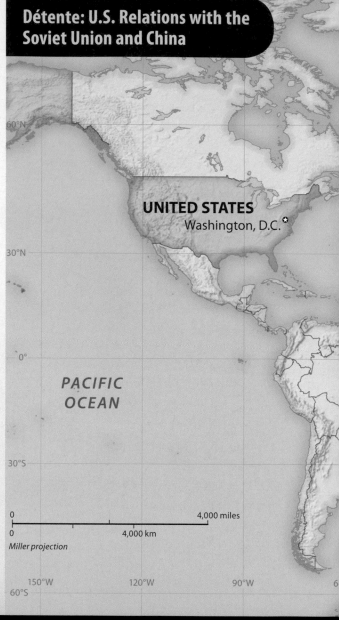

Détente: U.S. Relations with the Soviet Union and China

UNITED STATES
Washington, D.C.

PACIFIC OCEAN

0   4,000 miles
0   4,000 km
Miller projection

60°N
30°N
0°
30°S
30°S
60°S

150°W   120°W   90°W   6

Step Into the Time

Choose an event from the time line and write a paragraph predicting the general social, political, and economic consequences that event might have on political power, civil rights, or the environment.

U.S. PRESIDENTS

UNITED STATES

WORLD

Nixon
1969–1974

April 22, 1970 First Earth Day observed

December 1970 Environmental Protection Agency established

1972 Nixon visits China and the Soviet Union

June 1972 Watergate burglars are arrested

1968   1970   1972

1971 People's Republic of China admitted to UN

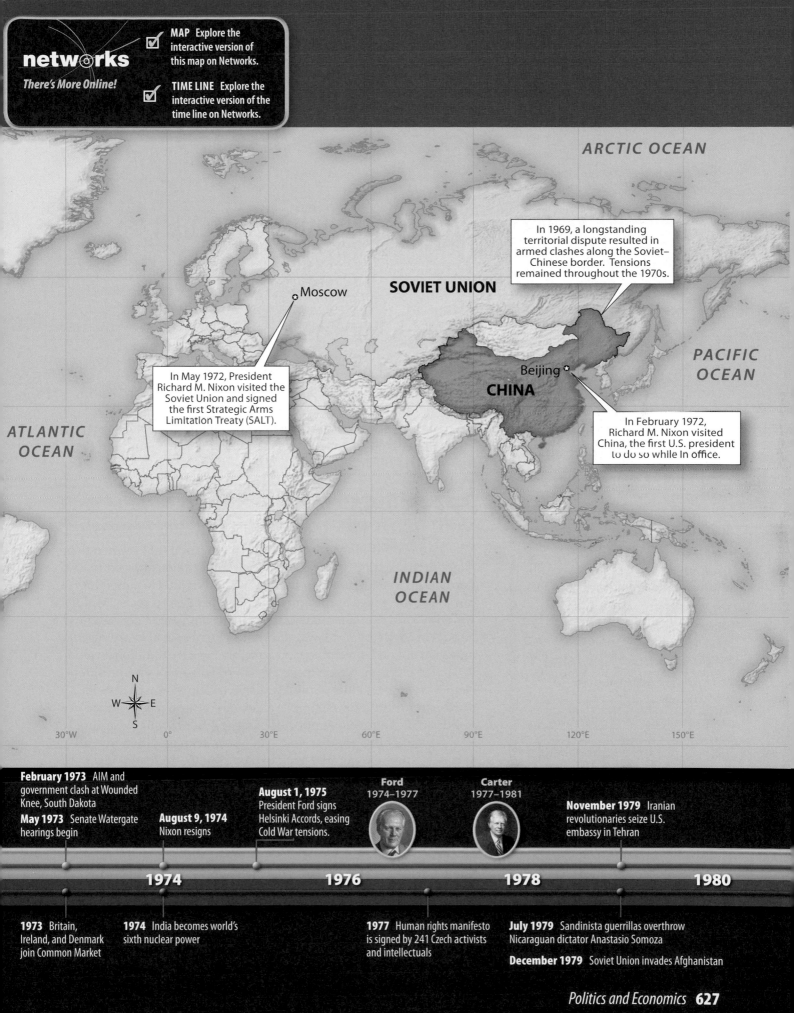

ARCTIC OCEAN

SOVIET UNION

∘ Moscow

In 1969, a longstanding territorial dispute resulted in armed clashes along the Soviet–Chinese border. Tensions remained throughout the 1970s.

In May 1972, President Richard M. Nixon visited the Soviet Union and signed the first Strategic Arms Limitation Treaty (SALT).

PACIFIC OCEAN

Beijing ✪

CHINA

In February 1972, Richard M. Nixon visited China, the first U.S. president to do so while in office.

ATLANTIC OCEAN

INDIAN OCEAN

N
W   E
S

30°W   0°   30°E   60°E   90°E   120°E   150°E

February 1973 AIM and government clash at Wounded Knee, South Dakota

May 1973 Senate Watergate hearings begin

August 9, 1974 Nixon resigns

August 1, 1975 President Ford signs Helsinki Accords, easing Cold War tensions.

Ford 1974–1977

Carter 1977–1981

November 1979 Iranian revolutionaries seize U.S. embassy in Tehran

1974   1976   1978   1980

1973 Britain, Ireland, and Denmark join Common Market

1974 India becomes world's sixth nuclear power

1977 Human rights manifesto is signed by 241 Czech activists and intellectuals

July 1979 Sandinista guerrillas overthrow Nicaraguan dictator Anastasio Somoza

December 1979 Soviet Union invades Afghanistan

Reading **HELP**DESK

Content Vocabulary

- **revenue sharing**
- **impound** • **summit**
- **détente**

Academic Vocabulary

- **welfare** • **liberal**

TAKING NOTES: *Organizing*

ACTIVITY As you read, complete a graphic organizer similar to the one below by listing Nixon's domestic and foreign policies.

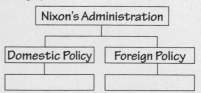

Nixon's Administration

Domestic Policy   Foreign Policy

LESSON 1
The Nixon Administration

ESSENTIAL QUESTIONS • *How do you think the Nixon administration affected people's attitudes toward government?* • *How does society change the shape of itself over time?*

IT MATTERS BECAUSE

After he won the 1968 election, President Richard Nixon sought to restore law and order at home. His greatest accomplishments, however, were in foreign policy, where he worked to ease Cold War tensions with China and the Soviet Union.

Appealing to Middle America

GUIDING QUESTION *What were Nixon's keys to victory in the 1968 presidential election?*

Many Americans longed for an end to the turmoil that seemed to be plaguing the nation. In 1968 these frustrated citizens turned to Republican presidential candidate Richard Nixon. He aimed his campaign messages at this group, whom he referred to as "Middle America" and the "silent majority." Nixon promised "peace with honor" in Vietnam and law and order at home. He also promised a more streamlined government and a return to more traditional values.

In the election, Nixon faced President Johnson's vice president, Democrat Hubert Humphrey. He also went up against a strong third-party candidate, George Wallace, an experienced Southern politician and avowed supporter of segregation. Wallace captured 13.5 percent of the popular vote. Yet Nixon managed to win with 43.4 percent of the popular vote to Humphrey's 42.7, and 301 electoral votes to Humphrey's 191.

The Southern Strategy

Nixon partially owed his victory to a surprisingly strong showing in the South. The South had long been a Democratic stronghold, but Nixon worked hard to get its support. He had met with powerful South Carolina senator Strom Thurmond and won his support by promising several things. Nixon agreed to appoint only conservatives to the federal courts and to name a Southerner to the Supreme Court. He also promised to oppose court-ordered busing and to choose a vice-presidential candidate that the South could support. (Nixon chose Spiro Agnew, governor of the state of Maryland.)

Nixon's efforts paid off on Election Day. Large numbers of white Southerners left the Democratic Party. Humphrey's only Southern victory was in Lyndon Johnson's home state of Texas. Wallace claimed most of the states in the Deep South, but Nixon captured Virginia, Tennessee, Kentucky, and North Carolina. Thurmond's support delivered his state of South Carolina for the Republicans as well.

After his victory, Nixon set out to attract more Southerners to the Republican Party. This effort became known as the Southern strategy. He took steps to slow desegregation and worked to overturn civil rights policies. He also reversed a program that had cut off funds for racially segregated schools.

A Law-and-Order President

Nixon had promised to uphold law and order, and his administration went after antiwar protesters. Attorney General John Mitchell warned that he stood ready to prosecute anyone who crossed state lines to start riots. His deputy, Richard Kleindienst, declared, "We're going to enforce the law against draft evaders, against radical students, against deserters, against civil disorders, against organized crime, and against street crime."

President Nixon also attacked the recent Supreme Court rulings that expanded the rights of accused criminals. Nixon openly criticized the Court and its chief justice, Earl Warren. The president promised to fill vacancies on the Court with judges who would support the rights of law enforcement over the rights of suspected criminals.

Warren retired soon after Nixon took office. The president replaced him with respected conservative judge Warren Burger. He placed three other conservative justices on the Court, including one from the South. The Burger Court did not reverse Warren Court rulings on suspects' rights, but it refused to expand those rights. For example, in *Stone* v. *Powell* (1976), it limited defendants' rights to appeal state convictions to the federal judiciary. The Burger Court also reaffirmed capital punishment.

GEOGRAPHY CONNECTION

Republican Richard Nixon defeated Democrat Hubert Humphrey and third-party candidate George Wallace in the election of 1968.

1 **PLACES AND REGIONS** *In which region did Nixon receive the most support?*

2 **THE WORLD IN SPATIAL TERMS** *Which states' electoral votes went wholly or in part to Wallace?*

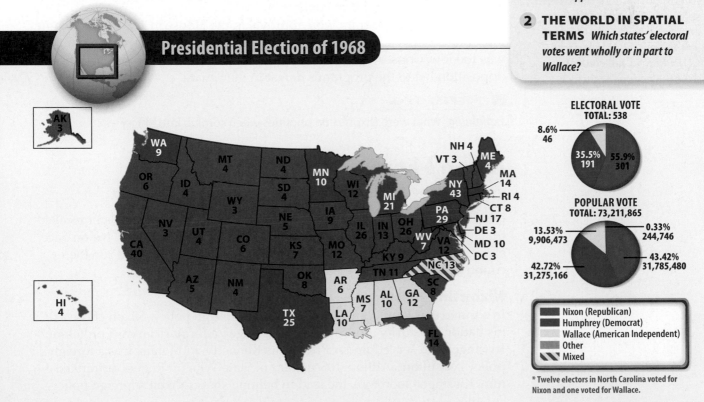

Presidential Election of 1968

ELECTORAL VOTE
TOTAL: 538

8.6% 46
35.5% 191
55.9% 301

POPULAR VOTE
TOTAL: 73,211,865

13.53% 9,906,473
42.72% 31,275,166
0.33% 244,746
43.42% 31,785,480

■ Nixon (Republican)
■ Humphrey (Democrat)
▨ Wallace (American Independent)
■ Other
▧ Mixed

* Twelve electors in North Carolina voted for Nixon and one voted for Wallace.

revenue sharing federal tax money that is distributed among the states

impound to take possession of

welfare aid in the form of money or necessities for those in need, especially disadvantaged social groups

liberal a person who generally believes the government should take an active role in the economy and in social programs but should not dictate social behavior

Connections to **TODAY**

Removal of U.S. Troops From Iraq

Just as Vietnamization called for the South Vietnamese military to take over duties from American troops, the gradual close of American involvement in Iraq has seen American troops give increased responsibility to Iraqi security forces. Although American combat troops officially left Iraq in August 2010, some 50,000 soldiers remained in the country. Their primary duty was to help the Iraqi army as it assumed full control over the nation's security.

The New Federalism

Nixon had also promised to reduce the size of the federal government. He planned to end several federal programs and give more control to state and local governments. Nixon called this the "New Federalism." He argued that such an approach would make government more effective. "I reject the patronizing idea that government in Washington, D.C., is inevitably more wise, more honest and more efficient than government at the local or State level," Nixon declared. "The idea that a bureaucratic elite in Washington knows what's best for people . . . is really a contention that people cannot govern themselves."

Under Nixon's New Federalism plan, Congress passed a series of **revenue-sharing** bills granting federal funds to state and local agencies. As states came to depend on federal funds, the federal government could impose conditions on states. Unless states met those conditions, funds would be cut off.

As part of the New Federalism, Nixon wanted to end many of Johnson's Great Society programs. He vetoed funding for the Department of Housing and Urban Development. He eliminated the Office of Economic Opportunity, and tried unsuccessfully to shut down the Job Corps. When Congress appropriated money for programs he opposed, Nixon **impounded,** or refused to release, the funds. By 1973, it was estimated that he had impounded as much as $18 billion. The Supreme Court eventually declared the practice of impoundment unconstitutional.

The Family Assistance Plan

One federal program Nixon wanted to reform was the nation's **welfare** system—Aid to Families with Dependent Children (AFDC). The program had many critics. In 1969 Nixon proposed replacing the AFDC with the Family Assistance Plan. The plan called for providing needy families a yearly grant of $1,600, which could be supplemented by outside earnings. Many **liberals** applauded the plan as a significant step toward expanding federal responsibility for the poor.

Although the program won approval in the House in 1970, it soon came under harsh attack. Welfare recipients complained that the federal grant was too low. Conservatives disapproved of guaranteed income. Such opposition led to the program's defeat in the Senate.

☑ **PROGRESS CHECK**

Explaining What were Nixon's first priorities when coming into office?

Nixon's Foreign Policy

GUIDING QUESTION *What do you think was Nixon's greatest foreign policy achievement?*

Despite Nixon's domestic initiatives, a State Department official later recalled that Nixon had a "monumental disinterest in domestic policies." Nixon once expressed his hope that a "competent cabinet" of advisers could run the country, allowing him to focus on foreign affairs.

Nixon and Kissinger

In a move that would greatly influence his foreign policy, Nixon chose as his national security advisor Henry Kissinger, a former Harvard professor. Kissinger had served under Presidents Kennedy and Johnson as a foreign policy consultant. Although Secretary of State William Rogers outranked him, Kissinger soon took the lead in helping shape Nixon's foreign policy.

The Nixon Doctrine Nixon and Kissinger shared many views. Both believed abandoning the war in Vietnam would damage the nation's position in the world. Thus, they worked toward a gradual withdrawal while also training the South Vietnamese to defend themselves.

This policy of Vietnamization, as it was called, was extended globally in what came to be known as the Nixon Doctrine. In July 1969, only six months after taking office, Nixon announced that the United States would honor all of the alliances it had signed. The nation would continue to provide military aid and training to allies. Yet, it would no longer "conceive all the plans, design all the programs, execute all the decisions and undertake all the defense of the free nations of the world." America's allies would have to take responsibility for maintaining peace and stability in their own areas of the world.

The New Policy of Détente The Soviet Union was not pleased when Nixon became president. He was known to be strongly anti-Communist. Yet Nixon and Kissinger believed the United States needed to adjust to the growing role of China, Japan, and Western Europe. This emerging "multipolar" world demanded a different approach to American foreign policy.

Both Nixon and Kissinger wanted to continue to contain communism, but they believed that negotiation with Communists was a better way for the United States to achieve its international goals. They developed a new approach called **détente,** or relaxation of tensions, between the United States and its two major Communist rivals, the Soviet Union and China. Nixon said that the nation had to build a better relationship with its main rivals for world peace:

détente a policy that attempts to relax or ease tensions between nations

PRIMARY SOURCE

❝We must understand that détente is not a love fest. It is an understanding between nations that have opposite purposes, but which share common interests, including the avoidance of a nuclear war. Such an understanding can work—that is, restrain aggression and deter war—only as long as the potential aggressor is made to recognize that neither aggression nor war will be profitable.❞

—quoted in *The Limits of Power,* 1992

The successes of détente were diminished due to upheavals in smaller nations. In Chile, President Salvador Allende was killed during a coup supported by the American CIA. Similarly, the Angolan Civil War, which began in 1975, featured secret aid from the United States. The conflicts in Chile and Angola were examples of proxy wars—conflicts during the Cold War that did not directly involve the United States and the Soviet Union but pursued Cold War aims of the two superpowers.

Mao Zedong, leader of China, greets President Nixon in Beijing on February 21, 1972.

▶ **CRITICAL THINKING**
Identifying Central Issues What was the primary goal of the policy of détente?

Nixon Visits China

Détente began with an effort to improve American-Chinese relations. Since 1949, when Communists took power in China, the United States had refused to recognize the Communists as the legitimate rulers. Instead, the U.S. government recognized the exiled regime on the island of Taiwan as the Chinese government. Having long supported this policy, Nixon now set out to reverse it.

Henry Kissinger (1923–)

Henry Kissinger and his family left Germany for the United States in 1938 to escape Nazi anti-Jewish restrictions. Kissinger served in U.S. military intelligence during World War II, then attended Harvard University, later joining its faculty. He was a consultant on national security under Presidents Kennedy and Johnson, before becoming Nixon's national security advisor and later secretary of state. He helped establish the policy of détente with the Soviet Union and China. Kissinger negotiated the cease-fire with North Vietnam and was awarded the Nobel Peace Prize in 1973. In 1977 Kissinger received the Presidential Medal of Freedom.

▶ **CRITICAL THINKING**
Drawing Inferences How did Henry Kissinger influence foreign policy in the 1970s?

summit a meeting between heads of government

After a series of highly secret negotiations between Kissinger and Chinese leaders, Nixon announced that he would visit China in February 1972. During the historic trip, the leaders of both nations agreed to establish "more normal" relations between their countries. In a statement Nixon told his Chinese hosts during a banquet toast:

PRIMARY SOURCE

❝[S]o let us, in these next five days, start a long march together. Not in lockstep, but on different roads leading to the same goal: the goal of building a world structure of peace and justice in which all may stand together with equal dignity.❞

—quoted in the *New York Times*, February 22, 1972

United States–Soviet Tensions Ease

Nixon's strategy toward the Soviet Union worked. Shortly after the public learned of American negotiations with China, the Soviets proposed an American-Soviet **summit,** or high-level diplomatic meeting, to be held in May 1972. On May 22, President Nixon flew to Moscow for a weeklong summit. Nixon was the first American president since World War II to visit the Soviet Union.

During the historic Moscow summit, the two superpowers signed the first Strategic Arms Limitation Treaty, or SALT I, a plan the two nations had been working on for years. The treaty temporarily froze the number of strategic nuclear weapons. Nixon and Soviet premier Leonid Brezhnev also agreed to increase trade and the exchange of scientific information. Détente had helped ease tensions between the two countries. One Soviet official admitted that by the end of Nixon's presidency, "the United States and the Soviet Union had their best relationship of the whole Cold War period."

Another highlight of détente was a series of meetings that created the Helsinki Accords. In 1975 the United States, Canada, and most of the countries of Eastern and Western Europe committed to three sets of recommendations focusing on security, economic, and human rights issues. In one section, the signing states agreed to "respect human rights and fundamental freedoms, including the freedom of thought, conscience, religion or belief, for all without distinction as to race, sex, language or religion."

President Nixon indeed had made his mark on the world stage. However, a scandal was about to engulf his presidency and plunge the nation into one of its greatest constitutional crises.

✓ **PROGRESS CHECK**

Defining What was the policy of Vietnamization, and how did it relate to the Nixon Doctrine?

LESSON 1 REVIEW

Reviewing Vocabulary

1. ***Explaining*** How does revenue sharing work?

2. ***Identifying*** What takes place at a summit?

Using Your Notes

3. ***Summarizing*** Review the notes that you completed throughout the lesson to summarize Nixon's major domestic and foreign policy initiatives.

Answering the Guiding Questions

4. ***Stating*** What were Nixon's keys to victory in the 1968 presidential election?

5. ***Evaluating*** What do you think was Nixon's greatest foreign policy achievement?

Writing Activity

6. **EXPOSITORY** Take on the role of a journalist assigned to cover the 1972 Moscow summit. Write a newspaper article about the events and outcomes of this meeting.

Reading **HELP**DESK

Content Vocabulary

- **executive privilege**
- **special prosecutor**

Academic Vocabulary

- **incident**   • **challenger**

TAKING NOTES: *Outlining*

ACTIVITY Use the headings in this lesson to create an outline similar to the one below by recording information about the Watergate scandal.

> The Watergate Scandal
> I. The Roots of Watergate
>   A.
>   B.
> II.
>   A.
>   B.

LESSON 2
The Watergate Scandal

ESSENTIAL QUESTIONS • *How do you think the Nixon administration affected people's attitudes toward government?* • *How does society change the shape of itself over time?*

IT MATTERS BECAUSE

Despite a successful first term, Richard Nixon and his supporters worried about reelection. The tactics they resorted to led to the Watergate scandal, one of the nation's great constitutional crises.

The Roots of Watergate

GUIDING QUESTION *Why did Nixon's advisers order a break-in at the Democratic Party's headquarters?*

The Watergate scandal led to the only time in the nation's history when the president of the United States was forced to resign from office. It began on the morning of June 17, 1972, when a young *Washington Post* reporter named Bob Woodward was assigned to cover a seemingly insignificant but bizarre **incident.** Early that morning, five men had broken into the Democratic National Committee (DNC) headquarters in the city's Watergate apartment office complex. Woodward attended the arraignment. He was asked to go to see if there was a story worth reporting.

As Woodward sat near the back of the courtroom listening to the bail proceedings for the five defendants, the judge asked each man his occupation. One of the men, James McCord, answered that he was retired from government service. "Where in government?" asked the judge. "CIA," McCord whispered. Woodward sprang to attention. Why was a former CIA agent involved in what seemed to be just a burglary? Over the next two years, Woodward and another reporter, Carl Bernstein, investigated this question. They uncovered a scandal that helped trigger a constitutional crisis and eventually forced Nixon to resign.

Mounting a Reelection Fight

The Watergate scandal directly involved the Nixon administration's efforts to cover up its involvement in the break-in at the Democratic National Committee headquarters. It also included other illegal actions. Many scholars believe the roots of the scandal, however, lay in Nixon's character and the atmosphere of the White House.

Richard Nixon had fought hard to become president, battling back from numerous political defeats. Along the way, he had grown defensive, secretive, and often resentful of his critics. He became president amid race riots, war protests, and other turmoil. He became so consumed with his opponents that he made an "enemies list" of people whom he considered a threat to his presidency.

As the 1972 presidential election approached, Nixon's reelection prospects seemed promising, but not certain. He had just finished triumphant trips to China and the Soviet Union. Former governor George Wallace had dropped out of the race after an assassin's bullet paralyzed him. And many considered Democratic **challenger** Senator George McGovern too liberal. But the Vietnam War still raged, and staffers remembered the close 1968 election. Determined to win, they began spying on opposition rallies and spreading rumors about opponents.

Trying to help the president, Nixon's advisers ordered five men to break into the Democratic Party's headquarters at the Watergate complex and steal sensitive campaign information. They were also to place wiretaps on the office telephones. While the burglars worked, a security guard spotted a piece of tape holding a door lock. The guard removed the tape, but when he passed the door later, he saw that it had been replaced. He quickly called police, who arrived shortly and arrested the men.

The Cover-Up Begins

After the break-in, the media discovered that one burglar, James McCord, was not only an ex-CIA officer but also a member of the Committee for the Re-election of the President (CRP). Reports surfaced that the burglars had been paid from a secret CRP fund controlled by the White House.

Nixon may not have ordered the break-in, but he did order a cover-up. White House officials destroyed incriminating documents and gave investigators false testimony. With Nixon's consent, administration officials asked the CIA to stop the FBI from investigating the source of money paid to the burglars. The CIA told the FBI that the investigation threatened national security. FBI deputy director W. Mark Felt then secretly leaked information about Watergate to the *Washington Post*.

Meanwhile, Nixon's press secretary dismissed the incident, and the president told the American public, "The White House has had no involvement whatever in this particular incident." It worked. Most Americans believed Nixon. Despite efforts by the media to keep the story alive, few people paid much attention during the 1972 presidential campaign. Nixon won reelection by one of the largest margins in history.

✔ **PROGRESS CHECK**

Explaining What effect did the CIA have on the FBI's investigation of the burglars in the Watergate break-in?

James McCord shows the Senate Watergate Committee the bugging device he installed.

▶ **CRITICAL THINKING**
Identifying Central Issues
What made the Watergate scandal so damaging to the Nixon administration?

The Cover-Up Unravels

GUIDING QUESTION *How much power can a president wield to ensure national security?*

In early 1973, the Watergate burglars went on trial. Under relentless prodding from federal judge John J. Sirica, McCord agreed to cooperate with the grand jury investigation and to testify before the newly created Senate Select Committee on Presidential Campaign Activities. The chairman of the committee was Democratic senator Sam J. Ervin from North Carolina.

A Summer of Shocking Testimony

McCord's testimony opened a floodgate of confessions. Presidential counsel John Dean, who had testified in June 1973, confessed that former attorney general John Mitchell had ordered the Watergate break-in and that Nixon had taken part in the cover-up.

The Nixon administration strongly denied the charges. Dean had no evidence, and the Senate committee spent weeks trying to determine who was telling the truth. The answer appeared on July 16. White House aide Alexander Butterfield testified that Nixon had ordered a taping system installed in the White House to record all conversations to help him write his memoirs after leaving office. The tapes would tell the committee what Nixon knew and when he knew it—if the president released them.

The Case of the Tapes

At first, Nixon refused to hand over the tapes, pleading **executive privilege,** the principle that White House conversations should remain confidential to protect national security. **Special Prosecutor** Archibald Cox took Nixon to court in October 1973 to make him give up the tapes. Nixon ordered Attorney General Elliot Richardson to fire Cox, but Richardson refused and resigned. Nixon then ordered Richardson's deputy to fire Cox, but he, too, resigned. Nixon's solicitor general, Robert Bork, finally fired Cox, but the incident badly damaged Nixon's reputation.

The fall of 1973 proved disastrous for other reasons as well. Vice President Spiro Agnew resigned in disgrace after investigators found that he had taken

executive privilege
principle stating that communications of the executive branch should remain confidential to protect national security

special prosecutor a lawyer from outside the government

🏛 ANALYZING SUPREME COURT CASES

UNITED STATES v. *NIXON,* 1974

Background to the Case

In 1974 Special Prosecutor Leon Jaworski issued a subpoena to gain access to audio tape recordings President Nixon had made of conversations. Jaworski believed that the tapes would prove the active involvement of the president in the Watergate cover-up. Nixon filed a motion to prevent the subpoena, claiming executive privilege. The case went to district court, but that court withheld judgment pending the decision of the Supreme Court.

How the Court Ruled

In a unanimous 8-to-0 decision (Justice Rehnquist did not take part), the Supreme Court found that executive privilege did not protect Nixon's tape recordings. The ruling stated that while the president has a right to protect military secrets and other sensitive material and has a right to some confidentiality, the needs of a criminal trial must take precedence. In the Court's opinion Chief Justice Warren Burger wrote, "We conclude that when the ground for asserting privilege as to subpoenaed materials sought for use in a criminal trial is based only on the generalized interest in confidentiality, it cannot prevail over the fundamental demands of due process of law in the fair administration of criminal justice. . . ."

The Senate committee overseeing the Watergate investigation, chaired by Senator Sam Ervin (fourth from left at the table), wanted access to Nixon's White House tape recordings.

▶ CRITICAL THINKING

❶ *Identifying Central Issues* What was the purpose or central issue of the case?

❷ *Constructing Arguments* Do you agree with the Supreme Court's decision in this case? Explain.

Rose Mary Woods was Nixon's personal secretary. She claimed that an 18½ minute gap in the Watergate tapes was the result of an accidental erasure.

▶ **CRITICAL THINKING**
Drawing Conclusions Why might Woods's explanation of the gap in the tapes have been doubted?

bribes while governor of Maryland and while serving in office in Washington. Gerald Ford, Republican leader of the House of Representatives, became the new vice president.

Nixon Resigns

Nixon tried to quell outrage by appointing a new special prosecutor, Leon Jaworski, who also proved determined to obtain the tapes. In July the Supreme Court ruled that Nixon had to surrender them. He complied. Days later, the House Judiciary Committee voted to impeach Nixon, or officially charge him with misconduct. Charges included obstructing justice, misusing federal agencies to violate the rights of citizens, and defying the authority of Congress. Then new evidence emerged: a tape revealed that Nixon had ordered the CIA to stop the FBI probe into the Watergate burglary on June 23, 1972. Impeachment and conviction were inevitable. On August 9, 1974, Nixon resigned in disgrace.

Vice President Gerald Ford took office as president of the United States after Nixon's resignation. He urged Americans to put the scandal behind them, saying, "Our long national nightmare is over." On September 8, 1974, Ford announced a full pardon for Nixon. Ford's pardon of Nixon drew public criticism and diminished his popularity.

The Impact of Watergate

The constitutional crisis led to new laws intended to limit the power of the executive branch. The Federal Campaign Act Amendments of 1974 limited campaign contributions and set up an independent agency to enforce strict election laws. The Ethics in Government Act required financial disclosure by high government officials throughout all branches of government. The FBI Domestic Security Investigation Guidelines Act restricted the FBI's political intelligence-gathering activities. Congress also laid out a means to appoint an independent counsel to investigate and prosecute wrongdoing by high government officials.

Many Americans developed a distrust of public officials. Others, such as Bob Woodward, believed the affair proved that no one is above the law: "Watergate was probably a good thing for the country. . . . The problem with kings, and prime ministers, and presidents, is that they think . . . that they have some special rights. . . . We have our laws and believe them, and they apply to everyone, [which] is a very good thing."

✓ **PROGRESS CHECK**

Assessing What role did the Nixon tapes play in discovering the truth about the Watergate scandal?

LESSON 2 REVIEW

Reviewing Vocabulary
1. *Defining* What is executive privilege?

2. *Stating* What do special prosecutors do?

Using Your Notes
3. *Sequencing* Use your notes to write a description of the major events of the Watergate scandal in order.

Answering the Guiding Questions
4. *Explaining* Why did Nixon's advisers order a break-in at the Democratic Party's headquarters?

5. *Analyzing Ethical Issues* How much power can a president wield to ensure national security?

Writing Activity
6. PERSUASIVE Shortly after taking office, President Ford granted Nixon a full pardon for any crimes he may have been involved in or committed. Use the Internet to find two or more reactions to this action and identify the author and time period when the reaction was written. Evaluate the validity, reliability, and bias of the reactions and write a paragraph comparing which is the best source to understand Ford's actions.

netw⊙rks

There's More Online!

☑ **IMAGE** Camp David Accords

☑ **IMAGE** Ayatollah Khomeini

☑ **IMAGE** Soviet Invasion of Afghanistan

☑ **VIDEO** Ford and Carter

☑ **INTERACTIVE SELF-CHECK QUIZ**

Reading **HELP**DESK

Content Vocabulary

- **inflation**
- **stagflation**
- **embargo**

Academic Vocabulary

- **theory**
- **deregulation**

TAKING NOTES: *Identifying Cause and Effect*

ACTIVITY As you read, complete a graphic organizer similar to the one below by listing the causes of economic problems in the 1970s.

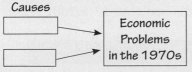

Causes → Economic Problems in the 1970s

LESSON 3

Ford and Carter

ESSENTIAL QUESTIONS · *How do you think the Nixon administration affected people's attitudes toward government?* · *How does society change the shape of itself over time?*

IT MATTERS BECAUSE

By the time Richard Nixon resigned, the postwar economic boom period Americans had experienced was ending. Presidents Gerald R. Ford and Jimmy Carter attempted to lead the United States through both domestic and foreign crises.

The Economic Crisis of the 1970s

GUIDING QUESTION *What economic conditions or problems led to a stagnant economy during the 1970s?*

After World War II, American prosperity seemed normal. It relied on easy access to global raw materials and a strong manufacturing base at home. In the 1970s, however, prosperity gave way to a decade of hard times.

A Mighty Economic Machine Slows

Economic troubles began in the mid-1960s. President Johnson increased deficit spending, to fund the Vietnam War and the Great Society, without raising taxes. This pumped money into the economy, but by the 1970s, this spending caused rapid **inflation.**

Rising oil prices dealt another blow. By 1970, the United States had become dependent on imported oil. In 1973 the Organization of the Petroleum Exporting Countries (OPEC)—a cartel dominated by Arab countries—used oil as a political weapon when war erupted between Israel and its Arab neighbors. OPEC announced an **embargo,** or trade ban, on petroleum to countries that supported Israel. OPEC raised the price of crude oil by 70 percent and then by another 130 percent a few months later. After the embargo ended, oil prices continued to rise, from $3 per barrel in 1973 to $30 per barrel in 1980. This meant that Americans had less money for other goods, which contributed to a recession.

A Stagnant Economy

Declining manufacturing was another economic problem. By 1970, many American factories were old and less efficient than those in competing countries. In 1971 the nation imported more than it

Comparing and Contrasting

Historians can examine economic data when they are trying to analyze history and to better understand the actions and choices made during a particular period of history. They can draw conclusions from comparing and contrasting the price of oil from two different time periods. They can evaluate how global or local historic events or changes in supply and demand may have contributed to a decline or rise in oil prices. For example, in 1981 crude oil prices for refiners hit a high of about $39 per barrel. They declined slowly and then sharply until the early 2000s. Then, in 2008, oil prices rose dramatically, to about $131 per barrel. In order to analyze the similar data for oil prices in 1981 and 2008, historians might look at related local and world events that could have affected this soar in prices in both years.

inflation the loss of value of money

exported for the first time since 1889. Many factories closed. Millions of workers lost their jobs. In the early 1970s, Nixon thus faced a new economic problem nicknamed **"stagflation"**—a combination of inflation and a stagnant economy with high unemployment.

Because some economists supported the **theory** that inflation could only occur when demand for goods was high, they were not sure what fiscal policy the government should follow in order to fight inflation and the recession. Nixon wanted to control inflation. The government first tried to cut spending and raise taxes, and then tried to get the Federal Reserve to raise interest rates. When these methods failed, Nixon imposed a 90-day wage and price freeze. He also issued regulations limiting future increases. This met with little success.

✓ PROGRESS CHECK

Identifying Cause and Effect Why were some economists unsure of how to fight stagflation?

Ford and Carter Battle the Economic Crisis

GUIDING QUESTION *How did Ford and Carter try to resolve the nation's domestic issues?*

When Nixon resigned in 1974, inflation was still high. Meanwhile, the unemployment rate was over 5 percent. It would now be up to the new president, Gerald Ford, to confront stagflation.

Ford Tries to "Whip" Inflation

By 1975, unemployment had risen to nearly 9 percent. Ford launched a plan called WIN—"Whip Inflation Now"—but it had little impact on the economic situation. He tried other measures to reduce inflation, including keeping taxes low, but these plans also failed to revive the economy.

Ford's Foreign Policy

Ford continued Nixon's general foreign policy strategy. He kept Kissinger on as secretary of state and continued to pursue détente. In August 1975, Ford met with leaders of NATO and the Warsaw Pact to sign the Helsinki Accords. Under the accords, the parties recognized the post–World War II borders of Eastern Europe. The Soviets promised to uphold certain human rights, although this did not always happen.

In May 1975, soon after Communists seized power in Cambodia, Cambodian forces captured the *Mayaguez,* an American cargo ship. Ford sent U.S. Marines to retrieve the ship, but Cambodia had already secretly

CHARTS/GRAPHS

President Ford failed to solve the nation's lingering economic problems.

▶ CRITICAL THINKING

1 *Analyzing Information* What was the trend for both unemployment and inflation in the late 1970s?

2 *Drawing Conclusions* What effect do you think levels of inflation and unemployment had on Ford's presidential bid in 1976?

INFLATION AND UNEMPLOYMENT RATES

Source: U.S. Department of Labor; Bureau of Labor Statistics.

released the crew. Unaware of the crew's safety, the marines recaptured the ship, and 41 servicemen died in the battle.

The Election of 1976

The presidential race pitted Ford against former Georgia governor Jimmy Carter, who had no experience in Washington. Carter ran as an outsider promising to restore honesty to the federal government. He also promised to create or reform several domestic programs. Carter's image as a moral and upstanding individual attracted many voters, and he narrowly defeated Ford.

Carter's Economic Policies

Carter tried to use domestic policies to fix the economy. At first he tried to end the recession and reduce unemployment by increasing government spending and cutting taxes. Then he tried to ease inflation by reducing the money supply and raising interest rates. These measures did not work.

Carter believed that the nation's most serious economic problem was its dependence on foreign oil. He asked Americans to fight against rising energy consumption. He also proposed a national energy program to conserve oil and to promote the use of coal and renewable energy sources. Carter even convinced Congress to create a Department of Energy, and asked Americans to reduce energy consumption. Some argued that Carter should deregulate the domestic oil industry to decrease dependence on imported oil. Carter agreed to support **deregulation** but called for a special tax to keep oil companies from overcharging.

In the summer of 1979, instability in the Middle East produced a second major fuel shortage. Under pressure, Carter spoke in a televised address. He warned about a "crisis of confidence" that had struck "at the very heart and soul and spirit of our national will." The address became known as the "malaise" speech, although Carter had not used that word. Many Americans felt that Carter was blaming them for his failures.

President Carter's difficulties in solving the nation's economic problems lay partly in his inexperience and inability to work with Congress. He made little effort to reach out to Washington's legislative leaders, and many of his energy proposals failed. By 1979, public opinion polls showed that Carter's popularity had dropped.

☑ **PROGRESS CHECK**

Summarizing How did President Carter try to change the domestic oil industry?

Although Jimmy Carter's outsider status had made him an appealing candidate, his inexperience in Washington proved problematic.

▶ **CRITICAL THINKING**
Drawing Conclusions How might a lack of experience in Washington have made it difficult for Carter to achieve his goals?

embargo a government ban on trade with other countries

stagflation persistent inflation combined with stagnant consumer demand and relatively high unemployment

theory a hypothesis meant for argument or investigation

deregulation the act or process of removing restrictions or regulations

Carter's Foreign Policy

GUIDING QUESTION *What were President Carter's greatest foreign policy success and his greatest failure?*

A man of strong religious beliefs, President Carter argued that the United States must try to be "right and honest and truthful and decent" in dealing with other nations. Yet it was on the international front that Carter suffered a devastating defeat.

Morality in Foreign Policy

In his Inaugural Address, Carter gave his foreign policy a focus by saying:

PRIMARY SOURCE

❝Our commitment to human rights must be absolute . . . the powerful must not persecute the weak, and human dignity must be enhanced. . . . We pledge perseverance and wisdom in our efforts to limit the world's armaments to those necessary for each nation's own domestic safety.❞

—from his Inaugural Address, January 20, 1977

PHOTO: Library of Congress

❝He looked exhausted and careworn, sitting behind the big wooden desk in the Oval Office as he spoke. 'It was my decision to attempt the rescue operation. It was my decision to cancel it when problems developed. . . . The responsibility is fully my own.'

The mood at the senior staff meeting was somber and awkward. I sensed that we were all uncomfortable, like when a loved one dies and friends don't know quite what to say.❞

—Chief of Staff Hamilton Jordan, *Crisis*, 1982

DBQ *ANALYZING PRIMARY SOURCES* Why did Carter consider the rescue operation's failure his responsibility?

Carter and his foreign policy team—including Andrew Young, the first African American ambassador to the United Nations—strove to achieve these goals.

To remove a major symbol of American interventionism, Carter agreed to give Panama control of the Panama Canal, which the United States had built and operated for over 60 years. In 1978 the Senate ratified two Panama Canal treaties, which transferred control of the canal from the United States to Panama on December 31, 1999. Carter also singled out the Soviet Union as a human rights violator. Relations between the two superpowers suffered a further setback when Soviet troops invaded Afghanistan in December 1979. Carter responded by imposing an embargo on the sale of grain to the Soviet Union and boycotting the 1980 Summer Olympic Games in Moscow. Détente was crumbling.

Triumph and Failure in the Middle East

In 1978 Carter helped broker a historic peace treaty, known as the Camp David Accords. The agreement was signed between Israel and Egypt—two nations that had been bitter enemies for decades. Although many Arab nations did not support the treaty, it helped begin the slow peace process in the Middle East.

Just months after the treaty was signed in 1979, Carter faced a crisis in Iran. The United States had long supported Iran's monarch, the shah, because Iran was a major oil supplier and a buffer against Soviet expansion. The shah had grown increasingly unpopular in Iran due to his repressive rule and Westernizing reforms. The Islamic clergy opposed the shah's reforms. In January 1979, protesters forced him to flee. An Islamic republic was then declared.

Led by religious leader Ayatollah Khomeini, this new regime distrusted the United States because of its support of the shah. In November 1979, revolutionaries stormed the American embassy in Tehran and took 52 Americans hostage. The Carter administration unsuccessfully tried to negotiate the hostages' release. In April 1980, Carter approved a daring rescue attempt that failed when several helicopters malfunctioned and one crashed in the desert. Eight servicemen died in the accident.

The crisis continued. Every night, news programs reminded viewers how many days the hostages had been held. Carter's inability to free them cost him support in the 1980 election. On January 20, 1981, the day Carter left office, Iran released the Americans, ending their 444 days in captivity.

☑ **PROGRESS CHECK**

Evaluating How would you describe the philosophy of Carter's foreign policy?

LESSON 3 REVIEW

Reviewing Vocabulary
1. *Stating* What are the pros and cons of an embargo?

2. *Contrasting* How does inflation differ from stagflation?

Using Your Notes
3. *Making Generalizations* Use your notes to write a generalization about the causes of economic problems in the 1970s.

Answering the Guiding Questions
4. *Analyzing Cause and Effect* What economic conditions or problems led to a stagnant economy during the 1970s?

5. *Explaining* How did Ford and Carter try to resolve the nation's domestic issues?

6. *Assessing* What were Carter's greatest foreign policy success and his greatest failure? Why?

Writing Activity
7. **NARRATIVE** Assume the role of a journalist during the conclusion of the Iran hostage crisis. Write a script for a radio broadcast, recapping the events of the crisis, to be aired the day of the hostages' release.

networks

There's More Online!

☑ **BIOGRAPHY** Jesse Jackson

☑ **IMAGE** Pro-Busing and Anti-Busing

☑ **IMAGE** Protests at Wounded Knee

☑ **VIDEO** New Approaches to Civil Rights

☑ **INTERACTIVE SELF-CHECK QUIZ**

Reading **HELP**DESK

Content Vocabulary

• busing
• affirmative action

Academic Vocabulary

• criteria   • appropriate

TAKING NOTES: *Sequencing*

ACTIVITY Complete a time line similar to the one below by recording groups in the civil rights movement and their actions.

```
          ┌── 1971 ──┐
  ┌───────┤          ├───────┐
 1969      │          │      1977
          └── 1973 ──┘
```

PHOTOS: (l to r) Scherl/SV-Bilderdienst/The Image Works, Dave Bartruff/Documentary/Corbis, AP Images, Ed Kashi/Corbis News/Corbis, AP Images

LESSON 4
New Approaches to Civil Rights

ESSENTIAL QUESTIONS • *How do you think the Nixon administration affected people's attitudes toward government?* • *How does society change the shape of itself over time?*

IT MATTERS BECAUSE

Throughout the 1960s and 1970s, minority groups such as African Americans, Native Americans, and persons with disabilities began to develop new ways to expand opportunities and assert their civil rights.

African Americans Seek Greater Opportunity

GUIDING QUESTION *How did African American civil rights leaders change their reform focus?*

Although various forms of racial discrimination had become illegal, many African Americans saw little improvement in their daily lives. Access to good jobs and schooling remained issues. Civil rights leaders began to focus on these problems.

Equal Access to Education

In the 1970s, African Americans began to push harder for improvements in public education and access to good schools. In the 1954 case *Brown* v. *Board of Education*, the Supreme Court had ordered an end to segregated public schools. In the 1960s, however, many schools remained segregated as communities moved slowly to comply with the Court. Since children usually attended a school in their neighborhood, segregation in public schools reflected the racial segregation of neighborhoods.

In many cases where such de facto segregation existed, the white schools were superior, as Ruth Baston of the NAACP noted in 1965 after visiting Boston schools:

PRIMARY SOURCE

❝When we would go to white schools, we'd see . . . a small number of children in each class. The teachers were permanent. We'd see wonderful materials. When we'd go to our schools, we would see overcrowded classrooms, children sitting out in the corridors, and so forth. And so then we decided that where there were a large number of white students, that's where the care went. That's where the books went. That's where the money went.❞

—quoted in *Voices of Freedom*, 1990

The National March on Boston in 1975 marked the anniversary of the *Brown* v. *Board of Education* decision.

▶ **CRITICAL THINKING**

Making Inferences Why are protesters holding signs that read "21 years is too long to wait"?

busing a policy of transporting children to schools outside their neighborhoods to achieve greater racial balance

affirmative action an active effort to improve employment or educational opportunities for minorities and women

Courts began ordering local governments to bus children to schools outside their neighborhoods to achieve greater racial balance. The practice led to protests and even riots in several white communities. The Supreme Court, however, upheld the constitutionality of **busing** in the 1971 case *Swann* v. *Charlotte-Mecklenburg Board of Education*.

In response, many white parents took their children out of public schools or moved to districts with no busing. For example, thousands of white students left Boston's public school system to attend parochial and private schools. By late 1976, minorities made up the majority of Boston's public school students. This "white flight" also occurred in other cities. Detroit tried to bus students from one district to another in 1974. The plan was challenged, however, and the Court ruled in *Milliken* v. *Bradley* that busing across district lines was unconstitutional unless districts had been purposely drawn to create segregation.

Affirmative Action

In addition to supporting busing, civil rights leaders began advocating **affirmative action** as a new way to solve discrimination. Affirmative action was enforced through executive orders and federal policies. It called for companies, schools, and institutions doing business with the federal government to recruit African Americans. The hope was that this would lead to improved social and economic status. Officials later expanded affirmative action to include other minority groups and women.

Through affirmative action, Atlanta witnessed a significant increase in minority job opportunities. In 1974 Maynard Jackson took office as Atlanta's first African American mayor. When Jackson was elected, African Americans made up a large part of Atlanta's population. Few city contracts went to African American companies, however. Jackson worked to change this imbalance. Through his efforts, small companies and minority firms took on a higher percentage of all city contracts.

The *Bakke* Case

Critics viewed affirmative action programs as a form of reverse discrimination. They claimed that qualified white male workers and students were kept from jobs, promotions, and places in schools because of the slots set aside for minorities or women. In 1978 the Supreme Court addressed affirmative action in *Regents of the University of California* v. *Bakke*. Officials at the University of California at Davis medical school had twice turned down the application of a white applicant named Allan Bakke. When Bakke learned that slots had been set aside for minorities, he sued the school. Bakke pointed out that the school had admitted minority applicants with lower exam scores than his. He claimed that the school had discriminated against him based on his race.

In a 5-to-4 ruling, the Supreme Court declared that the university had violated Bakke's civil rights. It added, though, that schools had an interest in having racial diversity and could consider race as part of their admissions **criteria.** They could not, however, use "fixed quotas," or slots reserved for minority students.

New Political Leaders

New political leaders emerged in the African American community in the 1970s. For the first time since Reconstruction, African Americans became more influential in national politics. Jesse Jackson, a former aide to Martin Luther King, Jr., was among this new generation of activists. In 1971 Jackson founded Operation PUSH (People United to Save Humanity). Operation PUSH was dedicated to developing African American businesses, educational opportunities, and social and political development. In 1984 and 1988, Jackson sought the Democratic presidential nomination and lost. Yet he won over millions of voters.

In 1971 African American members of Congress organized the Congressional Black Caucus (CBC) to more clearly represent their concerns. One of the CBC's founding members was Shirley Chisholm of New York, the first African American woman to serve in Congress. In 1977 another former assistant to Dr. King, U.S. representative Andrew Young, became the first African American to serve as U.S. ambassador to the United Nations. He later served as the mayor of Atlanta. By the mid-1980s, African American mayors had been elected in Atlanta, Detroit, Chicago, Los Angeles, New Orleans, Philadelphia, and Washington, D.C.

Another leader who emerged in the 1980s was Louis Farrakhan, a prominent minister of the Nation of Islam. He organized the Million Man March on October 16, 1995. His goal for the march was to promote self-reliance and responsibility among African American men. Speakers at the event included Jesse Jackson and poet Maya Angelou.

In 1990 Virginia voters elected L. Douglas Wilder, who became the first African American governor of a state. That same year, David Dinkins took office as the first African American mayor of New York City.

☑ **PROGRESS CHECK**

Explaining What was the goal of affirmative action?

Native Americans Raise Their Voices

GUIDING QUESTION *What civil rights gains have Native Americans achieved since the 1960s?*

In 1970 Native Americans were one of the nation's smallest minority groups, yet they faced enormous problems. The unemployment rate for Native Americans was ten times the national rate. Unemployment was particularly high on reservations, where nearly half of all Native Americans lived. Little education or training was available. Their average annual family income was $1,000 less than that of African Americans. In addition, statistics showed that the life expectancy of Native Americans was seven years below that of whites.

A Protest Movement Emerges

In 1961 more than 400 members of 67 Native American groups gathered in Chicago to discuss their problems. They developed a Declaration of Indian Purpose asking for federal programs to create greater economic opportunities for all Native Americans. In 1968 Congress passed the Indian Civil Rights Act. The legislation guaranteed reservation residents the protections of the Bill of Rights while still recognizing tribal courts.

Native Americans who viewed the government's efforts as too modest formed more militant groups, such as the American Indian Movement (AIM). In 1969 Native Americans occupied the closed federal prison on Alcatraz Island in San Francisco Bay for 19 months, claiming ownership "by right of discovery."

BIOGRAPHY

Ben Nighthorse Campbell (1933–)

A member and chief of the Northern Cheyenne tribe, Ben Nighthorse Campbell entered politics in the early 1980s as a Colorado state legislator. He was elected to the U.S. Senate in 1992, serving as the governing body's only Native American member until he chose not to run for reelection in 2004. In addition to his political career, Campbell has also been a successful jewelry designer, rancher, and horse trainer.

▶ **CRITICAL THINKING**
Interpreting Significance Why was Campbell's election to the U.S. Senate significant?

criteria standards on which a judgment or action may be based

The American Indian Movement, with leaders Russell Means (left) and Dennis Banks, staged a protest at Wounded Knee, South Dakota, in 1973.

▶ **CRITICAL THINKING**

Comparing and Contrasting How were the goals of the Native American movement similar to the goals of other movements in the 1960s and 1970s?

Analyzing PRIMARY SOURCES

Letter Protesting Mining on Hopi Lands

❝Today the sacred lands where the Hopi live are being desecrated by men who seek coal and water from our soil that they may create more power for the white man's cities. This must not be allowed to continue. . . . The Great Spirit said not to take from the Earth. . . . Your government has almost destroyed our basic religion which is actually a way of life for all our people in this land of the Great Spirit.❞

—quoted in *Touch the Earth,* 1971

DBQ *ANALYZING PRIMARY SOURCES* Why do the Hopi claim that coal mining on their lands is wrong?

AIM's most famous protest took place at Wounded Knee, South Dakota. U.S. troops had killed hundreds of Sioux there in 1890. In February 1973, AIM members seized the town for 70 days. They demanded that the government honor its past treaty obligations, insisting on changes in reservation administration. Before the siege between AIM and the FBI ended, two Native Americans were killed and both sides suffered injuries.

Other groups, such as the Hopi and the Navajo, objected to land leases to mining companies that scoured the land, displaced families, and posed a threat to sacred places. They wrote letters of protest to the government.

Native American Gains

By the mid-1970s, the Native American movement had begun to achieve some of its goals. In 1975 Congress passed the Indian Self-Determination and Educational Assistance Act. This act encouraged tribal participation in and management of federal programs, such as social services, law enforcement, and health services, which the Bureau of Indian Affairs and Health and Human Services' Indian Health Service had previously administered. It also increased funds for Native American education.

Native Americans won several court cases involving land and water rights. The Pueblo of Taos, New Mexico, regained property rights to Blue Lake, a place sacred to their religion. In 1980 the government paid the Passamaquoddy and the Penobscot peoples $81.5 million to give up their claim to land in Maine. Other court decisions gave tribal governments the power to tax businesses on reservations.

Since Native Americans began to organize, many reservations have improved their economic conditions. Businesses such as electric plants, resorts, cattle ranches, and oil and gas wells have been developed. More recently, gambling casinos have become a successful activity. Rulings on sovereignty have allowed some Native Americans to operate casinos under their own laws even though state laws prevent others from doing so.

☑ **PROGRESS CHECK**

Summarizing Why did Native Americans protest for their civil rights to be recognized?

The Disability Rights Movement

GUIDING QUESTION *How did federal legislation protect the civil rights of people with disabilities?*

The struggle for disability rights had its early expression in the independent living movement that began at the University of California at Berkeley in the early 1970s. The movement advocated for the right of people of all

levels of abilities to choose to live freely in society. This was part of a new attitude that encouraged people who had disabilities to move out of institutions and live independently.

People with disabilities also looked to the federal government to protect their civil rights. They sought access to public facilities. They also demanded bans on discrimination in employment. One victory was the 1968 Architectural Barriers Act. This act required that new buildings constructed with federal funds be accessible to persons with disabilities. The Rehabilitation Act of 1973 was even more significant. Section 504 states that no person with a disability can be discriminated against in any way by an entity that receives federal funding.

Passage of the Rehabilitation Act meant little, however, until procedures for enforcing it were established. As of 1977, the Department of Health, Education, and Welfare (HEW) had no such procedures. Frustrated, the American Coalition of Citizens with Disabilities organized protests. On April 5, 1977, some 2,000 persons with disabilities in 10 cities began sit-ins at regional HEW offices. Protesters in San Francisco kept up their sit-in for over three weeks, until HEW's director signed the regulations banning discrimination.

Changes also occurred in special education. In 1966 Congress created the Bureau for the Education of the Handicapped, which provided grants to develop programs for educating children with disabilities. In 1975 the Education for All Handicapped Children Act required that all students with disabilities receive a free, **appropriate** education. One trend was to mainstream, or bring into the regular classroom, students with disabilities.

In 1990 Congress enacted the Americans with Disabilities Act. This far-reaching legislation banned discrimination against persons with disabilities in employment, transportation, public education, and telecommunications. Today, technologies such as closed-captioned television broadcasts, devices for telephones, and screen readers help people with disabilities access information in new ways.

Section 504 of the Rehabilitation Act and, later, the Americans with Disabilities Act specified that people with disabilities must have equal access to public facilities, such as transportation and parking.

▶ **CRITICAL THINKING**
Identifying Central Issues What rights did people with disabilities struggle for in the 1970s?

appropriate especially suitable or compatible

✓ **PROGRESS CHECK**

Explaining What tactics did people with disabilities use to protest that were also used by other minority groups? Were they effective? Explain.

LESSON 4 REVIEW

Reviewing Vocabulary
1. *Identifying* What was the purpose of busing?

Using Your Notes
2. *Comparing* Use your notes to write a paragraph identifying similarities among the gains made by African Americans, Native Americans, and people with disabilities.

Answering the Guiding Questions
3. *Evaluating* How did African American civil rights leaders change their reform focus?

4. *Describing* What civil rights gains have Native Americans achieved since the 1960s?

5. *Summarizing* How did federal legislation protect the civil rights of people with disabilities?

Writing Activity
6. **EXPOSITORY** Write a paragraph in which you summarize the issues involved in the Supreme Court cases of *Swann* v. *Charlotte-Mecklenburg Board of Education* and *Regents of the University of California* v. *Bakke*.

networks

There's More Online!

- ☑ **BIOGRAPHY** Rachel Carson
- ☑ **IMAGE** Earth Day
- ☑ **MAP** Recent Environmental Problems
- ☑ **SLIDE SHOW** Endangered Species List
- ☑ **VIDEO** Environmentalism
- ☑ **INTERACTIVE SELF-CHECK QUIZ**

Reading **HELP**DESK

Content Vocabulary
- smog
- fossil fuel

Academic Vocabulary
- intensify
- alternative

TAKING NOTES: *Organizing*

ACTIVITY As you read, complete a graphic organizer similar to the one below by including actions taken to combat the nation's environmental problems in the 1960s and 1970s.

Actions Taken

LESSON 5
Environmentalism

ESSENTIAL QUESTIONS • *How do you think the Nixon administration affected people's attitudes toward government?* • *How does society change the shape of itself over time?*

IT MATTERS BECAUSE

Americans became increasingly aware of the damage being done to the environment. Soon, environmental issues became national concerns, and individuals, local groups, and the government acted to address the damage and protect natural resources.

The Origins of Environmentalism

GUIDING QUESTION *What concerns inspired the environmental movement?*

In 1966 Carol Yannacone of Patchogue, a small community on Long Island, New York, learned that officials were using the powerful pesticide DDT as part of a mosquito control operation at a local lake. Yannacone and her husband Victor, an attorney, were concerned that the pesticide might be poisonous. They decided to contact local scientists, who confirmed their suspicions.

The Yannacones then successfully sued to halt the use of the pesticide. In so doing, they had discovered a new strategy for addressing environmental concerns. Shortly after the Yannacones' court victory, the scientists involved in the case established the Environmental Defense Fund. They used its contributions for a series of legal actions across the country to halt DDT spraying. Along with those of other environmental organizations, their efforts led to a nationwide ban on DDT in 1972.

The effort to ban DDT was only one part of a new environmental movement that took shape in the 1960s and 1970s. The person who helped trigger this new movement was a soft-spoken marine biologist named Rachel Carson. Carson's 1962 book *Silent Spring* assailed the increasing use of pesticides, particularly DDT. She argued that while pesticides curbed insect populations, they also killed birds, fish, and other creatures that might ingest them. Carson warned Americans of a "silent spring," in which there would be no birds left to usher spring in with their songs. "No . . . enemy action had silenced the rebirth of new life in this stricken world. The people had done it themselves. . . . A grim specter has crept upon us almost unnoticed, and this imagined tragedy may easily become a stark reality we all shall know," she warned.

Silent Spring became a best seller and one of the most controversial and influential books of the 1960s. The chemical industry was outraged and began an intense campaign to discredit Carson and her arguments. Many Americans believed Carson's warnings, however, largely because of what they were seeing around them and reading in news reports.

Rivers across the nation were no longer safe for fishing or swimming. **Smog,** or fog made heavier and darker by smoke and chemical fumes, hung over many major cities. In the Northwest, timber companies were cutting down acres of forest. In 1969 a major oil spill off Santa Barbara, California, ruined miles of beach and killed many birds and aquatic animals. Land development in Florida's Everglades contributed to the destruction of much of the original natural area. Pollution and garbage caused many fish to die in Lake Erie. By 1970, many citizens were convinced it was time to do something about protecting the environment.

A Grassroots Effort Begins

Many observers point to April 1970 as the unofficial beginning of the environmentalist movement. That month, the nation first observed Earth Day, a day devoted to environmental concerns. The national response was overwhelming. On college campuses, in secondary schools, and in communities, Americans actively showed their environmental awareness.

After Earth Day, many citizens formed local environmental groups, adding new voices to those of organizations such as the Audubon Society, the Sierra Club, and the Wilderness Society. These organizations worked to protect the environment and promote the conservation of natural resources. In 1970 activists started the Natural Resources Defense Council to coordinate a nationwide network of scientists, lawyers, and activists.

Many communities and businesses responded to these organizations. They tried to make communities and buildings more environmentally friendly, and worked to restore damaged natural spaces.

☑ **PROGRESS CHECK**

Identifying Cause and Effect How did the environmental movement affect the rise of smaller grassroots efforts?

The Environmental Movement Blossoms

GUIDING QUESTION *How did new laws passed in this time period protect the environment?*

As the environmental movement gained support, the federal government took action. In 1970 President Nixon signed the National Environmental Policy Act, which created the Environmental Protection Agency (EPA). The EPA set and enforced pollution standards, promoted research, and directed antipollution activities with state and local governments.

In 1970 President Nixon signed a new Clean Air Act into law. This act established emissions standards for factories and automobiles. It aimed to improve national air quality within five years, and set guidelines and timetables for states and cities to meet.

In the following years, Congress passed two more pieces of significant environmental legislation. The Clean Water Act of 1972 restricted the discharge of pollutants into the nation's lakes and rivers. The other act was

smog fog made heavier and darker by smoke and chemical fumes

The publication of *Silent Spring* made biologist Rachel Carson one of the early environmental movement's important figures. The book's warnings about the dangers of pollution drew fire from the chemical industry but won over many readers.

▶ **CRITICAL THINKING**
Making Generalizations What was Carson's greatest contribution to the environmental movement?

Smog heavily polluted the air around major cities, heightening residents' awareness of environmental problems.

▶ **CRITICAL THINKING**

Analyzing Primary Sources Based on this photograph, what might be a main contributor to the problem of smog?

the Endangered Species Act of 1973, which established measures for saving threatened animal and plant species. These laws succeeded in reducing smog, and the pollution of many lakes, streams, and rivers declined.

Love Canal

Despite increasing federal legislation, Americans also worked for change at the community level throughout the 1970s. One of the most powerful displays of community activism occurred in a housing development near Niagara Falls, New York, known as Love Canal.

During the 1970s, residents of Love Canal began to notice an increasingly high number of health problems in their community. The people in the community were suffering from nerve damage, blood diseases, cancer, miscarriages, and birth defects. The residents soon learned that their community sat atop a decades-old toxic waste dump. Over time, its hazardous contents had spread through the ground. Led by a local woman, Lois Gibbs, the residents joined together and demanded that the government take steps to address these health threats. Gibbs later wrote about the importance of organizing to protect the environment:

> **PRIMARY SOURCE**
>
> ❝ It will take a massive effort to move society from corporate domination, in which industry's rights to pollute and damage human health and the environment supersede the public's right to live, work, and play in a safe environment. This is a political fight, since the science is already there showing that people's health is being placed at risk. To win the political fight, we need to continue to build the movement, to network with one another, and to plan, strategize, and keep moving forward. ❞
>
> —from *Love Canal: The Story Continues . . .*, 1998

Residents struggled against uncooperative officials and worked to increase awareness of their plight. The state finally relocated more than 200 families in 1978.

The same year, President Carter declared Love Canal a limited disaster area. In 1980 he called for emergency aid and moved approximately 500 families who remained to new locations. In 1983 Love Canal residents sued the company that had created the dump site and settled the case for around $20 million. The site was cleaned up by sealing the waste within an underground bunker and demolishing homes located above the dumping ground.

Concerns About Nuclear Energy

Also during the 1970s, a number of citizens became concerned about the use of nuclear reactors to generate electricity. As nuclear power plants began to dot the nation's landscape, the debate over their use **intensified.** Supporters of nuclear energy hailed it as a cleaner and less expensive **alternative** to **fossil fuels,** such as coal, oil, and natural gas, which are in limited supply. Opponents warned of the risks nuclear energy posed, particularly the devastating consequences of radiation released into the air.

The nuclear debate gained national attention in a shocking fashion in 1979. In the early hours of March 28, one of the reactors at the Three Mile Island nuclear facility outside Harrisburg, Pennsylvania, overheated. The

intensify to become more frequent and powerful

alternative another choice

fossil fuel a fuel formed in the Earth from decayed plant or animal remains

PHOTO: Designp cs.com/PunchStock

problem occurred after its cooling system failed. That night, as plant officials scrambled to fix the problem, low levels of radiation began to escape from the reactor.

Officials evacuated many nearby residents, while others fled on their own. Citizens and community groups expressed outrage at protest rallies. Officials closed down the reactor and sealed the leak. The Nuclear Regulatory Commission, the federal agency that regulates the nuclear power industry, eventually declared that the plant was safe. President Carter even arranged a visit to the site to allay the public's concerns.

The accident at Three Mile Island had a powerful impact politically. It left much of the public with grave doubts about the safety of nuclear energy. Such doubts have continued.

✔ **PROGRESS CHECK**

Evaluating Was the national government's response to the environmental movement effective? Why?

In the aftermath of the accident at Three Mile Island, residents held protests that questioned the safety of nuclear energy.

▶ **CRITICAL THINKING**
Constructing Arguments Are the residents justified in their concerns about nuclear energy? Explain why or why not.

PHOTO: Wally McNamee/Historical/CORBIS

LESSON 5 REVIEW

Reviewing Vocabulary
1. *Describing* What is smog?

2. *Listing* What are some examples of fossil fuels?

Using Your Notes
3. *Naming* Review the notes that you completed throughout the lesson to list some environmental protection initiatives that were begun during this period.

Answering the Guiding Questions
4. *Identifying* What concerns inspired the environmental movement?

5. *Assessing* How did new laws passed in this time period protect the environment?

Writing Activity
6. DESCRIPTIVE Take on the role of an investigative reporter, and describe the environmental disaster at either Love Canal or Three Mile Island. Explain how community activism brought the issue to the nation's attention.

Directions: On a separate sheet of paper, answer the questions below. Make sure you read carefully and answer all parts to the question.

Lesson Review

Lesson 1

1 *Analyzing* How were both federal and state governments affected by Nixon's New Federalism?

2 *Explaining* How was détente a factor in Nixon's visit to China?

Lesson 2

3 *Describing* What role did James McCord play in the Watergate scandal?

4 *Identifying Cause and Effect* How was the FBI Domestic Security Investigation Guidelines Act a result of the Watergate scandal?

Lesson 3

5 *Explaining* Explain the significance of the Camp David Accords.

6 *Considering Perspectives* Why did Ayatollah Khomeini not trust the United States?

Lesson 4

7 *Explaining* What was the purpose of the Americans with Disabilities Act?

8 *Making Connections* What events made Wounded Knee, South Dakota, an important location in 1890 and 1973?

Lesson 5

9 *Identifying Perspectives* What group was in favor of the message in *Silent Spring*, and what group opposed it?

10 *Describing* What are two key acts of legislation enacted in 1970 to help protect the environment?

21st Century Skills

11 IDENTIFYING PERSPECTIVES AND DIFFERING INTERPRETATIONS Explain why you think Nixon used the term "silent majority."

12 IDENTIFYING CAUSE AND EFFECT What motivated people to break into the Watergate apartment complex?

13 UNDERSTANDING RELATIONSHIPS AMONG EVENTS How can an embargo be used for political purposes?

14 EXPLAINING CONTINUITY AND CHANGE Explain the role that Carol and Victor Yannacone played in the origins of environmentalism.

Exploring the Essential Questions

15 *Drawing Conclusions* Give an oral presentation on turmoil in the 1970s. The presentation should answer two questions: How did the Nixon administration's actions affect people's attitudes toward government? How did society change during the 1970s?

DBQ Document-Based Questions

Use the cartoon to answer the following questions.

This political cartoon provides commentary about the 1972 talks on the Strategic Arms Limitation Treaty, or SALT I.

PRIMARY SOURCE

16 *Analyzing Visuals* What do the two men wearing hats represent?

17 *Analyzing Visuals* What message does this cartoon convey about taxpayers and the buildup of weapons?

Extended-Response Question

18 *Drawing Conclusions* Write an essay explaining how the Watergate scandal challenged people's ideas about executive privilege. Your essay should contain an introduction and at least two paragraphs.

Need Extra Help?

If You've Missed Question	1	2	3	4	5	6	7	8	9	10	11	12	13	14	15	16	17	18
Go to page	630	631	633	636	640	640	645	644	646	647	628	633	637	646	628	650	650	635

The Resurgence of Conservatism

1980–1992

ESSENTIAL QUESTION • *How do you think the resurgence of conservative ideas has changed society?*

The Story Matters...

After several decades in which progressive and liberal ideas dominated American politics, conservatism began making a comeback in the 1970s. In 1980 voters elected the conservative Ronald Reagan as president. Reagan's commitment to less government regulation, a stronger military, and uncompromising anticommunism seemed to meet voters' concerns.

◄ Ronald Reagan was hailed by many Americans as a conservative hero who would lead the country to prosperity after two decades of social change and turmoil.

PHOTO: Tony Korody/Sygma/CORBIS

651

CHAPTER 29

Place and Time: Eastern Europe 1979–1991

In the 1980s, President Ronald Reagan took a tough stance against the Soviet Union and Eastern Bloc nations by building up weapons and supporting anticommunist movements. By the end of the 1980s, the Soviet Union was greatly weakened, fell, and broke apart into separate republics. Other Communist governments in the Eastern Bloc fell as well. The Cold War was over. With his successor George H. W. Bush calling for a "new world order," the United States prepared to take on a leading role in a complicated world of new alliances.

Step Into the Place

Read the quotes and look at the information presented on the map.

 What do the quotes and the information on the map indicate about democratic movements in Eastern Europe and the political climate that resulted?

PRIMARY SOURCE

❝We are witnessing most profound social change. Whether in the East or the South, the West or the North, hundreds of millions of people, new nations and States, new public movements and ideologies have moved to the forefront of history. Broad-based and frequently turbulent popular movements have given expression . . . to a longing for independence, democracy and social justice. The idea of democratizing the entire world order has become a powerful socio-political force.❞

—Mikhail Gorbachev, from a speech to the UN General Assembly, December 7, 1988

PRIMARY SOURCE

❝This is an historic moment. We have in this past year made great progress in ending the long era of conflict and cold war. We have before us the opportunity to forge for ourselves and for future generations a new world order—a world where the rule of law, not the law of the jungle, governs the conduct of nations.❞

—George H. W. Bush, from a televised broadcast to the nation, January 16, 1991

Step Into the Time

Choose an event from the time line and write a paragraph that predicts the social, political, or economic consequences that event might have on the resurgence of conservatism.

U.S. PRESIDENTS

Carter 1977–1981

Reagan 1981–1989

1981 American hostages released from Iran

1982 Boland Amendment keeps the U. S. from giving aid to the contras

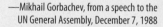

UNITED STATES

WORLD

1978	1980	1982

April 1979 Islamic Republic of Iran declared

1980 War begins between Iran and Iraq

December 1979 Soviets invade Afghanistan

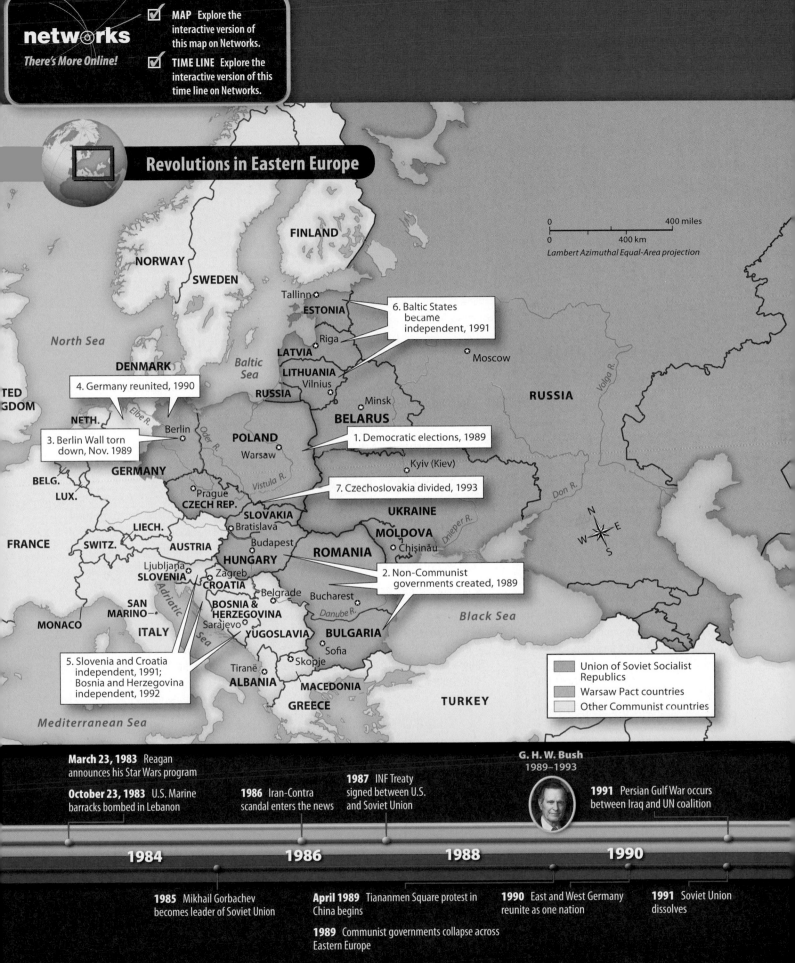

networks
There's More Online!

☑ **MAP** Explore the interactive version of this map on Networks.

☑ **TIME LINE** Explore the interactive version of this time line on Networks.

Revolutions in Eastern Europe

0   400 miles
0   400 km
Lambert Azimuthal Equal-Area projection

6. Baltic States became independent, 1991

4. Germany reunited, 1990

3. Berlin Wall torn down, Nov. 1989

1. Democratic elections, 1989

7. Czechoslovakia divided, 1993

2. Non-Communist governments created, 1989

5. Slovenia and Croatia independent, 1991; Bosnia and Herzegovina independent, 1992

NORWAY
SWEDEN
FINLAND
North Sea
DENMARK
Baltic Sea
ESTONIA — Tallinn
LATVIA — Riga
LITHUANIA — Vilnius
RUSSIA
Moscow
Minsk
BELARUS
RUSSIA
Volga R.
NETH.
Berlin
Elbe R.
Oder R.
POLAND
Warsaw
Vistula R.
GERMANY
BELG.
LUX.
Prague
CZECH REP.
SLOVAKIA
Bratislava
Kyiv (Kiev)
UKRAINE
Don R.
Dnieper R.
LIECH.
Budapest
MOLDOVA
Chişinău
FRANCE
SWITZ.
AUSTRIA
HUNGARY
ROMANIA
Ljubljana
Zagreb
SLOVENIA
CROATIA
Belgrade
Bucharest
Danube R.
Black Sea
SAN MARINO
BOSNIA & HERZEGOVINA
Sarajevo
YUGOSLAVIA
BULGARIA
MONACO
ITALY
Adriatic Sea
Sofia
Skopje
Tiranë
ALBANIA
MACEDONIA
GREECE
TURKEY
Mediterranean Sea

N E S W (compass)

Union of Soviet Socialist Republics
Warsaw Pact countries
Other Communist countries

March 23, 1983 Reagan announces his Star Wars program

October 23, 1983 U.S. Marine barracks bombed in Lebanon

1986 Iran-Contra scandal enters the news

1987 INF Treaty signed between U.S. and Soviet Union

G. H. W. Bush 1989–1993

1991 Persian Gulf War occurs between Iraq and UN coalition

1984   1986   1988   1990

1985 Mikhail Gorbachev becomes leader of Soviet Union

April 1989 Tiananmen Square protest in China begins

1989 Communist governments collapse across Eastern Europe

1990 East and West Germany reunite as one nation

1991 Soviet Union dissolves

networks

There's More Online!

☑ **BIOGRAPHY** William F. Buckley

☑ **BIOGRAPHY** Billy Graham

☑ **IMAGE** Higher Taxes Protest

☑ **IMAGE** Moral Majority

☑ **VIDEO** The New Conservatism

☑ **INTERACTIVE SELF-CHECK QUIZ**

Reading **HELP**DESK

Content Vocabulary

• liberal   • televangelist
• conservative

Academic Vocabulary

• indicate   • stability

TAKING NOTES: *Outlining*

ACTIVITY As you read about the resurgence of conservatism, complete a graphic organizer similar to the one below. Use the major headings of this section to outline information about the rise of the new conservatism in the United States.

> The New Conservatism
> I. Liberalism and Conservatism
>   A.
>   B.
> II.
>   A.

LESSON 1
The New Conservatism

ESSENTIAL QUESTION • *How do you think the resurgence of conservative ideas has changed society?*

IT MATTERS BECAUSE

By the 1980s, new levels of discontent with government and society had left many Americans concerned about the direction of the nation. Some began to call for a return to more conservative approaches and values.

Liberalism and Conservatism

GUIDING QUESTION *Do you consider yourself liberal or conservative?*

Conservative writer Midge Decter was appalled at the looting and arson that rocked New York City during a blackout on the night of July 13, 1977. City officials and the media blamed the events on the anger and despair of youth in neglected areas. Decter disagreed:

PRIMARY SOURCE

❝[T]hose young men went on their spree of looting because they had been given permission to do so. They had been given permission to do so by all the papers and magazines, movies and documentaries—all the outlets for the purveying of enlightened liberal attitude and progressive liberal policy—which had for years and years been proclaiming that race and poverty were sufficient excuses for lawlessness. ❞

—from "Looting and Liberal Racism," *Commentary,* September 1977

Midge Decter's article blaming liberalism for the New York riots illustrates one side of a debate in American politics that still continues. On one side are people who call themselves **liberals;** on the other side are those who identify themselves as **conservatives.** In the 1960s, liberal ideas dominated U.S. politics. Conservative ideas gained support in the 1970s. In 1980 conservative Ronald Reagan was elected president.

Liberalism

In general, modern liberals believe that government should regulate the economy to protect people from the power of corporations and wealthy elites. Liberals also believe that the federal government should help disadvantaged Americans through social programs and by putting more of society's tax burden on wealthier people. They believe that those with greater assets should take on more of the costs of government.

Although liberals favor government intervention in the economy, they do not support the government regulating social behavior. They are opposed to the government supporting or endorsing religious beliefs, no matter how indirectly. They believe that a society with ethnic and cultural diversity tends to be more creative and energetic.

Conservatism

Conservatives distrust the power of government and wish to limit it. They also believe that government regulation makes the economy less efficient, and that free enterprise is the best economic system. They argue that increased economic regulation could lead to regulation in every aspect of people's behavior. Conservatives fear the government will so restrict people's economic freedom that Americans will no longer be able to improve their standard of living. They generally oppose high taxes and government programs that redistribute wealth.

Many conservatives believe that most social problems result from issues of morality and character. They argue that such issues are best addressed through commitment to a religious faith and through the private efforts of churches, individuals, and communities to help those in need. Despite this general belief, conservatives often support the use of police powers to regulate social behavior.

✓ **PROGRESS CHECK**

Contrasting How do liberals and conservatives view government?

Conservatism Revives

GUIDING QUESTION *Why are some regions of the country more conservative or liberal than other areas?*

During the New Deal era of the 1930s, conservative ideas lost influence in national politics. After World War II, however, conservatism began to revive.

The Role of the Cold War

The Cold War helped revive support for conservative ideas. First, the struggle against communism revived the debate about the role of the government in the economy. Some Americans believed that liberal economic ideas were slowly leading the United States toward communism and set out to stop this trend. They also thought the United States had failed to stop the spread of Soviet power because liberals did not fully understand the need for a strong anticommunist foreign policy. At the same time, some Americans viewed the Cold War in religious terms, seeing the struggle against communism as a struggle between good and evil. Liberalism gradually lost the support of these Americans as they increasingly turned to conservatism.

Conservatives Organize

In 1955 a young conservative, William F. Buckley, founded a magazine called *National Review,* which helped revive conservative ideas in the United States. Buckley worked to spread conservative ideas to a wider audience. In 1960 some 90 young conservative leaders met at Buckley's family estate and founded Young Americans for Freedom (YAF). This independent conservative group pushed for their ideas and supported conservative candidates. By 1964, the new conservative movement had achieved enough influence within the Republican Party to enable the conservative Barry Goldwater to win the nomination for president. President Lyndon Johnson defeated him and won by a landslide.

The Rise of the Sunbelt

In the 1950s and early 1960s, the South and the West were more conservative than other regions. Southern conservatives, however, generally voted for the Democrats, while conservatives in the West voted for the Republicans.

liberal a person who generally believes the government should take an active role in the economy and in social programs but should not dictate social behavior

conservative a person who believes government power, particularly in the economy, should be limited in order to maximize individual freedom

— *Thinking Like a* —
HISTORIAN

Contrasting

Throughout history, the terms *liberal* and *conservative* have not always had the same sense as they do today. Culture and history have influenced their meanings. For example, after the Napoleonic Wars, European leaders met at the Congress of Vienna (1814–1815) to reconstruct Europe. Conservatives included monarchs, nobles, and church leaders who supported the idea that Europe should return to its pre-Napoleonic political and social order, a hierarchical one in which the lower class submitted to the rule of the upper class. There was fear that democratic "rule by many" would lead to rule by an uneducated mob. On the other hand, liberals represented the middle class and advocated a separation of powers, natural rights, and a republic. Understanding that a word's definition may change over time is important for a clear reading of history.

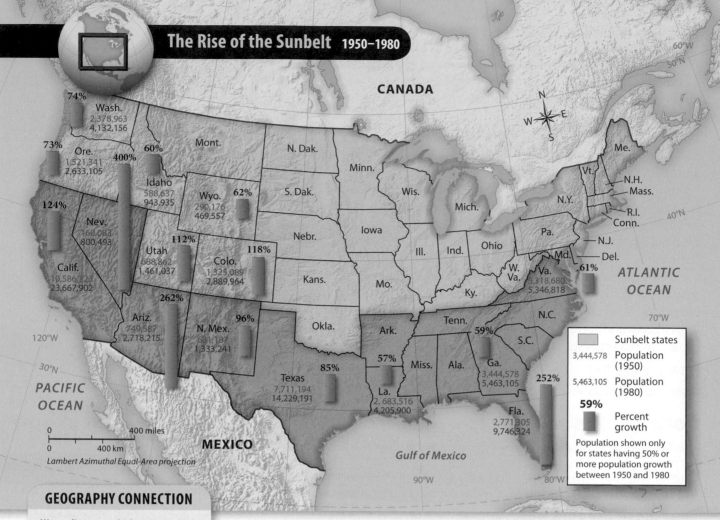

The Rise of the Sunbelt 1950–1980

CANADA

74%
Wash.
2,378,963
4,132,156

73%
Ore.
1,521,341
2,633,105

Mont.

N. Dak.

Minn.

Me.

60%

400%

Idaho
588,637
943,935

Wyo.
290,176
469,557

62%

S. Dak.

Wis.

Mich.

Vt.
N.H.
Mass.
N.Y.
R.I.
Conn.

124%

Nev.
160,083
800,493

112%
Utah
688,862
1,461,037

Colo.
1,325,089
2,889,964

118%

Nebr.

Iowa

Ill.   Ind.   Ohio

Pa.

N.J.
Md.   Del.

Calif.
10,586,223
23,667,902

262%

Kans.

Mo.

Ky.

W.
Va.

Va.
3,318,680
5,346,818

.61%

ATLANTIC
OCEAN

120°W

Ariz.
749,587
2,718,215

96%

N. Mex.
681,187
1,333,241

Okla.

Ark.

Tenn.

59%

N.C.

S.C.

70°W

30°N

PACIFIC
OCEAN

85%

Texas
7,711,194
14,229,191

57%

La.
2,683,516
4,205,900

Miss. Ala.

Ga.
3,444,578
5,463,105

252%

40°N

0   400 miles

0   400 km
Lambert Azimuthal Equal-Area projection

MEXICO

Gulf of Mexico

Fla.
2,771,305
9,746,324

90°W

80°W

	Sunbelt states
3,444,578	Population (1950)
5,463,105	Population (1980)
59%	Percent growth

Population shown only for states having 50% or more population growth between 1950 and 1980

GEOGRAPHY CONNECTION

Warm climates and job opportunities contributed to population growth in the Sunbelt.

1. **THE WORLD IN SPATIAL TERMS** *Which Sunbelt states had more than 8 million residents in 1980?*

2. **ENVIRONMENT AND SOCIETY** *What factors may explain why some Sunbelt states experienced strong growth while others did not?*

Thus, the party that won the populous Northeast would win the presidential election. Since the Northeast strongly supported liberal ideas, both parties leaned toward liberal policies.

This pattern began to change during World War II, when large numbers of Americans moved south and west for jobs in war factories. These Sunbelt states experienced dramatic population growth. For instance, Census Bureau data showed Florida's population growing every year from 1946 until 2009. The movement was fueled by warmer climates and increasing job opportunities. Florida's weather and expanding tourist industry met both criteria. As the Sunbelt's economy expanded, these residents began thinking differently about the government than people in the Northeast did.

Sunbelt and Suburban Conservatism

Industry in the Northeast was in decline, leading to the region's nickname, the Rust Belt. Northeasterners looked to the government to help them solve problems of unemployment, congestion, and pollution. In contrast, many Americans in the Sunbelt opposed high taxes and federal regulations that might interfere with their region's growth. Many white Southerners were also angry with the Democrats for supporting civil rights, which they saw as the federal government's effort to impose its policies on the South.

When Barry Goldwater argued that the federal government was becoming too strong, many Southerners agreed. For the first time since Reconstruction, they began voting Republican in large numbers. Although Goldwater lost, he showed that supporting conservative policies attracted Southern voters.

Americans living in the West also responded to conservative criticism of the government. Westerners resented federal environmental regulations that limited ranching, controlled water use, and restricted the development of natural resources. By 1980, the Sunbelt's population had surpassed that of the Northeast, giving these conservative regions more electoral votes.

During the 1960s and 1970s, many Americans moved to suburbs to escape urban chaos. Even there, however, they found the middle-class lifestyle they desired was in danger. Rapid inflation had caused their buying power to shrink while taxes remained high. Tax cuts became a national issue. As conservatives called for tax cuts, middle-class voters flocked to their cause.

The Religious Right

Some people were drawn to conservatism because they feared that American society had lost touch with its traditional values. Some Americans with conservative religious faith were shocked by Supreme Court decisions protecting the right to an abortion, limiting prayer in public schools, and expanding protections for people accused of crimes. The feminist movement's push for the Equal Rights Amendment (ERA) also upset some religious conservatives because it challenged aspects of the traditional family. In addition, student protesters' contempt for authority seemed to **indicate** a general breakdown in American values and morality. These concerns helped expand the conservative cause into a mass movement.

Protestant evangelicals were the largest group of religious conservatives. After World War II, a religious revival began in the United States among this group. Ministers such as Billy Graham and Oral Roberts built national followings, and some owned their own newspapers, magazines, radio stations, and television networks. With television, evangelical ministers reached a nationwide audience. These **televangelists** included Marion "Pat" Robertson and Jerry Falwell, who founded a group called the Moral Majority. The Moral Majority built up a network of ministers to register new voters who backed conservative candidates and issues. The group registered 2 million new voters in the 1980 election.

A New Coalition

A new conservative coalition began to believe that society had lost its way. Political scandal, economic worries, and social turmoil seemed to plague the nation. International events such as the withdrawal from Vietnam seemed to make the nation look weak. Many Americans were tired of upheaval. They wanted **stability** and a return to what they remembered as better times.

✓ **PROGRESS CHECK**

Making Connections How did economic factors cause a shift in ideas about the government among residents in the Sunbelt?

Jerry Falwell related to the concerns of conservative Christians and organized them into a conservative voting bloc.

▶ **CRITICAL THINKING**
Making Connections How might the Cold War have encouraged Americans to join the religious right?

indicate to point out, point to, or demonstrate the necessity of

televangelist an evangelist who conducts regularly televised religious programs

stability a state of peace; condition resistant to change or upheaval

PHOTO: Diana Walker/Time & Life Pictures/Getty Images

LESSON 1 REVIEW

Reviewing Vocabulary

1. *Listing* What are some core ideas of conservatives?

2. *Identifying* Where would you expect to see the message of a televangelist?

Using Your Notes

3. *Identifying Cause and Effect* Use your notes to write a paragraph describing the factors that led to the revival of conservatism.

Answering the Guiding Questions

4. *Classifying* Do you consider yourself liberal or conservative?

5. *Analyzing Cause and Effect* Why are some regions of the country more conservative or liberal than other areas?

Writing Activity

6. NARRATIVE Suppose that you are a magazine journalist. Write a narrative article about the revival of conservatism from the period after World War II to 1980.

networks

There's More Online!

☑ **BIOGRAPHY** Mikhail Gorbachev

☑ **BIOGRAPHY** Sandra Day O'Connor

☑ **CHART/GRAPH** Tax Rates

☑ **VIDEO** The Reagan Years

☑ **INTERACTIVE SELF-CHECK QUIZ**

LESSON 2
The Reagan Years

Reading **HELP**DESK

Content Vocabulary

- supply-side economics
- deficit
- mutual assured destruction

Academic Vocabulary

- confirmation • visible

TAKING NOTES: *Organizing*

ACTIVITY As you read about the resurgence of conservatism, complete a graphic organizer similar to the one below by filling in the major points of the supply-side theory of economics.

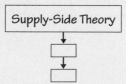

ESSENTIAL QUESTION · *How do you think the resurgence of conservative ideas has changed society?*

IT MATTERS BECAUSE

In 1981 Ronald Reagan became president. He cut taxes, deregulated several industries, and appointed conservative justices. He began a massive military buildup that greatly increased the deficit and sent aid to insurgent groups fighting communism.

The Road to the White House

GUIDING QUESTION *How did Reagan's early personal experiences influence his political beliefs?*

At age 15, Ronald Reagan worked as a lifeguard on the Rock River in Illinois. Reagan later wrote that this experience taught him quite a bit about human nature:

PRIMARY SOURCE

❝Lifeguarding provides one of the best vantage points in the world to learn about people. During my career at the park, I saved seventy-seven people. I guarantee you they needed saving—no lifeguard gets wet without good reason. . . . Not many thanked me, much less gave me a reward. . . . They felt insulted. . . . I got to recognize that people hate to be saved.❞
—from *Where's the Rest of Me?*, 1965

Along with a philosophy of self-reliance and independence, Reagan took the belief that people do not want to be saved to the White House.

Becoming a Conservative

Reagan's adult experiences also swayed him toward conservative views. After graduating from Eureka College in 1932, he worked as a radio broadcaster and became a Hollywood actor in the late 1930s. In 1947 Reagan became the president of the Screen Actors Guild—the actors' union. As president of the Screen Actors Guild, he testified before the House Un-American Activities Committee. Reagan had been a liberal Democrat, but dealing with Communists in the union shifted him toward conservative Republican ideas.

In the 1950s, Reagan traveled the nation to promote a television program that he hosted. During these travels, he said, he met many people who complained about big government. By the time he ran for governor of California in 1966, Reagan was a committed conservative. Reagan won the election and was reelected in 1970. Ten years later, he won the Republican presidential nomination.

The Election of 1980

Reagan's campaign appealed to frustrated Americans by promising to cut taxes and increase defense spending. He won the support of social conservatives by calling for a constitutional amendment banning abortion. Reagan won the election easily. For the first time since 1954, Republicans also gained control of the Senate.

☑ **PROGRESS CHECK**

Assessing How did Reagan's travels around the country affect his political beliefs?

Domestic Policies

GUIDING QUESTION *If you were president, how would you fight stagflation?*

Ronald Reagan believed that the key to restoring the economy and overcoming problems in society was to get Americans to believe in themselves again. "In this present crisis," he claimed, "government is not the solution to our problem; government is the problem."

Reaganomics

Reagan first turned to the lingering problem of stagflation. Conservative economists offered two competing ideas for fixing the economy. One group supported raising interest rates to combat inflation. The other group supported **supply-side economics.** They believed that high taxes took too much money away from investors, and that tax cuts could provide extra money to expand businesses and create new jobs. The result would be a larger supply of goods for consumers, who would now have more money to spend because of the tax cuts.

Reagan adopted supply-side economics. He encouraged the Federal Reserve to keep interest rates high and asked Congress to pass a massive 25 percent tax cut. Critics called his approach Reaganomics or "trickle-down economics." They believed Reagan's policy would help corporations and wealthy Americans, but little wealth would "trickle down" to middle-class or poor Americans.

PHOTO: Mark Lennihan/AP Images

THE BUDGET DEFICIT

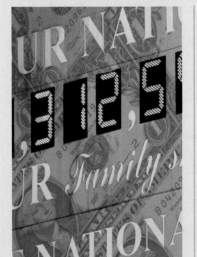

CHARTS/GRAPHS

As a result of Reagan's economic policies, the national debt increased rapidly.

▶ **CRITICAL THINKING**

1 *Analyzing Information* When does the budget deficit begin its greatest increase?

2 *Drawing Inferences* Why do you think the federal debt rose more sharply over time than total federal expenses did?

In Hundreds of Billions of Dollars

— Federal Debt
— Total Federal Expenses
— National Defense

40
35
30
25
20
15
10
5
0

1980 1981 1982 1983 1984 1985 1986 1987 1988 1989 1990 1991 1992

Source: Departments of Commerce and Treasury; Office of Management and Budget.

PHOTOS: (l) Wally McNamee/Historical/CORBIS, (r)Roger Ressmeyer/Roger Ressmeyer - Starlight/CORBIS

deficit the amount by which expenses exceed income

Cutting Programs Lower taxes increased the budget **deficit**—the amount by which expenditures exceed income. To keep the deficit under control, Reagan proposed cuts to social programs, including food stamps, school lunches, Medicare payments, unemployment compensation, and student loans.

After a struggle, Congress passed most of these cuts, but the fight convinced Reagan that Congress would never cut spending enough to balance the budget. He decided that cutting taxes and building up the military were more important than balancing the budget.

Deregulation Reagan believed that excessive government regulation was another cause of the economy's problems. His first act as president was to sign an executive order to end price controls on oil and gasoline. Other deregulation in broadcasting, banking, and automotive industries soon followed. Increased oil drilling, mining, and logging on public land angered environmentalists, as did EPA decisions to ease regulations on pollution-control equipment and to reduce safety checks on chemicals and pesticides.

Reagan Wins Reelection By 1984, the nation had begun the biggest economic expansion in its history. Incomes climbed and unemployment fell. The recovery made Reagan very popular, and he won the 1984 presidential election in a landslide against Democrats Walter Mondale and Representative Geraldine Ferraro, the first woman nominated to run for vice president for a major party.

Shifting the Judicial Balance

Reagan tried to bring a strict constructionist outlook to the federal judiciary, wanting judges there who followed the original intent of the Constitution.

ANALYZING PRIMARY SOURCES

Debating Tax Cuts

During the 1984 presidential campaign, President Ronald Reagan and Democratic candidate Walter Mondale presented opposing ideas about taxes, government spending, and the budget deficit.

❝[T]he plan that we have had and that we are following is a plan that is based on growth in the economy.... Our tax cut, we think, was very instrumental in bringing about this economic recovery.... So, we believe that as we continue to reduce the level of government spending . . . and, at the same time, as the growth in the economy increases the revenues the government gets, without raising taxes, those two lines will meet.... The deficit is the result of excessive government spending.... I don't believe that Mr. Mondale has a plan for balancing the budget; he has a plan for raising taxes.... And for the 5 years previous to our taking office, taxes doubled in the United States, and the budgets increased $318 billion. So, there is no ratio between taxing and balancing a budget.❞

—Ronald Reagan, from the presidential debate, October 7, 1984

❝[E]ven with historically high levels of economic growth, we will suffer a $263 billion deficit.... Real interest rates—the real cost of interest—will remain very, very high, and many economists are predicting that we're moving into a period of very slow growth.... I proposed over a hundred billion dollars in cuts in federal spending over 4 years, but I am not going to cut it out of Social Security and Medicare and student assistance and things . . . that people need.... The rate of defense spending increase can be slowed.... And there are other ways of squeezing this budget without constantly picking on our senior citizens and the most vulnerable in American life.❞

—Walter Mondale, from the presidential debate, October 7, 1984

DBQ **Document Based Questions**

① *Specifying* How does Reagan propose to balance the federal budget?

② *Summarizing* How does Mondale respond to Reagan's plan? What effects does he foresee from that course?

He changed the Supreme Court by nominating moderate conservative Sandra Day O'Connor, who became the first female justice in 1981. In 1986 Reagan chose conservative associate justice William Rehnquist to succeed retiring chief justice Warren Burger, and named conservative judge Antonin Scalia to fill Rehnquist's vacancy. After the Senate denied the **confirmation** of conservative Robert Bork in 1987, Reagan nominated moderate Anthony Kennedy as a new associate justice.

☑ **PROGRESS CHECK**

Expressing What factors led to the reelection of President Reagan?

Reagan Oversees a Military Buildup

GUIDING QUESTION *Why did Reagan build up the military?*

Reagan also adopted a new foreign policy that rejected both containment and détente. He called the Soviet Union "an evil empire." In his view, the United States should try to defeat evil, not contain or negotiate with it.

"Peace Through Strength"

In Reagan's opinion, the only option in dealing with the Soviet Union was "peace through strength," a phrase he used during his campaign. Reagan launched a $1.5 trillion military buildup meant to bankrupt and destroy the Soviet Union if it tried to keep up. The United States also tried to stop nations from supporting terrorism. After Libya backed a terrorist bombing in Berlin, the United States launched an air attack on Libya on April 14, 1986.

Reagan's military buildup created new jobs in defense industries. Supply-side economists had predicted that, despite the spending, lower taxes and cuts in government programs would generate enough revenue growth to balance the budget. Although tax revenues rose, Reagan could not cut popular programs significantly. The annual budget deficit went from $80 billion to more than $200 billion.

The Reagan Doctrine

Reagan believed that the United States should support guerrilla groups who were fighting to overthrow Communist or pro-Soviet governments. This policy became known as the Reagan Doctrine.

Aid to Afghan Rebels Perhaps the most **visible** example of the Reagan Doctrine was in Afghanistan. In 1979 Soviet troops had invaded Afghanistan. Reagan sent hundreds of millions of dollars in covert military aid to Afghan guerrillas who were fighting the Soviets. As casualties mounted, the war strained the Soviet economy, and in 1988 the Soviets decided to withdraw.

Nicaragua and Grenada Reagan was also concerned about Soviet influence in Nicaragua. Rebels known as the Sandinistas had overthrown a pro-American dictator in Nicaragua in 1979, set up a socialist government, and accepted Cuban and Soviet aid. The Reagan administration responded by secretly arming an anti-Sandinista guerrilla force known as the contras. When Congress learned of this policy, it banned further aid to the contras. In Grenada, radical Marxists overthrew the left-wing government in 1983. Reagan sent in troops, who quickly defeated the Grenadian and Cuban soldiers, and a new anti-Communist government was put in place.

The Iran-Contra Scandal Despite the congressional ban, individuals in Reagan's administration illegally continued to support the Nicaraguan rebels. They also secretly sold weapons to Iran, considered an enemy and sponsor of terrorism, in exchange for the release of American hostages in the Middle East.

BIOGRAPHY

Ronald Reagan (1911–2004)
During his two terms as president, Reagan used the charm and communication skills he learned as a Hollywood actor to gain a great deal of popularity with voters. Reagan's legacy as president includes his negotiations with Mikhail Gorbachev and the Soviet Union that contributed to the end of the Cold War. Reagan's popularity and his administration's policies have served as a basis for much of today's Republican Party philosophy.

▶ **CRITICAL THINKING**
Drawing Conclusions How might Reagan's legacy have been different had communism not fallen in the Soviet Union shortly after his tenure as president?

confirmation the formal approval of an executive act by a legislature

visible what can be seen

The B-52 Stratofortress can carry nuclear or precision-guided conventional weapons, including air-launched cruise missiles.

▶ **CRITICAL THINKING**
Drawing Inferences How could an arms control agreement benefit both the United States and the Soviet Union?

mutual assured destruction the strategy assuming that, as long as two countries can destroy each other with nuclear weapons, they will be afraid to use them

Profits from the weapons sales were then sent to the contras. News of these operations broke in November 1986. U.S. Marine colonel Oliver North and senior National Security Council members and CIA officials admitted before Congress to covering up their actions. President Reagan had approved the sale of arms to Iran, but the congressional investigation concluded that he had had no direct knowledge about the diversion of the money to the contras.

Arms Control

As part of the military buildup, Reagan decided to place missiles in Western Europe to counter Soviet missiles. When protest erupted worldwide, he offered to cancel the new missiles if the Soviets removed their missiles from Eastern Europe. He also proposed Strategic Arms Reduction Talks (START) to cut the number of missiles on both sides in half. The Soviets refused.

"Star Wars" Reagan disagreed with the military strategy known as nuclear deterrence, sometimes called **"mutual assured destruction."** He knew that if nuclear war did begin, there would be no way to defend the United States. In March 1983, he proposed the Strategic Defense Initiative (SDI), nicknamed "Star Wars," to develop weapons that could intercept incoming missiles.

A New Soviet Leader In 1985 Mikhail Gorbachev became the leader of the Soviet Union and agreed to resume arms-control talks. Gorbachev believed that the Soviet Union could not afford another arms race with the United States. Reagan and Gorbachev met in a series of summits. The first ended in a stalemate, as Gorbachev promised to cut back nuclear forces if Reagan gave up SDI, but Reagan refused. Reagan then challenged Gorbachev to make reforms. In West Berlin, Reagan stood at the Brandenburg Gate of the Berlin Wall—the symbol of divided Europe—and declared: "General Secretary Gorbachev, if you seek peace, if you seek prosperity for the Soviet Union and Eastern Europe . . . tear down this wall!"

Relations Improve In December 1987, the two leaders signed the Intermediate Range Nuclear Forces (INF) Treaty. With an arms control deal in place, Gorbachev pushed ahead with economic and political reforms, which eventually led to the collapse of the Soviet Union. In the United States, the economy was booming, the military was strong, and relations with the Soviet Union rapidly improving as Ronald Reagan's second term came to an end.

✓ **PROGRESS CHECK**

Explaining Why did President Reagan not favor a policy of détente?

PHOTO: Tech. Sgt. Robert J. Horstman/U.S. Air Force

LESSON 2 REVIEW

Reviewing Vocabulary
1. *Making Connections* Why did supply-side economics appeal to conservatives?

2. *Identifying Cause and Effect* Why did the budget deficit rise during the Reagan presidency?

Using Your Notes
3. *Explaining* Use your notes to write a paragraph explaining the theory of supply-side economics.

Answering the Guiding Questions
4. *Making Connections* How did Reagan's early personal experiences influence his political beliefs?

5. *Hypothesizing* If you were president, how would you fight stagflation?

6. *Summarizing* Why did Reagan build up the military?

Writing Activity
7. PERSONAL Do you think that the benefits of supply-side economics outweighed the costs? Write a short essay in which you present your opinion about the question. Be sure to back up your opinion with facts and information from the lesson.

networks

There's More Online!

- ☑ **BIOGRAPHY** Toni Morrison
- ☑ **BIOGRAPHY** Amy Tan
- ☑ **BIOGRAPHY** Ted Turner
- ☑ **BIOGRAPHY** Sam Walton
- ☑ **SLIDE SHOW** Space Shuttle Launch
- ☑ **VIDEO** Life in the 1980s
- ☑ **INTERACTIVE SELF-CHECK QUIZ**

Reading **HELP**DESK

Content Vocabulary

- **yuppie**
- **discount retailing**

Academic Vocabulary

- **via**
- **orientation**

TAKING NOTES: *Organizing*

ACTIVITY Complete a graphic organizer similar to the one below by listing the kinds of social issues that Americans faced in the 1980s.

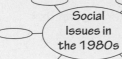

Social Issues in the 1980s

LESSON 3
Life in the 1980s

ESSENTIAL QUESTION · *How do you think the resurgence of conservative ideas has changed society?*

IT MATTERS BECAUSE

The 1980s was a period of increased wealth for many, as areas of the economy improved and new technologies appeared. Cuts in social programs, however, left many Americans in need, leading to new activism.

A Booming Economy

GUIDING QUESTION *How did discount retailing and new forms of media contribute to the economic boom of the 1980s?*

By late 1983, stagflation had largely ended and stock prices soared as many companies reported record profits. Stockbrokers, speculators, and real estate developers made multimillion-dollar deals. Many of the new moneymakers were young, ambitious, and hardworking. They were nicknamed **yuppies,** short for "young urban professionals."

The rapid economic growth and emphasis on accumulating wealth in the 1980s was partly caused by the baby boom. By then, most baby boomers had finished college, entered the job market, and begun building their careers. Because baby boomers were so numerous, their concerns tended to shape the culture.

The strong economic growth of the 1980s mostly benefited middle- and upper-class Americans. As a result, the emphasis on acquiring wealth had another effect on society. From 1967 to 1986, the amount of money earned by the top 5 percent of Americans fluctuated between 14.4 and 16.5 percent of the nation's aggregate family income. In the late 1980s, their share of the nation's income began to rise. By the mid-1990s, the top 5 percent of Americans earned over 20 percent of the nation's income.

A Retail Revolution

In addition to the booming real estate and stock markets, the economy witnessed a revolution in retail sales with the growth of **discount retailing.** This type of selling had actually begun to emerge in the 1960s, but did not have a major impact on the economy until the 1980s. Discount retailers sell large quantities at very low prices, trying to sell the goods fast to turn over their entire inventory in a short period.

yuppie a young, college-educated adult employed in a well-paying profession and living in or near a large city

discount retailing selling large quantities of goods at very low prices and trying to sell the goods quickly to turn over the entire inventory in a short period of time

via by way of or through

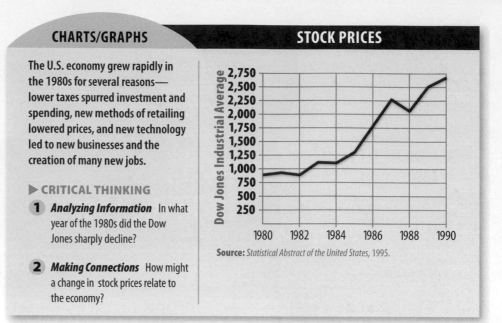

CHARTS/GRAPHS | **STOCK PRICES**

The U.S. economy grew rapidly in the 1980s for several reasons—lower taxes spurred investment and spending, new methods of retailing lowered prices, and new technology led to new businesses and the creation of many new jobs.

▶ **CRITICAL THINKING**

1 *Analyzing Information* In what year of the 1980s did the Dow Jones sharply decline?

2 *Making Connections* How might a change in stock prices relate to the economy?

Source: *Statistical Abstract of the United States, 1995.*

Discount retailers could make more money than traditional retailers who sold fewer products at higher prices. The most successful discount retailer was Sam Walton, the founder of Wal-Mart. Annual sales at Wal-Mart increased from about $2 billion in 1980 to over $20 billion by 1988. By 1985, he was the richest person in the United States.

Walton was one of the first retailers to track inventory and sales with a computer database. He also used a system of distribution centers to resupply stores. Others soon copied this approach. By the late 1970s, discount retailers such as Home Depot and Best Buy had begun to build "superstores." Their innovations created millions of new jobs in the 1980s and helped fuel the era's rapid economic growth.

A Revolution in Media

In the 1980s, other entrepreneurs began changing the news and entertainment industries. Until the late 1970s, television viewers were limited to three national networks, local stations, and the public television network. In 1970 a businessman named Ted Turner bought a failing television station in Atlanta, Georgia. He pioneered a new type of broadcasting by creating WTBS in 1975. WTBS was the first "superstation"—a television station that sold low-cost sports and entertainment programs **via** satellite to cable companies across the nation.

The Rise of Cable Television Turner's innovation changed broadcasting and helped spread cable television. Other new cable networks focused on specific audiences, such as churchgoers, shoppers, or minorities. In 1980 entrepreneur Robert Johnson created Black Entertainment Television (BET). In 1981 music and technology merged when Music Television (MTV) went on the air to broadcast performances of songs and images, or music videos. Although the videos were often criticized for their content, MTV was a hit. Music videos boosted the careers of artists such as Madonna and Michael Jackson.

Rap music was the new sound of the 1980s. Originating in local clubs in New York City's South Bronx, rap emphasized heavy bass and rhythmic sounds and lyrics that frequently focused on the African American experience in the inner city. Its rapid rise in popularity made rap into a multimillion-dollar industry.

Technology and Media Technology also transformed how people accessed entertainment. Until the 1980s, most people listened to music on large stereo systems that played records in their homes and relied on the car radio when they were driving. The new Sony Walkman made music portable, marking the beginning of a new way for people to access music. In the 1990s, portable compact disc (CD) players replaced the Walkman, and in the early 2000s, digital audio players, such as the iPod and MP3 players, advanced the technology even further.

Videocassette recorders (VCRs) allowed people to tape television shows or watch taped films whenever they wished. By the early 2000s, digital video disk (DVD) recorders began replacing VCRs.

Technology also brought about a new form of entertainment—the video game. Early video games grew out of military computer technology. The first video arcade game was a game called *Pong,* released in 1972. Home video games developed quickly. In the early 1980s, sales reached about $3 billion with the popularity of games such as *Pac-Man* and *Space Invaders.* By the mid-1980s, home video games competed with arcade games in graphics and speed. Video games have continued to grow in popularity to the present day.

☑ PROGRESS CHECK

Comparing and Contrasting Of the new media and technology that emerged in the 1980s, which are still in use today?

New Social Activism

GUIDING QUESTION *Why did new activist groups form in the 1980s?*

The 1980s was a decade of wealth and prosperity. Yet social problems, such as drugs, poverty, homelessness, and disease, continued.

Social Problems

Drug abuse in the 1980s made many city neighborhoods dangerous. Drug users often committed crimes in order to get money for drugs. Drug use spread from cities to suburbs, small towns, and rural areas.

Fighting Drugs and Alcohol In an effort to reduce teen drug use, some schools began searching student bags and lockers for drugs. In 1984 one teen who had been arrested for selling drugs challenged the school's right to search her purse without a warrant. In 1985 the Supreme Court case *New Jersey* v. *T.L.O.* upheld the school's right to search without a warrant if it had probable cause. Similarly, the 1995 case of *Vernonia School District* v. *Acton* held that random drug tests do not violate students' Fourth Amendment rights.

Abuse of alcohol was also a serious concern. In 1980 Mothers Against Drunk Driving (MADD) was founded to try to stop underage drinking and drunk driving in general, and "[t]o aid the victims of crimes performed by individuals driving under the influence of alcohol or drugs, to aid the families of such victims and to increase public awareness of the problem of drinking and drugged driving." In 1984 Congress cut highway funds to any state that did not raise the legal drinking age to 21.

The AIDS Epidemic In 1981 researchers identified a deadly disease that they named "acquired immunodeficiency syndrome," or AIDS. AIDS weakens the immune system. In the United States, AIDS was first noticed among homosexual men.

AIDS quilts became ways for people to share the story and the loss of their loved ones to the disease. Typically, the names of AIDS victims are sewn onto the quilt squares.

▶ **CRITICAL THINKING**
Analyzing Primary Sources
What is the impact of having the names of victims on AIDS quilts?

Soon, though, it spread among heterosexual men and women. Many people were infected by sexual partners. Between 1981 and 1988, the Centers for Disease Control and Prevention identified more than 100,000 cases in the United States.

New Activist Groups

AIDS increased the visibility of the country's gay and lesbian community, but some homosexuals had been engaged in efforts to defend their civil rights since the 1960s. On June 27, 1969, New York City police raided a nightclub called the Stonewall Inn. The police had often raided the nightclub because of the sexual **orientation** of its patrons. Frustration among the gay and lesbian onlookers led to a riot. The Stonewall Riot marked the beginning of the gay activist movement. Soon after, organizations such as the Gay Liberation Front began efforts to increase tolerance of homosexuality.

orientation a position relative to a standard

Rock 'n' Rollers Become Activists Many musicians and entertainers in the 1980s began using their celebrity to raise awareness about social issues. To help starving people in Ethiopia, Irish rocker Bob Geldof organized musicians in England to present "Band Aid" concerts in 1984. In the next year, the event grew into "Live Aid." People in some 100 countries watched benefit concerts televised from London, Philadelphia, and Sydney, Australia. The organization's theme song, "We Are the World," was a best seller. In the same year, country singer Willie Nelson organized "Farm Aid" to help American farmers who were going through hard times. Musicians also publicized efforts to end the segregated apartheid social system in South Africa. In the late 1980s, the United States and other nations were attempting to end apartheid in South Africa by imposing economic sanctions against the country.

Senior Citizens Begin To Lobby Another group that became politically active in the 1980s was senior citizens. Decades of improvements in medicine had resulted in more Americans surviving to an older age. In addition, the birthrate had declined, so younger people represented a comparatively smaller proportion of the population. The fact that more Americans were receiving Social Security payments created budget pressures for the government. Older Americans became very vocal in the political arena, opposing cuts in Social Security or Medicare. Because they tend to vote in large numbers, senior citizens are an influential interest group. Their major lobbying organization is AARP (which originally stood for the American Association of Retired Persons).

✓ **PROGRESS CHECK**

Explaining What role did the government take in supporting efforts to remedy social problems?

LESSON 3 REVIEW

Reviewing Vocabulary

1. *Listing* What were the characteristics of yuppies?

2. *Classifying* What are some major discount retailers?

Using Your Notes

3. *Contrasting* Use your notes to write a description of the main tensions in American society during the 1980s.

Answering the Guiding Questions

4. *Making Connections* How did discount retailing and new forms of media contribute to the economic boom of the 1980s?

5. *Analyzing Cause and Effect* Why did new activist groups form in the 1980s?

Writing Activity

6. **DESCRIPTIVE** Select one technological innovation from the 1980s and describe how it continues to have an influence on life today. Be sure to include descriptive words to show how that innovation affects modern life.

netw⊙rks

There's More Online!

- ☑ **BIOGRAPHY** Saddam Hussein
- ☑ **BIOGRAPHY** Colin Powell
- ☑ **BIOGRAPHY** Boris Yeltsin
- ☑ **IMAGE** Persian Gulf War
- ☑ **VIDEO** End of the Cold War
- ☑ **INTERACTIVE SELF-CHECK QUIZ**

Reading **HELP**DESK

Content Vocabulary

- **perestroika**
- **glasnost**
- **downsizing**
- **capital gains tax**
- **grassroots movement**

Academic Vocabulary

- **repress**
- **retain**

TAKING NOTES: *Categorizing*

ACTIVITY As you read, complete a graphic organizer similar to the one below by describing U.S. foreign policy in each of the places listed.

Place	Foreign Policy
Soviet Union	
China	
Panama	
Middle East	

LESSON 4
The End of the Cold War

ESSENTIAL QUESTION · *How do you think the resurgence of conservative ideas has changed society?*

IT MATTERS BECAUSE

In the late 1980s, the United States faced a series of international crises. The Cold War came to an end in Europe, but events in the Middle East soon led the United States into its first major war since Vietnam.

The Soviet Union Collapses

GUIDING QUESTION *How did Gorbachev's attempts to revive the Soviet Union's economy lead to a revolution?*

When Ronald Reagan left office, many Americans wanted his domestic policies to be continued. In 1988 Republicans nominated George H. W. Bush, who reassured Americans that he would do just that:

> **PRIMARY SOURCE**
>
> ❝My opponent won't rule out raising taxes. But I will. And the Congress will push me to raise taxes and I'll say 'no.' And they'll push, and I'll say 'no,' and they'll push again, and I'll say to them: 'Read my lips: no new taxes.'❞
>
> —from his acceptance address at the Republican National Convention, August 18, 1988

The Democrats hoped to regain the White House in 1988 by promising to help minorities as well as working-class and poor Americans. Civil rights leader Jesse Jackson tried to create a "rainbow coalition" of those groups, and although unsuccessful, he became the first African American to make a serious run for the presidential nomination. The Democrats nominated Michael Dukakis, who was the governor of Massachusetts, but with Reagan's endorsement and a strong economy, Bush easily won the general election. Though voters had focused on domestic issues during the election campaign, President Bush had to focus on foreign policy soon after taking office.

Revolution in Eastern Europe

As president, Bush continued Reagan's policy of cooperation with Soviet leader Mikhail Gorbachev. By the late 1980s, the Soviet economy was suffering from years of inefficient central planning and huge expenditures on the arms race. To save the economy, Gorbachev instituted **perestroika,** or "restructuring," which allowed some private enterprise and profit making.

Gorbachev also established **glasnost,** or "openness," to allow more freedom of religion and speech. Glasnost spread to Eastern Europe, and in 1989 revolutions replaced Communist rulers with democratic governments in Bulgaria, Czechoslovakia, Hungary, Poland, and Romania. At midnight on November 9, 1989, guards at the Berlin Wall opened the gates. Soon, bulldozers began leveling the symbol of Communist repression. East Germany and West Germany soon reunited.

The End of the Soviet Union

As Eastern Europe abandoned communism, Gorbachev faced mounting criticism at home. In August 1991, a group of Communist Party officials and army officers tried to stage a coup. They arrested Gorbachev and sent troops into Moscow. In Moscow, Russian president Boris Yeltsin defied the coup leaders from his offices in the Russian Parliament. President Bush telephoned Yeltsin to express U.S. support. The coup soon collapsed and Gorbachev returned to Moscow. All 15 Soviet republics declared their independence from the Soviet Union. In late December 1991, Gorbachev announced the end of the Soviet Union. Most of the former Soviet republics joined in a federation called the Commonwealth of Independent States (CIS). Although member states remained independent, they formed a common economic zone in 1993.

✓ **PROGRESS CHECK**

Explaining Why do you think glasnost spread to Eastern Europe?

A New World Order

GUIDING QUESTION *How did the end of the Cold War lead to more global U.S. military conflicts?*

After the Cold War, President Bush noted that a "new world order" was emerging. As he told Congress in a speech, "We stand today at a unique and extraordinary moment. . . . Out of these troubled times . . . a new world order . . . can emerge: a new era—freer from the threat of terror, stronger in the pursuit of justice, and more secure in the quest for peace." The new world order introduced new military challenges around the globe. For example, U.S. troops led Operation Restore Hope, providing humanitarian assistance and famine relief to refugees in Somalia. Western aid had supported that country during the 1980s due to its strategic location near Middle Eastern oil fields, but with the end of the Cold War, its importance—and U.S. aid—had waned.

Tiananmen Square

Despite the collapse of communism elsewhere, China's Communist leaders were determined to stay in power. China's government had relaxed controls on the economy, but continued to **repress** political speech. In April and May 1989, Chinese students and workers held pro-democracy demonstrations at Tiananmen Square in Beijing, China's capital. In early June, government tanks and soldiers crushed the protests. Many people were killed. Hundreds of pro-democracy activists were arrested and later sentenced to death. Shocked, the United States and several European countries halted arms sales and reduced diplomatic contacts with China. The World Bank suspended loans. Bush resisted harsher sanctions. He thought that trade and diplomacy would change China's behavior.

The Tiananmen Square protests ended in bloodshed when the Chinese government sent in the army to crush the demonstrations.

▶ **CRITICAL THINKING**
Comparing and Contrasting How did the results of the Tiananmen Square protests differ from those of the revolutions in Eastern Europe?

Panama

In 1978 the United States had agreed to give Panama control over the Panama Canal by the year 2000. Because of the canal's importance, American officials wanted to make sure Panama's government was both stable and pro–United States. But by 1989, Panama's dictator, General Manuel Noriega, was aiding drug traffickers and harassing American military personnel defending the canal. In December 1989, Bush ordered U.S. troops to invade Panama. The troops seized Noriega, who was sent to the United States to stand trial on drug charges. The troops then helped the Panamanians hold elections and organize a new government.

The Persian Gulf War

President Bush faced perhaps his most serious crisis in the Middle East. In August 1990, Iraqi dictator Saddam Hussein sent his army to invade oil-rich Kuwait. U.S. officials feared that the invasion might be only the first step and that Iraq's ultimate goal was to capture Saudi Arabia and its vast oil reserves. President Bush persuaded other United Nations member countries from Europe, the Middle East, and Canada to join a coalition to stop Iraq. The United Nations set a deadline for Iraqi withdrawal from Kuwait, after which the coalition would use force to remove them. Congress voted to authorize the use of force if Iraq did not withdraw.

On October 31, 1990, General Colin Powell, chairman of the Joint Chiefs of Staff, Secretary of Defense Dick Cheney, and other high-ranking officials met with President Bush. It was clear that Iraq would not obey the UN deadline. Powell presented the plan for attacking Iraq. "Mr. President," Powell began, "[w]e've gotta take the initiative out of the enemy's hands if

GEOGRAPHY CONNECTION

After its invasion of Kuwait, Iraq was defeated by a U.S.-led coalition of troops.

1 **PLACES AND REGIONS** *Why do you think that Allied troops staged their invasion of Iraq from Saudi Arabia?*

2 **THE WORLD IN SPATIAL TERMS** *What nations did Iraq attack with SCUD missiles during the war?*

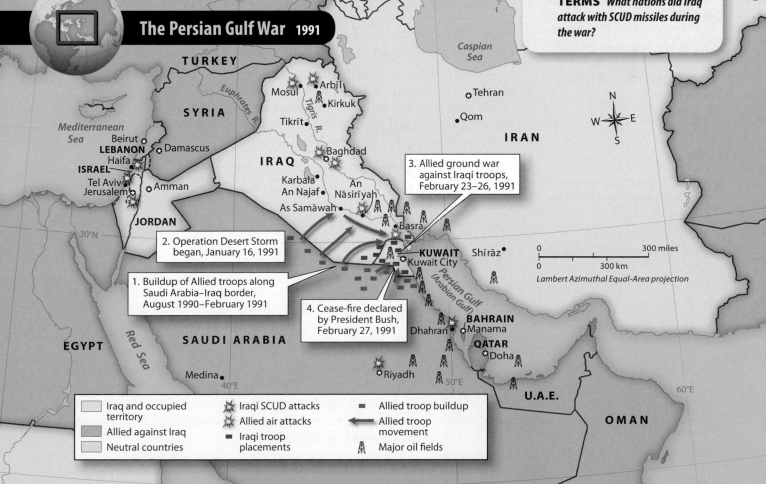

The Persian Gulf War 1991

we're going to go to war." Cheney later recalled that Bush "never hesitated." He looked up from the plans and simply said, "Do it."

On January 16, 1991, coalition forces launched Operation Desert Storm. Cruise missiles and laser-guided bombs fell on Iraq, destroying its air defenses, bridges, artillery, and other military targets. After about six weeks, the coalition launched a massive ground attack. Thousands of Iraqi soldiers died. Fewer than 300 coalition troops were killed. Just 100 hours after the ground war began, Bush declared Kuwait to be liberated. Iraq accepted the cease-fire terms, and American troops returned home to cheering crowds.

☑ PROGRESS CHECK

Assessing Why did President Bush persuade United Nation members to join together to stop Iraq's invasion of Kuwait?

Domestic Challenges

GUIDING QUESTION *Why did President George H. W. Bush lose his bid for reelection in 1992?*

President Bush spent much of his time dealing with foreign policy, but he could not ignore domestic issues. He inherited a growing deficit and a slowing economy. With the Persian Gulf crisis, the economy plunged into a recession and unemployment rose.

The Economy Slows

The recession that began in 1990 was partly caused by the end of the Cold War. As the Soviet threat faded, the nation cut back on military spending. Soldiers and defense industry workers were laid off. Other companies also began **downsizing,** or laying off workers to become more efficient. The nation's high level of debt made the recession worse.

The huge deficit forced the government to borrow money to pay for its programs, keeping money from being available to businesses. The government also had to pay interest on its debt, using money that might otherwise have helped fund programs or boost the economy.

Many savings and loan institutions had collapsed, making the deficit worse. After President Reagan allowed them to be deregulated, many had made risky or even dishonest investments. When these investments failed, depositors collected from federal programs that insured deposits. The cost to the public may have reached $500 billion.

Gridlock in the Government

President Bush tried to improve the economy. He called for a cut in the **capital gains tax**—the tax paid by businesses and investors when they sell stocks or real estate for a profit. Bush believed that the tax cut would encourage businesses to expand. Calling the idea a tax break for the rich, Democrats in Congress defeated it.

Aware that the growing federal deficit was hurting the economy, Bush broke his "no new taxes" campaign pledge. After meeting with congressional leaders, he agreed to a tax increase in exchange for cuts in spending. This decision turned many voters against Bush.

The 1992 Election

Although the recession had hurt his popularity, Bush won the Republican nomination. Bush promised to address voters' economic concerns. He blamed congressional Democrats for the government's gridlock.

downsizing reducing a company in size by laying off workers and managers to become more efficient

capital gains tax a federal tax paid by businesses and investors when they sell stocks or real estate

Many businesses laid off workers as the economy slowed for the first time in almost a decade.

▶ CRITICAL THINKING

Predicting Consequences How would you expect the downsizing trend to affect Bush's reelection prospects?

Ross Perot's inclusion in the televised presidential debate was unusual for a third-party candidate.

This cartoon makes reference to frequent third-party presidential candidate Ralph Nader as well as a Clinton campaign catchphrase, "It's the economy, stupid."

The election of 1992 marked the first time since 1968 that no candidate won at least 50 percent of the popular vote, and for a similar reason: in 1992 a strong third-party challenger, Ross Perot, took votes from both major candidates.

▶ **CRITICAL THINKING**

1 *Analyzing Primary Sources* What does the cartoon suggest about independent candidates?

2 *Making Connections* From which candidate was Perot more likely to take votes? Why?

The Democrats nominated Arkansas governor William Jefferson Clinton, despite stories that questioned his character and his evasion of military service. Calling himself a "New Democrat," Clinton promised to cut middle-class taxes, reduce government spending, and reform the nation's health care and welfare programs. His campaign repeatedly blamed Bush for the recession.

An independent candidate, billionaire Texas businessman H. Ross Perot, also made a strong challenge. He stressed the need to end deficit spending. His no-nonsense style appealed to many Americans, and a **grassroots movement**—groups of people organizing at the local level—put Perot on the ballot in all 50 states.

Clinton won the election with 43 percent of the popular vote and 370 electoral votes. Bush won 37 percent of the popular vote, and Perot 19 percent. The Democrats also **retained** control of Congress.

The 46-year-old Clinton was the first person from the baby boomer generation to occupy the White House. It was his task to revive the economy and guide the United States in a rapidly changing world.

grassroots movement
a group of people organizing at the local or community level, away from political or cultural centers

retain to keep in possession

✔ **PROGRESS CHECK**

Identifying What campaign promise did Bush break? Why?

PHOTO: (l)Wally McNamee/Corbis News/CORBIS, (r)©2004 Mike Lane and PoliticalCartoons.com

LESSON 4 REVIEW

Reviewing Vocabulary

1. *Defining* What was perestroika?

2. *Determining Cause and Effect* What was one effect of glasnost?

3. *Locating* Where does a grassroots movement begin?

Using Your Notes

4. *Describing* Use your notes to write a paragraph describing the role the United States played in world affairs during the Bush presidency.

Answering the Guiding Questions

5. *Making Connections* How did Gorbachev's attempts to revive the Soviet Union's economy lead to a revolution?

6. *Analyzing Cause and Effect* How did the end of the Cold War lead to more global U.S. military conflicts?

7. *Explaining* Why did President George H. W. Bush lose his bid for reelection in 1992?

Writing Activity

8. PERSUASIVE Suppose that you are a television political commentator. Write a short speech persuading viewers to support Bush, Clinton, or Perot in the 1992 presidential election.

Directions: On a separate sheet of paper, answer the questions below. Make sure you read carefully and answer all parts to the question.

Lesson Review

Lesson 1

1 *Identifying Central Issues* What caused a revival of conservatism after World War II?

2 *Comparing and Contrasting* How are the ideas of liberals different from those of conservatives?

Lesson 2

3 *Interpreting Significance* Why was Reagan's solution to the economic problems called Reaganomics?

4 *Identifying Cause and Effect* What caused Reagan to begin a massive military buildup, and what was its effect on the spread of communism?

Lesson 3

5 *Explaining* How did entrepreneurs help transform the news and entertainment industries?

6 *Comparing and Contrasting* How did activist groups work to help cure social problems in the 1980s?

Lesson 4

7 *Analyzing* Why did the United States launch Operation Desert Storm?

4 *Identifying Cause and Effect* How did glasnost contribute to the collapse of the Soviet Union?

21st Century Skills

9 **EXPLAINING CONTINUITY AND CHANGE** How did population shifts in the Sunbelt affect conservatism?

10 **ECONOMICS** Why did Reagan encourage tax cuts and deregulation? What impact did his economic policy have on the environment?

11 **ECONOMICS** How did the VCR and the development of home video games affect the U.S. economy in the 1980s?

Exploring the Essential Question

12 *Identifying Bias* Write the script for a political TV advertisement that describes positive ways that conservative ideas have changed society. Then consider the counterarguments, and write the script for a political TV advertisement that criticizes conservative ideas.

DBQ Document-Based Questions

Use the document to answer the following questions.

President Ronald Reagan addressed the American people at the end of his presidency. The following is an excerpt from that address:

PRIMARY SOURCE

❝The way I see it, there were two great triumphs, two things that I'm proudest of. One is the economic recovery, in which the people of America created—and filled—19 million new jobs. The other is the recovery of our morale. America is respected again. . . .

Common sense told us that when you put a big tax on something, the people will produce less of it. So, we cut the people's tax rates, and the people produced more than ever before. The economy bloomed. . . . Common sense told us that to preserve the peace, we'd have to become strong again after years of weakness and confusion. So, we rebuilt our defenses, and this New Year we toasted the new peacefulness around the globe.❞

—from his Farewell Address to the nation, January 11, 1989

13 *Analyzing Primary Sources* What did Reagan believe were his greatest accomplishments?

14 *Drawing Inferences* How did Reagan feel his administration preserved peace?

Extended-Response Question

15 *Assessing* Was Reagan's conservative revolution that began in 1980 successful or unsuccessful in meeting its goals of shrinking the federal government, restoring U.S. military prestige, and electing conservative politicians?

Need Extra Help?

If You've Missed Question	1	2	3	4	5	6	7	8	9	10	11	12	13	14	15
Go to page	655	654	659	661	664	665	669	668	656	659	665	654	672	672	654

A Time of Change

1980–2000

ESSENTIAL QUESTIONS • *How have improvements in science and technology helped change society?* • *How have immigration, technology, and global trade changed the world?*

networks

There's More Online about how life changed quickly during the last two decades of the twentieth century.

CHAPTER 30

The Story Matters...

Immigration made the United States increasingly interconnected with the rest of the world. It also brought a growing awareness of Hispanic influence on American culture, as immigration from Latin America began to swell in the 1980s. Rookie pitcher for the Los Angeles Dodgers Fernando Valenzuela, a recent immigrant from Mexico, attracted an unprecedented number of fans to Dodgers games and became a cultural icon in the Latino community.

◄ Los Angeles Dodgers pitcher Fernando Valenzuela became a symbol of Hispanic success, winning Rookie of the Year and the Cy Young Award in 1981.

PHOTO: Vince Streano/CORBIS

Place and Time: United States 1981–1999

The economic growth and technological innovations experienced by the United States under the Reagan administration were soon surpassed by those that took place under President Bill Clinton. As the economy became more global and less segmented, cheaper labor in other countries made it more challenging for American companies to compete with goods made overseas that were sold at a lower price. With an interconnected world and a new wave of immigration, the United States continued to change.

Step Into the Place

Read the quote and look at the information presented on the map.

What do the quote and the information on the map indicate about the trend toward globalization in the late twentieth century?

PRIMARY SOURCE

❝ . . . Even as people take pride in their national independence, we know we are becoming more and more interdependent. The movement of people, money, and ideas across borders, frankly, breeds suspicion among many good people in every country. They are worried about globalization because of its unsettling and unpredictable consequences.

Yet, globalization is not something we can hold off or turn off. It is the economic equivalent of a force of nature, like wind or water. We can harness wind to fill a sail. We can use water to generate energy. We can work hard to protect people and property from storms and floods. But there is no point in denying the existence of wind or water, or trying to make them go away. The same is true for globalization. We can work to maximize its benefits and minimize its risks, but we cannot ignore it and it is not going away. ❞

—President Bill Clinton, from an address at
Vietnam National University, November 17, 2000

Step Into the Time

Choose an event from the time line and write a paragraph suggesting the ways that event might reflect or influence how the countries of the world became increasingly connected during the last decades of the twentieth century.

Reagan
1981–1989

U.S. PRESIDENTS

UNITED STATES

WORLD

1981 IBM introduces its version of the PC or personal computer

1984 Apple's Macintosh introduces the mouse and on-screen icons

1986 Immigration Reform and Control Act passed

1981

1984

1987

1983 Finnish company Nokia begins concentrating on producing cell phones

1987 Soviet Union and United States sign INF treaty

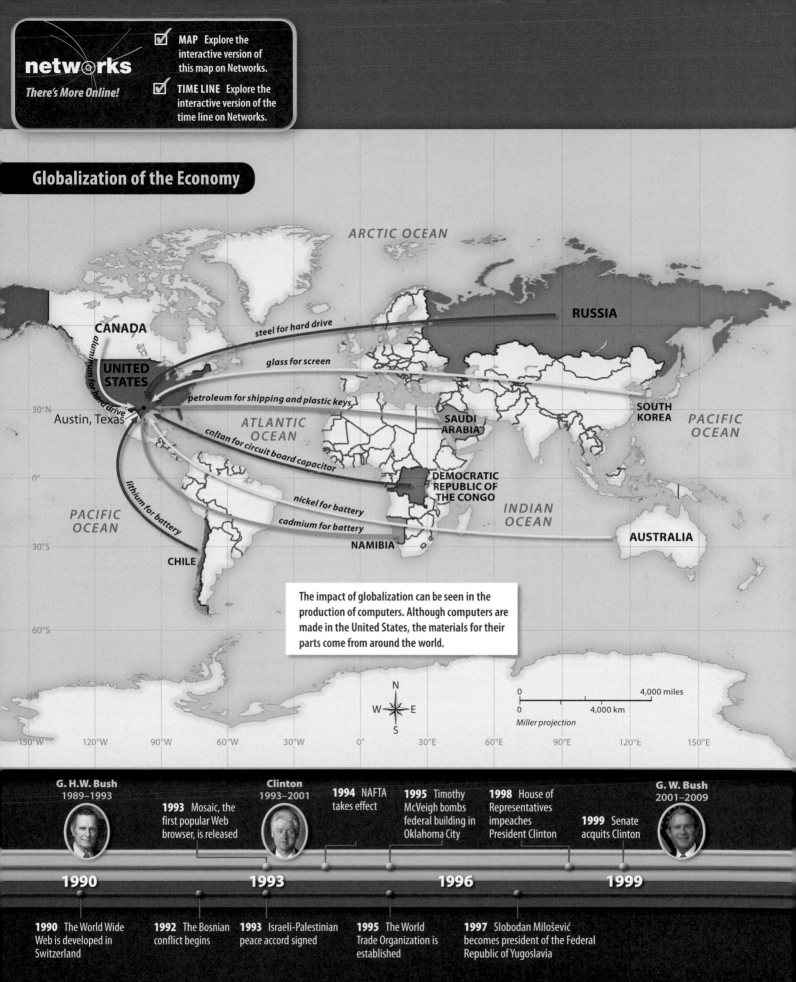

networks

There's More Online!

☑ **MAP** Explore the interactive version of this map on Networks.

☑ **TIME LINE** Explore the interactive version of the time line on Networks.

Globalization of the Economy

ARCTIC OCEAN

RUSSIA

CANADA

steel for hard drive

UNITED STATES

glass for screen

aluminum for hard drive

Austin, Texas

petroleum for shipping and plastic keys

SOUTH KOREA

PACIFIC OCEAN

SAUDI ARABIA

ATLANTIC OCEAN

coltan for circuit board capacitor

DEMOCRATIC REPUBLIC OF THE CONGO

INDIAN OCEAN

lithium for battery

nickel for battery

PACIFIC OCEAN

cadmium for battery

AUSTRALIA

NAMIBIA

CHILE

The impact of globalization can be seen in the production of computers. Although computers are made in the United States, the materials for their parts come from around the world.

N W E S

0 — 4,000 miles
0 — 4,000 km
Miller projection

150°W 120°W 90°W 60°W 30°W 0° 30°E 60°E 90°E 120°E 150°E

60°N · 30°N · 0° · 30°S · 60°S

G. H.W. Bush 1989–1993

Clinton 1993–2001

1994 NAFTA takes effect

1995 Timothy McVeigh bombs federal building in Oklahoma City

1998 House of Representatives impeaches President Clinton

G. W. Bush 2001–2009

1993 Mosaic, the first popular Web browser, is released

1999 Senate acquits Clinton

1990

1993

1996

1999

1990 The World Wide Web is developed in Switzerland

1992 The Bosnian conflict begins

1993 Israeli-Palestinian peace accord signed

1995 The World Trade Organization is established

1997 Slobodan Milošević becomes president of the Federal Republic of Yugoslavia

networks

There's More Online!

☑ **BIOGRAPHY** Hillary Clinton

☑ **BIOGRAPHY** Newt Gingrich

☑ **BIOGRAPHY** Ruth Bader Ginsburg

☑ **IMAGE** Chief Justice Rehnquist

☑ **IMAGE** Soldiers and Serbians

☑ **VIDEO** The Clinton Years

☑ **INTERACTIVE SELF-CHECK QUIZ**

Reading **HELP**DESK

Content Vocabulary

• **perjury**
• **ethnic cleansing**

Academic Vocabulary

• **modify**
• **unprecedented**
• **participant**

TAKING NOTES: *Outlining*

ACTIVITY As you read about the administration of President Clinton, use the headings of the section to create an outline similar to the one below.

The Clinton Years
  I. Clinton's Agenda
     A.
     B.
     C.
     D.
  II.

LESSON 1
The Clinton Years

ESSENTIAL QUESTIONS • *How have improvements in science and technology helped change society?* • *How have immigration, technology, and global trade changed the world?*

IT MATTERS BECAUSE

When William Jefferson Clinton was elected in 1992, he became the first Democrat to win the presidency in 12 years. After achieving only part of his agenda, he faced a Republican Congress that had very different plans.

Clinton's Agenda

GUIDING QUESTION *During his first presidential term, what domestic policy areas did Clinton focus on?*

Just 46 years old when he took office, Bill Clinton was the first baby boomer to reach the Oval Office. He set out an ambitious domestic agenda focusing on the economy, the family, education, crime, and health care.

Raising Taxes, Cutting Spending

Clinton first focused on the economy. He saw the massive federal deficit as the main source of the economy's weakness. It forced the government to borrow heavily, which helped drive up interest rates. Clinton believed that lowering interest rates would enable businesses and consumers to borrow more money for business investment and increased consumer purchasing, which would then promote growth.

About half of all government spending went to entitlement programs—such as Social Security and veterans' benefits—that could not easily be cut because so many people relied on them. Facing these constraints, Clinton's 1993 plan for reducing the deficit proposed raising taxes on middle and upper incomes and placing new taxes on gasoline, heating oil, and natural gas. Congressional Republicans refused to support the unpopular tax increases. Clinton pressured Democrats, however, and after many amendments, a **modified** version of the plan narrowly passed.

Stumbling on Health Care

During his campaign, Clinton had promised to reform the health care system. Some 40 million Americans, or roughly 15 percent of the nation, did not have health insurance. The president created a task force and appointed his wife, Hillary Rodham Clinton, to head it—an **unprecedented** role for a First Lady. The task force developed a plan that put much of the burden of paying for the benefits on employers. Small business owners feared they could not afford it. The insurance industry and doctors' organizations mounted a nationwide advertising campaign to build public opposition to the plan. Republican opposition and a divided Democratic Party led to the death of the plan without a vote.

Families and Education

During his campaign, Clinton had stressed the need to help American families. His first success was the Family Medical Leave Act. This law gave workers up to 12 weeks per year of unpaid leave for the birth or adoption of a child or for the illness of a family member. He also persuaded Congress to create the AmeriCorps program. This program puts students to work improving low-income housing, teaching children to read, and cleaning up the environment. AmeriCorps incorporated the VISTA program that John F. Kennedy had created. AmeriCorps volunteers earn a salary and are awarded a scholarship to continue their education. In September 1994, some 20,000 AmeriCorps volunteers began serving in more than 1,000 communities.

Crime and Gun Control

Clinton strongly endorsed new gun-control laws. Despite opposition from many Republicans and the National Rifle Association (NRA), Congress passed a gun-control law known as the Brady Bill. This law established a waiting period and required a criminal background check before selling someone a handgun. The following year, Clinton introduced another bill to fund new prisons and add 100,000 more police officers. It also banned 19 kinds of assault weapons and funded crime prevention programs.

☑ **PROGRESS CHECK**

Summarizing How did Clinton help stimulate the economy and handle the massive federal deficit?

Republicans Gain Control of Congress

GUIDING QUESTION *How did the Republican Party respond to the victory in the 1994 midterm elections?*

Clinton's popularity was low by late 1994. He had raised taxes and failed to fix health care. The economy was improving, but many companies were still downsizing. Personal issues involving Clinton further weakened public confidence in him. In response, many Americans decided to vote Republican.

The Contract With America

In the 1994 midterm elections, congressional Republicans, led by Representative Newt Gingrich of Georgia, proposed the "Contract with America." This program proposed changes including lower taxes, welfare reform, tougher anticrime laws, and a balanced budget amendment. Republicans won a majority in both houses of Congress for the first time in 40 years. House Republicans quickly passed almost the entire program, but the Senate defeated several proposals, and the president vetoed others.

The Budget Battle

In 1995 Republicans and Clinton clashed over the new federal budget. Clinton vetoed several Republican budget proposals, saying they cut into social programs too much. Gingrich believed if Republicans stood firm, Clinton would approve the budget rather than let the government shut down for lack of funds. Clinton, however, allowed the federal government to close.

modify to make changes or alter

unprecedented having no earlier occurrence of something similar

President Clinton explains the proposed Health Security card in a speech to Congress in October 1993.

▶ **CRITICAL THINKING**
Identifying Cause and Effect What factors contributed to the failure of Clinton's health care plan?

By standing firm, Clinton regained much of the support he had lost. Congressional Republicans realized that they needed to work with the president to pass legislation. Soon afterward, they reached an agreement with Clinton to balance the budget. The next year, Congress passed the Health Insurance Portability Act to improve health coverage for people who changed jobs and to reduce discrimination against those with pre-existing illnesses. Congress also passed the Welfare Reform Act, which limited people to no more than two consecutive years on welfare and required them to work to receive benefits. The law also increased child-care spending and gave tax breaks to companies hiring new employees who had been on welfare.

Clinton Wins Reelection

The economic boom of the 1990s was the longest sustained peacetime expansion in American history, and Clinton took credit for it. Inflation and unemployment fell to their lowest levels in 40 years. A booming economy helped Clinton's popularity climb rapidly.

In April 1995, however, an act of domestic terrorism shocked the nation. Timothy McVeigh, formerly a soldier in the U.S. Army, planted a massive homemade bomb in a rental truck near a federal building in Oklahoma City. The explosion killed 168 people and injured more than 500 others. As a result, American officials began investigating right-wing militant groups who shared views like McVeigh's, and membership in those groups declined.

PHOTOS: (l)Terry Ashe/Time Life Pictures/Getty Images, (r)Georgia General Assembly

ANALYZING PRIMARY SOURCES

Is a Balanced Budget Amendment a Good Idea?

One of the ideas that congressional Republicans put forth in the "Contract with America" was a balanced budget amendment to the Constitution. Would such an amendment force Congress to be more responsible in how it spends the taxpayers' money? Or would it dangerously limit Congress's ability to respond to economic and national security emergencies?

——— YES ———

66While Congress could achieve a balanced budget by statute, past efforts ... have failed. It is simply too easy for Congress to change its mind. ... The constitutional amendment is unyielding in its imposition of discipline on Congress to make the tough decisions necessary to balance the federal budget. Over the past half-century, Congress has demonstrated a total lack of fiscal discipline evidenced by an irrational and irresponsible pattern of spending. This reckless approach has seriously jeopardized the Federal government and threatens the very future of this Nation. As a result, I believe we must look to constitutional protection from a firmly entrenched fiscal policy which threatens the liberties and opportunities of our present and future citizens.99

Strom Thurmond
U.S. Senator

—statement to the Judiciary Committee, February 16, 1994

——— NO ———

66And I thought the amendment simply a political ploy to erroneously make Americans think we were actually doing something about the deficit. In fact, we knew how to truly balance the budget but lacked the political courage to do so. Instead, this amendment had a hidden escape valve, saying we could all ignore it with a three-fifth Congressional vote. And ... this [amendment] could have taken up to seven years to be adopted. We didn't have that long. ... I wanted a balanced budget with all these kinks worked out. I've been quoted as saying, 'I pray for the integrity, justice, and courage to vote the correct vote, not the political vote,' and this was no time for change.99

Mark Hatfield
U.S. Senator

—from *Against the Grain: Reflections of a Rebel Republican*, 2001

DBQ Document Based Questions

❶ *Analyzing Primary Sources* How might an "irresponsible pattern of spending" by Congress threaten the nation's future?

❷ *Drawing Conclusions* Which argument do you find more convincing? Why?

In 1995 a clash between congressional Republicans and President Clinton over the federal budget led to a shutdown of the federal government.

▶ **CRITICAL THINKING**

1 *Identifying Central Issues* Why do you think the cartoonist says that both Clinton and Gingrich might be non-essential federal employees?

2 *Drawing Inferences* What is the significance of depicting rain and puddles in the cartoon?

In 1996 Republicans nominated Senator Bob Dole to run against Clinton. H. Ross Perot also ran again. Despite two opponents, Clinton won reelection with more than 49 percent of the popular vote and 379 electoral votes. Republicans, however, retained control of Congress.

✓ **PROGRESS CHECK**

Drawing Conclusions What were the political consequences of the budget battle?

Clinton's Second Term

GUIDING QUESTION *Why was President Clinton's domestic agenda less aggressive during his second term?*

During Clinton's second term, the economy continued to expand. In 1997 he submitted a balanced budget to Congress. In 1998 the government began to run a surplus—that is, it collected more money than it spent. Despite these achievements, Clinton devoted much of his second term to foreign policy and struggling against personal scandal.

Putting Children First

One area of domestic policy Clinton did focus on during his second term was helping the nation's children. He asked Congress for a $500 per child tax credit. He also signed the Adoption and Safe Families Act and asked Congress to ban cigarette advertising aimed at children. In August 1997, Clinton signed the Children's Health Insurance Program to provide health insurance for children whose parents could not afford it.

Clinton also focused on students. "I came from a family where nobody had ever gone to college before. . . . When I became President, I was determined to do what I could to give every student that chance. I am well aware, if it hadn't been for that chance . . . I wouldn't be standing here today," he told graduating college students. Clinton asked for a tax credit, a large increase in student grants, and expansion of Head Start for disadvantaged preschoolers.

Clinton Is Impeached

Clinton's popularity soon faltered, however. During his first term, he was accused of arranging illegal loans for Whitewater Development, an Arkansas real estate company, as governor of that state. Attorney General Janet Reno called for an independent counsel to investigate. A three-judge panel appointed former federal judge Kenneth Starr to this role.

Thinking Like a
HISTORIAN

Comparing and Contrasting

Bill Clinton became only the second American president to be impeached. The first was Andrew Johnson, the Reconstruction-era president who succeeded Abraham Lincoln. In both cases, political opposition to the president by Congress played a role in bringing the Chief Executive to trial. Unlike Clinton's case, however, Johnson's crisis stemmed from a political, rather than personal, scandal: he fired the secretary of war without Senate approval, a violation of the Tenure of Office Act. Although Congress failed to remove either leader, historians generally agree that political motivations contributed to their trials.

Clinton's impeachment trial captured the attention of the nation.

► **CRITICAL THINKING**
Predicting Consequences What influence might public opinion have on the outcome of an impeachment trial?

perjury lying when one has sworn under oath to tell the truth

ethnic cleansing the expulsion, imprisonment, or killing of ethnic minorities by a dominant majority group

participant one who takes part or shares in something

Haitians gather outside the fence of the U.S. camp to talk to American peacekeepers.

► **CRITICAL THINKING**
Drawing Inferences What can you conclude about the Haitian people's hope for peace from the way they are clustered at the fence?

In early 1998, new allegations emerged about Clinton's relationship with a White House intern. Some evidence suggested that he had committed **perjury,** or had lied under oath, about the relationship. In September 1998, Starr argued that Clinton had obstructed justice, abused his power as president, and committed perjury. Starr found no evidence to formally charge Clinton regarding the Whitewater accusations, however.

Clinton's supporters argued that Starr was playing politics. Opponents claimed Clinton should face charges if he had committed a crime. On December 19, 1998, the House of Representatives passed two articles of impeachment, one for perjury and one for obstruction of justice. The vote split along party lines, and the case moved to the Senate. On February 12, 1999, the senators voted 55 to 45 that Clinton was not guilty of perjury, and 50–50 on obstruction of justice. Both votes fell short of the two-thirds needed to remove Clinton from office, but his reputation suffered.

☑ **PROGRESS CHECK**

Examining What impact did impeachment have on Clinton's second term?

Clinton's Foreign Policy

GUIDING QUESTION *How did the Clinton administration provide foreign aid to areas of conflict around the world?*

Although Clinton's domestic policies became bogged down in struggles with Congress, he was able to engage in a series of major foreign policy initiatives. Several times he used force to try to resolve regional conflicts.

The Haitian Intervention

In 1991 military leaders in Haiti overthrew democratically elected president Jean-Bertrand Aristide. Seeking to restore democracy, the Clinton administration convinced the United Nations to impose a trade embargo on Haiti. The embargo caused a severe economic crisis in that country, and many Haitians fled to the United States. Clinton then ordered an invasion of Haiti. However, former president Carter convinced Haiti's rulers to step aside, and American troops landed to serve as peacekeepers.

Bosnia and Kosovo

The United States also was concerned about mounting tensions in southeastern Europe. During the Cold War, Yugoslavia had been a nation of many ethnic groups under a strong Communist government. In 1991 Yugoslavia began to split apart. In the new republic of Bosnia and Herzegovina, a civil war erupted among Orthodox Christian Serbs, Catholic Croatians, and Bosnian Muslims. The Serbs began what they called **ethnic cleansing**—the brutal expulsion of non-Serbs from a geographic area. In some cases, Serbian troops slaughtered Bosnian Muslims instead of moving them.

The United States convinced its NATO allies to take military action. NATO warplanes attacked the Serbs in Bosnia, forcing them to negotiate. The Clinton administration arranged peace talks in Dayton, Ohio, where the **participants** signed a peace plan known as the Dayton Accords. In 1996 about 60,000 NATO troops entered Bosnia to enforce the plan.

In 1998 another war erupted, this time in the Serbian province of Kosovo. Kosovo has two major ethnic groups—Serbs and Albanians. Many Albanians wanted Kosovo to separate from Serbia. To keep Kosovo in Serbia, Serbian leader Slobodan Milošević ordered a crackdown. Worried by Serbian violence against Albanian civilians, Clinton asked European leaders to intervene. In March 1999, NATO began bombing Serbia, and Serbia pulled its troops out of Kosovo.

Peacemaking in the Middle East

Although Iraq was defeated in the Persian Gulf War, Iraqi president Saddam Hussein was determined to hang onto power. In 1996 Iraqi forces attacked the Kurds, an ethnic group whose homeland lies in northern Iraq. To stop the attacks, the United States fired cruise missiles at Iraqi military targets.

Relations between Israel and the Palestinians were even more volatile. In 1993 Israeli prime minister Yitzhak Rabin and Palestine Liberation Organization (PLO) leader Yasir Arafat reached an agreement. The PLO recognized Israel's right to exist, and Israel recognized the PLO as the representative of the Palestinians. President Clinton then invited Arafat and Rabin to the White House, where they signed the Declaration of Principles—a plan for creating a Palestinian government. Extremist opposition to the peace plan emerged on both sides. Radical Palestinians exploded bombs in Israel, killing 256. In 1995 a right-wing Israeli assassinated Prime Minister Rabin.

In 1994, with help from the United States, Jordan and Israel signed a peace treaty. In 1998 Israeli and Palestinian leaders met with President Clinton at the Wye River Plantation in Maryland. The agreement they reached, however, did not address the contested status of Jerusalem or the ultimate dimensions of a projected Israeli withdrawal from the West Bank and Gaza.

In July 2000, President Clinton invited Arafat and Israeli prime minister Ehud Barak to Camp David to discuss unresolved issues. Barak agreed to the creation of a Palestinian state in all of Gaza and over 90 percent of the West Bank, but Arafat rejected the deal. In late September 2000, a Palestinian uprising began. The region was as far from peace as ever.

Israeli prime minster Yitzhak Rabin (left) and Palestinian leader Yasir Arafat shake hands after signing the 1993 Declaration of Principles.

▶ **CRITICAL THINKING**
Constructing Arguments Do you think that the United States should intervene in world conflicts? Why or why not?

✓ **PROGRESS CHECK**

Drawing Inferences Why did the Clinton administration intervene in conflicts such as Haiti, the former Yugoslavia, and the Middle East?

LESSON 1 REVIEW

Reviewing Vocabulary
1. ***Defining*** How is perjury different from lying?

2. ***Identifying*** For what purpose did Bosnian Serbs practice ethnic cleansing?

Using Your Notes
3. ***Evaluating*** Review the notes you took during the lesson. Write a paragraph telling whether President Clinton was more successful in domestic policy or in foreign policy. Support your opinion with specific details from the lesson.

Answering the Guiding Questions
4. ***Identifying*** During his first presidential term, what domestic policy areas did Clinton focus on?

5. ***Describing*** How did the Republican Party respond to the victory in the 1994 midterm elections?

6. ***Assessing*** Why was President Clinton's domestic agenda less aggressive during his second term?

7. ***Explaining*** How did the Clinton administration provide foreign aid to areas of conflict around the world?

Writing Activity
8. **PERSUASIVE** Suppose that you are a member of Congress. Write a speech in which you attempt to persuade other lawmakers to vote for or against Clinton's impeachment.

netw⊙rks

There's More Online!

- ☑ **CHART/GRAPH** Illegal Border Crossing Deaths
- ☑ **IMAGE** Jorge Urbina
- ☑ **PRIMARY SOURCE** Citizenship Challenged
- ☑ **VIDEO** A New Wave of Immigration
- ☑ **INTERACTIVE SELF-CHECK QUIZ**

Reading **HELP**DESK

Content Vocabulary

- **migration chains**
- **refugee** • **amnesty**

Academic Vocabulary

- **illegal** • **resident**
- **allocate**

TAKING NOTES: *Determining Cause and Effect*

ACTIVITY As you read the lesson, complete a graphic organizer similar to the one below to list the effects of the Immigration Act of 1965.

Effects of the
Immigration Act of 1965

LESSON 2
A New Wave of Immigration

ESSENTIAL QUESTIONS • *How have improvements in science and technology helped change society?* • *How have immigration, technology, and global trade changed the world?*

IT MATTERS BECAUSE

In the late twentieth century, the number of immigrants to the United States hit an all-time high. Large numbers of non-European immigrants changed the nation's ethnic composition. Immigration, both legal and illegal, became a difficult political issue.

Changes in Immigration Law

GUIDING QUESTION *How have important immigration laws affected legal and illegal immigration to the United States?*

After the introduction of the national origins quota system in the 1920s, the sources and character of immigration to the United States changed dramatically. For the next few decades, the total number of immigrants arriving annually remained markedly lower. The quota system, which favored immigrants from northern and western Europe, remained largely unchanged until the mid-1960s.

The Immigration Act of 1965 abolished the national origins quota system. It gave preference to skilled persons and persons with close relatives who are U.S. citizens—policies that remain in place today. The preference given to the children, spouses, and parents of U.S. citizens meant that **migration chains** were established. As newcomers became citizens, they could send for relatives in their home country. Also, the legislation introduced the first limits on immigration from the Western Hemisphere. The act further provided that immigrants could apply for U.S. citizenship after five years of legal residency.

At the time of its passage, few people expected that the new law would cause much change in the pattern or volume of immigration to the United States. Supporters of the law presented it as an extension of America's growing commitment to equal rights for all people, regardless of race or ethnicity. As U.S. Representative Philip Burton of California explained:

PHOTOS: (l to r)Stanley Rogouski, Carlos Barria/Reuters/CORBIS

"Just as we sought to eliminate discrimination in our land through the Civil Rights Act, today we seek by phasing out the national origins quotas to eliminate discrimination in immigration to this Nation composed of the descendants of immigrants."

—from a speech before Congress, August 25, 1965

Supporters of the new law also assumed that the new equal quotas for non-European nations would generally go unfilled. In fact, immigration from non-European countries soared. Some newcomers arrived in the United States as **refugees.** Beginning in 1948, refugees from countries ravaged by World War II were admitted, although they were counted as part of their nation's quota. The Cold War brought more refugees. According to the McCarran-Walter Act of 1952, anyone who was fleeing a Communist regime could be admitted as a refugee. The Refugee Act of 1980 further broadened U.S. policy by defining a refugee as anyone leaving his or her country due to a "well-founded fear of persecution on account of race, religion, nationality, membership in a particular group, or political opinion."

The growing problem of **illegal** immigration also prompted changes in immigration law. During the Reagan administration, Congress passed the Immigration Reform and Control Act of 1986, which established penalties for employers who knowingly hired unauthorized immigrants. This law strengthened border controls to prevent illegal entry into the United States. It also set up a process to grant **amnesty,** or a pardon, to any undocumented alien who could prove that he or she had entered the country before January 1, 1982, and had since lived in the United States.

migration chains the process by which immigrants who have acquired U.S. citizenship can send for relatives in their home country to join them

refugee someone leaving his or her country due to a well-founded fear of persecution on account of race, religion, nationality, membership in a particular group, or political opinion

illegal not according to or authorized by law

GEOGRAPHY CONNECTION

In 2000 there were an estimated 8.4 million unauthorized residents in the United States.

1 PLACES AND REGIONS *According to the map, which states have the largest numbers of unauthorized residents?*

2 HUMAN SYSTEMS *What are some geographic factors that could explain why some states attract more immigrants than others?*

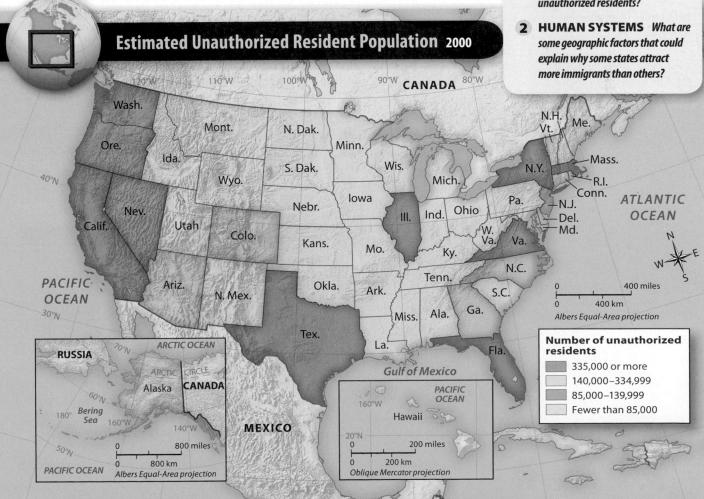

Estimated Unauthorized Resident Population 2000

Number of unauthorized residents
- 335,000 or more
- 140,000–334,999
- 85,000–139,999
- Fewer than 85,000

Illegal immigration has long been a divisive issue.

▶ **CRITICAL THINKING**
Using Context Clues In what sense is this woman using the term *aliens*?

amnesty the act of granting a pardon to a large group of people

allocate to set apart for something specific

resident one who lives in a place for some length of time

Despite these changes, illegal immigration persisted, and the number of unauthorized immigrants grew. By 1990 an estimated 3.5 million unauthorized immigrants resided in the United States. By the mid-1990s, Congress was debating new ways to combat illegal immigration. It passed the Illegal Immigration Reform and Immigrant Responsibility Act of 1996, which made several changes to American immigration law.

First, it required families sponsoring an immigrant to have an income above the poverty level. Second, it **allocated** more resources to stop illegal immigration, authorizing an additional 5,000 U.S. Border Patrol agents and calling for the construction of a 14-mile fence along the border near San Diego. Third, the law toughened penalties for smuggling people or providing fraudulent documents. Finally, the law made it easier for immigration authorities to deport undocumented aliens.

Another change in immigration law was spurred by the terrorist attacks of September 11, 2001. The USA PATRIOT Act of 2001 put immigration under the control of the newly created Department of Homeland Security. It also tripled the number of Border Patrol agents, Customs Service inspectors, and Immigration and Naturalization Service inspectors along the Canadian border.

☑ PROGRESS CHECK

Sequencing How did the Immigration Reform and Control Act of 1986 attempt to control illegal immigration?

Recent Immigration

GUIDING QUESTION *How has the federal government addressed immigration reform in the twenty-first century?*

Certain states experienced a larger influx of immigrants than others. In 1990 California, Texas, New York, New Jersey, and Florida had the largest populations of foreign-born **residents.** High numbers of immigrants also increased the ethnic diversity of these states, as their Latino and Asian populations grew. Among the immigrants who arrived during the 1990s, just over 10 percent came from Europe. More than half of new immigrants came from Latin America, while about another 25 percent came from Asia. By 2001 the top five countries of origin for legal immigrants to the United States were Mexico, India, China, the Philippines, and Vietnam.

Refugees added to the growing immigrant population. In the 25 years following the Cuban Revolution of 1959, more than 800,000 Cubans arrived in the United States. So many settled in the Miami, Florida, area that the only city that is home to more Cubans is Havana, Cuba. Also, the Vietnam War

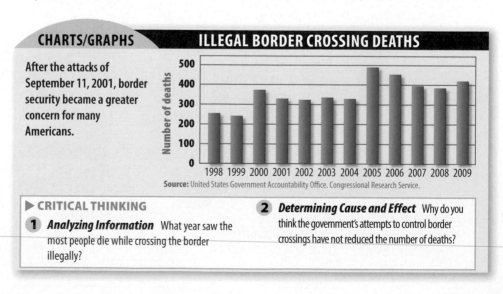

CHARTS/GRAPHS | **ILLEGAL BORDER CROSSING DEATHS**

After the attacks of September 11, 2001, border security became a greater concern for many Americans.

Source: United States Government Accountability Office. Congressional Research Service.

▶ **CRITICAL THINKING**

1 *Analyzing Information* What year saw the most people die while crossing the border illegally?

2 *Determining Cause and Effect* Why do you think the government's attempts to control border crossings have not reduced the number of deaths?

684

PHOTO: Stanley Rocouski

created refugees. Some 600,000 immigrants from Vietnam, Laos, and Cambodia arrived in the decade after 1974.

Other immigrants arrived without official permission. The largest number of unauthorized immigrants came from Mexico, El Salvador, and Guatemala. The amnesty program established in 1986 had been designed to solve the problem of illegal immigration. Yet, over the next 20 years, the number of unauthorized immigrants more than tripled. Americans were divided over whether unauthorized immigrants should be able to obtain driver's licenses or send their children to public schools and receive other government services.

Some believed that unauthorized immigrants should be deported. Others favored allowing them to apply for temporary work visas so the government could keep track of them. Some supported permitting them to earn permanent residence if they learned English, paid back taxes, and had no criminal record.

In 2006 President George W. Bush made immigration reform a top priority, but members of Congress strongly disagreed over how to solve the problem. A bipartisan majority of the Senate favored legislation that blended tougher enforcement of immigration laws with some form of earned citizenship.

The Senate bill included a provision that allowed undocumented aliens who grew up in the United States and graduated from high school to apply for citizenship. Conservative Republicans who held the majority in the House objected that this would reward illegal behavior. "Granting amnesty to people who broke the law penalizes the millions of people who are waiting to come to America legally," argued Republican senator Phil Gramm of Texas.

The House rejected any form of amnesty and called for the United States to build a wall along its Mexican border. By this time, the United States had already tripled the size of its border patrol without reducing illegal immigration. As Congress debated a bill that would subject undocumented aliens to criminal prosecution, Latinos held rallies across the country, carrying signs that read: "We are not criminals."

Advocates of immigration reform promoted alternatives such as expanding quotas through a guest-worker program and establishing a legalization process for those already in the country. Some undocumented immigrants had lived in the United States for years and had raised families. Deporting them would mean separating husbands, wives, and children. Some had arrived as children and had lived in the United States most of their lives. Their own children, born in the United States, were native-born citizens even though their parents lacked legal status. Among those who became legal citizens, most wanted other family members to join them.

✓ PROGRESS CHECK

Constructing a Thesis How would you solve the problem of illegal immigration?

LESSON 2 REVIEW

Reviewing Vocabulary

1. ***Defining*** Why were people who came to the United States as a result of World War II and the Cold War considered refugees?

2. ***Explaining*** How might migration chains affect the immigration patterns or numbers of immigrants entering the country?

Using Your Notes

3. ***Summarizing*** Review the notes that you completed during the lesson. Then write a paragraph summarizing the effects of the Immigration Act of 1965.

Answering the Guiding Questions

4. ***Evaluating*** How have important immigration laws affected legal and illegal immigration to the United States?

5. ***Describing*** How has the federal government addressed immigration reform in the twenty-first century?

Writing Activity

6. **PERSUASIVE** After reading about the problem of illegal immigration, write a letter to your representative in Congress explaining what you feel he or she should do about the problem.

networks

There's More Online!

☑ **BIOGRAPHY** Bill Gates

☑ **BIOGRAPHY** Steve Jobs

☑ **GRAPHIC NOVEL** "All Work and No Play"

☑ **IMAGE** Kyoto Accords

☑ **VIDEO** Technology and Globalization

☑ **INTERACTIVE SELF-CHECK QUIZ**

Reading **HELP**DESK

Content Vocabulary
- telecommute
- euro
- global warming

Academic Vocabulary
- cited
- awareness

TAKING NOTES: *Organizing*

ACTIVITY As you read the lesson, complete the graphic organizer below to show ways new technology and trade brought the world closer together during the 1990s.

Globalism

LESSON 3

Technology and Globalization

ESSENTIAL QUESTIONS · *How have improvements in science and technology helped change society?* · *How have immigration, technology, and global trade changed the world?*

IT MATTERS BECAUSE

Since the 1980s, computer technology has advanced greatly, with the creation of home computers and the expansion of the Internet. Trade barriers have fallen, and the environment has become a global concern.

The Computer Changes Society

GUIDING QUESTION *How did the computer revolution change the workplace?*

The first electronic digital computer began operation in 1946 and was the size of a small house. In 1959 Robert Noyce designed the first integrated circuit—a whole electronic circuit on a single silicon chip. In 1968 Noyce's company, Intel, put several integrated circuits on a single chip. This made circuits much smaller and easy to manufacture. By the late 1960s, manufacturers were making microprocessors, or single chips with many integrated circuits containing both memory and computing functions. These microprocessors made computers even smaller and faster.

Using microprocessor technology, Steve Jobs and Stephen Wozniak set out to build a small computer suitable for personal use. They founded Apple Computer in 1976. The following year they launched the Apple II, the first practical and affordable home computer. In 1981 International Business Machines (IBM) introduced the "Personal Computer," or PC. In 1984 Apple put out the Macintosh, which used on-screen symbols called icons that users could manipulate with a hand-operated device called a mouse.

As Jobs and Wozniak were creating Apple, Bill Gates cofounded Microsoft. In 1980 IBM hired Microsoft to make an operating system for its new PC. The system was called MS-DOS. Microsoft came out with the "Windows" operating system in 1985. Computers became essential tools in almost all businesses. By the late 1990s, many workers were able to **telecommute,** or work from home via computer.

Telecommunications also underwent a revolution. In 1996 Congress passed a law allowing phone companies to compete with one another and to send television signals. It also allowed cable companies to offer telephone service. Soon wireless digital technology made it possible to make small, inexpensive satellite dishes for home use. Cell phones, invented in the 1940s, became popular as wireless digital technology made phones smaller and service cheaper. As this technology became more advanced, companies developed interconnectable digital music players, cameras, radios, televisions, and music and video recorders.

✓ **PROGRESS CHECK**

Describing What advantage did microprocessors give to computers?

The Rise of the Internet

GUIDING QUESTION *How have advances in telecommunications and the rise of the Internet affected the U.S. standard of living?*

The Internet began as a system of networked computers of a U.S. Defense Department agency that linked to a system of networked supercomputers of the National Science Foundation. Similar networks grew across the world, and this communications system became known as the Internet. As personal computer ownership rose, individuals—rather than just government agencies—began connecting to the Internet. By 2007, more than 1 billion people around the world were regularly using the Internet.

Birth of the World Wide Web

In 1990 researchers in Switzerland developed a new way to present information on Internet-linked computers. Known as the World Wide Web, this system used hypertext, or "links," and was accessed with Web browser software. Users could post information on Web pages and use links to move between sites.

Enthusiasm for the World Wide Web spawned a "dot-com" economy. The stock of Internet-related companies helped fuel the prosperity of the 1990s. It fell dramatically in 2000 when many unprofitable online companies failed. A few "dot-com" companies were very successful. This new economy also required American workers to acquire new skills. This retraining increased productivity as well as the nation's GDP. Driven by the information technology industry, the GDP rose more than 20 percent during the mid- to late 1990s.

The Internet Changes Society

For many people, the World Wide Web builds a sense of community. People with common interests visit the same Web sites to post comments and interact with one another. They share stories and photos about themselves on blogs— short for Web logs. "People read and publish blogs because they recognize that there is a way to put themselves into this virtual world and interact within it. With every new sign-up . . . our world gets a little smaller—and the web gets more character," explained Internet entrepreneur Biz Stone.

✓ **PROGRESS CHECK**

Analyzing How has digital technology affected the U.S. economy?

The New Global Economy

GUIDING QUESTION *How did NAFTA and other regional trading blocs affect the global economy?*

In the 1990s, economies of individual nations were becoming more interdependent as new technology helped link the world together economically and culturally. Also, many world leaders were convinced that free trade and the global exchange of goods contributed to prosperity and economic growth. This idea that the world is becoming increasingly interconnected is called globalism, and the process is globalization.

telecommute to work at home by means of an electronic linkup with a central office

Selling American-made goods abroad had long been important to U.S. prosperity. American businesses make money selling goods abroad, and consumers benefit by having the option to buy cheaper imported goods. Opponents, however, argued that global trade could cost American workers jobs. The debate became an important part of American politics.

Regional Blocs

Regional trade pacts, like the North American Free Trade Agreement (NAFTA), increase international trade. Approved by Congress in 1993, NAFTA linked Canada, the United States, and Mexico in a free-trade zone. Many Americans feared that NAFTA would cause industrial jobs to move to Mexico, where labor costs were lower. Although some jobs were lost, the U.S. unemployment rate fell as wages rose. Many American businesses upgraded their technology, and workers shifted to more skilled jobs or to the service industry.

In 1993 the European Union (EU) was created to promote economic and political cooperation among many European nations. It created a common bank, encouraged free trade, and created a common currency called the **euro.** The Asia-Pacific Economic Cooperation (APEC) came together in 1989 to promote economic cooperation and lower trade barriers. Major political differences, however, kept its members from acting together.

The World Trade Organization

In 1995 the World Trade Organization (WTO) formed to represent some 120 nations in efforts to negotiate international trade agreements and trade disputes. Supporters of the WTO **cited** benefits for American consumers, including cheaper imports, new markets, and copyright protection. Opponents argued that the United States would have to accept the WTO's rulings in trade disputes even if they hurt the American economy.

euro the basic currency shared by the countries of the European Union since 1999

cite to point out as an example in an argument or debate

GEOGRAPHY CONNECTION

Global trading blocs have formed to increase international trade.

1 **THE WORLD IN SPATIAL TERMS** *What large countries make up the Asia-Pacific Economic Cooperation?*

2 **HUMAN SYSTEMS** *Why might it be beneficial for countries within a region to join in a free-trade agreement?*

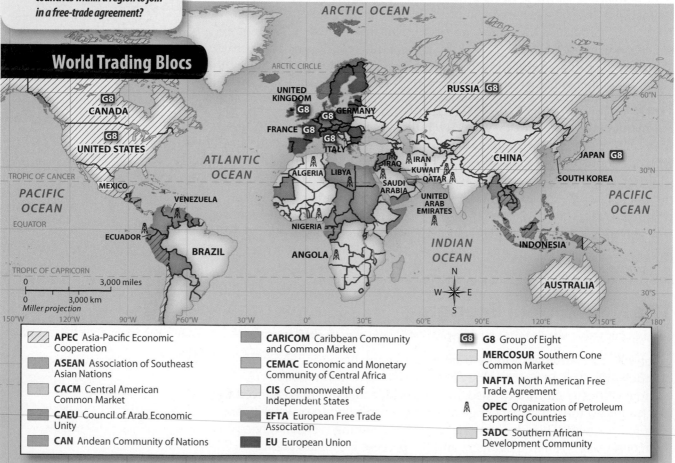

World Trading Blocs

APEC Asia-Pacific Economic Cooperation

ASEAN Association of Southeast Asian Nations

CACM Central American Common Market

CAEU Council of Arab Economic Unity

CAN Andean Community of Nations

CARICOM Caribbean Community and Common Market

CEMAC Economic and Monetary Community of Central Africa

CIS Commonwealth of Independent States

EFTA European Free Trade Association

EU European Union

G8 Group of Eight

MERCOSUR Southern Cone Common Market

NAFTA North American Free Trade Agreement

OPEC Organization of Petroleum Exporting Countries

SADC Southern African Development Community

Trade With China

China presented a huge potential market for American goods, but some were wary of trading with China due to its poor record on human rights. President Clinton urged Congress to grant China permanent normal trade relation status to bring it into the world community. Although many groups objected, Congress passed the bill in late 2000.

☑ **PROGRESS CHECK**

Identifying What trade agreements and organizations promoted globalization?

Global Environmentalism

GUIDING QUESTION *How have the United States and other nations responded to global environmental concerns?*

The rise of a global economy also increased **awareness** of environmental issues. Environmentalists began thinking of the environment as a global system and addressing issues they believed were of global concern. In the 1980s, scientists discovered that chlorofluorocarbons (CFCs) were affecting the layer of ozone in Earth's atmosphere. Ozone blocks many of the sun's ultraviolet rays. At that time, CFCs were widely used in air conditioners and refrigerators. In that same decade, scientists documented a large hole in the ozone layer over Antarctica. In 1987 the United States and many other nations agreed to phase out CFCs and other chemicals that might be weakening the ozone layer.

During this time, another environmental issue emerged when some scientists warned that **global warming** could lead to more droughts and other forms of extreme weather. Many experts concluded that carbon dioxide emissions from factories and power plants caused global warming, but others disagreed. The issue became controversial because of the cost of controlling emissions. Industries would have to pay the cost of reducing emissions, and these costs would be passed on to consumers. Developing nations trying to industrialize would be hurt the most. Economic growth in wealthier nations would be hurt as well. Concern about global warming led the EU and many other nations to sign the Kyoto Protocol in 1997, promising to reduce emissions. President Clinton did not submit the protocol for ratification because most senators opposed it. President George W. Bush withdrew the United States from the agreement entirely, citing flaws in the treaty.

awareness the state of having or showing realization, perception, or knowledge

global warming an increase in average world temperatures over time

☑ **PROGRESS CHECK**

Describing What scientific data encouraged nations to protect the environment?

LESSON 3 REVIEW

Reviewing Vocabulary

1. *Defining* How can telecommuting be an easier option for some employees?

2. *Explaining* Why are scientists concerned about the effects of global warming?

Using Your Notes

3. *Explaining* Review the notes you took during the lesson and explain why many people felt that the world came closer together during the 1990s.

Answering the Guiding Questions

4. *Analyzing* How did the computer revolution change the workplace?

5. *Determining Cause and Effect* How have advances in telecommunications and the rise of the Internet affected the U.S. standard of living?

6. *Making Connections* How did NAFTA and other regional trading blocs affect the global economy?

7. *Describing* How have the United States and other nations responded to global environmental concerns?

Writing Activity

8. **NARRATIVE** Imagine what your life would be like without technological developments such as the Internet and the cell phone. Write a short narrative in which you describe how your typical day would be different without this type of technology.

Directions: On a separate sheet of paper, answer the questions below. Make sure you read carefully and answer all parts to the question.

Lesson Review

Lesson 1

1 *Interpreting Significance* What was the significance of the Brady Bill?

2 *Identifying Cause and Effect* How did NATO respond to the process of ethnic cleansing?

Lesson 2

3 *Summarizing* What were two key points of the Illegal Immigration Reform and Immigrant Responsibility Act of 1996? How were they different from the key points of the Immigration Act of 1965?

4 *Analyzing* Why did many refugees from Europe come to the United States in the late 1940s and early 1950s?

Lesson 3

5 *Explaining* How have technological improvements changed how people use digital technology?

6 *Evaluating* How has the involvement of the United States in trade agreements and globalization affected the average American?

21st Century Skills

7 **EXPLAINING CONTINUITY AND CHANGE** What does the acronym CFCs stand for, and how did CFCs affect the ozone layer?

8 **TIME, CHRONOLOGY, AND SEQUENCING** List the following developments in computer technology in chronological order: Apple II, integrated circuit, and wireless digital technology. Then explain the role of entrepreneurship and innovation in the development of computer technology.

9 **UNDERSTANDING RELATIONSHIPS AMONG EVENTS** How was perjury a factor in the impeachment of President Clinton?

10 **CREATE AND ANALYZE ARGUMENTS AND DRAW CONCLUSIONS** What was one advantage of President Clinton's decision to appoint Hillary Rodham Clinton to

head a task force on health care? What was one disadvantage of appointing her?

11 **IDENTIFYING PERSPECTIVES AND DIFFERING INTERPRETATIONS** From a manufacturer's perspective, what are the advantages and disadvantages of trying to reduce a factory's carbon dioxide emissions?

Exploring the Essential Questions

12 *Exploring Issues* Write a short report that could be published as a Web page. The report should explain the global impact of technology, immigration, or international trade. Underline four words that could be made into hypertext links. Include four footnotes to describe what the viewer would see by clicking on the hypertext.

DBQ Document-Based Questions

Use the graph to answer the following questions.

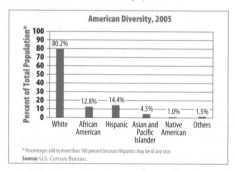

American Diversity, 2005

White 80.2%, African American 12.8%, Hispanic 14.4%, Asian and Pacific Islander 4.5%, Native American 1.0%, Others 1.5%

* Percentages add to more than 100 percent because Hispanics may be of any race.
Source: U.S. Census Bureau.

13 *Analyzing Visuals* Which group accounted for the smallest percentage of the total population in 2005?

14 *Making Predictions* In the year 2020, do you think the percentage of Hispanic people in the United States will be higher or lower than it was in 2005? Why?

Extended-Response Question

15 *Making Connections* Television commentators often use this expression: "The world is getting smaller." Write an essay explaining how globalization, computer technology, and immigration have made the world seem like a "smaller" place. Use examples from the chapter to support your argument.

Need Extra Help?

If You've Missed Question	**1**	**2**	**3**	**4**	**5**	**6**	**7**	**8**	**9**	**10**	**11**	**12**	**13**	**14**	**15**
Go to page	677	680	684	683	686	687	689	686	680	677	689	683	690	690	676

America's Challenges for a New Century

2001–Present

ESSENTIAL QUESTIONS · *How is American culture shaped by a set of common values and practices?* · *How have disputes over ideas, values, and politics resulted in change?*

The Story Matters...

As the United States entered the twenty-first century, a new collection of challenges emerged. Terrorists launched devastating attacks on September 11, 2001 that led to wars in Afghanistan and Iraq. The economy slowed and then crashed. In 2008 Barack Obama became the first African American to be elected president of the United States. His campaign promised hope to a country swept up in a time of great challenges.

◀ Barack Obama took office in January 2009. His first tasks were leading two wars, improving a declining economy, and reshaping a political system filled with partisanship.

As the United States entered the twenty-first century, combating terrorism at home and abroad became a national priority. The attacks on the World Trade Center and the Pentagon resulted in wars in Afghanistan and Iraq, where Islamic fundamentalist militants trained to use terrorism to overthrow pro-Western governments. The wars as well as new security policies led to great controversy in American politics.

Step Into the Place

Read the quote and look at the information presented on the map.

 According to President Obama, what strategy will help the United States win the wars in Afghanistan and Iraq?

PRIMARY SOURCE

66I think there are achievable goals in Afghanistan. . . . Our goal in the region is to keep the American people safe. And I think that the more we can accomplish that through diplomacy, and the more we can accomplish that by partnering with actors in the region, rather than simply applying U.S. military forces, the better off we're going to be. . . .

A lot of the ultimate outcome in Iraq now is going to depend on how the political issues that have dogged Iraq for a very long time get resolved. . . . There are a whole host of political issues between the various factions and between Sunni, Shia and Kurd in Iraq that still have to be worked on. . . . We've got to redouble our efforts when it comes to the diplomatic side if we're going to be successful.99

—Barack Obama, *Interview with Jim Lehrer,*
February 27, 2009

PHOTOS: left page (t)Brooks Kraft/Corbis News/Corbis, (b)Eric Draper, White House/U.S. Department of Defense; right page Pete Souza/Obama Transition Team/Handout/Corbis News/CORBIS

Step Into the Time

Choose an event from the time line and write a paragraph explaining how that event might contribute to America's challenges.

U.S. PRESIDENTS

UNITED STATES

WORLD

2000   2002   2004

November 2000 A close vote in Florida causes a contested presidential election

G. W. Bush 2001–2009

September 11, 2001 Terrorists attack the World Trade Center and the Pentagon

2003 The United States invades Iraq

2001 Terrorists attack the Indian Parliament

May 2003 Terrorists bombings in Casablanca, Morocco

March 2004 Terrorists bomb trains in Spain

December 2004 Tsunami in Indian Ocean devastates Indonesia and surrounding regions

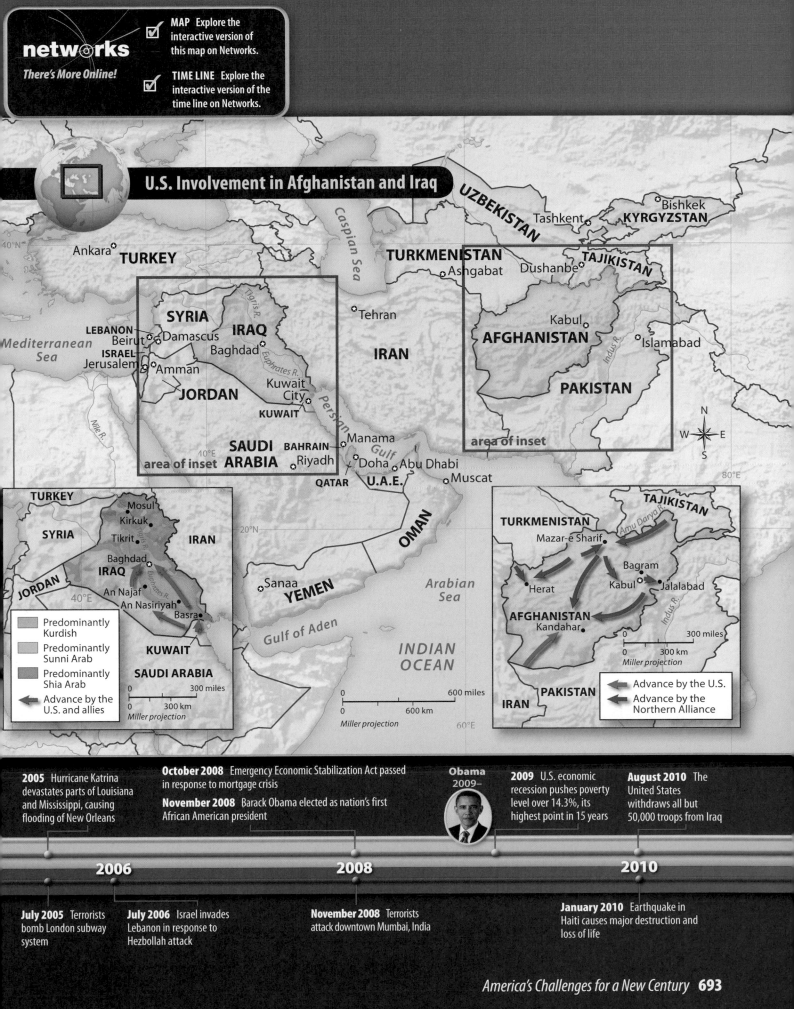

networks
There's More Online!

☑ MAP Explore the interactive version of this map on Networks.

☑ TIME LINE Explore the interactive version of the time line on Networks.

U.S. Involvement in Afghanistan and Iraq

UZBEKISTAN

Bishkek
Tashkent ○ KYRGYZSTAN

40°N

Ankara ○ TURKEY

TURKMENISTAN
Ashgabat ○

Dushanbe ○ TAJIKISTAN

Caspian Sea

Tehran ○

SYRIA
IRAQ
LEBANON
Beirut ○ Damascus ○
Baghdad ○
ISRAEL
Jerusalem ○ Amman ○
JORDAN

Kabul ○
AFGHANISTAN
Islamabad ○

IRAN

PAKISTAN

Mediterranean Sea

Nile R.

Tigris R.

Euphrates R.

Indus R.

Kuwait City
KUWAIT

area of inset

40°E

SAUDI ARABIA
area of inset

BAHRAIN
Manama ○
Doha ○
QATAR

Riyadh ○
Gulf
Abu Dhabi ○
U.A.E.

Muscat ○

Persian Gulf

N
W E
S

80°E

Iraq inset

TURKEY

SYRIA

Mosul
Kirkuk

Tikrit

IRAN

Baghdad
IRAQ

JORDAN

An Najaf
An Nasiriyah
Basra

40°E

KUWAIT

SAUDI ARABIA

☐ Predominantly Kurdish
☐ Predominantly Sunni Arab
☐ Predominantly Shia Arab
← Advance by the U.S. and allies

0   300 miles
0   300 km
Miller projection

20°N

OMAN

Sanaa ○ YEMEN

Arabian Sea

Gulf of Aden

INDIAN OCEAN

0   600 miles
0   600 km
Miller projection

60°E

Afghanistan inset

TAJIKISTAN

TURKMENISTAN
Mazar-e Sharif

Amu Darya R.

Bagram
Kabul
Jalalabad

Herat

AFGHANISTAN
Kandahar

Indus R.

0   300 miles
0   300 km
Miller projection

PAKISTAN

IRAN

← Advance by the U.S.
← Advance by the Northern Alliance

2005 Hurricane Katrina devastates parts of Louisiana and Mississippi, causing flooding of New Orleans

October 2008 Emergency Economic Stabilization Act passed in response to mortgage crisis

November 2008 Barack Obama elected as nation's first African American president

Obama 2009–

2009 U.S. economic recession pushes poverty level over 14.3%, its highest point in 15 years

August 2010 The United States withdraws all but 50,000 troops from Iraq

2006   2008   2010

July 2005 Terrorists bomb London subway system

July 2006 Israel invades Lebanon in response to Hezbollah attack

November 2008 Terrorists attack downtown Mumbai, India

January 2010 Earthquake in Haiti causes major destruction and loss of life

Reading HELPDESK

Content Vocabulary

- **chad**
- **terrorism**
- **state-sponsored terrorism**
- **anthrax**

Academic Vocabulary

- **resolve** • **obtain**
- **interpretation**

TAKING NOTES: *Organizing*

ACTIVITY Use the following graphic organizer to show causes of terrorism.

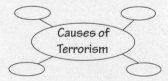

Causes of Terrorism

LESSON 1
Bush's Global Challenges

ESSENTIAL QUESTIONS • *How is American culture shaped by a set of common values and practices?* • *How have disputes over ideas, values, and politics resulted in change?*

IT MATTERS BECAUSE

After a disputed outcome in the election of 2000, George W. Bush became president. On September 11, 2001, terrorists attacked the United States. In response, Bush and Congress launched a war on terrorism.

The Election of 2000

GUIDING QUESTION *Why was the presidential election of 2000 controversial?*

In the election of 2000, the division between liberals and conservatives widened. The election itself was one of the closest in American history.

The Candidates Campaign

The Democrats nominated Vice President Al Gore for president. For his running mate, Gore chose Senator Joseph Lieberman, the first Jewish American to run for vice president on a major party ticket. The Republican candidate was Texas governor George W. Bush, son of former president George H. W. Bush. For his vice-presidential candidate, Bush chose Dick Cheney, who had served as George H. W. Bush's secretary of defense. Well-known consumer advocate Ralph Nader also entered the race on the Green Party ticket.

The election campaign revolved around the question of what to do with surplus tax revenues. Both Bush and Gore agreed that Social Security needed reform, but they disagreed on the details. Both promised to cut taxes, to improve public education, and to support plans to help senior citizens pay for prescription drugs.

A Close Vote

No candidate won a majority in the 2000 election, but Gore received the most votes, with 48.4 percent of the popular vote compared to 47.9 percent for Bush. To win the presidency, however, candidates must win a majority of votes in the Electoral College.

The election came down to the results in Florida—both men needed its 25 electoral votes to win. The counts in Florida were so close that state law required a recount of the ballots using vote-counting machines. There were, however, thousands of ballots the machines could not read. Gore then asked for a recount of ballots in several strongly Democratic counties. After the machine recount showed Bush still ahead, a battle began over the manual recounts.

Most Florida ballots required voters to cast a vote by punching a small piece of cardboard out of the ballot beside the candidate's name. This small piece is called a **chad.** Vote counters had to determine how to count a ballot if the chad was still partially attached. On some, the chad was still in place, and the voter had left only a dimple on the ballot's surface. Vote counters thus had to determine what the voter intended—and different counties used different standards.

chad a small piece of cardboard produced by punching a data card

Under state law, Florida officials had to certify the results by a certain date. When it became clear that not all of the recounts could be finished in time, Gore went to court to challenge the deadline. The Florida Supreme Court agreed to set a new deadline. At Bush's request, the U.S. Supreme Court intervened to decide whether the Florida Supreme Court had acted constitutionally. The hand recounts continued, but not all of the counties were able to meet the new deadline. On November 26, Florida officials certified Bush the winner by 537 votes.

🏛 ANALYZING SUPREME COURT CASES

BUSH v. *GORE*, 2000

Background of the Case

The outcome of the 2000 presidential election hinged on Florida's 25 electoral votes. When the polls closed on November 7, the vote in Florida was so close that it triggered an automatic recount. Bush led by only 1,784 out of more than 6 million votes cast. When ballots were again run through tabulation machines, Bush's lead shrank to fewer than 200 votes. Gore requested hand recounts of ballots in four predominantly Democratic counties where thousands of punch-card ballots had recorded no vote for president. Bush asked the U.S. District Court to block any further recounts.

While the manual recount was still in progress, the Florida secretary of state certified Bush as the winner by 537 votes. Gore appealed this action, and the Florida Supreme Court authorized manual recounts of disputed ballots to begin immediately. Bush appealed the ruling to the U.S. Supreme Court, which ordered the recount to stop.

An election worker inspects a ballot during the Florida recount.

How the Court Ruled

The Florida Supreme Court ordered any recounts to use a general standard set forth in Florida law to discern the "clear intent of the voter." In a 7-2 ruling, the U.S. Supreme Court declared that because different vote counters used different standards, the recount did not treat all voters equally.

In addition, both federal law and the Constitution require the electoral votes for president to be cast on a certain day. If Florida missed that deadline, its electoral votes would not count. The Court ruled 5-4 that there was not enough time left to conduct a manual recount that would pass constitutional standards.

▶ **CRITICAL THINKING**

❶ *Identifying Central Issues* If it is the electoral votes that count in the election of the president, why is it important to count the popular vote?

❷ *Drawing Conclusions* What made the decision in *Bush* v. *Gore* controversial?

PHOTO: Robert King/Getty Images News/Getty Images

resolve fixity of purpose, or resoluteness

terrorism the use of violence by nongovernmental groups against civilians to achieve a political goal by instilling fear and frightening governments into changing policies

interpretation the act or process of explaining or telling the meaning of

Bush v. Gore

Gore's lawyers returned to court, arguing that thousands of ballots remained uncounted. The Florida Supreme Court ordered all state counties to begin a hand recount of ballots rejected by the machines. As counting began, the U.S. Supreme Court ordered the recount to stop until it had issued its ruling. On December 12 in *Bush* v. *Gore*, the U.S. Supreme Court ruled 7–2 that because identical ballots might be treated differently by different vote counters, the recount violated the U.S. Constitution's equal protection clause. Bush remained the certified winner in Florida.

✓ **PROGRESS CHECK**

Exploring Issues Do you think that Gore winning the popular vote but not the electoral vote is controversial? Why?

September 11, 2001

GUIDING QUESTION *What contributed to the rise in terrorist groups, and why did these groups resort to violent attacks?*

On September 11, 2001, two passenger jets slammed into the two towers of the World Trade Center in New York City. Soon afterward, a third plane crashed into the Pentagon in Washington, D.C. Within about two hours, the World Trade Center collapsed in a billow of dust and debris, killing nearly 3,000 people. The airplanes did not crash accidentally. Hijackers deliberately flew them into the buildings. Hijackers had also seized a fourth airplane. Passengers on that flight had cell phones and had learned of the earlier attacks. Four passengers decided to fight the hijackers, and the plane crashed in a field in Pennsylvania.

A National Emergency

The attacks shocked Americans. Citizens donated food, money, supplies, and their own time toward the recovery effort. They rallied together to show their unity and **resolve.** On September 14, President Bush declared a national emergency. Congress authorized the use of force to fight whoever had attacked the nation. Osama bin Laden and his organization, al-Qaeda (al KY•duh), were soon identified as the plotters behind the attacks.

The South Tower of the World Trade Center bursts into flames after being struck by an airliner while the North Tower burns from an attack a few minutes earlier.

Middle East Terrorism and the United States

The 9/11 attacks were acts of **terrorism,** the use of violence by nongovernmental groups to achieve a political goal. Most terrorist attacks on Americans since World War II have been carried out by Middle Eastern groups.

In the 1920s, the United States invested in Middle East oil. The ruling families in some kingdoms grew wealthy, but most other people remained poor. Many Muslims feared their traditional values were weakening as the oil industrialists also brought Western ideas into the region. New movements arose calling for a strict **interpretation** of the Quran—the Muslim holy book—and a return to traditional religious laws. Some militant supporters began using terrorism to achieve their goals.

The United States's support of Israel also angered many in the Middle East. In 1947, as a response to global outrage over the Holocaust, the UN proposed to divide the British Mandate of Palestine into an Arab state and a Jewish state. The Jews accepted the UN plan and established Israel in 1948. Arab states responded by attacking Israel. The territory that the UN had proposed as an Arab state came under the control of Israel, Jordan, and Egypt. In the 1950s, Palestinians

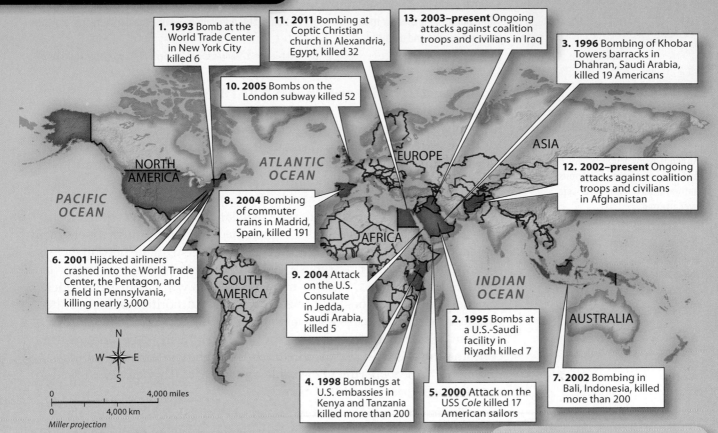

1. **1993** Bomb at the World Trade Center in New York City killed 6

11. **2011** Bombing at Coptic Christian church in Alexandria, Egypt, killed 32

13. **2003–present** Ongoing attacks against coalition troops and civilians in Iraq

3. **1996** Bombing of Khobar Towers barracks in Dhahran, Saudi Arabia, killed 19 Americans

10. **2005** Bombs on the London subway killed 52

12. **2002–present** Ongoing attacks against coalition troops and civilians in Afghanistan

8. **2004** Bombing of commuter trains in Madrid, Spain, killed 191

6. **2001** Hijacked airliners crashed into the World Trade Center, the Pentagon, and a field in Pennsylvania, killing nearly 3,000

9. **2004** Attack on the U.S. Consulate in Jedda, Saudi Arabia, killed 5

2. **1995** Bombs at a U.S.-Saudi facility in Riyadh killed 7

4. **1998** Bombings at U.S. embassies in Kenya and Tanzania killed more than 200

5. **2000** Attack on the USS *Cole* killed 17 American sailors

7. **2002** Bombing in Bali, Indonesia, killed more than 200

0 —— 4,000 miles
0 —— 4,000 km
Miller projection

began staging guerrilla raids and terrorist attacks against Israel. Since the United States gave aid to Israel, it became the target of Muslim hostility. In the 1970s, several Middle Eastern nations realized they could fight Israel and the United States by providing terrorists with money, weapons, and training. This is called **state-sponsored terrorism.** The governments of Libya, Syria, Iraq, and Iran have all sponsored terrorists.

The Rise of Al-Qaeda

In 1979 the Soviet Union invaded Afghanistan, and Muslims from across the world headed there to help fight the Soviets. Among them was Osama bin Laden. In 1988 bin Laden founded the organization called al-Qaeda or "the Base." This organization carried out attacks on U.S. embassies and other targets in the years leading up to the 9/11 attacks.

✔ **PROGRESS CHECK**

Analyzing Cause and Effect Why did Muslim hostility grow against the United States in the Middle East?

The War on Terrorism Begins

GUIDING QUESTION *What major actions marked the beginning of the United States's war on terrorism?*

On September 20, 2001, President Bush demanded that the Taliban regime in Afghanistan turn over bin Laden and his supporters and shut down all terrorist camps. The United States began building international support against terrorism and began deploying troops to the Middle East. The war would not end quickly, but it was a war the nation had to fight:

GEOGRAPHY CONNECTION

Terrorism is a worldwide threat that usually occurs without any warning and harms innocent people.

1 THE WORLD IN SPATIAL TERMS *On what continents have attacks occurred?*

2 HUMAN SYSTEMS *What can you infer about terrorist networks by the many targets that have been attacked?*

state-sponsored terrorism violent acts against civilians that are secretly supported by a government in order to attack other nations without going to war

Although many people were sickened and some died from a bioterrorist anthrax attack, no suspects were ever arrested.

▶ **CRITICAL THINKING**

Drawing Inferences Why did law enforcement officials determine that the appearance of anthrax was a terrorist attack?

obtain to gain possession of

anthrax a bacteria causing serious infection or death used to create biological weapons

PRIMARY SOURCE

❝Great harm has been done to us. We have suffered great loss. And in our grief and anger we have found our mission and our moment. . . . Our Nation—this generation—will lift a dark threat of violence from our people and our future.❞

—President George W. Bush, *Address to Joint Session of Congress,* September 20, 2001

Homeland Security and the USA PATRIOT Act

One effective way to fight terrorist groups is to cut off their funding. On September 24, President Bush issued an executive order freezing the financial assets of individuals and groups suspected of terrorism. He asked other nations to help, and soon some 80 nations had issued orders freezing the assets of the organizations and individuals on the American list.

To protect against further attacks, Bush created the Office of Homeland Security and asked Congress to pass legislation to help law enforcement agencies locate terrorist suspects. Congress had to balance Fourth Amendment protections against unreasonable search and seizure with the need to increase security, but in October 2001, Bush signed into law the antiterrorist bill called the USA PATRIOT Act. The law made it easier to wiretap suspects, track Internet communications, and seize voice mail. Authorities were permitted to conduct secret searches and were allowed to **obtain** a nationwide search warrant usable in any jurisdiction. In June 2002, Bush asked Congress to combine the agencies responsible for public safety into a new cabinet department, the Department of Homeland Security. This agency worked to coordinate efforts to fight terrorism.

Bioterrorism Strikes the United States On October 5, 2001, a new threat arose when a newspaper editor in Florida died from an anthrax infection. **Anthrax,** a type of bacteria, has been used to create biological weapons. Antibiotics can cure anthrax, but if left untreated, it can quickly become lethal. Anthrax was also found in offices in New York and Washington, D.C. It became clear that these anthrax attacks were being delivered via the postal service. As a result of these attacks, 5 people died and 17 were sickened.

The War in Afghanistan Begins On October 7, 2001, the United States began bombing al-Qaeda camps and Taliban military forces in Afghanistan. Addressing the nation, Bush explained that Islam and the Afghan people were not the enemy, and that the United States would send aid to refugees. He also declared that the war on terrorism would continue until victory was achieved.

✅ **PROGRESS CHECK**

Identifying What was the purpose of the Office of Homeland Security?

LESSON 1 REVIEW

Reviewing Vocabulary

1. *Stating* Why is anthrax a bioterrorism threat?

Using Your Notes

2. *Explaining* Review the notes that you took during this lesson and write a paragraph explaining why some groups in the Middle East disagree with U.S. foreign policy.

Answering the Guiding Questions

3. *Interpreting* Why was the presidential election of 2000 controversial?

4. *Listing* What contributed to the rise in terrorist groups, and why did these groups resort to violent attacks?

5. *Identifying* What major actions marked the beginning of the United States's war on terrorism?

Writing Activity

6. PERSUASIVE The USA PATRIOT Act gave law enforcement new ways to fight terrorism. Write a letter to a newspaper explaining why you are either for or against giving up some freedoms in exchange for increased security.

netw⊙rks

There's More Online!

☑ **IMAGE** Desolate Iran

☑ **TIME LINE** The Global War on Terrorism

☑ **VIDEO** Focusing on Afghanistan and Iraq

☑ **INTERACTIVE SELF-CHECK QUIZ**

Reading **HELP**DESK

Content Vocabulary

- **weapons of mass destruction (WMD)**

Academic Vocabulary

- **inspectors** • **eliminate**
- **significantly**

TAKING NOTES: *Organizing*

ACTIVITY As you read, use the following graphic organizer to show the different groups in Iraq.

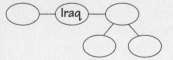

PHOTOS: (l to r)David Guttenfelder/AP Images, Scott Nelson/Getty Images News/Getty Images, Wathiq Khuzaie/Getty Images News/Getty Images, ALI YUSSEF/AFP/Getty Images, Murad Sezer/AP Images

LESSON 2
Focusing on Afghanistan and Iraq

ESSENTIAL QUESTIONS • *How is American culture shaped by a set of common values and practices?* • *How have disputes over ideas, values, and politics resulted in change?*

IT MATTERS BECAUSE

After the attacks of September 11, 2001, U.S. forces invaded Afghanistan, the Central Asian nation that had sheltered many al-Qaeda members. In 2003, troops invaded Iraq and toppled the regime of Saddam Hussein.

The Taliban and WMD

GUIDING QUESTION *Why did the United States want to overthrow the Taliban regime?*

Soon after the September 11 attacks, the United States launched a war in Afghanistan to bring down the Taliban regime that had sheltered Osama bin Laden and other members of al-Qaeda. U.S. warplanes bombed Taliban forces as the United States began sending military aid to the Northern Alliance, a coalition of Afghan groups that had been fighting the Taliban for several years. The U.S. bombing campaign quickly shattered the Taliban's defenses, and the Northern Alliance launched a massive attack. In December 2001, the Taliban government fell, and surviving members fled to the mountains of Afghanistan. Afghanistan slowly began to recover from decades of war.

Rebuilding Afghanistan

After the Taliban fled, the United States and its allies helped local Afghan leaders create a new government. Meanwhile, thousands of U.S. and allied troops arrived to act as peacekeepers. In 2003 NATO took command of the peacekeeping. Afghanistan held its first nationwide democratic election in December 2004, and Hamid Karzai was elected president. One year later, the Afghan people elected a National Assembly. Despite these successes, Afghanistan continued to suffer from violence. The U.S. military has remained in Afghanistan in an effort to help stabilize the country.

The Search for Bin Laden

U.S. intelligence agencies believed Osama bin Laden had fled to Pakistan. Reports in the summer of 2010 suggested he was hiding north of Pakistan's capital city of Islamabad. In May 2011, bin Laden's

Hamid Karzai (1957–)

Hamid Karzai was elected president in Afghanistan's first democratic election on October 9, 2004. He had worked to remove the Taliban and its supporters from Afghanistan. In 2001, participants of the UN-sponsored Bonn Conference elected him Chairman of the Interim Administration. He was then elected President of the Transitional Government on June 13, 2002, by members of the Emergency Loya Jirga (grand council). Karzai had been a strong proponent of establishing a Loya Jirga, believing it to be the only way to resolve the differences among the various Afghan factions. Though there have been charges of corruption in his administration, as president, Karzai has been an advocate of human rights and has appointed several women to his cabinet.

▶ **CRITICAL THINKING**
Drawing Conclusions Why do you think Hamid Karzai was elected president of Afghanistan?

weapons of mass destruction (WMD) weapons—including nuclear, chemical, and biological—capable of killing large numbers of people all at once

inspector a person appointed to examine facilities, usually in search of specific items, in regard to safety or quality

exact location was verified and President Obama ordered U.S. troops to attack. Bin Laden was killed after a brief fight and DNA tests verified his identity. President Obama announced to the nation that "justice has been done."

Tracking Down Al-Qaeda

Former President George W. Bush responded to bin Laden's death by reminding the nation that "the fight against terror goes on, but . . . [n]o matter how long it takes, justice will be done." During the almost decade-long search for bin Laden, the U.S. and its allies captured or killed hundreds of al-Qaeda members. In 2003, Pakistani and U.S. forces captured Khalid Shaikh Mohammed, the man suspected of planning the September 11 attacks. Between 2002 and 2006, the U.S. government believes to have prevented at least 10 major al-Qaeda attacks, including at least three on the United States and two on Great Britain.

Iraq and Weapons of Mass Destruction

The terrorist attacks of 9/11 showed that groups such as al-Qaeda were determined to kill as many Americans as possible. President Bush and his advisers were deeply concerned that terrorists might acquire **weapons of mass destruction (WMD)**—including nuclear, chemical, and biological weapons—that could kill large numbers of people all at once.

During the Cold War, the United States relied upon a policy of deterrence to prevent the use of such weapons. The rise of state-sponsored terrorism created a new problem. If a nation secretly gave weapons to terrorists who then used them against the United States, the U.S. military might not know whom to attack in response to their use.

The "Axis of Evil"

In his 2002 State of the Union address, President Bush warned that an "axis of evil" made up of Iraq, Iran, and North Korea posed a grave threat. Each nation had been known to sponsor terrorism and was suspected of developing weapons of mass destruction. Bush warned that the United States "will not permit the world's most dangerous regimes to threaten us with the world's most destructive weapons."

The president and his advisers believed Iraq to be the most immediate danger. It had used chemical weapons against the Kurds, an ethnic group in northern Iraq. After the 1991 Gulf War, UN **inspectors** found evidence that Iraq had developed biological weapons and had been working on a nuclear bomb. Between 1991 and 1998, Iraq appeared to be hiding weapons of mass destruction from UN inspectors. In 1998 the Iraqi government expelled the inspectors. In response, President Clinton ordered a massive bombing attack on Iraq to destroy its ability to make such weapons. Despite the attack, intelligence agencies continued to believe Iraq was hiding weapons of mass destruction.

An Ultimatum to Iraq

In 2002 President Bush decided to deal with Iraq. On September 12, he asked the United Nations for a new resolution against Iraq. If Iraq's dictator, Saddam Hussein, wanted peace, he would have to give up Iraq's weapons of mass destruction, readmit the UN weapons inspectors, stop supporting terrorism, and stop oppressing his people. Although he was asking the United Nations to pass a resolution, the president made it clear that the United States would act with or without UN support. Bush asked

PHOTO: David Guttenfelder/AP Images; TEXT: Statement by President George W. Bush on bin Laden's Death, May 1, 2011.

Congress to authorize the use of force against Iraq, which it did. Later, the United Nations approved a new resolution against Iraq that threatened "serious consequences" if Iraq did not comply.

significantly in a way that is important enough to have an effect

✓ **PROGRESS CHECK**

Identifying Why did President Bush call Iraq, Iran, and North Korea the "axis of evil"?

Confronting Iraq

GUIDING QUESTION *What factors led to the U.S. invasion of Iraq?*

In November 2002, Iraq agreed to readmit UN weapons inspectors. It then submitted a statement admitting it had weapons of mass destruction before the Gulf War, but denying it currently had them. Secretary of State Colin Powell said that Iraq's declaration contained lies and was in "material breach" of the UN resolution.

As the United States and a coalition of some 30 nations prepared for war with Iraq, others in the UN Security Council argued that the inspectors should be given more time to find evidence of Iraq's WMD programs. By March 2003, inspectors still had found nothing, and the United States began pressing the United Nations to authorize the use of force.

France and Russia, two UN Security Council members with veto power, refused to back such a resolution. As war became imminent, world opinion divided between those who supported the United States and those who opposed an attack on Iraq. Around the world, antiwar protesters staged rallies and marches. Several nations that had supported the United States in its war on terror and had sent troops to Afghanistan—including France, Germany, and Canada—refused to join the coalition against Iraq. Saudi Arabia and Turkey—both American allies—refused to allow the United States to attack Iraq from their territories. The only nation bordering Iraq that granted permission to use its territory was Kuwait.

The Invasion Begins

On March 20, 2003, the U.S.-led coalition forces attacked Iraq. More than 150,000 U.S. troops, some 45,000 British troops, as well as a few hundred special forces from Australia and Poland took part in the invasion. Much of the Iraqi army dissolved as soldiers refused to risk their lives for Saddam Hussein. A few fierce battles took place, but the Iraqis were unable to slow the coalition advance **significantly.** On May 1, President Bush declared that the major combat was over. About 140 Americans and several thousand Iraqis had died. Hussein was captured in late 2003. After a prolonged trial, an Iraqi court found him guilty of ordering mass executions. He was executed in 2006.

Insurgents and Reconstruction

Soon after the coalition took control of the country, small groups of Iraqis began staging bombings, sniper attacks, and sporadic battles against coalition forces. Some carrying out the attacks were former members of Saddam Hussein's military. Others were affiliated with al-Qaeda and other radical Muslim groups who believed the invasion offered a chance to build support in the Muslim world by organizing resistance to the United States. Militias belonging to the different religious and ethnic groups in Iraq also carried out some attacks.

The war in Iraq relied heavily on advanced technology. U.S. forces used new tools such as remote-controlled drone bombers and laser-guided pointers to precisely target enemy bunkers.

▶ **CRITICAL THINKING**

Interpreting What advantages does this soldier seem to have over the enemy?

The majority of Iraq's population is Shia Muslim, but there is also a large Sunni Muslim minority. The Sunni are themselves divided between Sunni Arabs, who ruled the country under Saddam Hussein's leadership, and Sunni Kurds. The collapse of Hussein's dictatorship renewed old hostilities among these groups, forcing coalition troops to protect them from attacks from each other's militias.

Having aimed to overthrow a tyrant and **eliminate** the possibility of weapons of mass destruction being given to terrorists, the United States found itself trying to suppress an insurgency, prevent a civil war, and establish a new Iraqi government. The United States and its allies spent more than $30 billion to improve infrastructure, but insurgent attacks slowed these efforts. Despite the problems, Iraq's economy began to grow rapidly and a substantial improvement in living standards took place.

U.S. policy makers now faced a dilemma. If they pulled troops out too soon, Iraq might fall into civil war and provide a safe haven and breeding ground for terrorist groups. At the same time, the longer the United States stayed, the more its presence might stir resentment and support for terrorist groups. The best solution seemed to be to get a functioning, democratic Iraqi government in place as quickly as possible and then train its forces to take over the country's security. To do this, in January 2005, the Iraqi people went to the polls in huge numbers for the first free elections in their country's history. After much debate, voters then overwhelmingly approved a new constitution in October 2005.

Problems in Iraq

Many Americans were encouraged when large numbers of Iraqis turned out to vote in democratic elections, but hope for peace in Iraq soon faded. Many Americans had expected the war to end quickly, but between 2003 and 2006, insurgents killed more than 3,000 U.S. soldiers. As the fighting dragged on, support for the war began to decline. Also, the failure to find any WMD added to growing controversy as to whether the war had been a mistake.

The elections were followed by a rise in sectarian violence as Sunni and Shia militias turned against each other. Ongoing suicide bombings, kidnappings, and attacks on U.S. soldiers set a majority of Americans against the war. As a *New York Times* editorial argued:

> **PRIMARY SOURCE**
>
> ❝Iraq is becoming a country that America should be ashamed to support, let alone occupy. The nation as a whole is sliding closer to open civil war. In its capital, thugs kidnap and torture innocent civilians with impunity, then murder them for their religious beliefs. . . . The stories about innocent homeowners and storekeepers who are dragged from their screaming families and killed by . . . militias are heartbreaking, as is the thought that the United States, in its hubris, helped bring all this to pass.❞
>
> —from the *New York Times*, April 2, 2006

eliminate to remove or get rid of

In 2005 Iraqis were able to vote in their first free elections.

▶ **CRITICAL THINKING**
Making Predictions Will regular elections lead to a more stable national government in Iraq?

Despite problems of lingering violence and uncertainty, many began to rebuild a shattered Iraq.

▶ **CRITICAL THINKING**
Constructing Arguments What was the most important U.S. accomplishment in Iraq? Why?

PHOTOS: (t)Wathiq Khuzaie/Getty Images News/Getty Images, (b)ALI YUSSEF/AFP/Getty Images

A U.S. Army soldier plays soccer with Iraqi children while on patrol in Baghdad.

▶ **CRITICAL THINKING**
Constructing Arguments Was Operation Iraqi Freedom a success? Why or why not?

PHOTO: Murad Sezer/AP Images

Democrats demanded the president set a timetable for withdrawing U.S. troops, a policy that President Bush described as "cut and run."

Troops Surge to Iraq

In 2006 Secretary of Defense Donald Rumsfeld resigned, and President Bush appointed Robert Gates to replace him. Bush then announced a plan to send a "surge" of some 20,000 more troops to Iraq to restore order in Baghdad, where the violence was concentrated. With the additional surge of troops, General David Petraeus began clearing and holding areas of Baghdad that had been plagued by crime and insurgent attacks. His forces also began reaching out to Sunni groups in western Iraq that had been opposed to the American presence.

In the western province of Anbar, a militant group known as al-Qaeda in Iraq (AQI) was trying to impose a militant version of Islam through murder and intimidation. The Sunni groups in that area began working with U.S. forces to fight AQI. These actions helped change the course of the war.

By the fall of 2008, violence in Iraq had been dramatically reduced. Coalition forces had handed over control of 12 of Iraq's 18 provinces to the Iraqi government and coalition casualties were lower than at any time since the war began in 2003. In August 2010, Operation Iraqi Freedom officially ended as the number of U.S. troops remaining in Iraq was reduced to about 50,000. Their job was primarily to train Iraqi troops.

✓ **PROGRESS CHECK**

Summarizing What dilemmas did the United States face if troops were pulled out of Iraq too soon?

LESSON 2 REVIEW

Reviewing Vocabulary

1. **Defining** What are weapons of mass destruction?

2. **Comparing and Contrasting** What is the difference between terrorism and state-sponsored terrorism?

Using Your Notes

3. **Explaining** Review the notes you have taken describing the different groups in Iraq. Then explain why the fighting continued in Iraq after President Bush declared the major combat was over.

Answering the Guiding Questions

4. **Summarizing** Why did the United States want to overthrow the Taliban regime?

5. **Identifying** What factors led to the U.S. invasion of Iraq?

Writing Activity

6. **DESCRIPTIVE** Suppose that you are an Iraqi who has recently voted in your first election. Write a journal entry that explains how you feel following your vote.

networks

There's More Online!

- ☑ **BIOGRAPHY** Condoleezza Rice
- ☑ **BIOGRAPHY** Nancy Pelosi
- ☑ **IMAGE** PATRIOT Act Protests
- ☑ **IMAGE** Hurricane Katrina
- ☑ **VIDEO** Domestic Challenges
- ☑ **INTERACTIVE SELF-CHECK QUIZ**

Reading **HELP**DESK

Content Vocabulary

- swing vote

Academic Vocabulary

- controversial

TAKING NOTES: *Outlining*

ACTIVITY Use the following graphic organizer to create an outline using the major headings of the lesson.

Domestic Challenges
I. Security vs. Liberty
A.
B.
II.

LESSON 3
Domestic Challenges

ESSENTIAL QUESTIONS · *How is American culture shaped by a set of common values and practices?* · *How have disputes over ideas, values, and politics resulted in change?*

IT MATTERS BECAUSE

After a close campaign, President Bush was reelected in 2004, but scandals and continued difficulties in Iraq helped Democrats win control of Congress in 2006.

Security vs. Liberty

GUIDING QUESTION *How did the September 11th terrorist attacks and the wars in Afghanistan and Iraq increase tension between the need for national security and protecting civil liberties?*

In early 2004, President Bush's approval ratings began to fall. The ongoing war in Iraq and the failure of inspectors to find any weapons of mass destruction weakened his support, as did the scandal at the Iraqi prison of Abu Ghraib, where some prisoners were abused by American soldiers. These events gave Democrats the opportunity to mount a serious challenge in the 2004 election.

President Bush and Vice President Cheney were renominated by the Republicans. The Democrats nominated Massachusetts senator John Kerry for president and North Carolina senator John Edwards for vice president. Despite the problems in Iraq, voters felt it safer to stay with the incumbent. Nationwide, Bush won both the popular and the electoral vote.

Prisoners at Guantanamo

The war on terror heightened the tension between national security and civil liberties. People questioned whether terrorist attacks justified limits on civil liberties and whether captured terrorists had any rights at all.

In 2004 President Bush decided to hold captured members of al-Qaeda at the American military base in Guantanamo Bay, Cuba, where they could be interrogated. This decision was very **controversial.** Some people argued that the prisoners should have the right to a lawyer, formal charges, and a proper trial. The Bush administration insisted that the prisoners were enemy combatants, not suspects charged with a crime, and did not have the right to appeal their detentions to an American court. The administration also declared that the procedures regarding the treatment of prisoners, as specified in the Geneva Conventions, did not apply to terrorists since they were not part of any nation's armed forces.

The Supreme Court disagreed. In *Rasul* v. *Bush* (2004), the Court ruled that foreign prisoners who claimed that they were unlawfully imprisoned had the right to have their cases heard in court. In response, the Bush administration created military tribunals to hear detainee cases. The Supreme Court struck this plan down in 2006 in *Hamdan* v. *Rumsfeld*.

Bush then asked Congress to establish new tribunals that met the Court's objections. Congress passed the Military Commissions Act, which stated that noncitizens captured as enemy combatants had no right to file writs of habeas corpus. In 2008, in *Boumediene* v. *Bush,* the Supreme Court ruled that the detainees had a right to habeas corpus and declared that section of the Military Commissions Act unconstitutional.

Domestic Surveillance

As part of the war on terror, the National Security Agency (NSA) began wiretapping domestic telephone calls made to overseas locations when they believed one party in the call was a member of al-Qaeda or affiliated with al-Qaeda. When the monitoring program became public in 2005, it created a controversy. Civil rights groups argued that the program violated the Fourth Amendment. In 2006 a federal judge declared the wiretapping to be unconstitutional, but the following year an appeals court overturned the judge's decision. When Congress began drafting legislation to address the issue, the Bush administration suspended the program and announced that future wiretaps would require a warrant from the Foreign Intelligence Surveillance Court.

☑ **PROGRESS CHECK**

Constructing Arguments Do you agree with the Supreme Court's decision about the rights of detainees at Guantanamo Bay? Why or why not?

A Stormy Second Term

GUIDING QUESTION *What were the successes and failures of President George W. Bush's second term?*

President Bush's reelection convinced him that he had a mandate to continue his policies. He explained in a press conference: "[W]hen you win, there is a feeling that the people have spoken and embraced your point of view. And that's what I intend to tell the Congress. . . . I earned capital in the campaign, political capital. And now I intend to spend it."

Debating Social Security

One priority of Bush's second term domestic policy was Social Security reform. He proposed that workers be allowed to put 4 percent of their income in private accounts rather than in Social Security. He believed that private accounts would grow rapidly and help cover the expected shortfall in Social Security accounts. Democrats argued that privatizing any part of Social Security was dangerous. With the public unenthusiastic, the plan was never brought to a vote in Congress. Although this plan failed, Bush did convince Congress to enact a new prescription drug program for seniors. Under the new program, provided by Medicare, people age 65 and older can sign up for insurance that helps cover the cost of prescription drugs.

PHOTO: Mike Simons/Corbis News/CORBIS

controversial given to controversy, disputable

Critics charged that the Bush administration's national security actions violated people's civil liberties.

▶ **CRITICAL THINKING**
Drawing Inferences What civil liberties did opponents of the national security program believe were being violated?

Hurricane Katrina ravaged New Orleans, Louisiana. During the flooding, people wrote messages on their roofs in the hope that rescuers would see them.

▶ **CRITICAL THINKING**

Identifying Central Issues Why were Americans angered over President Bush's response to Hurricane Katrina?

swing vote a vote that may sometimes lean conservative and other times liberal

Hurricane Katrina

On August 29, 2005, Hurricane Katrina smashed into the Gulf Coast of the United States, spreading devastation from Florida to Louisiana. The fierce winds, rain, high tides, and storm surges destroyed buildings, roads, and electrical lines, left thousands of people homeless, and cost at least 1,200 lives. After the hurricane had passed, rising waters breached levees protecting New Orleans and flooded the low-lying city, causing thousands to flee to rooftops and for shelter in the convention center and at the Superdome. Waiting for days with little food, clean water, or information from authorities, survivors were shown on television news in deplorable conditions.

Reporters asked why the government was not responding more quickly. The mayor of New Orleans was faulted for not issuing a mandatory evacuation until the storm was less than a day away and for having failed to provide public transportation. The Federal Emergency Management Agency (FEMA) seemed unprepared in its response. With polls showing a sharp drop in confidence in his administration, President Bush fired the head of FEMA and traveled to New Orleans to pledge federal funds for rebuilding the city. Congress approved $200 billion for the massive task.

New Supreme Court Judges

In 2005 President Bush filled two vacancies on the Supreme Court. In the spring of 2005, Justice Sandra Day O'Connor announced her retirement. Although appointed by President Reagan, Justice O'Connor had been a pivotal **swing vote** on the Court, sometimes siding with conservatives, sometimes with liberals. As her replacement, Bush nominated federal judge John G. Roberts, Jr., a conservative who was well regarded in the Senate. Before the Senate could act, however, Chief Justice William Rehnquist died. Bush then named Roberts to replace him. Again attempting to fill Justice O'Connor's vacancy, President Bush nominated federal judge Samuel Alito, Jr., a well-known conservative justice. Roberts and Alito were confirmed by the Senate.

The 2006 Midterm Elections

The first two years of President Bush's second term had not gone well. At the same time, Americans had also grown frustrated with Congress. The Republican majority seemed awash in scandals. Two Republicans had resigned from Congress after being convicted of corruption, and House majority leader Tom DeLay had resigned after being indicted for violating campaign finance laws. Congress seemed unable to control spending, partly because Republicans and Democrats had been adding an increasing number of special funding requests to spending bills.

Voters expressed their unhappiness with the president and the Republican Congress in 2006. The Democrats won a majority in both the House and the Senate for the first time since 1992. House Democrats then elected California representative Nancy Pelosi to be the first female Speaker of the House of Representatives. She summed up Democrats' interpretation of their victory:

PRIMARY SOURCE

❝The election of 2006 was a call to change, not merely to change the control of Congress, but for a new direction for our country. . . . Our Founders envisioned a new America driven by optimism, opportunity, and courage. . . . Now it is our responsibility to carry forth that vision of a new America into the 21st century.❞

—from a speech to the House of Representatives, January 4, 2007

Despite promises to end the war and change how Congress operated, Speaker Pelosi and other Democrats were not able to get enough votes to cut funding, set a deadline for pulling troops out of Iraq, or reduce spending. The American economy was on a downturn.

Economic Recession

By 2008, the American economy was in crisis. In 2007 many people with low incomes or poor credit began defaulting on their mortgage payments. At the same time, housing prices began to fall. People could no longer borrow against their home values, and banks across the country that had relied on mortgage-backed investments did not know what their investments were worth. Without adequate "real" funds to lend, banks reduced the amounts they lent, and many businesses feared they could not borrow enough money to keep operating. This led to a long recession and caused a number of well-known investment banking firms to face bankruptcy and collapse. Companies began laying off workers in response to the financial crisis. By January 2009, the unemployment rate was up to 7.2%. The country was in an economic recession.

✓ **PROGRESS CHECK**

Making Inferences What effect did Hurricane Katrina have on the Bush administration?

Thinking Like a
HISTORIAN

Evaluating Information

Suppose you needed to write a report about an election. The Internet might be the first place you would look for information. How do you evaluate if the information you find is valid and unbiased? You should check to see if the organization or author is identified. If you are unable to verify the creator of the site, be wary of trusting the information. If a site refers to sources, that is a clue that the information is reliable. Also, the information should be presented factually and objectively, without bias.

LESSON 3 REVIEW

Reviewing Vocabulary
1. *Explaining* What is meant by the term *swing vote*?

Using Your Notes
2. *Summarizing* Review your notes and write a summary of the major domestic events of President Bush's second term.

Answering the Guiding Questions
3. *Making Connections* How did the September 11th terrorist attacks and the wars in Afghanistan and Iraq increase tension between the need for national security and protecting civil liberties?

4. *Evaluating* What were the successes and failures of President George W. Bush's second term?

Writing Activity
5. NARRATIVE Write a journal entry describing President Bush's second term that will be read by students 50 years in the future. Be clear and concise with your descriptions of these events.

networks

There's More Online!

- ☑ **CHART/GRAPH** GDP
- ☑ **CHART/GRAPH** S&P 500 Stock Index
- ☑ **CHART/GRAPH** Unemployment
- ☑ **SLIDE SHOW** BP Oil Spill
- ☑ **MAP** 2008 Presidential Election
- ☑ **VIDEO** The Obama Presidency
- ☑ **INTERACTIVE SELF-CHECK QUIZ**

Reading **HELP**DESK

Content Vocabulary
- **earmark**

Academic Vocabulary
- **monitor**
- **procedure**

TAKING NOTES: *Outlining*

ACTIVITY As you read about key events in the Obama candidacy and presidency, use the major headings of the lesson to create an outline similar to the one below.

```
      The Obama Presidency
  I. The Election of 2008
     A.
     B.
  II.
     A.
     B.
```

LESSON 4
The Obama Presidency

ESSENTIAL QUESTIONS · *How is American culture shaped by a set of common values and practices?* · *How have disputes over ideas, values, and politics resulted in change?*

IT MATTERS BECAUSE
The 2008 election of Barack Obama as the nation's first African American president was a watershed event. The nation became increasingly polarized, however, as he began to carry out his agenda. After the 2010 midterm elections, the Republicans regained control of the House.

The Election of 2008

GUIDING QUESTION *What issues and events attracted support for Barack Obama's presidential campaign?*

In 2007 a major financial crisis developed. Millions of Americans found themselves unable to make payments on their home mortgages. Financial institutions failed. As the 2008 election approached, the economy had replaced the war in Iraq as the most important issue for most Americans.

Choosing the Candidates

Senator John McCain of Arizona, a widely admired hero of the Vietnam War, won the Republican nomination for president. He chose Sarah Palin, the conservative governor of Alaska, as his running mate.

Illinois senator Barack Obama bested New York senator Hillary Clinton to win the Democratic nomination. Obama had delivered the keynote address at the 2004 Democratic National Convention. His speech impressed Democrats and made him a national political figure. Senator Joe Biden of Delaware was his running mate. Biden's 35 years in the Senate helped balance criticism of Obama's relative inexperience.

Obama Wins

In October 2008, President Bush and Congress passed a $700 billion bailout for the nation's financial institutions, intended to help the worsening crisis. Americans opposed it. With the approval ratings of the president and Congress at all-time lows, McCain and Obama both promised change. Obama made good use of the Internet and formed a strong grassroots network of young supporters. On Election Day, Obama won 53 percent of the popular vote and 365 electoral votes.

It was the biggest victory for a Democratic candidate since 1964. Obama, the first African American to win the presidency, exulted:

Barack Obama waves to the crowd in Chicago's Grant Park on election night.

PRIMARY SOURCE

❝ This is our moment . . . to put our people back to work and open doors of opportunity for our kids; to restore prosperity and promote the cause of peace; to reclaim the American Dream and reaffirm that fundamental truth—that out of many, we are one; that . . . where we are met with . . . those who tell us that we can't, we will respond with that timeless creed that sums up the spirit of a people: Yes We Can. ❞
—from the Address at Grant Park, November 4, 2008

✓ **PROGRESS CHECK**

Analyzing How did the passing of the $700 billion bailout affect the 2008 election?

Financial Meltdown

GUIDING QUESTION *How did the economic recession and housing crisis affect Obama's domestic goals?*

When Americans voted President Obama into office, many expected him to improve the shaky economy. Obama's domestic agenda proposed to create jobs, relieve suffering families, assist home owners, and ease the financial crisis. Yet as the economy worsened, Obama's specific plans to solve the nation's problems drew criticism. Some people believed he was not doing enough, while others argued that he was misusing government authority by doing too much.

The Economy in 2009

Despite the Bush administration's bailout of financial institutions and insurance companies, the American economy continued to weaken. More Americans lost their homes, and banks closed. Many large companies reported record losses. They laid off workers, contributing to a spike in unemployment. With fewer workers, less money went into Social Security, threatening the sustainability of the program. As the crisis spread worldwide, global trade lessened and the world economy shrank.

Obama's Response

In response to the failing economy, Obama signed the American Recovery and Reinvestment Act in February 2009. The act aimed to stimulate the economy by providing tax cuts to working families and small businesses. It allocated federal funds for growth and investment as well as for education, health, and other entitlement programs. Many Americans were still angry about Bush's bailout plan. They believed it favored large businesses at the expense of ordinary people. To counter this anger, the act set up a system to **monitor** how the recovery money was spent. Obama pushed additional legislation through the Democrat-controlled Congress in July 2010. Among other things, this financial reform bill provided protection for consumers. It also called for more government oversight of financial institutions and large companies.

monitor to observe, oversee, or regulate

By the end of 2009, there were signs that some of Obama's measures were working. The nation's gross domestic product (GDP) had climbed. Some of the large businesses that had accepted stimulus funds were reporting gains. The unemployment rate, however, continued to rise, as did the federal deficit. And many Americans were uncomfortable with what they viewed as a rapidly growing role for the federal government in the economy.

✓ **PROGRESS CHECK**

Identifying Central Issues Do you think the American Recovery and Reinvestment Act helped stimulate the economy?

PHOTO: Chris McGrath/Getty Images News/Getty Images

Foreclosures averaged between 4–6% for many years.

▶ CRITICAL THINKING

1 *Evaluating* What was the percentage increase in foreclosures between 2007 and 2009?

2 *Making Generalizations* Why was there a steady rise in foreclosures beginning in 2007?

The weak economy caused many people to struggle financially. As a result, many Americans either sold their homes or lost them to foreclosure.

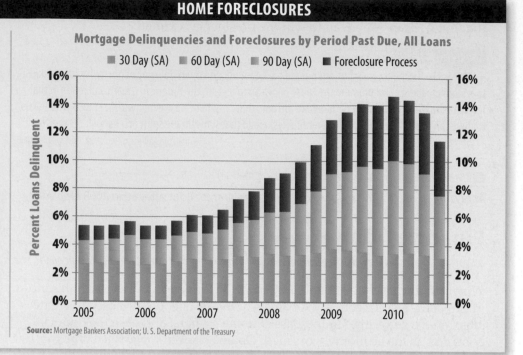

Mortgage Delinquencies and Foreclosures by Period Past Due, All Loans

■ 30 Day (SA)   ■ 60 Day (SA)   ■ 90 Day (SA)   ■ Foreclosure Process

Percent Loans Delinquent

2005   2006   2007   2008   2009   2010

Source: Mortgage Bankers Association; U. S. Department of the Treasury

Health Care Reform, Energy, and the Environment

GUIDING QUESTION *What other major domestic events defined Obama's first years as president?*

As a candidate and president-elect, Obama stressed many other domestic issues. Two priorities were to reform and expand the health care system and to solve the nation's energy and environmental problems.

Health Care Reform

Obama's health care reform plan aimed to lower health care costs, introduce better **procedures** for delivering care, and insure all Americans. In a speech to Congress delivered in 2009, he said, "We are the only advanced democracy on Earth—the only wealthy nation—that allows such hardships for millions of its people. There are now more than thirty million American citizens who cannot get coverage."

procedure a particular way of conducting or engaging in an activity

Obama wanted to pay for the plan through higher taxes on the wealthy and by reducing wasteful spending. Yet some Americans opposed what they saw as another expensive government intrusion. Months of heated partisan debate took place within Congress. No Republican voted for the final bill that passed in March 2010, and many vowed to overturn it. Though Obama had promised to reform the system of **earmarks,** the bill contained many.

earmarks specifications added by both Republicans and Democrats for the expenditure of federal money for particular projects

The bill extended coverage to about 32 million more Americans who could not previously afford it. It prevented insurers from denying insurance to people who had preexisting medical conditions. It also gave tax credits to small businesses that provide health care to their employees. According to the White House, it would lower costs, strengthen the Medicare program, and expand the Medicaid program.

Energy Policy and the Environment

President Obama's energy plan enforced limits on the amount of pollution companies could emit. Conservatives who opposed the idea stalled the bill in Congress. Then, an environmental disaster struck the Gulf of Mexico

PHOTO: Tannen Maury/epa/CORBIS

in April 2010. A British Petroleum (BP) oil rig exploded, sending nearly 5 million barrels of oil into the Gulf. It was the worst marine oil spill in history. Commercial fishing and tourism in the Gulf region suffered. Obama required BP to create a $20 billion fund to assist people affected by the oil spill. Federal agencies directed the recovery, which lasted through October.

✔ **PROGRESS CHECK**

Drawing Conclusions How did the British Petroleum disaster in the Gulf of Mexico affect the environment?

2010 Midterm Elections

GUIDING QUESTION *What did the results of the elections say about the mood of the nation at that time?*

As the 2010 midterm elections approached, Obama's approval rating was at a low point. Many Americans felt that the stimulus and health care bills had been too expensive and had not strengthened the economy. A grassroots movement called the "Tea Party" sprang up to protest the Obama administration. The movement took its name from a reference to the Boston Tea Party protests against British taxation. Most in the movement opposed what they called "big government"—including taxes, the health care program, and the economic stimulus plans of Bush and Obama. Yet they disagreed on many other issues.

Republicans gained a rousing win in the midterm elections. Republicans gained 60 seats in the House of Representatives and took back control of that House of Congress. It was the biggest shift in power in over 60 years. The Republicans also captured six Senate seats, though the Democrats maintained the majority. It was clear that Americans of all political beliefs needed to work together to solve the issues facing the nation. In a White House conference a day after the election, President Obama said, "Over the last two years, we've made progress. But, clearly, too many Americans haven't felt that progress yet, and they told us that yesterday." The United States had obstacles to overcome: the worst economic depression in 70 years and two ongoing wars. Yet opportunities to innovate in the nation's economic system gave new challenges. The commitment remained to strengthen the nation's political institutions as a foundation to address any future conflict.

✔ **PROGRESS CHECK**

Synthesizing What issues were raised by the Tea Party movement?

Thinking Like a
HISTORIAN

Interpreting Significance

When President Obama chose Sonia Sotomayor and Elena Kagan to fill vacancies on the U. S. Supreme Court, he became the first president to successfully nominate two women to the nation's highest court. These women are now the third and fourth female justices in the nation's history. Born and raised in a Puerto Rican family in the Bronx, New York, Sotomayor is the nation's first justice of Latin American descent. Determining the significance of both women's service to the Supreme Court will be based on their interpretations of the legal questions that come before the Court.

LESSON 4 REVIEW

Reviewing Vocabulary

1. *Making Inferences* Why did Obama sign a bill with earmarks when he had opposed them at one time?

Using Your Notes

2. *Summarizing* Use your notes to write a paragraph summarizing the main domestic issues of the Obama presidency.

Answering the Guiding Questions

3. *Identifying Central Issues* What issues and events attracted support for Barack Obama's presidential campaign?

4. *Identifying Cause and Effect* How did the economic recession and housing crisis affect Obama's domestic goals?

5. *Specifying* What other major domestic events defined Obama's first years as president?

6. *Interpreting* What did the results of the elections say about the mood of the nation at that time?

Writing Activity

7. PERSUASIVE Write a persuasive journal entry describing current events that will be read by students 50 years in the future. Be clear and concise with your description of these events.

Directions: On a separate sheet of paper, answer the questions below. Make sure you read carefully and answer all parts to the question.

Lesson Review

Lesson 1

1 *Drawing Conclusions* Why were chads and voter intentions two key issues in the Florida recount during the 2000 presidential election?

2 *Identifying Cause and Effect* What security-related changes did the federal government make after the attacks of September 11, 2001?

Lesson 2

3 *Explaining* Why did the United States launch a war in Afghanistan in 2001?

4 *Analyzing* What was the significance of the UN weapons inspectors' activities when the United States was attempting to negotiate with Iraq in 2002 and early 2003?

Lesson 3

5 *Analyzing* Why did the National Security Agency wiretap domestic phone calls, and why was this action controversial?

6 *Listing* Which members of the Supreme Court were added during President Bush's second term as president?

Lesson 4

7 *Evaluating* What are two aspects of the recession that the American Recovery and Reinvestment Act of 2009 was designed to combat?

8 *Identifying Cause and Effect* How was the membership of the House of Representatives affected by the 2010 midterm elections?

21st Century Skills

9 **EXPLAINING CONTINUITY AND CHANGE** How did the September 11 attacks lead to the USA PATRIOT Act?

10 **EXPLAINING CONTINUITY AND CHANGE** Explain why you think Barack Obama's election as president in 2008 was historically significant.

Exploring the Essential Questions

11 *Evaluating Counter Arguments* Write the text for a short debate on a political or legal issue. Describe two conflicting views on the issue, and present counter arguments. Then write a paragraph about the role of disputes in creating change, and the ways in which American culture is shaped by a set of common values and practices.

DBQ Document-Based Questions

Use the documents to answer the following questions.

Below are comments about the controversial USA PATRIOT Act.

PRIMARY SOURCE

❝If we were to take the position, reflected in provisions in the USA PATRIOT Act, that the government can invade our privacy and gather evidence that can be used against us based on no suspicion whatsoever that we've done anything wrong, but simply because the government wants to gather evidence . . . then we will have rendered that Fourth Amendment principle essentially meaningless.❞

—Congressman Bob Barr (R-GA),
from "Problems with the USA PATRIOT Act," December 6, 2005

❝Zero. That's the number of substantiated USA PATRIOT Act civil liberties violations. Extensive congressional oversight found no violations.❞

—Congressman James Sensenbrenner (R-WI),
from "No rights have been violated," March 1, 2006

12 *Analyzing Primary Sources* According to Congressman Barr, which constitutional right does the PATRIOT Act violate, and how does it do this?

13 *Evaluating Counter Arguments* What is Congressman Sensenbrenner's response to the accusation that the PATRIOT Act violates civil rights?

Extended-Response Question

14 *Making Connections* Write an essay that describes upheaval in U.S. domestic and foreign policy in the twenty-first century. How have controversial events challenged both political leaders and the general public?

Need Extra Help?

If You've Missed Question	**1**	**2**	**3**	**4**	**5**	**6**	**7**	**8**	**9**	**10**	**11**	**12**	**13**	**14**
Go to page	695	698	699	700	705	706	709	711	698	708	694	712	712	694

- Content vocabulary are words that relate to American history content.
- Words that have an asterisk (*) are academic vocabulary. They help you understand your school subjects.
- All vocabulary words are **boldfaced** or **highlighted in yellow** in your textbook.

ENGLISH — A — ESPAÑOL

ENGLISH	ESPAÑOL
*abandon to withdraw protection, support, or help (p. 540)	***abandonar** retirar la protección, el apoyo o la ayuda (pág. 540)
abolition the immediate ending of slavery (p. 177)	**abolición** finalización inmediata de la esclavitud (pág. 177)
*academic associated with higher learning at a scholarly institution (p. 369)	***académico** asociado con el aprendizaje superior en una institución educativa (pág. 369)
*access freedom or ability to obtain or make use of (p. 347)	***acceso** libertad o capacidad de obtener o usar (pág. 347)
*acquire to get as one's own; to come into possession or control of (p. 11)	*** adquirir** obtener como propiedad; tomar posesión o control de (pág. 11)
*adapt to change in order to meet the demands of a certain environment or circumstance (p. 271)	***adaptar** cambiar para satisfacer las necesidades de un ambiente o circunstancia determinados (pág. 271)
*adequate sufficient for a specific requirement; completed to its minimum requirements (p. 622)	***adecuado** suficiente para un requisito específico; que cumple con los requisitos mínimos (pág. 622)
*adequately sufficiently; completed to its minimum requirements (p. 390)	***adecuadamente** suficientemente; que cumple con los requisitos mínimos (pág. 390)
*advocate to propose a certain position or viewpoint (p. 361)	***defender** proponer una posición o un punto de vista determinados (pág. 361)
affirmative action an active effort to improve employment or educational opportunities for minorities and women (p. 642)	**acción afirmativa** esfuerzo activo por mejorar las oportunidades de empleo o de educación para las minorías y las mujeres (pág. 642)
Agent Orange a chemical defoliant used to clear Vietnamese jungles during the Vietnam War (p. 599)	**Agente Naranja** defoliante químico usado para limpiar las selvas vietnamitas durante la guerra de Vietnam (pág. 599)
agrarianism the philosophy that agriculture and owning land is the backbone of the economy (p. 123)	**agrarismo** filosofía según la cual la agricultura y la tenencia de tierras son la columna vertebral de la economía (pág. 123)
agricultural revolution period when early peoples learned how to plant and raise crops (p. 4)	**revolución agrícola** periodo en que los primeros pueblos aprendieron a plantar y cultivar (pág. 4)
alien a person living in a country who is not a citizen of that country (p. 126)	**extranjero** persona que vive en un país del cual no es ciudadano (pág. 126)
*allocate to set apart for something specific (p. 684)	***asignar** reservar para algo específico (pág. 684)
allotment a plot of land assigned to an individual or a family for cultivation (p. 281)	**parcela** porción de terreno asignada a un individuo o familia para el cultivo (pág. 281)
*alternative another choice (p. 648)	***alternativa** otra opción (pág. 648)
*ambiguous to lack a definitive purpose (p. 153)	***ambiguo** que carece de un propósito definitivo (pág. 153)
amendment a change to the Constitution (p. 80)	**enmienda** reforma a la Constitución (pág. 80)

Glossary/Glosario

ENGLISH

ESPAÑOL

Americanization process of acquiring or causing a person to acquire American traits and characteristics (p. 320)

americanización proceso por el cual una e persona adquiere o hace que otra adquiera rasgos y características americanos (pág. 320)

amnesty the act of granting a pardon to a large group of people (pp. 251, 683)

amnistía acto de otorgar un perdón a un gran número de personas (págs. 251, 683)

amphtrac an amphibious tractor used to move troops from ships to shore (p. 493)

amtrac vehículo anfibio utilizado para trasladar tropas de los barcos hasta la orilla (pág. 493)

anarchist a person who believes there should be no government (p. 412)

anarquista persona que cree que no debería haber gobierno (pág. 412)

annexation incorporating a territory within the domain of a country (p. 194)

anexión incorporación de un territorio al dominio de un país (pág. 194)

*annual occurring or happening every year (p. 150)

*anual que ocurre o sucede cada año (pág. 150)

annuity money paid by contract at regular intervals (p. 277)

anualidad dinero que se paga por contrato a intervalos regulares (pág. 277)

anthrax a bacteria used to create biological weapons (p. 698)

ántrax bacterias usadas para crear armas biológicas (pág. 698)

*apparent appearing to be fact as far as can be understood (p. 443)

*aparente que parece ser un hecho hasta donde se puede entender (pág. 433)

appeasement giving in to the unjust demands of a belligerent leader in order to avoid war (p. 463)

apaciguamiento ceder a exigencias injustas de un líder beligerante para evitar la guerra (pág. 463)

*appropriate especially suitable or compatible (p. 645)

*apropiado especialmente adecuado o compatible (pág. 645)

*approximately an estimate of a figure that is close to the actual figure (p. 281)

*aproximadamente estimado de una cifra que se acerca a la cifra real (pág. 281)

*arbitrary existing or coming about seemingly at random or as an unfair or unreasonable act of will (p. 559)

*arbitrario que existe o se produce al parecer por azar o como una acción injusta o poco razonable de la voluntad (pág. 559)

arbitration settling a dispute by agreeing to accept the decision of an impartial outsider (pp. 301, 364)

arbitraje resolución de una disputa mediante un acuerdo para aceptar la decisión de una tercera persona imparcial (págs. 301, 364)

armistice a temporary agreement to end fighting (p. 391)

armisticio acuerdo temporal para poner fin a una lucha (pág. 391)

*assemble to bring together in a certain place for a particular purpose (p. 230)

*congregar reunir en un lugar determinado para un propósito en particular (pág. 230)

assembly line a production system with machines and workers arranged so that each person performs an assigned task again and again as the item passes before him or her (p. 406)

cadena de montaje sistema de producción con máquinas y obreros dispuestos de manera que cada persona realiza una tarea asignada una y otra vez a medida que el producto pasa frente a ella (pág. 406)

assimilate to absorb a group into the culture of another population (p. 281)

asimilar incorporar a un grupo en la cultura de otra población (pág. 281)

*assume to take for granted or as true (p. 472)

*asumir dar por sentado o por cierto (pág. 472)

astrolabe a device used to determine direction, latitude, and local time (p. 11)

astrolabio aparato usado para determinar la dirección, la latitud y la hora local (pág. 11)

attrition the act of wearing down by constant harassment or attack (p. 227)

desgaste acción de menoscabar mediante el acoso y los ataques permanentes (pág. 227)

*authorities those who have control over determining and enforcing what is right or wrong (p. 397)

*autoridades personas que tienen el control para determinar qué está bien o mal y hacerlo cumplir (pág. 397)

autonomy the quality of or state of being self-governing (p. 341)

autonomía calidad o estado de autogobernarse (pág. 341)

*awareness the state of having or showing realization, perception, or knowledge (p. 689)

*conciencia tener o mostrar comprensión, percepción o conocimiento (pág. 689)

B

baby boom a marked rise in birthrate, such as occurred in the United States following World War II (p. 544)

***boom* de natalidad** marcado aumento en la tasa de nacimientos, como el que ocurrió en Estados Unidos después de la Segunda Guerra Mundial (pág. 544)

bailiff minor officer of the courts (p. 432)

alguacil oficial inferior de las cortes (pág. 432)

bank holiday closing of banks during the Great Depression to avoid bank runs (p. 444)

cierre bancario cierre de bancos durante la Gran Depresión para evitar el pánico bancario (pág. 444)

bank run persistent and heavy demands by a bank's depositors, creditors, or customers to withdraw money (p. 428)

pánico bancario demandas persistentes y considerables por parte de los depositantes, acreedores o clientes de un banco para retirar dinero (pág. 428)

barrios Spanish-speaking neighborhoods in a town or city (p. 273)

barrios vecindarios de habla hispana en un pueblo o una ciudad (pág. 273)

*benefit something that promotes well-being or is a useful aid (p. 450)

*prestación algo que promueve el bienestar o es una ayuda útil (pág. 450)

benevolent society an association focusing on spreading the word of God and combating social problems (p. 171)

sociedad benévola asociación que se ocupa de dar a conocer la palabra de Dios y combatir los problemas sociales (pág. 171)

bilingualism the practice of teaching immigrant students in their own language (p. 623)

bilingüismo práctica de enseñar a los estudiantes inmigrantes en su propio idioma (pág. 623)

bill of rights a summary of fundamental rights and privileges guaranteed to a people against violation by the state (p. 83)

carta de derechos resumen de los derechos y privilegios fundamentales que el estado garantiza al pueblo que no se violarán (pág. 83)

binding arbitration process whereby a neutral party hears arguments from two opposing sides and makes a decision that both must accept (p. 451)

arbitraje obligatorio proceso mediante el cual una parte neutral oye los argumentos de dos partes opuestas y toma una decisión que ambas partes deben aceptar (pág. 451)

black codes laws passed in the South just after the Civil War aimed at controlling freedmen and enabling plantation owners to exploit African American workers (p. 253)

códigos negros leyes aprobadas en el Sur inmediatamente después de la Guerra Civil, que buscaban controlar a los hombres liberados y permitir a los dueños de las plantaciones explotar a los trabajadores afroamericanos (pág. 253)

black power the mobilization of the political and economic power of African Americans, especially to compel respect for their rights and to improve their condition (p. 588)

poder negro movilización del poder político y económico de los afroamericanos, en especial para exigir respeto a sus derechos y mejorar su situación (pág. 588)

blockade runner ship that runs through a blockade, usually to smuggle goods through a protected area (p. 229)

evasor de bloqueo barco que evade un bloqueo, por lo general para contrabandear mercancías a través de un área protegida (pág. 229)

blue-collar worker workers in the manual labor field, particularly those requiring protective clothing (p. 544)

operarios obreros que realizan actividades manuales, en particular aquellos que requieren usar ropa de protección (pág. 544)

Glossary/Glosario

Glossary/Glosario **715**

ENGLISH	ESPAÑOL
blues style of music evolving from African American spirituals and noted for its melancholy sound (p. 419)	*blues* estilo de música que evoluciona a partir de la música espiritual afroamericana, caracterizado por su sonido melancólico (pág. 419)
bohemian a person (as an artist or a writer) leading an unconventional lifestyle (p. 415)	**bohemio** persona (por ejemplo un artista o un escritor) que lleva un estilo de vida poco convencional (pág. 415)
bonanza farm a large, highly profitable wheat farm (p. 275)	**granja en bonanza** granja de trigo extensa y de alta rentabilidad (pág. 275)
bond a note issued by the government that promises to pay off a loan with interest (p. 121)	**bono** título emitido por el gobierno en el que se compromete a pagar un préstamo con intereses (pág. 121)
bounty money given as a reward, as to encourage enlistment in the army (p. 228)	**bonificación** dinero entregado como recompensa, por ejemplo para incentivar el alistamiento en el ejército (pág. 228)
*briefly for a short time (p. 500)	***brevemente** por poco tiempo (pág. 500)
brinkmanship the willingness to go to the brink of war to force an opponent to back down (p. 530)	**política arriesgada** disposición de ir hasta el borde de una guerra para obligar al oponente a retractarse (pág. 530)
broker state role of the government to work out conflicts among competing interest groups (p. 455)	**estado intermediario** papel del gobierno para resolver conflictos entre grupos con conflictos de intereses (pág. 455)
bull market a long period of rising stock prices (p. 427)	**mercado alcista** periodo prolongado de alzas en el valor de las acciones (pág. 427)
busing a policy of transporting children to schools outside their neighborhoods to achieve greater racial balance (p. 642)	**transporte de escolares** política que consiste en trasladar a los niños a escuelas fuera de sus vecindarios para alcanzar mayor equilibrio racial (pág. 642)

C

ENGLISH	ESPAÑOL
cabinet a group of advisers to the president (p. 120)	**gabinete** grupo de consejeros del presidente (pág. 120)
capital gains tax a federal tax paid by businesses and investors when they sell stocks or real estate (p. 670)	**impuesto a las ganancias de capital** impuesto federal que pagan los comerciantes e inversionistas cuando venden acciones o bienes raíces (pág. 670)
caravel sailing ship capable of long-distance exploration (p. 11)	**carabela** embarcación capaz de explorar a largas distancias (pág. 11)
carpetbagger name given to many Northerners who moved to the South after the Civil War and supported the Republicans (p. 256)	**explotador político** (*carpetbagger*) nombre dado a muchos norteños que se trasladaron al Sur después de la Guerra Civil y apoyaron a los Republicanos (pág. 256)
caucus system a system in which members of a political party meet to choose their party's candidate for president or decide policy (p. 163)	**sistema de comité electoral** sistema en el cual los miembros de un partido político se reúnen para elegir el candidato de su partido para la presidencia o decidir sobre políticas (pág. 163)
cede to give up by treaty (p. 199)	**ceder** rendirse mediante un tratado (pág. 199)
censure to express a formal disapproval of an action (p. 527)	**censura** expresar formalmente la desaprobación de una acción (pág. 527)

chad a small piece of cardboard produced by punching a data card (p. 695)

confeti pequeño pedazo de cartulina que se produce al perforar una tarjeta de datos (pág. 695)

*challenger one who enters a competition (p. 634)

*retador persona que entra en una competencia (pág. 634)

charter a constitution (p. 512)

carta constitucional una constitución (pág. 512)

checks and balances the system in which each branch of government has the ability to limit the power of the other branches to prevent any from becoming too powerful (p. 79)

equilibrio de poderes sistema en el cual cada rama del gobierno tiene la capacidad de limitar el poder de las otras ramas para evitar que alguna de ellas se vuelva demasiado poderosa (pág. 79)

circumnavigate to sail around (p. 13)

circunnavegar navegar alrededor (pág. 13)

*circumstance a factor in a problem that determines its solution (p. 263)

*circunstancia factor en un problema que determina su solución (pág. 263)

*cite to point out as an example in an argument or debate (p. 688)

*citar señalar como ejemplo en un argumento o debate (pág. 688)

*civil of or relating to citizens (p. 187)

*civil de o relativo a los ciudadanos (pág. 187)

closed shop an agreement in which a company agrees to hire only union members (pp. 302, 539)

taller cerrado acuerdo en el cual una compañía sólo contrata miembros del sindicato (págs. 302, 539)

cloture a motion that ends debate and calls for an immediate vote (p. 584)

clausura moción que pone fin a un debate y requiere una votación inmediata (pág. 584)

*code a signal or symbol used to represent something that is to be kept secret (p. 490)

*código señal o símbolo usado para representar algo que se debe guardar en secreto (pág. 490)

*collapse a sudden loss of force, value, or effect (p. 426)

*colapso pérdida repentina de fuerza, valor o efecto (pág. 426)

*colleague a person who works in the same, or a similar, profession (p. 433)

*colega persona que trabaja en la misma profesión o en una similar (pág. 433)

collective a farm, especially in Communist countries, formed from many small holdings collected into a single unit for joint operation under governmental supervision (p. 461)

granja colectiva granja, especialmente en los países comunistas, formada por muchas propiedades pequeñas reunidas en una sola para operar conjuntamente bajo supervisión gubernamental (pág. 461)

*command to be in control of, to have full power (p. 462)

*mandar tener el control, tener facultades plenas (pág. 462)

*commentator one who explains, discusses, or reports in an expository manner, especially news on radio or television (p. 556)

*comentarista persona que explica, analiza o informa de manera expositiva, en especial las noticias en la radio o la televisión (pág. 556)

*commissioner the officer in charge of a department or bureau of the public service (p. 257)

*comisionado funcionario a cargo de un departamento u oficina del servicio público (pág. 257)

*commitment an agreement or pledge to do something in the future (p. 218)

*compromiso acuerdo o empeño de hacer algo en el futuro (pág. 218)

committee of correspondence committee organized in each colony to communicate with and unify the colonies (p. 44)

comité de correspondencia comité organizado en cada colonia para comunicarse con las colonias y unificarlas (pág. 44)

communes group living arrangements in which members share everything and work together (p. 614)

comuna organización de vivienda en grupos, en la cual sus integrantes comparten todo y trabajan juntos (pág. 614)

*community people with common characteristics living in the same area (p. 435)

*comunidad personas con características comunes que viven en la misma área (pág. 435)

Glossary/Glosario

ENGLISH	ESPAÑOL
*compatible capable of existing in harmony (p. 619)	***compatible** que puede existir en armonía (pág. 619)
*compensate to offset an error, defect or undesired effect (p. 176)	***compensar** resarcir un error, defecto o efecto no deseado (pág. 176)
*comprehensive covering a broad range of topics (p. 258)	***integral** que cubre una amplia variedad de temas (pág. 258)
concentration camp a camp where persons are detained or confined (p. 473)	**campo de concentración** campo donde se detienen y confinan personas (pág. 473)
*conference a meeting of two or more persons for discussing matters of common concern (p. 339)	***conferencia** reunión entre dos o más personas para analizar temas de interés común (pág. 339)
*confine to enclose or restrain (p. 568)	***confinar** encerrar o restringir (pág. 568)
*confirmation the formal approval of an executive act by a legislative body (p. 661)	***confirmación** aprobación formal de un acto legislativo por parte de la Asamblea Legislativa (pág. 661)
*conform to change in a way that fits a standard or authority (p. 544)	***adecuar** cambiar de manera que se ajuste a un patrón o una autoridad (pág. 544)
*conformity agreement in form, manner, or character (p. 612)	***conformidad** acuerdo en la forma, el modo o el carácter (pág. 612)
conquistador Spanish for "conqueror"; the men who led the expeditions to conquer the Americas (p. 14)	**conquistador** hombre que lideraba las expediciones para la conquista de América (pág. 14)
conscription requiring people to enter military service (p. 225)	**conscripción** requisito de que las personas ingresen al servicio militar (pág. 225)
consensus general agreement (p. 566)	**consenso** acuerdo general (pág. 566)
conservative a person who believes government power, particularly in the economy, should be limited in order to maximize individual freedom (p. 654)	**conservador** persona que cree que el poder del gobierno, particularmente en la economía, debe ser limitado para maximizar la libertad individual (pág. 654)
*constitute to be composed of, made up of, or formed from (p. 303)	***constituirse** que está compuesto de, que consta o esta hecho de (pág. 303)
*consumer a person who buys what is produced by an economy (p. 295)	***consumidor** persona que compra lo que produce una economía (pág. 295)
containment the policy or process of preventing the expansion of a hostile power (p. 517)	**contención** política o proceso para evitar la expansión de una potencia hostil (pág. 517)
contraband goods whose importation, exportation, or possession is illegal (p. 381)	**contrabando** bienes cuya importación, exportación o posesión es ilegal (pág. 381)
*contract a binding legal document between two parties (p. 31)	***contrato** documento legal vinculante entre dos partes (pág. 31)
*contradiction a situation in which inherent factors, actions, or propositions are inconsistent or contrary to one another (p. 63)	***contradicción** situación en la cual factores, acciones o proposiciones inherentes son incompatibles o contrarios entre sí (pág. 63)
*controversial relating to a prolonged public dispute (p. 704)	***controvertido** relativo a una disputa pública prolongada (pág. 704)
*controversy a prolonged public dispute (p. 156)	***controversia** disputa pública prolongada (pág. 156)

convention an assembly of persons who meet for a common purpose (p. 192)

convención reunión de personas que tienen un mismo propósito (pág. 192)

*conventional nonnuclear (p. 561)

*convencional que no es de tipo nuclear (pág. 561)

*convert to bring over from one belief, view, or party to another (p. 185)

*convertirse cambiar de una creencia, opinión o partido a otro (pág. 185)

*convince to bring to belief, consent, or a course of action (p. 525)

*convencer hacer que alguien crea algo, lo consienta, o realice una acción (pág. 525)

convoy a group that travels with something, such as a ship, to protect it (p. 390)

convoy grupo que viaja con algo, como un barco, para protegerlo (pág. 390)

convoy system a system in which merchant ships travel with naval vessels for protection (p. 496)

sistema de convoy sistema en el cual las embarcaciones comerciales viajan con naves de la armada para garantizar su protección (pág. 496)

cooperative a store where farmers buy products from each other; an enterprise owned and operated by those who use its services (p. 324)

cooperativa tienda donde los agricultores compran productos entre sí; empresa de propiedad de aquellos que usan sus servicios, quienes también la operan (pág. 324)

cooperative individualism President Hoover's policy of encouraging manufacturers and distributors to form their own organizations and volunteer information to the federal government in an effort to stimulate the economy (p. 404)

individualismo cooperativo política del presidente Hoover que estimulaba a los fabricantes y distribuidores a formar sus propias organizaciones y a dar información voluntaria al gobierno federal en un esfuerzo para estimular la economía (pág. 404)

*coordinate to harmonize or bring into common action, movement, or condition (p. 486)

*coordinar armonizar o realizar acciones o movimientos comunes, o tener las mismas condiciones (pág. 486)

corporation an organization that is authorized by law to carry on an activity but treated as though it were a single person (p. 294)

sociedad anónima organización autorizada por la ley para desarrollar una actividad, pero que recibe el tratamiento de un individuo particular (pág. 294)

*correspondence communication by letters (p. 210)

*correspondencia comunicación por medio de cartas (pág. 210)

corrupt bargain an illegitimate agreement between politicians (p. 157)

trato corrupto acuerdo ilegítimo entre políticos (pág. 157)

cost of living the cost of purchasing goods and services essential for survival (p. 394)

costo de la vida costo de comprar bienes y servicios esenciales para la supervivencia (pág. 394)

cost-plus a government contract to pay a manufacturer the cost to produce an item plus a guaranteed percentage (p. 483)

contrato de margen fijo contrato del gobierno para pagar a un fabricante el costo de producir un artículo más un porcentaje garantizado (pág. 483)

cotton gin a machine that removed seeds from cotton fiber (p. 150)

desmotadora de algodón máquina que quitaba las semillas de la fibra de algodón (pág. 150)

counterculture a culture with values and beliefs different than those of the mainstream (p. 614)

contracultura cultura con valores y creencias que difieren de los de la cultura principal (pág. 614)

court-packing the act of changing the political balance of power in a nation's judiciary system whereby a national leader, such as the president of the United States, appoints judges who will rule in favor of his or her policies (p. 454)

reorganización de la corte acción de cambiar el equilibrio político del poder en el sistema judicial de una nación mediante la cual un líder nacional, como el presidente de Estados Unidos, nombra a los jueces que fallarán a favor de sus políticas (pág. 454)

covert not openly shown or engaged in; secret (p. 531)

encubierto que no se muestra o compromete abiertamente; secreto (pág. 531)

ENGLISH

creationism the belief that God created the world and everything in it, usually in the way described in Genesis (p. 413)

credibility gap lack of trust or believability (p. 600)

***credit** an amount or sum of money placed at a person's disposal by a bank on condition that it will be repaid with interest (p. 408)

***creditor** one to whom a debt is owed (p. 121)

***criteria** standards on which a judgment or action may be based (p. 642)

crop lien obligation placed on a farmer to repay a debt with crops (p. 263)

***crucial** something considered important or essential (p. 232)

***currency** paper money used as a medium of exchange (p. 324)

customs duty a tax on imports and exports (p. 40)

ESPAÑOL

creacionismo creencia de que Dios creó el mundo y todo lo que hay en él, por lo general de la manera en que se describe en el Génesis (pág. 413)

barrera de credibilidad falta de confianza (pág. 600)

***crédito** suma de dinero que un banco pone a disposición de una persona con la condición de que ésta la pague con intereses (pág. 408)

***acreedor** persona a quien se le adeuda algo (pág. 121)

***criterios** estándares en los cuales se basa un juicio o una acción (pág. 642)

gravamen de cultivo obligación que adquiere un agricultor para cancelar una deuda con cultivos (pág. 263)

***crucial** algo que se considera importante o esencial (pág. 232)

***moneda** papel moneda usado como medio de cambio (pág. 324)

arancel aduanero impuesto a las importaciones y exportaciones (pág. 40)

D

debt peonage condition of sharecroppers who could not pay off their debts and, therefore, could not leave the property they worked (p. 263)

***decline** a change to a lower state or level (p. 5)

de facto segregation segregation by custom and tradition (p. 574)

deficit the amount by which expenses exceed income (p. 660)

deficit spending government practice of spending borrowed money rather than raising taxes, usually in an attempt to boost the economy (p. 449)

deflation a decline in the volume of available money or credit that results in lower prices, and, therefore, increases the buying power of money (pp. 298, 324)

***demonstration** an outward expression or display (p. 177)

***denial** refusal to satisfy a request or desire (p. 235)

***deny** to declare untrue (p. 414)

deport to expel an individual from the country (p. 396)

***deregulation** the act or process of removing restrictions or regulations (p. 639)

esclavitud deudora condición de los aparceros que no podían pagar sus deudas y, por lo tanto, no podían abandonar la propiedad donde trabajaban (pág. 263)

***descenso** cambio hacia un estado o nivel inferior (pág. 5)

segregación *de facto* segregación por costumbre y tradición (pág. 574)

déficit cantidad en la cual los gastos superan a los ingresos (pág. 660)

gasto deficitario práctica gubernamental de gastar dinero prestado en lugar de aumentar los impuestos, por lo general en un esfuerzo por estimular la economía (pág. 449)

deflación caída en el volumen de dinero disponible o crédito, que da lugar a precios más bajos y, en consecuencia, aumenta el poder adquisitivo del dinero (págs. 298, 324)

***demostración** expresión o manifestación abierta (pág. 177)

***negativa** rechazo a satisfacer una solicitud o un deseo (pág. 235)

***negar** declarar como falso (pág. 414)

deportar expulsar a un individuo de un país (pág. 396)

***desregulación** acto o proceso de eliminar restricciones o regulaciones (pág. 639)

Glossary/Glosario

*despite in spite of (p. 503)

détente a policy that attempts to relax or ease tensions between nations (p. 631)

developing nation a nation whose economy is primarily agricultural (p. 531)

direct primary a vote held by all members of a political party to decide their candidate for public office (p. 358)

discount retailing selling large quantities of goods at very low prices and trying to sell the goods quickly to turn over the entire inventory in a short period of time (p. 663)

*discrimination different treatment or preference on a basis other than individual merit (p. 329)

disenfranchise to deprive of the right to vote (p. 481)

*disposable referring to the money remaining to an individual after deduction of taxes (p. 407)

*disproportionate lacking regularity or symmetry in size, degree, or intensity (p. 601)

*distinct separate, apart, or different from others (p. 24)

*distribution the act or process of being given out or disbursed to clients, consumers, or members of a group (p. 295)

*diverse being different from one another (p. 415)

dollar diplomacy a policy of joining the business interests of a country with its diplomatic interests abroad (p. 350)

*dominance being in a state or position of command or control over all others (p. 38)

*dominate to be in a state or position of command or control over all others (p. 461)

domino theory the belief that if one nation in Asia fell to the Communists, neighboring countries would follow (p. 595)

dove a person in favor of the United States withdrawing from the Vietnam War (p. 602)

downsizing reducing a company in size by laying off workers and managers to become more efficient (p. 670)

*draft to select a person at random for mandatory military service (p. 386)

*draft a system used for choosing people from the population to serve in the military (p. 480)

dry farming a way of farming dry land in which seeds are planted deep in the ground where there is some moisture (p. 275)

*a pesar de pese a que (pág. 503)

distensión política orientada a suavizar o aliviar las tensiones entre las naciones (pág. 631)

nación en vías de desarrollo nación cuya economía es principalmente agrícola (pág. 531)

elección primaria votación de todos los miembros de un partido político para elegir su candidato a un cargo público (pág. 358)

venta al por menor con descuento vender grandes cantidades de bienes a precios muy bajos y tratar de hacerlo rápidamente para rotar todo el inventario en un corto periodo de tiempo (pág. 663)

*discriminación tratamiento diferente o preferencial por razones distintas al mérito individual (pág. 329)

privación del voto negar el derecho al voto (pág. 481)

*disponible relativo al dinero que le sobra a un individuo después de las deducciones de sus impuestos (pág. 407)

*desproporcionado que carece de regularidad o simetría en tamaño, grado o intensidad (pág. 601)

*distinto separado, aparte o diferente de otros (pág. 24)

*distribución acción o proceso de entregar o desembolsar a los clientes, consumidores o integrantes de un grupo (pág. 295)

*diverso diferente uno de otro (pág. 415)

diplomacia del dólar política que une los intereses comerciales de un país con sus intereses diplomáticos en el extranjero (pág. 350)

*dominación que se halla en estado o posición de mando o control sobre los demás (pág. 38)

*dominar hallarse en un estado o posición de mando o control sobre los demás (pág. 461)

teoría dominó creencia de que si una nación asiática caía ante los comunistas, los países vecinos también lo harían (pág. 595)

paloma persona que apoyaba el retiro de Estados Unidos de la guerra de Vietnam (pág. 602)

reducción de personal reducir el tamaño de una compañía despidiendo empleados y directivos para volverla más eficiente (pág. 670)

*conscribir elegir a una persona al azar para el servicio militar obligatorio (pág. 386)

*conscripción sistema usado para elegir a una persona al azar para el servicio militar obligatorio (pág. 480)

agricultura de secano forma de cultivar terreno seco en la cual las semillas se plantan a grandes profundidades en el terreno donde hay un poco de humedad (pág. 275)

ENGLISH	ESPAÑOL
due process a judicial requirement that laws may not treat individuals unfairly, arbitrarily, or unreasonably, and that courts must follow proper procedures and rules when trying cases (p. 560)	**debido proceso** requisito judicial según el cual las leyes no pueden tratar a los individuos de manera injusta, arbitraria o poco razonable, y los tribunales deben seguir los procedimientos y normas apropiados al ver las causas (pág. 560)
duty a tax on imports (p. 74)	**arancel** impuesto a las importaciones (pág. 74)
dynamic conservatism policy of balancing economic conservatism with some activism (p. 541)	**conservadurismo dinámico** política que consiste en equilibrar el conservadurismo económico con algún activismo (pág. 541)

E

ENGLISH	ESPAÑOL
earmark specifications added by both Republicans and Democrats for the expenditure of federal money for particular projects (p. 710)	**asignación de fondos** especificaciones de republicanos y demócratas para que el dinero federal se gaste en proyectos específicos (pág. 710)
economies of scale the reduction in the cost of a good brought about especially by increased production at a given facility (p. 294)	**economías de escala** reducción en el costo de un bien ocasionada por un aumento en la producción en un sector determinado (pág. 294)
*eliminate to remove or get rid of (p. 702)	***eliminar** quitar o deshacerse de algo (pág. 702)
emancipation the act or process of freeing enslaved persons (pp. 65, 177)	**emancipación** acción o proceso de liberar a los esclavos (págs. 65, 177)
embargo a government ban on trade with other countries (pp. 131, 638)	**embargo** prohibición gubernamental de comerciar con otros países (págs. 131, 638)
*emphasis a special importance given to an object or idea (p. 379)	***énfasis** importancia especial que se da a un objeto o a una idea (pág. 379)
empresario person who arranged for the settlement of Texas in the 1800s (p. 190)	**empresario** persona que hacía arreglos para el asentamiento de tierras en Texas en el siglo XIX (pág. 190)
*enable to make possible, practical, or easy (p. 133)	***facultar** hacer posible, práctico o fácil (pág. 133)
*encounter to come upon face-to-face as an enemy or adversary (p. 238)	***confrontar** enfrentarse cara a cara con un enemigo o adversario (pág. 238)
*enforce to urge or carry out using force (p. 46)	***hacer cumplir** instar o llevar a cabo por medio de la fuerza (pág. 46)
*enforcement the act of urging or carrying out by force (p. 589)	***aplicación de la ley** la acción de instar o llevar a cabo por medio de la fuerza (pág. 589)
*ensure to guarantee or make certain (p. 278)	***asegurar** garantizar o cerciorarse de algo (pág. 278)
*entity something having independent, separate, or self-contained existence (p. 550)	***entidad** algo que existe de manera independiente, separada o autónoma (pág. 550)
entrepreneur one who organizes, manages, and assumes the risks of a business or enterprise (p. 289)	**emprendedor** quien organiza, administra o asume los riesgos de un negocio o una empresa (pág. 289)

enumerated powers powers listed in the Constitution as belonging to the federal government (p. 121)

poderes enumerados poderes que se enumeran en la Constitución como pertenecientes al gobierno federal (pág. 121)

*environmental relating to the environment; the complex system of plants, animals, water, and soil (p. 365)

*medioambiental relativo al medioambiente; el complejo sistema de plantas, animales, agua y suelo (pág. 365)

envoy a person delegated to represent one country to another (p. 196)

enviado persona delegada para representar a un país frente a otro (pág. 196)

*equip to furnish with provisions; to make ready for action (p. 57)

*equipar suministrar provisiones; preparar para poner en acción (pág. 57)

*equipment the articles or physical resources prepared or furnished for a specific task (p. 514)

*equipo artículos o recursos físicos preparados o suministrados para una tarea específica (pág. 514)

*erode to wear away at something until it fades (p. 381)

*erosionar desgastar algo hasta hacerlo desaparecer (pág. 381)

espionage spying, especially to gain government secrets (p. 385)

espionaje espiar, especialmente para conocer secretos del gobierno (pág. 385)

*ethnic relating to large groups of people classed according to common racial, national, tribal, religious, linguistic, or cultural origin or background (p. 309)

*étnico relativo a grandes grupos de personas clasificadas porque comparten el mismo origen o entorno racial, nacional, tribal, religioso, lingüístico o cultural (pág. 309)

ethnic cleansing the expulsion, imprisonment, or killing of ethnic minorities by a dominant majority group (p. 680)

limpieza étnica expulsión, encarcelamiento o asesinato de minorías étnicas por parte de una mayoría dominante (pág. 680)

euro the basic currency shared by the countries of the European Union since 1999 (p. 688)

euro moneda de todos los países de la Unión Europea desde 1999 (pág. 688)

*eventually at an unspecified time or day; in the end (p. 8)

*con el tiempo en una hora o día no específicos; al final (pág. 8)

*evident obvious, clear (p. 162)

*evidente obvio, claro (pág. 162)

*evolution the scientific theory that humans and other forms of life have evolved over time (pp. 317, 413)

*evolución teoría científica según la cual los seres humanos y otras formas de vida han evolucionado con el tiempo (págs. 317, 413)

executive privilege principle stating that communications of the executive branch should remain confidential to protect national security (p. 635)

privilegio ejecutivo principio que establece que las comunicaciones de la rama ejecutiva deben ser confidenciales para proteger la seguridad nacional (pág. 635)

*expansion the act or process of increasing or enlarging the extent, number, volume, or scope (p. 336)

*expansión acción o proceso de aumentar o ampliar la extensión, el número, el volumen o el alcance (pág. 336)

*explicit fully revealed or expressed and leaving no question as to meaning (p. 72)

*explícito totalmente revelado o expresado y que no deja dudas en cuanto a su significado (pág. 72)

*exploit to take unfair advantage of (p. 460)

*explotar tomar una ventaja injusta (pág. 460)

*exposure the condition of being unprotected, especially from severe weather (p. 165)

*exposición que carece de protección, en especial contra las inclemencias del tiempo (pág. 165)

extermination camp a camp where men, women, and children were sent to be executed (p. 473)

campo de exterminio campo adonde se enviaban hombres, mujeres y niños para que los ejecutaran (pág. 473)

*extract to remove by force (p. 270)

*arrancar sacar por la fuerza (pág. 270)

*extraction the act or process of drawing or pulling something out (p. 146)

*extracción acción o proceso de sacar o retirar algo (pág. 146)

Glossary/Glosario

ENGLISH F	ESPAÑOL

*facility something that is built, installed, or established to serve a particular purpose (p. 574)

*instalación algo que se construye, instala o establece con un propósito en particular (pág. 574)

fallout radioactive particles dispersed by a nuclear explosion (p. 528)

lluvia radiactiva partículas radiactivas dispersas debido a una explosión nuclear (pág. 528)

fascism a political system headed by a dictator that calls for extreme nationalism and often racism and no tolerance of opposition (p. 460)

fascismo sistema político encabezado por un dictador que llama al nacionalismo extremo y a menudo al racismo y a la falta de tolerancia hacia la oposición (pág. 460)

favorite sons men who enjoyed the support of leaders from their own state and region (p. 156)

hijos favoritos hombres que contaban con el apoyo de los líderes de su propio estado y región (pág. 156)

federalism political system in which power is divided between the national and state governments (p. 79)

federalismo sistema político en el cual el poder se divide entre los gobiernos nacional y estatal (pág. 79)

feminism the belief that men and women should be equal politically, economically, and socially (p. 615)

feminismo creencia según la cual hombres y mujeres deben ser iguales en lo político, lo económico y lo social (pág. 615)

filibuster an attempt to kill a bill by having a group of senators take turns speaking continuously so that a vote cannot take place (p. 584)

obstruccionista intento de impedir la aprobación de un proyecto de ley haciendo que un grupo de senadores se turnen para hablar continuamente para que la votación no pueda tener lugar (pág. 584)

*finalize to put in finished form (p. 144)

*finalizar llevar a término (pág. 144)

*finance to provide money for a project (p. 450)

*financiar proveer dinero para un proyecto (pág. 450)

*financier one who deals with finance and investment on a large scale (p. 76)

*financista persona que se ocupa de las finanzas e inversiones a gran escala (pág. 76)

fireside chats radio broadcasts made by FDR to the American people to explain his initiatives (p. 445)

charlas íntimas transmisiones de radio que hacía el presidente Roosevelt para explicar a los estadounidenses sus iniciativas (pág. 445)

flexible response the buildup of conventional troops and weapons to allow a nation to fight a limited war without using nuclear weapons (p. 561)

respuesta flexible concentración de tropas y armas convencionales para permitir que una nación participe en una guerra limitada sin emplear armas nucleares (pág. 561)

forage to search or raid for food (p. 237)

forrajear buscar o asaltar en busca de alimento (pág. 237)

foreclose to take possession of a property from a mortgagor because of defaults on payments (p. 436)

ejecutar tomar posesión de una propiedad de un deudor hipotecario debido al incumplimiento en los pagos (pág. 436)

*formulate to prepare or devise according to a systemized statement or formula (p. 213)

*formular preparar o diseñar de acuerdo con una declaración o fórmula sistematizadas (pág. 213)

fossil fuel a fuel formed in the Earth from decayed plant or animal remains (p. 648)

combustible fósil combustible formado en la Tierra a partir de la descomposición de restos vegetales o animales (pág. 648)

*framework a set of guidelines to be followed (p. 82)

estructura conjunto de directrices que se han de seguir (pág. 82)

franchise the right or license to market a company's goods or services in an area, such as a store of a chain operation (p. 544)

franquicia derecho o licencia para comercializar los bienes o servicios de una compañía en un área, por ejemplo una tienda de una cadena (pág. 544)

free enterprise system market economy in which privately owned businesses have the freedom to operate for a profit with limited government intervention (p. 147)

sistema de libre empresa economía de mercado en la cual las empresas privadas tienen la libertad de operar para obtener ganancias con una intervención gubernamental limitada (pág. 147)

*fundamental being of central importance (p. 446)

*fundamental de importancia central (pág. 446)

G

*gender term applied to the characteristics of a male or female (p. 616)

general strike a strike involving all the workers in a particular geographic location (p. 394)

*generation a classification of people who share the same experience throughout their lives (p. 604)

generation gap a cultural separation between parents and their children (p. 547)

glasnost a Soviet policy permitting open discussion of political and social issues and freer dissemination of news and information (p. 668)

global warming an increase in average world temperatures over time (p. 689)

gold standard a monetary standard in which one ounce of gold equals a set number of dollars (p. 444)

gradualism the theory that slavery should be ended gradually (p. 176)

graduated income tax a tax based on the net income of an individual or business and which taxes different income levels at different rates (p. 325)

graft the acquisition of money in dishonest ways, as in bribing a politician (pp. 257, 315)

*grant to give or bestow upon, especially by a formal act (p. 17)

grassroots movement a group of people organizing at the local or community level, away from political or cultural centers (p. 671)

greenback unit of paper currency first issued by the federal government during the Civil War (pp. 225, 324)

gross national product the total value of goods and services produced by a country during a year (p. 286)

*guarantee a statement of assurance (p. 184)

guerrilla member of an armed band that carries out surprise attacks and sabotage rather than open warfare (pp. 351, 595)

guerrilla warfare a hit-and-run technique used in fighting a war; fighting by small bands of warriors using tactics such as sudden ambushes (p. 58)

*género término aplicado a las características masculinas o femeninas (pág. 616)

huelga general huelga que involucra a todos los trabajadores de un punto geográfico en particular (pág. 394)

*generación clasificación de personas que comparten las mismas experiencias durante su vida (pág. 604)

brecha generacional separación cultural entre padres e hijos (pág. 547)

glasnot política soviética que permitió la discusión abierta de temas políticos y sociales y la libre difusión de noticias e información (pág. 668)

calentamiento global aumento en la temperatura promedio mundial a través del tiempo (pág. 689)

patrón oro estándar monetario en el cual una onza de oro equivale a un número de dólares determinado (pág. 444)

gradualismo teoría según la cual la esclavitud debía terminarse de manera gradual (pág. 176)

Impuesto graduado sobre la renta impuesto que se basa en los ingresos netos de un individuo o empresa, el cual grava con diferentes tasas niveles diferentes de ingreso (pág. 325)

corrupción adquisición de dinero en forma deshonesta, por ejemplo mediante el soborno a un político (págs. 257, 315)

*otorgar dar o conferir, especialmente mediante un acto formal (pág. 17)

movimiento de base grupo de personas que se organiza a nivel local o comunitario, lejos de los centros políticos o culturales (pág. 671)

greenback primer papel moneda emitido por el gobierno federal durante la Guerra Civil (págs. 225, 324)

producto nacional bruto valor total de los bienes y servicios que produce un país durante un año (pág. 286)

*garantía declaración de aseguramiento (pág. 184)

guerrilla miembro de un grupo armado que lleva a cabo ataques sorpresivos y sabotajes en vez de entrar en una batalla abierta (págs. 351, 595)

guerra de guerrillas técnica de ataques rápidos y sorpresivos que se usa durante la guerra; pelear en pequeños grupos de combatientes usando tácticas tales como las emboscadas repentinas (pág. 58)

Glossary/Glosario

ENGLISH | H | ESPAÑOL

Glossary/Glosario

habeas corpus a legal order for an inquiry to determine whether a person has been lawfully imprisoned (p. 225)

habeas corpus orden legal para realizar una investigación que determine si una persona ha sido apresada de manera legal (pág. 225)

hacienda a huge ranch (p. 272)

hacienda rancho grande (pág. 272)

hardtack a hard biscuit made of wheat flour (p. 235)

galleta náutica galleta dura preparada con harina de trigo (pág. 235)

hawk someone who believed the United States should continue its military efforts in Vietnam (p. 602)

halcón persona que creía que Estados Unidos debía continuar sus esfuerzos militares en Vietnam (pág. 602)

headright system in which settlers were granted land in exchange for settling in Virginia (p. 17)

derecho de terreno sistema en el cual a los colonos se les otorgaba tierra a cambio de establecerse en Virginia (pág. 17)

hedgerow an enclosure made of dirt walls built to fence in cattle and crops (p. 502)

cerco de setos cerco construido con muros de tierra para encerrar ganado y cultivos (pág. 502)

hippies refers to young Americans, especially during the 1960s, who rejected the conventions of established society (p. 614)

hippies relativo a los jóvenes estadounidenses que, especialmente de 1960 a 1970, rechazaron las convenciones establecidas por la sociedad (pág. 614)

hobo a homeless and usually penniless wanderer (p. 431)

vagabundo persona errante sin hogar y por lo general sin dinero (pág. 431)

holding company a company whose primary business is owning a controlling share of stock in other companies (p. 297)

sociedad de cartera compañía cuya actividad principal es poseer una participación accionaria mayoritaria en otras compañías (pág. 297)

homestead a piece of U.S. public land acquired by filing a record and living on and cultivating it (p. 275)

posesión de tierras una porción de terreno público estadounidense adquirió mediante la presentación y que viven en y cultivaría (pág. 275)

hydraulic mining method of mining by which water is sprayed at a very high pressure against a hill or mountain, washing away large quantities of dirt, gravel, and rock and exposing the minerals beneath the surface (p. 270)

minería hidráulica método de minería mediante el cual se riega con agua a elevadísima presión una colina o montaña; este lavado elimina grandes cantidades de suciedad, grava y roca, y expone los minerales que están bajo la superficie (pág. 270)

I

*ideology a system of thought that is held by an individual, group, or culture (p. 444)

*ideología sistema de pensamiento de un individuo, un grupo o una cultura (pág. 444)

*ignorance the state of being uneducated, uninformed, or unaware (p. 157)

*ignorancia que carece de educación, información o conciencia (pág. 157)

*illegal not according to or authorized by law (p. 683)

*ilegal que no está de acuerdo o autorizado por la ley (pág. 683)

*immigrant one who enters and becomes established in a country other than that of his or her original nationality (p. 308)

*inmigrante persona que ingresa y se radica en un país diferente de aquel del cual es natural (pág. 308)

*impact a lasting impression upon an individual or group (p. 420)

*impacto impresión duradera en un individuo o grupo (pág. 420)

impeach to formally charge a public official with misconduct in office (p. 255)

imputar acusar formalmente a un funcionario público por mala conducta en su cargo (pág. 255)

Glossary/Glosario

imperialism the actions used by one nation to exercise political or economic control over a smaller or weaker nation (p. 336)

imperialismo acciones que emplea una nación para ejercer control político o económico sobre una nación más pequeña o más débil (pág. 336)

*implement to put into action (p. 227)

*implementar poner en práctica (pág. 227)

implied powers powers not specifically listed in the Constitution but claimed by the federal government (p. 121)

poderes implícitos poderes que no están enumerados específicamente en la Constitución, pero que el gobierno federal reclama (pág. 121)

*imply to express indirectly (p. 532)

*implicar expresar en forma indirecta (pág. 532)

*impose to establish authority by force (p. 219)

*imponer establecer la autoridad mediante el uso de la fuerza (pág. 219)

*imposition something established or brought about as if by force (p. 172)

*imposición algo establecido o alcanzado mediante el uso de la fuerza (pág. 172)

impound to take possession of (p. 630)

incautar tomar posesión (pág. 630)

*incentive something that motivates a person into action (p. 312)

*incentivo algo que motiva a una persona a actuar (pág. 312)

*incident single occurrence of a happening or situation (p. 633)

*incidente suceso o situación que ocurre una sola vez (pág. 633)

*income a gain or recurrent benefit usually measured in money derived from capital or labor (p. 549)

*ingreso ganancia o beneficio recurrente que por lo general se mide en dinero y proviene de capital o trabajo (pág. 549)

income tax a tax based on the net income of a person or business (p. 371)

impuesto a la renta impuesto que se basa en los ingresos netos de una persona o negocio (pág. 371)

indentured servant an individual who contracts to work for a colonist for a specified number of years in exchange for transportation to the colonies, food, clothing, and shelter (p. 25)

sirviente por contrato individuo que firma un contrato para trabajar para un colono durante un número específico de años a cambio de transporte a las colonias, alimentación, vestuario y vivienda (pág. 25)

*indicate to point out, point to, or demonstrate the necessity of (p. 657)

*indicar señalar, describir o demostrar la necesidad de algo (pág. 657)

individualism the belief that no matter what a person's background is, the person can still become successful through effort (p. 316)

individualismo creencia según la cual sin importar cuál sea el entorno de una persona, ésta puede llegar a tener éxito si se esfuerza (pág. 316)

industrial union an organization of common laborers and craft workers in a particular industry (p. 299)

sindicato industrial organización de obreros comunes y trabajadores calificados de una industria particular (pág. 299)

inflation an ongoing increase in prices and decrease in the value of money (pp. 40, 324, 638)

inflación aumento continuo de los precios y disminución del valor del dinero (págs. 40, 324, 638)

*initially of or relating to the beginning (p. 520)

*inicialmente relativo al principio (pág. 520)

initiative the right of citizens to place a measure or issue before the voters or the legislature for approval (p. 358)

iniciativa derecho que tienen los ciudadanos de presentar una propuesta o un tema ante los electores o la Asamblea Legislativa para su aprobación (pág. 358)

injunction a court order whereby one is required to do or to refrain from doing a specified act (p. 302)

orden judicial orden judicial por la cual se le exige o prohíbe a alguien que realice una acción determinada (pág. 302)

*innovation a new idea or method (p. 275)

*innovación idea o método nuevos (pág. 275)

*insecurity the state of not being confident or sure (p. 517)

*inseguridad no tener confianza o no estar seguro (pág. 517)

Glossary/Glosario

ENGLISH

*inspector a person appointed to examine foreign facilities, usually in search of weapons (p. 700)

installment monthly plan made to pay off the cost of an item when buying it on credit (p. 429)

*institute to initiate or establish something (p. 563)

*institution an established organization or corporation (p. 171)

insubordination disobedience to authority (p. 367)

insurrection an act of rebellion against the established government (p. 214)

*integrate to combine two previously separate things (p. 291)

*intense existing in an extreme degree (p. 501)

*intensify to become more frequent and powerful (p. 648)

interchangeable parts uniform pieces that can be made in large quantities to replace other identical pieces (p. 147)

internationalism a national policy of actively trading with foreign countries to foster peace and prosperity (p. 466)

interposition theory that a state should be able to intervene between the federal government and the people to stop an illegal action (p. 127)

*interpret to explain the meaning of complex material (p. 142)

*interpretation the act or process of explaining or telling the meaning of (p. 696)

*intervene to get involved in the affairs of another (p. 341)

*invest to put money into a company in order to gain a future financial reward (p. 427)

*investigation a systematic examination or official inquiry (p. 403)

*investor one who puts money into a company in order to gain a future financial reward (p. 292)

Iron Curtain the political and military barrier that isolated Soviet-controlled countries of Eastern Europe after World War II (p. 516)

*isolationism a national policy of avoiding involvement in world affairs (p. 404)

ESPAÑOL

*inspector persona designada para examinar instalaciones extranjeras, por lo general en busca de armas (pág. 700)

cuota plan de pagos mensuales para cubrir el costo de un artículo que se compra a crédito (pág. 429)

*instituir iniciar o establecer algo (pág. 563)

*institución organización o corporación establecida (pág. 171)

insubordinación desobediencia a la autoridad (pág. 367)

insurrección acto de rebelión contra el gobierno establecido (pág. 214)

*integrar unir dos cosas que antes estaban separadas (pág. 291)

*intenso que existe en grado extremo (pág. 501)

*intensificar volverse más frecuente y poderoso (pág. 648)

partes intercambiables piezas uniformes que se pueden fabricar en grandes cantidades para reemplazar otras piezas idénticas (pág. 147)

internacionalismo política nacional de comercio activo con países extranjeros para fomentar la paz y la prosperidad (pág. 466)

interposición teoría que afirma que un Estado debe ser capaz de intervenir entre el gobierno federal y el pueblo para detener una acción ilegal (pág. 127)

*interpretar explicar el significado de material complejo (pág. 142)

*interpretación acción o proceso de explicar o decir el significado de algo (pág. 696)

*intervenir involucrarse en los asuntos de otro (pág. 341)

*invertir colocar dinero en una compañía para obtener una retribución financiera en el futuro (pág. 427)

*investigación examen sistemático o indagación oficial (pág. 403)

*inversionista quien invierte dinero en una compañía con el fin de obtener una retribución económica en el futuro (pág. 292)

Cortina de Hierro barrera política y militar que aisló a los países controlados por la Unión Soviética de Europa del Este durante la Segunda Guerra Mundial (pág. 516)

*aislacionismo política nacional de evitar involucrarse en asuntos internacionales (pág. 404)

J

jazz American style of music that developed from ragtime and blues and that uses syncopated rhythms and melodies (p. 419)

jazz estilo de música estadounidense que se desarrolló a partir del *ragtime* y el *blues* y que usa ritmos y melodías sincopados (pág. 419)

Jim Crow laws statutes enacted to enforce segregation (p. 329)

leyes Jim Crow conjunto de leyes promulgadas para hacer cumplir políticas de segregación (pág. 329)

jingoism extreme nationalism marked by aggressive foreign policy (p. 341)

jingoísmo nacionalismo extremo marcado por una política exterior radical (pág. 341)

joint-stock company form of business organization in which many investors pool funds to raise large amounts of money for large projects (p. 17)

sociedad comanditaria por acciones forma de organización empresarial en la cual muchos inversionistas hacen un fondo común para recaudar grandes sumas de dinero con el fin de realizar grandes proyectos (pág. 17)

judicial review power of the Supreme Court to determine whether laws of Congress are constitutional and to strike down those that are not (p. 130)

revisión judicial facultad de la Corte Suprema para determinar si las leyes expedidas por el Congreso son constitucionales y anular aquellas que no lo son (pág. 130)

*justify to prove or to show to be just, right, or reasonable (p. 486)

*justificar probar o demostrar que algo es justo, correcto o razonable (pág. 486)

juvenile delinquency antisocial or criminal behavior of young people (p. 551)

delincuencia juvenil conducta antisocial o criminal de los adolescentes (pág. 551)

K

kamikaze during World War II, a Japanese suicide pilot whose mission was to crash into his target (p. 494)

kamikaze durante la Segunda Guerra Mundial, piloto suicida japonés cuya misión era estrellarse contra su objetivo (pág. 494)

kiva circular ceremonial room built by the Anasazi (p. 7)

*kiva habitación ceremonial en forma de círculo construida por los anasazi (pág. 7)

L

*labor an action that produces a good or service (p. 12)

*mano de obra acción que produce un bien o servicio (pág. 12)

labor union an organization of workers formed for the purpose of advancing its members' interests (p. 147)

sindicato organización de trabajadores formada con el fin de promover los intereses de sus miembros (pág. 147)

laissez-faire a policy that government should interfere as little as possible in the nation's economy (p. 289)

laissez-faire política según la cual el gobierno debe intervenir lo menos posible en la economía de la nación (pág. 289)

land grant a grant of land by the federal government, especially for roads, railroads, or agricultural colleges (p. 292)

concesión de tierras terrenos que el gobierno federal cede, especialmente para carreteras, vías férreas o escuelas agrarias (pág. 292)

*legislation a proposed law to be voted on by a governing body (p. 358)

*legislación ley propuesta para someterla a la votación de un órgano directivo (pág. 358)

Glossary/Glosario

ENGLISH	ESPAÑOL
*legislator one who makes laws as a member of a political, legislative body (p. 539)	***legislador** quien hace las leyes, por ejemplo un miembro de un órgano legislativo o político (pág. 539)
*liberal a person who generally believes the government should take an active role in the economy and in social programs but should not dictate social behavior (pp. 630, 655)	***liberal** persona que cree que el gobierno debe tener un papel activo en la economía y en los programas sociales, pero no debe dictar cuál debe ser la conducta social (págs. 630, 655)
*liberate to set free (p. 513)	***liberar** poner en libertad (pág. 513)
*license permission or freedom to act (p. 131)	***licencia** permiso o libertad para actuar (pág. 131)
*likewise in the same way; similarly (p. 620)	***asimismo** de la misma manera; de modo semejante (pág. 620)
limited war a war fought with limited commitment of resources to achieve a limited objective, such as containing communism (p. 522)	**guerra limitada** guerra que en la que se participa comprometiendo pocos recursos para alcanzar un objetivo limitado, como contener el comunismo (pág. 522)
linkage policy of improving relations with the Soviet Union and China in hopes of persuading them to cut back their aid to North Vietnam (p. 604)	**enlace** política orientada a mejorar las relaciones con la Unión Soviética y China con la esperanza de persuadirlas de suspender sus ayudas a Vietnam del Norte (pág. 604)
lockout a company tool to fight union demands by refusing to allow employees to enter its facilities to work (p. 299)	**cierre patronal** estrategia de una compañía para frenar las exigencias de los sindicatos negándose a permitir que los empleados ingresen a trabajar en sus instalaciones (pág. 299)
loyalty review program a policy established by President Truman that authorized the screening of all federal employees to determine their loyalty to the U.S. government (p. 524)	**programa de verificación de la lealtad** política establecida por el presidente Truman que autorizaba investigar a todos los empleados federales para determinar si eran leales al gobierno de Estados Unidos (pág. 524)
lynch to execute, by hanging, without lawful approval (p. 330)	**linchar** ejecutar en la horca sin autorización legal (pág. 330)

M

mandate authorization to act given to a representative (p. 244)	**mandato** autorización para actuar que se otorga a un representante (pág. 244)
*manipulate to operate or arrange manually to achieve a desired effect (p. 525)	***manipular** operar o acomodar manualmente para alcanzar un efecto deseado (pág. 525)
manumission the voluntary freeing of enslaved persons (p. 66)	**manumisión** liberación voluntaria de esclavos (pág. 66)
margin buying a stock by paying only a fraction of the stock price and borrowing the rest (p. 427)	**margen** comprar acciones pagando sólo una fracción de su precio y pidiendo en préstamo el saldo (pág. 427)
margin call demand by a broker that investors pay back loans made for stocks purchased on margin (p. 427)	**margen de garantía** exigencia de un corredor de bolsa para que los inversionistas paguen los préstamos hechos para la compra de acciones al margen (pág. 427)
martial law the law administered by military forces that is invoked by a government in an emergency (p. 219)	**ley marcial** ley administrada por las fuerzas militares invocada por el gobierno durante una emergencia (pág. 219)
massive retaliation a policy of threatening a massive response, including the use of nuclear weapons, against a Communist state trying to seize a peaceful state by force (p. 530)	**retaliación masiva** política consistente en amenazar con una respuesta masiva, incluido el uso de armas nucleares, contra un estado comunista que busca apoderarse de un estado pacífico por la fuerza (pág. 530)

mass media medium of communication (as in television and radio) intended to reach a wide audience (p. 417)

medios masivos de comunicación medios de comunicación (como la televisión y la radio) que buscan llegar a una amplia audiencia (pág. 417)

mass production the production of large quantities of goods using machinery and often an assembly line (p. 407)

producción masiva producción de grandes cantidades de bienes usando maquinaria y a menudo una cadena de montaje (pág. 407)

*media a means of expression or communication, especially in reference to the agencies of mass communication—newspapers, radio, television, and the Internet (p. 600)

*medios de comunicación medios de expresión o comunicación, en especial las agencias de comunicación de masas: periódicos, radio, televisión e Internet (pág. 600)

*mediate an attempt to resolve conflict between hostile people or groups (p. 455)

*mediar intento de resolver conflictos entre grupos o personas hostiles (pág. 455)

mercantilism the theory that a state's power depends on its wealth (p. 29)

mercantilismo teoría según la cual el poder de un Estado depende de su riqueza (pág. 29)

mestizo a person of mixed blood or ancestry (p. 188)

mestizo persona de sangre o ascendencia mixtas (pág. 188)

*migrate to move from one location to another (p. 384)

*migrar desplazarse de un lugar a otro (pág. 384)

*migration movement from one location to another (p. 16)

*migración trasladarse de un lugar a otro (pág. 16)

migration chain the process by which immigrants who have acquired U.S. citizenship can send for relatives in their home country to join them (p. 682)

cadena migratoria proceso por el cual los inmigrantes que han obtenido la ciudadanía estadounidense pueden enviar por sus familiares en su ciudad natal para reunirse con ellos (pág. 682)

militarism a policy of aggressive military preparedness (p. 378)

militarismo política de preparación militar radical (pág. 378)

military-industrial complex an informal relationship that some people believe exists between the military and the defense industry to promote greater military spending and influence government policy (p. 533)

complejo militar e industrial relación informal que algunas personas creen que existe entre el ejército y la industria de defensa para incentivar el gasto militar e influir en las políticas del gobierno (pág. 533)

minutemen companies of civilian soldiers who boasted they were ready to fight at a minute's notice (p. 47)

minutemen compañías de soldados civiles que se jactaban de estar listos para combatir en cuestión de minutos (pág. 47)

missile gap the belief that the Soviet Union had more nuclear weapons than the United States (p. 556)

diferencia de misiles creencia de que la Unión Soviética tenía más armas nucleares que Estados Unidos (pág. 556)

Model T automobile built by the Ford Motor Company from 1908 until 1927 (p. 406)

Modelo T automóvil construido por la Compañía Automotriz Ford desde 1908 hasta 1927 (pág. 406)

*modify to make changes or alter (p. 676)

*modificar hacer cambios o alterar (pág. 676)

*monitor to observe, oversee, or regulate (p. 709)

*monitorear observar, supervisar o regular (pág. 709)

monopoly total control of a type of industry by one person or one company (p. 296)

monopolio control total de un tipo de industria por parte de una persona o compañía (pág. 296)

morale a feeling of confidence or enthusiasm (p. 59)

moral sensación de confianza o entusiasmo (pág. 59)

most-favored nation a policy between countries ensuring fair trading practices (p. 125)

nación más favorecida política entre los países que asegura prácticas comerciales justas (pág. 125)

muckraker a journalist who uncovers abuses and corruption in a society (p. 357)

muckracker periodista que descubre abusos y corrupción en una sociedad (pág. 357)

mudslinging attempt to ruin an opponent's reputation with insults (p. 157)

injuria intento de arruinar la reputación de un oponente con insultos (pág. 157)

multinational corporation large corporation with overseas investments (p. 544)

multinacional gran corporación con inversiones en el extranjero (pág. 544)

mutual-assured destruction the strategy assuming that, as long as two countries can destroy each other with nuclear weapons, they will be afraid to use them (p. 662)

destrucción mutua asegurada estrategia que asume que siempre y cuando dos países puedan destruirse entre sí con armas nucleares, ambos estarán temerosos de usarlas (pág. 662)

N

napalm a jellied gasoline used for bombs (pp. 504, 599)

napalm gasolina gelatinosa usada para fabricar bombas (págs. 504, 599)

nationalism loyalty and devotion to a nation (pp. 135, 379)

nacionalismo lealtad y devoción a una nación (págs. 135, 379)

national self-determination the free choice by the people of a nation of their own future political status (p. 392)

autodeterminación de los pueblos libre elección por parte de los habitantes de una nación de su situación política futura (pág. 392)

nativism hostility toward immigrants (pp. 168, 310, 412)

nativismo hostilidad hacia los inmigrantes (págs. 168, 310, 412)

***network** an interconnected system (p. 388)

***red** sistema interconectado (pág. 388)

***neutral** not aligned with any political or ideological group (p. 124)

***neutral** que no está alineado con ningún grupo político o ideológico (pág. 124)

nomad a person who continually moves from place to place, usually in search of food (p. 277)

nómada persona que se traslada continuamente de un lugar a otro, por lo general en busca de alimentos (pág. 277)

nonimportation agreement a pledge by merchants not to buy imported goods from a particular source (p. 41)

acuerdo contra la importación compromiso de los comerciantes de no comprar bienes importados de una fuente en particular (pág. 41)

***nuclear** relating to the nucleus of an atom (p. 505)

***nuclear** relativo al núcleo de un átomo (pág. 505)

nullification theory that states have the right to declare a federal law invalid (p. 126)

invalidación teoría según la cual los estados tienen derecho a declarar inválida una ley federal (pág. 126)

O

***objective** strategic position to be attained or a purpose to be achieved by a military operation (p. 61)

***objetivo** posición estratégica que se quiere alcanzar o propósito por lograr mediante una operación militar (pág. 61)

***obtain** to gain possession of (p. 698)

***obtener** lograr la posesión de algo (pág. 698)

***occupy** to take control or possession of a location (p. 74)

***ocupar** tomar control o posesión de un territorio (pág. 74)

***ongoing** being in process; continuing (p. 421)

***en curso** que se halla en proceso; que continúa (pág. 421)

Open Door policy a policy that allowed each foreign nation in China to trade freely in the other nations' spheres of influence (p. 347)

política de Puertas Abiertas política que permitía que toda nación extranjera en la China negociara libremente en la esfera de influencia de las otras naciones (pág. 347)

open range vast areas of grassland owned by the federal government (p. 271)

terreno abierto vastas áreas de praderas de propiedad del gobierno federal (pág. 271)

*orientation a position relative to a standard (p. 666)

*outcome something that follows as a result or consequence (p. 262)

overlander someone who travels overland to the West (p. 185)

*overseas situated, originating in, or relating to lands beyond the sea (p. 133)

*orientación posición con relación a un estándar (pág. 666)

*resultado algo que ocurre como producto o consecuencia (pág. 262)

viajero terrestre persona que viaja por tierra hacia el Oeste (pág. 185)

*en el extranjero que se sitúa, origina o relaciona con territorios que están al otro lado del mar (pág. 133)

P

Pan-Americanism the idea that the United States and Latin American nations should work together (p. 339)

*participant one who takes part or shares in something (p. 680)

party boss the person in control of a political machine (p. 314)

penitentiary prison whose purpose is to reform prisoners (p. 172)

*perception comprehension or understanding influenced by observation, interpretation, and attitude (p. 207)

perestroika a policy of economic and government restructuring instituted by Mikhail Gorbachev in the Soviet Union in the 1980s (p. 668)

periphery the outer boundary of something (p. 495)

perjury lying when one has sworn under oath to tell the truth (pp. 525, 680)

*phenomenon an exceptional, unusual, or abnormal person, thing, or occurrence (p. 543)

philanthropy providing money to support humanitarian or social goals (p. 317)

*philosopher a person who seeks wisdom or enlightenment (p. 170)

pietism movement in the 1700s that stressed an individual's piety and an emotional union with God (p. 33)

pillage to loot or plunder (p. 244)

pocket veto indirectly vetoing a bill by letting a session of Congress expire without signing the bill (p. 251)

polio abbreviated term for poliomyelitis, an acute infectious disease affecting the skeletal muscles, often resulting in permanent disability and deformity (p. 442)

Panamericanismo idea según la cual Estados Unidos y las naciones latinoamericanas deberían trabajar unidas (pág. 339)

*participante persona que toma parte en algo o lo comparte (pág. 680)

jefe político persona que controla la maquinaria política (pág. 314)

penitenciaria prisión cuyo propósito es reformar prisioneros (pág. 172)

*percepción comprensión o conocimiento influenciado por la observación, la interpretación y la actitud (pág. 207)

perestroika política de reestructuración económica y gubernamental instituida por Mijaíl Gorbachov en la Unión Soviética de 1980 a 1990 (pág. 668)

periferia límite exterior de algo (pág. 495)

perjurio mentir cuando se ha jurado decir la verdad (págs. 525, 680)

*fenómeno persona, cosa o suceso excepcional, poco usual o anormal (pág. 543)

filantropía aportar dinero para apoyar causas humanitarias o sociales (pág. 317)

*filósofo persona que busca sabiduría o ilustración (pág. 170)

pietismo movimiento del siglo XVII que ponía de relieve la piedad y la unión emocional del individuo con Dios (pág. 33)

saquear apoderarse de todo lo que se encuentra o robar (pág. 244)

veto indirecto imponer un veto indirecto a un proyecto de ley dejando que una sesión del Congreso termine sin que se firme el proyecto de ley (pág. 251)

polio abreviatura de poliomielitis, una enfermedad infecciosa aguda que afecta los músculos esqueléticos y a menudo produce discapacidad y deformidad permanentes (pág. 442)

Glossary/Glosario

political machine an organization linked to a political party that often controlled local government (p. 314)

maquinaria política organización vinculada a un partido político que a menudo es controlada por el gobierno local (pág. 314)

poll tax a tax of a fixed amount per person that had to be paid before the person could vote (p. 328)

impuesto de capitación impuesto de una cantidad fija por persona que debía pagarse para poder votar (pág. 328)

popular sovereignty government subject to the will of the people (p. 79); before the Civil War, the idea that people living in a territory had the right to decide by voting whether slavery would be allowed there (p. 205)

soberanía popular gobierno sujeto a la voluntad del pueblo (pág. 79); antes de la Guerra Civil, la idea de que las personas que vivían en un territorio tenían derecho a votar para decidir si se debía permitir la esclavitud ahí (pág. 205)

populism political movement founded in the 1890s representing mainly farmers that favored free coinage of silver and government control of railroads and other large industries (p. 324)

populismo movimiento político fundado en el siglo XIX que representaba principalmente a los agricultores que estaban a favor de la libre acuñación de plata y del control gubernamental de los ferrocarriles y otras grandes industrias (pág. 324)

poverty line a level of personal or family income below which one is classified as poor by the federal government (p. 549)

límite de pobreza nivel de ingresos personales o familiares por debajo del cual el gobierno federal lo clasifica como pobre (pág. 549)

*practice to do something repeatedly so it becomes the standard (p. 289)

*practicar hacer algo en repetidas ocasiones, de manera que se vuelva el estándar (pág. 289)

*precedent an earlier occurrence of something that may serve as a model for similar occurrences in the future (p. 255)

*precedente algo que ha ocurrido con anterioridad y puede servir como modelo para situaciones similares en el futuro (pág. 255)

*predominantly being most frequent or common (p. 168)

*predominantemente con gran frecuencia o muy común (pág. 168)

*prior happening before an event (p. 271)

*previo que sucede antes de un evento (pág. 271)

prisoner of war a person captured in war (p. 236)

prisionero de guerra persona capturada en guerra (pág. 236)

*procedure a particular way of conducting or engaging in an activity (p. 710)

*procedimiento manera particular de realizar una actividad o participar en ella (pág. 710)

*prohibit to make illegal by an authority (p. 472)

*prohibir cuando una autoridad establece que algo es ilegal (pág. 472)

prohibition laws banning the manufacture, transportation, and sale of alcoholic beverages (p. 362)

Prohibición leyes que prohibían la fabricación, el transporte y la venta de bebidas alcohólicas (pág. 362)

*promote to advance in station, rank, or honor (p. 241)

*promover avanzar en estación, rango u honor (pág. 241)

propaganda the spreading of ideas about an institution or individual for the purpose of influencing opinion (p. 380)

propaganda difusión de ideas sobre una institución o un individuo con el propósito de influenciar a la opinión (pág. 380)

proprietary colony a colony owned by an individual (p. 18)

colonia propietaria colonia de propiedad de un individuo (pág. 18)

*prospective to be likely to, or have intentions to, perform an act (p. 275)

*potencial que es probable que, o tiene intenciones de, realizar una acción (pág. 275)

protective tariff a tax on imports designed to protect American manufacturers (p. 141)

arancel proteccionista impuesto sobre las importaciones diseñado para proteger a los fabricantes estadounidenses (pág. 141)

protectorate a country that is technically independent but is actually under the control of another country (p. 336)

protectorado país independiente desde el punto de vista técnico pero que en realidad está bajo el control de otro país (pág. 336)

public works projects such as highways, parks, and libraries built with public funds for public use (p. 435)

obras públicas proyectos como carreteras, parques y bibliotecas construidos con fondos públicos para uso público (pág. 435)

*publish to make a document available to the general public (p. 320)

*publicar hacer que un documento esté disponible al público (pág. 320)

pueblo Spanish for "village"; term used by early Spanish explorers to denote large housing structures built by the Anasazi (p. 7)

pueblo villa; término usado por los exploradores españoles para denotar grandes estructuras de vivienda construidas por los anasazi (pág. 7)

*purchase something obtained especially for a price in money or its equivalent (p. 467)

*compra algo obtenido especialmente a cambio de un precio en dinero o su equivalente (pág. 467)

R

racism prejudice or discrimination against someone because of his or her race (p. 586)

racismo prejuicio o discriminación contra alguien por su raza (pág. 586)

*radical one whose political views, practices, or policies are considered extreme (p. 124)

*radical persona cuyas opiniones, prácticas o doctrinas políticas se consideran extremas (pág. 124)

rationalism philosophy that emphasizes the role of logic and reason in gaining knowledge (p. 31)

racionalismo filosofía que pone de relieve el papel de la lógica y la razón en la adquisición del conocimiento (pág. 31)

*rationality the quality or state of being agreeable to reason (p. 614)

*racionalidad cualidad o condición de estar dispuesto a razonar (pág. 614)

rationing restricting the amount of an item an individual can have due to a limited supply (p. 487)

racionar restringir la cantidad de un artículo que un individuo puede tener, debido a la escasez de provisiones (pág. 487)

reapportionment the method states use to draw up political districts based on changes in population (p. 559)

redistribución método que usan los estados para conformar distritos políticos con base en los cambios demográficos (pág. 559)

recall the right that enables voters to remove unsatisfactory elected officials from office (p. 358)

revocatoria derecho que permite a los electores remover del cargo a funcionarios elegidos cuyo desempeño es insatisfactorio (pág. 358)

recession an economic slowdown (p. 74)

recesión desaceleración económica (pág. 74)

*recovery an economic upturn, as after a depression (p. 454)

*recuperación mejoría económica, por ejemplo después de una depresión (pág. 454)

referendum the practice of letting voters accept or reject measures proposed by the legislature (pp. 213, 358)

referendo práctica de permitir que los electores acepten o rechacen medidas propuestas por el legislativo (págs. 213, 358)

refugee someone leaving his or her country due to a well-founded fear of persecution on account of race, religion, nationality, membership in a particular group, or political opinion (p. 683)

refugiado persona que deja su país debido a un temor bien fundado de persecución a causa de su raza, religión, nacionalidad, pertenencia a un grupo particular u opinión política (pág. 683)

*register to file personal information in order to become eligible for an official event (p. 581)

*inscribirse entregar información personal con el fin de ser elegible para un evento oficial (pág. 581)

*regulate to govern or direct according to rule (p. 365)

*regular gobernar o dirigir ciñéndose a las normas (pág. 365)

*reinforcement additional assistance, material, or support to strengthen an existing situation (p. 193)

*refuerzo ayuda, material o apoyo adicionales para fortalecer una situación existente (pág. 193)

Glossary/Glosario

ENGLISH	ESPAÑOL
*reliable dependable; giving the same results on successive trials (p. 25)	***confiable** digno de confianza; que da los mismos resultados en sucesivos intentos (pág. 25)
relief aid for the needy; welfare (p. 435)	**auxilio** ayuda para los necesitados; asistencia social (pág. 435)
*relocate to move to a new place (p. 277)	***trasladar** pasar a un nuevo lugar (pág. 277)
*remove to change the location or position (p. 564)	***remover** cambiar de ubicación o posición (pág. 564)
reparations payment by the losing country in a war to the winner for the damages caused by the war (p. 392)	**indemnización** pago que el país perdedor en una guerra hace al ganador para compensar los daños ocasionados por la guerra (pág. 392)
repatriation being restored or returned to the country of origin, allegiance, or citizenship (p. 621)	**repatriación** acción por la cual se devuelve o regresa a una persona al país de origen, lealtad o ciudadanía (pág. 621)
*repress to stop something by force (p. 668)	***reprimir** detener algo mediante el uso de la fuerza (pág. 668)
republic form of government in which power resides in a body of citizens entitled to vote (p. 63)	**república** forma de gobierno en la cual el poder reside en un cuerpo de ciudadanos que tienen derecho al voto (pág. 63)
*requirement something essential to the existence or occurrence of something else (p. 254)	***requisito** algo esencial para que exista u ocurra algo más (pág. 254)
*resident one who lives in a place for some length of time (p. 684)	***residente** persona que vive en un lugar durante cierto tiempo (pág. 684)
*resolution a formal expression of opinion, will, or intent voted by an official body or assembly (p. 196)	***resolución** expresión formal de una opinión, deseo o intención por la cual vota una asamblea u organismo oficial (pág. 196)
*resolve to come to an agreement (p. 392)	***resolver** llegar a un acuerdo (pág. 392)
*resolve fixity of purpose, or resoluteness (p. 696)	***determinación** con un propósito fijo o resolución (pág. 696)
*resources materials used in the production process, such as money, people, land, wood, or steel (p. 286)	***recursos** materiales utilizados en el proceso de producción, tales como dinero, personal, tierras, madera o acero (pág. 286)
*response something said or done as a reaction (p. 533)	***respuesta** lo que se dice o se hace como reacción (pág. 533)
*restraint the act of limiting, restricting, or keeping under control (p. 299)	***restricción** acción de limitar, restringir o mantener bajo control (pág. 299)
*retain to keep in possession (p. 671)	***retener** mantener la posesión (pág. 671)
*revelation an act of revealing to view or making known (p. 404)	***revelación** acción de revelar para ver o dar a conocer (pág. 404)
*revenue the total income produced by a given source (p. 120)	***renta** ingresos totales producidos por una fuente determinada (pág. 120)
revenue sharing federal tax money that is distributed among the states (p. 630)	**participación en los ingresos** dinero proveniente de los impuestos federales que se distribuye entre los estados (pág. 630)
revenue tariff a tax on imports for the purpose of raising money (p. 141)	**arancel financiero** impuesto sobre las importaciones con el fin de recaudar dinero (pág. 141)
*revise to make changes to an original document (p. 467)	***modificar** hacer cambios a un documento original (pág. 467)
revival large public meeting for preaching and prayer (p. 33)	**asamblea** gran reunión pública para predicar y orar (pág. 33)

*revolutionary constituting or bringing about a major or fundamental change (p. 65)

*revolucionario que constituye o provoca un cambio considerable o fundamental (pág. 65)

right-to-work laws a law making it illegal to require employees to join a union (p. 539)

leyes de derecho al trabajo leyes que hacen ilegal exigir que los empleados se unan a un sindicato (pág. 539)

rock 'n' roll popular music usually played on electronically amplified instruments and characterized by a persistent, heavily accented beat, much repetition of simple phrases, and often country, folk, and blues elements (p. 547)

rock and roll música popular que por lo general se interpreta con instrumentos amplificados electrónicamente; se caracteriza por un compás persistente y bastante acentuado, muchas repeticiones de frases sencillas y, a menudo, elementos de música *country*, *folk* y *blues* (pág. 547)

romanticism a literary, artistic, and philosophical movement in the late 1700s and early 1800s emphasizing the imagination, the emotions, and the individual above society (p. 170)

Romanticismo movimiento literario, artístico y filosófico del siglo XVIII que pone énfasis en la imaginación y los sentimientos, defendiendo el sentimiento sobre la razón, la espiritualidad interior sobre las reglas externas, al individuo sobre la sociedad y la naturaleza sobre los entornos creados por los seres humanos (pág. 170)

*route an established or selected course of travel or action (p. 11)

*ruta curso de viaje o acción establecido o escogido (pág. 11)

S

safety net something that provides security against misfortune; specifically, government relief programs intended to protect against economic disaster (p. 455)

red de protección algo que brinda seguridad contra las calamidades; en particular, programas de ayuda del gobierno que buscan proteger contra un desastre económico (pág. 455)

satellite nations nations politically and economically dominated or controlled by another more powerful country (p. 516)

naciones satélite naciones que están bajo el dominio o control político y económico de un país más poderoso (pág. 516)

scalawag name given to Southerners who supported Republican Reconstruction of the South (p. 256)

scalawag nombre dado a los sureños que apoyaban la Reconstrucción Republicana del Sur (pág. 256)

secede to leave or withdraw (p. 163)

separarse dejar o retirarse (pág. 163)

secession withdrawal from the Union (p. 206)

secesión retiro de la Unión (pág. 206)

secularize to transfer the use, possession, or control of something from church to civil authority (p. 187)

secularizar transferir a la autoridad civil el uso, la posesión o el control de bienes de la iglesia (pág. 187)

*secure free from risk of loss (p. 198)

*seguro que no tiene riesgo de perderse (pág. 198)

sedition incitement to rebellion (p. 126)

sedición incitación a la rebelión (pág. 126)

segregation the separation or isolation of a race, class, or group (p. 329)

segregación separación o aislamiento de una raza, clase o grupo (pág. 329)

"separate but equal" doctrine established by the 1896 Supreme Court case *Plessy* v. *Ferguson* that permitted laws segregating African Americans as long as equal facilities were provided (p. 574)

"separados pero iguales" doctrina establecida por la Corte Suprema en el caso *Plessy contra Ferguson* de 1896, que permitía las leyes que segregaban a la población afroamericana siempre que se brindaran instalaciones iguales (pág. 574)

separation of powers government principle in which power is divided among different branches (p. 79)

separación de poderes principio de gobierno en el cual el poder está dividido en diferentes ramas (pág. 79)

*series a number of events that come one after another (p. 435)

*serie conjunto de eventos que vienen uno después del otro (pág. 435)

Glossary/Glosario

ENGLISH	ESPAÑOL
settlement house institution located in a poor neighborhood that provided numerous community services such as medical care, child care, libraries, and classes in English (p. 319)	**centro comunitario** institución localizada en un vecindario pobre que presta numerosos servicios a la comunidad, tales como atención médica, cuidado de niños, bibliotecas y clases en inglés (pág. 319)
sharecropper farmer who works land for an owner who provides equipment and seed and receives a share of the crop (p. 263)	**aparcero** agricultor que trabaja la tierra para un propietario que provee equipos y semillas y recibe a cambio una parte de la cosecha (pág. 263)
siege a military blockade of a city or fortified place to force it to surrender (p. 238)	**sitio** bloqueo militar de una ciudad o lugar fortificado para obligarlo a rendirse (pág. 238)
*significantly in a manner likely to have influence or effect (p. 701)	***considerablemente** de manera que puede influir o tener efecto (pág. 701)
"sin tax" federal tax on alcohol and tobacco (p. 260)	**impuesto a los vicios** impuesto federal al alcohol y el tabaco (pág. 260)
sit-down strike method of boycotting work by sitting down at work and refusing to leave the establishment (p. 451)	**huelga de brazos caídos** método de boicotear el trabajo sentándose en el puesto de trabajo y negándose a abandonar el establecimiento (pág. 451)
skyscraper a very tall building (p. 312)	**rascacielos** edificio muy alto (pág. 312)
smog fog made heavier and darker by smoke and chemical fumes (p. 647)	**esmog** niebla que se hace más densa y oscura debido al humo y a los vapores químicos (pág. 647)
soap opera a serial drama on television or radio using melodramatic situations (p. 433)	**telenovela** drama seriado en televisión o radio que presenta situaciones melodramáticas (pág. 433)
Social Darwinism a philosophy based on Charles Darwin's theories of evolution and natural selection, asserting that humans have developed through competition and natural selection with only the strongest surviving (pp. 317, 363)	**Darwinismo Social** filosofía basada en las teorías de Charles Darwin sobre la evolución y la selección natural, la cual afirma que los seres humanos se han desarrollado por la competencia y la selección natural y sólo los más fuertes han sobrevivido (págs. 317, 363)
sodbuster a name given to Great Plains farmers (p. 275)	**rompeterreno** nombre dado a los granjeros de las Grandes Llanuras (pág. 275)
*source the point at which something is provided (p. 412)	***fuente** punto en el cual se proporciona algo (pág. 412)
space race refers to the Cold War competition over dominance of space exploration capability (p. 562)	**carrera espacial** relativo a la competencia que se dio durante la Guerra Fría por el dominio de la capacidad de exploración espacial (pág. 562)
speakeasy a place where alcoholic beverages are sold illegally (p. 414)	**clandestino** lugar en el que se venden bebidas alcohólicas ilegalmente (pág. 414)
special prosecutor a lawyer from outside the government (p. 635)	**fiscal especial** abogado externo al gobierno (pág. 635)
*specific related to a particular individual, situation, relation, or effect (p. 83)	***específico** relativo a un individuo, una situación, una relación o un efecto en particular (pág. 83)
speculation act of buying stocks at great risk with the anticipation that the prices will rise (p. 427)	**especulación** compra de acciones con gran riesgo con la expectativa de que los precios subirán (pág. 427)

Glossary/Glosario

738

speculator a person who risks money in hopes of a financial profit (p. 121)

especulador persona que arriesga dinero con la esperanza de obtener un beneficio económico (pág. 121)

sphere of influence section of a country where a foreign nation enjoys special rights and powers (p. 347)

esfera de influencia sección de un país donde una nación extranjera goza de derechos y facultades especiales (pág. 347)

spoils system practice of handing out government jobs to supporters; replacing government employees with the winning candidate's supporters (p. 163)

sistema de sinecuras práctica de dar trabajos gubernamentales a los partidarios; sustitución de los empleados del gobierno por partidarios del candidato ganador (pág. 163)

squatter someone who settles on public land under government regulation with the hope of acquiring title to the land (p. 184)

ocupante ilegal persona que se instala en tierras públicas bajo las normas del gobierno con la esperanza de adquirir el título de la tierra (pág. 184)

*stability a state of peace; condition resistant to change or upheaval (p. 657)

*estabilidad estado de paz, resistencia al cambio o la agitación (pág. 657)

stagflation persistent inflation combined with stagnant consumer demand and relatively high unemployment (p. 638)

estanflación inflación persistente en combinación con un estancamiento de la demanda y un desempleo relativamente alto (pág. 638)

state-sponsored terrorism violent acts against civilians that are secretly supported by a government in order to attack other nations without going to war (p. 697)

terrorismo de Estado actos violentos contra los civiles, que son apoyados en secreto por un gobierno con el fin de atacar a otras naciones sin entrar en guerra (pág. 697)

stock market a system for buying and selling stocks in corporations (p. 426)

mercado de valores sistema de compra y venta de acciones en las sociedades anónimas (pág. 426)

*strategic related to long-term interests and how to achieve them (p. 596)

*estratégico relacionado con intereses de largo plazo y cómo lograrlos (pág. 596)

strategic materials materials needed for fighting a war (p. 468)

materiales estratégicos materiales necesarios para participar en una guerra (pág. 468)

*strategy a plan or method for achieving a goal (p. 324)

*estrategia plan o método para alcanzar un objetivo (pág. 324)

strike work stoppage by workers to force an employer to meet demands (p. 148)

huelga interrupción en las labores por parte de los trabajadores para obligar a un empleador a satisfacer sus peticiones (pág. 148)

*structure something that is composed or arranged into a unified whole, as a building or edifice (p. 244)

*estructura algo compuesto o dispuesto como un todo, por ejemplo una construcción o edificio (pág. 244)

*submit to put forward for consideration or judgment (p. 51)

*proponer someter a consideración o fallo (pág. 51)

*subordinate one who is under the authority of a superior (p. 242)

*subordinado alguien que está bajo la autoridad de un superior (pág. 242)

*subsidy money granted by the government to achieve a specific goal that is beneficial to society (p. 569)

*subsidio dinero que el gobierno entrega para alcanzar un objetivo específico que beneficia a la sociedad (pág. 569)

*substitute to put or use in the place of another (p. 41)

*sustituir poner o usar en lugar de otra persona o cosa (pág. 41)

subversion a systematic attempt to overthrow a government by using persons working secretly from within (p. 524)

subversión intento sistemático de derrocar un gobierno valiéndose de personas que trabajan en secreto dentro de ese gobierno (pág. 524)

*sufficient enough, adequate (p. 225)

*suficiente adecuado (pág. 225)

suffrage the right to vote (pp. 162, 359)

sufragio derecho al voto (págs. 162, 359)

Glossary/Glosario

ENGLISH	ESPAÑOL
*sum a specified amount of money (p. 427)	***suma** cantidad específica de dinero (pág. 427)
summit a meeting between heads of government (p. 632)	**cumbre** reunión entre los jefes de gobierno (pág. 632)
Sunbelt a new industrial region in southern California and the Deep South, developing during World War II (p. 485)	**Cinturón del Sol** nueva región industrial al sur de California y el Bajo Sur, que se desarrolló durante la Segunda Guerra Mundial (pág. 485)
*supplemented added to (p. 235)	***complementado** agregado a (pág. 235)
supply-side economics economic theory that lower tax rates will boost the economy as businesses and individuals invest their money, thereby creating higher tax revenue (pp. 404, 659)	**economía de oferta** teoría económica según la cual los impuestos más bajos estimulan la economía en la medida que las empresas y los individuos invierten su dinero, en consecuencia se crea una renta tributaria más alta (págs. 404, 659)
*survival the continuation of life or existence (p. 205)	***supervivencia** continuación de la vida o existencia (pág. 205)
*suspend to cease or stop (p. 431)	***suspender** cesar o detener (pág. 431)
swing vote a vote that may sometimes lean conservative and other times liberal (p. 706)	**voto flotante** voto que unas veces puede ser conservador y otras veces liberal (pág. 706)
*symbolize to represent, express, or identify by a symbol (p. 419)	***simbolizar** representar, expresar o identificar mediante un símbolo (pág. 419)

T

ENGLISH	ESPAÑOL
*target something or someone fired on or marked for attack (p. 496)	***objetivo** algo o alguien a quien se le dispara o se marca para atacar (pág. 496)
task system a method of organizing enslaved labor wherein workers were given a specific set of jobs to accomplish every day, after which they were allowed to spend their time as they chose (p. 153)	**sistema de tareas** método de organización del trabajo esclavo en el cual los trabajadores recibían una serie específica de tareas que debían realizar a diario, después de las cuales podían pasar el tiempo como quisieran (pág. 153)
teach-in an extended meeting or class held to discuss a social or political issue (p. 600)	**foro** asamblea o clase prolongadas para tratar un tema social o político (pág. 600)
*technique a method of achieving a desired aim (p. 433)	***técnica** método para alcanzar un objetivo trazado (pág. 433)
*technology the manner of accomplishing a task using specialized methods, processes, or knowledge (p. 6)	**tecnología** manera de realizar una tarea usando métodos, procesos o conocimientos especializados (pág. 6)
telecommute to work at home by means of an electronic linkup with a central office (p. 686)	**teletrabajo** trabajar en casa mediante una conexión electrónica con una oficina central (pág. 686)
televangelist an evangelist who conducts regularly televised religious programs (p. 657)	**telepredicador** predicador que conduce habitualmente programas religiosos por televisión (pág. 657)
temperance moderation in or abstinence from alcohol (p. 172)	**templanza** moderación o abstinencia en el uso del alcohol (pág. 172)
tenant farmer farmer who works land owned by another and pays rent either in cash or crops (p. 263)	**granjero arrendatario** agricultor que trabaja la tierra que pertenece a otro y le paga una renta ya sea en efectivo o con sus cosechas (pág. 263)

Glossary/Glosario

tenement multifamily apartments, usually dark, crowded, and barely meeting minimum living standards (p. 313)

casa de vecindad apartamentos multifamiliares, por lo general oscuros, hacinados y que apenas cumplen los estándares mínimos de vivienda (pág. 313)

***tension** friction or opposition between groups (p. 348)

***tensión** fricción u oposición entre grupos (pág. 348)

termination policy a government policy to bring Native Americans into mainstream society by withdrawing recognition of Native American groups as legal entities (p. 550)

política de terminación política gubernamental para incorporar a los indígenas americanos a la sociedad predominante cancelando el reconocimiento de los grupos indígenas americanos como entidades legales (pág. 550)

terrorism the use of violence by non-governmental groups against civilians to achieve a political goal by instilling fear and frightening governments into changing policies (p. 696)

terrorismo uso de la violencia por parte de grupos no gubernamentales contra los civiles para alcanzar un objetivo político, atemorizando e intimidando a los gobiernos para que cambien sus políticas (pág. 696)

***theory** a hypothesis meant for argument or investigation (p. 638)

***teoría** hipótesis planteada para argumentar o investigar (pág. 638)

***thereby** because of that (p. 451)

***por consiguiente** por esta razón (pág. 451)

time zone a geographic region in which the same standard time is kept (p. 292)

huso horario región geográfica en la cual se mantiene la misma hora estándar (pág. 292)

town meeting a gathering of free men in a New England town to elect leaders, which developed into the local town government (p. 23)

asamblea popular reunión de hombres libres en Nueva Inglaterra para elegir líderes, que se desarrollaba en las oficinas del gobierno municipal (pág. 23)

***traditional** the usual way of doing things (p. 596)

***tradicional** manera usual de hacer las cosas (pág. 596)

transcendentalism a philosophy stressing the relationship between human beings and nature, spiritual things over material things, and the importance of the individual conscience (p. 170)

Transcendentalismo filosofía que destaca la relación entre los seres humanos y la naturaleza, lo espiritual sobre lo material y la importancia de la conciencia individual (pág. 170)

transcontinental railroad a railway system extending across the continent (p. 208)

ferrocarril transcontinental sistema ferroviario que atraviesa el continente (pág. 208)

***transportation** method of travel from one place to another (p. 145)

***transporte** forma de viaje de un lugar a otro (pág. 145)

triangular trade a three-way trade route for exchanging goods between the Americas, Europe, and Africa (p. 26)

comercio triangular ruta comercial de tres vías para intercambiar productos entre las Américas, Europa y África (pág. 26)

tribute a payment by one ruler or nation to another in acknowledgment of submission or as the price of protection (p. 5)

tributo pago de un gobernante o nación a otra en reconocimiento por su sumisión o como precio por su protección (pág. 5)

***trigger** to cause an action that causes a greater reaction (p. 314)

***desencadenar** provocar una acción que provoca una reacción mayor (pág. 314)

trust a combination of firms or corporations formed by a legal agreement, especially to reduce competition (p. 296)

trust asociación de firmas o sociedades anónimas formadas por un acuerdo legal, especialmente para reducir la competencia (pág. 296)

U

***ultimately** in the end, finally, or eventually (p. 189)

***en última instancia** al final, finalmente o a la larga (pág. 189)

***unconstitutional** not in accordance with or authorized by the constitution of a state or society (p. 372)

***inconstitucional** no conforme con o autorizado por la Constitución de un Estado o la sociedad (pág. 372)

ENGLISH

*underestimate to estimate lower than the real amount or number (p. 469)

unfair trade practices trading practices that derive a gain at the expense of competition (p. 371)

*unify to bring a group together with a similar goal or thought pattern (p. 417)

union shop a business that requires employees to join a union (p. 539)

*unprecedented having no earlier occurrence of something similar (p. 677)

*unresolved not cleared up, understandable, or dealt with successfully (p. 607)

urban renewal government programs that attempt to eliminate poverty and revitalize urban areas (p. 550)

utopia a community based on a vision of a perfect society sought by reformers (p. 169)

ESPAÑOL

*subestimar estimar en un valor más bajo que la cantidad o el número reales (pág. 469)

prácticas comerciales desleales prácticas comerciales que generan ganancias a expensas del bienestar de la competencia (pág. 371)

*unificar juntar un grupo con un objetivo o un patrón de pensamiento similares (pág. 417)

empresa de afiliación sindical obligatoria empresa que exige que los empleados se unan a un sindicato (pág. 539)

*sin precedentes que no ha ocurrido algo similar antes (pág. 677)

*sin resolver que no se ha aclarado, hecho comprensible o tratado con buenos resultados (pág. 607)

renovación urbana programas gubernamentales que buscan eliminar la pobreza y revitalizar las áreas urbanas (pág. 550)

utopía comunidad que se basa en una visión de una sociedad perfecta que buscan los reformistas (pág. 169)

V

vaqueros men who herded cattle on haciendas (p. 188)

veto power of the chief executive to reject laws passed by the legislature (p. 80)

*via to come by way of, or through (p. 664)

victory garden a garden planted by civilians during war to raise vegetables for home use, leaving more of other foods for the troops (pp. 383, 487)

victory suit a men's suit with no vest, no cuffs, a short jacket, and narrow lapels, worn during World War II in order to save fabric for the war effort (p. 486)

Vietnamization the process of making South Vietnam assume more of the war effort by slowly withdrawing American troops from Vietnam (p. 604)

vigilance committee group of ordinary citizens formed by local law enforcement officers whose goal is to find criminals and bring them to justice (p. 269)

*virtually almost entirely; nearly (p. 475)

*visible what can be seen (p. 661)

*volunteer person who joins the military by choice (p. 342)

vaqueros hombres que pastoreaban el ganado en las haciendas (pág. 188)

veto facultad del Ejecutivo de rechazar leyes aprobadas por el Legislativo (pág. 80)

*vía llegar por medio de o mediante (pág. 664)

huerta de la victoria huerta plantada por los civiles durante la guerra con el fin de cultivar vegetales para uso doméstico, y dejar más de otros alimentos para las tropas (págs. 383, 487)

traje de la victoria traje de hombre sin chaleco ni puños, con chaqueta corta y solapas pequeñas que se usó durante la Segunda Guerra Mundial con el fin de ahorrar tela para la guerra (pág. 486)

vietnamización proceso por el cual se hizo que Vietnam del Sur asumiera mayor parte del esfuerzo bélico retirando lentamente las tropas estadounidenses de Vietnam (pág. 604)

comité de vigilancia grupo de ciudadanos del común integrado por funcionarios locales que hacen cumplir las leyes, cuyo objetivo es hallar a los criminales y ponerlos a órdenes de la justicia (pág. 269)

*prácticamente casi todo; estrechamente (pág. 475)

*visible que se puede ver (pág. 661)

*voluntario persona que elige enlistarse en la milicia (pág. 342)

W

weapons of mass destruction (WMD) weapons—including nuclear, chemical, and biological—that can kill large numbers of people all at once (p. 700)

armas de destrucción masiva (ADM) armas nucleares, químicas y biológicas, entre otras, que pueden matar a un gran número de personas a la vez (pág. 700)

*welfare aid in the form of money or necessities for those in need, especially disadvantaged social groups (p. 630)

*asistencia social ayuda en dinero o en especies para los necesitados, en especial para grupos en desventaja social (pág. 630)

white-collar job jobs in fields not requiring work clothes or protective clothing, such as sales (p. 544)

empleado de oficina trabajos en cargos que no requieren el uso de ropa de protección, como en ventas (pág. 544)

*widespread having influence on or affecting a large group; widely diffused or prevalent (p. 33)

*extendido que tiene influencia sobre o que afecta un grupo grande; común o muy difundido (pág. 33)

writs of assistance a search warrant enabling customs officers to enter any location to look for evidence of smuggling (p. 42)

interdicto de despojo orden de allanamiento que permite a los funcionarios de aduana ingresar a un lugar en busca de evidencia de contrabando (pág. 42)

*widespread widely diffused or prevalent (p. 395)

*extendido ampliamente difundido o frecuente (pág. 395)

Y

yellow journalism type of sensational, biased, and often false reporting for the sake of attracting readers (p. 341)

prensa sensacionalista tipo de periodismo exagerado, tendencioso y a menudo falso con el fin de atraer lectores (pág. 341)

yeoman farmer owner of a small farm with four or fewer enslaved persons, and usually none (p. 152)

terrateniente rural propietario de una granja pequeña con cuatro o menos personas esclavizadas, y por lo general ninguna (pág. 152)

yuppie a young, college-educated adult employed in a well-paying profession and living in or near a large city (p. 663)

yupi adulto joven con educación universitaria que tiene una profesión bien remunerada y vive en una ciudad grande o cerca de ella (pág. 663)

Z

zoot suit men's clothing of extreme cut typically consisting of a thigh-length jacket with wide padded shoulders and baggy, pleated pants with narrow cuffs (p. 486)

traje zoot prenda de hombre de corte extremo que por lo general consta de una chaqueta larga y apretada con hombreras anchas y pantalones sueltos con pliegues y dobladillos angostos (pág. 486)

Glossary/Glosario

Italicized page numbers refer to illustrations. The following abbreviations are used in the index: m = map; c = chart; p = photograph, painting, or picture; g = graph; crt = cartoon; q = quote

Index

Index

Index

Index

Index

Index

Index

Index

Index

U

V

Index

Index